THE BLOOMSBURY
HANDBOOK OF LITERARY
AND CULTURAL THEORY

THE BLOOMSBURY HANDBOOK OF LITERARY AND CULTURAL THEORY

Edited by Jeffrey R. Di Leo

BLOOMSBURY ACADEMIC
LONDON • NEW YORK • OXFORD • NEW DELHI • SYDNEY

BLOOMSBURY ACADEMIC
Bloomsbury Publishing Plc
50 Bedford Square, London, WC1B 3DP, UK
1385 Broadway, New York, NY 10018, USA

BLOOMSBURY, BLOOMSBURY ACADEMIC and the Diana logo are trademarks
of Bloomsbury Publishing Plc

First published in Great Britain 2019

Cover design: Eleanor Rose
Cover photograph © Chris Barbalis / Unsplash

A catalogue record for this book is available from the British Library.

A catalog record for this book is available from the Library of Congress.

ISBN: HB: 978-1-3500-1280-6
ePDF: 978-1-3500-1282-0
eBook: 978-1-3500-1281-3

Typeset by Deanta Global Publishing Services, Chennai, India
Printed and bound in Great Britain

To find out more about our authors and books visit www.bloomsbury.com
and sign up for our newsletters.

CONTENTS

ACKNOWLEDGMENTS

Many of the contributors to this book I have come to know and admire through my work as editor of *symplokē,* and executive director of the Society for Critical Exchange and its Winter Theory Institute. To them is my greatest debt of gratitude.

The notion that theory is a community offered in the introduction to this book is their fault—not mine. Their collegiality and collaboration in pursuit of theory has led me to this conclusion. It is an unshakeable one that has only grown stronger over the years. Though we may differ in our views as to theory's strengths and weaknesses, heroes and villains, the shared pursuit of theory trumps these differences.

I'd also like to thank all of those who have contributed to this book that I have come to know through our collaborative work on this handbook. The experience of getting to know so many distinguished scholars and practitioners of theory from around the world primarily through correspondence on this book has been a rewarding and special experience for me. Thank you for sharing your insights on theory—and for working within the time and space constraints of this book—which as I know from many of you was not an easy thing. Your collective good will is much appreciated.

The idea for this Handbook was presented to me by David Avital of Bloomsbury. While working together on another project, we started to discuss this one over coffee in Vienna. The notion that it would not be a memorial to theory in the sense of just looking back at its past, but rather a more vibrant book that looks forward to its futures was one upon which we agreed. So too was a balance between the old and the new in theory. And so work on the book began. I deeply appreciate his unflagging encouragement regarding this project, and support in shepherding it through the peer review and publication process.

I am also grateful to Keri Farnsworth for her assistance in the production of this book, particularly in the early stages when I was facing the organizational challenges of a book that would involve hundreds of entries and contributors; to Vikki Fitzpatrick for her administrative support, especially in securing materials used for the development of this book; and to the late John Fizer of Rutgers University for introducing me to literary theory.

Finally, I would like to thank my wife Nina, for her unfailing encouragement, support, and patience.

LIST OF CONTRIBUTORS

A

Daniela Agostinho, *University of Copenhagen (Denmark)*
Manuel Aguirre, *Universidad Autónoma de Madrid (Spain)*
Thomas Allen, *University of Ottawa (Canada)*
Charles Altieri, *University of California, Berkeley (United States)*
Carlos M. Amador, *Michigan Technological University (United States)*
Eyal Amiran, *University of California, Irvine (United States)*
Michael Amrozowicz, *University at Albany, SUNY (United States)*
Myrdene Anderson, *Purdue University (United States)*
Sean Johnson Andrews, *Columbia College Chicago (United States)*
Paul Ardoin, *University of Texas, San Antonio (United States)*

B

Andrew Baerg, *University of Houston-Victoria (United States)*
Ian Balfour, *York University (Canada)*
Ian Barnard, *Chapman University (United States)*
Kiff Bamford, *Leeds Beckett University (United Kingdom)*
Jae Basiliere, *Grand Valley State University (United States)*
Jason M. Baskin, *University of Exeter (United Kingdom)*
Megan Becker-Leckrone, *University of Nevada, Las Vegas (United States)*
Alexander Beecroft, *University of South Carolina (United States)*
Michael C. Behrent, *Appalachian State University (United States)*
Charles Bernstein, *University of Pennsylvania (United States)*
R. M. Berry, *Florida State University (United States)*
Greg Bird, *Wilfrid Laurier University (Canada)*
Jacob Blevins, *Sam Houston State University (United States)*
Ronald Bogue, *University of Georgia (United States)*
Jay David Bolter, *Georgia Institute of Technology (United States)*
Marc Bousquet, *Emory University (United States)*
Michael Boylan, *Marymount University (United States)*
Christopher Breu, *Illinois State University (United States)*
Sarah Brouillette, *Carleton University (Canada)*
Bill Brown, *University of Chicago (United States)*
Carolyn E. Brown, *University of San Francisco (United States)*
Nicholas Brown, *University of Illinois, Chicago (United States)*
Gerald L. Bruns, *The University of Notre Dame (United States)*
Ashley Byock, *Edgewood College (United States)*

C

Mark Canuel, *University of Illinois, Chicago (United States)*
Sarah Phillips Casteel, *Carleton University (Canada)*
Nicholas Chare, *Université de Montréal (Canada)*
Szu-Ying Chen, *University at Albany, SUNY (United States)*
Flore Chevaillier, *Texas State University (United States)*
Keridiana Chez, *City University of New York (United States)*
Robert Chodat, *Boston University (United States)*
Ralph Clare, *Boise State University (United States)*
Richard A. Cohen, *University at Buffalo (United States)*
Tom Cohen, *University at Albany, SUNY (United States)*
Vincent Colapietro, *Penn State University (United States)*
Andrew Cole, *Princeton University (United States)*
Claire Colebrook, *Penn State University (United States)*
Daniel Conway, *Texas A&M University (United States)*
Eleanor Courtemanche, *University of Illinois, Urbana-Champaign (United States)*
Clayton Crockett, *University of Central Arkansas (United States)*

D

Lennard Davis, *University of Illinois, Chicago (United States)*
Leland De la Durantaye, *Claremont McKenna College (United States)*
Steven Delmagori, *University at Albany, SUNY (United States)*
Shane Denson, *Stanford University (United States)*
Jeffrey R. Di Leo, *University of Houston-Victoria (United States)*
Robert Doran, *University of Rochester (United States)*
David B. Downing, *Indiana University of Pennsylvania (United States)*
Alan R. Dunn, *University of Tennessee (United States)*
John N. Duvall, *Purdue University (United States)*

E

Andrew Edgar, *Cardiff University (United Kingdom)*
John R. Ehrenberg, *Long Island University (United States)*
Stuart Elden, *University of Warwick (United Kingdom)*
Caryl Emerson, *Princeton University (United States)*
Jeremy David Engels, *Penn State University (United States)*
Brad Evans, *University of Bristol (United Kingdom)*
Mary Evans, *University at Albany, SUNY (United States)*
Tom Eyers, *Duquesne University (United States)*

F

Horace Fairlamb, *University of Houston-Victoria (United States)*
Krzysztof Fijalkowski, *Norwick University of the Arts (United Kingdom)*
Gregory Flaxman, *University of North Carolina, Chapel Hill (United States)*
William Franke, *Vanderbilt University (United States)*
Rosa Freedman, *University of Reading (United Kingdom)*
John Frow, *University of Sydney (Australia)*

G

D. Christopher Gabbard, *University of North Florida (United States)*
Patrick Gamez, *Missouri S&T (United States)*
Samir Gandesha, *Simon Fraser University (Canada)*
Amanpal Garcha, *Ohio State University (United States)*
Ranjan Ghosh, *University of North Bengal (India)*
Jeremy Gilbert, *University of East London (United Kingdom)*
Henry A. Giroux, *McMaster University (Canada)*
Robin Truth Goodman, *Florida State University (United States)*
Dinda L. Gorlée, *University of Bergen (Norway)*
Sean Grattan, *University of Kent (United Kingdom)*
Jesper Gulddal, *University of Newcastle (Australia)*
David J. Gunkel, *Northern Illinois University (United States)*

H

Ross Haenfler, *Grinnell College (United States)*
Christian P. Haines, *Dartmouth College (United States)*
W. David Hall, *Centre College (United States)*
Francis Halsall, *National College of Art and Design, Dublin (Ireland) and University of the Free State, Bloemfontaine (South Africa)*
Faye Hammill, *University of Glasgow (United Kingdom)*
Charles Harris, *Illinois State University (United States)*
Salah D. Hassan, *Michigan State University (United States)*
Eric Hayot, *Penn State University (United States)*
Ursula K. Heise, *University of California, Los Angeles (United States)*
Andrea Henderson, *University of California, Irvine (United States)*
Mike Hill, *University at Albany, SUNY (United States)*
Peter Hitchcock, *City University of New York (United States)*
Andrew Hoberek, *University of Missouri (United States)*
Patrick Colm Hogan, *University of Connecticut (United States)*
W. Lawrence Hogue, *University of Houston (United States)*
Derek Hook, *Duquesne University (United States)*
Tom Huhn, *School of Visual Arts, New York City (United States)*
Mark Hussey, *Pace University (United States)*
Linda Hutcheon, *University of Toronto (Canada)*

J

Aaron Jaffe, *Florida State University (United States)*
Ian James, *Cambridge University (United Kingdom)*
Adeline Johns-Putra, *University of Surrey (United Kingdom)*
Charles Johnson, *University of Washington, Seattle (United States)*
Keith Leslie Johnson, *College of William and Mary (United States)*

K

Ubaraj Katawal, *Valdosta State University (United States)*
Joshua Kates, *Indiana University, Bloomington (United States)*
Vicki Kirby, *University of New South Wales (Australia)*
Marcia Klotz, *University of Arizona (United States)*

Alexander Kozin, *University of Sussex (United Kingdom)*
Colleen Kropp, *Temple University (United States)*
Kir Kuiken, *University at Albany, SUNY (United States)*

L
Pierre Lamarche, *Utah Valley University (United States)*
Gregg Lambert, *Syracuse University (United States) and Kyung Hee University (South Korea)*
Vincent B. Leitch, *University of Oklahoma (United States)*
Nicolas Lemay-Hébert, *University of Birmingham (United Kingdom)*
Brian Lennon, *Penn State University (United States)*
Jeffrey S. Librett, *University of Oregon (United States)*
James Liner, *University of Washington Tacoma (United States)*
Catherine Liu, *University of California, Irvine (United States)*
David Palumbo Liu, *Stanford University (United States)*
Jessica Lockrem, *Rice University (United States)*
Valérie Loichot, *Emory University (United States)*

M
Gina Masucci Mackenzie, *Holy Family University (United States)*
Steven Mailloux, *Loyola Marymount University (United States)*
Padma D. Maitland, *University of California, Berkeley (United States)*
Charlene Makley, *Reed College (United States)*
T. J. Martinson, *Indiana University, Bloomington (United States)*
Robert P. Marzac, *Purdue University (United States)*
Graham J. Matthews, *Nanyang Technological University (Singapore)*
Laci Mattison, *Florida Gulf Coast University (United States)*
Todd May, *Clemson University (United States)*
William McBride, *Purdue University (United States)*
Bruce McComiskey, *University of Alabama at Birmingham (United States)*
Marina McCoy, *Boston College (United States)*
John McGowan, *University of North Carolina, Chapel Hill (United States)*
Brian McHale, *Ohio State University (United States)*
David W. McIvor, *Colorado State University (United States)*
Tracey McNulty, *Cornell University (United States)*
Hassan Melehy, *University of North Carolina, Chapel Hill (United States)*
John Michael, *University of Rochester (United States)*
Christopher Patrick Miller, *University of California, Berkeley (United States)*
J. Hillis Miller, *University of California, Irvine (United States)*
Jason Miller, *Warren Wilson College (United States)*
Michael Miller, *Rice University (United States)*
Paul Allen Miller, *University of South Carolina (United States)*
Toby Miller, *Universidad del Norte, Barranquilla (Columbia)*
Charles Mills, *Graduate Center, City University of New York (United States)*
Nathaniel Mills, *University of Minnesota (United States)*
Rita Mookerjee, *Florida State University (United States)*
Alexandra S. Moore, *Binghamton University (United States)*
Christian Moraru, *University of North Carolina, Greensboro (United States)*

Warren Motte, *University of Colorado, Boulder (United States)*
John Mowitt, *University of Leeds (United States)*
Matthew Mullins, *Southeastern Baptist Theological Seminary (United States)*
Stuart J. Murray, *Carleton University (Canada)*

N
Jeffrey T. Nealon, *Penn State University (United States)*
Kalliopi Nikolopoulou, *University at Buffalo (United States)*
Mathias Nilges, *St. Francis Xavier University (Canada)*
Dany Nobus, *Brunel University London (United Kingdom)*
Daniel Rosenberg Nutters, *Temple University (United States)*

O
Phil O'Brien, *University of Manchester (United Kingdom)*
Sharon O'Dair, *University of Alabama (United States)*
Daniel T. O'Hara, *Temple University (United States)*
Brian O'Keeffe, *Barnard College (United States)*
Dorothea Olkowski, *University of Colorado, Colorado Springs (United States)*

P
Jussi Parikka, *Winchester School of Art, University of Southampton (United Kingdom)*
John W. P. Phillips, *National University of Singapore (Singapore)*
Charles Platter, *University of Georgia (United States)*
Simon Porzak, *Columbia University (United States)*
Gerald Prince, *University of Pennsylvania (United States)*

R
Jean-Michel Rabaté, *University of Pennsylvania (United States)*
Swapnil Rai, *Brown University (United States)*
Masood Raja, *University of North Texas (United States)*
Herman Rapaport, *Wake Forest University (United States)*
Scott Rettberg, *University of Bergen (Norway)*
Carlin Romano, *Urinus College (United States)*
Amit Ron, *Arizona State University (United States)*
Arthur Rose, *Durham University (United Kingdom)*

S
Kenneth J. Saltman, *University of Massachusetts, Dartmouth (United States)*
Jeffrey A. Sartain, *University of Houston-Victoria (United States)*
Laura Savu, *Columbia College, South Carolina (United States)*
Sean Sayers, *University of Kent (United Kingdom)*
Darrow Schecter, *University of Sussex (United Kingdom)*
Matthew Schilleman, *University of Massachusetts, Amherst (United States)*
Marta Segarra, Universitat de Barcelona (Spain)
Joshua Shaw, *Penn State University (United States)*
Charles Shepherdson, *University at Albany, SUNY (United States)*
David R. Shumway, *Carnegie Mellon University (United States)*

Nicole Simek, *Whitman College (United States)*
Alan Singer, *Temple University (United States)*
Joseph R. Slaughter, *Columbia University (United States)*
Richard G. Smith, *Swansea University (United Kingdom)*
Joel P. Sodano, *Keele University (United Kingdom)*
William Spanos, *Binghamton University (United States)*
C. Allen Speight, *Boston University (United States)*
Tanja Staehler, *University of Sussex (United Kingdom)*
Lara Stevens, *University of Melbourne (Australia)*
Ted Stolze, *Cerritos College (United States)*
Brad Elliott Stone, *Loyola Marymount University (United States)*
Henry Sussman, *Yale University (United States)*
Imre Szeman, *University of Waterloo (Canada)*

T
Joseph Tabbi, *University of Illinois, Chicago (United States)*
Robert J. Tally Jr., *Texas State University (United States)*
Lian Tanguay, *University of Houston-Victoria (United States)*
Zachary Tavlin, *School of the Art Institute of Chicago (United States)*
Paul J. Thibault, *University of Agder, Kristiansand (Norway)*
Calvin Thomas, *Georgia State University (United States)*
Dominic Thomas, *University of California, Los Angeles (United States)*
David Trend, *University of California, Irvine (United States)*
Stephen Tumino, *Fordham University (United States)*
Aidan Tynan, *Cardiff University (United Kingdom)*

U
Gregory L. Ulmer, *University of Florida (United States)*
Steven Ungar, *University of Iowa (United States)*

V
Georges Van Den Abbeele, *University of California, Irvine (United States)*
Pol Vandevelde, *Marquette University (United States)*
Harold Aram Veeser, *City University of New York (United States)*

W
Michael Wayne, *Brunel University London (United Kingdom)*
Jamieson Webster, *Eugene Lang College at The New School (United States)*
Phillip E. Wegner, *University of Florida (United States)*
Donald R. Wehrs, *Auburn University (United States)*
Charles Wells, *Wilfrid Laurier University (Canada)*
Jeffrey J. Williams, *Carnegie Mellon University (United States)*
Alden Sajor Wood, *University of California, Irvine (United States)*
Simon Morgan Wortham, *Kingston University (United Kingdom)*

Z
Zahi Zalloua, *Whitman College (United States)*

Introduction: Theory in the New Millennium

JEFFREY R. DI LEO

Theory is stronger now than it ever was in the twentieth century. The reason for this is not necessarily a deepening or intensification of the work of theory in traditional areas such as literary criticism and critique (though arguments may be made here), but rather a widening or broadening of its reach and domain. This book aims to illustrate this by bringing together original contributions from 230 theorists from across the globe.

Through twenty-seven chapters on topics ranging from theory's engagement with the ancient world (Chapter 1, Early Theory) to a survey of various efforts to challenge some versions of theory (Chapter 27, Antitheory), a vibrant working portrait of theory in the twenty-first century begins to take shape. While the focus in these chapters is to provide insight into many of the major concerns of twenty-first-century theory and theorists, an effort is also made to acknowledge the shape of twentieth-century theory and earlier for context and inspiration. Chapter contributors were encouraged to not just look backward regarding their topic, but to look forward as well and to entertain the possibilities for theory in the new millennium in their area of concern. They were also asked for a listing of key terms and figures related to their chapter topic. These lists were then culled to form the basis for the three hundred and nine term-and-figure entries that comprise the second half of this book.

Consequently, the three hundred-plus terms and figures in Part 2 of this book complement the chapters in Part 1. The two hundred and fifty-eight entries on some of the key terms utilized by theorists in the new millennium, and the fifty-one entries on central figures in twenty-first-century theory provide a finer grained portrait of theory in the new millennium, one that supplements the chapters in Part 1. Most of the term-and-figure entries though are written by a different group of contributors than those who penned the chapters. These briefer entries provide a gallery of micro-pictures of theory in the new millennium to consider alongside the macro-portraits of the chapters. Together the two halves of this book are in effect two separate galleries of theory. Though about equal in length, they present varying ways to portray theory in the new millennium.

By limiting the word counts on the terms and figures in Part 2, contributors were encouraged to write less encyclopedically and more essayistically. Unlike encyclopedia entries that are intended to give the air of "objectivity," the term-and-figure entries in this book, where appropriate, reveal openly the interests and concerns of their author—whose name and affiliation is clearly noted after each entry. Moreover, it is no coincidence that many of the term-and-figure contributors are themselves authors of work on this term or figure. And rather than hiding this, they were encouraged to foreground it in either the entry itself or the suggestions for further reading. In addition, each of the term-and-figure entries is generously cross-listed with other entries as well as with the chapters to facilitate a dynamic and open-ended vision of theory in the new millennium. Tracking terms and figures through their network of associations and affiliations allows one to discover not only the breadth of theory today, but also new possibilities for it.

The possibilities for theory in the new millennium are directly connected more than anything else to its disciplinary shape and identity within the academy. After all, unlike, say, novelists who often are not members of the academy, theorists in the new millennium are more often than not *members* of the academy (though perhaps less by choice than fiscal necessity). Therefore, it is not unreasonable to consider theory as primarily situated in the academic context of disciplinarity and departments. So, what then is its disciplinary context? Is it narrow like philosophy or broad like interdisciplinary studies? Fortunately, for theory it is more like the latter than the former.

Theory in the new millennium is a multi- and interdisciplinary endeavor that operates within and among the humanities (particularly, history, languages, linguistics, the arts, philosophy, and religion, in addition to literature), the social sciences (including anthropology, ethnic and cultural studies, economics, political science, psychology, and sociology), and many of the professions (e.g., architecture, business, communication, education, environmental studies, journalism, law, museum studies, media studies, military science, public policy, and sport science, among others). In addition to its now somewhat more standard-fare work in these areas, of which prime examples may be found throughout this book, it has also made some substantial inroads into the natural sciences (e.g., biology, physics, the earth sciences, and the space sciences) and the formal sciences (especially mathematics, computer science, and systems science).[1] To be sure, more disciplines from across the academy have integrated theory into their practice than at any other time in history—and, in many ways, theory today is the id of the disciplines and the engine of interdisciplinary studies. This, of course, is good news for theorists and theory at large.

Moreover, the academic community that engages, supports, and uses theory in the twenty-first century is not only much larger in number than it ever was in the twentieth century, for many the presumed "heyday of theory," it is also, in part as a consequence of its multi- and interdisciplinary reach, more diverse with respect to the objects and subjects of its attention. In addition to traditional objects of theoretical engagement such as literary, philosophical, and artistic texts, many others are now becoming commonplace such as new media, the environment, and even the university itself. But theory has also extended the range of *subjects* of its attention. In addition to more commonplace ones such as narrative, identity, translation, and rhetoric, subjects such as affect, globalization, biopolitics, political economy, and institutions have emerged as major concerns for theory. Many of these new and emerging objects and subjects of theory are discussed in the chapters, and term-and-figure entries in this book. For that matter, this introduction itself deals with one of the major concerns of theory and theorists today, namely, its institutionalization and place within the academy, which is itself a field of theory.

The popularity and strength of theory in the new millennium is directly related to the fearlessness it engenders in individuals and communities to question the precepts and extend the boundaries of individual disciplines as well as to draw the disciplines into dialogue with each other. In addition, theory's willingness to turn its critical powers toward the problems facing society and the world at large—as well as upon itself—proves to be still another point of attraction. This is why there seems to be nary a subject or object that has not been engaged in some way or another by theory today. To be sure, most everything is fair game for theory—even theory itself.

Still, while more academics than ever before use theory today in their critical practices, only a small percentage of them self-affiliate as "theorists." This is a problem for theory because affiliations confer value and identity on individuals, disciplines, and institutions. They also have a formative role in determining the status and self-image of theory.[2] As such, through the lens of affiliation, the theory community itself is a small one that is getting smaller, particularly as the older generation of theorists change tense. Without the influx of a new generation of theorists, theory appears on the brink of demise. But all here is not as it appears. Part of the explanation of this apparent decline is that theory is undergoing a sort of identity crisis. The kind of theory that dominates the new century is very different from the kind of theory presented in the textbooks of the previous one.

Late twentieth-century literary and cultural theory charted its identity and progress through a series of schools and movements designated by "-isms": formalism, structuralism, new criticism, psychoanalytic criticism, post-structuralism, linguistic criticism, Marxism, feminism, cultural materialism, New Historicism, new pragmatism, reader-response criticism, postcolonialism, postmodernism, and so on. The adjectives "new" and "post" added to these "-isms" were major points of discussion and disagreement. Also discussed was whether any of these "-isms" could be reduced to a method or system. Progress and development in theory was denoted by the "invention" of new "-isms," the appending of these two adjectives to outdated "-isms," and the success of efforts to find a method in the madness of key theorists such as Roland Barthes, Jacques Derrida, and Michel Foucault—and sharing it with others.

For many today, the problem seems to be not the importance, significance, and relevance of theory to subjects of concern and objects of study, but rather the identification of oneself as a "theorist"—a term with closer associations to the critical schools and movements of the twentieth century than the emerging and energetic forms of theory of the twenty-first century. Like the great American thinker, Charles Peirce, who wanted nothing more to do with "pragmatism" after William James popularized it and refused to be called a "pragmatist," preferring instead to be called a "pragma*ti*cist," theorists today seem to be distancing themselves from the general term used to describe their work.[3] However, unlike Peirce who thought James dumbed down pragmatism by popularizing it, many "theorists" in the new millennium are moving in the opposite direction. Namely, they are moving to more populist instantiations of theory by taking on subjects and objects of more general concern and access.

As such, for them, there is some discomfort and inappropriateness in being called or considered a "theorist." In addition, the term "posttheorist," which may seem an appropriate one and may have served some transitional need to describe the emergence of new forms of theory in the 1990s, is today an anachronistic and inaccurate one. Finally, the term "theore*ti*cist" a la Peirce is a really ugly one, so it too is probably off the table as an option. We are left then with a naming problem. To self-identify as a "theorist" today is for many to put oneself in the company of the past, rather than the present. However, there is not a better term to describe the current and copious work that has followed in the footsteps, at least in an historical sense, of the movements and schools of the twentieth century.

Still, the self-affiliation problems of "theorists" do not change the fact that the community in the new millennium that uses and engages the work of theory is larger and more diverse in its interests than ever. Perhaps reluctant theorists today need to do like the pop musician and singer Prince and take up a glyph as their common name, rather than the apparently outdated designation "theorist." Though as this did not last very long for the man from Paisley Park—he gave up on the glyph and returned to his real name—there is not much hope that it will solve theorist's problem's either (even though it would be cool to do so).[4]

If anything has died in the world of theory in the twenty-first century, then it is the dominance of its "-isms." There was a time in the previous century when affiliation with an "-ism" was the required badge of entry into the theory world. One was not just a "theorist," but a member of a specific subcommunity of theory designated by an "-ism." Just as the world of religion has Catholicism, Judaism, and Buddhism, the world of theory had structuralism, Marxism, and feminism. And the lines of division between them within the theory community were at times no less flexible than those within the religious community. One of the most celebrated of all of the theory communities was "deconstruction's 'community,'" which Henry Sussman identifies in Chapter 9 as including "Hélène Cixous, Paul de Man, J. Hillis Miller, Jean-Luc Nancy, Philippe Lacoue-Labarthe, Bernard Stiegler, Samuel Weber, Jonathan Culler, Gayatri Chakravorty Spivak, Rodolphe Gasché, Carol Jacobs, Werner Hamacher, Catherine Malabou, Avital Ronell, John Sallis, Geoff Bennington, Robert Bernasconi, and Tom Cohen." Reports Sussman, "for all that its convener [Jacques Derrida] looked askance at this term [deconstruction], has held remarkably tight to its inaugural specifications."

But community "tightness" in theory also had another side. Think about how search committees used to badger job candidates with parochial questions about their theoretical affiliation? To do so today almost seems like a violation of FERPA laws. And woe be to the job candidate who professed the wrong theoretical affiliation. Or confessed to the right one, but was not in line with the preferred house of postmodernism or version of feminism? Though the late twentieth century may have been the heyday of "high" theory, in retrospect, it appears much more provincial and doctrinaire compared to the world of theory in the new millennium—one that is not only much more pluralistic and amorphous but also less tight and divisive than the previous one.[5]

Whereas in the past, fault lines between and distinctions within "-isms" often became feuding points among theorists, the new object- or subject-centered world of theory is a much less divisive one. Who today is going to argue that the object or subject of your theoretical affection (say, pop music or affect) is the wrong one? Or that working on "debt" is superior to working on "masculinity"? Though there is still some bickering about "whose" debt and "which" masculinity is the right, valid, or true one, such complaints seem more reactionary than progressive, scholastic than pluralistic—and ultimately thus less acceptable—after the demise of the big house of new-, post-, and original flavor "-isms." Theoretical attention to objects or subjects allows for more pluralism and toleration in the theory world compared to its previous incarnation as a world of schools, movements, and -isms. Though, as we will see below, the new object- and subject-centric world of theory has many more *divisions* than the theory world of "-isms," it is also a much less *divisive* one.

The shift from high theory to low theory lessened the divisiveness among theorists. Twentieth-century theory invested a lot in its "-isms," but most all have fallen on hard times in the new millennium—even if a few new ones have surfaced. For one thing, the theory world of the twentieth century often appeared as a war of all against all. Macho theorists wielded their -isms against each other both as a primary way of theoretical life and as a way to achieve power and dominance within the academy. In doing so, the world of theory came to look more and more like the world of philosophy, where disputes and disagreements are viewed as the modus operandi of the field—and professional power is afforded to those who battle their way to being the last man standing.

No area of theory in the twentieth century attracted, if not also welcomed, dispute more than the high or grand theory exemplified through the work of figures such as Jacques Lacan, Julia Kristeva, Hélène Cixous, Jean-François Lyotard, Gilles Deleuze, Michel Foucault, and Jacques Derrida. These structuralist and post-structuralist thinkers set an impressive high-profile agenda for theory in the late twentieth century. It was also, though, a very divisive one, that is, one that met with, if not also encouraged, opposition from many different quarters.

A strong case may be made that post-structuralist responses to social and political events such as Jean Baudrillard's to the Gulf War in *The Gulf War Did Not Take Place* (*La Guerre du Golfe n'a pas eu lieu* [1991]), and then again to the events of September 11, 2001, in "L'esprit du terrorisme" (2002) and "Requiem pour les Twin Towers" (2002) were some of the straws that broke the camel's back of twentieth-century theory—and presaged the major changes in the temper of theory to come, which is to say, theory in the new millennium.[6] I still remember the negative reactions of students who were or knew veterans of the Gulf War, and of those grieving the death and destruction of September 11, 2001, to these works by Baudrillard—and of the feeling I had at the time that high theory responses like Baudrillard's to major current events might not be a good thing in the long run for theory. It is one thing to speculate on simulation while watching *The Matrix*, but quite another to try to present a case to students that the towers fell on their own while at the same time being respectful to the names and lives of those who died in the plane crashes that brought the towers down.

Vincent Leitch, one the contributors to this book, notes that the opposition to high theory came "from not only conservative scholars, but also a broad array of contending liberal and left theorists, indicting it (particularly post-structuralism) for philosophical idealism, nominalism, obscurantism, and quietism, charges early made famous by certain Marxists, feminists, critical race theorists, and cultural studies scholars."[7] Work like Baudrillard's in the wake of the events of September 11, 2001, only added fuel to the fire.

I mention the *divisiveness* not as a character flaw of high theory (for some it was and still is one of its endearing qualities, especially for those relishing the role of enfant terrible, as Richard G. Smith, for example, describes Baudrillard in his figure entry on him for this book[8]), but rather as a point of differentiation with the world of theory that succeeded it. As we now know, the high or grand theory exemplified by the work of Deleuze, Foucault, and Kristeva was eclipsed in the 1990s by both low theory, which found its form in a multitude of "studies," and posttheory, "a pragmatic approach to theory which leads them to assess various theoretical models on the basis of the socio-cultural and political understanding that these models bring about."[9] To be sure, the modus operandi of "studies" and "posttheory" was anything but a divisive one. The aim of the studies and posttheory generation that followed in the wake of the high road of twentieth-century theory was less to put down differing projects, than to vigorously and interdisciplinarily pursue and study the object or subject of its theoretical attention. In fact, differing projects appear to the studies and posttheory generation not as *competition*, but rather as extensions of a common critical or theoretical spirit signified by their shared use of the term "studies."

Moreover, the succeeding generation of theorists were much less obsessed with *how* they accomplished the study of the object or subject at hand, than *why* they were pursuing it. In other words, method took a backseat to things such as public interest, social and political activism, and ethics. It is a trend in theory that continues today, namely, to do theory with an eye toward making the world a better place, rather than avoiding it or trying to deny its existence.

In a way then, theory "after theory" never changed tense, it just changed focus. Since the ascent of high theory (or the even higher, so-called sky-high theory or "theoreticism"[10]) and the emergence of various forms of opposition to it, rumors of and statements about the demise of theory have persisted. Even today, closure regarding the issue seems remote. It is often said that "theory is dead"—superseded by a multitude of studies. Gone are theory stalwarts such as deconstruction, Marxism, and feminism. They have been replaced by studies of everything and anything from Barbie dolls and Beyonce to biopolitics and books. In fact, a significant number of the 258 term entries in this book are themselves "studies"[11] areas including affect, archive, canon, class, critical climate, cyborg, debt, diaspora, disability, ethnicity, gender, genre, globalization, labor, law, materialism, memory, migration, minority, multiculturalism, neoliberalism, object, performativity, pop culture, postcolonial, posthuman, print culture, queer, race, reading, reception, resistance, rights, sexuality, sound, subaltern, subculture, surveillance, translation, trauma, university, whiteness, and many others.[12]

This emerging and expanding multitude of literary and cultural theory in the twenty-first century leaves little or no room for the more dominant outline of literary theory and criticism, namely, one which divides it into schools and movements. Designators of the outlines of theory and criticism such as Russian formalism, New Criticism, psychoanalysis, feminism, Marxism, structuralism, post-structuralism, queer theory, New Historicism, and postcolonial theory are strictly a twentieth-century phenomenon. Though these designators were important to the emergence of "theory" in the last quarter of the twentieth century, they have outlived their usefulness for mapping literary and cultural theory in the twenty-first century. The explosion of "studies" in the first quarter of the twenty-first century leaves little opportunity for organizing literary and cultural theory into the older matrix of schools and movements. Or, alternately stated, studies as sub-species of the "twentieth-century" schools and movements make for a very messy and confusing outline. Hence, why bother? Better to just leave it to the historians of theory to trace the legacies of theory amid the "studies" multitude.

What then to do with "theory," that is, the sum body of the twentieth century's schools and movements in the wake of the explosion of twenty-first-century "studies"? For me, the answer, as evidenced through the title and organization of this book, is one of enthusiastic embrace, rather than rejection. The heterogeneity of "theory" today is a sign of its strength, rather than an indication of its weakness or failure. The aim of this book is to provide a resource to theory in the new millennium. It does so by offering hundreds of different doors to enter the new millennial world of theory. While some of these doors are recognizable schools or movements in theory such as structuralism, feminism, and Marxism, many of these doors are not—and they are open to nascent worlds of millennial theory.

In short, because there is no other term that adequately captures the "proliferation" of objects and subjects of critical attention today, the designator "theory" needs to continue to be used. This approach to theory in the twenty-first century is the proper one and as a whole represents a powerful, collective response to the so-called death of theory.[13] Not only is theory not dead—in spite of the recent passing of many of its major progenitors— it is undergoing a "reinvention" of sorts today. To put it bluntly, the death of theory is an illusion—and the future of this illusion, through efforts such as this book, will hopefully be short-lived.[14]

Still, what happens if we replace all of the uses of "studies" in conjunction with the multitude of objects and subjects now associated with it with the term "theory" and make its implicit references explicit? For one thing, doing so would end the charade that all of these "studies" are not second-generation theory—or dare we say, "*new* theory"? For transitional purposes, it was important at the end of the twentieth century to designate this work with a term other than theory. But a quarter-century later it just seems silly and is needlessly confusing. Theory is not dead—it just changed its name when its focus and the objects of its attention began to broaden and change. Calling theory "theory," rather than "studies," allows the larger and committed community dedicated to it to regroup and retool their identity in the wake of major changes in the theory world. It is past time that this was done.

Theorists today, much like the "deconstruction community" noted above by Sussman, still work in affiliation with communities of shared interest and concern. This notion has at times been expressed by the statement "theorists run in packs," one most commonly associated with Stanley Fish's idea of "interpretive communities." Fish uses the notion of "interpretive communities" to answer the question as to "why will different readers execute the same interpretive strategies when faced with the 'same' text?," particularly as "*they don't have to.*"[15] "Interpretive communities," writes Fish, "are made up of those who share interpretive strategies not for reading (in the conventional sense) but for writing texts, for constituting their properties and assigning their intentions."[16] Borrowing from his idea of "community" in theory, it is here being extended well beyond just "interpretive strategies" for "writing texts"—to all of the ways in which theory brings critics and activists together around shared interests and into networks of concern, that is, engages them with common subjects and objects of theoretical attention.

The notion of communities (or networks) of theorists applies equally to men and women; to students and teachers; to the high priests and low practitioners of theory. It has no sexual preference, requires no specific pedigree, and is blind to race and class. It always already reminds us that in spite of the individuality of our voices and the perceived solitude of scholarly pursuits, there is a form of affiliational collectivity that underlies the work of theory—and its multitude of areas of concern and interest. To argue for the validity of this statement is to argue for theory in the best sense of the term—for its continuing relevance; for its continued existence. It is an argument that can be made simply by observing the ways in which theory materializes and comes to be. It asks us to see individuals within the academy affiliating, rather than atomizing; as forming both relations with others, and relationships to distinct places or regions of critical exchange.

The most basic forms of affiliation are the groups and organizations we join in the name of theory. One need look no further than the Allied Organization Directory of the Modern Language Association of America (MLA) to catch a sense of their depth and diversity: the American Comparative Literature Association, the American Name Society, the American Psychoanalytic Association, the American Translators Association, the Association for Computers and the Humanities, the Association for the Study of Literature and the Environment, the Conference on Christianity and Literature, Feministas Unidas, the GL/Q Caucus for the Modern Languages, the Graduate Student Caucus, the International Society for the Study of Narrative, the Marxist Literary Group, the Modernist Studies Association, the Radical Caucus in English and Modern Languages, the Reception Study Society, the Rhetoric Society of America, the Society for Medieval Feminist Scholarship, and the Society for Critical Exchange.

Each of these organizations have allied with the MLA in an effort to further their theoretical interests.[17] Panels are offered each year at the MLA to forward the theoretical agendas of each organization. While there are many societies and organizations affiliated with specific authors (e.g., Thoreau, Faulkner, and Goethe), languages (e.g., Italian, Portuguese), periods (e.g., eighteenth century, medieval), and areas of teaching (e.g., teachers of German, teachers of technical writing), the presence of distinctly theory-based organizations affiliated with the MLA attests to one of the more important forms of theoretical affiliation.[18] But there are many others aside from professional organizations.

Academic journals, for example, are a form of theoretical affiliation. Communities of theorists gravitate around one or more of them with respect to their specific interests. They write articles and book reviews for them; they peer-review each other's work; and they serve as editors and advisers to them; so too are scholarly presses, conference proceedings, blogs, discussion groups, reading groups, colloquia, symposiums, and institutes. Theoretical affiliation has many different venues and far too many are supported by active and passionate communities of scholars to even posit that theory is not alive and well. If one turns to each of the areas of theoretical concern and interest, they will find that each in turn has numerous venues and communities that support, encourage, and facilitate work in the area. Some support multiple areas of concern and interest, while others only support one though their relative inclusivity and exclusivity does not impede their role in or support of theoretical affiliation.

To really kill theory, one would need to shut down all of these venues. To make it sick, start diminishing their overall number. But fortunately, such acts of academic terrorism against theory are not occurring with great frequency. In fact, the opposite seems to be happening. There are more venues now than ever to engage in theory. Some are traditional, such as conferences and journals, but others are new, such as blogs and online discussion groups. These venues multiply as theory expands its reach into new disciplines, subjects, and objects, if not also the commons itself. Not only is the community for theory alive and well, it is continuously growing and expanding in a variety of ways.

Theorists today often affiliate simultaneously with different areas of concern and interest. For example, it is not uncommon to see a theorist committed to critically exploring neoliberalism *and* one or more other zones of critical inquiry. Debt or university studies, for example, are often paired with neoliberalism to produce more specialized zones of critical exchange like *critical* debt studies. But so too are many other zones of critical exchange paired like empire, postcolonial studies, and academic labor studies.

Working in several different areas of theoretical interest at the same time albeit with differing intensities is part of the strength of millennial theory. One of the major differences say between twentieth-century theory and twenty-first-century theory is the more exclusive nature of theoretical work in the previous century. If in the twentieth century, psychoanalysis, semiotics, deconstruction, and feminism had any meaning, then it was generated through the common work of a particular area of theory. To be a theorist was to associate strongly with at least one school or movement of criticism or theory. If one self-identified as a working theorist during this period, it would not be unusual, as noted before, to be asked to *what* school of criticism or theory one belonged. Each school had a more or less distinct identity, and several leaders and master texts. For example, there was no way to affiliate with psychoanalysis *without* Freud and/or Lacan, no way to be a semiotician *without* Saussure and/or Peirce. The same, however, cannot be said of those who affiliate with the subjects and objects of the new millennial theoretical multitude. Take, for example, two of the more fruitful and well-known zones in the theoretical multitude today, neoliberalism and disability.

Sure, one can say that in the twenty-first century it is impossible to affiliate with neoliberalism without also affiliating with Milton Friedman, Friedrich von Hayek, and John Maynard Keynes, or that disability without Michael Berube, Lennard Davis, and Tobin Siebers is empty, the scale of affiliation is much different than it was in the twentieth century. To do semiotic theory without Saussure or Peirce was *impossible* in the twentieth century. However, to do disability studies without Berube or Davis today is not a mortal wound. Though your work may be impoverished without the presence of one of the leaders of your area of concern, it is not immediately invalidated. So too is the case with Milton Friedman, Friedrich von Hayek, and John Maynard Keynes in neoliberal theory.

The ability of theorists to work in different areas of theory at the same time is one the strengths of theory in the new millennium. When such opportunities presented themselves in the 1990s, the nervous reaction to them was to call them "posttheory."[19] The fear was that theorists who worked in several different areas were in some way watering down or destroying the purity of theory. This may have been true in the 1990s when theoretical work was more insular, but in the twenty-first century, not only is it acceptable as a theorist to work in several different areas of theoretical inquiry, *it is more the norm than the exception.*

So if theory is united through communities or networks of shared interest and concern, then one of the ways to destroy theory is to pull apart or atomize them. John Ellis sensed this when he wrote back in the late 1990s in support of his version of "antitheory" that "theorists do not run in packs."[20] His proposal was that

> they are individuals who set out to crack particular theoretical problems by thinking hard about them. Their work is solitary; it is never fashionable and must always be estranged from orthodoxies. It follows that a theory elite can arise only when theory has ceased to function effectively and when the individuals who are a part of it no longer act like theorists. Real theorists thrive on the concept of argument and counterargument that is central to theoretical analysis, but race-class-gender scholars show a marked tendency to avoid facing the substance of the arguments of the critics.[21]

While there are many things with which to take issue in this statement by Ellis, perhaps the most important one is the notion that the work of theorists is "solitary." Nothing is further from the truth.

Though some theoretical communities are smaller than others, a community of one is not a community. Theoretical problems do require hard thinking, and making arguments and counterarguments as a theorist is a common practice, but to pursue problems and arguments outside of a community is like trying to play chess without an opponent. It may seem like chess, but it isn't. The same is true with theory.

With a community comes the critical exchange that is necessary for theory to adapt to better meet the needs of the community. Without critical exchange, theoretical communities risk becoming frozen in time or crystalized—that is, they hazard establishing orthodoxies that are impervious to critique and never develop or change. But orthodoxy in itself is not the problem.

Orthodoxies bring communities together. They give them a sense of self-identity and shared-momentum. They put theory in motion. Sometimes they bring it down roads well traveled, whereas other times they do not. It is often the interplay between orthodoxy and community that makes the theoretical journey a productive and progressive one. All of this is not to say that theorists cannot or should not be trailblazers. Original and heterodox theory is not only important for progress in theory, but also for challenging the status quo. Nevertheless, it is only possible against the backdrop of orthodoxies shared by communities. If Ellis's point is that there are pioneers in theory, then I have no problem with this. If his point though is that theorists must work in a vacuum, which he seems to be saying, then he is wrong. Working in a theoretical community may result in the creation of new directions for theory, but theory that is not the consequence of some type of community life is better left on its own and ignored.

"Fashionable theory" or the "latest big thing in theory" may not be everyone's preference. But it is also not a bad thing for people to be excited about new directions or trends in theory. Again, "fashionable" or heterodox theory is only intelligible within the context of "unfashionable" or orthodox theory. Moreover, if no one believes in a proposed "theory" and if no community forms around it, isn't this just solipsism? Or worse yet, narcissism? For Ellis, theory that builds a community around it is "a degraded and corrupt shadow of what theory should be."[22] I strongly disagree.

When theory does not work within a community, it risks irrelevance or worse yet, death. The best way to destroy a theory is for no one to believe in it. Theoretical innovation may begin with the unorthodox work of one individual, but it will end there if it continues to lurk in the shadows of the theory community. Moreover, there is nothing wrong or elite with being the leader of a community of theorists. After all, communities without leadership inevitably fail.

In sum, theory without community is dead theory. Community helps it to survive, thrive, and stay relevant. Theorists without community lapse into esotericism and risk becoming irrelevant. The solitary theorist is nothing to be celebrated. Rather it is something to be mourned. But still, the flourishing and multiplication of subjects and objects of theoretical intrigue in the twenty-first century presents a challenge to creating and sustaining community in theory. If one does not have the relatively limited number of schools and movements around which to build community, but rather have the scores of objects and subjects such as those listed above and in Part 2 of this book, then creating community around this multitude can be a challenge.

If there is any problem with theory in the new millennium, it is that the multitude of theoretical objects and subjects today leaves theorists with too many choices for theoretical affiliation. There are so many, in fact, that the whole notion of affiliation can become as overwhelming as trying to visualize the whole field of theory today. Let us again take, for example, affiliation with neoliberalism, one of the few -isms still in vogue today.

In twenty-first-century theory, "neoliberalism" has become one of our most visible and productive sites for critical exchange. For many, it implies both a critique of late capitalism and the belief that political economy is something that is worthy of our critical attention. Theorists who affiliate with this subject both explore differing ways to define its terms and defend its territories as well as survey alternative histories and extensions of it.

However, theorists who work on neoliberal theory and who find this subject a valuable point of or nexus for critical inquiry, again, more than likely have interests in one or more other areas of theory as well. Moreover, there may also be other subjects and objects and along with them their communities of inquirers that also fit well with the interests of neoliberal inquiry. This is one of the exciting features of the brave new world of twenty-first-century theory: namely, the way in which it encourages different communities to network with each other in the shared pursuit of theory. It is also one of the more intimidating features of theory in the new millennium, for it is often unclear where affiliations should begin—and where they should end.

The community activity of theorists involves reading and commenting on each other's work. It also involves using the theoretical work of others as a launching pad for your own work either positively as a source of critical insight—or negatively as a foil. Sometimes, theorists praise each other. Other times they disagree with each other. Some theoretical communities have recognizable leaders, while others don't. Regardless, community is essential to the well-being of theory.

Theory today is a community, or, more precisely, a set of communities. They may not go by recognizable names like the feminism, deconstruction, and psychoanalysis of the last century, but theory still is driven by communities of individuals who share common bonds of theoretical pursuit and interest. Like all communities, theoretical ones go through periods of growth and popularity—and periods of decline and unpopularity. Some become fashionable, while others languish in relative obscurity. For example, few today seem to want to live in the structuralist community. Though it was once a thriving and active one, arguments and disagreements within the community led many to move to other communities or to take part in the formation of new ones. And this, of course, is not a bad thing. Just look at what the legacies of structuralism gave to the world of theory, including, most significantly, post-structuralism, the roots of which still branch through much millennial theory.

While community is not unique to theorists, it does not diminish its importance in understanding how theory works, flourishes, and even sometimes fails. Theory today has a large, robust, and strong community, one that anyone who values it needs to support. Without the support of communities, theory risks becoming the solitary and esoteric entity envisioned by Ellis. Working in one or several communities of theorists allows theory to flourish and thrive in the new millennium as it continues the process of refiguring or remapping its purview. The chapters, and term-and-figure entries, in this book energetically demonstrate that theory in the new millennium is neither isolated nor dead. Rather, it is supported and strengthened by a global network of scholars committed to not just the survival of theory—but to its continued development and relevancy, particularly in dark times.

University of Houston, Victoria (United States)

NOTES

1. I will leave it up to the reader to explore the various connections of all of these areas to theory. While the bibliography in the natural sciences and formal sciences is much less extensive than in the humanities, social sciences, and professions, there are still examples in all of these areas of the multi- and interdisciplinary inroads of theory into these areas. The challenge is not so much to find examples as to determine ways to assess the impact or value of the specific examples.

2. See Jeffrey R. Di Leo, ed., *Affiliations: Identity in Academic Culture* (Lincoln: University of Nebraska Press, 2003), for an introduction to the role of "affiliation" in academic culture.

3. Here is Peirce writing on why he adopts the term "pragmaticism" instead of the more common "pragmatism," a term which he also coined:

    His [Peirce's] word "pragmatism" has gained general recognition in a generalized sense that seems to argue power of growth and vitality. The famed psychologist, James, first took it up, seeing that his "radical empiricism" substantially answered to the writer's definition of pragmatism, albeit with a certain difference in the point of view. Next, the admirably clear and brilliant thinker, Mr. Ferdinand C. S. Schiller, casting about for a more attractive name for the "anthropomorphism" of his *Riddle of the Sphinx*, lit, in that most remarkable paper of his on *Axioms as Postulates*, upon the same designation "pragmatism," which in its original sense was in generic agreement with his own doctrine, for which he has since found the more appropriate specification "humanism," while he still retains 'pragmatism' in a somewhat wider sense. So far all went happily. But at present, the word begins to be met with occasionally in the literary journals, where it gets abused in the merciless way that words have to expect when they fall into literary clutches. Sometimes the manners of the British have effloresced in scolding at the word as ill-chosen—ill-chosen, that is, to express some meaning that it was rather designed to exclude. So then, the writer, finding his bantling "pragmatism" so promoted, feels that it is time to kiss his child good-by and relinquish it to its higher destiny; while to serve the precise purpose of expressing the original definition, he begs to announce the birth of the word "pragmaticism," which is ugly enough to be safe from kidnappers.

Charles S. Peirce, *Collected Papers of Charles Sanders Peirce*, six vols., eds. Charles Hartshorne and Paul Weiss (Cambridge: Harvard University Press, 1931–35), vol. 5, para. 414.

4. In 1993, Prince Rogers Nelson changed his name to a glyph as an act of defiance toward his record label, Warner Brothers, which was trying to slow down his creative output to suit its marketing schedule. He dropped the glyph in 2000 when his record deal with Warner Brothers ended. *Rolling Stone* magazine lists it as the fourth boldest move in the history of rock. See Margaret Rhodes, "The Fascinating Origin Story of Prince's Iconic Symbol," *Wired* (April 22, 2016). https://www.wired.com/2016/04/designers-came-princes-love-symbol-one-night/

5. See Jeffrey R. Di Leo, "On Being and Becoming Affiliated," in *Affiliations: Identity in Academic Culture*, 101–14, for a discussion of affiliating with philosophy versus comparative literature, a case with similarities to the ones proposed here for affiliating with "theory" versus "studies."

6. Or, decidedly turned the academic momentum from theory to studies, or, alternately, from critique to criticism. French theorist Jean Baudrillard's responses, for example, to these two particular events in works like *La Guerre du Golfe n'a pas en lieu* (Paris: Éditions Galilée, 1991), and "L'esprit du terrorisme" (2002) and "Requiem pour les Twin Towers" (2002) (both of which are translated and collected in Jean Baudrillard's *The Spirit of Terrorism* [London: Verso, 2012]) were widely criticized and the subject of much debate. See, Jeffrey R. Di Leo, "The Ruins of Critique," in *Criticism After Critique: Aesthetics, Literature, and the Political*, ed. Jeffrey R. Di Leo (New York: Palgrave, 2014), 1–4.

7. Vincent Leitch, *Living with Theory* (Malden, MA: Blackwell Publishing, 2008), 10.

8. Or as Gary A. Olson terms Stanley Fish in his biography, *Stanley Fish: America's Enfant Terrible, The Authorized Biography* (Carbondale: Southern Illinois University Press, 2016).

9. Jeffrey R. Di Leo and Christian Moraru, "Posttheory Postscriptum," *symplokē* 3.1 (1995): 120. For us, posttheorists both critique extant theory as well as use it to position their work both on and off campus. See also, my entry on "Posttheory" in this book.

10. See, Dominic LaCapra, *History in Transit: Experience, Identity, Critical Theory* (Ithaca, NY: Cornell University Press, 2004), 156.

11. These "studies" often find their way into university curriculums either as individual courses, concentrations, minors, or sometimes even majors. Some, like "disability studies" and "translation studies," have become more mainstream; others like "Beyonce studies,"

an undergraduate degree concentration that was proposed at my own university are less so, but still they reveal the immense range of these "studies" as curricular opportunities.

12. In *Literary Theory in the 21st Century: Theory Renaissance* (New York: Bloomsbury, 2014), Vincent Leitch maps out literary and cultural theory into ninety-four subdisciplines and fields circling around twelve major topics reminiscent of planets and satellites in their relationship. I see, however, a much more amorphosis and extensive relationship among the terms and figures subject to studies. Still, both Leitch and I concur that the galaxy that is theory today is expansive. The first recto of his book contains a chart of the state of "theory" circa 2014.

13. See, for example, Terry Eagleton, *After Theory* (New York: Basic Books, 2003), Nicholas Birns, *Theory after Theory: An Intellectual History of Literary Theory from 1950 to the Early 21st Century* (Buffalo: Broadview Press, 2010), *Theory after "Theory,"* eds. Jane Elliott and Derek Attridge (New York: Routledge, 2011), and, most recently, Vincent Leitch's *Literary Theory in the 21st Century*, for a representative sample.

14. Related to the death of theory is the legacy of theory after the death of so many of its leading lights, from Roland Barthes to Jacques Derrida. Not only has the question of the death of theory haunted theory from its beginnings, but so too has the specter of death. See Jeffrey R. Di Leo, ed., *Dead Theory: Derrida, Death, and the Afterlife of Theory* (London: Bloomsbury, 2016).

15. Stanley Fish, "Interpreting the *Variorum*," in *Is There a Text in This Class?: The Authority of Interpretive Communities* (Cambridge: Harvard University Press, 1980), 170, a chapter first published though in the second volume of *Critical Inquiry* four years earlier.

16. Fish, "Interpreting the *Variorum*," 171.

17. According to the MLA, "Allied organizations are learned societies or professional associations whose interests encompass disciplines represented by the MLA and whose purposes and activities are closely allied to those of the MLA. Since many of their members may also be MLA members, holding sessions during the MLA convention helps attract the maximum number of persons who share their interests. Further, these sessions enrich the range and diversity of the convention offerings. Allied organizations are, however, independent of the association and thus may not use the MLA logo or other trademarked material that would suggest MLA oversight or sponsorship." https://www.mla.org/Convention/Planning-a-Convention-Session/Policies-for-Forums-and-Allied-Organizations

18. https://apps.mla.org/orginfo_directory

19. See more on the state of posttheory in the late 1990s, see Jeffrey R. Di Leo and Christian Moraru, "Posttheory Postscriptum," and "Posttheory, Cultural Studies, and the Classroom: Fragments of a New Pedagogical Discourse," in *Class Issues: Pedagogy, Cultural Studies and the Public Sphere,* ed. Amitava Kumar (New York: New York University Press, 1997), 237–46; and Jeffrey Williams, "The Posttheory Generation," *symplokē* 3.1 (1995): 55–76.

20. John Ellis, *Literature Lost: Social Agendas and the Corruption of the Humanities* (New Haven: Yale University Press, 1997), 202.

21. Ellis, *Literature Lost*, 202.

22. Ibid., 203.

WORKS CITED

Baudrillard, Jean. *La Guerre du Golfe n'a pas en lieu.* Paris: Éditions Galilée, 1991.
Baudrillard, Jean. *The Spirit of Terrorism.* London: Verso, 2012.

Birns, Nicholas. *Theory after Theory: An Intellectual History of Literary Theory from 1950 to the Early 21st Century*. Buffalo: Broadview Press, 2010.

Di Leo, Jeffrey R. "On Being and Becoming Affiliated." In *Affiliations: Identity in Academic Culture*. Ed. Jeffrey R. Di Leo. Lincoln: University of Nebraska Press, 2003. 101–14.

Di Leo, Jeffrey R., ed. *Affiliations: Identity in Academic Culture*. Lincoln: University of Nebraska Press, 2003.

Di Leo, Jeffrey R. "The Ruins of Critique." In *Criticism after Critique: Aesthetics, Literature, and the Political*. Ed. Jeffrey R. Di Leo. New York: Palgrave, 2014. 1–12.

Di Leo, Jeffrey R., ed. *Dead Theory: Derrida, Death, and the Afterlife of Theory*. London: Bloomsbury, 2016.

Di Leo, Jeffrey R., and Christian Moraru. "Posttheory Postscriptum." *symplokē* 3.1 (1995): 119–22.

Di Leo, Jeffrey R., and Christian Moraru. "Posttheory, Cultural Studies, and the Classroom: Fragments of a New Pedagogical Discourse." In *Class Issues: Pedagogy, Cultural Studies and the Public Sphere*. Ed. Amitava Kumar. New York: New York University Press, 1997. 237–46.

Eagleton, Terry. *After Theory*. New York: Basic Books, 2003.

Elliott, Jane, and Derek Attridge, eds. *Theory after "Theory."* New York: Routledge, 2011.

Ellis, John. *Literature Lost: Social Agendas and the Corruption of the Humanities*. New Haven: Yale University Press, 1997.

Fish, Stanley. "Interpreting the *Variorum*." *Critical Inquiry* 2 (1976): 465–85.

Fish, Stanley. *Is There a Text in This Class?: The Authority of Interpretive Communities*. Cambridge: Harvard University Press, 1980.

LaCapra, Dominic. *History in Transit: Experience, Identity, Critical Theory*. Ithaca: Cornell University Press, 2004.

Leitch, Vincent. *Living with Theory*. Malden: Blackwell Publishing, 2008.

Leitch, Vincent. *Literary Theory in the 21st Century: Theory Renaissance*. New York: Bloomsbury, 2014.

Olson, Gary A. *Stanley Fish: America's Enfant Terrible, The Authorized Biography*. Carbondale: Southern Illinois University Press, 2016.

Peirce, Charles S. *Collected Papers of Charles Sanders Peirce*. Six vols. Eds. Charles Hartshorne and Paul Weiss. Cambridge: Harvard University Press, 1931–35.

Rhodes, Margaret. "The Fascinating Origin Story of Prince's Iconic Symbol." *Wired* (April 22, 2016). https://www.wired.com/2016/04/designers-came-princes-love-symbol-one-night/

Williams, Jeffrey. "The Posttheory Generation." *symplokē* 3.1 (1995): 55–76.

PART ONE

Essays

CHAPTER ONE

Early Theory

PAUL ALLEN MILLER

Theory is often considered to be a critical practice of relatively recent vintage. We speak of the linguistic or the theoretical "turn." The problem of course is that "theory" as a separate "thing" is largely a disciplinary fiction. Having begun life in the American university system as "literary theory," in the 1970s and 1980s it represented an attempt to come to terms with the rapid developments in linguistics, philosophy, psychoanalysis, the social sciences, and the formal study of literary and rhetorical technique that were known as structuralism and post-structuralism. These theoretical interventions, mostly centered in post-1968 France,[1] but drawing on traditions of linguistic and literary scholarship that originated in the former Soviet Union, Czechoslovakia, and Denmark, were often combined with the Hegelian Marxism of Frankfurt school critical theory, Georg Lukács, and Bertolt Brecht. The result was a heady mixture of diverse traditions and focused debates. Comparative and general literature programs were at the center of this intellectual ferment in the United States. They combined a traditional interest in the definitional problems of literary form with the cosmopolitan and multilingual perspective necessary to engage these issues. At the same time, philosophy departments in the United States remained tied for the most part to a tradition of Anglo-American logical positivism and scientific empiricism that left little room for the speculatory flights of their continental confrères. Theory was new. Theory was avant-garde. Theory was opposed to traditional scholarship. These were all the truisms of the age.

In fact, however, if one returns to the texts of those who were considered the leading lights of post-structuralist theory, a very different vision emerges. Of course, in many cases, these thinkers offer new insights and contest traditional readings of the texts they examined and of the topics they engaged. But they do so very much from within the dominant traditions of Western thought and by engaging many of the central texts of the Western canon. A number of books and articles have been published in the last twenty years demonstrating the deep engagement of the major thinkers of French post-structuralist theory with the classic texts of Western thought.[2] If theory is a dissident movement within Western thought, it is one with a very long and well-attested pedigree.

In what follows I will offer what limited space demands to be a cursory chronicle of these thinkers' engagement with what we can only call "early theory." I will survey the work of Lacan, Derrida, Cixous, Irigaray, Foucault, and Kristeva in terms of their engagement with the classical past. In each case, we will see that their commitment to early theory is substantive and extensive, offering less a rejection of traditional scholarship than a continuing engagement with it.

There was from the beginning a strong affinity between Lacan's work and philology. As Jean-Michel Rabaté observes, "Lacan . . . stood out among his immediate contemporaries and colleagues in psychiatry as a philosopher who could read Greek and German fluently and who put to good use his knowledge of the classics."[3] For Lacan the study of the Classics was central. His return to Freud sought not to found a series of timeless truths, but to "re-found" the subject in relation to the discrete forms of meaning that structured its desire. It is paradigmatic of Lacan's engagement with Greco-Roman antiquity that in 1959, when searching for a model of pure desire for his seminar on "The Ethics of Psychoanalysis," he chose Sophocles's *Antigone*. His reading of the tragedy represents the climax of a three-year engagement with the tragic genre that had begun with *Hamlet* and would end with Claudel's Coûfontaine trilogy. Throughout this period there are references in the seminars to *Oedipus Tyrannus* and *Oedipus at Colonus*. Nonetheless, it is the reading of the character of Antigone as one who does not cede on her desire that is considered a masterpiece by classicists like Nicole Loraux.

The following year, Lacan focused on Plato's *Symposium* for his seminar on "transference." Socrates, like Antigone, represents for Lacan a purity that exceeds the bounds of communally acknowledged goods. His *atopia*, as Alcibiades terms it,[4] places him beyond the bounds of the order defined by the Athenian *polis*, and it is that singularity that is the basis of his purity. What Lacan sought in the figure of Socrates as portrayed in the *Symposium* was a model for elaborating a theory of Eros as a response to the fundamental lack in our being that Freudian theory sees as the root of human desire. These two seminars formed a pair, and both Lacan's ethics and his reading of the *Symposium* became touchstones in later postmodernist debates. Whereas the seminar on the ethics asks what do we owe our desire, that on transference asks what do we owe the other as both the cause and the object of that desire.

The Platonic corpus, particularly dialogues such as the *Phaedrus* and the *Symposium*, which interrogate the relationship between desire and truth, are a central concern for all the major figures in post-structuralism. Lacan's readings of the *Antigone* and the *Symposium* helped inaugurate a dialogic space that not only made post-structuralism possible but also anticipated the later investigations of antiquity that characterized the works of Derrida and Foucault, as well as Irigaray, Kristeva, and Cixous.

The *Phaedrus* was a crucial text for Derrida. Derrida's vocabulary and set of concerns, unlike Lacan's, are more conceptual than experiential. His task is not to train the next generation of analysts, which was the purpose of Lacan's seminars, but to analyze the possible formations of the psyche and of reason per se as they are instantiated in the textual tradition that constitutes Western philosophy. In Derrida's 1972 essay on the *Phaedrus*, "Plato's Pharmacy," the ambiguous figure of the *pharmakos/pharmakon* functions as the primary exemplar of the problematic status of writing, intentionality, and meaning within the Western metaphysical tradition. Plato's aversion to writing, which is plainly stated in the *Phaedrus*'s declaration that the true philosopher would never entrust anything serious to writing, unless it were that special writing inscribed upon the soul, is interpreted by Derrida as symptomatic of a more general tendency in philosophy to banish the external and the material from the essence of meaning and value, and to posit a realm of pure presence, an absolute origin.[5] The deconstruction of the fantasy of such a moment of plenitude and undivided origin is the central task of Derridian philosophy as a whole.

Plato and Socrates play a large role in Derrida's *La carte postale*. The postcard of the title is a reproduction of the frontispiece to a thirteenth-century work of fortune telling. The image depicts two figures: one is seated at a desk producing a manuscript; the other is standing behind the first and giving directions, perhaps even dictating what is being written. They are labeled, respectively, Socrates and Plato. Among the many ironies noted by Derrida is the reversal of roles found in the postcard's depiction of Plato and Socrates. By tradition, Socrates did not write. He is the first philosopher in the West, the one from whom all subsequent ancient schools claimed their descent, and yet he left no writings. Most famously, we know Socrates from the writings of Plato. The Socrates of modern philosophy and theory is very much Plato's creation. He did, in a real sense, take Plato's dictation. He received the young philosopher's inscription to precisely the extent that Plato was the faithful disciple able to receive his.

In *Khôra* at the beginning of the 1990s, Derrida reads Plato's *Timaeus*. This dialogue consists of an introductory conversation[6] followed by a long speech in which Timaeus tells how a divine craftsman created the universe through imitating a set of preexisting eternal essences or forms.[7] Halfway through, however, our speaker must pause and begin again.[8] If the divine Demiurge creates perfect copies of the intelligible essences in the world of sense, then how, he asks, would those imitations differ from the originals, and if they were indeed perfect copies, then how are we to explain the manifest change and corruption of the world of our experience? A new beginning must be made, which makes possible the Demiurge's labor of reproducing the intelligible order in the world of sense. This "cause" is the famous *khôra*, the mother or womb of creation.[9]

Written as a homage to Jean-Pierre Vernant, *Khôra*, like all works of Derrida, seeks simultaneously to accept and go beyond the terms of the text being read. In *Mythe et société en Grèce ancienne*, Vernant had posited a fundamental opposition between *muthos* and *logos*, with the latter representing a discourse founded on noncontradiction, a quasi-Aristotelian logic of the excluded middle, and the former being a narrative discourse that thrives on ambiguity and indeterminacy. For Derrida it is the *Timaeus*'s formulation of the *khôra* that calls this opposition into question. *Khôra* stands as the prephilosophical, prenarrative moment that makes the construction of both *muthos* and *logos* possible, even as it reveals their essential complicity. It is that which neither participates in the intelligible essences per se nor constitutes the realm of their mimetic instantiation. As such, it is neither being nor becoming, neither essence nor appearance, neither proof nor tale.

Derrida's engagement with antiquity is not limited to Plato. Aristotle and Cicero both play major roles in 1994's *Politics of Friendship*. *Politics of Friendship* is a book about the history of the concept of friendship from Plato to Blanchot by way of Cicero. It is also a book about the inseparability of politics from a concept of both the friend and the enemy. It returns again and again to a possibly apocryphal saying of Aristotle's, "Oh my friends, there is no friend." The true friend, as the saying makes apparent, is the impossible exception. That rare true friend is portrayed in Cicero as a second self, as the other of myself who reflects my self to myself. And yet my friend, as friend, remains other. And insofar as my friend remains other, he or she, as my second self, has the potential to call the integrity, the sufficiency, of my self into question. There is a potential violence in friendship: a violence that recalls the passion of love. Thus, Derrida notes, Cicero observes that *amicitia* receives its name from love (*amor*) and that each sets the soul aflame. Yet, the flames of passion only too easily become those of hatred.

The Belgian-born philosopher, Luce Irigaray, exploded into the intellectual consciousness of the French, English, and Italian-speaking world with the publication of her doctoral dissertation in philosophy, *Speculum, de l'autre femme* (1974). Along with Kristeva and Cixous, Irigaray's name became synonymous with a psychoanalytically inflected "French" feminism that not only saw woman as the other of man, but also saw that otherness as going beyond a simple dialectical negation to posit her own identity. For the post-1968 generation of French feminists, woman was not simply man's counterpart, but a being in her own right, possessing distinct relations to desire, language, and the body.

Speculum is a comprehensive investigation of the role woman plays as the constitutive other in the history of Western thought beginning with Plato. Woman is the object of man's speculative gaze, the mirror in which he sees himself, and thus the other who is always already recuperated into the logic of the Same. The task, then, for Irigaray is in the first instance an archaeological one, a patient sifting through of the accumulated layers of discourse to uncover the ways in which woman is recuperated into the logic of the Same through "regimes of property, systematic philosophies, [and] religious mythologies."[10] *Speculum*, therefore, begins with a lengthy reading of Freud, then passes through short central sections on Plato, Aristotle, Plotinus, Descartes, Christian mysticism, Kant, and Hegel's reading of the *Antigone*, before reaching its end, which is also its beginning, "L'hystera de Platon." This final section consists of a lengthy reading of Plato's myth of the cave, which constitutes the intellectual center of the entire project. It argues that what the myth of the cave institutes, or at least stands as synecdoche for, is the institution of a world picture, in which woman as such becomes invisible. Woman is the wall of the cave against which man projects the images of his identity. It is Irigaray's task to make that wall visible.

Although Cixous and Irigaray are often lumped together as French feminists, and both undertake a serious engagement with antiquity, Cixous's strategy of writing is very different. She is a novelist, a dramatist, a poet, and a critic where Irigaray is a philosopher, a psychoanalyst, and a linguist. Cixous's approach can be seen in the following quotation from a 2006 interview. The subject is her continuing fascination with the first poet of the ancient mythic tradition:

> Cixous: It seems to me that initially I lived "Orpheus" in a structurally ambiguous way ("Orpheus" is a man, in the myth and therefore not me. "Orpheus" is the singer— therefore me. It's her. It's him.). . . . What I tell myself is that Orpheus is a being with a woman inside, but a large woman, great big life with death. . . . Orpheus is any creature who writes, and divides itself in two, dies in writing, lives in writing, dies living in writing. But in Ovid the whole myth can be read minutely. Obviously, one should always think the couple as One (male)-One (female), handed down from the Platonic Androgyne.[11]

A number of important features of Cixous's thought are made evident in this quotation. First, Orpheus is not a topic *that* Cixous thinks *about*. He is not an external object toward which Cixous takes up a definite attitude, but rather *he* is something *she* "lives" and "*lives* . . . in a structurally ambiguous way." That ambiguity occurs on two axes simultaneously: that of masculinity and femininity and that of inside versus outside. And while these axes are inseparable from one another, they are never strictly homologous (i.e., inside = masculine, outside = feminine, or vice versa). Orpheus is instead both masculine and feminine, like Plato's Androgyne in the *Symposium* but also like Cixous herself on this telling. Moreover, Cixous, in living Orpheus, does not simply absorb and sublimate his masculinity, nor does he appropriate her femininity, but each becomes a lived aspect of the other and each comes to internalize the other, defining their internality by the other's momentary externality. "Orpheus is a being with a woman inside, but a large woman, great big life with death," and insofar as this is true then Orpheus is a writer who lives by externalizing a part of the self, by dying a little bit through that externalization, through this moment of giving birth, through the production of a text, a song. Orpheus is at once an externality, a figure from the past whose narrative can be found in Ovid and Vergil, and an immediate reality of Cixous's existence.

Orpheus is not the lone such figure in Cixous's Imaginary. Aeschylus's *Oresteia* represents another touchstone for her. It is a primary reference in "Sorties," which appeared in a joint work with Cathérine Clément, *La jeune née* (1975). The *Oresteia*, moreover, continues to occupy an important place in her thought until at least the beginning of the nineties, when she is commissioned by the Théâtre du Soleil to produce a translation of the *Euménides* (1992). The year after, she produced a sequel, *La ville parjure ou le reveil des Erinyes* (1994). In the preface to her translation, Cixous makes clear what is at stake in this work for her. Following Bachofen, she sees in the *Oresteia* a dramatization of the beginning of patriarchy and of the overthrow of the goddesses who presided over early matriarchal culture.[12] Her belief or nonbelief in the historical accuracy of Bachofen's claims is less important than the opportunity the *Oresteia* presents Cixous for imagining a world otherwise, a world beyond the hierarchies and oppositions of the present, a world of Orphic ambiguities. Aeschylus in the *Euménides*, she contends, presents a world that is at once our origin and our other, our remote past and our unconscious present:

> He gives us a vision of the Erinyes-Euménides. Who?
>
> That's the enigma. Nobody has ever seen them. No creatures more strange.
>
> Everything about them is strange, strange to think, a stranger to our thought, to our experience, to our perception. But not to our unconscious. Powers, Terrors, infernal countries that we have never seen but whose presence gnaws and makes us weak in the knees, our Dreams see them. But they escape description.[13]

The *Euménides* for Cixous function as the repressed other of contemporary patriarchal culture. They represent a world of feminized madness and terror, from the perspective of our dominant symbolic order, but they also reveal a fundamentally different fashion of relating to the world, one in which the oppositions of subject and object, masculine and feminine, no longer mark stable points of reference, but dissolve into an open field of relations that is at once exhilarating and terrifying. They call forth madness and rapture, *jouissance*: the possibility of a fundamentally different relation to being, to the repressed that is constitutive of our present psychic order.

For many years, if one thought about Foucault's interest in the ancient world, the point of reference was the last two volumes of *The History of Sexuality*. The topic of Foucault's final published works was the ancient world's conception of the place of sexual object choice in determining the subject's self relation. This premodern conception was reflected in a wide variety of topics, including pederasty, marriage, dietary and physical regimens, and the practice of medicine. Foucault spent the last five years of his life lecturing on antiquity at the Collège de France, and while some of those lectures do find their way into *The History of Sexuality*, most do not. Indeed in 1980, Michel Foucault's lectures at the Collège de France take a decisive turn. And while, there are clear overlaps between the work he was presenting in his course and the last books he published, the lectures have a different focus.

On January 7, 1980, Foucault began his lectures for the year by describing an audience hall in the palace of Septimius Severus. On the ceiling was painted an image of the night sky as it appeared on the day of the emperor's birth: a representation of cosmic truth that served to legitimate and actualize his power. Foucault asks us to imagine the purpose of this manifestation of truth in the constitution of an absolute imperial power. While the title of the course, *The Government of the Living*, seems to indicate a continuation of Foucault's concerns with biopower, governmentality, and their implication within systems of knowledge, which had been Foucault's primary subject matter since 1976, the shift of scene to the display of power in late imperial Rome announces an inflection point in his thought. It is not so much that Foucault has left his previous concerns behind as that he had determined that their adequate investigation required a more profound historical depth. *The Government of the Living* asks the question: why is a manifestation of the truth necessary for the government of human beings? Such a question is clearly related to Foucault's earlier concern with knowledge and power, but it is not precisely identical to the previous problematic in all aspects. This new topic is explored through a close reading of, first, *Oedipus Tyrannus* and, then, of a variety of texts from the primitive church on baptism, penitence, and confession. In each case, the question Foucault poses is: what relation obtains between the subject, its acts of manifesting or producing truth, and that subject's adhesion to a larger institutional structure, which both makes the truth possible and is made possible by the truth: that is, the *polis*, the church, a government?

The questions of the subject's relation to its own truth and of the production of that truth through processes of confession and self-examination have certain ties both to the problematic of volume one of *The History of Sexuality* (1976) and to Foucault's larger critique of normalizing disciplinary and psychotherapeutic structures, which he had undertaken beginning with *Histoire de la folie*. The primary topic, indeed, of volume two of *The History of Sexuality* (1984) is how the truth of the subject in Western culture comes to be defined as that subject's desire. The shift to antiquity is designed to produce a genealogy of the desiring subject, who ultimately becomes the modern subject of sexuality and psychoanalysis. Foucault's course for 1981, *Subjectivity and Truth*, is the series of lectures at the Collège de France that most clearly captures the concerns of *The History of Sexuality* and of its turn to antiquity. Indeed, the entire project of the last volumes of *The History of Sexuality*, including the never published final volume on early Christianity, is outlined in this year's series of lectures. The topics explored include Artemidorus's *Oneirocriticon*, classical Greek pederasty, Xenophon's *Oikinomikos* on the governing of the classical household, Plutarch's *Erotikos* and ancient sexual ethics, Hellenistic and Roman discourses on marriage under the empire, and the evolution of ancient arts of existence. These discussions, however, which closely parallel Foucault's published work, are able to be read in a fundamentally different light, however, when they are seen not only as a new point of departure for *The History of Sexuality*, but also as a way station in Foucault's larger investigation of truth, power, and the subject. *Subjectivity and Truth* both continues the previous year's investigation and prepares for the following year's lectures, in which sexuality plays only a small part.

In 1982's the *Hermeneutics of the Subject*, Foucault introduces his concept of spiritual practices, which, following the work of Pierre Hadot, he defines as "the body of researches, practices, and experiences, which can be purifications, practices, renouncements, turning of the gaze, and modifications of existence that constitute, not for knowledge, but for the subject, for the very being of the subject, the price to pay for access to the truth." The primary example of such a practice might well be the passage from Plato's *Seventh Letter* in which authentic knowledge is described as coming not from written summaries of things known—and hence from the mere truth or falsity of the statements contained therein—but from the continual interaction between master and student (*tribē*) that produces the spark of enlightenment. These practices are directly linked with philosophy in the ancient world as the condition of possibility for access to the truth, from Plato's *tribē* to Plutarch's *hypomnemata* and Seneca's nightly examination of conscience (also discussed in 1980). Many of these practices are repurposed in later Christian forms of self-examination, confession, and penitence. Yet as spirituality becomes increasingly a property of faith as opposed to a practice of truth, then spiritual practice likewise becomes something undertaken only as a result of the prior acceptance of that truth. The truth is no longer a product of the practice but rather its condition. Truth thus becomes separable from the practices undertaken by the subject to access it. Hence, to the extent that these spiritual practices survive into the modern world as does their corollary, a form of truth that is not dependent on an autonomous observing subject—as opposed to an embodied practicing subject—then those practices and their truth become relegated to the realms of art, poetry, music, and religion, as opposed to science and philosophy: the privileged discourses of modernity's truth.

In his 1983 course, *Le gouvernement de soi et des autres*, Foucault lectured on the relation between *parrhēsia*, "truth-telling" and the constitution of the subject in relation to historically discrete structures of power. More particularly, he traced a fundamental shift that occurred in the way *parrhēsia* was conceived: from the inherited right of democratic speech in the agonistic politics of fifth-century Athens to the honest speech offered by the philosophical counselor to the prince or other instances of aristocratic and sovereign power in the fourth century and later Hellenistic and imperial periods. The lectures for this year concentrate on Plato and Euripides, with a lesser amount of attention being paid to Polybius and Thucydides. They pick up on the previous year's discussion of *parrhēsia* as a spiritual practice, a tool of personal transformation in which the philosopher participates to insure the spiritual health of both his students and the state. Where in 1982's *Hermeneutics of the Subject* Foucault had examined *parrhēsia* merely as one form of spiritual practice, here he focuses on the genealogy of *parrhēsia* itself. He asks: how did the act of truth-telling became a technology of the self and thus a means of both resistance and legitimation in the government of the self and of others? In both courses, however, *parrhēsia* is examined as the embodiment of the frank speech of philosophy as opposed to the rhetoric and flattery of the court. It is not only a method of giving honest counsel to princes and to those to whom one owes spiritual guidance, but also a guarantor and embodiment of one's own authenticity: *parrhēsia* is the means whereby—as well as the manifest sign that—the subject coincides with itself. Truth-telling is not only an instrument to be used in philosophical protreptic and political criticism but also a technology that creates a self defined by its *actes de vérité*.

In 1984, Foucault gave his final course. He was already profoundly ill, not beginning his course till February, as opposed to his usual start date at the beginning of January, and finishing on March 28 with what in retrospect appear to be the prophetic words, "But in the end it is too late. So, thank you." The course picks up where the previous year had left off with an examination of *parrhēsia* or the act of telling the truth. As it develops, Socrates assumes the role of the philosopher and truth-teller par excellence, with special emphasis on the *Apology*, *Laches*, and the *Crito*, while also returning to the *Seventh Letter* and the *Alcibiades*, which had occupied central positions in Foucault's lectures the two previous years. The Socratic commitment to unvarnished truth-telling in turn, Foucault argues in the last half of the course, find its true continuation among the Cynics. He closes with an examination of the use of *parrhēsia* in the New Testament and among the early Church Fathers, thus returning to the relation between acts of truth and the constitution of the subject in its institutional setting, first broached in 1980.

In 1966, Julia Kristeva, a young Bulgarian student arrived in Paris. In the late sixties and early seventies, she, like many intellectuals of the day attended Lacan's seminar. Kristeva produces two major engagements with Platonic texts. The first is the concept of the *chora* in *The Revolution in Poetic Language* (*RPL*), the second, her reading of the *Phaedrus* and the *Symposium* in *Tales of Love* (*Histoires d'amour*), both works represent dialogic engagements with the writers already discussed. *RPL* is Kristeva's doctoral dissertation and the major theoretical statement of the first part of her career. Her reading of the *Timaeus*, while central to her own critical project, is also part and parcel of a larger series of debates on writing, materialism, Marxism-Leninism, and the role of the maternal feminine in the constitution of the speaking subject that were central to the post-1968 Paris intellectual scene.

RPL falls into two parts. The first half offers an account of language's relation to the subject. It presents a radical synthesis of formal linguistics, psychoanalysis, and phenomenology. It aims to provide an account not only of normal language acquisition but also of poetic language and its political implications. The second half is a case study meant to offer empirical confirmation of the theoretical argument made in the first half. The semiotic *chora* in Kristeva's work, which appears in the initial theoretical portion of the work, is said to represent the primary matrix from which the later intelligible forms of linguistic and literary creation arose. It is the womb from which the intelligible universe of the symbolic order is born, in much the same way that Plato refers to the *khôra* as the womb of creation. Kristeva's concept of the *chora,* however, is deeply concerned with the maternal, with desire, and with the possibility of women's discourse related to the nonrational and the mystical.[14]

In 1983, Kristeva published *Tales of Love*, a psychoanalytically inspired genealogy of love in the Western world, from Plato's *Phaedrus* and *Symposium* to Baudelaire, Stendahl, and Bataille. At this same time, Michel Foucault was lecturing at the Collège de France on the care of the self and *parrhēsia* in ancient philosophy was putting the final touches on volumes two and three of the *Histoire de la sexualité*. Kristeva's work clearly positions itself as a rejoinder to Foucault's. Both works contain important readings of Plato's texts, while focusing on the problematics of sexuality, gender, and desire. Both respond to Lacan's readings of the *Antigone* and the *Symposium*. The reading of the *Phaedrus* and the *Symposium* contained in the first chapter of *Histoires d'amour* remains one of Kristeva's most sustained engagements with ancient philosophy. It is immediately followed by a reading of the "Song of Songs" and a chapter on the figure of Narcissus in Ovid and in Plotinus.

Of course, other figures could be added to this brief survey: Deleuze, Serres, Wittig, and Kofman from the French tradition; Adorno, Benjamin, and Horkheimer from the German; in Russia the Bakhtin circle's knowledge of the ancient world was profound; and contemporary examples could be found in the work of Butler, Žižek, and Badiou. The point, however, is clear. Theory is part of a much larger series of conversations that began neither in 1968 nor in the post–World War world. It is only the modernist prejudice toward "making it new" that mandates seeing each new link in the dialogic chain as an apocalyptic break with the past.

University of South Carolina (United States)

NOTES

1. In the period after the repression of the student and worker uprisings in 1968, there was an astonishing proliferation of discourses, which sought not only to define new identities in relation to the institutions of the state, the family, and the educational system, but also to analyze why the revolutionary moment of 1968 had ultimately failed. This was a period in which the discourses of feminism, Marxism, Maoism, Nietzschean and Heideggerian

philosophy, psychoanalysis, and structural linguistics interacted with a kind of polymorphic promiscuity easy to underestimate.

2. Paul Allen Miller, "The Classical Roots of Poststructuralism: Lacan, Derrida, and Foucault," *International Journal of the Classical Tradition* 5 (1999): 204–25; Paul Allen Miller, "Truth-Telling in Foucault's 'Le gouvernement de soi et des autres' and Persius 1: The Subject, Rhetoric, and Power," *Parrhesia* (2006): 27–61; Paul Allen Miller, *Postmodern Spiritual Practices: The Construction of the Subject and the Reception of Plato in Lacan, Derrida, and Foucault* (Columbus: Ohio State University Press, 2007); Paul Allen Miller, "The Platonic Remainder: *Khôra* and the *Corpus Platonicum*," in *Derrida and Antiquity*, ed. Miriam Leonard (Oxford: Oxford University Press, 2010); Paul Allen Miller, *Diotima at the Barricades: French Feminists Read Plato* (Oxford: Oxford University Press, 2016); Miriam Leonard, "Irigaray's Cave: Feminist Theory and the Politics of French Classicism," *Ramus* 28 (1999): 152–68; Miriam Leonard, "Creating Dawn: Writing Through Antiquity in the Works of Helene Cixous," *Arethusa* 33 (2000): 121–48; Miriam Leonard, "Antigone, The Political and the Ethics of Psychoanalysis," *Proceedings of The Cambridge Philological Society* 49 (2003): 130–54; Miriam Leonard, *Athens in Paris: Ancient Greece and the Political in Post-War French Thought* (Oxford: Oxford University Press, 2005); Miriam Leonard, "Oedipus in the Accusative: Derrida and Levinas," *Comparative Literature Studies* 43 (2006): 224–52; and Miriam Leonard, "Derrida Between 'Greek' and 'Jew,'" in *Derrida and Antiquity*, ed. Miriam Leonard (Oxford: Oxford University Press, 2010), 135–58.

3. Jean-Michel Rabaté, "Lacan's Turn to Freud," in *Cambridge Companion to Lacan*, ed. Jean-Michel Rabaté (Cambridge: Cambridge University Press, 2003), 12.

4. Jacques Lacan, *Le séminaire livre VIII: Le transfert*, ed. Jacques-Alain Miller (Paris: Seuil, 1991), 215a2.

5. Jacques Derrida, "La pharmacie de Platon," in *La dissémination* (Paris: Seuil, 1972), 182–83.

6. Jacques Derrida, *Khôra* (Paris: Galilée, 1993); *Timaeus* 17a–27b.

7. *Timaeus*, 27c–92c.

8. Ibid., 47e.

9. Ibid., 50a–51b.

10. Luce Irigaray, *Speculum, De l'autre femme* (Paris: Minuit, 1974), 161.

11. Frédéric-Yves Jeannet, "The Book that You Will Not Write: An Interview with Hélène Cixous," trans. Thomas Dutoit, *New Literary History* 37 (2006): 251.

12. Hélène Cixous, *Les Euménides d'Eschyle* (Paris: Théâtre du Soleil, 1992), 5–7.

13. Cixous, *Les Euménides d'Eschyle* (Paris: Théâtre du Soleil), 10–11.

14. Julia Kristeva, *Histoires d'amour* (Paris: Denoël, 1983), 226, 246–47.

WORKS CITED

Cixous, Hélène. "Sorties." In *La jeune née*. Ed. Hélène Cixous and Catherine Clément. Paris: Union Génerale d'Edition, 1975. 114–245.

Cixous, Hélène. *Les Euménides d'Eschyle*. Paris: Théâtre du Soleil, 1992.

Cixous, Hélène. *La ville parjure ou le reveil des Erinyes*. Paris: Théâtre du Soleil, 1994.

Derrida, Jacques. "La pharmacie de Platon [1968]." In *La dissémination*. Ed. Jacques Derrida. Paris: Seuil, 1972. 74–196.

Derrida, Jacques. *La carte postale: de Socrate à Freud et au-delà*. Paris: Aubier-Flammarion, 1980.

Derrida, Jacques. *Khôra*. Paris: Galilée, 1993.

Derrida, Jacques. *Politiques de l'amitié, suivi de L'oreille de Heidegger*. Paris: Galilée, 1994.

Foucault, Michel. *La volonté de savoir. Histoire de la sexualité*, vol. 1. Paris: Gallimard, 1976.

Foucault, Michel. *L'usage des plaisirs. Histoire de la sexualité*, vol. 2. Paris: Gallimard, 1984.

Foucault, Michel. *Le souci de soi. Histoire de la sexualité*, vol. 3. Paris: Gallimard, 1984.

Foucault, Michel. *L'Herméneutique du sujet: Cours au Collège de France 1981-82*. Ed. Frédéric Gros. Paris: Gallimard/Seuil, 2001.

Foucault, Michel. *Le gouvernement de soi et des autres: Cours au Collège de France 1982-83*. Ed. Frédéric Gros. Paris: Gallimard/Seuil, 2008.

Foucault, Michel. *Le Courage de la vérité. Le gouvernement de soi et des autres II: Cours au Collège de France 1983-84*. Ed. Frédéric Gros. Paris: Gallimard/Seuil, 2009.

Foucault, Michel. *Du gouvernement de vivants: Cours au Collège de France 1979-80*. Ed. Michel Senellart. Paris: Gallimard/Seuil, 2012.

Foucault, Michel. *Subjectivité et verité: Cours au Collège de France 1980-81*. Ed. Frédéric Gros. Paris: Gallimard/Seuil, 2014.

Irigaray, Luce. *Speculum, De l'autre femme*. Paris: Minuit, 1974.

Jeannet, Frédéric-Yves. "The Book that You Will Not Write: An Interview with Hélène Cixous." Trans. Thomas Dutoit. *New Literary History* 37 (2006): 249–61.

Kristeva, Julia. *La révolution du langage poétique: L'avant-garde à la fin du XIXe siècle: Lautréamont et Mallarmé*. Paris: Seuil, 1985. Original, 1974.

Kristeva, Julia. *Histoires d'amour*. Paris: Denoël, 1983.

Lacan, Jacques. *Le séminaire livre VII: L'éthique de la psychanalyse*. Ed. Jacques-Alain Miller. Paris: Seuil, 1986.

Lacan, Jacques. *Le séminaire livre VIII: Le transfert*. Ed. Jacques-Alain Miller. Paris: Seuil, 1991.

Leonard, Miriam. "Irigaray's Cave: Feminist Theory and the Politics of French Classicism." *Ramus* 28 (1999): 152–68.

Leonard, Miriam. "Creating Dawn: Writing through Antiquity in the Works of Helene Cixous." *Arethusa* 33 (2000): 121–48.

Leonard, Miriam. "Antigone, The Political and the Ethics of Psychoanalysis." *Proceedings of the Cambridge Philological Society* 49 (2003): 130–54.

Leonard, Miriam. *Athens in Paris: Ancient Greece and the Political in Post-War French Thought*. Oxford: Oxford University Press, 2005.

Leonard, Miriam. "Oedipus in the Accusative: Derrida and Levinas." *Comparative Literature Studies* 43 (2006): 224–52.

Leonard, Miriam. "Derrida Between 'Greek' and 'Jew.'" In *Derrida and Antiquity*. Ed. Miriam Leonard. Oxford: Oxford University Press, 2010. 135–58.

Miller, Paul Allen. "The Classical Roots of Poststructuralism: Lacan, Derrida, and Foucault." *International Journal of the Classical Tradition* 5 (1999): 204–25.

Miller, Paul Allen. "Truth-Telling in Foucault's 'Le gouvernement de soi et des autres' and Persius 1: The Subject, Rhetoric, and Power." *Parrhesia* 1 (2006): 27–61.

Miller, Paul Allen. *Postmodern Spiritual Practices: The Construction of the Subject and the Reception of Plato in Lacan, Derrida, and Foucault*. Columbus: Ohio State University Press, 2007.

Miller, Paul Allen. "The Platonic Remainder: *Khôra* and the *Corpus Platonicum*." In *Derrida and Antiquity*. Ed. Miriam Leonard. Oxford: Oxford University Press, 2010. 321–41.

Miller, Paul Allen. *Diotima at the Barricades: French Feminists Read Plato*. Oxford: Oxford University Press, 2016.

Rabaté, Jean-Michel. "Lacan's Turn to Freud." In *Cambridge Companion to Lacan*. Ed. Jean-Michel Rabaté. Cambridge: Cambridge University Press, 2003. 1–24.

CHAPTER TWO

Structuralism and Semiotics

HERMAN RAPAPORT

Whereas structuralism is the study of signifying systems at the macro-level, semiotics operates as the study of signifying elements at the micro-level, including but not limited to signs, signals, icons, indices, codes, and information (the statistical properties of a message separate from its meaning). Whereas semiotics is defined in various linguistic encyclopedias as simply "the study of signs," which speaks to how signs signify in terms of the various systems in which signs can be said to occur, structuralism has been defined as "the perception and description of structures."[1] In their authoritative *Dictionnaire de linguistique*, Jean Dubois et al. write that "the term structuralism is applied and applies itself, with respect to moments and individuals, to different schools of linguistics [which] have in common a certain number of conceptions and methods that involve the definition of linguistic structures."[2] Generative grammar, distributionism, functionalism, and glossematics are among the different approaches, whereas notable structuralist movements are said to include Russian formalism, the Jakobson school of linguistics, Saussurean semiology, and American structuralism.

Debatable has been whether structuralism or semiotics, for that matter, are positivist or not. The linguist Ferdinand de Saussure, founder of French structuralism, coined the word *semiology* (the study of signs and their structuration) and called it a *science*, as many subsequent practitioners have. However, Roland Barthes, an exponent of what he called "the structuralist activity," argued that structuralism is hypothetical or theoretical. "The goal of all structuralist activity, whether reflexive or poetic, is to reconstruct the 'object' in such a way as to manifest thereby the rules of functioning (the 'functions') of this object. Structure is therefore a *simulacrum* [a virtual representation] of the object, but a directed, interested simulacrum, since the imitated object makes something appear which remained invisible or, if one prefers, unintelligible in the natural object."[3] For Barthes, structure is more theoretical than empirical, not that there isn't concrete evidence upon which to base one's structural models. In books such as the *Empire of Signs*, Barthes imagined the structuralist activity as one of observing in terms of dichotomous structural principles in order to arrange perception along the lines of a model or system. Reality, then, is never seen as an absolute thing in itself, but in terms of rules and principles that systematically construct and model reality. Questions of logical entailment, symmetry, permutation, stratification, embeddedness, consistency, contradiction, and discrepancies in self-referentiality are typical concerns with respect to modeling that were treated differently by the various practitioners of structuralism. As François Dosse noted in *History of Structuralism*, Barthes himself was a "receptacle for the multiple variations" within the diverse structuralisms that converged in Paris in the 1950s and 1960s, which is why he became as influential as he was.[4]

If my account of structuralism and semiotics privileges this interdisciplinary convergence of various structuralist activities, it is not in order to forget that structuralism and semiotics were based in the field of linguistics out of which principles of semiotics and structuralism have been transposed and adapted to other disciplines, among them, communications, anthropology, psychoanalysis, Marxism, literary criticism, cultural studies, feminism, and film studies. That is, linguistics has to be given credit for having given birth to an interdisciplinary venture in which structuralism assumes a world comprised of implicit and explicit structural patterns and systems that people can rationally extrapolate and codify. Of course, such structural analysis was already well under way in Aristotle who had an interest in modeling structures that have a logical, formal identity that is not only consistent and functional, but also produces predictable outcomes. However, structuralism differs from such familiar, well-established structural analysis, which influenced American New Criticism, insofar as structuralism is predicated upon semiotics which emphasizes *the priority of the sign*.

A good way to imagine such prioritization is by way of French literary writers of the *nouveau roman* who in the 1950s were participating in what Barthes called the *structuralist activity* to the extent that for them phenomena were posited mainly as physical signs that make up an implicit structure. For example, in the novels of Alain Robbe-Grillet things are presented not as occasional depictions of objects for the sake of verisimilitude but as a collection or set of signs that will be repeated and permutated. In *The Voyeur*, which is a novel about a door-to-door salesman whose visit to an island coincides with the murder of a girl, we read about Matthias entering someone's home in order to demonstrate and sell his watches.

> [Matthias] managed to reach the kitchen and its oval table, and set his suitcase on it while continuing the conversation. Then there was the oilcloth and the little flowers of its pattern. . . . There was the pressure of his fingers on the clasp of the suitcase, the cover opening wide, the memorandum book lying on the pile of cardboard strips, the dolls printed on the lining, the memorandum book inside the open cover, the piece of cord rolled into a figure eight on top of the pile of cardboard strips.[5]

Somewhat earlier the reader was told, "The table was covered by an oilcloth with a pattern of little flowers, a pattern that might have been like the one on the lining of his suitcase." And "instead of the memorandum book spread conspicuously over the sheet of paper that protected the first row of watches, appeared the wad of cord rolled into a figure eight."[6] Apparently the pattern on the lining of the suitcase (it is a sign) isn't identical in the two descriptions. In the one instance the pattern is that of dolls and in the other the pattern is *perhaps* that of the little flowers on the oilcloth. Reality in this novel lacks the certainty of verisimilitude because its signifiers "float" somewhat, depriving us of a fixed sense of reference, that is, of what is and isn't the case and hence of what is and isn't real. In Robbe-Grillet, reality is constructed by the ordering of signs that like cards in a pack can be rearranged in different groups or sets. At a later point when a girl's body is found at the bottom of a cliff by the sea, we're told, "it might as well have been a stuffed doll thrown over the cliff."[7] This is an analogy or metaphor, certainly, but in the context of the novel the word doll has a sort of life of its own as a sign that keeps turning up here and there without any fixed or essential correlation. We saw it turn up in the description above of the suitcase whose lining has dolls printed on it—or was that the lining of the memorandum book? It would seem that in the passage above the word doll and the girl's body converge as if by accident. In Robbe-Grillet, then, the word "doll" functions largely as a mark, tag, or sign whose significance is to be grasped in terms of the places of its emergence that make one suppose it could have the function of evidence whereby logical connections can be made with respect to subjects, actions, and things. That the signs don't actually have the status of concrete evidence can be read as a critique of detective fiction in which we are to assume that signs have the function of evidence of definitively established truths.

During the 1970s when structuralism and semiotics became of considerable interest in the United Kingdom and the United States, it was mainly critics in cinema studies, Stephen Heath among them, who appreciated the complicity between structuralism and the *nouveau roman*.[8] However, most researchers in the United Kingdom and the United States with an interest in structuralism were putting considerable effort into defining and redefining the sign and its constituent parts, the signifier and the signified. The hope was that by understanding these concepts, some sort of major transformation of how to think about literature and culture would take place that could revolutionize the humanities. Of course, everyone was careful to reread de Saussure who had originally formulated these concepts in his *Course in General Linguistics*, which had been given circa 1915 and written down by his students. Treated for a time as if it were Holy Writ, attempts were made to derive a doctrine or dogma from the *Course* that would scientifically ground the humanities and social sciences. Dubois et al. offered a useful corrective to a dogmatic reading of Saussure when they pointed out that structuralists such as Saussure advanced significant insights that had become formalized as related individual topics that only loosely referred to an overall theoretical horizon whereby the various topics of structuralist analysis converged. These topics included (1) a definition of the sign in terms of its constituent parts, the signifier and the signified; (2) the distinction of *langue* from *parole* (i.e., language from speech); (3) arbitrariness of the sign; (4) the synchronic-diachronic axis; (5) the establishment of value by means of exchange; (6) the conviction that the whole of a system or structure precedes any of its parts; (7) the establishment of identity by way of difference; and (8) the view that language speaks man and not the other way around. Given the importance of these Saussurean concepts and principles, explication of them is required, beginning with the sign.

1. Simply put, a "sign" is made up of the "signifier" (the expression) and the "signified" (the meaning). Consider that phrases such as Gertrude Stein's "Why will they disturb me to disturb not me as they do" from *Stanzas in Meditation* or "A season in yellow sold extra strings makes lying places" from *Tender Buttons* are easy to decipher word for word, because the relation of signifier to signified is self-evident, but that when taken together as a single phrasal unit we can't quite establish a self-evident signified, because the phrases appear illogical and counterfactual.[9] Some structuralists, the psychoanalyst Jacques Lacan among them, called such phrases signifiers when they are used as expressions whose signified is suppressed (or "repressed," in Lacan's parlance). Even in phrases that seem to make self-evident sense, as in the case of poet Charles Bernstein's title *The Pitch of Poetry*, we don't know what the signifier "pitch" expresses. Does the signifier refer to the pitch of a boat or plane, the pitch as baseball or sales pitch, the pitch on which a game is played, or the pitch of a musical note? Here, again, the signified is suppressed, and the reader is put in the role of having to *return*

what has been obscured by re-reading the phrase. In Lacan's understanding of Saussure, the signifier is rendered formulaically as a capital *S* over a bar beneath which is a small *s* that represents the repression of the signified that the addressee has to retrieve, if he or she can. As Lacan expressed this in the 1950s, there is a sliding of the signifier over the signified. Notice how one has to perform this sliding as one reads and rereads "the pitch of poetry" or "a season in yellow sold extra strings makes lying places" or even just a single word such as Lewis Carroll's signifier "Bandersnatch" in the poem "Jabberwocky." Our eyes have to slide over the words back and forth to glimpse their signified, as if the signifiers themselves were traveling. According to Lacan, the signified in this case is the latent content of the signifier and should be considered as the signifier's unconscious. As it happens, even straightforward sentences require a certain scansion which we perform subconsciously. As Lacan pointed out, only once we come to the end of a phrase do we retroactively make sense of the whole.

2. Saussure's language/speech distinction has also received considerable attention, particularly by figures such as Roman Jakobson and Roland Barthes. It is important to recall that in French one actually refers to *langage*, *langue*, and *parole*, which complicates matters a bit for English speakers. Language (*langage*) is a system of values, a social institution, an abstract signifying structure governed by rules. Speech (*parole*) is the actualization of language by an individual's performance of it. *Langue* is the tongue derived by means of *parole* from language in the abstract, whether dialect, idiosyncratic manners of speaking, or what in writing would be called *style*. As an improvised, combinative activity expressing personal thoughts and attitudes, speech (*parole*) is heard as *langue*. Both *langue* and *parole* exist in dialectical relation with language as a general social, nationalist institution. As Barthes has pointed out, extended speech is what we know as discourse, which presumes the sustained attention of an addressee; discourse may be descriptive, argumentative, persuasive, poetic, and so on. Extended speech necessitates rhetoric, recognizable ready-made verbal devices that are appropriated by *parole* into *langue*.

3. Saussure's notion of the arbitrariness of the sign presumes an *a priori* system that can accept any made-up element as long as it fits the rules. *Tree, arbre, Baum* . . . it doesn't matter whether we use English, French, or German as long as the rules established by a specific language are met and the addressee knows what is being denoted. *Über* (over, super) is a preposition in German, but when carried over into English it can work as a proper noun (*Uber* the cab service). There is no *essential* connection between the word and its grammatical function or its meaning. Here it is structure that establishes meaning. This means that a word doesn't imitate its referent. Were words to do so, they would be independent entities. Rather, they are the expression of a preexisting system, the organization of a rule-governed network that is determinative. This speaks to a central principle of structuralism, namely that system and not reference governs meaning. Of course, it is easy to see that arbitrariness is not absolute. Certain possibilities (combinations) are excluded by the rules, which is why Japanese sounds like Japanese and not French: at the phonemic level not all sounds are permitted or made possible by the system.

4. Saussure's distinction between the synchronic and the diachronic considers the present state of a system in its entirety as a fixed configuration versus its

temporal execution whereby the state of a system is in play and is subject to change and evolution. Roman Jakobson used this distinction in order to discuss relations between combination and selection. Combination implies metonymy, that signs are parts of a whole which is their combinative structure, whereas selection implies metaphor or substitution. "Combination. Any sign is made up of constituent signs and/or occurs only in combination with other signs. This means that any linguistic unit at one and the same time serves as a context for simpler units and/or finds its own context in a more complex linguistic unit. . . . Combination and contexture are two faces of the same operation." As to selection, "A selection between alternatives implies the possibility of substituting one for the other, equivalent in one respect and different in another. Actually selection and substitution are two faces of the same operation." Addressing Saussure, Jakobson adds, "the fundamental role which these two operations play in language was clearly realized by Ferdinand de Saussure. Yet of the two varieties of combination—concurrence and concatenation—it was only the latter, the temporal sequence, which was recognized by the Geneva linguist. Despite his own insight into the phoneme as a set of concurrent distinctive features (*éléments différentiels des phonèmes*), the scholar succumbed . . . in the linear character of language 'which excludes the possibility of pronouncing two elements at the same time.'"[10]

5. Saussurian linguistics was embraced by French Marxists in the 1960s, because Saussure argued that language was a mode of production based upon processes of exchange that constructed value. Saussure famously offered the economic analogy between signs and bank notes: a five-franc note can be exchanged for a thing one buys at the store, which gives the note a certain value, and it can, on another register, be exchanged for other denominations of money. In that context signs as words can be said to have a certain exchange value too, because their value is established within the system of language by means of the speaker's ability to select words in a mode that exchanges them for one another. The word *perchance* can be exchanged into the words *maybe, perhaps, possibly, for all one knows, conceivably*, or even the word *peradventure*. This speaks to both combination (synchrony) and selection (diachrony). But it also speaks to the value of the word in relation to adequately conveying reference. In that sense, *peradventure* may have a value that *perhaps* does not, given the contextual occasion. The upshot of Saussure's emphasis upon exchange is that it enabled Claude Lévi-Strauss, Jean Baudrillard, and others to view language in terms of what was sometimes called an *economy* (a system of exchange and value production) that could be viewed culturally in other domains besides language alone. Barthes's *The Fashion System* and Jean Baudrillard's *Société de consommation* explored a structuralist approach to how signs were produced, distributed, and consumed in the context of capitalist economy relative to the commodity.

6. Closely related to Saussure's economic understanding of language was his understanding that the meaning of the sign was established in terms of difference and identity. We generally think of difference and identity according to what philosophers call positive terms. A table is an entity that has certain features that identify it as such and that sets it apart from chairs and sofas. Saussure looked at this in reverse. A sign has the identity it does not on account of characteristics it

has but because of what it is not. As we will see later, Lacan brought this out in his psychoanalytical work by arguing that gender identity is not established in positive terms, but rather by means of ascertaining what one is not by means of semiotic mediation. In Saussure and by extension Lacan, the no-go or taboo concerns the constraints imposed on linguistic elements by the laws of the system.

7. The last two crucial teachings of Saussure are the principles that (a) the whole precedes the parts: "It is from the interdependent whole that one must start and through analysis obtain its elements"; and (b) that man doesn't speak language, language speaks man.[11] We are the effect of language, not its cause. The idea that man is the effect of language is demonstrated at length by Michel Foucault when he makes the argument, discussed later, that the author is a discursive bureaucratic construction, the effect of a semiotic set of systems that have been institutionalized in order to produce the object of their inquiry. In *The Order of Things*, Foucault made a somewhat parallel argument for the invention of man, which he saw as a discursive construction required for observing and objectifying the world for the sake of managing and controlling it. The idea that language speaks man (and by implication woman) was indicative of a linguistic turn that characterized much critical theoretical thinking in the 1960s.

Saussurean linguistics hardly stops here. Roman Jakobson built on the idea of value production in order to show that one could decompose words into elementary bits in order to show that it was by way of the coupling of contrastive linguistic elements that meanings were made possible by way of displacement and substitution (differentiation and identification). Along with C. Gunnar Fant and Maurice Halle, Jakobson would refine this insight in terms of advancing the concept of the distinctive feature, which has become an essential empirical finding in linguistics, namely the encoding of sound by means of a small set of binary oppositions (i.e., such sound differentials as p/b, s/z, t/f, v/w). For structuralists the discovery of the principle of the distinctive feature was to linguistics what the discovery of DNA was to genetics, a point relevant to work by Claude Lévi-Strauss who saw language not just mirrored in the binary apparatus of DNA, but programmed there.

Commonplace in anthropology textbooks has been the idea that language is a tool invented by human beings for utilitarian reasons. This often presupposes someone coming out of their cave in prehistoric times with a bright idea. "Wouldn't it be great," caveman thinks, "if we could all talk to each other by utilizing our vocal cords, tongues, and mouths in order to sound out words to which we could give meanings in order to designate objects and describe actions?" The idea that someone must have invented language the way someone invented bows and arrows seems commonsensical enough. But the problem with language invention is that one would have to be in possession of it first in order to invent it, which is logically absurd. More plausible is the hypothesis that language evolved out of simpler communication systems, for example, those we see among birds, wolves, and chimpanzees. It seems likely that like the primates, hominoids were on the way to language. The point that language has been in some sense inherent has been amply demonstrated by researchers teaching chimpanzees how to communicate by using language through the manipulation of signs, though quite recently researchers have also learned that some bats don't just send out calls, but formulate communications that are addressed to a particular individual. Researches know this because when the bats communicate, they reserve a particular way of communicating for the particular bat they are addressing. Dolphins behave similarly.

In the "Finale" to the fourth volume of *Mythologies*, subtitled *Naked Man*, Claude Lévi-Strauss points out that structural linguistics

has been given a natural and objective status through the discovery and the cracking of the genetic code: the universal language used by all forms of life, from micro-organisms to the higher mammals, as well as by plants, and which can be seen as the absolute prototype, the model of which is echoed, on a different level, by articulate language: the model itself consisting, at the outset, of a finite group of discrete units, chemical bases or phonemes, themselves devoid of meaning but which, when variously combined into more complex units—the words of language or triplets of nucleotides—specify a definite meaning or a definite chemical substance. Similarly, the words of language or the triplets of the genetic code combine in turn to form "sentences," that life composes in the molecular form of DNA, this form being the bearer of a differential meaning, the message of which specifies such and such a protein of a given type.[12]

Lévi-Strauss's underlying conviction is that language inheres in the biochemistry of all things and that it is therefore not surprising that the anthropologist's science of decoding Amerindian mythology isn't really different in kind from decoding DNA. Hence Lévi-Strauss says that "when Nature, several thousand million years ago, was looking for a model, she borrowed in advance, and without hesitation, from the human sciences: this is the model which, for us, is associated with the names of Trubetskoy and Jakobson [members of the Prague Circle of linguistics]." Elsewhere in the "Finale," Lévi-Strauss shows how structuralist principles are at work in the body's physical perception of the outside world. "The eye does not simply photograph visible objects; it codifies their relationships, and what it transmits to the brain is not so much figurative images as a system of binary oppositions between immobility and movement, the presence or absence of color, movement occurring in one direction rather than in others." The principles of visualization are biologically programmed in ways remarkably correlative to the programming of language throughout all of human societies, given that both depend upon "a system of binary oppositions."[13] Given Lévi-Strauss's biological point of view, for him structural linguistics is not simply one critical method among others, but currently the only scientifically valid method for conducting social-cultural analyses.

In the 1960s a much younger generation of structuralist thinkers came into prominence; among them was Julia Kristeva, a major practitioner of structuralist linguistics, who came to Paris from communist Bulgaria. In a recent interview she recalls,

My formation as a linguist would not have been sufficient had I not included semiology [*la sémiologie*]: Saussure, Benveniste, Griemas, Barthes. I had the chance, at a very young age, of participating in this opening up of the study of meaning through the linguists' object of "language," and of heading into translinguistic "signifying practices": initially literature, but also that of the image, along with painting, cinema, music, and gesture, etc. This period and its studies, which today are so easily forgotten, ridiculed, or often closed off by means of a technical esotericism, nevertheless appear to me as being among the high points of contemporary thought.[14]

Kristeva notes that during the 1960s she had imagined "meaning as a dynamic process, a *signifiance* [signifyingness], which mobilizes, along with language, other means of signification."[15] Her project at the time was to amplify structuralism by looking at what semiology had ignored, for example, matter or stuff (*hylé*) and the "other."

Simultaneously, she was aiming at rehabilitating the Freudian understanding of drive and desire in terms of interpreting poetic enunciation. What she retained from the world of structuralism was the idea of revolution in terms of textual mutation and transformation, which for Kristeva was the consequence of the Freudian return of the repressed, rather than the consequence of linguistic permutations whereby the speaker behavioristically adapts language to his or her world as a matter of everyday language use. Creole might be a good example in which adaptation and psychological impulses work together in order to deform or mutate normative language practices, both syntactic and semantic. Unlike Lévi-Strauss who abjured the psychologization of linguistics (in *Naked Man* he rejects Lacan), Kristeva says she introduced subjectivization which she examined in terms of "les facettes hétérogènes" whereby the stabilizations of language are disrupted by pulsions (the Freudian drives).

Kristeva's example points to a key distinction within structuralism that concerns the acceptance or rejection of psychology, often as reflected in creative semiotic activities (literature, painting, etc.). Saussure noticeably avoided mention of literature in the *Course*, thereby avoiding the kind of subjectivization one encounters in literary works. However, unlike Saussure, Kristeva has been of the view that (1) the diachrony of language *can* be interrupted and mutated by the artist, that (2) language is not just a social fact, but a psychological process that includes a prelinguistic sensorial experience related to the mother in very early child development, and that (3) Saussure's genderless depiction of the speaking subject as neuter is gender blind and requires revision.

Whereas Lévi-Strauss has been accused of being far too rationalistic in his approach to myth, Kristeva is vulnerable to the charge that she has promoted a mystical approach to its study (in the context, say, of Christian legend) as well as of language, particularly in terms of her stress upon mystical union with the mother. In her later work on *Génie feminine* (female genius), she insists that for a woman the divisions between body and soul, eros and agape, self and other are insupportable.[16] In the book *Polylogue*, the linguistic expression of such union was termed the *sémiotique*, whereas the term *symbolique* was reserved for the sort of structuralist view of language maintained by Saussure. The two were said by Kristeva to be in polyphonic relation. To see this, one can turn to James Joyce's *Finnegans Wake* in which the semiotic overruns the symbolic, as in the following well-known passage: "Calling all downs. Calling all downs to dayne. Array! Surrection! Eireweeker to the wohld bludyn world. O rally, O rally, O rally!"[17] In this case, the semiotic is visible in terms of the lyrical construction of sounds and rhythm that are draped over ordinary language such as "Calling all Cars! Calling all Cars!" which alludes to the Dick Tracy radio show of the 1930s. Also in play is "Calling all dawns today," which we know was on Joyce's mind because in the first draft of the *Wake* "downs" was originally written as "dawns." The passage is a call to arms. "O rally" is a hidden word inside the proper name Persse O'Reilly, a balladeer in Joyce's novel. Despite all these deformations whereby language seems to melt down, the rules of English are upheld such that we can decipher the text based on distinguishing identities and differences.

Indeed, the contrast between Lévi-Strauss and Kristeva generally points to what are, in effect, two types of structuralist thinkers: conservative technicians who tend toward abstract, formal, logical analysis, informed by attention to binary distinctions, and concerned largely with structure per se, and liberal implementers who carry structuralist thinking into domains where either its principles are called into question, as in the case of deconstruction as developed by Jacques Derrida, or where its application is extended, as in the case of Lacan's adaptation of structuralism to Freudian psychoanalysis, an approach that Kristeva also adopted. Among what one might call the purely analytical structuralists and semioticians are Charles Sanders Peirce, A. J. Griemas, Juri Lotman, Christian Metz, and Umberto Eco. Among the liberal implementers and innovators of structuralism and semiotics are Jacques Lacan, Roland Barthes, Tzvetan Todorov, Michael Riffaterre, Gérard Genette, and Jean Baudrillard. Michel Foucault, Gilles Deleuze, Jacques Derrida, and Louis Althusser are outliers who were clearly influenced by structuralist ideas. Roman Jakobson, it has to be said, bridged the hard-nosed analytical approach to structuralism with more liberal approaches, given that he was quite open to issues bearing on the psychology of language, particularly with respect to sound.

Given that it's not possible to discuss in depth all the major figures just cited above, we will focus at some length on just the three most relevant figures, at present in the languages and literatures, who incorporated structuralist thinking in their work. Barthes has already been mentioned, given his centrality, but he requires much more commentary. A belletristically inclined critic, he brought to literary and cultural analysis an effortless and seemingly instantaneous capacity to derive rules and laws from whatever he was observing, once he looked at his object as a discourse made up of signs that stood in place of phenomena. The capacity to discriminate in order to set up signifying oppositions occurs in Barthes the way wit occurs in the writings of Oscar Wilde. In a piece entitled "Adamov and Language," Barthes immediately notices that "the pinball machine in [Adamov's] *Ping Pong* symbolizes nothing at all; it does not express, it produces; it is a literal object, whose function is to engender, by its very objectivity, certain situations. But once again our criticism is misled, in its thirst for depth: these situations are not psychological, they are essentially *language situations*."[18] In such passages we can see Barthes observing in terms of binaries that are not transcendental to the text but embedded within it. Symbolization versus non-symbolization, expression versus production, depth versus surface, and psychology versus language-situation are inherent to the critic's perception as well as to the object of perception.

In terms of cultural critique, Barthes's aptly named book on Japan, *The Empire of Signs*, is part structuralist investigation and part travelogue. In it we can see how binary oppositions are redistributed in Tokyo in contrast with Paris or some other major European city. Speaking of Japanese cuisine, Barthes writes "Entirely visible (thought through, concerted, arranged to be seen, even from the point of view of painting, of the graphic) [Japanese food] is not deep or profound: what is edible lacks a precious heart, hidden force, a vital secret. No Japanese dish is provided with a *center* . . . it is all an ornament of another ornament."[19] According to Barthes, Japanese food is essentially a collection of fragments appropriate to indirection and detachment. As in the fiction of Robbe-Grillet mentioned above, signs are revealed in and as the materiality of things and become apparent to the naked eye in terms of their value distinctions: image versus substance, absent versus present center, ornamentation versus plainness, fragmentation versus wholeness, direction versus indirection, detachment versus attachment, and so on. Barthes doesn't systematize these oppositions into a full-blown structuralist chart of binary oppositions whereby Japanese culture can be decoded in terms of its underlying semiotic operating system, because his aim is simply to describe the world semiotically in a way that resembles the food he is talking about in terms of his offering a collection of fragments appropriate to indirection and detachment. As if in imitation of his analysis, his various sections in *Empire* are more ornamental than not, and the travelogue consists of mainly a visualization of Japan as a semiotic landscape, much as a prepared Japanese dish. Notable, however, is the derivation of not only semiotic dichotomies but Barthes's intuitive and almost immediate understanding of how the dichotomies are experienced in terms of personal likes and dislikes, attractions and repulsions, feelings and thoughts. In short, Barthes introduced issues of taste into structuralist analysis from both a subjective and objective orientation.

Barthes's overall oeuvre is vast and to his credit consists of all manner of studies that developed highly innovative strategies of investigation. The study *S/Z* on Balzac is celebrated for being probably the only literary critical work in existence that has commented on literally every sentence of a prose work. In line with structuralist thinking, Barthes analyzed Balzac's story "Sarrasine" about a transgendered person in terms of five codes (action, hermeneutic, culture, semantic, symbolic) and their interplay, hence bringing to light various crucially important structures that otherwise would pass by unnoticed. In *A Lover's Discourse*, Barthes conducted a loosely structuralist reading of lovers' tropes in literature that are arranged as if in a lexicon. In *The Fashion System*, a book on women's clothing ensembles, Barthes engaged in the kind of rigorous structuralism typical of Griemas and Eco. Barthes revealed the extraordinary application that structuralism has to literature and consumer culture as an insightful analytic, provided the critic has an especially acute sensibility, extraordinary powers of observation, and polymathic abilities, in addition to which one finds a writing style embodying what Barthes called "brio."

Lacan has also been mentioned, but requires much more commentary because his structuralist orientation is still being promulgated by figures such as Slavoj Žižek, Alenka Zupancic, Alain Badiou, and Jacques-Alain Miller. Indeed, it was during the mid-1950s that Lacan's applications of structuralism began to have revolutionary consequences for French thought, consequences Lacan himself built upon in subsequent years. Joël Dor describes the core of Lacan's structuralist revolution as follows:

> [Because] it is through the signifying order that the subject arises, he is always merely represented in the language that caused him. The foremost consequence of this, one that inserts the subject into the order of discourse, is that *a signifier is that which represents a subject for another signifier*. This consequence is inevitably brought about by the intrinsic structure of the language system. If the subject figures in discourse only as a representative, and if, moreover, it is a signifier that gives him the status of subject in discourse, then this can only be in relation to another signifier. *This is why the subject is an effect of the signifier, and only an effect*. In no way can he be the cause of the signifier.[20]

Lacan himself puts the matter this way in his *Écrits*:

> The effect of language is the cause introduced into the subject. By virtue of this effect, he is not the cause of himself: he bears within himself the worm of the cause that splits him. For this cause is the signifier, without which there would be no subject in the real. But this subject is what this signifier represents, and it can never represent anything except for another signifier, to which, from that point on, the listening subject is reduced. So we don't speak of the subject. That speaks of him, and it is there that he apprehends himself—and all the more necessarily so since, before he disappears as a subject beneath the signifier that he becomes because of the sole fact that *that* addresses him, he was absolutely nothing.[21]

As Alain Badiou has put it, the difference between Lacan's writings and the writings of his explicators is that he insisted on a discourse in which *not everything* is enigmatic. In Lacan's passage we are required to ponder the meaning of "the worm of the cause that splits him," which forces us to go over the passage retroactively, perhaps even many times. But not everything in the passage is quite so obscure. It is because the signifier addresses me that I disappear beneath it, on the one hand, or find myself represented by it, on the other hand. Our identity isn't based on our proper name but on all the words, pictures, documents, and so on that situate that proper name in relation to us. No doubt, our identity disappears or is retracted beneath this mass of signification even as it appears in various guises depending on the signifiers presented. Our identity papers produce us as an effect, one that is different each time, even though we could say we are their singular cause, having applied for them. Privileging oneself as cause alone is an imaginary trap of self-mirroring or apprehension that, in Lacan's view, led ego-psychologists astray. What they couldn't see is the worm underground that splits the subject as agent/effect by means of breaking up the Cartesian soil upon which the subject rests. Here the subject as an imaginary agency and cause of events that constitute his or her world is being mediated and broken up by the subject as the signifying effect of a symbolic order into which the subject is born. This modifies the structuralist doctrine that the subject is only an effect of language.

Among Lacan's most conspicuous structuralist writings is "The Instance of the Letter in the Unconscious" which revises Saussure's well-known image of a tree above which is placed a horizontal bar (or divisor) and above that the word "tree." Lacan's version of this "faulty illustration," as he calls it, is the depiction of two closed doors, one next to the other, and a horizontal bar above them. Over the bar we see the words "Gentleman" above the left door and "Ladies" above the right door. The doors themselves are blank and identical. The words are in binary differential opposition. The doors are the signifieds that receive their signification from the signifiers that are defined in terms of what they are not ("Gentlemen" not being "Ladies" and vice versa). For Lacan this means that the signifier has a structural relation that is transferred onto the blank doors such that each becomes a door of admission for one sex and prohibition for the other. The doors as signifieds therefore represent a law of difference that each sex experiences in terms of a taboo. This is why Lacan tells us the following story: "A train arrives at a station. A little boy and a little girl, brother and sister, are seated across from each other in a compartment next to the outside window that provides a view of the station platform buildings going by as the train comes to a stop. 'Look,' says the brother, 'we're at Ladies!' 'Imbecile!' replies his sister, 'Don't you see that we're at Gentlemen'"[22]. The brother and sister are like the blank doors until they arrive at the respective signifiers which in each case represents what each is not and socially constitutes a taboo or no-go for each child respectively. Lacan is saying that one comes to know one's sex not positively (inclusively) but in terms of a taboo (exclusion), which manifests difference under threat of punishment. The little girl arrives at "Ladies" only because she is banned from "Gentlemen" and the boy arrives at "Gentlemen" only because he is banned from "Ladies." The signifiers here are more than helpful labels, for in fact they are the expression of a *social law* that when materialized as signifieds on restroom doors carries the threat of social reprisal if their rule for inclusion/exclusion (endogamy/exogamy) is broken. Of central importance for Lacan is that difference is entirely symbolic, given that the doors, the restrooms, words, and even people are not essentially differentiated, only *culturally marked* as different, thanks to the signifier. Here *sexual difference is the effect of the signifier; it has no essential positivity.*

Last, we will consider Michel Foucault, in particular, his "Discourse on Language" which had been enormously influential on the new historians and American cultural critics of the late twentieth century. Like Lacan, Foucault understood signification in terms of constraint, exclusion, and the no-go or taboo. Indeed, at the time of its delivery at the Collège de France in 1970, Foucault's "Discourse on Language" was viewed as a major position paper with the import of a structuralist manifesto. Its argument concluded, "and now . . . let those with little comprehension of theory call all this—if its appeal is stronger than its meaning for them—structuralism."[23]

Foucault's starting point is that "In every society the production of discourse is at once controlled, selected, organized, and redistributed according to a certain number of procedures."[24] Foucault terms these procedures *prohibitions* and *exclusions*. That "we are not free to say just anything" is historically not so much the consequence of direct authoritarian repression, not that this hasn't occurred, than it is the result of socially instituting divisions or oppositions that make up systems that constrain and regulate discourse.[25] Such oppositions establish rules that exercise control. For example, distinctions between truth and falsehood have a regulative function. Internal to discourse, the exclusion of the unsupported assumption, the nonsequitur, the ungrammatical sentence, illogical reasoning, and so on make up a system of taboos of which discourse is the effect. From an external point of view, such internal rules establish norms of sense-making considered socially acceptable as opposed to the expression of nonsensical or irrational discourse that will be ignored.

The binary opposition of truth versus falsehood complements another fundamental principle of exclusion, the binary distinction between reason and folly. "From the depths of the Middle Ages, a man was mad if his speech could not be said to form part of the common discourse of men."[26] Historically, this principle of exclusion undergoes modification when folly begins to undergo a transformation whereby what used to be called madness is suddenly considered to be art. *Hamlet's* mad scenes already point to this revalorization whereby madness is transformed into the literary. In this way, madness comes into appearance as "masked truth," not that this does away with the reason/folly opposition. Reason/folly, truth/falsehood, sense/nonsense, logic/illogic make up a series of kindred oppositions, made operative both within and outside the discourse, that enforce a boundary, limit, or threshold that determines the validity or respectability of a discourse.

From an external point of view, the author, too, is a regulatory principle whose function is to unify writings and statements. As external cause, the author accounts for the internal origin of a discourse's production (its "genealogy" in Foucault's vocabulary) and significance and thereby accounts for a discourse's meaning, which the author principle unifies and identifies. In terms of the reason/folly distinction, "the author [is] the index of the work's truthfulness. A proposition [is] held to derive its scientific value from its author."[27] Foucault is thinking about scientific discourse whereby the truth/falsehood distinction is resolved by the greatness of the author's genius in relation to factual proofs that were predicted by the author before they were actually established, often by others. But the author principle can just as easily validate the creativity or genius of a work of art that violates the truth/falsehood distinction or sense/nonsense distinction as long as the author principle gives consistency and meaning to the violation or crossing of the threshold.

Commentary, which is also seen as largely external to a primary text, also has its prohibitions if only in terms of what discourses it selects to address and hence reinforce. "Commentary limit[s] the hazards of discourse through the action of an identity taking the form of repetition and sameness."[28] Through commentary the primary text reappears in its identity as something shared, familiar, finite, but also potentially inexhaustible and capable of infinite recommencement, modification, and reframing. Yet, "commentary averts the chance element of discourse by giving it its due: it gives us the opportunity to say something other than the text itself, but on condition that it is the text itself which is uttered and, in some ways, finalized."[29] Externally, commentary guarantees the identity or self-sameness of the primary text, while internal to the primary text's discourse, such commentary serves the purpose of making the discourse reappear as something new and different. The novelty of a text "lies no longer in what is said, but in its reappearance" as commentary.[30] Is the primary text the effect of its secondary commentaries? That would be the structuralist thesis. Internal to a discourse, commentary, similar to the author principle, governs an interplay of differences—of ideas, values, perspectives, techniques, styles, intentions—but whereas the author principle does so by means of establishing the supposition of individuality and selfhood, commentary does so by means of repeating a text differently through multiple commentators. In that sense commentary and authorship themselves make up a fundamental binary opposition.

To complicate matters, Foucault observes that the commentary/authorship opposition is itself opposed by "the organization of disciplines." The disciplines are opposed to the author principle because "disciplines are defined by groups of objects, methods, their corpus of propositions considered to be true, the interplay of rules and definitions, of techniques and tools."[31] Therefore, not the individual but an instituted field now occupies the place of what Lacan called the "subject-who-is-supposed-to-know," a conception dear to Foucault. In opposition to commentary, disciplines are not interested in "meanings which must be rediscovered, nor an identity to be reiterated," because a discipline's function is the possibility for "the construction of new statements." Hence, "for a discipline to exist, there must be the possibility of formulating—and of doing so ad infinitum—fresh propositions."[32] Disciplines are clearly external to the discourses they manage by means of imposing rules of inclusion and exclusion: that is, rules of identification, classification, ordering, and distribution. Foucault doesn't mention it, but disciplines in their classificatory role relate rather closely to the archive (library science, for example). Of course, whether a discourse is poetry or prose, mimetic or abstract, satirical or farcical concerns the implementation of barriers, limits, and thresholds requiring internal analysis of a discourse. Foucault notes that criticism, or close reading, is more integral to disciplinarity and the archive than one might be led to think, given the bias toward forensics.

Taken altogether, of chief interest to Foucault are the "principles of analysis" of which discursivity is the effect rather than the cause. This conforms to Foucault's argument, derived from the fields of both phenomenology and structuralism, that objects of knowledge do not exist independently of the analytical procedures whereby those objects are constituted or constructed. This too was well anticipated by Lacan who some twenty years before Foucault had been lecturing on the illusory supposition of the subject *and* the object on the part of the signifier. As Foucault put this, discourse itself is nullified "in placing itself at the disposal of the signifier" and that discourse "never involves anything but signs."[33] This is precisely the point Lacan was trying to make in the story mentioned above about the brother and sister arriving by train at the restroom doors. The signifiers "Gentlemen" and "Ladies" (the distinctive feature of sex and gender) *presuppose* a subject defined in terms of its exclusion that the subject derives not from the signifiers themselves but from an object world that is assumed to exist *a priori*. This means that for the subjects arriving on the train, heteronormativity appears to be predetermined by an independent order of things that the children, not unlike most grown-ups, will uncritically assume is a matter of nature. That the object is only *supposed* by the signifier escapes the children's attention. In Foucault, there is the slight modification that the object is supposed *a priori* by a *discourse* and that it is not accidental that the exclusionary principles of discourse analysis have been set up to conceal this sleight of hand. This is but a modification of what is essentially the structuralist insight that people mistakenly treat subjects and objects as if they were more fundamental than the signs with which they are represented. This can be summarized in Lacan's formulation that a signifier represents (i.e., supposes, supports) a subject in relation to another signifier, though what Foucault himself will emphasize in work after the "Discourse on Language" is how the social subject, however mediated by the signifier, accedes to being a practitioner of the very signifier that presupposes and hence constitutes him or her.

Wake Forest University (United States)

NOTES

1. Terence Hawkes, *Structuralism and Semiotics* (Berkeley: University of California Press, 1977), 17.

2. Jean Dubois, Mathée Giacomo, Louis Guespin, Christiane Marcellesi, Jean-Baptiste Marcellesi, and Jean-Pierre Mével, *Dictionnaire de linguistique* (Paris: Librairie Larousse, 1973), 432.

3. Roland Barthes, "The Structuralist Activity," in *Critical Essays*, trans. Richard Howard (Evanston: Northwestern University Press, 1972), 214–15.

4. Francois Dosse, *History of Structuralism*, vol. 1, trans. Deborah Glassman (Minneapolis: Minnesota University Press, 1997), 71.

5. Alain Robbe-Grillet, *The Voyeur* (New York: Grove Press, 1967), 31.

6. Robbe-Grillet, *The Voyeur*, 29.

7. Ibid., 150.

8. Stephen Heath, *The Nouveau Roman* (Philadelphia: Temple University Press, 1971); Stephen Heath, *Questions of Cinema* (London: McMillan, 1981).

9. Gertrude Stein, *Stanzas in Meditation* (New Haven: Yale University Press, 2012), 143; Gertrude Stein, "Tender Buttons," in *Selected Writings of Gertrude Stein*, ed. Carl Van Vechten (New York: Modern Library, 1945), 471.

10. Roman Jakobson, "Two Aspects of Language and Two Types of Aphasic Disturbances," in *On Language* (Cambridge, MA: Harvard University Press, 1990), 119.

11. Ferdinand de Saussure, *Course in General Linguistics*, trans. Wade Baskin (New York: McGraw-Hill Blook Company, 1966), 113.

12. Claude Lévi-Strauss, *The Naked Man*, trans. John and Doreen Weightman (New York: Harper and Row, Publishers, 1981), 684–85.

13. Lévi-Strauss, *The Naked Man*, 678.

14. Julia Kristeva, *Pulsions du temps* (Paris: Fayard, 2013), 159. Translation mine.

15. Kristeva, *Pulsions du temps*, 159.

16. Ibid., 169.

17. James Joyce, *Finnegans Wake* (New York: Viking, 1980), 593.

18. Roland Barthes, "Adamov and Language," in *The Eiffel Tower and Other Mythologies*, trans. Richard Howard (New York: Hill and Wang, 1979), 55–56.

19. Roland Barthes, *L'empire des signes* (Paris: Flammarion, 1970), 32. Translation mine.

20. Joël Dor, *Introduction to the Reading of Lacan*, ed. Judith Feher Gurewich (New York: The Other Press, 1998), 137.

21. Dor, *Introduction to the Reading of Lacan*, 138. The citation, quoted in Dor's book, is taken from Lacan's "Position de l'inconscient" in *Écrits* (Paris: Seuil, 1966): 829–850.

22. Jacques Lacan, *Écrits*, trans. Bruce Fink (New York: Norton, 2002), 417.

23. Michel Foucault, "The Discourse on Language," in *The Archaeology of Knowledge*, trans. A. M. Sheridan Smith (New York: Pantheon Books, 1971), 234.

24. Foucault, "The Discourse on Language," 216.

25. Ibid.

26. Ibid., 217.

27. Ibid., 222.

28. Ibid.

29. Ibid., 221.

30. Ibid.

31. Ibid., 222.

32. Ibid., 223.

33. Ibid., 228.

WORKS CITED

Barthes, Roland. *L'empire des signes*. Paris: Flammarion, 1970.

Barthes, Roland. "The Structuralist Activity." In *Critical Essays*. Trans. Richard Howard. Evanston: Northwestern University Press, 1972. 213–20.

Barthes, Roland. *S/Z* [1970]. Trans. Richard Howard. New York: Hill and Wang, 1974.

Barthes, Roland. *A Lover's Discourse* [1977]. Trans. Richard Howard. New York: Hill and Wang, 1978.

Barthes, Roland. "Adamov and Language." In *The Eiffel Tower and Other Mythologies*. Trans. Richard Howard. New York: Hill and Wang, 1979. 55–58.

Barthes, Roland. *The Fashion System* [1967]. Trans. Richard Howard. New York: Hill and Wang, 1983.

Baudrillard, Jean. *La société de consummation*. Paris: SEGP, 1970.

Bernstein, Charles. *The Pitch of Poetry*. Chicago: University of Chicago Press, 2016.

Dor, Joël. *Introduction to the Reading of Lacan*. Ed. Judith Feher Gurewich. New York: The Other Press, 1998.

Dosse, Françoise. *History of Structuralism, vol. 1* [1991]. Trans. Deborah Glassman. Minneapolis: Minnesota University Press, 1997.

Dubois, Jean, Mathée Giacomo, Louis Guespin, Christiane Marcellesi, Jean-Baptiste Marcellesi, and Jean-Pierre Mével. *Dictionnaire de linguistique*. Paris: Librairie Larousse, 1973.

Foucault, Michel. *The Order of Things* [1966]. London: Tavistock, 1970.

Foucault, Michel. "The Discourse on Language." In *The Archaeology of Knowledge* [1969]. Trans. A. M. Sheridan Smith. New York: Pantheon Books, 1971. 215–37.

Hawkes, Terence. *Structuralism and Semiotics*. Berkeley: University of California Press, 1977.

Heath, Stephen. *The Nouveau Roman*. Philadelphia: Temple University Press, 1971.

Heath, Stephen. *Questions of Cinema*. London: McMillan, 1981.

Jakobson, Roman. "Two Aspects of Language and Two Types of Aphasic Disturbances [1956]."
    In *On Language*. Eds. Linda R. Waugh and Monique Monville-Burston. Cambridge, MA:
    Harvard University Press, 1990. 115–33.
Joyce, James. *Finnegans Wake* [1939]. New York: Viking, 1982.
Kristeva, Julia. *Polylogue*. Paris: Seuil, 1977.
Kristeva, Julia. *Pulsions du temps*. Paris: Fayard, 2013.
Lacan, Jacques. *Écrits* [1966]. Trans. Bruce Fink. New York: Norton, 2002.
Lévi-Strauss, Claude. *The Naked Man: Introduction to the Science of Mythology, IV*. Trans. John
    Weightman and Doreen Weightman. New York: Harper and Row Publishers. 1981.
Robbe-Grillet, Alain. *The Voyeur* [1955]. Trans. Richard Howard. New York: Grove Press,
    1967.
Saussure, Ferdinand de. *Course in General Linguistics* [1916]. Trans. Wade Baskin. New York:
    McGraw-Hill Book Company, 1966.
Stein, Gertrude. "Tender Buttons" [1914]. In *Selected Writings of Gertrude Stein*. Ed. Carl Van
    Vechten. New York: Modern Library, 1945. 407–52.
Stein, Gertrude. *Stanzas in Meditation* [1956]. Eds. Susannah Hollister and Emily Setina.
    New Haven: Yale University Press, 2012.
Žižek, Slavoj. *The Sublime Object of Ideology*. New York: Verso, 1989.

CHAPTER THREE

Narrative and Narratology

GERALD PRINCE

A narrative is an entity taken to constitute the representation of at least two related asynchronous events (or one state of affairs and one event) that do not presuppose or imply each other ("John tried to keep his balance but Peter pushed him off the ledge"; "Mary was always optimistic and then she lost her job"). This definition, which agrees (or does not radically conflict) with commonly held views about the nature of narrative,[1] evokes the *semantic* rather than *semiotic* character of narratives: the latter, unlike signs, are not *recognized* but *understood*. The definition also allows for a distinction between narrative and nonnarrative (a purely phatic comment, say, an existential statement, a syllogism, or the mere description of an action or event like "John ate" or "It rained") and it makes room for a substantial amount of diversity by not stipulating the medium of narrative representations (language, for example, still or moving pictures, gestures, or a combination thereof), not mentioning their content and its relation to anthropomorphic experience, not specifying their truth or falsehood, fictionality or factuality, ordinariness or literariness, spontaneity or deliberateness.

Narratology, which was structuralist-inspired and which focused on narrative as an autonomous subject of inquiry, studies what all and only possible narratives have in common as well as what enables them to differ from one another *qua* narratives and it aims to describe the rules and operations involved in narrative production and processing. It counts among early representatives its French or Francophonic founders—Roland Barthes,[2] Tzvetan Todorov,[3] Gérard Genette,[4] A. J. Greimas,[5] Claude Bremond[6]—and continuators like Mieke Bal,[7] Seymour Chatman,[8] and Gerald Prince.[9] As for precursors and relatives, they include Claude-Edmonde Magny and Jean Pouillon, Vladimir Propp and the Russian Formalists, German and Austrian scholars like Käte Friedemann, Käte Hamburger, Eberhard Lämmert, or Franz Stanzel, English and American scholars like Percy Lubbock, Wayne C. Booth, Robert Scholes, and Robert Kellogg, not to mention Greeks like Plato and Aristotle.

In its first decades—from the mid-1960s to the mid-1980s—narratology devoted most of its attention to isolating and describing the universal constitutive elements of the narrated (the story reported, the events depicted, the "what" that is represented) and the narrating (the discourse or the way the story is reported and the events are depicted) as well as the principles governing their modes of combination. For example, narratologists characterized such basic constituents of the narrated as states and processes, goal-directed actions and mere happenings, accomplishments or achievements and they distinguished those essential to the coherence of the story from those not essential to it.[10] They examined the (syntagmatic and paradigmatic, spatiotemporal, thematic, logical, functional, transformational) relations between the basic units.[11] They showed that ever more complex narrative sequences can be said to result from the combining of simpler ones through operations like conjunction, embedding, or alternation.[12] They explored the ways stories can be semantically analyzed as possible worlds consisting of domains (sets of events pertaining to given actors) and the ways each domain is governed by alethic, epistemic, axiological, or deontic modal constraints that establish what is or could be the case in the represented world, govern the actors' knowledge, set their values, duties, and objectives, guide their course of action, and determine what takes place.[13]

Narratologists also explored the narrating, describing the temporal order that narrative representations can follow, for instance, investigating narrative speed and its canonical tempos (ellipsis, summary, scene, stretch, pause), studying narrative perspective, the extent of narrative mediation, and the major modes of narration (ulterior, anterior, simultaneous, intercalated), specifying the signs referring to the narrator or to the narratee, and analyzing the possible distances (physical, social, intellectual, emotional) between the narrational actants as well as the distances separating them from the characters and events in the story.[14]

In fact, though narratology was concerned with the governing principles of narrative, though it tried to describe what allows narratives to have meanings instead of what meanings particular narratives have, and though it was or aspired to be an autonomous branch of poetics rather than a basis for critical commentary, narratological features and categories constitute a toolkit for the exploration of particular sets of texts and they have fostered an important body of narratological criticism. After all, as Genette's *Narrative Discourse* and a critical tradition concentrating on narrative technique and going back to Henry James demonstrate, any narratological characterization of a text can provide a starting point for a reading, any technical feature can induce the construction of meaning, any "how" can yield a "why." Narratological description can help to account for the uniqueness of a given narrative, to compare and contrast (sets of) narratives, to establish classes of narratives according to narratively relevant traits, and it can also help to devise interpretations, to buttress interpretive arguments, or to illumine various reactions to narrative texts. Besides, by focusing on the narrative dimension of texts, narratology typically encourages the study of narrative as thematic frame and theme. This led to the analysis of the theme of narrative in many texts (from *The Odyssey* and *The Quest of the Holy Grail* to *Candide, Sarrasine, Nausea*) and contributed to the so-called narrative turn, the reliance on the notion of "narrative" to discuss not only artistic, literary, or verbal texts but any number of practices and domains: political ideas, for instance, family meals, psychoanalytic sessions, or scientific endeavors.[15]

Noting that (narrative) representations exhibit different degrees of narrativity, that the importance of a narrative structure in their economy varies, that they are more or less narrative, as it were, narratologists analyzed the factors responsible for this phenomenon. Gerald Prince, for example, argued that the narrativity of a representation depends on the extent to which that representation constitutes an autonomous whole consisting of discrete, specific, and positive situations and events, concerning some kind of conflict that involves human entities, and including alternative courses of action that do not take place but could have been followed by these entities.[16] Didier Coste[17] adopted a similar scalar view of narrativity. Apart from maintaining that the latter varies with the degree of narrative dominance in a representation and that this dominance can be quantitative or hierarchic, he specified that the presence in a text of singular (rather than banal) actions involving both an agent and a patient as well as deep or remote causality and the presence of references to possible but unrealized events positively affect narrativity. Likewise, Marie-Laure Ryan[18] contended that some configurations of events are more narrative than others. For her, narrativity depends on the richness and variety of virtual embedded narratives (representations produced in the minds of characters and fashioned in terms of their knowledge, duties, wishes, intentions, or fantasies); it is a function of unrealized strings of events (unsuccessful actions, broken promises, crushed hopes); and it increases as the narrative goes back and forth between the characters' competing plans. Ryan[19] would also sketch a taxonomy of different modes of narrativity, including the simple narrativity of fairy tales and urban legends, the complex narrativity of Dickens or Dumas, the figural narrativity of lyric, historiographic, or philosophic texts, and the instrumental narrativity of debates and sermons.[20]

In an attempt to systematize or integrate their results, and no doubt because of the influence of structuralism and, more particularly, linguistics on their discipline, narratologists sometimes proposed models of narrative and its different dimensions that took the shape of grammars or sets of statements and formulas linked by an ordered series of rules.[21] According to Prince, the most comprehensive of these grammars would ideally comprise a (syntactic) component generating the macro- and microstructures of all and only sequences of narrated situations and events; a (semantic) component interpreting these structures (characterizing their content); a component consisting of rules operating on the interpreted structures and accounting for the narrating; and a (pragmatic) component specifying the factors affecting the narrativity of the output of the first three components.[22]

Most generally, in line with the narrative turn that they helped to bring about and like other students of narrative,[23] narratologists made it clear that, while narrative can fulfill any number of functions, from informing to diverting attention, there are functions that it excels at or is unique in fulfilling. As etymology suggests, narrative constitutes a particular kind of knowledge. It does not simply reflect what takes place; it discovers and invents what can take place. It does not merely report changes of state; it establishes them and interprets them as meaningful parts of signifying wholes and can thus illuminate individual fate or group destiny, the unity of a self as well as the nature of a society. By showing that disparate events and states of affairs can compose one signifying structure (or vice versa) and by providing a particular kind of order and coherence to a possible reality, narrative gives examples for that reality's redescription or transformation and mediates between what is and what may be. Above all, by instituting and linking distinct temporal moments, by exposing the meaning of time and imposing meaning on it, narrative reads time, shows how to read it, and sheds light on temporality and on human beings as temporal beings. Indeed, narratologists emphasized how studying narrative, its constituent parts, and the way it can be constructed, paraphrased, summarized, or expanded is studying one of the basic and singularly human means of making sense.[24]

If, in its initial phase, narratology concentrated on narrative invariants; if it focused on questions pertaining to form, technique, and poiesis instead of questions pertaining to authorial intentions, receiver reactions, or contextual situations and functions; if it favored the synchronic over the diachronic and system over history, it slowly underwent significant transformations. This was, no doubt, in part because of the influence of other (sub-)disciplines (feminist theory, for instance, or reader-response criticism), in part because of increased awareness of its limitations, biases, or flaws (scientism, say, or disregard for communicative practices or representational media), and, perhaps most important, in part because of its own interests, goals, and results. For example, underlining the semantic as opposed to semiotic character of narrative leads to an interest in it not only as product but also as production and meaning-making instrument or grid. Similarly, aiming to describe the rules that govern narrative processing and to characterize narrative competence leads to an interest in processors (listeners, spectators, readers). Moreover, attending to features that affect narrativity prompts consideration of circumstances that direct attention to these features. Supplying tools that help to analyze particular texts or to shed light on responses to them encourages the exploration of *what* rather than *how* these texts can mean. Gradually, what could be called *classical narratology* turned into what David Herman[25] called *postclassical narratology*.

As its name suggests, postclassical narratology is not a mere negation or rejection of classical narratology but more of a prolongation, an expansion, a refinement, a diversification of it. If postclassical narratology asks the questions asked by classical narratology—what is narrative as opposed to nonnarrative, for instance, or what are the possible kinds of narrative—it also raises many other questions pertaining, for example, to their cognitive and affective dimensions, to their function and not merely their functioning, to their history as much as to the system underlying them, and to what particular narratives mean in particular contexts. Indeed, it can even seem that no question, nothing in narrative texts or their indefinitely numerous contexts is alien to postclassical narratology and that the very phrase is more or less synonymous with "narrative studies."[26]

In its expansion and diversification, postclassical narratology utilizes a more varied corpus. It relies on many more instruments: not just linguistics and its various inflections, but all the tools afforded by the textual, cultural, communicational, and cognitive sciences. It is plural, as evidenced by the recurrent use of compound or hyphenated expressions to characterize its different manifestations (e.g., feminist narratology, rhetorical narratology, postcolonial narratology, socio-narratology). It is more given to interdisciplinarity. It is more inclined to formulating relativistic arguments. It is more attentive to hermeneutic concerns and more cognizant of the role of the receiver. For example, rhetorical narratology, as developed by James Phelan[27] and Peter Rabinowitz,[28] proves mindful of the ideological functioning of texts and interested in the ethical and aesthetic judgments of readers. Similarly, the feminist narratology associated with Susan Lanser,[29] Robyn Warhol,[30] Ruth Page,[31] or Susan Stanford Friedman[32] insists on the ways sex, gender, or sexuality affect the shape of narratives and it does not separate text from context.

Among the many other approaches to narrative study subsumed under postclassical narratology, *cognitive narratology* has attracted a good deal of attention and produced a good deal of research. Introduced by Manfred Jahn,[33] the term refers to the examination of those aspects of mind pertaining to narrative production and processing. Cognitive narratology focuses on the activities and operations involved in the construction and understanding of narrative as well as on narrative as an instrument for making sense of self and world. Exploiting the resources provided by the cognitive sciences, by literary studies, or by classical narratology, it is presaged by a variety of work in these fields. For instance, psychologists like Perry Thorndyke,[34] David Rumelhart,[35] and Jean Mandler[36] constructed story grammars accounting for important structural elements of stories and useful for the exploration of narrative understanding, memorization, summarization, and storage. A philosopher like Roman Ingarden examined, as early as 1931, the ways readers concretize literary works and transform mere sets of words and phrases into esthetic objects.[37] Another phenomenologist, Paul Ricœur, developed a tripartite model of mimesis in which the temporal configurations represented by narrative plots are prefigured in the field of life and refigured through narrative reception.[38] Researchers in artificial intelligence studied the role played in textual processing by various kinds of stereotypical mental representations of sets of events and states of affairs, various frames, schemas, scripts, and plans.[39] Building on William Labov's analyses of narratives of personal experience, which provided a basis for understanding the organization and tellability of narratives,[40] linguists and anthropologists studied ways in which narrative functions as a tool for making sense of different kinds of phenomena.[41]

There were precursors among literary scholars too. Roland Barthes described in *S/Z* the major codes in terms of which narrative representations can be read.[42] Jonathan Culler, in *Structuralist Poetics*, discussed the knowledge of literary conventions and operations that allows readers to read poems and fictions literally and that constitutes a kind of literary competence.[43] In the 1960s and 1970s reader-response theorists and critics argued that readers, with their psychological makeup, their horizons of expectations, their assumptions and knowledge, played an essential role in the interpretation, evaluation, and very constitution of texts. Particularly interesting to narratologists was Wolfgang Iser's work on the implied reader in prose fiction.[44] Like Ingarden, Iser used a phenomenological approach and made a distinction between the text, its concretizing, and its transformation into a work of art. To take both text and reading activity into account, he devised the implied reader. The latter is an entity deducible from the text as well as a meaning-producing tool, a set of mental operations used in sense-making (e.g., choosing and arranging information, relating past and present knowledge, eliminating textual areas of indeterminacy or gaps). It encompasses the constraints and directions set by the text as well as the mental activities involved in reading.

Narratologists themselves, including some classical ones, did not ignore the operations at work in narrative processing. Thus, Meir Sternberg[45] showed how assessments of and responses to narrated situations and events are affected by the serial positioning, the primacy and recency, of various textual clues;[46] Peter Rabinowitz's characterization of the different reception positions that readers adopt when reading narrative fiction and James Phelan's clarification of it in his analysis of narrative as rhetoric captured the interaction of different belief systems involved in processing;[47] and Gerald Prince[48] concluded his study of the form and functioning of narrative by opting for a cognitive rather than textual definition of narrative and proposing that narrative is not only or not so much a certain kind of representation but also and even more so a certain kind of grid for processing representations.

A particularly influential kind of postclassical narratology that makes significant use of cognitive concepts, categories, and activities is the natural narratology elaborated by Monika Fludernik. According to Fludernik, experientiality—"the quasi-mimetic evocation of 'real-life' experience"[49]—rather than plot, which is only one of its manifestations, is the defining element of narrativity. Experientiality involves cognitive parameters based on one's embodied presence and engagement in the world and it constitutes the foundation of the so-called natural, spontaneous narratives occurring in everyday life as well as of more sophisticated narratives and, indeed, of narrativization, of the processing of texts as narratives. Fludernik model may not be powerful enough since it does not take into account representations of sequences of events that do not refer to human beings and their experience (e.g., "It snowed and then it rained and the snow melted"). It may also be too powerful and include in its domain representations of human experiences that do not refer to any action or change of state (e.g., "I feel pretty, Oh, so pretty!"). But it has the virtue of conforming to the common view that stories crucially involve and are interpreted in terms of anthropomorphic concerns and anthropomorphic projects.

Continuing and developing various exploitations of cognitive parameters in order to illuminate narrative functioning, cognitive narratologists and their cousins have investigated, in narrative texts as well as in encounters between texts and receivers, aspects of what Herman called "the nexus of narrative and mind."[50] For instance, in the important essay in which Jahn[51] points to the elaboration of a cognitive narratology, he shows how cognitive frames govern the interpretation of a text and are modified or replaced by other frames when textual features call for it. Alan Palmer too draws on the cognitive sciences in focusing on how the minds of fictional characters are constructed by authors or their readers and in stressing that fictional mental functioning is revealed not only through depictions or presentations of a character's consciousness but also through the character's actions, reactions, and interactions.[52] In particular, he demonstrates the importance of the continuing-consciousness frame in fashioning characters' minds, a frame which allows for the creation of a consciousness on the basis of different textual passages and of subframes involving intermental (shared, joint) thinking or the continuum between thought and action. In her exploration of readers' interest in fictional texts, Lisa Zunshine invokes theory of mind and human mind-reading capacities as well as the capacity to monitor representational sources (keep track of who said, thought, or felt what in what context) and characters' states of mind. She argues that reading fiction can promote the intricate use of these capacities, constitute a learning experience, and increase mental ability.[53] Furthermore, at least some of the abundant and varied production of Marie-Laure Ryan—who has examined such topics as linguistic models in narratology, possible worlds and narrative semantics, the nature of narrative fiction, space in narrative and narrative in space[54] and who has expressed reservations about the tendency of cognitive narratologists to adopt ready-made notions from cognitive science and to make exaggerated claims about the cognitive importance of narrative[55]—can be put under the banner of cognitive narratology: think of her study of mental immersion and the way receivers update mental models, for example, or of her work in transmedial narratology and her view of narrative as a frame that enables the (more or less efficient) processing of texts.[56] Last but by no means least, David Herman has helped both to expound and to develop cognitive narratology by characterizing the various factors, dimensions, and research areas pertinent to it and by studying some of the operations that underlie inferences about storyworlds or their constituent elements, by examining the relation between textual features and responses to texts, and by exploring narrative as an interpretive tool.[57]

Another postclassical approach to narrative study that has given rise to a lot of work is unnatural narratology or unnatural narrative theory. According to some of its practitioners, including Brian Richardson[58] who was among the very first to explore systematically "unnatural" aspects of narrative representations (e.g., unnatural temporalities or unnatural narrators), unnatural narratology focuses on anti-mimetic narratives (as distinct from mimetic ones and from nonmimetic ones which simply expand the domain of mimetic conventions from the natural to the supernatural, say, or from planet Earth to Jupiter or Mars). Anti-mimetic narratives are anti-illusionistic and, above all, unconventional. They relish unexpectedness, they (intentionally) contravene the basic foundations and assumptions of conversational, nonfictional, natural narratives, and they violate the precepts of realism and mimeticism. Other practitioners, who consider narratives to be unnatural if they involve elements that cannot (or do not) exist in the real world (e.g., talking animals, telepathy, or time travel), include nonmimetic narratives in the set of unnatural narrative representations but make a distinction between unnatural aspects that are conventional and unnatural aspects that have not (yet) been (entirely) conventionalized.[59] In any case, regardless of their definition of unnatural narrative; regardless of whether they prove mainly interested in identifying and appreciating the transgression of mimetic principles or whether they are primarily concerned with the difficulties this transgression occasions or with the strategies that might resolve them; and regardless of their dependence on such fuzzy notions as unexpectedness and unconventionality, "unnatural narratologists" have discussed a large number of representations that challenge the soundness or accuracy of narratological categories, discriminations, and arguments, that point to more or less significant elements which (classical) narratology, in its quest for universals, may have ignored or misconstrued, and that (should) result in alterations of narratological models. Some *fabulas* and *syuzhets* are inconsistent, some narrators and narratees multiform and contradictory, some focalizations weird, some characters ontologically diverse, and narratology must account for them too.

There are several other postclassical narratologies that, in recent years, have generated considerable interest: historical or diachronic narratology,[60] for example, which examines the diachronic development of narrative elements (unreliable narration, free indirect discourse, internal point of view) and their functioning in particular time periods, or affective narratology, which focuses on the links between narrative and emotions, including the role of the latter in stories, the ways in which they condition the very structure of representations, or receivers' emotional engagement with narrative.[61] There are also narratologies that should be developed. Geographical narratology, for instance, would explore the relations between geography and narrative forms or traits; neuronarratology or bionarratology, apart from studying biological correlates of emotions, their activation, their fluctuations, their valences, would map brain areas, say, to specific (sets of) narrative features or their interplay and would analyze narrative disorders like the inability to order experiences in story form or to consider virtualities in the unfolding of event sequences; and evolutionary narratology would investigate the ways narrative and its diversification fit within evolutionary theory, the kinds of survival advantage that they afford, the aspects of evolutionary fitness that they represent, the types of adaptive traits that they constitute, the relations with evolutionary features, mechanisms, and processes that they have.

Whatever the particular kind or branch of narratology involved and whether classical or postclassical glasses are worn and synchronic or diachronic, formalist or cognitive, natural or unnatural approaches and interests are operating, some of the future tasks of the discipline seem clear. Narratologists should continue to refine and systematize narratological knowledge; they should further specify what narrative understanding entails; they should further explore the functions, the "why" (rather than the "what" or the "how") of narrative; and they should develop models of narrative or sets of narratives that are explicit and complete (accounting for all and only narratives in the relevant set) but that are also realistic, that is, grounded on empirical or experimental (cross-cultural and cross-media) study. After all, theory should agree with reality, the map should conform to the territory, the description should correspond to the phenomena, and such models can only facilitate the systematic examination of narratology's singularly human object.

University of Pennsylvania (United States)

NOTES

1. See, for example, William Labov, *Language in the Inner City* (Philadelphia: University of Pennsylvania Press, 1972); Brian Richardson, *Unnatural Narrative: Theory, History, and*

Practice (Columbus: The Ohio State University Press, 2015); Marie-Laure Ryan, "Narrative," in *Routledge Encyclopedia of Narrative Theory*, eds. David Herman, Manfred Jahn, and Marie-Laure Ryan (London: Routledge, 2005), 344–48; and Tzvetan Todorov, *Introduction to Poetics*, trans. Richard Howard (Minneapolis: University of Minnesota Press, 1981).

2. Roland Barthes, "An Introduction to the Structural Analysis of Narrative," *New Literary History* 6 (1975): 237–62.

3. Tzvetan Todorov, *Grammaire du Décaméron* (The Hague: Mouton, 1969).

4. Gérard Genette, "Boundaries of Narrative," *New Literary History* 8 (1976): 1–15; Gérard Genette, *Narrative Discourse: An Essay in Method*, trans. Jane E. Lewin (Ithaca: Cornell University Press, 1980).

5. A. J. Greimas, *Structural Semantics: An Attempt at a Method*, trans. Daniele McDowell, Ronald Schleifer, and Alan Velie (Lincoln: University of Nebraska Press, 1983).

6. Claude Bremond, *Logique du récit* (Paris: Seuil, 1973).

7. Mieke Bal, *Narratologie: essais sur la signification narrative dans quatre romans modernes* (Paris: Klincksieck, 1977); and Mieke Bal, *Narratology: Introduction to the Theory of Narrative*, trans. Christine van Boheemen (Toronto: University of Toronto Press, 1985).

8. Seymour Chatman, *Story and Discourse: Narrative Structure in Fiction and Film* (Ithaca: Cornell University Press, 1978).

9. Gerald Prince, *A Grammar of Stories: An Introduction* (The Hague: Mouton, 1973); and Gerald Prince, *Narratology: The Form and Functioning of Narrative* (Berlin: De Gruyter, 1982).

10. Roland Barthes, "An Introduction to the Structural Analysis of Narrative," 1975; Chatman, *Story and Discourse*, 1978.

11. Chatman, *Story and Discourse*, 1978; Prince, *Narratology*, 1982; and Tzvetan Todorov, *Introduction to Poetics*, 1981.

12. Bal, *Narratology*, 1985; Claude Bremond, *Logique du récit*, 1973; Prince, *A Grammar of Stories*, 1973; Tzvetan Todorov, "Les Catégories du récit littéraire," *Communications* 8 (1966): 125–51; and Tzvetan Todorov, *Introduction to Poetics*, 1981.

13. See, for example, Lubomír Doležel, "Narrative Semantics," *PTL* 1 (1976): 129–51; Thomas Pavel, "Narrative Domains," *Poetics Today* 1 (1980): 105–14; and Marie-Laure Ryan, "The Modal Structure of Narrative Universes," *Poetics Today* 6 (1985): 717–55.

14. Bal, *Narratology*, 1985; Chatman, *Story and Discourse*, 1978; Gérard Genette, *Narrative Discourse*, 1980; Gérard Genette, *Narrative Discourse Revisited*, trans. Jane E. Lewin (Ithaca: Cornell University Press, 1988); Gerald Prince, "Notes Towards a Preliminary Categorization of Fictional 'Narratees,'" *Genre* 4 (1971): 100–06; and Gerald Prince, "Introduction to the Study of the Narratee," *Reader-Response Criticism*, ed. Jane Tompkins (Baltimore: Johns Hopkins University Press, 1980), 7–25.

15. See Roland Barthes, *S/Z: An Essay*, trans. Richard Miller (New York: Hill and Wang, 1974); Martin Kreiswirth, "Trusting the Tale: The Narrativist Turn in the Human Sciences," *New Literary History* 23 (1992): 629–57; Gerald Prince, "Le Thème du récit," *Communications* 47 (1988): 199–208; Gerald Prince, *Narrative as Theme: Studies in French Fiction* (Lincoln: University of Nebraska Press, 1992); and Tzvetan Todorov, *The Poetics of Prose*, trans. Richard Howard (Ithaca: Cornell University Press, 1978).

16. Gerald Prince, "Narrativity," eds. Daniel Rancour-Laferrière and Karl Menges, *Axia. Davis Symposium on Literary Evaluation* (Stuttgart: Akademischer Verlag, 1981), 61–76; Prince, *Narratology*, 1982; and Gerald Prince, "Remarks on Narratology (Past, Present, Future)," *Narratology and Narrative*, eds. A. Maynor Hardee and Freeman G. Henry (Columbia, SC: University of South Carolina, 1990), 1–14.

17. Didier Coste, *Narrative as Communication* (Minneapolis: University of Minnesota Press, 1989).

18. Ryan, "The Modal Structure of Narrative Universes," 1985; Marie-Laure Ryan, *Possible Worlds, Artificial Intelligence, and Narrative Theory* (Bloomington: Indiana University Press, 1991).

19. Marie-Laure Ryan, "The Modes of Narrativity and Their Visual Metaphors," *Style* 26 (1992): 368–87.

20. See also H. Porter Abbott, "Narrativity," in *Handbook of Narratology*, vol. 2, eds. Peter Hühn, JohnPier, Wolf Schmid, and Jörg Schönert (Berlin: De Gruyter, 2014), 587–607.

21. Gérard Genot, *Elements of Narrativics: Grammar in Narrative, Narrative in Grammar* (Hamburg: Helmut Buske Verlag, 1979); Thomas Pavel, *La Syntaxe narrative des tragédies de Corneille* (Paris: Klincksieck, 1976); Thomas Pavel, *The Poetics of Plot: The Case of English Renaissance Drama* (Minneapolis: University of Minnesota Press, 1985); Prince, *A Grammar of Stories*, 1973; Prince, *Narratology*, 1982; and Gerald Prince, "On Formalist Narratology," *Languages of Design* 1 (1993): 303–19.

22. Gerald Prince, "Narrative Analysis and Narratology," *New Literary History* 13 (1982): 179–88; Gerald Prince, "Narrative Pragmatics, Message, and Point," *Poetics* 12 (1983): 527–36; and Gerald Prince, *A Dictionary of Narratology*, rev. ed. (Lincoln: University of Nebraska Press, 2003).

23. Jerome Bruner, *Actual Minds, Possible Worlds* (Cambridge, MA: Harvard University Press, 1986); Paul Ricœur, *Time and Narrative*, vols. 1–3, trans. Kathleen McLaughlin (Blarney) and David Pellauer (Chicago: University of Chicago Press, 1984–88); Hayden White, *Metahistory: The Historic Imagination in Nineteenth-Century Europe* (Baltimore: Johns Hopkins University Press, 1973); Hayden White, "The Value of Narrativity in the Representation of Reality," *Critical Inquiry* 7 (1980): 9–27; and Hayden White, *The Content of the Form: Narrative Discourse and Historical Representation* (Baltimore: The Johns Hopkins University Press, 1987).

24. See, for example, Barthes, "An Introduction to the Structural Analysis of Narrative," 1975; Prince, *Narratology*, 1982; and Prince, *A Dictionary of Narratology*, 2003.

25. David Herman, "Scripts, Sequences, and Stories: Elements of a Postclassical Narratology," *PMLA* 112 (1997): 1046–59.

26. See Herman, "Scripts, Sequences, and Stories," 1997; David Herman, ed., *Narratologies: New Perspectives on Narrative Analysis* (Columbus: Ohio State University Press, 1999); Ansgar Nünning, "Narratology or Narratologies? Taking Stock of Recent Developments, Critique and Modest Proposals for Future Usages of the Term," in *What Is Narratology? Questions and Answers Regarding the Status of a Theory*, eds. Tom Kindt and Hans-Harald Müller (Berlin: De Gruyter, 2003), 239–75; Ansgar Nünning and Vera Nünning, "Von der strukturalischen Narratologie zur 'postklassischen' Erzähltheorie: Ein Überblick über Ansätze und Entwicklungstendenzen," in *Neue Ansätze in der Erzähltheorie*, eds. Ansgar Nünning and Vera Nünning (Trier: Wissenschaftlicher Verlag, 2002), 1–33; and Gerald Prince, "Classical and/or Postclassical Narratology," *L'Esprit Créateur* 48 (2008): 115–23.

27. James Phelan, *Reading People, Reading Plots: Character, Progression, and the Interpretation of Narrative* (Chicago: University of Chicago Press, 1989); James Phelan, *Narrative as Rhetoric: Technique, Audiences, Ethics, Ideology* (Columbus: Ohio State University Press, 1996); and James Phelan, *Living to Tell About It: A Rhetoric and Ethics of Character Narration* (Ithaca: Cornell University Press, 2005).

28. Peter J. Rabinowitz, "Truth in Fiction: A Reexamination of Audiences," *Critical Inquiry* 4 (1977): 121–41; Peter J. Rabinowitz, *Before Reading: Narrative Conventions and the Politics of Interpretation* (Ithaca: Cornell University Press, 1987).

29. Susan Sniader Lanser, "Toward a Feminist Narratology," *Style* 20 (1986): 341–63; Susan Sniader Lanser, *Fictions of Authority: Women Writers and Narrative Voice* (Ithaca: Cornell University Press, 1992).

30. Robyn Warhol, *Gendered Interventions: Narrative Discourse in the Victorian Novel* (New Brunswick: Rutgers University Press, 1989).

31. Ruth E. Page, *Literary and Linguistic Approaches to Feminist Narratology* (New York: Palgrave MacMillan, 2006).

32. Susan Stanford Friedman, *Mappings: Feminism and the Cultural Geographies of Encounter* (Princeton: Princeton University Press, 1998).

33. Manfred Jahn, "Frames, References, and the Reading of Third-Person Narratives: Towards a Cognitive Narratology," *Poetics Today* 18 (1997): 441–68.

34. Perry W. Thorndyke, "Cognitive Structures in Comprehension and Memory of Narrative Discourse," *Cognitive Psychology* 9 (1977): 77–110.

35. David E. Rumelhart, "Notes on a Schema for Stories," in *Representation and Understanding: Studies in Cognitive Science*, eds. Daniel G. Bobrow and Allan Collins (New York: Academic Press, 1975), 211–36.

36. Jean Matter Mandler, *Stories, Scripts, and Scenes: Aspects of Schema Theory* (Hillsdale: Lawrence Erlbaum, 1984).

37. Roman Ingarden, *The Literary Work of Art: An Investigation on the Borderlines of Ontology, Logic, and Theory of Literature*, trans. George G. Grabowicz (Evanston: Northwestern University Press, 1973).

38. Ricœur, *Time and Narrative*, 1984–88.

39. Roger Schank and Robert Abelson, *Scripts, Plans, Goals, and Understanding* (Hillsdale: Lawrence Erlbaum Associates, 1977); Robert Wilensky, *Understanding Goal-Based Stories*, Research Report no. 140, Department of Computer Science (New Haven: Yale University,1978).

40. Labov, *Language in the Inner City*, 1972.

41. Charlotte Linde, *Life Stories: The Creation of Coherence* (Oxford: Oxford University Press, 1993); Elinor Ochs, Carolyn Taylor, Dina Rudolph, and Ruth Smith, "Storytelling as Theory-Building Activity," *Discourse Processes* 15 (1992): 37–72.

42. Barthes, *S/Z*, 1974.

43. Jonathan Culler, *Structuralist Poetics: Structuralism, Linguistics, and the Study of Literature* (Ithaca: Cornell University Press, 1975).

44. Wolfgang Iser, *The Implied Reader: Patterns of Communication in Prose Fiction from Bunyan to Beckett* (Baltimore: Johns Hopkins University Press, 1974).

45. Meir Sternberg, *Expositional Modes and Temporal Ordering in Fiction* (Baltimore: Johns Hopkins University Press, 1978).

46. See also Meir Sternberg, "Telling in Time (I): Chronology and Narrative Theory," *Poetics Today* 11 (1990): 901–48; Meir Sternberg, "Telling in Time (II): Chronology, Teleology, Narrativity," *Poetics Today* 13 (1992): 463–541.

47. Rabinowitz "Truth in Fiction," 1977; Rabinowitz, *Before Reading*, 1987; Phelan, *Reading People, Reading Plots*, 1989; Phelan, *Narrative as Rhetoric*, 1996.

48. Prince, *Narratology*, 1982.

49. Monika Fludernik, *Towards a "Natural" Narratology* (London: Routledge, 1996), 12.

50. David Herman, "Cognitive Narratology," in *Handbook of Narratology*, vol. 1, eds. Peter Hühn, John Pier, Wolf Schmid, and Jörg Schönert (Berlin: De Gruyter, 2014), 46.

51. Jahn, "Frames, References, and the Reading of Third-Person Narratives," 1997.

52. Alan Palmer, *Fictional Minds* (Lincoln: University of Nebraska Press, 2004).

53. Lisa Zunshine, *Why We Read Fiction: Theory of Mind and the Novel* (Columbus: Ohio State University Press, 2006).

54. See Marie-Laure Ryan, "Linguistic Models in Narratology," *Semiotica* 28 (1979): 127–55; Marie-Laure Ryan, "Fiction as a Logical, Ontological, and Illocutionary Issue," *Style* 18 (1984): 121–39; Ryan, *Possible Worlds, Artificial Intelligence, and Narrative Theory*, 1991; Marie-Laure Ryan, "Space," in *Handbook of Narratology*, vol. 2, eds. Peter Hühn, John Pier, Wold Schmid, and Jörg Schönert (Berlin: De Gruyter, 2014), 796–811; and Marie-Laure Ryan, Kenneth Foote, and Maoz Azaryahu, *Narrating Space, Spatializing Narrative: Where Narrative Theory and Geography Meet* (Columbus: Ohio State University Press, 2016).

55. Marie-Laure Ryan, "Narratology and Cognitive Science: A Problematic Relation," *Style* 44 (2010): 469–95.

56. Marie-Laure Ryan, *Narrative as Virtual Reality: Immersion and Interactivity in Literature and Electronic Media* (Baltimore: Johns Hopkins University Press, 2001); Marie-Laure Ryan, ed., *Narrative Across Media: The Languages of Storytelling* (Lincoln: University of Nebraska Press, 2004); Marie-Laure Ryan, *Avatars of Story: Narrative Modes in Old and New Media* (Minneapolis: University of Minnesota Press, 2006); and Marie-Laure Ryan, *Narrative as Virtual Reality 2: Revisiting Immersion and Interactivity in Literature and Electronic Media* (Baltimore: Johns Hopkins University Press, 2015).

57. David Herman, "Narratology as a Cognitive Science," in *Image & Narrative*, vol. 1, 2000; David Herman, *Story Logic: Problems and Possibilities of Narrative* (Lincoln: University of Nebraska Press, 2002); David Herman, ed., *Narrative Theory and the Cognitive Sciences* (Chicago: University of Chicago Press, 2003); David Herman, *Storytelling and the Sciences of Mind* (Cambridge, MA: MIT Press, 2013); and Herman, "Cognitive Narratology," 2014.

58. Brian Richardson, "Narrative Poetics and Postmodern Transgression: Theorizing the Collapse of Time, Voice, and Frame," *Narrative* 8 (2000): 23–42; Brian Richardson, *Unnatural Voices: Extreme Narration in Modern and Contemporary Fiction* (Columbus: Ohio State University Press, 2006); Brian Richardson, "What Is Unnatural Narratology?," in *Unnatural Narratives: Unnatural Narratology*, eds. Jan Alber and Rüdiger Heinze (Berlin: De Gruyter, 2011), 23–40; and Richardson, *Unnatural Narrative*, 2015.

59. See, for example, Jan Alber, "Impossible Storyworlds: And What to Do with Them," *Storyworlds* 1 (2009): 79–96; Jan Alber, "Unnatural Narrative," in *Handbook of Narratology*, vol. 1, eds. Peter Hühn, John Pier, Wolf Schmid, and Jörg Schönert (Berlin: De Gruyter, 2014), 887–95; Jan Alber and Rüdiger Heinze, eds., *Unnatural Narratives: Unnatural Narratology* (Berlin: De Gruyter, 2011); Jan Alber, Stefan Iversen, Henrik Skov Nielsen, and Brian Richardson, "What Is Unnatural about Unnatural Narratology? A Response to Monika Fludernik," *Narrative* 20 (2012): 371–82; and Jan Alber, Henrik Skov Nielsen, and Brian Richardson, eds., *A Poetics of Unnatural Narrative* (Columbus: Ohio State University Press, 2013).

60. Jan Alber, "The Diachronic Development of Unnaturalness: A New View on Genre," in *Unnatural Narratives: Unnatural Narratology*, eds. Jan Alber and Rüdiger Heinze (Berlin: De Gruyter, 2011), 41–70; Monika Fludernik, "The Diachronization of Narratology," *Narrative* 11 (2003): 331–48; Ansgar Nünning, "Towards a Cultural and Historical Narratology: A Survey of Diachronic Approaches, Concepts, and Research Projects," in *Anglistentag 1999 Mainz: Proceedings*, eds. Bernhard Reitz and Sigrid Rieuwerts (Trier: Wissenschaftlicher Verlag, 2000), 345–73.

61. David Herman, "Cognition, Emotion, and Consciousness," in *The Cambridge Companion to Narrative*, ed. David Herman (Cambridge: Cambridge University Press, 2007), 245–59; Patrick Colm Hogan, *The Mind and Its Stories: Narrative Universals and Human Emotion* (Cambridge: Cambridge University Press, 2003); Patrick Colm Hogan, *Affective Narratology: The Emotional Structure of Stories* (Lincoln: University of Nebraska Press, 2011); and David S. Miall, "Emotions and the Structuring of Narrative Responses," *Poetics Today* 32 (2011): 323–48.

WORKS CITED

Abbott, H. Porter. "Narrativity." In *Handbook of Narratology*. Eds. Peter Hühn, John Pier, Wolf Schmid, and Jörg Schönert. Vol. 2. Berlin: De Gruyter, 2014. 587–607.

Alber, Jan. "Impossible Storyworlds: And What to Do with Them." *Storyworlds* 1 (2009): 79–96.

Alber, Jan. "The Diachronic Development of Unnaturalness: A New View on Genre." Eds. Jan Alber and Rüdiger Heinze. *Unnatural Narratives: Unnatural Narratology*. Berlin: De Gruyter, 2011. 41–70.

Alber, Jan. "Unnatural Narrative." In *Handbook of Narratology*. Vol. 1. Eds. Peter Hühn, John Pier, Wolf Schmid, and Jörg Schönert. Berlin: De Gruyter, 2014. 887–95.

Alber, Jan, and Rüdiger Heinze, eds. *Unnatural Narratives: Unnatural Narratology*. Berlin: De Gruyter, 2011.

Alber, Jan, Stefan Iversen, Henrik Skov Nielsen, and Brian Richardson. "What Is Unnatural about Unnatural Narratology? A Response to Monika Fludernik." *Narrative* 20 (2012): 371–82.

Alber, Jan, Henrik Skov Nielsen, and Brian Richardson, eds. *A Poetics of Unnatural Narrative*. Columbus: Ohio State University Press, 2013.

Bal, Mieke. *Narratologie: essais sur la signification narrative dans quatre romans modernes*. Paris: Klincksieck, 1977.

Bal, Mieke. *Narratology: Introduction to the Theory of Narrative*. Trans. Christine van Boheemen. Toronto: University of Toronto Press, 1985.

Barthes, Roland. *S/Z* [1970]. Trans. Richard Miller. New York: Hill and Wang, 1974.

Barthes, Roland. "An Introduction to the Structural Analysis of Narrative." *New Literary History* 6 (1975): 237–62.

Bremond, Claude. *Logique du récit*. Paris: Seuil, 1973.

Bruner, Jerome. *Actual Minds, Possible Worlds*. Cambridge, MA: Harvard University Press, 1986.

Chatman, Seymour. *Story and Discourse: Narrative Structure in Fiction and Film*. Ithaca: Cornell University Press, 1978.

Coste, Didier. *Narrative as Communication*. Minneapolis: University of Minnesota Press, 1989.

Culler, Jonathan. *Structuralist Poetics: Structuralism, Linguistics, and the Study of Literature*. Ithaca: Cornell University Press, 1975.

Doležel, Lubomír. "Narrative Semantics." *PTL* 1 (1976): 129–51.

Fludernik, Monika. *Towards a "Natural" Narratology*. London: Routledge, 1996.

Fludernik, Monika. "The Diachronization of Narratology." *Narrative* 11 (2003): 331–48.

Friedman, Susan Stanford. *Mappings: Feminism and the Cultural Geographies of Encounter*. Princeton: Princeton University Press, 1998.

Genette, Gérard. "Boundaries of Narrative." *New Literary History* 8 (1976): 1–15.

Genette, Gérard. *Narrative Discourse: An Essay in Method.* Trans. Jane E. Lewin. Ithaca: Cornell University Press, 1980.

Genette, Gérard. *Narrative Discourse Revisited.* Trans. Jane E. Lewin. Ithaca: Cornell University Press, 1988.

Genot, Gérard. *Elements of Narrativics: Grammar in Narrative, Narrative in Grammar.* Hamburg: Helmut Buske Verlag, 1979.

Greimas, A. J. *Structural Semantics: An Attempt at a Method.* Trans. Daniele McDowell, Ronald Schleifer, and Alan Velie. Lincoln: University of Nebraska Press, 1983.

Herman, David. "Scripts, Sequences, and Stories: Elements of a Postclassical Narratology." *PMLA* 112 (1997): 1046–59.

Herman, David, ed. *Narratologies: New Perspectives on Narrative Analysis.* Columbus: Ohio State University Press, 1999.

Herman, David. "Narratology as a Cognitive Science." *Image & Narrative* 1 (2000). www.imageandnarrative.be/inarchive/narratology/davidherman.htm

Herman, David. *Story Logic: Problems and Possibilities of Narrative.* Lincoln: University of Nebraska Press, 2002.

Herman, David, ed. *Narrative Theory and the Cognitive Sciences.* Chicago: University of Chicago Press, 2003.

Herman, David. "Cognition, Emotion, and Consciousness." In *The Cambridge Companion to Narrative.* Ed. David Herman. Cambridge: Cambridge University Press, 2007. 245–59.

Herman, David. *Storytelling and the Sciences of Mind.* Cambridge, MA: MIT Press, 2013.

Herman, David. "Cognitive Narratology." In *Handbook of Narratology.* Vol. 1. Eds. Peter Hühn, John Pier, Wolf Schmid, and Jörg Schönert. Berlin: De Gruyter, 2014. 46–64.

Hogan, Patrick Colm. *The Mind and Its Stories: Narrative Universals and Human Emotion.* Cambridge: Cambridge University Press, 2003.

Hogan, Patrick Colm. *Affective Narratology: The Emotional Structure of Stories.* Lincoln: University of Nebraska Press, 2011.

Ingarden, Roman. *The Literary Work of Art: An Investigation on the Borderlines of Ontology, Logic, and Theory of Literature* [1965]. Trans. George G. Grabowicz. Evanston: Northwestern University Press, 1973.

Iser, Wolfgang. *The Implied Reader: Patterns of Communication in Prose Fiction from Bunyan to Beckett.* Baltimore: Johns Hopkins University Press, 1974.

Jahn, Manfred. "Frames, References, and the Reading of Third-Person Narratives: Towards a Cognitive Narratology." *Poetics Today* 18 (1997): 441–68.

Kreiswirth, Martin. "Trusting the Tale: The Narrativist Turn in the Human Sciences." *New Literary History* 23 (1992): 629–57.

Labov, William. *Language in the Inner City.* Philadelphia: University of Pennsylvania Press, 1972.

Lanser, Susan Sniader. "Toward a Feminist Narratology." *Style* 20 (1986): 341–63.

Lanser, Susan Sniader. *Fictions of Authority: Women Writers and Narrative Voice.* Ithaca: Cornell University Press, 1992.

Linde, Charlotte. *Life Stories: The Creation of Coherence.* Oxford: Oxford University Press, 1993.

Mandler, Jean Matter. *Stories, Scripts, and Scenes: Aspects of Schema Theory.* Hillsdale: Lawrence Erlbaum, 1984.

Miall, David S. "Emotions and the Structuring of Narrative Responses." *Poetics Today* 32 (2011): 323–48.

Nünning, Ansgar. "Towards a Cultural and Historical Narratology: A Survey of Diachronic Approaches, Concepts, and Research Projects." In *Anglistentag 1999 Mainz: Proceedings.* Eds. Bernhard Reitz and Sigrid Rieuwerts. Trier: Wissenschaftlicher Verlag, 2000. 345–73.

Nünning, Ansgar. "Narratology or Narratologies? Taking Stock of Recent Developments, Critique and Modest Proposals for Future Usages of the Term." In *What Is Narratology? Questions and Answers Regarding the Status of a Theory.* Eds. Tom Kindt and Hans-Harald Müller. Berlin: De Gruyter, 2003. 239–75.

Nünning, Ansgar, and Vera Nünning. "Von der strukturalischen Narratologie zur 'postklassischen' Erzähltheorie: Ein Überblick über Ansätze und Entwicklungstendenzen." In *Neue Ansätze in der Erzähltheorie.* Eds. Ansgar Nünning and Vera Nünning. Trier: Wissenschaftlicher Verlag, 2002. 1–33.

Ochs, Elinor, Carolyn Taylor, Dina Rudolph, and Ruth Smith. "Storytelling as Theory-Building Activity." *Discourse Processes* 15 (1992): 37–72.

Page, Ruth E. *Literary and Linguistic Approaches to Feminist Narratology.* New York: Palgrave MacMillan, 2006.

Palmer, Alan. *Fictional Minds.* Lincoln: University of Nebraska Press, 2004.

Pavel, Thomas. *La Syntaxe narrative des tragédies de Corneille.* Paris: Klincksieck, 1976.

Pavel, Thomas. "Narrative Domains." *Poetics Today* 1 (1980): 105–14.

Pavel, Thomas. *The Poetics of Plot: The Case of English Renaissance Drama.* Minneapolis: University of Minnesota Press, 1985.

Phelan, James. *Reading People, Reading Plots: Character, Progression, and the Interpretation of Narrative.* Chicago: University of Chicago Press, 1989.

Phelan, James. *Narrative as Rhetoric: Technique, Audiences, Ethics, Ideology.* Columbus: Ohio State University Press, 1996.

Phelan, James. *Living to Tell About It: A Rhetoric and Ethics of Character Narration.* Ithaca: Cornell University Press, 2005.

Prince, Gerald. "Notes Towards a Preliminary Categorization of Fictional 'Narratees.'" *Genre* 4 (1971): 100–06.

Prince, Gerald. *A Grammar of Stories: An Introduction.* The Hague: Mouton, 1973.

Prince, Gerald. "Introduction to the Study of the Narratee." In *Reader-Response Criticism.* Ed. Jane P. Tompkins. Baltimore: Johns Hopkins University Press, 1980. 7–25.

Prince, Gerald. "Narrativity." In *Axia. Davis Symposium on Literary Evaluation.* Eds. Daniel Rancour-Laferrière and Karl Menges. Stuttgart: Akademischer Verlag, 1981. 61–76.

Prince, Gerald. "Narrative Analysis and Narratology." *New Literary History* 13 (1982): 179–88.

Prince, Gerald. *Narratology: The Form and Functioning of Narrative.* Berlin: De Gruyter, 1982.

Prince, Gerald. "Narrative Pragmatics, Message, and Point." *Poetics* 12 (1983): 527–36.

Prince, Gerald. "Le Thème du récit." *Communications* 47 (1988): 199–208.

Prince, Gerald. "Remarks on Narratology (Past, Present, Future)." In *Narratology and Narrative.* Eds. A. Maynor Hardee and Freeman G. Henry. Columbia: University of South Carolina Press, 1990. 1–14.

Prince, Gerald. *Narrative as Theme: Studies in French Fiction.* Lincoln: University of Nebraska Press, 1992.

Prince, Gerald. "On Formalist Narratology." *Languages of Design* 1 (1993): 303–19.

Prince, Gerald. *A Dictionary of Narratology*, rev. ed. Lincoln: University of Nebraska Press, 2003.

Prince, Gerald. "Classical and/or Postclassical Narratology." *L'Esprit Créateur* 48 (2008): 115–23.

Rabinowitz, Peter J. "Truth in Fiction: A Reexamination of Audiences." *Critical Inquiry* 4 (1977): 121–41.

Rabinowitz, Peter J. *Before Reading: Narrative Conventions and the Politics of Interpretation.* Ithaca: Cornell University Press, 1987.

Richardson, Brian. "Narrative Poetics and Postmodern Transgression. Theorizing the Collapse of Time, Voice, and Frame." *Narrative* 8 (2000): 23–42.

Richardson, Brian. *Unnatural Voices: Extreme Narration in Modern and Contemporary Fiction.* Columbus: Ohio State University Press, 2006.

Richardson, Brian. "What Is Unnatural Narratology?" In *Unnatural Narratives: Unnatural Narratology.* Eds. Jan Alber and Rüdiger Heinze. Berlin: De Gruyter, 2011. 23–40.

Richardson, Brian. *Unnatural Narrative: Theory, History, and Practice.* Columbus: The Ohio State University Press, 2015.

Ricœur, Paul. *Time and Narrative.* Vols. 1–3. Trans. Kathleen McLaughlin (Blarney) and David Pellauer. Chicago: University of Chicago Press, 1984–88.

Rumelhart, David E. "Notes on a Schema for Stories." In *Representation and Understanding: Studies in Cognitive Science.* Eds. Daniel G. Bobrow and Allan Collins. New York: Academic Press, 1975. 211–36.

Ryan, Marie-Laure. "Linguistic Models in Narratology." *Semiotica* 28 (1979): 127–55.

Ryan, Marie-Laure. "Fiction as a Logical, Ontological, and Illocutionary Issue." *Style* 18 (1984): 121–39.

Ryan, Marie-Laure. "The Modal Structure of Narrative Universes." *Poetics Today* 6 (1985): 717–55.

Ryan, Marie-Laure. *Possible Worlds, Artificial Intelligence, and Narrative Theory.* Bloomington: Indiana University Press, 1991.

Ryan, Marie-Laure. "The Modes of Narrativity and Their Visual Metaphors." *Style* 26 (1992): 368–87.

Ryan, Marie-Laure. *Narrative as Virtual Reality: Immersion and Interactivity in Literature and Electronic Media.* Baltimore: Johns Hopkins University Press, 2001.

Ryan, Marie-Laure, ed. *Narrative Across Media: The Languages of Storytelling.* Lincoln: University of Nebraska Press, 2004.

Ryan, Marie-Laure. "Narrative." In *Routledge Encyclopedia of Narrative Theory.* Eds. David Herman, Manfred Jahn, and Marie-Laure Ryan. London: Routledge, 2005. 344–48.

Ryan, Marie-Laure. *Avatars of Story: Narrative Modes in Old and New Media.* Minneapolis: University of Minnesota Press, 2006.

Ryan, Marie-Laure. "Narratology and Cognitive Science: A Problematic Relation." *Style* 44 (2010): 469–95.

Ryan, Marie-Laure. "Space." In *Handbook of Narratology.* Vol. 2. Eds. Peter Hühn, John Pier, Wold Schmid, and Jörg Schönert. Berlin: De Gruyter, 2014. 796–811.

Ryan, Marie-Laure. *Narrative as Virtual reality 2: Revisiting Immersion and Interactivity in Literature and Electronic Media.* Baltimore: Johns Hopkins University Press, 2015.

Ryan, Marie-Laure, Kenneth Foote, and Maoz Azaryahu. *Narrating Space, Spatializing Narrative: Where Narrative Theory and Geography Meet.* Columbus: Ohio State University Press, 2016.

Schank, Roger, and Robert Abelson. *Scripts, Plans, Goals, and Understanding.* Hillsdale: Lawrence Erlbaum Associates, 1977.

Sternberg, Meir. *Expositional Modes and Temporal Ordering in Fiction.* Baltimore: Johns Hopkins University Press, 1978.

Sternberg, Meir. "Telling in Time (I): Chronology and Narrative Theory." *Poetics Today* 11 (1990): 901–48.

Sternberg, Meir. "Telling in Time (II): Chronology, Teleology, Narrativity." *Poetics Today* 13 (1992): 463–541.

Thorndyke, Perry W. "Cognitive Structures in Comprehension and Memory of Narrative Discourse." *Cognitive Psychology* 9 (1977): 77–110.

Todorov, Tzvetan. "Les Catégories du récit littéraire." *Communications* 8 (1966): 125–51.

Todorov, Tzvetan. *Grammaire du Décaméron*. The Hague: Mouton, 1969.

Todorov, Tzvetan. *The Poetics of Prose*. Trans. Richard Howard. Ithaca: Cornell University Press, 1978.

Todorov, Tzvetan. *Introduction to Poetics*. Trans. Richard Howard. Minneapolis: University of Minnesota Press, 1981.

Warhol, Robyn. *Gendered Interventions: Narrative Discourse in the Victorian Novel*. New Brunswick: Rutgers University Press, 1989.

White, Hayden. *Metahistory: The Historic Imagination in Nineteenth-Century Europe*. Baltimore: Johns Hopkins University Press, 1973.

White, Hayden. "The Value of Narrativity in the Representation of Reality." *Critical Inquiry* 7 (1980): 9–27.

White, Hayden. *The Content of the Form: Narrative Discourse and Historical Representation*. Baltimore: The Johns Hopkins University Press, 1987.

Wilensky, Robert. *Understanding Goal-Based Stories*. Research Report no. 140, Department of Computer Science. New Haven: Yale University, 1978.

Zunshine, Lisa. *Why We Read Fiction: Theory of Mind and the Novel*. Columbus: Ohio State University Press, 2006.

CHAPTER FOUR

Marxism

PETER HITCHCOCK

Attempting to frame the extent and breadth of Marxist literary criticism is as daunting as offering to encapsulate the complex contours of Marxism itself, but let us briefly consider the challenge according to the terms of their relationship. Marxism, as a body of ideas building on Marx's critique of political economy, *Capital* (1867), concerns itself primarily with an economic understanding of society and intends to show how socioeconomic relations are formed and maintained by class divisions across history. Regarding capitalism, Marxism provides not just an understanding of the fraught connections of labor and capital as relations but, in its analysis of economic and social contradiction, dares to fathom how capitalism might be overcome as a whole. Because the conditions of capitalism are material and historical, and because capitalism is an economic system of the social, it is hardly far-fetched to believe that it has literary, cultural, and by all means aesthetic ramifications. In true dialectical style, however, Marxist literary criticism holds that cultural production and consumption are not simply effects of capital as an economic base, and that culture, as a "whole way of life" as Raymond Williams put it, mediates economic logic and understanding at every level. One of the great debates in materialist criticism is the extent to which culture undoes all thoughts of economic determinism, but this is far from being a rejection of economic explanation per se. Both Marxism and Marxist literary criticism attend to processes of social production and reproduction even if their methodologies must necessarily differ by degree if not in kind.

Just as critiques of political economy do not begin with Marx, so a materialist understanding of culture does not spring spontaneously from Marxism. Marx himself begins to formulate his revolutionary paradigm not just by reading economists against the grain (David Ricardo, Adam Smith) but by linking this to philosophical structures of thought (the attention to revolutionizing Hegelian dialectics being foremost). Marx's collaboration with Friedrich Engels elaborates and deepens various aspects of materialist possibility, and their collective works represent a massive intervention in how humans understand and change their conditions of socialization. That both Marx and Engels wrote extensively on literature and alluded to it still more is not a coincidence: simply put, a materialist conception of history sees culture as an integral part of reality, as a complex process, as vital to the ways in which social change may be affected and produced. Unfortunately, of course, neither Marx nor Engels systematized their literary critique along the lines of their approaches to political economy, yet this has proved to offer a distinctly theoretical challenge that has been met on a number of pertinent and provocative levels. Indeed, one could argue that a genealogy of Marxist literary criticism does not appear in the shadow of Marxist economic theory, but is now Marxism's most vibrant composite, a dynamic space of cultural and political possibility. While the following notes cannot possibly do justice to this tradition of inspirational imbrication, I hope to indicate along the way how cultural Marxism comes to assume this significant position.

Among the earlier Marxist attempts to wrestle with art's relationship to social change (a list that includes Georgi Plekhanov's *Art and Social Life* [1912] and the compilation, *Lenin on Literature and Art* [1970]) was Leon Trotsky's *Literature and Revolution* (1924). While appreciating "Proletkult," Trotsky urged that, in a period of revolutionary tumult, the Soviet Communist Party should also pay attention to writers and works broadly sympathetic to the aims of the revolution tout court. Proletarian consciousness was not the sole provider of proletarian or revolutionary literature, so Marxism should be sensitive to a variety of cultural expression and not just art that appeared in accord with specific class interests. As the epochal 1917 revolution hardened into dogma what counted as literary began to shrink into typologies, or into formulas like socialist realism. Joseph Stalin's cultural enforcer, A. A. Zhdanov, used concrete reality to pour over the jouissance of experimentation leaving great artists of modernism like James Joyce buried and vilified. Zhdanov is little read today but his kind of "art to order" approach seriously damaged the aesthetic credentials of Marxist criticism. While Trotsky warned of the pernicious effects of reactionary art, he remained dedicated to the idea that the best art was free enough to be revolutionary in its own ways, unencumbered by prescriptions and parroting. The realism/modernism debate in the 1920s and 1930s was typified by the exchanges of Georg Lukács and Bertolt Brecht,[1] but they focused more on important questions of consciousness and alienation, rather than fixating on cultural absolutes. How is social totality to be intimated? How are questions of socioeconomic contradiction articulated or explained away by cultural expression? Seen historically, such debates today appear much more open-ended than they might have seemed in their present, when acute political divisions seemed to hang on polemical ripostes. Indeed, this is one way we might view the greater impress of contemporary Marxist cultural criticism, when such distinctions no longer impact party profiles or five-year plans. I will return to this point in my conclusion.

A significant flowering of Marxist criticism at the edge or beyond the imperatives of party or state grew from a more general concern with structuralism after the Second World War. Claude Lévi-Strauss may not have been a Marxist but his thoughts on symbolic functions spoke to materialists less inclined to favor economic determinism sui generis (especially when the latter was increasingly tied to the disasters of Stalinism). Coupled with structuralist approaches to psychoanalysis (Jacques Lacan) and history (Michel Foucault), structuralist Marxism sought to rethink the elements of radical knowledge while diminishing what they thought of as the limits of Hegelian humanism. Chief among theorists in this regard was Louis Althusser who, in a series of key interventions (*Lenin and Philosophy and Other Essays* [1968], *For Marx* [1965], *Reading Capital* [1965]) realigned Marxist critique with its scientific lineaments. In the Lenin collection, he advanced new conceptual categories for materialist analysis. The notion of an "ideological state apparatus," for instance, underlined that subjective self-consciousness was not a given, and that a social subject might be interpellated or hailed according to the needs of a dominant structure. Indeed, rather than a crude socioeconomic framework, in which an economic infrastructure conditioned institutional and cultural formations, Althusser suggests a panoply of fields of contradiction whereby social change is distinctly overdetermined, but where ideology saturates the socius. The key impact for Marxist literary criticism lies in Althusser's *Reading Capital* project developed with his graduate students, several of whom went on to become significant thinkers in their own right (Etienne Balibar,

Pierre Macherey, Jacques Rancière). The basic idea is not only to recognize the material conditions of Marx's key text but to understand its methodology as an epistemological challenge. In Althusser's contribution to the "reading" he emphasizes the symptom: specifically, where the text is constrained not to speak its truths. There are several ways in which this might be interpreted, both in Marx's reading practices—he elaborates an answer to a question David Ricardo and Adam Smith cannot bring themselves to ask ("What is the value of labor?")—and in Althusser's reading of Marx, particularly where he separates the mature scientist of political economy from the youthful Hegelian Marx of the early philosophical manuscripts of 1844. Regarding the Hegelian work, Althusser sees only symptoms of idealism, whereas in the subsequent critique of capitalism he recognizes a Marxism replete with scientific practices ("theoretical practices" as Althusser would come to call them). Sometimes the symptom of science manifests itself as a neologism or as an acronym, but the main tension in Althusser's reading is between Marx's acute understanding of the unspoken and the ideological in his contemporary counterparts, and the relative lack of contamination in Marx's own science, burdened mostly by the understanding that it is true (as science).

Balibar's reading methodology will maintain a philosophical bent less determined to argue for its status as science (and follows Spinozist trajectories shared with Althusser). Macherey, both in *Lire Capital* (1965) and in his *A Theory of Literary Production* (1966), cleaves more closely to a distinctly literary critique that, while hardly letting go of philosophical principles, is deeply concerned to explicate what is literary in the literary text that yet cannot speak its historical possibilities (seen in his readings of Borges, Balzac, Tolstoy, Verne, and Defoe). Here the symptom comes alive as more than a repressive hypothesis but as a full-fledged materialist condition of the literary. This notion of the text bearing a dimension not legible in its empirical surfaces was a way both to complicate notions of realism, reality, and the real while releasing the literary from the dominance of authorial consciousness (moves that would have both class and aesthetic implications). The acronymic emphasis in symptomatic reading would not last long[2] but the general parameters of Althusserian approaches would be highly influential. There was, however, another strand of Marxist criticism that emerged in the middle of the twentieth century that took a very different tack on what constituted the materiality of the literary.

What became known as the "Frankfurt School" began in the 1920s as a loose association of intellectuals with the Frankfurt Institute for Social Research, a think tank of Marxist theory. Both Karl Korsch and Georg Lukács were linked to the institute in its early days but it is now known chiefly through the work of Eric Fromm, Herbert Marcuse, Ernst Bloch, Theodor Adorno, and Max Horkheimer. Horkheimer and Adorno in particular focused on a materialist understanding of philosophy, history, and culture, and their *Dialectic of Enlightenment* (1947) set out the terms for a critical theory that could account for the persistence of domination beyond moments of revolution. They saw the power of culture as being complicit in such hegemony, especially through what they called the "culture industry," which described capitalist processes of homogenization and standardization that they argued reinforced docility, acquiescence, and conformity. The function of mass-produced culture and technologies of cultural mediation continue to stir key debates in materialist thinking, although perhaps with a tad more optimism than the initial diagnosis would permit. This too should be read as a remark on material conditions since Adorno and Horkheimer had seen culture used as a weapon by fascism and totalitarianism, as if the whole discourse of Enlightenment itself was a parody of freedom and equality. For Adorno, this necessitated a negative dialectics, one that could probe the limits of thought itself and not just the objects and time arrayed before it. Of course, there are connections to the Althusserian problematic, especially regarding a radical interrogation of what constitutes the subject, as human, as cultural, as an agent of history. Both theoretical approaches eschew Hegelian concepts of the whole, and of teleology, but along distinct methodological principles and philosophical concerns. If, for Althusserianism, the literary text is constrained by what it ideologically cannot say, for Adornian aesthetics, literature is caught within a broader field of contradictions that it cannot simply sublate or overcome—it is textured by constitutive limits of thought itself.

Among the "associates" of the Frankfurt School, none has been more influential for literary and cultural study than Walter Benjamin. If the mode of production saturates the social, Benjamin detailed how it was culturally manifested across forms, structures, and language. Benjamin's "Theses on the Philosophy of History" contains the notion that "there is no document of culture which is not at the same time a document of barbarism." Like Adorno, Benjamin opposed the pieties that informed principles of progress and sought to engage social contradiction at every level. Yet Benjamin's approach was highly idiosyncratic, a kind of Messianic materialism that produced brilliant cultural exegesis in prose at once informative and spiritually dense. His unfinished work, *The Arcades Project* (2002), piled up cultural examples juxtaposed with commentary, aphorisms, citations, and historical markers. Ostensibly, the text is about the history and culture of Parisian arcades, the Ur-form of the shopping mall, but as one engages its frantic surfaces, page after page, one finds oneself immersed in the substance of socialization itself. Occasionally, one is transported by what Benjamin explicates as a dialectical image, a kind of freeze frame of philosophy, but the process of reading becomes its own form of awakening and reveals, if not what one could describe as full-fledged Marxism, a materialism at one with the challenge of fragmentation under capitalism, a critique of poetics that is itself poetic.

Both Althusserian and Frankfurt School forms of Marxist criticism distance a cultural understanding of capitalism premised on state or party precepts, typologies, or norms. There are ways to read this as anti-Marxist, of course, but the lesson is about critical reflexivity and the idea that Marxism must be as dynamic in its protocols and instincts as capitalism is in its constant revolutions. It should be emphasized that such thinking does not simply occur outside or blissfully beyond actually existing socialism—one could argue, for instance, that the Bakhtin Circle in the Soviet Union (Bakhtin, Volosinov, Medvedev, Kagan, etc.) also produced a dynamism whose Marxist inconsistencies and contradictions enabled Marxism, despite itself, to deepen its sociopolitical understanding. You cannot square dialogics with dialectics and that, perhaps, is the tragedy and possibility in both. Driven by its exceptions more than conformism, what became known as the New Left also embraced a Marxism beside itself, skeptical of its truth claims but no less critical of the class divisions capitalism tirelessly worked to reproduce.

Raymond Williams is a good example of a Marxist critic who cleaved to a creative critical nonconformism. Hardly an heir to Frankfurt School critique and no mere apostle of French structuralism, Williams's work accentuates a deep concern for the socially lived, the actual experiences and expressions that compose the ordinariness of the cultural everyday. While it is true that in *Culture and Society* (1958), *The English Novel from Dickens to Lawrence* (1970), and *Marxism and Literature* (1977), Williams does not shy away from either the main currents of British literary tradition or the abstractions of literary theory, his acuity lies in elaborating a critical vocabulary of materialist means (to some extent formalized in *Keywords*), whereby the literary for Marxism becomes thoroughly enmeshed, correlated, and engaged consciously or not with what makes up the social from one moment to the next. As a novelist, playwright, and short story author, Williams had an intuitive sense of literary production that he brought to his literary criticism without fuss or abstractions as their own reward. Reading *Marxism and Literature* today, one senses a critic who begins with his political commitments as a kind of affective embrace that bridges inexorably with cultural concerns. Again, one must keep in mind the historical coordinates of Williams's intervention. Broadly associated with the New Left (and partly responsible for it), Williams built extensively on his acknowledged forebears (including those mentioned above) and fostered an open materialism that would both enlarge and complicate the contours of a common culture. Thus, *Marxism and Literature* not only details the basic components of Marxist theory (base/superstructure, determination, productive forces) but pushes one to think of new ways to approach cultural interaction (including his burgeoning attention to cultural formation analysis under the rubric of dominant, residual, and emergent—as well as Williams's highly influential understanding of "structures of feeling"). True, this is not a book that directly engages with a great range of radical politics, especially the massive contributions of feminism and anti-colonial critiques in and around Marxism at the time (to be discussed below), but it remains a key reference and a provocation about critical possibility. Here, for instance, is Williams on writing:

> Writing is often a new articulation and in effect a new formation, extending beyond its own modes. But to separate this as art, which in practice includes, always partly and sometimes wholly, elements elsewhere in the continuum, is to lose contact with the substantive creative process and then to idealize it; to put it above or below the social, when it is in fact the social in one of its most distinctive, durable, and total forms.[3]

Such a view is one way to understand the materialism of Marxist literary criticism: by thinking of creative processes as enmeshed in the social, such criticism turns its back on neither the economic nor the aesthetic, but pivots on how cultural expressivity mediates the social in its most profound extent and complexity. This does not mean a work like Daniel Defoe's *Robinson Crusoe* or Toni Morrison's *Beloved* are best read as novelized ideologies. Far from it. The point of Williams's examination of Marxism and literature is that neither exhausts the truths of their interrelation. For this too means to live history in changing it.

For some it is the parochialism of Williams's "literary" that limits the reach of his critical categories, although it has to be said that in general the half-life of any literary criticism or theory is a good deal shorter than the intellectual history on which it may be based. Perhaps it is because of the close attention to the time and place of social change that reveals Marxism as a basis for understanding literary criticism today. Terry Eagleton, who studied with Williams, brought this engagement to literary theory, defamiliarizing its pretensions and unmasking its ideological configurations. Along the way he produced what is still considered the best primer (*Literary Theory* [1983]) about what literary theory represents. In part, its success rests on the tools Eagleton developed in two previous materialist critiques, *Marxism and Literary Criticism* (1976) and *Criticism and Ideology* (1976): the first, a survey of the roots of cultural Marxism in the tensions of literature and history; the second, as mentioned, an Althusserian moment of structural Marxism invested in the possibilities of reading as materialist science. If the first text, like here, offers a genealogy of Marxist criticism, the second book is an example of how Marxism might intervene on its own terms as a critical method. If the enthusiasm for Althusserianism has waned (aesthetics being somewhat prickly for science), ideas of form and content being linked to historical context, and art as also production have remained key elements of Marxist analysis. Eagleton's work in general has expanded these claims. He has also acknowledged the influence of the Frankfurt School in his thinking, albeit through the aforementioned Walter Benjamin.[4] Eagleton's magnum opus is *The Ideology of the Aesthetic*, which is both an examination of the claims of ideological critique and a materialist history of ideas (and, not coincidentally, features a chapter on Benjamin and the "Marxist sublime"). While many of Eagleton's books are witty capsules of materialist analysis (*Ideology, Materialism, Postmodernism*, etc.), *The Ideology of the Aesthetic* puts these elements to work and rewrites critical history in the process.

Eagleton's writing represents a consolidation of Marxist literary criticism within the New Left. All of the major concerns of such criticism, including economic hierarchy, class structure, institutions of knowledge, imperialism, cultural forms, come into play in his work. Fredric Jameson can also be interpreted in this vein, but he has also pushed the boundaries of what can be considered materialist criticism and how we might comprehend culture from a Marxist perspective. Like Eagleton, Jameson reveals the influence of Althusserianism (particularly its Lacanian dimensions) and the Frankfurt School (Adornian aesthetics above all others), but his intervention and impact have been deeper and more lasting. *Marxism and Form* (2016), *The Political Unconscious* (1982), and *Postmodernism, or, The Cultural Logic of Late Capitalism* (1992) are core texts of Marxist cultural criticism that, even at their most abstract, confront the implications of a materialist problematic head on. How do cultural forms produce and mediate the material conditions of their time? Is narrative a specific form of action and what would this mean for (political) praxis? How might one characterize the cultural constellations of global capitalism, and do these actually permit a symptomatic understanding of hegemonic ideas of time and space? A comparatist and a polymath of cultural genre, Jameson's oeuvre epitomizes the sagacity of dialectical critique (and in dialectical sentences, no less). His reading of "Third World Literature" is in many ways a missed opportunity among the range of his interests, although it is fair to say this challenge has been more than met within materialist analyses of postcoloniality and the Global South.

There is much that is obvious but also displaced in Marxism's cultural understanding of globality. Often, such critique attends to primarily Western formations of material culture or pivots upon specifically national paradigms of literary tradition. If the notes above reflect these emphases they also indicate that such shortfalls have been in some sense constitutive even though a history of revolutions against, for instance, imperialism and/or capitalism have for the most part occurred outside or at the edge of Eurocentric purviews. A key work like Roberto Fernandez Retamar's *Caliban and Other Essays* (the central essay is from 1971—the English translation appears in book form in 1989 with an introduction by Jameson) underlines that a Marxist imperative in literary understanding bears within it antinomies of the world system as such, a combined and uneven development in which socioeconomic exploitation requires distinctly global frameworks of critique. Retamar's Marxism attends to the revolutionary movements of Latin America as an important ground for new cultural articulations of solidarity and opposition. Rather than see this as tendentious or reductive, the point is to fathom literature's organic relationship to social change, much of which has to challenge traditional genealogies, including those fostered by Marxism itself. Retamar takes a classic figure of othering and marginalization, Shakespeare's Caliban, and recomposes his cultural symbolic in decolonizing Western precepts. Caliban emerges not simply as a character or as a recurring motif, but as an interruption in how a cultural knowledge of Latin America is constellated.

Among other pivotal critics concerned to decenter the priorities of Western criticism, Ngũgĩ Wa Thiong'o and Gayatri Chakravorty Spivak are exemplary. Like Retamar, Ngũgĩ's key works are born of a revolutionary moment and possibility, one that helps to explain a flowering of Marxist literary criticism after the Second World War when major empires were challenged and disintegrated. Like Williams, Ngũgĩ writes literature as well as criticism, yet *Decolonizing the Mind* (1986) and *Globalectics: Theory and the Politics of Knowing* (2012) stand in their own right as a materialist understanding of literature in an anti- and postimperialist world. Rather than read Marxism as a checklist of state and party prerogatives, Ngũgĩ exudes a critical reflexivity both local and global in thinking the situatedness of literary expression. In *Globalectics* this entails an overreaching of both Marxism and the postcolonial, yet in the spirit of their own questioning. The global, then, is a heuristic in discussing culture on a world scale, although this is a paradigm of possibility rather than an established critical practice. For Spivak, the operative term would now be "planetarity," although it does not refer to a methodology as such but to what she has termed "planet thought" (thinking the planet as different from being its custodian). Earlier in her writing, however, particularly in the collection, *In Other Worlds* (2012), and in the essay, "Can the Subaltern Speak?" Spivak's work was active in a highly nuanced and influential interrogation of postcolonial worlds and worlding (the latter an indication of how hegemony shapes the world in its own image). Writing in a complex intersection of Marxism, feminism, and deconstruction, Spivak elucidates the deep structures of colonial thought and its undoing. The subaltern analysis, perhaps one of the most famous essays of decolonization, explores how the figure of the subaltern destabilizes subject reason and the voice it is meant to assume. Using history, philosophy, and political acuity Spivak does not pretend to speak for the subaltern but questions the world in which her silence is predicated.

This is, of course, also a profoundly feminist intervention and much of the essay deconstructs masculinist shibboleths in philosophy and "radical" thinking in general. While this may not be explicitly read as Marxist feminism, Spivak's contribution is nevertheless crucially active in explicating the ties that bind social production and social reproduction, links between class and gender under-theorized in the materialist concerns detailed above. Michèle Barrett's *Women's Oppression Today* (1980; new edition 2014) offers a forthright critique of Marxism in this vein and enjoins feminist debates on Marxist feminism going back at least to the work of Alexandra Kollontai and Rosa Luxemburg. Toril Moi's *Sexual/Textual Politics* (1985) also intervenes in such debates, while clearly establishing a critical distance from the main currents of Marxist thought.[5] Rosemary Hennessy's *Materialist Feminism and the Politics of Discourse* (1992) marks this difference from the gendered lacunae in Marxism, yet Hennessy is mainly concerned with reestablishing materialist principles in the face of a broad discursive, cultural, and postmodern "turn" and her project therefore exists in tension with Moi's contribution. This links both to critical work that elaborates cultural Marxism at the heart of feminist readings of the literary like Barbara Foley's *Radical Representations* (1993), and to a long-standing attention to women's working-class writing that problematizes authorship, subjectivity, and how to "represent" the material divisions and differences of class and gender. This genealogy itself questions what has best "represented" Marxist literary criticism in the last half century (with a simultaneously correlative and disjunct philosophical thread between Simone de Beauvoir and Judith Butler).

If a basic premise of Marxism is to reveal and challenge socioeconomic conditions of inequality through history, then the destabilization and deconstruction of material formations of patriarchy are not merely adjunct to social transformation but vital to its central dynamic. Literature does not just describe these conditions but is active in changing them by coming to terms with how they may be articulated aesthetically, formally, and historically. Yet, again using Spivak's prescient relay between philosophy, literature, and history in her subaltern essay, other elements of Marxism's materialist foundations are also indicated and elaborated. Chief among these is a demystification of the relationship between Western philosophical concepts of the subject and the production of colonialism and imperialism. Like feminism, such concern is not an extension of Marxism but has deeper implications for its reconceptualization. If, for instance, postcolonialism has historically attended to the production and decolonization of an imperial episteme, this has also been a measure of the complex imbrication between Marxism and the liberation struggles of the Global South. Spivak's literary critiques, from *In Other Worlds* through *An Aesthetic Education in the Era of Globalization* (2013), have never flinched from examining these connections and, if postcolonial critique is now closely associated with Marxism (seen in the work of Parry, Lazarus, and Ganguly among others), it is in part a product of reflection on what makes materialism when colonialist and capitalist matrices are brought to account. Certainly, the anti-colonial writings of, for instance, Cabral, Césaire, Fanon, and James constitute the real foundations of this challenge, but it took somewhat longer for such Marxist interventions to be elaborated in literary criticism itself. Similarly, a materialist understanding of imperialism is definitively co-extensive with the history of Marxist theory, but it is in the anti-colonial movements of the mid- to late twentieth century that the question of race foregrounds the economic and social categories of subjugation. Again, this must be seen not as some kind of extension of Marxism or simply as a supplement, but as a radical challenge to what constitutes materialist suppositions themselves. Cedric Robinson's *Black Marxism* (1983) not only questioned some of the major assumptions of Marxist analysis, but offered, in the concept of racial capitalism, a new paradigm for thinking political economy. Intimations of such understanding about race and empire, for instance, certainly appeared in literary representations of decolonization, but if analyses of these constellations are more prevalent now in Marxist literary criticism it is because it is not seen as somehow outside or beyond the substance of political economy proper. Indeed, it might be said to accentuate the force of dialectical thinking as a whole.

It is often suggested today that Marxism, like politics in general, is a preeminently cultural endeavor and that, further, a literary critique of neoliberal capitalism is somehow easier to make than posing the question of its attenuation or transformation. This would seem to misunderstand the social dynamics of capitalism at any one moment in its history. It is true, for instance, that a class analysis of, say, *Pride and Prejudice*, might seem a luxurious pursuit when the contradictions of contemporary capitalism are so acute, yet if we take variegations of Marxism as themselves symptomatic of an alternative vision of socialization, then a materialist understanding of the literary is surely part of this possibility, its constitutive imaginary. Such "Marxism beyond Marxism" can be assessed in a number of ways[6] and remains a provocation for further critique. By thinking about the imaginative constraints and creativity of the literary across a history of class struggles and structures, one not only comes to terms with the meaning of aesthetic difference, but also the role of social division in the ways art is expressed. The prevalence of culturalism and cultural politics today is overdetermined by a whole host of factors, including the manner in which the political in general is mediated. If the contradictions of contemporary capitalism appear to warrant greater Marxist critique, within literary criticism there are many access points for radical readings, on affect, on identity, on nature for example, that do not have to begin necessarily with political economy. Indeed, even the use of "materialism" as a catch-all can signal important differences from what might be deemed conventional Marxist categorizations alongside antagonisms not primed by class or capitalist contradiction. Perhaps, dialectically, this is further evidence of what Trotsky once described as combined and uneven development, but at the level of literary criticism itself. This could mean that after the collapse of "actually existing socialism" Marxist literary criticism becomes almost literally detached; yet, in its manifest attention to the conditions of knowledge in which the literary takes place, it plays a vital role in keeping the knowledge and possibility of change alive.

City University of New York (United States)

NOTES

1. See, for instance, Ernst Bloch, et al., *Aesthetics and Politics* [1977], trans. Rodney Livingstone (London: Verso, 2007).

2. Terry Eagleton, for instance, only really tried it for one book, *Criticism and Ideology* (London: Verso, 1976).

3. Raymond Williams, *Marxism and Literature* (Oxford: Oxford University Press, 1977), 211–12.

4. See, for instance, Terry Eagleton, *Walter Benjamin, or Towards a Revolutionary Criticism* (London: Verso, 2009).

5. A distance that has increased in more recent work where one reads an incredulity about the theoretical and political in general. See Toril Moi, *Revolution of the Ordinary* (Chicago: University of Chicago Press, 2017).

6. Both Nicholas Brown's *Utopian Generations: The Political Horizons of Twentieth Century Literature* (Princeton: Princeton University Press, 2005) and Sonali Perera's *No Country: Working-Class Writing in the Age of Globalization* (New York: Columbia University Press, 2014), for instance, re-constellate "real foundations" between the economic and the cultural by looking at modernity and globalization, respectively.

WORKS CITED

Adorno, Theodor W., and Max Horkheimer. *Dialectic of Enlightenment* [1947]. Trans. Edmund Jephcott. Palo Alto: Stanford University Press, 2007.

Althusser, Louis. *Lenin and Philosophy and Other Essays* [1968]. Trans. Ben Brewster. New York: Monthly Review Press, 2001.

Althusser, Louis. *For Marx* [1965]. Trans. Ben Brewster. London: Verso, 2006.

Althusser, Louis, Étienne Balibar, Roger Establet, Pierre Macherey, and Jacques Rancière. *Lire le Capital*. Paris: Maspero, 1965.

Althusser, Louis, Étienne Balibar, Roger Establet, Pierre Macherey, and Jacques Rancière. *Reading Capital: The Complete Edition* [1965]. Trans. Ben Brewster and David Fernbach. New York: Verso, 2016.

Bakhtin, Mikhail. *The Dialogic Imagination: Four Essays*. Trans. Caryl Emerson and Michael Holquist. Austin: University of Texas Press, 1981.

Barrett, Michele. *Women's Oppression Today: The Marxist/Feminist Encounter*. London: Verso, 2014.

Benjamin, Walter. *The Arcades Project*. Trans. Howard Eiland and Kevin McLaughlin. Cambridge: Belknap Press, 2002.

Bloch, Ernst, Georg Lukács, Bertolt Brecht, Walter Benjamin, and Theodor Adorno. *Aesthetics and Politics* [1977]. Trans. Rodney Livingstone. London: Verso, 2007.

Brown, Nicholas. *Utopian Generations: The Political Horizons of Twentieth Century Literature*. Princeton: Princeton University Press, 2005.

Eagleton, Terry. *Criticism and Ideology*. London: Verso, 1976.

Eagleton, Terry. *Marxism and Literary Criticism*. Berkeley: University of California Press, 1976.

Eagleton, Terry. *Literary Theory*. Oxford: Blackwell, 1983.

Eagleton, Terry. *The Ideology of the Aesthetic*. Oxford: Blackwell, 1991.

Eagleton, Terry. *Walter Benjamin, or Towards a Revolutionary Criticism*. London: Verso, 2009.

Hennessy, Rosemary. *Materialist Feminism and the Politics of Discourse*. London: Routledge, 1992.

Jameson, Fredric. *The Political Unconscious: Narrative as a Socially Symbolic Act*. Ithaca: Cornell University Press, 1982.

Jameson, Fredric. "Third-World Literature in the Age of Multinational Capitalism." *Social Text* 15 (1986): 65–88.

Jameson, Fredric. *Postmodernism, or, The Cultural Logic of Late Capitalism*. Durham, NC: Duke University Press, 1992.

Jameson, Fredric. *Marxism and Form*. Princeton: Princeton University Press, 2016.

Lenin, Vladimir I. *Lenin on Literature and Art*. New York: Wildside Press, 2008.

Macherey, Pierre. *A Theory of Literary Production* [1966]. Trans. Geoffrey Wall. New York: Routledge, 2006.

Marx, Karl. *Capital* [1867]. Vol. 1. Trans. Ben Fowkes. Intro. Ernest Mandel. New York: Penguin, 1976.

Marx, Karl. *Economic and Philosophic Manuscripts of 1844*. Trans. Martin Milligan. New York: Prometheus, 2009.

Medvedev, Pavel. *The Formal Method in Literary Scholarship*. Trans. Albert J. Wehrle. Baltimore: Johns Hopkins, 1991.

Moi, Toril. *Sexual/Textual Politics*. New York: Routledge, 2002.

Moi, Toril. *Revolution of the Ordinary*. Chicago: University of Chicago Press, 2017.

Ngũgĩ Wa Thiong'o. *Decolonizing the Mind*. London: Heinemann, 1986.

Ngũgĩ Wa Thiong'o. *Globalectics: Theory and the Politics of Knowing*. New York: Columbia University Press, 2012.

Perera, Sonali. *No Country: Working-Class Writing in the Age of Globalization*. New York: Columbia University Press, 2014.

Plekhanov, Georgi. *Art and Social Life*. New York: Aakar Books, 2011.

Retamar, Roberto Fernández. *Caliban and Other Essays*. Trans. Edward Baker. Minneapolis: University of Minnesota Press, 1989.

Robinson, Cedric. *Black Marxism*. Chapel Hill: University of North Carolina Press, 2000.

Spivak, Gayatri. "Can the Subaltern Speak?" In *Can the Subaltern Speak?: Reflections on the History of an Idea*. Ed. Rosalind Morris. New York: Columbia University Press, 2010. 21–80.

Spivak, Gayatri. *In Other Worlds*. New York: Routledge, 2012.

Spivak, Gayatri. *An Aesthetic Education in the Era of Globalization*. Cambridge: Harvard University Press, 2013.

Trotsky, Leon. *Literature and Revolution*. New York: Haymarket Books, 2005.

Volosinov. V. *Marxism and the Philosophy of Language* [1929]. Trans. Ladislav Matejka and
    I. R. Titunik. Cambridge, MA: Harvard University Press, 1986.
Williams, Raymond. *Marxism and Literature*. Oxford: Oxford University Press, 1977.
Williams, Raymond. *Culture and Society* [1958]. New York: Columbia University Press, 1983.
Williams, Raymond. *The English Novel from Dickens to Lawrence* [1970]. London: Hogarth
    Press, 1987.
Williams, Raymond. *Keywords* [1976]. London: Oxford: Oxford University Press, 2014.

CHAPTER FIVE

Post-Structuralism

DANIEL T. O'HARA

To understand post-structuralism, one must understand at least some basic elements of structuralism. Applying the linguistic model of analysis derived from Ferdinand de Saussure, structuralists such as Roman Jacobson in poetics, Claude Lévi-Strauss in anthropology, and Jacques Lacan in psychoanalysis (among many others in the humanities and social sciences) demonstrated what appeared to be a new general method for the human sciences, on a par with the scientific method in the STEM disciplines. The structuralists treated texts, social institutions, or unconscious symptoms as differentially related elements (as if they were signs) in a synchronic system (as if it were *langue*) arbitrarily imposed (*bricolage*) upon phenomena (as if *parole* or spoken words) for the purpose of producing (as in making appear theatrically) a largely hidden but effective order operating automatically like literary conventions, marriage laws, or unconscious phenomena. As such, this theory of Saussure's would serve as a meta-theory in the human sciences, a general law of all possible theories and readings in these fields, for now and as if for all time. Method and meta-theory were one and the same. Left out of this picture, of course, was history, change: diachrony.

A perfect exemplification of structuralism at work in literary studies is Lacan's notorious seminar on Edgar Allan Poe's "The Purloined Letter." Reducing the story to its bare-bones plot, he shows how its two main events—the theft and the return of the letter, whose contents are never made known—replicate the same elementary structure of subject positions, as if being a subject were being a signifier in an allegorical waltz. In the first scene, when the Police Prefect reports to Dupin on his reason for consulting Poe's famous detective, we learn how the letter has been stolen under the very eyes of the Queen, who can say nothing due to the presence of her husband, the King. Minister D, who swipes the letter, recognizes the writing on the envelope and immediately understands that it is a clandestine communication between the Queen and one of his rivals at court.

Here we find, Lacan argues, the nexus of three gazes that define the subject positions of *unseeing authority* figure (King), *seeing victim* (Queen), and *transgressor* (Minister D). This triangulation of positions repeats itself piecemeal throughout the second half of the story, even as here in the initial report, the Prefect of Police stands in the position of the King, Minister D is in that of the Queen, and Dupin is in that of the Minister, his double (both are mathematical and poetic geniuses) and bitter rival, as it turns out. For Lacan, this replication of what he sees as an Oedipal structure shows how any subject is defined and constituted by the position it occupies in a repeating symbolic chain of signifiers that is essentially a binary opposition, not triangular, between two of the seers: the one who sees and is the victim and the one who sees and victimizes. And the subsequent series of revisionary critiques of Lacan's reading shows us, too, how this chain is potentially infinite in its repetitions. It may or may not be that, as Lacan says in the last line of his seminar that "a letter always arrives at its destination,"[1] but given such infinite possibility, it may take a very long time indeed. And at the center of these repeating circuits stands the letter whose meaning remains unknown but whose function is key to the socially symbolic enterprise.

What so many structuralist analysts do, as here in Lacan, is to treat the elements of the texts, institutions, or other cultural phenomena they read as if the text (or intertext), the institution (the fashion industry, say, as in Roland Barthes), or the advertising industry in question were structures of signs, specifically signifiers, whose patterns and movements can be mapped a priori like a semiological system that is virtually a schema of one's own mind. So when Lacan declares that Poe's tale tells the story of the inevitable return of the letter to its destination, the destination can only be that of his own mind, that is, his own theory. Cutting and pasting a worldly phenomenon so as to materialize one's own imaginary structures may be lots of fun, but hardly substitutes for effective and credible analysis.

As Jacques Derrida in his scathing critique "The Purveyor of Truth" demonstrates, to produce such a reading so faithful to his own structuralist theory of the symbolic, Lacan must ignore the literary facts of "The Purloined Letter," such as the entire story is being told by the unnamed narrator, Dupin's companion, and that it proceeds by two similar acts of reporting, the Police Prefect's and Dupin's himself after he retrieves the letter and reveals it. What Derrida argues is that there is always another (in this case fourth) position in literature, not simply as here three, and this supplemental literary position is that of the narrator, so that fiction is always the fiction of accurate reporting, the fiction of fiction "telling the truth."[2] So rather than simply telling the truth, Poe's tale tells the story of how stories would always tell that story as a fiction we recognize as such. The writer, the story, and the reader of literature are not occupying one of Lacan's three positions, but instead are occupying that of the literary subject spectrally inhabiting the tale as a shifting, composite, virtually anonymous iteration, the trace of *ecriture*, of *differance*. This fourth imaginative "gaze" (as if of the dead) comprehending the other three gazes without repeating them but instead playing ironically among them and yet still so different from them is the essence of literature and what Lacan sacrifices to the truth of his structural theory of psychoanalysis he would purvey.

We can say fairly enough, in this view, that Lacan's symbolic reading demonstrates how structuralism as a theory and method reduces a field of differences ultimately to a weighted hierarchy of binary oppositions atop of which sits the theory itself, smiling down upon its own creation to see, as if a newly installed imaginary king or god. Derrida's deconstruction of every such structuralist activity, as in his sustained critique of Lévi-Strauss in *Of Grammatology* (1976), marks the "posting," as it were, of structuralism by post-structuralism. When lined up with the history of philosophy before its arrival on the scene, structuralism represents the last phase of the tradition of ontotheology, logocentrism, and the privileging of timeless presence and certain speech over mortifying temporality and ambiguous writing from Plato to Lacan before its explosive interruption by post-structuralisms of all sorts.

The poster boy for post-structuralism could be Derrida, especially in this context, but for most commentators it is in fact Michel Foucault. Always ambivalent about his work being lumped in with structuralism, especially due to his 1966 bestselling *Les Mots et Les Choses* (*The Order of Things* in English), which actually critiques the prehistory of structuralisms in economics, linguistics, and anthropology, Foucault is so well focused on the mapping and time-freezing dimensions of its targets therein that the book appears to be to many at the time a species of that which it claims to critique. As I argued at length in both *Radical Parody* (1992) and *Empire Burlesque* (2003), Foucault is a world-historical parodist, whose range of writing styles is so great, whose virtuosity so magnificent, his work is often more exacting a version of what he actually opposes as to make it hard to distinguish it as such. This is because Foucault emphasizes that discursive practices and disciplines are not synchronic spectacles of antithesis but systems of power under repeated challenges, displacements, and reassertions by differential forces and movements turning over and returning without end. This vision arises from the ground of his own prose upward like smoke from Western Man's self-immolate auto de fe, the death of god being the death of man for Foucault in *The Order of Things*.

As practiced by Foucault, post-structuralism is the war among discursive practices for the purpose of reshaping the historical field, disrupting and reversing hierarchies, and carrying this anarchic process to the point where the original multiplicity of differential relations among the elements, whatever they may be, returns. As Gilles Deleuze in *Nietzsche and Philosophy* says about Nietzsche's troubling doctrine of the eternal recurrence of the same, what returns eternally is ever the same *difference,* not simply the same.[3] Post-structuralism in this form reminds one of "creative destruction," that "incessant product and process innovation mechanism by which new production units replace outdated ones, according to Joseph Schumpeter who considered it 'the essential fact about capitalism.'"[4] The main difference is that Foucault is more radical than that, as he would take things further, well beyond any "innovation mechanism," to the point where it were as if the anonymous multiplicities of the state of nature itself would return perpetually.

We can see this quintessential post-structuralist move operative most influentially in Foucault's most famous book, *Discipline and Punish* (1975). Here's how he summarizes the differences between discipline and punishment under the king where sovereign violent spectacle rules and those silent saturating social practices function in the age of Jeremy Bentham's Panopticon, that is, in our modern age:

> The panoptic schema, without disappearing as such or losing any of its properties, was destined to spread throughout the social body [in the later nineteenth century]; its vocation was to become a generalized function. The plague-stricken town [in early times] provided an exceptional disciplinary model [under the king]: perfect, but absolutely violent; to the disease that brought death, power opposed its perpetual threat of death; life inside it was reduced to its simplest expression; it was, against the power of death, the meticulous exercise of the right of the sword [in leper houses for the soon-to-die]. The Panopticon, on the other hand, has a role of amplification; although it arranges power, although it is intended to make it more economic and more effective, it does so not for power itself, nor for the immediate salvation of a threatened society: its aim is to strengthen the social forces—to increase production, to develop the economy, spread education, raise the level of public morality; to increase and multiply. How is power to be strengthened in such a way that, far from impeding progress, far from weighing upon it with its rules and regulations, it actually facilitates such progress. What intensificator of power will be able at the same time to be a multiplicator of production? How will power, by increasing its forces, be able to increase those of society instead of confiscating them or impeding them? The Panopticon's solution to this problem is that the productive increase of power can be assured only if, on the

one hand, it can be exercised continuously in the very foundations of society, in the subtlest possible way, and if, on the other hand, it functions outside these sudden, violent, discontinuous forms that are bound up with the exercise of sovereignty. The body of the king, with its strange material and physical presence, with the force that he himself deploys or transmits to some few others, is at the opposite extreme of this new physics of power represented by panopticism; the domain of panopticism is, on the contrary, that whole lower region, that region of irregular bodies, with their details, their multiple movements, their heterogeneous forces, their spatial relations; what are required are mechanisms that analyze distributions, gaps, series, combinations, and which use instruments that render visible, record, differentiate and compare: a physics of a relational and multiple power, which has its maximum intensity not in the person of the king, but in the bodies that can be individualized by these relations. At the theoretical level, Bentham defines another way of analyzing the social body and the power relations that traverse it; in terms of practice, he defines—a procedure of subordination of bodies and forces that must increase the utility of power while practising the economy of the prince. Panopticism is the general principle of a new "political anatomy" whose object and end are not the relations of sovereignty but the relations of discipline. The celebrated, transparent, circular cage, with its high towers powerful and knowing, may have been for Bentham a project of perfect disciplinary institution; but he also set out to show how one may "unlock" the disciplines and get them to function in a diffused, multiple, polyvalent way throughout the whole social body. These disciplines, which the classical age had elaborated in specific, relatively enclosed places—barracks, schools, workshops—and whose total implementation had been imagined only at the limited and temporary scale of a plague-stricken town, Bentham dreamt of transforming into a network of mechanisms that would be everywhere and always alert, running through society without interruption in space or in time. The panoptic arrangement provides the formula for this generalization. It programmes, at the level of an elementary and easily transferable mechanism, the basic functioning of a society penetrated through and through with disciplinary mechanisms. There are two images, then, of discipline. At one extreme, the discipline-blockade, the enclosed institution, established on the edges of society, turned inwards towards negative functions: arresting evil, breaking communications, suspending time. At the other extreme, with panopticism, is the discipline-mechanism: a functional mechanism that must improve the exercise of power by making it lighter, more rapid, more effective, a design of subtle coercion for a society to come. The movement from one project to the other, from a schema of exceptional discipline to one of a generalized surveillance, rests on a historical transformation: the gradual extension of the mechanisms of discipline throughout the seventeenth and eighteenth centuries, their spread throughout the whole social body, the formation of what might be called in general the disciplinary society.[5]

The sovereign expression of absolute power is a violent spectacle of total unproductive expenditure, as seen in Figure 1.

The Panopticon is a model of saturating power that works for prisons, factories, schools, and barracks, with equal success and only slight modifications [see Figure 2].

By bringing these radically opposing extremes together in his analysis, Foucault evacuates the field of possibilities of all mediating in-between alternatives; thereby, as his representative post-structuralism does every time, it returns the scene of power to

FIGURE 1: *Damien's Execution* Marten Kuilman, "DOC11/1465—The execution (quartered by horses) of Damiens," *flickr,* April 30, 2014. https://www.flickr.com/photos/quadralectics/13889911770

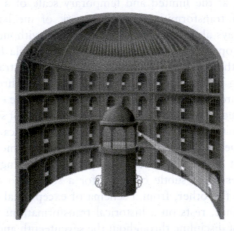

FIGURE 2: *Bentham's Panopticon* Sascha Matuszak, "Panopticon," *Chenguliving,* February 28, 2015. http://www.chenguliving.com/escaping-conformity/panopticon/

chaotic nothingness, as in the beginning of all things. By adding time, change, history, politics to the synchronic formalism of structuralism, Foucault, as post-structuralists do, explodes structuralist forms to reveal in repeated negative apocalypses, prepared for by meticulous details of analytic presentations, modernity's definitive, constituting break with the recognizable human past, on the way to unknown, posthuman futures.

While structuralist thinkers espouse or at least assume a radical intellectual stance, at times complementing it with a leftish political viewpoint, such as Roland Barthes throughout his many pre-1968 texts, from *Writing Degree Zero* and *Mythologies* (1957) to *Elements of Semiology* (1964) or *The Fashion System* (1967), post-structuralists write as if the emerging future were postapocalyptic, postmodernist, and posthuman, in which the anonymous murmur of the global multitudes drown out the self-important, perhaps violent displays of the once rich and advanced North. While structuralism coincides with the full emergence of Euro-American late capitalism, post-structuralism marks the new final phase of nomadic, transnational, planetary capital, globalization with a vengeance.

In this context, only Nietzsche can serve as the most complete representative of post-structuralism, nearly a century before its advent. Consider his conclusion to *Twilight of the Idols* (1889), in which for five numbered sections he analyses what he terms "The Problem of Socrates." As the first four sections lay out the dialectic of perspectives Nietzsche has had on this founding figure of Western philosophy (whose details need not detain us here), the reader expects either some trans-valuating albeit parodic synthesis or even more, perhaps, a suspension of judgment, leaving the dialectic ironically open to the future. Both of these critical moves are familiar to readers of Nietzsche and the post-structuralists he fathered. But instead, the reader finds Nietzsche returning to an even earlier point in his own career, to double-down on his original position in *The Birth of Tragedy* (1872) about "the psychology of the orgiastic," the Dionysian:

> The psychology of the orgiastic as an overflowing feeling of life and strength, where even pain still has the effect of a stimulus, gave me the key to the concept of tragic feeling, which had been misunderstood both by Aristotle and even more by modern pessimists. Tragedy is so far from being a proof of the pessimism (in Schopenhauer's sense) of the Greeks that it may, on the contrary, be considered a decisive rebuttal and counterexample. Saying Yes to life even in its strangest and most painful episodes, the will to life rejoicing in its own inexhaustible vitality even as it witnesses the destruction of its greatest heroes—that is what I called Dionysian, that is what I guessed to be the bridge to the psychology of the tragic poet. Not in order to be liberated from terror and pity, not in order to purge oneself of a dangerous affect by its vehement discharge—which is how Aristotle understood tragedy—but in order to celebrate oneself the eternal joy of becoming, beyond all terror and pity—that tragic joy included even joy in destruction.[6]

And with that I again touch on my earliest point of departure: *The Birth of Tragedy* was my first revaluation of all values. And on that point I again stand on the earth out of which my intention, my ability grows—I, the last disciple of the philosopher Dionysus—I, the teacher of the eternal recurrence. The Dionysian herein summoned—contra many commentators—does not include an Apollonian component, but rather assumes an ultimate point of new origin characteristic of apocalyptic re-visionaries such as Nietzsche and, I would argue, his true post-structuralist disciples George Bataille, Foucault, Gilles Deleuze, and Felix Guattari, and many other lesser lights. The internalization of apocalypse to the point where what is left to be summoned for analysis are the micro-physics, the micro-politics, and now the micro-data of power, hegemony, difference, and the anonymous histories of "revolting" multitudes—such are the remnants of post-structuralism, that mindless state of nature we are all still trying to live through.

To end on a somewhat different note, I want to conclude with a passage from Roland Barthes's *S/Z* (1970), perhaps the greatest post-structuralist literary analysis of them all, and his equally superb but neglected *Sade/Fourier/Loyola* (1971), Barthes's favorite "logothetes," or founders of their own unique "words" or discourses, even virtually private languages.

An essay originating in a two-year seminar reading of Balzac's short novel "Sarrasine" about a castrato La Zambinella, whose feminine masquerade as La Zambinella so fooled the title character to the point of suicide that (s)he retreats from life save to endow Sarrasine's relatives with his riches while living his newly ascetic life to its own grizzled and twisted fate, S/Z is often misread, especially initially, as a structuralist classic because of its elaboration of five codes for reading (hermeneutic, semantic, proairetic, cultural, and symbolic) or its famous distinction of two fundamental narrative kinds, the readerly text and the writerly text—that is, the classic text that would suppress (unsuccessfully) all multiple significations in favor of a single realistic one, and the modern text that disseminates multiplicities of all kinds. In fact, this last distinction of the writerly text defines the goal of S/Z itself, which if anything is a readerly text repeating shown apocalyptically dissolving into the writerly text to end all such texts. For example, what but itself is the following passage, commenting on "It was a man" from "Sarrasine," most vehemently characterizing?

XX. The Dissolve of Voices

Who is speaking [here]? Is it a scientific voice from the type "personage" infers, in passing, a species, "man," in order later to give it another species, "castrato"? Is it a phenomenalist voice naming what it sees, the wholly masculine garb of the old man? Here it is impossible to attribute an origin, a point of view, to the statement. Now, this impossibility is one of the ways in which the plural nature of a text can be appreciated. The more indeterminate the origin of the statement, the more plural the text. In modern texts, the voices are so treated that any reference is impossible: the discourse, or better, the language, speaks: nothing more. By contrast, in the classic text the majority of the utterances are assigned an origin, we can identify their parentage, who is speaking: either a consciousness (of a character, of the author) or a culture (the anonymous is still an origin, a voice, the voice we find, for example, in the gnomic code [a subset of the hermeneutic code]); however, it may happen that in the classic text, always haunted by the appropriation of speech, the voice gets lost, as though it had leaked out through a hole in the discourse. The best way to conceive the classical plural is then to listen to the text as an iridescent exchange carried on by multiple voices, on different wavelengths and subject from time to time to a sudden *dissolve*, leaving a gap which enables the utterance to shift from one point of view to another, without warning: the writing is set up across this tonal instability (which in the modern text becomes atonality), which makes it a glistening texture of ephemeral origins.[7]

With the synesthesia, the radical diction ("a hole in the discourse"), and the other avant-garde experimental signs, Barthes is pulling out many if not all stops here.

Earlier in S/Z, in a section called "The Starred Text," Barthes characterizes how he sees, as in a visionary scene, what he (and originally his two-year seminar) is doing in reading together Balzac's text, and in doing so manages to convey a model for reading a la post-structuralist protocols generally into the future of our own time and beyond:

We shall therefore star the text, separating, in the manner of a minor earthquake, the blocks of signification of which reading grasps only the smooth surface, imperceptibly soldered by the movement of sentences, the flowing discourse of narration, the "naturalness" of ordinary language. The tutor signifier will be cut up into a series of brief, contiguous fragments, which we shall call *lexias,* since they are units of reading. This cutting up, admittedly, will be arbitrary in the extreme; it will imply no methodological responsibility, since it will bear on the signifier, whereas proposed analysis bears solely on the signified. The lexia will include sometimes a few words, sometimes several sentences; it will be a matter of convenience: it will suffice that the lexia be the best possible space in which we can observe meanings; its dimension, empirically determined, estimated, will depend on the density of connotations, variable according to the moments of the text: all we require is that each lexia should have at most three or four meaning to be enumerated. The text, in its mass, is comparable to a sky, at once flat and smooth, deep, without edges and without landmarks; like the soothsayer drawing on it with the tip of his staff an imaginary rectangle wherein to consult, according to certain principles, the flight of birds, the commentator traces through the text certain zones of reading, in order to observe the migration of meanings, the outcropping of codes, the passage of citations.[8]

This scene marks the return of the original state of reading, perhaps, or at least it does within the horizon of Barthes's and our own post-structuralist positioning in time. Reading, after post-structuralism, after what often is synonymously named the moment of "high theory" in the Anglo-American culture of literary criticism anyway, comes down to attempting, via various improvised and standardized moves alike, to define the imaginary subject of reading and sketch out its possible futures ever emerging from the starred texts of our postmodern condition.

In this context, the final sentences of this section of Barthes's *S/Z* cast a chilling specter over our present moment:

The lexia is only the wrapping of a semantic volume, the crest line of the plural text, arranged like a berm of possible (but controlled, attested by a systematic reading) meanings under the flux of discourse: the lexia and its units will thereby form a kind of polyhedron faceted by the word, the group of words, the sentence or the paragraph, i.e., with the language which is its "natural" excipient.[9]

In 1971, when *Sade/Fourier/Loyola* is originally published in French, Barthes comments on system and systematics, cited from Marx and Engel's *The German Ideology,* in order to distinguish between Fourier and his disciples, with respect to how their texts function. In the process, he reveals the legacy of post-structuralism par excellence:

Systematics is the play of the *system*: it is language that is open, infinite, free from any referential illusion (pretension); its mode of appearance, its constituency, is not "development" but pulverization, dissemination (the gold dust of the signifier); it is a discourse without "object" (it only speaks of a thing obliquely, by approaching it indirectly: Civilization in Fourier) and without "subject" (in writing, the author does not allow himself to be involved in the imaginary subject, for he "performs" his enunciatory role in such a manner that we cannot decide whether it is serious or parody). It is a vast madness which does not end, but permutates.[10]

As one sees here, the translator of Barthes, like the author himself and his subjects, must be a bit of a logothete, too.

Post-structuralism arises out of structuralism, and spreading beyond the compass of professional intellectuals, clears the would-be radical fields of the human sciences and their real-world attachments of all theories worthy of the name, leaving in its wake the debris that once was known as New Historicism, ideology critique, and most lately and worst of all, digital humanities. This debris of the vast wave that was post-structuralism bears witness, then, to a revisionary madness to end all revisionism:

> Here there is a sort of question, call it historical, of which we are only glimpsing today the conception, the formation, the gestation, the labor. I employ these words, I admit, with a glance toward the business of childbearing—but also with a glance toward those who, in a company from which I do not exclude myself, turn their eyes away in the face of the as yet unnameable which is proclaiming itself and which can do so, as is necessary whenever a birth is in the offing, only under the species of the non-species, in the formless, mute, infant, and terrifying form of monstrosity.[11]

Temple University (United States)

NOTES

1. Jacques Lacan, quoted in John Muller and William J. Richardson, eds., *The Purloined Poe: Lacan, Derrida and Psychoanalytic Reading* (Baltimore: The Johns Hopkins University Press, 1987), 43.

2. Muller and Richardson, *The Purloined Poe*, 97.

3. Gilles Deleuze, *Nietzsche and Philosophy*, trans. Hugh Tomlinson (New York: Columbia University Press, 1983), 45.

4. Ricardo J. Caballero, "Creative Destruction," economics.mit.edu/files/1785.

5. Michel Foucault, *Discipline and Punish: The Birth of the Prison*, trans. Alan Sheridan (New York: Vintage, 1995), 95.

6. Fredrick Nietzsche, *The Twilight of the Idols*, trans. R. J. Hollingdale and Walter Kaufmann (New York: Create Space Independent Publishing Platform, 2016).

7. Barthes, *S/Z*, 41–42.

8. Ibid., 13–14.

9. Ibid., 14.

10. Roland Barthes, *Sade/Fourier/Loyola*, trans. Richard Miller (Berkeley and Los Angeles: University of California Press, 1976), 110.

11. Jacques Derrida, quoted in Richard A. Macksey, ed., *The Structuralist Controversy: The Languages of Criticism and the Sciences of Man*, 40th Anniversary Edition (Baltimore: The Johns Hopkins University Press, 2007), 95.

WORKS CITED

Barthes, Roland. *Elements of Semiology* [1964]. Trans. Annette Lavers and Colin Smith. New York: Hill and Wang, 1968.

Barthes, Roland. *Writing Degree Zero* [1953]. Trans. Annette Lavers and Colin Smith. New York: Hill and Wang, 1968.

Barthes, Roland. *Mythologies* [1957]. Trans. Annette Lavers. New York: Hill and Wang, 1972.

Barthes, Roland. *S/Z: An Essay* [1970]. Trans. Richard Miller. New York: Hill and Wang, 1974.

Barthes, Roland. *Sade/Fourier/Loyola* [1971]. Trans. Richard Miller. Berkeley and Los Angeles: University of California Press, 1976.

Barthes, Roland. *The Fashion System* [1967]. Trans. Matthew Ward and Richard Howard.
    Berkeley: University of California Press, 1990.

Caballero, Ricardo J. "Creative Destruction." economics.mit.edu/files/1785

Deleuze, Gilles. *Nietzsche and Philosophy* [1962]. Trans. Hugh Tomlinson. New York:
    Columbia University Press, 1983.

Derrida, Jacques. *Of Grammatology* [1967]. Trans. Gayatri Chakravorty Spivak. Baltimore:
    Johns Hopkins University Press, 1976.

Foucault, Michel. *Discipline and Punish: The Birth of the Prison* [1975]. Trans. Alan Sheridan.
    New York: Vintage, 1995.

Kuilman, Marten. "DOC11/1465—The execution (quartered by horses) of Damiens." *flickr.*
    April 30, 2014. https://www.flickr.com/photos/quadralectics/13889911770

Macksey, Richard A., ed. *The Structuralist Controversy: The Languages of Criticism and the
    Sciences of Man.* 40th Anniversary Edition. Baltimore: The Johns Hopkins University Press,
    2007.

Matuszak, Sascha. "Panopticon." *Chengduliving.* February 28, 2015. http://www.chengduliving.
    com/escaping-conformity/panopticon/

Muller, John P., and William J. Richardson, eds. *The Purloined Poe: Lacan, Derrida and
    Psychoanalytic Reading.* Baltimore: The Johns Hopkins University Press, 1987.

Nietzsche, Friedrich. *The Birth of Tragedy* [1872]. Trans. Walter Kaufman. New York: Vintage
    Books, 1967.

Nietzsche, Fredrick. *The Twilight of the Idols* [1889]. Trans. R. J. Hollingdale and Walter
    Kaufmann. New York: Create Space Independent Publishing Platform, 2016.

O'Hara, Daniel. *Radical Parody: American Culture and Critical Agency After Foucault.*
    New York: Columbia University Press, 1992.

O'Hara, Daniel. *Empire Burlesque: The Fate of Critical Culture in Global America.* Durham:
    Duke, 2003.

CHAPTER SIX

Historicisms

HAROLD ARAM VEESER

"I began with the desire to speak with the dead." While not startling in itself, this statement was unexpected as the lead sentence of Stephen Greenblatt's 1987 book, *Shakespearean Negotiations*. Granted that Greenblatt was based in New Age mecca northern California, home of Werner Erhard's EST movement, the Haight-Ashbury Summer of Love, and the Manson family, so an element of craziness was understandable—but not from the intellectual heavyweight who had mounted the first significant challenge to the ruling class of literary ideas, the big brain who in 1982 had christened his movement "the new historicism." Now here he was talking crazy about the underworld, the dead, and resurrection, calling himself "a middle-class shaman," and telling weird anecdotes about excrement, garbage, and transgender plays. But the surprising effect of all this was to install a new reign of historicism that, in effect, still remains the dominant literary critical mode to this very day.

The "desire to speak with the dead" was the kind of superstition you'd expect the *National Geographic* to feature, with bare-breasted photographs, among lost tribes of the Amazon basin. And yet the appeal to hidden powers made a certain kind of sense in 1988, a year of eroding respect for literature and indeed all the humanities disciplines. English departments seemed to be becoming little more than "mounds marking the edge of another age, illusions of eternity."[1] Few people were any longer inclined to read books in order to understand themselves. As recently as the mid-century, English had been the most popular college major and many students eagerly traced the rise of the novel in order to learn how their own middle-class society had come into being. But by the late 1980s, works of genius could no longer claim to have their former "synecdochic relation to history." In fact by 1988 when *Shakespearean Negotiations* appeared, "mid-20th-century audiences [had] stopped pretending to care about high culture."[2] History, downsized, had its market niche as a commercial product, cut up into periods and packaged and sold as retro style.[3] Museums, archives, cemeteries, festivals, monuments, fraternal orders, and anniversaries were ponderous, elephantine, and out of touch, suitable perhaps for clueless tourists, like Times Square. Today, "memory exists only in sites of memory—*lieux de mémoire*—from Proust's madeleine to the defunct revolutionary calendar."[4] By the second decade of the twenty-first century, the best historicist critics had switched their attention to the Anthropocene, "deep time," and what the current editor of *PMLA* called *antihumanist humanism*. As the importance of human history lost people's respect and interest, the vastly expanded scales of geological, technological, mathematical, and climatological time gained persuasive power. The present chapter will trace this momentous change, from the New Criticism through New Historicism up to the huge enlargements of scale that underwrite the radically different historical theories today.

The Old Historicism, based on scrupulous archival research, had been under attack for some time. From the Annales school, to the Warburg-Courtauld Institute, to Carlo Ginzberg-style social history, to Geertzian interpretive anthropology, Foucaultian archaeologies, and the discontinuous histories of epistemic rupture, exciting new paradigms continually rotated into view. The effect has been that of a Google map, zooming out to a satellite view of earth. Consider Fernand Braudel and the Annales group that he helped to found. He emphasized the *longue durée* focused on climate change and centuries-long developments of trade routes. Or think of Wai Chee Dimock's postmodern historiographies based on the Albert Einstein's theory of relativity, and her resulting thoughts about the Anthropocene and "deep time." Some literary historians are still New Historicists, of course. There is James Shapiro, who draws on the work of social historians, inspired by Peter Laslett, who points out, for example, that in late sixteenth-century England both men and women did not marry at fourteen, on average (as had been believed) but at the average age of twenty-four—leaving a twelve-year gap when women were more or less unaccounted for, a situation that profoundly changes our conception of the Elizabethan theater. But Shapiro is an outlier; most literary historians are thinking about eons, not parish records or margin notes in the Calendar of State Papers. As for what was big in the old historiography, namely the master narratives from Marx to Freud to Lévi-Strauss, these have been thoroughly hammered, modified, split apart, and discarded as hopelessly inflated fictions. "We live now, especially when it comes to historiography, after the age of the *grand récit*, i.e., in an epoch for which the large story of the exigent unfolding of beginning, through middle, to end, no longer carries any urgency."[5] All the sweeping accounts of civilization, whether they are stories of advancement (Hegel, Marx) or degeneration (Oswald Spengler), indeed all the confident enumerations of historical stages, lie in ruins.

Grand récit devotées survive: smart people, not merely Evangelicals confidently awaiting the end of days, but also the likes of theoretical genius Fredric Jameson, the Marxist literary critic of immeasurable fecundity. "The cultural past is momentarily returned to life and warmth and allowed to speak," warns Jameson, "only if they are grasped as episodes in a single vast unfinished plot." His plot is an old one: a progression from tribal hordes, to Neolithic kinship-based societies, to Oriental despotisms, to slave-owning societies of antiquity, to feudalism, primitive accumulation, capitalism, and finally communism. Only a thinker affectionately known as "the last Marxist" could still believe this neat linear narration. But other totalizing theories and enabling fictions abound. Structuralism in its myriad forms underwrote, for example, thousands of books in many fields from linguistics to interpretive anthropology, in each case ferreting out the submerged and hidden center that organized all the details and arrangements of a given system. The structuralism of Claude Lévi-Strauss could posit the same fundamental structural logic underwriting the intricate system of kinship ties and the street-plan of the village and the architecture of the houses. This kind of immanence is now fully discredited.[6] The unities and universals of Freudian psychoanalysis have come under devastating attack, for example by Deleuze and Guattari in *Anti-Oedipus* (1972). Indeed, no master narrative, no centered structure or immanent principle, has withstood the test of time. For most historians, there can be no transcendental plot or plan. The very thought is absurd. And yet this skepticism poses a real problem. For without such a transcendent pattern, how can a historian make sense of the infinite, chaotic details that fill even a brief moment of time? Some kind of master plan or teleology seems necessary if we are not simply to abandon the attempt to explain what the poet called the immense panorama of anarchy and futility that is modern life.

The ancients had their historical mythologies. Fifth-century BC Greek historian Thucydides, for example, had an overarching theory of Athenian supremacy that allowed him to sort particular events into the intelligible whole of a sequential, framing narrative.[7] This frankly prejudiced standpoint made Thucydides a stark realist, however, when compared to his peer, Herodotus, whose memorializing historiography was openly receptive to myths, entertaining stories, and praise for great men. (Epideictic history always maintained a following, given the enduring appetite of the great for commemorative tributes.) Commemorative histories written in the epideictic mode arguably preponderate throughout history: think only of Carlyle's or Trevelyan's histories of Great Britain, Gibbons's of Rome, or Arthur Schlesinger's history of the United States.

But the hymns to progress and great men came to be shadowed by critics who preferred history conceived as a science. Considerable skepticism about Enlightenment hopes for human improvement was devastatingly pointed in J. G. Herder's book, *Yet Another Philosophy of History for the Enlightenment of Mankind* (1774). Giambattista Vico offered a totalizing history in his book *The New Science*, and the early nineteenth-century founder of objective historiography, Leopold von Ranke, counseled: *Wie es eigentlich gewesen*—write only that which has actually happened. But stepping outside one's own culture and beliefs, as Ranke advised historians, was more easily said than done. Critical historians already had intimations that all "facts" were constructed. Would-be scientific historians rejected Ranke as simplistic and relativistic. They preferred to track history through its iron laws—in Marx's case, the dialectical laws of class struggle, in Freud's, the dictates of instinct. More conventional liberal historians also had their master narratives. The Whigs believed in steady progress, a belief that flourished when times were good but that faltered when the First World War broke out. But the various progressive and evolutionary historiographies were always on the defensive. Common sense held that history, as one wag put it, to "one damn thing after another"—a classic put-down leveled at Whig historians.

Literary critics faced the same challenges that plagued historians: to get outside one's own potentially distorting beliefs while trying to comprehend an alien culture, to wrestle with overwhelming data without, in desperation, imposing arbitrary patterns, to tell a story without succumbing to storytelling fictions. Into this turbulent, unorganized setting, stepped the New Criticism, a method of literary interpretation that must have seemed like reason itself. New Criticism began with Agrarian Christian humanists. These men handled the messy complications of historical method by ignoring history altogether.

> During its triumphant ascent—from the Marxist thirties to the academic canonization of the fifties—the New Criticism encountered very few "theories" on its path. The intellectual atmosphere was still relatively unpolluted by the theoretical proliferation that set in with a vengeance in subsequent years; even the philosophy departments had yet to feel the first fresh stirrings of the gale-force winds unleashed by existentialism. Only an old-fashioned communism and an old-fashioned psychoanalysis stood out upon the agrarian landscape like immense and ugly foreign bodies, history itself (equally old-fashioned in those days) being very effectively consigned to the dusty ash can of "scholarship."[8]

With feeble opponents like these, the New Criticism enjoyed a remarkably unobstructed march to power.

Uncontaminated by any "extrinsic" information such as the author's biography or intentions, the historical context, or the urgencies of the time, the New Criticism eventually became synonymous with the explication of the text alone. Political and ethical principles were ruled out of bounds. Anyone who proposed such considerations was dismissed as a mere journalist or sociologist who had an axe to grind.[9] Shrinking and scaling-down were second nature to the New Criticism. Whatever the literary work under consideration, for example, the New Critics generically called it "the poem" even if it happened to be a novel or a play. New Criticism was good for English department pride. The permitted topics for analysis, after everything historical was ruled out of bounds, comprised a very short list ("irony," "paradox," "tension," "unity"). All were established properties of the English department; no other department was interested in them. New Critics took a hard line. Any department that allowed discussion of extra-literary contexts might "almost as well announce that it does not regard itself as entirely autonomous but as a branch of the department of history."[10] Text-centered, formalist New Criticism had strong institutional bases in the Gauss Seminars at Princeton and, later, in the Kenyon School of English, funded by the Rockefeller Foundation. As this blindered formalism won ever more adherents, journalists such as Edmund Wilson taxed it with the "impossible attempt to make aesthetic values independent of all other values."[11] More important, resistance formed within the English department itself. The text itself was finally just not enough. Historicist resistance began to form.

Even while New Criticism gained control of one English department after another, historicist English professors began to resist. But they were not in mid-season form. They needed a new idea. The existing schools of historical criticism were two: the history of ideas and the Old Historicism. History of ideas was easily attacked. Their trick was to assign to an "age" a universal set of beliefs, and then proceed to "discover" those beliefs in the period's literary works. Its champions had essentially opted out of the English department altogether. "The ideas in serious reflective literature are of course in great part philosophical ideas in dilution," explained A. O. Lovejoy, author of a history of ideas bestseller. So then literature is just "the water added to philosophy,"[12] tartly replied René Wellek, one of the leading New Critics. History of ideas was and is demeaning to literature. To history of ideas people—to a Lovejoy or an E. M. W. Tillyard—*Hamlet* and *Tommy the Tow Truck* were equal. Ideas could be found and explicated in both works. All the imagery and mimesis just got in the way. Another feature that undermined history of ideas was its tendency to attract unimaginative pedants. It appealed to the kind of professor who clung to a bedrock of over-simplified philosophy and a rigid canon of great thinkers. The history of ideas was not a valuable enterprise.

The other branch of the old literary historicism devoted itself to minutiae. Historical facts, no matter how chaotic, were their topic. Literary historians could seem petty and nit-picking, especially when they policed the historically uninformed New Critics, calling them out on their many anachronisms. When the poet Andrew Marvell dreamed that "our vegetable love should grow," for example, historical critics were there to point out that he meant the third or vegetative soul of Aristotle, not "some monstrous and expanding cabbage."[13] The old historicists also objected that New Critics had a single, uninflected standard. "Mr. Brooks [a prominent New Critic] gave the impression that nearly all poetry between Marvell and Pound was a mistake," observed historical critic Douglas Bush.[14] But the old historicists also revived the important complaint of Hans-Georg Gadamer: New Critics were unable to stage a dialogue between the past and the present. They lived in a timeless vacuum except for the eternal structures of language, such as irony, tension, paradox, and symmetry. Since these tensions and tropes could be found, with enough digging, in any "poem," the New Criticism had little credibility in the still-respected English department's main task of evaluating, measuring, and hierarchizing literary works. New Critics had little patience with the historicists. "Every English professor is diligently devoting himself to discovering what porridge had John Keats,"[15] the New Critics complained. Meanwhile, both factions made adjustments as the students flocked into English. With so many Ph.D. students in English, at Yale, Chicago, and Princeton, the New Critics had to open new fields in search of raw materials for their students' dissertations. It was imprudent to dismiss all romantic poetry as a mistake. Meanwhile, historians searched for more inventive ways to reverse the triumph of unabashed formalism.

The near-total victory of formalism over historicism, while it lasted, owed much to the G. I. bill and general prosperity. The universities were overrun, it was D-Day on the Omaha Beach of English. But the solution was the New Critics': the text itself. As one professor remembered his earliest teaching job, "By concentrating on the text itself I could get a good discussion going about almost any literary work without having to know anything about its author, its circumstances of composition, or the history of its reception. . . . Given the vast unknowns on both sides of the lectern, the work itself was indeed our salvation."[16] The New Criticism was therefore both intelligible to students and easy for professors. But times were a-changing, and as the universities built Quonset huts to hold the overpopulation, a more complex, less seat-of-the-pants instructional model emerged.

What changed all this was the arrival of new literary theories from the Continent. Pioneers such as Edward Said were beginning by the mid-1960s to experiment with the Geneva School of phenomenology and the humanistic Marxism of Georg Lukács. The two ugly giants, Marxism and psychoanalysis, were themselves undergoing makeovers, transforming their methods piece by piece even while they were, like Jason's ship, the Argo, still under sail. The fascinating Michel Foucault announced that "history has no meaning" but yet is intelligible and "susceptible of analysis down to the smallest detail."[17] Those details were ultimately words. No facts were unmediated by texts. The decisive moment had come. The linguistic turn was underway.

Marxism and Freudian psychoanalysis could now be seen as structures of language: they had the same ontology as any other work of fiction. Hayden White provides the most sweeping linguistic reinterpretation of *grands récits*. With his crucial *Metahistory* (1975), he demonstrated that master narratives were entirely works of fiction. "Every account of the past is mediated by the language mode in which the historian casts his [sic] original description of the historical field prior to any analysis, explanation, or interpretation he may offer of it."[18] All the great historical accounts of the nineteenth century modeled themselves on genres such as comedy, tragedy, satire, and romance. As soon as White said this, it was obvious to all: Marx wrote comedy, ending with the workers' paradise and the leveling of class differences, while Burckhardt wrote satire, Nietzsche wrote tragedy, and Tocqueville romance. Marx, Nietzsche, Freud, and the rest were largely unaware that they were following thoroughly conventional templates. White was a structuralist, and he was convincing. He proved time and again how "those fields of study which, like historiography, seek to be 'objective' and 'realistic' in their representations of the world but which, by virtue of the unacknowledged poetic element in their discourse, hide their own 'subjectivity' and 'culture-boundedness' from themselves."[19] Structuralism helped White to discover this quality in so-called objective history. A similar demonstration had occurred much earlier, when Vladimir Propp showed how all Russian folktales are constructed by shuffling the same forty-four "functions" (example: the donor gives the hero a magical aid) and putting them into one of a very finite set of patterns. But White had a foot equally in post-structuralism as well.

If White was correct and all narratives molded themselves in the shape of the accepted fictional templates of their time, should we therefore expect that our contemporary historians will unconsciously give history the contours of an HBO series, a sitcom, or a video game? The New Historicism, for example, originating among the California dreamers of Berkeley and the University of San Diego, might embody some of the narratological norms of its era—the mid-1970s through the mid-1990s and beyond. Certainly, the New Historicism was a creature of its time in rejecting all structures. It was true to the New Age shamanism proclaimed by Greenblatt, readily going down to the archival underworld and sipping the warm blood preserved in vials found among the Calendar of State Papers. Greenblatt, Louis Montrose, Catherine Gallagher, and Jerome McGann were tomb raiders who dug out these precious deposits and incanted the spells that brought them to life. They would seize upon an event or anecdote—colonist John Rolfe's conversation with Pocahontas' father, a note found among Nietzsche's papers to the effect that "I have lost my umbrella"—and reread it in such a way as to reveal through the analysis of tiny particulars the behavioral codes, logics, and motive forces controlling a whole society.

"Controlling a whole society" is too strong, reminiscent of Lévi-Strauss or Victor Turner-vintage structural anthropology. Though I saw it that way in 1989, I was wrong. New Historicism was never a structuralism. It tried to avoid any hint of a centered or hidden structure that could be got at through hermeneutics. One of the founding members of New Historicism, the late, Berkeley-based Joel Fineman, noticed "its characteristic air of reporting, haplessly, the discoveries it happened serendipitously to stumble upon, in the course of undirected, idle rambles through the historical archives."[20] While Fineman correctly understood this supposed aimlessness as a way to strangle, with destabilizing anecdotes, any fetal development of a totalizing analysis (so uncool!) Jameson predictably gave a totalizing account of the practice. The goal was, in Jameson's brilliant analysis, to "open up a whole post-theoretical set of operations that retain the discursive conquest of a range of heterogeneous materials while quietly abandoning the theoretical component that once justified that enlargement, omitting the transcendental interpretations that had once seemed to be the very aim and purpose of homologies in the first place."[21] New Historicism would never seek a deep structure such as the forty-four invariable functions of the Russian folk tale (as had Vladimir Propp). They took the anthropology but threw out the structure.

To many, this structuralism-without-structures amounted to a sensationalist pursuit of "direct access to history's gritty, ground-level texture."[22] To others, the New Historicists' extended conceits and yoking of unlike things finally amount to little more than "a relation of pure suggestiveness."[23] Jameson was typical of grand narrative loyalists in dismissing the movement as a frivolous montage of attractions.

New Historicists were undeterred. Suspicious of any criticism predetermined by a Marxist or liberal grid, New Historicists eschewed overarching hypothetical constructs in favor of surprising coincidences. The New Historicist essay was a cabinet of wonders. For example, Suffragette street actions and the "hobble skirt" presented by the Parisian fashion house of Worth adorn one essay; a seventeenth-century French hermaphrodite's criminal trial, Shakespeare's *Twelfth Night*, and leather and rubber gloves adorn another; population theories of Malthus, the nineteenth-century hygienic movement, changing conceptions of the vital, and the disposal of sewage conjoin in a third essay. Is this a "montage of historical attractions," as per Jameson, an idle showing off, wherein "elegance here consists" in constructing bridge passages over the greatest possible distances, for example, from Malthus to sewage or hermaphrodites to Sir Toby Belch? To put it in less disparaging terms, and also to acknowledge the Renaissance origins of the movement, is New Historicism literary criticism now put in the old form of metaphysical conceits? Conceits were annoying then, too: "Their thoughts are often new, but seldom natural; they are not obvious, but neither are they just; and the reader, far from wondering that he missed them, wonders more frequently by what perverseness of industry they were ever found."[24] But these vintage stylistic habits of New Historicism, while significant, hardly account for the more programmatic and decidedly postmodern thrust of the movement. This thrust asserted that

a. every expressive act is embedded in a network of material practices;

b. every act of unmasking, critique, and opposition uses the tools it condemns and risks falling prey to the practice it exposes;

c. literary and non-literary "texts" circulate inseparably;

d. no discourse, imaginative or archival, gives access to unchanging truths or expresses inalterable human nature;

e. finally, a critical method and a language adequate to describe culture under capitalism participate in the economy they describe.

These ambitions go beyond the titillations of yoking heterogeneous objects together, as for example yoking Norman Mailer's novel *The Executioner's Song* to a stabbing death in New Orleans, or tying the ritual of eating offal by Zuni tribesmen with analyses of scatology in writings by Martin Luther and Sir Thomas More. Substantial content, really valuable lessons, began coming out of New Historicism as early as Louis Montrose's exemplary New Historicist essay, "'The Place of a Brother' in *As You Like It*: Social Process and Comic Form."[25] This study entails evidence taken from the literary and autobiographical subgenre of "advice to a son"; a social historian's data on the endowments, inheritances, and marriage patterns of younger brothers; and the rites of pastoral sequestration and initiation performed by tribal adolescents, as reported by ethnographers and anthropologists; all these may be summoned to contextualize the Shakespearean comedy. The montage of attractions is there, but so are analytical speculations that seem remarkably prescient. A seeming fixed social given like masculinity, for example, reemerges as a tenuous value that its possessors must unendingly strive to keep in place. The enduring condition of gender becomes the volatile act of gendering.

Anticipatory shades of Judith Butler! But Montrose published it in 1981, a good nine years before *Gender Trouble* appeared. Nor was this a unique instance of New Historicism opening lines of inquiry that would just a few years later expand into new subdisciplines and suggest the contours of entirely new fields of study.

A structural analysis of the typical New Historicist essay is counter to the movement's fierce anti-structuralism bias. But for that reason alone, it is a useful exercise, a procedure that can cut through the camouflage. The New Historicist essay typically falls into five stages. In "Marlowe and the Will to Absolute Play,"[26] these steps might be called, somewhat reductively, *anecdote, outrage, resistance, containment,* and the *critic's autobiography.* These phases unfold over a sequence of twenty-five pages.

The opening passage acts "less as explanatory illustration than as disturbance, that which required explanation."[27] The chapter begins laconically: "On 26 June 1586 a small

fleet, financed by the Earl of Cumberland, set out from Gravesend for the South Seas."
With the fleet under sail and the twice-terminal *Gravesend* named as the ominous port of
embarkation, Greenblatt hands the mic to an actual historical merchant-adventurer, John
Sarracoll, who continues the narrative. The English fleet is set in Sierra Leone, merchants
and crew admiring a beautiful "town of the Negroes . . . of about two hundred houses,
and walled about with stakes so thick, that a rat could hardly get in or out." A postscript
drops this final surprise: "Our men at their departure set the town on fire" and burned
it to ashes.

No easy answers here. The English admire the beauty of the town and then casually
burn down the object of their admiration. Greenblatt channels our puzzlement and
outrage. He tries to imagine what Sarracoll thought, why he wrote as he wrote. Does an
"aesthetic element" in the Englishmen's response to the village "conflict with or somehow
fuel the destructiveness?" And if Sarracoll feels no uneasiness at all, which seems to be the
case given his bland impassivity, "Why does he suddenly shift and write not *we* but *our
men?* . . . When he recalls the invasion, why does he think of rats?" Although Sarracoll's
rats and his change of we to our men would attract few historians' attention, Greenblatt
displays his English department loyalties as he pries at these hairline verbal fractures
to get an inside look at the psychology of the narrator Sarracoll and notes "the moral
blankness that rests like thick snow on Sarracoll's sentences."[28]

Greenblatt now introduces stage three, a resistor who opposes the moral vacancy
that underwrites this imperialist atrocity. That resistant figure is Marlowe himself, the
playwright whose "life suggests the very opposite of that 'peculiar equilibrium' [of
Sarracoll's]" and "rushes to embrace the tragic with a strange eagerness." Marlowe's play,
The Jew of Malta, is now introduced. Greenblatt holds the play to be a critical exploration
of the "essential meaninglessness of theatrical space, the vacancy that is the dark side of
its power to imitate any place." Marlowe stands outside his society and delivers sharp
critiques of rapacious and amoral characters very much resembling the real-life Sarracoll.

Stage four ensues with the strong containment move: the mechanism familiar in
Foucault's account of the futility of resistance. Every system of power incites, uses, and
co-opts to its own benefit all manner of resistances and rebellions. At this point, Greenblatt
specifies that all Marlowe's attacks on social norms—Tamburlaine's excessive violence,
Barabas's amorality, Edward's homosexuality, Faustus's skepticism—are "exposed as
unwitting tributes to that social construction of identity against which they struggle." By
embracing what society deems evil, "they have unwittingly accepted [society's] crucial
structural elements." Then comes a further turn of the screw: Marlowe is a true rebel
nonetheless, because his "unwitting tributes to society" undermine the liberal, Modernist-
nurtured consensus that great art is oppositional. In this sequence of dizzying turns,
Marlowe has gone from rebel, to conformist, finally back to rebel.

The final, fifth move is confessional and self-referential. Praising Marlowe's heroes for
their love of the outlandish and absurd, their delight in role-playing and "entire absorption
in the game at hand and consequent indifference to what lies outside the boundaries
of the game,"[29] Greenblatt describes, as he quickly makes clear, both himself and the
New Historicism. He now provides, alarmingly, a personal, illustrative anecdote: he once
silently watched a man—who winked at him!—steal a tourist's camera in Naples. We see
that the absorbing game of criticism supersedes outrage, that the delights of playing the
game offset political impotence, that the more important matters lying outside the game
leave a critic indifferent. This penchant for playful, aggressive forgetfulness sounds like
Nietzschean amorality or postmodern play at its worst. (What if Greenblatt had silently

watched a rape in Naples?) Yet, this stunning meta-critique and confession confirm what a reader has suspected: that Sarracoll's weird fusion of admiration and destruction models the New Historicism's response to iconic literary works: admire them, but burn them down.

In the twenty-five years that elapsed between the New Historicism and the current historiography of "deep time," the status of history itself has utterly changed. No longer does anyone believe that "collective memory is stronger than death." *Pace* Shakespeare and Ovid, no one will gain immortality from a poem. New Historicism put its heart into literary study. It married postmodern theory and primitive belief. For a time, literary study was jolted back into life. But the bizarre juxtapositions and startling self-revelations that became stock features of historical criticism have lost much of their freshness and charm. Today, the historical study of literature has passed into different hands. Arguably, postcolonial studies, post-feminism, queer studies, disability studies, and a revived Old Historicism have opened new ways of making texts exciting again. The wider, globalizing perspectives on the Anthropocene and deep time offer an entirely different kind of historicism. While the strikingly dramatic conceits of New Historicism seem to be a thing of the past, we can be reassured that the whole world lies open before us.

City University of New York (United States)

NOTES

1. See Pierre Nora, *Realms of Memory: Rethinking the French Past*, ed. Lawrence D. Kritzman, trans. Arthur Goldhammer (New York: Columbia University Press, 1996).

2. Ted Underwood, "Stories of Parallel Lives and the Status Anxieties of Contemporary Historicism," *Representations* 85.1 (Winter 2004): 3.

3. Fredric Jameson, *Postmodernism; or, The Cultural Logic of Late Capitalism* (Durham: Duke University Press, 1999).

4. Underwood, "Stories of Parallel Lives and the Status Anxieties of Contemporary Historicism."

5. Joel Fineman, "The History of the Anecdote: Fiction and Fiction," *The New Historicism,* ed. H. Aram Veeser (New York: Routledge. 1989), 57.

6. Though see Timothy Mitchell, *Colonizing Egypt* (Berkeley: University of California Press, 1988).

7. Joel Fineman, "The History of the Anecdote," 52.

8. Fredric Jameson, *Postmodernism,* 183–84.

9. Gerald Graff, *Professing Literature: An Institutional History* (Chicago and London: University of Chicago Press, 1987), 147.

10. John Crowe Ransom, "Criticism, Inc." quoted in Gerald Graff, *Professing Literature,* 148.

11. Graff, *Professing Literature,* 151.

12. Ibid., 185.

13. T. S. Eliot, qtd. in Gerald Graff, *Professing Literature,* 201.

14. Graff, *Professing Literature,* 204.

15. Cleanth Brooks, quoted in Gerald Graff, *Professing Literature,* 188.

16. Graff, *Professing Literature,* 179.

17. Paul Hamilton, *Historicism* (New York: Routledge, 1995), 138.

18. Hayden White, "Historicism, History, and the Figurative Imagination," in *Tropics of Discourse*, ed. Hayden White (Baltimore and London, The Johns Hopkins University Press, 1978), 117.

19. White, "Historicism, History, and the Figurative Imagination," 104.

20. H. Aram Veeser, ed., *The New Historicism* (New York: Routledge, 1989), 52.

21. Jameson, *Postmodernism,* 188.

22. Frank Lentricchia, "Foucault's Legacy: A New Historicism?," in *The New Historicism,* ed. H. Aram Veeser (New York: Routledge, 1989), 234.

23. Alan Liu, "The Power of Formalism: The New Historicism," *ELH* 56 (1989): 743.

24. Dr. Samuel Johnson quoted in John Rumrich and Gregory Chaplin, eds., *Seventeenth-Century Poetry, 1603-1660: A Norton Critical Edition* (New York: W.W. Norton & Co., 2006), 740. The editors are quoting Johnson from his "Lives of the English Poets," specifically the text of G. Birkbeck Hill's editions, 3 vols. (Oxford, 1905).

25. Louis Adrian Montrose, "'The Place of a Brother' in *As You Like It*: Social Process and Comic Form," *Shakespeare Quarterly* 32 (1981): 28–54.

26. Stephen Greenblatt, *Renaissance Self-Fashioning: From More to Shakespeare* (Chicago: University of Chicago Press, 1980), chapter 5.

27. Stephen Greenblatt, *Learning to Curse: Essays in Early Modern Culture* (New York: Routledge, 1990), 5.

28. Greenblatt, *Learning to Curse*, 194.

29. Ibid., 220.

WORKS CITED

Deleuze, Gilles, and Félix Guattari. *Anti-Oedipus: Capitalism and Schizophrenia* [1972]. Trans. Robert Hurley, Mark Seem, and Helen R. Lane. Minneapolis: University of Minnesota Press, 1992.

Fineman, Joel. "The History of the Anecdote: Fiction and Fiction." In *The New Historicism.* Ed. H. Aram Veeser. New York: Routledge, 1989. 49–76.

Graff, Gerald. *Professing Literature: An Institutional History*. Chicago and London: University of Chicago Press, 1987.

Greenblatt, Stephen. *Renaissance Self-Fashioning: From More to Shakespeare*. Chicago and London: University of Chicago Press, 1980.

Greenblatt, Stephen. *Learning to Curse: Essays in Early Modern Culture*. New York: Routledge, 1990.

Greenblatt, Stephen. *Shakespearean Negotiations: The Circulation of Social Energy in Renaissance England*. Oxford: Clarendon Press, 1987.

Hamilton, Paul. *Historicism*. New York: Routledge, 1995.

Jameson, Fredric. *Postmodernism; or, The Cultural Logic of Late Capitalism*. Durham: Duke University Press, 1999.

Lentricchia, Frank. "Foucault's Legacy: A New Historicism?" In *The New Historicism*. Ed. H. Aram Veeser. New York: Routledge, 1989. 231–42.

Liu, Alan. "The Power of Formalism: The New Historicism." *ELH* 56 (1989): 721–71.

Montrose, Louis Adrian. "'The Place of a Brother' in *As You Like It*: Social Process and Comic Form." *Shakespeare Quarterly* 32 (1981): 28–54.

Mitchell, Timothy. *Colonizing Egypt*. Berkeley: University of California Press, 1988.

Nora, Pierre. *Realms of Memory: Rethinking the French Past*. Ed. Lawrence D. Kritzman. Trans. Arthur Goldhammer. New York: Columbia University Press, 1996.

Rumrich, John P., and Gregory Chaplin, eds. *Seventeenth-Century Poetry, 1603-1660: A Norton Critical Edition*. New York: W.W. Norton & Co., 2006.

Underwood, Ted. "Stories of Parallel Lives and the Status Anxieties of Contemporary Historicism." *Representations* 85.1 (Winter 2004): 1–20.

Veeser, H. Aram, ed. *The New Historicism*. New York: Routledge, 1989.

White, Hayden. *Metahistory: The Historical Imagination in Nineteenth-Century Europe*. Baltimore and London: The Johns Hopkins University Press, 1975.

White, Hayden. "Historicism, History, and the Figurative Imagination." *Tropics of Discourse*. Baltimore and London: The Johns Hopkins University Press, 1978. 101–20.

CHAPTER SEVEN

Psychoanalytic Theory

JEAN-MICHEL RABATÉ

There are two cardinal human sins from which all others derive: impatience and indolence. Because of impatience they were expelled from Paradise, because of indolence they do not return. But perhaps there is only one cardinal sin: impatience. Because of impatience they were expelled, because of impatience they do not return.[1]

I will start from a psychoanalytic paradigm predicated upon the application of literature to psychoanalysis,[2] the case of Hamlet as read by major psychoanalysts, in order to understand what a concept like the *Unconscious* means. Then I will try to generalize by moving from Freud's interpretation to Lacan's objection to a certain epistemological impatience that has marked psychoanalytic discourse. Finally, I will argue that there is some value to be found in post-Freudian impatience.

Freud, who had a life-long passion for Shakespeare, and quoted from memory lines and entire passages from more than twenty plays in his letters and essays, took the bard not only as a guide to help him discover the existence of a cultural unconscious but also to provide early identifications. Freud's letter to his friend Fliess from September 21, 1897, parallels an awareness of his identification with Hamlet and the sense of an epistemological breakthrough, when he was reshaping his theory of neuroses. Freud had believed that neuroses were created by an actual sexual trauma, often perpetrated by perverse fathers, uncles, or close parents—their molestations would produce the notable hysterical symptoms observed in their sons and daughters. In 1897, Freud realized that many of these accusations were fantasmatic constructions. Deciding to take a new departure, he slightly misquoted *Hamlet*'s "The readiness is all."[3] Like Hamlet, Freud was full of doubts when he made the decision to recast his psychological theory. He was glimpsing the Unconscious as an "other" theatrical stage, a behind-the-scenes mechanism of hidden forces. Desire could not be caused by a reaction to stimulus, it would be founded upon psychological determinations to which subjects have no access.

The allusion to *Hamlet* segues into a Jewish *Witz* offering a wry comment on the fate of Ophelia. The climax of the joke shows a man telling the prospective bride: "Rebecca, take off your gown, you are no longer a bride."[4] Like the Prince of Denmark who balances betrayal, murder, and the repudiation of his fiancée, Freud is torn but refuses to despair. In spite of the collapse of his certainties, feeling naked and destitute as Rebecca must have been, he reaches a core of truth, for "the psychological alone has remained untouched."[5] Hamlet turns into a picky Jewish bridegroom opting, like Kafka, for the solitude of the writer, in order to untangle the knots of the Unconscious.

Analyzing himself relentlessly, Freud explains to Fliess his sexual desire for his mother and the jealousy experienced facing his father in early childhood: "I have found, in my own case too, [the phenomenon of] being in love with my mother and jealous of my father, and I now consider it a universal event in early childhood, even if not so early as in children who have been made hysterical. . . . If this is so, we can understand the gripping power of *Oedipus Rex*. . . . Fleetingly, the thought passed through my head that the same thing might be at the bottom of *Hamlet* as well. I am not thinking of Shakespeare's conscious intention, but believe, rather, that a real event stimulated the poet to his representation, in that his unconscious understood the unconscious of the hero."[6] Here lies the foundation of Freud's theory of the unconscious. The idea can be universalized for it discloses a universal law: because of our life in human groups, a specific type of repression prevents the erotic link between parents and children of the opposite sex. Freud's predicament leads him to the Oedipus complex, the keystone of his theory. The edifice of psychoanalytical concepts is founded upon an enthusiastic, almost hysterical reading of two literary texts, *Hamlet* and *Oedipus Rex*. Freud's immersion in the authors he has absorbed bypasses the intentions of Sophocles and Shakespeare in order to reach the Unconscious itself. The concatenation of *Hamlet* and *Oedipus Rex* gives access to a fundamental law of society, the law of the prohibition of incest.

Freud looked for a confirmation of his insights in the author's biography. Georg Brandes's book on Shakespeare told him that *Hamlet* had been composed shortly after the demise of the playwright's father. This suggested that Hamlet the character was a projection of the author's inner turmoil. In the interpretive process, Hamlet turned into one of the hysterics Freud has treated in Paris and Vienna: "How does Hamlet the hysteric justify his words, 'Thus conscience does make cowards of us all'?" How does he explain his irresolution in avenging his father by the murder of his uncle—the same man who sends his courtiers to their death without a scruple and who is positively precipitate in murdering Laertes? How better than through the torment he suffers from the obscure memory that he himself had contemplated the same deed against his father out of passion for his mother, and— "use every man after his desert, and who should 'scape whipping?'"[7] The Shakespearean tag recurs often under Freud's pen, as it does in a letter to Arnold Zweig from May 1936. Zweig considered writing a biography of Freud, who rejected this idea because a biographer has to disentangle too many lies:

> Anyone turning biographer commits himself to lies, to concealment, to hypocrisy, to flattery, and even to hiding his own lack of understanding, for biographical truth is not to be had, and even if it were it couldn't be used. Truth is unobtainable; humanity does not deserve it, and incidentally, wasn't our Prince Hamlet right when he asked whether anyone would escape a whipping if he got what he deserved?[8]

Freud remained a Hamlet until the end.

In the October 15, 1897, letter to Fliess, Freud's precipitation appears in a slight mistake: he unwittingly replaces Polonius with Laertes. In the play, Polonius, Ophelia's father, is dispatched by Hamlet who is then killed at the end in a duel with Laertes. The slip of the pen betrays Freud's uncertainty facing genealogies, which follows a pattern discernible in other symptomatic mistakes. The *Psychopathology of Everyday Life* discusses errors on names in the *Interpretation of Dreams*. Freud had mixed up Hasdrubal and Hamilcar Barca as the father of Hannibal; he had written that Zeus had castrated his father Kronos, whereas Kronos castrated his father Uranus.[9] The confusion on Laertes and Polonius is of the same type. Freud's hysteria is thus predicated on a similar uncertainty facing family relations and family rituals (as Hamlet observes, the wedding follows too quickly after the burial of his father).

The passage from the letter to Fliess contains the insight upon which the theory of unconscious desire will rest, as systematized in the *Interpretation of Dreams*. In a footnote, Freud develops the comparison between Sophocles and Shakespeare:

> Another great creation of tragic poetry is rooted in the same soil as *Oedipus the King*: Shakespeare's *Hamlet*. But the change in treatment of the same material reveals the difference in the inner life of these two cultural periods so remote from each other: the advance of repression over the centuries in mankind's emotional life. In *Oedipus* the child's wishful fantasy on which it is based is out in the open and realized—as it is in dreams; in *Hamlet* it remains repressed, and we learn of its existence—as we learn of a neurosis—only through the inhibiting effect it produces.[10]

Shakespeare's play is universal because it teaches something fundamental about human sexuality, desire, and the evolution of culture. Reading *Hamlet,* we become aware of a change in morality and ethics. The Greeks were less repressed than us "moderns." What was accomplished thoughtlessly and effortlessly by Oedipus became impossible for Hamlet. The most obvious features of the plot, its hesitations, procrastinations, its sadistic games interspersed with sudden outbursts of violence, touch a nerve in us all, in our identical belatedness and inability to act upon our deepest impulses.

Freud continues his analysis:

> Hamlet can do anything—except take revenge on the man who removed his father and took the latter's place beside his mother, the man who shows him his own repressed infant wishes realized. The revulsion that should urge him to revenge is thus replaced by self-recrimination, by the scruples of conscience which accuse him of being, quite literally, no better than the sinner he has to punish. . . . If anyone wants to call Hamlet a hysteric, I can only acknowledge that it is an inference my interpretation admits. The sexual revulsion which Hamlet expressed in the dialogue with Ophelia is congruent with it.[11]

Freud evinces no hesitation about speaking of the "unconscious" of Hamlet. Hamlet's revulsion facing sexuality is hidden by a "conscience" that conceals the unconscious knowledge of his incestuous desire for his mother. Hamlet ends up defeated by his own moralism. His self-reproaches tell him he is no better than an uncle who has had the courage to act, to kill so as to achieve the possession of Gertrude. His sexual coldness facing Ophelia, his rejection of paternity, and the displacement of aggression from his uncle to the feminine pole are all signs of Freud's notion of hysteria. Hamlet is a male version of Dora: he refuses to know the truth about his role in a perverted sexual exchange, and he precipitates a crisis instead of solving it. He brings down the punishment on himself: he dies in the same way as his father, both poisoned by the Oedipal rival.

Ernest Jones systematized Freud's theory of Hamlet with "The Oedipus Complex as an Explanation of Hamlet's Mystery" published in *The American Journal of Psychology* in 1910 then expanded as *Hamlet and Oedipus*.[12] Jones offered a few insights of his own about "matricide": he wondered whether Hamlet had not wanted to kill his mother instead of his uncle. Gertrude's hurried remarriage hints of her guilt, and this guilt had to be called "incest" (she married someone too close of kin) in the language of the times. If "incest" becomes a feature shared by Gertrude and Hamlet, Hamlet can then disobey the ghost's request.[13] A subtler variation upon Freud's concept came through Ella Freeman Sharpe, whose 1929 paper on the impatience of Hamlet reversed the pattern of previous glosses insisting on the hero's procrastination. Instead, Sharpe foregrounded haste and precipitation. Her provocative thesis of *Hamlet* is not the tragedy of procrastination but a "tragedy of impatience."[14] In spite of the protracted denouement of the last act, the main symptom exhibited by the play's eponymous hero is the melancholia caused by a failed mourning.

Mourning requires time, and melancholia freezes time. Because time is denied to Hamlet, time, because it is "out of joint," is similarly withdrawn from the other protagonists. This accounts for the accelerations of the plot and the murders culminating in a general slaughter. Then Hamlet exclaims:

> Had I but time—as this fell sergeant, death,
> Is strict in his arrest—O, I could tell you—
> But let it be.[15]

Hamlet's tragedy of haste finds its counterpart in the fate of Ophelia, the feminine side of Hamlet, whereas Gertrude is a castrating mother, which explains why there are traps everywhere—castration's many guises, "oral frustration, oral impatience and oral sadism."[16] Sharpe resists Freud's equation of Shakespeare and Hamlet: "The poet is not Hamlet. Hamlet is what he might have been if he had not written the play of *Hamlet.*"[17]

Lacan was reading Sharpe when tackling *Hamlet* and he similarly stressed the function of haste in interpreting *Hamlet*. Lacan decided to examine critically the core of Freud's argument, the idea that Hamlet could not kill Claudius because of their common Oedipal longing. Lacan revisited Freud's contention that Hamlet presented a modern-day version of an uninhibited Oedipus by pointing out Freud's reliance upon an unexamined psychology. Indeed, Freud's Oedipal model was predicated upon a reasoning that could be reversed:

> What does the psychoanalytic tradition tell us? That everything hinges around the desire for the mother, that this desire is repressed, and that this is the cause for which the hero could not approach the act that is requested of him, namely the revenge against a man who is the current possessor, how illegitimate because a criminal, of the maternal object. If he cannot strike the person who has been pointed out for his vindication, it is because he himself has already committed the crime to be avenged. In as much as there is in the background the memory of an infantile desire for the mother, of the Oedipal desire to murder the father, Hamlet would in a sense become an accomplice of the current owner, *beatus possidens*, in his eyes. He could not attack this owner without attacking himself. Is this what they mean?—or he could not attack this possessor without reawakening in himself the old desire, felt as a guilty desire, in a mechanism that one feels everywhere in the play.[18]

Lacan questioned the pseudo-evidence of the psychological mechanism: "Couldn't we say as well that everything can be reversed? If Hamlet was to jump immediately on his father-in-law, could one not say that he finds in this an opportunity to quench his guilt finding a culprit outside of himself?"[19]

Lacan rejects Freud's contention that Hamlet could not kill his uncle because Claudius enacted his own repressed wish because that interpretation presupposes a psychology of imitation that can be read differently. Freud's psychologization of the "French triangle" with two rivals for one woman relies on a commonsense view that can be turned into its opposite easily. Why not imagine that Hamlet would want to punish a rival all the more as Claudius has got what he was prevented from having? Such a reversal was made possible by Lacan's analysis of the "mirror stage" in 1936, and his 1948 study of "aggressiveness in psychoanalysis."[20] When I discover that other subjects show features similar to mine, I face what Freud called the "narcissism of small differences" and react with aggressiveness. This aggressiveness is deployed in *Hamlet*. In order to read *Hamlet*, one should thus operate a strategic shift from a subjective genitive (the "mother's desire" means "desire for the mother") to an objective genitive (the "mother's desire" is read as "her desire for another man") is a dialectical reversal that abandons the psychology of mimetic desire assuming that one will not want to kill a rival who has acted out one's deepest longings. Thanks to this conceptual reversal, Hamlet's inhibition will be seen coming from desire in his mother, but not as an object of desire. The mother is indeed the main source of desire, but here Hamlet's paralysis derives from his bafflement at witnessing his mother's desire for another man.

Lacan reads the text closely, slowly, paying attention to recurring signifiers. One of these is the echo between Ophelia and "phallus," an echo soon turning into a *"Knotenpunkt,"* a verbal node allowing for the overdetermination of images in dreams, similar to those mentioned by Freud in the *Interpretation of Dreams*. Hamlet's failure as a desiring subject is explained by the fact that he has put into question the source of all desire and thus of truth. Is the ghost telling the truth? Is his mother lying? Can Ophelia be honest if women are suspected of treachery? The solution lies in an other desire found in his mother, but he will only understand this by paying with his life.

Hamlet moves beyond the archaic desire for his mother and comes to terms with the phallic object embodied by Ophelia before finally encountering the lethal phallus of the swords. Freud's psychology of mimetic doubling—I cannot attack someone who has acted out my deepest longings—should be replaced by an ethics of desire. The key scene is the moment when Hamlet attempts to make Gertrude renounce Claudius and confess her guilt. He seems to have won but suddenly sends her back to her lover:

> Let the bloat king tempt you again to bed,
> Pinch wanton on your cheek, call you his mouse,
> And let him for a pair of reeky kisses,
> Or paddling in your neck with his damned fingers,
> Make you to ravel all this matter out[21]

Hamlet's effort collapses: he cannot make his mother move from her desire. Hamlet is overwhelmed by his mother's excessive enjoyment in love-making, a sexual desire that he can neither fathom nor displace.

Hamlet retrieves his desire only after he comes back from England and sees Laertes standing in Ophelia's open tomb. Hamlet abandons his melancholic position and asserts his identity: "This I, Hamlet the Dane."[22] He states this because of the impact of Ophelia's death by drowning. By dying, Ophelia fulfills her role as an impossible object of desire. Ophelia embodied the phallus hinted at by her name when she gave erotic names for the flowers used for her funeral garland. Once absent, Ophelia is indeed the phallus, a symbol of tumescence, an impossibly sublime erection that calls up its antithesis, namely castration and death.

Lacan restates Sharpe's thesis about the impatience of Hamlet with a difference. For him, the analysis of Hamlet's desire is inscribed in a symbolic logic underpinned by the Other, the law upon which culture is founded. When Hamlet jumped into Ophelia's freshly dug tomb, he was able to mourn the object and to escape from the power of his mother's desire. His own death allows him to respond to the dead father's demand.

Because of the original "haste" evinced by all the protagonists, even the dead father reached the kingdom of the dead with an open wound and an open debt.

Reading the scene of the duel, Lacan underlines the word "foils" meaning swords ("Let the foils be brought")[23] and the occasion of Hamlet's last pun: "I'll be your foil, Laertes."[24] Laertes is a better swordsman and more handsome, which brings us to the mirror stage: Hamlet and Laertes are caught up in an imaginary rivalry. A new phallus appears, uniting Hamlet, Laertes, and the guilty king. This phallus will not stop the hole opened for Hamlet when he jumped into Ophelia's tomb.

Lacan's interpretation does not discard the basic tenets of Freudian theory, but points out the moment of haste and hysterical identification in Freud. If *Hamlet* is the tragedy of desire, and if the key is an insufficient mourning, it follows that it is the phallus that has to be mourned. As Freud argued about the "decline of the Oedipus complex" (1924),[25] the only way for the subject to accept castration and resolve the Oedipus complex is to mourn the phallus. The phallus evokes the narcissism that the subject must abandon. One cannot "kill" the phallus because, like Hamlet's king, it is a "thing of nothing." Hamlet is able to desire and kill his rivals because he has relinquished his narcissistic attachments. Mortally wounded, knowing that he is going to die, Hamlet and Laertes exchange mutual blessings. They want to prevent other deaths to follow, unlike the situation of *Oedipus,* in which the tragic *ate* is perpetuated and passed on to the next generation. By positing Hamlet caught up in his mother's desire until he traverses death and comes to terms with the phallus, thanks to Ophelia's sad fate, Lacan has nevertheless pushed his reading of the play beyond the idea that it restages the Oedipus complex.

Lacan wished less to interpret *Hamlet* differently than learn from it, and learn how to read with it.[26] Reading literature remains a pedagogical process. We as readers are taught something about our connection to language, desire, society, gender in so far as our desire is questioned. Hamlet's hysteria is contagious: it hystericizes us by forcing us to pose the question of our own desire. The unconscious, that obscure part of knowledge unavailable to the writer, contains an injunction to make sense of our desires. After having read *Hamlet* or seen it performed on stage, we are told to interpret the world and see our position in it. Much as when Freud felt the urge to interpret why Michelangelo's Moses exerted such a fascination on him, we, readers of *Hamlet*, must "know something which is by hypothesis unknowable"—having met the Other in "an experience which exceeds the facts."[27] We have the daunting task of trying to understand those things that Shakespeare could not understand himself.

Such an understanding entails a certain role of haste in reaching a conclusion. Lacan's critique of Freud's reading of *Hamlet* recalls his 1945 essay on "Logical Time and the Assertion of Anticipated Certainty," a text that analyzes at some length a simple logical game. Three prisoners in a jail are told that only one of them will be set free if he can guess correctly the color of a disk that will be put on his back. They learn that there are three white disks and two black disks. Each prisoner can see the others' disks but not his own. The director promises that the first prisoner who can tell the color of his disk will be allowed to leave the room freely. In reality, each prisoner is given a white disk. Each sees the two white disks on the others' backs and concludes from the fact that they all hesitate for a while that their own disk has to be white and not black. Ideally, each subject should reason in the same way, thinking: "If I was black, the two whites I see would deduce quickly that they are white. But they hesitate, which proves that they are white as well." Will they reach the same conclusion at the same time? Logically, yes. In practice, the fastest and smartest of the three will win. His haste in coming to a conclusion will be decisive. This situation recalls the mirror stage but triangulates it. Each subject is caught up in a game of rivalry dominated by jealousy. The only solution is via the agency of haste—one of the prisoners, or perhaps all three at once, will rush to the door. Haste will make them assert their color, as the "I" has been produced at the end of the mirror stage.

Lacan pays attention to the "moment of concluding."[28] Each subject concludes that he must be white when he sees the others hesitate, but at the same time each prisoner acts in a hurry in order to get out first. Since each makes the same deduction and affirms with certainty that he is white, urgency is a determining factor: "It is not because of some dramatic contingency, the seriousness of the stakes, or the competitiveness of the game, that time presses; it is owing to the urgency of the logical movement that the subject *precipitates* both his judgment and his departure ("precipitates" in the etymological sense of the verb: headlong)."[29]

One can only act—and any interpretation is an act—in a moment of haste. This precipitation is the condition for a progression that will go beyond the limitations of a specular image, but also for any interpretation that is based on my certainty of having understood a text because it relates to my own subjective position in life. Such an initial identification, that I have called "enthusiastic" is necessary to reach a certain truth about a text, but it is predicated on a certain function of haste. Such haste is related to the function of the collective agreement as to what defines truth. This is also the place in which we see the link between private images, our own family romances, and our collective identifications via a social "I-deal." In a note added to his essay in 1966, Lacan quotes Freud's 1920 analysis of collective psychology in *Group Psychology and the Analysis of the Ego* and concludes: "The collective is nothing but the subject of the individual."[30]

Was Freud's impatience such a bad thing? Not necessarily. One can often catch him in some type of conceptual impatience, but this is often when his insights are the deepest and the most productive. I might give as an example the almost surreptitiously introduced term of *das Ding* into the core of the subject's psychic structure in an early text linking the issue of the "fellow-creature," the neighbor, to the emergence of the Thing:

> It is on his fellow-creatures that a human being first learn to cognize. . . . Thus the complex of a fellow-creature falls into two portions. One of these gives the impression of being a constant structure and remains as a coherent thing; while the other can be understood by the activity of memory—that is, can be traced back to information about the subject's body. This process of analyzing a perceptual complex is described as *cognizing* it; it involves a *judgment* and is brought to an end when that has been achieved.[31]

We face the terminological problems of Freud's "Project for a Scientific Psychology" from 1895, this unpublished draft attempting to link the unconscious with a mapping of the brain's different neurons.

Freud developed the concept of "the Thing" when tackling an important problem. If the aim of all thought process is to establish a state of identity, why is there a principle of reality? Why don't we hallucinate all the time, if we are ruled by an Unconscious whose main objective is the attainment of pleasure? It is because thought recognizes that there is something like reality that is impervious to its encroachments. There is thus a judgment about the reality of things that is based upon libidinal investments. This is where the Thing intervenes, since it marks a pole of exteriority within the subject; it is the trace of the Other in us. One could also mention *Beyond the Pleasure Principle* in which Freud "speculates" first that there is something like a "death drive," and then that one can think of life as persisting beyond it. What Derrida used to call "speculation" in Freud can also be described as his conceptual impatience.

Freud was impatient because he wanted to link his experience as a psychoanalyst listening to his analysands with a need to generalize and elaborate a theory of the unconscious. In the cure itself, time was of the essence, and Freud often set a term to an analysis beforehand, as we can see with the case of the Wolfman: "I decided—not without allowing myself to be guided by reliable signs that the timing was right—that the treatment would have to end by a certain date, no matter what progress had been made."[32] Here is a good occasion to recall that for Freud, most psychoanalyses were meant to last less than one year, often six months.

This impatience had a strong ethical motivation—it was the wish not to reduce his analysands to the status of medical patients. Not being patients although suffering all the same, Freud's analysands were given the tools to work out their neuroses themselves, using the only weapons he allowed to them and to himself: words and time. To the psychoanalyst were given other tools, those of literature and myth.

Freud listed literature as one of the fields that a psychoanalyst should master in order to be trained fully. This is clear in *The Question of Lay Analysis,* a book in which Freud rejects the idea that medical training is a prerequisite for psychoanalysts. Instead, he promotes the humanities. The analytical curriculum has to "include subjects which are far removed from medicine and which a doctor would never require in his practice: the history of civilization, mythology, the psychology of religion, and literature."[33] Freud was not simply alluding to the familiarity with culture provided by contact with poems, novels, and plays when he sketched a *"Literaturwissenschaft,"*[34] a science of literature combining literary expertise and a science including hermeneutics and literary criticism.

A science of literature encompasses techniques of interpretation moving from the literary field to include the living characters, situations, and jokes derived from individual diagnoses. This is the science that allowed Freud to dig deeply into the dramas of his patients' lives, and also to take into account the chronicles of ancient gods and heroes, their mythical paradigms offering ways of understanding trans-generational dramas. Literature informs a new pedagogy and underpins a training that combines the medical and the humanistic. It offers a privileged entrance into culture and a way of recapturing the old patience of language, this ancient memory of all the traumas of the past. The effort to capture this web of interrelated allusions is underpinned by an impatience leading to new insights, new perceptions, and an open future time necessary to understand it all. Because of impatience we were expelled, because of impatience we cannot return, but thanks to impatience we can write and make sense of our structural shortcomings as speaking subjects.

University of Pennsylvania (United States)

NOTES

1. Franz Kafka, "The Collected Aphorisms," *The Great Wall of China and Other Stories,* trans. Malcolm Pasley (London: Penguin, 1973), 79.

2. In Jean-Michel Rabaté, *Introduction to Literature and Psychoanalysis* (Cambridge: Cambridge University Press, 2015), 2–5; I allude to Pierre Bayard who claims that instead of applying psychoanalysis to literature, we should apply literature to psychoanalysis. See Pierre Bayard, *Peut-on appliquer la littérature à la psychanalyse?* (Paris: Minuit, 2004).

3. Sigmund Freud, *The Complete Letters to Wilhelm Fliess (1887-1904)*, ed. and trans. Jeffrey Moussaieff Masson (Cambridge, MA: Harvard University Press, 1985), 265.

4. Freud, *The Complete Letters to Wilhelm Fliess*, 266.

5. Ibid.

6. Ibid., 272.

7. Letter from October 15, 1897; Freud, *The Complete Letters to Wilhelm Fliess*, 272–73.

8. Sigmund Freud, *Letters of Sigmund Freud 1873-1939*, ed. Ernst L. Freud, trans. Tania and James Stern (London: Hogarth Press, 1961), 430.

9. Sigmund Freud, *The Psychopathology of Everyday Life*, trans. Anthea Bell (New York: Penguin, 2002), 208–09.

10. Sigmund Freud, *The Interpretation of Dreams: The Original Text*, trans. Joyce Crick (Oxford: Oxford University Press, 1999), 204.

11. Freud, *The Interpretation of Dreams*, 204.

12. Ernest Jones, *Hamlet and Oedipus* (New York: Doubleday, 1954).

13. Jones, *Hamlet and Oedipus*, 109. He refers to Dover Wilson's influential reading of *Hamlet*; Dover J. Wilson, *What Happens in Hamlet*, second ed. (Cambridge: Cambridge University Press, 1959).

14. Ella Freeman Sharpe, "The Impatience of Hamlet," in *Collected Papers on Psycho-Analysis* (London: Hogarth Press, 1950), 203.

15. William Shakespeare, *Hamlet*, ed. Philip Edwards (Cambridge: Cambridge University Press, 1985), V, 2, 314–16.

16. Sharpe, "The Impatience of Hamlet," 211.

17. Ibid., 205.

18. Jacques Lacan, *Le désir et son interpretation*, ed. Jacques-Alain Miller (Paris: Editions de la Martiniere, 2013), 330. Translations are mine.

19. Lacan, *Le désir et son interpretation*, 330.

20. See Jacques Lacan, *Écrits*, trans. Bruce Fink (New York: Norton, 2006). Specifically see the chapters "The Mirror Stage as Formative of the *I* Function" and "Aggressiveness in Psychoanalysis" (75–101).

21. Shakespeare, *Hamlet*, III, 4, 182–87.

22. Ibid., V, 1, 223–24.

23. Ibid., V, 2, 155.

24. Ibid., V, 2, 227–29.

25. Sigmund Freud, "The Passing of the Oedipus-Complex," *Sexuality and the Psychology of Love* (New York: Collier, 1978), 176–82.

26. Bruce Fink, "Reading Hamlet with Lacan," in *Lacan, Politics, Aesthetics*, eds. Willy Apollon and Richard Feldstein (Albany: State University of New York Press, 1996), 182. See Julia Reinhard Lupton and Kenneth Reinhard, *After Oedipus: Shakespeare in Psychoanalysis* (Ithaca: Cornell University Press, 1993), 60–118.

27. See T. S. Eliot, "Hamlet and His Problems," *The Sacred Wood* (1920) (London: Methuen, 1972), 103.

28. Lacan, *Écrits*, 168.

29. Ibid., 169.

30. Ibid., 175.

31. Sigmund Freud, "Project for a Scientific Psychology," in *The Origins of Psychoanalysis,* trans. Eric Mosbacher and James Strachey (New York: Basic Books, 1977), 393–94.

32. Sigmund Freud, "From the History of an Infantile Neurosis," in *The "Wolfman" and Other Cases,* trans. Louise Adey Huish (London: Penguin, 2002), 208.

33. Sigmund Freud, *The Question of Lay Analysis,* trans. Nancy Procter-Gregg (New York: Norton, 1950), 118.

34. Sigmund Freud, *Die Frage der Laienanalyse (VII). Studienausgabe, Schriften zur Behandlungstechnik* (Frankfurt: Fischer, 1982), 337.

WORKS CITED

Bayard, Pierre. *Peut-on appliquer la littérature à la psychanalyse?* Paris: Minuit, 2004.

Eliot, T. S. "Hamlet and His Problems." In *The Sacred Wood* [1920]. Ed. T. S. Eliot. London: Methuen, 1972. 95–103.

Fink, Bruce. "Reading Hamlet with Lacan." In *Lacan, Politics, Aesthetics.* Eds. Willy Apollon and Richard Feldstein. Albany: State University of New York Press, 1996. 181–98.

Freud, Sigmund. *The Question of Lay Analysis* [1926]. Trans. Nancy Procter-Gregg. New York: Norton, 1950.

Freud, Sigmund. *Letters of Sigmund Freud 1873-1939.* Ed. Ernst L. Freud. Trans. Tania Stern and James Stern. London: Hogarth Press, 1961.

Freud, Sigmund. "Project for a Scientific Psychology." In *The Origins of Psychoanalysis: Letters to Wilhelm Fliess, Drafts and Notes, 1887–1902.* Trans. Eric Mosbacher and James Strachey. New York: Basic Books, 1977.

Freud, Sigmund. "The Passing of the Oedipus-Complex." In *Sexuality and the Psychology of Love.* Trans. Joan Riviere. New York: Collier, 1978. 176–82.

Freud, Sigmund. *Die Frage der Laienanalyse (VII). Studienausgabe. Schriften zur Behandlungstechnik.* Frankfurt: Fischer, 1982.

Freud, Sigmund. *The Complete Letters to Wilhelm Fliess (1887-1904).* Ed. and trans. Jeffrey Moussaieff Masson. Cambridge: Harvard University Press, 1985.

Freud, Sigmund. *The Interpretation of Dreams: The Original Text* [1899]. Trans. Joyce Crick. Oxford: Oxford University Press, 1999.

Freud, Sigmund. "From the History of an Infantile Neurosis." In *The "Wolfman" and Other Cases.* Trans. Louise Adey Huish. London: Penguin, 2002. 203–320.

Freud, Sigmund. *The Psychopathology of Everyday Life* [1901]. Trans. Anthea Bell. New York: Penguin, 2002.

Jones, Ernest. *Hamlet and Oedipus.* New York: Doubleday, 1954.

Kafka, Franz. "The Collected Aphorisms." In *The Great Wall of China and Other Stories* [1931]. Trans. Malcolm Pasley. London: Penguin, 1973.

Lacan, Jacques. "Aggressiveness in Psychoanalysis." In *Écrits* [1966]. Trans. Bruce Fink. New York: Norton, 2006. 82–101.

Lacan, Jacques. "The Mirror Stage as Formative of the *I* Function" and "Aggressiveness in Psychoanalysis." In *Écrits* [1966]. Trans. Bruce Fink. New York: Norton, 2006. 75–81.

Lacan, Jacques. *Le désir et son interpretation.* Ed. Jacques-Alain Miller. Paris: Editions de la Martiniere, 2013.

Lupton, Julia Reinhard, and Kenneth Reinhard. *After Oedipus: Shakespeare in Psychoanalysis.* Ithaca: Cornell University Press, 1993.

Rabaté, Jean-Michel. *Introduction to Literature and Psychoanalysis*. Cambridge: Cambridge University Press, 2015.

Shakespeare, William. *Hamlet*. Ed. Philip Edwards. Cambridge: Cambridge University Press, 1985.

Sharpe, Ella Freeman. "The Impatience of Hamlet." In Ella Freeman Sharpe, *Collected Papers on Psycho-Analysis*. Ed. Marjorie Brierly. London: Hogarth Press, 1950. 203–13.

Wilson, J. Dover. *What Happens in Hamlet*. Second ed. Cambridge: Cambridge University Press, 1959.

CHAPTER EIGHT

Rhetoric

STEVEN MAILLOUX

Rhetoric provides both a framework encompassing literary-cultural studies and one approach among many within those studies.[1] As a larger architectonic framework, rhetoric defines a long intellectual tradition dealing with uses of language in a range of cultural domains from theology, philosophy, and law to literature, history, and politics.[2] Today it also includes the transdisciplinary study of the human sciences, analyzing and comparing the tropes, arguments, and narratives constituting disciplinary matrices and interdisciplinary networks, such as those of literary and cultural studies.[3] But rhetoric also represents identifiable historical movements and theoretical approaches within literary-cultural studies itself, schools and perspectives influential throughout the twentieth century and emergent in the twenty-first. This chapter will focus primarily on those rhetorical movements and approaches to literature and culture developing over the last few decades while it also assumes rhetorical studies as a metacritical framework.

Most broadly, rhetoric can be viewed as *the use of language in a context to have effects*, language here understood to include not only words but also physical gestures, visual images, and all other symbolic instruments. Historically, rhetorical effects have been conceptualized as *effects on audiences*, such as persuasion, and *effects on language* itself, often called *figuration*. Throughout the twentieth-century persuasion and figuration, arguing and troping, were practices described and analyzed by a diverse array of literary-cultural approaches. Such approaches either explicitly self-identified as rhetorical or implicitly relied on theoretical traditions of rhetoric. An example of the former was the Chicago school of neo-Aristotelian criticism, some of which evolved into rhetorical forms of narratology; an example of the latter was reader-response criticism, whose influence can be seen in contemporary rhetorical-oriented reception study. We can begin with a selective overview of some of these earlier rhetorical approaches, which set the stage for those consolidating or emerging in the present day.

The last century's most influential rhetorician, Kenneth Burke began his career as an editor, translator, poet, fiction writer, and literary and music critic in the 1920s. In his early *Counter-Statement* (1931), Burke explained drama in terms of its psychology of form, the particular ways literary works arouse audience's desires and then fulfill them (thus anticipating the reader-response criticism developed in the sixties). In books such as *Permanence and Change: An Anatomy of Purpose* (1935) and *Attitudes Toward History* (1937), Burke as cultural critic analyzed the dominant pieties of American society and engaged the sociopolitical controversies of the period. Later, he developed a dramatistic model of symbolic action, working out in *A Grammar of Motives* (1945) and *A Rhetoric of Motives* (1950) how all action can be analyzed through a pentad of terms for attributing motives: an *agent* uses an *agency* to perform an *act* for a *purpose* in a *scene*. Burke's preoccupation with the power of language—with the literal and figurative, logical and associative functions of symbolic action—led him to dramatistic analyses and logological explorations that included rhetorical theorizing about persuasion and identification, as well as critical interpretations of small bits of figurative language and the tropological dynamics of entire philosophical systems. Sometimes Burke emphasized literature as rhetorical inducement to an attitude, offering strategies for encompassing situations and providing readers with "equipment for living"; at other times, he followed through the interpretive implications of a single trope in a literary text or used the "four master tropes" (metaphor, metonymy, synecdoche, and irony) to characterize the figurative processes through which humans discover and describe "the truth." With such rhetorical crossings everywhere in his work, it is not surprising that Burke ended one of his mid-career lectures by noting that he was more interested "in bringing the full resources of Poetics and [Rhetoric] to bear upon the study of a text than in trying to draw a *strict* line of demarcation between Rhetoric and Poetics, particularly in view of the fact that the full history of the subject has necessarily kept such a distinction forever on the move."[4]

In *The Rhetoric of Religion* (1961) Burke made a significant contribution to the study of political theology. Here Burke tracked terminological analogies and orderings across the verbal realms of the sociopolitical and the supernatural. In his *logology*—words about words—Burke emphasized the same secular borrowings from theology and the parallel reversals of the profane back into the sacred that function at the core of what Robert Esposito calls the "political-theological machine," the conceptual apparatus enacted and debated by such figures as Carl Schmitt and Eric Peterson in post–First World War Germany.[5] Like those political-theological precursors, Burke too attempted to apply his rhetorical-hermeneutic analysis to contemporary political events, in his case those of the Cold War. As he put it in the introduction to *The Rhetoric of Religion*, he "propose[d] to replace the present political stress upon men in rival international situations by a 'logological' reaffirmation of the foibles and quandaries that all men (in their role as 'symbol using animals') have in common." Rhetorical perspectives on political theology have continued to develop in the twenty-first century and promise to become even more useful in offering critical opportunities for analyzing the national and international scene in our post-secular age.

The Rhetoric of Religion was a favorite book of Wayne Booth, the most influential literary-rhetorician after Burke in the twentieth century.[6] An admirer and correspondent with Burke, Booth's rhetorical approach to literature was strongly shaped by figures associated with Chicago neo-Aristotelianism such as Richard McKeon and R. S. Crane. In his *The Rhetoric of Fiction* (1961), Booth set out to inventory "the rhetorical resources available to the writer of epic, novel, or short story as he tries, consciously or unconsciously, to impose his fictional world upon the reader." Viewing "the techniques of nondidactic fiction" as "the art of communicating with readers," Booth wrote within the tradition of rhetoric as persuasion, which in his later work he developed explicitly into a rhetoric of good reasons.[7] *The Rhetoric of Fiction* describes how authors convince readers to accept the fictional facts and various aesthetic, moral, and other values of their narratives. Through such descriptions, Booth developed a useful critical vocabulary for interpreting the rhetorical effects of narrative, proposing a handy set of practical distinctions: between narrator and implied author, between reliable and unreliable narrators, and between observers and narrative agents. This scheme allowed him to provide persuasive accounts of how narrative techniques relate to rhetorical effects in a wide range of fictions, charting these effects from the overt rhetoric of earlier authorial commentary to the "disguised rhetoric of modern fiction."

In his work on the rhetoric of narrative, Booth influenced later theorists of narratology, including those with an explicitly rhetorical take on the field such as James Phelan (*Narrative as Rhetoric*, 1996) and those developing directly out of reader-oriented criticism such as Peter Rabinowitz (*Before Reading*, 1998). Various approaches to narrative theory and practice remain rich examples of contemporary rhetorical approaches to literary culture as seen in the journal *Narrative* and the conferences of the International Society for the Study of Narrative. As Phelan wrote in his useful revisionist history, "Rhetorical theory is an ongoing enterprise that has a major place in contemporary narrative theory, itself an increasingly important field in the age of the Narrative Turn."[8]

Over the last decade we continue to see such cross-influences and mutual borrowings between contemporary rhetorical studies and ongoing and emergent approaches within critical theory and cultural studies. An example I have already mentioned is the rhetorically oriented work in twentieth-century reader-oriented theory and contemporary reception study. Again, a bit of history: in explaining his theory of narrative rhetoric, Booth distinguished his focus on formal techniques from psychological and sociological attention to authors and readers in history. This formalist orientation was in keeping with the Anglo-American new critical proscriptions, dominant in the mid-twentieth century, against talking about authorial intention and reader response as causes and effects of literary meaning and value. Later rhetorical approaches treating literature as affecting readers also wrestled with these purported "Intentional and Affective Fallacies." In the late 1960s and early 1970s, for example, reader-response critics such as Stanley Fish and Wolfgang Iser proposed their own implicitly rhetorical approaches to literature by distinguishing their reader theories both from the objective formalism of Anglo-American New Criticism and sometimes from the explicitly rhetorical but primarily holistic criticism of Booth.[9] Fish's affective stylistics claimed to be demonstrating that the *affective fallacy* is itself a fallacy, as he focused not on the final rhetorical effect of a text as a whole but on the moment-by-moment lived reading experience of a hypothetical informed reader. Iser also took account of formalist proscriptions and attended to the temporal reading experience in his phenomenological criticism, but he negotiated the affective fallacy by describing the workings of the implied reader posited by a text, citing the work of Booth. Neither Fish nor Iser emphasized the rhetorical character of their early criticism, but both were plainly dealing with the suasive and other effects of literature in their interpretations.[10]

Most of these twentieth-century rhetorical approaches to artistic techniques and narrative conventions dealt primarily with readers addressed in or assumed by the interpreted text. That is, the rhetorical effects of literature were primarily "read off" the text itself, even when what was purportedly being described was the reading experience the text provided. Sometimes, however, reader-response critics used as evidence for the work's rhetorical effects the interpretations or reported experiences of other readers, whether popular reviewers or other professional literary critics. In such cases, reader-response criticism tended toward another kind of literary-critical approach that might also be characterized as rhetorical: reception study. Often influenced by the *Rezeptionsästhetik* of Hans Robert Jauss, reception critics describe the way literary texts affect readers in specific historical contexts of reading conventions, literary traditions, cultural politics, or material conditions of publication, distribution, and consumption.[11] Such rhetorically inflected reception study continues to develop in this century as can be seen in the conferences of the Reception Studies Society and its journal *Reception: Texts, Readers, Audiences, History*.

Rhetorical pragmatism is another current development in rhetorical studies with deep roots in the twentieth century. Back in the 1930s Louise Rosenblatt published her *Literature as Exploration* (1938), which went through five editions, the latest published in 1996 by the Modern Language Association with a foreword by Wayne Booth. Her critical and pedagogical focus on the "transaction" between readers and texts was influenced by John Dewey's pragmatist instrumentalism that called into question traditional epistemology's foundationalist assumption of a subject-object, knower-known opposition. In the later twentieth century, during the so-called revival of pragmatism in the humanities and social sciences, Richard Rorty combined Dewey with the later Wittgenstein and early Heidegger to produce a neopragmatism with strong rhetorical affiliations, replacing a confrontational model between knower and world with a conversational model among knowers in the world.[12] Various forms of rhetorical pragmatism are currently being developed as approaches to critical theory and cultural studies, especially in contemporary communication studies, with several attempts to retrieve and repurpose explicit and implicit rhetorical aspects in the work of William James, Dewey, and others in the classical pragmatist tradition.[13]

Contemporary rhetorical hermeneutics combines this rhetorical pragmatism in critical theory with reception study in cultural criticism to provide a theoretical framework and interpretive resource for literary and cultural studies. As a critical perspective on using language and making sense, rhetorical hermeneutics contributes to two broad interdisciplinary domains. Engaging current theoretical debates about literature and culture, it represents a rhetoricized form of neopragmatism organized around rhetoric and interpretation; in practicing historical interpretation, it exemplifies a cultural studies interpreting the production, circulation, and reception of rhetorical effects. Combining rhetorical pragmatism with cultural rhetoric study, rhetorical hermeneutics often uses rhetoric to practice theory by doing history, whether analyzing the cultural reception of *Huckleberry Finn* within the 1880s Bad Boy Boom or the assumptions about ideology in debates within the cross-cultural reception of Azar Nafizi's *Reading Lolita in Tehran* (2003) or the conceptions of the human-made problematic in the controversial receptions of animal liberation manifestos or understandings of political theology in media coverage of contemporary exchanges between Pope Francis and US president Donald Trump.[14]

Cultural rhetoric studies has been developed further by rhetoricians working at the intersections of composition studies, technical communication, digital media, and engaged cultural studies. This "cultural rhetorics" scholarship emphasizes connections with political approaches studying the interaction of culture and rhetoric and identifies with contributions made by minoritized scholars within writing studies and beyond. This rhetorical perspective emphasizes interpretive categories of embodied actions, global decolonization, personal narratives, and the cultural specificity of constellated meaning-practices.[15] The Cultural Rhetorics Consortium and its conferences attempt to provide "intellectual and community space for academics, activists, artists, teachers, and community members who practice cultural rhetorics."[16]

Like literary-cultural studies more generally, contemporary rhetoric study continues to build and extend approaches developed within and outside the humanities during the twentieth century: studies in feminism and gender, Marxism and post-Marxism, psychoanalytic and especially Lacanian theories, colonialism and postcolonialism, critical race theory, and other theoretical positions and interpretive practices applied throughout the human sciences. Such "traditional" perspectives adopted and adapted within rhetoric are combined with emergent approaches to form new intersectional rhetorics. For example, in *Race, Rhetoric, and Technology* (2006), Adam Banks rhetorically reads new media technologies through the lens of African American studies by presenting "the Digital Divide" both as a literal description of the socioeconomic condition of technological access and as a figurative representation of the historical and political situation of race relations in the United States. Banks then builds on his proposal for "transformative access" in a second book, *Digital Griots: African American Rhetoric in a Multimedia Age* (2010). Here he proposes a new theoretical framework for rhetorically reading contemporary media—through the figure of the DJ as griot—and uses new digital and multimedia strategies, such as mixing, remixing, and mixtaping, as descriptive tropes and concrete writing practices. Thus, Banks employs technological innovations to reinterpret African American rhetorical traditions and uses those rhetorical traditions to repurpose new technologies, nicely illustrating the self-reflexive utility of current rhetorical theory.

Many contemporary rhetoricians have joined the debates over the posthuman in critical cultural studies. Coming out of a Third Sophistic with a Derridean ethical shift, Diane Davis and Michelle Ballif have organized and contributed to discussions of extra-human rhetorics, including those addressing the animal, the object, the dead, and the divine. Extra-human rhetorical relations include all "scenes of responsive engagement with or among nonhuman others." In focusing on such relations, rhetoricians examine ways in which "the human" has been constituted through "ahuman and inhuman communication" and sometimes theorize the workings of "a generalized notion of rhetoricity—a fundamental affect*ability*, persuad*ability*, or respons*ivity*—that remains irreducible to 'speech' and symbolic exchange more generally."[17] Davis argues that this rhetoricity constitutes a primordial ethico-rhetorical imperative, an openness to others, a kind of "inessential solidarity" that precedes and enables every persuasive discourse or communicative practice, every conscious rhetorical activity as traditionally understood. Ballif takes the ethico-rhetorical turn into the theorizing of rhetorical historiography and, more specifically, into a Derridean "hauntology," a historiographic method of "conversing with the dead" that disturbs our understanding of the "past" and invites us to refigure the "future" ethically as "not-yet."

Among the most popular new rhetorical approaches have been those tied to the new materialisms. Borrowing from thing theory, object-oriented ontology, alien phenomenology, and related philosophical thinking, the new materialist rhetorics challenge some of the most basic assumptions of contemporary rhetorical studies such as the privileging of a human agent's symbolic practices and dualisms of rhetor/audience, intelligibility/materiality, and reason/affect. Focusing on the thingness of rhetoric and the rhetoric of things, these new materialist rhetorics displace the human from the center of theoretical and critical attention while still attending to human relations with and within networks of objects. As described by the editors of *Rhetoric, Through Everyday Things* (2016), "Turning our attention back to things may constitute a *post*human turn, but it need not be an *anti*human one."[18]

Sometimes inspired by reinterpretations of Heidegger on "tool-being" in *Being and Time* (1927) or his later essay, "The Thing" (1950), such approaches ascribe rhetorical agency to physical objects and describe the suasive effects of material environs. For example, Thomas Rickert's *Ambient Rhetoric: The Attunements of Rhetorical Being* (2013) insists on rethinking the rhetorical role of material environments, an argument that is both theoretical and historical. It is theoretical in that it calls into question certain traditional ontological claims about the passivity of material contexts in the performance of rhetorical acts, but the argument is also historical in that it asks us to reconsider the role of external environments in prehistoric peoples' artistic practices and to engage more fully the changes in human being in today's age of new media and other emergent technologies. Combining theoretical insights from, among others, Kenneth Burke and the later Heidegger, Rickert's book illustrates the way current rhetorical studies absorbs and extends other contemporary intellectual-cultural movements, in his case hermeneutic phenomenology, cognitive science, speculative materialism, and ambient music aesthetics. Similar kinds of adaptations can be seen in contemporary rhetorical study's appropriations and contributions to an array of emergent approaches, including actor network theory, assemblage theory, affect theory, emotion history, body theory, and disability studies.[19]

In surveying old and new approaches to the rhetorical study of literature and culture, I have pointed out that contemporary rhetorical studies, like every established academic discipline and interdiscipline, continues to borrow from other fields to develop its interpretive strategies and theoretical positions. Thus, I have indicated how emergent rhetorics are interconnected in their genealogies and adaptations of past intellectual movements as well as in their mutual borrowings among themselves in the present. But I also want to emphasize that rhetorical study offers special resources to literary-cultural studies for doing its versions of interdisciplinary work. Those resources include specific case studies of cultural events and the language arts in relation to their intellectual, material, and other historical contexts as well as terminology, models, and histories useful to any field doing interpretive work on symbolic action.

Rhetorical study also provides metacritical, transdisciplinary perspectives useful for literary-cultural studies in making sense of its own critical and theoretical inquiries. It does this by presenting frameworks for analyzing the disciplinary matrices of literary and cultural studies, including their vocabularies, tropes, narratives, argumentative topoi, evidentiary proofs, enabling fictions, ongoing debates, institutional supports, and so on. In addition, the field of rhetoric stages in a particularly pointed way various conflicts and paradoxes continuing to energize literary-cultural studies. Take the ongoing debate, in its various versions, between approaches directed at aesthetic form and those aimed at sociopolitical diagnostics, close textual reading versus new historical contextualization, what used to be characterized as intrinsic versus extrinsic criticism. Rhetorical study requires both: rhetoric is formally inside the text as it also circulates outside in various contexts; it is intrinsic and extrinsic to texts and historically constitutive of the boundary between the two domains. In various ways, then, rhetoric continues to serve as both a set of interpretive strategies and theoretical positions for doing literary-cultural studies as well as an architectonic framework for understanding the past, present, and future of the study of literature and culture.

Loyola Marymount University (United States)

NOTES

1. Portions of the first half of this chapter update an earlier piece, Steven Mailloux, "Rhetoric and Literature," in *International Encyclopedia of Linguistics*, second ed., ed. William Frawley (New York: Oxford University Press, 2003), 2: 472–75.

2. Cf. Richard McKeon, "The Uses of Rhetoric in a Technological Age: Architectonic Productive Arts," in *The Prospect of Rhetoric*, eds. Lloyd F. Bitzer and Edwin Black (Englewood Cliffs: Prentice-Hall, 1971), 44–63.

3. See Steven Mailloux, *Rhetoric's Pragmatism: Essays in Rhetorical Hermeneutics* (State College: Penn State University Press, 2017), 2, 8.

4. Kenneth Burke, *Language as Symbolic Action: Essays on Life, Literature, and Method* (Berkeley: University of California Press, 1966), 307.

5. Robert Esposito, *Two: The Machine of Political Theology and the Place of Thought*, trans. Zakiya Hanafi (New York: Fordham University Press, 2015).

6. See Wayne C. Booth, "The Many Voices of Kenneth Burke, Theologian and Prophet, as Revealed in His Letters to Me," in *Unending Conversations: New Writings by and about Kenneth Burke*, eds. Greig Henderson and David Cratis Williams (Carbondale: Southern Illinois University Press, 2001), 179–201; Wayne C. Booth, "Kenneth Burke's Religious Rhetoric: 'God-terms' and the Ontological Proof," in *Rhetorical Invention and Religious Inquiry: New Perspectives*, eds. Walter Jost and Windy Olmsted (New Haven: Yale University Press, 2000), 25–46.

7. See Wayne C. Booth, *Modern Dogma and the Rhetoric of Assent* (Chicago: University of Chicago Press, 1974).

8. James Phelan, "The Chicago School: From Neo-Aristotelian Poetics to the Rhetorical Theory of Narrative," in *Theoretical Schools and Circles in the Twentieth-Century Humanities: Literary Theory, History, Philosophy*, eds. Marina Grishakova and Silvi Salupere (New York: Routledge, 2015), 133–51.

9. See Wolfgang Iser, *The Implied Reader: Patterns of Communication in Prose Fiction from Bunyan to Beckett* (Baltimore: Johns Hopkins University Press, 1974); Stanley Fish, *Is There a Text in This Class? The Authority of Interpretive Communities* (Cambridge: Harvard University Press, 1980), 21–67; Jane P. Tompkins, ed., *Reader-Response Criticism: From Formalism to Post-Structuralism* (Baltimore: Johns Hopkins University Press, 1980); Steven Mailloux, *Interpretive Conventions: The Reader in the Study of American Fiction* (Ithaca: Cornell University Press, 1982), 19–65; and Peter Rabinowitz, "Other Reader-Oriented Theories," in *The Cambridge History of Literary Criticism, Vol. 8: From Formalism to Post-structuralism*, ed. Raman Selden (Cambridge: Cambridge University Press, 1995), 375–403.

10. Fish focused explicitly on the rhetorical aspects of his later theory of interpretive communities; see Fish, *Is There a Text in This Class?*, 336–71 and "Rhetoric," in *The Stanley Fish Reader*, ed. H. Aram Veeser (Oxford: Blackwell, 1999), 116–44.

11. See James L. Machor and Philip Goldstein, eds., *Reception Study: From Literary Theory to Cultural Studies* (New York: Routledge, 2001); Philip Goldstein and James L. Machor, eds., *New Directions in American Reception Study* (Oxford: Oxford University Press, 2008).

12. See Richard Rorty, *Contingency, Irony, and Solidarity* (Cambridge: Cambridge University Press, 1989) and *Philosophy and the Mirror of Nature* (Princeton: Princeton University Press, 1979).

13. See Keith Gilyard, *Composition and Cornel West: Notes Toward a Deep Democracy* (Carbondale: Southern Illinois University Press, 2008); Paul Stob, *William James and the Art of Popular Statement* (East Lansing: Michigan State University Press, 2013); Brian Jackson and Gregory Clark, eds., *Trained Capacities: John Dewey, Rhetoric, and Democratic Practice* (Columbia: University of South Carolina Press, 2014); and Robert Danisch, *Building a Social Democracy: The Promise of Rhetorical Pragmatism* (New York: Lexington Books, 2015).

14. For some of these examples and others, see William E. Cain, ed., *Reconceptualizing American Literary/Cultural Studies* (New York: Garland, 1996); Mailloux, *Rhetoric's Pragmatism*; Kristian Bjørkdahl, "Enlarging the *Ethnos*: Rorty, Redescription, and the Rhetorical Labor of Moral Progress," Ph. D. dissertation (University of Oslo, 2016); James Zeigler, *Red Scare Racism and Cold War Black Radicalism* (Jackson: University Press of Mississippi, 2015).

15. Phil Bratta and Malea Powell, "Entering the Cultural Rhetorics Conversation," *Enculturation* (2016) http://enculturation.net/entering-the-cultural-rhetorics-conversations.

16. http://cultrhetconsortium.org/

17. Diane Davis and Michelle Ballif, "Pushing the Limits of the Anthropos," *Philosophy and Rhetoric* 47.4 (2014): 349. Also see Diane Davis, *Inessential Solidarity: Rhetoric and Foreigner Relations* (Pittsburgh: University of Pittsburgh Press, 2010); Diane Davis, "Autozoography: Notes Toward a Rhetoricity of the Living," *Philosophy and Rhetoric* 47.4 (2014): 533–53; Michelle Ballif, "Historiography as Hauntology: Paranormal Investigations into the History of Rhetoric," in *Theorizing Histories of Rhetoric*, ed. Michelle Ballif (Carbondale: Southern Illinois University Press, 2013), 139–53; and Michelle Ballif, "Regarding the Dead," *Philosophy and Rhetoric* 47.4 (2014): 455–71. On the Third Sophistic, see Victor Vitanza, "'Some More' Notes, Towards a Third Sophistic," *Argumentation* 5 (1991): 117–39, and *Negation, Subjectivity, and the History of Rhetoric* (Albany: State University of New York Press, 1997).

18. Scot Barnett, and Casey Boyle, eds., *Rhetoric, through Everyday Things* (Tuscaloosa: University of Alabama Press, 2016).

19. See, for example, Paul Lynch and Nathaniel Rivers, eds., *Thinking with Bruno Latour in Rhetoric and Composition* (Carbondale: Southern Illinois University Press, 2015); Debra Hawhee, *Moving Bodies: Kenneth Burke at the Edges of Language* (Columbia: University of South Carolina Press, 2009); Debra Hawhee, *Rhetoric in Tooth and Claw: Animals, Language, Sensation* (Chicago: University of Chicago Press, 2017); Daniel M. Gross, *The Secret History of Emotion: From Aristotle's* Rhetoric *to Modern Brain Science* (Chicago: University of Chicago Press, 2006); and Stephanie Kerschbaum, *Toward a New Rhetoric of Difference* (Urbana: NCTE, 2014).

WORKS CITED

Ballif, Michelle. "Historiography as Hauntology: Paranormal Investigations into the History of Rhetoric." In *Theorizing Histories of Rhetoric*. Ed. Michelle Ballif. Carbondale: Southern Illinois University Press, 2013. 139–53

Ballif, Michelle. "Regarding the Dead." *Philosophy and Rhetoric* 47.4 (2014): 455–71.

Banks, Adam J. *Race, Rhetoric, and Technology: Searching for Higher Ground.* Mahwah and Urbana: Lawrence Erlbaum and NCTE, 2006.

Banks, Adam J. *Digital Griots: African American Rhetoric in a Multimedia Age.* Urbana: CCCC and NCTE, 2010.

Barnett, Scot and Casey Boyle, eds. *Rhetoric, through Everyday Things.* Tuscaloosa: University of Alabama Press, 2016.

Bjørkdahl, Kristian. "Enlarging the *Ethnos*: Rorty, Redescription, and the Rhetorical Labor of Moral Progress." Ph. D. dissertation. University of Oslo, 2016.

Booth, Wayne C. *The Rhetoric of Fiction.* Chicago: University of Chicago, 1961.

Booth, Wayne C. *Modern Dogma and the Rhetoric of Assent.* Chicago: University of Chicago Press, 1974.

Booth, Wayne C. "Kenneth Burke's Religious Rhetoric: 'God-terms' and the Ontological Proof." In *Rhetorical Invention and Religious Inquiry: New Perspectives.* Eds. Walter Jost and Windy Olmsted. New Haven: Yale University Press, 2000. 25–46.

Booth, Wayne C. "The Many Voices of Kenneth Burke, Theologian and Prophet, as Revealed in His Letters to Me." In *Unending Conversations: New Writings by and about Kenneth Burke.* Eds. Greig Henderson and David Cratis Williams. Carbondale: Southern Illinois University Press, 2001. 179–201.

Bratta, Phil, and Malea Powell. "Entering the Cultural Rhetorics Conversation." *enculturation* (2016). http://enculturation.net/entering-the-cultural-rhetorics-conversations.

Burke, Kenneth. *Counter-Statement*. New York: Harcourt, Brace, 1931.

Burke, Kenneth. *Permanence and Change: An Anatomy of Purpose*. New York: New Republic, 1935.

Burke, Kenneth. *Attitudes Toward History*. Two vols. New York: New Republic, 1937.

Burke, Kenneth. *A Grammar of Motives*. New York: Prentice-Hall, 1945.

Burke, Kenneth. *A Rhetoric of Motives*. New York: Prentice-Hall, 1950.

Burke, Kenneth. *The Rhetoric of Religion: Studies in Logology*. Boston: Beacon Press, 1961.

Burke, Kenneth. *Language as Symbolic Action: Essays on Life, Literature, and Method*. Berkeley: University of California Press, 1966.

Cain, William E., ed. *Reconceptualizing American Literary/Cultural Studies*. New York: Garland, 1996.

Danisch, Robert. *Building a Social Democracy: The Promise of Rhetorical Pragmatism*. New York: Lexington Books, 2015.

Davis, Diane. *Inessential Solidarity: Rhetoric and Foreigner Relations*. Pittsburgh: University of Pittsburgh Press, 2010.

Davis, Diane. "Autozoography: Notes Toward a Rhetoricity of the Living." *Philosophy and Rhetoric* 47.4 (2014): 533–53.

Davis, Diane, and Michelle Ballif. "Pushing the Limits of the Anthropos." *Philosophy and Rhetoric* 47.4 (2014): 346–53.

Esposito, Robert. *Two: The Machine of Political Theology and the Place of Thought*. Trans. Zakiya Hanafi. New York: Fordham University Press, 2015.

Fish, Stanley. *Is There a Text in This Class? The Authority of Interpretive Communities*. Cambridge: Harvard University Press, 1980.

Fish, Stanley. "Rhetoric." In *The Stanley Fish Reader*. Ed. H. Aram Veeser. Oxford: Blackwell, 1999. 116–44.

Frawley, William. *Rhetoric's Pragmatism: Essays in Rhetorical Hermeneutics*. University Park: The Pennsylvania State University Press, 2017.

Gilyard, Keith. *Composition and Cornel West: Notes toward a Deep Democracy*. Carbondale: Southern Illinois University Press, 2008.

Goldstein, Philip, and James L. Machor, eds. *New Directions in American Reception Study*. Oxford: Oxford University Press, 2008.

Gross, Daniel M. *The Secret History of Emotion: From Aristotle's Rhetoric to Modern Brain Science*. Chicago: University of Chicago Press, 2006.

Hawhee, Debra. *Moving Bodies: Kenneth Burke at the Edges of Language*. Columbia: University of South Carolina Press, 2009.

Hawhee, Debra. *Rhetoric in Tooth and Claw: Animals, Language, Sensation*. Chicago: University of Chicago Press, 2017.

Heidegger, Martin. *Being and Time* [1927]. Trans. John Macquarrie and Edward Robinson. New York: Harper and Row, 1962.

Heidegger, Martin. "The Thing [1951]." In *Poetry, Language, Thought*. Trans. Albert Hofstadter. New York: Harper and Row, 1971. 165–86.

Iser, Wolfgang. *The Implied Reader: Patterns of Communication in Prose Fiction from Bunyan to Beckett*. Baltimore: Johns Hopkins University Press, 1974.

Jackson, Brian, and Gregory Clark, eds. *Trained Capacities: John Dewey, Rhetoric, and Democratic Practice*. Columbia: University of South Carolina Press, 2014.

Kerschbaum, Stephanie. *Toward a New Rhetoric of Difference*. Urbana: NCTE, 2014.

Lynch, Paul, and Nathaniel Rivers, eds. *Thinking with Bruno Latour in Rhetoric and Composition*. Carbondale: Southern Illinois University Press, 2015.

Machor, James L., and Philip Goldstein, eds. *Reception Study: From Literary Theory to Cultural Studies*. New York: Routledge, 2001.

Mailloux, Steven. *Interpretive Conventions: The Reader in the Study of American Fiction*. Ithaca: Cornell University Press, 1982.

Mailloux, Steven. "Rhetoric and Literature." In *International Encyclopedia of Linguistics*. Second ed. Ed. William Frawley. New York: Oxford University Press, 2003. 2: 472–75.

Mailloux, Steven. *Rhetoric's Pragmatism: Essays in Rhetorical Hermeneutics*. State College: Penn State University Press, 2017.

McKeon, Richard. "The Uses of Rhetoric in a Technological Age: Architectonic Productive Arts." In *The Prospect of Rhetoric*. Eds. Lloyd F. Bitzer and Edwin Black. Englewood Cliffs: Prentice-Hall, 1971. 44–63.

Phelan, James. *Narrative as Rhetoric: Technique, Audiences, Ethics, Ideology*. Columbus: Ohio State University Press, 1996.

Phelan, James. "The Chicago School: From Neo-Aristotelian Poetics to the Rhetorical Theory of Narrative." In *Theoretical Schools and Circles in the Twentieth-Century Humanities: Literary Theory, History, Philosophy*. Eds. Marina Grishakova and Silvi Salupere. New York: Routledge, 2015. 133–51.

Rabinowitz, Peter. "Other Reader-Oriented Theories." In *The Cambridge History of Literary Criticism, Vol. 8: From Formalism to Poststructuralism*. Ed. Raman Selden. Cambridge, UK: Cambridge University Press, 1995. 375–403.

Rabinowitz, Peter. *Before Reading: Narrative Conventions and the Politics of Interpretation*. Second ed. Columbus: Ohio State University Press, 1998.

Rickert, Thomas. *Ambient Rhetoric: The Attunements of Rhetorical Being*. Pittsburgh: University of Pittsburgh Press, 2013.

Rorty, Richard. *Philosophy and the Mirror of Nature*. Princeton: Princeton University Press, 1979.

Rorty, Richard. *Contingency, Irony, and Solidarity*. Cambridge: Cambridge University Press, 1989.

Rosenblatt, Louise M. *Literature as Exploration*. Fifth ed. New York: Modern Language Association of America, 1995.

Stob, Paul. *William James and the Art of Popular Statement*. East Lansing: Michigan State University Press, 2013.

Tompkins, Jane P., ed. *Reader-Response Criticism: From Formalism to Post-Structuralism*. Baltimore: Johns Hopkins University Press, 1980.

Vitanza, Victor. "'Some More' Notes, Towards a Third Sophistic." *Argumentation* 5 (1991): 117–39.

Vitanza, Victor. *Negation, Subjectivity, and the History of Rhetoric*. Albany: State University of New York Press, 1997.

Zeigler, James. *Red Scare Racism and Cold War Black Radicalism*. Jackson: University Press of Mississippi, 2015.

CHAPTER NINE

Deconstruction

HENRY SUSSMAN

With demagogues of the Far Right (Steve Bannon)[1] and conservative intellectuals (Charles Hill)[2] currently vying over deployment rights to the complex signifier, "deconstruction," this fabled figure in the rise and preeminence of contemporary critical theory has by now come full turn. No single term, in the late twentieth century and on into the twenty-first, is more responsible for placing critical analysis and exegesis in the forefront of public scrutiny than "deconstruction." The term has remained hotly contested ever since it was placed into critical service by the French-Algerian Parisian philosopher (but also globetrotting, with especially meaningful collaborations and affiliations in the United States) Jacques Derrida in 1965–66.[3] "Deconstruction," as a general epithet for cultural debunking and the demolition of long-standing core-concepts in the operating systems of Western philosophy and culture, has indeed wandered far from the readings in Enlightenment and German idealistic philosophies, twentieth-century phenomenology, psychoanalysis, and a broad swathe of modern experimental fiction and poetry—the textual environment in which Derrida initially launched it. As a descriptive term for subversive practices often running counter to deeply entrenched styles and conventions, "deconstruction" has also been applied to fashion, architecture, cuisine, and even hairstyles. Yet, to a sprawling "pack" of literary authors and critics, cultural theorists, philosophers, social scientists, theologians, architects, and historians who have generated critical illumination under its aegis and inspiration, deconstruction is hardly exhausted through its popular designation as a cultural tactic of resistance against totalistic politics and thinking. Deconstruction is far more demanding, rigorous, and even technical than that. Deconstruction started out as a philologically and etymologically informed, demandingly erudite way of reading the conceptual linchpins of philosophical, social, and scientific systems and texts against their "grain," their purported meanings, and their historically assigned significance and centrality. In the course of three-some decades of elaboration, refinement, and extension supplied by Derrida himself, and in the hands of a devoted and remarkably gifted and erudite cadre of collaborators and students, among which are Hélène Cixous, Paul de Man, J. Hillis Miller, Jean-Luc Nancy, Philippe Lacoue-Labarthe, Bernard Stiegler, Samuel Weber, Jonathan Culler, Gayatri Chakravorty Spivak, Rodolphe Gasché, Carol Jacobs, Werner Hamacher, Catherine Malabou, Avital Ronell, John Sallis, Geoff Bennington, Robert Bernasconi, and Tom Cohen, deconstruction's "community," for all that its convener looked askance at this term, has held remarkably tight to its inaugural specifications.

As will be detailed below, deconstruction in practice is far less glamorous than "deconstruction," the antipodal pose beloved by skeptics and hipsters of many stripes and now contested by the Alt-Right. It is certainly at the most radical remove possible from the idea of simple dismantling, destruction, or shutting down that Steve Bannon would like to apply to governmental function and interactivity with the public. Deconstruction's commitment to the truth, albeit of a certain kind, and to the disclosure of every arbitrariness in the structure and exercise of power, marks precisely the point where it separates paths from demagoguery of every persuasion. To the end, Derrida insisted that each deconstructive reading was text-specific and that the range of its implications was no greater than the textual environment (or "local difference")[4] in which it had highlighted the *contresens* of what might have otherwise seemed patent, well-established, and self-evident.

The widest swathe that Derrida allowed for the premise of the "deconstructibility" of all canons of authority in religion, ideology, and culture was an overarching ambivalence, from civilization to civilization, toward the linguistic medium itself. Extending from the early studies of Edmund Husserl and twentieth-century phenomenology that were to prove crucial over Derrida's entire career was a double-vision of language both as an impersonal communications system and as the very "platform" for subjectivity's experience of itself, its possibility for "auto-affection." Against the backdrop of this linguistically driven investigation into phenomenological complexity, in instance after instance of canonical texts that he parsed on a microscopic level, Derrida discerned a counterpoint: of naïve acceptance of language's service as a handmaiden to "higher" truths and foundations to social and epistemological order. On the ideological level, this attribution of *purely representational* and *instrumental* functions and values to language alternated with a pitched skepticism and even horror at language's unavoidable uncertainties, multiple (even conflicting) meanings and suggestions, and manifest artificiality. The franchise that culture extended to language when it was official, when it "represented" the interests and authority of the deity, spirit, state, or hegemonic class, when it expressed itself only as a subservient house-organ, Derrida called "voice" and related to the cultural activity of "Speech." "Writing," on the other hand, became the linguistic scapegoat (literally, in "Plato's Pharmacy"), onto which culture projects its profound misgivings toward the slippage, inexactitude, and even subterfuge, intentional or not, endemic to language and its deployment.

As Derrida branched off from the linguistic and phenomenological foci of his doctoral and postdoctoral study, the authors who consistently fascinated him were the ones who came closest to discerning the fullest open-ended and self-engendering play of language for its own sake (as under the aura of "Writing")—yet who eventually succumbed, somewhere and somehow, to some manifestation of misgivings, disenchantment, or outright contempt toward language as expressed in surveillance and "closure" applied to it in culturally specific fashion. With Derrida's intense early engagement with the writings of Husserl and Martin Heidegger still fresh in mind (the latter still quite controversial in the 1960s and 1970s), language, in all its media and artifacts, fluctuated in its status between the very source and bastion of ideological self-certainty and a "supplement" (or counterculture) to itself: playful, confused, dysfunctional, unreliable, manifestly "unnatural" and artificial.

Paris, in the early 1960s, when Derrida launched his career, having stunned such mentors as Jean Hyppolite, Maurice de Gandillac, Louis Althusser, and Lucien Goldmann with his erudition and innovation, was in no short supply of luminaries. (Among others, Roland Barthes, Michel Foucault, Althusser himself, Maurice Blanchot, Jacques Lacan, and Claude Lévi-Strauss were all active, still at the peak of their respective theoretical and writerly practices.) Yet what set Derrida's work apart from the outset was, in choreographing the counterpoint between "Speech" and "Writing," in extrapolating the "supplemental" status to which the latter had been relegated, the uniquely broad bandwidth on which he was able to place both the monuments of Western metaphysics[5] (works by, among others, Plato, Aristotle, Rousseau, Kant, Hegel, Nietzsche, and Heidegger) and his contemporaries (Lévi-Strauss, Francis Ponge, Blanchot, Emmanuel Levinas) in intimate conversation. Centering deconstructive discourse around the linguistic medium (above all as manifest as the pivotal tropes or figures of speech both making specific works possible and exemplifying their own and textual multidimensionality) enabled writers as diverse as Freud, Stéphane Mallarmé, Joyce, Antonin Artaud, Jean Genet, and Paul Celan to be read as philosophers of language and the media; conversely, it enabled philosophers and social thinkers, Marx as well as Kant, Hegel, Nietzsche, and Heidegger, to be fully appreciated as literary innovators, if not specifically as poets. Although in an idiosyncratic and highly improvisational textual medium, Derrida personified the insistence that critical discourse itself rise to exemplify and even stretch the highest poetico-aesthetic criteria. This had been Walter Benjamin's rallying cry to the public intellectuals of a previous generation— one addressing the radical theoretical breakthrough and artistic innovation managing against all odds to coincide with the twentieth century's global death-trip and devolution into violence on the industrial (or even postindustrial) scale.

A powerful instance of deconstructive virtuosity may literally bring the house down (in the sense of radically debunking elements of widely accepted cant regarding specific institutions, ideologies, works of art, or writers), but its effect is anything but violent, simplistic, or numbing. There is a telling way in which the "signature" tropes of deconstruction, such as the supplement, the trace, the wheel, and even Writing itself, rhizomatically loop back upon one another, in interpretative acts of mutual illumination. Yet no single act of deconstruction authoritatively "speaks" for any other. It remains nevertheless worthwhile to pause at the richness, complexity, and even contradictory nuance that Derrida was able to infuse into the figure of the *pharmakon* that he culled, in an act of uncanny selection, from Plato's *Phaedo* (among other dialogues). Not only does *pharmakon* reorient, in a stunningly radical way, the venerable stereotype of Plato as a purveyor of the Good, the True, and the Beautiful, as a pivotal trope, or possibly, infrastructure; the figure also *performs* the debunking to the Platonic "logocentrism" (its drift in the direction of Speech) that the term, in multiple contexts, and its variants, *signify*. The performativity that Derrida is able to choreograph into *pharmakon* as it careens through the Platonic bedrock into Western mores and metaphysics is *concurrent* to the exegetical task that Derrida assigns it—namely serving as a previously undisclosed pivot (or "strange attractor")[6] within the system of Platonic argumentation. Today we would say that the *explanatory* function of *pharmakon* relates in a "strange loop" (Douglas R. Hofstadter)[7] to the *rhetorical performance* that Derrida has added to the specifications of fully outfitted critique. And no element of this performance is more crucial than exposing the *vilification* of the full range of linguistic nuance and complexity (again: "Logocentrism") also taking a lead role in Plato's historical placement at the very "bedrock" of Western thinking and in his ongoing persistence as an icon of Western civilization and values.

Deconstruction is a leading branch of contemporary systems theory conducted under an aura of nonchalance that is merely the disguise both for the comprehensiveness and scholarly rigor of its analyses and its situation at the microscopic level of linguistic and semiotic articulation (committing it to joint-processing at the "lower" as well as "upper" levels). The seeming nonchalance also bears witness to the personal modesty and intimacy that characterized, over the years, Derrida's personal interactions with close friends, fellow top French intellectuals, academic colleagues, and students alike. Derrida's most notable pieces of writing often begin with a rambling "exergue" or preamble that—akin to the prolonged exploration of a harmonic "neighborhood" at the head of an Indian raga—seems to go nowhere. Upon a second reading, though, the exergue, more often than not, bristles with what will emerge as the operative vocabulary in a text and context-specific unraveling of a pivotal work of philosophical or cultural programming, with all the historical "baggage" that it may bear, making crucial conceptual connections that will pertain throughout the critico-philosophical readout at hand. The seemingly whimsical exergue serves as prelude to a performance highlighting both the isolation and the freeing up of the points of fixity defining an influential work's historical persistence and distinction.[8] It is precisely upon these figurative and conceptual vertebrae that canonical works base their claims to authority.

A crucial correlative to deconstruction's pronounced bearing of nonchalance is stylistic. Not very far along in his published oeuvre Derrida realizes that it is fully in keeping with a philosophical inquiry driven by the contingencies and associative leaps in the language making it up to make provision and space for the *double entendres*, homonymies, and other linguistic epiphenomena bubbling up from the discussion at hand—above all as they pertain to the figural tropes that have emerged as "operative" for the particular "case study." The result is a highly distinctive textual medium, critique with the density of a thick pastry studded with instances of linguistic play and variation, in no particular hurry to bring home a point or crown an argument. In the overall playfulness of his script, in its susceptibility to the deep etymology of the word-clusters to which he was led by any particular text or texts under his scrutiny, Derrida's primary "writing master" was indeed Heidegger. (Such an observation in no way diminishes Husserl's centrality to his work: this as manifest in an uncanny ability to "chunk" vast sets of micro-phenomena into the most trenchant inferences and boundaries imaginable, and through this process, to set aside some of philosophy's more flamboyant constructs, whether the sublime or "original genius.") And deconstruction manifests the audacity to deploy a textual medium with "resistance" written all over it in the service of cultural reception, scholarship, and the refinement of philosophy's ages-old battery of logical and conceptual instruments, an academic utility most often shrouded in dignity, if not outright sanctimony. The result, stylistically, is as outrageous as it is instructive. Even in a hand-instrument of reference, the deconstructive textual medium grounded in such premises best speaks for itself. The writerly performance of deconstruction carries through to the latest phase of Derrida's writings, as the following citation from the 2005 *Rogues* makes abundantly clear:

> There is always a wheel [*roue*] in torture. Torture always puts to work an encircling violence and an insistent repetition, a relentlessness, the turn and return of a cycle.
>
> The torture of the wheel belongs to a long juridical and political history. It sets into motion not only the turning apparatus of a wheel but the quartering of the alleged criminal. The subject being punished is quartered, his bound body forming one body with the wheel, subjected to its rotation. When I speak of a double question whose torture returns, when I say that this question was at the same time and/or by turns historical and conceptual, or semantic, I am describing torturing and quartering on the wheel.[9]
>
> But I don't imagine it was ever possible to think and say, even if only in Greek, "democracy," before the rotation of some *wheel*. When I say "wheel," I am not yet or not

necessarily referring to the technical possibility of the *wheel*, but, rather, rather earlier, to the roundness of a rotating movement, the rondure of a return to self before any distinction between *physis* and *technē*, *physis* and *nomos*, *physis* and *thesis*, and so on.[10]

Indeed, it seems difficult to think such a desire for or naming of democratic space without the rotary motion of some quasi-circular return or rotation toward the self, toward the origin itself, toward and upon the self of the origin, whenever it is a question, for example, of sovereign self-determination, of the autonomy of the self, of the *ipse*, namely, of the one-self that gives itself its own law, of autofinality, self-relation as being in view of the self. . . . For the sake of economy in language, let me simply announce in a word that, from now on, each time I say *ipse*, *metipse*, or *ipseity*, relying at once on their accepted meaning in Latin, their meaning within the philosophical code, and their etymology, I also want to suggest the self, the one-self, being properly oneself, indeed being in person.[11]

In this compendium of extracts from the outset of *Rogues*, the figure of the wheel itself is the "loose cannon," cutting a dazzling trajectory from torture, through democracy, to the circular (and self-fulfilling) structure of selfhood, which plays, unpredictably, at the very foundation of national sovereignty and its spinoffs. (The critique here of the closed circuits of selfhood via the brute exercise of sovereign self-interest comes through just as strongly as its counter-rhythm.) The demonstration, one of several culminations to Derrida's political thought, goes on to establish the forces of multinational corporatism and forced "bailouts" and "loans" as the true candidates for "roguery" on the stage of global economics and political coercion.

In these multiple deconstructive parameters—exegetical, stylistic, even tonal—"Plato's Pharmacy" is already fully on (or is that off-?) course. At the heart of an argument that is every bit as much a masterful philosophical allegory, stands the figure of the *pharmakon*. Dancing the stutter-step characteristic of other mega-tropes or radical poetic figures, including the hymen, the heliotrope, the specter, and the wheel that Derrida situated both at the center and in the disreputable *banlieux* of Western metaphysics, the *pharmakon* combines and establishes rapport between multiple, often conflicting definitions and motifs affording the Platonic discourse its stereotypical profile.

> Hence, for example, the word *pharmakon*. In this way we hope to display in the most striking manner the regular, ordered polysemy that has, through skewing, indetermination, or overdetermination, but without mistranslation, permitted the rendering of the same word by "remedy," "recipe," "poison," "drug, "philter," etc. It will also be seen to what extent the malleable unity of this concept, or rather its rules and strange logic that links it with its signifier, has been dispersed, masked, obliterated, and rendered almost unreadable not only by the imprudence or empiricism of the translators, but first and foremost by the redoubtable, irreducible difficulty of translation. It is a difficulty inherent in its very principle, situated less in the passage from one language to another, than already, as we shall see, in the tradition between Greek and Greek; a violent difficulty in the transference of a nonphilosopheme into a philosopheme.[12]
>
> In this way, writing, touted by Theuth as a remedy, a beneficial drug, is later overturned and denounced by the king and then, in the king's place, by Socrates, as a harmful substance, a philter of forgetfulness. Inversely, and although in a less immediately readable manner, the hemlock, that potion which in the *Phaedo* is never called anything but a *pharmakon*, is presented to Socrates as a poison; yet it is transformed, through the effects of the Socratic *logos* and of the philosophical

demonstration of the *Phaedo*. . . . There is certainly *play* in such a movement, and this chiasmus is authorized, even prescribed, by the ambivalence of the *pharmakon*. Not only by the polarity good/evil, but by the double participation in the distinct regions of the soul and the body, the invisible and the visible. This double participation, once again, does not mix together two previous separate elements; it refers back to a *same* that is not the identical. . . . Thus, writing is given as the sensible, visible, spatial surrogate of the *mnēmē*; it later turns out to be harmful and benumbing to the invisible interior of the soul, memory and truth. Inversely, the hemlock is given as a poison that harms and benumbs the body. But it later turns out to be helpful to the soul. . . . If the *pharmakon* is "ambivalent," it is because it constitutes the medium in which the opposites are opposed, the movement and the play that links them among themselves, reverses them or makes one side cross over into the other (soul/body, good/evil, inside/outside, memory/forgetfulness, speech/writing, etc.). It is on the basis of this play or movement that the opposites or differences are stopped by Plato. The *pharmakon* is the movement, the locus, and the play: (the production of) difference. It is the difference of difference.[13]

Cannily, in its suppleness, *pharmakon* spans the gap, opens a feedback loop, between "nonphilosopheme" and "philosopheme." As a term to which Plato, in his pronouncements on knowledge and ethics, repeatedly devolves, *pharmakon* is at the nexus of a volatile constellation of words whose inflections extend to artificiality (in memory as well as self-presentation), illegitimacy, falsehood, exile, and even death. In each of these capacities, *pharmakon* is the occasion and locus of an irrepressible play: one "opposing opposites," "reverses them or makes one side cross over to the other." In its own ambivalence and diversity of suggestion, *pharmakon* is an *agent provocateur* of what Derrida terms polysemy, the ability of signifiers, in the plurality of their meanings, even to revert to their presumed opposites. Yet, at the same time that the term is an encapsulation and derivative of a particular figural (poetic) vocabulary, in this case highly idealized, it is also a "philosopheme." Through this attribution, Derrida explicitly places *pharmakon* alongside other of his key meta-tropes as "supplement," "difference," "trace," and "writing" itself in a compendium of poetically charged, philosophically driven figures underscoring the swerves constantly besetting language—both as it vacillates between conceptual rigor and poetic invention and between the dual approbation and censure tendered by the various social systems of authority.

Now that Derrida has interposed it, *pharmakon*, the new (and doubled) focal point of Platonic philosophy, fans out without restriction in the collection, linkage, and reorientation of the "classical" terminologies and disciplinary bearings that have hitherto addressed the phenomenon of Greek idealism. In the second of the extracts immediately above, Derrida pauses at the implications of *pharmakon* for the agonizing Western tension between "natural" (*mnēmē*) and artificial memory (*hypomnēmē*), a cultural ambivalence much on his mind at this period as he approaches Freud.[14] (Less the modern Plato as authoritative spelunker of the soul, Freud emerges: architect of the subconscious as an *archive*, with its full cybernetic implications, the very bastion of a memory replete with its contrivance and artificiality—yet no less indispensable a force in thinking and living.) Derrida continues, in this extract, exploring the uncanny doubling by which the medication, as life-saver, could assimilate the toxic qualities of a poison. Each new entry in the complex of "logocentrism," Western metaphysics' inevitable and relentless gravitation toward the interests (and politics) of speech—whether "nature"/"artificiality," "remedy"/"poison," "legitimacy"/"illegitimacy," or "memory"/"artificial memory," falls under the sway of the *pharmakon*. And this Platonic meta-textual trope thus rescued from obscurity, in the thrust of its *performance* (remembering that Derrida insisted on a performative "swerve" to the nuanced reading-process), freely fluctuates between the opposed gravitational fields of classical categories and values. Under today's regime of cybernetic organization and binary languages, *pharmakon* serves the function of a *digital switch*: "It reverses them [the opposed belief systems], or makes one side cross over into the other."

The vast store of volatile intellectual energy, broad scholarly erudition and fascination, and penetrating insight that Derrida unleashed in the derivation of the *pharmakon* sets the agenda for the remainder of Derrida's work, whether delegated to the formal arguments, concepts, and structures at the heart of Kant, Hegel, Hermann Cohen,[15] Husserl, Heidegger, Levinas, and other philosophers, or in celebration of the awesome creativities of Shakespeare, Mallarmé, Ponge, Artaud, Genet, Celan, and perhaps above all, Joyce. The *pharmakon* also sets the writerly and conceptual bar for Derrida's published work at a dauntingly high level, a mark never placed in jeopardy by his prolific production, set for some three decades at a feverish pace in order to keep up with a taxing round of writing commitments and conferences all over the world.

Derrida's emergent writing scenario, the loose tracking of a meta-figure or trope within a particularly prominent or persistent textual "local climate" (otherwise: "environment" or "ground") of cultural inscription—with meticulous attention to the singularities of its linguistic provenance, articulation, and variance from itself, in effect secured for deconstruction a passport enabling itself to freely cross the boundaries and finesse the protective tariffs imposed by academic disciplines and discursive genres. The composite "discipline," with elements of mainstream philosophy, deep philology, twentieth-century linguistics, psychoanalytical apprehension, French *sciences humaines*, the emergent cultural studies already embedded in the margins of Barthes and Foucault, and sheer dogged scholarship fully at work in "Plato's Pharmacy," extends to the studies encompassed within the early essay collections, from the inaugural *Writing and Difference* (1967; English, 1978) to *Margins of Philosophy* (1972; English, 1982), and *Dissemination* (1972; English, 1981). Whatever the issuing agencies for the categories that the Derridean approach stridently overstepped—prose, drama, poetry, or letters; cultural studies, sociology, philosophy, law, or architecture; metaphysics, ethics, logic, aesthetics, or ontology—deconstructive reading isolated the operative figures on which telling documents and works both founded their distinction and foundered in their explicit design. In the wake of Derrida's early period (1965–80) during which he both establishes the modality of deconstruction as a contrapuntal *bearing* and assembles a vast network of writers and works placed into communication by deconstructive exegeses, he develops no less than eight distinctive critical sub-literatures all consistent with practices evolved during the early studies of Husserl and in the initial contributions to *Critique, Tel Quel, Glyph*, and related publications:

1. following from the analysis of writing systems and their early modern mythologies in *Of Grammatology*, a body of work on media, memory and its storage, and modalities of reproduction and representation in culture and technology. Not only does this dimension of scrutiny pervade his "Ulysses Gramophone";[16] it sets the agenda for such further writings as "Typewriter Ribbon: Limited Ink (2)";[17]

2. a collection of in-depth theoretical studies on literary authors and works, arising on the occasions of Shakespeare, Mallarmé, Ponge, and Joyce among others,

following very much along the lines of "Plato's Pharmacy," always with the specific figurations conjured and synthesized by their authors as "strange loops" or "pivots";

3. from early on, an impact study of the implications of deconstructive apprehensions and measures upon the prevailing academic division of labor, whether the Papal line of demarcation, in philosophy, between the "analytic" tradition (in critique as well as philosophy proper) and a philologically and poetically immanent counterpoint, emergent from "Continental" sources; or the twentieth-century correlative to the Kantian "battle of the faculties." For example, the very early piece from *Writing and Difference* on "restricted" and "general economy" (otherwise put: open and closed system)[18] in Georges Bataille,[19] a vibrant critic whose disciplinary calling card of convenience may well have been sociology, is a bellwether to deconstruction's vast disciplinary outreach. Derrida's overarching inquiry into the logic and ideology underlying the territoriality of various academic subjects and aesthetic genres is inextricable from another ongoing trajectory of his writing, the declaration of a performative dimension in discourse, indicative of a collaboration with aesthetics reaching far beyond what is possible by means of scholastic categorization and paraphrase. Such early works as "Signature Event Context"[20] and "Limited Inc abc. . ."[21] are infused with a precise calculation of what is at stake in the late twentieth-century philosophical turf-wars. At the same time, they articulate the deconstructive position with regard to several key arguments espoused by the contemporary analytical philosopher John Searle, along with John Austin, whose logical analysis-inspired *How to Do Things with Words* had impacted powerfully on criticism as disseminated through English departments. While Derrida can only applaud (and even one-up) the rigorous isolation of the irreducibly performative dimension of vows, curses, declarations, and the like, he takes strong issue with the assertion that a proper analysis could account for entire categories of speech acts. His insistence on the distortion effects accruing from the *context* in which locutions are made and speech acts generated is akin to his cognizance of the singularity that "local difference" infuses into theories of writing and instances of literary exegesis alike;[22]

4. contributions to the study of aesthetics, addressing, in Derrida's writings on Kant (in *Truth in Painting*),[23] the contradictory status of the ornament; with respect to Blanchot, an inspired response to the arbitrariness of genre categories, literary and otherwise.[24] It is within the framework of his aesthetic writings that Derrida's work on the visual arts, whether his commentary on the painter Valerio Adami or the architectural projects and commentaries done in conjunction with Peter Eisenman,[25] would need to be placed;

5. political writings, beginning with early meditations on his native Algeria's independence from French colonial rule.[26] Also including major works devoted to the "specter" of Marx as a congenitally "out of joint" call to democracy, justice, and radical reappropriation persisting to the present day; on the momentous impact and ideological aporias surrounding the designation of Hebrew as *the* national language of the State of Israel;[27] and concerning the ideological, figural underpinnings beneath the coercive practices of such supra-national agencies as the World Bank and IMF as they bring less stable economies in check and in step;

6. theological writings, beginning with the early essay on Jabès and continuing in his attentiveness to Levinas.[28] Within this framework, Derrida is both capable of questioning such deep-seated beliefs and practices as circumcision[29] and sacrificing one's life for another;[30] and of "chunking" the overarching tenets of the three major monotheistic world religions into a shared conceptual platform, thus highlighting the tenuousness of sectarian strife and violence, whether between Judaism, Christianity, and Islam or between their sub-sects;

7. ethical writings, in many respects congruent with (5), in which Derrida can broach questions of responsibility in critique and cultural participation as well as in conduct. In this conjunction, the essay "Faith and Knowledge" is particularly compelling, as is *Politics of Friendship*.[31] The former pursues a vertiginous sequence of cultural ramifications extending from the complex signifier, "religion," which in deconstructive parlance itself fluctuates atop a doubled etymology. Among the semantic byways that Derrida charts in the essay, through which religion exerts a massive impact, inchoate as well as explicit, on Western societies, are its tightly woven links to responsibility, sacrifice, faith, belief, and violence;

8. experimental writings, beginning with the frontispiece to *Margins of Philosophy*, entitled "Tympan," but mutating with a vengeance in the epistolary "Envois" section of *The Post Card* (1980; 1987 English translation): here the performative "secret sharer" in the process of deconstructive inscription manages to gain the upper hand. The "occasion" for this celebration of the conjunctions between Greek philosophy, active eroticism, a growing worldwide intellectual "web" (or community) of deconstruction, and psychoanalysis happens to be an engraving that Derrida has discovered at the Bodleian Library, Oxford, the frontispiece of the thirteenth-century *Prognostica Socratis basilei* by Matthew Paris, a fortune-telling book; or rather, a postcard version of the artwork, sent to various recipients as a vital sign of this explosive moment in Derrida's creativity. Outrageous, self-indulgent, overflowing with the pleasures of a life that has caught up with the balletic pyrotechnics of deconstruction, "Envois," included in a volume also containing Derrida's feedback to Lacanian psychoanalysis, a text also pirouetting around texts transmitted by post (in this case Poe's "The Purloined Letter")[32] is an instance, along with key passages of "Plato's Pharmacy" and the extended Mallarmé essay, "The Double Session," where critique crosses the frontier into literary composition for its own sake and pleasure. It would be remiss not to also mention in this regard the other major radically experimental work of this period, in fact referenced in *The Post Card*: *Glas* (1974; 1986, English translation). *Glas* sustains two simultaneous lines of critique: one, highlighting the ambiguities surrounding the Hegelian *Philosophy of Right*, typeset as the left column of every page; and counterbalanced, on the right, by an extended celebration of the radically transgressive ethics (ironically, of a higher spirituality than the Hegelian) embodied by Jean Genet, whom Derrida had met at Parisian dinners hosted by Paule and Yves Thevénin in the mid-1960s. What may well be most unique about *Glas* is the fashion in which Derrida manages to correlate strategic variations in the bicolumnar typesetting with substantial correlations, divergences, and counterpoints transpiring in the interstitial zone between the texts (and *bearings*) of Hegel and Genet.

It remains for cultural history to determine whether the pitched controversies that deconstruction had a way of setting off were substantial or overblown "tempests in teapots." But in their multiple venues, from Paris to Yale, where Derrida was declared a non-philosopher, to Prague, where he was arrested for participating in a philosophical seminar deemed subversive, and to Oxford, where he was denied an honorary degree, deconstruction's pugilistic side-shows, in their day, drew sharp attention to the Humanities and to the broader sociopolitical issues under its academic stewardship. That the Alt-Right would "raid" the term for the purposes of legitimating a regime notable for the violence of its reductionism and its anti-intellectualism is a notable, and to some degree notorious attestation to the wide swathe that "deconstruction" cut. This bizarre, fleeting cultural epiphenomenon only underscores the pressing need for the "task of deconstruction" to be carried on and diversified with even greater resolve than ever, and in keeping with the consummate conceptual and ethical rigor and finitude that Derrida embedded at the outset within its "practice."

Yale University (United States)

NOTES

1. Max Fisher, "Stephen K. Bannon's CPAC Comments, Annotated and Explained," *New York Times*, The Interpreter. https://www.nytimes.com/2017/02/24/us/politics/stephen-bannon-cpac-speech.html

2. "The Next Four Years," *Yale Alumni Magazine* (January–February 2017): 48. https://yalealumnimagazine.com/articles/4425-the-next-four-years

3. According to the current authoritative biography of Derrida, by Benoît Peeters, Derrida inaugurated the rhetoric of *deconstruction* in "Writing Before the Letter" (*L'Écriture avant la léttre*), an extended review-article published in the esteemed Parisian journal, *Critique*, in December 1965 and January 1966. The term, bearing its fully nuanced palette of senses, would be in full force throughout the presentation pieces of 1967, notably in *Speech and Phenomena* (*La Voix et le phénomène*) and *Of Grammatology* (*De la Grammatologie*). See Benoît Peeters, *Derrida: A Biography* (Cambridge: Polity, 2013), 159–60.

4. Jacques Derrida, *Of Grammatology*, trans. Gayatri Chakravorty Spivak (Baltimore: Johns Hopkins University Press, 1976); 251, 260, 268, 280–81.

5. A "minority report," on the Derridean sub-literature keyed to the *counter-rhythm* to this particular scenario, demands issue at this very juncture. If not debunking masterworks that have already, through cant generalization, or sheer overlooking, "outgrown their breeches" within the compass of Western culture's compilation volume of itself, deconstructive writing keys on the most "minor" productions, ones at the threshold of oblivion, but in fact signposting a highroad to deeper philosophical deliberation than had been previously undertaken.

6. This is a term that contemporary physics has developed to characterize the pattern, that eventually intervenes in situations of physical turbulence, for example, in liquid or states. Through the phenomenon of "strange attractors," science and technology thus gain the leverage to characterize and to some degree predict, if not to manage, highly turbulent physical conditions, whether liquid or gaseous. In effect correlatives from the physical world to highly volatile, polysemic figures of speech, the relevance of strange attractors to deconstructive mega-tropes or "infrastructures" should be readily apparent. See James Gleick, *Chaos: Making a New Science* (London: Penguin, 1988), 122–53.

7. The immense playfulness that Douglas R. Hofstadter was able to access and deploy in accounting for the immense sea-changes that were about to take place in "advanced"

societies through the widespread dissemination of cybernetic technologies is an intellectual achievement well deserving to be placed alongside the illuminations furnished by deconstruction—many of which arose at roughly the same time. This in spite of the techno-quantitative nature of the phenomena that he observed and to a significant degree inaugurated. The figure of the "strange loop" is above all a phenomenon by which a script of writing (musical notes, drawing, and numeration, as well as discourse as he profoundly demonstrates in *Gödel Escher Bach*), stretches against the limitations of its own dimensionality in attaining a meta-operational level, one capable of commenting upon and modifying itself. The overall drift of "strange loops," then, is in the direction of what systems theorists term "autopoiesis." See Douglas R. Hofstadter, *Gödel, Escher, Bach: An Eternal Golden Braid* (New York: Vintage, 1979). For what is perhaps Hofstadter's most graphic illumination of the phenomenon of "strange loops," see Douglas R. Hofstadter, *I Am a Strange Loop* (New York: Basic Books, 2007), 99–104.

8. The systolic/diastolic rhythm between "open" and "closed" systems as entertained by the radical social sciences of the 1960s and 1970s and by the forerunners to contemporary computer science is a most fruitful context in which to gauge Derrida's mega-intervention. My thoughts here run to Gregory Bateson, whose encomia to what he called "loose thinking" and whose insight into the systematic production of (and reliance upon) difference might without exaggeration be called *proto-deconstructive*; also to Anthony Wilden, who melded the radical anthropology of Bateson and the antipodal psychoanalysis of Jacques Lacan into an uncannily prescient progress report on the status of systematic organizations at the outset of the cybernetic age. See Gregory Bateson, *Steps to an Ecology of Mind* (Chicago: University of Chicago Press, 2000); Anthony Wilden, *System and Structure* (London: Tavistock, 1972), 172–74, 178–88, 202–10, 354, 357–64, 367–70.

9. Jacques Derrida, *Rogues: Two Essays on Reason*, trans. Pascale-Anne Brault and Michael Naas (Stanford: Stanford University Press, 2005), 8.

10. Derrida, *Rogues*, 9.

11. Ibid., 10–11.

12. Jacques Derrida, "Plato's Pharmacy," *Dissemination*, trans. Barbara Johnson (Chicago: University of Chicago Press, 1983), 71–72.

13. Derrida, "Plato's Pharmacy," 126–27.

14. "Freud and the Scene of Writing," in Jacques Derrida, *Writing and Difference,* trans. Alan Bass (Chicago: University of Chicago Press, 1978), 196–231.

15. "Interpretation at War: Kant, the Jew, the German," in Jacques Derrida, *Acts of Religion,* ed. Gil Anidjar (New York: Routledge, 2002), 137–88.

16. "Ulysses Gramophone," in Jacques Derrida, *Acts of Literature,* ed. Derek Attridge (New York: Routledge, 1991), 353–309.

17. In Jacques Derrida, *Without Alibi*, ed. and trans. Peggy Kamuf (Stanford: Stanford University Press, 2000), 71–160.

18. See footnote 8.

19. "From Restricted to General Economy: A Hegelianism without Reserve," in Jacques Derrida, *Writing and Difference*, trans. Alan Bass (Chicago: University of Chicago Press, 1978), 251–77.

20. Jacques Derrida, "Signature Event Context," in *Glyph 1* (Baltimore: Johns Hopkins University Press, 1977), 172–97.

21. Jacques Derrida, "Limited Inc abc...," in *Glyph 2* (Baltimore: Johns Hopkins University Press, 1977), 162–253.

22. Also see, with respect to speech acts and performatives, "Le Parjure, Perhaps" in Jacques Derrida, *Without Alibi*, ed. and trans. Peggy Kamuf (Stanford: Stanford University Press, 2002), 161–201.

23. Jacques Derrida, *The Truth in Painting*, trans. Geoffrey Bennington and Ian McLeod (Chicago: University of Chicago Press, 1987).

24. "The Law of Genre," in Jacques Derrida, *Acts of Literature*, ed. Derek Attridge (New York: Routledge, 1991), 221–52.

25. Jacques Derrida and Peter Eisenman, *Chora L Works* (New York: Monacelli Press, 1997).

26. "Taking a Stand for Algeria," in Jacques Derrida, *Acts of Religion,* ed. Gil Anidjar (New York: Routledge, 2002), 299–308.

27. "The Eyes of Language: The Abyss and the Volcano," in Jacques Derrida, *Acts of Religion*, 189–227.

28. "Edmond Jabès and the Question of the Book," in Jacques Derrida, *Writing and Difference*, 64–78; "Violence and Metaphysics: An Essay on the thought of Emmanuel Levinas," in Jacques Derrida, *Writing and Difference*, 79–153.

29. Jacques Derrida and Geoffrey Bennington, *Jacques Derrida: Derrida Base/Circumfession* (Chicago: University of Chicago Press, 1993). Also see "A Silkworm of One's Own," in Jacques Derrida, *Acts of Religion*, 309–55.

30. See, on this latter point, Jacques Derrida, *The Gift of Death,* trans. David Wills (Chicago: University of Chicago Press, 1995). French version, 1992.

31. "Faith and Knowledge," in Jacques Derrida, *Acts of Religion*, 40–101. Jacques Derrida, *Politics of Friendship,* trans. George Collins (New York: Verso, 1997).

32. "Le Facteur de la Vérité," in Jacques Derrida, *The Post Card,* trans. Alan Bass (Chicago: University of Chicago Press, 1987), 411–96.

WORKS CITED

Bateson, Gregory. *Steps to an Ecology of Mind.* Chicago: University of Chicago Press, 2000.

Derrida, Jacques. *Of Grammatology* [1967]. Trans. Gayatri Chakravorty Spivak. Baltimore: Johns Hopkins University Press, 1976.

Derrida, Jacques. "Limited Inc abc..." In *Glyph 2*. Baltimore: Johns Hopkins University Press, 1977. 162–253.

Derrida, Jacques. "Signature Event Context." In *Glyph 1*. Baltimore: Johns Hopkins University Press, 1977. 172–97

Derrida, Jacques. *Writing and Difference* [1967]. Trans. Alan Bass. Chicago: University of Chicago Press, 1978.

Derrida, Jacques. "Plato's Pharmacy." In *Dissemination* [1972]. Trans. Barbara Johnson. Chicago: University of Chicago Press, 1981. 61–172.

Derrida, Jacques. *Margins of Philosophy* [1972]. Trans. Alan Bass. Chicago: Chicago University Press, 1982.

Derrida, Jacques. *The Truth in Painting* [1978]. Trans. Geoffrey Bennington and Ian McLeod. Chicago: University of Chicago Press, 1987.

Derrida, Jacques. *The Post Card* [1980]. Trans. Alan Bass. Chicago: University of Chicago Press, 1987.

Derrida, Jacques. *Acts of Literature.* Ed. Derek Attridge. New York: Routledge, 1991.

Derrida, Jacques. *The Gift of Death* [1992]. Trans. David Wills. Chicago: University of Chicago Press, 1995.

Derrida, Jacques. *Politics of Friendship* [1994]. Trans. George Collins. New York: Verso, 1997.

Derrida, Jacques. *Acts of Religion*. Ed. Gil Anidjar. New York: Routledge, 2002.

Derrida, Jacques. *Without Alibi* [2000]. Ed. and trans. Peggy Kamuf. Stanford: Stanford University Press, 2002.

Derrida, Jacques. *Rogues: Two Essays on Reason* [2003]. Trans. Pascale-Anne Brault and Michael Naas. Stanford: Stanford University Press, 2005.

Derrida, Jacques, and Geoffrey Bennington. *Jacques Derrida: Derrida Base/Circumfession* [1991]. Chicago: University of Chicago Press, 1993.

Derrida, Jacques, and Peter Eisenman. *Chora L Works*. New York: Monacelli Press, 1997.

Fisher, Max. "Stephen K. Bannon's CPAC Comments, Annotated and Explained." *New York Times*. The Interpreter. https://www.nytimes.com/2017/02/24/us/politics/stephen-bannon-cpac-speech.html

Gleick, James. *Chaos: Making a New Science*. London: Penguin, 1988.

Hofstadter, Douglas R. *Gödel, Escher, Bach: An Eternal Golden Braid*. New York: Vintage, 1979.

Hofstadter, Douglas R. *I Am a Strange Loop*. New York: Basic Books, 2007.

Peeters, Benoît. *Derrida: A Biography* [2010]. Trans. Andrew Brown. Cambridge: Polity, 2013.

"The Next Four Years." *Yale Alumni Magazine* (January–February 2017). https://yalealumnimagazine.com/articles/4425-the-next-four-years

Wilden, Anthony. *System and Structure*. London: Tavistock, 1972.

CHAPTER TEN

Feminism

ROBIN TRUTH GOODMAN

We are used to hearing about the history of feminism as a story about waves. First, there was the "First Wave," often starting with Mary Astell or Mary Wollstonecraft's revisions of rights. The "First Wave" includes women's agitations for educational (e.g., Virginia Woolf), religious (e.g., Sarah Moore Grimké and Angelina Emily Grimké), economic (e.g., Charlotte Perkins Gilman), health (e.g., Margaret Sanger, Marie Stopes), civic (e.g., Jane Addams), and political access in suffrage (e.g., Susan B. Anthony, Elizabeth Cady Stanton). After the vote was won, feminism went into abeyance, with some telltale clues of the continued gestation of its commitments: for example, Margaret Meade's theories of sex roles in the 1930s and, prominently, the publication of Simone de Beauvoir's *The Second Sex* in the 1940s as well as Betty Friedan's exposition of women's secret malady in the early 1960s.

Then came the "Second Wave," following on the Sexual Revolution of the 1960s with its leftist orientations, and advocating for equal rights, equal wages, equal representation, and sexual liberation. The "Second Wave" included Kate Millet's crushing attack on literary sexism and Juliette Mitchell's articulation in the early 1970s of the importance of psychoanalysis as a counter-ideological feminist tool, where feminism would share with the psychoanalytic Unconscious the analytical presumption that "something persists that is incommensurate with the real social situation."[1] At the same time, the Combahee River Collective of black feminists was formed "most obviously," as they write in their foundational statement, "in connection with the second wave of the American women's movement beginning in the late 1960s."[2] They note that "Black, other Third World, and working women have been involved in the feminist movement from the start"[3] but have been marginalized because of elitism in the movement. Even so, the feminist "political analysis and practice that we women use to struggle against our oppression"[4] was what inspired the formation of a separate group of black feminists with an eye toward ending oppressions of all sorts while lending credibility to the movement as a whole.

In the late 1970s and 1980s, during the fervor of the Women's Liberation Movement, women's studies was institutionalized in universities even as feminism took on many glosses and political frameworks, from a "radical feminism" that fervently opposed violence against women and the legal systems that defended and even encouraged it (e.g., Andrea Dworkin, Catherine MacKinnon), to a "liberal feminism" with its faith in equality, recognition, and a broader inclusion (e.g., Elaine Showalter, Sandra Gilbert, Susan Gubar), to a "difference feminism" (e.g., bell hooks, This-Bridge-Called-My-Back Collective). As the story goes, though energetic in thinking and action, the "Second Wave" was soon riddled by deep schisms as black, queer, Chicana, transnational, postcolonial, and other feminisms shook up its subjective unity and universalisms. Additionally, science studies (e.g., Donna Haraway, Sandra Harding, Anne Fausto-Sterling) put into doubt long-standing conceptions of nature and divisions between consciousness, on the one hand, and, on the other, bodies, empirical fact, or matter.

New perspectives deemed earlier analyses—which, supposedly, assumed the identity of "women" as sharing a singular empirical experience of oppression—as "essentialist"—that is, as assuming social meanings as carried naturally in bodies, as though physical fact (like bodies) and consciousness (ideology, or the social-symbolic) were inextricably imbricated. Postmodernism weighed in, with its abstraction of "difference" into a linguistic effect, its skepticism about representation altogether, its adamant anti-essentialism, its fierce social constructivism based in structural linguistics, psychoanalysis, and deconstruction, making the very idea of an identity called "woman" seem like a throw-back to patriarchy. In other words, feminists started to question the word "woman" for its representational value, exposing how "women's experiences" were constructed falsely as self-evident forms of living—through such institutions as medicine, biology, and psychoanalysis, the meanings of the word "women" were made to seem ingrained in women's bodies, determining their experiences, when they were actually expressions of social hierarchies, discursive structures, and distributions of power. As historian Joan Scott astutely clarifies, "When the evidence offered is the evidence of 'experience,' the claim for referentiality is further buttressed—what could be truer, after all, than a subject's own account of what he or she has lived through? It is precisely this kind of appeal to experience as uncontestable evidence and as an originary point of explanation—as a foundation upon which analysis is based—that weakens the critical thrust of histories of difference."[5] Scott challenges researchers to consider the language forms that brought identities into existence at certain historical moments—like the universalism of rights discourse—rather than to assume that identities like "women," recognized as a certain type of experience, always existed as such.

In the 1990s, we are told, a new generation of feminists entered the scene who saw the "Second Wave" as restrictive, too serious, and too white, and interpreted the postmodern "turn" as devoid of politics. The reaction was a "materialist turn," a quasi-rejection of the "linguistic" or "cultural turn" of the postmodern moment. "Dominant constructivist orientation to social analysis," note, for example, the editors of *The New Materialisms,* referring to the "cultural turn," "is inadequate for thinking about matter, materiality, and politics."[6] This "materialist turn" coincides with an interest in contexts outside of Western philosophical tradition, an ascendance of social science over the humanities, and a greater attention to empiricism, objects, and "real experience." Thus a "Third Wave" developed, focused on difference, bodies, and their pleasures, unbound by a discourse of representation and rights and seemingly more global, partly because of its embrace of commodity culture as a means to independent, singular self-expression and identity formation. "Media texts like *Buffy the Vampire Slayer* are moving to the forefront of critical inquiry and are being taken seriously by third wave feminists," writes, for example, Michele Byers in the field-defining anthology *Catching a Wave.* "One of our jobs is to recognize feminist moments in these texts."[7] This inclination toward popular culture coincides with what some have called "post-feminism," with some women declaring that feminism has outlived its need, or that equality has been achieved and feminism is over, and turning to a celebration of the womanness of individual women and their choice. As Alison Phipps has remarked, "Elements of the feminist critique of feminism, namely those focused on cultural and identity-based recognition, have been co-opted in the current political context,"[8] so that identity itself has become a marketable form to further a consumerism that empties subjectivity and reduces politics to aesthetics or entertainment.

This historical scheme roughly traces the three generations of feminists outlined in Julia Kristeva's famous essay "Women's Time": the first stage is composed of "suffragists and existential feminists" and "was deeply rooted in the sociopolitical life of nations";[9] the second stage is associated with "aesthetic or psychoanalytic experiences"[10] with a "highly pronounced mistrust of political life," more interested in "the specificity of feminine psychology," issues of representation and language;[11] the third stage brings into play a new generation, dismissive of socialism and collective identity representations, and steeped in the unique singularity of subjects depicted in Freudian configurations of difference—"the singularity of each woman, her complexities, her many languages"[12] taking the place of the religious iconicity that universal Woman adopted in her opposition to universal Man.

WAIVING THE WAVES

The "wave" story, then, frames a critical feminist theory's history where racial and sexual diversity enters at a certain point as a rejection of the past and as a corrective. Black feminists, we have learned, suddenly burst into the open, blaming the "Second Wave" for positing a universal experience of oppression for all those seemingly marked equally by the term "woman," and creating a better discursive structure out of the ashes. Unlike the "First and Second Waves," we learn from the "Third Wave," for the first time (such theorists believe), the diversity of a possible feminism that could claim the legacy of civil rights. Though certainly such criticisms voiced a substantial grievance against some of feminism's universalist tendencies, they at times seemed to bind together all of feminist innovation under a generalized simplification where every feminist assertion might be read as bounded by and making sense only through racism. "Racism abounds in the writings of white feminists," declares, for example, bell hooks, "reinforcing white supremacy and negating the possibility that women will bond politically across ethnic and racial boundaries. Past feminist refusal to draw attention to and attack racial hierarchies suppressed the link between race and class."[13] "In trying to become 'objective,'" adds Chicana queer feminist Gloria Anzaldúa, describing what she calls *mestiza* consciousness, "Western culture" including feminism, "made 'objects' of things and people when it distanced itself from them, thereby losing 'touch' with them. This dichotomy is the root of all violence."[14]

In this perspective, "Third World feminism" intersects with the "Third Wave," showing that the "First and Second Waves" inhibited feminism from realizing its true self as radically polyglot, racially proliferating, global and individualizing at the same time, making any total narrative impossible. Publishing what is considered a groundbreaking work in transnational feminism, Inderpal Grewal and Caren Kaplan, for example, propose, "We are interested in problematizing theory; more specifically, feminist theory. In many locations in the United States and Europe, theory often tends to be a homogenizing move by many First World women and men. That is, theory seems unable to deal with alterity at all or falls into a kind of relativism."[15] Such assertions were interpreted as a condemnation and a rejection, though a more careful reading might have shown that hooks's, Anzaldúa's, and many postcolonial critics' relation to feminism was more complicated. bell hooks, for example, often refers to feminism as a necessary if unfinished critique of domination and authority even as she lambasts some feminists for speaking in the place of minorities or not paying proper attention to perspectives and articulations of nonwhites. "Third wave feminist movements," Kyoo Lee characterizes rejectionist readings in a recent volume critical of the "Third Wave," "highlight and mobilize what was not fully registered or even completely ignored by the first and second wave feminists, namely that women are diverse."[16] Yet, instead of rejecting all prior feminist thought as corrupted under feminism's essentializing and racist past, Lee understands how feminism might reappropriate and retemporalize its reflective terms, building out from its own narratives and critiques like rereading Simone de Beauvoir's "invisible grammar"[17] as receptive to alterity.

Allegations that feminism is thoroughly corrupted (even worse than cancer, as some have declared), instead of partial or in process, have, indeed, been appropriated and twisted by a far right contingent. "There is a need now," write, for example, Phyllis Chesler and Donna M. Hughes in the *Washington Post* (2004), "in the opening years of the twenty-first century, to rethink feminism."[18] Chesler and Hughes talk about feminism's lack of attention to Third World issues, particularly in the face of Islamic fundamentalism, and the only way to combat women's oppression is to extend war. Those making such arguments—former First Lady Laura Bush among them—are not generally radical advocates of women's rights and safety on other issues such as abortion access or marriage equality.

Writers of the "First and Second Waves" are identified in much "Third Wave" analyses as assuming that all women share a similar, essential experience of being in women's bodies even if the social positioning of those bodies were culturally constructed rather than biologically determined. In such criticisms, "race" comes to represent all that is blind in the "First and Second Waves," and thus to become in itself the true sign that proves earlier inequality. The "Third Wave" can thus promote itself as a better, faster, improved version that overcomes a sordid and shameful past. Earlier versions of feminism, particularly socialist feminism (e.g., Selma James, Sheila Rowbotham, Sylvia Federici), that considered where women and their work stood in relation to the wage economy, became part of the "old bad" feminism, too Western and too white and too universalist (e.g., a field-consolidating book like *Third Wave Feminism: A Critical Exploration* barely discusses class).

I would never contest—in fact, I would severely oppose—any claim that earlier feminisms were devoid of racism. However, even as past feminist texts may have clear indications of racist, provincial, and/or essentialist inclinations or, at best, an indefensible lack of awareness, to box-in *all past feminism* as racist and as expressive only of racism homogenizes feminism's traditions as reduced to one of its traits while throwing away as unrecoverable all the concepts that those traditions have developed. This move repeats the kinds of exclusionary gestures that these critics seem to reject in the "First and Second Waves." As Diana Fuss has asked, "Has essentialism received a bad rap? Few other words in the vocabulary of contemporary critical theory are so persistently maligned, so little interrogated, and so predictably summoned as a term of infallible critique."[19]

Part of the problem of the "wave" picture, too, is that the stages are unclearly delineated, so that different perspectives sometimes get conferred on one wave and sometimes on another, the dividing lines between stages are ambivalently placed and often contradictory, or parts of a text get ignored to make the defining mode of the stage seem prevalent. Judith Butler, for example, developed a theory of "gender as performance" that has become ubiquitous in many different kinds of feminist arguments. Yet, her place in the "wave" parameters is nearly impossible to determine: she might be claimed as "postfeminist" (as she herself suggests), because she puts into doubt whether there is anything essential in the identity of "woman" and whether feminism can have a subject;[20] or as "Second Wave," because many of the references and antecedents through which she constructs her feminist theory belong to the "Second Wave" and particularly to Beauvoir's legacy; or as "post-structuralist," because of her reliance on theories of language and representation, though she herself does not adopt that rubric to describe her work; or as not even engaged with feminism but with "queer theory," because she introduces sexuality as a construction, though she builds on traditions of feminist thought. And who cares about any of these questions anyway—how does our thinking advance by gathering ideas into stagnant academic categories?

The "wave" narrative has other implications as well. Barbara Johnson warns that the framing of feminist history through generations cannot "achieve a full elaboration of any discursive position other than that of child,"[21] restoring women to the singular biological essentialism of the maternal body, while Hemming cautions that the generational account of feminist history places scholarly debate "within a *family drama*,"[22] riddled by psychoanalytic conflicts, melancholia, and lack that were dominantly heterosexualizing. As Stacy Gillis, Gillian Howie, and Rebecca Munford argue, the wave analogy "reduces the complexity of each of these three waves"[23] and the social antagonisms that inhabit them, marking each stage as unified in itself. What might happen if we were to admit that this accepted vision of feminist history is wrong, Hemming asks, in that it erases the connection of feminism's liberating impulses with decolonizing histories and marginalizes the connection of feminism to lesbian history by equating sexuality with the mistakes of the "cultural turn"?

Additionally, the triumphalism of the "Third Wave" has adopted, perhaps inadvertently, a perspective that dovetails with a commercial and politically cynical attack on feminist history's advance. Speaking of the "Third Wave" as not opposed to the "Second" but rather existing alongside it, Leslie Heywood and Jennifer Drake nevertheless define their "Third Wave" project being "hard at work on a feminism that strategically combines elements of [equity feminism, gender feminism, and post-structuralism], and are now hard at work on a feminism that strategically combines elements of these feminisms, along with black feminism, women-of-color feminism, working-class feminism, pro-sex feminism, and so on."[24] There is no work cited here to show that equity, gender, and post-structuralist feminisms were devoid of black, women-of-color, working-class, or pro-sex feminisms, nor that they were somehow necessarily incapable, blinded from, or closed off to such challenges. Nor is there work cited to show what is "new"—how the "Third Wave" has broached something never before tried that bridges insurmountable gaps and developed techniques where the previously excluded can now, newly, play a part. Rather, the idea projected here is that "these feminisms" did not acknowledge the existence of the politics of race and, indeed, could not acknowledge this existence because of the essentialism embedded in what they defined as feminist goals and in the universalist subject they claimed for feminism, and that the present feminism is doing something different in kind. This staging of feminist history gives the "Third Wave" the power to characterize the "First and Second Waves" retrospectively in order to differentiate the past from the triumphal self-congratulations of a feminism having learned its lessons that its mothers could not learn (though what those lessons were remain obscure). Shutting down the radical momentum of the "First and Second Waves" by attributing it to the trash-heap of history's mistakes, such versions of the "Third Wave" promise the new and the transcendent like a shiny advertisement: you, too, can be Buffy in ways your mother never could!

The "Third Wave" might, then, be said to stake its claims by falsely unifying, settling, and boxing in the "First and Second Waves" at the expense of the impetus of feminism's incomplete project. As a feminist, such a perspective assumes, I am locked into my own subjective, locational, and generational experience, where what I can know is increasingly narrowed to my own (either biological or socially constructed) experience, and where I must be at the same time claiming to represent all other women's experience. Often, claims for recognition or calls for "voice" fix or naturalize identities within representations, attributing "authenticity" that makes the personal—particularly personal suffering—stand in for the whole. As, in the 1970s, feminists rallied around the slogan "the personal is political," now, seemingly, the personal is all that is left of the political.

Feminist theorists have pointed to the importance to feminism of, precisely, not nailing down meanings and of respecting that concepts engaged with social histories are necessarily going to be messy. Joan Scott, for example, teaches us that feminist history has to refuse "the certainty of disciplined history's categories" in order to take into account "the elusive pursuit of language" with its "emphasis on the unknowable";[25] gender is always in process, mixing perspectives, interrupting its own linearities, engaged in fantasies. Is the Third Wave's declaration of itself as "new," more diverse, and more inventive serving to pin down, realign, and malign a feminist history that never was, while disregarding the political breakthroughs of the one that was?

Beyond the "Third Wave"'s declarations that past feminisms are over, feminism sees itself as an open book, radical in its very openness, as Jürgen Habermas saw modernity as "the very celebration of dynamism" that "lives on the experience of rebelling against all that is normative."[26] For Habermas, the process of rational development and critique that was tied part and parcel to modernity was confiscated by the bureaucratic apparatus and commercial enterprises to the extent that this rebellion had to take the form of reason's turning against reason itself. The outcome was a triumphal celebration of the elusive, the contingent, the discontinuous, and the transitory that resisted connections to grand narratives but, because of this, allowed the narratives that sustained the present to remain "undefiled,"[27] while the vision of "the infinite advance towards social and moral betterment"[28] got derailed. Though certainly the ideal of universal progress has served imperialist interests and has been instrumental in reproducing inequalities, the promise of human emancipation still might be heralded as the power behind feminism's project. As Wendy Brown puts it, how does feminism and feminist scholarship live "without a revolutionary horizon?"[29] Whether or not one agrees with Habermas, one might still wonder if feminism similarly gave up too early on the radical and resistant strains in its discourse, and if those breaking into a new "stage" justified this break by mischaracterizing what was left behind as unworthy of its future. As Winifred Woodhull remarks, such feminists "appear to have forgotten second wave feminism's roots not only in the U.S. Civil Rights Movement but also in third world liberation movements as well, in which radical feminists of the 1960s and 1970s considered their own struggles to be inextricably implicated."[30] If we do not want to surrender feminism's political edge and anti-capitalist tendencies to commercialization, administered reason, and corporate complicity, it is imperative to ask what other stories we can tell.

SHE CAME TO STAY

Feminism cannot avoid the charge that its past had universalizing tendencies. Consider the "sex/gender system," a concept that for the last forty years has shaped feminist debate, where "sex" is the physical body and "gender" its cultural or discursive manifestation, independent of its anatomy. The "sex/gender system" was developed as a mode of explanation for the interactions between nature and culture, between bodies and the normalizing symbolic frameworks associated with them. Even as Gayle Rubin, an anthropologist who first coined the "sex/gender" concept, presents a variety of rituals and kinship systems that oppress women in a variety of ways, her stated goal is to find out the singular and original cause of patriarchy, explaining why women as women are oppressed everywhere and always: "One begins to have a sense of a systematic social apparatus which takes up females as raw materials and fashions domesticated women as products."[31] The conviction of a single origin of women's singular experience of oppression underlays the parallel conviction that a single solution would fix it. All we have to do, Rubin would conclude, is, "simply," to change culture, and women's oppression would end.

Rubin's version of the "sex/gender system" has limitations. For example, if "gender" is cultural and "sex" is the material substance of bodies, then why do we only have two genders or, for that matter, an understanding of "sex" based in a dimorphism? Even with the separation of the matter of the body from its cultural ideal or symbolic form, "sex" is still attached to "gender," and "gender" is ultimately locked into binary codes of sexual difference, so that "gender" seemed to precede the dualism of "sex," as its ontology. As one of the primary critics to put "queer theory" on the critical theory map, Judith Butler develops this point: "Gender ought not to be conceived merely as the cultural inscription of meaning on a pregiven sex. . . . Gender must also designate the very apparatus of production whereby the sexes themselves are established. As a result, gender is not to culture as sex is to nature; gender is also the discursive/cultural means by which 'sexed nature' or 'a natural sex' is produced and established as 'prediscursive,' prior to culture, a politically neutral surface *on which* culture acts."[32] Gender is the cultural system that makes bodies look like they belong to a unified sex. The resiliency of nature, the way it seems always to reassert its presence as "natural" within the constructivist logic of culture, is a problem for feminism because it implies that women are stuck in roles determined by their bodies. Giving up on nature, though, is also a predicament for feminism, because feminism at its core would seem to depend on a subject called "women." How, then, has feminism confronted such a paradox?

After Rubin's famous essay, the "sex/gender" system developed, as what Elizabeth Grosz has called, a "concept": concepts, she says, "are not means of control, but forms that carve out for us a space and time in which we may become capable of responding to the indeterminate particularity of events."[33] They are "ways of addressing the future, and in this sense are the conditions under which a future different from the present—the goal of every radical politics—becomes possible."[34] Concepts for Grosz are mixtures of culture and matter that clear space in the present for expressing the work of difference and the possible even as they are bound to the present. They are akin to what Jacqueline Rose has called "the 'failure' of identity,"[35] where our experiences are underrepresented and alienated within the cultural and symbolic apparatuses to which we belong, or what Emily Apter has termed "the Untranslatable," that is, "the limits of reference" and "the outer reach of thinkability"[36] brought to bear by language that is always in movement across time and space. "Untranslatability" insists that the concept cannot be secluded in a particular territory but is necessarily engaged across sites that are incomparable and disconnected, not belonging where it is, unamenable to being made the property of those that claim its authorship. The questions raised in these feminist interventions is whether the content of the concept coheres over time, or whether concepts operate to disrupt the present and its descriptions of itself, allowing the formation of alternatives to social and political oppression. That is, do concepts like the "sex/gender system" or even "women" have a determined content or can their terms of reference have a history and a future detachment from that history that returns as critique?

The treatment of gender as a social system precedes Rubin, already evident in the work of Simone de Beauvoir who many would name as the foremother of the "Second Wave." Some would accuse Beauvoir of, like Rubin, trapping women in the singular meaning of their biology, in universal opposition to biological men. For Beauvoir, women are, after all, "immanent," that is, immersed in the cycles of material nature, whereas men are "transcendent," free of the body and so able to freely pursue an idea. "Woman," she says, "has ovaries, a uterus; these particularities imprison her in her subjectivity, circumscribe her within the limits of her own nature."[37]

Yet, Beauvoir begins her book with a series of questions that suggest that such a situation is not inevitable: "One wonders," she admits "if women still exist, if they will always exist, whether or not it is desirable that they should, what place they occupy in this world, what their place has been."[38] "In speaking of certain women," she goes on, "connoisseurs declare that they are not women, although they are equipped with a uterus like the rest."[39] In the first chapter, on biology, Beauvoir concedes that, even though women's bodies are the place where the species asserts itself over and above the woman's capacities for individuation, sexuation is incomplete, "accidental or contingent"[40] and could be otherwise, while sexual difference and its hierarchies are environmentally variable, and sexual dimorphism for the purposes of species reproduction may someday become unnecessary. Here, Beauvoir is pushing the biological concept through translation and mistranslation, explaining sex as it appears in toads, birds, and honeybees in order to argue that sex moves, changes, and takes on multiple forms not only as constricted by nature and context but also responding to history's inducements. As Butler interprets it, women for Beauvoir are falsely represented because "the entire structure of representation [is] inadequate."[41] "Biology is not enough," Beauvoir states quite clearly, "to find out what humanity has made of the human female."[42] As Toril Moi interprets Beauvoir, "a woman defines herself through the way she lives her embodied situation in the world, or in other words, through the way in which she makes something of what the world makes her."[43] Steeped in social, symbolic, and material interactions, the body is not an inert mass receptive to the imprint of culture at a particular time or within a particular stream of time but rather is a set of lived meanings active in relation to an active world.

"Woman" or sex, then, is a concept that exists in translation. As Apter specifies, "The way in which [*The Second Sex*] pressed *sexe* into service as a multi-use term prepared the way for thinking about it as a philosophical Untranslatable that lends itself to the *contrasens,* a translation that reverses the logic or meaning of the original sentence."[44] Translation comes first rather than ontology. In fact, *The Second Sex* has inspired intense debates over its own translation because, Apter continues, its terminology tends to err, its word usage impossible to pin down. A leading voice in these debates, Moi has faulted the first translation as a "mangling of syntax, sentence structure and punctuation"[45] which fundamentally alters the intention and misses the point, turning the word "woman" into a synonym for culture when it is meant to remain untranslatable within culture (Moi thinks the second English translation is even worse). The terms that have couched "sex" within feminist theory are unamenable to ownership within a particular cultural formation or historical tradition, unconflatable to a singular meaning even within a single language, constantly speaking multiple conflicting languages at once, irresolvable.

THE WILD WOMAN

"The black abolitionist and freed slave, Sojourner Truth, spoke out at the Akron convention in 1851," begins Denise Riley's 1988 groundbreaking, influential work *Am I That Name?* in the heyday of the "Second Wave." "She rested her case on her refrain 'Ain't I a woman?'"[46] Riley is writing about the development of a historical situation, from the seventeenth century on, where "women" come to be seen as a particular identity that can advocate for a particular politics—in other words, the condition for feminism. This condition arises only after a long historical process. As different scientific, religious, social, and political discourses vie over the constitution of "the human," the identity of "women" forms both inside and outside these realignments so that "'women' is a simultaneous foundation of and an irritant to feminism."[47] By starting this tale in the words of a former slave who is, already in the nineteenth century, engaging with feminism through her discomfort with its subject, and even titling this major inaugural contribution to post-structuralist feminism in echoes of Sojourner's words, Riley exhibits the subject of feminism as a representation that is partial and excessive at once.

For Riley, "women" as an identity is difficult and disrupted: "Argued, stretched, dismembered, dragged hither and thither, re-aligned in every possible direction"[48] and never homogenized. "It is rarely, if ever, the case that all women will step forward as completely unified candidates for emancipation."[49] Feminism here is not complete because its concept has to contend with its impossible pretensions of a future universal ascription, always failing. This is what makes "women" an incoherent category as well as a category worthy of a feminist politics. Feminism's representation fails because it has to allude to a future alliance, a future self, that is determinant in the present but is at the same time unpredictable.

Other feminists have likewise seen the subject of feminism as vying for a coherence that can never be because its symbolic structure is contested by its representational contents. Julia Kristeva, for example, formulates the social-symbolic as a cultural imposition, a stable linguistic set of categories that is constantly antagonized and destabilized by unrepresentable, prelinguistic instinctual drives and psychosomatic functions connected to the mother. Kristeva calls these gestures and guttural sounds "the semiotic," using anthropology as well as psychoanalysis to show the violence that inhabits representations because of the "detritus" that representations expel, the unrepresentable inside. Mary Orr shows how Kristeva's trip to China with the *Tel Quel* group during the 1960s influenced this construction of the pre-symbolic, a translinguistic state or model of subjective production, linked to the maternal, that Kristeva develops in response to Mao's work policies excluding women as they became "reference points . . . for . . . the particularity of women's sexuality."[50] The symbolic of gender is, for Kristeva, doubled by "a dominant 'destructive wave' that is the drive's most characteristic trait" composed of "waves of attack against stases."[51] Words like "women" are torn apart by the destructive forces that bring them into being anew.

Maybe one of the "sex/gender" feminists generally understood as most essentialist, Hélène Cixous is best known for her theory of *écriture féminine*, or "feminine writing," which she put on the critical theory map in "The Laugh of the Medusa" and *The Newly Born Woman. Écriture féminine* is predominantly read as a theory that connects "feminine writing" to the experience of women's sexed bodies. Cixous says that women are barred from their bodies, "a world all her own which has been secretly haunting since early childhood."[52] Writing, or *écriture,* answers to this repression of women's sexed bodies with waves of substitutions that never lead back to the missing body but produce constantly mobilizing, emancipating, translating, and re-mashing textual motifs.

Less well known, perhaps, are Cixous's autobiographical texts about her childhood in Algeria in the 1950s, before the war of decolonization against the French (e.g., *Reveries of a Wild Woman: Primal Scenes, So Close, The Day I Wasn't There*, "My Algeriance, in Other Words: To Depart Not to Arrive from Algeria," "Letter to Zohra Drif," "The Names of Oran"). Growing up in Algiers where her family had immigrated to escape French anti-Semitism and then the Nazis, Cixous and her family lived outside the French quarter in an Arab neighborhood, when the French government denied French citizenship to her family as Jews as well as to Arabs and restricted educational access, even though her father was a military doctor. Robert Young has remarked on the importance of Algeria to the deconstructive project (many French theorists had experience in Algeria), attributing the split, decentered subject to the decolonizing "violence [that] makes subject double, doubly subject. . . an outsider to his or her own being. . . . It is by becoming a subject of violence that the dehumanized colonized subject becomes a subject for the first time."[53] The suppressed, unrepresented body of sex in *écriture* is a reverberation of a memory of her Algerian childhood, made inaccessible to symbolic form because of the war: "In the Casbah," she writes in "Letter to Zohra Drif," "the oldest of Algiers's cities, the most folded up, the convoluted one, the cascade of alleyways with the odours of urine and spices, the secret of Algiers, and, if I had been able to name it then by its hidden name, I would have called it the savage genitals, the antique femininity," she says, "vaginality."[54] The memory of her Algerian childhood lost (like the feminine body in *écriture*), Cixous makes a substitution by writing a letter to one of her Algerian schoolmates. The inaccessible that defines her bodily subjectivity (like the Unconscious or "need" in the psychoanalysis that she is interpreting) appears in the form of the inaccessible Algerian woman that is the identity of her future. Cixous, like Kristeva and Riley, foregrounds "women" as an unresolvable, unrepresentable identity—an identity caught up in language's inadequacies of symbolization never settling in their global travels; they are fractured because they develop inside historical ruptures like colonialism. Cixous wants her lost friend to answer the letter that she has addressed to her, but the school friend from Algeria cannot be located at that address (she has joined the resistance), so (even after Hélène meets Zohra Drif, now senator) the letter is permanently set adrift.

Those who constellate the "First and Second Waves" of feminism as defined by a neglect of race experience and contributors of color also are undervaluing the critique of world-historical racism that influences the construction of feminism's subject in many cases. Fredric Jameson has praised feminism for developing a theory of oppression that does not constrict it inside of the categories of self-knowing that the oppression itself imposes: "The emphases here," he states, "include an experience of the body radically distinct from that of men . . . [and] . . . a capacity for non-reified consciousness . . . which itself 'leaps over' a certain historical stage of psychic division of labor to which men have historically had to submit."[55] Jameson sees some feminism tending toward reification (stasis) in standpoints, or points of view, that he, at the same time, understands feminism as distinctly able to counter. Saying that a racialized woman can replace the subject of feminism leads either to a radical individualism, where everybody is singular beyond political constellation, or to replacement of some universalizing tendencies with others, with the body being the source of all available meaning. The possibility that a racial experience of gender or sexuality would replace the old, ugly essentialisms only repeats those old, ugly essentialisms unless representation makes its own critique visible.

Feminism relies on "women" being more than what "women" are, for those who see in "women" the potential of a better world. In other words, the attribution of essentialism—that the subject of feminism is stuck in a defined set of values and meanings to be rejected or celebrated in toto—is a gesture of objectification and othering that denies feminism its history, its conceptual thought and incompleteness, its foregrounding of critique and self-critique, and its creative emancipatory intent.

Florida State University (United States)

NOTES

1. Juliet Mitchell, *Psychoanalysis and Feminism: A Radical Reassessment of Freudian Psychoanalysis* (New York: Basic Books, 2000), xvii.

2. Combahee River Collective, "Combahee River Collective Statement," in *Feminism in Our Times: The Essential Writings, World War II to the Present,* ed. Miriam Schneir (New York: Vintage Books, 1994), 177.

3. Combahee River Collective, "Combahee River Collective Statement," 177–78.

4. Ibid., 178.

5. Joan Wallace Scott, "Experience," in *Feminists Theorize the Political,* eds. Judith Butler and Joan W. Scott (New York: Routledge, 1992), 24.

6. Diana Coole and Samantha Frost, "Introducing the New Materialisms," in *New Materialisms: Ontology, Agency, and Politics,* eds. Diana Coole and Samantha Frost (Durham and London: Duke University Press, 2010), 6.

7. Michele Byers, "*Buffy the Vampire Slayer:* The Next Generation of Television," in *Catching a Wave: Reclaiming Feminism for the 21st Century,* eds. Rory Dicker and Alison Piepmeier (Boston: Northeastern University Press, 2003), 171.

8. Alison Phipps, *The Politics of the Body: Gender in a Neoliberal and Neoconservative Age* (Malden: Polity, 2014), 4.

9. Julia Kristeva, "Women's Time," in *French Feminism Reader,* ed. Kelly Oliver (Lanham: Rowman & Littlefield, 2000), 186.

10. Kristeva, "Women's Time."

11. Ibid., 187.

12. Ibid., 197.

13. bell hooks, *Feminist Theory: From Margin to Center* (Boston: South End Press, 1984), 3.

14. Gloria Anzaldúa, *Borderlands/La Frontera: The New Mestiza* (San Francisco: Aunt Lute Books, 1987), 37.

15. Inderpal Grewal and Caren Kaplan, "Introduction: Transnational Feminist Practices and Questions of Postmodernity," in *Scattered Hegemonies: Postmodernity and Transnational Feminist Practices,* eds. Inderpal Grewal and Caren Kaplan (Minneapolis and London: University of Minnesota Press, 1994), 2.

16. Kyoo Lee, "(Un)naming the Third Sex After Beauvoir: Toward a Third-Dimensional Feminism," in *Undutiful Daughters: New Directions in Feminist Thought and Practice,* eds. Henriette Gunkel, Chrysanthi Nigianni, and Fanny Söderbäck (New York: Palgrave, 2012), 198.

17. Lee, "(Un)naming the Third Sex After Beauvoir," 202.

18. As cited in Elora Shehabuddin, "Gender and the Figure of the 'Moderate Muslim'" Feminism in the Twenty-First Century," in *The Question of Gender: Joan W. Scott's Critical*

Feminism, eds. Judith Butler and Elizabeth Weed (Bloomington and Indianapolis: Indiana University Press, 2011), 114.

19. Diana Fuss, *Essentially Speaking: Feminism, Nature & Difference* (New York: Routledge, 1989), xi.

20. Judith Butler, *Gender Trouble: Feminism and the Subversion of Identity* (New York: Routledge, 2006), 7.

21. Barbara Johnson, "Apostrophe, Animation, and Abortion," in *Feminisms: An Anthology of Literary Theory and Criticism,* eds. Robyn R. Warhol and Diane Price Herndl (New Brunswick: Rutgers University Press, 1997), 706.

22. Clare Hemming, *Why Stories Matter: The Political Grammar of Feminist Theory* (Durham and London: Duke University Press, 2011), 148.

23. Stacy Gillis, Gillian Howie, and Rebecca Munford, "Introduction," in *Third Wave Feminism: A Critical Exploration,* eds. Stacy Gillis, Gillian Howie, and Rebecca Munford (New York: Palgrave, 2007), xxii.

24. Leslie Heywood and Jennifer Drake, "Introduction," in *Third Wave Agenda: Being Feminist, Doing Feminism* (Minneapolis and London: University of Minnesota Press, 1997), 3.

25. Joan Wallace Scott, *The Fantasy of Feminist History* (Durham and London: Duke University Press, 2011), 21.

26. Jürgen Habermas, "Modernity—An Incomplete Project," in *The Anti-Aesthetic: Essays on Postmodern Culture,* ed. Hal Foster (Port Townsend: Bay Press, 1983), 5.

27. Habermas, "Modernity—An Incomplete Project," 5.

28. Ibid., 4.

29. Wendy Brown, *Edgework: Critical Essays on Knowledge and Politics* (Princeton and Oxford: Princeton University Press, 2005), 99.

30. Winifred Woodhull, "Global Feminisms, Transnational Political Economies, Third World Cultural Production," in *Third Wave Feminism: A Critical Exploration,* eds. Stacy Gillis, Gillian Howie, and Rebecca Munford (New York: Palgrave, 2007), 157–58.

31. Gayle Rubin, "The Traffic in Women: Notes on the 'Political Economy' of Sex," in *Towards an Anthropology of Women,* ed. Rayna R. Reiter (New York: Monthly Review Press, 1976), 158.

32. Butler, *Gender Trouble,* 10.

33. Elizabeth Grosz, "The Future of Feminist Theory: Dreams for New Knowledges," in *Undutiful Daughters: New Directions in Feminist Thought and Practice,* eds. Henriette Gunkel, Chrysanthi Nigianni, and Fanny Söderbäck (New York: Palgrave, 2012), 15.

34. Grosz, "The Future of Feminist Theory."

35. Jacqueline Rose, *Sexuality in the Field of Vision* (London: Verso, 1986), 90.

36. Emily Apter, *Against World Literature: On the Politics of Untranslatability* (London: Verso, 2013), 11.

37. Simone de Beauvoir, *The Second Sex,* trans. H. M. Parshley (New York: Vintage Books, 1989), xxi.

38. Beauvoir, *The Second Sex,* xix.

39. Ibid., xix.

40. Ibid., 6.

41. Butler, *Gender Trouble,* 13.

42. Beauvoir, *The Second Sex*, 37.

43. Toril Moi, *What Is a Woman?* (Oxford and New York: Oxford University Press, 1999), 72.

44. Apter, *Against World Literature*, 157.

45. Toril Moi, "The Adultress Wife," *London Review of Books* 32.3 (February 11, 2010): 3–6.

46. Denise Riley, *"Am I That Name": Feminism and the Category of "Women" in History* (Minneapolis: University of Minnesota Press, 1988), 1.

47. Riley, *"Am I That Name,"* 17.

48. Ibid., 93.

49. Ibid., 94.

50. Mary Orr, "Kristeva and the Trans-Missions of the Intertext: Signs, Mothers and Speaking in Tongues," in *Third Wave Feminism: A Critical Exploration,* eds. Stacy Gillis, Gillian Howie, and Rebecca Munford (New York: Palgrave, 2007), 37.

51. Julia Kristeva, *Revolution in Poetic Language,* trans. Margaret Waller (Columbia University Press, 1984), 28.

52. Hélène Cixous, "The Laugh of the Medusa," in *Feminisms: An Anthology of Literary Theory and Criticism,* eds. Robyn R. Warhol and Diane Price Herndle (New Brunswick: Rutgers University Press, 1993), 334.

53. Cixous, "The Laugh of the Medusa," 294–95.

54. Hélène Cixous, "Letter to Zohra Drif," in *Volleys of Humanity: Essays 1972-2009*, ed. Eric Prenowitz (Edinburgh: Edinburgh University Press, 2011), 107.

55. Fredric Jameson, *"History and Class Consciousness* as an 'Unfinished Project,'" in *The Feminist Standpoint Theory Reader: Intellectual and Political Controversies,* ed. Sandra Harding (New York: Routledge, 2004), 147.

WORKS CITED

Anzaldúa, Gloria. *Borderlands/La Frontera: The New Mestiza.* San Francisco: Aunt Lute Books, 1987.

Apter, Emily. *Against World Literature: On the Politics of Untranslatability.* London: Verso, 2013.

Beauvoir, Simone de. *The Second Sex* [1949]. Trans. H. M. Parshley. New York: Vintage Books, 1989.

Brown, Wendy. *Edgework: Critical Essays on Knowledge and Politics.* Princeton and Oxford: Princeton University Press, 2005.

Butler, Judith. *Gender Trouble: Feminism and the Subversion of Identity.* New York: Routledge, 2006.

Byers, Michele. *"Buffy the Vampire Slayer:* The Next Generation of Television." In *Catching a Wave: Reclaiming Feminism for the 21st Century.* Eds. Rory Dicker and Alison Piepmeier. Boston: Northeastern University Press, 2003. 171–87.

Cixous, Hélène. "The Laugh of the Medusa." In *Feminisms: An Anthology of Literary Theory and Criticism.* Eds. Robyn R. Warhol and Diane Price Herndle. New Brunswick: Rutgers University Press, 1993. 334–49.

Cixous, Hélène. "Letter to Zohra Drif." In *Volleys of Humanity: Essays 1972-2009.* Ed. Eric Prenowitz. Edinburgh: Edinburgh University Press, 2011. 106–14.

Combahee River Collective. "Combahee River Collective Statement." In *Feminism in Our Times: The Essential Writings, World War II to the Present.* Ed. Miriam Schneir. New York: Vintage Books, 1994.

Coole, Diana, and Samantha Frost. "Introducing the New Materialisms." In *New Materialisms: Ontology, Agency, and Politics*. Eds. Diana Coole and Samantha Frost. Durham, NC and London: Duke University Press, 2010. 1–43.

Fraser, Nancy. *Unruly Practices: Power, Discourse and Gender in Contemporary Social Theory*. Minneapolis: University of Minnesota Press, 1989.

Fuss, Diana. *Essentially Speaking: Feminism, Nature & Difference*. New York: Routledge, 1989.

Gillis, Stacy, Gillian Howie, and Rebecca Munford. "Introduction." In *Third Wave Feminism: A Critical Exploration*. Eds. Stacy Gillis, Gillian Howie, and Rebecca Munford. New York: Palgrave, 2007. xxi–xxxiv.

Grewal, Inderpal, and Caren Kaplan. "Introduction: Transnational Feminist Practices and Questions of Postmodernity." In *Scattered Hegemonies: Postmodernity and Transnational Feminist Practices*. Eds. Inderpal Grewal and Caren Kaplan. Minneapolis and London: University of Minnesota Press, 1994. 1–33.

Grosz, Elizabeth. "The Future of Feminist Theory: Dreams for New Knowledges." In *Undutiful Daughters: New Directions in Feminist Thought and Practice*. Eds. Henriette Gunkel, Chrysanthi Nigianni, and Fanny Söderbäck. New York: Palgrave, 2012. 13–22.

Habermas, Jürgen. "Modernity—An Incomplete Project." In *The Anti-Aesthetic: Essays on Postmodern Culture*. Ed. Hal Foster. Port Townsend: Bay Press, 1983. 3–15.

Hemming, Clare. *Why Stories Matter: The Political Grammar of Feminist Theory*. Durham and London: Duke University Press, 2011.

Heywood, Leslie, and Jennifer Drake. "Introduction." In *Third Wave Agenda: Being Feminist, Doing Feminism*. Eds. Leslie Heywood and Jennifer Drake. Minneapolis and London: University of Minnesota Press, 1997. 1–20.

hooks, bell. *Feminist Theory: From Margin to Center*. Boston: South End Press, 1984.

Jameson, Fredric. "*History and Class Consciousness* as an 'Unfinished Project.'" In *The Feminist Standpoint Theory Reader: Intellectual and Political Controversies*. Ed. Sandra Harding. New York: Routledge, 2004. 143–51.

Johnson, Barbara. "Apostrophe, Animation, and Abortion." In *Feminisms: An Anthology of Literary Theory and Criticism*. Eds. Robyn R. Warhol and Diane Price Herndl. New Brunswick: Rutgers University Press, 1997. 694–707.

Kristeva, Julia. *Revolution in Poetic Language* [1974]. Trans. Margaret Waller. New York: Columbia University Press, 1984.

Kristeva, Julia. "Women's Time." In *French Feminism Reader*. Ed. Kelly Oliver. Lanham, MD: Rowman & Littlefield, 2000. 181–200.

Lee, Kyoo. "(Un)naming the Third Sex After Beauvoir: Toward a Third-Dimensional Feminism." In *Undutiful Daughters: New Directions in Feminist Thought and Practice*. Eds. Henriette Gunkel, Chrysanthi Nigianni, and Fanny Söderbäck. New York: Palgrave, 2012. 195–207.

Mitchell, Juliet. *Psychoanalysis and Feminism: A Radical Reassessment of Freudian Psychoanalysis*. New York: Basic Books, 1974, 2000.

Moi, Toril. *What Is a Woman?* Oxford and New York: Oxford University Press, 1999.

Moi, Toril. "The Adultress Wife." *London Review of Books* 32.3 (February 11, 2010): 3–6.

Orr, Mary. "Kristeva and the Trans-Missions of the Intertext: Signs, Mothers and Speaking in Tongues." In *Third Wave Feminism: A Critical Exploration*. Eds. Stacy Gillis, Gillian Howie, and Rebecca Munford. New York: Palgrave, 2007. 30–45.

Phipps, Alison. *The Politics of the Body: Gender in a Neoliberal and Neoconservative Age*. Malden: Polity, 2014.

Riley, Denise. *"Am I That Name": Feminism and the Category of "Women" in History.* Minneapolis: University of Minnesota Press, 1988.

Rose, Jacqueline. *Sexuality in the Field of Vision.* London: Verso, 1986.

Rubin, Gayle. "The Traffic in Women: Notes on the 'Political Economy' of Sex." In *Towards an Anthropology of Women.* Ed. Rayna R. Reiter. New York: Monthly Review Press, 1976. 157–210.

Scott, Joan Wallace. "Experience." In *Feminists Theorize the Political.* Eds. Judith Butler and Joan W. Scott. New York: Routledge, 1992. 22–40.

Scott, Joan Wallace. *The Fantasy of Feminist History.* Durham and London: Duke University Press, 2011.

Shehabuddin, Elora. "Gender and the Figure of the Moderate Muslim'" Feminism in the Twenty-First Century." In *The Question of Gender: Joan W. Scott's Critical Feminism.* Eds. Judith Butler and Elizabeth Weed. Bloomington and Indianapolis: Indiana University Press, 2011. 102–42.

Woodhull, Winifred. "Global Feminisms, Transnational Political Economies, Third World Cultural Production." In *Third Wave Feminism: A Critical Exploration.* Eds. Stacy Gillis, Gillian Howie, and Rebecca Munford. New York: Palgrave, 2007. 156–67.

Young, Robert J. C. *Postcolonialism: An Historical Introduction.* Malden: Blackwell, 2001.

CHAPTER ELEVEN

Cultural Studies

JOHN FROW

ONE

Talking about the origins of an academic discipline doesn't necessarily tell us much about how the field has evolved or what might give it its bounded shape. In the case of the discipline of cultural studies, however (for it is in the formal sense very much a discipline, with its own institutional infrastructure of academic departments, national and international conferences, specialist journals, and publishers' lists), the early history is important for working out what the coherence of the field might be. My argument in what follows is that cultural studies does indeed delineate a coherent object of knowledge—I call it for short the social life of cultural forms—but that it possesses no coherent methodology or ensemble of methodologies, and that much of what is done in its name falls short of the early promise of a genuine fusion of textual with sociological and politically engaged approaches to the world of cultural forms.

The discipline that cultural studies most closely resembles, and from which it has frequently borrowed, is doubtless anthropology; and what they most obviously have in common is a concern with the materials and organization of culture understood not as "high" aesthetic culture but as the set of symbolic practices within which social life is embedded. A clear line of filiation runs from Edward Tylor's evolutionary conception of culture as a "complex whole which includes knowledge, belief, art, morals, law, custom, and any other capabilities and habits acquired by man as a member of society,"[1] through the Boasian notion of a plurality of internally coherent cultures corresponding to distinct national or social groups and T. S. Eliot's quasi-anthropological description of culture as "the way of life of a particular people living together in one place," the core of which is religion as "the whole way of life of a people,"[2] to Raymond Williams's understanding of culture, in *The Long Revolution* (1961), as "the relationships between elements in a whole way of life," and as the "patterns" formed by those relationships.[3]

Williams's holistic take on the organization of culture as covering the whole range of practices and representations through which a social group's reality (or realities) is constructed and maintained has been foundational for cultural studies. Understood by way of opposition to the normative Kantian and Arnoldian tradition of an essentially aesthetic understanding of culture, it seeks to valorize the meanings and values expressed not only in art and learning but also in institutions and in ordinary behavior; Williams takes the category of culture to include "the organization of production, the structure of the family, the structure of institutions which express or govern social relationships, [and] the characteristic forms through which members of the society communicate,"[4] and this way of formulating the concept seems to radically disable the normative value systems that underpin traditional aesthetics.

Yet, as many later critics have argued, this critical move remained incomplete, and in many ways Williams's work remained hostage to those older accounts of culture; Tony Bennett, who has traced the genealogy of the concept of culture in some detail, argues that "many of the early formulations of cultural studies owe a good deal more to the intellectual legacy of the post-Boasian trajectories of the culture concept than they do to Tylor"; in connecting "the concept of culture as a way of life to the analysis of class relations," Williams "translated post-Kantian aesthetic conceptions into the politico-aesthetic project of the creation of a common culture";[5] and in drawing on a tradition stretching from Herder to Leavis that sees cultures as particularized expressions of the coherence of organic communities, Williams posits a notion of the experientially established closure of a "community" which has dangerous connotations of cultural purity.

TWO

Arguably, much of the uptake of Williams's work (and to a lesser extent that of Richard Hoggart) by the first generation of cultural studies practitioners at the University of Birmingham's Centre for Contemporary Cultural Studies[6] repeated Williams's idealization of an organic working-class or subcultural community. At the same time, Williams's broadening of the concept of culture to include the practices and institutions of everyday life opened up a rather different set of questions. *Culture and Society* (1958) and *The Long Revolution* were grappling, among other things, with the legacy of the Marxist metaphor of the relation between an economic "base" and a cultural and political "superstructure"; the question Williams seeks to answer is that of how the economic and political spheres of successive English social formations are culturally embedded; how the "way of life" coincides with its cultural expression. For the main intellectual driver of the cultural studies project, Stuart Hall, by contrast, the central question is much more urgently political: how is the political domination of one class secured culturally—and, more directly, how is the hegemony of the British ruling class secured by means of those cultural forms that the "popular" classes have made their own?

The paradox that Hall tries to confront is one that has haunted liberal democracies throughout the twentieth century: how is it that those who are most materially disadvantaged by capitalism have given their support to value systems and to political organizations which seem to directly contradict their own material interests? For Hall the key test case is that of Thatcherism and of the neoliberal turn more generally, with its undermining of the welfare state, of trade unions, and of the public domain, and its commitment to privatization, deregulation, and financial austerity. The classic Marxist theory that the masses are blinded by false consciousness is inadequate to explain the acceptance of Thatcherism by large sections of the British working class, or of Nixon and Reagan by blue-collar American workers: it seems to Hall to be the height of arrogance to assume that ordinary people can be systematically duped into misrecognizing their real interests in a way that we privileged intellectuals cannot be. If an ideological formation like Thatcherism can attract working-class voters we should ask "not what is *false* about it but what about it is *true*"—that is, what there is about it that "makes good sense" of people's experience of the world.[7]

It is true that Thatcherism didn't appear from nowhere: it has deep ideological roots, and it was the product of years of institution-building by right-wing ideologues, such that it penetrated deep into the bureaucracy, the universities, and the media. But these were not (as Althusserian theory would have it) just *state* ideological apparatuses: the battle over neoliberalism was fought out as much in civil society as in the organs of state, and it was in part a battle for the "consent of the governed": Gramsci's phrase evokes the extent to which the hegemony of one class over others is dependent on the winning of approval, however grudging and conditional, for its core values, from which alone the legitimacy of its leadership in the political and economic spheres is derived.

What "made good sense" in the time and place of Thatcherism was a cluster of values that made up a "common sense" through which the more doctrinal aspects of neoliberalism could be promoted: the values of the individual, the family, the nation and "Englishness," respectability, prudence in the management of the household budget, and the "natural" hierarchies of gender, race, and sexuality. These values implicitly and sometimes explicitly excluded others: society, the common good, the welfare state, the structural antagonism of capital and labor, the history of working-class resistance to exploitation, and the values of the countercultures and new social movements of the 1960s and 1970s. The success of Thatcherism lay in its reversal of the postwar social-democratic consensus in order to institute a new economic order of deregulated markets, privatized state monopolies, and the restoration of "the prerogatives of management, capital, and control";[8] and it did so by effectively becoming "a populist political force, enlisting popular consent among significant sections of the dominated classes, successfully presenting itself as a force on the side of the people."[9]

Popular culture—the tabloid press, television and the movies, talkback radio, popular music, sport, the world of consumer goods, shared cultures of talk and recreation and dress—is one of the crucial domains in which this struggle of values is negotiated; in the contest between what Hall (problematically, I think)[10] calls "the power bloc" and "the people," popular culture is not expressive either of a popular will or of ruling-class values but is, rather, the *ground* on which a tension, negotiation, and accommodation of values take place, and thus on which popular values may be articulated to the political interests of the dominant class.[11] Popular culture is important because, and only to the extent that, it is capable of *forming* popular experience, providing "elements of recognition and identification, something approaching a recreation of recognisable experiences and attitudes to which people are responding."[12]

If popular culture is a site of struggle rather than an expression of fixed-class values, then it follows that it has no inherent meaning or value. Most cultural forms are

> composed of antagonistic and unstable elements. The meaning of a cultural form and its place or position in the cultural field is *not* inscribed inside its form. Nor is its position fixed once and forever. . . . The meaning of a cultural symbol is given in part by the social field into which it is incorporated, the practices with which it articulates and is made to resonate.[13]

There can therefore be no fixed inventory of forms, describing the novel, for example, as a "bourgeois" form, as though it could never be anything else, or rap as a "resistant" form, as though it could never be appropriated to commercial ends and made part of a musical mainstream. The effects of cultural texts and practices have to do with the particular conjuncture in which they occur and the kind of work that is performed on them. The metaphor of "articulation" is used here to express that relational existence of cultural texts and practices: their position in a context, and the constant reshapings to which they are liable; it expresses the complexity of the shifting field of forces within which they operate.[14]

THREE

While some of the early collective publications of the Centre for Contemporary Cultural Studies (e.g., *Policing the Crisis: Mugging, the State and Law and Order*, 1978) retained the directly political focus and the nuanced sense of the relation between cultural forms and class formations that is found in Hall's best work, much of the Centre's research continued to rely upon the figure of an organic link between a community and its expressive culture. Some research explored the notion of a distinctive working-class culture; Paul Willis's *Learning to Labour* (1977), for example, was an extended ethnographic study of the language and the social interactions of a group of working-class "lads" in a Midlands secondary school whose hostility to the formal culture of learning and to the "ear'oles" who accept its norms builds a group solidarity based on the refusal of authority, assertive masculinity, and racism; paradoxically, it is precisely their proud resistance to dominant norms that dooms them to an entrapment in dead-end working-class jobs and allows for the reproduction of capitalist relations of production, a reproduction that they see as freely chosen.[15]

More influential, perhaps, for the later development of cultural studies was the notion of the subcultural community. Designating the tightly knit identity of a social group bonded above all by a restricted and highly loaded choice of stylistic markers, the concept of the subculture ties the principle of bonding and exclusion not so much to the familiar demographic variables of class, region, or even ethnicity—although the age cohort remains crucial—as to cultural choice itself. In Phil Cohen's essay "Subcultural Conflict and Working-Class Community" the emphasis is firmly on the relation between youth subculture and its "parent" (i.e., class) culture, and in particular on the way the former seeks to effect a "magical" resolution to the contradictions of a declining working-class community.[16] Dick Hebdige's *Subculture*, by contrast, shifts the emphasis, especially in the case of punk subculture, away from this socially expressive function and toward the more stylized and reflexive function of representing "the experience of contradiction itself."[17] Hebdige's opposition of stylistic innovators to epigonal followers, however, or the opposition mooted in the introduction to the collective publication *Resistance Through Rituals* between direct peer-group socialization and the "vicarious peer-group experience" provided by commercial culture,[18] both promote a normative notion of the authenticity of subcultural expression. "Style" becomes a figure of the organic relation to a community (or an anti-community), rather than of the self-conscious production of authenticity within a highly industrialized fashion system.

At the heart of the cultural studies project in its early phases is a conception of cultural practices as ways of dealing actively and often subversively with texts and institutions; members of a culture are not "cultural dupes" (Hall's phrase closely echoes Harold Garfinkel's "cultural dopes") but seek to shape texts and institutions to their own ends in ways that embody values that may differ from those of the dominant culture. Hall's account of reading as a process in which the "decoding" of texts may be at odds with the values "encoded" in a text, while rather mechanical in its use of the metaphor of a disjunction between an input and an output, was widely influential in placing the focus of analysis on the uses of texts rather than on supposedly inherent meanings.[19] David Morley's *The "Nationwide" Audience* (1980), for example, conducted an ethnography of the audience of a BBC current affairs program by way of focus-group discussions with groups of viewers selected according to a range of different class, gender, educational, or occupational affiliations; its aim was to analyze the relation between different ("dominant," "resistant," or "negotiated") readings of the same text and the social location of the different groups, and it found that, while readings split along broadly class-based lines, there was no simple correlation between the ways in which individual members of the same social groups made sense of the program's "preferred" codes.[20]

One of the problems that flows from Hall's replacement of a differentiated class analysis with the broad categories of "the people" and "the power bloc" is that it tends to reduce this kind of nuanced analysis of a diversity of overlapping and intersecting social positions and its complex relation to texts to a simpler set of binary oppositions and an overly politicized account of practices of interpretation. The work of John Fiske, which came to be widely influential in the late 1980s and the 1990s, is exemplary in this respect.

For Fiske, the category of popular culture in advanced capitalist societies is defined not by its industrial mode of production but by the extent to which cultural products are able to "bear the interests of the people."[21] On the basis of a strategic separation between the industrial and cultural economies, between commodities and the uses made of them, Fiske can then perform a further act of purification by protecting popular readings from any contamination by hegemonic values: "There can be no popular dominant culture, for popular culture is formed always in reaction to, and never as part of, the forces of domination."[22] Any non-oppositional reading of a text (e.g., a reading of the television show *Dallas* that accepts its "capitalist, consumerist, sexist, racist values")[23] is *therefore* not a popular reading. "The people," that is to say, by definition subscribe to none of these values; incorrect values come only from the dominant class. The popular is sanitized by the expulsion from it of all ambivalence, all complexity, all forms of perverse pleasure; it expresses a homogeneous will, and all its expressions are by definition politically virtuous. At the same time, cultural variation comes to bear an immediate political significance. Thus the wearing of torn jeans, or listening to rock music, or going shopping all work as models of political resistance and opposition to "the power bloc." Any purely bodily pleasure, such as that given by hard drugs or loud rock music, is *a priori* subversive since it breaks down the socially constructed self,[24] and simply to watch television is to make "scandalous, oppositional meanings."[25] This is a politics without effects (summed up, perhaps, in the purely *psychological* orientation of the category of "empowerment") which offers a magical solution to the political contradictions it claims to address. And while it seeks to oppose the privileged aesthetics of "high" culture, it tends to valorize those forms of youth culture that it takes to be most resistant to a dominant social order.

Too much work in cultural studies, Nick Couldry complains, is characterized by "the ignoring of the cultural experience of the old; the downplaying of the 'middlebrow' or of any cultural experience which is not 'spectacular' or 'resistant'; the lack of attention to the cultural experience of elites . . .; [and] the limited research . . . on the cultures of work, business and science."[26] It is not popular culture as a whole, then, but rather those practices of cultural engagement that are taken to be both resistant to dominant values and in some sense aesthetically cutting-edge that have come to form the usual theoretical object of study for the mainstream of cultural studies. The "organic community" that it takes as its privileged object has increasingly come to be that of a marginalized (racial or sexual or ethnic) identity, and the celebration of the culture of this group then functions as the site of a fantasy politics conducted entirely on a cultural ground, "a form of resistance through ritual"[27] where "the people" or the marginalized group acts as "the textually delegated, allegorical emblem of the critic's own activity."[28] Cultural studies has been prolific of attempts to reconcile the division of knowledge, to overcome the split between reflexive knowledge and its others. The characteristic masks in which it performs have been those of the organic intellectual, the fan, the participant observer; or, more deceptively, it has worn the invisible mask of a humanism which supposes the common identity and the common interests of the knower and the known.

FOUR

What is nevertheless potentially radical in the project of cultural studies is its combination of an engagement with the "ordinary" cultural forms of the present (similar in this respect to the archives of past experience explored by oral history and history "from below") with a methodological commitment to understanding the mesh of textual and social relations with which those forms are articulated and which give them their historically particular value. Cultural studies, as Lawrence Grossberg puts it, "is most certainly not the celebration and empirical elaboration, in all its detail, of popular culture and everyday life,"[29] but it undertakes the difficult task of exploring that present which has not yet sedimented into fixed meanings and hierarchies of worth, and of which the analyst is never simply a detached observer:

> Analysis cannot start by dividing up the terrain according to the analyst's own map of tastes and distastes (although their travelogues are always contaminated by them), or their own sense of some imaginary boundary which divides a mythic (and always dominant) mainstream from a magical (and always resistant) marginality, or of an assumed impassable gulf between their intellectual self and their daily self, with only the latter invested in the alliances of popular culture.[30]

The archive of the present, at once banal, ephemeral, and repetitious and yet (perhaps precisely because of this) packed with historicity, presents a challenge of interpretation that mirrors the challenge faced by our "daily selves" in making sense of the worlds of meaning we inhabit. The challenge is, in the first place, simply to accept that the practices and institutions of everyday life are worth our attention, are capable of yielding a significance that is more than trivial, or indeed that "the very ephemerality of an archive makes it worth reading"[31]—something that is often contested by the established disciplines of knowledge.

Beyond this initial point of engagement, however, the challenge to cultural studies is to develop a methodological stance that is, of necessity, always ad hoc and yet which must correspond to the complexity of its objects. Lauren Berlant puts it like this:

> Dedicated to engaging with and writing the history of the present, cultural studies seeks to address and explicate the geopolitical specificity of cultural forms and practices; to describe not only the hierarchical mechanisms that produce identities of all kinds but also the contexts for agential practice, resistance, and experience articulated around those mechanisms; to track in particular people's ordinary lives the effects of discursive and institutional practices of domination, subordination, and hegemony; to appraise technologies of intimacy, longing, aversion, and ecstasy; and to historicize political spaces and forms like bodies, schools, cities, nations, and transnational corporations.[32]

What kinds of objects does cultural studies deal with? Typically it starts from condensed points of concentration of social meaning, scraps of ordinary or banal existence from which it then seeks to unpack the density of relations and of intersecting social domains that inform it. You could call these scraps of existence "sites," or you could use the traditional term "text"—but these scraps of the archive of the present are not textual in the sense of designating a place where meanings are constructed in a single point of inscription (writing, speech, film, dress, etc.) but rather are read as an interleaving of multiple levels of inscription. Richard Johnson thus writes that the object of knowledge for cultural studies is not the text "but the social life of subjective forms at each moment of their circulation, including their textual embodiments."[33]

Some years ago Meaghan Morris and I made a similar argument about an example of the kind of thing we thought cultural studies might work on: the shopping mall. If it is conceived on the model of textuality, we wrote,

> then this "text" involves practices, institutional structures and the complex forms of agency they entail, legal, political, and financial conditions of existence, and particular flows of power and knowledge, as well as a particular multilayered semantic organisation; it is an ontologically mixed entity, and one for which there can be no privileged or "correct" form of reading. It is this, more than anything else, that forces cultural studies' attention to the diversity of audiences for or users of the structures of textuality it analyses—that is, to the open-ended social life of texts—and that forces it, thereby, to question the authority or finality of its own readings.[34]

Because the conditions of existence of a complex object like this are diverse, its study requires a cross-disciplinary perspective: you might need to draw (for example) on economic discourses to do with the profit structures of malls, marketing strategies, and the flow of shoppers through space, as well as more theoretical discourses about commodity production and circulation; on aesthetic discourses to do with architecture and advertising and mood control; on political discourses to do with zoning permits and town planning and with the politics of concentrating and dispersing bodies through the mall; a legal discourse of contracts and liabilities; a discourse about the gendering of marketing and employment and childcare; an ethnographic discourse that can get at the lived experience of using a mall; a discourse of history that can analyze changes in the retail trade and in the formation of transient communities of consumption; and a more general hermeneutics that can relate these specific modes of analysis to questions of perspective and of analytic interest—that is, questions about the kinds of investment and payoff that drive any research project and determine what might fall within its scope.

FIVE

This, I think, is a program for cultural studies rather than an account of any single actually existing practice. Indeed, there is no "single" received model of cultural studies, but rather a heterogeneous and uneven plethora of objects and approaches. A quick and unsystematic trawl through current journals and publishers' lists yielded the following clusters of broad areas of research:

Economy: neoliberalism, financialization, debt, precarity, women's work, prostitution
Ethnicity: whiteness, indigeneity, marginality, hybridity
Media: convergence, music piracy, digital sampling, celebrity cultures
Body: anorexia, AIDS, narratives of illness, disability, masculinity, transgender studies
Experience: intimacy, memorialization, synaesthesia, life-writing
Space: mobility, scenes, deterritorialization, borders
Knowledge: disciplinarity, technology, laboratories, local knowledges

At the last major cultural studies conference I attended I heard papers that engaged with biology and the neurosciences, with the ontology of markets and with organization theory, with water resources and the commodification of water, with health services, with digital economies, with tourism, with the archive, with the limits of the human, with religion, with social media, with class, with social justice, with biometrics, with the production and distribution of food, with ethical economies, as well as papers devoted to questions of methodology: papers on the status of objects of enquiry, or on the empirical methodologies of actor network theory; on affect theory and the critique of affect theory; on the new materialism and the critique of the new materialism.

These two different kinds of papers—those that move outwards to objects associated with other disciplines, and papers that move inwards to think about the methodological concerns of cultural studies—exemplify two vectors that define the scope of the discipline and what most matters to it; I'll call them an extensive and an intensive vector. The driving force of cultural studies, the reason it remains a productive site of intellectual work, is, I think, primarily that centrifugal drive toward an engagement with a range of objects of enquiry and a range of other disciplines. Cultural studies has always prided itself on transgressing disciplinary boundaries, on stepping into places where it's not welcome. It is and always has been a powerful force for questioning the settled assumptions of the more traditional disciplines on which it has been productively parasitic, in Michel Serres's sense of that word. Yet that productive parasitism is also the source of an inherent and continuing problem for cultural studies, the weakness of its intensive vector, its lack of disciplinary specificity: that is, on the one hand the uncertainty of its object of analysis, and on the other its lack of a methodology which would be specific to its own work.

Is this a problem? It may not be, or not for the time being. One of the things that has always marked cultural studies is the potentially radical nature of its pedagogy—its assumption that its students are likely to know just as much as its teachers about its subject matter. But knowledge doesn't float free; it is grounded in institutions, and it acquires its force and its place in the world, its authority and its legitimacy, from its ability to persuade other institutions—for example, those that fund its activities and those that employ its graduates—that its work is serious and valuable. There is a trade-off to be made between that grounding of knowledge in disciplines and institutions, on the one hand, and, on the other, the imaginative, ad hoc, and multidisciplinary solutions that cultural studies has so often found in its exploration of the archive of the present. It is still an open question how that trade-off will work out.

University of Sydney (Australia)

NOTES

1. Edward Burnett Tylor, *Primitive Culture: Researches into the Development of Mythology, Philosophy, Religion, Language, Art and Custom* (London: J. Murray, 1871), 1.

2. T. S. Eliot, *Notes Towards the Definition of Culture* (London: Faber and Faber, 1948), Appendix: "The Unity of European Culture," 120.

3. Raymond Williams, *The Long Revolution* (New York: Harper and Row, 1961; revised ed. 1965), 46.

4. Williams, *The Long Revolution*, 42.

5. Tony Bennett, "Cultural Studies and the Culture Concept," *Cultural Studies* 29.4 (2015): 547, 548; cf. Tony Bennett, *Culture: A Reformer's Science* (London: Sage, 1998), 101.

6. Richard Hoggart was appointed as the Centre's first director in 1964, and he was succeeded by his deputy, Stuart Hall, in 1969; the key "culturalist" texts of that moment were Williams's *Culture and Society 1780-1950* (1958) (New York: Columbia University Press, 1983) and *The Long Revolution* (1961), revised ed. (New York: Harper and Row, 1965); Hoggart's *The Uses of Literacy* (1957) (New York: Routledge, 2017); and E. P. Thompson's *The Making of the English Working Class* (New York: Pantheon, 1964).

7. Stuart Hall, "The Toad in the Garden: Thatcherism Among the Theorists," in *Marxism and the Interpretation of Culture*, ed. Cary Nelson and Lawrence Grossberg (London: Macmillan, 1988), 46.

8. Hall, "The Toad in the Garden," 39.

9. Ibid., 40.

10. For my own extended critique, cf. John Frow, *Cultural Studies and Cultural Value* (Oxford: Clarendon Press, 1995), 70–80.

11. Graeme Turner, *British Cultural Studies: An Introduction* (1990; rpt. London: Routledge, 1996), 195.

12. Stuart Hall, "Notes on Deconstructing 'the Popular,'" in *People's History and Socialist Theory*, ed. Raphael Samuel (London: Routledge, 1981), 233.

13. Hall, "Notes on Deconstructing 'the Popular,'" 235.

14. Lawrence Grossberg, *We Gotta Get Out of this Place: Popular Conservatism and Postmodern Culture* (New York: Routledge, 1992), 56.

15. Paul Willis, *Learning to Labour: How Working Class Kids Get Working Class Jobs* (London: Saxon House, 1977).

16. Phil Cohen, "Subcultural Conflict and Working-Class Community (1972)," in *Culture, Media, Language: Working Papers in Cultural Studies, 1972-79,* eds. Stuart Hall, Dorothy Hobson, Andrew Lowe, and Paul Willis (London: Hutchinson, 1980).

17. Dick Hebdige, *Subculture: The Meaning of Style* (London: Methuen, 1979), 121.

18. John Clarke, Stuart Hall, Tony Jefferson, and Brian Roberts, "Subcultures, Cultures and Class: A Theoretical Overview," in *Resistance Through Rituals: Youth Subcultures in Post-War Britain*, eds. Stuart Hall and Tony Jefferson (London: HarperCollins, 1976), 52.

19. Stuart Hall, "Encoding/Decoding," in *Culture, Media, Language: Working Papers in Cultural Studies, 1972-79*, eds. Stuart Hall, Dorothy Hobson, Andrew Lowe, and Paul Willis (London: Hutchinson, 1980), 117–27.

20. David Morley, *The "Nationwide" Audience* (London: BFI, 1980).

21. John Fiske, *Understanding Popular Culture* (Boston: Unwin Hyman, 1989), 23.

22. Fiske, *Understanding Popular Culture*, 45.

23. Ibid., 44.

24. Ibid., 50.

25. Ibid., 36.

26. Nick Couldry, *Inside Culture: Re-Imagining the Method of Cultural Studies* (London: Sage, 2000), 3.

27. Francis Mulhern, *Culture/Metaculture* (London: Routledge, 2000), 168.

28. Meaghan Morris, "Banality in Cultural Studies," *Discourse* 10.2 (1988): 17.

29. Lawrence Grossberg, *Cultural Studies in the Future Tense* (Durham: Duke University Press, 2010), 2.

30. Lawrence Grossberg, *We Gotta Get Out of This Place*, 111.

31. Lauren Berlant, "Collegiality, Crisis, and Cultural Studies," *Profession* (1998), 109.

32. Berlant, "Collegiality, Crisis, and Cultural Studies," 106.

33. Cited in John Storey, ed., *What Is Cultural Studies? A Reader* (London: Arnold, 1996), 2.

34. John Frow and Meaghan Morris, "Introduction," in *Australian Cultural Studies: A Reader*, eds. John Frow and Meaghan Morris (Sydney: Allen and Unwin, 1993), xix.

WORKS CITED

Bennett, Tony. *Culture: A Reformer's Science*. London: Sage, 1998.

Bennett, Tony. "Cultural Studies and the Culture Concept." *Cultural Studies* 29.4 (2015): 546–68.

Berlant, Lauren. "Collegiality, Crisis, and Cultural Studies." *Profession* (1998): 105–16.

Clarke, John, Stuart Hall, Tony Jefferson, and Brian Roberts. "Subcultures, Cultures and Class: A Theoretical Overview." In *Resistance Through Rituals: Youth Subcultures in Post-War Britain*. Eds. Stuart Hall and Tony Jefferson. London: HarperCollins, 1976. 3–59.

Cohen, Phil. "Subcultural Conflict and Working-Class Community [1972]." In *Culture, Media, Language: Working Papers in Cultural Studies, 1972-79*. Eds. Stuart Hall, Dorothy Hobson, Andrew Lowe, and Paul Willis. London: Hutchinson, 1980. 66–75.

Couldry, Nick. *Inside Culture: Re-Imagining the Method of Cultural Studies*. London: Sage, 2000.

Eliot, T. S. [Thomas Stearns]. *Notes Towards the Definition of Culture*. London: Faber and Faber, 1948.

Fiske, John. *Understanding Popular Culture*. Boston: Unwin Hyman, 1989.

Frow, John. *Cultural Studies and Cultural Value*. Oxford: Clarendon Press, 1995.

Frow, John, and Meaghan Morris, eds. *Australian Cultural Studies: A Reader*. Sydney: Allen and Unwin, 1993.

Grossberg, Lawrence. *We Gotta Get Out of this Place: Popular Conservatism and Postmodern Culture*. New York: Routledge, 1992.

Grossberg, Lawrence. *Cultural Studies in the Future Tense*. Durham: Duke University Press, 2010.

Hall, Stuart. "Encoding/Decoding." In *Culture, Media, Language: Working Papers in Cultural Studies, 1972-79*. Eds. Stuart Hall, Dorothy Hobson, Andrew Lowe, and Paul Willis. London: Hutchinson, 1980. 117–27.

Hall, Stuart. "Notes on Deconstructing 'the Popular'." In *People's History and Socialist Theory*. Ed. Raphael Samuel. London: Routledge, 1981. 227–41.

Hall, Stuart. "The Toad in the Garden: Thatcherism Among the Theorists." In *Marxism and the Interpretation of Culture*. Ed. Cary Nelson and Lawrence Grossberg. London: Macmillan, 1988. 35–57.

Hebdige, Dick. *Subculture: The Meaning of Style*. London: Methuen, 1979.

Hoggart, Richard. *The Uses of Literacy* [1957]. New York: Routledge, 2017.

Morley, David. *The "Nationwide" Audience*. London: BFI, 1980.

Morris, Meaghan. "Banality in Cultural Studies." *Discourse* 10.2 (1988): 3–29.

Mulhern, Francis. *Culture/Metaculture*. London: Routledge, 2000.

Storey, John, ed. *What Is Cultural Studies? A Reader*. London: Arnold, 1996.

Thompson, E. P. [Edward Palmer]. *The Making of the English Working Class*. New York: Pantheon, 1964.

Turner, Graeme. *British Cultural Studies: An Introduction* [1990]. London: Routledge, 1996.

Tylor, Edward Burnett. *Primitive Culture: Researches into the Development of Mythology, Philosophy, Religion, Language, Art and Custom*. London: J. Murray, 1871.

Williams, Raymond. *The Long Revolution* [1961]. Revised ed. New York: Harper and Row, 1965.

Williams, Raymond. *Culture and Society 1780-1950* [1958]. New York: Columbia University Press, 1983.

Willis, Paul. *Learning to Labour: How Working Class Kids Get Working Class Jobs*. London: Saxon House, 1977.

CHAPTER TWELVE

Postmodernism

JEFFREY T. NEALON

"Postmodern" is an adjective that loomed heavily over late twentieth-century academic discourse on cultural production. We're perhaps used to "postmodern" as a word used to describe fiction like Thomas Pynchon's or Ishmael Reed's, but it's also noteworthy that Clint Eastwood's film *Unforgiven* was hailed as a "postmodern Western"; *Seinfeld* has been called postmodern television; Stanley Tigerman, who designed several Hard Rock Cafes, is routinely called a "postmodern" architect; and visual artists Barbara Kruger (who splashes provocative words across her photographs) and Andy Warhol are called "postmodern" in the same breath. Performance artist and former porn star Annie Sprinkle calls one of her performances "Post-Porn-Modern." And poet Kevin Young remarks that when he first heard Public Enemy's *It Takes a Nation*, he finally understood what postmodernism sounded like.[1] The possible references go on and on: from free jazz to the films of the Coen Brothers, the lists of things labeled "postmodern" were myriad in the late twentieth century.

What, one might wonder, could all these disparate art forms have in common? How could "postmodern" (or any category, for that matter) possibly encompass a wildly diverse grouping of artists like Chuck D, Clint Eastwood, Jerry Seinfeld, Annie Sprinkle, and Andy Warhol? It seems impossible, but on further reflection, some general connections might be made. There seems to be a certain sense of style shared by many of the things labeled "postmodern," a sense of disjunction or deliberate confusion, irony, playfulness, reflexivity, a kind of cool detachment, a deliberate foregrounding of constructedness, a suspicion concerning neat or easy conclusions. Following up this preliminary sense of postmodern, we might note that Eastwood's *Unforgiven* is postmodern insofar as it plays with the good/evil dichotomy running through so many westerns; it coolly and ironically exposes the constructedness of the Western myth, and in the process challenges this myth's seemingly natural validity. The gunslinger is not a hero or a God; he's just a hired killer. Similarly, *Seinfeld* is postmodern insofar as it is par excellence the sitcom that foregrounds and plays with the fact that nothing ever happens on sitcoms; the show doesn't even pretend to have a plot most of the time, and when it does, the plot is so contrived and full of planned "coincidences" as to be obviously and deliberately ridiculous. And the rap practice of sampling—patchworking sounds from other recordings—always emphasizes the fact that the music is constructed, put together in a certain way in the hope of producing a certain set of effects in the listener. As producer Hank Shocklee says, "Music is nothing but organized noise. You can take anything—street sounds, us talking, whatever you want—and make it music by organizing it."[2]

Maybe all this suggests a postmodern insistence on process rather than product. A "postmodern" cultural artifact is one that consistently questions itself and the context that it seems to fit within. Perhaps, preliminarily, we could say that postmodern cultural artifacts are constantly calling attention to the ways in which both the work and the viewer are constructing, deconstructing, and reconstructing meaning. In the end, then, one might say that *Seinfeld* is "postmodern" insofar as it's a sitcom about sitcoms, and *Unforgiven* is a postmodern "western about westerns," while rap and hip-hop are forms dedicated to remixing existing sounds. Similarly, Warhol's art is primarily about producing art (or walking the fine line that separates museum art from other commodities like soup cans or Hollywood movies), and postmodern architects might be said to produce buildings that are about buildings. The hallways that go nowhere, the exposed beams, and the see-through elevators that characterize postmodern buildings all point to the fact that space is constructed rather than merely found. And these deliberately difficult architectural constructions challenge the user of the building to think about the ways in which his or her movements are unconsciously channeled (one might even say controlled) by architects and other urban planners.

But as any academic trend or "cultural dominant" discovers sooner or later, success doesn't last forever. At the twilight of the twentieth century, or dawn of the twenty-first century, critics and theorists overtly began to wonder over the immanent demise of postmodernism, and began to raise the related question of the "next big thing" in cultural production: what comes after postmodernism? We were told that the notoriously difficult David Foster Wallace was the last postmodernist fiction writer, with the novel turning away from linguistic experimentation and toward a new realism or a new sincerity (in, for example, Karl Ove Knausgaard's scrupulously realist *My Struggle*, or the work of the various Jonathans in American fiction—Jonathan Frantzen, Jonathan Lethem, and Jonathan Safran-Foer). In American experimental poetry, the postmodern linguistic provocations of the "Language" poets gave way to the stark post-postmodern realism of so-called Conceptual Writing (which merely copies preexisting documents).[3] Architecture took the post-postmodern turn as early as 1995, and the *New York Times* has in the twenty-first century taken to using the word *post-postmodern* to refer to everything from Marvel superhero movies to dance performances in which there's no dancing.

Although this description gives us a beginning handle on postmodernism and what might come after, at the same time this initial characterization of the situation surrounding postmodernism raises a host of questions. Most pressing among them, perhaps, is not so much figuring out what the "posts-" mean, but rather understanding what the "modern" means. If postmodern signifies, at least in part, "after the modern," then what is or was "modern"? And in the adolescence of the twenty-first century, are we still postmodern? Or have we become post-postmodern, whatever that might mean? It's to those questions that we now turn.

MODERNISM AND POSTMODERNISM AS A HISTORICAL PERIOD OR STYLE

In literary history, "modernism" tends to signify an international aesthetic movement that began to take hold in the late nineteenth and early twentieth centuries in Europe and America and ended sometime after the Second World War. As a reaction to the European romanticism of the early and middle nineteenth century, modernism as a literary and artistic movement tended to stress form over romantic feeling; hence, the poetry of Ezra Pound is modern insofar as it is impersonal, complex, and allusive, especially when compared with the romantic verse of Wordsworth. Likewise, Hemingway's short and clipped modernist prose style stands in stark contrast to the voluminous Victorian novel of the late nineteenth century. It's not so much that modernism abandons the subjective feeling of romanticism or the narrative heft of Victorianism, but the subject or self in a modern work is troubled, psychologically and physically. The kind of fragmented subjective vision that one sees in Picasso's modernist work, for example, stands in marked contrast to the gentle color schemes of Monet's neo-romanticism, just as Eliot's highly fragmented practice of writing poetry in "The Waste Land" stands in stark contrast to Wordsworth's formula for producing romantic poetry, which requires tapping into what he calls the "spontaneous overflow of powerful feelings."[4]

If you step outside the literature department, and head over to the philosophy department and sign up for "Modern Philosophy," you're not going to encounter the same definition of modernism. In fact, in philosophical parlance, the "modern" period begins not in the late nineteenth century, but with René Descartes (born in 1596) and ends in the early nineteenth century, which in practice means that modern philosophy covers the philosophy of subjectivity from Descartes to Kant or Hegel. Likewise, if you go to the history department and sign up for a course in "Early Modern Europe," you'll be looking at the beginning of the sixteenth or seventeenth centuries, not the beginning of the twentieth. In historical parlance, "modern" tends to mean the history of industrialization and the rise of towns and commerce, beginning after the medieval or feudal period. And, just to make things really confusing, in literary and visual arts, as we saw above, "modern" tends to mean a historical period following the Victorians, beginning around the turn of the twentieth century and ending in 1945. So if you take the "Modern American Novel" course at my university, you're taking "American Novel 1890–1945"; after 1945, the course is called "Contemporary American Novel," or perhaps one might call it the "postmodern" novel course. But, all that considered, we seem to find ourselves farther from—rather than closer to—a concrete definition of either modernism or postmodernism.

In his essay "Toward a Concept of Postmodernism,"[5] critic Ihab Hassan lays out a list of "schematic differences" between modernism and postmodernism in literature and the arts. Perhaps highlighting certain of Hassan's differences will bring the question more clearly into focus:

Modernism	Postmodernism
Form (closed)	Anti-form (open)
Purpose	Play
Design	Chance
Hierarchy	Anarchy
Finished Art Object	Process/Performance
Distance	Participation
Totalization	Deconstruction
Centering	Dispersal
Metaphor	Metonymy
Depth	Surface
Determinacy	Indeterminacy
Signified	Signifier

Hassan's list tends to emphasize very concisely the stylistic differences between modernism and postmodernism. As we saw above, the unexpected, questioning, or process-oriented form of *Seinfeld* or Public Enemy is the thing that makes people call them "postmodern," in contradistinction to the highly designed, totalized, "consumable" quality of traditional TV shows or most popular songs. It is some deliberate sense of open-endedness, self-reflexiveness, indeterminacy, or uncertainty that would seem to make an artifact "postmodern." However, this list—as convenient as it is—introduces a truckload of problems. For example, T. S. Eliot's 1922 poem "The Waste Land" is a landmark of modernism, but it seems to have all the artistic markers of postmodernism: the poem seems to have an incredibly "open" form that relies much more heavily on "dispersal" than on "centering," with the poem as a whole depending a lot more on "anarchy" than it does on "hierarchy."

One could say much the same thing for famous modernists Gertrude Stein and William Faulkner, whose works seem to have all the markers of "postmodernism." This gets even trickier if we consider the incredibly open and dispersed character of an eighteenth-century novel like *Tristram Shandy*, or even the decentering maneuvers of Chaucer's *Canterbury Tales*. Perhaps one could solve this problem, though, by insisting on the more literal, historical meaning of postmodern: after the modern period, after the end of the Second World War, roughly after 1945. Of course, the problem there is that not everything produced in this period is "postmodern" in the sense outlined by Hassan's list. For example, the fiction of John Updike or Joyce Carol Oates, or the poetry of Sylvia Plath, doesn't easily fit the "postmodern" suit. So maybe the most cogent definition of "postmodern" as an artistic style is using it to refer to disjunctive, ironic, and/or reflexive artistic work produced after 1945. And, as we've seen, it is a rejection of this hyper-reflexive, self-undercutting artistic maneuver that most intensely characterizes the new realist stylistics of the post-postmodern period in the twenty-first century.

MODERNISM AND POSTMODERNISM AS CULTURAL DOMINANT; OR POSTMODERNISM AND CAPITALISM

The other principle way that modernism and postmodernism have been conceptualized comes out of the work of Fredric Jameson, whose conception of postmodernism as a "cultural dominant" was worked out in his highly influential essays throughout the 1970s and 1980s, culminating in his 1991 book *Postmodernism: or, The Cultural Logic of Late Capitalism*. As is clear from the subtitle, Jameson is not primarily interested in defining modernism and postmodernism by offering a slate of stylistic phenomena that would characterize their differences (as we see, for example, with Hassan's characterization of modernism versus postmodernism according to their formal artistic features). While not merely ignoring these stylistic features, Jameson looks more closely at the changing *function* of art in the twentieth century: the first historical era where we saw the commodification and mass technological distribution of art. Twentieth century marks the moment when cultural production became what Theodor Adorno famously called an "industry" that manufactures mass-produced art commodities—blockbuster films, popular music hits, bestseller paperbacks—just as a factory manufactures cars, toasters, or hair brushes. In that kind of economic world, where factory production is the economic dominant mode, there's still room for art, but for something to be deemed art (to be innovative, new, startling), it has to work against the cultural or economic dominant of fordist factory production. So, for example, while the 1950s television variety shows, or teen films, or radio hit parade remained clearly in tune with the economic dominant of factory production (mass producing a more-or-less identical product), the more adventurous artists of the time were producing work that attempted to remain "other" to that cultural dominant of factory-produced culture. For example, the abstract expressionist painting of Jackson Pollock, the be-bop and free jazz of Charlie Parker or John Coltrane, or the art cinema of Orson Welles all remain resolutely hostile (or in an oppositional relationship) to the cultural dominant of factory fordism. If Ezra Pound suggested modernist poetry's slogan was "Make it new!," that's at least in part because a dominant factory economy is in the business of "making it the same" each and every time. Thereby, if art wishes to be something other than a mass-produced commodity, it's charged in the modern era with innovating forms, boldly transgressing expectations, and challenging the viewer or listener with something "new." And thereby the function of authentic art, in the modernist era of mass production, is to innovate; precisely insofar as any given art form follows that imperative to create new forms, experiences, techniques, ideas, it's considered authentic precisely because it's *not* following the culturally dominant dictates of mass factory production.

Fast forward from the middle of the twentieth century to today, and we see that the "cultural dominant" of American society has shifted considerably, and with those social changes, so must change the function of a formerly resistant notion of modernist artistic innovation. As anyone living in or traveling through the rust belt states of the American Midwest can attest, largely gone are the factories that dominated those landscapes only a generation ago. Any quick trip though the airport bookstore will show you that the economic dominant of American capitalism is no longer mass-produced sameness, but an almost slavish dedication to the new, the innovative, the alternative. Even neo-Nazis these days call themselves the alternative or "alt-right." Today, nobody wants to be thought about in terms of your grandfather's anything, and that newly structuring position of economic innovation (rather than factory re-production) is precisely the concept that Jameson foregrounds in his discussion of postmodernism. As he writes concisely of the shift from modernism to postmodernism, "What has happened is that aesthetic production today has become integrated into commodity production generally: the frantic economic urgency of producing fresh waves of ever more novel-seeming goods (from clothing to airplanes), at ever greater rates of turnover, now assigns an increasingly essential structural function and position to aesthetic innovation and experimentation."[6] Which is maybe simply to say that innovation, which could be counted upon in the modernist era to define art and aesthetic experience (as "other" to the dictates of mainstream factory culture), has in the present become the business norm or the cultural dominant, and thereby, artistic innovation can no longer be counted upon to oppose, negate, or even be other than the dominant mode of economic production in a service, finance, or entertainment-based economy (which is forever innovating, just as poetry and painting did in the modernist era).

So at the end of the day, is postmodernism primarily a dominant artistic style deployed during a particular historical period? Or is postmodernism better understood as a moment in the development of modern capitalism, from a kind of factory economy in the early to mid-twentieth century to the computerized finance-driven capitalism of our day? Jameson makes a useful distinction here between postmodernism and postmodernity that may help in sorting this out. He defines postmodernism much as we've seen Hassan define it, as an artistic movement or style characteristic of the late twentieth century—a style that is surely waning or mutating in the adolescence of the twenty-first century. On the other hand, postmodernity for Jameson is defined as the entire historical and economic climate of an era (the unique socioeconomic situation that defines an era, as opposed to an artistic style among others). Thereby postmodernity on Jameson's view constitutes a state of affairs that's not prone to quick transformation. As Jameson says in an interview, postmodernism as a dominant style can and does change very quickly, as new generations of artists reject and rework the styles that came before them. However, postmodernity (understood as the current socioeconomic climate of globalization) is much more resistant to quick mutation, and postmodernity is likely to be a very long affair indeed.[7] As I've suggested in my book *Post-Postmodernism,* what's going on in the adolescence of the twenty-first century is much better understood as an intensification or deepening (rather than a rejection or overcoming) of Jameson's culturally dominant socioeconomic sense of "postmodernity."[8]

POSTMODERNISM AND/AS "THE LINGUISTIC TURN": POSTMODERNISM AS THEORY

In its heyday, postmodernism was also known by philosopher Richard Rorty's phrase "the linguistic turn,"[9] a set of philosophical movements held together by the sense that language was the overarching paradigm that could be used to understand everything from kinship systems of primitive peoples (Claude Lévi-Strauss), to contemporary Marxism (Louis Althusser) or gender performance (Judith Butler), all the way to the workings of the unconscious itself (Jacques Lacan). Indeed, perhaps the paradigmatic discourse for understanding postmodernism's philosophical movements is the linguistics of Ferdinand de Saussure, summed up in his *Course in General Linguistics.* In the course of this lecture series, Saussure distinguishes between the material sign or speech act and the underlying structures that render such symbolic acts intelligible, the movement from the particular (the *signifier,* the individual word) to the structure that governs it (the *signified,* what the word means). For Saussure, and for the generations of postmodernists who followed in his footsteps, both the signifier and the signified are "arbitrary": there is no essential (or structural) connection between a word and what that word means. We know this, as Saussure argues, because different languages have different signifiers that all stand in for the same signified: for example, the word "dog" in English is "perro" in Spanish, "Hund" in German, "chien" in French, "gou" in Mandarin Chinese, and so on. These are all different signifiers or words, but they share the same signified or meaning, which demonstrates that there's no essential or natural connection between the thing in the world and the name that we give to it in differing languages. It is this notion of "essentialism" (the idea that meaning is found within the essence of things, rather than in the social relations that configure the things) that postmodernism as theory most forcefully rejected.

However, to say that meaning is "arbitrary" generally suggests that it's based on a somewhat flimsy set of connections, and therefore easy to change. In this sense, naming your favorite NBA basketball player is a largely "arbitrary" exercise—which is to say, your favorite player is a personal preference that can easily change from month to month. Of course, this is certainly not the sense in which the Saussurean signifier is "arbitrary." The linguistic signifier, although it is "arbitrary" in its connection to a particular referent or meaning, is far from being merely an idiosyncratic individual preference. Individual persons don't get to decide what we call that plot of land between the sidewalk and the street, even though it's called different things in different parts of the United States (a median, a parkway, even a Devil's Strip). If you boldly decide to call it a "babosphere," no one's going to understand what you're talking about. Like the name for dogs in different languages or strips of grass in English, any given signified doesn't have a "natural" name that corresponds to it; but neither does that mean that each and every person has a different name for each and every thing. Language doesn't work like that—it's a mass phenomenon that's very slow to change over time, not an individual one that can fluctuate from day to day. As such, postmodernism as linguistic-turn theory was never a celebration of anything-goes anarchy and out-of-control subjective determination, but it was rather a discourse dedicated to dealing first and foremost with social constraint.

In fact, as Saussure writes, the "arbitrary nature of the sign is really what protects language from any attempt to modify it,"[10] which initially seems pretty strange. If the "arbitrary" nature of the signifier means that there is no "natural" connection between signifier and signified (that the relation is "culturally constructed" as opposed to "essential"), wouldn't that also suggest that the relation is easier to change or modify? If the relation between word and meaning is "arbitrary" rather than "essential," then isn't every word subject to easy "modification" in this way? And doesn't this open the way to what comedian Stephen Colbert has called "truthiness" (the idea that truth or meaning or the signified can be endlessly reconfigured), or what political spokespeople for Donald Trump have called "alternative facts"? Is postmodernism and its linguistic turn, as some have suggested, responsible for the war on truth that seems to have taken over much political discourse in the first decades of the twenty-first century? If facts are merely cultural constructions, rather than transhistorical realities, doesn't that make them liable to quick and merciless manipulation? Indeed, to say something is "culturally constructed" rather than "essential" or "natural" has somehow come to suggest that it's easy to change: if meaning is not essential or natural, then it should be really easy to modify, right?

As Saussure counterintuitively suggests when he argues that the arbitrary nature of the signifier actually protects it from modification, it doesn't follow that socially constructed means easy to change. For example, most people would agree that the pressing problems of our day are socially constructed: poverty, crime, discrimination, high taxes, wars. Everyone knows that these things are socially constructed; discrimination is not a "natural" phenomenon, any more than high taxes or wars are. People become bigots; they are not born bigots. This fact, however, doesn't seem to have much effect on the discourse of racism or gender discrimination, and certainly doesn't make hatred or discrimination disappear overnight. As feminist theorist Eve Kosofsky Sedgwick ironically recalls, "I remember the buoyant enthusiasm with which feminist scholars used to greet the finding that one or another brutal form of oppression was not biological but 'only' cultural! I have often wondered what the basis was for our optimism about the malleability of culture by any one group or program."[11] In fact, if discrimination were a "natural" thing, and it could be somehow scientifically invalidated, it would in fact be much easier to "change" it than if one agrees that discrimination is and has been a socially constructed phenomenon from the start. Social habits are in fact notoriously difficult to change, and not because they're "essential" but precisely because we're so used to them. Social conventions are a powerful force working against quick or wholesale social change.

In sum, since "arbitrary" means "socially constructed" for the postmodern linguistic turn, it then necessarily also means "resistant to change." To point out that something is constructed or structured is not the same thing as being able somehow to change it wholesale—especially not by individual action. You can't reform language, any more than you can other social systems, all by yourself. This highly constrained sense of the social construction of subjectivity, agency, and political action was one of the hallmarks of postmodernism and the linguistic turn of theory.

POST-POSTMODERNISM AND THE RETURNS OF ESSENTIALIST REALISM

As we've seen, the polar opposite of postmodernism's "social constructionism" is comprised by what used to be called "essentialism," or what's called today a return to "realism" ("real" here being the opposite of something that's constructed by social or political conditions). Post-postmodernism, or the period after postmodernism, has been characterized as just such a return of realism—and one that was fueled, ironically enough, at least partly due to social and political factors since 2001. Certainly, a return to prestige for transhistorical, realist facts was fueled by George W. Bush's largely fabricated (or more generously, socially constructed) case to get the United States into the Iraq war, and certainly it was intensified in the war on facts waged by the campaign of Donald Trump and his advisors—who reminded us that what used to be called the *real* or the *truth* is merely the product of "alternative facts." Or maybe you can blame it all on postmodernist par excellence the Dude, from *The Big Lebowski*, who infamously retorts to a taunt with: "Yeah, well, you know, that's just, like, your opinion, man," in what the poster who put the clip up on YouTube brands the "Best Comeback of All Time."[12] Indeed, it's become a kind of internet meme that Donald Trump is the first openly "postmodern" president, one who assails essentialist truths and the realism of facts, preferring the open-ended processes of alternative facts that are re-spun daily by his handlers.[13]

But as much as many people have nostalgia for essentialist truth (a real that is purely and pristinely true, outside or without political or social or linguistic intervention), postmodernism had one thing completely right: the question of truth is and remains a political question, and facts (scientific ones as well as cultural ones) are the outcome of a discovery process. However much we yearn for a return to some kind of more reality-based political discourse worldwide, it remains the case, as Michel Foucault puts it, that "truth is a thing of this world . . . and it induces regular effects of power. Each society has its regime of truth, its 'general politics' of truth: that is, the types of discourse which it accepts and makes function as true; the mechanisms and instances which enable one to distinguish true and false statements . . . [and] the status of those who are charged with saying what counts as true."[14] Here, Foucault reminds us that, in the postmodern period or any period for that matter, truth is primarily a *political* question, one that we all have to fight over each and every day. And there's no end in sight for those fights, so we'd better get used to them, whether we're modern, postmodern, or post-postmodern.

Indeed, one could hesitate here to wonder about the larger cultural or academic return of what looks like several unrelated strands of realism (movements that only half a generation ago would have been branded naïve or, worse yet, essentialist). Take, for example, recent fiction and its returns to realism. As Robert L. McLaughlin writes in his essay on "Post-Postmodernism," "Where postmodern authors often used self-reference to expose their own fiction's artificiality, . . . post-postmodern authors tend to offer an idiosyncratic respect for the suspension of disbelief, spending less time reflecting on their narratives as narrative . . . and more on exploring the protean and fractious nature of what their characters consider to be reality. This change of focus is the main reason why many critics have noted a sea change in fiction, a transition from postmodernism to something that seems to be different. It is also the reason that some critics and reviewers define this sea change as a return to some kind of realism."[15]

Pivoting from the returns of realism in contemporary fiction, we could note a series of comebacks for so-called essentialisms and other rejections of the postmodern linguistic turn's social constructionism. In philosophy, we could note the vehement anti-linguistic turn in object-oriented philosophy and speculative realism (in the work of Graham Harman, for example), as well as various forms of vibrant or agential Matter (Jane Bennett and Karen Barad); gender studies, which was ruled a generation ago by the sign- and language-based theories of performativity (Eve Sedgwick and Judith Butler), has gone in a series of other "new materialist" directions; in literature departments, think of the recent anti-hermeneutic methodological rise of data analysis, most convincingly thematized as distant reading (Franco Moretti), not to mention emergent methods of surface reading (Stephen Best and Sharon Marcus) or post-critical reading (Rita Felski); or consider various kinds of scientific, neuroscientific, and new media approaches to literature—examining everything from the nonhuman networks in which we act (Bruno Latour), to the brain chemistry of reading or the evolutionary functions of storytelling (Lisa Zunshine). All the way to animal studies and posthumanism, with their stinging critiques of linguistic anthropomorphism (say, Cary Wolfe's work). Cinema studies, the home of so much foundational work in sign theory, must note with anxiety that Jean-Luc Godard named his final film *Farewell to Language*; or consider the MP3-fueled rise of Ubiquitous Listening and Poptimism in Music Criticism (which doesn't critique or interpret individual songs, artists, or albums, but rather downloads them all, and lets the iPod shuffle sort them out).[16] If we look closely at the signposts concerning the present, it begins to look like we are post-signs, on the other side of the postmodern linguistic turn.

In the end, to return to Jameson's distinction between postmodernism as a style and postmodernity as a socioeconomic situation, it does seem that postmodernism is in the process of being eclipsed as a historical period, as the dominant artistic style, and even as the primary philosophical linguistic-turn theory of our day. On the other side of the coin, however, postmodernity in Jameson's sense (as the socioeconomic cultural dominant of the capitalist neoliberal era) is still very much with us, and seems likely to remain so for many years to come.

Penn State University (USA)

NOTES

1. Kevin Young, *The Grey Album: On the Blackness of Blackness* (Minneapolis: Graywolf, 2012), 348.

2. Quoted in Tricia Rose, *Black Noise* (Middletown: Wesleyan University Press, 1994), 82.

3. See "A Brief Guide to Conceptual Poetry," *Poets.org* (February 20, 2014). https://www.poets.org/poetsorg/text/brief-guide-conceptual-poetry

4. William Wordsworth, "Preface to Lyrical Ballads," *Bartleby.com*. http://www.bartleby.com/39/36.html

5. Ihab Hassan, "Toward a Concept of Postmodernism," in *The Postmodern Turn* (Columbus: Ohio State University Press, 1987).

6. Fredric Jameson, *Postmodernism, or, The Cultural Logic of Late Capitalism* (Durham: Duke University Press, 1991), 5.

7. See Jameson discuss this distinction here: Fronteiras do Pensamento, "Fredric Jameson—Pós-modernismo ou pós-modernidade?" Online video clip, *YouTube*, July 5, 2013. https://www.youtube.com/watch?v=nSNAhib3B_M

8. See Jeffrey T. Nealon, *Post-Postmodernism; or, The Cultural Logic of Just-In-Time Capitalism* (Stanford: Stanford University Press, 2012), especially chapters 1 and 2.

9. See Richard Rorty, *The Linguistic Turn* (Chicago: University of Chicago Press, 1967).

10. Saussure, *Course in General Linguistics*, 73.

11. Eve Kosofsky Sedgwick, *Epistemology of the Closet* (Berkeley: University of California Press, 1990), 41.

12. Watch it here: "Best Comeback of All Time," *YouTube,* Uploaded by Daniel Lopez DiMarco, March 11, 2012. https://www.youtube.com/watch?v=XkADiJCYS2k

13. See, for example, Peter McKnight, "Trump as Postmodernist: Truth No Longer Bound by Facts," *The Globe and Mail* (January 28, 2017). http://www.theglobeandmail.com/opinion/trump-as-postmodernist-truth-no-longer-bound-by-facts/article33796581/; or Victor Davis Hansen, "Donald Trump, Postmodernist Candidate," *National Review* (August 4, 2016). http://www.nationalreview.com/article/438647/donald-trump-destroys-normal-politics-first-postmodern-candidate

14. Michel Foucault, "Truth and Power," in *Power/Knowledge: Selected Interviews and Other Writings*, ed. Colin Gordon (New York: Pantheon Books, 1980), 131.

15. Joe Bray, Alison Gibbons, and Brian McHale, eds., *The Routledge Companion to Experimental Literature* (New York: Routledge, 2012), 218–19.

16. Just to scratch the surface of these various "new realist" or "new materialist" movements, see Graham Harman et al., eds, *The Speculative Turn: Continental Materialism and Realism* (Melbourne: re.press, 2011); Jane Bennett, *Vibrant Matter: A Political Ecology of Things* (Durham: Duke University Press, 2010); Karen Barad, *Meeting the Universe Halfway* (Durham: Duke University Press, 2007); Iris van der Tuin, *Generational Feminism: A New Materialist Introduction to a Generative Approach* (Lanham: Lexington Books, 2014); Franco Moretti, *Distant Reading* (Brooklyn: Verso, 2013); Stephen Best and Sharon Marcus, "Surface Reading: An Introduction," *Representations* 108.1 (2009): 1–21; Rita Felski, *The Limits of Critique* (Chicago: University of Chicago Press, 2015); Bruno Latour, "Why Has Critique Run Out of Steam? From Matters of Fact to Matters of Concern," *Critical Inquiry* 30.2 (2004): 225–48; Lisa Zunshine, *Oxford Handbook of Cognitive Literary Studies* (Oxford: Oxford University Press, 2015); and Anahid Kassabian, *Ubiquitous Listening: Affect, Attention, and Distributed Subjectivity* (Berkeley: University of California Press, 2013).

WORKS CITED

Barad, Karen. *Meeting the Universe Halfway*. Durham: Duke University Press, 2007.

Bennett, Jane. *Vibrant Matter: A Political Ecology of Things*. Durham: Duke University Press, 2010.

"Best Comeback of All Time." *YouTube*. Uploaded by Daniel Lopez DiMarco. March 11, 2012. https://www.youtube.com/watch?v=XkADiJCYS2k

Best, Stephen, and Sharon Marcus. "Surface Reading: An Introduction." *Representations* 108.1 (2009): 1–21.

Bray, Joe, Alison Gibbons, and Brian McHale, eds. *The Routledge Companion to Experimental Literature*. New York: Routledge, 2012.

"A Brief Guide to Conceptual Poetry." *Poets.org*. February 20, 2014. https://www.poets.org/poetsorg/text/brief-guide-conceptual-poetry

Bryant, Levi, Nick Srnicek, and Graham Harman, eds. *The Speculative Turn: Continental Materialism and Realism*. Melbourne: re.press, 2011.

Felski, Rita. *The Limits of Critique*. Chicago: University of Chicago Press, 2015.

Foucault, Michel. "Truth and Power." In *Power/Knowledge: Selected Interviews and Other Writings 1972-1977*. Ed. Colin Gordon. Trans. Colin Gordon, Leo Marshall, John Mepham, and Kate Soper. New York: Pantheon, 1980.

"Fredric Jameson—Pós-modernismo ou pós-modernidade?" *YouTube*. Uploaded by Fronteiras do Pensamento. July 5, 2013. https://www.youtube.com/watch?v=nSNAhib3B_M

Hansen, Victor Davis. "Donald Trump, Postmodernist Candidate." *National Review* (August 4, 2016). http://www.nationalreview.com/article/438647/donald-trump-destroys-normal-politics-first-postmodern-candidate

Hassan, Ihab. "Toward a Concept of Postmodernism." In *The Postmodern Turn*. Ed. Ihab Hassan. Columbus: Ohio State University Press, 1987. 84–96.

Jameson, Fredric. *Postmodernism, or, The Cultural Logic of Late Capitalism*. Durham: Duke University Press, 1991.

Kassabian, Anahid. *Ubiquitous Listening: Affect, Attention, and Distributed Subjectivity*. Berkeley: University of California Press, 2013.

Latour, Bruno. "Why Has Critique Run Out of Steam? From Matters of Fact to Matters of Concern." *Critical Inquiry* 30.2 (2004): 225–248.

McKnight, Peter. "Trump as Postmodernist: Truth No Longer Bound by Facts." *The Globe and Mail* (January 28, 2017). http://www.theglobeandmail.com/opinion/trump-as-postmodernist-truth-no-longer-bound-by-facts/article33796581/

Moretti, Franco. *Distant Reading*. Brooklyn: Verso, 2013.

Nealon, Jeffrey T. *Post-Postmodernism; or, The Cultural Logic of Just-In-Time Capitalism*. Stanford: Stanford University Press, 2012.

Rorty, Richard. *The Linguistic Turn*. Chicago: University of Chicago Press, 1967.

Rose, Tricia. *Black Noise*. Middletown: Wesleyan University Press, 1994.

Saussure, Ferdinand de. *Course in General Linguistics* [1916]. Trans.Wade Baskin. New York: McGraw-Hill, 1966.

Sedgwick, Eve Kosofsky. *Epistemology of the Closet*. Berkeley: University of California Press, 1990.

Tuin, Iris van der. *Generational Feminism: A New Materialist Introduction to a Generative Approach*. Lanham: Lexington Books, 2014.

Wordsworth, William. "Preface to Lyrical Ballads [1801]." *Bartleby.com*. http://www.bartleby.com/39/36.html

Young, Kevin. *The Grey Album: On the Blackness of Blackness*. Minneapolis: Graywolf Press, 2012.

Zunshine, Lisa. *Oxford Handbook of Cognitive Literary Studies*. Oxford: Oxford University Press, 2015.

CHAPTER THIRTEEN

Race and Postcolonial Studies

NICOLE SIMEK

To study race as a force shaping social, political, and economic life is to study more than its role in modern European colonization, where many locate its origins as a concept. Likewise, in order to understand the past and present-day impacts of colonization, postcolonial studies scholars must address a wide range of issues beyond race and racism alone. Yet colonialism has played such an important part in shaping notions of race, and race such a central one in the colonial project, that we cannot productively study either in isolation from the other. Touching every aspect of modern life, from intimate personal and sexual relations to global trade and political institutions, from gender norms and family structures to science, medicine, and ecology, race and colonialism have drawn the interest of scholars in numerous academic disciplines. Analyzing phenomena with such an extensive impact on so many different facets of life in fact requires multiple critical lenses and tools. Critical interest in race and postcolonial studies did not emerge as a single, defined project or field of study, however, but rather as a diffuse set of questions arising across the humanities and social sciences. Gathering these concerns together under the name "Postcolonial Studies" highlights at once the important scope and interrelated nature of these questions, the desire among similarly motivated scholars to make the field of study visible as such and more open to deliberate collaboration, but also the multiplicity of the field, the divergences and frictions between scholars who vary in the emphases, priorities, and methods they bring to their analysis of race and postcoloniality.

Naming, as foundational postcolonial thinker Edward Said has pointed out, involves exercising power, giving shape to concepts and identities in ways that do not simply reflect the world, but that impact perception and action. What we mean when we use the terms "race," "colonization," or "postcoloniality"—which phenomena we include in these categories, which we do not, what relationships we see between them, and how we interpret their function and importance—represents itself a fundamental and persistent question for postcolonial studies scholars. Today, "postcolonial studies" has commonly come to refer to the study of European colonization and its impacts, from the imperial conquests and colonial settlements that began in the fifteenth century through the accession of former colonies to independent statehood in the mid-twentieth century and beyond. If in earlier decades, arguments over terminology in the field often revolved around the nature of the "post-" in "postcolonial," and whether it should refer to postindependence literature and scholarship, or rather to post-invasion cultural relationships more broadly, debates today have shifted focus, with wider acceptance of an expansive understanding of the field's potential scope. Yet, the concerns animating earlier disputes over postcolonial studies' purview have not gone away, for they are tied to the field's critical orientation: its prioritization of critique in the service of political progress and social justice, and its understanding of scholarship as an activity necessarily implicated in politics, economics, and culture, rather than a neutral or objective practice that can be separated from these other spheres of human activity. The goal for postcolonial studies, as for Marxist theory before it, is not merely to interpret the world, but to change it. More than a concern to accurately describe the breaks and continuities between colonization and what followed, to document the persistence or alteration of colonial patterns in the political, economic, and cultural relations that succeeded colonization for the sake of understanding itself, disputes over postcolonial studies' periodizations and characterizations of its subject matter reflect scholars' desire to intervene in the world and effectuate sociopolitical change. Today's debates seek to make these animating assumptions more explicit, and to evaluate the field's successes and shortcomings in its attempts to critique postcolonial conditions and transform them.

The definitional and political challenges facing postcolonial studies in the twenty-first century intersect with those encountered by critical race studies. Scholars of race have similarly sought to put their work to social and political use, though the causes they have served have differed radically over time. Nineteenth- and early twentieth-century investigations of race that assumed the validity of racial distinctions bolstered repressive programs of colonization, segregation, eugenics, and genocide, while countervailing studies of racial differences as socially constructed but ultimately foundationless led to different conclusions about the best ways in which to organize social and political life. Critical race studies, drawing on centuries-long traditions of anti-racist activism, philosophy, theology, and political thought, as well as modern research methods from across the humanities, social sciences, and natural sciences, have sought to further address the injustices of racism and the consequences of racial thinking. One conundrum facing scholars of race, like those in postcolonial studies, is the difficulty of working with a term that must be flexible enough to encompass shifting meanings of race, while remaining specific enough to distinguish between related but differing phenomena.

Ta-Nehisi Coates captures well today's academic attitude toward the relationship between race and racism: "Race is the child of racism, not the father."[1] The impulse to discriminate—to distinguish and categorize groups—comes before the categories themselves that we develop. The value and meaning imputed to race emerge in historically specific conditions, and thus remain open to transformation and reconfiguration. Today, as Ania Loomba has noted, the term "race" stands for "various combinations of ethnic, geographic, cultural, class, and religious differences."[2] Yet despite its malleability, the term does convey specific meanings that feel accurate and urgent to those who use it to conceptualize conflict. "While the colour issue is particularly prominent in the United States and to the history of slavery," Loomba explains, "anti-Jewish or anti-Arab prejudice has always turned on the question of religious or cultural difference. The conflicts in Rwanda between Tutsis and Hutus, or the caste wars in India, have not primarily centered on colour, but the victims in each case feel they are racial in nature."[3] Understanding the specificity of the content various people give to the term "race" is important to identifying the source of conflict and responding to demands for redress against racial violence. Yet, if the elasticity of the term "race" poses one conceptual problem, its dominant association with nineteenth-century European views of race as a biological category poses another.

As the conception of race as a social construction has come to supplant this "scientific" or "pseudo-scientific" view of race—the notion that humans belong to racial groups distinguishable by their physical characteristics, and that these biological traits determine intellectual and moral qualities—so too has recognition of race and racism's persistence dwindled.

Conceiving of racism narrowly as the belief in the superiority of certain racial groups over others, and focusing on the affirmative expression of this belief in individual attitudes, in discriminatory laws, or employment practices has led some to contend that Western societies have entered a "postracial" period, that these societies have finally left race, and racism, behind. Because legal statutes permitting racial discrimination have largely been outlawed and protections against discrimination put in place in their stead (extending, in some countries, to prohibitions or restrictions on the collection of statistics or census data relating to race), racism has come to be seen by many as a matter of individual prejudice and individual criminal action to be dealt with on a case-by-case basis. Yet discrediting biology as the origin of "race" does not put an end to racial thinking. As Seyla Benhabib puts it, "We live in a 'post-racial' society only in the sense that we are all generalized others in the eyes of the law; but as we learn painfully, not in the eyes of those who administer the law."[4] Dispensing with biological notions of race on a conceptual level does not automatically shift long-standing thought patterns and emotional habits.

If we define racism narrowly as the explicit, pseudo-scientific belief in the superiority of one "biological" group over another, we risk overlooking other forms of racial discrimination, such as implicit or unintentional bias, or positive stereotyping. Even when one form of racism becomes less common in public discourse, other characteristics—such as culture or religion—are marshaled to justify, implicitly or explicitly, the perception that racial differences exist. The basis for racial discrimination does not so much disappear as it gets displaced onto other foundations, which continue to underpin the perception that human groups are differentiated along racial lines. Moreover, definitions of racism tend to make it a private matter, a matter of individual attitude, obscuring the ongoing structural levers and effects of past and present discrimination, such as income inequality, structural barriers to accessing education, housing, or employment, and differing rates of exposure to environmental hazards.

For scholars of both race and postcoloniality, therefore, work remains to be done. The structural inequalities, conceptual hierarchies, and cognitive-affective habits instituted in earlier eras have not simply been overcome in the new millennium. The very persistence of these problems speaks, however, to the need for scholars to question the frames and role of their work, and the means by which to keep their critical edge sharp. How might comparative studies of colonialisms better elucidate linkages and shifts between "pre-modern" and "modern" forms of domination? How do various forms of colonization come to assume or promote particular modes of sociopolitical organization (such as nation-states), and of what consequence are these structures today? How has globalization shifted political and economic power relationships? Do the terms "postcolonial" or "neocolonial" adequately channel our critical attention today, or do we risk overlooking new modes of agency, relationship, and oppression by projecting past configurations onto a different historical moment with its own particular characteristics? How restrictive or expansive a definition of "race" adequately represents the ways societies have conceptualized human differences as differences? How do we understand the continuums between biology and a host of other markers of difference, such as culture, religion, and ethnicity, or caste, class, lineage, and bloodline?

One tack scholars have taken in order to sharpen their critical tools involves shifting objects of study, in order to build on earlier work by nuancing and altering existing paradigms. Recognizing, for example, that Eurocentric frameworks continue to structure postcolonial studies, despite the field's efforts to critique Eurocentrism, scholars have set out to push past these limitations, asking what objects of study we have inadvertently left aside. Commenting, for example, on postcolonial studies' focus on the modern period and the notion of modernity (a tenet of nineteenth-century colonial policies), Peter Hulme notes that even while criticizing the assumption that societies progress through primitive modes of life to more technologically and politically advanced modes of social organization, postcolonial studies has tended to reproduce and remain bound by Eurocentric chronologies. "Even when postcolonial studies has looked back beyond the nineteenth century," he writes, "it has tended to thump into the backstop of 1492, reinforcing the idea of the Middle Ages as some kind of dark hole out of which modernity magically emerged."[5] New work by postcolonial medievalists seeks to push beyond such limitations, which not only restrict the scope of postcolonial investigation, but also weaken the ability of postcolonial studies to address contemporary issues. Hulme points out, for example, the consequences of reiterating assumptions about the Middle Ages in contemporary discourse about Islam, which is frequently labeled "medieval" as a shorthand for primitive, savage, unenlightened—in short, as an identity in need of "modernization."

Questioning chronologies and opening the field up to a "wider and longer history"[6] shifts not only colonial assumptions about historical progress, but also insufficiently critical attempts to retrieve from the pre-colonial past a more harmonious model for the future. The effort to demonstrate that race can be historicized, that it is not an essential and inevitable category dividing humanity, can prompt critics to underestimate its longevity or to idealize cultures in which notions of race appear to have been absent. "As we strive towards a future where racial thinking has less destructive power in our lives, it is enabling to find a past where it had not yet acquired that power," explains Ania Loomba. Yet, she continues, in the interest of better attending to race's malleability and durability alike, "it is as necessary to confront the long histories of race as it is to show that racial thinking has a history and is not a fixed or universal."[7] In opening ourselves up to the stubborn persistence of racial thinking, we do not legitimate its existence, but rather gain insight into its operations.

Loomba's comparative work on racial ideologies has shown, for example, that biology, culture, religion, and class have not always functioned as separable and distinct concepts, but rather mingle together and inform one another in both older and contemporary understandings of race. In medieval and early modern England, for instance, class status was conceived as rooted in family lineage and in the blood itself ("blue blood" accounted for one's nobility and character), while religion and skin color were frequently viewed as linked ("religious outsiders, minorities, as well as people from a vast spectrum of non-European lands were routinely described in terms of colour," and their conversion was depicted in medieval texts as altering the body: "Upon conversion, black Moors fantastically become white, and unbelievers find their deformed offspring transformed"[8]). Recognizing these interconnections in the past—recognizing that "'biology' itself has a history," and that "the separation of 'biology' from 'culture' is the outcome of this very history"[9]—casts contemporary assumptions about race and racism in a different light. Insisting on a sharp distinction between "racism" and other forms of hierarchical differentiation obscures the ways in which phenomena such as color prejudice, caste, anti-Semitism, Islamophobia, or Zionism are mutually implicated on conceptual, social, political, and economic levels. Teasing out not just the differences, but also the continuities between these issues, as Loomba stresses, creates possibilities for solidarity and activism that would otherwise go unexplored.

Loomba's work on comparative methodology and its critical and political efficacy takes part in a wider movement to bring methodological assumptions and motivations to the forefront of postcolonial and critical race studies, in order to challenge the field to meet its goals. While continuing to deepen their engagement with the instantiations of race and colonial settlement that have dominated critical interest, scholars are also continually taking stock of the questions that arise from the work of past decades, to refine these questions and put them to new use. "Postcolonial is a way of reading," argues Bill Ashcroft,[10] and thinking of it as such prompts us to ask not only what we are reading, but how we are reading, and why. To what ends can and should reading be put?

David Scott has put these questions pointedly in his work, asking at the turn of the millennium whether the critical paradigms postcolonial studies scholars have fought to bring about have lost their critical potential in their very normalization itself. In his 2004 book, *Conscripts of Modernity*, Scott argues that keeping the concept of problem-space in view in postcolonial work can help maintain its critical vitality. A problem-space is first "a discursive context, a context of language," but more than that, it is a horizon of investment and struggle, "an ensemble of questions and answers around which a horizon of identifiable stakes (conceptual as well as ideological-political stakes) hangs."[11] If we recall that a problem-space is "a context of argument and, therefore, one of *intervention*," we can begin to shift our interpretation of the past—the objects we choose to analyze and, especially, the *questions* we ask about them, in ways that help us intervene in the present.[12] Criticism's capacity to effect change hinges first, Scott contends, on the questions we ask, not just the answers we develop. We need to be concerned not just about truth, but, strategically, about which truths—which questions and answers—most urgently need exploration and argument. "Problem-spaces alter historically, because problems are not timeless and do not have everlasting shapes," writes Scott. "In new historical conditions old questions may lose their salience, their bite." Thus, postcolonial criticism "ought always to seek to clarify whether and to what extent the questions it is trying to answer continue to be questions worth having answers to."[13]

Over the last decade, postcolonial and critical race scholars have increasingly turned attention to these issues. What are the contours of the problem-spaces in which we are working today? What are the stakes, and how do these stakes shape the questions we need to ask in our scholarship? How do we best orient our critical interventions into what Boaventura de Sousa Santos has described as the complex "constellations of oppression" through which various forms of domination function?[14] The following sections take up a few of the major lines of inquiry motivating scholars today.

IS CULTURAL RESISTANCE STILL RESISTANT?

Bill Ashcroft identifies an ability to analyze cultural practices as one of the most important contributions of postcolonial studies in the late twentieth century. One reason postcolonial theory sparked great interest in this period of accelerating globalization, Ashcroft argues, was that it satisfied a world "hungry for a language to describe the diversity of cultures and the intersecting global range of cultural production" characterizing the moment. In the face of fears about the free-market ideologies increasingly governing state and global financial institution policies, postcolonial studies offered hope for alternatives, through its focus on local and cultural responses and resistance to globalization's homogenizing and dispossessing effects. "It was through *cultural* practices," Ashcroft asserts, "that difference and hybridity, diffusion and the imaginary, concepts that undermined the Eurocentric narrative of modernity, were evident."[15] Postcolonial studies took culture as its field of struggle, and directed its attentions to the ways in which cultural production and cultural practices both reflect and reshape political and economic spheres. In the 1980s and 1990s, postcolonial art and literature increasingly gained acceptance in the canons of academic criticism, while the major critical investments and paradigms of postcolonial thought—anti-essentialism, an insistence on historicizing, a concern for relations of domination and resistance[16]—became increasingly visible and influential across academic fields.

Yet, critics like Peter Hallward or Nicholas Harrison have recalled that postcolonial studies—and more specifically postcolonial literary criticism—must take account of the gap between its intended effects and the reality of material developments on the ground. Noting postcolonial literary critics' predilection for textual analysis, Harrison points out that such analysis alone does not suffice either to identify or to bring about revolutionary effects. Rather, "critics who wish to discuss a text's politics and to claim, for example, that a particular text is 'subversive,' or conservative, often need logically to consider reception, in order to give real political weight to their claims. (*Whose* views or behaviour, if anyone's, does or did the text reinforce or subvert?)"[17] Hallward takes an even more admonitory position, asserting that "postcolonial theory emerged as the dominant paradigm for understanding collective 'struggle' over the same years that witnessed the massive and sustained asset-stripping of the third world."[18] Not only, then, have postcolonial critics mistaken cultural processes and performances for effective political action, but, in so doing, they have unwittingly colluded with commodification and co-optation, the very forces they purport to combat. In arguing this point, Hallward redefines the contours of the problem-space, the context of intervention, to which postcolonial critics should attend. In the face of increasing economic and political inequalities across the globe, is the question of how artistic texts subvert dominant conceptual paradigms still the question worth answering? Is there a role for aesthetics in postcolonial studies, or should critical attention be given instead to the material conditions underpinning social and political life?

For some contemporary critics, as Chris Bongie says, the answer to the question, "What's literature got to do with it?" is, "Not much of anything."[19] Literary studies should renounce its attempts to read politics schematically into literature, and postcolonial studies should attend instead to the material dimensions of discourse. Yet, the very separation between literature and politics—between the undecidability of the literary and the need for decisive action required of politics—perhaps provides, Bongie argues, the conditions for literature's disruption of contemporary political logics. In its "singular unverifiability," literature (following Gayatri Spivak), foregrounds the undecidability of meaning, and erupts as something uncontainable (or, following Jacques Derrida, "intolerable") within a logic that does not tolerate ambiguity, that requires certain decisions and actions.[20] On this view, analyzing what exactly literariness interrupts (which totalizing systems, which hegemonic convictions), how exactly it does so (through which affective and conceptual maneuvers), and how it sustains its interruptive force remains an important endeavor in our contemporary historical conjunction.

Such insights into the qualities and limitations of the aesthetic shift both the objects critics prioritize, and, when they examine literature, the kinds of questions critics ask about literature's political work. As Jane Hiddleston argues, rather than mistaking texts to be representative of colonial experience or immediately subversive in their political effects, critics need to attend to the specificity of literature as literature, to "the ways in which form and genre can engage with the political."[21] That is, rather than doing away with the political altogether in literary analysis, literary critics should produce more accurate, precise accounts of literature's effects, investigating "how texts offer multiple distinct ways of responding to political and historical questions," as well as "the ways in which literature can alter the way we think, can constitute a mode of thought of its own."[22]

NEOLIBERALISM'S NEW NORMAL

One particularly pressing political and historical question imposing itself across the fields of postcolonial and critical race studies is that of neoliberalism. More than an economic policy, an intensification of liberal principles—the values of free-market competition, privatization, and consumer choice, premised on conceptions of the individual, and individualism, as the fundamental units or levers of economic and social action—neoliberalism represents, Wendy Brown argues, a "profoundly destructive" governing rationality, one that "transmogrifies every human domain and endeavor, along with humans themselves, according to a specific image of the economic."[23] In that image, Brown continues, "all conduct is economic conduct; all spheres of existence are framed and measured by economic terms and metrics, even when those spheres are not directly monetized."[24] In casting every sphere of life as a marketplace, in conceiving of people as "human capital," and in valuing the market freedom of the private individual to the exclusion of other forms of freedom, neoliberalism alters "the meaning of democracy *tout court*," reducing democracy's language, a language of "inclusive and shared political equality, freedom, and popular sovereignty," to a language of market values alone.[25]

While postcolonial and critical race studies are only two of the many fields engaged in the study and critique of neoliberalism today, they bring particularly trenchant tools and perspectives to that analysis because of their long engagement with discourses about capitalism, modernity, human value, and "the global flow of persons, commodities, and ideas" across uneven political and economic terrains.[26] Scholars attentive to difference and uneven power relations, like Brown, have been quick to note that neoliberalism affects different populations unequally, exacerbating inequality and segregation. As neoliberal states shrink public services, converting publically funded education, research, social security, or infrastructure into privately purchased services, individuals without means must finance these goods through debt, or forego them. Neoliberal privatization, as Brown puts it, "further constrains the liberty of neoliberalized subjects required to procure individually what was once provisioned in common."[27]

David Theo Goldberg also stresses the crucial stakes involved in struggles to liberalize the state, drawing out the process by which neoliberalism reinforces racialized social rifts. More than an ideology theorizing individuals universally in the abstract as market actors enhancing their human capital, neoliberal discourses and policies rely on racialized notions of the deserving and the lazy, the competent and the corrupt, on distinctions between whom state services are for, and whom they are not for. Goldberg points out that it was at the same moment when countries with robust welfare programs became demographically more diverse, when the caretaking functions of the state were perceived as covering the socially marginalized, that doubts about this state function captured public attention and motivated cutbacks. "The neoliberal attack on the caretaker state," Goldberg maintains, "is the simultaneous commitment to racial neoliberalization."[28] The neoliberal ideology of individual choice privatizes racism and thereby masks structural inequalities, with dire consequences: in construing racisms "as personal preferences, as a habit of the heart, as choices individuals make not choices structured by social arrangement, by predefined state possibilities and impossibilities," neoliberal privatization policies reduce one's quality of life, and even the possibility of living itself.[29] "The U.S.," Goldberg warns, "has become a country that in repeatedly committing people to this form of constrained freedom is condemning them in the last instance to die."[30]

In observing the ways in which neoliberal discourses operate, Boaventura de Sousa Santos sees continuities between them and colonial discourses before them. Defining colonialism as a system that naturalizes difference, that makes differences appear natural rather than historically produced, Santos points out that such discourses confuse cause and effect. Like neoliberalism, which views the individual as inherently in need of market incentive to stimulate productivity, or sexism, which takes unequal access to be a result of natural differences between genders, colonialism viewed its own hierarchies and modes of domination as "a *product* of the inferiority of certain people, and not the *cause* of their inferiority."[31] In addition to justifying genocide, such perceptions also served to legitimize what Santos describes as "epistemicide," or the destruction of knowledge, of ways of knowing. Epistemicide kills off "culture, memories, ancestries," and also the ways in which people conceive of social life: how they think of each other, how they conceive of nature, ecology, political relations, and the law.[32]

Given that knowledge itself is a battlefield, one urgent task and responsibility for postcolonial studies is to decolonize its own modes of producing knowledge—how it conceives of knowledge, expertise, and intellectual property. Decolonizing scholarship involves teasing out conceptual limitations in one's work and better tracing the global genealogy of what are often taken as "Western" inventions or innovations ("Who invented printing? Who invented gunpowder?" asks Santos. "If you go on and on, you will see that many achievements that are attributed to the West, not to mention the zero, are not Western"[33]). Decolonizing also involves, however, taking other forms of knowing, and other collaborators, seriously. It means asking: Who might we work with in generating knowledge? How can scholars help create healthier "ecologies of knowledges?"[34] How can scholars recognize and collaborate with those who produce knowledge outside their own disciplines, in locations beyond the West or the Global North, or outside the academy—from indigenous, anti-racism, and anti-capitalist activists to people living their everyday lives?

UNDERSTANDING, LIBERATION, DIFFERENCE

In the face of economic liberalizations that pass for liberations, in the face of structural racisms made private and invisible to many, how can critique gain purchase, find a foothold for questioning the status quo? For many scholars, the path forward involves both questioning the terms of neoliberalism itself, opening up ideas like "freedom" to scrutiny and alternative definitions, and shifting the ways in which scholarship enters public discourse. Postcolonial writers participate in social movements, collaborate with artists, and make use of various media outlets. Solidarity movements like Black Lives Matter reach across national boundaries and involve creative cultural producers, community members, educators, and political representatives in a collective effort to reshape discourse and material conditions. Scholars, too, seek out new venues and modes of speech in an effort to engage wider audiences. For scholars like Santos, political activism serves not just as the outcome of scholarship or a complement to it, but as an integral part of that scholarship itself. Describing himself as a "rearguard" rather than "vanguard" intellectual, Santos views his role not as bringing knowledge to the people, but instead as learning from activists and contributing his own perspective as a sociologist and legal scholar, in a collaborative effort to move forward together.[35]

Martinican poet and theorist Édouard Glissant has similarly taken a strong interest in the ethical and political dimensions of epistemology, of ways of knowing others. In *Poetics of Relation*, Glissant proposes a mode of knowledge that he calls "donner-avec," or "giving-on-and-with," a way of interpreting offered as an ethical alternative to the grasping, appropriative logic of "comprehension" underpinning instrumental rationality broadly, and colonial or neocolonial political projects more specifically.[36] To comprehend, etymologically, meant to "seize" or "grasp." If comprehension designates, for Glissant, an attitude or "gesture of enclosure, if not appropriation," "giving-on-and-with" names a form of understanding that relinquishes the quest for conquest or total mastery, in order to open oneself to other modes of relation to the self and to the other.[37] The chief impact of this shift from grasping to "giving with" is that one abandons the attempt to "reduce [human] behaviors to . . . preconceived [and transparent] universal models."[38]

Significantly, not immediately understanding others in our own terms does not mean that we have to abandon our efforts to relate to them, because, as Glissant puts it, "To feel in solidarity with [the other] or to build with him or to like what he does, it is not necessary to grasp him . . . nor to 'make' him in my image."[39] That is, living and working together do not require that we fully understand one another according to a single, universal measure, according to the same terms by which we understand ourselves. The absence of a single metric of understanding, the absence of a common, clear language in which we might come to consensus points both to the difficulties of any critical project but should not be understood as merely an obstacle or a loss. Multiplicity and difference mean that perfect consensus is unattainable, friction unavoidable, and the future unpredictable, but these are also conditions for creativity, for the possibility of change, for a life that is unconstrained by sameness. How to direct friction and difference to the benefit of all remains a difficult but necessary and urgent task for scholars invested in truly postcolonial and postracial futures.

Whitman College (United States)

NOTES

1. Ania Loomba, "Race and the Possibilities of Comparative Critique," *New Literary History* 40.3 (2009): 7.

2. Ania Loomba, *Shakespeare, Race, and Colonialism* (Oxford: Oxford University Press, 2002), 2.

3. Ibid.

4. George Yancy and Seyla Benhabib, "Whom Does Philosophy Speak For?" *New York Times* (October 29, 2015). http://opinionator.blogs.nytimes.com/2015/10/29/who-does-philosophy-speak-for/

5. Peter Hulme, "Beyond the Straits: Postcolonial Allegories of the Globe," in *Postcolonial Studies and Beyond*, eds. Ania Loomba, Suvir Kaul, Matti Bunzl, Antoinette Burton, and Jed Esty (Durham: Duke University Press, 2005), 42.

6. Ania Loomba, "Race and the Possibilities of Comparative Critique," 503.

7. Ania Loomba, *Shakespeare, Race, and Colonialism*, 5.

8. Ania Loomba, "Race and the Possibilities of Comparative Critique," 504.

9. Ibid., 503.

10. Bill Ashcroft, "Future Thinking: Postcolonial Utopianism," in *The Future of Postcolonial Studies*, ed. Chantal Zabus (New York: Routledge, 2015), 235.

11. David Scott, *Conscripts of Modernity: The Tragedy of Colonial Enlightenment* (Durham: Duke University Press, 2004), 4.

12. Scott, *Conscripts of Modernity*.

13. Ibid.

14. Boaventura de Sousa Santos, "Boaventura de Sousa Santos," in *Conversations in Postcolonial Thought*, ed. Katy Sian (New York: Palgrave Macmillan, 2014), 69.

15. Bill Ashcroft, "Future Thinking," 236.

16. David Theo Goldberg, "David Theo Goldberg," in *Conversations in Postcolonial Thought*, ed. Katy Sian (New York: Palgrave Macmillan, 2014), 41.

17. Nicholas Harrison, "Metaphorical Memories: Freud, Conrad, and the Dark Continent," in *Postcolonial Poetics: Genre and Form*, eds. Patrick Crowley and Jane Hiddleston (Liverpool: Liverpool University Press, 2011), 50.

18. Peter Hallward, *Absolutely Postcolonial: Writing Between the Singular and the Specific* (New York: Palgrave, 2001), 64.

19. Chris Bongie, *Friends and Enemies: The Scribal Politics of Post/colonial Literature* (Liverpool: Liverpool University Press, 2008), 22.

20. Bongie, *Friends and Enemies*, 23.

21. Jane Hiddleston, "Introduction," in *Postcolonial Poetics: Genre and Form*, eds. Patrick Crowley and Jane Hiddleston (Liverpool: Liverpool University Press, 2011), 1.

22. Hiddleston, "Introduction," 1–2.

23. Wendy Brown, *Undoing the Demos: Neoliberalism's Stealth Revolution* (Cambridge: MIT Press, 2015), 9–10.

24. Brown, *Undoing the Demos*, 10.

25. Ibid., 44.

26. Ania Loomba, Suvir Kaul, Matti Bunzl, Antoinette Burton, and Jed Esty, eds., *Postcolonial Studies and Beyond* (Durham: Duke University Press, 2005), 16.

27. Brown, *Undoing the Demos*, 42.

28. David Theo Goldberg and Susan Searls Giroux, *Sites of Race: Conversations with Susan Searls Giroux* (Cambridge: Polity Press, 2014), 75.

29. Goldberg and Giroux, *Sites of Race*, 80.

30. Ibid.

31. Boaventura de Sousa Santos, "Boaventura de Sousa Santos," 68.

32. Ibid., 69.

33. Ibid., 78.

34. Ibid., 77.

35. Ibid., 75.

36. Édouard Glissant, *Poetics of Relation*, trans. Betsy Wing (Ann Arbor: University of Michigan Press, 1997), 191–92.

37. Glissant, *Poetics of Relation*, 192.

38. Ibid., 193.

39. Ibid.

WORKS CITED

Ashcroft, Bill. "Future Thinking: Postcolonial Utopianism." In *The Future of Postcolonial Studies*. Ed. Chantal Zabus. New York: Routledge, 2015. 235–53.

Bongie, Chris. *Friends and Enemies: The Scribal Politics of Post/colonial Literature*. Liverpool: Liverpool University Press, 2008.

Brown, Wendy. *Undoing the Demos: Neoliberalism's Stealth Revolution*. Cambridge: MIT Press, 2015.

Coates, Ta-Nehisi. *Between the World and Me*. New York: Spiegel & Grau, 2015.

Comaroff, Jean. "The End of History, Again? Pursuing the Past in the Postcolony." In *Postcolonial Studies and Beyond*. Eds. Ania Loomba, Suvir Kaul, Matti Bunzl, Antoinette Burton, and Jed Esty. Durham: Duke University Press, 2005. 125–44.

Glissant, Édouard. *Poetics of Relation* [1990]. Trans. Betsy Wing. Ann Arbor: University of Michigan Press, 1997.

Goldberg, David Theo. "David Theo Goldberg." In *Conversations in Postcolonial Thought*. Ed. Katy P. Sian. New York: Palgrave Macmillan, 2014. 35–47.

Goldberg, David Theo, and Susan Searls Giroux. *Sites of Race: Conversations with Susan Searls Giroux*. Cambridge: Polity Press, 2014.

Hallward, Peter. *Absolutely Postcolonial: Writing Between the Singular and the Specific*. New York: Palgrave, 2001.

Harrison, Nicholas. "Metaphorical Memories: Freud, Conrad, and the Dark Continent." In *Postcolonial Poetics: Genre and Form*. Eds. Patrick Crowley and Jane Hiddleston. Liverpool: Liverpool University Press, 2011. 49–70.

Hiddleston, Jane. "Introduction." In *Postcolonial Poetics: Genre and Form*. Eds. Patrick Crowley and Jane Hiddleston. Liverpool: Liverpool University Press, 2011. 1–9.

Hulme, Peter. "Beyond the Straits: Postcolonial Allegories of the Globe." In *Postcolonial Studies and Beyond*. Eds. Ania Loomba, Suvir Kaul, Matti Bunzl, Antoinette Burton, and Jed Esty. Durham: Duke University Press, 2005. 41–61.

Loomba, Ania. *Shakespeare, Race, and Colonialism*. Oxford: Oxford University Press, 2002.

Loomba, Ania. "Race and the Possibilities of Comparative Critique." *New Literary History* 40.3 (2009): 501–22.

Loomba, Ania, Suvir Kaul, Matti Bunzl, Antoinette Burton, and Jed Esty, eds. *Postcolonial Studies and Beyond*. Durham: Duke University Press, 2005.

Santos, Boaventura de Sousa. "Boaventura de Sousa Santos." In *Conversations in Postcolonial Thought*. Ed. Katy P. Sian. New York: Palgrave Macmillan, 2014. 63–80.

Scott, David. *Conscripts of Modernity: The Tragedy of Colonial Enlightenment*. Durham: Duke University Press, 2004.

Yancy, George, and Seyla Benhabib. "Whom Does Philosophy Speak For?" *New York Times*. October 29, 2015. http://opinionator.blogs.nytimes.com/2015/10/29/who-does-philosophy-speak-for/

CHAPTER FOURTEEN

Ecocriticism

CLAIRE COLEBROOK

It is possible to argue that all literary criticism is ecocriticism: in order to read a text, the marks on the page must gesture or intimate a life, world, and environ beyond the text itself. Just what counts as a text's context, world, or environment would then be a matter of dispute. Do texts refer to something as general as life, history, sex, gender, class—or perhaps the most general context of all, the planet? At the same time, there is something essentially counter-ecological in the very notion of the *literary*: for American New Criticism a text needs to be read on its own terms, as though the text itself were a bounded whole, akin to a living being or organism with no reference to anything other than itself. More recently, new materialism—though primarily a philosophical movement concerned with the things of this world, rather than our knowledge of them—has nevertheless argued for a form of criticism that isolates the physical text as an object.[1] One might argue that there is an ecological tension or problem both in the concept of text, *and* in the concept of *oikos* from which both "ecology" and "economy" derive. First, a text is (especially in its literary mode) akin to a living being or organism; insofar as it is woven from interrelated aspects that make sense in their relation to a whole, a text seems to possess a certain autonomy or apartness. As early as the seventeenth century, John Milton was comparing books to living organisms: "Books are not absolutely dead things but do contain a potency of life in them to be as active as that soul whose progeny they are . . . a good book is the precious lifeblood of a master spirit, embalmed and treasured up on purpose to a life beyond life."[2] For the American New Critic Cleanth Brooks, who argued that a text ought to be treated as a distinct and autonomous whole, master of its own relations, there is no single feature or quality that all poems share; what makes a poem a poem is its organic organization. As a *literary* text, then, a poem is an ecology unto itself:

> The attempt to locate the "poetry" in a special doctrine or a special subject matter or a special kind of imagery . . . speedily breaks down. It must break down, if literature exists as literature; for different poems state what are apparently contradictory doctrines and employ very different materials. Yet if we are to emphasize, not the special subject matter, but the way in which the poem is built, or—to change the metaphor—the form which it has taken as it grew in the poet's mind, we shall necessarily raise questions of formal structure and rhetorical organization: we shall be forced to talk about levels of meanings, symbolizations, clashes of connotations, paradoxes, ironies, etc.
>
> Moreover, however inadequate these terms may be, even so, such terms do bring us closer, I feel, to the structure of the poem as an organism—the formal structure as it is related to the relatively complex effect which even a simple poem gives.[3]

On the one hand, *literary* criticism focuses on the internal relations and ennabling connections of the text itself, treating the text as something like an organism or living object. And yet at the same time to treat a text as *literary* is to set it apart from the day-to-day life of communicating and circulating language. A text is at once like a living body, an ecology unto itself with its own self-constituting relations, at the same time as the text is cut off from life: no longer tied to the author, and allowed to circulate, be copied, transmitted and ultimately (possibly) to decay. The word *oikos,* originally referring to a household, suggests that an ecology is like a relatively enclosed whole with its internal hierarchies and relations, like the well-woven organism; but *oikos* is also like an economy—an open and unbounded network or text of relations. When Jacques Derrida argued that there was "nothing outside the text" he offered an *economic*-ecological account of texts.[4] Even deconstruction, which was often criticized for being "textualist" in its refusal of any simple referent, insisted that a text's *context* is unlimited. One cannot delimit or cut the text off from its milieu; the context of a text cannot stop with the author, the audience, or the simple historical period, but would encompass all possible relations, including the "play of the world."[5] Just as the concept of "text" at once signals a material object *and* a network of relations, so the "eco" of ecocriticism at once refers to ecology in the sense of an enclosed living system, but also ecology-economy as an open whole of relations. Thinking of a text *as an ecology* (like a living organism) precludes thinking of a text *ecologically*—or as bound up with a world beyond itself. Textualist approaches that focus on the book or matter itself would appear to be opposed to ecological approaches that open the text toward the world. There would seem to be an opposition between formalist and referential approaches, between isolating the text as literature or seeing the text as part of a broader whole. Ecocriticism, even before its explicit manifestation as a movement renders such an opposition both explicit and problematic. This is because of the very ecological nature of texts, and the textual nature of ecologies.

In fact, one of the ways to think about ecocriticism is *not* as one more expansion of the context of texts to include the "environment." Ecocriticism would not be the *addition* of environmental concerns to, say, Marxist or Feminist approaches. Nor would ecocriticism open formalism to the milieu of nature from which texts emerge. Such approaches were already thoroughly oriented toward nature and *ecology.* As I have already suggested, formalist and textualist notions drew upon a conception of the text as a living body; by seeing the text as an ecological whole, as a self-organizing relation among dynamic forces, the problem of how such relations emerge and might be sustained was never questioned. F. R. Leavis's classic *New Bearings in English Poetry* tellingly saw the *poem's* life as a way of making up for humanity's "uprooting" from nature: "What we are witnessing today is the final uprooting of the immemorial ways of life, of life rooted in the soil."[6] The poem's "achieved harmony" and life was necessary because of the separation from nature that constitutes modernity. A much later text, Jonathan Bate's *A Song of the Earth* (2000) expresses its dream of deep ecology as a utopian idea that—not unlike Leavis's lament of "uprooting"—focuses upon the human predicament of diremption from the earth. His "environmentalism" is (as Ursula Heise would later argue in her claims for a *critical* ecocriticism) an assumption of something as broad as *the earth* to which we humans may or may not be connected; even though he refuses the task of poetry as a recompense for the loss of nature, he nevertheless argues for a *thought experiment* that would have as its ideal a profound, if impossible, connectedness for the sake of *our species*:

> Central to the dilemma of environmentalism is the fact that the act of identifying the presumption of human apartness from nature as the problem is itself a symptom of that

very apartness. The identification is the product of an instrumental way of thinking and of using language. It may therefore be that a necessary step in overcoming the apartness is to think and to use language in a different way. Let us begin by supposing that we cannot do without thought experiments and language-experiments which imagine a return to nature, a reintegration of the human and the Other. The dream of deep ecology will never be realized upon the earth, but our survival as a species may be dependent on our capacity to dream it in the work of our imagination.[7]

The environment, nature, and ecology have not only been present in literary forms from the earliest genesis myths to contemporary cli-fi and postapocalyptic mournings of a nature irretrievably lost (and we might think here of Cormac McCarthy's *The Road* (2006), where the "end of the world" is presented as the continuation of human existence without any other forms of life), but also have been crucial, beyond formalism, to political literary theory. In Marxist forms of literary criticism, "nature" was a problem but only insofar as it appeared *either* as a nostalgic and compensating paradise lost, *or* as a force that would need to be reintegrated in a modern and just future. For Raymond Williams, nature has always been humanized, mourned, and rendered in anthropomorphic terms that become increasingly problematic with the intensification of industrialism. By the end of the nineteenth-century "nature" was a product of the idyllic urban imagination. Writing about H. G. Wells's *The Time Machine* of 1899, Williams notes

> what Wells calls "human ecology": a new collective consciousness, scientific and social, which is capable of taking control of an environment in a total way and directing it to human achievement. This dimension of thought is new, and it is provoked by observation of what has been done to men and animals, to the country and the city, by unplanned and ignorant and aggressive development. The new city, when it comes, will be a new world, directed by the new kind of science.[8]

More recently, but still well before the efflorescence of ecocriticism, the radical feminist critic Shulamith Firestone insisted that patriarchy's domination of nature was intertwined with the oppression of women; like Marxist critics she saw a renovated relationship to nature and technology as a universal and necessary good. Her vision for a more just future required a nature reconfigured *for human felicity*:

> Humanity can no longer afford to remain in the transitional stage between simple animal existence and full control of nature. And we are much closer to a major evolutionary jump, indeed, to direction of our own evolution, than we are to a return to the animal kingdom through which we evolved. Thus in view of accelerating technology, a revolutionary ecological movement would have the same aim as the feminist movement: control of the new technology for humane purposes, the establishment of a new equilibrium between man and the artificial environment he is creating, to replace the destroyed "natural" balance.[9]

If Marxism looked toward a progress of technology that would end human servitude and allow the human species to reach a liberated maturity, eco-feminism would attend to the interrelation between occlusion of nature and oppression of women. But in both these cases, as with broader forms of environmentalism, nature is the milieu for human history, and human history has as its task an ongoing transformation of nature for its own liberation. Ecocriticism, by contrast, has adopted a *critical* relation to what has been constituted in Western literary history as the environment. Rather than accepting the inclusion of one more contextual factor—adding nature to the considerations of class, sex, gender, history, race, disability, or ethnicity—ecocriticism adopts a reflexive attitude to what has been inscribed as nature. For Ursula Heise any appeal to connectedness, environment, sense of place, or nature needs to be rendered multiple, such that a literary critical task would have a sense of the global and historical ways in which the planet has been figured and allegorized:

> the environmentalist emphasis on restoring individuals' sense of place, while it might function as one useful tool among others for environmentally oriented arguments, becomes a visionary dead end if it is understood as a founding ideological principle or a principally didactic means of guiding individuals and communities back to nature. Rather than focusing on the recuperation of a sense of place, environmentalism needs to foster an understanding of how a wide variety of both natural and cultural places and processes are connected and shape each other around the world, and how human impact affects and changes this connectedness.[10]

Given the complexity of ecocriticism, and its ongoing self-differentiation from seemingly straightforward environmentalist approaches, it is not surprising that what counts as ecocriticism is very much a work in progress. According to Lawrence Buell who authored a magisterial study of the "environmental imagination" that encompassed the history of American literature from Thoreau onward,[11] environmental *criticism* is a very recent theoretical event. If nature and the environment have inevitably been a backdrop for literary history, and if "first wave" ecocriticism assumed that the "environment" was coterminous with "nature,"[12] ecocriticism today is a hybrid formation. Buell therefore rejects the concept of "eco" criticism and favors environmental criticism:

> I believe that "environmental" approximates better than "eco" the hybridity of the subject at issue—all "environments" in practice involving fusions of "natural" and "constructed" elements—as well as the movement's increasingly heterogeneous foci, especially in its increasing engagements with metropolitan and/or toxified landscapes and with issues of environmental equity that challenge early ecocriticism's concentration on the literatures of nature and preservationist environmentalism. . . . "environmental" criticism somewhat better captures the interdisciplinary mix of literature-and-environment studies, which has always drawn on the human as well as the natural sciences and in recent years cross-pollinated more with cultural studies than with the sciences.[13]

For Buell, the "eco" of ecocriticism suggests an unproblematic notion of "intellectually shallow nature worshippers."[14] Yet, as I have already suggested, the "eco" of ecology harbors a fruitful ambivalence, not only because it suggests the bounded relations of household alongside the unbounded relations of an economy, but because its deployment in ecocriticism itself has done much to destroy the milieu, habitat, or "environing" figures of "environment." Timothy Morton has argued for an "ecology without nature": *all* we have are relations and no single terms or things that enter into relations.[15] MacKenzie Wark, however, has argued precisely the opposite:

> There is only nature without ecology.
>   This nature is recalcitrant, enervating, unpredictable, only ever partially known, and if known at all, known badly, through the metaphors of the time. It has no ecology, in the sense that it is nature without guarantees. It has no necessary tendency to

stability or order, no bias toward homeostasis. Its history is a history of metabolic rifts, of varied cosmological, geological, and biological causes. God is dead, and so too is ecology. Disingression awaits. Stabilities are temporary and haphazard organizations.[16]

Rather than decide between these two options—Morton's relations without any terms or Wark's nature that stays insistently out of reach—the "eco" of literature requires *both* these approaches. A literary text can be read *as literary* by being cut off from everyday relations; it can be opened in multiple contexts across time and no longer tied to its original *oikos*. A text is literary insofar as it is detached from its original environs or world—such that Shakespeare's *Hamlet* can be read as a text on something as universal as "the subject"—and yet that same universality can be seen as part of a broader economy and ecology, the entire Western trajectory of the self, or even—as with the most radical forms of ecocriticism—as a document in the history of the "man" of the Anthropocene. A text is at once an ecology (like a house or *oikos*), a system of its own, *and* an economy or an ongoing proliferation of relations. The problem, to quote Timothy Clark, is one of scale: the most local and enclosed events open to the cosmos, while the cosmos is a concept of such reach that local actions *cannot* have any singular effect:

> One symptom of a now widespread crisis of scale is a derangement of linguistic and intellectual proportion in the way people often talk about the environment, a breakdown of "decorum" in the strict sense. Thus a sentence about the possible collapse of civilization can end, no less solemnly, with the injunction never to leave a TV on standby or forget to recycle a cardboard box. A headline in *New Scientist* magazine reads "To save the planet, chow down on a caterpillar." An item in the same journal for 3 March 2014 proclaims, "Captains of industry, listen up. There is a fortune to be made from saving the planet." A motorist who occasionally takes a bus prides herself on helping "save the planet." Jonathan Bate claims "poetry is the place where we save the earth."
>
> This ubiquitous phrase, used as shorthand for so many environmentally informed actions (even buying a slightly more efficient fridge) condenses in itself a set of mutually implicated but contradictory notions of the Earth, of humanity, of language and of ethics.[17]

What Clark identifies as a derangement of scale that occurs when thinking about the relations among individual actions and events and the broader whole of which they are a complex part is at once what makes ecocriticism revolutionary and yet also intensifies an ongoing problem of literary theory. Those forms of criticism that appear to be the *least* ecological, such as the formalism that demands we read the text on its own terms, nevertheless use the language of life and living organisms to describe how texts work as autonomous, self-organized wholes. And those approaches that would seem to be manifestly ecological (even before the first self-declared eco-critical theories emerged in the late twentieth century) more often than not assume that nature or the environment is there to be found, rather than emerging through the practices of inscription from which texts and persons emerge. From its very inception—going back to Aristotle, through to eighteenth-century theories of aesthetics and the sublime, and up to contemporary formalism—texts have been regarded as akin to living organisms (with the understanding of the whole being drawn from the dynamic relations among parts). Even a theory as ruthlessly materialist as the deconstruction of Paul de Man argued that once we accept that something like the "state of nature" is a fiction, and once we try to focus on the purely literal, or purely material textual object, we will ultimately end up positing something like the text as a natural object.[18] Gestures, such as Timothy Morton's, that argue for an ecology *without nature*, nevertheless allow ecology to be the "ground" or "nature" from which all things emanate. Erasing "nature" as a fiction, a lure, or a mere textual artifact is ultimately a naturalizing gesture. This is why, for de Man, the "sublime" which is commonly thought to be *nature's* capacity to exceed any image we have of it, should ultimately be understood as a textual event: when matter itself appears *as it is*.[19] If one wishes to isolate the text itself, in its simple matter, then books, poems, and all other texts become things of the world or natural objects. To think of the text *naturally* or *materially* would be counter-ecological insofar as it severs the text from relations, seeing it as nothing more than itself. And yet criticism of that type—pure formalist criticism—has tended to animate and render organic-ecological the text itself.

If literary criticism can be, at one extreme, a demand that texts be considered in themselves and not in terms of anything else, then this is because texts themselves are ecologies, and because *literary* criticism demands that texts be considered not simply as objects that circulate in the world, but as bearing their own internal dynamic. From formalism to deconstruction to new formalism, even though it is the text *itself* that is the object of focus, this very isolation requires that the text be considered as a set of generative and interdependent relations: an ecology. At the other extreme, if movements such as feminism, critical race theory, Marxism, postcolonialism, queer theory or various ethical, inhuman, affective, and materialist turns refuse to isolate the text, they do so by opening the text outward toward the conditions and relations from which it emerges. To consider a text in terms of the environment, or more accurately *ecology* (the interconnections that compose the environment) opens texts to forces well beyond human intentions, well beyond human history, and well beyond the identities of race, class, gender, and sexuality. In that respect, ecocriticism would appear to bring the history of literary criticism to its natural fulfillment: from Aristotle's consideration of how texts produce catharsis, to ever further openings of the text to the social-economic world (Marxism), patriarchy (feminism), sexuality (queer theory), and what we deem to be human or inhuman (postcolonialism); ecocriticism is now the consideration of the text in its relation to the earth. And yet ecocriticism is also radical insofar as it brings into play not only forces that lie beyond the human world and human bodies and structures, but a new conception of textuality.

Nowhere is this more evident than in ecocriticism's most recent expression in the consideration of the Anthropocene. Here, it is not nature or even climate change that provides a way to forces that enrich its sense, but the earth as a living system. As I have already suggested, the most fruitful way of thinking about the Anthropocene in terms of its inflection of criticism and literary criticism is through Tim Clark's conception of derangements of scale. If one were lost in a town and approached a local resident for directions, and were given a map only then to discover that it's a map of the world, one would have received the right information but at the wrong scale. Clark goes on to discuss how a text might be deranged if one were to read the highly local narratives of twentieth-century American culture in terms of a humanity fueled by fossil energies that allow "nature" to appear as nothing more than a backdrop for an ever-expanding horizon of man's self-formation. What makes Clark's argument so compelling is its pertinence both for the Anthropocene and for ecocriticism more generally. The Anthropocene is a distinct shift of scale and register: not simply a difference of degree but a difference of kind. Geologists propose that human activity has not only generated climate change by destroying certain ecosystems or warming the planet, it has also altered the earth as a living system, to the point where it is now appropriate to mark the end of the Holocene and the beginning of a new era that would be discernible as a distinct strata in the composition of the earth's layers. If one accepts the claims of stratigraphic time, several consequences for literature follow.

First, as demonstrated by Clark, the world of human time and action would appear to be possible because of a broader milieu of an earth and its inhuman past. At the same time, local human actions transform the earth geologically. The life of cars, fridges, mobile phones, and global interconnectivity is at once a human narrative to do with the polity, but also opens out onto a dynamism and temporality beyond the standard frames of reference for critique:

> Viewed on very long time scales, human history and culture can take on unfamiliar shapes, as work in environmental history repeatedly demonstrates, altering conceptions of what makes something "important" and what does not. Nonhuman entities take on a decisive agency. Thus some would argue that, globally, the two major events of the past three centuries have been the industrial exploitation of fossil fuels and a worldwide supplanting of local biota in favor of an imported portmanteau of profitable species: cattle, wheat, sheep, maize, sugar, coffee, eucalyptus, palm oil, etc. Thus it is that most of the world's wheat, a crop originally from the middle east, now comes from other areas—Canada, the United States, Argentina, Australia—just as people of originally European descent now dominate a large proportion of the earth's surface. This huge shift in human populations, including slaves as well as domesticated animals and plants, has largely determined the modern world, with its close connections between destructive monocultures in food production, exploitative systems of international trade and exchange and the institution of the modern state. At its bleakest, an ecological overview of the current state of the planet shows a huge bubble of population and consumption in one species intensifying exponentially and expanding at a rate that cannot be supported by the planet's resources for long. It is the transitory world of this bizarre, destructive and temporary energy imbalance that Western populations currently inhabit and take for a stable and familiar reality.[20]

Second, the very conception of scale has ramifications well beyond the geological time frame of the Anthropocene and ecocriticism in its narrow sense. If one accepts the challenge of ecocriticism and opens the text to "our" relation to nature, just what nature are we attending to? A nature that we imagine as cyclic, eternal, harmonious, and fecund in opposition to the changing and brutish world of human affairs, a nature that provides abundant recompense in the face of human finitude, or a nature that is red in tooth and claw and that reminds us that what we know as civility and humanity is fragile and fleeting? Is nature the earth prior to or beyond human labor and industry, or is nature always bound up with the actions and lives of the various human worlds that make up history? In short, opening the text to a nature that it appears to express or represent— even without the deep time of the Anthropocene—raises the question of the threshold between nature and "nature," between a natural world that seems to admonish us in being radically other than our human concerns and interests, and a "nature" that is an imaginary projection of an always human and always historicized world. Here again we might follow Timothy Morton and argue that we have ecology without nature. However we conceive the human world, it is bound up with relations beyond human bodies and interests; there is no nature-in-itself that would exist as some pure form outside the temporalities and systems through which it operates. Despite that necessary relationality or economy, what the Anthropocene discloses is a certain closure of ecology, where this specific earth system operates beyond our experience and intentionality.

Finally, even supposedly non-ecological literary-critical contexts—such as feminist or Marxist criticism—are ultimately inflected, or deranged by thinking of the ecological scale. Kate Millett's argument for sexual politics—that the personal is *political*—takes on quite a different force if one opens the scale of the polity.[21] Where feminist criticism would demand that we think of everything from the novel to the lyric as part of a history of patriarchy and the sexual division of labor, it would be necessary in turn to think of the gender system (of men, women, marriage, and the family) as a reproductive apparatus that relies upon and transforms the composition of the earth. Similarly, if the Marxist imperative is "always historicize!"[22] then such a command opens, rather than closes, the question of scale: Is the history that would provide the context for the seemingly subjective and lyric moments of literary lives the history of large-scale shifts from feudalism to capitalism to late monopoly capitalism (which would, in turn, still include the increasing extraction of the planet's finite resources), or is materialist history only achieved with attention to the nuances of day-to-day practices and the formations of bodies in various disciplines and technologies? (And here, again, any history of bodies would need to include the way bodies are constituted through habits of hyper-consumption and the appropriation of nature). The history of the human relations of labor, class, industry, and technology must also include the forces of fossil fuels, rising sea levels, and the ongoing plunder of the planet's resources. Consider, for example, a few stanzas from what might at first appear to be one of the most enclosed, private, and psychically singular literary expressions of experience, Sylvia Plath's "Daddy" (1965; usually interpreted through the frame of the fraught biography of Plath's tragic life):

> But they pulled me out of the sack,
> And they stuck me together with glue.
> And then I knew what to do.
> I made a model of you,
> A man in black with a Meinkampf look
>
> And a love of the rack and the screw.
> And I said I do, I do.
> So daddy, I'm finally through.
> The black telephone's off at the root,
> The voices just can't worm through.
>
> If I've killed one man, I've killed two—
> The vampire who said he was you
> And drank my blood for a year,
> Seven years, if you want to know.
> Daddy, you can lie back now.
>
> There's a stake in your fat black heart
> And the villagers never liked you.
> They are dancing and stamping on you.
> They always knew it was you.
> Daddy, daddy, you bastard, I'm through.[23]

It is not too difficult to see how the personal (and sexual) is political in Plath's poem. The speaker's relation to her father is likened both to a village's relation to a terrorizing vampire and to an even more intense position of subjection and abjection in the Jewish people's annihilation by the Nazis ("Chuffing me off like a Jew" . . . "A man in black with a Meinkampf look.") The anonymous "they" who continue to reassemble the broken self ("they stuck me together with glue"), and who do so for an authoritarian "you" (Daddy, tyrant, God, vampire) *can* be interpreted in terms of the poet's own life, where a relation to the suffocating and even exterminating authority of one's father is inextricably intertwined with a broader milieu of patriarchy that ultimately needs to be thrown off ("I'm through"). One could either see the figures of the village vampire, Nazi, or simply "man" ("If I've killed one man, I've killed two") as ongoing variants of an originally prohibiting father figure, *or* one could see the terror elicited by "Daddy" as possible only because of a long history of paternal/patriarchal authority. In either case, this seemingly sexual or personal relation of daughter to father opens out to a broader history not only of male authority, but of a certain desire for subjection, as though (to follow psychoanalysis) one must imagine a prohibiting authority in order to deal with the sheer loss of plenitude that constitutes individual existence. It is precisely here, though, in its enclosure within the psyche and a sexual-political history that ecocriticism would intervene. How is it possible that the intensity of individual suffering is imagined in terms of an apparently global history (from village vampires to Nazism) *without any sense of a world or earth*? How does this highly personal "I," along with the practice of lyric poetry intertwined with personal biography demand an interrogation of a highly individuated subject? If one were to thoroughly or absolutely be eco-critical one would need to ask about the planetary composition of this "I" for whom the world is given in political/historical figures—vampires and Nazis—without any sense of the earth. There seems to be nothing at all ecological about this personal/political poem, and to engage in ecocriticism would seem to demand turning to more obviously nature-engaged texts, such as romanticism's explicit appeals to nature or even high Modernism's laments of urban life. Politicizing Plath's work would seem to require turning to gender and sexuality, rather than nature. It is, however, a specifically Western and modern literary history that forms a certain type of subjectivity that has no world other than a history of human power. The speaker in Plath's poem whose inner trauma maps onto a world of "man" and history, for all its pain and abjection, relies upon a long history of colonization, industrialism, and "nature"-plundering that ultimately results in the individual liberal subject and "psyche." The conditions for a poem such as Plath's are at once literary, political, and environmental. In order to have "a" subject who thinks of herself as an isolated and singular "I," there must be a long history of increasingly intense agriculture and enslaved or indentured labor. The condition for the possibility of the self who appears to have no relation to "nature" whatsoever is that nature must have already been mastered, erased, "humanized," or invented as *nature*. Plath's isolated poetic self has been preceded by centuries of literary history where nature is imagined as reflective of some divine power that will ultimately realize itself harmoniously or as a vehicle for human meaning and expression. One can think of John Milton's depiction of the garden of Eden in *Paradise Lost* as typical of already nostalgic visions of an uncorrupted and thoroughly spiritualized nature. Milton describes Satan entering a garden of Eden that takes the form of a beautifully tended, balanced, landscaped, imperial, and *ordered* paradise, as though the world before fallen humanity was the world humanity would aim to manufacture for itself:

> *Eden*, where delicious Paradise,
> Now nearer, Crowns with her enclosure green,
> As with a rural mound the champain head
> Of a steep wilderness, whose hairie sides
> With thicket overgrown, grottesque and wilde,
> Access deni'd; and over head up grew
> Insuperable highth of loftiest shade,
> Cedar, and Pine, and Firr, and branching Palm
> A Silvan Scene, and as the ranks ascend
> Shade above shade, a woodie Theatre
> Of stateliest view. Yet higher then thir tops
> The verdurous wall of paradise up sprung:
> Which to our general Sire gave prospect large
> Into his neather Empire neighbouring round.
> And higher then that Wall a circling row
> Of goodliest Trees loaden with fairest Fruit,
> Blossoms and Fruits at once of golden hue
> Appeerd, with gay enameld colours mixt:
> On which the Sun more glad impress'd his beams
> Then in fair Evening Cloud, or humid Bow
> When God hath showrd the earth; so lovely seemd
> That Lantskip[24]

If one looks forward from *Paradise Lost* to Margaret Atwood's 2009 *The Year of the Flood* it is possible to read the ways in which paradisiacal figures of nature as a landscape and empire for "man's" fruitful becoming are inextricably intertwined with a history of subjectivity defined by production, self-expression, fecundity, and futurity. In *The Year of the Flood* two postapocalyptic enterprises govern the earth, a biotech company determined to manufacture and streamline life, and an Adamic cult who worship a nature of fruitful and abundant production. What Atwood, ecocritically, sets against both eco-worship and eco-management are new forms of self, art, and futurity that do not fetishize ongoing production. The central female characters in her novel are bonded by affiliation, not by blood, and are oriented toward forms of care and creation that are fragile and fleeting. Here is how the female narrator describes her friend Amanda:

> Then Amanda broke up with Jimmy. She let me know about it in a roundabout way. She'd already told me about her landscape installation series called The Living Word— how she was spelling words out in giant letters, using bioforms to make the words appear and then disappear, just like the words she used to do with ants and syrup when we were kids. Now, she said, "I'm up to the four-letter words." And I said, "You mean the dirty ones like *shit*?" And she laughed and said, "Worse ones than that." And I said, "You mean the c-word and the f-word?" and she said, "No. Like *love*."[25]

Amanda's art is literally a destruction of the living word that also includes "dirty" words, as though an expressive nature would utter expletives, and then the "even worse" notion of "love" that has held together the romance structures that have sustained the novel, patriarchy, and the division of labor. In *The Year of the Flood* two enterprises that fetishize the flourishing of life at all costs—the biotech corporation and the Adamic nature cult—are contrasted with female friendships and forms of art that are evanescent and fragile. Between Milton's pastoral of the seventeenth century and Atwood's eco-critical presentation of figures of nature, one can see William Wordsworth's romantic turn to nature for solace and "abundant recompense" as part of a long poetic history that creates nature as a landscape for imaginative human projection.[26] And this literary history is possible (and necessary) only because a certain type of self has been formed for whom the world is fully humanized, and fully historicized in solely "human" terms, where what counts as "humanity" is ultimately Western colonizing humanity and where what counts as "nature" is already given in the form of a landscape. In this respect, one could consider three registers of ecocriticism. The first would take the form of expanding the range of a text's context to include nature, not merely as the backdrop for human history, but as a force in its own right. The second would be genealogical, and would critique the anthropomorphism and manufacture of nature. The third would recognize that every critical destruction of "nature" nevertheless generates a presupposed *real* nature that always recedes from textual capture.

Penn State University (United States)

NOTES

1. Michael H. Epp, "Object Lessons: The New Materialism in U.S. Literature and Culture," *Canadian Review of American Studies* 34.3 (2004): 305–13.

2. John Milton, *Complete Prose Works: Volume 2,* ed. Ernest Sirluck (New Haven: Yale University Press, 1958), 492–93.

3. Cleanth Brooks, *The Well-Wrought Urn: Studies in the Structure of Poetry* (New York: Harcourt Brace, 1947), 199.

4. Jacques Derrida, *Of Grammatology*, trans. Gayatri Chakravorty Spivak (Baltimore: Johns Hopkins, 1972), 158.

5. Derrida, *Of Grammatology,* 287.

6. F. R. Leavis, *New Bearings in English Poetry* (London: Faber and Faber, 1932), 131.

7. Johnathan Bate, *The Song of the Earth* (Cambridge: Harvard University Press, 2000), 37–380.

8. Raymond Williams, *The Country and the City* (London: Chatto and Windus, 1974).

9. Shulamith Firestone, *The Dialectic of Sex* (New York: Bantam, 1971), 193.

10. Ursula K. Heise, *Sense of Place and Sense of Planet: The Environmental Imagination of the Global* (Oxford: Oxford University Press, 2008), 21.

11. Lawrence Buell, *The Environmental Imagination: Thoreau, Nature Writing and the Formation of American Culture* (Cambridge: Harvard University Press, 1995).

12. Buell, *The Environmental Imagination,* 27.

13. Lawrence Buell, *The Future of Environmental Criticism: Environmental Crisis and Literary Imagination* (Oxford: Blackwell, 2005), viii.

14. Buell, *The Future of Environmental Criticism*, viii.

15. Timothy Morton, *Ecology Without Nature: Rethinking Environmental Aesthetics* (Cambridge: Harvard University Press, 2009).

16. McKenzie Wark, *Molecular Red: Theory for the Anthropocene* (London: Verso, 2015), 82.

17. Timothy Clark, *Ecocriticism on the Edge: The Anthropocene as a Threshold Concept* (London: Bloomsbury, 2015), 37.

18. Paul de Man, *Allegories of Reading: Figural Language in Rousseau, Nietzsche, Rilke, and Proust* (New Haven: Yale University Press, 1979), 137.

19. Paul de Man, *Aesthetic Ideology,* ed. Andrzej Warminski (Minneapolis: University of Minnesota Press, 1996), 76.

20. Timothy Clark, "Scale," in *Telemorphosis: Theory in the Era of Climate Change, Vol. 1,* ed. Tom Cohen (Ann Arbor: Open Humanities Press, 2012). https://quod.lib.umich.edu/o/ohp/10539563.0001.001/1:8/—telemorphosis-theory-in-the-era-of-climate-change-vol-1?rgn=div1;view=fulltext

21. Kate Millett, *Sexual Politics* (Urbana: University of Illinois Press, 1969).

22. Fredric Jameson, *The Political Unconscious: Narrative as a Socially Symbolic Act* (Ithaca: Cornell University Press, 1981), 9.

23. Sylvia Plath, "Daddy," in *Collected Poems* (New York: Harper Perennial Modern Classics, 2008), 183.

24. John Milton, *The Complete Poetry of John Milton,* ed. John T. Shawcross (New York: Anchor, 1971), 4.132–153.

25. Margaret Atwood, *The Year of the Flood* (New York: Random House, 2009), 304.

26. William Wordsworth, "The Excursion," in *Wordsworth: Poetical Works, With Introduction and Notes,* ed. Ernest de Selincourt (Oxford: Oxford University Press, 1936), 650.

WORKS CITED

Atwood, Margaret. *The Year of the Flood.* New York: Random House, 2009.

Bate, Johnathan. *The Song of the Earth.* Cambridge: Harvard University Press, 2000.

Brooks, Cleanth. *The Well-Wrought Urn: Studies in the Structure of Poetry.* New York: Harcourt Brace, 1947.

Buell, Lawrence. *The Environmental Imagination: Thoreau, Nature Writing and the Formation of American Culture.* Cambridge: Harvard University Press, 1995.

Buell, Lawrence. *The Future of Environmental Criticism: Environmental Crisis and Literary Imagination.* Oxford: Blackwell, 2005.

Clark, Timothy. "Scale." In *Telemorphosis: Theory in the Era of Climate Change, Vol. 1.* Ed. Tom Cohen. Ann Arbor: Open Humanities Press, 2012. https://quod.lib.umich.edu/o/ohp/10539563.0001.001/1:8/—telemorphosis-theory-in-the-era-of-climate-change-vol-1?rgn=div1;view=fulltext

Clark, Timothy. *Ecocriticism on the Edge: The Anthropocene as a Threshold Concept.* London: Bloomsbury, 2015.

De Man, Paul. *Allegories of Reading: Figural Language in Rousseau, Nietzsche, Rilke, and Proust.* New Haven: Yale University Press, 1979.

De Man, Paul. *Aesthetic Ideology.* Ed. Andrzej Warminski. Minneapolis: University of Minnesota Press, 1996.

Derrida, Jacques. *Of Grammatology* [1967]. Trans. Gayatri Chakravorty Spivak. Baltimore: Johns Hopkins, 1972.

Derrida, Jacques. *Writing and Difference* [1967]. Trans. Alan Bass. London: Routledge, 1978.

Epp, Michael H. "Object Lessons: The New Materialism in U.S. Literature and Culture." *Canadian Review of American Studies* 34.3 (2004): 305–13.

Firestone, Shulamith. *The Dialectic of Sex*. New York: Bantam, 1971.

Heise, Ursula K. *Sense of Place and Sense of Planet: The Environmental Imagination of the Global*. Oxford: Oxford University Press, 2008.

Jameson, Fredric. *The Political Unconscious: Narrative as a Socially Symbolic Act*. Ithaca: Cornell University Press, 1981.

Leavis, Frank Raymond. *New Bearings in English Poetry*. London: Faber and Faber, 1932.

Lukács, Georg. *History and Class Consciousness: Studies in Marxist Dialectics* [1968]. Trans. Rodney Livingstone. London: Merlin, 1971.

Millett, Kate. *Sexual Politics*. Urbana: University of Illinois Press, 1969.

Milton, John. *Complete Prose Works: Volume 2*. Ed. Ernest Sirluck. New Haven: Yale University Press, 1958.

Milton, John. *The Complete Poetry of John Milton*. Ed. John T. Shawcross. New York: Anchor, 1971.

Morton, Timothy. *Ecology Without Nature: Rethinking Environmental Aesthetics*. Cambridge: Harvard University Press, 2009.

Plath, Sylvia. "Daddy [1965]." In *Collected Poems*. Ed. Ted Hughes. New York: Harper Perennial Modern Classics, 2008. 183.

Wark, McKenzie. *Molecular Red: Theory for the Anthropocene*. London: Verso, 2015.

Williams, Raymond. *The Country and the City*. London: Chatto and Windus, 1974.

Wordsworth, William. "The Excursion [1814]." In *Wordsworth: Poetical Works. With Introduction and Notes*. Ed. Ernest de Selincourt. Oxford: Oxford University Press, 1936. 589–689.

CHAPTER FIFTEEN

Biopower and Biopolitics

GREGG LAMBERT

THE "SUBJECT OF POWER" (CIRCA 1975–76)

Anytime one begins to define the genealogy concept in Michel Foucault, one must first address the question of his method. Consequently, let me begin my definition of the concepts of biopolitics and biopower by highlighting the importance of Foucault's two great methodological reversals in the analysis of the subject of power: first, to no longer define power through a traditional theory of sovereignty or philosophy of right. Secondly, as Foucault states at many points throughout his analysis of the subject of power, we must not imagine that power is neither an eternal form or a natural being. Rather, it is an artifice, a device, a technique, or a strategy. Therefore, after subtracting the natural and historical representations of power—first of all, that power is not an attribute, that is, neither substance, as in Spinoza, nor subject, as in Hegel and Marx—we are initially given a strictly nominalist definition first given in the first volume of *The History of Sexuality* (1976): "Power is not an institution, and not a structure; neither is it a certain strength we are endowed with; it is the name that one attributes to a complex strategic situation in a particular society."[1]

Beginning with the lectures of 1975–76, in his analysis of the subject of power Foucault announces that he will no longer privilege the juridical model of contract theory—which was always a speculative fiction at best, or a romance, as in Rousseau—since power is not something that can be possessed and thereby consequently "alienated" like a property or a commodity. He underscores the fact that the traditional philosophical and juridical theory of right has always begun with the definition of the right to property in which both legitimate and illegitimate power relations—that is, the actual occasions and forms of possession, ownership, use, usury, violation, and transgression—are then interpreted and defined in terms of the constitution of a legitimate subject of rights (i.e., the Bourgeois subject). Therefore, the description of "power as a right that can be possessed in the same way one possesses a commodity," only functions in reference to a juridical model that rationalizes the transfer and accumulation of power in certain social subjects and its alienation (or "scarcity") in others; as a result, beginning in the nineteenth century, "political power finds its historical *raison d'etre* in the economy."[2]

Therefore, if the economy is indeed "world-making" or "world-forming," as classical liberalism claims, beginning with Smith's theory of the invisible hand, then all the degrees of human capital from the alienation to the satisfaction of interest will be determined in its domain. These are the principles at the basis of what Foucault later describes in the lectures on "The Birth of Biopolitics," following Hume and British empiricism, as a new subject beginning in the eighteenth century, *homo economicus*, in distinction from *homo juridicus*, the subject of rights.[3] The question, as Foucault will constantly underline throughout his analysis of discipline, is whether this new subject can be brought into coordination with the juridical subject of rights, and whether the techniques and knowledges operated by modern states are equipped to fashion this correspondence, or whether new juridical mechanisms will serve this purpose. Another way of posing the same question, in more Kantian terms, is whether the economic subject motivated by self-interest can be brought into harmony with the subject of right, duty, and the rule of law?

This introduces a second problem, since the traditional analysis of power merely rests on an empirical analogy that can either be reinforced, as in the case of neoliberalist arguments put forward later by Hayek and others, or challenged and critiqued, as in the history of Marxist critique. Regardless, the actual mechanisms that perpetuate and reproduce power relations are outside the control of normal and everyday citizens, given the fact that the great historical state actors of the nation-states are the only subjects who are capable of possessing or seizing control of these mechanisms of juridical right and employing them strategically in targeting populations both internal and external (particularly in the development of international law and commerce from the eighteenth century onward), while the vast multitude of those who exist within already-established power relations are permanently located in a subjective position of alienation (a fact which, in some ways, is reflected in the philosophies of alienation and oppression that have dominated the twentieth century).

Turning now to the first appearance of the concepts of the "biopolitical" and "biopower," in the lectures of 1975 Foucault introduces the presence of "a new character" of power—as one might say in a novel—something he goes on to define variously as both a new element and a new technology "of which the theory of right and disciplinary practice knew nothing."[4] This is because the theory of right only treated individuals (in particular, "individual citizens") and the assumption of an implicit social contract between them, and disciplines only treated their bodies in practical terms (as living, laboring, reproducing, etc.); whereas, as Foucault states, "what we are dealing with in the new technology of power is not exactly society . . . nor the individual-as-body," but rather an entirely new and multiple body of the population as both a statistical and biological problem of power from that point onward. It is at this point, Foucault announces, that biopolitics emerges sometime between the late eighteenth century and the first half of the nineteenth century.[5]

Foucault's understanding of the character of power announced above is primarily drawn from the biologist-philosopher Georges Canguilhem, who first argued that the emergence of Bourgeois society is not the result of the fixed ratio of labor time as it is the gradual mechanization of the different parts of labor into the form of a machine. In other words, it is only based on this prior mechanization that the total process can be standardized, numerically determined—that is, the parts or elements must already be made disposable to being standardized, they must in some manner be homogenized.[6] For example, as Canguilhem argues in an early article on "Machine and Organism" (1953), the soul cannot move the body unless the body is already predisposed to movement.[7] Foucault applies this same principle in *Discipline and Punish*; an army, which is assembled from heterogeneous elements, cannot move as one body unless they are already disposed to be made from the same mettle. Thus, a new demand appears to which discipline must respond: "To construct a machine whose effect will be maximized by the concerted articulation of the elementary parts of which it is composed. Discipline is no longer simply an art of distributing bodies, of extracting time from them and accumulating it, but of composing forces to obtain an efficient machine."[8]

As Matteo Pasquinelli has observed, the concept of normalization is pivotal to Foucault's thought from this period and assumes a central place in *Discipline and Punish*, which was published that same year at the lectures on *The Abnormal* (1975).[9] Both in the lecture course and in the book, Foucault explains the process of normalization by applying Canguilhem's groundbreaking interpretation in *The Normal and the Pathological* (1966), where the power of the norm is first defined as something that operates differently from law, since the norm's function is not to exclude and reject, but rather, "it is always linked to a positive technique of intervention and transformation, to a sort of normative project."[10] This insight directly leads to Foucault's adaptation of the evolution of the norm to determine the technical apparatus of discipline as something that is partly "artificial," like a machine, which, like any machine, demands constant reinvention, adaptation, correction, new techniques and tactics, but is also vulnerable to sudden interruptions, appropriations, breakdowns, and even reversals with the introduction of new power relations.

At the same time, it is also at this point that a model of biological normalization is substituted for mechanical causality to determine the evolutionary path of any normative order as also being open to the moments of rupture and discontinuity, or, at least, the sudden appearance of new elements and techniques as part of a generalized struggle to maintain its consistency and unity. As Canguilhem argued, the unity of an organism in its encounter with the environment can only be defined as one of a constant agnostic struggle; for example, in its encounter with illness, the organism attempts to invent a new norm that will be able to maintain its integrity and restore balance in its relation to its environment—both interior and exterior.[11] Foucault employs this new model as a lever to pry the analysis of power away from a classical mechanistic and even modern structural determinations; hence, the subject of power no longer exclusively refers to a positive and heterogeneous agency of the law, or to a sovereign figure, but also functions as a "normative autonomous agent."[12] It is here, moreover, where we find the convergence of two techniques that will later be employed to define the dual object of biopolitical order: strategies directed at the level of populations; concrete techniques directed at the "micrological" level of living bodies.

THE "DEPLOYMENT" (*DISPOSITIF*) OF SEXUALITY (1976)

A year later in the first volume of *The History of Sexuality*, Foucault will nevertheless recount a different starting point for his genealogy of biopower, which indicates a different direction of his research as well as a different problem, which is the abstract body that suddenly appears at the end of the process defined above as the nexus of all the disciplinary techniques and apparatuses (schools, barracks, prisons, clinics, but also colonies and administrated territories), and then just as suddenly disappears into the real enigma of sexuality itself. In other words, as Foucault refines his earlier statement, following the explosion of numerous and diverse techniques for subjugating bodies, the "age of biopower" could be said to have properly commenced only when these two directions that were still separated by the end of the eighteenth century, and were only joined at the level of discourse (e.g., "Ideology"), gradually converged in the form of "concrete assemblages" (*agencements concrets*) that will make up the great technology of power in the nineteenth century; "the deployment (*dispositif*) of sexuality would be one of them, and one of the most important."[13]

To account for this sudden convergence and transformation, however, we must again highlight Foucault's dual use of the terms "element" and "technique" in his presentation of the concept of biopower. For example, sexuality can be described as both an element (in the sense of a medium) that is crucial to the incipient development of later capitalism (the insertion of actual bodies into the machinery of production and, at the same time, the optimization of life, habits, and health of general populations) and as a technique that is deployed as part of an overall strategy of power. This would imply, as Foucault goes on to argue, that what is called "sexuality" from the nineteenth century onward can no longer be understood to belong to the "body" as an exterior domain to which power is applied, but rather the effect of "a complex idea" that takes shape inside the different strategies of power that will determine the role that it has played therein—that is, being both "the effect of a result and an instrument (*dispositif*) of power's designs."[14]

If only to add further confusion to variation of the definition of biopower between an "element," an "effect," and a definite "technique," in the quotation of the passages above, I have enumerated the different translations of the concrete arrangement of biopower, for which Foucault employs the French term *dispositif*, but which in the English translations has been rendered sometimes as an "instrument," at other times, as an "apparatus," and in the English translation of *The History of Sexuality*, as "deployment" or "design." Although all these translations are technically correct, in many ways it is the lexical ambiguity of the term itself that has been the source of the misunderstandings that have surrounded the history of the concept.

In an interview that occurs after the publication of *Discipline and Punish* and *The History of Sexuality*, Foucault offers one of the few explanations of his use of the term:

> What I'm trying to single out with this term is, first and foremost, a thoroughly heterogeneous set consisting of discourses, institutions, architectural forms, regulatory decisions, laws, administrative measures, scientific statements, philosophical, moral, and philanthropic propositions—in short, the said as much as the unsaid. Such are the elements of the *dispositif*. . . . It is the network that can be established between these elements.[15]

To illustrate, let us examine more closely the elements that make up the *dispositif* of sexuality (from Chapter 4 of the first volume of *The History of Sexuality*). First, beginning in the nineteenth century, there is a concerted elaboration of the idea of sexuality as something that is not anatomically determined by biology, but rather is discovered to have intrinsic properties and laws of its own, properties and laws that were formerly either repressed or shrouded in secrecy, but now promises to define the essence of Man. Second, Foucault alludes here to the early birth of the clinic which was already the subject of an earlier study; thus, this undiscovered continent of sexuality is immediately coupled with a concrete strategy of "hystericizing" women, which produces three kinds of sexuality: biologically and anatomically, as that which belongs in common to men and women; culturally, as that which belongs, par excellence, to men, and hence is lacking in women; pathologically, pertaining to the specific physiology of women, as that which by itself constitutes woman's body, ordering it wholly in terms of the functions of reproduction and keeping it in constant agitation through the effects of that very function. Accordingly, from this strategy follows a consequent hysterization of children, which was deployed by Freud and his followers in the interpretation of the perversions as the latent sexuality of the child that would later appear in adult life as the effects of the early sexualization and which became the basis for understanding and classifying the modern neuroses.

Finally, recalling Foucault's observation above, the reality of "sex" was given a universal and cosmological signification as the expression of the Thanatos-Eros, or the economic determination of the drives and the "constant tendency of the pleasure principle to elude this determinism."[16]

In each of these developments, Foucault provides us with a complete description of the concrete *dispositif* of sexuality, which is initially defined as an "artificial unity" of heterogeneous elements in more generalizable strategies of subjection and subjectification, thus vividly demonstrating the deployment of sexuality as emerging and one of the most powerful *"biopolitical dispositifs"* (albeit not the only one, as he will argue in the lecture course of the following year, which I will address below). However, it is also important to recall, at the very moment that Foucault was writing in the early 1970s, that sexuality was being hailed as the very fulcrum of subjectivity given that its practical and theoretical function established by psychoanalysis is an imaginary point that the individual must pass through to have access to her own intelligibility as a person, including access to her own body and subjective identity. However, this is not necessarily a liberation of the individual, since "we have arrived at the point where we expect our intelligibility to come from what was for many centuries thought of as madness; the plenitude of our body from what was long considered its stigma and likened to a wound; our identity from what was perceived as an obscure and nameless urge. Hence the importance we ascribe to it, the reverential fear with which we surround it, the care we take to know it."[17]

Finally, recalling another famous hypothesis that also appears in the opening of *The History of Sexuality*, the forms of subjectification (*formes d'assujettissement*) do not always appear in the form of repression or inhibition (based largely on an earlier theory of the instincts), but rather also through recent and more positive forms such as incitement, seduction, multiplication, and expansion. "The irony of this deployment," he concludes, "is in having us believe that our 'liberation' is in the balance."[18] He will return to this hypothesis in 1982, two years before his death, to announce a new problem of power that concerns precisely the explosion of new forms of subjectification, in some sense echoing his earlier observations regarding a similar explosion of new disciplinary techniques at the end of the eighteenth century. Although, he says, "the struggle against forms of domination and oppression have certainly not disappeared—in fact, quite the opposite!"—it is the "submission to subjectivity itself" (i.e., under the earlier normative forms of subjection of populations and individuals, such as race and sexuality) that is responsible for producing the greatest resistances today.[19]

THE GOVERNMENT OF THE LIVING:
THE BIRTH OF BIOPOLITICS (1978–1979)

From the relatively short period of a few years following the publication of the first volume of *The History of Sexuality* and the lecture course on *Security, Territory, Population* of 1977–78, there is a parallel thesis—perhaps even a certain "correlationism"—established between the evolution of disciplinary and security apparatuses (*dispositifs*) that are directed either at the level of populations or species-being, and the concept of freedom transferred first to the individual substance under liberalism, but gradually become identified with the multiple and micrological processes of life itself. As Foucault emphasizes, "Freedom is nothing else but the correlative deployment of the apparatuses of security."[20] In other words, "there is a very tight correlation of biopolitical security apparatuses" (i.e., health, sexuality, deviancy, hygiene, etc.) with the forces of contingency, discontinuity, economy, and circulation that will come to the forefront of the 1978–79 lectures that comprise *The Birth of Biopolitics*.[21]

This brings us to Foucault's initial discussions of neoliberalism when Foucault first addresses the concept of "biopolitics" explicitly in relation to what he accounts for as the influence of some of the principles of German ordoliberalism during the postwar period, but primarily from the influence on national economic policies of Great Britain and the United States by members of the MPS (Hayek, Friedman, Stigler, Popper, Polanyi, Einaudi).[22] However, it is important to point out in the 1979 seminars beginning in January, that, while Foucault promises a complete picture of the different national and economic arrangements that result from what he identified as the "dispersion" of the German ordoliberal model, including the hybrid form which neoliberalism assumes in American society through the influence of the Chicago school that was taking place also at precisely this moment, he eventually restricts his analysis mostly to the key figures of the earlier Frieburg school, and especially those aspects that are consistent with his earlier work on disciplinary society, such as the analysis of criminality and juvenile delinquency.[23]

In the 1978–79 seminars, Foucault's own examples of biopolitics concerns and areas where we see the growth of new techniques are birth rate in national populations, child-rearing in the family, juvenile delinquency in civil society, to which we might also add several other values of human capital including education, hygiene, mental health, and so on. In other words, this constitutes the program that is generally identified with the economization of the private sphere of society, which became the hallmark of what ordoliberal economist Wilhelm Röpke called *Gesellschaftspolitik*, and Alexander von Rüstow called *Vitalpolitik*. What Foucault will conclude from these policies is the extension of new techniques of governing living bodies and populations, techniques and their corresponding knowledges that "cross the threshold of the traditional political sciences" and extend the problem of governmentality "beyond its former limits, including all the spheres of life in the government's political activity," including, I might add, the life of other species and "non-human animals within the bio political frame."[24]

As Foucault quotes from Bilger's *La Pensée économique liberale de L'Allemagne contemporaine* (1966), upon which he relies for much of his own understanding of German ordoliberal theory, "Rüstow defined *Vitalpolitik* [as] a policy of life, which is not essentially orientated to increased earnings and reduced hours for the worker, like traditional social policy of labor time, but which takes cognizance of the worker's whole vital situation, his real, concrete situation, from morning to night and from night to morning" (including material and moral hygiene, sense of property and social integration, etc.).[25] In other words, the major problem posed by postwar German ordoliberalist theories was how to redefine a market society made up from purely "raw" or "cold" values (i.e., the principle of unrestrained economic competition) without this principle itself causing the fabric of civil society to unravel. In large part, this represents a critique of the classical principles of free-market economy, often leading to a laissez-faire state that in some ways resembles a Hobbesian state of nature. Rüstow, who, along with Erhard and Röpke, is considered one of the primary economic theorists of "social market theory," proposed to resolve this ambiguity in the following manner: "Since competition is a principle that dissolves more than it unifies," "we have to organize the economy of the social body according to the rules of the market economy," but at the same time, to infuse these principles a number of "light" or "warm" values must be created to buffer the individual from the disintegrating and atomistic effects of "pure, raw, or *cold* competition."[26] Consequently, the primary concern of *Vitalpolitik* was in shaping the subjective value of human capital in its individuated form, that is, to normalize subjectification so that it is intergraded into the free-market society without overt coercion or the potentially disintegrating reaction caused by power's overt manifestation as a violent, dominating, or repressive force. These positive values can be understood as corollaries to Foucault's version of biopolitics that enhances the productive forces of life, rather than premised on sovereign violence, that is, upon a "government of the living."

However, both in reference to Rüstow's argument concerning a positive *Vitalpoliik*, or in Foucault's analysis of the growth of nineteenth century *Poliziewissenschafften*—"police sciences," taken in its broadest sense, including the laws of commerce and circulation— that forms the basis of his own investigation into the problem of neoliberalism, these new knowledges or techniques are not immediately assumed to already function as the official organs of state power, but rather to constitute an array of knowledges and that emerged alongside the new form of governmentality. For Rüstow, these knowledges constitute a special region of the social policies and mostly stem from what he often refers to as the "new anthropology," which in the 1950s corresponded with the emergence of sociology as an official academic discipline in the Western university. Given Foucault's own interest in the emergence of new knowledges in the social sciences and statistical arts that are gradually incorporated into the "contemporary art of governmentality," these new knowledges and techniques that compose the biopolitical frame could be taken as expressions of "a new political economy" (i.e., a government of the living) that will form the primary problem of what Foucault will henceforth call "governmentality." As he announced in the previous year, "What is important for our modernity, that is to say, for our present, is not then the takeover (*étatisation*) of society, so much as what I would call the 'governmentalization' of the state."[27] In other words, what Foucault is first calling attention to is the emergence of neoliberal policies, knowledges, as well as new juridical mechanisms that actually seek to restrict the power of the state to intervene into the economy—and often in the name of life, security, and individual freedoms!

At the same time, it is important to point out that while Foucault first sets out to examine the emergence of this new political economy in its contemporary biopolitical frame, by the mid-point of the year he restricts his analysis to only one model. This is clearly announced in the March 7, 1979, lecture when he announces: "I would have liked to assure you that, in spite of everything, I really did intend to talk about biopolitics, and then, things being what they are, I have ended up talking at length, and maybe too long, about neo-liberalism and neo-liberalism in its German form."[28] This last observation raises the question of whether the lectures course of 1978–79 actually provides us with a complete picture of the "birth of biopolitics," and thus, a coherent theory of the *biopolitical dispositif* that governs contemporary neoliberal societies—as many of Foucault's readers have assumed? Of course, if only from a historical perspective, the answer would be "no." In fact, Foucault's own analysis might also be viewed as dated since it cannot account for significant divergences in neoliberal doctrine that did not occur until the mid-1980s, along with the rise of Thatcherism and Reagonomics in the mid-1980s. Consequently, his analysis of American neoliberalism extends only to the end of the Carter administration and cannot address current neoliberalism policy— especially, after 2004 and leading up to the fiscal recession of 2008—or the new waves of libertarianism in the United States from the 1980s to the contemporary Tea Party movement. On the other hand, does this fact necessarily imply that Foucault's analysis provides us with no tools for understanding the nature of neoliberal governmentality today? The answer would also be negative, if we estimate the value of Foucault's analysis is providing us what he himself calls a "grid of intelligibility" for studying the "new model of economic rationality" within the space opened by new strategies and tactics of power that take life as their object. In many respects, this highlights the fact that Foucault's system is not philosophical, but epistemological and historical, even though recent scholarship tends to apply Foucault's theories ontologically (i.e., paradigmatically), rather than as descriptions of finite genealogical arrangements that can undergo quite sudden transformations following another famous hypothesis of Foucault: the discontinuity, or rupture, between epochal formations of knowledge and power.

THE MAJOR MUTATIONS OF THE CONCEPT OF BIOPOWER (1984–): DELEUZE AND AGAMBEN

Since Foucault's untimely death in 1984, there have been many interpretations of Foucault's concepts of "biopolitics" and "biopower," and this trend has only intensified recently with the publication of the lecture courses beginning with "Society Must be Defended" in 2003. In concluding my brief itinerary through the genealogy of these concepts and their sources, I will highlight two dominant interpretations of the concept of biopower, in particular, that in many ways have reshaped its original application to social phenomena, either causing a mutation of its historical specificity, according to the major interpretation offered by French philosopher Gilles Deleuze, or perhaps even the deformation of its positive genealogical sense in favor of a more ontologically inflected reading offered by Italian philosopher Giorgio Agamben. For example, it is not simply by accident that in 1988 and in 2006, respectively, each addressed Foucault's major concept in essays that are both titled with that very question: "What is a dispositif?"[29] While both philosophers agreed that the term refers to the heterogeneous mechanisms of "capturing" and "transforming" living beings by a process in which the "dimension of power" plays a crucial role, they differed in terms of whether this dimension already belonged to sovereign power in the production of the "biopolitical body," according to Agamben, or may usher in an entirely new form of "control" that directly takes charge of life as "a political object," according to Deleuze.[30]

In the year immediately following Foucault's death, Deleuze, who was a longtime interlocutor and former colleague, conducts his own seminar on Foucault's major concepts, which is published in 1986 and described as "a portrait of the philosopher and his work."[31] However, it is not until a postscript that appears several years later do we find a description of a new biopolitical order of "control" that is emerging to replace disciplinary society.[32] Deleuze explicitly proposes a program to identify the new mechanisms of control in terms of the following problem: how does one locate and identify all the elements of a multiplicity in an open, or relative unlimited and "smooth" space? This is contrasted to the social problem of a disciplinary order, much like the one described earlier on Foucault, which is how to locate a relative number of elements of a finite multiplicity within a closed space (the factory, the school, the prison, the hospital). Thus, a spatiotemporal "diagram" is introduced into Foucault's earlier analysis of disciplinary society, supplanting the positive role of concrete dispositifs of Foucault's earlier analysis of sexuality and security, which now serves to distinguish a society of discipline from a society of control. For Deleuze, moreover, the emphasis is no longer placed on the emergence of biopolitics sometime in the nineteenth century, but rather on the creation of a program for outlining the potential of future forms of resistance, that is, the shape of the power relations to come, which in the present moment constitute the "outside" of disciplinary enclosures and are composed of purely virtual and unformed power relations and new, yet-to-be-determined subjectivities.

Of course, throughout his analysis Foucault nowhere presents the distinction between disciplinary apparatuses and biopolitical dispositifs in terms of their spatiotemporal relations, nor is "resistance" described in terms of smooth or unformed power relations that will emerge from an indeterminate "outside." To be fair, perhaps what Deleuze is attempting to describe is also what Foucault had addressed in the statement quoted above: that the greatest source of new resistance is the submission to the earlier normative and disciplinary forms of subjectivity. In the conclusion of his brief "postscript," however, Deleuze himself worries whether these new forms of resistance will only lead to a more powerful form of confinement than discipline could ever dream—a confinement by the continuous process of subjectification through the production of new forms of human capital demanded by late-capitalist societies. For example, Deleuze sees this danger in what he observes as "the strange craving" of the youth to be motivated, or in the demands for new vocational training and "special courses for continuing education."[33] (Although after making these observations, he immediately confesses himself as an old mole, maybe a little too blind to see "the intricacies of a snake's coils.")[34] A more progressive interpretation will later be found in the work of Hardt and Negri, who, in the trilogy beginning with *Empire* (2000), enlist both Deleuze and Foucault's theories in the construction of an "affirmative biopolitics" premised on the continuous production and reproduction of new forms of living labor, that is, when the subjectification of life itself is equal to resistance.[35]

Given the identification of resistance with the new forms of living labor, perhaps a more accurate term for what Deleuze called "control" is simply the term "enterprise," which Foucault himself employs to distinguish between disciplinary and biopolitical techniques of subjectification and their concrete dispositifs. What then is the relationship between what Foucault calls "Enterprise Society" (a.k.a. "Control Society") and a Judicial Society (a.k.a. "Disciplinary Society")? After discussing the principles of *Vitalipolitik* in the seminar of February 14, 1979, Foucault answers: "An enterprise society and a judicial society framed by the multiplicity of juridical institutions, are two faces of a single phenomenon."[36] In other words, here we see a very different relationship between so-called discipline and so-called control that cannot be represented by historical periodicity or succession (e.g., "We are quitting disciplinary society and arriving at something new"), but rather something like the multiplication of centers of action, all of which belong to the present. For example, today we continue to witness the multiplication of new juridical and normative mechanisms that have emerged to limit—or, at least, to mediate—the growing number of conflicts engendered by capitalist production and reproduction, which Foucault early on described as the multiplication of surfaces of friction and potential legal disputes that emerge between the private and the public (as well as political) spheres. Of course, it also follows that many of these mechanisms expand beyond the threshold of political authority (or national sovereignty) and can no longer be centralized on the state-form, as later exemplified in Hardt and Negri's refashioning of the concept of civil society to now exist "outside" of the historical nation-states.

Although these "multiple surfaces of friction" that emerge within contemporary neoliberal society might be compared to patches of Riemannian space (Deleuze), they do not necessarily represent new points of resistance, or "counter attack," that is, according to perhaps too formalist an analogy that Deleuze often makes with the emergence of serialization in music, or to the syntactic and linguistic discoveries of writers like Melville, Proust, but especially Roussel, who Deleuze often employs as a kind of code for deciphering Foucault's writings on power after *The Order of Things* and *Discipline and Punish*. In the end, concerning the late "postscript," we might come to simply understand Deleuze's own vision of control society as historically dated, since it hails from the early introduction of neoliberal policies into French society during the period of the early 1980s (e.g., the break with the *dirigiste* model in 1983). As a regional and somewhat parochial point of view of the impact of globalization on one society alone, therefore, it cannot be employed paradigmatically as an image of the society to come.

And yet, perhaps the most paradigmatic and influential reinterpretation of the concept of biopower is the one offered by Giorgio Agamben in his groundbreaking *Homo Sacer* (1995). As is well known, in the opening pages of his major argument concerning the intimate relationship between sovereign power and bare life, founded upon the Greek concepts of *bios* and *zoe*, Agamben stages a direct confrontation with Foucault's genealogy of biopolitics, from the final chapter of *The History of Sexuality* (vol. 1) to the last seminar on "the subject of power" given at University of Vermont in 1982, both of which I have recounted above. Returning to the question of Foucault's method, Agamben explicitly challenges what he perceives as "the decisive abandonment of the traditional approach to power, which is based on juridico-institutional models (the definition of sovereignty, the theory of the State)" in favor of the study of new political techniques and technologies of subjectification that are present throughout Foucault's later works and lectures.[37] "Clearly," he writes, "these two lines [of research] (which carry on two tendencies present in Foucault's work from the very beginning) intersect in many points and refer back to a common center."[38]

What is this "common center," and what would be the function of a center in the above description? Since Descartes and Leibniz, the question of philosophical method is based on the art of geometry; the function of a center is the virtual point where at least three lines converge or intersect. However, the diagram of Foucault's method that Agamben provides is of two lines that may intersect at many points, and may "refer to a common center," but in fact, never converge, "but is something like a vanishing point that the different lines of Foucault's inquiry (*and, more generally, of the entire Western reflection on power*) converge toward without ever reaching."[39] Therefore, if Foucault's method contests the traditional approach to power, he asks, then where is the point of their intersection?

It is here, of course, that Agamben famously locates a "blind spot in the eye of the researcher."[40] In perhaps one of the most remarkably counterintuitive statements in the history of contemporary philosophy, Agamben claims that in fact there is nothing new in Foucault's "reflection on power." (Here, he completely disregards Foucault's emphasis upon the array of disciplinary knowledges that will compose the new political techniques, "such as the police sciences," which in the later essay on the concept of the *dispositif*, he will characterize as merely the process of the "secularization" of knowledge-power in modernity that "profanes, in the most problematic manner," what is essentially a theological genealogy of biopolitical apparatuses.)[41] In other words, despite all his supposed innovation, Foucault's reflections only manage to extend the perspectival lines that already belong to "the entire Western reflection on power" a little farther out toward a distant point where "the hidden meaning of the political itself gets lost on that same horizon," and thus its "practical calling" also remains to this day in a state of "concealment." Here, in this very blindness that appears at the very end of this reflection, if not in the eye of Foucault himself, Agamben reveals the original—if still concealed—"nucleus of sovereign power" that will henceforth function as the point of intersection between the juridico-institutional and biopolitical models of power.[42]

Turning now to Foucault's own diagram, let us recall the earlier statement from *The History of Sexuality* (immediately following the sections on "method, domain, and periodization") that, indeed, the "age of biopower" could be said to have properly commenced only when the two lines defined above (i.e., disciplinary techniques and the new knowledges of political economy), which were still separated by the end of the eighteenth century, and were only joined at the level of discourse (e.g., "Ideology"), gradually converged in the form of "concrete assemblages" (*agencements concrets*) forming the dispositifs of sexuality, security, and governmentality. Thus, it is the center of each dispositif that the subject power emerges as a "complex idea," one that can no longer be completely "rationalized" by the traditional forms of sovereignty, or a theory of the state. Certainly, in response one may ask the questions "Where is sovereignty?" or "Where is the state?" but no longer according to the classical coordinates belonging to the previous diagram of sovereignty by asking "Where is the center?" In fact, Foucault will return to this point at the beginning of each year if only to qualify and further refine his methodology—and, of course, to defend his decision, beginning in the 1975 lectures, to "bypass or get around the problem of sovereignty . . . and to reveal the problem of domination and subjugation instead." Therefore, as he immediately adds in the first of a series of "methodology precautions," "our objective is not to analyze rule-governed and legitimate forms of power that have a single center [i.e., sovereignty], or to look at what its general mechanisms or its overall effects might be [i.e., the state, juridico-legal institutions, etc.]."[43]

As a result of this "decisive abandonment of the traditional approach to power," does this mean that the question concerning sovereignty in particular disappears entirely from Foucault's reflections on power? Not if we listen to Foucault's response to the very same objection at the beginning of the lecture course of 1978—seventeen years before Agamben even thought to make it—that, in fact, "the problem sovereignty is not eliminated by the emergence of a new art of government that has crossed the threshold of the political sciences . . . ; on the contrary, it is made more acute than ever."[44] At this point, I will conclude my own reflections on the major mutations introduced into the original concepts of biopolitics and biopower by quoting the following passage, which I believe, addresses both the problem of periodization in Deleuze's account, as well as the specific diagram that Foucault has in mind:

> Consequently, the idea of government as a government of population makes the problem of the foundation of sovereignty even more acute (and we have Rousseau) and it makes the need to develop disciplines even more acute (and we have the history of disciplines that I have tried to analyze elsewhere). So, we should not see things as the replacement of the society of sovereignty by the society of discipline, and then of a society of discipline by a society of, say, government [or, say, "a society of control"—GL]. In fact, we have a triangle: sovereignty, discipline, and governmental management, which has population as its main target and apparatuses of security as its essential mechanism (*dispositif*).[45]

To conclude our brief tour through the genealogy of these concepts, let us return to the first instance where Foucault first introduces this pivotal distinction between discipline and biopolitics in the 1975 lecture course on *The Abnormal*. What does he say exactly? He says that this year, instead of the mechanics of the disciplinary apparatus, I will be looking at the "effects of normalization," which are defined as the effective function of various *dispositifs*. This does not imply that organism replaces mechanism, that biopower replaces discipline, but that both coexist in a total social organization and operate according to different principles that both separates them and, at the same time, combines them in an "art of governmentality."[46] In other words, as he clarified this relationship a year later, normative biopolitics is simply the other side of juridical and political structures of representation and is the condition of its functioning and effectiveness.[47] If the disciplinary technique of subjection functions all the more effectively as a general form of subjectification, "by which concrete individuals are thereby transformed into subjects," to quote an earlier line from Althusser, it is because the generalized strategy of biopolitics becomes typical, ordinary, common, that is, as the "complex idea" of power that everyone in the social field both possesses and is possessed by.[48] It is here again we see Foucault's favorite pair of conceptual terms for the emergence of new strategies of power and their concrete *dispositifs*—*dispersion* and *generality*, rather than *universality and totalization*.

Syracuse University (United States) and Kyung Hee University (South Korea)

NOTES

1. Michel Foucault, *The History of Sexuality, Vol. 1: An Introduction* (New York: Vintage Books, 1980), 152.

2. Michel Foucault, *"Society must be Defended": Lectures at the College of France 1975-1976*, eds. Mauro Bertani and Allessandro Fontana (Basingstoke: Palgrave Macmillan, 2003), 14.

3. Michel Foucault, *The Birth of Biopolitics: Lectures at the College of France, 1978-1979*, eds. Michael Senellart, Francois Ewald and Alessandro Fontana (Basingstoke: Palgrave Macmillan, 2008), 271.

4. Foucault, *The Birth of Biopolitics*, 245.

5. Ibid.

6. Georges Canguilhem, *Knowledge of Life*, eds. Paola Marrati and Todd Meyers (New York: Fordham, 2008), 84ff.

7. Canguilhem, *Knowledge of Life*.

8. Michel Foucault, *Discipline and Punish: The Birth of the Prison* (New York: Vintage Books, 1977), 164.

9. Matteo Pasquinelli, "What an Apparatus is Not: On the Archeology of the Norm in Foucault, Canguilhem, and Goldstein," *Parrehesia* 22 (2015): 81.

10. Michel Foucault, *Abnormal: Lectures at the College of France 1974-1975*, eds. Valerio Marchetti and Antonella Salomoni, trans. Graham Burchell (Basingstoke: Palgrave Macmillan, 2003), 50.

11. Georges Canguilhem, *Knowledge of Life*, 111ff.

12. Matteo Pasquinelli, "What an Apparatus is Not," 82.

13. Michel Foucault, *The History of Sexuality, Vol. 1*, 140. Of course, in the final chapter on the "Right of Death and the Power over Life," the specific populations of the colony and the camp are identified as alternative starting points of the same genealogy, but according to a different set of disciplinary knowledges (including modern biology and anthropology)

that make up the biopolitical dispositif of race, something that is already announced ten years earlier in the conclusion of *The Order of Things* in addressing the convergence of psychoanalysis and ethnology at the end of the nineteenth century. See Michel Foucault, *The Order of Things* (New York: Random House, 1970), 373ff.

14. Ibid.

15. Michel Foucault, *Power/Knowledge: Selected Interviews and Other Writings, 1972-1977*, ed. C. Gordon (New York: Pantheon Books, 1980), 94.

16. Michel Foucault, *The History of Sexuality, Vol. 1*, 156.

17. Ibid., 156.

18. Ibid., 159.

19. Michel Foucault, *Dit et écrits*, vol. 4 (Paris: Éditions Gallimard, 1994), 228.

20. Michel Foucault, *Security, Territory, Population: Lectures at the College of France, 1977-1978*, ed. Michael Senellart (Basingstoke: Palgrave Macmillan, 2007), 48.

21. See also Chapter 2 of Michael Dillon, *Biopolitics of Security: A Political Analytic of Finitude* (London: Routledge, 2015), 45–75.

22. Foucault, *The Birth of Biopolitics*, 80ff. See also Philip Mirowski and Dieter Plehwe, eds., *The Road from Mont Pelerin: The Making of a Neoliberal Thought Collective* (Cambridge: Harvard University Press, 2009).

23. Ibid., 185ff. Also see 218ff for a brief comparison of the different national forms of neoliberalism up to this period.

24. Michel Foucault, *Security, Territory, Population*, 107. Concerning the inclusion of animals and other species in the problem of the government of the living, see Cary Wolfe, *Before the Law: Humans and Other Animals in a Biopolitical Frame* (Chicago: University of Chicago Press, 2012).

25. Quoted in Michel Foucault, *The Birth of Biopolitics*, 157.

26. Ibid., 148.

27. Michel Foucault, *Security, Territory, Population*, 109.

28. Ibid., 185.

29. See Giorgio Agamben, *What is an Apparatus?* (Palo Alto: Stanford University Press, 2009), 1–24; Gilles Deleuze, *Two Regimes of Madness: Texts and Interviews 1975-1995* (New York: Semiotexte, 2006), 338–48.

30. Giorgio Agamben, *Homo Sacer: Sovereign Power and Bare Life* (Palo Alto: Stanford University Press, 1995), 6; Gilles Deleuze, *Foucault* (Minneapolis: University of Minnesota Press, 1988), 92.

31. Gilles Deleuze, *Foucault*; see also "A Portrait of Foucault," in Gilles Deleuze, *Negotiations: 1972-1990* (New York: Columbia University Press, 1995), 102–18.

32. Gilles Deleuze's "Postscript to Society of Control" first appears in *L'Autre Journal* 1 (May 1990). Deleuze *Negotiations*, 177–82.

33. Gilles Deleuze, *Negotiations*, 182. For the best description of this new form of confinement, the intensification of confinement by the form of subjectification itself, see Jeffrey T. Nealon's account in Chapter 5 of *Foucault Beyond Foucault: Power and its Intensifications since 1984* (Palo Alto: Stanford University Press, 2008), 94–112.

34. Gilles Deleuze, *Negotiations*, 182.

35. Michael Hardt and Antonio Negri, *Commonwealth* (Cambridge: Harvard University Press, 2009), 59.

36. Michel Foucault, *The Birth of Biopolitics*, 150.

37. Giorgio Agamben, *Homo Sacer*, 5.

38. Ibid.

39. Ibid., 6.

40. Ibid.

41. Giorgio Agamben, *What is an Apparatus?* 19.

42. Giorgio Agamben, *Homo Sacer*, 6.

43. Michel Foucault, *"Society must be defended,"* 27.

44. Michel Foucault, *Security, Territory, Population*, 107.

45. Ibid., 107–08.

46. Ibid., 48. See also Pasquinelli, "What an Apparatus is Not."

47. Michel Foucault, *The Birth of Biopolitics*, 175.

48. Louis Althusser, *Lenin and Philosophy and Other Essays* (New York: Monthly Review Press, 2001), 117.

WORKS CITED

Agamben, Giorgio, *Homo Sacer: Sovereign Power and Bare Life* [1995]. Trans. Daniel Heller-Roazen. Stanford: Stanford University Press, 1998.

Agamben, Giorgio. *What is an Apparatus?* Trans. David Kishik and Stefan Pedatella. Palo Alto: Stanford University Press, 2009.

Althusser, Louis. *Lenin and Philosophy and Other Essays* [1968]. Trans. Ben Brewster. New York: Monthly Review Press, 2001.

Canguilhem, Georges. *Knowledge of Life* [1965]. Eds. Paola Marrati and Todd Meyers. Trans. Stefanos Geroulanos and Daniela Ginsburg. New York: Fordham, 2008.

Deleuze, Gilles. *Foucault* [1986]. Trans. Seán Hand. Minneapolis: University of Minnesota Press, 1988.

Deleuze, Gilles. *Negotiations: 1972-1990*. New York: Columbia University Press, 1995.

Deleuze, Gilles. *Two Regimes of Madness: Texts and Interviews 1975-1995*. New York: Semiotexte, 2006.

Dillon, Michael. *Biopolitics of Security: A Political Analytic of Finitude*. London: Routledge, 2015.

Foucault, Michel. *The Order of Things* [1966]. New York: Random House, 1970.

Foucault, Michel. *Discipline and Punish: The Birth of the Prison* [1975]. Trans. Alan Sheridan. New York: Vintage Books, 1977.

Foucault, Michel. *The History of Sexuality, Volume I: An Introduction* [1976]. Trans. Robert Hurley. New York: Vintage Books, 1978.

Foucault, Michel. *Power/Knowledge: Selected Interviews and Other Writings 1972-1977*. Ed. Colin Gordon. Trans. Coling Gordon, Leo Marshall, John Mepham, and Kate Soper. New York: Pantheon, 1980.

Foucault, Michel. *Dit et écrits*, vol. 4. Paris: Éditions Gallimard, 1994.

Foucault, Michel. *Abnormal: Lectures at the College of France 1974-1975*. Eds. Valerio Marchetti and Antonella Salomoni. Trans. Graham Burchell. Basingstoke: Palgrave Macmillan, 2003.

Foucault, Michel. *"Society Must Be Defended": Lectures at the College of France 1975-1976*. Eds. Mauro Bertani and Alessandro Fontana. Trans. David Macey. Basingstoke: Palgrave Macmillan, 2003.

Foucault, Michel. *Security, Territory, Population: Lectures at the College of France, 1977-1978.*
     Ed. Michael Senellart. Trans. Graham Burchell. Basingstoke: Palgrave Macmillan, 2007.
Foucault, Michel. *The Birth of Biopolitics: Lectures at the College of France, 1978-1979.* Eds.
     Michael Senellart. Trans. Graham Burchell. Basingstoke: Palgrave Macmillan, 2008.
Hardt, Michael, and Antonio Negri. *Commonwealth.* Cambridge: Harvard University Press,
     2009.
Mirowski, Philip, and Dieter Plehwe, eds. *The Road from Mont Pelerin: The Making of a
     Neoliberal Thought Collective.* Cambridge: Harvard University Press, 2009.
Nealon, Jeffrey T. *Foucault Beyond Foucault: Power and its Intensifications since 1984.*
     Palo Alto: Stanford University Press, 2008.
Pasquinelli, Matteo. "What an Apparatus is Not: On the Archeology of the Norm in Foucault,
     Canguilhem, and Goldstein." *Parrehesia* 22 (2015): 79–89.
Wolfe, Cary. *Before the Law: Humans and Other Animals in a Biopolitical Frame.* Chicago:
     University of Chicago Press, 2012.

CHAPTER SIXTEEN

Pop Culture

AARON JAFFE

PLASTIC MAN, WHERE ARE YOU?

Not long ago an announcement about a screening of *Metropolis* came across my social-media feed. The municipal art museum was sponsoring a summer series on films that had inspired *Star Wars*. The very first comment someone wrote under the post was as follows: "Hitler's favorite movie . . . I'll pass." It's a strange thing for someone to assert peremptorily that Hitler's favorite movie was *Metropolis*, that it should be avoided for this reason. For one thing, it is not true. That prize goes to—according to Martin Bormann, at least, who recorded this and other of tidbits of table chatter from Hitler—*King Kong*:[1] more on Kong later. But, first, where does this pseudo-proposition come from, why does it have so much currency, what sense can we make from it? Fritz Lang's expressionist masterpiece, made in 1927, wasn't a Nazi film, after all. Nor was Lang a Nazi.[2] In fact, he fled the Nazis. The *Gleichschaltung* was clearly the cause of his flight. *Gleich* means the same, *schaltung* means something like circuitry, wiring, configuration. Lang wanted no part of the coming reconfiguration of society and culture under the repressive controls and authoritarian idiocies of the Nazis.

The distributive principle—pop-cultural connectivity—is what I wish to explore: the meaning of the statement that *Metropolis* was Hitler's favorite movie. It's a sloppy version of Siegfried Kracauer, I suppose—for which the director's actual politics—his particular enmity to Nazis—is irrelevant.[3] The concept of a cultural telephone game makes the pseudo-statement *Metropolis was Hitler's favorite movie* . . . true. Why do people like this mistaken notion? Click, like, the idea, Hitler's favorite movie, is what I mean. Leslie Fiedler's point is something else. Fiedler, the pioneering commentator on popular culture, "unrestructured dilettante," in his words, notes he too likes *King Kong* and makes what he calls a disconcerting "discovery" about connectivity, the popular, and the aesthetic:

> It not only joins together the poor and the rich, the educated and the uneducated, male and female, children and adults, but the good and bad as well; that in the enjoyment of popular literature one is joined to those people who are felt to be socially reprehensible, wicked, whatever your social code and values may be. Popular literature joins you and your worst enemies as well as your worst self![4]

The field of consumption is a plane of risky connectivity, a technical interface, a platform for bringing popular things and favorite things together in a toxic purge outside the laws of critical intelligence.

What does it mean to call one movie your favorite anyway? Does it mean that you watch it over and over again? That you think other people should watch it this same way on repeat? Or, is it more like the setting of preferences, exteriorizing them, making them conspicuous as yourself to others? That you'd like them to check it out, to test if it could be one of their favorite things, too? That you'll go back to it? Or else, it signals the hazards of consumption—*raindrops on roses and whiskers on kittens*—these things may also be fascist? What-Hitler-likes is an odd metric. Fielder points to the sudden appearance of the popular in the aesthetic, the discovery of significance in the consumption of popular culture in the sense of all things touched by the aesthetic in the collaborative admixture of the monstrous and the trivial. Beware what you like or you may like Adolf Hitler—once described by Theodor Adorno as "a mixture of King Kong and a suburban hairdresser"[5]; the colossal reality-warping character of a zone made of, in Jacques Rancière's words, "free and equal individuals . . . dragged together into a ceaseless whirl in search of an excitement that was nothing but the mere internalization of the endless and purposeless agitation of the whole social body."[6] Excitement gives way to connectivity—an unbounded, hyper-synchronized infinite distraction, as Dominic Pettmann puts it, in which "we never feel the same way as other potential allies and affines at the same moment? While one person is fuming about economic injustice or climate change denial, another is giggling at a cute cat video."[7] In effect, this platform optimizes distraction as a massified aggregate reception horizon.

"Torn from its obviousness in order to become a hieroglyph, a mythological or phantasmagoric figure," "the ordinary becomes beautiful as a trace of the true," Rancière notes in *The Politics of Aesthetics*, describing what we might call pop culture degree zero.[8] Enter King Kong, the "tallest, darkest leading man in Hollywood."[9] Meet the Campbell Soup Can: "I used to drink it. I used to have the same lunch every day, for twenty years, I guess, the same thing over and over again."[10] Presto change-o! the Las Vegas Strip becomes the postmodern apotheosis of complexity and contradiction in architecture.[11] The reason *visibility* might be preferred to *legibility* in these references is that the aesthetic is not a discursive field to be read—or interpreted—but a platform to be suddenly seen, accessed, or processed, to be seen looking for exciting objects of attention and affection. The person being somebody is only completed by connections with the kitsch that arrives on her threshold, kitsch that is now given a strictly agnostic valence—as the cultural given, the data. Data ("flows . . . more vast than anything the world has seen," Pynchon writes) seem "jumbled up together" in mixtures of "profane and sacred, uncivilized and cultured, antique and modern, that each sum up a world."[12] Too much data (online) replace more life (in literature). Agency is located not within a single human being per se, as a condition of exemplary personhood, but gets distributed outside: the emancipation of the zone. Broadcast in and through a newly sensible popular domain, a connected platform—"graffiti, shop signs, or catalogues of out-of-date merchandise" and so forth— it is administered in and as aesthetic-bureaucratic smegma, to recall Tyrone Slothrop's desk in Psysection, in the great novel about these themes, Thomas Pynchon's *Gravity's Rainbow*.[13] Blissful ignorance, benighted stupidity, determined prejudice give way to an animate tissue of dissatisfactions, disruptions, interruptions. In the ruins of Europe, the last months of the Second World War, Pynchon's antihero sits in the wreckage reading a *Plastic Man* comic, gathering more counsel from its pages about how to adapt to this setting than from any of the official briefings from HQ.[14]

From about a century earlier it is Emma Bovary who provides Rancière's hero as networked aesthetic receiver: "The heroine of a certain aesthetic democracy . . . Bovary wants to bring art into her life, both into her love life and into the décor of her house. The novel is constructed as a constant polemic against a farm girl's desire to bring art into life. It contrasts 'art in life' (this will later be called the aestheticization of daily life) with a form of art that is in books and only in books." Bovary's *agon* is the waste land of freely appropriated total sensibility—"paths of communications opened up in the earth itself" (i.e., popular content wants to be free)—ripe with all kinds of banalities and stupidities. Here, the accounting he has in mind is un-literary *pars pro toto*—not merely against "the chatter of newspapers" but also the nullification of all "fatal words written on paper."[15] Opposing this is what Rancière nominates as "a good form of writing . . . inscribed in things themselves," a "form of writing [that] can only mean, in the end, the self-cancellation of literature." That he calls this ruined condition for literature writing is weird, for there are no pure criteria left for inscription—besides the "excitement" of jostling in the heterogeneous aesthetic whirlwind. While not necessarily invested in technicity, Rancière is indeed dreaming of his modernism without moderns, a dark Kantianism that provides the imaginative preconditions for a total connectivity network of distraction and interruption: "The sensible framework defined by a network of meanings, an expression does not find its place in the system of visible coordinates where it appears. The dream of a suitable political work of art is in fact the dream of disrupting the relationship between the visible, the sayable, and the thinkable without having to use the terms of a message as a vehicle."[16]

Instead of a Kantian *sensus communis*, the heroic idea that everyone has access to the same perception of the aesthetic, the sudden appearance of the popular as an aesthetic platform entails zones of attention and inattention and calls forth something different. Enter Rancière's virtuous dissensus ("being together apart") that I would propose as something like being distracted together.[17] Dissensus dismantles criteria around itself, dissolving the literary into distributed sensibilities ("fusing literature and life and making any source of excitement equal to any other," he writes), and pricking itself with various inoculations of ignorance, dissatisfaction, stupidity, distraction, favorites, popularity, readily "incorporated into anybody's life" and "become part of the scenery and the furnishings of everyday life."[18] In his response to Alain Badiou's *Handbook of Inaesthetics*, Rancière points to a modernism without modernism—the modernist variant described in *The Politics of Aesthetics* as the "mode of sensible being proper to artistic products"—that arrives specially defined by its necessity for explication from outside— the cultural thing arrives intertwined, as it were, with the literary-philosophical operator manuals that provide "orientation[s] for thought." "Such is the paradox of the aesthetic regime in the arts," he writes: "It posits the radical autonomy of art, its independence of any external rule. But it posits it in the same gesture that abolishes the mimetic closure separating the rationale of fictions from that of facts, the sphere of representation from other spheres of existence." Rancière's pure "aesthetic regime," made of impure stuff (disrupting the "Romantic quagmire . . . bogged down in the humus of fossils"), might be usefully compared to Arthur Danto's Artworld. Less an autonomous preserve for aesthetic purity, it calls attention to the institutionalized ways of seeing heteronymous ingredients aesthetically that don't get noticed otherwise.[19] "To see something as art," writes Danto, "requires something the eye cannot decry [*sic*, descry]—an atmosphere of artistic theory, a knowledge of the history of art: an Artworld."[20] Instead of a totaled Berlin, Slothrop envisions a totalized "apescape," inserting uncanny pop-cultural references as a multi-mediated alibi into the ruined literary-historical environment:

> Well, what it is—is? what's "is"?—is that King Kong, or some creature closely allied, squatting down, evidently just, taking a shit, right in the street! and everything! a-and

being ignored, by truckload after truckload of Russian enlisted men in pisscutter caps and dazed smiles, grinding right on by-"Hey!" Slothrop wants to shout, "hey lookit that giant ape! or whatever it is. You guys? Hey . . ." But he doesn't, luckily. On closer inspection, the crouching monster turns out to be the Reichstag building, shelled out, airbrushed, fire-brushed powdery black on all blastward curves and projections, chalked over its hardechoing carbon insides with Cyrillic initials, and many names of comrades killed in May.[21]

Only King Kong is "Bad and Big enough to take part in transcendent doings," Pynchon writes elsewhere.[22] The precarity of common social existence is, in this sense, the animate background noise of modernity—"not dysfunctional or a 'strange creature' in the global economy, but rather . . . functionally constitutive."[23] To detect a human form-factor (a husk of humanism) against the technical backdrop of pervasive precarity ("full of tricks," as Pynchon has it) isn't an additive process—a version of the social-political life in which everyone gets ceremoniously counted together.[24] Rather, it means subtracting a form of aesthetic signal detection from already damaged conditions available in popular culture.

The background is foregrounding itself.

Those who may or may not be working—the global pool of the "precarious"—make precarity a perversely privileged position—that is, an opportunity and also "a determinable condition." Beyond its role as a would-be "identificatory emblem," precarity operates as its own ambivalent theme. It is the stranger at the door of the denizen who is enjoined endlessly to prepare for its arrival.[25] Opportunity knocks. Approaching precarity is experienced as a kind aesthetic address—critical positioning and aesthetic risk taking—as much as anything else. A point about the functionality of these words as risky criteria: the precarity of criteria signals a vortex of ambivalence that isn't so much about shoring up would-be identities—not least, aggregate identities—as it heralds something like the arrival of modernity as an inhuman format for dividing individuals into individual units of apprehension and further division of these into derivative risk positions. Vilém Flusser puts it this way: "One has to possess criteria—the units of measurements and rules—to be able to critique: the yardstick that one applies to the thing one critiques, to judge and decide over it. The tradition knows three kinds of measurement standards: the epistemological ('true-false'), the ethical ('good-bad'), and the aesthetic ('beautiful-ugly')."[26] Just now, criticism about the epistemological, the ethical, and the aesthetic is the ultimate contingent labor nobody wants.

At a distance—from outer space, as it were—pop-cultural precarity is the ruined condition for criteria, and risk is the hidden calculation that includes all standards by excluding judgment about the true, the good, and the beautiful from a present situation. It is this calculation about the format of criteria in modernity that is rarely mentioned by name, either positively or negatively. Lately, the known forms of criticism seem precariously confined to precipitously shrinking surfaces. Professions of critical humility abound, commonsensical, descriptive lessons about realism, flat ontologies, the mortifications of theory, denunciations of the folly of hermeneutics, etc., are legion. What we need now, we're told, is to get back in queue behind the more empirically sensitive/vulnerable denizens in front of us, attend only to what is readily "evident, perceptible, apprehensible [to them] . . . what insists on being looked at rather than what we must train ourselves to see through."[27] The face of the denizen is itself a precarious surface, a surface that provokes surface reading as surely as any text. What's on the face, like what's in the text, seems to solicit a desire for nothing more than imprecations of epistemological modesty, for confirmations about the value of spending all our time with bogus realism. It's all right there on the face of it. Nevertheless, the surface is inscrutable, it also wants to be read as something else, a screen, a search engine bar. What I have in mind is that we must face up to for criticism at the present time to what Alexander Galloway calls an interface effect: the interface, he writes, is an "agitation" or generative friction between different precarious formats, a "fertile nexus between insides and outsides," across scales, sizes, membranes, and platforms. Criticism might be conceived as an attempt to work through the unworkably precarious criteria of popular culture.[28]

In "Notes on Deconstructing the Popular," Stuart Hall observes that popular culture is a "pretty horrendous" category.[29] Each word—popular and culture—presents distinct conceptual difficulties, further complicated by joining them together. Chief among these shared difficulties is periodizing the conjunction, imagining life before popular culture, as it were, as a Skull Island fossil of the age before *popular* and *culture* were considered praiseworthy or even key critical concepts. They both promise massive inclusivity without conditions. The pleonastic aspect is striking—*popular culture*—as if underscoring that much of what gets called *culture* isn't particularly *popular*, and much of what's *popular* isn't especially valued or visible as *culture* per se. The adjective "popular" comes from the Latin *popularis*, meaning "belonging to the people"—not surprisingly, *populus* means people.[30] Part of what's at issue here is the question of *to whom culture properly belongs*. Popular culture, possessed and prepossessed by its consumers, foregrounds problems of property and propriety. *Voxpop*—to borrow a word from Meaghan Morris—is the voice of the pop cultural dispossessed (disposed through assorted functionaries and the admin-cult of spokespersonship).[31] The sense of the word "popular" being "suited to ordinary people" comes from the late sixteenth century, and it retains a sense of aristocratic disapprobation. What is "popular" is "well-liked [or] admired by the people," and the particular association with ostensibly inconsequential arts and entertainment, in the sense of a "popular song," for example, was already well-established in the nineteenth century.[32]

Insofar as popularity becomes associated with new democratic virtues, new audience formations, cultural pluralism, and so forth, it also indexes inflationary dangers in this (quasi-)capitalist system, not least, that, in a democracy of goods the price of good goods is correlated with their scarcity. Critical ambivalences such as these are baked in—into the concept of popular culture itself, that is—as Hall explains: a given popular cultural object is coded with "struggle and resistance—but also, of course, appropriation and ex-propriation."[33] Too often, popular culture entails the "active destruction of particular ways of life," as he puts it.[34] The colloquialism *pop* culture—that somewhat archaic abbreviation—gets at this capacity: pop culture *pops*. It has a special capacity to arrest, to shock, to surprise, to sting, to zing. Here, I'm thinking of Rancière's point about the sudden visibility of "Emma Bovary" as an exemplary cultural consumer, and the threatening meaning that Flaubert ascribes to it. In other words, pop culture designates an approach, an aesthetic instantiated in a sentimental education about things as objects of affection. It is, following Morris, "a way of operating—rather than as a set of contents, a marketing category, a reflected expression of social position, or even a 'terrain' of struggle."[35]

In *Heart of Darkness*, Marlow stumbling around the Congo Free State happens upon "an extraordinary find," a single, discarded book about seamanship near "a heap of rubbish reposed in a dark corner" of an abandoned hut. What arrests him most about his discovery is that someone has annotated it in code: "Yes, it looked like cipher. Fancy a man lugging with him a book of that description into this nowhere and studying it—and making notes—in cipher at that! It was an extravagant mystery."[36] Marlow is astounded to discover a literary artifact of modernity in this context, a critical annotation, evidence of someone's attempt to sort useful information from useless noise (thinking of seamanship, cybernetics comes from the Greek word for the helmsman). Here, Marlow is an improbable modernist reader looking for something different to read, except Conrad has created a fictional world in which something different to read is also something to read at all. It is a scene of reading in a forensic sense, a reader reconstructing an imaginary scene of another reader before a book. In the anonymous, sedulous reader—the ciphering note-taker—he has found a secret sharer. One of the most difficult things of Conrad's novella is coming to terms with Marlow's irresistible need to flatter, adulate, stroke, and tickle this toxic document—not least in this scene, when a reader would be forgiven for assenting to its suppression. Slothrop, reading his *Plastic Man* comic, gives us a related scene, in this version, cybernetic notation no longer hides from view; pop culture comes into the open as a tool of thought charting a way out of the lettered world and into the universe of technical images and Ben-Day dots: "Four-color Plasticman goes oozing out of a keyhole, around a corner and up through piping that leads to a sink in the mad Nazi scientist's lab, out of whose faucet Plas's head now, blank carapaced eyes and un-plastic jaw, is just emerging."[37] Later, Pynchon makes clear that this is also a path into distributed paranoia, "nothing less than the onset, the leading edge, of the discovery that everything is connected, everything in the Creation, a secondary illumination—not yet blindingly One, but at least connected."[38]

To some extent, the critical conception of pop culture at work here is a creature of very recent provenance, sustained by forms of academic attention and zones of interest associated with cultural studies.[39] Nevertheless, it is worth noting not only that popular culture exists well before its recent academic invention but also that it exists as an event that forms critical reflexivity. As countless commentators have observed, Rancière included, votes and factories were decisive factors for making popular and culture mutually articulated concepts. Dennis R. Hall shows that Dr. Johnson in the mid-seventeenth century, for example, "seriously poses a question [that is still] common in popular culture studies: 'do the producers of popular culture create a taste in their audience or do they response to a taste already existing in their audience?' Surely, each modifies the other."[40] Enthusiastically writing for a "populous" literary marketplace becomes for Dr. Johnson an exercise of connecting "the ridiculous" and "the profound."[41] As pop culture collapses the cultural producer and the cultural consumer, it also blurs differences between pop-cultural fandom and aesthetic-critical environment.[42] Popular culture flickers into self-reflexivity much like Molière's bourgeois gentleman who discovers he's been speaking prose all along. The sense that much of pop culture is readily available for second-order administration is at the center of its legitimacy struggles for visibility and prestige (as well as a continuous parade of pop-cultural adepts). Patrick Brantlinger and James Naremore include Popular in their heuristic of six co-articulated artistic "cultures" in modernity: High, Modernist, Avant-garde, Folk, Mass, and Popular.[43] In their taxonomy, each presents a durable disposition emphasizing different constellations of production, consumption, meaning, sensibility, and reflexivity.[44] As predicate for redeeming Mass with Folk, the Popular resituates Modernism, Avant-garde, and Folk with risk positions and risky ambitions, and so on. It's important to note that forms of connectivity—indeed, plasticity, popular, or otherwise—stretch across all dispositions. Indeed, in the formulation, these are not discrete, graduated domains one might be led to suspect, but "an unsettled mixture": "If they are real, they partake of one another, sometimes overlapping, blurring together or speaking dialogically—and sometimes, like figures on a chessboard, living in antagonistic relation."[45]

Unsettled and unsettling, the pop culture game (often more Trivial Pursuit than 3D chess) has been up for "serious" scrutiny for a long time. Instead of the seven classic arts—Architecture, Sculpture, Painting, Music, Poetry, Dance, Performing—in 1924, Gilbert Seldes proposes a taxonomy of seven "lively" arts—comics, movies, musicals, vaudeville, radio, popular music, dance—as all "worthy of a second look."[46] With cultural studies, the heat lamps of reflexive secondary illumination warm a heteronomous variety of phenomena, happenings, scenes, and practices: advertising, fashion, leisure, entertainment, celebrity, music, sports, fashion, gaming, vernacular intellectuals, zines, superheroes, shopping, cosplay, collecting, stand-up, hipsters, guerilla gardening, nerds, King Kong cultism, television, chat rooms, sitcoms, reality TV, cocktail culture, slang, pulp, crazes, memes. Recognizing the co-emergence of criticality in pop-cultural connectivity is crucial. Good pop culture research can't stand apart—or, wholly apart—from the objects of its study nor can it legitimately condescend to them (sweetening lesson plans with homiletic spoonfuls of *The Simpsons* or *Star Trek*), because it is *in the mix*. It is in the mix not just in what pop culture artifacts mean in terms of textual dynamics—coding and decoding signs, for instance—but also how they work as signals and how they matter in different situations, contexts, and environments. Ideally, attention to meaning and mattering expands hermeneutics to the actual forces and flows of value, information, tech, feeling, power, and so on.[47] Putting emphasis on the particular rather than the general, this kind of activity explores the idiosyncrasies of specific audience structures and the emergence of the aesthetic objects and cult artifacts that define them. Working through issues of production as well as consumption, mashing-up academic and nonacademic ways of thinking into novel configurations of thought and gesture, pop culture might be best understood as a laboratory of cultural methodology.[48] Making matter *matter* is a strategically important element of an approach that pays attention to the extended thing, with all the immanent or prognostic powers adduced, *res extensa*, from assorted pop-cultural things, fossils, totems, talismans, findings, commodities, jokers, novelties, and trash.[49]

In a bad way, Dwight MacDonald's most popular essay, "Masscult and Midcult," illustrates the workings of the critical legitimacy crisis I have in mind.[50] "The recent [1958] centenaries of Poe and Melville passed without undue excitement in the press," he writes, "but *Sports Illustrated* devoted four pages to the fiftieth anniversary of Fred ('Bonehead') Merkle's failure to touch second base in a World Series game" (65).[51] MacDonald is concerned that the press (Midcult) is more exercised about sports (the epitome of Masscult) than literature (the epigone of High Culture). Today, outside rarified circles of the baseball antiquarian, Bonehead Merkel is an all but forgotten footnote while Poe and Melville remain famous. People honor their birthplaces and graves, read from their works, read translations, watch adaptations, consume product tie-ins and assorted merchandise. The audience for Bonehead Merkle's notorious base-running error were the spectators in attendance at a late season game in a tight pennant race in the fall of 1908 as well as those reading about it in the *New York Times* in which Merkel was mercilessly scapegoated (*apescaped*, as Pynchon would have it). The controversy surrounding the irregular umpiring of the incident may have led the commissioner of baseball to commit suicide, some speculate, and Merkle never could escape his unjust association with it. Many fans of the New York Giants held Bonehead Merkel responsible for the team's late season collapse. Some fans of the Chicago Cubs took the Merkel Boner as the totemic cause of the Cubs' legendary curses. Deep unpopularity is itself a sign of popularity. *Is it better to be somebody than it is to be nobody or anybody?* to paraphrase Terry Malloy in *On the Waterfront*. Bonehead Merkel provides a real-life ready-made parable of unpopular pop culture—modern notoriety—as a failure to touch base. No eyewitnesses survive. For almost everybody now, Bonehead Merkel is a nobody. Posterity in Literature may or may not be more difficult to achieve than other forms of fame, but once achieved, it is more durable. This, for MacDonald, isn't the issue (though it may be too soon for him to tell about Merkel's Boner); the problem is that Midcult always hits its mark: "A tepid ooze . . . spreading everywhere."[52]

Again, the issue is that the popular implies connectivity understood as anonymous and heteronomous touching:

The danger to High Culture is not so much from Masscult [writes MacDonald] as from a peculiar hybrid bred from the latter's unnatural intercourse with the former. A whole middle culture has come into existence and it threatens to absorb both its parents. This intermediate form—let us call it Midcult—has the essential qualities of Masscult— the formula, the built-in reaction, the lack of any standard except popularity—but it decently covers them with a cultural figleaf. In Masscult the trick is plain—to please the crowd by any means. But Midcult has it both ways: it pretends to respect the standards of High Culture while in fact it waters them down and vulgarizes them.[53]

Displaced anxieties about "unnatural intercourse" aside, the essay resembles nothing less than a Midcult version of Adorno—*the enemy within* being administrative functionary whose self-appointed task is to report upon "what-the-public-wants," and the voxpop ventriloquism confuses evaluation, measurement, and management at every turn (either by applause-meter or by collecting "1,036 pages of data and interpretations without offending any religious, racial, political or social group").[54] Measurement facilitates domination; value gets attributed in the rear view mirror. In a zone where pop culture retrofits "value" to popularity, Plas and Anton Webern are equally obscure (either reference presupposes a high level of erudition); MacDonald's essay is symptomatic of the very hegemony of hybrid and heteronomy he wishes to avert. In the universe of pop-cultural annotation, Bonehead Merkle shakes hands with Herman Melville and Edgar Allan Poe right here before your eyes as Dwight MacDonald makes the introductions.

Let's end this foray into pop culture notation as a form of critical thought amid the animate ooze of a televised debate from the 1980s (on Nightline) about the merits of the latest cinematic box-office juggernaut in the *Star Wars* franchise, a video artifact someone uploaded online as a relic of the rapidly fading past.[55] The anonymous comments section, that pop-cultural trash compactor at the end of history, alternates between those scandalized by pop-cultural sacrilege (who belittles *Star Wars*?) to those lamenting the loss of high-minded critical civility from our primetime national discourse to those who marvel at the astute judgments by the loyal pop-cultural opposition combating kitsch in space. It's 1983, with the much-anticipated third installment of a trilogy mere days away, the debate itself consists of a mild give-and-take between three men, a tandem of sweater-wearing movie critics (the "Sweater Guys"), with their own television show and newspaper columns, proudly swearing allegiance to the popular, on the one hand, and a solitary film and drama critic of a starchier bent, who writes for serious papers and newsweeklies, on the other, and who pronounces himself deeply defiant. (It should be noted that these three discussants are not academics in any sense.)

The host gets at things quickly: *Was the original* Star Wars *good or bad*, he pointedly asks? And, later, to the heart of things: *okay, but, is it great cinema?* The site of struggle over critical frontiers of the Good, the Bad, and the Great—conflict over the popular—comes down to marking out particular zones for a virtuous affective response concerning the aesthetic, marking out relations to audience enthusiasm, in particular. Right out of the gate, the hostile critic (dubbed "Mr. Grouchy McHighbrow," by one commenter), plays pop-cultural killjoy, a villain who dares to disparage a much-loved cultural object as "malodorous offal," deriding the cult-like response it stimulates. His aversion, he says, is directly proportional to the wild responses of fans as well as the (Masscult) critics who emulate them: "The raves [are] so violent and extravagant one cannot afford to mince one's words if one dislikes these things." For him, the films are bad because they "dehumanize" audiences, and fans and critics alike are subject to their ploys. The word *dehumanize* is significance not least because it really means *infantilize*. *Think of the children*—as Helen Lovejoy would have it on *The Simpsons*. Children, from this vantage, are either subjects for uplift into fully enlightened human adulthood or potential victims for dehumanization through aesthetic desensitization: "Let's face it," he says, Star Wars movies "are for children or for childish adults. They are not for adult mentalities, which unfortunately means that they are not for a lot of my fellow critics who also lack adult mentalities." The first of the two pop-cultural enthusiast critics says he "totally disagrees." The disagreement is not premised on any stated position but an inferred relation between acclaim (even among children) and cultural value. In other words, to dislike *Star Wars* is to dislike children, insinuates Sweater Guy #1, recalling a childhood spent watching "serials and Saturday matinees" and having his "imagination stimulated." Star Wars is virtuous because it helps you stay "young at heart." In truth, he basically presents another version of Lovejoy's *think of the children* reaction. Children are people, too! Sweater Guy #2, his partner, backs him up by describing a viewing in a movie theatre full of rapt and "ecstatic" children whose imaginative hyper drive was fully operational by the administration of moral value (in "asking each other who's who," "rooting for the right guys, booing the bad guys," etc.).

Both sides, it must be noted, have remarkably little to say about the film itself (or, "the normal standards by which we judge movies is this a great film," as the host puts it), despite arguing about the merits of special effects ("when you have a film that's 90% special effects, you might as well be watching an animated cartoon," according to Starchy McHighbrow). Yet, the idea of critical reflexivity as a gateway to the rare air of high cultural prestige, however old-fashioned, is anything but defunct. Both sides of the *Star Wars* debate eagerly play the part of gatekeepers to the human zoo—what George Yúdice has described as culture-as-resource—as a pseudo-place that simultaneously legitimizes, preserves, and enshrines the durable value of popular enthusiasms as an exploitable standing reserve.[56] Once upon a time, this site might have been a debate about *Star Wars* on *Nightline*, now it happens with every reposted listicle on social media. Even though the Sweater Guys don't self-consciously position themselves as cultural gatekeepers in this venue—mere spokespeople for what's popular, whatever hits its mark—their oft-performed role of Masscult apologists trades on the bread and butter of respectable Midcult administration.

The laboratory upstairs is brightly lit, well-ordered, crammed with blown glass, work *tables, lights of many colors, speckled boxes, green folders—a mad Nazi scientist lab!* *Plasticman, where are you?*[57]

Florida State University (United States)

NOTES

1. For selections from this material, see Adolf Hitler, *Hitler's Table Talk, 1941-1944: His Private Conversations*, trans. Norman Cameron and R. H. Stevens, intro. H. R. Trevor-Roper (New York City: Enigma Books, 2000). For confirmation that Hitler was a fan of *King Kong*, see Ernst Hanfstaengl, *Hitler: The Missing Years* [1957] (New York: Arcade, 1994), 221; as well as Volker Koop, *Warum Hitler King Kong liebte, aber den Deutschen Mickey Maus verbot* (Berlin: be.bra verlag, 2015).

2. Leaving aside the complicated issue of possible toxic subtexts in *Metropolis* and their etiology (including the error of calling the director a fascist for representing a (quasi-) fascist dystopia in his film)—Lang exited Nazi Germany on July 31, 1933, claiming later that his departure was motivated by an uncomfortable meeting with the Reich minister of propaganda, Joseph Goebbels, in which Goebbels, Lang claimed, expressed his admiration for his films and tried to draft him to the cause of chief Nazi film propagandist. See Gösta Werner, "Fritz Lang and Goebbels: Myth and Facts," *Film Quarterly* 43.3 (Spring 1990): 24–27. It is also worth mentioning that Lang's mother was Jewish. For a discussion of the anecdote, see Tom Gunning, *The Films of Fritz Lang: Allegories of Vision and Modernity* (London: British Film Institute, 2000), 8–11.

3. Siegfried Kracauer cites Hitler's interest in *Metropolis* specifically—gleaned from another interview with Lang—but the thrust of his argument concerns the role of Weimar cinema in preparing the ground for Nazism, by externalizing "deep psychological dispositions" toward obedience to authoritarian domination through "subterranean content that, like contraband [crosses] the borders of consciousness without being questioned." Siegfried Kracauer, *From Caligari to Hitler: A Psychological History of the German Film* [1947] (Princeton: Princeton University Press, 2004), 163–64.

4. Leslie Fiedler, *The Devil Gets His Due: The Uncollected Essays of Leslie Fiedler* (Berkeley: Counterpoint, 2008), 22.

5. Quoted in Stefan Müller-Doohm, *Adorno: A Biography* (Cambridge: Polity, 2005), 182.

6. Jacques Rancière, "Why Emma Bovary Had to Be Killed," *Critical Inquiry* 34.2 (Winter 2008), 233–48.

7. Dominic Pettman, *Infinite Distraction* (Cambridge: Polity, 2016), 29.

8. Jacques Rancière, *The Politics of Aesthetics* (New York: Bloomsbury, 2013), 52, 30.

9. Thomas Pynchon, *Gravity's Rainbow* (New York: Penguin, 1995), 179.

10. Andy Warhol, *I'll Be Your Mirror: The Selected Andy Warhol Interviews*, ed. Kenneth Goldsmith (New York: Carroll and Graf, 2004), 18.

11. Robert Venturi, Steven Izenour, and Denise Scott Brown, *Learning from Las Vegas* (Cambridge, MA: MIT Press, 1972).

12. Rancière, *The Politics of Aesthetics*, 37.

13. Ibid., 54.

14. Pynchon, *Gravity's Rainbow*, 206.

15. Rancière, *The Politics of Aesthetics*, 54. See Janice Radway, *Reading the Romance: Women, Patriarchy, and Popular Literature* (Chapel Hill: University of North Carolina Press, 1984). On the relation between Bovary's reading habits and popular reading practices around popular romance novels, see Dorothee Birke, *Writing the Reader: Configurations of a Cultural Practice in the English Novel* (Berlin: DeGruyter, 2016).

16. Rancière, *The Politics of Aesthetics*, 51.

17. Ibid., 54.

18. Rancière, "Why Emma Bovary Had to Be Killed," 240.

19. Arthur Danto, "The Artworld," *The Journal of Philosophy* 61.19 (October 15, 1964): 571–84.

20. Danto, "The Artworld."

21. Pynchon, *Gravity's Rainbow*, 368.

22. Thomas Pynchon, "Is It Okay to be a Luddite?" *New York Times* (October 28, 1984), www.nytimes.com/books/97/05/18/reviews/pynchon-luddite.html. Referencing a slogan of the 1960s counterculture ("King Kong Died for Our Sins"), Pynchon describes "Kong" as the "classic Luddite saint," the only "countercritter Bad and Big enough" to countermand "what would happen in a nuclear war." The implication is that even Kong's terrible beauty (killed for beauty not by airplanes, Pynchon reminds us) as the anxious and "irresponsible" apotheosis of "our" toxified pop-cultural coprophelia can't expiate "us" from the death cult of the military-industrial war machine.

23. Martin Bak Jørgensen, "The Precariat Strikes Back: Precarity Struggles in Practice," in *Politics of Precarity: Migrant Conditions, Struggles and Experiences*, eds. Carl-Ulrik Schierup and Martin Bak Jørgensen (Amsterdam: Brill, 2016), 55.

24. Pynchon, "Is It Okay to be a Luddite?"

25. Philip Armstrong, "Precarity/abandonment," in *Nancy and the Political*, ed. Sanja Dejanovic (Edinburgh: Edinburgh University Press, 2015).

26. Vilém Flusser, *Writings* (Minneapolis: University of Minnesota Press, 2002), 44.

27. Felski, *The Limits of Critique*, 55.

28. Alexander Galloway, *The Interface Effect* (Malden, MA: Polity, 2012), 52.

29. Stuart Hall, "Notes on Deconstructing the Popular," in *Cultural Theory and Popular Culture: A Reader*, ed. John Storey (London: Pearson, 1998), 442.

30. *Oxford English Dictionary*.

31. Meaghan Morris, "Banality in Cultural Studies," in *Logics of Television: Essays in Cultural Criticism*, ed. Patricia Mellencamp (Bloomington: Indiana University Press, 1990), 22.

32. *Oxford English Dictionary*.

33. Hall, "Notes on Deconstructing the Popular," 442.

34. Ibid.," 443.

35. Morris, "Banality in Cultural Studies," 30. She is drawing on and repurposing Michel de Certeau.

36. Joseph Conrad, *Heart of Darkness* (Oxford: Oxford University Press, 2008), 141.

37. Pynchon, *Gravity's Rainbow*, 206.

38. Ibid., 703.

39. Numerous accounts—and scores of anthologies of key foundational texts—are readily available for tracing the complex genesis and contentious terrain of the cultural studies approach to popular culture. Cultural studies stabilized in the 1980s and 1990s around a range of concurrent debates held by faculty more or less trained in literary interpretation in language and literature departments. It eventually developed into a kind of elastic third-space stretching across the humanities and humanities-inclined units of the social sciences (women's studies, race and ethnic studies, postcolonial studies, area studies, speech and communications, film, media and digital studies, to name several). Much of the common ground concerns the ways collective identities are negotiated in and through objects of pop-cultural attention, as arenas "of consent and resistance," in Stuart Hall's words, preeminently through class, race, ethnicity, gender, sexuality, and various modes of intersectionality. Cultural studies simultaneously provides an intellectual clearinghouse

"between post-structuralism and humanism," as Patrick Brantlinger and James Naremore put it; a vanishing mediator between assorted controversies about Modernism/postmodernism and media theory; and, an incubator for the identitarian investments of the neoliberal academy (1). In broad strokes, Brantlinger and Naremore are generally still correct to observe that cultural studies is built on consensus about a "dynamic model of the social subject" and the generic application of more sociologically inclined strains of post-1968 continental thought: Antonio Gramsci, Michel Foucault, Michel de Certeau, and Pierre Bourdieu, in particular, with various additions from the Grand Theory bookshelf, including Edward Said, Judith Butler, and other notable guests. On the cultural studies syllabus, they rightly underscore the importance of the British cultural materialists associated with the Birmingham School—Raymond Williams, Stuart Hall, Dick Hebdige—as well as the influences of earlier generations of intellectuals especially Frankfurt School Critical Theorists—Walter Benjamin and Theodor Adorno. Hovering around the study of pop culture, like animating ectoplasm, is the inspiring presence of Roland Barthes, not only the glittering example of his *Mythologies* but also the prevailing sense that the canon wars had dethroned the Greats ("killing the author") and perhaps more importantly diminished the centrality the Literary itself (moving from "work to text").

40. Dennis Hall, "Signs of Life in the Eighteenth Century: Dr. Johnson and the Invention of Popular Culture," *Kentucky Philological Review* 19 (2005): 14–15. Incidentally, Hall sees Donald Duck *not* King Kong as the pop culture egregore par excellence for the "American" century.

41. Compare Meaghan Morris: "'Banality' is one of a group of words—including 'trivial' and 'mundane'—whose modern history inscribes the disintegration of old ideals about the common people, the common place, the common culture. In medieval French, the 'banal' fields, mills, and ovens were those used communally. It is only in the late eighteenth century that these words begin to accumulate their modern sense of the trite, the platitudinous, and the unoriginal. So it's a banal observation that if banality, like triviality, is an irritant that returns again and again to trouble cultural theory, it is because the very concept is part of the modern history of taste, value, and critique of judgement, that constitutes the polemical field within which cultural studies takes issue with classical aesthetics" (40).

42. For a paradigmatic example, see Janice Radway: "Commodities . . . are selected, purchased, constructed and used by real people with previously existing needs, desires, intentions, and interpretive strategies. By reinstating those active individuals and their creative, constructive activities in the heart of our interpretive enterprise, we avoid blinding ourselves to the fact that the essentially human practice of making meaning goes on even in a world increasingly dominated by things and by consumption. In thus recalling the interactive character of operations like reading, we restore time, process, and action to our account of human endeavour and therefore increase the possibility of doing justice to its essential complexity and ambiguity as practice" (221).

43. Patrick Brantlinger and James Naremore, eds., *Modernity and Mass Culture* (Bloomington: Indiana University Press, 1991), 8–13.

44. Brantlinger and Naremore, *Modernity and Mass Culture*. Importantly, Brantlinger and Naremore observe that each operates in particular relations with the others as well as through symptomatic aporia, generating "ideologies, reading practices, and forms of subjectivity through which art can be received and understood." Defined by overly narrow elitism and strained ambitions for heroic literary supremacy, High splinters into Modernism and Avant-garde. Folk mutates into Mass and Popular. Mass, defined by its ravenous, vertically integrated cash nexus, provides the cornerstone of the Frankfurt School's powerful account of the Culture Industry as a form of domination and manipulation. Raymond Williams famously observed that "there are in fact no

masses, but only ways of seeing people as masses." This is an important corrective to the preoccupation with the vices of Mass Culture in Kulturkritik, but understanding Mass in terms of mass mediation is another fact, the issue being—in a word—scale: Masses of cultural consumers, standing in reserve, provide battery packs of value for energizing the mode and means of pop culture akin to the human bodies stored in pods in *The Matrix*. Cultural studies has sought to do justice to forms of resistance and feedback, giving social meaning to consumption in terms of communities, practices, and critical environments. The Popular is, in a sense, the category to rule them all; it designates the reception horizon with the greatest plasticity. Does its inclusiveness compromise its critical powers?

45. Ibid., 8.

46. Gilbert Seldes, *The 7 Lively Arts* (New York: Dover, 2001).

47. Inevitably, the pop culture ladder gets pulled up completely away from the literary—and various attenuated forms of literary-style criticism, interpretation or textual analysis, are set aside for the style of empiricism promised by archival materials, survey research, or ethnographic methods. Pop-cultural work in sociology or communication departments often takes on an empiricist cast formed by vocational-minded positivism or the pursuit of grants or contracts.

48. See especially Steven Connor, "Cultural Phenomenology, CP: or, A Few Don'ts By A Cultural Phenomenologist," *parallax* 5.2 (1999): 17–31.

49. This list borrows from the taxonomy proposed by Joshua Glenn and Rob Walker, *Significant Objects*, http://significantobjects.com. See also Aaron Jaffe, *The Way Things Go* (Minneapolis: University of Minnesota Press, 2014).

50. Dwight MacDonald, "Masscult and Midcult," *Against the Grain* (New York: Da Capo, 1983).

51. MacDonald, "Masscult and Midcult," 65.

52. Ibid., 54; on the misogynistic matrix of the semiotics of High and Low, esp. the tendency to equate mass culture and amorphous ooze, see Andreas Huyssen, *After the Great Divide: Modernism, Mass Culture, Postmodernism* (Bloomington: Indiana University Press, 1986).

53. Ibid., 37.

54. Ibid., 54.

55. "Siskel and Ebert defend Star Wars," *YouTube,* uploaded by grebmops (April 5, 2013), https://www.youtube.com/watch?v=Ky9-eIlHzAE.

56. See George Yúdice, *The Expediency of Culture: Uses of Culture in the Global Era* (Durham: Duke University Press, 2003). My reading of Yúdice is influenced by Mulhern, *Culture/ Metaculture*, and Peter Osborne "'Whoever Speaks of Culture Speaks of Administration as Well': Disputing Pragmatism in Cultural Studies." *Cultural Studies* 20.1 (2006): 33–47.

57. Pynchon, *Gravity's Rainbow*, 314.

WORKS CITED

Armstrong, Philip. "Precarity/Abandonment." In *Nancy and the Political*. Ed. Sanja Dejanovic. Edinburgh: Edinburgh University Press, 2015.

Birke, Dorothee. *Writing the Reader: Configurations of a Cultural Practice in the English Novel.* Berlin: DeGruyter, 2016.

Brantlinger, Patrick, and James Naremore, eds. *Modernity and Mass Culture.* Bloomington: Indiana University Press, 1991.

Connor, Steven. "Cultural Phenomenology, CP: or, A Few Don'ts by A Cultural Phenomenologist." *Parallax* 5.2 (1999): 17–31.

Conrad, Joseph. *Heart of Darkness*. Oxford: Oxford University Press, 2008.

Danto, Arthur. "The Artworld." *The Journal of Philosophy* 61.19 (October 15, 1964): 571–84.

Felski, Rita. *The Limits of Critique*. Chicago: University of Chicago Press, 2015.

Fiedler, Leslie. *The Devil Gets His Due: The Uncollected Essays of Leslie Fiedler*. Berkeley: Counterpoint, 2008.

Flusser, Vilém. *Writings*. Minneapolis: University of Minnesota Press, 2002.

Galloway, Alexander. *The Interface Effect*. Malden: Polity, 2012.

Glenn, Joshua, and Rob Walker. *Significant Objects*. http://significantobjects.com

Gunning, Tom. *The Films of Fritz Lang: Allegories of Vision and Modernity*. London: British Film Institute, 2000.

Hall, Dennis. "Signs of Life in the Eighteenth Century: Dr. Johnson and the Invention of Popular Culture." *Kentucky Philological Review* 19 (2005): 14–15.

Hall, Stuart. "Notes on Deconstructing the Popular." In *Cultural Theory and Popular Culture: A Reader*. Ed. John Storey. London: Pearson, 1998.

Hanfstaengl, Ernst. *Hitler: The Missing Years* [1957]. New York: Arcade, 1994.

Hitler, Adolf. *Hitler's Table Talk, 1941-1944: His Private Conversations*. Trans. Norman Cameron, and R. H. Stevens. Intro. H. R. Trevor-Roper. New York: Enigma Books, 2000.

Huyssen, Andreas. *After the Great Divide: Modernism, Mass Culture, Postmodernism*. Bloomington: Indiana University Press, 1986.

Jaffe, Aaron. *The Way Things Go*. Minneapolis: University of Minnesota Press, 2014.

Jørgensen, Martin Bak. "The Precariat Strikes Back: Precarity Struggles in Practice." In *Politics of Precarity: Migrant Conditions, Struggles and Experiences*. Eds. Carl-Ulrik Schierup, and Martin Bak Jørgensen. Amsterdam: Brill, 2016.

Koop, Volker. *Warum Hitler King Kong liebte, aber den Deutschen Mickey Maus verbot*. Berlin: be.bra verlag, 2015.

Kracauer, Siegfried. *From Caligari to Hitler: A Psychological History of the German Film* [1947]. Princeton: Princeton University Press, 2004.

MacDonald, Dwight. "Masscult and Midcult [1960]." In *Against the Grain*. New York: Da Capo, 1983. 3–75.

Morris, Meaghan. "Banality in Cultural Studies." In *Logics of Television: Essays in Cultural Criticism*. Ed. Patricia Mellencamp. Bloomington: Indiana University Press, 1990.

Mulhern, Francis. *Culture/Metaculture*. New York: Routledge, 2000.

Müller-Doohm, Stefan. *Adorno: A Biography*. Cambridge: Polity, 2005.

Osborne, Peter. "'Whoever Speaks of Culture Speaks of Administration as Well': Disputing Pragmatism in Cultural Studies." *Cultural Studies* 20.1 (2006): 33–47.

Pettmann, Dominic. *Infinite Distraction*. Cambridge: Polity, 2016.

Pynchon, Thomas. "Is It Okay to be a Luddite?" *New York Times* (October 28, 1984). www.nytimes.com/books/97/05/18/reviews/pynchon-luddite.html

Pynchon, Thomas. *Gravity's Rainbow*. New York: Penguin, 1995.

Radway, Janice. *Reading the Romance: Women, Patriarchy, and Popular Literature*. Chapel Hill: University of North Carolina Press, 1984.

Rancière, Jacques. "Why Emma Bovary Had to Be Killed." *Critical Inquiry* 34.2 (Winter 2008): 233–48.

Rancière, Jacques. *The Politics of Aesthetics*. New York: Bloomsbury, 2013.

Seldes, Gilbert. *The 7 Lively Arts*. New York: Dover, 2001.

"Siskel and Ebert defend Star Wars." *YouTube*. Uploaded by grebmops (April 5, 2013). https://www.youtube.com/watch?v=Ky9-eIlHzAE

Venturi, Robert, Steven Izenour, and Denise Scott Brown. *Learning from Las Vegas*. Cambridge, MA: MIT Press, 1972.

Warhol, Andy. *I'll Be Your Mirror: The Selected Andy Warhol Interviews*. Ed. Kenneth Goldsmith. New York: Carroll and Graf, 2004.

Werner, Gösta. "Fritz Lang and Goebbels: Myth and Facts." *Film Quarterly* 43.3 (Spring 1990): 24–27.

Yúdice, George. *The Expediency of Culture: Uses of Culture in the Global Era*. Durham: Duke University Press, 2003.

CHAPTER SEVENTEEN

Comparativisms

ALEXANDER BEECROFT

From its nineteenth-century origins, comparative literature was notoriously a discipline built around the concept of the national literature, and the European national literature at that.[1] In order for comparison to take place, the reasoning went, one must begin with discrete objects which can be put into comparison, and the nation-state, presumed to map onto language and culture in a one-to-one fashion, provided the most ready basis for the distinguishing of literatures as distinct objects. Comparative literature emerged precisely as national literatures were taking firm shape, and as the first literary histories were being written, generally along national lines. This structure of the field of comparative literature was put with a distinctive precision by Hugo Meltzl de Lomnitz, in his historically important 1877 "Vorläufige Aufgaben der vergleichenden Literatur," or "The Present Tasks for Comparative Literature," an essay in the first volume of his journal the *Zeitschrift für vergleichende Literatur*.[2] This essay establishes the ten languages which, in Meltzl's view, have achieved sufficient levels of classicism to warrant entry into the field of comparative literature: German, French, English, Italian, Spanish, Portuguese, Dutch, Swedish, Icelandic, and Hungarian. Even Russian, it seems, despite isolated flashes of brilliance like Pushkin, had not reached this level, let alone the languages of non-European peoples (though in fact those languages do from time to time feature in Meltzl's journal), so the objects to be compared are not only discrete, but relatively few in number. Meltzl argued, furthermore, that the goal of comparative literature should be precisely to resist cosmopolitanizing theories, and to cultivate the "purely national of all nations," to reveal, in other words, the national particularities of each literary tradition through comparison with the others.

Not every later scholar of comparative literature, of course, has adhered rigidly to Meltzl's proclamations, but the model of a meta-discipline which gathers together the respective national traditions of Europe (and its overseas imperial extensions), while maintaining the integrity of those traditions, has held enduring significance, and is reflected in the organizational structure of many US universities to this day, with a comparative literature program or department often organizationally distinct from the various national-literature departments, the former's faculty selected as part-time visitors from the latter. Such a model necessarily privileges those texts and authors which rest most easily within the bosom of the nation-state, and all the more those which form the core of the national canon (the better with which to observe that which is "purely national"). Hybrid texts, texts from the national periphery (linguistically, geographically, or racially), or texts in any way from the margins of literary history, are harder to fit into this model.

Non-European languages have likewise been fit into this paradigm of comparative literature only with difficulty, and for the most part only as those literatures enter into a (European) modernity, rendering their contents more readily assimilable to European models. As Gayatri Spivak has observed,[3] when non-European languages and literatures are included in the comparative paradigm, it has often been through the vehicle of area studies. The story of the emergence of area studies programs, with their social-scientist and presentist proclivities, out of a Cold War–era desire to better understand America's enemies and rivals, has been well documented.[4] This approach has not always been conducive to comparative study, particularly over the *longue durée*, though Spivak offers an alternative perspective, where the emphases of area studies allow for a greater focus on the political dimensions of literary texts than is possible with conventional comparative literature methods. Spivak's qualified enthusiasm notwithstanding, the area studies model presents considerable challenges to literary study, among which one might mention that the borders of "Areas," dictated as they are by trade or by national-security concerns, may or may not correspond with coherent linguistic or cultural units, and do not coincide with the nation. Where in area studies, for example, do we fit the Persianate poetry of south Indian courts (caught between Middle Eastern and South Asian studies), or the Tibetan epic of Gesar (caught between South Asian and East Asian, and benefiting as well from the assistance of an all-too-tiny Central Asian studies)? Where the areas of area studies do happen to map onto regions of cultural circulation, as with East and South Asia to varying extents, the language competencies required to address these areas as a whole pose formidable obstacles, and with a few notable exceptions[5] work in these fields is necessarily collaborative.[6]

Both nation and area, then, have always been somewhat unsatisfactory geographic principles around which to organize literary study. And with the twenty-first-century advent of globalization and its discontents, the inadequacy of both the nation-state and the Cold War–based Area to organize the study of literary and cultural production has become only more apparent. One response to this perceived inadequacy of existing geographic paradigms has been the exponential growth in World Literature, both as a pedagogical enterprise and as a scholarly question.[7] Such a move is both necessary and desirable, as a means of capturing literary circulations on their broadest possible scales, and as the most potent disruptor of national-literature models. World Literature, whose day has been proclaimed now for 190 years since Goethe's famous conversation with Eckermann, seems finally to have arrived.

And yet it should also be clear that the "world" of world literature is not enough, conceptually speaking. Thinking on a global scale obscures as much as it reveals, relying as it necessarily does on work read in translation, on collaboration, and on the reading of secondary scholarship. The finer grained aspects of a literary network need to be seen up close to be understood with any precision, and if world literature merely rests atop essentially undisturbed fields of national-literature scholarship, then the new discipline will inevitably and uncritically absorb many of the conceptual failings of the old: privileging centers over peripheries, essentialist notions of cultural purity over hybridity, stasis over change. The desire to move beyond a national- and area-based model of literary circulation requires not only a move upward in scale to the globe, but also a lateral shift to new ways of examining literary networks, built neither on the Westphalian model of the nation-state, nor on Cold War–era national-security interests, but, one hopes, on bases more closely reflecting actually existing literary circulations.

And such models have indeed proliferated in the twenty-first century, especially in the years since the economic crisis of 2008. Many of these models have affinities with the rubric of the "transnational," a concept whose prehistory draws on the work of the Cuban anthropologist Fernando Ortiz on the concept of "transculturation."[8] For Ortiz, transculturation was the process by which cultures in dynamic interaction mutually transformed each other, frequently creating new cultural formations in the process, as in the case of his native, Cuba, whose indigenous culture was overlain with Spanish, African, and other influences. Beginning in the late 1990s, Ortiz's work began to reshape the discipline of American studies—itself always a somewhat unusual variation of the area studies model, turned inward on the United States itself—to allow that discipline to reimagine the study of the United States through what came to be called a *transnational* perspective, in which individuals, identities, processes, and flows move through borders rather than being fully described by them.[9] This notion of the transnational is both produced by the desire to transcend the limitations of the nation-state as a theoretical model, and by its very nature itself implicated in the nation-state, always already present within it if only as the thing to be transcended. So while transnational studies has been an active and growing field of study in its own right, my focus here will be on a series of frameworks which more completely dispense with the nation-state as their point of reference.

As a first-order approximation, these new models for literary circulation can be divided into two categories: the linguistic and the geographic. Where the national and area studies models presumed (even as they often knew otherwise) a rough homology between the two, more contemporary thought has tended to view linguistic and spatial structurings of literary space as at the least not entirely congruent, even when they are not wholly distinct. On the linguistic level, "-spheres" and "-phones" have proliferated: the Anglosphere, the Francophone, Hispanophone, Lusophone, and Sinophone.[10] Such zones, deliberately fuzzy on a geographic level, seek to integrate the entire body of work somehow associated with a major language, frequently privileging the hybrid and the marginal. In geographic terms, we have seen a proliferation of oceans and hemispheres: from the Black Atlantic to the Indian Ocean; from hemispheric studies in the Americas to the Global South. Such spaces denote the operative regions of complex and unequal flows, neither contained nor regulated by nations, but shaped according to the logics of trade, capital, and empire.

Such conceptual innovations are clearly long overdue. But every model has its limitations, its blind spots, the ground beneath its feet which it cannot see clearly. I will take the Sinophone as an example, since it has been theorized with considerable sophistication. Shu-mei Shih has described Sinophone studies as "the study of Sinitic-language cultures on the margins of geopolitical nation-states and their hegemonic productions [locating] its objects of attention at the conjuncture of China's internal colonialism and Sinophone communities everywhere immigrants from China have settled."[11] The Sinophone does not, then, simply encompass all cultural production in "Chinese" (i.e., in the family of Sinitic languages including both Classical Chinese and Modern Standard Mandarin, as well as the myriad spoken "dialects," many of them more divergent phonetically, semantically, and even syntactically than the members of the romance language family). Or at least, the focus of the Sinophone is not so much on that totality, and rather on its limits: as Shih argues, on the continental colonial fringes of the Chinese state; in the settler-colonial Chinese-language communities of Southeast Asia; in the immigrant communities in North America, Australia, and everywhere.

Importantly, each of these limits is itself a multilingual space. Sinophone writers in Tibet, Xinjiang, Manchuria, Inner Mongolia, or the mountainous southwest of China may be native speakers of their local languages, many of which have centuries of literary tradition in their own right. Writers from Chinese communities in Thailand, Malaysia, Singapore, Indonesia, and so on are necessarily implicated in the national languages and literatures of those nations, often themselves polyglot and involving other settler communities (South Asians in particular), as well as the languages of maritime European colonists, especially English. Immigrant communities in the United States and Canada, among other places, must also contend with the local languages of their new homes. The distinctive cases of Hong Kong and Taiwan offer their own multilingual complexities as well.

So if the Sinophone is not (or not especially) the center, and is located rather on the periphery of the Sinitic world, it is also always necessarily elsewhere: on the periphery, or at times even at the center, of other cultural worlds. This means that the Sinophone (and the categories like it) cannot effectively be described using maps or statistics. Census data may tell us, for example, that ethnically Chinese people formed 43 percent of the population of Kuala Lumpur in 2010, and 28 percent of the population of Vancouver in 2011. This bare information, however, tells us nothing about the relative situations of Sinitic languages in both places: about the relative statuses of different dialects and of the standardized forms of the language; about the cultural situation of "Chinese" as compared with other immigrant or local languages; about how any or all of these languages relate to English. What motivates the choice to express oneself in Chinese, as opposed to any of these other options, in each city? How, in other words, does each city participate in the Sinophone, and how does that engagement connect with other cultural engagements: with South Asian diasporas, a Malayo-Indonesian continuum, and Global English in the case of Kuala Lumpur; with South Asian and other diasporas, the fringes of the Francophone world, First Nations peoples and an Anglophone settler colony in the case of Vancouver? Thick description will be needed here to limn the complex relations among cultural and political dynamics.

Moving beyond the specific case of the Sinophone, are each of these -phones created equal? Following Shih's characterization of the Chinese presence in Southeast Asia as resembling a "settler colony," that presence actually resembles a very particular class of settler colonies worldwide: those later subjected to other imperialisms of their own, and thus always caught between their own exploitation of the lands they entered and their subjugation in turn to a newer and mightier imperial authority: a productive comparison might exist in that sense among the Chinese in Southeast Asia; the French in Canada; the Afrikaans in South Africa. And yet each of these cases would also reveal its distinctive differences, having to do with the relative power and prestige of various ethnic groups in various modern states; different forms of domination engaged in by imperial powers and by their post-independence heirs; varying degrees of access to audiences in the metropolis or elsewhere. More broadly, each -phone or -sphere is distinct: the Sinophone by virtue of China never having been a maritime colonizing power; the Francophone by the continued cultural dominance of the old metropolitan center (and by the status of French as a minority language in Belgium, Canada, and Switzerland);[12] the Hispanophone by the multilingual character of Spain and complex and varied forms of indigeneity and creolism across Latin America;[13] the Lusophone by the peripheral and dominated quality of Portugal within Europe and by Lusotropical fantasies of *mestiçagem*.[14]

Further, each of these sets of dynamics are contested, creating the need for still more nuanced analysis. A key question, articulated to varying degrees in various linguaspheres, has been whether the -phone or -sphere terminology should include or exclude the metropolitan center (however defined). The 2007 manifesto, "Pour une littérature-monde en français," for example, advocated for the abolition of the distinction between "French" and "Francophone" literature, arguing that the latter category marginalized an increasingly vital dimension of French-language literature.[15] Others have critiqued the manifesto, suggesting that it asserts the privilege of the publishing industry in France, and therefore reinscribes the very notion of inferiority it seeks to erase.[16] Scholars and public intellectuals on all sides of the French debate frequently cite, as model to be emulated or avoided, the increasingly prominent role of postcolonial literature within the English-language canon, consecrated through institutions such as the Booker Prize. It is, however, striking how comparatively undertheorized the Anglosphere seems to be in comparison with its Chinese and French equivalents:[17] the power of English as a universal language (and the centrality of English departments within the humanities as constructed in US and UK universities) seems to have directed theoretical energies rather in the directions of postcolonial theory or world literature, each often heavily Anglophone in practice, without fully accounting for that Anglocentrism in theory. Even a basic vocabulary is missing in the case of English—our language lacks, among other things:

1. A clear way of identifying the difference between "English" literature (i.e., the literature of the UK country of England) and "English" literature (i.e., literature in English).

2. Distinct terms for the literatures of geographic regions, along the lines of Peninsular and Latin American literatures in Spanish, or Francophone literature versus that of Metropolitan France or "the Hexagon."

3. Indeed, a clear sense of what the core and the periphery of the English-language literary system might be. The United States and the United Kingdom both belong within that core in some sense (with possible question marks about, say, Scottish literature, or regional literatures within the US, whose access to cultural capital in New York or London may be weak compared to that for writers active in those cities). But what about Ireland? Canada? Australia? India?

There has been a tendency to talk about "postcolonial literature in English" as if it were a national literary category of its own,[18] again without clearly demarcating which nations count (or better, which writers, since the writers of the postcolonial canon frequently divide their time among various Anglophone nations). Can the settler colonies of Canada, Australia, and New Zealand be subsumed under the label of "postcolonial," and if they can, why not the settler colony of the United States? The newer term, "World Literature in English," is equally vague in its implications, sometimes being used for all literature written in English; sometimes exempting the United States and all or parts of the islands of Great Britain and Ireland; sometimes restricted to the literature of Africa, the Caribbean, and India. There has been a history, thanks to publishing traditions, of vaguely thinking of English-language writing from outside the United States as belonging in some way to a single literature, but this too lacks a name. "Commonwealth literature" leaves out Ireland (and currently Zimbabwe; at other times Nigeria and/or Fiji, and before that South Africa). "Booker Prize-eligible literature" would have been a viable category before the extension of Man Booker Prize eligibility to all novels written in English, in 2014. With fifty-four nations and twenty-seven other territories using English as an official language (*de iure* or, like the United States and the United Kingdom, *de facto*), it would be cumbersome to treat each Anglophone national literature as a discrete entity, not to mention the complicating factors of transnational writers in English and of the complex multilingual environments in many of these nations. The simplest solution—a single literature consisting of all works written in English, regardless of the ethnic identity or legal residency of the author—seems the least commonly used. All of the disparate and inchoate terminology used in the case of the Anglophone, then, insists on the need to distinguish between core and periphery, without being terribly clear on the limits of each. As with the critique of the *"littérature-monde en français"* manifesto, it seems that our efforts to integrate the full range of literary production in the language into our scholarly purview may merely repeat the very act of separation it was designed to erase.

An additional danger lurks in the -sphere/-phone model: the Sinophone, Francophone, Hispanophone, Lusophone, Anglophone worlds, and their equivalents in other languages, are all deeply and inherently multilingual in both theory and practice. The imposition of a colonial language always implies the presence of indigenous languages of one kind or another, and very often of other colonial languages as well, while immigrant and diasporic communities necessarily interact with local languages both dominant and subaltern. Moreover, none of these great world languages is entirely one: Chinese in particular, as we have seen, is a vast family of languages rather than a single language, and each of the great European imperial languages developed regional variations, ranging from orthographic differences to full-on creolization, as they traveled. There is therefore much room, and much need, for multilingual scholarship on each of the -phones, although in general the need has been recognized theoretically more than it has been realized in practice. Scholarship on the -phones can in fact provide a vehicle for admitting more marginal literary traditions into the purview of Euro-American scholarship: contemporary writing in Uyghur, Tibetan or Yi, for example, has a clear place in Sinophone discussions of the periphery of the PRC, and literature in Thai or Malay, similarly lacking in institutional academic homes, might gain more recognition through comparative work on the Sinophone diaspora. Slowly, the number of faculty in French departments making use of Wolof or Arabic in their work, and of those in English departments using Bengali or Yoruba, are increasing, and as their numbers grow we should see increasing scholarship in which literatures in these languages are brought into dialogue with French and English works. These developments offer at least a limited access, from a very particular perspective, for works which have otherwise languished in the US academy, despite the surge of interest in postcolonial writing in English and French.[19]

What are the limits to the -sphere/-phone phenomenon? Interest in the margins of the linguistic community has grown in the scholarship on many languages, perhaps in all of those which generate significant bodies of scholarly analysis. Not all such languages possess the full panoply of linguistic situations displayed by major world languages such as Chinese, English, French, or Spanish, but everywhere today there is a renewed interest in texts by and about empire (whether that language was used to promote, or to resist, imperialism); in texts by diasporic and/or immigrant writers; in texts by regional or minority writers, and by writers in smaller nations in which a given language is present. Such issues are increasingly prominent in the study of, for example, German,[20] Arabic,[21] Japanese,[22] and Russian[23] literature, and can be found even in the scholarship on smaller, less globalized, European languages such as Italian,[24] Dutch,[25] and the Scandinavian[26] languages. At the same time, there has been the beginnings of a critical rethinking of the idea of "Europe" itself, recognizing that the continent as a geographic expression has its own core and periphery, its own construction of an internal Mediterranean Other to the imperialist northwestern Europe taken as paradigmatic of the whole continent when viewed from afar.[27] All this activity notwithstanding, a -sphere/-phone approach is clearly more salient for some languages than for others, and each language will require careful attention to the specifics of its case, including the overlap with other linguistic communities. As such, the project at its best seems to rely inherently on a comparative model, even if a rather different model from that of a Goethe or a Meltzl.

So, too, for the new models based on geographic spaces which have likewise come into their own in the past two decades. Where the "Areas" of area studies were continental expanses of territory, assembled in part out of the military concerns they generated, but frequently possessing some kind of shared large-scale cultural circulation, the new geographies have generally worked on a different basis, their origins less in Toynbee's notion of the civilization[28] and more in the Mediterranean of Braudel.[29]

An early model here is that of the "Black Atlantic," articulated by Paul Gilroy in 1995: where more traditional scholarship had tended to separate the experiences of Africans, the peoples of the Caribbean, and their descendants in the United States and the United Kingdom, into discrete objects of study, Gilroy argued for the fundamental coherence of a modern Black Atlantic culture incorporating them all.[30] At around the same time,[31] the model of "Transatlantic Studies" began to emerge in English departments, exploring connections between US and UK literary traditions rather than studying the two in comparative isolation. Similar transatlantics have begun to spring up in the other major European languages found on both sides of the ocean. Christopher Miller has explored the "French Atlantic Triangle" created by the slave trade, drawing both on Anglophone work on the Black Atlantic and on the existing Franco-Caribbean intellectual models offered by Édouard Glissant and others.[32] In Spanish, scholars like Julio Ortega have pioneered the exploration of the Spanish transatlantic, emphasizing the role of European traditions in constructing a creole sense of self in Latin America.[33] This transatlantic scholarship is open to various sorts of critique: some have found it too heavily focused on readings of texts from the Americas, rather than transforming our understanding of the European canon; for being insufficiently comparative among the European transatlanticisms; for underplaying the significance of indigenous pre-Columbian cultures and traditions.[34] Each of these critiques, in fact, offers a rich and suggestive program for the ongoing vitality of the transatlantic field, whose potential insights have just begun to be tapped.

The Atlantic is not, of course, the only ocean, though it is the ocean whose history is most accessible for those whose research relies on European languages. The general field of oceanic studies has enjoyed a recent boom, indexed in part by the essays collected in the May 2010 issue of the *PMLA*. In addition to the expected contributions on the Atlantic, the other major oceans are represented, with essays on the Arctic,[35] Pacific[36], and Indian Oceans.[37] Each of these oceans figures rather differently in the discussion. The Arctic is visible mostly as a site of European exploration and discovery; the Pacific as a further zone of exploration and colonization, but also as a region from which the postcolonists write back, focused on the South Pacific. The "Pacific Rim" of major contemporary economies, from Russia to New Zealand on the west and from Canada to Chile on the east, has not yet received the attention it might merit as an object for cultural analysis. The Indian Ocean has a rather more complicated role to play, as both a major site of European (particularly British) imperialism and, prior to that, as a major locus for earlier phases of globalization in which Europe played a comparatively small role.[38] As such, the recent rise in oceanic studies elsewhere in the North American academy has in the case of the Indian Ocean joined in progress a rich existing discourse.[39] Indian Ocean studies, whether premodern or modern, have a particularly rich potential to open up new vistas for thinking through literatures and cultures, and their circulations, in a way which does not pass through Europe or North America, a potential matched to be sure by the linguistic demands imposed on those who would study the region.

Alongside the ocean, the hemisphere has become a new frame for intellectual inquiry. Strikingly, it is the so-called Western Hemisphere ("so-called" because neither hemisphere can be east or west in any absolute sense), that is, the Americas, which has attracted scholarly attention as an object of study. That other hemisphere, the eastern one which includes the continuous landmass of Europe, Africa, and Asia, might become an object of study someday, approximating the scale of the world itself (and being entirely equivalent to the world, prior to the fifteenth century, for most of its inhabitants).[40] The term "hemispheric studies" has acquired particular currency as a means of opening up the existing discipline of "American Studies" (in its origins implicitly "U.S. Studies"), to transnational perspectives, incorporating the work of Latin Americanists as well as scholars of American studies and of the various ethnic studies disciplines within the United States.[41] As a term, "hemispheric studies" has the advantage of evading the ambiguity between the double meaning of "American" in English as pertaining either to the United States or to the whole of North and South America together. This emergent field has developed in parallel to, and for entirely different reasons than, the existing inter-American discourses in comparative literature as represented by scholars such as Lois Parkinson Zamora.[42] In principle, this hemispheric project should be deeply multilingual: certainly involving Spanish, and ideally also English, Portuguese, and French, with the possible additions of minor colonial languages such as Dutch, indigenous languages, or the languages of diasporic immigrant communities who have found their way to the Americas. In practice, hemispheric studies is frequently invoked in specifically Anglophone contexts, significantly limiting its reach beyond the United States. With its focus on opening up the study of the United States to transnational perspectives, this Hemispheric turn runs the risk (seen elsewhere in this survey) of reinscribing the dynamic of center and periphery it earnestly seeks to erase, where it does not fully embrace the multilingual realities of the Western Hemisphere.

In a phrase echoing Voltaire's famous dictum about God, the Czech historian and nationalist František Palacký (1798–1876) is said to have proclaimed, roughly, that if Austria did not exist, then she would have had to be invented. ("Wahrlich, existierte der österreichische Kaiserstat nicht schon längst, man müsste im Interesse Europas, im Interesse der Humanität selbst sich beeilen, ihn zu schaffen.") Palacký was writing about the transnational Hapsburg Empire in a letter addressed to the revolutionary German parliament at Frankfurt in 1848, proclaiming that as a Czech he had no stake in incipient German nationalism. Early twenty-first-century thought has been haunted by the notion that the nation-state is past its prime, that forces larger, smaller, other than the nation increasingly shape our world, and the study of culture has increasingly shared in this perception that the nation-state is no longer (and perhaps never was) the optimal scale on which to study literature and culture. And yet if the nation-state does not exist, we must still invent it—or at least some equivalent manageable enough for the kind of detailed analysis that cannot take place at the global scale alone. The proliferation of -phones and -spheres, of transnational studies of minor languages, of oceans and hemispheres, is invigorating the comparative study of cultures worldwide, but always risks return to the monolingual, to the canonical, to the static, merely under a new guise. These new spaces and structures could in time become as rigid and inflexible as the old nation-state paradigm, and to maintain their vigor it will be necessary to keep multiple frames of reference (old and new alike) in play. Ottamar Ette has suggested, with his concept of Transarea studies, the need to transcend these new geographies, much as the old comparative literature of Meltzl emerged to transcend the then-new geography of the nation-state, and to think of these geographies themselves as collections of movements rather than as static spaces.[43] It is that gesture, I would suggest—the gesture of treating all geographies as provisional and ad hoc, and not the replacement of old geographies by new—that must define the parameters of cultural studies.

University of South Carolina (United States)

NOTES

1. Alexander Beecroft, "Greek, Latin, and the Origins of 'World Literature,'" *CLCWeb: Comparative Literature and Culture* 15.5 (December 31, 2013). doi:10.7771/1481-4374.2334

2. Cited at Haun Saussy, *Comparative Literature in an Age of Globalization* (Baltimore: Johns Hopkins University Press, 2006), 36.

3. Gayatri Chakravorty Spivak, *Death of a Discipline* (New York: Columbia University Press, 2005), 75–76.

4. Harry Harootunian, *Learning Places: The Afterlives of Area Studies* (Durham: Duke University Press, 2002).

5. Karen Laura Thornber, *Empire of Texts in Motion: Chinese, Korean, and Taiwanese Transculturations of Japanese Literature* (Cambridge: Harvard University Asia Center, 2009).

6. See, for example, the essays gathered in Sheldon Pollock, *Literary Cultures in History: Reconstructions from South Asia* (Berkeley: University of California Press, 2003).

7. Pascale Casanova, *La République mondiale des lettres* (Paris: Editions du Seuil, 1999); Franco Moretti, "Conjectures on World Literature," *New Left Review* 1 (February 2000): 54–68; and Alexander Beecroft, *An Ecology of World Literature: From Antiquity to the Present Day* (New York: Verso, 2015).

8. Fernando Ortiz, *Cuban Counterpoint, Tobacco and Sugar* (Durham: Duke University Press, 1995).

9. For a survey of the early stages of this process, see Robert A. Gross, "The Transnational Turn: Rediscovering American Studies in a Wider World," *Journal of American Studies* 34.3 (2000): 373–93.

10. I discuss some important works in each of the -phones and -spheres below. The essays gathered in Françoise Lionnet and Shu-mei Shih, *Minor Transnationalism* (Durham: Duke University Press, 2005) are also an indispensable resource.

11. Shu-mei Shih, "The Concept of the Sinophone," *PMLA* 126.3 (2011): 710.

12. For an elegant but critical sketch of the existing Francophone literary space, see Jean-Marc Moura, "French-Language Writing and the Francophone Literary System," *Contemporary French and Francophone Studies* 14.1 (2010): 29–38. doi:10.1080/17409290903412664

13. José Del Valle, *A Political History of Spanish: The Making of a Language* (Cambridge: Cambridge University Press, 2013).

14. Luís Madureira, "Nation, Identity and Loss of Footing: Mia Couto's 'O Outro Pé Da Sereia' and the Question of Lusophone Postcolonialism," *NOVEL: A Forum on Fiction* 41.2/3 (2008): 200–28.

15. Michel Le Bris, Jean Rouaud, and Collectif, *Pour une littérature-monde* (Paris: Editions Gallimard, 2007); the essays in the (earlier) Farid Laroussi and Christopher L. Miller, eds., *French and Francophone: The Challenge of Expanding Horizons*, Vol. 103, Yale French Studies (New Haven: Yale University Press, 2003) explore the same theme from a more scholarly perspective.

16. For a wide-ranging discussion, see the essays in Alec G. Hargreaves, Charles Forsdick, David Murphy, and Society for Francophone Postcolonial Studies, *Transnational French Studies: Postcolonialism and Littérature-Monde* (Liverpool: Liverpool University Press, 2010).

17. Though see, for example, Paul Jay, "Beyond Discipline? Globalization and the Future of English," *PMLA* 116.1 (2001): 32–47; Paul Jay, *Global Matters: The Transnational Turn in Literary Studies* (Ithica: Cornell University Press, 2010); and Michael Bérubé, "Introduction: Worldly English," *MFS Modern Fiction Studies* 48.1 (2002): 1–17; all of which acknowledge the need for further theoretical work on the Anglosphere.

18. See the discussion at Beecroft, *An Ecology of World Literature*, 337.

19. A point long made by at least some critics operating in a postcolonial context; see, for example, Gayatri Chakravorty Spivak, "Woman in Difference: Mahasweta Devi's 'Douloti the Bountiful,'" *Cultural Critique* 14 (1989): 105–28. doi:10.2307/1354294

20. The "literature of migration" has been a major topic of study in German literature since at least Leslie A. Adelson, "Migrants' Literature or German Literature? TORKAN's Tufan: Brief an Einen Islamischen Bruder," *German Quarterly* (1990): 382–89.

21. Zahia Smail Salhi and Ian Richard Netton, *The Arab Diaspora: Voices of an Anguished Scream* (New York: Routledge, 2006).

22. Faye Yuan Kleeman, *Under an Imperial Sun: Japanese Colonial Literature of Taiwan and the South* (Honolulu: University of Hawaii Press, 2003).

23. Harsha Ram, *The Imperial Sublime: A Russian Poetics of Empire* (Madison: University of Wisconsin Press, 2006); Naomi Beth Caffee, "Russophonia: Towards a Transnational Conception of Russian-Language Literature," *eScholarship.org*, 2013. http://www.escholarship.org/uc/item/3z86s82v

24. Sandra Ponzanesi, "The Postcolonial Turn in Italian Studies," in *Postcolonial Italy: Challenging National Homogeneity*, eds. Cristina Lombardi-Diop and Caterina Romeo (New York: Palgrave Macmillan, 2012), 51–69.

25. Elleke Boehmer and Frances Gouda, "Postcolonial Studies in the Context of the 'diasporic' Netherlands," *Comparing Postcolonial Diasporas* (New York: Springer, 2009), 37–55.

26. Bolette B. Blaagaard, "Whose Freedom? Whose Memories? Commemorating Danish Colonialism in St. Croix," *Social Identities* 17.1 (2011): 61–72.

27. Roberto Dainotto, *Europe (in Theory)* (Durham: Duke University Press, 2007).

28. Arnold Joseph Toynbee, *A Study of History* (London: Oxford University Press, 1935).

29. Fernand Braudel, *La Mediterranee et le monde mediterraneen a l'epoque de Philippe II* (Paris: Armand Colin, 1990); for the medieval Mediterranean itself as a literary space, see for example, Karla Mallette, *The Kingdom of Sicily, 1100-1250: A Literary History* (Philadelphia: University of Pennsylvania Press, 2011); and David Wacks, *Framing Iberia: Maqamat and Frametale Narratives in Medieval Spain* (Leiden: BRILL, 2007).

30. Paul Gilroy, *The Black Atlantic: Modernity and Double-Consciousness*, reissue edition (Cambridge, MA: Harvard University Press, 1993).

31. Susan Manning and Andrew Taylor, *Transatlantic Literary Studies: A Reader* (Edinburgh: Edinburgh University Press, 2007), 4; discusses the significant role of a 1997 Ford

Foundation grant to Duke for the "Oceans Connect" project in the evolution of Transatlantic Studies in English.

32. Christopher L. Miller, *The French Atlantic Triangle: Literature and Culture of the Slave Trade* (Durham: Duke University Press, 2007).

33. Julio Ortega, *Transatlantic Translations: Dialogues in Latin American Literature* (Islington: Reaktion Books, 2006).

34. Adam Lifshey, *Specters of Conquest: Indigenous Absence in Transatlantic Literatures* (New York: Fordham University Press, 2010).

35. Adriana Craciun, "The Frozen Ocean," *PMLA* 125.3 (2010): 693–702.

36. Noelani Arista, "Navigating Uncharted Oceans of Meaning: Kaona as Historical and Interpretive Method," *PMLA* 125.3 (2010): 663–69; Teresia Teaiwa, "What Remains to Be Seen: Reclaiming the Visual Roots of Pacific Literature," *PMLA* 125.3 (2010): 730–36.

37. Gaurav Desai, "Oceans Connect: The Indian Ocean and African Identities," *PMLA* 125.3 (2010): 713–20; Isabel Hofmeyr, "Universalizing the Indian Ocean," *PMLA* 125.3 (2010): 721–29. The bibliographies of each of these articles offer rich introductions to their respective fields.

38. Janet L. Abu-Lughod, *Before European Hegemony: The World System A.D. 1250-1350* (New York: Oxford University Press, 1989).

39. See, among many others, Sanjay Subrahmanyam, "Connected Histories: Notes towards a Reconfiguration of Early Modern Eurasia," *Modern Asian Studies* 31.3 (1997): 735–62; Edward A. Alpers, *The Indian Ocean in World History* (Oxford: Oxford University Press, 2014); and Markus PM Vink, "Indian Ocean Studies and the 'new Thalassology,'" *Journal of Global History* 2.1 (2007): 41–62.

40. Alexander Beecroft, "Eurafrasiachronologies," *Journal of World Literature* 1.1 (2016): 17–28.

41. Caroline F. Levander and Robert S. Levine, *Hemispheric American Studies* (New Brunswick: Rutgers University Press, 2007).

42. Lois Parkinson Zamora, *The Usable Past: The Imagination of History in Recent Fiction of the Americas* (Cambridge: Cambridge University Press, 1997). As a revealing index of the parallel and distinct nature of hemispheric American studies and Comparative Inter-American studies, one might notice that there is no overlap between the contributors to Levander and Levine, *Hemispheric American Studies*; and to Lois Parkinson Zamora and Silvia Spitta, eds., *The Americas, Otherwise*, special issue, *Comparative Literature* 61.3 (Summer 2009).

43. Ottmar Ette, *TransArea: A Literary History of Globalization* (Berlin: Walter de Gruyter GmbH & Co KG, 2016).

WORKS CITED

Abu-Lughod, Janet L. *Before European Hegemony: The World System A.D. 1250-1350.* New York: Oxford University Press, 1989.

Adelson, Leslie A. "Migrants' Literature or German Literature? TORKAN's Tufan: Brief an Einen Islamischen Bruder." *German Quarterly* (1990): 382–89.

Alpers, Edward A. *The Indian Ocean in World History.* Oxford: Oxford University Press, 2014.

Arista, Noelani. "Navigating Uncharted Oceans of Meaning: Kaona as Historical and Interpretive Method." *PMLA* 125.3 (2010): 663–69.

Beecroft, Alexander. "Greek, Latin, and the Origins of 'World Literature.'" *CLCWeb: Comparative Literature and Culture* 15.5 (December 31, 2013). doi:10.7771/1481-4374.2334

Beecroft, Alexander. *An Ecology of World Literature: From Antiquity to the Present Day*.
   New York: Verso, 2015.

Beecroft, Alexander. "Eurafrasiachronologies." *Journal of World Literature* 1.1 (2016): 17–28.

Bérubé, Michael. "Introduction: Worldly English." *MFS Modern Fiction Studies* 48.1 (2002): 1–17.

Blaagaard, Bolette B. "Whose Freedom? Whose Memories? Commemorating Danish
   Colonialism in St. Croix." *Social Identities* 17.1 (2011): 61–72.

Boehmer, Elleke, and Frances Gouda. "Postcolonial Studies in the Context of the 'Diasporic'
   Netherlands." In *Comparing Postcolonial Diasporas*. Eds. Michelle Keown, David Murphy,
   and James Procter. New York: Springer, 2009. 37–55.

Braudel, Fernand. *La Mediterranee et le monde mediterraneen a l'epoque de Philippe II*.
   Paris: Armand Colin, 1990.

Bris, Michel Le, Jean Rouaud, and Collectif. *Pour une littérature-monde*. Paris: Editions
   Gallimard, 2007.

Caffee, Naomi Beth. "Russophonia: Towards a Transnational Conception of Russian-Language
   Literature." *eScholarship.org* (2013). http://www.escholarship.org/uc/item/3z86s82v

Casanova, Pascale. *La République mondiale des lettres*. Paris: Editions du Seuil, 1999.

Craciun, Adriana. "The Frozen Ocean." *PMLA* 125.3 (2010): 693–702.

Dainotto, Roberto. *Europe (in Theory)*. Durham: Duke University Press, 2007.

Damrosch, David. *What Is World Literature?* Illustrated edition. Princeton: Princeton University
   Press, 2003.

Desai, Gaurav. "Oceans Connect: The Indian Ocean and African Identities." *PMLA* 125.3
   (2010): 713–20.

Ette, Ottmar. *TransArea: A Literary History of Globalization*. Berlin: Walter de Gruyter GmbH
   & Co KG, 2016.

Gilroy, Paul. *The Black Atlantic: Modernity and Double-Consciousness*. Reissue edition.
   Cambridge, MA: Harvard University Press, 1993.

Gross, Robert A. "The Transnational Turn: Rediscovering American Studies in a Wider World."
   Journal of American Studies 34.3 (2000): 373–93.

Hargreaves, Alec G., Charles Forsdick, David Murphy, and Society for Francophone
   Postcolonial Studies. *Transnational French Studies: Postcolonialism and Littérature-Monde*.
   Liverpool: Liverpool University Press, 2010.

Harootunian, Harry. *Learning Places: The Afterlives of Area Studies*. Durham: Duke University
   Press, 2002.

Hofmeyr, Isabel. "Universalizing the Indian Ocean." *PMLA* 125.3 (2010): 721–29.

Jay, Paul. "Beyond Discipline? Globalization and the Future of English." *PMLA* 116.1 (2001):
   32–47.

Jay, Paul. *Global Matters: The Transnational Turn in Literary Studies*. Ithaca: Cornell University
   Press, 2010.

Kleeman, Faye Yuan. *Under an Imperial Sun: Japanese Colonial Literature of Taiwan and the
   South*. Honolulu: University of Hawaii Press, 2003.

Kono, Kimberly. *Romance, Family, and Nation in Japanese Colonial Literature*. New York:
   Springer, 2010.

Laroussi, Farid, and Christopher L. Miller, eds. *French and Francophone: The Challenge of
   Expanding Horizons*, vol. 103. Yale French Studies. New Haven: Yale University Press, 2003.

Levander, Caroline F., and Robert S. Levine. *Hemispheric American Studies*. New Brunswick:
   Rutgers University Press, 2007.

Lifshey, Adam. *Specters of Conquest: Indigenous Absence in Transatlantic Literatures*. New York:
   Fordham University Press, 2010.

Lionnet, Françoise, and Shumei Shih. *Minor Transnationalism*. Durham: Duke University Press, 2005.

Madureira, Luís. "Nation, Identity and Loss of Footing: Mia Couto's 'O Outro Pé Da Sereia' and the Question of Lusophone Postcolonialism." *NOVEL: A Forum on Fiction* 41.2/3 (2008): 200–28.

Mallette, Karla. *The Kingdom of Sicily, 1100-1250: A Literary History*. Philadelphia: University of Pennsylvania Press, 2011.

Manning, Susan, and Andrew Taylor. *Transatlantic Literary Studies: A Reader*. Edinburgh: Edinburgh University Press, 2007.

Miller, Christopher L. *The French Atlantic Triangle: Literature and Culture of the Slave Trade*. Durham: Duke University Press, 2007.

Moretti, Franco. "Conjectures on World Literature." *New Left Review* 1 (February 2000): 54–68.

Moura, Jean-Marc. "French-Language Writing and the Francophone Literary System." *Contemporary French and Francophone Studies* 14.1 (2010): 29–38. doi:10.1080/17409290903412664

Ortega, Julio. *Transatlantic Translations: Dialogues in Latin American Literature*. Islington: Reaktion Books, 2006.

Ortiz, Fernando. *Cuban Counterpoint, Tobacco and Sugar*. Durham: Duke University Press, 1995.

Pollock, Sheldon. *Literary Cultures in History: Reconstructions from South Asia*. Berkeley: University of California Press, 2003.

Ponzanesi, Sandra. "The Postcolonial Turn in Italian Studies." In *Postcolonial Italy: Challenging National Homogeneity*. Eds. Cristina Lombardi-Diop, and Caterina Romeo. New York: Palgrave Macmillan, 2012. 51–69.

Ram, Harsha. *The Imperial Sublime: A Russian Poetics of Empire*. Madison: University of Wisconsin Press, 2006.

Salhi, Zahia Smail, and Ian Richard Netton. *The Arab Diaspora: Voices of an Anguished Scream*. New York: Routledge, 2006.

Saussy, Haun. *Comparative Literature in an Age of Globalization*. Baltimore: Johns Hopkins University Press, 2006.

Shih, Shu-mei. "The Concept of the Sinophone." *PMLA* 126.3 (2011): 709–18.

Spivak, Gayatri Chakravorty. "Woman in Difference: Mahasweta Devi's 'Douloti the Bountiful.'" *Cultural Critique* 14 (1989): 105–28. doi:10.2307/1354294

Spivak, Gayatri Chakravorty. *Death of a Discipline*. New York: Columbia University Press, 2005.

Subrahmanyam, Sanjay. "Connected Histories: Notes towards a Reconfiguration of Early Modern Eurasia." *Modern Asian Studies* 31.3 (1997): 735–62.

Teaiwa, Teresia. "What Remains to Be Seen: Reclaiming the Visual Roots of Pacific Literature." *PMLA* 125.3 (2010): 730–36.

Thornber, Karen Laura. *Empire of Texts in Motion: Chinese, Korean, and Taiwanese Transculturations of Japanese Literature*. Cambridge, MA: Harvard University Asia Center, 2009.

Toynbee, Arnold Joseph. *A Study of History*. London: Oxford University Press, 1935.

Valle, José Del. *A Political History of Spanish: The Making of a Language*. Cambridge: Cambridge University Press, 2013.

Vink, Markus P. M. "Indian Ocean Studies and the 'New Thalassology.'" *Journal of Global History* 2.1 (2007): 41–62.

Wacks, David. *Framing Iberia: Maqamat and Frametale Narratives in Medieval Spain*. Leiden: BRILL, 2007.

Zamora, Lois Parkinson. *The Usable Past: The Imagination of History in Recent Fiction of the Americas*. Cambridge: Cambridge University Press, 1997.

Zamora, Lois Parkinson, and Silvia Spitta, eds. *The Americas, Otherwise*. Special Issue. *Comparative Literature* 61.3 (Summer 2009).

CHAPTER EIGHTEEN

Translation

BRIAN O'KEEFFE

ONE

Vladimir Nabokov once described translation as a journey between two countries named From and To.[1] The author (John From) supplies the text, and the translator (John To) transports it to the farther country—the destination point of translation. Here, already, is translation's ideal: translation as the twinning of two Johns, an onomastic double-act where the protagonists are identically named, where two are one. Shared authorship is part of translation's dream of equivalence: the journey of translation sets out toward a shimmering horizon of sameness, where the ideal of a perfect transfer of meaning is achieved, where nothing is lost in translation, where the translation clinches itself as an identical reproduction of the original text.

Translation studies has moved swiftly upon its own ideal. The experience of practicing translators shows that judicious approximations are the best one can hope for. Paul Ricoeur,[2] replacing hope by melancholy, suggested that the translator "mourns" what is inevitably lost, sighs in disappointment that ideal translation is impossible. Yet, the more positive view is that translation finds its freedom once it abandons its aspiration to exact fidelity. A better approach involves a "transcoding" model—a flexible exercise in finding expressive compatibilities between the two texts. A corollary is the "creative" model of translation, which isn't afraid to take a degree of poetic license, and make evident such liberties taken. This model is not willing to hide its art in accordance with the notion that a translation should never draw attention to itself. For it would imply that the interplay between texts and languages occurs without any impact on the host language. Yet it surely does. The host language, the translation that receives the foreign text, is often obliged to "foreignize" itself—to become different, in order to sensitively register what is different about that other text. As translations become more visible, translators themselves become less self-effacing, less deferential toward the source text. Translators are active interpreters; they no longer need to be especially shy about appropriating the idiom of the original. They are vigorous participants in the recontextualization and revitalization of cultural products.

The move away from equivalence-based approaches has been key to raising the profile of translation and translators. An important book in this regard is Lawrence Venuti's *The Translator's Invisibility*,[3] a book deeply mindful of the tendency to undervalue translation, despite the vital contribution it makes to the transmission and circulation of knowledge. But translation studies hasn't quite escaped the gravitational pull of equivalence—in areas like medical translation, it is still important to ensure an accurate translation. More consequentially for defining translation "theory," the pull of terms like equivalence, adequacy, imitation, and identity is exerted especially forcefully in two contexts, namely philosophy and literary studies. At issue, in this respect, is whether translation studies remains indebted to these two disciplines, or must liberate itself from them in the name of greater interdisciplinarity. At issue, moreover, is whether the principal theorizations of these terms, especially in and around attitudes to the imitative practice of translation, inevitably move translation studies toward Western thinking on philosophy, literature, and art. Marc Froment-Meurice has written that "the theory of translation follows that of imitation, of mimesis, which in turn determines every theory of Occidental art."[4] This need not be true for translation theory everywhere. But if this is true for Western translation theory, then imitation, replication, and reproduction remain the terms to be reckoned with. Translation may have to acknowledge its "determination" as a mimetic exercise. Yet if that determination keeps translation in touch with theories of Western art, it also keeps translation within the purview of Western philosophy, and subject thereby to the contending views philosophy has adopted vis-à-vis mimesis. One of these views is suspicion: is it that translation, like mimesis in general, counterfeits the original, reproduces it like an imposter? Or, to deploy the vocabulary of "property" (frequently used in translation theory), is it that translation jeopardizes what is proper to the original—its own idiom, its original meaning—in a ruinous exercise of illegitimate appropriation? The further question then arises (it is very much Western philosophy's question) as to whether certain provisos must be imposed upon translation, much like they have been imposed on Western art. Translation must become subject to the order of mimesis and regard its exclusive task to produce imitations. It must respect the priority of the original, come in order, after the original text, thereby ensuring that the priority of the original to *be* original remains in place.

Is philosophy the unacknowledged legislator of translation? The idea is thoroughly debatable. But perhaps what explains philosophy's keen interest in translation is that philosophy desires the transportation of a meaning or a truth to occur without loss. A truth cannot be one such if it changes its meaning from one language to another. As Jacques Derrida observes, "Philosophy [is] the thesis of translatability."[5] This thesis lays down the law to translation, requiring it to achieve ideal equivalence. One response to this might well be disobedience, a refusal to be true to truth, true to the original text. Yet for every claim to poetic license or free creativity, there are examples where this fidelity still commands the activity of translation, where the commitment to true translation holds sway. That commitment can inspire ethical despair, expressed by the unhappy saying *traduttore, traditore* (translator, traitor). Or else it inspires an *amour fou*—a mad desire to wed translation to the original so completely that imitation becomes perfect, and difference is erased.

Madness, rather than impossible fidelity, is more illustrative here. Let me present two literary examples. The first concerns Hölderlin's translations from Sophocles. They have been deemed failures that played a role in his descent into madness. Philippe Lacoue-Labarthe has argued that Hölderlin's difficulty was that Sophocles's plays could not perform their function as conduits through which a certain "Greece" would flow and emerge into German language and letters. But there was no Greece offering itself to Hölderlin via the intermediary of Sophocles. This is because Greece withdrew into mystery, leaving only vestiges of itself, offering vain temptations to those who would imitate—or translate—what Greece might have been. Greece simply names what cannot be recovered, what is permanently lacking, and Hölderlin experienced this lack as the absence of a stable model his translations could reliably imitate. What he experienced is translation in want of a model. He confronted the tragedy of translation, or else, in his failed translations, expressed tragedy itself: "Greece will have been, for Hölderlin, this inimitable. . . . The tragic as such, if it is true that the tragic begins with the ruin of the imitable and the disappearance of models."[6] The order of mimesis is orderly when there is first a model and then a copy, but now mimesis is in free fall. Like an archaeologist digging forever and in vain, Hölderlin's etymological investigations and archaizing coinages tried to imitate a source model that simply was not there, or which could only offer itself as a gulf no translation could ever bridge.

In my second example, Borges's "Pierre Menard, Author of the *Quixote*," the opposite is true: the original source text is all too evident. Menard, a fictitious French poet, finding that Cervantes's *Don Quixote* lacks the definite status that would make it untranslatable, undertakes the project to achieve "total identification"[7] with Cervantes and his text. We have but few fragments of this undertaking; as reproduced by the narrator, they are verbatim excerpts from *Don Quixote*. This is a purloined *Quixote*, an original text hidden in plain sight. Or else, a palimpsest so ideal it is no longer a palimpsest. These "translations" come close to perfect equivalence only to tip over into what translation is not: translation's ideal realized at the moment of its nullification. Yet the ironic commentary supplied by the narrator insists on the differences between Menard's version and Cervantes—Menard's work is almost better than the original. If so, the ideal of translation, namely to be as one, at one with the original, is here joined with translation's mad desire to outdo the original, to offer itself as the original's superlative.

Here, then, are two instances where translation, if it is determined by the logic of imitation or mimesis, breaks down. Hölderlin loses the model; Menard finds it all too well. But both experience the desire for similitude, absolute sameness with the original. This is hubris, or else a kind of madness. Maurice Blanchot, writing of Hölderlin, observed with blunt precision, "To translate, in the end, is madness."[8] This is perturbing, but registering the strange desires of translation is fundamental to describing what John Sallis calls its "ineradicable errancy."[9] At issue, on the one hand, is translation's drift beyond the stable trajectory of From and To into freewheeling creative adaptation. On the other, there is a drift into vain dreams and compellingly impossible ideals.

TWO

This constitutive errancy suggests something of the difficulty of talking about translation. But we can gain more stable purchase on the topic by classifying the different types of translation. A useful point of departure is provided by Roman Jakobson:[10] intralingual translation ("rewording") is the interpretation of verbal signs by other signs of the same language; interlingual translation ("translation proper") is the interpretation of verbal signs by some other language; intersemiotic translation ("transmutation") is the interpretation of verbal signs by nonverbal systems, like music or dance.

"Translation proper" is revealingly categorical. It seeks to name an essence of translation, despite alternatives (especially transmutation) which could easily fold translation proper into a more general definition. In any case, the question is how this interpretive exchange of signs is to occur. A word-for-word swap would be ideal but, as Cicero observed, a word-for-word rendering isn't necessary, provided one preserves the sense of what is said: "For I did not think I ought to count them out to the reader like coins, but to pay them by weight."[11] The numismatic or chrematistic metaphor is significant: do translations offer payment in kind, or simply shortchange the original? What are the weights and measures of translation? At least one consideration translators are often bidden to bear in mind is an economy of means: do not let the translation sprawl into periphrases and glosses. A translation should match, as far as possible, the number of words in the original. While Cicero freed translators from the word-for-word translation, that is to say, one should still strive for a one word *by* one word translation.

In the various (often tripartite) classifications of translation, restriction often contends with liberation. Taking the *measure* of that liberty is what matters. Consider John Dryden: metaphrase involves "turning an author word by word, and line by line, from one language into another." Paraphrase, or "translation with latitude," allows a translator to amplify, but not alter the original text. The third way is imitation, "where the translator (if now he has not lost that name) assumes the liberty, not only to vary from the words and sense, but to forsake them both as he sees occasion."[12] We risk losing the name "translator" when latitude becomes untrammeled liberty. Imitation loses its model such that translation becomes something other than translation. The indistinctness of translation is a constant concern. Hölderlin and Menard both show that generalized "imitation" can lose everyone—the original author, the original work, the difference between the original and the translation. The imitation game is a dangerous one to play in the vicinity of originality. Safer terrain is provided by hermeneutics, because it considers matters not in terms of imitation, but rather in the context of a philosophy of interpretation. Hermeneutics is underpinned by an analogy—interpretation is like a conversation between two parties who remain distinct from one another. The dialogical model stabilizes difference; generalized imitation threatens to dissolve it. For Gadamer, writing in *Truth and Method*,[13] what is sought by true interpretation is common ground, and following the tactful protocols of well-intentioned conversation gives us a sense of how that can be achieved. Interpretive tact is a matter of respecting mutual difference, and when this is transposed into the scenarios where a translator is relating to a text, we have two horizons (the contexts—linguistic, cultural, and historical—in which each party is necessarily situated), but a "fusion" is possible, Gadamer avers, if mutual respect accompanies the dialogical operations of translation.

Earlier than Gadamer, Schleiermacher also represented translation as a matter of mediating between the mutual foreignness of author and reader. Here, however, the dialogical scenario is resolved into an exchange between two poles, where what matters is which pole to go toward. "Either the translator leaves the writer alone as much as possible and moves the reader toward the writer, or he leaves the reader alone as much as possible and moves the writer towards the reader."[14] If one moves toward the writer, to the foreign text, the question is how far into the foreign to go. One can go too far, and reduce the translation to a linguistic hodgepodge. This is one danger. The other is madness: a wholesale foreignizing can lead to Menard's desire to vicariously inhabit the foreign text so absolutely that difference—upon which all *relational* models of translation rely—disappears.

Translation's exposure to the foreign text has to be carefully managed. But hermeneutics valuably shows us what is at stake when foreignness goads the translator into overcoming that foreignness, and learning from it. At stake is the awakening to difference that the dialogical activity of translation can elicit. Translation activates thought, refreshes language, and vivifies culture. Translations import words and ideas that enrich a host language. Goethe, for example, heartily agreed: translations expose us to otherness, and this is a good thing. He also produced a triune classification of translation types (or epochs). "The first acquaints us with the foreign country on our own terms."[15] In the second, "the translator endeavors to transport himself into the foreign situation but actually only appropriates the foreign idea and represents it as his own."[16] Goethe's third epoch expresses the abiding fantasy of perfect translation: "The goal of the translation is to achieve perfect identity with the original, so that the one does not exist instead of the other but in the other's place."[17]

Is there a difference between existing instead of the other and existing in the other's place? In fact, Goethe envisages translation's ideal as an interlinear textual product where the translation does not erase the original; rather, each is visible as they both occupy the same page.

> A translation that attempts to identify itself with the original ultimately comes close to an interlinear version and greatly facilitates our understanding of the original. We are led, yes, compelled as it were, back to the source text: the circle, within which the approximation of the foreign and the familiar, the known and the unknown constantly move, is finally complete.[18]

Consider the geometry of translation's ideal: a closed circle, a seamless conjunction of translation and source text. Translation, when it imagines its completion, thinks in terms of loops and rotations in order to envisage its journey. To turn back to the source is to be instantly propelled forward and along toward the host language. Or vice versa of course—such is the logic of circular thinking.

The problem is whether this ideal generates a harmonious or a vicious circle. Perhaps the source text might wish to resist this translatory completion, break out of its circular enclosures, and insist not on turns that always return, but on taking the translator on a permanent detour. Less a turn and turn about, more a turn away, where the foreign remains foreign, and the unknown remains categorically permanent—a bar to translation's overweening will-to-knowledge, rather than a spur to ever more complete approximations.

THREE

I turn now to two important theoretical arguments about translation: to Derrida, and first, to Benjamin's essay "The Task of the Translator." Benjamin's central proposition is this: "Translatability is an essential quality of certain works, which is not to say that it is essential for the works themselves that they be translated; it means, rather, that a specific significance inherent in the original manifests itself in its translatability."[19] For Benjamin, the task is to consider translation's ability to unlock a potential residing within the original text. The original does not participate in the activities of translation, but nonetheless, translation realizes something "essential" in the original—a latent ability to become something else.[20]

Benjamin imagines texts appealing for their potential to be realized. They appeal for a higher life, an afterlife, survival. Texts submit to translation, Benjamin observes, like seeds offer themselves to the process of ripening. But this germinative metaphor breeds odd elaborations: the relationship between an original's content and its exterior form or linguistic sheath, Benjamin writes, is so tight as to be indivisible, like a fruit and its skin. The relationship a translation has to the content of the original text is also a matter of envelopment, but when Benjamin pictures this kind of enfolding, the image is different: "Whereas content and language form a certain unity in the original, like a fruit and its skin, the language of the translation envelops its content like a royal robe with ample folds."[21]

The thought here is of skins and mantles enveloping a core, or indeed, a regal body. But how should a translation enfold the original text? "A real translation is transparent; it does not cover the original, does not block its light, but allows the pure language, as though reinforced by its own medium, to shine upon the original more fully."[22] "Transparency" returns us, controversially, to the ideal of perfect equivalence, but the image itself refers to a transparent film, enfolding but not concealing the original—an image I have somewhat imprudently likened to a piece of Saran wrap.[23] But what is more controversial is what Benjamin means by "the pure language," by *reine Sprache*. It is language stripped of all communicative intent so as to leave the Word. "In this pure language—which no longer means or expresses anything but is, as expressionless and creative Word, that which is meant in all languages—all information, all sense, and all intention finally encounter a stratum in which they are destined to be extinguished."[24]

What is meant by all languages is meaningfulness itself, a verbal plenitude, a Word that has gathered all words to itself. This idea returns us to God's Word perhaps, to language before the fall of Babel and to the Garden of Eden. But it also forces us to move forward, to look toward a linguistic achievement that has not yet come. In the meantime, translation hears the accords and harmonies that bring any given language into harmony with *reine Sprache*; translation weds all contingent languages to what Benjamin calls a suprahistorical kinship. Translation intimates something of the pure language, expresses that intimation each time an original text is borne up to the higher linguistic plane where translation's promise—a reconciliation of tongues—gets a little more fulfilled, a little easier to discern. Yet there remains that meantime, that wait time, and during such time, translation fails and fails again, but ever better. Whence another metaphorical image, that of the broken vase: each language is a shard which translation must glue together. There are fragments (Babel splintered the harmony of languages into confusion), but translation's patient reconstruction nonetheless gives us some image of what we are waiting for: a complete vase.

Reaction to Benjamin's essay has been ambivalent. For some, Benjamin's text is too theoretical, too "messianic," too cluttered by metaphors. For others—especially Derrida—it is the metaphorical register in Benjamin that draws the attention. In "Des tours de Babel," Derrida wonders (archly) about the status of Benjamin's kernels and seed pips. Is there something core-hard that resists translation, whatever the claims Benjamin makes for translation's germinative capacities? Derrida writes, "The always intact, the intangible, the untouchable is what fascinates and orients the work of the translator."[25] He wonders about the possibility of a text remaining "intact and virgin in spite of the labor of translation."[26] Transposed into another register, where a putative virginity is at issue, not to mention impregnability, Derrida permits himself to consider an erotics of translation—forbidden fruit. The erotic theme reemerges in "What Is a 'Relevant' Translation?" in the context of a desirous fascination for the intact idiom of the original. That desire is an amorous flame of passion:

> If I love the word, it is only in the body of its idiomatic singularity, that is, where a passion for translation comes to lick it as a flame or an amorous tongue might: approaching as closely as possible while refusing at the last moment to threaten or to reduce, to consume or to consummate, . . . on the very brink of this refusal or withdrawal—and after having aroused or excited a desire for the idiom, for the unique body of the other, in the flame's flicker or through a tongue's caress.[27]

Derrida's flame resembles the flames of Pentecost, when all spoke in tongues. But Derrida's fiery kiss is also an all-consuming desire where translation reduces the original to ashes, or to nothing at all. A holocaust of translation—a horrible thought. But the kiss of entwined tongues apparently stays on the brink—the vague place where the translator's desire is checked by last-ditch refusals. Perhaps "fidelity" to the original enjoins the translator to hold back. Perhaps it is a love for the "idiom," for the textual "body," as if love mates desire at the last, and proposes less a consummation, and more a tactful touching at a distance, a conjoining of partners, rather than an excitedly reckless consumption of the textual other.

Embedded in Derrida's account of amorous rapture is the vivid profile of a question: what happens when the translator's brinkmanship verges on the realization that there is something that remains, and must remain untranslatable, intact, and untouched? Another question: what is that "something?" Perhaps we might approach the matter by proposing something and nothing, or else, everything and nothing. These polarizing statements, introduced in "What Is a 'Relevant' Translation?" have become famous: "Nothing is translatable." And then, "Everything is translatable."[28] It wouldn't do to assume Derrida is being entirely serious—there is always the possibility that these are feigned axioms, truth-seeming truths. James Joyce's tart humor glosses Derrida best: "Untranslatable? Nothing."[29] There is nothing that shouldn't already be the work of a translator, nothing that isn't already calling for translation. Everything is therefore subject to translation; there is nothing that isn't already in translation. Even when we are speaking (or writing) in our mother tongues, we are still translating ideas into language.

The risk, however, is that "translation" becomes so general that nothing seems capable of resisting translation. Yet there is something that is commonly declared to be untranslatable, namely poetry. In "Rams," Derrida seems to agree: "The poem no doubt is the only place propitious to the experience of language, that is to say, of an idiom that forever defies translation and therefore demands a translation that will do the impossible, make the impossible possible in an unheard-of event."[30] The "idiom" apparently renders translation impossible. Yet Derrida also resists impossibility in the name of time itself— time is always open to a limitless future, and if we avoid foreclosing on what time may bring, perhaps an unprecedented event of translation will rout premature declarations of impossibility. We shouldn't prematurely restrict translation, given that it is, as Benjamin says, a process of maturation. Derrida, like Benjamin, opens translation to the to-come, to the coming of an event. For all Derrida's theses of translatability and untranslatability, theses which, if they are true, define what is possible and impossible for translation once and for all, infinite time can unpick the lock engineered upon translation, nonetheless.

Yet if the poem still forbids translation in the meantime, it seems that in doing so, it shields the idiom from the translator. Perhaps it is the exemplary task of translation to discover that there is an intact idiom—something immune, unassimilable, singular, and proper to the poem. We need to figure the intact, the impervious, or untouchable, Derrida suggests, in order to apprehend the primal scene of translation, namely the provocation of the idiom itself, its capacity to provoke the translator to desire and love. The "thesis" of desire is that there must be an intact kernel. There must be, in order to arouse the translator to his or her ardent kiss.

FOUR

Octavio Paz found the claim that poetry is untranslatable "offensive."[31] But the idea still exerts considerable fascination (if not covetous desire) on translators. Yet poetry is not the only source of fascination. Another is philosophy: *The Dictionary of Untranslatables: A*

Philosophical Lexicon,[32] for instance, provides entries for a wide range of terms that resist translation. Attitudes to "the untranslatable"[33] vary, however. For some, the insistence on untranslatability scants the relative successes of translation. For others, the real question is this: what is the point of declaring that there are untranslatable poems, concepts and words, or indeed, that there is something designated as *the* untranslatable? One answer might be that translation needs boundaries, needs to acknowledge resistance to its activities, lest translation become a bully, wrestling all languages into transparency. Another answer lies in another question: does the field of translation studies need its parameters defined by categorical statements, unarguable truths? It is a dangerous question, since it challenges translation studies to perform a "critique" in the Kantian sense. This might involve granting philosophy (a discourse that specializes in making categorical statements) the prerogative to police the perimeters and parameters of translation studies, granting to philosophy the right to say (as Derrida dares to put it so axiomatically) what is categorically possible or not, categorically translatable or not.

In this respect, Derrida's axioms have proven especially provocative because they have been seen as a way of inviting translation studies to subordinate itself to philosophy. Contrariwise, and paradoxically, Derrida's deconstructive approach has been seen less as an attempt to impose starkly unambiguous truths upon translation studies, and more as a way to force it into the ambiguous embrace of postmodernism. The idea that there are objective value criteria for measuring the successes of a translation (its fidelity, the clarity of its rendering, its truth) is severely challenged by postmodernism's radical skepticism about all validity criteria, especially in the context of linguistic transfer—the postmodern insistence is that meaning is perpetually in flux, or "indeterminate." In this sense, the idea of untranslatability, because it seems to disable translation and cast it into hapless flux, emerges from the postmodern and post-structuralist configurations of twentieth-century "continental" philosophy in particular.

Other theories, rooted in disciplines far removed from continental philosophy, stress the ability of translators to convey meaning intact. The professional obligation to translate a medical or legal document accurately is such that, quite obviously, postmodernist appeals to the indeterminacy of meaning would be a grievous liability (or a breach of contract). These approaches can be called instrumentalist, relying on linguistics, discourse analysis, and digital technologies. They tend to find their greatest applicability in professional contexts, working less well in the domains of literary and philosophical translation. The contrast between postmodernist/post-structuralist and instrumentalist approaches is too stark, of course, but the matter for contemporary translation theory remains one of finding middle ground, where ambiguity is not impatiently brushed aside in the name of clarity, where untranslatability is grappled with as a meaningful exercise in considering the limits of translation, and where the search for translation methods does not become a narrow, un-theoretical pragmatism. In the search to find a framework which could offer some hope of mediation, some have proposed hermeneutics. For it is hospitable to the idea that interpretation will always induce certain indeterminacies of meaning, given that interpretation has to negotiate more than one perspective, and tactfully allow some perspectives to remain unreconciled. But hermeneutics, especially when it appeals to tact, holds out some hope for a common ground, the achievement of which represents the joint overcoming of mutual "alienation," as Gadamer puts it. Moreover, hermeneutics, because it reflects on what it means to interpret and to translate, enables the translator-interpreter to achieve a degree of theoretical self-awareness. This emerges the moment a translator is conscious of the different horizon in which he or she is situated; it emerges when the translator inspects his or her ethical standards—agrees, that is, to enter into the dialogical relationship of translation in the spirit of a respect for difference.

These ethical protocols matter, insofar as the relationship between a translator and a text (but not just a text) can be described as an encounter with otherness. The injunctions to respect the otherness of the other, and pledge fidelity to difference, have become watchwords in translation studies, as they have elsewhere in what has been described as "the ethical turn" in contemporary theory. If translation enhances our awareness of other cultures, other languages, that is to say, it can only be enhancing if the respect for otherness motivates the operations of translation, since they still remain exercises in making the other more familiar, the foreign less foreign, the unknown more known.

As the category of the Other has become a requisite theoretical concept, the material upon which translators work on has widened beyond words and texts to encompass cultures, and indeed, all manifestations of so-called foreignness. As Susan Bassnett and André Lefevere have observed, "'Culture' has become the operational unit of translation."[34] But if this is the case, then the task set before translation is so vast as to be unmanageable. Examining the activities of translation as it occurs in multifarious social, cultural, economic, and political contexts makes for an impossibly complex field of study. A different and more optimistic approach, however, is to consider "complexity" itself, especially in terms of complex systems. In the literary domain, proponents of Itamar Even-Zohar's polysystem theory,[35] for example, locate translated literature within a multiplex, "poly" system called "literature." Similar attempts to gain purchase on the multilayered, highly ramified arena into which one might place translations have deployed Hans Robert Jauss's reception theory, and Pierre Bourdieu's concept of the "literary field." More broadly, theoretical reference points include the systems theory of Friedrich Kittler or Niklas Luhmann, information theory, and Gilles Deleuze's deployment of the "rhizome" (in botany, a network of bulbs and tubers). The task is to envisage how translations *spread*. We can visualize this as a filigree, a lattice, or a grid, or else as a flow along circuits and pathways. But these visualizations also depict networks and concentrations of power, whether it is the power held by publishing houses and their commissioning editors, or the power held by "major" languages. The more densely depicted the map of translation becomes, in fact, the more the landscape of translation embeds the five scapes described by Arjun Appadurai: the ethnoscape, mediascape, technoscape, financescape, and ideoscape.[36]

The vocabulary of maps, scapes, and places reminds translation studies of one of its foundational scenarios, that of a journey from one place to another. Current locations for translation studies on the map of "theory" vary from the local to the global. But perhaps, as Emily Apter suggests,[37] if the "translation zone" is to be found anywhere, it is surely at the border, at the checkpoint. Yet as translation studies negotiates the border crossings, and lodges itself in the interstices, the major theoretical concepts remain much more global, or, to put it another way, the "globe" has become a theoretical concept, particularly if the matter under consideration is whether translation enables the forces of globalization (isn't the supreme triumph of translation the fact we are all suborned by the international language of finance?) or offers a means to resist (can acts of deliberate untranslatability glitch and disrupt the smooth activities of internationalization?). In the latter case, translation studies may yet need the idea of untranslatability, albeit now considered from the angle of a politics of translation, or indeed, a politics of resistance. It may also be that translation studies needs to weigh up the implications of its vaster purview—consider its use of such terms as globe, planet, and world.

Most particularly, the spread of translation across the world, or globe, has often been enabled by the brutal drives of colonializing imperialism. The most compelling reminders of the dangers of translation have come from colonial contexts. Here it can be a matter of celebrating the expressive potential of creoles and pidgins, or of giving (with barbed intent) English, French, and Spanish back to the home countries, richly re-rendered by those forced to write and speak those languages in the countries where Empire spread. It can also be a matter of dramatizing the violence of colonization as a moment of equally violent translation.

My example is *Omeros*, by the Caribbean poet Derek Walcott. He chants the name of Homer, and each invocation says his name in Greek. Walcott respects the idiomaticity of his proper name—the authoritative name cosigning all true poems, perhaps. But he also translates that name into Antillean French, even as the poem writes itself in English: "I said, 'Omeros,' and O was the conch-shell's invocation, *mer* was both mother and sea in our Antillean patois, *os*, a grey bone, and the white surf as it crashes and spreads its sibilant collar on a lace shore."[38] Here is Homer translated. In between the O and the *os*, there is *mer* (sea) but also *mère* (mother), both wedded in an acoustic partnership only available in French. The mother-sea is not Homer's wine-dark sea, nor necessarily the *thalassa* of Joyce's *Ulysses*, nor necessarily the womb or matrix of poetry itself. For what the mingling of Homer's Mediterranean and Walcott's Caribbean Sea brings are not necessarily the galleys of Western civilization, but also slave ships. The spray of the filigree tide can also be a "collar" of iron lace—the heavy cuff of a slave's shackle (just later, Walcott speaks of "manacled ankles" and "coffled feet,"[39] horror poetry's lyre must still find the resources to hymn). So the mouth that opens to begin the articulation of Homer's name, the proper origin of poetry, perhaps the source of Western civilization itself, resonates in the echo chamber of a language Homer did not speak, in the hollow of a shell he couldn't have picked up and held to his ear. What Walcott hears, in French, is the nasty sibilance of *os*—a bone. On his beach, we might not only find canoes, fishing nets, and shells, but also find a sea-shore ossuary of the victimized dead of colonizing Empire.

Here, then, is translation's journey From and To narrated by a poem that preserves the name of Homer in order to propitiate the fatherly muse of all true poetry, while still hearing another language in order to supply a mouth to voice the lamentable moan of woe. Postcolonial experiments in translation offer eloquent proof that translation is important because it offers expressive resources, a vital theme, and a way to testify. It is one context, perhaps the most important context, where literary and cultural theory presently intersects with history and memory, even as that theory still cultivates the future journey to come. Poetry knows this intersection all too well: translation is a Homeric Odyssey, where the home shores are always in the vicinity, beckoning poets to originality as well as to the Siren shores of derivativeness. But it is also an anti-Odyssey, where the homecoming is replaced by perpetual expatriation—there is no father- or mother-comfort to be had as the *mer*-crossing is undertaken, no comfort in the exile that is perhaps the true destiny and vocation of the translator.

Barnard College (United States)

NOTES

1. Vladimir Nabokov, "The Art of Translation," in *Verses and Versions: Three Centuries of Russian Poetry*, eds. Brian Boyd and Stanislav Shvabrin (New York: Harcourt Books, 2008), 14–15.

2. Paul Ricoeur, *On Translation*, trans. Eileen Brennan (New York: Routledge, 2006), 3.

3. See Lawrence Venuti, *The Translator's Invisibility: A History of Translation* (New York: Routledge, 2008).

4. Marc Froment-Meurice, *That is To Say: Heidegger's Poetics*, trans. Jan Plug (Stanford: Stanford University Press, 1998), 36–37.

5. Jacques Derrida, *The Ear of the Other: Otobiography, Transference, Translation*, trans. Avital Ronell and Peggy Kamuf (Lincoln: University of Nebraska Press, 1998), 140.

6. Philippe Lacoue-Labarthe, "Hölderlin and the Greeks," *Typography: Mimesis, Philosophy, Politics*, trans. Christopher Fynsk (Stanford: Stanford University Press, 1998), 247.

7. Jorge Luis Borges, "Pierre Menard, Author of the Quixote," in *Collected Fictions*, trans. Andrew Hurley (New York: Penguin Books, 1999), 90.

8. Maurice Blanchot, *Political Writings, 1953-1993*, trans. Zakir Paul (New York: Fordham University Press, 2010), 62.

9. John Sallis, *On Translation* (Bloomington: Indiana University Press, 2002), xi.

10. Roman Jakobson, "On Linguistic Aspects of Translation," in *Theories of Translation: An Anthology of Essays from Dryden to Derrida*, eds. Rainer Schulte and John Biguenet (Chicago: Chicago University Press, 1992), 145.

11. Quoted in Sallis, *On Translation*, 66.

12. John Dryden, "On Translation," in *Theories of Translation: An Anthology of Essays from Dryden to Derrida*, 17.

13. See Hans-Georg Gadamer, *Truth and Method*, trans. Joel Weinsheimer and Donald G. Marshall (New York: Continuum, 1996).

14. Friedrich Schleiermacher, "On the Different Methods of Translating," in *Theories of Translation: An Anthology of Essays from Dryden to Derrida*, 42.

15. Johann Wolfgang von Goethe, "Translations," in *Theories of Translation: An Anthology of Essays from Dryden to Derrida*, 60.

16. von Goethe, "Translations," 60.

17. Ibid., 61.

18. Ibid., 63.

19. Walter Benjamin, "The Task of the Translator," trans. Harry Zohn, in *Walter Benjamin. Selected Writings, Volume 1, 1913-1926*, eds. Marcus Bullock and Michael W. Jennings (Cambridge: The Belknap Press of Harvard University Press, 1996), 254.

20. For more on the cluster of terms used by Benjamin, and which involve a thought of "ability," see Samuel Weber, *Benjamin's—abilities* (Cambridge, MA: Harvard University Press, 2010).

21. Benjamin, "The Task of the Translator," 258.

22. Ibid., 260.

23. I permit myself to refer to my essay "The 'Saran Wrap' Theory of Translation: Transparency and Invisibility, or the Kernel and the Shell," *symplokē* 23.1–2 (2015): 375–92.

24. Benjamin, "The Task of the Translator," 261.

25. Jacques Derrida, "Des tours de Babel," trans. Joseph F. Graham, in *Psyche: Inventions of the Other, Volume 1*, eds. Peggy Kamuf and Elizabeth Rottenberg (Stanford: Stanford University Press, 2007), 214.

26. Derrida, "Des tours de Babel," 214.

27. Jacques Derrida, "What is a 'Relevant' Translation?," trans. Lawrence Venuti, in *Signature Derrida / Jacques Derrida*, ed. Jay Williams (Chicago: Chicago University Press, 2013), 351.

28. Derrida, "What is a 'Relevant' Translation?" 355.

29. Joyce's remark is quoted in Blanchot, *Political Writings, 1953-1993,* 155.

30. Jacques Derrida, "Rams: Uninterrupted Dialogue—Between Two Infinities, the Poem," trans. Thomas Dutoit and Philippe Romanski, in *Sovereignties in Question: The Poetics of Paul Celan,* eds. Thomas Dutoit and Onti Pasanen (New York: Fordham University Press, 2005), 137.

31. Octavio Paz, "Translation: Literature and Letters," in *Theories of Translation: An Anthology of Essays from Dryden to Derrida,* 155.

32. *Dictionary of Untranslatables: A Philosophical Lexicon,* eds. Barbara Cassin, Emily Apter, Jacques Lezra, and Michael Wood, trans. Stephen Rendall et al. (Princeton: Princeton University Press, 2014).

33. See Apter, *Against World Literature,* 3.

34. *Translation, History and Culture,* eds. Susan Bassnett and André Lefevere (London: Bloomsbury Academic, 1998), 8.

35. See, for example, Itamar Even-Zohar, "The Position of Translated Literature within the Literary Polysystem," *Poetics Today* 11.1 (1990), 45–51. See also Edwin Gentzler, *Contemporary Translation Theories,* chapter 5, "Polysystem Theory" (New York: Routledge, 1993).

36. See Arjun Appadurai, *Modernity at Large: Cultural Dimensions of Globalization* (Minneapolis: University of Minnesota Press, 1996).

37. See Emily Apter, *The Translation Zone: A New Comparative Literature* (Princeton: Princeton University Press, 2006).

38. Derek Walcott, *Omeros* (New York: Farrar, Straus and Giroux, 1990), 14.

39. Walcott, *Omeros,* 15.

WORKS CITED

Appadurai, Arjun. *Modernity at Large: Cultural Dimensions of Globalization.* Minneapolis: University of Minnesota Press, 1996.

Apter, Emily. *The Translation Zone: A New Comparative Literature.* Princeton: Princeton University Press, 2006.

Apter, Emily. *Against World Literature: On the Politics of Untranslatability.* New York: Verso, 2013.

Bassnett, Susan, and André Lefevere. *Translation, History and Culture.* London: Bloomsbury Academic, 1998.

Benjamin, Walter. "The Task of the Translator." In *Walter Benjamin: Selected Writings, Volume 1, 1913-1926.* Trans. Harry Zohn. Eds. Marcus Bullock, and Michael W. Jennings. Cambridge, MA: The Belknap Press of Harvard University Press, 1996.

Blanchot, Maurice. *Political Writings, 1953-1993.* Trans. Zakir Paul. New York: Fordham University Press, 2010.

Borges, Jorge Luis. "Pierre Menard, Author of the Quixote [1939]." In *Collected Fictions.* Trans. Andrew Hurley. New York: Penguin Books, 1999.

Cassin, Barbara. *Dictionary of Untranslatables: A Philosophical Lexicon* [2004]. Trans. Stephen Rendall, Christian Hubert, Jeffrey Mehlman, Nathanael Stein, and Michael Syrotinski. Eds. Emily Apter, Jacques Lezra, and Michael Wood. Princeton: Princeton University Press, 2014.

Derrida, Jacques. *The Ear of the Other: Otobiography, Transference, Translation* [1982]. Trans. Avital Ronell, and Peggy Kamuf. Lincoln: University of Nebraska Press, 1998.

Derrida, Jacques. "Rams: Uninterrupted Dialogue—Between Two Infinities, the Poem [2003]." *Sovereignties in Question: The Poetics of Paul Celan.* Trans. Thomas Dutoit, and Philippe Romanski. Eds. Thomas Dutoit, and Onti Pasanen. New York: Fordham University Press, 2005.

Derrida, Jacques. "Des tours de Babel." In *Psyche: Inventions of the Other, Volume 1* [1987]. Trans. Joseph F. Graham. Eds. Peggy Kamuf, and Elizabeth Rottenberg. Stanford: Stanford University Press, 2007.

Derrida, Jacques. "What is a 'Relevant' Translation?" *Signature Derrida/Jacques Derrida.* Trans. Lawrence Venuti. Ed. Jay Williams. Chicago: Chicago University Press, 2013.

Even-Zohar, Itamar. "The Position of Translated Literature within the Literary Polysystem." *Poetics Today* 11.1 (1990): 45–51.

Froment-Meurice, Marc. *That is To Say: Heidegger's Poetics.* Trans. Jan Plug. Stanford: Stanford University Press, 1998.

Gadamer, Hans-Georg. *Truth and Method* [1960]. Trans. Joel Weinsheimer, and Donald G. Marshall. New York: Continuum, 1996.

Gentzler, Edwin. *Contemporary Translation Theories.* New York: Routledge, 1993.

Lacoue-Labarthe, Philippe. "Hölderlin and the Greeks." In *Typography: Mimesis, Philosophy, Politics.* Trans. Christopher Fynsk. Stanford: Stanford University Press, 1998.

Nabokov, Vladimir. "The Art of Translation." *Verses and Versions: Three Centuries of Russian Poetry.* Eds. Brian Boyd, and Stanislav Shvabrin. New York: Harcourt Books, 2008.

O'Keeffe, Brian. "The 'Saran Wrap' Theory of Translation: Transparency and Invisibility, or the Kernel and the Shell." *symplokē* 23.1–2 (2015): 375–92.

Ricoeur, Paul. *On Translation.* Trans. Eileen Brennan. New York: Routledge, 2006.

Sallis, John. *On Translation.* Bloomington: Indiana University Press, 2002.

Schulte, Rainer, and Biguenet, John, eds. *Theories of Translation: An Anthology of Essays from Dryden to Derrida.* Chicago: Chicago University Press, 1992.

Venuti, Lawrence. *The Translator's Invisibility: A History of Translation.* New York: Routledge, 2008.

Walcott, Derek. *Omeros.* New York: Farrar, Straus and Giroux, 1990.

Weber, Samuel. *Benjamin's—Abilities.* Cambridge, MA: Harvard University Press, 2010.

CHAPTER NINETEEN

Media Studies

TOBY MILLER

INTRODUCTION

Media studies has several differing genealogies. Those histories and family resemblances affect how it is defined, conducted, and understood. Unsurprisingly, "media" is a *portmanteau* word that covers a multitude of cultural and communications machines, processes, and genres. There is increasing overlap within this multitude, as seemingly black-box techniques and technologies, once set away from audiences, increasingly become part of public debate and utilization as consumer electronics connect to information and communication technologies and *vice versa*. So televisions resemble computers; books are read on telephones; newspapers are written through clouds; and so on. Genres and gadgets that were once separate are now linked.

That said, the media constitute and are constituted by

- technologies, which form their conditions of possibility;
- policies, which determine the field in which they operate;
- genres, such as drama, music, sports, and information;
- workers, who make texts in performance and recording;
- audiences, who receive the ensuing content; and
- the environment, which houses their detritus.

The media inevitably connect with the social identities of spectators, readers, and players. These include gender, race, class, age, religion, and disability, inter alia. That link has led to many extreme reactions to the emergent success of media technologies and genres. During the Industrial Revolution, anxieties about a suddenly urbanized and educated population raised the prospect of a long-feared "ochlocracy" of "the worthless mob" driven by unscrupulous demagogues through speeches, tracts, and journalism.[1]

By the early twentieth century, academic experts had decreed media audiences to be passive consumers, thanks to the missions of literary criticism (distinguishing the aesthetically cultivated from others) and psychology (distinguishing the socially competent from others). Decades of social science have analyzed audience reactions to audiovisual entertainment.[2]

HISTORY

Media studies was founded in the United States a century ago via speech communication and rhetoric to assist with the assimilation of white, non-English-speaking migrants into the emergent manufacturing workforce. Then the engineering professors who founded radio stations in colleges during the 1920s needed program content, and drew volunteers from speech communication and rhetoric when literature departments reacted to their suits with disdain. These stations became laboratories, with research undertaken into technology, content, and reception.

This period of massively complex urbanization and the spread of adult literacy, democratic rights, labor organization, and socialist ideas then gave rise to a social-science equivalent to the study of speech: mass communication. First radio, then cinema, then TV were simultaneously prized and damned for their demagogic qualities, which it was hoped and feared could turn people into consumers or communists alike.

Such tendencies have continued to thrive, as we shall see. Theorists from both right and left argued that newly literate publics would be vulnerable to manipulation by demagogues. Bourgeois economics assumes that rational consumers determine what is popular in the media, but is concerned that people can be bamboozled by unscrupulously fluent ones have recurred throughout the modern period. Marxism has often viewed the media as a route to false consciousness that diverts the working class from recognizing its economic oppression; feminist approaches have moved between condemning the media as a similar distraction from gendered consciousness and celebrating it as a distinctive part of women's culture; and cultural studies has regarded it as a key location for the symbolic resistance of class, race, and gender oppression alike.[3]

As a consequence, there has been an emphasis on the origin, number, and conduct of audiences to the media, from an array of political and epistemological perspectives: where spectators came from, how many there were, and what they did as a consequence of being present. Such concerns are coupled with a focus on content: *what* were audiences watching when they——? And so both audiences and texts are conceived as empirical entities that can be known, via research instruments derived from sociology, psychology, literary criticism, demography, linguistics, communications, anthropology, accountancy, economics, and marketing.[4]

APPROACHES

The media have thereby given rise to three related topics of scholarly inquiry:

- technology, ownership, and control—their political economy;
- textuality—their meaning; and
- audiences—their public.

Within these categories lie three further divisions:

- approaches to technology, ownership, and control vary between neoliberal endorsements of limited regulation by the state in the interests of protecting property and guaranteeing market entry for new competitors, Marxist critiques of the bourgeois media for controlling the sociopolitical agenda, and environmental investigations of the impact of media gadgetry on energy use and electronic waste;
- approaches to textuality vary between hermeneutics, which unearths the meaning of individual programs and links them to broader social formations and problems, such as the way that social identities are represented, and content analysis, which

establishes patterns across significant numbers of similar texts, rather than close readings of individual ones; and

- approaches to audiences vary between social-psychological attempts to validate correlations between television and social conduct, political-economic critiques of imported texts threatening national culture, and celebrations of spectators' interpretations.

The media are addressed differently from different parts of campus. In today's humanities theater, film, television, radio, art, craft, writing, music, dance, and electronic gaming are judged by criteria of representativeness and quality, as framed by practices of cultural criticism and history. For their part, the social sciences focus on the languages, religions, customs, times, spaces, and exchanges of different groups, as explored ethnographically or statistically.

So, whereas the humanities articulate differences within populations, through symbolic norms (e.g., providing some of us with the cultural capital to appreciate high culture) the social sciences articulate such differences through social norms (e.g., legitimizing inequality through doctrines of human capital).[5]

An aesthetic discourse about the media sees culture elevating people above ordinary life, transcending body, time, and place. Conversely, an anthropological and psychological discourse expects the media to settle us into society through the wellsprings of community, as part of daily existence. And a discourse about pop idealizes media fun, promising secular transcendence through joy.[6]

And media studies within the liberal arts in turn articulate both to particular academic disciplines, which are tied to particular interests of state and capital, and may arc across campus beyond the humanities and social sciences:

- Engineering, computing, public policy, journalism, and "film" schools create and run media production and reception via business, the military, the community, and the public service.

- Communication studies focuses on propaganda, marketing, and citizenship.

- Economics theorizes and polices doctrines of scarcity, as well as managing over-production through overseas expansion.

- The psy-function (pediatrics, psychology, and psychiatry) examines child development and such social issues as sexual violence and gender representation in relation to media exposure.

- Sociology, political science, and the law look at media regulation, violence, contracts, and treaties.

- Literature, cinema studies, television studies, languages, and cultural studies evaluate representation, justify protectionism, and call for content provision.

There are seven principal forms of inquiry within the specialist areas that entirely focus on the media. They

- borrow ethnography from sociology and anthropology to investigate the experiences of audiences;

- use experimentation and testing methods from psychology to establish cause-and-effect relations between media use and subsequent conduct;

- adapt content analysis from sociology and communication studies to evaluate texts in terms of generic patterns;

- adopt textual analysis from literary theory and linguistics to identify the ideological tenor of content;

- apply textual and audience interpretation from psychoanalysis to speculate on psychic processes;

- deploy political economy to examine ownership, control, regulation, and international exchange; and

- utilize archival, curatorial, and historiographic methods to give the media a record of their past.

More than half a century ago, Dallas Smythe explained that audience attention—presumed or measured—was the commodity that TV and radio stations sold to advertisers.[7] Programs were therefore not so much consumer items as "symbols for time."[8] Media audiences participate in the most global (but local) communal (yet individual) and time-consuming practice of making meaning in the history of the world. The concept and the occasion of being an audience are links between society and person, at the same time as viewing and listening involve solitary interpretation as well as collective behavior.

Production executives invoke the audience to measure success and claim knowledge of what people want, regulators to organize administration, psychologists to produce proofs, and lobby groups to change content. Hence the link to panics about education, violence and apathy supposedly engendered by the media and routinely investigated by the state, psychology, Marxism, feminism, conservatism, religion, and others. The audience as consumer, student, felon, voter, sexist, heathen, progressive, and fool engages such groups. Effects and ratings research traverses the industry, the state, and criticism. Academic, commercial, and regulatory approaches focus most expansively on audiences as citizens and consumers, far more than media technology, law, or even content.[9]

This focus on the public and how to corral and control it is in keeping with anxieties that time and technology increase rather than erase. The pattern has been that when new media technologies emerge, young people in particular are identified as both pioneers and victims, simultaneously endowed by manufacturers and critics alike with power and vulnerability—the first to know yet the last to understand cheap novels during the 1900s, silent then sound film during the teens and 1920s, radio in the 1930s, comic books of the 1940s and 1950s, pop music and television from the 1950s and 1960s, satanic rock as per the 1970s and 1980s, video cassette recorders in the 1980s, and rap music, video games, and the internet since the 1990s.[10]

Each new media innovation since the advent of print has brought an expanded horizon of texts to audiences. In keeping with this history, texts and viewers come to be defined in both market terms and through a regulatory morality of conscience and taste, because "a new practice of piety" accompanies each "new communications technology."[11] As a consequence, moral panics are common among the denizens of communication studies, pediatrics, psychology, and education, who largely abjure cultural and political matters to do with television in favor of experimenting on its viewers. This is the psy-function at work.[12]

Media studies also covers political economy, which focuses on ownership and control rather than audience responses. Because the demand for the media is dispersed but much of their supply is centralized, political economy argues that the media are one more industrial process subordinated to dominant economic forces within society that seek standardization of production. Far from reflecting already-established and already-revealed preferences of consumers in reaction to tastes and desires, the media manipulate audiences from the economic apex of production, with coercion mistaken for free will. The only element that might stand against this leveling sameness is said to be individual consciousness. But that consciousness has itself been customized to the requirements of the economy and media production: maximization of sameness through repetition and minimization of innovation and newness in order to diminish risk and cost.[13]

There are significant ties between critical theory, which calls for a resistive consciousness through artisanal rather than industrial created texts, and political economy, which calls for diverse ownership and control of the industry. The first trend is philosophical and aesthetic in its desire to develop modernism and the avant-garde, the second policy-oriented and political in its focus on institutional power. But they began as one with lamentations for the loss of a self-critical philosophical address and the triumph of industrialized cultural production. The two approaches continue to be linked via a shared distaste for what is still often regarded as mass culture.[14] The media are said to force people to turn away from precious artistic and social traces of authentic intersubjectivity as they take control of individual consciousness. Like the psy-function, this part of media studies is frequently functionalist, neglecting struggle, dissonance, and conflict in favor of a totalizing narrative in which its object of study dominates everyday life and is all-powerful.

NEW DIRECTIONS

Something happened in the mid-1960s to counter these forms of knowledge: the advent of a more conflictual version of media studies. The Italian medievalist, semiotician, columnist, and novelist Umberto Eco developed notions of encoding-decoding, open texts, and aberrant readings by audiences.[15] He looked at differences between the way meanings were put into Italian TV programs by producers and how they were deciphered by viewers. Eco's insights were picked up by the British political sociologist Frank Parkin[16] and the Jamaican cultural studies theorist Stuart Hall.[17]

There have been two principal methodological iterations of the encoding-decoding approach: uses and gratifications (U&G) and ethnography/cultural studies. U&G operates from a psychological model of needs and pleasures; cultural studies from a political one of needs and pleasures. U&G focuses on what are regarded as fundamental psychological drives that define how people use the media to gratify themselves. Conversely, cultural studies' ethnographic work has shown some of the limitations to claims that viewers are stitched into certain perspectives by the interplay of narrative, dialogue, and image. Together, they have brought into question the notion that audiences are blank slates ready to be written on by media messages.[18]

Drawing upon these findings, some denizens of media studies argue that today's new media represent the apex of modernity, the first moment in history when central, political, and commercial organs and agendas became receptive to the popular classes. This perspective differs from the idea that the apparatus is all-powerful. It maintains instead that the all-powerful agent is the audience: the public is so clever and able that it makes its own meanings, outwitting institutions of the state, academia, and capitalism that seek to measure and control it. In the case of children and the media, anxieties about turning Edenic innocents into rabid monsters or capitalist dupes are dismissed.[19]

Faith in the active audience reaches cosmic proportions, such that the media is not responsible for anything. Consumption is the key, with production discounted, work neglected, consumers sovereign and research undertaken by observing one's own practices of viewing and one's friends and children. This is narcissography at work, with the critic's *persona* a guarantor of assumed audience revelry and Dionysian joy.[20] Welcome to "Readers Liberation Movement" media studies:[21] everyone is creative and no one is a spectator. Internally divided—but happily so—each person is "a consumer on the one hand, but . . . also a producer."[22]

The media supposedly obliterate geography, sovereignty, and hierarchy in an alchemy of truth and beauty. Today's deregulated, individuated media world allegedly makes consumers into producers, frees the disabled from confinement, encourages new subjectivities, rewards intellect and competitiveness, links people across cultures, and allows billions of flowers to bloom in a post-political cornucopia.

In one sense, then, media studies buys into corporate fantasies of control—the political economist's arid nightmare of music, movies, television, and everything else converging under the sign of empowered firms. In another, it incarnates individualist fantasies of reader, audience, consumer, or player autonomy—the libertarian intellectual's wet dream of music, movies, television, and everything else converging under the sign of empowered fans. Those antinomies shadow the fetish of innovation that informs much talk of media technology and consumerism while ignoring the environmental destruction and centralized power that underpin them.[23]

Media studies today thrives in the context of a reformist, even reactionary formation, which rejects the field's past in favor of hitching itself to the new surge in cultural industries represented by public policies and investment patterns. This has involved consultancies on behalf of the media, museums, copyright, pornography, schooling, and cultural precincts. Instrumental policy people and scholars argue for an efflorescence of creativity, cultural difference, import substitution, and national and regional pride and influence, thanks to new technologies and innovative firms—with capitalism an ally, not a foe.[24]

The discourse takes one or several of the following tacks:

- Because of new technology and inventive practices of consumption, concentration of media ownership and control no longer matters—information is finally free, thanks to multipoint distribution and destabilized hierarchies.

- Consumers are sovereign and can transcend class and other categories.

- Young people are liberated from media control.

- Journalism is dying as everyone and their owl become sources of both news and reporting.

- Creative destruction is an accurate and desirable description of economic innovation.

- When scholars observe media workers and audiences, they discover that ideology critique is inappropriate.

- Marxist political economy denies the power of audiences and users and the irrelevance of boundaries—it is pessimistic and hidebound.

- Cultural imperialism critiques miss the creativity and resilience of national and subnational forms of life against industrial products.

- Media effects studies are inconsequential—audiences outwit corporate plans and psy-function norms.

What is left out of these seemingly dynamic and innovative but in fact tired and venerable lines?

- the ecological impact of the media;
- questions of labor and life in the cognitariat;
- those who essentially live outside consumption, beyond multinational markets—beyond an electricity grid and potable water, for example;
- citizenship;
- concentrated ownership and obedient regulation;
- cultural imperialism's resonance with populations and activists;
- the supposedly new vulnerability of media organizations to the power of the young, the rebelliousness of consumers, and the force of new technology is as old as these organizations themselves;
- the expansion of newspapers outside the Global North—people still line up in Barranquilla by the dozen each morning to place classified advertisements in the local paper, for instance; and
- the *real* use of new technologies—for example, people citing one another's sexting or swearing on smart phones in family courts to undermine claims to parental responsibility, leading to judgments that deny people custody of their children.[25]

THE FUTURE

In its uneasy blend of these perspectives, media studies is being partially recharacterized by a progressive agenda that is skeptical without being cynical, rigorous without losing optimism, and committed to popular democracy. The result has seen analyses devoted to some key issues that go beyond the psy-function, political economy, and active audiences, while drawing on their insights. A brief list might include

- feminist concerns over the representation of women, both on- and off-screen;
- critics' desires to reach beyond bourgeois-individualistic accounts of creativity in favor of generic analysis;
- studies of postimperial social control in the Global South via domestic and global media dominance;
- Marxist aesthetics reading story against ideology;
- evaluations of the media's environmental impact; and
- voices from below, heard through the participant observation of workers and audiences.

Such staples as cultural imperialism critique and national media history have been supplemented by work on national, regional, global, diasporic, First People's, women's, and activist textuality and ideology critique has been enriched by Gramscianism, racialization analysis, queer theory, and policy studies. This is in keeping with intellectual developments and political trends, such as social movements, the globalization and privatization of the media in the wake of the Cold War, and the rise of neoliberalism. Foundational debates since 1990 have put leftist, queer, disabled, feminist, multicultural, and postcolonial formations in play.

But this is no Whiggish teleology charging toward freedom of inquiry and open access to new approaches. As higher education has grown and opened up to these critical tendencies within the human sciences, social movements, and more instrumental, conservatory-style training, media studies has often been deemed simultaneously too progressive, too applied, and insufficiently scientific by many traditionalists.[26] Robert W. McChesney laments that the study of the media is "regarded by the pooh-bahs in history, political science, and sociology as having roughly the same intellectual merit as, say, driver's education."[27] Similar bigotries occur in the humanities.[28] Such hostility may fade over time.

One ongoing problem, however, is that so many analysts of the media undertake research in purely national, or solely English-language, contexts. These professional norms have served them well in terms of publication and pedagogy. But technological, migratory, linguistic, and politico-economic changes now make it imperative that media studies operates in a global context, sloughing off monolingual disciplinary parthenogenesis. The complexity of processes subsumed by the media makes linguistically, analytically, and geographically narrow approaches to the topic simply untenable.

So at a moment when the Global North uses culture as a selling point for deindustrialized societies, and the Global South does so for never-industrialized ones, scholars must adopt a nimble, hybrid approach that is governed neither by the humanities or the social sciences, nor by the parent disciplines mentioned above—and assuredly not by one language—but by a critical agenda that inquires *cui bono*: who benefits and loses from governmental and corporate maneuvers, who complains about the fact, and how can we learn from them?

"Global media studies" is an interdisciplinary concept that emerged in the late 1990s to describe the convergence of areas of study traditionally known as "international communication" and "comparative media systems" (in the social sciences) versus "national cinema" and "world cinema" (in the humanities). It also reflected a more developed appreciation of culture within the political-economy tradition via a literature that mixed the theories and methods of political economy and cultural studies.[29]

This perspective, and the knowledge it produces, has led analysts across the humanities and social sciences to criticize the widespread neoliberal dismissal of the state as an inappropriate arbiter of media regulation and control. They argue that the market and civil society are not the same thing, thus challenging neoclassical assertions that laissez-faire policies best serve the interests of society at large. This does not mean a return to the critiques of left-wing cultural commentators that transnational culture perverts pure indigenous traditions; indeed, theories of hybridity preclude such analyses.[30] Nor does this position support rather aristocratic complaints that mass dissemination corrupts high art. However, it does challenge neoliberal policymakers who assert that the free-market facilitates cultural products produced in the periphery circulating globally. Without reviving a chauvinistic nationalism, there must be a critical state intervention which recognizes that "culture is too important to be relinquished exclusively to the competition among international markets."[31]

The new position is justly wary of cybertarian temptations about the imagined autonomy of networked societies via the apparent openness of the internet. For beyond the Global North, revelations of technocentric, cybertarian failures of explanation proliferate, as the reality of successive liberatory "springs" supposedly unleashed by social-media networks is exposed as the work of long-laid plans of organized and very material revolutionary groups.[32]

Such grounded cosmopolitanism refuses the blandishments of both *revanchisme* and cybertarianism. It gives real hope to a new form of media studies that transcends the divisions and obsessions of the past in favor of democratizing the media worldwide.

Universidad del Norte, Barranquilla (Columbia)

NOTES

1. Samuel Pufendorf, *On the Duty of Man and Citizen According to Natural Law*, trans. Michael Silverthorne, ed. James Tully (Cambridge: Cambridge University Press, 2000), 144.

2. Toby Miller, "Media Effects and Cultural Studies: A Contentious Relationship," in *The Sage Handbook of Media Processes and Effects*, eds. Robin L. Nabi and Mary Beth Oliver (Thousand Oaks: Sage Publications, 2009), 131–43.

3. Dorothy E. Smith, *The Everyday World as Problematic: A Feminist Sociology* (Boston: Northeastern University Press, 1987); Stuart Hall and Tony Jefferson, eds., *Resistance Through Rituals: Youth Subcultures in Post-War Britain* (London: Hutchinson, 1976).

4. Silvio Waisbord, ed., *Media Sociology: A Reappraisal* (Cambridge: Polity Press, 2014).

5. Immanuel Wallerstein, "Culture as the Ideological Battleground of the Modern World-System," *Hitotsubashi Journal of Social Studies* 21.1 (1989): 5–22; Pierre Bourdieu, *Distinction: A Social Critique of the Judgement of Taste*, trans. Richard Nice (Cambridge, MA: Harvard University Press, 1984).

6. Simon Frith, "The Good, the Bad, and the Indifferent: Defending Popular Culture from the Populists," *diacritics* 21.4 (1991): 102–15.

7. Dallas Smythe, "The Consumer's Stake in Radio and Television," *Quarterly of Film Radio and Television* 6.2 (1951): 109–28.

8. John Hartley, "Invisible Fictions: Television Audiences, Paedocracy, Pleasure," *Textual Practice* 1.2 (1987): 133.

9. Ien Ang, *Desperately Seeking the Audience* (London: Routledge, 1991).

10. Toby Miller, *Technologies of Truth: Cultural Citizenship and the Popular Media* (Minneapolis: University of Minnesota Press, 1998).

11. Ian Hunter, "Providence and Profit: Speculations in the Genre Market," *Southern Review* 22.3 (1988): 220.

12. Charles Krinsky, ed., *The Ashgate Research Companion to Moral Panics* (Farnham: Ashgate, 2013).

13. Theodor W. Adorno and Max Horkheimer, "The Culture Industry: Enlightenment as Mass Deception," in *Mass Communication and Society*, eds. James Curran, Michael Gurevitch, and Janet Woollacott (London: Edward Arnold, 1977), 349–83.

14. Nicholas Garnham, "Concepts of Culture: Public Policy and the Cultural Industries," *Cultural Studies* 1.1 (1987): 23–37.

15. Umberto Eco, "Towards a Semiotic Inquiry into the Television Message," trans. Paolo Splendore, *Working Papers in Cultural Studies* 3 (1972): 103–21.

16. Frank Parkin, *Class Inequality and Political Order* (London: MacGibbon & Kee, 1971).

17. Stuart Hall, "Encoding/Decoding," in *Culture, Media, Language*, eds. Stuart Hall, Dorothy Hobson, Andrew Lowe, and Paul Willis (London: Hutchinson, 1980), 128–39.

18. Lawrence A. Wenner and Walter Gantz, "Watching Sports on Television: Audience Experience, Gender, Fanship, and Marriage," in *MediaSport*, ed. Lawrence A. Wenner (London: Routledge, 1998), 233–51; Ang, *Desperately Seeking the Audience*.

19. Perhaps there should be more of a focus on the material dangers posed to children by TVs: well over 385,000 young people have been admitted to US emergency rooms in the last two decades due to physical injuries caused by sets. See Ana C. De Roo, Thiphalak Chounthirath, and Gary A. Smith, "Television-Related Injuries to Children in the United States, 1990-2011," *Pediatrics* 132.2 (2013): 267–74.

20. Meaghan Morris, "The Banality of Cultural Studies," in *Logics of Television: Essays in Cultural Criticism*, ed. Patricia Mellencamp (Bloomington: Indiana University Press, 1990), 14–43.

21. Terry Eagleton, "The Revolt of the Reader," *New Literary History* 13.3 (1982): 449–52.

22. Michel Foucault, *The Birth of Biopolitics: Lectures at the Collège de France, 1978-79*, trans. Graham Burchell, ed. Michel Senellart (Houndmills: Palgrave Macmillan, 2008), 226.

23. Richard Maxwell and Toby Miller, *Greening the Media* (New York: Oxford University Press, 2012).

24. John Hartley, ed., *Creative Industries* (Malden: Blackwell, 2005); Richard Florida, *The Rise of the Creative Class: And How It's Transforming Work, Leisure, Community and Everyday Life* (New York: Basic Books, 2002).

25. "Child Custody: Family Court and Social Media." *MaleyInvestigations*. 2017. http://maleyinvestigations.com/child-custody.asp?tip=45

26. Graeme Paton, "Media Studies Wastes Good Brains, Says Sugar," *Telegraph* (May 7, 2007), http://www.telegraph.co.uk/news/uknews/1550580/Media-studies-wastes-good-brains-says-Sugar.html; Graeme Paton, "Ofqal: Dozens of 'Soft' GCSEs and A-levels to be Axed," *Telegraph* (June 4, 2014), http://www.telegraph.co.uk/education/educationnews/10873368/Ofqual-dozens-of-soft-GCSEs-and-A-levels-to-be-axed.html; and Andreas Whittam Smith, "Media Studies is No Preparation for Journalism," *Independent* (February 25, 2008), http://www.independent.co.uk/voices/commentators/andreas-whittam-smith/andreas-whittam-smith-media-studies-is-no-preparation-for-journalism-786785.html

27. Robert W. McChesney, *Communication Revolution: Critical Junctures and the Future of Media* (New York: New Press, 2007), 16.

28. Michele Hilmes, "The Bad Object: Television in the American Academy," *Cinema Journal* 45.1 (2005): 113.

29. Marwan M. Kraidy, "Ferment in Global Media Studies," *Journal of Broadcasting & Electronic Media* 46.4 (2002): 630–40; Marwan M. Kraidy, *Hybridity, or the Cultural Logic of Globalization* (Philadelphia: Temple University Press, 2005); Yuezhi Zhao and Paula Chakravartty, eds., *Global Communications: Towards a Transcultural Political Economy* (Boulder: Rowman and Littlefield, 2007); Vincent Mosco and Dan Schiller, eds., *Continental Order? Integrating North America for Cybercapitalism* (Lanham: Rowman and Littlefield, 2001); Vincent Mosco, *The Digital Sublime* (Cambridge, MA: MIT Press, 2004); and Vincent Mosco, *To the Cloud: Big Data in a Turbulent World* (Boulder: Paradigm Publishers, 2014).

30. Néstor García Canclini, *Hybrid Cultures: Strategies for Entering and Leaving Modernity*, trans. Christopher L. Chiappari and Silvia L. López (Minneapolis: University of Minnesota Press, 1995).

31. Néstor García Canclini, "North Americans or Latin Americans? The Redefinition of Mexican Identity and the Free Trade Agreements," in *Mass Media and Free Trade: NAFTA and the Culture Industries*, eds. Emile D. McAnany and Kenton T. Wilkinson (Austin: University of Texas Press, 1996), 155.

32. Néstor García Canclini, *El mundo entero como lugar extraño* (Buenos Aires: Gedisa, 2014).

WORKS CITED

Adorno, Theodor W., and Max Horkheimer. "The Culture Industry: Enlightenment as Mass Deception." In *Mass Communication and Society*. Eds. James Curran, Michael Gurevitch, and Janet Woollacott. London: Edward Arnold, 1977. 349–83.

Ang, Ien. *Desperately Seeking the Audience*. London: Routledge, 1991.

Bourdieu, Pierre. *Distinction: A Social Critique of the Judgement of Taste* [1979]. Trans. Richard Nice. Cambridge, MA: Harvard University Press, 1984.

"Child Custody: Family Court and Social Media." *Maley Investigations*. 2017. http://maleyinvestigations.com/child-custody.asp?tip=45

De Roo, Ana C., Thiphalak Chounthirath, and Gary A. Smith. "Television-Related Injuries to Children in the United States, 1990-2011." *Pediatrics* 132.2 (2013): 267–74.

Eagleton, Terry. "The Revolt of the Reader." *New Literary History* 13.3 (1982): 449–52.

Eco, Umberto. "Towards a Semiotic Inquiry into the Television Message." Trans. Paolo Splendore. *Working Papers in Cultural Studies* 3 (1972): 103–21.

Florida, Richard. *The Rise of the Creative Class: And How It's Transforming Work, Leisure, Community and Everyday Life*. New York: Basic Books, 2002.

Foucault, Michel. *The Birth of Biopolitics: Lectures at the Collège de France, 1978-79*. Trans. Graham Burchell. Ed. Michel Senellart. Houndmills: Palgrave Macmillan, 2008.

Frith, Simon. "The Good, the Bad, and the Indifferent: Defending Popular Culture from the Populists." *Diacritics* 21.4 (1991): 102–15.

García Canclini, Néstor. *Hybrid Cultures: Strategies for Entering and Leaving Modernity*. Trans. Christopher L. Chiappari, and Silvia L. López. Minneapolis: University of Minnesota Press, 1995.

García Canclini, Néstor. "North Americans or Latin Americans? The Redefinition of Mexican Identity and the Free Trade Agreements." In *Mass Media and Free Trade: NAFTA and the Culture Industries*. Eds. Emile D. McAnany, and Kenton T. Wilkinson. Austin: University of Texas Press, 1996. 142–56.

García Canclini, Néstor. *El mundo entero como lugar extraño*. Buenos Aires: Gedisa, 2014.

Garnham, Nicholas. "Concepts of Culture: Public Policy and the Cultural Industries." *Cultural Studies* 1.1 (1987): 23–37.

Hall, Stuart. "Encoding/Decoding." In *Culture, Media, Language*. Eds. Stuart Hall, Dorothy Hobson, Andrew Lowe, and Paul Willis. London: Hutchinson, 1980. 128–39.

Hall, Stuart, and Tony Jefferson, eds. *Resistance Through Rituals: Youth Subcultures in Post-War Britain*. London: Hutchinson, 1976.

Hartley, John. "Invisible Fictions: Television Audiences, Paedocracy, Pleasure." *Textual Practice* 1.2 (1987): 121–38.

Hartley, John, ed. *Creative Industries*. Malden: Blackwell, 2005.

Hilmes, Michele. "The Bad Object: Television in the American Academy." *Cinema Journal* 45.1 (2005): 111–17.

Hunter, Ian. "Providence and Profit: Speculations in the Genre Market." *Southern Review* 22.3 (1988): 211–23.

Kraidy, Marwan M. "Ferment in Global Media Studies." *Journal of Broadcasting & Electronic Media* 46.4 (2002): 630–40.

Kraidy, Marwan M. *Hybridity, or the Cultural Logic of Globalization*. Philadelphia: Temple University Press, 2005.

Krinsky, Charles, ed. *The Ashgate Research Companion to Moral Panics*. Farnham: Ashgate, 2013.

Maxwell, Richard, and Toby Miller. *Greening the Media*. New York: Oxford University Press, 2012.

McChesney, Robert W. *Communication Revolution: Critical Junctures and the Future of Media*. New York: New Press, 2007.

Miller, Toby. *Technologies of Truth: Cultural Citizenship and the Popular Media*. Minneapolis: University of Minnesota Press, 1998.

Miller, Toby. "Media Effects and Cultural Studies: A Contentious Relationship." In *The Sage Handbook of Media Processes and Effects*. Eds. Robin L. Nabi, and Mary Beth Oliver. Thousand Oaks: Sage Publications, 2009. 131–43.

Morris, Meaghan. "The Banality of Cultural Studies." In *Logics of Television: Essays in Cultural Criticism*. Ed. Patricia Mellencamp. Bloomington: Indiana University Press, 1990. 14–43.

Mosco, Vincent. *The Digital Sublime*. Cambridge, MA: MIT Press, 2004.

Mosco, Vincent. *To the Cloud: Big Data in a Turbulent World*. Boulder: Paradigm Publishers, 2014.

Mosco, Vincent, and Dan Schiller, eds. *Continental Order? Integrating North America for Cybercapitalism*. Lanham: Rowman and Littlefield, 2001.

Parkin, Frank. *Class Inequality and Political Order*. London: MacGibbon & Kee, 1971.

Paton, Graeme. "Media Studies Wastes Good Brains, Says Sugar." *Telegraph* (May 7, 2007). http://www.telegraph.co.uk/news/uknews/1550580/Media-studies-wastes-good-brains-says-Sugar.html

Paton, Graeme. "Ofqal: Dozens of 'Soft' GCSEs and A-levels to be Axed." *Telegraph* (June 4, 2014). http://www.telegraph.co.uk/education/educationnews/10873368/Ofqual-dozens-of-soft-GCSEs-and-A-levels-to-be-axed.html

Pufendorf, Samuel. *On the Duty of Man and Citizen According to Natural Law*. Trans. Michael Silverthorne. Ed. James Tully. Cambridge: Cambridge University Press, 2000.

Smith, Dorothy E. *The Everyday World as Problematic: A Feminist Sociology*. Boston: Northeastern University Press, 1987.

Smythe, Dallas. "The Consumer's Stake in Radio and Television." *Quarterly of Film Radio and Television* 6.2 (1951): 109–28.

Waisbord, Silvio, ed. *Media Sociology: A Reappraisal*. Cambridge: Polity Press, 2014.

Wallerstein, Immanuel. "Culture as the Ideological Battleground of the Modern World-System." *Hitotsubashi Journal of Social Studies* 21.1 (1989): 5–22.

Wenner, Lawrence A., and Walter Gantz. "Watching Sports on Television: Audience Experience, Gender, Fanship, and Marriage." In *Media Sport*. Ed. Lawrence A. Wenner. London: Routledge, 1998. 233–51.

Whittam Smith, Andreas. "Media Studies is No Preparation for Journalism." *Independent* (February 25, 2008). http://www.independent.co.uk/voices/commentators/andreas-whittam-smith/andreas-whittam-smith-media-studies-is-no-preparation-for-journalism-786785.html

Zhao, Yuezhi, and Paula Chakravartty, eds. *Global Communications: Towards a Transcultural Political Economy*. Boulder: Rowman and Littlefield, 2007.

CHAPTER TWENTY

Digital Humanities

JOSEPH TABBI

We might have expected, following the first wave of hypertext fictions written for the stand-alone desktop computer, that a literary genre was likely in formation. The professional networks were all in place by the mid-1980s and so were the necessary, marginal formations. Lines of communication opened between print and digital practitioners; critical encounters were sustained, and these were, at times, edgy. The digital practitioners were aware of academia but they were careful not to self-identify programmatically as a part of literary theory or creative writing—whose rise was contemporaneous and whose principled, respectful, and professional noncommunication was mutual. In the meantime, in the second decade of the twenty-first century both theory and creative writing have been each untouched by a subsequent rise in the digital humanities. That process of institutional, functional differentiation, more than the production of literary genres and the renewal of an audience for literary writing in digital media, will be as much a part of any history of "digital literary arts," as the identification, evaluation, reproduction, and recirculation of works themselves.

When hypertext entered the scene in the 1980s, a metafictional awareness and postmodernist sensibility were prevalent. It would be a mistake, however, to regard the experimentation in new media as a continuation of the previous generation of print fictions, for example by Thomas Pynchon, Don DeLillo, William Gaddis, Joseph McElroy, and, notably, Robert Coover, who, unlike his compeers took an active interest in writing for the stand-alone computer, then the 3 dimensional (CAVE) environments and, eventually networked devices. Though Coover knew enough (as he approached his seventies) to restrict his own experimental creative practice to print fiction, he was instrumental in his support of the founding (by Scott Rettberg and Jeff Ballowe) of an Electronic Literature Organization (ELO) and at the same time he brought many emerging digital talents to his program in Literary Arts at Brown University. I recall Coover remarking, during the Q & A at a 2007 colloquium in Paris,[1] that all of the writers who would become known as "postmodern" arrived independently, through very different topical and stylistic practices at a common understanding: they all realized for reasons of their own that the modernist project was finished; that the works they'd been weaned on needed to be totally reconfigured in a postwar, filmic, broadcast radio, and televisual world where mass media was no longer a novelty; not Walter Benjamin's "mechanical reproduction" nor Baudrillard's "simulation culture." Our media environment had become more a reality in and of itself, a powerful way of shaping consciousness and organizing lived experience and increasingly licensed communication. Neither were media a nuisance that could be kept at bay through critique and creative deviation, the "detournement" practiced by Situationists of the second half of the twentieth century. By the time Coover and his contemporaries came on the scene, the modernist project was no longer itself a driver of innovation and that was the thing, modernism itself, that needed to be reconfigured if not dismantled.[2] But if the theorists gave this common project a name—"postmodernism"— the literary creators themselves never regarded that practice (as many modernists did) self-consciously as a "movement." It was more a commitment to continued formal and stylistic experimentation, for a while consistent with alternative lifeways, identities, and social formations that emerged in the 1960s and 1970s, until these alternatives, eventually became a cultural mainstream: economized, commercialized, and domesticated.

Apart from systematically imposed, professional separations, what kept postmodern print and early hypertextual practices separate, materially, was a recognition of the need for hypertext authors to explore their medium (and not just reflect on it)—for authors to engage the digital at the operative level. Many literary practitioners became proficient at programming and this in turn encouraged transformations in their literary practice as the medium itself followed a path of continuous platform upgrades, the computers became networked and the software more user friendly—without regard for the interests of literary experimentation, necessarily. An independent publishing concern did emerge with Mark Bernstein's Eastgate Systems. Its Storyspace platform (1987) for composition was created by an established literary scholar, Jay David Bolter, together with an accomplished practitioner, Michael Joyce. But this at once commercially and technologically innovative, self-consciously non-populist venue for "Serious Hypertext" was neither an academic press nor a conventional commercial enterprise: it turned out to be, like so much of the intermedial hybridity of first-generation hypertext, the only one. Apart from Storyspace and John McDaid's "HyperEarthTM," which anticipates Google Earth by fifteen years, not so many literary authors have attempted to innovate with the software and textual content simultaneously or scale the upgrade path that is likely to render their own work unreadable.

A series of influential and recognized narratives nonetheless issued forth, but there were few followers in any given storytelling mode; few ways for a creative artist to enter a collective of like-minded or productively contrarian practitioners, of the sort that Coover and his fellow experimentalists had stumbled upon independently in print a decade or two earlier. Scholars at conferences began to speak of the "one Afternoon: A Story" phenomenon. The "one Patchwork Girl" problem. These are works that continue to be studied and read in classrooms (along with McDaid's Uncle Buddie's Funhouse, Stuart Moulthrop's Victory Garden and the work of Judy Malloy and Deena Larson, William Bly and Kate Pullinger, among others); recently some of the works written for stand-alone computers have been replayed by the authors themselves on carefully reconstructed Apple IIe's and IBM 286s where they first emerged, in homes and offices. The retrospective performances are described in a 2017 MIT Press collection of essays, Traversals, and interviews, Pathfinders, put together by Mouthrop and Dene Grigar. Malloy's dream dialogue with near contemporaries Carolee Schneemann, Chris Burden, and Kathy Acker; the ancient Greek (and later Roman) texts collected in the Project Perseus that inform the work of Bly—each of these re-visionings, rewritings, and (not least) relocations of past practices in digital media constitute much that's distinctively literary about electronic literature. And the conversations just as often cross national and linguistic borders even as they enter digital pathways that can alter the course of literary criticism.

Coover may have understood this "creative and technical ebullience" as a unique convergence not merely of two fields, the technological and the aesthetic, but of two definitively modernist formations that were each freshly available for innovation and renewal on the part of an incoming generation of authorial and technological practice; yet the entirely actualizable aesthetic and "technical ebullience," no less than a concurrent "irrational exuberance"[3] in the economic sphere, turned out to be short-lived and unreproduceable. "The End of Books" that Coover formulated, as more of a thought experiment in his widely cited *New York Times Book Review* essay (1992), would be reconsidered by Coover less than a decade later as a "Golden Era" of hypertext experimentation.[4] The "complex textual webworks of multilinear narrative and, to a much lesser extent, lyrical or poetic webworks,"[5] however radical they might have been as means of disrupting and possibly reshaping habits of readerly attention, were nonetheless constrained by the digital formats of the day. Designed for shelvable floppy disks, UNIX Shell Scripts or CD-ROMs (*Read Only* in more than one sense of the word), the first-generation hypertexts for all their open-ended narrative formats were, materially, "mostly discrete objects like books."[6] That gave authors and readers from both domains, print, and digital, an opportunity for the most part textually to trace and cognize radical diversions from linear narrative in the new medium; habits of reading might change, to be sure, yet reading as such (not viewing or listening) remained the primary activity, and the alternative sequencings and linkages made possible by the computer, were gathered into one place—not distributed in networks.

In 1999, it may have been too soon to anticipate just how thoroughgoing restrictions would be on access to commercially monitored digital platforms; and how increasingly distanced readers of "user friendly," handheld apps would be from any awareness of the underlying software architecture (except when a system slowed down or crashed). Though Coover doesn't say so explicitly, the move to networked multimedia would make DIY technical experimentation on the same order as "creative" writing unlikely, even by litterateurs with some programming savvy. Michael Joyce and Shelley Jackson, regarded by Coover and many others as the most accomplished hypertexualists, would each shift or (in Joyce's case, return) to print for their continuing experimental practice.

The early hypertexts are part of literary history but they never became an avant-garde or a *movement*, along the modernist model for literature, sound, and visual arts of the previous turn of the century. The nonlinear or nonsequential hypertext narrative made possible by the computer, unlike (for example) the novel, poem, or short story in print, never became a *genre*. The process was unified by an experimental tendency that flourished briefly, with the same stand-alone Apple and IBM computers on which they can now be read in a few curated labs (notably in Dene Grigar's program at the University of Washington, Victoria, Matt Kirshenbaum's Human-Computer Interaction Lab at Maryland, and Lori Emerson's lab at the University of Colorado, Boulder). Subsequent platforms such as *Twine* and Erik Loyer's open source *Stepworks Library* (http://step.works/, dedicated to a form of "one button storytelling") are unlike *Storyspace* in that the reader is expected not just to click or tap or scroll and see what alternative pathways the author has set in place; readers tend, rather, to be engaged as coauthors who can themselves enter a work and adjust its content at will, and then pass their own versionings on to others.[7] In such networked hypertextual practices, the above cited "dream dialogues" among near contemporaries (enacted by Judy Malloy) can now be opened to a general readership and expanded to authors more distant in time; there is no longer a self-contained product that the artist circulates, it's rather a series of processual pages and platforms "available for you to perform, modify, or replace with your own content. You can remix the content of any story with the look and feel of any other."[8]

John Cayley emerged as a digital literary artist just a few years after the *Storyspace* era, when the internet was in place and he was appointed to direct the same Brown University writing program that had been attended by *Patchwork Girl* author Shelley Jackson along with early net artists such as Mark Amerika and Noah Wardrip-Fruin. Cayley is well placed, then, to comment on the early reception and never realized potential of a hypertextual literary practice: since then, "the myth of computational media's indeterminacy, openness, freedom has . . . become just that, still affectively powerful, but merely a story from the hyper-distant recent past. The actual world of computation within which we now dwell has an architecture that is as substantial and determinative as that of bricks and mortar."[9] The materiality may be softer, more a matter of programming and information flows, but the digital infrastructure (what Cayley terms "Big Software") is by now no less necessary for the construction and maintenance of buildings, institutions, and (not least) communicative pathways within a tightly controlled corporate lifeworld. While that particular corporate transformation transpired within little more than a decade, it is not easy to describe any similar or concurrent transformation in the literary arts: to the contrary, the corporate expansion of text based writing for mainly commercial purposes (and the predominance of digital data mining in the humanities) arguably helped to sideline the internet's literary affordances and may continue to do so. Just as it took centuries, not decades, for the novel to emerge after the installation of (for example) the Gutenberg press, and lifetimes following the Industrial Revolution for the realist novel of Austin, Dickens, and George Eliot to emerge, we should perhaps not expect a speedier emergence of a digitally structured literary practice, whether for popular or professional audiences or emerging arts networks in the gallery system.

What we can say, for sure, is that as yet no known economy (not even the "gift economy" of academic writing made freely available in return for an author's promotion and tenure), has emerged to support and sustain the development of literary genres and practices in new media. As Martin Eve argues in his essay, "Scarcity and Abundance," we have not yet put in place a "discovery space" for the act of reading, and writing online:

> For what, we might ask, are the quality markers that make it possible to discern where one should direct one's time within the electronic world? Guides, such as those produced by the Electronic Literature Organization (ELO) are one such signal. Indeed, the ELO Showcase and Electronic Literature Collection act as signposts of value, while admitting their own non-comprehensivity.[10] However, the fact that the ELO brackets the works in which it is interested under a medium of form—however hard this may be to define[11]—means that a given piece of electronic literature will only be discovered here by those seeking it through the medium, rather than it being an honest competition with print. In other words, only readers who seek "electronic literature" will find electronic literature.[12]

We may nonetheless postulate, given the growing corpus of born digital literary objects, what an emergent electronic literary practice (and economy) might look like, whose innovations no longer take place so much through direct literary applications of technologies under development (as happened with *Storyspace*). As I'll argue momentarily, current practices tend rather to set themselves *against* the material emplacements of a digital infrastructure that is now pervasive and unavoidable, and whose innovative power, such as it is, is not so often or so openly made available as before. But first, so that we have a sense of what it is literary scholars should be looking for by way of a post-digital corpus, we might look further into some of the specifically literary sources of that "still affectively powerful" narrative of a transmedial, breakaway writing practice. Robert Coover himself, in a little-known essay (occasioned by a 1986 collection titled *Sudden Fictions*) sought to link the potential of a nonlinear, post-digital practice not so much to innovation as to a perennial persistence of deviant storytelling. Noting his own inspiration in the preceding generation of Kafka, Beckett, and Borges, but also recalling the prehistory through millennia of what would eventually settle into present forms of storytelling and novel writing, Coover lists—not many, but a number of past practitioners, some of them working singly but many more in collaboration, who "have taken short fictions and linked them up . . . , moving from disparate short narratives toward longer, more Complex ones."[13] Such is the mode of the Book of Genesis, which was "done by gathering up a mass of traditional tales, widely available, and attaching them, linking them to a name, to a character" (Abraham). And so it has been for all our mythical heroes and (in Coover's United States) national frontiersmen: "And thus Odysseus, thus King Arthur, thus Br'er Rabbit and the Saturday morning TV cartoons: webworks of borrowed fragments."

One might have expected the reformulation of such "webworks" using fictions short enough to be viewed on a single computer screen, whose networks are custom made not just for linking but the carrying over (i.e., the "borrowing") of fragments, their redistribution, and a consequent expansion of such practices to a newly forming, popular reading audience. The latter, unprecedented audience expansion did in fact happen but with much more conventional realist (and often racy) narratives such as E. L. James's *Fifty Shades of Gray* that were self-published by individual authors on fan fiction sites and Amazon.com. But there was also the prospect, similarly unrealized, of the revival and wider circulation of classic (and classically deviant) framed narratives on the order of Boccaccio's *Decameron*, Basile's *Pentameron*, Chaucer's *Canterbury Tales*, and (in Coover's words) the "freer, less programmatic approach" of Cretien de Troyes, whose "own loose narratives are much more playful and full of unexpected, sometimes dissonant, but often very creative juxtapositions, including a number of wildly improbable linkages that through creative displacement helped to generate a whole new literary form." Never mind that the newness was the discovery of an "ancient idea of books buried in books": Cervantes used "all of these devices," often parodically, in the invention of a different sort of book; namely, the literary novel: "*Don Quixote* Part I is still essentially a loosely linked collection of short fictions based on sequential parodies of contemporary literary forms, but Cervantes gets the whole package integrated and put together in Part II, and the novel, the classic form of the Gutenberg era, is born."[14]

What then, has held back a comparable literary formation in the post-digital era? Coover is able to cite the self-described "hypernovel," *Invisible Cities* (1972) whose author, Italo Calvino, was able (albeit in print) "to concentrate all [his] reflections, experiments, and conjectures on a single symbol." Calvino says that he was able to "build up," in this volume "a many-faceted structure in which each brief text is close to the others in a series that does not imply logical sequence or a hierarchy, but a network in which one can follow multiple routes and draw multiple, ramified conclusions."[15]

But that was all done exclusively in print, in Calvino's published work as in Coover's own. The series of "sudden link[s]" made by Coover in this one short essay, he recognizes, would be much easier to follow on a screen, and so presumably would the "deeper mainstream" of proto-, parodic, and persisting novelistic fictions that Coover traces. Calvino sets out, and realizes notionally in *Invisible Cities* multiple routes "aimed at tracing the lightning flashes of the mental circuits that capture and link points distant from each other in space and time." But the current digital media that embody such linkages, operationally, have yet to produce anything quite like the literary mainstream these experimental authors (Calvino, Coover) imagine in print.

There's another aspect, however, to Calvino's art that Coover doesn't mention—one that moves the discussion past the organization of story elements (whether in print, on stand-alone computers, or the internet) toward a more generalized consideration of literary writing as *writing under constraint*. Calvino after all was a part of the Oulipo, the *Ouvroir de littérature potentielle*, which looked to the materiality of literary arts, and more generally to the mathematics of inscription, frequencies of words and letters and also spacings; mental linkages generated not so much by unconscious or affective states as by material constraints: the determination to write a novel without the letter "e," for example (*La Disparition*; Perec 1968; translated as *A Void* by Gilbert Adair in 1995; *A Vanishing* by Ian Monk; *Vanish'd!* by John Lee; and *Omissions* by Julian West), or the recombination of the fourteen lines in ten sonnets that produces, potentially, 10 to the 14th or *Cent Mille Milliards de Poèmes* (A Hundred Thousand Billion Poems).[16] Comparable endeavors using computational means have been accomplished by Nick Montfort and Stephanie Strickland, whose mining of texts by Emily Dickinson and Herman Melville can be, not only read but also *rewritten* by interested readers. The same is true of Jhave Johnston's *BDP: Big Data Poetry* ("Almost poems generated from almost big data by an almost programmer-poet").[17] Jhave's remix of "some 10,557 poems from the Poetry Foundation, 57,000+ hip-hop rap songs from Ohhla.com, and over 7,000 pop lyrics," however freewheeling they might appear, has struck critics Davin Heckman and James O'Sullivan as a precise enactment of writing under constraint within an internet environment. Jhave presents himself as reading "along with the machine, verbally stitching and improvising spoken poems," an activity that is, for Heckman and O'Sullivan, perhaps "the only possibility of overwriting" the machine's own "writing constraint."

Another approach, by John Cayley and Daniel Howe,[18] is to locate in the everyday speech and writing posted to the internet, sequences of text that happen to repeat phrases or lines in the published writing of Samuel Beckett: "We address," Cayley and Howe write, "the association of phrases with an authorized text, exploding its integrity and discovering the same words 'in the wild,' so to speak—among fragments of feral language both human and posthuman, in the common tongues that are proper to the contemporary linguistic commons." Here the conscious creative participation of the reader is neither expected nor needed, since what we say collectively, is likely over time to iterate all that has been said by Beckett or for that matter any published author. The gist of all these engagements, is not so much to keep alive a tradition by acknowledging its "influence" (the framework advanced by T. S. Eliot in his essay, "Tradition and the Individual Talent"); rather, it's a way for each of these writers to engage both the corpus and the vernacular *as data*, and so to demonstrate accidents and coincidences of machinic processing whose patterns actually have little at all to do with (for example) Calvino's "multi-faceted" structures and "lightning flashes of the mental circuits." Unlike the Oulipian constraints whose authorial imposition and embrace are *generative* of unexpected mental connections on the part of human authors and readers, the machinic, enacted computational constraints tend rather to make us aware of our distance from a literary corpus that has relocated *as data*: the "linguistic commons" thus conceived has the capacity to reproduce all past poetries, stories, and novelistic sentences, if the net is cast widely enough, and our access is kept open. But this latter requirement (Open Access), though it can be found in databases such as Poetry.org is never certain (not for long) when our linguistic "commons" increasingly is enclosed, as Cayley and Howe again emphasize: "Big software that are, as we speak, enclosing language, in order to find the words of an authorized text where they are still, if only momentarily, associating freely."[19]

The constraints within which writers of internet self-consciously work, are thus (again) significantly different from those of the preceding generation of constraint-based writing, as the hypertext innovators differed from their immediate postmodern predecessors. Queneau, who studied mathematics as well as "Letters" as a graduate student in the Sorbonne, was no doubt fully aware of the instrumentalist applications of the emerging digital media in particular; he was also, in the words of the *Encyclopedia Brittanica*, "a reader for the prestigious *Encyclopédie de la Pléiade*, a scholarly edition of past and present classical authors, and by 1955 was its director" (Wikipedia). Grounded in the classics as much as Robert Coover or Italo Calvino, Queneau resisted the idea of a literary "movement" (after early encounters with the French Surrealists and Dadaists), but he was devoted to the idea of sustained collaborations among a persisting communicative cohort.[20] The resonances, the capacity for linkage and reiteration of older forms, are however quite different when these are *generated* by machinic processes, not introduced (however arbitrarily) by the authors.

The introduction, *into the literary* of material and mathematical formalisms, is also consistent with a now unavoidable collocation on the internet of text, sound, and image—a co-presencing that has very real implications not only for how we cognize the work and its boundaries, but also for the professional structure and performative practice of literary arts. Freedom in such practice ceases to be associated with individual choices within a bounded field determined by an author, but is more to do with a recognition of nonhuman material constraints on all medial and mental linkages, and this recognition is as relevant to sound and visual elements as it is to the generation of text, for a strain of authors and artists larger than the literary centered Oulipo but never so large as the mainstream commercial practitioners in literature and the arts. Hence, Manuel Portela, in his essay "Writing Under Constraint,"[21] is able to cite Igor Stravinsky[22] as readily as Queneau or Calvino. "I shall go even further," Stravinsky writes:

> My freedom will be so much the greater and more meaningful the more narrowly I limit my field of action and the more I surround myself with obstacles. Whatever diminishes constraint, diminishes strength. The more constraints one imposes, the more one frees one's self of the chains that shackle the spirit.

What is noticeable about many such experiments in constrained writing, no less than acts of visual and sonic composition, is the way that they self-consciously *deviate* from established means of organizing the aesthetic experience—away from story and plot lines in fiction, and against harmony in music, for example; opening the composition to folkways and aesthetic forerunners on the one hand, and also to accidents, noises, or (as in the work of John Cage) silences that take on new qualities as they are brought into a highly structured work. In music, such off modern, off kilter practices never supplanted the classical or popular, folk or bluesy modes; the rioting audience on the opening night in Paris 1913 of *The Right of Spring* (compellingly reimagined by Thomas Pynchon in his debut novel, *V.* [1963]), may have established an avant-garde credibility but as the disruption, inevitably, recedes and the often equally compelling, performative practitioners pass on, the constraints that enabled such experimentation carry on and inspire other, often lasting expression.

Such practices, as they resumed for example in the work of John Cage in the sixties, have in fact found a surprisingly wide acceptance. As Philip Clark notes at the end of a *London Review of Books* essay on John Cage, "many assumed his work would die with him. Cage's quixotic ideas, they believed, required his presence and charm if they were to be sold to a skeptical audience hungry for Beethoven and Mahler. Yet in the years following his death the message of his silence roared ever louder. As if to vindicate Cage's faith in technology, the compact disc arrived: the new medium's absence of background hiss suited the often delicate textures of his music better than vinyl, and his music began to appear in abundance on CD."[23] And there were others—never a mainstream, but always more—who followed in his wake: Brian Eno (who brought so many commercially successful artists from David Bowie to Devo to the Talking Heads into areas they might not have reached on their own); "Cosey Fanni Tutti, the British post-punk group Throbbing Gristle," and "the Wandelweiser Group, a collective of composers and improvisers who to this day grapple with the question: after silence, what next?" (Clark).

When the "myth of great composers and the stories their music told" is stripped away, what's left is "sound. Then listening becomes a proactive responsibility. Music is no longer entertainment. You must sit, sometimes in silence, and listen hard" (Clark). It is a lot to ask, and less and less likely to happen the more and more mediated input succeeding generations are asked, and more often required, to process. (Coover himself recognized, even as he noted the passing of hypertext's "Golden Age," that an author's imagination of "the patient reader, if there are any left in the world," was nonetheless the foundation to literary creation in any media.) But Stravinski and Cage and enough others show that such a mediatic, environmentally open approach can indeed find and sustain an audience in spite of all the danger (and distraction). Does the present exploration under way in literary experimentation give us reason to believe that something similarly off kilter and off modern can emerge in post-digital literary writing?

In a sense, on the literary side we may be moving toward a *return* to the open-ended prehistoric, proto-novelistic explorations in the exemplars and antecedents listed by Coover. None of these can be said to form anything like a formalized storytelling practice (of the sort advocated in commercial publishing and creative writing programs) or the settled practices of nineteenth-century-realist fiction. Yet they offered something more, a practice much older than stories or novels that runs against the grain of generic practices and genre fictions; a tradition that never settles into fixed forms, but instead deviates from the norm at any given time.

That we should look not solely to the literary canon but to experimental practices in the sound and visual spheres that textual writing now encounters, opens literary practice to the same kind of citational aesthetic that brought environmental sounds and silences into experimental music; and for this we may expect to find more written works conceived not for this or that computer or some other device, but for (and with) the internet. Here, too, Michael Joyce's print fiction *Was: A Novel of Internet* gestures in the same direction: "A highly elliptical, discontinuous, polyglot work that clearly has its own genetic relationship to the experimental tradition of modernism, though more in the line of Stein or Pound than Fitzgerald."[24] Joyce's novel also appropriates lines from the internet, as often (or as readily) as it sets down lines that the author himself thought up (to the extent that the language we form in our minds is ever our own). Joyce's print novel is thus "part of an extended intercourse" that now includes the internet as much as spoken conversation or written signage, and so are several born or genetically digital works that take the print canon or corpus not so much as a living "tradition" and not even as "Big Data," in the sense that we may now regard the thirty million books scanned by Google (as of this writing, circa March 2017; over 140 million are expected to fill out Google's Library Project). As Nick Montfort points out in conversation,[25] however, there is nothing inherently "big" about the corpus of all books available everywhere now in databases:

> It only seems big because we have been focused on much smaller data sets. Our discussion of "big data" does not pertain to how much data there is, but rather what our traditional means of data collection and analysis have led us to expect. When those expectations change, what seems like "big data" now will no longer seem big. It will just be "data."

And that data can be, in turn, resituated at will by authors with the programming knowledge and access to the sites, the collections, and not least the software that organizes databases. The literary, as such can be present only so long as authors can go on engaging not data and not conventional traditions but I would say, rather, cohering and continuing literary practices—through direct and indirect citations, reorganization, and the cognitive dissonance of continually comparing our internalized speech and thought patterns with the written, recorded speech and thought of others (including past authors).

Montfort and Stephanie Strickland's own *Toroko Gorge* (2012) illustrates this recombinant conversation clearly, by steadily and continuously working variations on lines from Emily Dickinson and Herman Melville (together with input from readers). We are able to see the results (which are infinite) at any moment forming in front of us on the screen. The mechanism underlying each of these clearly articulated, unrealizable (never to be finished and sometimes unreadable) projects are nonetheless entirely accessible and available—no less than the formerly, largely notional recombination of textual elements was essential to our experience of Queneau's and Calvino's antecedents.

At the same time, all works within the Dickinson and Melville corpus that are reworked by Strickland and Montfort are out of copyright, and the database from which they have been retrieved is Open Access. There is no reason to suppose, to stay with our current example, that Google's scanned corpus of thirty-plus million (and growing, albeit haltingly[26]) will be similarly available for such recombinant reading. Cayley's "Big Software," with its infrastructural constraints, might well be the greater challenge than any concern with the tracking, counting, and accounting for "Big Data" that has preoccupied so many humanities researchers. And as the mechanisms become more and more hidden, our creative attentions today turn more to errors, liminalities, and glitches that reveal our mediatically determined situation; these are what now define a contemporary digital "Glitch Poetics,"[27] a kind of accidental writing that at once reveals potentialities that are (and have to be) passed over by commercial digitization. The glitch (for Nathan Jones) and what John Cayley describes as a lapse of designation, or "Grammalepsy," are terms that remind us of the arbitrariness of any act of signification, in writing on a page no less than coding on silicon. There is no reason why the latter, so different from our neurological circuits, should be better than any other conventional designation at encapsulating and communicating thought. The fact that literary theorists (and also makers like Cayley and Jones) place their work and thought self-consciously in the margins of what is now a digital consensus, suggests the presence of a long-standing (and continuing) literary counter-history to the Digital Humanities, that are too often characterized by datafication, single-entendre designation, and instrumentalist tendencies.[28]

A networked literary practice that enters easily into "dream dialogues" with near contemporaries and canonical cousins, to recall Judy Malloy's early formulation, is one promise of the internet that is currently realizable. It will engage massive data, for sure, but it won't be a continuation of the maximalist ambitions of the postmodern fiction authors of the previous generation, Coover among them, who assembled "sudden stories" into epical, enveloping world fictions. Something quite different, if in some ways more worldly would appear to be in formation in the sphere of digital literary arts. Coover's intuitive focus on an unbounded interconnection of "short fictions," closer to the prehistory of the novel is a valuable first pass at describing this development; Calvino's many-faceted, nonhierarchical, and nonlinear structure that sought to invoke "mental circuits," and Cayley and Howe's rediscovery of Beckett's sentences in found texts on the internet, all point to another characterization—one that we might identify as a "minor" literature of a sort that was recognized by another key precursor to digital aesthetic and cultural theory, namely, Gilles Deleuze. As Laura Shackelford and Laura Marks have recently noted, Deleuze's "minor science" takes us toward "emerging, immanent, practice-based methods for diagnosing and pursuing the shifts in language and poetics and their larger literary, symbolic, and political economies."[29]

For Shackelford, discerning a "minor" literature involves our "retracing these digital literary strains of inquiry into language and emerging, computation-based digital media, and their bioinformatic symbolic and political economies and circulatory regimes." For Rob Wittig, who in 1989 attended a seminar with Jacques Derrida and has practiced an alternative, improvisational mode of digital writing since the early days of the *In.S.Omnia* project in Seattle, a thing called "Netprov" represents a hitherto unrecognized practice ("minor" by design) that recalls emergent practices in print by Defoe, Sterne, H. G. Wells and Mark C. Danielewski, even as its embrace and detournment of any and all social media sets it squarely in "contrast to high literary forms such as the holy trinity of poem, short story and novel." Where much that is innovative and avant-garde in electronic literature has found a limited audience mostly in academia, Wittig's collaborative and contrarian Netprov remains

> *informal* in contrast to works vetted, edited and published in major journals, *interactive* because reactions from readers are expected and can rapidly be published alongside the text, and *vernacular* because they are cultural practices that develop from everyday use and are not, or not yet, taught in schools and universities. (Note that I use the word "vernacular" here not as linguists do, but as graphic designers do. In design scholarship it means design done by untrained creators. Such work is beloved in graphic design culture, sometimes with a camp sensibility, more often with genuine admiration.)

Wittig's elaboration points to the necessarily populist, potentially but not necessarily commercially popular aspect of Netprov, and to an internet whose restrictions, once noted, can occasion improvisational writing under constraint. His reference to "graphic design culture," like our previous invocation of experimental music, helps to fill out the affective and sensual multiplicity that is the likely environment for reading activity, going forward. A self-consciously "minor" practice that situates itself in neither commercial "discovery spaces" nor the academic gift economy: here is the place where experimental writers have come closest to realizing the literary/human potential of the internet.

University of Illinois, Chicago (United States)

NOTES

1. The (March 22–24, 2007) colloquium was held in honor of Marc Chenetier on the occasion of his retirement from the University Paris 8.
2. I cannot recall the exact terms used by Coover, but the sense at that 2007 conference— there are no tweets or proceedings that I know of—was that postmodernism had been undergoing some as yet unnamed transformation in the new, digital environments.

The continued inability to name or periodize the present moment, and a spate of "new" practices—Media, Materialisms, Medievalisms, even the "New IRS" that preoccupies David Foster Wallace in *The Pale King* (2011)—all are symptomatic of the incomplete establishment of a post-print, predominantly digital practice in professional communication and the literary arts.

3. The term was advanced by then chair of the Federal Reserve, Alan Greenspan, in "a speech given at the American Enterprise institute during the dot-com bubble of the 1990s" (Wikipedia).

4. October 29, 1999, Keynote Address, Digital Arts and Culture, Atlanta, Georgia. Coover's speech was also published in *Feed* magazine in 2000.

5. Robert Coover, "Storying in Hyperspace: Linkages," in *The Tales We Tell: Perspectives on the Short Story*, eds. Barbara Lounsberry, Susan Lohafer, Mary Rohrberger, Stephen Pett, and R. C. Feddersen (Westport: Praeger, 1998).

6. Coover, "Storying in Hyperspace."

7. Apart from the interactivity that readers can practice, the act of reading in *Stepwise* remains very much on the model of turning pages. As Loyer and Marino write:

> These actions are like turning pages in a book. They're digital ways of saying "next, please."
> "Press SPACE BAR to continue."
> "Click to continue."
> "Tap to continue."

8. Erik Loyer and Mark Marino; email circulated March 10, 2017, via the Electronic Literature Organization listserv.

9. John Cayley, "The Advent of Aurature and the End of (Electronic) Literature," in *The Bloomsbury Handbook of Electronic Literature*, ed. Joseph Tabbi (London: Bloomsbury Press, 2017). Cayley's recognition of an unfulfilled promise is echoed by his younger contemporary, Nick Monfort. As Cayley (and I) acknowledge and wish to specify a lost promise when a term, and practice such as "hypertext" is supplanted, we can also see this happening with so many other terms, such as "push media" and "cyberspace" which, as Montfort notes "sound very outmoded now, but I don't mean to be dismissive when I refer to them; some of those underlying ideas have been important and remain so, and yet, obviously, everything promised by such terms did not persist (or never came to be in the first place). How do terms such as these represent hopes, imaginations, fascinations, and also misconceptions." That question posed by Montfort (Nick Montfort, "Self-Monitoring and Corporate Interests," Interview with Roberto Simanowski, *Digital Humanities and Digital Media: Conversations on Politics, Culture, Aesthetics and Literacy* [Ann Arbor: Open Humanities Press, 2016], 209), seems to me a worthwhile research agenda for the incoming generation of scholars taking a *literary* interest in modes of digital expression, an interest that can run counter to the upgrade path and at times meme-happy pursuits of first-order digital production.

10. "Showcase." *eliterature.org*. 2006. https://eliterature.org/news/showcase/

11. "For an indication of the difficulties here," Eve references Caroline Levine, *Forms: Whole, Rhythm, Hierarchy, Network* (Princeton: Princeton University Press, 2015), 1–23.

12. Martin Paul Eve, "Scarcity and Abundance," in *The Bloomsbury Handbook of Electronic Literature*, ed. Joseph Tabbi (London: Bloomsbury Press, 2017).

13. Robert Coover, "A Sudden Story," in *Sudden Fictions*, eds. Robert Shapard and James Thomas (Salt Lake City: G. M. Smith, 1986), vii–xii.

14. Coover, "A Sudden Story."

15. Italo Calvino, *Invisible Cities,* trans. William Weaver (New York: Harcourt, Inc., 1974).

16. Raymond Queneau, *Cent Mille Milliards de Poèmes* (Paris: Gallimard, 1961).

17. David Jhave Johnston, "About," *BDP: Big Data Poetry,* http://bdp.glia.ca/about/

18. John Cayley and Daniel Howe, "'How It Is in Common Tongues': An Interview with John Cayley and Daniel Howe," Scott Rettberg, *Vimeo* (November 3, 2012). https://vimeo.com/59669354

19. Cayley and Howe are cited in the entry on John Cayley and Daniel Howe, "Common Tongues," *ELMCIP,* Posted by Elisabeth Nesheim, https://elmcip.net/node/4677

20. Members of Oulipo were admitted for life, and they remain members after their passing.

21. Manuel Portela, "Writing Under Constraint," in *Bloomsbury Handbook of Electronic Literature,* ed. Joseph Tabbi (London: Bloomsbury Press, 2017).

22. Igor Stravinsky, *The Poetics of Music in the Form of Six Lessons* (Cambridge: Harvard University Press, 1947), 65.

23. Philip Clark, "I have Nothing to Say, and I am Saying It," *London Review of Books* 38.24 (December 15, 2016): 31.

24. Stuart Moulthrop, "Lift This End: Electronic Literature in a Blue Light," in *Bloomsbury Handbook of Electronic Literature,* ed. Joseph Tabbi (London: Bloomsbury Press, 2017).

25. Montfort, "Self-monitoring and corporate interests," 210.

26. Jeffrey R. Di Leo sees the slowdown in Google's acquisitions (mostly from books gathered and scanned from US lending libraries), as a sign of "digital fatique" (Jeffrey R. Di Leo, "Digital Fatigue," *American Book Review* 37.6 [September/October 2016]). This may be so, but Google has been patient, it has so far successfully waited out the unresolved legal objections to its practice and could do so for as long as it takes to complete the scanning of an anticipated corpus numbering well over a hundred million. As Montfort suggests, the data thus obtained is not so "big" if one is handling only the numbers, the page and word and sentence counts and so forth (assuming these will be made accessible). But if the current practice of accessing (and fragmentary reading) continues, one book at a time on the Google Book site with occasional purchases of the entire print copy, then the majority of readers will be right back where we started: dipping in and then reading another self-contained artifact, be it online or in print.

27. Nathan Jones, "Glitch Poetics," in *Bloomsbury Handbook of Electronic Literature,* ed. Joseph Tabbi (London: Bloomsbury Press, 2017).

28. Cayley's book, *Grammalepsy,* is in press at the time of this writing (Bloomsbury 2018). In the preface, Cayley notes how his titular term "eschews the tendency of literary critics and writers, including theorists and critics of electronic literature, to reduce aesthetic linguistic making—even when it has multimedia affordances—to 'writing.'" A conveyance of philosophy, and not least Derridean theory, is for Cayley precisely what's needed for the "digital literary arts" to be recognized as literary. His book is a welcome counter to the sidelining of literary theory that too often characterizes university writing programs.

29. Qtd. by Laura Shackelford, "Postmodern, Posthuman, Postdigital," in *Bloomsbury Handbook of Electronic Literature,* ed. Joseph Tabbi (London: Bloomsbury Press, 2017). Shackelford is here drawing on Laura U. Marks' work (Laura Marks, *Touch: Sensuous Theory and Multisensory Media* [Minneapolis: University of Minnesota Press, 2002], xiv), in which she applies the term *minor science* to her discussion of experimental film, video, and digital art.

WORKS CITED

Calvino, Italo. *Invisible Cities* [1972]. Trans. William Weaver. New York: Harcourt, Inc., 1974.

Cayley, John. *Grammalepsy*. London: Bloomsbury, 2018.

Cayley, John. "The Advent of Aurature and the End of (Electronic) Literature." In *The Bloomsbury Handbook of Electronic Literature*. Ed. Joseph Tabbi. London: Bloomsbury, 2017. 73–94.

Cayley, John, and Daniel Howe. "'How It Is in Common Tongues': An Interview with John Cayley and Daniel Howe." Scott Rettberg. *Vimeo* (November 3, 2012). https://vimeo.com/59669354

Cayley, John, and Daniel Howe. "Common Tongues." *ELMCIP*. Posted by Elisabeth Nesheim. https://elmcip.net/node/4677

Clark, Philip. "I have nothing to say, and I am saying it." *London Review of Books* 38.24 (December 15, 2016): 29–31.

Coover, Robert. "A Sudden Story." In *Sudden Fictions*. Eds. Shapard, Robert, and James Thomas. Salt Lake City: G. M. Smith, 1986. vii–xii.

Coover, Robert. "Storying in Hyperspace: Linkages." In *The Tales We Tell: Perspectives on the Short Story*. Eds. Barbara Lounsberry, Susan Lohafer, Mary Rohrberger, Stephen Pett, and R. C. Feddersen. Westport: Praeger, 1998. 133–38.

Deleuze, Gilles, and Felix Guattari. "1227: Treatise on Nomadology:—The War Machine." In *A Thousand Plateaus*. Minneapolis: University of Minnesota Press, 1987. 351–423.

Derrida, Jacques. "Structure, Sign and Play." In *Writing and Difference*. London: Routledge, 2006. 351–70.

Di Leo, Jeffrey R. "Digital Fatigue." *American Book Review* 37.6 (September/October 2016): 2, 14.

Eve, Martin Paul. "Scarcity and Abundance." In *The Bloomsbury Handbook of Electronic Literature*. Ed. Joseph Tabbi. London: Bloomsbury, 2017. 385–98.

Johnston, David Jhave. "About." In *BDP: Big Data Poetry*. http://bdp.glia.ca/about/

Jones, Nathan. "Glitch Poetics." In *Bloomsbury Handbook of Electronic Literature*. Ed. Joseph Tabbi. London: Bloomsbury, 2017. 237–54.

Levine, Caroline. *Forms: Whole, Rhythm, Hierarchy, Network*. Princeton: Princeton University Press, 2015.

Marks, Laura. *Touch: Sensuous Theory and Multisensory Media*. Minneapolis: University of Minnesota Press, 2002.

Montfort, Nick. "Self-Monitoring and Corporate Interests." Interview with Roberto Simanowski. *Digital Humanities and Digital Media: Conversations on Politics, Culture, Aesthetics and Literacy*. Ann Arbor: Open Humanities Press, 2016. 206–27.

Moulthrop, Stuart. "Lift This End: Electronic Literature in a Blue Light." In *Bloomsbury Handbook of Electronic Literature*. Ed. Joseph Tabbi. London: Bloomsbury, 2017. 59–72.

Portela, Manuel. "Writing Under Constraint." In *Bloomsbury Handbook of Electronic Literature*. Ed. Joseph Tabbi. London: Bloomsbury, 2017. 181–200.

Queneau, Raymond. *Cent Mille Milliards de Poèmes*. Paris: Gallimard, 1961.

Shackelford, Laura. "Postmodern, Posthuman, Postdigital." In *Bloomsbury Handbook of Electronic Literature*. Ed. Joseph Tabbi. London: Bloomsbury, 2017. 335–60.

"Showcase." *eliterature.org* (2006). https://eliterature.org/news/showcase/

Stravinsky, Igor. *The Poetics of Music in the Form of Six Lessons*. Cambridge: Harvard University Press, 1947.

CHAPTER TWENTY-ONE

Late Capitalism

HENRY A. GIROUX

In August 2016, Donald Trump lowered the bar even further than he has in the past when he called Mexicans who illegally entered the country rapists and drug dealers, stated he wanted to ban Muslims from coming into the United States, defamed Fox News host Megyn Kelly by referring to her menstrual cycle, and questioning the heroism and bravery of former prisoner of war Senator John McCain. In what can only be described as unimaginable, Trump urged Russia to hack Hilary Clinton's emails, and attacked the Muslim parents of Capt. Humayan Khan, who was killed in 2004 by a suicide bomber while he was trying to save the lives of the men in his unit. In addition, during a campaign rally in North Carolina, Trump suggested that "Second Amendment people" would take care of Hilary Clinton for picking Supreme Court judges who favor stricter gun laws. The Clinton campaign and many others saw this as a veiled endorsement of an assassination attempt. These stunts were just one of the many examples of his chillingly successful media strategy, which is based not on changing public consciousness but on titillating and infantilizing it within a flood of shocks, sensations, and simplistic views. It is a strategy that only succeeds due to the deep cultural and political effects of a savage form of casino capitalism in our society—effects that include widespread atomization and depoliticization.

Prior to his election as president of the United States, Trump was caught bragging on a 2005-recorded tape about sexually assaulting women. He states, shamelessly, on the surfaced recording: "Grab them by the pussy. You can do anything," he said, as well as "I just start kissing them. It's like a magnet. Just kiss. I don't even wait. And when you're a star they let you do it. You can do anything."[1] He later dismissed the repugnant comment as just locker talk. He was accused publicly by a number of women of sexual misconduct, and he lied endlessly about everything ranging from his business dealings to a fake story about Muslims in New Jersey celebrating the attack on the Twin Towers. Trump rode into the election on a scandal sheet that, because it was so extensive, bordered on science fiction. Yet, none of these violations of public integrity, trust, and the truth prevented him from being elected. In this particular instance, politics was emptied of any substance, reason gave way to the spectacle, and the lure of celebrity culture conferred the ultimate authority and legitimation for creating a mass and largely civically challenged public following.[2] Within the first few days of his presidency, Trump lied over and over again about the size of the attendance at his inaugural speech claiming it was much larger than the media reported. He also claimed without any evidence that he lost the popular vote to Hillary Clinton because millions of unauthorized immigrants had voted illegally.[3] Instead of dealing with complex social and economic issues, Trump mimics the tactics of the financial elite and Republican Party extremists by turning to fear while promoting spectacularized panicked rage that channels anger into the wrong places. As David Dillard-Wright observes, Trump

> drowns the listener in fear and then reaches out a helping hand from the threat that he, himself, has conjured. This verbal waterboarding breaks down the Trump fan into a panicked rage and then channels that fear and anger into the pretend solution of a giant wall or jailing Hillary Clinton, which not incidentally, also places Trump at the center of power and control over his fans' lives. Fear actually short-circuits rational thought and gets the rally-goer to accept the strongman as the only way to avoid the perceived threat.[4]

In trying to understand how the "protean elements of totalitarianism are still with us, particularly loneliness as the normal register of social life,"[5] I have recently returned to reading Leo Lowenthal, particularly his insightful essay, "Terror's Atomization of Man," first published in *Commentary* in January 1, 1946, and reprinted in his book, *False Prophets: Studies in Authoritarianism*.[6] Lowenthal writes about the atomization of human beings under a state of fear that approximates a kind of updated fascist terror. What he understood with great insight, even in 1946, is that democracy cannot exist without the educational, political, and formative cultures and institutions that make it possible. He observed that atomized individuals are prone not only to the forces of depoliticization but also to the poisonous visions and spirit of demagogues, to discourses of hate, and to appeals that demonize and objectify the Other. What Lowenthal realized is that democracy cannot function without a collective subject.

Lowenthal is helpful in illuminating the relationship between the underlying isolation individuals feel in an age of precarity, uncertainty, and disposability, and the dark shadows of authoritarianism threatening to overcome the United States. Within this new historical conjuncture, finance capital rules, producing extremes of wealth for the 1 percent, promoting cuts to government services and defunding investments in public goods, such as public and higher education, in order to offset tax reductions for the ultra-rich and big corporations. Paul Buchheit claims rightly that these are the real terrorists in America.[7] Meanwhile, millions are plunged into either the end-station of poverty or become part of the mass incarceration state. Mass fear is normalized as violence increasingly becomes the default logic for handling social problems. In an age where everything is for sale, ethical accountability is rendered a liability and the vocabulary of empathy is viewed as a weakness, reinforced by the view that individual happiness and its endless search for instant gratification are more important than supporting the public good and embracing an obligation to care for others. Americans are now pitted against each other as a form of neoliberal fascism puts a premium on competitive cage-like relations that degrade collaboration, solidarity, and the public spheres that support such relationships.

Within neoliberal ideology, an emphasis on competition in every sphere of life promotes a winner-take-all ethos that finds its ultimate expression in the assertion that fairness has no place in a society dominated by winners and losers. As William Davies points out, competition in a market-driven social order allows a small group of winners to emerge while at the same time sorting out and condemning the vast majority of institutions, organizations, and individuals "to the status of losers."[8]

As has been made clear in the much publicized language of Donald Trump, both as a reality TV host of "The Apprentice" and as a former presidential candidate, calling someone a "loser" has little to do with them losing in the more general sense of the term. On the contrary, in a culture that trades in cruelty and divorces politics from matters of ethics and social responsibility, "loser" is now elevated to a pejorative insult that humiliates and justifies not only symbolic violence, but also (as Trump has made clear in many of his rallies and as the current president) real acts of violence waged against his critics, such as members of the movement for Black lives. As Greg Elmer and Paula Todd observe, "To lose is possible, but to be a 'loser' is the ultimate humiliation that justifies taking extreme, even immoral measures."[9] They write:

> We argue that the Trumpesque "loser" serves as a potent new political symbol, a caricature that Trump has previously deployed in his television and business careers to sidestep complex social issues and justify winning at all costs. As the commercial for his 1980s board game "Trump" enthused, "It's not whether you win or lose, but whether you win!" Indeed, in Trump's world, for some to win many more must lose, which helps explain the breath-taking embrace by some of his racist, xenophobic, and misogynist communication strategy. The more losers—delineated by Trump based on every form of "otherism"—the better the odds of victory. . . . We argue that the Trumpesque "loser" serves as a potent new political symbol, a caricature that Trump has previously deployed in his television and business careers to sidestep complex social issues and justify winning at all costs. As the commercial for his 1980s board game Trump" enthused, "It's not whether you win or lose, but whether you win!"[10]

As president of the United States, Trump has assembled an administration filled not only with incompetents, militarists, white supremacists, billionaires, and strident market-driven ideologues, he has also put into place policies driven by an apocalyptic vision of America that is as dystopian as it is dangerous. Under Trump's reign of terror, *losers* not only becomes a pejorative label that points to the terminal exclusion, social abandonment, and humiliation of those deemed other, but also marks this vulnerable and dissenting population that becomes the object of policies that reek of retribution and revenge.[11] Fear and uncertainty in an age of precarity offers the perfect mix for the rise of demagogues, but that is only part of the reason that America is descending into a neofascist state. Since the 1970s, the United States has been in the grip of a neoliberal ideology that believes that the market should shape all social relations, that profit making and consuming are the essence of citizenship, and that the social contract is a pathology. Couple these ideological beliefs with the notion that economics should drive politics, that everything should be privatized, that markets must regulate themselves, the welfare state should be dismantled, and that self-interest is the highest ideal along with the competitive attitudes it promotes and a society is created ripe for authoritarianism. The consequences of such a poisonous ideology, set of values, policies, and mode of pedagogy are hard to miss.

Money has corrupted politics at the state and national levels. Civic culture and civic literacy have been undermined paving the way for the erosion of any sense of public trust, truth, and shared citizenship. The aesthetics of vulgarity now drives the spectacle that makes up politics and degrades the culture of entertainment. The assault on public and higher education produces a new kind of stupidity in which the line between fact and fiction is blurred giving rise to the empty and deceptive slogans, fake news and post-truth. As language is emptied out of any substantive meaning, moral relativism provides support for a culture of immediacy, self-absorption, and privatization. Is it any wonder that Trump rode to victory in the presidential race, given the collapse of any commanding democratic vision in America?

Atomization fueled by a fervor for unbridled individualism produces a pathological disdain for community, public values, the public good, and the notion of the social. As democratic pressures are weakened, authoritarian societies resort to fear so as to ward off any room for ideals, visions and hope. Efforts to keep this space open are made all the more difficult by the ethically tranquilizing presence of a celebrity and commodity culture that works to depoliticize people. The realms of the political and the social imagination wither as shared responsibilities and obligations give way to an individualized society that elevates selfishness, avarice, consumption, and militaristic modes of competition as its highest organizing principles.

Under such circumstances, the foundations for a modicum of security and stability are being destroyed, with jobs being shipped overseas, social provisions destroyed, the social state hollowed out, public servants and workers under a relentless attack, students burdened with the rise of a neoliberal debt machine, and many groups considered disposable. At the same time, these acts of permanent repression are coupled with new configurations of power and militarization normalized by a neoliberal regime in which an ideology of political and economic savagery has become unaccountable; under such conditions, one dispenses with any notion of compassion and holds others individuals solely responsible for problems they face, problems over which they have no control. In this case, shared responsibilities and hopes have been replaced by the isolating logic of individual responsibility, a false notion of resiliency, and a growing resentment toward those viewed as strangers.

We live in an age of death-dealing loneliness, isolation, and militarized atomization. If you believe the popular press, loneliness is reaching epidemic proportions[12] in advanced industrial societies. A few indices include the climbing suicide rate of adolescent girls;[13] the rising deaths of working class, less-educated white men;[14] and the growing drug overdose crises raging across small towns and cities throughout America.[15] Meanwhile, many people often interact more with their cell phones, tablets, and computers than they do with embodied subjects. Disembodiment in this view is at the heart of a deeply alienating neoliberal society in which people shun in-person relationships for virtual ones. In this view, the warm glow of the computer screen can produce and reinforce a new type of alienation, isolation, and a sense of loneliness. At the same time, it is important to note that in some cases digital technologies have also enabled young people who are hyper-connected to their peers online to increase their face-to-face time by coordinating spontaneous meetups, in addition to staying connected with each other near-constantly virtually. How this dialectic plays out will in part be determined by the degree to which young people can be educated to embrace modes of agency in which a connection to other human beings, however diverse, becomes central to their understanding of the value of creating bonds of sociality. Late capitalism has become a mecca for dissolving social bonds and elevating isolation, loneliness, and an ossified view of the self to the center of American culture and the primary register of everyday life. Within this context and the deeply embedded isolation many Americans experience, Trump is a tragedy for democracy and a triumph for the financial elite and the second Gilded Age, but, as Frank Rich observes, he also, and more importantly, poses a great threat to America and that "the great task before us is to stop him from taking down with him all that remains good about America, before his reign comes to its inevitable bad end."[16]

Needless to say, however, blaming Trump alone misses the mark. Some have argued that the growing isolation and despair in American life can be laid at the door of the internet itself, which is far from a new pillar of democracy. Yet, for all of its flaws, including its undercutting of embodied relations and its acceleration of a culture of conformity, instantaneity, and speed, it has also helped forge connections, and has facilitated movement-building and provided much wider accessibility of information to millions of people. Blaming the internet is too easy. The landscape of disembodiment, celebrity culture, and flight from community exceeds the power and influence of the internet. We live in a society in which notions of dependence, compassion, mutuality, care for the other and sociality are undermined by a neoliberal ethic in which self-interest and unchecked avarice have become the central principles of one's life and a survival-of-the fittest ethic breeds a culture that at best promotes an indifference to the plight of others and at worse a disdain for the less fortunate and support for a widespread culture of cruelty. Isolated individuals do not make up a healthy democratic society.

NEW FORMS OF ALIENATION AND ISOLATION

A more theoretical language produced by Marx talked about alienation as a separation from the fruits of one's labor. While that insight is certainly truer than ever, the separation and isolation is now more extensive and governs the entirety of social life in a privatized and consumer-based society run by the demands of commerce and the financialization of everything. Isolation, privatization, and the cold logic of instrumental rationality have created a new kind of social formation and social order in which it becomes difficult to form communal bonds, deep connections, a sense of intimacy, and long-term commitments.

Neoliberalism fosters the viewing of pain and suffering as entertainment, warfare a permanent state of existence, and militarism as the most powerful force shaping masculinity. Politics has taken an exit from ethics and thus the issue of social costs is divorced from any form of intervention in the world. For example, under neoliberalism, economic activity is removed from its ethical and social consequences and takes a flight from any type of moral consideration. This is the ideological metrics of political zombies. The key word here is atomization, and it is the defining feature of neoliberal societies and the scourge of democracy.

At the heart of any type of politics wishing to challenge this flight into authoritarianism is not merely the recognition of economic structures of domination, but something more profound—a politics which points to the construction of particular identities, values, social relations, or more broadly, itself. Central to such a recognition is the fact that politics cannot exist without people investing something of themselves in the discourses, images, and representations that come at them daily. Rather than suffering alone, lured into the frenzy of hateful emotion, individuals need to be able to identify—see themselves and their daily lives—within progressive critiques of existing forms of domination and how they might address such issues not individually but collectively. This is a particularly difficult challenge today because the menace of atomization is reinforced daily not only by a coordinated neoliberal assault against any viable notion of the social but also by an authoritarian and finance-based culture that couples a rigid notion of privatization with a flight from any sense of social and moral responsibility.

The cultural apparatuses controlled by the 1 percent, including the mainstream media and entertainment industries, are the most powerful educational forces in society and they have become disimagination machines—apparatuses of mis-recognition and brutality. Collective agency is now atomized, devoid of any viable embrace of the democratic social imaginary. Consequently, domination does not merely repress through its apparatuses of terror and violence, but also—as Pierre Bourdieu argues—through the intellectual and pedagogical, which "lie on the side of belief and persuasion."[17] For instance, in an age in which the term "loser" denotes language in the service of humiliation, there is also a deeper structure of meaning that is indebted to the current fascistic embrace of "total war" and a "survival-of-the fittest" ethos in which winning and losing become the central organizing principles of a neoliberal society. As the discourse of war and excessive competition moves into the realm of the market place, consumption also serves to reward winners and debase losers based upon a fetishistic notion of consumption. Subjecting the majority of the polity to the discourse of humiliation and disdain and praise for the small number of winners who constitute the criminogenic 1 percent of the population serves to create an affective economy of misdirected rage, resentment, and retaliation, which finds its most egregious expression in the hateful and racist discourses of authoritarianism. The economic and pedagogical forces at work in the production of atomization, loneliness, and humiliation provide fertile ground for the rise of the fascistic sovereign. This was evident at the 2016 Republican National Convention when Donald Trump told his adoring crowd that "I am your voice. I alone can fix it. I will restore law and order." As Yoni Appelbaum points out in *The Atlantic*, Trump "did not appeal to prayer, or to God. He did not ask Americans to measure him against their values, or to hold him responsible for living up to them. He did not ask for their help. He asked them to place their faith in him."[18] And in doing so, he was greeted with sporadic emotional outburst that amounted to disturbing expressions of racism, hyper-nationalism and calls for lawlessness. According to Appelbaum, "When Trump said, 'I am your voice,' the delegates on the convention floor roared their approval. When he said, 'I alone can fix it,' they shouted their approbation. The crowd peppered his speech with chants of 'USA!' and 'Lock her up!' and 'Build the wall!' and 'Trump!' It booed on cue, and cheered when prompted."[19] In his inaugural address, Trump made references to America first signaling not just his support for an isolationist foreign policy, but also echoing the more ominous fascist elements of ultranationalism and a politics of disposability embraced in the 1930s by Charles Lindbergh, the anti-Semite and Nazi sympathizer.[20] More is on display in Trump's rhetoric than the fascistic celebration of the heroic leader; there is also a systemic attempt to empty politics of its democratic impulses, repress debate and dialogue, and construct an antipolitics that thrives on conflict, on an enemy/friend divide, fueled by a rhetoric of demonization, objectification, and hatred.

Under such circumstances, language becomes militarized, serving as an expression of politics in which persuasion becomes armed, wedded to the production of desires, modes of agency, and forms of identification compatible with political and economic forms of authoritarian domination. Trump's rhetoric echoes Hannah Arendt's insight that totalitarianism is produced, in part, by making human beings superfluous, ignoring their voices, and silencing them in fascistic discourses of certainty, absolutes, and unaccountability that allow no space for critical thinking and informed agency. Trump's speeches and off-the-cuff comments bear an eerie resemblance to what Arendt once called in her famous book on Adolf Eichmann "the banality of evil," which she defines as a type of thoughtlessness, the inability to think, and the disavowal of any form of self-reflection and critical inquiry.[21] For some theorists such as Richard J. Bernstein, Arendt was largely interested in understanding how ordinary people with banal motives can commit horrendous crimes and how such actions were connected making human beings superfluous as critical, thinking agents.[22] He is only partly right. Arendt connected the dethroning of the political to the emergence of a kind of antipolitics, based on the inability or reluctance of individuals to "imagine what the other person is experiencing. . . . A kind of stupidity (in which) obedience is idealized."[23]

What can be learned from the rise of the political and economic structures of domination is that they are deeply dependent upon the educative nature of a politics that cripples critical consciousness, stunts any viable notion of agency, and embraces view of war that thrives on demonization, exclusion, and the production of losers. Too many people on the left have defaulted on this enormous responsibility for recognizing the educative nature of politics and the need for appropriating the tools, if not weapons, provided by the symbolic and pedagogical for challenging various form of domination, working to change consciousness, and making education central to politics itself. Central to such a task is expanding the notion of the political to include a notion of pedagogy that would address matters of identity, consciousness, and agency. The inability to think, the elimination of institutions and public spheres that make thinking possible, and the connection between nonthinking, thoughtlessness, and the routinization of misery, human suffering, and the destruction of the eco system should be at the heart of any theory willing to address the distinctive challenges posed by the emergence of a digital age in which culture, power, and politics become more integrated and serve to reconstitute the ways in which people relate to themselves, others, and the larger world. The task of theory in the age of an overabundance of information and knowledge is not to make pedagogy an object of analysis but to understand theory as a political project of which pedagogy is central to how it understands, addresses, and shapes the world.

DONALD TRUMP'S MEDIA STRATEGY

Donald Trump plays the media because he gets all of this. His media strategy before and after his election has been aimed at erasing memory, thoughtfulness, and critical dialogue. For Trump, miseducation was the key to getting elected and for legitimating the horrendous policies he has and will continue to introduce under his presidency. The issue here is not about the existing reign of civic illiteracy, it is about the crisis of agency, the forces that produce it under late capitalism, and the failure of progressives and the left to take such a crisis seriously by working hard to address the ideological and pedagogical dimensions of struggle. All of which is necessary in order, at the very least, to get people to be able to translate private troubles into wider social issues. The latter may be the biggest political and educational challenge facing those who believe that the current political crisis was not simply about either the election of Trump, the ruling-class carnival barker, or whether or not they should have supported Clinton, the warmonger, both of whom are, in the end, different types of cheerleaders for the financial elite and big corporations.

At the same time, it is important to recognize that Trump represents the more immediate threat, especially for people of color, undocumented immigrants, Muslims, and young people. As the apotheosis of a brutal, racist, fascist expression of neoliberalism, Trump is implementing policies that threaten to eliminate twenty million people from the ranks of those insured under Obamacare, deport eleven million undocumented immigrants, and implement executive orders that resume the production of two controversial pipelines—Keystone and Dakota—while weakening regulations that would inhibit climate warming.[24] He has also promised before his election to restrict or jail dissident journalists, "withdraw U.S. from the Paris agreement on global warming, end enforcement of the voting rights act," legitimate state sanctioned torture, encourage the spread of nuclear weapons, and stack the Supreme Court with right-wing ideologues who would implement reactionary polices for the next few decades. And that is only the beginning of what would amount to a reign of terror.[25] Since elected he has carried through on his promise to withdraw from the Paris agreement and has stacked the federal courts with right wing reactionaries.

At stake here is a different type of conflict between those who believe in democracy and those who don't. The 2016 presidential election did not address the ensuing crisis, which is really a fight for the soul of democracy. One consequence will be that millions one way or another will once again bear the burden of a society that hates democracy and punishes all but the financial elite. Both candidates and the economic and political forces they represented were part of the problem and offer up different forms of domination, though Trump embodied a neofascist ethos that far exceeded the threat Clinton posed to democracy in the most immediate sense. What is crucial for progressives to recognize is that it is imperative to make clear that neoliberal economic structures register only one part of the logic of repression. The other side is the colonization of consciousness, the production of modes of agency complicity with their own oppression.

This dual register of politics, which has been highlighted by theorists extending from Hannah Arendt and Antonio Gramsci to Raymond Williams and C. Wright Mills, has a long history but has been pushed to the margins under neoliberal regimes of oppression. Once again any viable notion of collective resistance must take matters of consciousness, identity, desire, and persuasion seriously so as to speak to the underlying conditions of atomization that depoliticize and paralyze people within orbits of self-interest, greed, resentment, misdirected anger, and spiraling violence. Addressing the affective and ideological dimensions not only of neoliberalism but also of the radical imagination is crucial to waking us all up to our ability to work together, recognize the larger social and systemic structures that dominate our lives, and provide each other with the tools to translate private troubles into broader systemic issues. The power of the social does not only come together in social movements; it is also central to the educative force of a politics that embraces democratic social relations as the foundation for collective action.

Overcoming the atomization inherent in neoliberal regimes means making clear how they destroy pedagogically and politically every vestige of solidarity in the interest of amassing huge amounts of wealth and power while successfully paralyzing vast numbers of people in the depoliticizing orbits of privatization and self-interest. Of course, we see examples of movements that embrace solidarity as an act of collective resistance—most visibly, the movement for Black lives, the Women's March on Washington, D.C. demonstration, the teacher strikes, students demonstrating against gun violence, and a range of movements extending from those fighting for a decent minimum wage for workers to movements fighting to halt climate change and the possibility of a nuclear war. This is a model that needs to take on a more general political significance in which the violence of apparatuses of oppression can be connected to a politics of atomization that must be addressed as both an educational and political issue. Neoliberal precarity, austerity, and the militarization of society inflict violence not just on the body but on the psyche as well. This means that the dual crisis of economic structures must be understood as part of the crisis of memory, thinking, hope, and agency itself.

BEYOND DISIMAGINATION MACHINES

The presence of Donald Trump on the American political scene exemplifies how ignorance breeds corruption and endears a large number of people to falsehoods, venality, and carnival barking. The corruption of both the truth and politics is made all the easier since the American public has become habituated to overstimulation and lives in an ever-accelerating overflow of information and images. Experience no longer has the time to crystalize into mature and informed thought. Leon Wieseltier is right in stating that "words cannot wait for thoughts and patience [becomes] a liability."[26] Opinion outdoes reasoned and evidence-based arguments and the power of expression degenerates into a spectacle. News has become entertainment and echoes reality rather than interrogating it. Popular culture revels in the spectacles of shock and violence.[27] Universities now labor under the burden of a neoliberal regime that celebrates the corporate model made famous by McDonalds. Knowledge is now instrumentalized and standardized, collapsing the distinction between education and training. Knowledge is packaged for easy consumption resulting in curricula that resemble a fast-food menu.[28]

Many of the commanding institutions that produce and distribute ideas—from the media to higher education—have become disimagination machines, tools for legitimating ignorance, and central to the formation of an authoritarian politics that is gutting any vestige of democracy from the ideology, policies, and institutions that now shape American society. Education has lost its moral, political, and spiritual bearings just as teachers and other public servants across the country are being belittled and attacked by economic and religious fundamentalists. One consequence is that an increasing number of public spheres have become corporatized, employ a top-down authoritarian styles of power, mimic a business culture, and infantilizes the larger polity by removing the public from all forms of governance. Clearly all of these defining relations produced in a neoliberal social order have to be challenged and changed.

The rise of thoughtlessness and the inability to think has become a political epidemic and does not augur well for democracy. Americans live in a historical moment that annihilates thought. Ignorance now provides a sense of community; the brain has migrated to the dark pit of the spectacle; the only discourse that matters is about business; poverty is now viewed as a technical problem; thought chases after an emotion that can obliterate it. Donald Trump, during the Republican Party primary, declared that he liked "the uneducated"—implying that it is better that they stay ignorant than be critically engaged agents—and boasts that he doesn't read books. Fox News offers no apologies for suggesting that thinking is an act of stupidity. A culture of cruelty and a survival-of-the-fittest ethos in the United States is the new norm and one consequence is that democracy is on the verge of disappearing or has already disappeared! Where are the agents of democracy and the public spaces that offer hope in such dark times?

What role will theory play at a time when the very ability of the public's ability to translate private troubles into broader systemic issues is disappearing? What role should theory play as a pedagogy force in a time of increasing violence? What role should intellectuals, cultural workers, artists, writers, journalists, and others play as part of a broader struggle to reclaim a democratic imaginary and exercise a collective sense of civic courage? Theorists such as Antonio Gramsci, C. Wright Mills, Hannah Arendt, and Raymond Williams understood the importance of the educative force of the wider culture and how such an understanding posed a challenge to those theories that relegated pedagogy to the lower depths of theorizing. What is now clear is that pedagogy is linked not only to social change but also to the production of modes of agency and the institutions that make such change possible. Education as a political force makes us both the subjects of and subject to relations of power. The key is to expand that insight theoretically so as to make education central to politics itself as part of a larger collective effort to make radical change possible.

McMaster University (Canada)

NOTES

1. Cited in David A. Graham, "The Many Scandals of Donald Trump: A Cheat Sheet," *The Atlantic* (January 23, 2017). http://www.theatlantic.com/politics/archive/2017/01/donald-trump-scandals/474726/

2. Ibid. for an extensive list and analysis of Trump's scandals.

3. Michael D. Shear and Emmarie Huetteman, "Trump Repeats Lie About Popular Vote in Meeting With Lawmakers," *New York Times* (January 23, 2017). https://www.nytimes.com/2017/01/23/us/politics/donald-trump-congress-democrats.html

4. David Dillard-Wright, "Explaining the Cult of Trump," *AlterNet* (December 16, 2016). http://www.alternet.org/election-2016/explaining-cult-trump

5. Bill Dixon, "Totalitarianism and the Sand Storm," *Hannah Arendt Center* (February 3, 2014). http://www.hannaharendtcenter.org/?p=12466

6. Leo Lowenthal, "Atomization of Man," in *False Prophets: Studies in Authoritarianism* (New Brunswick: Transaction Books, 1987), 181–82.

7. Paul Buchheit "The Real Terrorists: The .01%," *CommonDreams* (January 11, 2016). http://www.commondreams.org/views/2016/01/11/real-terrorists-01

8. William Davies, "How 'Competitiveness' Became One of the Great Unquestioned Virtues of Contemporary Culture," Blog Post, *The London School of Economics and Political Science* (May 19, 2014). http://blogs.lse.ac.uk/politicsandpolicy/the-cult-of-competitiveness/

9. Greg Elmer and Paula Todd, "Don't Be a Loser: Or How Trump Turned the Republican Primaries into an Episode of *The Apprentice*," *Television and News Media* 17.7 (June 29, 2016): 660.

10. Elmer and Paula Todd, "Don't Be a Loser," 661.

11. Frank Rich, "Trump's Speech Gave Us America the Ugly: Don't Let It Become Prophesy," *Reader Supported News* (January 22, 2017). http://readersupportednews.org/opinion2/277-75/41524-focus-trumps-speech-gave-us-america-the-ugly-dont-let-it-become-prophesy

12. Michael Bader, "How Can We Stop America's Deadly Epidemic of Loneliness?" *AlterNet* (December 22, 2015). http://www.alternet.org/news-amp-politics/how-can-we-stop-americas-deadly-epidemic-loneliness

13. Rae Ellen Bichell, "Suicide Rates Climb In U.S., Especially Among Adolescent Girls," *NPR Org* (April 22, 2016). http://www.npr.org/sections/health-shots/2016/04/22/474888854/suicide-rates-climb-in-u-s-especially-among-adolescent-girls

14. Gina Kolatanov, "Death Rates Rising for Middle-Aged White Americans, Study Finds," *New York Times* (November 2, 2015). http://www.nytimes.com/2015/11/03/health/death-rates-rising-for-middle-aged-white-americans-study-finds.html

15. Nadja Popovich, "A Deadly Crisis: Mapping The Spread Of America's Drug Overdose Epidemic," *The Guardian* (May 25, 2016). http://www.theguardian.com/society/ng-interactive/2016/may/25/opioid-epidemic-overdose-deaths-map

16. Rich, "Trump's Speech Gave Us America the Ugly."

17. Pierre Bourdieu and Günter Grass. "The 'Progressive' Restoration: A Franco-German Dialogue," *New Left Review* 14 (March–April 2002). https://newleftreview.org/II/14/pierre-bourdieu-gunter-grass-the-progressive-restoration

18. Yoni Appelbaum, "I Alone Can Fix It," *The Atlantic* (July 21, 2016). http://www.theatlantic.com/politics/archive/2016/07/trump-rnc-speech-alone-fix-it/492557/

19. Appelbaum, "I Alone Can Fix It."

20. Lily Rothman, "The Long History Behind Donald Trump's 'America First' Foreign Policy," *Time* (March 28, 2016). http://time.com/4273812/america-first-donald-trump-history/

21. Hannah Arendt, *Eichmann in Jerusalem: A Report on the Banality of Evil* (New York: Penguin Books Classics, 2006).

22. Richard J. Bernstein, *The Abuse of Evil: The Corruption of Politics and Religion Since 9/11* (New York: Polity Press, 2005).

23. Hannah Arendt, *Hannah Arendt: The Last Interview and Other Conversations* (Brooklyn: Melville House Publishing, 2013), 50.

24. Peter Baker and Coral Davenport, "Trump Revives Keystone Pipeline Rejected by Obama," *New York Times* (January 24, 2017). https://www.nytimes.com/2017/01/24/us/politics/keystone-dakota-pipeline-trump.html?emc=edit_cn_20170125&nl=first-draft&nlid=51563793&te=1

25. Mark Kleiman, "How Much Damage Could Donald Trump Really Do, After All? *Huffington Post* (August 9, 2016). http://www.huffingtonpost.com/mark-kleiman/donald-trump-damage_b_11402038.html. Also, see Philip Bump and Aaron Blake, "Donald Trump's Dark Speech to the Republican National Convention, Annotated," *Washington Post* (July 21, 2016). https://www.washingtonpost.com/news/the-fix/wp/2016/07/21/full-text-donald-trumps-prepared-remarks-accepting-the-republican-nomination; and John Halle, "Noam Chomsky's 8-point Rationale for Voting fort the Lesser Evil Presidential Candidate," *Alter Net* (July 25, 2016). http://www.alternet.org/election-2016/noam-chomskys-8-point-rationale-voting-lesser evil-presidential-candidate.

26. Leon Wieseltier, "Among the Disrupted," *International New York Times* (January 7, 2015). http://www.nytimes.com/2015/01/18/books/review/among-the-disrupted.html?_r=0

27. Brad Evans and Henry A. Giroux, *Disposable Futures: The Seduction of Violence in the Age of the Spectacle* (San Francisco: City Lights, 2016).

28. Ulrich Beck, *Twenty Observations on a World in Turmoil* (London: Polity Press, 2010), especially, 53–59.

WORKS CITED

Applebaum, Yoni. "I Alone Can Fix it." *The Atlantic* (July 21, 2016). http://www.theatlantic.com/politics/archive/2016/07/trump-rnc-speech-alone-fix-it/492557/

Arendt, Hannah. *Eichmann in Jerusalem: A Report on the Banality of Evil* [1963]. New York: Penguin Books Classics, 2006.

Arendt, Hannah. *Hannah Arendt: The Last Interview and Other Conversations*. Brooklyn: Melville House Publishing, 2013.

Bader, Michael. "How Can We Stop America's Deadly Epidemic of Loneliness?" *AlterNet* (December 22, 2015). http://www.alternet.org/news-amp-politics/how-can-we-stop-americas-deadly-epidemic-loneliness

Baker, Peter, and Coral Davenport. "Trump Revives Keystone Pipeline Rejected by Obama." *New York Times* (January 24, 2017). https://www.nytimes.com/2017/01/24/us/politics/keystone-dakota-pipeline-trump.html?emc=edit_cn_20170125&nl=first-draft&nlid=51563793&te=1

Beck, Ulrich. *Twenty Observations on a World in Turmoil*. London: Polity Press, 2010.

Bernstein, Richard J. *The Abuse of Evil: The Corruption of Politics and Religion Since 9/11*. New York: Polity Press, 2005.

Bichell, Rae Ellen. "Suicide Rates Climb in U.S., Especially Among Adolescent Girls." *NPR.org* (April 22, 2016). http://www.npr.org/sections/health-shots/2016/04/22/474888854/suicide-rates-climb-in-u-s-especially-among-adolescent-girls

Bourdieu, Pierre, and Günter Grass. "The 'Progressive' Restoration: A Franco-German Dialogue." *New Left Review* 14 (March–April 2002). https://newleftreview.org/II/14/pierre-bourdieu-gunter-grass-the-progressive-restoration

Buchheit, Paul. "The Real Terrorists: The .01%." *Common Dreams* (January 11, 2016). http://www.commondreams.org/views/2016/01/11/real-terrorists-01

Bump, Philip, and Aaron Blake. "Donald Trump's Dark Speech to the Republican National Convention, Annotated." *Washington Post* (July 21, 2016). https://www.washingtonpost.com/news/the-fix/wp/2016/07/21/full-text-donald-trumps-prepared-remarks-accepting-the-republican-nomination

Davies, William. "How 'Competitiveness' Became One of the Great Unquestioned Virtues of Contemporary Culture." Blog Post. *The London School of Economics and Political Science.* (May 19, 2014). http://blogs.lse.ac.uk/politicsandpolicy/the-cult-of-competitiveness/

Dillard-Wright, David. "Explaining the Cult of Trump." *Alter Net* (December 16, 2016). http://www.alternet.org/election-2016/explaining-cult-trump

Dixon, Bill. "Totalitarianism and the Sand Storm." *Hannah Arendt Center* (February 3, 2014). http://www.hannaharendtcenter.org/?p=12466

Elmer, Greg, and Paula Todd. "Don't Be a Loser: Or How Trump Turned the Republican Primaries into an Episode of *The Apprentice*." *Television and News Media* 17.7 (June 29, 2016): 660–62.

Evans, Brad, and Henry A. Giroux. *Disposable Futures: The Seduction of Violence in the Age of the Spectacle.* San Francisco: City Lights, 2016.

Graham, David A. "The Many Scandals of Donald Trump: A Cheat Sheet." *The Atlantic* (January 23, 2017). http://www.theatlantic.com/politics/archive/2017/01/donald-trump-scandals/474726/

Halle, John. "Noam Chomsky's 8-point Rationale for Voting fort the Lesser Evil Presidential Candidate." *Alter Net* (July 25, 2016). http://www.alternet.org/election-2016/noam-chomskys-8-point-rationale-voting-lesser evil-presidential-candidate

Kleiman, Mark. "How Much Damage Could Donald Trump Really Do, After All?" *Huffington Post* (August 9, 2016). http://www.huffingtonpost.com/mark-kleiman/donald-trump-damage_b_11402038.html

Kolatanov, Gina. "Death Rates Rising for Middle-Aged White Americans, Study Finds." *New York Times* (November 2, 2015). http://www.nytimes.com/2015/11/03/health/death-rates-rising-for-middle-aged-white-americans-study-finds.html

Lowenthal, Leo. "Atomization of Man." In *False Prophets: Studies in Authoritarianism.* Ed. Leo Lowenthal. New Brunswick: Transaction Books, 1987. 181–82.

Popovich, Nadja. "A Deadly Crisis: Mapping the Spread of America's Drug Overdose Epidemic." *The Guardian* (May 25, 2016). http://www.theguardian.com/society/ng-interactive/2016/may/25/opioid-epidemic-overdose-deaths-map

Rich, Frank. "Trump's Speech Gave Us America the Ugly: Don't Let It Become Prophesy." *Reader Supported News* (January 22, 2017). http://readersupportednews.org/opinion2/277-75/41524-focus-trumps-speech-gave-us-america-the-ugly-dont-let-it-become-prophesy

Rothman, Lily. "The Long History behind Donald Trump's 'America First' Foreign Policy." *Time* (March 28, 2016). http://time.com/4273812/america-first-donald-trump-history/

Shear, Michael D., and Emmarie Huetteman. "Trump Repeats Lie About Popular Vote in Meeting With Lawmakers." *New York Times* (January 23, 2017). https://www.nytimes.com/2017/01/23/us/politics/donald-trump-congress-democrats.html

Wieseltier, Leon. "Among the Disrupted." In *International New York Times* (January 7, 2015). http://www.nytimes.com/2015/01/18/books/review/among-the-disrupted.html?_r=0

CHAPTER TWENTY-TWO

Identity Studies

MIKE HILL

The best way to begin thinking about "identity studies" is to focus not just on the first word in that capacious phrase but on the second one as well. This is because subjectivity, the individual, the person, and not least, those proto-democratic possibilities of selfhood that are attached to the identity question—citizenship, rights, equality, and the human being per se—are wrapped up in the history of knowledge that extends at least as far back in the West as the Enlightenment.[1] Identity and its subtending offshoots—good and bad, its power, and the possibility or even the need for claiming knowledge of one's self—began with a historical conjuncture between the rising ethical status of the private person and the political one of bringing people together in a way that corresponded to the representative state. Identity in the modern sense had a point of historical origin. Its origin was simultaneous with modernity itself: experience-based thinking and rational debate; freedom of expression, especially in the form of written text; civil society; elected government; and not least, private property and commercial exchange. The modern state as a political entity was conceived as the ethical substance of basically literate and rational people, a group of private individuals both desirous and capable of coming together in a normative way.

Jürgen Habermas thus describes a moment in late-seventeenth- and early eighteenth-century Britain where identity first began to matter in this modern, civil-society sense. In Habermas's influential account of the public sphere, the rights-bearing individual who could claim a private interest, and who, in so claiming, presumed to respect the privacy of others, challenged and eventually displaced the long-standing structures of fixed feudal hierarchies.[2] The rise of the middling orders—merchants, small entrepreneurs, and an emerging bourgeoisie—signaled the establishment of early modern capitalism in this period. Alongside the free market, wage labor, bank credit, and private property, the newly empowered individual *qua* citizen formed a decidedly critical relation to an aristocratic order about to collapse.[3] Having an identity that was one's own and also belonged to a more generic political totality was what connected the Glorious Revolution in England and the first Bill of Rights (1688), the American War of Independence (1776), and the French Revolution (1789), all as subjectively empowering Enlightenment achievements. Identity functioned first and foremost, in a socially committed sense, as a challenge to the lordly classes.

The management of individual consent that cumulatively produced a notion of something collectively coherent enough to be called society started with the idea, also revolutionary at the time, that there was a state of being—a moral, legal, and knowledge-producing entity—called the individual in the first place. For the first time, Habermas suggests, the private or domestic sphere of the conjugal patriarchal family established a basis upon which a new entity called the people could enjoy relative security of mind, body, and property.[4] Private individuals enjoyed these kinds of security, relative that is, to the retrograde lordly classes, with their improprieties and frippery, arbitrary egos, internecine blood feuds, and family lines reaching back beyond the modern state into a publicly unusable past. According to the Enlightenment blueprint of this new mutually reinforcing relationship between public and private spheres, personal interests could flow more or less freely as much at home as in town and market, even though those interests were always also subject to socially constructed standards of personal habit and decorum, and directed toward capitalist ends.

Identity was thus from the outset positioned in a double way, cordoned off from two different additional (i.e., non-private) realms that were in turn divided from each other: the domestic sphere = civil society/markets = modern nation-state. Identity existed at its most interior core, or was at least supposed to exist, in a relatively autonomous way both from your ability to win arguments against your traditionally designated social betters, and from the state's ability to grant individual families prerogatives merely by their privilege of birth. Selfhood was not supposed to be sutured to the ebb and flow of mere profit and loss (if you were modern, you married for love); and the threshold of a modern man's home was the red line over which the powers of the state were objectively forbidden to cross (my property is private, after all). This Enlightenment way of having an identity was, therefore, simultaneously personal and epistemic, as well as economic and legal, with aspirations to liberty, equality, and fraternity that resound to this day.

But the idea of having a *universal* community of *particular* identities contained a tension from the outset about sameness and difference with which Western modernity has struggled for over three hundred years. Identity at its point of historical origin meant that one was unique in one's individual capacity to reason, at least in the sense that one could (and indeed must) do so by starting with personal experience. More than that, individual experience was valued to the degree that it was available to a certain number of others in such a way that, collectively speaking, the minds of consensus-driven truth seekers could be opened to the possibility of change. An identity worth having in the Enlightenment sense meant that my will to know anything worth knowing, while based on my own thoughts and feelings about the world around me, had better be transferable to a set of identities other than mine. (The scope of that set, and the importance of generic likeness in maintaining both certain categories of peoples and of things, is given closer analysis below.) I ought to be able to express myself—and this would be confirmation enough for having a *self* to express—in a way that was convincing to rational people at large. The degree of generic likeness between identities as they were formed and readjusted through mutually respectable positions of debate—that is, the scale of that at largeness—is where the tension between particularity and universality comes in.

Nonetheless, according to identity studies' liberal origins in the eighteenth century, to care about what others experienced and thought in a way that granted them a humane ethical status was supposed to keep the balance between self and sociability from going too far one way or the other. Even Adam Smith, the most famous philosopher of modern capitalism, demanded moral sympathy between mutually self-interested parties, whether there was distributive equality between those parties or not. You ought to feel bad about the poor if you have money, which doesn't mean you shouldn't also be okay with the riches that you happen to have.[5] And you ought not to give way to taking money from others who have it, if you happen to be poor.

This willingness to debate before engaging in other forms of mass action when it comes to wealth inequalities was more difficult to make than you might think in an age replete with what the founder of scientific method, Francis Bacon, aptly called, "rebellions of the belly."[6] Historians like E. P. Thompson point out, *contra* Habermas, that the very popular (and effective) grain riot solved more disputes about poverty for a good part of the eighteenth century than socializing in a polite and deferential way with your betters did.[7] The issue of popular direct action aside, to use the words of Nancy Fraser, in the history of liberal democracy in its commercial stage, a politics of recognition was the preferable mode of behavior over a politics of redistribution.

If you accept the politics-of-recognition way of thinking and arguing (which is built into procedural democracy), if what you mean by political activity is being able to argue in a literate, informed, and civilized manner, then you have put your modern identity to good use in the form of what Habermas calls communicative reason. Everyone should have it, or at least be able to get it, some day. Intersubjectivity as a consensus-based way of thinking and of being was the end game of bringing your identity to the civil-society table, at least in the modern Enlightenment sense, and of working out what kind of ethical norms and legal policies could be agreed upon from there. One can look at the historical record to see how many and who got to do the debating, and to what effect. Here again we run into the question of *scale*: what's the number of communicative reasoners in any given formation of the so-called public, in fact? And how to move in a politically coherent way from the messy (because both large and categorically complicated) question of numbers to the supposedly more stable (because smaller and generically abstract) one of representation? Putting those questions to the side for a moment, it would be a mistake to think that the ethical and political power of identity—whatever paradoxes and hypocrisies happen to turn up—was invented as a static or immutable affair. As a point of historical record, being one's self was never meant to be something separate from engaging with another. Having an identity never meant being impervious to the proximity of other identities—with an indomitable emphasis on the plural—however that plurality was reasoned about (or reasoned away).

It's no wonder then with this kind of ambivalence hardwired to identity studies from the beginning that one particular kind of study—the literary kind—holds pride of place. In fact, literature, in the way it's traditionally understood as a canon of deeply private writing meant to be debated as a public concern, emerged at exactly the same time as the original identity/sociability relation. Raymond Williams, among others, has documented the etymology of the word literature before the Enlightenment to mean anything written at all, and not just the shared deeply personal stuff.[8] Writers before modernity were not necessarily authors in the sense later given to both terms—Shakespeare never published, let alone signed his work—but were more like anonymous artist-technicians, scriveners, IT workers of their day, or creative geniuses without the need to put their creativity in such an individuated and subjectivist manner. The takeoff of to literary studies in the sense we know it now helped make identity possible and, of course, enabled—or better, demanded, and even enforced—the study of identity not just in the deepest but also the widest, most publicly debatable, ways.

Benedict Anderson thus uses the phrase "imagined community" in his history of identity, particularly national identity, with an emphasis not only on the term *imagination* but also, crucially, on the determining role that print-based media played in making identity at once a personal issue and one of social organization.[9] He uses the term *imagined* in the famous phrase not to play down the *real* effects of coming together by artificial means, but instead, to play up the importance of the artifices—*writing* in this case—that we've used since the Enlightenment to make *community* possible in the first place.

The ability to communicate is therefore to *commune* in a specific sense, as media ecologists like Walter Ong and Marshall McLuhan would have it.[10] The *message* that is the *media*—to twist McLuhan's famous phrase—is this: the tools we use to make knowledge have a lot to do with not only the content of that knowledge but also (a) the ways in which we think of ourselves in relation to each other; and (b) the boundaries of scale that we give to that larger (but still bounded) social totality. The intersubjectively inspired state of being, *apropos* Habermas, is both fashioned and maintained by a specific form of media technology that was original to modern ways of producing and sharing knowledge. So identity studies became possible at the same historical moment when private reading went public in an unprecedented way. The ubiquity of print following the lapse of the Licensing Act in England in 1695—thanks to movable type, steam-driven presses, cheap ink and paper, dissenting academies that promoted independent (non-Anglican) debate over formerly inaccessible (because untranslated) texts, coffee houses, the leisure time acquired by an emerging middle-class who could afford to buy (or rent) books—was part of a revolutionary media change that in turn *mediated* a modern sense of self.[11] The idea that an identity could and should be had, and that identities put together comprised an informed, reasonable, and not least, a governable (and governing) collective political group, depended on a sense of interiority whose psychic contours were above all conditioned by writing.

Thus by the way of the first serial magazines and public papers, which appeared in the early decades of the eighteenth century, individuals found out about *news*. It was knowledge on a larger scale, relative to the coterie productions of the court. It was public information, greater both in the scope of what it covered and for how many and whom. More important, even than the invention of news, given greater popularity and the high level of contention you could find there, the critical journal now sorted plays, novels, and museums into experiences of personal pleasure that accorded (or failed to accord) with the standards of taste. The new circulating libraries brought novels—above all other print matter—to provincial country villages where even servants—above all women servants—read them for better or worse. Satirical tracts and political broadsheets could be thought to hold the Lords in check. Identities could be discovered, shared, and reconfigured, because print collated and conditioned private experience in a publicly oriented way.

Notably, for both Habermas and Anderson, a print-mediated sense of identity depended largely on a modern rendering of the experience of time. If print is to manifest a sense of self in a way that can be interchanged with other selves—identity, en masse, or audience-oriented subjectivity—then experience within one moment must be transferable over time to a different moment for some other person someplace else. In this sense, identity studies at the onset introduced a third layer of complexity to the first two. If complexity number one is the matter of *category* (who am I and in what relation to others?), and complexity number two is the matter of *scale* (how many others are there and how can I know?), then the complexity called *time* completes identity studies' philosophical triad. For an experience to matter to anybody except the person having one, the event just encountered must be presumed to be not only re-collectable *in* time (in a synchronic way), but also repeatable to others *over* time (in a diachronic way) as well.

Anderson's interest in the serial publication and the invention of newspapers as audience-oriented *written* recollection is therefore an equally technical, social, and psychological concern. He argues that linking writing to time in the literal sense of having dates attached to publication fosters serial thinking as a matter of personal and social habit. News is thus important in two *temporally* oriented ways: first, serial thinking fosters the continuity between moments in the sense of connecting past and present, cause and effect. Yesterday's war will affect today's markets; what happens over there in some distant land will determine what is likely to happen here; the advice column's suggestion might be just as relevant to her as to me; this ship has set sail and my shares may be profitable; these shoes are in season; and so on and so forth. Less trivially, this way of thinking about the event as credibly repeatable is what's behind the Enlightenment's biggest contribution: scientific method. Bacon legitimated rebellions of the belly not aside from but part and parcel with the idea that you must not ignore the connection between the material cause of unrest and its social manifestation. Second, the serial nature of the periodical fosters shared time according to specific (and usually undisclosed) principles of *selection*. You could think about this principle of selection as a matter of scientific control, or in the semiotician's terms, after Ferdinand de Saussure, of delimitation.[12] The literary term for category works as well. Newspapers—really, all writing to the extent that it conforms to a particular *genre*—cull events from an infinite mass of happenings that take place at any one moment and at any one place. It's just that a relatively infinitesimal number of events matter enough to be preserved by whatever genre is doing the work of classification, for whom, and to what ends.

Anderson thus uses the term *empty homogenous time*, which resonates with our modern sense of simultaneity, to express the collation of events according to the principles of printed news.[13] By this term he means to emphasize a condition of thinking according to the standardizing power of both calendar and clock. Anderson proposes to study the measurement of time as it provides a certain *heuristic*, a way of making local knowledge and experiences accountable on a larger scale that is monitored by society and state. Thus, planned temporal coincidence is by definition time controlled by somebody other than you alone. This is the most crucial step toward conceiving of time in the modern sense as a problem of productivity and management: enjoy yourself, but do so as directed by doctors, clergy, or critics; be punctual; work for wages and save money for later; demarcate labor from what gives you joy. And to you readers—you novel readers, especially—make sure to spend your so-called free time (if you are going to risk reading at all) doing so in a morally careful and selective way that also accords with good taste. Anderson uses the term *print capitalism* in tandem with imagined communities to emphasize the relationship between national identity and the preparation of selfhood for capitalist divisions of labor.

To entice you to your leisure, wisely or not, to divide it absolutely from the labor you are trying to sell, Habermas reminds us, was the province, above all other kinds of writing, of the early modern novel. What the middling and lower sorts were reading in their free time—that is, in the hours not harnessed to the implicitly *un*-free hours connected to their labor—was the Enlightenment's most prodigious genre: long-form fiction. Novels were being written and read in this period in remarkably higher numbers than any other forms of print media.[14] As Habermas says, psychological realism, the preferred feature of this morally reinforcing genre, meant by definition a thorough purging of the morally un-enforcing features of the earlier genre of romance. The improbable stories such as those revolving around court intrigue, green giants, knight errands, ghosts, promiscuous Monks, and the like were warned against in advance of the fictional representation of socially respectable personal behavior that pertained especially to the sexual safety of women, the sanctity of family, and the loyalty of servants.

When the *newly* conceived general reader was doing private reading in her *newly* public way, she held a mirror to herself, as Habermas says. This was especially true of the epistolary novel, which was among the most popular writing of the first truly popular kind of book in Western history. In exactly the manner of Anderson's cultivation of homogenous time as a consequence of the newspaper, for Habermas, having an identity that could be squared with others in a sociably suitable way depended on what he calls achieving a state of trans-temporal continuity. If your experience could be mirrored by a novel, and that mirroring could be mirrored at any time in the future for other people in more or less the same way, then you could be assured, at least in theory, that your identity was both *particular* enough to claim as yours, and *universal* enough to matter in a publicly relevant way.

But to ask the question already posed: how *universal* was universal, as one looks at the historical record? In the Enlightenment as today, empirical realities belie the libratory intent of discourse based strictly on identity's terms, even when identity exists in an audience-oriented way. In its *normative* capacity, subjectivity, even as it was intertwined with other consensus-minded subjects, failed to achieve the intended result of equality, that is, equality in the *distributive* sense.

In point of fact, the vast majority of identities under the British Empire during the Enlightenment did not enjoy the freedom of expression, the security of self, of money, and of property—let alone access to the literary public sphere that might get her these things—that the new, masculine, and propertied bourgeoisie did. The majority did not enjoy these things, though the work that they did (paid work, but also unpaid), which was as often extracted with violence as done so voluntarily, was essential to the production of freedoms enjoyed by a relative few. In that sense, the middle class was *middle* in a very lopsided way. It existed between the dwindling aristocratic classes on the one side; and, more dangerously, on the other side, the more numerous classes of peasants, laborers, slaves, and servants, whose activities gave individual freedom its contradictory charge.

In that sense, the commercially grounded conception of the human being per se began by being available to a group of people that was still too few in number, never reaching, as Habermas concedes, the intended fullness that peoplehood in theory had promised. The majority of British subjects and borderline subjects—commoners, masses, multitudes, the vulgar, there are lots of eighteenth-century terms for non- or insufficiently individuated groups—did not read during the Enlightenment. That same majority hardly had time for matters beyond the belly, which is not to say the lower orders were passive or never had fun. The matter of wanting or having an identity excluded most people under British rule during the time it was invented. This was true not only in the original conception of intersubjectivity but also, Habermas admits, after that blissful moment of Enlightenment potential had passed. Colonialism, slavery, genocide, imperialist domination of every sort and stripe, coincided with the commercial degradation of the press in the nineteenth century; and this coincided in turn with the perversion of identity-based discourse now conceived along medico-normative—racist, sexist—and other biologically essentialist lines.

Thus, counter to Habermas's liberal ideal, the relationship between the public and private spheres, the space of civil society itself, originated as a set of ideological relations. Sociability, among other things, adjoined identity to property, and to new forms of wealth accumulation and division, in spite of the suspension of lordly status and modernity's ethical gains. More dubious still, civility was used to the make disparities between rich and poor both legally enforceable and morally right. In this sense, identity gave over to what Louis Althusser calls interpellation on behalf of the dominant classes.[15] He means by this a way of identifying *and* being identified—like the police yelling: "Hey, You!"—a moment in which the individual self being hailed *as a self* reinforces a system of power that doesn't work on the majority's behalf. The normative goals of procedural democracy, to again evoke Foucault, may turn out in it historical effects to be so much discipline in disguise.[16] Intersubjectivity turns here into a kind of atomism by commercial default.

Habermas concedes that identity, given its commercially inflected origins and its less-than-equitable outcomes, is an ideological construct. Yet he also insists that the mediated nature of private experience for public ends means that subjectivity must be *more than* just ideology. The significance of his phrase *more than* becomes clear once you remember that identity studies was not, in the Enlightenment sense anyway, supposed to be a closed system, even though it was also always haunted by the pressure of large numbers. Self and other may *or may not* be brought fully to square. The issue is whether or not the gap between identity and otherness that may be opened up by non-civil-society activities is regarded as occasionally legitimate or something to be repressed at all costs. Their conflict can be traced to the power of collectivities other than civil-society ones (e.g., the mass demonstration, political theater, civil disobedience, the grain riot). The subject may *or may not* be adequated to its object, to again recall the language of Althusser, according to this way of thinking about the agency of masses. Not only can there be resistance within identification, identities can open up in surprising and not altogether self-consciously transparent ways. The public sphere must in principle be *open* to any and all comers as long as, Habermas warns, they are rational. Against the presumption that it was every fully open, and contrary to the idea that the public sphere operates exclusively by the dictates of reason, identity studies in the wake of Enlightenment begins to gain traction.

So identity is historically prefigured with all sorts of dangers and doubts. As ethically and legally worthwhile as it was to have an identity in the Enlightenment, having one not only depended on other people having one too but also required the exclusion of a whole lot others whose identities were a more nettlesome affair. There is in the history of identity as much *repulsion* as *attraction* to the other, to put the matter in psychoanalytical terms. As Jacques Lacan would put it in his theory of the mirror phase, that *frisson* of recognition we see in our reflection as a child (he says at about six months old) has both alienation and desire locked within it.[17] When we form an identity, he says, we do so at our peril in a binaristic way, opposing the self who is emerging as we mature to the mere opposite of us, otherness as a kind of inverted self-sameness. In the mirror phase there is me who is physically me on the one hand, and on the other, that reflection who is both not really me but is me in some unstable representative sense (he calls this the imago). In such a way, we both recognize ourselves in that mirror and *mis*-recognize ourselves at the same time. The element of misrecognition, which is counter to intersubjectivity in the consensus-seeking way, is not assessable exclusively by way of rational debate, at least not without a lot of affective indirection leaking in. It is, rather, more an affair of what Lacan calls libidinal dynamism: a process of identification that involves desire, ambivalence, and affect.

So the nature of the real in this Lacanian sense is hardly reducible to what's knowable as communicative reason alone. That self/other binary we get during the mirror phase is unstable. This is because as we move through our lives, as we enter history, Lacan says, as we go around trying to adequate the others we meet into some version of our selves, we're bound to run into the kind of drama he calls primordial discord. Selves depend on others, but in an irreducible way such that the other signifies some absent version of myself that is beyond the binary reduction of the other to me. And it's this irreducibility of the other-as-plural that Lacan calls the unconscious. I am myself but my identity is never wholly mine because it is haunted by a double that is not adequately reducible to a simple one-or-the-other kind of schema.

You can see how this theory of identity both connects to Habermas on the ideology question and diverges from it. Psychoanalysis and procedural liberalism both run counter to the idea that the self is autonomous from the other. Both accord with the notion that identity is interconnected to other identities and never complete on its own; but, *pace* Habermas, for Lacan, the *more than* of ideology manifests itself ways beyond what I think I know, even intersubjectivity. Ideology is at work where reason means unconsciousness. The Lacanian *real* is another way of saying we are always *more*—and other—than ourselves, even, perhaps especially, in our most intimate forms of self-expression, which include art as much as dreaming. In that sense, the opposite of identity is not sameness, but plurality, and from there the *masses*, over and beyond the *public*, offer the possibility of personal and political expression that is latent, not known to the self entirely, and waiting to achieve an undiscovered form through channels that identity cannot control in an ideal way. Frederic Jameson makes this point with the term *political unconscious*. Theorists like Gilles Deleuze, Antonio Negri and Michael Hardt, Étienne Balibar, Warren Montag, and a host of materialist feminist writers, like Judith Butler, affirm the agency of the *multitude* as the public sphere's silent partner and historical rival. They embrace the effects of social movements alongside epistemological ones. By doing so they propose to bring to the table of identity studies both the knowable and the unknown features of who one is or thinks one is; and therefore, they admit the affective aspects of shared selfhood as much the rational ones.

Theoretical development after the Enlightenment—or at least, traditional descriptions of it like those that overlap with an activist tradition—begin to see the establishment of identity-studies departments in academic institutions in the 1960s. Following the civil rights period in the United States, and concurrent with the expansion of public universities during the decades after the G.I. Bill, student leaders used various forms of mass action to push the question of university-wide multicultural requirements as well as the first black, Latino, and women's studies departments. In less than a generation, by the 1970s, there existed hundreds of such programs. But the questions already enumerated as inherent to the rise of identity studies in its historical setting did not disappear as a result. The keywords for the kind of liberal multiculturalism that dominated the academy within separate institutional enclaves—diversity, tolerance, and not least, the word *culture* itself—belied the transformative potential of identity studies to address issues of distributive justice according to leftist critics of identity studies in its professional form.

Thus in displacing WASP (viz., White Anglo-Saxon Protestant) homogeneity, Cornel West also warns against the polarization of blackness as merely the fixed opposite of white. In her notion of American Africanism, Toni Morrison similarly avoids the romanticization of Blackness that exists when one cordons off one literary canon from the other, as if American literature did not have the black experience at its very core.

The idea of separate groups (of color) lining up as commonly minor in relation to a supposedly stable majoritarian (white) category of people misses a twofold set of realities that were the same ones glossed over by liberal idealism in its originally British, male, and propertied sense: (a) the so-called majority called white was never really coherent or major in the numerical sense at all. It was a socially constructed abstraction designed to represent a false notion of universality in the interests of the few who were themselves divided by class and other divisions (Irish, Scottish, Welsh, etc.). Whiteness was and is a historical fiction—a lie—as James Baldwin famously said; therefore, (b) if the center by which marginality is supposed to be measured as the opposite of white is itself not really white at all, then the coherence of marginalized identities in relation to the center and each other must be sorted out in another way than being just univocally abstracted from so-called majority experience.

Black women activists and critics drew attention to this problem of whiteness and its correlated problems for identity studies in particularly compelling ways as third-wave feminism came to the fore in the 1980s. Writers such as Robin Morgan, Marilyn Frye, Toni Cade Bambara, Cherie Moraga, Gloria Anzaldúa, and groups of thinkers on identity studies around the Combahee River Collective were among the first to pursue the whiteness problem in a sustained and critical way.[18] By doing so, they dismissed [or critiqued] as misguided the idea that identity on its own, as marked by difference in overly general terms (e.g., woman, white, and straight), could be enough to challenge the status quo on its own terms in relation to specifically capitalist forms of patriarchy was misguided. It was misguided for the same reason identity study in its ideal liberal form was misguided from the very beginning. The moving together of sexuality and gender, along with race, was innovative in that these scholars refused to overlook the idea of margins within margins, something that could be focused on by critiquing the concept of whiteness attached to feminism in earlier iterations. But it was also true to a history of modernity, more or less forgotten, where identity studies was originally burdened with the (subjectively minded) inability of the politics of recognition to fulfill the (materially minded) obligations of redistribution.

For critics of whiteness who put labor and the divisions of wealth at the center of identity studies, which include the labor historians David Roediger, Theodore Allen, and Noel Ignatiev, the study of racial categorization should not be divorced from the larger critique of capitalist relations of inequality, whether in their liberal or neoliberal form.[19] The consequence of relativizing the idea of earlier, white, and heterosexual feminism, in a way that highlighted both the oppressive nature of patriarchy to marginalize women and the ways white women—so marginalized—nonetheless enjoyed privileges unique to the lie of whiteness, posits the need to rethink identity studies within the context of labor and the accumulation of wealth. And this need was there from the onset. What the entry of whiteness has opened up within the identity-studies domain reintroduces the *more than* conundrum, marked but incompletely analyzed by Habermas, which is at the core of modernity itself.

In postcolonial studies, the division between colonizer and colonized is theorized in a similarly innovative and forceful way. It should be regarded as significant that the issue of complexity, particularly, of the self-other equation rendered too simply along the lines of a white-not-white binary, goes back to the issue of time, category, and scale, noted with the link between identity and the Enlightenment. The freedoms promised to modern subjectivity at its inception depended on the un-freedom of a vast and diverse majority of—mostly colonized—others. No rise of the British middle class, in other words, without those highly profitable Jamaican sugar plantations. In the sense that master and slave are joined, to repeat a phrase from Hegel, but without the happy synthesis of the two as mere inversions of each other, identity and homogeneity were never really very far from multiplicity and difference. This is true through a postcolonial theoretical template even if it is something traditional renderings of modernity tend to cover up.

Thus Edward Said critiques the separatist politics of nationalism in favor of what he calls worldliness. By this he means to place identity in a global context—another example of an increase in scale—where my relation to others, and others to me, comprises a mixed and enormous variety of traditions and situations. Similarly, in the colonial context, James Clifford remarks upon the creative interpenetration between cultures, which leaves room for critical appropriation on the side of the colonized. To mobilize this variety on behalf of anti-colonialist resistance forbids the glorification of victimhood. In the first instance, Said and Clifford's theory of identity as a trans-individual composite of local, historical, and geological factors that exist on the world scale deconsecrates Eurocentrism. In the second, trans-individualism as such jettisons essentialist versions of colonial marginality.

When Gayatri Spivak famously asks whether or not the subaltern can speak, it's not only *not* a yes-or-no response, but also the fact that the simple binary that marks the opposition between a yes and a no is apposite to postcolonial studies' rejection of identity as reducible to the self = other dualism. There is a certain strand of deconstruction that says the same about language: no reduction of the relationship between word and object, sign and signified, is absolute or doesn't in turn refer by way of a sublimated logic to *any number* of other word = object arrangements. To put this in identity's terms, while difference may be (falsely) presumed absent in the identification process, that absence is generative of identity itself.

The exclusion of the other therefore also leaves a trace. In that sense, a *critical* encounter between who I think I *am* and who I say I am *not* is never fully cordoned off from my experience. It is rather merely differed, and dependent on some place and time that might surprise me one day. The tools of irony, mimicry, and other ways of disrupting what Homi K. Bhabha calls the synchronic self-presence of the colonialist mindset become crucial here, the way the notion of a coherent past of whiteness breaks with a future no white person can know and stay white. You can see here how the issue of temporality adjoins to the ones of category and scale, modernity's tripartite theoretical conundrum, when it comes to identity studies. Johannes Fabian thus insists that we focus on the other insofar as that process necessarily involves a disruption and reorientation of the experience of time. He uses the phrase *allo-chronic discourse*—literally, language that brings *another* time—to emphasize that state of *frisson*, of recognition and misrecognition, that comes about when I realize on behalf of a greater and more equitable totality that I am partly other to myself.

But even this admission of otherness on the global scale of postcolonial studies approaches to identity studies is limited by the very concept it means to open up: the human being per se as an ontological category. To say so is to beg a series of questions that pushes against the salience of humanity as biologically separate both from the world itself and the technology we not only use but also are starting to make part of our identities in the literal sense. This is an other-than-worldly turn, beyond Said's worldliness, one where the world *others* humanity, where the body gives over in some measure to the machine, and where objects take on a vitality that interpenetrate the *whole* biological and geophysical—rather than *merely* human—world.

Thus Donna Haraway's posthumanist turn in favor of the libratory potential of the cyborg posits a hybrid of machine and organism that counters the biological determinist ideology of race and gender. She does this by dispersing such categories along a spectrum that runs between physical and technological domains as with, for example, the microprocessor implant, brain machine interface, and like manifestations of command and control systems that originate in the cybernetic theory of Norbert Weiner. As such, human, animal, and machine are commonly linked as computational—rather than linguistically—based entities, what Wolfgang Ernst regards as non- or non-reductively discursive entities. As in the discipline of neuro-ontology, which established categories between and within the human species that are neither racial- or gender-based, life manifests itself among an open field of *mathematizable* things. From the print-based notion of the modern subject then, where otherness is manifest either in the form of intersubjective consensus or, in a more occulted manner, in the depths of the human unconscious, posthumanism takes identity studies in the direction of what Quentin Meillassoux refers to as a mathematical absolute.

If the world of things and people can be adjoined by data-dependent technologies like computers—think for example, of the common element of frequency that exists for the radio as well as the brain—then the idea of the human subject reaches its historical endpoint.

But preference for thing theory over humanistic discourse also marks for some a point of historical continuation. Identity studies is no longer limited, speculative realists argue, by the boundaries of co-relational thinking between the subject knowing the world and the world to be known. Rather, identity is of and in the world, and to the far-reaching extent that the category of being called humanity is merely a convenient—and inadequate—way of maintaining a false sense of separation between subjects and objects, well beyond the merely human realm that separates between other identities and mine. When Bruno Latour insists that we have never been modern, he means to overturn a bad reading of the Enlightenment where the human being per se is wrongly assumed to achieve dominance over the reality of an *archaic* physical universe of which identities and people are an infinitesimally small part. Object ontology thus moves the theoretical triad of identity studies—time, category, and scale—to a point of extremity where identity itself begins to *lose* its traditional powers. Then again, identity *gains* in the place of this loss a set of challenges that Latour would say were central to modernity in the first place, challenges that humanism in its least capacious forms worked to cover up. Among the categories of identity we ascribe to the Enlightenment, the divide between the world of things (Latour calls this *nature*) and the world of people (Latour calls this *culture*) has for too long limited a fuller realization of the countless meandering and practical arrangements that move between, within, and beyond the two. But rather than thinking of the posthuman turn as break from modernity, the re-embedding of humanity within the physical world should be thought about as a return to a version of modernity we never fully had.

University at Albany, SUNY (United States)

NOTES

1. Definitions, critiques, defenses, and qualifications of the Enlightenment are as old as the period itself, but nobody contends the significance of the early modern period (late seventeenth through the eighteenth centuries) as a crucial moment of change in all aspects of Western society: moral, aesthetic, and economic. A locus classicus for understanding the Enlightenment is Immanuel Kant, "An Answer to the Question: 'What is Enlightenment?'," in *Political Writings*, ed. H. S. Reiss (Cambridge: Cambridge University Press, 1991), 42–60. In response, see Theodore Adorno and Max Horkheimer, *Dialectic of Enlightenment*, trans. John Cumming (New York: Herder & Herder, 1972); Clifford Siskin and William Warner, *This is Enlightenment* (Chicago: University of Chicago Press, 2010); and Mike Hill and Warren Montag, *Masses, Classes, and the Public Sphere* (London: Verso, 2001) to name a few contemporary thinkers.

2. Jürgen Habermas's *The Structural Transformation of the Public Sphere* (Baltimore: MIT, 1989), provides the basic blueprint of the advance of Western bourgeoisie society. This book has had remarkable staying power given its original publication (in German) in 1962, and

translation (into English) in 1989. Responses to Haberamas range from the defensive, to various materialists and feminist critiques. In addition to those mentioned above, see Sheyla Benhabib, *Another Cosmopolitanism* (Oxford: Oxford University Press, 2008); Nancy Fraser, *Trans-nationalizing the Public Sphere* (London: Polity Books, 2014); and Bruce Robbins, ed., *The Phantom Public Sphere* (Minneapolis: University of Minnesota Press, 1993).

3. On the origins of a co-equivalence between individuality in the political, legal, and morally normative way, and private property imperative, see Thomas Hobbes, *Leviathan* (New York: Penguin, 1982); and John Locke, *Some Thoughts Concerning Education and Of the Conduct of Understanding* (Indianapolis: Hackett Classics, 1996).

4. For a critique of the division of masculine and feminine genders as historically concurrent with the division between the public and private spheres, see Nancy Armstrong, *Desire and Domestic Fiction: A Political History of the Novel* (Oxford: Oxford University Press, 1990).

5. It must be noted that Adam Smith, though regarded after the nineteenth century as a political economist, lectured broadly in what today we would call the humanities, as in moral philosophy, epistemology, history, and the fine arts. In this sense, the version of Smith that for a long time determined who and what could be said about his work was an effect until recently of institutional habit disciplinary blindness. See Adam Smith, *The Theory of Moral Sentiments* (New York: Penguin, 2010). For a critical account of Jupiter's "invisible hand," see Mike Hill and Warren Montag, *The Other Adam Smith* (Palo Alto: Stanford University Press, 2015).

6. It is important to remember that the first modern Western scientists were less than sanguine about the ability of self-interest alone to distribute economic wealth in an equitable, and therefore socially stable, way. Hobbes's fear of the "multitude" thus runs consistently through contemporary thinkers ranging from Bacon and Locke, to Kant and Smith, as noted above. On "rebellions of the belly," see Francis Bacon, "Of Sedition and Troubles," in *Major Works Including New Atlantis and the Essays* (Oxford: Oxford World Classics, 1998), 367. For an affirmation of the multitude, *contra* Hobbes et al., see Étienne Balibar, *Masses, Classes, Ideas: Studies on Politics and Philosophy Before and After Marx* (New York: Routledge, 1994); and Michael Hardt and Antonio Negri, *Multitude: War and Democracy in the Age of Empire* (New York: Penguin, 2005).

7. A whole movement of New Left writing, which was later subsumed within the emerging discipline of cultural studies, emerged from Thompson's legitimation of "riot," the agency of the lower orders to effect change outside social and juridical norms. See originally, E. P. Thompson, *The Making of the English Working Class* (New York: Vintage, 1996); and *Customs in Common* (New York: The New Press, 1993).

8. On the historical specificity of the term and the institution of Literature, see Raymond Williams, *Writing in Society* (London: Verso, 1985). Like Thompson, Williams was a member of the New Left and reluctant founding father of the cultural studies movement.

9. For a useful read alongside Habermas and as critical rejoinder to him, see Benedict Anderson, *Imagined Communities: Reflections on the Origins and Spread of Nationalism* (London: Verso, 2016). Whereas Habermas wishes to hold on to the unfinished project of the Enlightenment as the communicative ideal of procedural liberalism, Anderson works within an alternate materialist tradition, and focuses as well on issues of capitalist accumulation, and especially, the relationship between modern subjectivity, print technology, and nationalism.

10. See Marshal McLuhan, *The Gutenberg Galaxy* (Toronto: University of Toronto Press, 2014); and especially, Walter Ong, *An Ong Reader: Challenges for Further Inquiry*, eds. Thomas J. Farrell and Paul A. Soulcup (Cresskil: Hampton Press, 2002). Ong usefully revises the way in which traditional media history divides the history of print technology from other—namely computational—media problems.

11. For an empirical account of the history of print technology as the dominant media for the early modern period, see Alvin Kernan, *Samuel Johnson and the Impact of Print* (Princeton: University Press, 1989); and William St. Clair, *The Reading Nation in the Romantic Period* (Cambridge: Cambridge University Press, 2007).

12. On the term delimitation as it originates in linguistic theory, Saussure, *Course in General Linguistics* [1916], eds. Charles Bally and Albert Sechehaye, trans. W. Baskin (Glasgow: Fontana/Collins, 1977).

13. On the crucial relationship between temporal experience and identity formation in addition to Anderson and Habermas, as noted above, see Johannes Fabian, *Time and the Other: How Anthropology Makes its Object* (New York: Columbia University Press, 2002).

14. A full list of scholarship on the historical prominence of the early novel and its predominate role in modern identity formation would be too long to provide here. For a *locus classicus*, see Ian Watt, *The Rise of the Novel: Studies in Defoe, Richardson, and Fielding* (Berkeley: University of California Press, 1957); a more recent mainstay is Michael McKeon's *The Origins of the English Novel, 1600-1740* (Baltimore: Johns Hopkins University Press, 1987). For a range of writing on the topic, see Diedre Lynch and William Beatty Warner, eds., *Cultural Institutions of the Novel* (Durham: Duke University Press, 1996).

15. Althusser's writing on ideology must be considered beyond the flat reductions of "ideology" = "false consciousness" that are too often attributed to him. See the long-form version of the more famous "Ideology" essay, *On the Reproduction of Capital: Ideology and Ideological State Apparatuses* (London: Verso, 2014); and, for an appropriately nuanced reading of Althusser, see Warren Montag, *Althusser and His Contemporaries: Philosophy's Perpetual War* (Durham: Duke University Press, 2013).

16. See Michel Foucault, *Discipline and Punish: The Birth of the Prison*, trans. Alan Sheridan (New York: Vintage Books, 1995). This book provides the architectural analogue for the production of modern identity, which Foucault famously calls, after Bentham, "the Panoption."

17. Jacques Lacan's theorization of otherness as a matter of both desire and repudiation informs a great deal of more recent theory on identity, especially within queer and performative orientations to the issue. See Lacan, *Formations of the Unconscious: The Seminar of Jacques Lacan*, Book 5 (London: Polity Books, 2017); and Judith Butler, *The Psychic Life of Power: Theories in Subjection* (Palo Alto: Stanford University Press, 1997).

18. Combahee River Collective, "Combahee River Statement," in *Feminism in Our Time: The Essential Writings, World War II to the Present*, ed. Miriam Schneir (New York. Vintage Books, 1994).

19. Further, on unexamined whiteness as a fading historical fiction, see Theodore Allen, *The Invention of the White Race*, vols. 1 and 2 (London: Verso, 2012); Ruth Frankenberg, *White Women. Race Matters: The Social Construction of Whiteness* (Minneapolis: University of Minnesota Press, 1993); Mike Hill, *After Whiteness: Unmaking an American Majority* (New York: New York University Press, 2004); Mike Hill, *Whiteness: A Critical Reader* (New York, New York University Press, 1997); and David Roediger, *The Wages of Whiteness: Race and the Making of the American Working Class* (London: Verso, 2007).

WORKS CITED

Adorno, Theodore, and Max Horkheimer. *Dialectic of Enlightenment* [1944/1947]. Trans. John Cumming. New York: Herder & Herder, 1972.

Allen, Theodore. *The Invention of the White Race*, vols. 1 and 2. London: Verso, 2012.

Althusser, Louis. *On the Reproduction of Capitalism: Ideology and Ideological State Apparatuses* [1995]. Trans. G. M. Goshgarian. New York: Verso, 2014.

Anderson, Benedict. *Imagined Communities: Reflections on the Origins and Spread of Nationalism*. London: Verso, 2016.

Anzaldúa, Gloria. *Borderlands/La Frontera: The New Mestiza*. San Francisco: Aunt Lute Books, 1987.

Armstrong, Nancy. *Desire and Domestic Fiction: A Political History of the Novel*. Oxford: Oxford University Press, 1990.

Bacon, Francis. "Of Sedition and Troubles." In *Major Works Including New Atlantis and the Essays*. Ed. Brian Vickers. Oxford: Oxford World Classics, 1998. 366–71.

Baldwin, James. *Notes of a Native Son* [1955]. Boston: Beacon Press, 1983.

Balibar, Étienne. *Masses, Classes, Ideas: Studies on Politics and Philosophy Before and After Marx*. New York: Routledge, 1994.

Bender, John. *Imagining the Penitentiary: Fiction and the Architecture of the Mind in Eighteenth-Century England*. Chicago: University of Chicago Press, 1989.

Benhabib, Sheyla. *Another Cosmopolitanism*. Oxford: Oxford University Press, 2008.

Butler, Judith. *The Psychic Life of Power: Theories in Subjection*. Palo Alto: Stanford University Press, 1997.

Cade Bambara, Toni. "Forward" to Chérie Moraga and Gloria Anzaldúa, eds. *This Bridge Called my Back: Writings of Radical Women of Color*. Watertown: Persephone Press, 1981.

Clifford, James. *The Predicament of Culture: Twentieth-Century Ethnography, Literature, and Art*. Cambridge: Harvard University Press, 1988.

Combahee River Collective. "Combahee River Statement." In *Feminism in Our Time: The Essential Writings, World War II to the Present*. Ed. Miriam Schneir. New York. Vintage Books, 1994.

Deleuze, Gilles, and Felix Guattari. *A Thousand Plateaus: Capitalism and Schizophrenia* [1980]. Trans. Brian Massumi. Minneapolis: University of Minnesota Press, 1987.

Ernst, Wolfgang. *Digital Memory and the Archive (Electronic Mediations)*. Minneapolis: University of Minnesota Press, 2012.

Fabian, Johannes. *Time and the Other: How Anthropology Makes its Object*. New York: Columbia University Press, 2002.

Foucault, Michel. *Discipline and Punish: The Birth of the Prison* [1975]. Trans. Alan Sheridan. New York: Vintage Books, 1995.

Frankenberg, Ruth. *White Women. Race Matters: The Social Construction of Whiteness*. Minneapolis: University of Minnesota Press, 1993.

Fraser, Nancy. *Trans-nationalizing the Public Sphere*. London: Polity Books, 2014.

Frye, Marilyn. "On Being White: Thinking Toward a Feminist Understanding of Race and Race Supremacy." In *The Politics of Reality: Essays in Feminist Theory*. Trumansburg, NY: Crossing Press, 1983. 110–27.

Habermas, Jürgen. *The Structural Transformation of the Public Sphere: An Inquiry into a Category of Bourgeois Society* (1962). Trans. Thomas Burger and Frederick Lawrence. Cambridge, MA: MIT Press, 1989.

Haraway, Donna. *Simians, Cyborgs, and Women*. London: Free Association Books, 1996.

Hardt, Michael, and Antonio Negri. *Multitude: War and Democracy in the Age of Empire*. New York: Penguin, 2005.

Hill, Mike, ed. *Whiteness: A Critical Reader*. New York: New York University Press, 1997.

Hill, Mike. *After Whiteness: Unmaking an American Majority*. New York: New York University Press, 2004.

Hill, Mike, and Warren Montag, eds. *Masses, Classes, and the Public Sphere*. London: Verso, 2001.

Hill, Mike, and Warren Montag. *The Other Adam Smith*. Palo Alto: Stanford University Press, 2015.

Hobbes, Thomas. *Leviathan* [1651]. New York: Penguin, 1982.

Hume, David. *An Enquiry Concerning Human Understanding* [1748]. Indianapolis: Hackett Classics, 1993.

Ignatiev, Noel. *How the Irish Became White*. New York: Routledge, 1995.

Jameson, Frederic. *The Political Unconscious: Narrative as a Socially Symbolic Act*. Ithaca: Cornell University Press, 1982.

Kant, Immanuel. "An Answer to the Question: 'What is Enlightenment'? [1784]." *Political Writings*. Ed. H. S. Reiss. Cambridge: Cambridge University Press, 1991. 42–60.

Kernan, Alvin. *Samuel Johnson and the Impact of Print*. Princeton: Princeton University Press, 1989.

Lacan, Jacques. *Formations of the Unconscious: The Seminar of Jacques Lacan* [1957-58]. Book 5. Trans. Russell Grigg. Ed. Jacques-Alain Miller. London: Polity Books, 2017.

Latour, Bruno. *We Have Never Been Modern* [Michael McKeon's *The Origins of the English Novel, 1600-1740* (Baltimore: Johns Hopkins University Press, 1987). For a range of writing on the topic, see Diedre Lynch and William Beatty Warner, eds., *Cultural Institutions of the Novel* (Durham: Duke University Press, 1996)]. Cambridge: Harvard University Press, 1993.

Locke, John. *Some Thoughts Concerning Education [1693] and Of the Conduct of Understanding [1706]*. Indianapolis: Hackett Classics, 1996.

Lynch, Diedre, and William Beatty Warner, eds. *Cultural Institutions of the Novel*. Durham: Duke University Press, 1996.

McKeon, Michael. *The Origins of the English Novel, 1600-1740*. Baltimore: Johns Hopkins University Press, 1987.

McLuhan, Marshal. *The Gutenberg Galaxy* [1962]. Toronto: University of Toronto Press, 2014.

Meillassoux, Quentin. *After Finitude: An Essay on the Necessity of Contingency*. London: Bloomsbury, 2014.

Montag, Warren. *Althusser and His Contemporaries: Philosophy's Perpetual War*. Durham: Duke University Press, 2013.

Moraga, Cherie, and Robin Morgan. *This Bridge Called My Back: Writings of Radical Women of Color*. Watertown: Persephone Press, 1981.

Morrison, Toni. *Playing in the Dark: Whiteness and the Literary Imagination*. New York: Vintage, 1993.

Ong, Walter. *An Ong Reader: Challenges for Further Inquiry*. Eds. Thomas J. Farrell and Paul A. Soulcup. Cresskil: Hampton Press, 2002.

Robbins, Bruce, ed. *The Phantom Public Sphere*. Minneapolis: University of Minnesota Press, 1993.

Roediger, David. *The Wages of Whiteness: Race and the Making of the American Working Class*. London: Verso, 2007.

Said, Edward. *Orientalism*. New York: Vintage, 1979.

Saussure, Ferdinand de. *Course in General Linguistics* [1916]. Trans. W. Baskin. Eds. Charles Bally and Albert Sechehaye. Glasgow: Fontana/Collins, 1977.

Siskin, Clifford. *The Work of Writing: Literature and Social Change in Britain, 1700-1830*. Baltimore: Johns Hopkins University Press, 1999.

Siskin, Clifford, and William Warner, eds. *This is Enlightenment*. Chicago: University of Chicago Press, 2010.

Smith, Adam. *The Theory of Moral Sentiments* [1759]. New York: Penguin, 2010.

Spivak, Chakravorty Gayatri. "Can the Subaltern Speak?" *Can the Subaltern Speak?: Reflections on the History of an Idea*. Revised edition. Ed. Rosalind C. Morris. New York: Columbia University Press, 2010. 21–28.

St. Clair, William. *The Reading Nation in the Romantic Period*. Cambridge: Cambridge University Press, 2007.

Thompson, E. P. *Customs in Common*. New York: The New Press, 1993.

Thompson, E. P. *The Making of the English Working Class* [1963]. New York: Vintage, 1996.

Watt, Ian. *The Rise of the Novel: Studies in Defoe, Richardson and Fielding* [1957]. Berkeley: University of California Press, 2001.

Weiner, Norbert. *Cybernetics; or, the Control and Communication in the Animal and Machine*. Baltimore: MIT, 1965.

West, Cornel. *Race Matters*. New York: Vintage, 1994.

Williams, Raymond. *Writing in Society*. London: Verso, 1985.

CHAPTER TWENTY-THREE

Materialisms

CHRISTOPHER BREU

UNDERSTANDING MATERIALISM AND MATERIALITY

Materialism (as well as related concepts such as matter and materiality) is one of the theoretical master signifiers of the twenty-first century. Just as much late twentieth-century theory was organized around the signifiers "language" and "culture," much recent work is organized around the signifiers "materialism" or "materiality." The status of materialism as a master signifier has asserted itself ever more forcefully in the present, not only generating new approaches such as new materialism in critical theory and speculative realism in philosophy, but also shaping (and in turn being informed by) the trajectory of other parallel new movements, such as animal studies, biopolitics, and posthumanism.[1] It has also inflected the trajectory of older movements (including older forms of materialism) that have taken on different characteristics in the present moment (including ecotheory, Marxist theory, and cultural studies).

On one level, materialism presents itself as the master signifier to end all master signifiers, since it is a master signifier that promises to undo the reign of the signifier itself (as the latter is associated with the privileging of language in what has become known as the linguistic turn). On another level, there is nothing remotely new about the question of materialism. The topic itself is central to philosophical discourse stretching back to the pre-Socratics, and has recurrences and developments throughout the history of philosophy from the discussion of matter in Aristotle's physics, through the discussion of the body and nature in Spinoza, to Marxist materialism, Nietzschean vitalism, Darwinian evolutionary biology, accounts of the body and the object in psychoanalysis, phenomenology, post-phenomenological thinking, and so forth. Indeed, if idealism is the dominant current in Western philosophy, materialism is its dark and ever-returning double, presenting an uncanny and disruptive visage to the former's divinely etched features.[2]

In what follows, then, I will detail recent developments in materialist thought, while also indicating their roots in older forms of materialist thinking. As Sara Ahmed has pointed out, the "new materialisms" are more indebted to older materialisms than the discourse of novelty often allows.[3] The trajectory of this chapter, then, will be to attend to this continuity, while also marking what is genuinely new about the new materialisms and speculative realism. The chapter will conclude by suggesting the ways in which these new developments can be brought into dialogue as well as tension with older forms of more explicitly political materialism, such as Marxist theory and biopolitical theory.

NEW MATERIALISMS

Work in what is being called the "new materialisms" has been one of the defining developments in twenty-first-century theory. Those whose work is usually grouped under the heading of new materialisms include (but are not reducible to) Stacy Alaimo, Samantha Frost, Susan Hekman, Diana Coole, Elizabeth Grosz, Brian Massumi, Catherine Malabou, Kim Tallbear, Bruno Latour, Jane Bennett, Claire Colebrook, Sara Ahmed, Rosi Bradotti, and Karen Barad.[4] The range of work that falls under this heading can be gleaned from two collections that appeared within a few years of each other: *Material Feminisms*, edited by Alaimo and Hekman, and *New Materialisms*, edited by Coole and Frost. Each of these volumes worked to push theory beyond the limitations of what the theorists termed the "linguistic turn" or the "cultural turn" that is, work in the 1980s and 1990s that took language or culture to be its master signifiers. This turn to the material works to address what was absent, attenuated, or untheorizable during the ascendancy of the linguistic and cultural turns. Thus categories like nature, the biological, the infrastructural, the animal, aspects of the material body, and the ontological itself, which were seen as entirely constructed or were ignored altogether during the linguistic turn, can now be posited and theorized in all of their material force, resistance, and agency. Such an approach, as Alaimo and Hekman argue, represents an important move forward from the linguistic and cultural frameworks privileged by postmodernism, post-structuralism, and cultural studies:

> The theorists assembled here have been working to revise the paradigms of poststructuralism, postmodernism, and cultural studies in ways that can more productively account for the agency, semiotic force, and dynamics of bodies and natures. The most daunting aspect of such projects is to radically rethink materiality, the very "stuff" of bodies and natures. The innovative work of these theorists and many others constitutes what we are calling the "material turn" in feminist theory, a wave of feminist theory that is taking matter seriously.[5]

Thus, Alaimo and Hekman put forward the concept of the "material turn" to replace the now surpassed cultural and linguistic turns. It is interesting to note, though, that their emphasis on the semiosis of matter suggests not so much a rejection of the insights of the linguistic turn but rather a complication and rethinking of them from within a materialist framework. This emphasis on using what is valuable from the linguistic turn while situating the linguistic and cultural within a broader materialist framework is characteristic of new materialisms, and to a lesser degree, of speculative realism.

Coole and Frost advance a similar argument in their own introduction, but from the disciplinary framework of political theory. They make an even stronger distinction between the exhaustion of linguistic and cultural constructivism and the vitality of what they term "new materialisms." Yet even here, the constructivist approach is not entirely jettisoned but rather enfolded into the more recent framework:

> In terms of theory itself, we are summoning a new materialism in response to a sense that the radicalism of the dominant discourses which have flourished under the cultural turn is now more or less exhausted. We share the feeling current among many researchers that the dominant constructivist orientation to social analysis is inadequate for thinking about matter, materiality, and politics in ways that do justice to the contemporary context of biopolitics and global political economy. While we recognize

that radical constructivism has contributed considerable insight into the workings of power over recent years we are also aware that an allergy to "the real" that is characteristic of its more linguistic or discursive forms—whereby overtures to material reality are dismissed as an insidious foundationalism—has had the consequence of dissuading critical inquirers from the more empirical kinds of investigations that material process and structures require. While by no means are all the essays in this volume hostile to constructivism, and new materialists countenance no simple return to empiricism or positivism, we share the view current among many critics that our contemporary context demands a theoretical rapprochement with material realism.[6]

While this passage is particularly dense, it, along with the Alaimo and Hekman's passage, elucidates many of the key tenets and terms that define the new materialisms and even points toward some of the arguments of speculative realism (which I will address later in this chapter). If we work to unpack both of these passages we will have a much stronger sense of what is at stake in the new materialisms, how they define themselves, and what they define themselves against.

Alaimo and Hekman trace their material turn out of the impasses produced by the influences of "postmodernism, poststructuralism, and cultural studies" on feminist work of the 1980s and 1990s. While each of these terms has a very specific history and meaning (actually multiple ones) each can be said to privilege a form of what Coole and Frost describe as a "constructivism," one defined against "foundationalism." Post-structuralism privileged language itself as the locus of the construction of both subjectivity and the world that the subject inhabits. Yet language, in post-structuralism, not only constructs, but undoes, or to use one of its privileged terms, deconstructs. Language in this framework is always haunted by its own contradictions. It is traversed by power and produces oppositions and resistances in the very act of inscribing a dominant discourse. Similarly, while postmodernism has myriad definitions (artistic, theoretical, and historical), one thing that most versions of it share is an understanding of the social and artistic world as constructed through culture and language. Culture is in this context thoroughly privileged over nature. Works of art and theories are celebrated for their self-reflexivity and their rigorous critique of anything essentialist—that is, something that makes foundational assumptions about the essence of an entity (e.g., gender, the aesthetic, or human nature) that exists prior to any linguistic or cultural construction. Even the Marxist critiques of postmodernism tended to presume a world that was largely constructed through language and culture, even as it read the latter as a symptom of the specific dynamics of late capitalism with its organization around immaterial (i.e., intellectual, service, and affect) labor and financialization. Finally, cultural studies in the eighties and nineties situated itself as a form of constructivism, although in this case a form of cultural constructivism. In each of these contexts, culture and/or language became the locus of social construction. Indeed, agency seemed primarily to inhere to language and culture in this paradigm, with subjective agency merely being an effect of both. Thus the theory of the linguistic and cultural turn was constructivist, in the specific sense that language and culture were presented as constructing reality as such. They were also anti-foundationalist in assuming that there were no natural (or pre-cultural) foundations to human existence or knowledge. In this sense they bracketed ontological claims and privileged epistemology. However, in spite of these anti-essentialist moves, one might say that they were ironically foundationalist in their understanding of language and culture.

Such, indeed, is the charge made by much of the work in the material turn; the emphasis on language and culture as sole producers of what is has had the ironic effect of obscuring a number of aspects of social, economic, ecological, and, in fact, material existence. Materiality in the earlier context can only be an effect of discourse. To take two examples from the fields in which Alaimo and Heckman and Coole and Frost make their intervention, Judith Butler's conception of performativity in feminist theory and Laclau and Mouffe's conception of the political field as a site of discursive struggle and antagonism around hegemony in political theory both represent the power and the limits of the cultural and linguistic turns for theorizing both embodiment and the social.

To further engage Butler's conception of performativity, in her groundbreaking book *Gender Trouble*, she posited concepts of gender and sex as discursively constructed through a set of performative iterations. This performative logic shaped not only the lived perceptions and experience of gender (which from at least Simone de Beauvoir on was generally seen as cultural or at least culturally malleable) but also the very materiality of the sexed body. In her follow up book *Bodies That Matter*, Butler posited the body itself as produced by a process of materialization, one which is enacted through the repeated citation of symbolic laws. Thus for Butler matter is finally constituted by linguistic, cultural, and psychic forces. To this end, Butler importantly pushes beyond ideas of sex as binary (in a way that has been very productive for queer, trans, and intersex theory) but still posits matter as only a product of discourse (which is itself material, but is the only material entity that is given agency in this account).

It is the one-way model of the cultural or linguistic construction that is challenged by new materialists like Alaimo, Barad, Bennett, Latour, Grosz, Frost, and others. Central to their arguments is an attention to the biological and/or material dimensions of embodiment and of ecosystems that theories of cultural construction efface. Take, for example, Karen Barad's agential realism, which builds off of Butler's account of performativity but takes Butler to task for finally giving the material and the biological short shrift:

> It is not at all clear Butler succeeds in bringing the discursive and the material into closer proximity. . . . If discursive practices constitute a productive social or cultural field, then how much of the very matter of bodies, both human and nonhuman, can be accounted for? Is the matter of things completely social in nature? Are we to understand matter as purely a cultural phenomenon?[7]

She goes on to argue that "any robust theory of the materialization of bodies would necessarily take account of *how the body's materiality* (including, for example, its anatomy and physiology) *and other material forces as well* (including nonhuman ones) *actively matter to processes of materialization*."[8] Barad proposes just such a theory with her account of agential realism, which is also routed through her engagement with quantum physics and feminist science studies. Her account of agential realism emphasizes a realist ontology which foregrounds various material-discursive actors and attends to what she terms their "intra-activity." Thus she emphasizes not only the performativity of various forms of scientific knowledge, including the ways in which scientific instruments like the STM (or Scanning Tunneling Microscope) coproduce the materialities they record, but the ways in which those materialities also have their agential dimension and are also performative, thus intra-actively contributing their own agency to the materialities recorded.

I have focused on Barad's account here at some length because it undertakes a number of moves that are characteristic of new materialisms (even as each thinker constructs a different ontology and a different account of the material). These moves include the following:

1. Like other thinkers such as Grosz and Frost, as well as those influenced by Deleuze such as Claire Colebrook and Brian Massumi, Barad emphasizes ontology over epistemology while not fully effacing the latter. If epistemology was a central category in the linguistic and material turns, then ontology is necessarily a privileged concept in the material turn. In its emphasis on what is rather than just what humans construct, it enables theorists to posit forms of materiality that are in tension with or are intra-active with human actors. This ontology can take many different forms, including Bennett and Massumi's vitalism (which is in turn drawn from Spinoza via Deleuze), Latour and Bennett's assemblages (which are derived from Deluze and Guarttari); Grosz's radical naturalism (which she derives from a rereading of Darwin); Catherine Malabou's plasticity; Colebrook's non-vitalist Deleuzian ontology; and Barad's realism (which also puts her work in dialogue with the speculative realists).

2. Similarly, Barad's rejection of dualisms (including the subject-object dualism and the representation-reality dualism) is also characteristic of new materialisms. Most new materialist thinkers deploy a version of deconstruction's undoing of binary oppositions. Unlike in deconstruction, however, in new materialism the undoing of the opposition doesn't lead to endless textual differals and differences, but rather tends to produce a new synthetic term like Barad's notion of intra-activity, Alaimo's "transcorporeality," which emphasizes the ways in which bodies and environments, bodily and ecological materialities intertwine and interpenetrate, or Frost's "biocultural creatures" as a new non-exceptionalist way of defining human beings.[9]

3. New materialisms tend to emphasize becoming over being. They tend to imagine matter in terms of flows and virtuality more than as substance and fixity. In this they borrow from Deleuze who in turn derives it from Nietzsche. However, as Rosi Bradotti points out, the Nietzsche used by new materialists tends to restore the biological dimension of his thought that was largely ignored by post-structuralism, especially in its reception in the United States during the linguistic turn.[10]

4. Central to these notions of becoming are concepts of agency. For almost all new materialists, matter itself exerts agency. Bruno Latour makes this explicit in his actor-network theory where he proclaims "objects too have agency."[11] Jane Bennett also discusses the agency of objects in *Vibrant Matter*, while Malabou's concept of plasticity also enacts a neurobiological and embodied conception of agency, and, as we have seen, Barad theorizes the agency of matter in her concept of intra-activity.

5. Much new materialist work attempts to engage many of the political categories central to cultural studies but in a more materialist register. Thus, Kim Tallbear's work focuses on cultural constructions of race, the science of DNA, and issues of material embodiment, while Nancy Tuana addresses race, racialized and class-based ecological violence, and the devastation wrought by Hurricane Katrina and its aftermath. Similarly, Sara Ahmed deploys a materialist reworking of phenomenology to address both queer embodiment and intersubjective power relations.

SPECULATIVE REALISM

If new materialisms tend to represent a refutation of the linguistic and cultural turn, it is a refutation that still incorporates many of the best insights proffered by the privileging of language and culture. It is thus a reorientation (to echo Sarah Ahmed) as much as a refutation. It is a reorientation that takes matter seriously in its various forms, including bodily and ecological matters, yet it hangs onto the insights of the earlier turns even while situating them within or in relationship to the material as a new heuristic. The challenge represented by speculative realism to the linguistic and cultural turns is much more fundamental. Indeed, the challenge posed by speculative realism is not just to the cultural and linguistic turns of the 1980s and 1990s, but to philosophy after Kant as such (of which, according to the speculative realists, the cultural and linguistic turns are merely local manifestations). As with the new materialists, the speculative realists don't wholly jettison the philosophy of the past. They do reread it however to frame questions that were off-limits in Kant's canonical positing of things in themselves as forever removed from human access (e.g., Quentin Meillassoux's rereads Descartes as a theorist of objects with primary qualities while Graham Harman's understands Heidegger as a theorist of the real and sensual dimensions of objects).[12]

Not all versions of speculative realism are materialisms (e.g., Harman's most recent book is called *Immaterialism*), but the work that it has done to move past the Kantian bracketing of things in themselves has opened up new territory for a range of materialist theorizing. It has also made realism (the position that there is a real world or universe that can be philosophically posited) a dominant trend in twenty-first-century philosophy. There can be anti-realist materialisms that finally posit only aspects of materiality that are accessible by the theorizing subject (as in Merleau-Ponty's account of the embodied subject as the subject of perception—although late Merleau-Ponty, with his concept of the flesh, can be read as moving toward a realist position).[13] Such materialist anti-realism may situate the materiality of the epistemological apparatus as such (as in post-structuralist accounts of the materiality of language or of the signifier). Finally, they may situate themselves in terms of the materiality of what is humanly produced and structured (as in cultural studies and most versions of Marxist theory, which finally take a more agnostic approach to the question of realism). Yet a truly robust materialism, one that can integrate the insights of scientific knowledge and posit that which is outside the frame and immediate apprehension of the human, will be an equally powerful realism. Such a realist materialism presents itself as ever more necessary in our age defined by growing ecological devastation.

The philosophies conventionally grouped under speculative realism have emerged in the twenty-first century as just such robust realisms, ones that have spawned a number of different materialisms. The philosophers and theorists grouped under the banner of speculative realism (even as some resist this grouping) include Quentin Meillassoux, Ray Brassier, Ian Hamilton Grant, Isabelle Stengers, Steven Shaviro, Eugene Thacker, and the thinkers affiliated with Object-Oriented Ontology (OOO), including Graham Harman, Levi Bryant, Ian Bogost, and Timothy Morton.[14] Central to almost all speculative realism is Meillassoux's critique of what he terms "correlationism" or "the idea according to which we only ever have access to the correlation between thinking and being, and never to either term considered apart from each other."[15] This, then, is Meillassoux's critique of the Kantian bracketing of things in themselves, which Meillassoux describes as the "central notion of modern philosophy." In other words, the subject can only philosophize about that which she can subjectively apprehend. Thus we can describe the phenomenal dimensions of objects but cannot make any claims about their noumenal properties (or what objects are in themselves). Even poststructuralism, which did so much to critique idealism and Kant's concept of the transcendental subject maintains this prohibition. Thus while post-structuralism and postmodernism may be anti-idealist, they tend to still be anti-realist. The maintenance of this prohibition, then, produces the characteristic forms of discursive, linguistic, and cultural constructivism that are associated with the cultural and linguistic turn. Language and culture, in this framework, constitute the world we can know, and since we can only know this world it becomes the world that is. One of the problems with this model is that it posits no resistance or agency to anything that falls out of the purview of human language and culture. It also tends to posit that which is outside of the subject as being as constructed as the subject itself. So bodies, environments, infrastructures, and so on tend to be passive sites of discursive construction and inscription.

Perhaps the need to move beyond correlationism is clear (although many would contest this), but how is such a move undertaken philosophically? (Many would also contest that most speculative realism, for all its attempts, has yet to effectively move beyond correlationism.)[16] Well, Meillassoux does this in two ways. First, he revives a distinction first articulated by Descartes between primary and secondary qualities. Secondary qualities are the sensible. For example, when I bite into a sliver of a jalapeño pepper, I feel its heat in my mouth (a secondary quality). When a parrot bites a sliver from the same pepper, it feels no heat. This is because birds in general do not have the receptor that processes capsaicin (the chemical that makes hot peppers taste hot to mammals) as heat; they are immune to its hot properties. Thus, heat or any other subjectively (broadly defined here to include all animals) perceived quality is not a part of the entity itself. It is a secondary quality. What is primary is the chemical, capsaicin. Thus primary qualities are present in the object or material entity outside of any relationship to subjective perception. This doesn't mean that they can't be transformed or affected. It just means that they are part of the object as constituted in itself.

The other way Meillassoux moves beyond correlationism is via forms of scientific knowledge that exceed or resist human subjective cognition. Thus he points to what he terms "ancestrality," or real (i.e., scientifically verifiable) knowledge of events that took place (like the big bang and other astrophysical phenomena, as well as prehuman ice ages, etc.) before the history of humans.[17] Thus, while the particulars of this knowledge can sometimes change with changing evidence or different tools of perception, the events are scientifically verified as existing independently of human subjective perception.

Yet speculative realism is not the same thing as scientific empiricism. There is a reason it is called *speculative* realism. Even Ray Brassier's materialist nihilism, which is the version of speculative realism that is most invested in scientific empiricism, emphasizes the importance of speculation. Like Catherine Malabou, Brassier emphasizes the recent findings of neurobiology. Unlike her, though, he uses these findings to dismiss psychoanalysis and other theories of the mind for a neurobiological account of the workings of the brain. But it is precisely the limits of our brains and our necessarily finite existence as a species that gives credence to his nihilism. Because our brains are limited, they cannot apprehend the radically nonhuman contingency of what is without translating it into partially human terms. Moreover, this quest for knowledge is finally meaningless on a cosmic scale, given our inevitable extinction. But these limits don't negate what has existed, what exists, or what may exist. It just means our access to it and its meaning for us is limited.

This emphasis on limits of perception is characteristic of speculative realism, which may seem odd given its investment in moving beyond Kantian prohibition on positing noumena. Speculative realism wants to posit a real, but this real does not necessarily correlate with human access. So the central problem of Kantianism hasn't disappeared; it has just been partially evaded, enabling philosophy to posit objects that exceed subjective cognition. What emerges in speculative realism instead is a real to which humans have partial access. This emphasis on limited access is perhaps most striking in OOO.

OOO is a body of theory which emphasizes ontology and the being of objects. In a certain way, as Ian Bogost describes it, it can be likened to an "alien phenomenology" or a phenomenology that privileges and begins with the object rather than the subject.[18] Thus, OOO will often ask questions about how the object interacts with other objects. It also often proposes a "flat ontology" in which all entities are presumed equal and all (including various animals, humans, and nonhumans) are considered objects.[19] While it can often seem counterintuitive and oddly playful (the latter is particularly true of Bogost's work, sometimes to its detriment), it can also have real political and ecological consequences that demonstrate the power of a post-correlationist materialism. While the founder and key theorists of OOO, Graham Harman, argues for an "immaterialism" since materialism proper undermines objects, Bryant, Morton, and Bogost articulate OOO as a form of materialism (Harman, *Immaterialism*). For Harman, there are two dangers that apply to any theory of objects, overmining and undermining. Overmining diffuses the particularity of objects (which can be of any size and complexity) into systems or assemblages, while undermining reduces them to smaller, perhaps subatomic, phenomena. Harman warns against both of these moves. Both these warnings seem fraught. As I will argue further later, new materialism and speculative realism in general need a confrontation with the systematic. Similarly, it's not clear why subatomic phenomena are not objects in the sense that OOO uses the term.

Perhaps what is most powerful about OOO, though, is its emphasis on both the reality of objects and on their only partial accessibility via human subjects. Harman who posits, as we discussed earlier, both a "sensual" dimension of the object and the "real" dimension of the object (echoing Meillassoux's account of secondary and primary qualities), argues that the real dimensions of objects are "withdrawn."[20] As a kind of ontological formalism this claim has its problems (see the fourth feature in the following paragraph). As an epistemological injunction about ontological entities, it can be powerful. The claim would be that there is a *not all* at stake in any kind of empirical understanding of an object. Some aspect of it recedes. Thus, human fantasies of mastery, which have inflected forms of capitalist, colonial, and ecological domination, would be challenged and hopefully undone by such an epistemology. Something about material objects escapes full human knowledge and mastery. Something about them remains contingent and agential in ways that are not fully predictable by human forms of knowledge even as they remain crucial for human (and nonhuman) flourishing. Levi Bryant and Timothy Morton emphasize the ways in which objects exceed human apprehension of them and the ways in which the linguistic and cultural turns have limited our understanding of the power of nonhuman objects, entities, and systems in ways that have potentially devastating ecological consequences.

As I did with new materialism, I will conclude this section by listing some of the characteristic features of most speculative realism:

1. As the name suggests, speculative realism articulates a realist vision of a universe or a world independent of thought. It however maintains that philosophical speculation is crucial to gaining access to what we can know of this world or universe.

2. Like new materialism, speculative realism emphasizes ontology over epistemology. Indeed, as Rebekah Sheldon has demonstrated, speculative realism sometimes overlooks epistemological questions at its peril, turning epistemological questions, like the withdrawal of objects from human (and other forms of) perception into ontological ones.[21] At its best though, speculative realism represents a powerful return to realism and ontology after the ossification of philosophy into anti-realist, correlationist positions.

3. All forms of speculative realism turn on Meillassoux's critique of correlationism. This enables us to posit entities and objects that exist both within and against subjective perception and control.

4. In contrast to new materialism, speculative realism tends to emphasize the way in which discourse and materiality, subjects and objects, exceed each other or are defined, in part, by an absence of full access or contact. This emphasis can function as a kind of powerful recognition of the partial autonomy, agency, and unknowability of the material, but if taken too far it can also reify the material into a relatively static system, parts of which remain forever untouched or unchanging. This is the problem with Harman's notion of the withdrawn as an ontological claim. Yet it is also crucial to theorize what exceeds human mastery, knowledge, and control. It seems to me that the new materialist insight of the co-constitution of matter and discourse, subject and object, and the speculative realist one of their partial excess in relationship to each other need to be thought together.

5. Speculative realism marks a new embrace of science and scientific knowledge within continental philosophy. In contrast to twentieth-century anti-realisms, which were almost uniformly hostile to science, speculative realism embraces scientific findings, while also maintaining its commitment to speculative metaphysics.

CODA: THE FUTURE OF CONTEMPORARY MATERIALISMS

As this chapter has hopefully indicated, new materialisms and speculative realisms are vibrant and dynamic new intellectual approaches. As the twenty-first century unfolds, materialism has emerged as one of the master signifiers of contemporary theory. The linguistic and cultural turns are becoming distant memories. Such a moment in the emergence of a body of thought is marked by both possibility and danger. The danger, of course, is that the new forms of materialism will calcify into the same kind of doxa that the cultural and linguistic turns became in their later years. In place of a linguistic or cultural foundationalism we will have a material one. What was once productive and radically reorienting will become the stuff of academic cliché and grist for the publication mill. In place of a linguistic or cultural essentialism, we will have a material essentialism. There is also a distinct danger that while conceptually these new materialisms represent an important and necessary corrective to the excesses and impasses of the cultural and linguistic turns, they, also, in their more mystical and speculative iterations threaten to become a retreat from the forms of necessary political critique central to the linguistic and cultural turns (indeed as such they could represent part of the depoliticization of the academy under neoliberalism marked by the growth of apolitical approaches like post-critique, surface reading, and certain versions of the digital humanities).

However, there are possibilities in this moment too. Given all the work that new materialisms and speculative realisms have done to reorient thinking in the present and to provide a viable alternative to the settlements of the cultural turn, postmodernism, and neo-Kantianism, they could cross-pollinate with other forms of materialism (some of them older) that have not played a central role in the movements so far in order to strengthen some of their weaknesses.

While the new materialisms and speculative realisms have been very good at providing theories of materiality in its specific manifestations, they have been less effective at thinking about understandings of materialism that emphasize systematicity, such as Marxist theory, with its emphasis on collective possibility and constraint within the workings of the capitalist world system, biopolitical theory, with its account of the political and economic shaping of biological life in the aggregate, and forms of ecological systematicity that extend beyond the local or regional ecosystem such as Jason W. Moore's conception of "world ecology."

Similarly, an engagement with various materialist historicisms would also benefit new materialisms and speculative realisms. Such historicisms would potentially provide a history, perhaps modeled in part on Manuel de Landa's *A Thousand Years of Nonlinear History*, of various forms of materiality, from the ecological, the geological, the cosmic, the political economic, the bodily, the evolutionary, and the linguistic, to the history of various built environments. Given their vast scale, such historicisms would probably be uneven and recursive, providing a much richer understanding of both space and time than was standard in the generally linear historicisms of the cultural turn. Such historicisms would also be reflexive in the best spirit of the linguistic turn. Such a reflexive historicism might situate new materialisms and speculative realisms as a symptomatic reflection of the second moment of neoliberalism. If the first moment of neoliberalism was about expansion (along with the forms of immiseration and inequality it also produced), corresponding to the seeming weightlessness of the postmodern or constructivist moment, then the second phase of neoliberalism (after the 2008 financial meltdown) has been about contraction. This second phase has been about deprivation for all but the elite, the weight of crushing debt, the rhetoric of austerity, growing ecological devastation, the crashing back to earth of the financial system, and the latter's reemergence as an even farther remove from the economy organized (however exploitatively) for the sustenance and enhancement of life. It makes sense that if language and sign systems were part of the giddiness for certain class fractions (including academics) in the first part of neoliberalism, then the constraints and obduracy of materialism would come to define our present age. An awareness of this history and how specific moments in history have political and ideological possibilities and liabilities would help new materialism and speculative realism be more engaged with the temporality of its moment as well as longer, sometimes ancestral, temporalities. In sum, an engagement by new materialisms and speculative realisms with other materialisms would make it one of the most promising and politically generative developments in contemporary theory.

Illinois State University (United States)

NOTES

1. For excellent accounts of new materialisms see the essays and introductions to Stacy Alaimo and Susan Hekman, eds., *Material Feminisms* (Bloomington: Indiana University Press, 2008) and Diana Coole and Samantha Frost, eds., *New Materialisms: Ontology, Agency, and Politics* (Durham: Duke University Press, 2010).

2. While the range of books in that invented tradition we term Western philosophy on materialism is much too large to cite in its entirety, my references here are to the following texts: Philip Wheelwright, ed., *The Presocratics* (New York Macmillan, 1985); Aristotle, *Physics*, trans. R. P. Hardie and R. K. Gaye (Grinnell: Parapetetic Press, 1980); Benedict de Spinoza, *Ethics*, trans. Edwin Curley (New York: Penguin Classics, 1992); Karl Marx, *Capital*, vol. 1, trans. Ben Fowkes (New York: Vintage, 1976); Charles Darwin, *The Origin of Species* (New York: Bantam Classics, 1999); Friedrich Nietzsche, *Thus Spoke Zarathustra*, trans. Adrian Del Caro (Cambridge: Cambridge University Press, 2006); Sigmund Freud, "The Ego and the Id and Other Works," in *The Standard Edition of the Complete Psychological Works of Sigmund Freud XIX (1923-1925)*, trans. James Strachey [New London: Hogarth Press, 1975], 1–67); Jacques Lacan, *Anxiety: The Seminar of Jacques Lacan, Book X*, ed. Jacques-Alain Miller, trans. A. R. Price (Cambridge: Polity Press, 2014); Maurice Merleau-Ponty, *The Phenomenology of Perception*, trans. Donald Landes (New York: Routledge, 2013); and Maurice Merleau-Ponty, *The Visible and the Invisible*, trans. Alphonso Lingis (Evanston: Northwestern University Press, 1968).

3. Sara Ahmed, "Orientations Matter," *New Materialisms: Ontology, Agency, and Politics*, eds. Diana Coole and Samantha Frost (Durham: Duke University Press, 2010), 235.

4. Representative work by these authors include the following (I have limited each author to one text, although certain authors, like Haraway, Grosz, Malabou, Massumi, and Latour, have many books to their names and have exerted a considerable influence on the other writers cited here): Sara Ahmed, *Queer Phenomenology: Orientations, Objects, Others* (Durham: Duke University Press, 2006); Stacy Alaimo, *Bodily Natures: Science, Environment, and the Material Self* (Bloomington: University of Indiana Press, 2010); Karen Barad, *Meeting the Universe Halfway: Quantum Physics and the Entanglement of Matter and Meaning* (Durham: Duke University Press 2006); Bennett, *Vibrant Matter*; Rosi Braidotti, *The Posthuman* (Cambridge: Polity Press, 2013); Diana Coole, "The Inertia of Matter and the Generativity of the Flesh," in *New Materialisms: Ontology, Agency, and Politics*, eds. Diana Coole and Samantha Frost (Durham: Duke University Press, 2010), 92–115; Samantha Frost, *Biocultural Creatures: Toward a New Theory of the Human* (Durham: Duke University Press, 2016); Elizabeth Grosz, *Becoming Undone: Darwinian Reflections on Life, Politics, and Art* (Durham: Duke University Press, 2011); Susan Hekman, *The Material of Knowledge: Feminist Disclosures* (Bloomington: University of Indiana Press, 2010); Bruno Latour, *Reassembling the Social: An Introduction to Actor-Network-Theory* (Oxford: Oxford University Press, 2005); Catherine Malabou, *Ontology of the Accident: An Essay on Destructive Plasticity*, trans. Carolyn Shread (Cambridge: Polity Press, 2012); Brian Massumi, *Parables for the Virtual: Movement, Affect, Sensation* (Durham: Duke University Press, 2002); and Kim Tallbear, *Native American DNA: Tribal Belonging and the False Promise of Genetic Science* (Minneapolis: University of Minnesota Press, 2014).

5. Stacy Alaimo and Susan Hekman, "Introduction: Emerging Models of Materiality in Feminist Theory," in *Material Feminisms*, eds. Stacy Alaimo and Susan Hekman (Bloomington: University of Indiana Press, 2008), 6.

6. Coole and Frost, "Introducing the New Materialisms."

7. Barad, *Meeting the Universe Halfway*, 64.

8. Ibid., 65, Italics in original.

9. Alaimo, *Bodily Natures*, 2; Frost, *Biocultural Creatures*, 4.

10. Rosi Braidotti, "The Notion of the Univocity of Being or Single Matter Positions Difference as a Verb or Process of Becoming at the Heart of the Matter," in *New Materialism: Interviews and Cartographies*, eds. Rick Dophijn and Iris van der Tuin (Ann Arbor: Open Humanities Press, 2012), 22.

11. Latour, *Reassembling the Social,* 63.

12. For an excellent introduction to speculative realism see Peter Gratton, *Speculative Realism: Problems and Prospects* (London: Bloomsbury, 2014). For a powerful critique of Object-Oriented Ontology, see Peter Wolfendale, *Object-Oriented Philosophy: The Noumenon's New Clothes* (Falmouth: Urbanomic, 2014).

13. These different versions of Merleau-Ponty's project are captured in the shift in his thinking from *The Phenomenology of Perception* to *The Visible and the Invisible.*

14. Representative works from these authors include the following: Ian Bogost, *Alien Phenomenology, or What It's Like to Be a Thing* (Minneapolis: University of Minnesota Press, 2012); Ray Brassier, *Nihil Unbound: Enlightenment and Extinction* (New York: Palgrave, 2007); Levi Bryant, *The Democracy of Objects* (Ann Arbor: Open Humanities Press, 2011); Ian Hamilton Grant, *Philosophies of Nature after Schelling* (London: Bloomsbury, 2008); Graham Harman, *The Quadruple Object* (Winchester: Zero Books, 2011); Quentin Meillassoux, *After Finitude: An Essay on the Necessity of Contingency*, trans. Ray Brassier (London: Continuum, 2008); Timothy Morton, *Hyperobjects: Ecology after the End of the World* (Minneapolis: University of Minnesota Press, 2013); Steven Shaviro, *The Universe of Things: On Speculative Realism* (Mineapolis: University of Minnesota Press, 2014); Isabelle Stengers, *Cosmopolitics I*, trans. Robert Bononno (Minneapolis: University of Minnesota Press, 2010); Isabelle Stengers, *Cosmopolitics II*, trans. Robert Bononno (Minneapolis: University of Minnesota Press, 2011); and Eugene Thacker, *In the Dust of this Planet: The Horror of Philosophy V.1* (Winchester: Zero Books, 2011).

15. Meillassoux, *After Finitude,* 5.

16. This is a point made by both Wolfendale's *Object-Oriented Philosophy* and Sheldon's "Dark Correlationism" (Rebekah Sheldon, "Dark Correlationism," Special Section on "Materialisms," ed. Christopher Breu, *symplokē* 24.1–2 [2016]: 137–53).

17. Meillassoux, *After Finitude,* 9.

18. Bogost, *Alien Phenomenology,* 1.

19. Bryant, *The Democracy of Objects,* 245.

20. Harman, *The Quadruple Object*, 20, 35, 38.

21. Sheldon, "Dark Correlationism," 138–41.

WORKS CITED

Ahmed, Sara. *Queer Phenomenology: Orientations, Objects, Others*. Durham: Duke University Press, 2006.

Ahmed, Sara. "Orientations Matter." In *New Materialisms: Ontology, Agency, and Politics*. Eds. Diana Coole and Samantha Frost. Durham: Duke University Press, 2010. 234–57.

Alaimo, Stacy. *Bodily Natures: Science, Environment, and the Material Self*. Bloomington: University of Indiana Press, 2010.

Alaimo, Stacy, and Susan Hekman. "Introduction: Emerging Models of Materiality in Feminist Theory." In *Material Feminisms*. Eds. Stacy Alaimo and Susan Hekman. Bloomington: University of Indiana Press, 2008. 1–19.

Alaimo, Stacy, and Susan Hekman, eds. *Material Feminisms*. Bloomington: Indiana University Press, 2008.

Aristotle. *Physics*. Trans. R. P. Hardie and R. K. Gaye. Grinnell: Parapetetic Press, 1980.

Barad, Karen. *Meeting the Universe Halfway: Quantum Physics and the Entanglement of Matter and Meaning*. Durham: Duke University Press, 2006.

Bennett, Jane. *Vibrant Matter: A Political Ecology of Things.* Durham: Duke University Press, 2010.

Bogost, Ian. *Alien Phenomenology, or What It's Like to Be a Thing.* Minneapolis: University of Minnesota Press, 2012.

Braidotti, Rosi. "The Notion of the Univocity of Being or Single Matter Positions Difference as a Verb or Process of Becoming at the Heart of the Matter." In *New Materialism: Interviews and Cartographies.* Eds. Rick Dophijn and Iris van der Tuin. Ann Arbor: Open Humanities Press, 2012. 19–37.

Braidotti, Rosi. *The Posthuman.* Cambridge: Polity Press, 2013.

Brassier, Ray. *Nihil Unbound: Enlightenment and Extinction.* New York: Palgrave, 2007.

Bryant, Levi. *The Democracy of Objects.* Ann Arbor: Open Humanities Press, 2011.

Bryant, Levi, Nick Srnicek, and Graham Harman. *The Speculative Turn: Continental Materialism and Realism.* Melbourne: re.Press, 2011.

Butler, Judith. *Gender Trouble: Feminism and the Subversion of Identity.* New York: Routledge, 1990.

Butler, Judith. *Bodies That Matter: On the Discursive Limits of "Sex."* New York: Routledge, 1992.

Colebrook, Claire. "On Not Becoming Man: The Materialist Politics of Unactualized Potential." In *Material Feminisms.* Eds. Stacy Alaimo and Susan Hekman. Bloomington: Indiana University Press, 2008. 52–84.

Colebrook, Claire. *Death of the Post Human: Essays on Extinction*, vol. 1. Ann Arbor: Open Humanities Press, 2015.

Coole, Diana. "The Inertia of Matter and the Generativity of the Flesh." In *New Materialisms: Ontology, Agency, and Politics.* Eds. Diana Coole and Samantha Frost. Durham: Duke University Press, 2010. 92–115.

Coole, Diana, and Samantha Frost. "Introducing the New Materialisms." In *New Materialisms: Ontology, Agency, and Politics.* Eds. Diana Coole and Samantha Frost. Durham: Duke University Press, 2010. 1–43.

Coole, Diana, and Samantha Frost, eds. *New Materialisms: Ontology, Agency, and Politics.* Durham: Duke University Press, 2010.

Darwin, Charles. *The Origin of Species* [1859]. New York: Bantam Classics, 1999.

De Landa, Maneuel. *A Thousand Years of Nonlinear History.* New York: Zone, 2000.

Freud, Sigmund. "The Ego and the Id and Other Works." In *The Standard Edition of the Complete Psychological Works of Sigmund Freud XIX (1923-1925).* Trans. James Strachey. New London: Hogarth Press, 1975. 1–67.

Frost, Samantha. *Biocultural Creatures: Toward a New Theory of the Human.* Durham: Duke University Press, 2016.

Grant, Ian Hamilton. *Philosophies of Nature after Schelling.* London: Bloomsbury, 2008.

Gratton, Peter. *Speculative Realism: Problems and Prospects.* London: Bloomsbury, 2014.

Grosz, Elizabeth. *Becoming Undone: Darwinian Reflections on Life, Politics, and Art.* Durham: Duke University Press, 2011.

Harman, Graham. *The Quadruple Object.* Winchester: Zero Books, 2011.

Harman, Graham. *Immaterialism: Objects and Social Theory.* Cambridge: Polity, 2016.

Hekman, Susan. *The Material of Knowledge: Feminist Disclosures.* Bloomington: University of Indiana Press, 2010.

Lacan, Jacques. *Anxiety: The Seminar of Jacques Lacan, Book X* [1962–63]. Ed. Jacques-Alain Miller. Trans. A. R. Price. Cambridge: Polity Press, 2014.

Latour, Bruno. *Reassembling the Social: An Introduction to Actor-Network-Theory*. Oxford: Oxford University Press, 2005.

Malabou, Catherine. *Ontology of the Accident: An Essay on Destructive Plasticity*. Trans. Carolyn Shread. Cambridge: Polity Press, 2012.

Marx, Karl. *Capital*, vol. 1 [1867]. Trans. Ben Fowkes. New York: Vintage, 1976.

Massumi, Brian. *Parables for the Virtual: Movement, Affect, Sensation*. Durham: Duke University Press, 2002.

Meillassoux, Quentin. *After Finitude: An Essay on the Necessity of Contingency*. Trans. Ray Brassier. London: Continuum, 2008.

Merleau-Ponty, Maurice. *The Visible and the Invisible* [1964]. Trans. Alphonso Lingis. Evanston: Northwestern University Press, 1968.

Merleau-Ponty, Maurice. *The Phenomenology of Perception* [1945]. Trans. Donald Landes. New York: Routledge, 2013.

Moore, Jason W. *Capitalism in the Web of Life: Ecology and the Accumulation of Capital*. London: Verso, 2015.

Morton, Timothy. *Hyperobjects: Ecology after the End of the World*. Minneapolis: University of Minnesota Press, 2013.

Nietzsche, Freidrich. *Thus Spoke Zarathustra* [1883-85]. Trans. Adrian Del Caro. Cambridge: Cambridge University Press, 2006.

Shaviro, Steven. *The Universe of Things: On Speculative Realism*. Mineapolis: University of Minnesota Press, 2014.

Sheldon, Rebekah. "Dark Correlationism." Special Issue on "Materialisms." Ed. Christopher Breu. *symplokē* 24.1–2 (2016): 137–53.

Spinoza, Benedict de. *Ethics* [1677]. Trans. Edwin Curley. New York: Penguin Classics, 1992.

Stengers, Isabelle. *Cosmopolitics I*. Trans. Robert Bononno. Minneapolis: University of Minnesota Press, 2010.

Stengers, Isabelle. *Cosmopolitics II*. Trans. Robert Bononno. Minneapolis: University of Minnesota Press, 2011.

Tallbear, Kim. *Native American DNA: Tribal Belonging and the False Promise of Genetic Science*. Minneapolis: University of Minnesota Press, 2014.

Thacker, Eugene. *In the Dust of this Planet: The Horror of Philosophy V.1*. Winchester: Zero Books, 2011.

Wheelwright, Philip, ed. *The Presocratics*. New York: Macmillan, 1985.

Wolfendale, Peter. *Object-Oriented Philosophy: The Noumenon's New Clothes*. Falmouth: Urbanomic, 2014.

CHAPTER TWENTY-FOUR

Posthumanism

ZAHI ZALLOUA

The rhetoric of posthumanism is all around us; it has infiltrated popular culture and academia alike. The term suggests uneasiness with the representation of human subjectivity, registering doubt about the nature of the human self and its givenness. And, perhaps most importantly, it reflects a desire for a notion of the human (and humanism) that is otherwise than anthropomorphic. From Donna Haraway's model of the cyborg to the hit AMC show *The Walking Dead*, a posthumanist turn seemingly marks our cultural imaginary. But more than a description of the state of things, attesting, as it were, to a new Zeitgeist, posthumanism is increasingly being mobilized as a "generative tool,"[1] as a creative response to the bio-genetic age dubbed the "Anthropocene": an unprecedented global state in which human activity has now become the determining factor influencing the climate and the environment. So how did we become posthuman? Or conversely, and more skeptically, are "we" posthuman? And what does it mean to be posthuman? Inquiries into posthumanism's origins, goals, and fantasies quickly lead to a host of questions: If posthumanism is ostensibly a turn *away* from the human and humanism, what is it a turn *toward*? What about competing or alternative terms/turns of anti-humanism, transhumanism, and the nonhuman turn?[2] And, more fundamentally: what is humanism? What is the nature of its privileged unit, the human?

THE PERSISTENCE OF THE HUMAN

Humanism, in its most abstract or general sense, refers to a set of beliefs that place the human subject at the center of reflection and concern. Humanism has unquestionably supplied Western discourse with a resilient model of subjectivity. Vincent Descombes attests to humanism's strong mark on the philosophy of the subject, which affirms

> that the only conceivable suppositum of a "properly human" action is the being that identifies itself, not with the empirical person that it also is, but with the autonomous subject. Not the individual, taken up as he is in the tissue of the world, but a being capable of positing itself as *ideally* (or ultimately) different from everything that history has made, from everything that society has conditioned, from everything that institutions have fixed, from all the futures that past events have already marked or cleared the way for. But it is also the being that decided to conduct itself in such a way that it can think of itself, at the end of an infinite effort, as the author of all its worldly determinations.[3]

Humanism nurtures a philosophy of the subject, empowering the subject with agency and purpose.

In antiquity, we can trace this humanist sensibility in Protagoras's famous claim that "man is the measure of all things." Man displaces the gods as the center of discourse. In the Renaissance, humanism takes the form of an interest in identifying what distinguishes humans from other beings, a concern with the condition and singularity of "man" ("man" here stands ideologically for all human beings, occluding the fact it represented, and still continues to represent, unmarked white (European), heterosexual, able-bodied men). Take, for example, fifteenth-century Italian thinker Pico Della Mirandolla, for whom man's ontological specificity is tied to his malleability: "It is given to [man] to have that which he chooses and to be that which he wills."[4] Complementing this image of a self-forming self is Dutch humanist Desiderius Erasmus's dictum, "Homines non nascuntur, sed finguntur" (Men are not born, they are fashioned). As with Pico Della Mirandolla, Erasmus foregrounded the creative activity of self-fashioning, committed to the humanist belief that the human subject is not given and unchangeable, but is something to form, to cultivate, or create. Erasmus's open-ended definition of the subject becomes, as Thomas Greene puts it, "the motto of the Humanist revolution."[5] With such portraits of the Renaissance self, Pico and Erasmus helped to inaugurate the humanist myth of the self-made man, a man endowed with the capacity of cultivating himself and elevating himself to divine heights, particularly through the study of good letters (ancient literature, philosophy, rhetoric, philology, etc.). Only through the study of good letters, which became synonymous with the study of humanity (*studia humanitatis*), could human beings ever achieve their full humanity, and be who they truly are.

If the Renaissance made man's powers of eloquence and the study of letters essential to humanism (emphasizing powers and projects aimed at perfecting the self, in the etymological sense of "completing" the self), modern versions of humanism distanced themselves from such essentialism. Jean-Paul Sartre's existentialism shows this break most dramatically. In claiming that "existence precedes essence" (Sartre vulgarizes the meaning and explanation of humanism in "Existentialism is a Humanism"[6]), Sartre radicalizes Erasmus's motto, stressing the subject's radical freedom and its nausea-inducing reality, while also positing human consciousness as the source of meaning in the world.

Yet a new generation of French intellectuals, spurred by the tumultuous events of May 1968, broke with Sartrean existentialism and its model of humanism. While they upheld the transience and contingency of meaning (the world does not possess any inherent, stable meaning), they radically questioned the powers of consciousness, the elevated status of the human, of the subject as a *constituting* force, that is, a force capable of fixing meaning. Louis Althusser was the first to level a devastating blow to Sartrean humanism. The subject, he showed, is *constituted*; the individual is subjected to the play of language or power. He or she is an ideological construction, the effect of what Althusser calls "interpellation." You are first an individual, and then you become a subject endowed with agency: "*All ideology hails or interpellates concrete individuals as concrete subjects.*"[7] Your emergence as a subject is predicated on your recognizing yourself as a subject when you are hailed by another (Althusser's paradigmatic example is the police officer who calls out to you, *demanding* your response/confirmation). Ideology through interpellation humanizes the social world; it discloses a meaningful world, in which there is a place for you, where you count and your voice matters. For example, television viewers are repeatedly interpellated as mass viewing subjects, subjects who are polled and asked to weigh in on matters or tweet a response. Or in the case of CNN's I-Reports, spectators, armed with the latest smart phones, are solicited and given ample opportunity to "make" the news. This (fake) democratization, or we might say "wikipedification," of the news gives the appearance of empowering audience members—transforming them from passive consumers (individuals) into active coproducers (subjects) of news—but it also risks reinforcing the commodification of journalism: journalistic knowledge and in-depth analysis take a back seat to the entertaining value of superficial analysis and sound bite, while viewer participation feeds the narcissistic fantasy of their self-importance.

Anti-humanism reaches its conceptual apogee in Michel Foucault's *The Order Things*, in which he argues for doing away with philosophy's cherished universal or ahistorical subject when he boldly declares "the death of man" in his concluding pages.[8] Language precedes Man. To speak of the "death of man" is to recognize that language structures the reality of human beings, and not simply the other way around. Human beings are not the center of discourse. Embracing the death of man did not entail an irresponsible misanthropy—despite the claim to the contrary within the humanities and social sciences. But Foucault also insisted, in his later essay "What is an Author?," on the ways the humanist subject lives on in people's perceptions, even after its metaphysical death. It is not enough to declare, with Roland Barthes, "the death of the author."[9] This postmodern slogan can occlude the persistence of the author. Foucault points to its continuing presence in the discourse of literary criticism, to the ways the "author" operates as a "principle of thrift" or shorthand in the interpretive reception of a work.[10] So, on one hand, we can reject the idea of the Author as God, seeing it as an old relic, and, on the other, still be invested in a different—and arguably more insidious—form of authorship, whereby submitting a work to what Foucault dubs the "author function" involves seeing the work as fitting into the larger, coherent thought of a unified author: namely, the humanist author at the center of all his works.

Posthumanism responds to these different understandings of humanism and its historical and ongoing role in shaping Western thought. Yet one understanding of the prefix "post-" that we should nuance—but not necessarily repudiate—from the start is that "*post-*" simply means "after," with the assumption that what comes after has moved beyond or superseded what came before. According to this definition of "post," posthumanism would entail a clean break with humanism. Here we might keep in mind Jean-François Lyotard's caution against thinking of the "*post*" only in terms of a neat progression of events, or conversely as an instantiation of the same phenomena in a new guise. It "does not mean a process of coming back or flashing back, feeding back, but of *ana*-lysing, *ana*-mnesing, of reflecting."[11] So if posthumanism ostensibly names a new body of knowledge, it remains to be seen how antagonistic a relation it maintains with humanism, the human, and the tradition of liberal rights. Thinking about posthumanism through a consideration of the "post" highlights the necessity of thinking *with and against* humanism. I want to pursue this line of inquiry across two distinct, yet interrelated, fields of study: biotechnology and the animal. Both fields, I argue, exert interpretive pressure on the "human," scrutinizing its individualism, its metaphysical underpinnings, exposing the ideology of human "exceptionalism" (human speciesism).

SCIENCE, TRANSHUMANISM, AND THE RISE OF THE CYBORG

Science has transformed the very notion of perfection, redefining the means by which it can be achieved. In the West today, it is often science—like the spiritual imitation of Christ, the philosophical imitation of Socrates, or the study of good letters more generally, which were dominant ideas at other moments in Western history—that promises to perfect humans (in the etymological sense of "completing" human nature, helping humans realize their full potential). Gene therapy, cosmetic surgeries, and pharmaceutical solutions substitute for transcendence. Operating on the plane of immanence, posthumanists refuse to settle for what *is*. They do not accept old age, or rather the effects of aging. Cosmetic surgeries are being perfected and made available to a larger body of people, while Viagra and other drugs reconfigure prior understandings of sexuality. It is, however, gene therapy, along with cloning, which has set off alarm bells among liberal humanists who see biotechnology as threatening to change humanity at the ontological level. Take for example, Francis Fukuyama's alarming observation: "What will happen to political rights once we are able to, in effect, breed some people with saddles on their backs, and others with boots and spurs?"[12] Fukuyama's representation of the posthuman world we are living in is cautionary. On this view, posthumanism endangers human agency and self-determination. It represents a negative departure from humanist goals.

Other critics celebrate rather than fear these changes, however, which they name transhumanism in order to stress the ways the human agency persists rather than declines with these advances in technology. In his 2005 article, "In Defence of Posthuman Dignity," Nick Bostrom writes:

> Transhumanism is a loosely defined movement that has developed gradually over the past two decades, and can be viewed as an outgrowth of secular humanism and the Enlightenment. It holds that current human nature is improvable through the use of applied science and other rational methods, which may make it possible to increase human health-span, extend our intellectual and physical capacities, and give us increased control over our own mental states and moods. Technologies of concern include not only current ones, like genetic engineering and information technology, but also anticipated future developments such as fully immersive virtual reality, machine-phase nanotechnology, and artificial intelligence.[13]

Giving primacy to rationality, transhumanism privileges and elevates the mind while the body is devalued and thematized as a limitation, whose vulnerability technological innovation seeks to reduce if not eliminate.

Yet taking a pro or an antitechnology stance on the question is not the only option. Other critics frame the issue quite differently, arguing that instead of embracing the humanist goals of individual perfection and self-determination, posthumanism should radically question and redefine what it means to be human in the first place. For Cary Wolfe, for example, the posthumanist project must genuinely trouble the place of the human; accordingly, the posthumanist project is

> to fully comprehend what amounts to a new reality: that the human occupies a new place in the universe, a universe now populated by what I am prepared to call nonhuman subjects. And this is why, to me, posthumanism means not the triumphal surpassing or unmasking of something but an increase in the vigilance, responsibility, and humility that accompany living in a world so newly, and differently, inhabited.[14]

In this respect, posthumanism should be different from transhumanism, which is merely "an intensification of humanism" through technological means.[15]

Wolfe's gloss introduces an important distinction, laying the conceptual ground for a critique of transhumanism's aggressive humanism. Decoupling transhumanism and posthumanism is a precondition for thinking of an alternative form of posthumanism, a "critical" posthumanism that explores the full potential of a non-humancentric perspective.[16] These alternative models question, for example, the consumerism of transhumanism (the consequences of framing human transformations as commodities to be bought and sold), or, more radically still, the ways innovations in science have impacted our existential relations to ourselves, others, and the world. Social theorist Donna Haraway, author of *A Cyborg Manifesto*, has led efforts to think the hybridity of the human, its coexistence or fusion with the machine in the sci-fi image of the cyborg. Fascination with the human-machine relationship has deep roots in philosophy. Ever since Descartes identified the mind as what sets humans apart from animals, and the body (both the human and the animal body) as a mere machine, philosophers have been eager to correct this bias in favor of the mind by giving a more prominent role to the body, and to matter more generally.

Downgrading the mind means downgrading man's privileged status in the humanist order of things, in the hierarchy that places humans at the pinnacle, above animals, plants, and inanimate matter. This shift has already happened, writes Haraway in 1985: "By the late twentieth-century, our time, a mythic time, we are all chimeras, theorized and fabricated hybrids of machine and organism—in short, we are cyborgs."[17] The cyborg is an aberration, a monster, some*thing* out of joint with a humanist Zeitgeist. It perverts society's binary oppositions between human and nonhuman, animate and inanimate, man and woman, while stubbornly rejecting all temptations of wholeness and closure: "The cyborg is a creature in a postgender world; it has no truck with bisexuality, pre-oedipal symbiosis, unalienated labor, or other seductions to organic wholeness through a final appropriation of all the powers of the parts into a higher unity."[18]

Posthumanism avows this new reality; it invites us to adjust our understanding of human sovereignty—to rewrite the story of the human. Haraway ends her cyborg manifesto with its most memorable line: "I would rather be a cyborg than a goddess."[19] Unlike Descartes's story, this new story tells us that humans are no longer—and perhaps never were—"masters and possessors of nature,"[20] deploying the tools of science solely for their advantage and progress. Rather, the new posthumanist narrative reconceives the human as fundamentally relational and dependent, constituted by technologies.

(RE)TURNING TO THE ANIMAL

Thinking of the human not as a master but as a being existing in relationships with other beings implies profoundly reconceptualizing the way we think of humans and animals, and their shared ontologies and worlds. Wolfe explains the importance of the animal question for posthumanism: "The animal properly understood is a privileged figure for the problem of difference and subjectivity generally, because it foregrounds how the subject is always already multiple."[21] Yet how exactly we should reconceptionalize the human-animal relation that takes place continues to be a disputed matter. Humanist thought silences animals by appropriating the power to name them and to designate them as inferior and available for mastery. Even when humanists want to defend animals, they typically resort to animal rights discourse (on the model of human rights discourse), unwittingly sustaining the animals' status as objects, as mute beings who cannot speak but must be spoken for.[22]

Anthropologist and sociologist of science Bruno Latour tries to remedy this asymmetrical situation by enlarging our understanding of subjects, of who or what can act and ultimately speak. Latour's interests do not lie primarily in animals but in nonhuman others. Latour upholds a flat ontology, meaning that animals, plants, and machines all share the same ontological playing field as humans. The modern distinction between nature and culture often used to legitimatize our relation to nonhuman others is at the source of the problem.[23] This distinction severely limits our imagination of agency and the inanimate world, of what it means to be an actor. Latour offers an expansive definition of actor, locating agency not in intentions (and the capacity to act on these intentions to bring them about), but in the effects of action: "There is no other way to define an actor but through its action, and there is no other way to define an action but by asking what other actors are modified, transformed, perturbed, or created by the character that is the focus of attention."[24] All beings are agential objects, objects that are more than the way they appear to us (their ontology exceeds their epistemological rendering as objects-for-us). Objects escape our grasp and resist our interpretations, our hermeneutic habits. Agency is thus not an ontological privilege restricted to humans, but is far more widespread in the world. Indeed, once we unmake humans the central focus of our discourse—synonymous with the act of de-modernizing the human—we can finally make or hear objects speak.

A different kind of de-modernizing of the human and the animal takes place in Gilles Deleuze and Félix Guattari's writings. In their project to undo species identities, Deleuze and Guattari introduce the concept of "becoming-animal." This does not mean crudely mimicking animals: "Becoming-animal does not consist in playing animal or imitating an animal."[25] Rather, it involves changing modes of being. Gerald L. Bruns outlines the force of this concept:

> becoming-animal is a movement from major (the constant) to minor (the variable); it is a deterritorialization in which a subject no longer occupies a realm of stability and identity but is instead folded imperceptibly into a movement or into an amorphous *legion* whose mode of existence is nomadic or, alternatively, whose "structure" is rhizomatic rather than arborescent, that is, restless, insomniac, or in flight rather than settled, upright, at one with itself and at peace with others.[26]

The animal for Deleuze and Guattari must always be thought in the multiple: "A becoming-animal always involves a pack, a band, a population, a peopling, in short a multiplicity."[27] As Wolfe observes, this type of thinking complicates the comfort of humanist subjectivity, which tends to conceive of itself in identitarian terms, as a whole, complete, and rooted being. In offering the notion of becoming-animal, Deleuze and Guattari aim to scandalize humanism by insisting that there is no unified "Man" but that "the subject is always already multiple."[28] Consequently, the long cherished humanist values of autonomy, self-mastery, sovereignty, all become suspect, ideologically dubious.

Deleuze and Guattari also caution against projecting an all-too-humanized and humanizing image of the animal. They are in particular scornful of the family pet, an instrumentalized being, a docile animal available for human enjoyment:

> Individuated animals, family pets, sentimental, Oedipal animals each with its own petty history, "my" cat, "my" dog. These animals invite us to regress, draw us into a narcissistic contemplation, and they are the only kind of animal psychoanalysis understands, the better to discover a daddy, a mommy, a little brother behind them . . . : anyone who likes cats or dogs is a fool.[29]

The concept of becoming-animal insists on the exteriority of the animal; its alterity is encountered as "contagion."[30] The animal as *other-than-human* can only appear as a frightening otherness, as a significant disruption of my hermeneutic comfort, my sense of the world; or as Jacques Derrida puts it: "Monsters cannot be announced. One cannot say: 'Here are our monsters', without immediately turning them into pets."[31]

"But what is so wrong with pets?" asks Haraway. She criticizes Deleuze and Guattari's bias against family pets, deeming their vision to be too abstract, too disconnected from the lives of actual animals, and ultimately failing to imagine another kind of world: "This is a philosophy of the sublime, not the earthly, not the mud; becoming-animal is not an *autre-mondialisation* [an other-worlding]."[32] Haraway is more sympathetic to Derrida's reflections on animals. After finding himself interpellated and othered (his own animality disclosed) by his little female cat as he was naked and coming out of the shower,[33] Derrida meditates on his feline's singularity and the inadequacies of language to account for it:

> If I say "it is a real cat" that sees me naked, this is in order to mark its unsubstitutable singularity. When it responds in its name . . . it doesn't do so as the exemplar of a species called "cat," even less so of an "animal" genus or kingdom. It is true that I identify it as a male or female cat. But even before that identification, it comes to me as this irreplaceable living being that one day enters my space, into this place where it can encounter me, see me, even see me naked. Nothing can ever rob me of the certainty that what we have here is an existence that refuses to be conceptualized [*rebelle à tout concept*].[34]

Derrida follows here in the footsteps of the pre-Cartesian or anti-Cartesian Michel de Montaigne (or, we might say, the posthumanist Montaigne), who also challenges human exceptionalism ("the most vulnerable and frail of all creatures is man, and at the same time the most arrogant") by musing on his cat's understanding and affectivity: "When I play with my cat, who knows if I am not a pastime to her more than she is to me?"[35] Agentiality—enacted in the cat's "capacity to respond"[36]—is on the cat's side as much as on Montaigne's.

Yet Derrida also disappoints Haraway by shifting conceptual gears too quickly, leaving behind his cat for a more sustained deconstructive mediation on "the animal" and its ambivalent place in the history of Western philosophy.[37] Derrida scrutinizes philosophy's rhetoric of the proper, its "timeless" question of "what is proper to man?," and its philosophers' varied answers: language, thinking, trickery, laughter, awareness of death, the face, and so on. Rather than a wholesale assault on the sovereignty of human subjectivity, Haraway would have preferred more of a "becoming with" the animal. This is a project that she undertakes herself. As Braidotti puts it, Haraway invites us "to see the inter-*relation* human/animal as constitutive of the identity of *each*."[38] Human animals and nonhuman animals become who they are only in relation to one another, not in isolation. Unsatisfied with the sublime abstractions of "becoming-animal," and also with Derrida's staging of his encounter with his cat as an event, which similarly flirts with the rhetoric of the sublime, Haraway introduces her concept of "companion species" as a means for thinking about new possibilities for human-animal life. The concept of companion species reflects the ontological and material entanglement of humans and nonhumans, which foregrounds touch over abstraction in the interaction with her pet dog. Haraway rejects the idea that the designation of "pet" necessarily neutralizes the nonhuman animal: "If I have a dog, my dog has a human; what that means concretely is at stake."[39] She finds Deleuze and Guattari's statement "anyone who likes cats or dogs is a fool" at once arrogant and ignorant, and though Derrida is more open to his cat for what she teaches him about himself, Haraway also faults him for lacking curiosity about the details of animals' lives and experiences.[40]

At stake for Haraway is the danger of a posthumanism that does away with subjectivity altogether, leaving the human dispossessed, with nothing to offer nonhuman animals. This is why Haraway argues that she is not a posthumanist:

> I never wanted to be posthuman, or posthumanist, any more than I wanted to be postfeminist. For one thing, urgent work still needs to be done in reference to those who must inhabit the troubled categories of woman and human, properly pluralized, reformulated, and brought into constitutive intersection with other asymmetrical differences.[41]

Relationality trumps de-subjectivization. The relation between humans and their companions define and shape who they are: "*The partners do not precede their relating*; all that is, is the fruit of becoming with: those are the mantras of companion species."[42]

To sum up: Haraway's suspicion of posthumanism lies in its exclusive critique of subjectivity, when what is needed is a better appreciation of our relation to companion species. Simply stated, posthumanism in its post-structuralism mode always risks compounding the problem of humanism rather than effectively overcoming its self-centered metaphysics. I wonder, however, whether Haraway forecloses too neatly and quickly what Derrida's thinking can bring to an alternative posthumanism.

Derrida's posthumanist forays can and do accommodate relationality. Cognizant of the homogenizing potential of the single category of "the animal"—of the violence in being named, inscribed in the socio-symbolic network—Derrida coins the anti-speciesist term "animot," which at once evokes the idea of multiplicity (as a homonym of the French term "animaux" [animals]), and foregrounds its linguistic character: it is a word ("mot" means "word" in French) not to be confused with the thing, the nonhuman materiality, that it represents.[43] *Animot* enables Derrida to establish a "relation without relation" with his cat. The word applies to his cat, thematizing this nonhuman animal, but it also reflexively interrupts that designation, simultaneously registering the radical alterity of his cat, the unreadability of her gaze, her refusal "to be conceptualized," treating their encounter as nothing short of an event, provoking a linguistic, existential, and ethical crisis. In psychoanalytic terms, Derrida's cat is always more than her symbolic and imaginary rendering; she is also real, irreducible either to his phantasmatic projections or to society's gentrification of the cat into a "pet." As Derrida discovers, his cat remains a "monster," capable of provoking a radical disruption in his hermeneutic comfort. Erica Fudge puts the matter in slightly different terms:

> The pet crosses over species boundaries. It is an animal—it cannot speak—but it is also an ideal human—it says what we want it to say. It is only when the pet displays its animal nature—when it pees on the carpet, brings in a half-dead sparrow, destroys the furniture—that we lose the tranquility of the relation. Then, and only then, do we really confront the existence of something beyond our control in our home.[44]

Derrida's cat is both a pet and a monster. Her radical alterity is never fully contained within the symbolic order. She is capable of producing events, of reminding us that she can't quite be categorized or explained in human terms. But what happens after the event (after catching your cat looking at you while you are naked, as Derrida does, or experiencing your cat as a killer, as Fudge notes) merits equal attention. What *habits* we cultivate with our companion species is a question just as important (this is what I take to be Haraway's rejoinder).

HUMAN OR POSTHUMAN?: YES, PLEASE![45]

As with Derrida's cat—who complicates any designation of her as pet or monster—we must reject the standard questions informing the dialogue between humanists and posthumanists: are we human or posthuman? Should we remain human or embrace our posthumanity? Should we forego posthumaninity and adopt a postanimal perspective? To the question, "Human or Posthuman?" we must answer "Yes, Please!" We can detect the spirit of this answer in the original French title of Derrida's *L'animal donc que je suis*: which can be translated as both "the animal therefore that I am" and "the animal therefore that I follow." The ambiguity of the title complicates a straightforward choice between the two translations. The first can read autobiographically as an anti-Cartesian statement of Derrida's ontological animality, a radical reworking of Descartes' *je pense, donc je suis* (I think, therefore I am). The second suggests the promise of a hermeneutics of difference, a mode of interpretation that, mindful of the *animot*, implicates his cat as much as himself—human and nonhuman animals. In the first translation, we can see Derrida affirming a new humanism, a humanism that includes a recognition of human animality while also insisting on its difference from the animality of nonhuman animals: "*Everything I'll say will consist*, certainly not in effacing the limit, but in multiplying its figures, in complicating, thickening, delinearizing, folding, and dividing the line precisely by making it increase and multiply."[46] But this ontological distinction between the human and the animal is deemphasized (but not obliterated) by the posthuman hermeneutics of the second translation. A critical posthumanism might do well to refuse this logic of the either/or. We should reject the misleading terms of the question, the choice between human or posthuman. Posthumanism is neither more of the same, nor a simple celebration of the human as obsolete. To the questions that have haunted posthumanism from its inception—Are we human or cyborg? Are we human or animal?—we should answer, "Yes, Please!"

Whitman College (United States)

NOTES

1. Rosi Braidotti, *The Posthuman* (Cambridge: Polity Press, 2013), 5.

2. Richard Grusin designates as a "nonhuman turn" a motley of approaches "engaged in decentering the human in favor of a turn toward and a concern for the nonhuman, understood by variously in terms of animals, affectivity, bodies, materiality, or technologies" (Richard Grusin, "Introduction," in *The Nonhuman Turn*, ed. Richard Grusin [Minneapolis: University of Minnesota Press, 2015], vii).

3. Vincent Descombes, "Apropos of the 'Critique of the Subject' and the Critique of this Critique," in *Who comes after the Subject?*, eds. Eduardo Cadava, Peter Connor, and Jean-Luc Nancy (London: Routledge, 1991), 132.

4. Pico della Mirandola, *On the Dignity of Man*, trans. Charles Glenn Wallis (Indianapolis: Hackett, 1998), 5.

5. Thomas Greene, "The Flexibility of the Self in Renaissance Literature," in *The Disciplines of Criticism*, eds. Peter Demetz, Thomas Greene, and Lawry Nelson Jr. (New Haven: Yale University Press, 1968), 249.

6. Jean-Paul Sartre, *Existentialism is a Humanism*, trans. Carol Macomber (New Haven: Yale University Press, 2007).

7. Louis Althusser, "Ideology and Ideological State Apparatuses (Notes towards an Investigation)," in *Mapping Ideology*, ed. Slavoj Žižek (London: Verso, 1994), 130.

8. Michel Foucault, *The Order of Things: An Archaeology of the Human Sciences*, trans. Alan Sheridan (New York: Vintage, 1970), 387.

9. Roland Barthes, "Death of the Author," in *Image, Text, Music*, trans. Stephen Heath (New York: Hill and Wang, 1977), 142–48.

10. Michel Foucault, "What is an Author?" in *The Foucault Reader*, ed. Paul Rabinow (New York: Pantheon Books, 1984), 118.

11. Jean-François Lyotard, "Defining the Postmodern," in *The Cultural Studies Reader*, ed. Simon During (London: Routledge, 1993), 173.

12. Francis Fukuyama, *Our Posthuman Future: Consequences of the Biotechnology Revolution* (New York: Farrar, Straus and Giroux, 2002), 10.

13. Nick Bostrom, "In Defence of Posthuman Dignity," *Bioethics* 19.3 (2005): 202–03.

14. Cary Wolfe, *What is Posthumanism?* (Minneapolis: University of Minnesota Press, 2010), 47.

15. Wolfe, *What is Posthumanism?*, xv.

16. Pramod K. Nayar, *Posthumanism* (Cambridge: Polity Press, 2013), 8–11.

17. Donna Haraway, "A Cyborg Manifesto: Science, Technology, and Socialist-Feminism in the Late Twentieth Century," in *Manifestly Haraway*, ed. Donna J. Haraway (Minneapolis: University of Minnesota Press, 2016), 7.

18. Haraway, "A Cyborg Manifesto," 8.

19. Ibid., 68.

20. René Descartes, *Discourse on Method and Meditations on First Philosophy*, trans. Donald A. Cress (Indianapolis: Hackett, 1998), 35.

21. Cary Wolfe, *Animal Rites: American Culture, the Discourse of Species, and Posthumanist Theory* (Chicago: Chicago University Press, 2003), 161.

22. See, for example, Martha C. Nussbaum, "Beyond 'Compassion and Humanity': Justice for Nonhuman Animals," in *Animal Rights: Current Debates and New Directions*, eds. Cass R. Sunstein and Martha C. Nussbaum (Oxford: Oxford University Press, 2004), 299–320.

23. See Bruno Latour, *We Have Never Been Modern*, trans. Catherine Porter (Cambridge: Harvard University Press, 1993).

24. Bruno Latour, *Pandora's Hope: Essays in the Reality of Science Studies* (Cambridge: Harvard University Press, 1999), 122.

25. Gilles Deleuze and Félix Guattari, *A Thousand Plateaus: Capitalism and Schizophrenia*, trans. Brian Massumi (Minneapolis: University of Minnesota Press, 1987), 238.

26. Gerald L. Bruns, "Becoming-Animal (Some Simple Ways)," *New Literary History* 38.4 (2007): 703–04.

27. Deleuze and Guattari, *A Thousand Plateaus*, 239.

28. Wolfe, *Animal Rites*, 161.

29. Deleuze and Guattari, *A Thousand Plateaus*, 240.

30. Ibid., 242.

31. Jacques Derrida, "Some Statements and Truisms about Neologisms, Newisms, Postisms, Parasitisms, and other small Seismisms," in *The States of "Theory,"* ed. David Carroll (New York: Columbia University Press, 1989), 80.

32. Donna Haraway, *When Species Meet* (Minneapolis: University of Minnesota Press, 2008), 28. Christopher L. Miller condemns the project of becoming-animal as "a form of exoticism": "Becoming woman, becoming animal, becoming minoritarian and 'third world' is a masquerade invented expressly for white male majoritarian humans to

play" (Christopher L. Miller, *Nationalists and Nomads: Essays on Francophone African Literature and Culture* [Chicago: University of Chicago Press, 1998], 23).

33. Jacques Derrida, *The Animal that Therefore I Am*, trans. David Willis (New York: Fordham University Press, 2008), 6.

34. Derrida, *The Animal*, 9.

35. Michel de Montaigne, *The Complete Essays*, trans. Donald Frame (Stanford: Stanford University Press, 1957), 330, 331; Derrida, *The Animal*, 6.

36. Derrida, *The Animal*, 163n8.

37. Along the same lines, Braidotti accuses Derrida of "reduc[ing] animality to a general figuration of Alterity" (Rosi Braidotti, "Posthuman, All Too Human Towards a New Process Ontology," *Theory, Culture & Society* 23.7–8 [2006]: 200). Similarly, Cynthia Willett writes: "Derrida's cat remains a figure and not a character in his life" (Cynthia Willett, *Interspecies Ethics* [New York: Columbia University Press, 2014], 72). Haraway, Braidotti, and Willett flatten, however, what Derrida does with figuration. Figuration is never crudely opposed to materiality in Derrida's writings.

38. Braidotti, *The Posthuman*, 79.

39. Donna Haraway, "The Companion Species Manifesto," in *Manifestly Haraway*, 145.

40. Haraway, *When Species Meet*, 20.

41. Ibid., 17.

42. Ibid.

43. Derrida, *The Animal*, 41.

44. Erica Fudge, *Animal* (London: Reaktion, 2002).

45. I am indebted to Slavoj Žižek's following formulation: "In a well-known Marx Brothers joke Groucho answers the standard question 'Tea or coffee?' with 'Yes, please!'—a refusal of choice. . . . One should answer in the same way the false alternative today's critical theory seems to impose on us: either 'class struggle' (the outdated problematic of class antagonism, commodity production, etc.) or 'postmodernism' (the new world of dispersed multiple identities, of radical contingency, of an irreducible ludic plurality of struggles). Here, at least, we can have our cake and eat it" (Slavoj Žižek, "Class Struggle or Postmodernism? Yes, Please!" in *Contingency, Hegemony, Universality: Contemporary Dialogues on the Left*, eds. Judith Butler, Ernesto Laclau, and Slavoj Žižek [New York: Verso, 2000], 90).

46. Derrida, *The Animal*, 29.

WORKS CITED

Althusser, Louis. "Ideology and Ideological State Apparatuses (Notes towards an Investigation)." In *Mapping Ideology*. Ed. Slavoj Žižek. London: Verso, 1994. 100–40.

Barthes, Roland. "Death of the Author [1968]." In *Image, Text, Music*. Trans. Stephen Heath. New York: Hill and Wang, 1977. 142–48.

Bostrom, Nick. "In Defence of Posthuman Dignity." *Bioethics* 19.3 (2005): 202–14.

Braidotti, Rosi. "Posthuman, All Too Human Towards a New Process Ontology." *Theory, Culture & Society* 23.7–8 (2006): 197–208.

Braidotti, Rosi. *The Posthuman*. Cambridge: Polity Press, 2013.

Bruns, Gerald L. "Becoming-Animal (Some Simple Ways)." *New Literary History* 38.4 (2007): 703–20.

Deleuze, Gilles, and Félix Guattari. *A Thousand Plateaus: Capitalism and Schizophrenia* [1980]. Trans. Brian Massumi. Minneapolis: University of Minnesota Press, 1987.

Derrida, Jacques. "Some Statements and Truisms about Neologisms, Newisms, Postisms, Parasitisms, and Other Small Seismisms." In *The States of "Theory."* Ed. David Carroll. New York: Columbia University Press, 1989. 63–94.

Derrida, Jacques. *The Animal that Therefore I Am [2006].* Trans. David Willis. New York: Fordham University Press, 2008.

Descartes, René. *Discourse on Method [1637] and Meditations on First Philosophy [1641].* Trans. Donald A. Cress. Indianapolis: Hackett, 1998.

Descombes, Vincent. "Apropos of the 'Critique of the Subject' and the Critique of this Critique." In *Who Comes after the Subject?* Eds. Eduardo Cadava, Peter Connor, and Jean-Luc Nancy. London: Routledge, 1991. 120–34.

Foucault, Michel. *The Order of Things: An Archaeology of the Human Sciences* [1966]. Trans. Alan Sheridan. New York: Vintage, 1970.

Foucault, Michel. "What is an Author? [1969]." In *The Foucault Reader.* Ed. Paul Rabinow. New York: Pantheon Books, 1984. 101–20.

Fudge, Erica. *Animal.* London: Reaktion, 2002.

Fukuyama, Francis. *Our Posthuman Future: Consequences of the Biotechnology Revolution.* New York: Farrar, Straus and Giroux, 2002.

Greene, Thomas. "The Flexibility of the Self in Renaissance Literature." In *The Disciplines of Criticism.* Eds. Peter Demetz, Thomas Greene and Lawry Nelson Jr. New Haven: Yale University Press, 1968. 241–64.

Grusin, Richard. "Introduction." In *The Nonhuman Turn.* Ed. Richard Grusin. Minneapolis: University of Minnesota Press, 2015. vii–xxix.

Haraway, Donna. *When Species Meet.* Minneapolis: University of Minnesota Press, 2008.

Haraway, Donna. "The Companion Species Manifesto." In *Manifestly Haraway.* Minneapolis: University of Minnesota Press, 2016. 91–198.

Haraway, Donna. "A Cyborg Manifesto: Science, Technology, and Socialist-Feminism in the Late Twentieth Century." In *Manifestly Haraway: The Cyborg Manifesto. The Companion Species Manifesto. Companions in Conversation (with Cary Wolfe).* Minneapolis: University of Minnesota Press, 2016. 3–90.

Latour, Bruno. *We Have Never Been Modern* [1991]. Trans. Catherine Porter. Cambridge: Harvard University Press, 1993.

Latour, Bruno. *Pandora's Hope: Essays in the Reality of Science Studies.* Cambridge: Harvard University Press, 1999.

Lyotard, Jean-François. "Defining the Postmodern." In *The Cultural Studies Reader.* Ed. Simon During. London: Routledge, 1993. 170–73.

Miller, Christopher L. *Nationalists and Nomads: Essays on Francophone African Literature and Culture.* Chicago: University of Chicago Press, 1998.

Mirandola, Pico della. *On the Dignity of Man.* Trans. Charles Glenn Wallis. Indianapolis: Hackett, 1998.

Montaigne, Michel de. *The Complete Essays.* Trans. Donald Frame. Stanford: Stanford University Press, 1957.

Nayar, Pramod K. *Posthumanism.* Cambridge: Polity Press, 2013.

Nussbaum, Martha C. "Beyond 'Compassion and Humanity': Justice for Nonhuman Animals." In *Animal Rights: Current Debates and New Directions.* Eds. Cass R. Sunstein and Martha C. Nussbaum. Oxford: Oxford University Press, 2004. 299–320.

Sartre, Jean-Paul. *Existentialism is a Humanism* [1996]. Trans. Carol Macomber. New Haven: Yale University Press, 2007.

Willett, Cynthia. *Interspecies Ethics*. New York: Columbia University Press, 2014.

Wolfe, Cary. *Animal Rites: American Culture, the Discourse of Species, and Posthumanist Theory*. Chicago: Chicago University Press, 2003.

Wolfe, Cary. *What is Posthumanism?* Minneapolis: University of Minnesota Press, 2010.

Žižek, Slavoj. "Class Struggle or Postmodernism? Yes, Please!" *Contingency, Hegemony, Universality: Contemporary Dialogues on the Left*. Eds. Judith Butler, Ernesto Laclau, and Slavoj Žižek. New York: Verso, 2000. 90–135.

CHAPTER TWENTY-FIVE

University Studies

JEFFREY J. WILLIAMS

THE RISE OF CRITICAL UNIVERSITY STUDIES

Since the late 1990s, a new movement in criticism and theory has developed focusing on higher education. It has been called critical university studies (CUS) to foreground its critical perspective on a major social institution, similar to previous initiatives such as critical legal studies (CLS), as well as to distinguish it from conventional scholarly accounts in education, literary and cultural studies, or other disciplines. It turns its sights on changes over the past forty years, particularly in the United States and more recently in Britain and other countries, away from a strong public model of higher education to a neoliberal privatized model. It combines investigative research with theoretical critiques of neoliberalism, updating the humanistic legacy of the university.

The university is often minimized as an "Ivory Tower," but given the number of people who pass through its doors (70 percent of Americans attend college at some point), those who work in them (more than 6 million teachers, administrators, staff, and other workers in the United States—not to mention all the workers dependent on campuses), and its extensive interchange with business and industry, it is a major social and cultural institution of our time. CUS examines the role of higher education in contemporary society and its relations to culture, politics, and labor.

Unlike initiatives during the era of grand theory, such as structuralism in the 1960s or deconstruction in the 1970s, CUS focuses less on the theoretical understanding of a general concept like language and aims more for analysis of the actual practices of extant institutions. Thus, it adopts the rubric of "studies" rather than a singular concept, and it adds a new branch to contemporary cultural studies. Like other branches of recent theory and criticism, such as gay and lesbian studies, disability studies, and race studies, it draws on previous theory, and like deconstruction it points out problems with conventional thinking. But it also keeps sight of practical goals; for instance, if more than two-thirds of those who attend university in the United States leave with more than $30,000 of student debt, then higher education does not confer freedom or a public good but constraint and harm, and CUS advocates policies to remedy it, such as loan forgiveness or debt-free college.

One way to think of it is as an applied theory rather than pure theory. At core, it is motivated by concern for students, university workers, and the democratic future of higher education, rather than a more abstract focus on the influence of Western metaphysics, as deconstruction had. Like CLS or critical race studies, it analyzes how our social institutions foster injustice or perpetuate inequality, and it advocates for their fuller democratic possibilities. Accordingly, it often takes an oppositional stance to some of the central changes in contemporary higher education.

Thus far, CUS has targeted several areas, notably the new corporate protocols of higher education, as administrators have become progressively more oriented toward business goals rather than intellectual or egalitarian ones, promoting work that directly serves corporations and reconfiguring faculty as labor to be managed. A central policy directive that marked a shift in contemporary higher education was the Bayh-Dole Act of 1980, which granted patent rights to universities and thus encouraged them to adopt business aims. Before that there was more of a firewall between academic work and business results, as rights reverted to the funding body—if a grant came from the NEH, the patent would revert to the United States, in other words to the public commons rather than toward private accumulation. Universities gradually adapted to this new situation, shifting their emphases from undergraduate education and open-ended research toward graduate education and research with immediately profitable uses.

The usual assumption is that universities benefit from this business relationship; however, one of the founding figures of CUS, Christopher Newfield, has shown that, rather than a gain, these practices have actually cost far more than assumed and drained funds from undergraduate teaching and from humanistic rather than profit-seeking disciplines. While humanities disciplines like English don't receive significant "external" funds, they have little overhead costs and tend to earn more their costs, thus often generating a surplus. In other words, in an accurate accounting, the humanities typically support the applied sciences, not the other way around, and overall the university has become a conduit for private profit.

These shifts have also had great effect on the main constituents of the university: faculty and students. In a traditional framework, the faculty is the core of the university; they form its "corporate body," which is one of the original uses of the word *corporate*, making decisions on academic issues and maintaining stability over time. Likewise, students are obviously an essential constituent. However, in recent years it seems as if the focus of higher education has turned away from academic issues and general education to profit-seeking research. Moreover, in recent years faculty have been construed as contingent, managed labor. Formerly the large majority of faculty had permanent, full-time positions; since around 1980 that has shrunken, with less than one-third holding full-fledged positions and two-thirds not. This reconfiguration of academic jobs is called "casualization," so that those working often hold "casual," adjunct, temporary, or nonpermanent jobs, frequently without benefits or any security.

Regarding students, this has led to poorer conditions for a rising majority. Most notably, it has prompted an astronomical rise in student debt as well as student work hours. This shift derives directly from neoliberal policies that theorists such as David Harvey diagnoses in his *Brief History of Neoliberalism*: under the former model, higher education, especially at state schools, was conceived as a public service, paid largely from public (tax) funds, and tuitions were relatively low—and in some states, free. (Private universities, such as Harvard or Columbia, also received substantial public funds in student aid as well as research, so also had relatively inexpensive tuition.) But under the new regime of neoliberalism, such public services are construed as a private, individual good, so state funding has been reduced and each individual has to pay his or her own way. Consequently, tuitions have risen exponentially, and in response the average student at state schools (which includes community colleges as well as research universities) works twenty-five hours per week. This despite the fact that excessive work hours correlate with poor performance, failure to complete a degree, and other problems.

In conjunction with work hours, student debt has risen nearly fifteenfold since 1980, when the rate of inflation has gone up only about 2.5 times.[1] At the same rate, an average new Chevy would now cost about $150,000. Sometimes this is blamed on colleges themselves, but the study "The Great Cost Shift"[2] demonstrates that it directly derives from the shrinkage of public funding.

Since the 1990s, a first wave of CUS scholars has targeted the corporatization of higher education and the shift to "academic capitalism," the exploitation of academic labor, and the rise of student debt. Subsequently, they have been joined by a second generation which is expanding the range of criticism to include the use and abuse of technology, the dominance of entrepreneurial values at the expense of the public good, and the proprietary expansion of American institutions globally. They also look at specific facets of corporatization, such as the progressive racial segregation of current higher education, such that fewer minority students attend than in the 1970s.[3]

THE TRADITION OF RADICAL CRITICISM OF HIGHER EDUCATION

There is a long tradition of commentary on higher education, notably on "the idea of the university." It has been a mainstay of the philosophical tradition, although scholars in literary studies, history, and sociology have also contributed. Touchstones include Immanuel Kant's *The Conflict of the Faculties*,[4] that argues for its being based on philosophical reason over practical disciplines or state control, and Cardinal Newman's *The Idea of a University*,[5] that calls for the liberal exploration of knowledge by undergraduate students rather than professional training. More recently, philosophers such as Jacques Derrida have continued the argument for the independence of the university and its pursuits, in essays such as "The University without Condition."[6]

The modern radical tradition began in the United States in the period after the Civil War,[7] as the institution grew from small religious or liberal arts colleges to the modern university system, which developed in conjunction with modern science and industrial expansion. For the first time, it encouraged research rather than rote learning and, under impetuses like the Morrill "Land Grant" Acts of 1862 and 1890, it aimed to serve a wide breadth of students. It responded to the Gilded Age, the period in American history that saw the accumulation of vast fortunes like those of Carnegie and Rockefeller, often through unscrupulous practices and at the expense of labor, and generating massive inequality. Two important intellectual figures, Thorstein Veblen, a founder of sociology, and Upton Sinclair, a novelist and muckraker, wrote studies of the new institution. Veblen's *The Higher Learning in America: A Memorandum on the Conduct of Universities by Business Men*[8] criticizes the embrace of business and management principles, and Sinclair's *The Goose-Step: A Study of American Education*[9] presents an exposé, much as he did of the meat industry in *The Jungle* (1906), this time drawing on an investigative tour across the United States investigating the influence of new wealth on universities.

The barons of business, as Veblen might have termed them, contributed substantial amounts of money to burgeoning universities. While under the rubric of philanthropy, they also attempted to control the future of higher education through those putative gifts, and Sinclair reported on some of their unsavory doings. This suggests one lesson from the history: we should not idealize or have false nostalgia for an earlier time. As with any social institution, the university has responded to its time and circumstances, and some of its previous conditions were troubling or problematic. However, neither should we give in to resignation that problems are perpetual and that we can never solve them: there are better and worse solutions.

The first wave of radical criticism largely carried out the aims of the progressive politics of the time, taking the large corporate powers of its day to task. While there were sporadic moments of criticism thereafter, notably over academic freedom and political repression during the 1950s stemming from McCarthyism, the next major phase did not occur until the 1960s, amid that decade's social foment. Funding from new policies such as the National Defense Education Act of 1958 and subsequent versions of the National Education Act fueled the accelerated expansion of American higher education through the 1960s and 1970s, bringing in students from classes previously excluded and supporting unprecedented amounts of research, often open-ended and unbeholden to business. However, by the late 1960s, there was also significant controversy, particularly over the university's links to the military-industrial complex during the Vietnam conflict, as well as its training students for a conformist role in society. A substantial wing of protest of the war came from campuses, with students protesting and also criticizing other social practices, notably the lack of civil rights. The influential group Students for a Democratic Society, or SDS, arose organically from the expanding student body, and a central plank of their manifesto, the Port Huron Statement, called for education to be less regimented, more open, and more relevant to people's actual lives. Similarly, philosophical critiques like Robert Paul Wolff's *The Ideal of the University*[10] deride the role of the university as a "social service station" or an "assembly line" for the white-collar world, and those in the Critical Pedagogy movement, inspired by Paulo Friere, promoted less instrumental, more engaged, and more democratic education.

Another noteworthy wing of criticism of the time came from the emerging feminist movement, in texts such as Adrienne Rich's "Toward a Woman-Centered University."[11] Up until that time, higher education largely served men (in fact, at the time all the Ivy League colleges took in only men—they only became coed over the next two decades). In addition, takeovers at Columbia and Cornell centered on civil rights, particularly the suppression of African-Americans in US society. The feminist and civil rights movements inveighed to open American universities to a fair representation of women and people of color. This precipitated the drive for diversity and, coalescing in the 1980s, multiculturalism—which in turn catalyzed a backlash, resulting in the culture wars that sparked during the late 1980s and early 1990s. One could tell the story of higher education not only through its progress but through its backlashes.

The neoliberal turn in higher education started gaining momentum during the 1980s, following shifts in American politics toward deregulation, the shrinkage of public services, and privatization. By the 1990s scholars and critics began realizing that there was systematic change afoot, and the first forays were often exposés of the corporatization of higher education and the corruption of humanistic principles, as well as critiques of academic labor. CUS arose not from a particular school or group of theorists but from critics and also activists in various fields. In this, it differs from deconstruction, which originated from a more distinct academic cohort, notably of those scholars who became known as the Yale school, or from radical initiatives like CLS, which was a more deliberately organized academic movement.

A comparison with CLS might help shine more light on CUS. Like CLS, which arose in the late 1970s and early 1980s, CUS examined a major social institution and had an explicit political dimension to its work. CLS distinguished itself from standard legal history, arguing that law was not neutral or impartial but an instrument of its social hierarchy and aiming to correct it.[12] CUS distinguishes itself from the standard history of education or the humanistic tradition of "the idea of the university," analyzing how higher education is an instrument of its social structure and advocates ways that it might be reformed. In philosophical terms, CLS is realist rather than idealist in orientation, emphasizing what the legal theorist Mark Kelman calls "law-in-action" rather than "law-in-books." Similarly, CUS is realist rather than idealist, studying concrete practices of higher education. Both draw on critical theory, although CLS has drawn on deconstruction and other forms of post-structuralism, looking at the way that language creates indeterminacy in law,[13] whereas CUS is less tied to post-structural theory and turns to subsequent theory of neoliberal capitalism.

While similarly critical of social hierarchies, there are some striking differences. CLS was inaugurated by faculty largely at elite institutions, notably Harvard and Yale, and aimed to effect change through legal education. CUS comes from a more diffuse group, from a range of institutions, for the most part public colleges and universities, and from a range of positions, often graduate student or adjunct, and it aims to effect change in direct action in unions or the student loan movement as well as through reportage, analysis, and pragmatic proposals. A significant wing of it comes from the academic labor movement, both of graduate students and of adjuncts, represented by groups such as the New Faculty Majority.

There is also a historical difference: CLS was formed by scholars largely from the 1960s generation and reflected concerns of the civil rights and anti-war movements. Emerging two decades later, CUS enlists those from subsequent generations, responding to conditions of the neoliberal turn of the 1980s and 1990s and draining of social institutions, in particular the shrinkage of full-time, professional jobs. CLS was a critique of complacent mid-century liberalism, whereas CUS is a critique of neoliberalism and the conservative ascendancy.

TOUCHSTONES AND NEW CHALLENGES OF UNIVERSITY STUDIES

Touchstones of the emerging field of CUS include critiques of corporatization, the casualization of academic labor, and the indenturing of students in future debt. Its first wave saw exposés of corporatization, such as Lawrence Soley's *Leasing the Ivory Tower: The Corporate Takeover of Academia*[14] and Jennifer Washburn's *University, Inc.: The Corporate Corruption of Higher Education*,[15] which looked at the corruption of research through intensified commercialization. It also included more scholarly accounts of "academic capitalism," notably in Sheila Slaughter's series of books, beginning with Slaughter and Leslie's *Academic Capitalism: Politics, Policies, and the Entrepreneurial University*,[16] which closely examines "technology-transfer" to businesses and the rise of corporate managerial policies in place of traditional faculty governance.

The inaugural wave of CUS also included analyses of academic labor, as those working in higher education were faced with the shrinkage of decent jobs and realized it was not a short-term problem but systematic. Administrators put in place a sharply stratified system, with the majority of faculty, rather than a body of scholars with full-fledged positions as professors, now contingent, with little formal job security, inferior or absent benefits, and relatively low or sometimes poverty-level wages. Joe Berry's *Reclaiming the Ivory Tower: Organizing Adjuncts to Change Higher Education*[17] gives a unionist account of dealing with these new conditions. (See also Johnson.) Moreover, a significant portion of teachers, staffing the bulk of introductory courses like composition, are graduate students—who thus function not exclusively as students but as labor. Coming out of the graduate student union movement, Marc Bousquet exposed the perverse position of those students in an influential essay, "The Waste Product of Graduate Education,"[18] that reasoned that, if the majority of PhDs were not getting tenure-stream jobs, then they were actually byproducts of the current system rather than apprentices, and exploited as cheap labor. Bousquet extended his analysis to look at the way that undergraduates have also been exploited through work-study plans and full-time faculty in fields such as composition have been remade as management in his book *How the University Works: Higher Education and the Low-Wage Nation*.[19] A related development has been the explosion of administration, with its numbers moving from a small portion to exceeding permanent faculty, detailed in Benjamin Ginsberg's *The Fall of the Faculty: The Rise of the All-Administrative University and Why It Matters*.[20]

Alongside the analysis of faculty labor, another significant wing of CUS has called attention to the escalation of college student loan debt, notably Jeffrey J. Williams's essays "Debt Education" and "Student Debt and the Spirit of Indenture."[21] At first it seemed that it was just a matter of rising costs, but Williams shows how they rose exponentially, far beyond the rate of inflation, rising to average nearly $30,000 for graduating seniors, and given their predominance, how they will affect rough half of those in rising generations in the United States. Further, he analyzes how they redraw the social contract from seeing education as a service to the young and a benefit to society to a private expense borne by the individual that conscripts the young. Student debt has severe effects on those subjected to it, perverting the goals of open-ended education and, beyond a simple bill, permeating their lives. At its worst, Williams contends that student debt literally approaches a form of indentured servitude—for the figurative transport to a job, in an unbreakable contract that is secured by the individual himself or herself rather than by property, and because of its high amounts enduring for long periods. Even though current policies spurring the rampant growth of student loan debt began in the 1980s, the consequences fell under the radar until around 2008, in part because of the work that CUS researchers have done. Since the early 2010s, groups such as Out with Student Debt have lobbied for reform or forgiveness of student loan debt and put front and center the question of free tuition.

An important group of work draws from these critiques but more generally makes the case for how to reinvigorate public higher education. Christopher Newfield, in *Unmaking the Public University: The Forty-Year Assault on the Middle Class*,[22] diagnoses the policies that have undermined public education, and in his *The Great Mistake: How We Wrecked Public Universities and How We Can Fix Them*[23] he provides a holistic analysis of the current system, pointing out a series of choices that contribute to a cycle of decline of public education. His fundamental point is that higher education is a public good that should be wholeheartedly defended and, calling for public reinvestment, it has historically been good for business as well as the public commons. He has been joined by union leader and scholar Robert Samuels, whose *Why Public Higher Education Should Be Free: How to Decrease Cost and Increase Quality at American Universities*[24] makes a powerful argument for the pragmatic possibility of free tuition.

Alongside particular works, the field has seen the establishment of two new book series so-named CUS, one in the United States edited by Williams and Newfield from Johns Hopkins University Press, and one in the United Kingdom, published by Palgrave and edited by John Smyth. In addition, there are a number of online sites, such as Newfield's Remaking the University, that provide platforms for CUS work.

The debilitating effect of student loan debt, the case for low tuition, and the public importance of higher education will no doubt continue as major concerns of CUS. With them, a few other challenges have begun to draw more attention, notably the questions of technology, globalization, and unions. Sometimes technology, in the form of online courses, is held up as the wondrous future of higher education, but most tests show them to be far less effective than person-to-person learning. In a still-relevant analysis, *Digital Diploma Mills: The Automation of Higher Education*,[25] the historian David Noble demonstrated how they were essentially a contemporary version of shoddy correspondence courses. There have been a number of critiques of MOOC's (Massive Open Online Courses), but given the pressure for them because of their minimal cost, they remain a flashpoint. The problem is not technology per se, but the way that they reinforce class hierarchy, with the privileged few still receiving in-person education but the less privileged receiving inferior facsimiles. In conjunction, one avenue of analysis might be the effect not only of technology but of major tech companies, such as Google, Microsoft, Apple, and Facebook, on education, and how those businesses tacitly control it for their own goals and ideologies.

Another challenge that has come to the fore in the 2000s is what Andrew Ross has called "the rise of the global university." As with technology, globalization evokes futurist projections and hopes. But in practice it primarily entails the export of American higher education, for the benefit of US universities that effectively license or sell their services at a handsome profit. This represents a further stage in corporatization, gaining revenues not only from research and students at home but from overseas, largely in less developed countries, in lucrative cash deals and with little government oversight or tax. We might as well call it academic imperialism. Shouldn't the aim be that the country in question should develop its own universities? Globalization seems a virtue, but the nub is that this form of it reinforces inequality and installs a colonial relation. The extension of American and other Western universities tends to exploit global inequality, as richer first-world institutions make deals much to their advantage with less powerful or developed nations.

A third challenge is the development of the union movement, for graduate students as well as faculty in its various forms. Academic unions have existed in the United States for a century, albeit unevenly, but given the contemporary reconfiguration of and prospects for jobs, the conditions spurring unionization have only increased. There are a number of tensions within the union movement—for instance, whether faculty should be organized altogether or if contingent faculty remain separate from permanent faculty, or whether unionization should occur in micro-units, given that research jobs that grad students or others hold in practical sciences are often substantially different from those who are teaching courses—but it is a major activist dimension that aims to redress the power structure within universities.

Given the centrality of higher education to modern life, to science and technology as well as to humanistic thought, and to social opportunity as well as to cultural understanding, CUS has a significant role to play. One additional challenge that it might take up is, in the slogan of Jeffrey J. Williams, to "Teach the University!"[26] Such an initiative does not advocate one or another political course, but aims to put issues confronting higher education in front of students, as well as giving them relevant background in history and theory, so that they might decide for themselves. The university could be a topic in courses across a number of disciplines and at several levels, introductory as well as advanced. That would reach one crucial public, students, so they might get the best information and thus use it to help create the university to come.

Carnegie Mellon University (United States)

NOTES

1. See Jeffrey J. Williams, "Debt Education: Bad for the Young, Bad for America," *Dissent* (Summer 2006): 55–61.

2. See Robert Hiltonsmith and Tamara Draut, "The Great Cost Shift Continues: State Higher Education Funding After the Recession," *Demos* (March 21, 2014). http://www.demos. org/publication/great-cost-shift-continues-state-higher-education-funding-after-recession; also Michael J. Rizzo, "State Preferences for Higher Education Spending: A Panel Data Analysis, 1977-2001," in *What's Happening to Public Higher Education? The Shifting Financial Burden*, ed. Ronald G. Ehrenberg (Baltimore: Johns Hopkins University Press, 2006), 3–35.

3. See Tamara Draut, "The Growing College Gap," in *Inequality Matters: The Growing Economic Divide in America and Its Poisonous Consequences*, eds. James Lardner and David A. Smith (New York: New Press, 2005), 89–101.

4. Immanuel Kant, *The Conflict of the Faculties*, (1798), trans. Mary J. Gregor (Lincoln: University of Nebraska Press, 1992).

5. John Henry Newman, *The Idea of a University*, (1852), ed. Frank M. Turner (New Haven: Yale University Press, 1996).

6. Jacques Derrida, "The University Without Condition," in *Without Alibi*, trans. and ed. Peggy Kamuf (Stanford: Stanford University Press, 2002), 202–37.

7. See Heather Steffen, "Intellectual Proletarians in the 20th Century," *Chronicle of Higher Education* (November 28, 2010), http://www.chronicle.com/article/intellectual-proletarians/125477

8. Thorstein Veblen, *The Higher Learning in America: A Memorandum on the Conduct of Universities by Business Men* [1918], ed. Richard R. Teichgraeber III (Baltimore: Johns Hopkins University Press, 2015).

9. Upton Sinclair, *The Goose-Step: A Study of American Higher Education* [1923] (Whitefish: Kessinger, n.d.).

10. Robert Paul Wolff, *The Ideal of the University* (Boston: Beacon, 1969).

11. Adrienne Rich, "Toward a Woman-Centered University," in *On Lies, Secrets, and Silence: Selected Prose 1966-1978* (New York: Norton, 1979), 125–55.

12. Mark Kelman, *A Guide to Critical Legal Studies* (Cambridge: Harvard University Press, 1987), 297.

13. See Allan C. Hutchinson, ed., *Critical Legal Studies* (Totowa: Rowman and Littlefield, 1989).

14. Lawrence Soley, *Leasing the Ivory Tower: The Corporate Takeover of Academia* (Boston: South End, 1995).

15. Jennifer Washburn, *University, Inc.: The Corporate Corruption of Higher Education* (New York: Basic, 2005).

16. Sheila Slaughter and Larry L. Leslie, *Academic Capitalism: Politics, Policies, and the Entrepreneurial University* (Baltimore: Johns Hopkins University Press, 1997).

17. Joe Berry, *Reclaiming the Ivory Tower: Organizing Adjuncts to Change Higher Education* (New York: Monthly Review, 2005).

18. Marc Bousquet, "The Waste Product of Graduate Education: Toward a Dictatorship of the Flexible," *Social Text* 70 (2002): 81–104.

19. Marc Bousquet, *How the University Works: Higher Education and the Low-Wage Nation* (New York: New York University Press, 2006).

20. Benjamin Ginsberg, *The Fall of the Faculty: The Rise of the All-Administrative University and Why It Matters* (New York: Oxford University Press, 2011).

21. Williams, "Debt Education: Bad for the Young, Bad for America," 55–61, and "Student Debt and the Spirit of Indenture," *Dissent* 55.4 (Fall 2008): 73–78.

22. Christopher Newfield, *Unmaking the Public University: The Forty-Year Assault on the Middle Class* (Cambridge: Harvard University Press, 2008).

23. Christopher Newfield, *The Great Mistake: How We Wrecked Public Universities and How We Can Fix Them* (Baltimore: Johns Hopkins University Press, 2016).

24. Robert Samuels, *Why Public Higher Education Should Be Free: How to Decrease Cost and Increase Quality at American Universities* (New Brunswick: Rutgers University Press, 2013).

25. David Noble, *Digital Diploma Mills: The Automation of Higher Education* (New York: Monthly Review, 2001).

26. Jeffrey J. Williams, "Teach the University!" *Pedagogy* 8.1 (2007): 25–42.

WORKS CITED

Berry, Joe. *Reclaiming the Ivory Tower: Organizing Adjuncts to Change Higher Education.* New York: Monthly Review Press, 2005.

Bousquet, Marc. "The Waste Product of Graduate Education: Toward a Dictatorship of the Flexible." *Social Text* 70 (2002): 81–104.

Bousquet, Marc. *How the University Works: Higher Education and the Low-Wage Nation.* New York: New York University Press, 2006.

Derrida, Jacques. "The University Without Condition." In *Without Alibi* [2000]. Trans. and ed. Peggy Kamuf. Stanford: Stanford University Press, 2002. 202–37.

Draut, Tamara. "The Growing College Gap." In *Inequality Matters: The Growing Economic Divide in America and Its Poisonous Consequences.* Eds. James Lardner and David A. Smith. New York: New Press, 2005. 89–101.

Ginsberg, Benjamin. *The Fall of the Faculty: The Rise of the All-Administrative University and Why It Matters.* New York: Oxford University Press, 2011.

Harvey, David. *A Brief History of Neoliberalism.* New York: Oxford University Press, 2005.

Hiltonsmith, Robert, and Tamara Draut. "The Great Cost Shift Continues: State Higher Education Funding After the Recession." *Demos* (March 21, 2014). http://www.demos.org/publication/great-cost-shift-continues-state-higher-education-funding-after-recession

Hutchinson, Allan C., ed. *Critical Legal Studies.* Totowa: Rowman and Littlefield, 1989.

Johnson, Benjamin, Patrick Kavanagh, and Kevin Mattson, eds. *Steal This University: The Rise of the Corporate University and the Academic Labor Movement.* New York: Routledge, 2003.

Kant, Immanuel. *The Conflict of the Faculties* [1798]. Trans. Mary J. Gregor. Lincoln: University of Nebraska Press, 1992.

Kelman, Mark. *A Guide to Critical Legal Studies*. Cambridge: Harvard University Press, 1987.

Newfield, Christopher. *Unmaking the Public University: The Forty-Year Assault on the Middle Class*. Cambridge: Harvard University Press, 2008.

Newfield, Christopher. *The Great Mistake: How We Wrecked Public Universities and How We Can Fix Them*. Baltimore: Johns Hopkins University Press, 2016.

Newman, John Henry. *The Idea of a University* [1852]. Ed. Frank M. Turner. New Haven: Yale University Press, 1996.

Noble, David. *Digital Diploma Mills: The Automation of Higher Education*. New York: Monthly Review Press, 2001.

Rich, Adrienne. "Toward a Woman-Centered University." In *On Lies, Secrets, and Silence: Selected Prose 1966-1978*. Ed. Adrienne Rich. New York: Norton, 1979. 125–55.

Rizzo, Michael J. "State Preferences for Higher Education Spending: A Panel Data Analysis, 1977-2001." In *What's Happening to Public Higher Education? The Shifting Financial Burden*. Ed. Ronald G. Ehrenberg. Baltimore: Johns Hopkins University Press, 2006. 3–35.

Ross, Andrew. "The Rise of the Global University." In *Nice Work If You Can Get It*. New York: New York University Press, 2009. 189–205.

Samuels, Robert. *Why Public Higher Education Should Be Free: How to Decrease Cost and Increase Quality at American Universities*. New Brunswick: Rutgers University Press, 2013.

Sinclair, Upton. *The Goose-Step: A Study of American Higher Education* [1923]. Whitefish: Kessinger, n.d.

Slaughter, Sheila, and Larry L. Leslie. *Academic Capitalism: Politics, Policies, and the Entrepreneurial University*. Baltimore: Johns Hopkins University Press, 1997.

Soley, Lawrence. *Leasing the Ivory Tower: The Corporate Takeover of Academia*. Boston: South End, 1995.

Steffen, Heather. "Intellectual Proletarians in the 20th Century." *Chronicle of Higher Education* (November 28, 2010). http://www.chronicle.com/article/intellectual-proletarians/125477

Veblen, Thorstein. *The Higher Learning in America: A Memorandum on the Conduct of Universities by Business Men* [1918]. Ed. Richard R. Teichgraeber III. Baltimore: Johns Hopkins University Press, 2015.

Washburn, Jennifer. *University, Inc.: The Corporate Corruption of Higher Education*. New York: Basic, 2005.

Williams, Jeffrey J. "Debt Education: Bad for the Young, Bad for America." *Dissent* 53.3 (Summer 2006): 55–61.

Williams, Jeffrey J. "Teach the University!" *Pedagogy* 8.1 (2007): 25–42.

Williams, Jeffrey J. "Student Debt and the Spirit of Indenture." *Dissent* 55.4 (Fall 2008): 73–78.

Williams, Jeffrey J. "The Need for Critical University Studies." In *A New Deal for the Humanities: Liberal Arts and the Future of Public Higher Education*. Eds. Gordon Hutner and Feisal Mohammad. New Brunswick: Rutgers University Press, 2016. 145–59.

Wolff, Robert Paul. *The Ideal of the University*. Boston: Beacon, 1969.

CHAPTER TWENTY-SIX

Affect Studies

SEAN GRATTAN

In the introduction to *The Affect Theory Reader* Melissa Gregg and Greg Seigworth rhetorically ask: "How to begin when, after all, there is no pure or somehow originary state of affect?" After all, as they rightly note, "affect arises in the midst of *in-between-ness*."[1] Yet this is perhaps too cute, and it might be useful to begin at another beginning. Teresa Brennan opens *The Transmission of Affect* by asking, "Is there anyone who has not, at least once, walked into a room and 'felt the atmosphere'?"[2] Brennan's lucid beginning, rooted in an everyday phenomenological experience of the world, is perhaps the easiest introduction to a discussion about affect. The feeling of a room, of the atmosphere, profoundly shapes our experience of it, but modern literary and cultural theory does not often seem to have space for the feeling of a room, however friendly or hostile it might be. Affect theory is one of the organizing theoretical categories of the late twentieth and early-twenty-first centuries. Affect theory is an attempt at getting at the heft, shape, and borders of feelings, and how those feelings ineluctably shape our political, cultural, and aesthetic experiences of the world. Thus, at root, affect studies is a way of describing encounters. While this might seem straightforward, there has been a concerted effort to plump for Cartesian dualism and rationality since he thought and therefore was, which is distinctly troubled by a turn to a theorization of affect. In working against the mind/body dualism of Cartesian philosophy, affect also calls into question the space between subject and object, or person and world. The arc of affect theory described in this essay follows a line from seventeenth-century Dutch philosopher Baruch Spinoza to contemporary investigations into diverse fields of study like queer theory, ecocriticism, new materialism, and object-oriented ontology.

Eve Kosofsky Sedgwick and Adam Frank begin their 1995 "Shame and the Cybernetic Fold" by drawing a line in the sand: "Here are a few things theory knows today."[3] Sedgwick and Frank's list of what theory knows could, in many ways, get directly lifted and transported into the present. Put briefly, for Sedgwick and Frank, when theory offers "any account of human beings or cultures" it must distance itself from the biological, assume language is the most productive model for representation, sight is the sense most amicable to theorization and working to root out false dualism, and, finally, rely on binaries (even under the guise of breaking those binaries). Their four points demarcate a territory highlighting the obduracy of theory elevating the connection between language to subjectivity, rationality, and, most generally, thought. It is the continued attempt to theorize the imbrication of language and theory that concerns what has generally come to be called the affective turn.

The now canonical start date of the affective turn is 1995 when Brian Massumi and Eve Kosofsky Sedgwick (with Adam Frank) published their influential articles "The Autonomy of Affect" and "Shame in the Cybernetic Fold" respectively. These two articles do more than announce a new field of study; they also articulate the basic bifurcation that affect studies continues to tread. They come from very different theoretical schools, and Massumi's and Sedgwick's concerns, though overlapping, at least at this early moment in affect studies, seem to concentrate energies around Deleuzian inspired materialism and queer theory. While this is clearly a simplification, and many theorists trouble this, there is also a stark and very real divide between approaches to the study of affect. There has been a recent attempt at codifying the theoretical variations in a couple of anthologies (*The Affective Turn* and *The Affect Theory Reader*). Perhaps put most bluntly, and certainly not exhaustively, the intersection of affect and literature has a long history that might be unfortunately boiled down to: does this make me *feel* anything.[4] Of course, there is much more to it than this, and this condensation is often the cause of critics taking the turn to affect less seriously than perhaps they should. The contemporary ubiquity of affect studies leads Lauren Berlant to anecdotally quip about a conference on affect and feelings that "affect is the new trauma,"[5] in other words, trendy, academically suspect, and unserious. Berlant rightly notes, though, that we've been doing affect for a long time, and that there is no particular need to justify an interest in a philosophical tradition easily stretching back to the seventeenth century.

The theorization of affect has a long history and it by no means sprung up overnight. The seventeenth-century Dutch Jewish philosopher Baruch Spinoza is most often connected with the twentieth- and twenty-first-century move to affect. Spinoza, who was famously barred from the Jewish community in Amsterdam, circulated his book *The Ethics* among a select coterie of readers. It is perhaps this inauspicious beginning that is picked up and carried through into the present. And while space dictates glossing quickly over this beginning, crucially Spinoza describes affect as the ability to affect and be affected. It is in the Spinozist vein that affect exists materially and, importantly, resists becoming the same as emotion. In *The Ethics*, Spinoza writes what is certainly his most often quoted line: "Nobody as yet has determined the limits of the body's capabilities: that is, nobody has learned from experience what the body can and cannot do."[6] Crucially, the body for Spinoza is not a fixed, singular, or sovereign thing; instead, the body is constantly in flux and fully imbricated with other bodies. French philosopher Étienne Balibar usefully describes Spinoza's philosophy as a philosophy of encounters. I would argue that this definition might be expanded to the theory of affect more generally. If affect is the ability to affect or be affected and it is not bounded by the merely human, then affect becomes a way of describing the world.

In one of his two monographs dedicated to Spinoza, French philosopher Gilles Deleuze writes, "Spinoza did not believe in hope or even in courage; he believed only in joy and in vision. . . . He more than any other gave me the feeling of a gust of air from behind each time I read him, of a witch's broom that he makes one mount."[7] Deleuze is perhaps the philosopher most associated with and responsible for the contemporary interest in affect. He theorized that art works produce sensations that have material affects in the world. We owe a lot of one prong of the affective turn to Deleuze's interest in Spinoza, and he owes a lot of that interest to Louis Althusser.[8] In *What is Philosophy?*, Deleuze and Felix Guattari argue for the importance of considering the ways works of art produce affects that are "*beings* whose validity lies in themselves and exceeds any lived. They could be said to exist in the absence of man because man, as he is caught in stone, on the canvas, or by words, is himself a compound of percepts and affects. The work of art is a being of sensation and nothing else: it exists in itself."[9] In other words, the work of art exists simultaneously and separately from anyone experiencing it and whoever produced it.

But before we head down that road, it's crucial to investigate why and how the turn to affect came about. Was it merely exhaustion at and of the critical formations of the linguistic turn, or were there other forces at work that marked a need to look to affect as another way of engaging texts and the world? For instance, in Bruno Latour's "Has Critique Run Out of Steam" he asks, "Is it really possible to transform the critical urge in the ethos of someone who *adds* reality to matters of fact and not *subtract* reality?"[10] Does a turn to affect work to thicken, enrich, or expand a sensorium of the world that was declared by Fredric Jameson on the wane? Is it precisely this exhaustion with the insouciant language games of high postmodernism and its attendant theoretical concerns? In other words, in these moments when paranoid conspiracy fantasies seem to closely mirror critical modes for questioning the merits of received and naturalized ideological truths, when the term "alternative facts" has suddenly entered the political lexicon, then perhaps criticism needs other sets of theoretical strategies. What is the value of critique when James Inhofe, the chair of the Environment and Public Works committee, can stand in front of the US Senate and declare that global warming doesn't exist because he's managed to make a snowball in Washington, D.C.? Latour sees the act of criticism as no longer "fighting empiricism, but on the contrary, renewing empiricism."[11]

The turn to affect is a way of destabilizing the neoliberal privatized subject, but in a prelinguistic or nonlinguistic manner. Affect theory is not a codified, monumental, or totalized form of criticism, though the different strands, which I would separate awkwardly into Spinozist and queer, do have common ground in the destruction or dissolution of the individual subject. What are our boundaries? How do we structure the place between one person's skin and the person next to them? These are containers, tensely holding our guts, veins, tendons, and blood in place, but our feelings and our senses drift beyond this tense boundary.

AFFECT AND QUEER THEORY

One of the two main strands of affect theory is braided into a larger queer theory project. In part this is because of Sedgwick's early contribution, but it is also because affect might serve as a way of troubling various binaries, boundaries, and normativities that rest at the heart of the project of queer theory. The focus on the way feelings seep into the everyday, forcing us to reconceptualize our notions of ourselves, troubles the too easy dichotomies of inside and outside, subject and object, and so on. Yet if we take Sedgwick and Frank seriously this troubling doesn't get away from the binary as organizing theoretical force. To return to "Shame and the Cybernetic Fold," Sedgwick and Frank still offer one of the more compelling and nuanced versions of affect and queer theory. If there is some weight to the lazy stereotype of queer theory as purely about disruption, then Sedgwick's and Frank's engagement with affect as an antidote for binary thinking usefully develops Sedgwick's early work in *Epistemology of the Closet* and prefigures her later work on texture and affect.

In the introduction to *Touching Feeling*, Sedgwick combines texture and affect to articulate a world of affects that is deeply invested in shaking up ways that post-structuralists of deconstructive projects often maintain a spatial, temporal, or rhetorical relationship with their object of critique. In doing so, according to Sedgwick, they never fully manage the theoretical and conceptual escape they claim. Thus, Sedgwick rejects metaphoric language like: beneath, beyond, depth, or hiddenness as they move from a "spatial description into implicit narratives of . . . origin and telos."[12] Instead, Sedgwick offers another spatial metaphor—one that is closely indebted to affect—*beside*. Of course, theorizing the beside immediately troubles the easy dichotomy structuring this essay, as here she is combining a Deleuzian planarity that imagines a spatial and theoretical model that exists, partially, as Spinozist affectivity. In other words, she combines Deleuzian affects with the psychologist Sylvan Tomkins theory of drives and affects to create a model that might offer an alternative to linguistic methods of criticism. But what does texture have to do with affect? As Sedgwick herself points out, in some ways the connections between touch and affect are all too simplistic. Yet, her description of their relation is much more complex:

> If texture and affect, touching and feeling seem to belong together, then, it is not because they share a particular delicacy of scale, such as would necessarily call for "close reading" or "thick description." What they have in common is that *at whatever scale they are attended to*, both are irreducibly phenomenological. To describe them primarily in terms of structure is always a qualitative misrepresentation. Attending to psychology and materiality at the level of affect and texture is also to enter a conceptual realm that is not shaped by lack nor by commonsensical dualities of subject versus object or of means versus ends.[13]

The project of thinking affectively, then, is to think phenomenologically about how the world actually feels.

Marxist critic Raymond Williams might not be the first name on a list of important theorists to queer theory, but in *Marxism and Literature*, he describes the present as always operating under "structures of feeling." For Williams, structures of feeling are a way of defining a "particular quality of social experience and relationship, historically distinct from other particular qualities, which gives the sense of a generation or period."[14] The quality of the social experience emerges from varied cultural, political, and social practices. Heather Love has found fertile ground in her *Feeling Backward*. Love writes that structures of feeling have been "crucial to queer studies, where the analysis of uncodified subjective experiences is an important supplement to the study of the history of formal laws, practices, and ideologies. The saturation of experience with ideology is particularly important to queer critics because homophobia and heterosexism inflect everyday life in ways that can be difficult to name."[15] Love's focus on uncodified and difficult to name encounters with the world mark a particular territory where the insistence on an attunement to affect resonates. How do we describe minor discomforts around awkward glances, whispered slurs, or a potentially mocking gesture?

The texture of the world, the weight and heft of feelings, is part of the critical topography for queer theory, but this is also a place where more politicized versions of queer belonging take place. It's in these spaces of unbelonging or non-belonging where theorists like Lauren Berlant, José Muñoz, and Sara Ahmed work. To varying degrees all three are interested in what it might mean to be a citizen, and how attending to affect, feeling, or emotion might demarcate the boundaries of citizenship. So, for instance, Lauren Berlant has written a series of texts she's grouped under the heading the national sentimentality trilogy. Berlant mostly investigates the affects that lodge uncomfortably in the gut, that signal the abusive, traumatic, distasteful, or malignant affects generated by late capitalism in the United States. Her extensive work traverses the nineteenth and twentieth century and moves into the contemporary moment. One particular instantiation of her thinking about citizenship and publics is her coauthored work "Sex in Public" with Michael Warner. Though not the central thesis of the text, their theorization of a sexual public hinges on the affects circulating in places like a club where an exhibition of erotic feeding takes place.

Other than Sedgwick, perhaps the queer theorists most engaged in affect are José Muñoz and Sara Ahmed. Both imagine affect as central to any understanding of queer experience, and while Ahmed points more directly to different ways of feeling bad, Muñoz also strives to investigate the affective force of persisting with feeling badly. Similar to Brennan, Ahmed also stresses the feeling of a room and how easily those feelings work to disrupt comfort, safety, and ease. Yet these disruptions might also be constitutive of a kind of queerness. In *The Promise of Happiness*, Ahmed describes the feeling of alienation at being in a movie theater and listening to the people around you laugh at homophobic and racist jokes. This is a moment of affect, and a moment that calls into stark relief the difference between yourself and the heterosexist society around you. Ahmed sees this dissonance as a provocation to act, to become a "feminist killjoy."[16] In other words, affect becomes a site of confrontation between the subject and the world, but the world, in its homophobic, racist, and sexist discourses tests the fragility of the queer subject through the public performance of homophobia, racism, and sexism. Here affect functions as a way of theorizing minoritarian positions through the feeling of those positions.

Similar to Ahmed, Muñoz argues that "the depressive position" is uniquely qualified to act as a marker for political and aesthetic engagements from minoritarian positions. For Muñoz, the focus on affect is a means of shifting away from "identitarian models of relationality."[17] In doing so, Muñoz illustrates at least one way that affect might turn away from linguistic literary and culture theory by modifying Gayatri Chakravorty Spivak's "famous question 'can the subaltern speak?' to ask How does the subaltern feel? How might subalterns feel to each other?"[18] Thus for Muñoz, the affective sphere becomes a place of theorizing how groups might combat racism through generative engagement not as individuals, but as producing a series of affects he names "racial performativity."[19] For Muñoz, crucially, "minoritarian affect is always, no matter its register, partially illegible in relation to the normative affect performed by normative citizen subjects."[20] The partially unrevealed and illegible minoritarian affect points to the same frisson Ahmed describes as becoming an "affect alien." Becoming an affect alien can happen suddenly, just as the feeling of a room can change suddenly. She writes: "We can also feel alienated by forms of happiness that we think are inappropriate. Take the example of laughter at the cinema. How many times have I sunk desperately into my chair when the laughter has been expressed at points I find far from amusing!"[21] The feelings of affective alienation arise most clearly in the spaces of dissonance between different kinds of subject positions. Put most simply, in this example Ahmed sinks into her chair because through the audience's laughter the people around her actively deny her existence; this denial is felt. The moment in the darkness of the cinema is precisely the kind of encounter that affect theory is most—and best—equipped to describe.

AFFECT AND MATERIALISM

The other line of inquiry associated with and produced by affect studies is dominated by an engagement with Deleuzian materialism. Along with "Shame and the Cybernetic Fold," 1995 also featured the publication of Brian Massumi's "Autonomy of Affect."

Massumi's brand of Deleuzian ontology is interested in the somatic frisson captured by theorizing affect. Like queer theory's affective prong, Massumi is also interested in how affect works "differentially in relation" to language.[22] Massumi draws keywords from the work of Henri Bergson, Spinoza, Gilles Deleuze, and Felix Guattari—speaking of intensities, amplification, resonances, event, virtual, actual. Massumi equates intensity with affect, writing "there seems to be a growing feeling within media and literary and art theory that affect is central to an understanding of our information- and image-based late-capitalist culture, in which so-called master narratives are perceived to have foundered."[23] Massumi continues: "Our entire vocabulary has derived from theories of signification that are still wedded to structure even across irreconcilable differences (the divorce proceedings of poststructuralism: terminable or interminable?)."[24] As Massumi makes clear, he is responding to the same set of theoretical questions as Sedgwick, and also responding through an engagement with affect, but his affective focus emerges from a different genealogy. In the linguistic turn the "classical definition of the human as the rational animal returns in a new permutation: the human as chattering animal. Only the animal is bracketed: the human as the chattering of culture."[25] Massumi rightly notes that this creates a "rigid divide between the human and the nonhuman," that ends up "making the human culture the measure and meaning of all things."[26] It is the push into the nonhuman that distinguishes this strand of affect studies, while queer theory seems more interested in the human within the world.

Massumi stresses the importance of differentiating between affect and emotion. "Emotion" he writes "is a subjective content, the socio-linguistic fixing of the quality of an experience which is from that point onward defined as personal."[27] Massumi also describes affect through spatial metaphors that trouble binaries, and, rather than replace those binaries, experiences them as "levels."[28] Thus affect and intensity is immanent for Massumi; life is a constant buffeting of intensities that generate and regenerate constantly shifting new intensities. For Massumi, "affect . . . is precisely this two-sidedness, the simultaneous participation of the virtual in the actual and the actual in the virtual, as one arises from and returns to the other."[29] The final thing to press with Massumi is that the study of affect is about ethics; affect can produce political effects as it swirls around between people, through people: fear, anger, dismay, and hope are all affects that produce effects. Of course this is all too evident in the formation of crowd behavior.

Finally, Massumi's interest in neuroscience links to another strand of affect and materialism summed up by Antonio Damasio's texts *Descartes' Error* and *Looking for Spinoza*. In *Descartes' Error*, Damasio claims "that the reasoning system evolved as an extension of the automatic emotional system, with emotion playing diverse roles in the reasoning process."[30] For Damasio, then, affect operates as a thicker way of understanding the thought and reasoning process. In other words, the Cartesian cogito constitutes a misstep in understanding human cognition. This is a similar insight as made by Spinoza when he argued against the Cartesian dualism of mind and body.

Perhaps the authors most closely linked with affect and the political are Michael Hardt and Antonio Negri. At the turn of the century the publication of their book *Empire* seemed to speak directly to the Zeitgeist of the times. Shockingly popular for a book of cultural theory, the *New York Times* hyperbolically began its review: "It comes along only once every decade or so, typically arriving without much fanfare. But soon it is everywhere: dominating conferences, echoing in lecture halls, flooding scholarly journals. Every graduate student dreams of being the one to think it up: the Next Big Idea."[31] The Big Idea is that the mode of labor has changed in contemporary capitalism, and that this shift might be described as a move from industrial labor to affective labor. This shift was certainly one of the more controversial claims of the text, and Hardt and Negri were at pain to describe affective labor as the hegemonic form of labor in late capitalism. Shortly before the publication of *Empire*, Hardt described affective labor as "one face of what [he] will call 'immaterial labor,' which has assumed a dominant position with respect to the other forms of labor in the global capitalist economy."[32] While in *Empire*, he and Negri write that "any theoretical conception that regards reproduction as simply part of the circulation of capital (as classical economics, Marxian theory, and neoclassical theories have done) cannot deal critically with the conditions of our new situation, particularly those resulting from the political-economic relations of the world market in postmodernity."[33] For Hardt and Negri, affective labor consists of labor organized around the production, maintenance, and reproduction of affects and is tied closely to their concept of immaterial labor.

AFFECT AND THE PRESENT

Looming over these different strands of affect theory is the way the study of affect has been most useful—as a methodology for theorizing the present. While Love productively engages Williams for redescribing a moment in modernist literature, more recently Lauren Berlant has combined Williams and Harry Harootunian for what she has called the "affectosphere" of the present. Similarly, Jonathan Flatley describes the experience of the world in terms of "affective mapping," a concept he has modified from Fredric Jameson's theory of cognitive mapping. For Flatley, "affective mapping . . . represents the historicity of one's affective experience."[34] The affective map gives rise to a larger historic sense of the world—that the affective present emerges from larger historical structures. Sianne Ngai has theorized a series of minor affects in her books *Ugly Feelings* and *Our Aesthetic Categories: Zany, Cute, Interesting*. Perhaps one way to understand the present is by establishing links between how we feel and how we encounter the world. How does focusing on the small affective moments reorient our present world? In other words, if our lives are fully imbricated in global capitalism, isn't it important that we study not just the large, explosive, blockbuster affects, but also the tiny, quiet, but no less equally insistent affective charges of the small. In other words, if we take Hardt and Negri's understanding of the hegemonic position of affective labor to heart, then we need to be attuned to the ways our affects are structured around us. Mark Fisher has explicitly linked depression and late capitalism. In other words, the waning of affect Jameson recognized as an outcome of late capitalism is, in reality, the proliferation of affects, their study, codification, and mapping. And the focus on wellness at work should be understood as a means of instituting regimes of feelings demarcating negative and positive affects for the work environment. At the same time, we might look to the work of Kathleen Stewart who painstakingly evokes the affective everyday with short, stuttering vignettes that capture, precisely, what it seems to me that Williams means by a structure of feeling.

There has been a recent move toward the codification and anthologization of affect studies. The *Affect Theory Reader* appeared in 2010, but it is primarily concerned with the materialist line of affect studies. In their introduction the editors Melissa Gregg and Gregory J. Seigworth make a preliminary list of eight ways affect has been theorized: (1) phenomenology of human and nonhuman; (2) human and cybernetic; (3) Spinozist; (4) psychological and psychoanalytical; (5) the work of activists; (6) rejection of the linguistic turn; (7) criticism and emotions; and finally (8) science and science studies.[35] One way of seeing the interconnection of all these strands is by thinking of affect as primarily a way of understanding the present, which is to say, that each of these attempts at codification delineate particular ways of being attuned to and attending to the contours of the present. Said differently, perhaps a crucial turn in affect studies is thinking about what affect can tell us about the position of the human subject within the contemporary epoch of the Anthropocene. It might appear that a theory that has, on one hand, feelings at its core could tell us anything about the impersonal realm of objects, but in reality the study of affect is uniquely poised to investigate the connections between bodies. Recent books like Heather Houser's *Environmental Affects* or Rachel Greenwald Smith's *Affect and American Literature in the Age of Neoliberalism* both articulate in different ways the imbrication of the ecological and contemporary American literature. While John Protevi's *Political Affects* is another text that highlights ways the study of affect can inform an imbrication of the political, somatic, and environmental. He does so through careful attention to events like the response to Hurricane Katrina. Mel Y. Chen might make this point the most forcefully when she writes of the "animacy" of certain nonhuman things like lead, mercury, or oil. In other words, the circulation of lead from factories, or toys, into sickening bodies, radically alters an understanding of where the boundaries are between people and things.

Really, what we are looking at when studying affect is a shift in the kinds of questions asked of texts, the world, and the lines between subjectivity and objectivity. Affect theory is a theory of the encounter, both with the world and with others.

If we read the theorization of affect as primarily about a theorization of encounters— between people and things—then the two strands of affect theory begin to braid together. Public feelings are political and the study of affect is an attempt to attend to the ways feelings circulate in public, which, in turn, produces different kinds of publics. If affect is a way of describing an embodied experience of the world, then these embodied experiences always exist on the level of the encounter.

University of Kent (United Kingdom)

NOTES

1. Gregory Seigworth and Melissa Gregg, eds., *Affect Theory Reader* (Durham: Duke University Press, 2010), 1.

2. Teresa Brennan, *The Transmission of Affect* (Ithaca: Cornell University Press, 2004), 1.

3. Eve Kosofsky Sedgwick, *Touching Feeling: Affect, Pedagogy, Performativity* (Durham: Duke University Press, 2003), 93.

4. For an excellent critique of this mode of literary criticism, see Rachel Greenwald Smith, *Affect and Literature in the Age of Neoliberalism* (Cambridge: Cambridge University Press, 2015).

5. Lauren Berlant, "Affect is the New Trauma," *Minnesota Review* 71–72 (2009): 131.

6. Baruch Spinoza, *Complete Works*, trans. Samuel Shirley (Cambridge: Hackett Publishing, 2002), 280.

7. Gilles Deleuze, *Spinoza: Practical Philosophy,* trans. Robert Hurley (San Francisco: City Lights Books, 2001).

8. Warren Montag's work is incredibly helpful in tracing the influence of Spinoza on French philosophy since the 1960s and how Louis Althusser directly produced a generation of scholars engaged with the intersections between Marx and Spinoza.

9. Gilles Deleuze and Felix Guattari, *What is Philosophy?*, trans. Hugh Tomlinson and Graham Burchell (New York: Columbia University Press, 1994), 164.

10. Bruno Latour, "Why Has Critique Run out of Steam? From Matters of Fact to Matters of Concern," *Critical Inquiry* 30 (2004): 232.

11. Ibid., 231.

12. Sedgwick, *Touching Feeling*, 8.

13. Ibid., 21.

14. Raymond Williams, *Marxism and Literature* (Oxford: Oxford University Press, 1978), 131.

15. Heather Love, *Feeling Backward: Loss and the Politics of Queer History* (Cambridge, MA: Harvard University Press, 2009), 12.

16. Sara Ahmed, *The Promise of Happiness* (Durham: Duke University Press, 2010).

17. José Estaban Muñoz, "Feeling Brown, Feeling Down: Latina Affect, the Performativity of Race, and the Depressive Position," *Signs: Journal of Women in Culture* 31.3 (2006): 677.

18. Muñoz, "Feeling Brown, Feeling Down."

19. Ibid., 678.

20. Ibid., 679.

21. Ahmed, *The Promise of Happiness*, 42.

22. Brian Massumi, "Autonomy of Affect," *Cultural Critique* 31 (1995): 86.

23. Massumi, "Autonomy of Affect," 88.

24. Ibid.

25. Ibid., 100.

26. Ibid.

27. Ibid., 88.

28. Ibid., 94.

29. Ibid., 96.

30. Antonio Damasio, *Descartes Error: Emotion, Reason, and the Human Brain* (New York: Penguin Books, 2005), xi–xii.

31. Emily Eakin, "What is the Next Big Idea? The Buzz is Growing," *New York Times* (July 7, 2001), http://www.nytimes.com/2001/07/07/arts/what-is-the-next-big-idea-the-buzz-is-growing.html

32. Michael Hardt, "Affective Labor," *Boundary 2* 26.2 (1999): 90.

33. Michael Hardt and Antonio Negri, *Empire* (Cambridge, MA: Harvard University Press, 2000), 465.

34. Jonathan Flatley, *Affective Mapping: Melancholia and the Politics of Modernism* (Cambridge, MA: Harvard University Press, 2008), 4.

35. Seigworth and Melissa, *Affect Theory Reader*, 6–8.

WORKS CITED

Ahmed, Sara. *The Promise of Happiness*. Durham: Duke University Press, 2010.

Balibar, Étienne. *Spinoza and Politics* [1985]. Trans. Peter Snowdon. London: Verso Books, 2008.

Berlant, Lauren. "Affect is the New Trauma." *Minnesota Review* 71–72 (2009): 131–36.

Berlant, Lauren. *Cruel Optimism*. Durham: Duke University Press, 2011.

Brennan, Teresa. *The Transmission of Affect*. Ithaca: Cornell University Press, 2004.

Chen, Mel Y. *Animacies: Biopolitics, Racial Mattering, and Queer Affect*. Durham: Duke University Press, 2012.

Damasio, Antonio. *Descartes Error: Emotion, Reason, and the Human Brain*. New York: Penguin Books, 2005.

Deleuze, Gilles. *Spinoza: Practical Philosophy* [1970/1981]. Trans. Robert Hurley. San Francisco: City Lights Books, 2001.

Deleuze, Gilles, and Felix Guattari. *What is Philosophy?* [1991]. Trans. Hugh Tomlinson and Graham Burchell. New York: Columbia University Press, 1994.

Eakin, Emily. "What is the Next Big Idea? The Buzz is Growing." *New York Times* (July 7, 2001). http://www.nytimes.com/2001/07/07/arts/what-is-the-next-big-idea-the-buzz-is-growing.html

Flatley, Jonathan. *Affective Mapping: Melancholia and the Politics of Modernism*. Cambridge: Harvard University Press, 2008.

Hardt, Michael. "Affective Labor." *Boundary 2* 26.2 (1999): 89–100.

Hardt, Michael, and Antonio Negri. *Empire*. Cambridge: Harvard University Press, 2000.

Jameson, Fredric. *Postmodernism, or The Cultural Logic of Late Capitalism*. Durham: Duke University Press, 1991.

Latour, Bruno. "Why Has Critique Run out of Steam? From Matters of Fact to Matters of Concern." *Critical Inquiry* 30 (2004): 225–48.

Love, Heather. *Feeling Backward: Loss and the Politics of Queer History*. Cambridge: Harvard University Press, 2009.

Massumi, Brian. "Autonomy of Affect." *Cultural Critique* 31 (1995): 83–109.

Muñoz, José Estaban. "Feeling Brown, Feeling Down: Latina Affect, the Performativity of Race, and the Depressive Position." *Signs: Journal of Women in Culture* 31.3 (2006): 675–88.

Sedgwick, Eve Kosofsky. *Touching Feeling: Affect, Pedagogy, Performativity*. Duke University Press, 2003.

Seigworth, Gregory, and Melissa Gregg, eds. *Affect Theory Reader*. Durham: Duke University Press, 2010.

Smith, Rachel Greenwald. *Affect and Literature in the Age of Neoliberalism*. Cambridge: Cambridge University Press, 2015.

Spinoza, Baruch. *Complete Works*. Trans. Samuel Shirley. Cambridge: Hackett Publishing, 2002.

Williams, Raymond. *Marxism and Literature*. Oxford: Oxford University Press, 1978.

CHAPTER TWENTY-SEVEN

Antitheory

VINCENT B. LEITCH

There are a dozen or more identifiable contemporary antitheory factions in North America and the United Kingdom. It's an odd phalanx. Among them are traditional literary critics; aesthetes; political conservatives; ethnic separatists; formalists; some literary stylisticians, philologists, and hermeneuticists; certain neopragmatists; champions of low and middlebrow literature; creative writers; defenders of common sense and plain style; plus some committed leftists. What most characterizes many of the antitheory factions as well as independent and maverick critics of theory are arguments calling for a return to the close reading of canonical literature, for clear writing of critical prose that avoids obscurity and jargon, and for settling disagreements through reasoned argumentation rather than statements of personal beliefs. Antitheorists often complain bitterly about contemporary theory's commitments to social constructionism (vs. scientific truth and objectivity), to multiculturalism with its critical focus on race-class-gender analyses, and to ideology critique and the demystification of great literature. For their part, theorists refer to antitheorists as the "I love literature crowd." When tolerated at all by antitheorists, theory serves as a handmaiden to appreciation of literary texts. In no case should theory become autonomous, a separate field, or an academic discipline (or subdiscipline). This is a consecration to be accorded above all and only to literature itself.

With its forty-eight pieces written over three decades, *Theory's Empire: An Anthology of Dissent*, edited by Daphne Patai and Will H. Corral and published in 2005, remains to this day the bible of contemporary antitheory arguments. It is a hodgepodge, with selections from such notables as René Wellek, M. H. Abrams, Marjorie Perloff, Tzvetan Todorov, and Denis Donoghue. They are brought together to criticize theory, defend the canon of great works and literary analysis, uphold a commonsense realist theory of language, and excoriate the politicization of literary study characteristic of much contemporary theory. The general point of view is conservative, characteristically looking backward to earlier better times and approaches (the modern vs. the postmodern). As the title suggests, the thesis of this landmark collection is polemical: theory during the postmodern era from the 1960s onward has come to dominate literary studies, creating in the process an enduring empire and an orthodoxy. So the critics of theory are marshaled here as anti-imperialist dissenters against empire. It is a telling self-aggrandizing conceit.

In this chapter, I portray five of the best antitheorists and their arguments, offering my own critical assessments and developing along the way a defense of theory. My primary argument is that we should not have to choose between theory and antitheory, and my secondary argument is that a portrait of contemporary theory is incomplete without accounting for its many adversaries. The phenomenon of antitheory constitutes a revealing segment of the history of theory. To file it away under "culture wars" or the "battle of the ancients versus the moderns revisited," while provocative, is short sighted. Much can be learned from the antitheory phenomenon about contemporary literary studies, the corporate university, and cultural politics as well as theory.

Taken from his inflammatory book, *Literature Lost: Social Agendas and the Corruption of the Humanities*,[1] John Ellis's "Is Theory to Blame?" gathers the theory of the closing three decades of the twentieth century under the banner "race-gender-class theory." Starting in the 1980s, Ellis has been one of the most cited antitheorists. His explicit standpoint is postwar Euro-American formalist stylistics as embodied in the landmark book, *Theory of Literature* (1949), coauthored by René Wellek and Austin Warren. As a historian of theory, nothing attracts his favorable attention after the 1950s. On key issues of theory, such as the nature of authorial intention, literary quality, and historical context, mid-century theorists are purportedly far more complex, convincing, well-informed, committed to analysis, independent, and original than their thankless heirs. For Ellis, contemporary race-gender-class theory is simpleminded, ill informed, dogmatic, and conformist. Furthermore, the topics of real concern today, long debated in the history of criticism, receive unsophisticated handling. Nowadays, nothing is new, just diluted. Standards of argumentation and logic have deteriorated. John Ellis's pioneering mission is to save real theory from bad theory: "What now passes for theory is a degraded and corrupt shadow of what theory should be."[2] What has been especially disturbing, historically speaking, is the recent becoming fashionable of theory and its jargon: "As theory became fashionable, there arose a theory cult in literary studies, and its leadership became a kind of theory jet set, a professional elite with a carefully cultivated aura of au courant sophistication. In this atmosphere, only recent theory counted; anything from earlier times was wooden and outmoded. The persistent ignorance of prior theory was therefore no accident but an essential feature of this new development."[3]

Obviously lumping all post-1950s theory under the category race-gender-class is a problem. While it might apply in a way, however unflattering and homogenizing, to ethnopoetics, feminism, New Historicism, queer theory, Marxism, postcolonial theory, or cultural studies, it does not depict psychoanalysis, hermeneutics, structuralism, deconstruction, reception theory, or post-structuralism. Theory is not one thing.[4] So, the charge of "political correctness," proffered by Ellis, amounts to a dismissive as well as careless slur. Also, Ellis's definition of real theory and theorists is narrow and prescriptive.

> Real theorists do not run in packs; they are individuals who set out to crack particular problems by thinking hard about them. Their work is solitary; it is never fashionable and must always be estranged from orthodoxies. . . . Real theorists thrive on the concept of argument and counterargument that is central to theoretical analysis, but race-gender-class scholars show a marked tendency to avoid facing the substance of the arguments of their critics.[5]

This view proposes a Great Man and solitary genius theory of cultural history that not only dissolves historical context but also discounts forerunners. Ironically, it does not apply at all to Ellis's beloved formalists, who ran in packs and became fashionable members of a reigning orthodoxy. Ellis damns everything that comes after the 1950s, a time when he was a student. He positions himself as a resentful defender of the old guard, a curmudgeon.

Given that advocates of new paradigms often ignore earlier competing paradigms, Ellis is misguided to expect the formalist tradition to be carefully examined as opposed to rudely dismissed by postformalists. For example, Yale-educated theorists Harold Bloom, Stanley Fish, and Stephen Greenblatt were trained by leading formalists but turned away from them in three different directions with very little looking back or reasoned argumentation. They are prodigal sons.[6] Intellectual change is often abrupt; it need not be respectfully conformist. Ellis is a poor historiographer. Moreover, his antitheory attacks leave out of account larger social dynamics such as the contemporary corporatization of the university and its requirements for productivity and innovation, not to mention its related nurturing of an elite star system set atop a massive army of adjuncts. It makes little sense to form judgments on the role of contemporary theory in the absence of the historical transformation, for good and ill, of the university. Not surprisingly, the advent of multiculturalism, liberal diversity programs, and their theoreticians uniformly constitute disasters in Ellis's unnuanced account.

One of the earliest and most lucid contemporary antitheory arguments appears in M. H. Abrams's prescient short piece "The Deconstructive Angel." This paper was originally delivered in the 1970s at a session of the annual convention of the Modern Language Association. On the panel were Abrams (distinguished literary historian), Wayne Booth (renowned advocate of Chicago school critical pluralism), and J. Hillis Miller (leading deconstructive critic). What prompted the panel was an earlier hostile review by Miller of Abrams' book *Natural Supernaturalism*. Miller cast the book as an example of "the grand tradition of modern humanistic scholarship,"[7] whereupon he proceeded to critique mercilessly the tradition in the name of Derridean and de Manian deconstruction. Wayne Booth wanted the antagonists to debate their differences publicly. Abrams portrays himself on the panel as a traditional historian of Western culture and a critical pluralist, meaning someone tolerant of different approaches to linguistic and historical interpretation. In his presentation he offers, first, fair-minded and cogent accounts of both Derrida's and Miller's theories of language and interpretation. Second, he cleverly counterposes his own ideas.

Just before Miller is to make his presentation, the last of the three papers, Abrams concludes his argument with a telling witty prognostication about Miller's talk:

> I shall hazard a prediction as to what Miller will do then. He will have determinate things to say and will masterfully exploit the resources of language to express these things clearly and forcibly, addressing himself to us in the confidence that we, to the degree that we have mastered the constitutive norms of this kind of discourse, will approximate what he means. . . . What he says will manifest, by immediate inference, a thinking subject or ego and a distinctive and continuant ethos.[8]

Each feature of discourse singled out in this mock praise of Miller constitutes a component of Abrams's commonsensical pragmatic account of language posited over against deconstruction's counterintuitive theory of discourse. For Abrams, speakers and writers use norms and conventions of language, including professional language, to express more or less determinable thoughts and feelings. They can be masterful or not, clear or not, and we the audience will make sense of these utterances crafted by individual persons. These persons possess consciousness, distinctive identities, and certain intentions. They are capable not only of initiating discourse but also of mutual understanding.

Deconstructive accounts of language for their part highlight the potential indeterminacy of language, most notably in polysemous literary and philosophical texts. *Finnegans Wake* comes to mind. Connotations always precede the orderly denotations of the belated dictionary makers. Grammar compounded by rhetoric (tropes are ineradicable) introduces slippage and uncertainty in language. Beyond any accounting, innumerable bits of previous intertexts run through texts (historical assemblages). Moreover, authorial intentions are not so much objectively inferred as assigned in retrospect with certain interests and prejudices, conscious and unconscious, in reserve. Here is how Abrams, exaggerating more than slightly, characterizes the upshot of Miller's deconstructive theory: "What it comes to is that no text, in part or whole, can mean anything in particular, and that we can never say just what anyone means by anything he writes."[9] Such purported deconstructive critical skepticism weakens the grounds for objective literary and historical interpretation, Abrams's main concern to support and defend.

What bearing does this debate have on the antitheory phenomenon? Early on and up to the present moment—for five decades—the term *theory* for its opponents has often too simply meant deconstruction, that is, Derrida and his followers. The common phrases *after theory* and *posttheory*, echoed in so many titles of books and articles starting in the 1990s, signify both "after the triumph of deconstruction in the 1980s" and "after its supercession during the 90s" by the growing successes of postcolonial and ethnic theory, the spread of New Historicisms, and the emergence of queer theory and cultural studies. Occasionally, "posttheory" and "after theory" get broadened and designate what comes after "French theory." But actually what comes after is more theory, often more or less influenced by deconstruction. The ubiquity and dissemination of deconstruction's groundbreaking critiques of "binaries" testify to the survival and fecundity of this particular theory. I have in mind the many critical inquiries up to today scrutinizing and reconfiguring traditional hierarchical binary conceptual pairs, for example, nature/culture, masculine/feminine, human/animal, self/other, conscious/unconscious, and normal/abnormal. These pairs recur in major Western literary and philosophical discourses and are topics of contemporary concern. My point is that there is no after theory—or after deconstruction—pure and simple. What there is is a devout wish for theory's demise, meaning the eradication of deconstruction and post-structuralism, plus their legacies. For the editors of *Theory's Empire*, Abrams's paper furthers that cause and is all to the good.

Eugene Goodheart's disarming "Casualties of the Culture Wars"[10] is clear and straightforward in its defense of aesthetic criticism against ideology critique aka theory.[11] His ultimate goal is to make peace between these two warring camps by putting chastised ideology critique in a subordinate place. He presents himself as an elder statesman. The main job of literary criticism for Goodheart is the interpretation and evaluation of literary works in the context of history. He is a critical pluralist self-declaredly tolerant of other approaches and perspectives. The task of aesthetic criticism entails appreciation and discrimination not only of craft and content but also of personal experiences and emotions. The critic has a trained sensibility. Amateurs are out. Scholarship is the sine qua non of proper criticism. The distinctive features of literary aesthetics for Goodheart consist of several kinds (although he doesn't package them this direct way): (a) splendor and rightness of language, wit, and ingenuity; (b) imagination and beauty, pleasure and power especially familiar from the sublime in art; and (c) disinterest, free play, and ineffability. What distinguishes his treatment of aesthetics is an avowed openness to impurities and entanglements. He is wary of the mystifications coming from advocates of pure aesthetics and art for art's sake. While politics and morality admittedly play roles in aesthetics from Shaftesbury, Addison, and Hogarth to Kant, Schiller, and Arnold, Goodheart holds out for distinctive aesthetic experience. In this he joins related contemporaneous parallel turns to affect theory, new formalisms, a return to literature, and surface reading.

What most typifies American criticism and theory since the 1970s is, according to Goodheart, a shift from formalism to ideology critique. His emergent critique of critique is prescient.[12] But ultimately it's a stark Manichean vision Goodheart offers. "Ideology critique rules the roost,"[13] he declares ruefully. Thus the editors of *Theory's Empire* cast him as an antitheorist. The faults of ideology critique are many for Goodheart. It construes the task of criticism as the uncovering of hidden interests. This hermeneutics of suspicion is morally righteous and reductive. It refuses debate (argumentation, evidence, logic). It abjures and anathematizes aesthetics. It practices bad prose style without any concern for elegance or clarity. It has no interest in literary sensibility and taste other than to be suspicious of them. It disregards open-mindedness and objectivity, letting beliefs take the place of knowledge. Finally, "there is nothing more aggressive than the effort to demystify the supposed illusions of others."[14] Who are these practitioners of ideology critique, according to Goodheart? It's a loose, not to say violent, assemblage of theory-affiliated schools and movements: Marxism, structuralism, feminism, post-structuralism, deconstruction, New Historicism, postcolonial theory, and cultural studies. Goodheart paints with an impossibly broad brush creating caricatures.

Eugene Goodheart positions himself as a liberal centrist against the extremisms of left and right cultural camps and tendencies. One problem is he doesn't detail the problems of the right. Another is he doesn't define ideology as anything other than as interests (hidden, disguised, or open). There is a great deal more to this venerable concept, for example, the base/superstructure dialectical model of society. To get a sense of Goodheart's vehement antitheory stance, consider the progression in this statement: "Ideology critique can be a valuable activity if it knows its limits, discriminating between what requires and what does not require demystification. In contemporary practice in the academy, it has become an imperial obsession with disastrous consequences."[15] Here emerges the metaphor of theory as imperialist empire. There are a handful of revealing passages where Goodheart, the Manichean, tries to strike a balance between left and right, ideology and aesthetics, critique and criticism (his oppositions). "The critic need not, indeed cannot, avoid talking about ethical, political, religious, or historical issues. What is decisive is the way he speaks or writes about the work, the kind of attention he gives to what counts as aesthetic qualities. An aesthetic response foregrounds the work and doesn't allow it to be devalued by one or another discourse."[16] This is Goodheart's modest proposal. He is motivated to make it because he foresees no going back to earlier times of aesthetic criticism free from ideology critique. As with many other antitheorists, the tone here is a mixture of sadness and outrage. Still, Goodheart seeks balance and a middle way. The love of literature always comes first. That's the main point, plus of course the criticism of theory. These are the reasons he finds a role in the antitheory mission of *Theory's Empire*.

Among the sharpest critics of theory is Mark Bauerlein, high-profile cultural warrior, English professor, and defender of the humanities for two decades. In his cogent article, "Social Constructionism: Philosophy for the Academic Workplace," published in 2001 by *Partisan Review*, he notes unhappily that social constructionism has become the dominant epistemology of the contemporary humanities, especially literary theory. He defines social constructionism succinctly: "It is a simple belief system, founded upon the basic proposition that knowledge is never true per se, but true relative to a culture, a situation, a language, an ideology, or some other social condition."[17] Key terms of contemporary theory that embody this noxious standpoint include antifoundationalism, contingency, and situationism, plus the slogan of many theorists following Fredric Jameson's famous axiom "always historicize." Pitted against such relativisms are truth, objectivity, knowledge, and facts, all subject to verification, validity, and argumentation, none of which concepts and procedures social constructionism bothers with.[18] The latter is a belief system not an epistemology. Touchstones for Bauerlein are science and logic. In ignoring and refusing debate (logic, evidence, justification), social constructionism shows itself to be a dogma, a creed, replete with a party line and an attitude. Representative theorists (constructionists) singled out by Bauerlein include Michel Foucault, Richard Rorty, Terry Eagleton, Stanley Fish, Eve Sedgwick, and Paul Lauter. These social constructionists are committed to a morality of social justice not a real epistemology open to philosophical scrutiny. They do not label their concepts as opinions, hypotheses, or speculations. They should. In arguments, they operate through psychology not epistemology, proceeding ad hominem. It is no use, therefore, to point out that social constructionism commits the genetic fallacy or is a form of relativism.

Why has social constructionism, asks Bauerlein, been so successful in the humanities? He offers a persuasive hypothesis:

> What has emerged from social constructionism is not a philosophical school or a political position, but an institutional product, specifically, an outpouring of research publications, conference talks, and classroom presentations by subscribers. For many who have entered the humanities as teachers and researchers, social constructionism has been a liberating and serviceable implement of work, a standpoint that has enhanced the productivity of professors.[19]

Bauerlien explains further that the US academic tenure system today requires a beginning professor in the humanities to produce a book manuscript within three to four years of hiring. This speedup means long-term projects and careful methods no longer serve. He rues the day that humanities professors let the quick book become the main criteria for tenure ("lifetime security"). As a result, beginning "professors will avoid empirical methods, aware that it takes too much time to verify propositions about culture, to corroborate facts with multiple sources, to consult primary documents, and to compile evidence adequate to inductive conclusions."[20] Facts, objectivity, and truth fall by the wayside. In short, social constructionism has been successful because "it is the epistemology of scholarship in haste, of professors under the gun. As soon as the humanities embraced a productivity model of merit, empiricism and erudition became institutional dead ends, and constructionism emerged as the method of the fittest."[21]

Bauerlein positions himself here as both critical of the current period and nostalgic for slower, more deliberative yet unspecified earlier times. He appears in the role of conservative defender of traditional humanities and transcendental truths based on reasoned method. It's a "timeless" ideal yet borne of modernity. He is hostile to all manner of contemporary theory and postmodernity as his list of social constructionists suggests (against post-structuralism, neopragmatism, post-Marxism, reception theory, gender and queer theory, plus cultural studies). Nonetheless, he is a penetrating critic (unaffiliated) of the contemporary corporate research-oriented university—with its addiction to productivity, speedup, and short-term accountability. He presents his Darwinian theory—a mode of historical and ideological critique after all—that social constructionism is a fit response to savage productivity demands as a hypothesis, a hunch. Scientific method requires such a gesture of modesty, a much-touted virtue by antitheorists along with humility.

But Bauerlein has forgotten that the great leap forward in research and publication productivity was spawned by early Cold War–era formalism, especially New Criticism.

Its successful formula for book writing survives to this day: a first chapter on a critical approach or method followed by four or five chapters of close readings of individual literary works. Productivity does not stem from social constructionism. It derives from the competitive business management model undergirding the research university established in the 1950s and 1960s and culminating with the corporate university of recent decades.

The corporatization of the university associated with the dominant economic paradigm of extreme laissez-faire late capitalism is not Bauerlein's target, although it should be. Productivity demands come from where? Like most antitheorists in *Theory's Empire*, Bauerlein is no social critic, nor does he want to be. Yet social currents run through his as well as their arguments in very obvious yet repressed ways. For Mark Bauerlein, the standard of truth is Newton's law—true in all times and all places. Such knowledge is not relativistic social construct. The humanities today, rightly defensive and in a survival mode, need to emulate scientific truth. That is Bauerlein's main point, which ironically happens to be an anti-humanistic belief, one could argue. In any case, he finesses the significant tensions between science and culture, truth and history.

Given the dominance of cultural studies in recent decades, the wide-ranging insightful critique by Stephen Adam Schwartz, titled "Everyman as Übermensch: The Future of Cultural Studies," is both relevant and au courant. It's a good place to begin concluding this critical survey of exemplary antitheory sentiments and arguments. Published originally in 2000 in *SubStance*, a North American journal of contemporary French literary culture, Schwartz's essay targets cultural studies as theorized and practiced especially in US English departments. He is a professor of French language and literature, an interested but dispassionate outsider. What is wrong with cultural studies? Most of the piece is given to impersonal exposition and critique of its various features and faults. Many faults are cited. Nothing good is said. Cultural studies is anti-disciplinary and anti-methodology. Hélas. It promotes popular culture and explodes the literary canon, jettisoning aesthetic value and distinction. It remains suspicious of social institutions in their support of norms and their policing of deviances. It buys into social constructionism, regarding knowledge as always enmeshed with both interest and power. It reduces facts to mere values and points of view. There is no neutral epistemological space in its faulty perspective. Cultural studies sees all of reality as a social construct, including notably science, literature, and truth. It is committed to a project of demystification, not appreciation. It buys into cultural relativism. It is unremittingly hostile to all hierarchies. Most importantly, it has a flawed concept of culture entangled with idiosyncratic notions about politics.

The idea of culture propounded by contemporary culture studies, argues Schwartz, pits master narratives against particular ones. It is always a matter of hegemonic and counter-hegemonic forces in struggle, where cultural studies sides predictably with subaltern, subcultural, and multicultural minorities. It routinely celebrates resistance, transgression, and difference. In this sense it is reminiscent for Schwartz of modernist avant-gardes, especially surrealism: both end up with ineffectual content-poor politics and merely aesthetic vanguardist appeal. What most characterizes the culture concept of cultural studies, claims Schwartz, is its surprising foundation in "the *individual* and his or her preferences." "In other words, individuals—replete with a full set of interests, desires, and beliefs—come first and culture is something not only derived and secondary but pernicious and, therefore, ultimately unnecessary. Personal preferences—*someone's* choices—turn out to be lying behind all collectively shared categories."[22] This charge of individualism leads Schwartz to project for cultural studies its unspoken utopia. He portrays an anti-hierarchical and leveling cultural studies depicted as an incoherent polyphony, an indistinction, of equally valid voices. Cultural studies "ends up with an epistemological and political anarchism rooted in the purest individualist voluntarism."[23] In a final twist of his argument, Schwartz concludes that cultural studies, after all, promotes the modern Western ideas of egalitarianism and expressive individualism, being just one more seemingly radical form of individualism in our time.

It takes guesswork to know what Stephen Adam Schwartz's own standpoint might be. He keeps it tightly under wraps. His highly dramatized description of cultural studies is fair enough, except for the characterization of its ideas on culture and anarchism. Pace Schwartz, cultural studies exhibits distinctively leftist anarchism not disguised right-wing libertarianism: it privileges the community over the individual. That is the upshot of race-class-gender analyses. In addition, there is no way that culture is unnecessary or secondary in cultural studies theory. It is inescapable. It molds individuals ineradicably. We are born into culture, its norms, conventions, and prejudices. It is more or less clear that Schwartz wants to respect hierarchies and preserve canonical literature over against popular culture. He is a critic of social constructionism and apparently a believer in classical canons of objectivity, truth, and disinterestedness. All these are evidently more than enough to make him a dissenter from the contemporary empire of theory and a card-carrying antitheorist.

I myself have an array of complaints against contemporary theory. Too many theorists' writing style lacks clarity and economy, not to mention elegance. A related problem is a relative lack of attention to formal literary craft, stylistics, and aesthetics, not that I want criticism done by strict formalist checklists. Some theorists are righteous and pious to the point of stern intolerance, where tone veers off badly. I have no problem with pleasure reading, a life-enhancing mode of "nonacademic" criticism that some mandarin theorists discount or overlook. I understand but worry about the utilitarian tendency among academic theorists to reduce all theories to formulaic approaches and methods as quickly as possible. Then there is the problem of market vanguardism, that is, theorists jumping on the latest theoretical bandwagon no matter what it might be. Such theorists are more interested in being provocative than convincing; it should not be a choice between these two values.

Theory in the contemporary era has become, on one hand, a crossover interdiscipline fusing literary criticism, linguistics, philosophy, psychoanalysis, anthropology, sociology, history, and politics. It possesses a distinctive postmodern identity readily on display in the many contemporary theory anthologies. On the other hand, however, it remains a subdiscipline housed in traditional departments such as English and comparative literature. There are no autonomous departments and only a few semiautonomous programs of theory in the Anglophone world. In other words, theory remains subject to literature in most jurisdictions while maintaining a sense of independence, especially from the traditional service functions of criticism, specifically textual explication and aesthetic evaluation. Meanwhile, the modes of critical reading have multiplied and the high status of canonical literature has been broadly challenged under pressure from excluded minorities and from popular culture and media. So, it is in the name of pre-postmodern discipline and the old order that antitheorists call theory to its role as handmaiden to literature (defined adamantly as canonical belles lettres). Anathema, therefore, is theory as multiculturalism, populist cultural studies, ideology critique, speculation, posthumanism, intellectual vanguardism, academic celebrity culture or, worst of all, an interdiscipline engaged in explicit transdisciplinary projects. This is "big T Theory" swollen with grandiose ambitions, and for the humble editors of *Theory's Empire*, it signals a lamentable degeneration. They deplore the self-enclosed jargon-ridden arcane world of Theory and call it back to the proper love of literature:

> We believe that in the thirty years between the publication of the first edition of Hazard Adams's *Critical Theory since Plato* [1971] and the appearance of the *Norton Anthology of Theory and Criticism* [2001], much has been lost with respect not only to theory and criticism that actually illuminate literary texts but also to the appreciation of criticism's actual contributions to academic discourse. That time span also saw the dissemination of theoretical principles in innumerable books aiming to ease readers' way into the arcane world of Theory, while in no way encouraging a love of literature.[24]

The antitheory message to Theory is clear: get back where you belong, the appreciation of literature. Put first things first. Reverse the tragic decline. Restore the canon. Fall in line. Declare your love for literature. I love literature. Say it loud, I LOVE LITERATURE.

A big problem for antitheorists is that I, myself a self-declared Theorist (big T), love literature, and doubtlessly I represent most theorists in saying so. An even bigger problem for antitheorists is that we theorists insist on examining how the I (the subject) of "I love literature" works, and who gets to define "literature," and where and why certain critical oaths of allegiance and related condemnations come about and at what cost. Critical inquiry creates disruption. It can be accused of corrupting society especially students, as we know, which is the case with much accusatory antitheory. In the end, there are many ways to love literature. Attacking theory does not help.

University of Oklahoma (United States)

NOTES

1. John M. Ellis, *Literature Lost: Social Agendas and the Corruption of the Humanities* (New Haven: Yale University Press, 1997).

2. John M. Ellis, "Is Theory to Blame?" in *Theory's Empire: An Anthology of Dissent*, eds. Daphne Patai and Will H. Corral (New York: Columbia University Press, 2005), 106.

3. Ellis, "Is Theory to Blame?," 104–05. John Ellis emerged as a leading figure in the US culture wars that started during the 1980s and that bubble up sporadically to this day. Early on he occupied the roles of defender of traditional Western humanities and critic of theory. In 1994 he cofounded the Association of Literary Scholars, Critics, and Writers, an affiliate of the National Association of Scholars (NAS, founded 1987), both conservative organizations with anti-liberal agendas. The ALSCW had and has as a main goal to create an alternative organization to the Modern Language Association (MLA, founded 1883). Many antitheorists are hostile to the 28,000-member MLA for accommodating, not to say promoting, theory. In its initial years between 1994 and 2007, ALSCW received more than thirty grants from well-known right-wing foundations, primarily Bradley, Olin, and Scaife, reaching a million dollars. ALSCW and NAS maintain substantial Web sites.

4. For six different current definitions of theory, see the entry on "Theory" in this volume.

5. Ellis, "Is Theory to Blame?," 105–06.

6. Jeffrey J. Williams, "Prodigal Critics," *The Chronicle of Higher Education: The Chronicle Review* (December 6, 2009): 14–15.

7. J. Hillis Miller, "Tradition and Difference," *Diacritics* 2.4 (Winter 1972): 6.

8. M. H. Abrams, "The Deconstructive Angel," in *Theory's Empire: An Anthology of Dissent*, eds. Daphne Patai and Will H. Corral (New York: Columbia University Press, 2005), 209.

9. Abrams, "The Deconstructive Angel," 206.

10. Eugene Goodheart, "Casualties of the Culture Wars," in *Theory's Empire: An Anthology of Dissent*, eds. Daphne Patai and Will H. Corral (New York: Columbia University Press, 2005).

11. Eugene Goodheart's article in *Theory's Empire* melds extracts from two earlier works by him: *Does Literary Studies Have a Future?* (Madison: University of Wisconsin Press, 1999) and "Criticism in the Age of Discourse," *Clio* 32.2 (2003): 205–08.

12. See Vincent B. Leitch, *Literary Criticism in the 21st Century: Theory Renaissance* (London: Bloomsbury, 2014), chap. 3, where I critically assess a dozen twenty-first-century critiques of critique on the way to specifying the wide-ranging tasks of critical reading today. The leading twenty-first-century advocates of critique of critique—Eve Sedgwick and Rita Felski—are theory friendly distinguished theorists calling for a balance between literary appreciation and critique, not an end to theory or to critique. Critique of critique and antitheory are two separate phenomena with different timelines, leading figures, and relations to theory.

13. Goodheart, "Casualties of the Culture Wars," 510.

14. Ibid.

15. Ibid., 510–11.

16. Ibid., 513.

17. Mark Bauerlein, "Social Constructionism: Philosophy for the Academic Workplace," in *Theory's Empire: An Anthology of Dissent*, eds. Daphne Patai and Will H. Corral (New York: Columbia University Press, 2005), 341.

18. Compare Amanda Anderson, who examines the nature of argumentation among theorists, notably feminists, post-structuralists, and pragmatists, from a Kantian Habermassian perspective that promotes theory as critical reflection. From 2008 to 2014, Anderson was director of the School of Criticism and Theory, the venerable US summer institute that has trained 2,500 theorists since 1976.

19. Mark Bauerlein, "Social Constructionism," 348.

20. Ibid., 350.

21. Ibid., 353.

22. Stephen Adam Schwartz, "Everyman An Übermensch: The Culture Of Cultural Studies," in *Theory's Empire: An Anthology of Dissent*, eds. Daphne Patai and Will H. Corral (New York: Columbia University Press, 2005), 373.

23. Ibid., 376.

24. Daphne Patai and Will H. Corral, eds., *Theory's Empire: An Anthology of Dissent* (New York: Columbia University Press, 2005), 6.

WORKS CITED

Abrams, M. H. "The Deconstructive Angel." In *Theory's Empire: An Anthology of Dissent*. Eds. Daphne Patai and Will H. Corral. New York: Columbia University Press, 2005. 199–212.

Anderson, Amanda. *The Way We Argue Now: A Study in the Cultures of Theory*. Princeton: Princeton University Press, 2006.

Bauerlein, Mark. "Social Constructionism: Philosophy for the Academic Workplace." In *Theory's Empire: An Anthology of Dissent*. Eds. Daphne Patai and Will H. Corral. New York: Columbia University Press, 2005. 341–53.

Ellis, John M. *Literature Lost: Social Agendas and the Corruption of the Humanities*. New Haven: Yale University Press, 1997.

Ellis, John M. "Is Theory to Blame?" In *Theory's Empire: An Anthology of Dissent*. Eds. Daphne Patai and Will H. Corral. New York: Columbia University Press, 2005. 92–109.

Goodheart, Eugene. *Does Literary Studies Have a Future?* Madison: University of Wisconsin Press, 1999.

Goodheart, Eugene. "Criticism in the Age of Discourse." *Clio* 32.2 (2003): 205–08.

Goodheart, Eugene. "Casualties of the Culture Wars." In *Theory's Empire: An Anthology of Dissent*. Eds. Daphne Patai and Will H. Corral. New York: Columbia University Press, 2005. 508–22.

Leitch, Vincent B. *Literary Criticism in the 21st Century: Theory Renaissance*. London: Bloomsbury, 2014.

Miller, J. Hillis. "Tradition and Difference." *Diacritics* 2.4 (Winter 1972): 6–13.

Patai, Daphne, and Will H. Corral, eds. *Theory's Empire: An Anthology of Dissent*. New York: Columbia University Press, 2005.

Schwartz, S. Adam. "Everyman an Übermensch: The Culture of Cultural Studies." In *Theory's Empire: An Anthology of Dissent*. Eds. Daphne Patai and Will H. Corral. New York: Columbia University Press, 2005. 360–80.

Williams, Jeffrey J. "Prodigal Critics." *The Chronicle of Higher Education: The Chronicle Review* (December 6, 2009): 14–15.

Terms and Figures

A

Ableism

The term *ableism* has evolved, with a newer term *disablism* assuming its original signification. The *Oxford English Dictionary* lists *ableism*'s first recorded usage as occurring in 1981 and supplies a single definition for it: "Discrimination in favour of able-bodied people; prejudice against or disregard of the needs of disabled people." The definition's reference to disability prejudice reveals the term's provenance: disability activists in the 1960s and 1970s developed the expression to question the privileges accruing to the nondisabled and call attention to the negative treatment of disabled people. The word's formation, *-ism* attaching to *able,* parallels other terms (i.e., *sexism* and *racism)* referencing similar forms of systematic oppression.

More recently disablism, a word not yet in the *Oxford English Dictionary*, has entered circulation. Although ableism and disablism are associated and are sometimes used interchangeably, theorists distinguish the two. Gregor Wolbring, Dan Goodley, and Fiona Kumari Campbell argue that ableism should not be used solely with regard to disabled people but should be understood in terms of broader cultural perspectives. In the main, they contend that ableism—the ideology of ability—is a ubiquitous belief system that privileges a certain type of person above others. This model is a young, white, fully physically functional, healthy, reasonably intelligent, heterosexual male. As such, ableism should be considered one of the most socially entrenched and accepted of -isms. Wolbring writes that "ableism is an umbrella ism for other isms." Forms of ableism he singles out are "biological structure-based ableism," "cognition-based ableism," "social structure-based ableism," and "ableism inherent to a given economic system." Goodley likewise maintains that the expression designates an ideology from which hetero/sexism, racism, homophobia, as well as disability prejudice, cannot be divorced. And Campbell frames ableism in terms of identifying the promotion of a naturalized understanding of a species-typical human being whom everyone is expected to emulate. Queer and disability studies theorist Robert McRuer elaborates on this, describing ableism in terms of a mandatory adherence to standards of normativity, or what he calls "compulsory able-bodiedness." In this formulation, everyone in an ableist regime is tacitly called upon to embody species-typicality. However, McRuer and others stress that doing so is impossible because this idealized version of human form, function, and cognition is nothing but a figment of the ableist imagination.

Disablism has become the term for specifically addressing prejudice/discrimination on the basis of disability. Still, ableism and disablism can be seen as complementary processes: the former values certain abilities, while the latter leads to discrimination and prejudice against the "less able." McRuer offers a useful analogy: "Compulsory ableism is to disablism what compulsory heterosexuality is to homophobia."

The ableist idea(l) implicitly sets up criteria for separating the fully human from those deemed "less than." Disability studies theorist Tobin Siebers states that ableism establishes "the baseline by which humanness is determined, setting the measure of body and mind that gives or denies human status to individual citizens." Ableism also carries implications for the transhumanist project. Goodley, Wolbring, and Campbell raise important ethical and political questions about the kinds of transhumans—hybrids, cyborgs, technological humans—that will be valued in an ableist system. Campbell for one sees in transhumanism the potential for an unbridled ableism. Moreover, many who today would be considered "able" tomorrow may become "less able" when compared to their technologically enhanced peers.

(*See also* Capacity; Chapter 11, Cultural Studies; Chapter 19, Media Studies; Chapter 24, Posthumanism; Disability; *and* Reading)

D. Christopher Gabbard, *University of North Florida (United States)*

Further Reading

Campbell, Fiona Kumari. *Contours of Ableism: The Production of Disability and Abledness.* New York: Palgrave Macmillan, 2009.

Goodley, Dan. *Dis/Ability Studies: Theorizing Disablism and Ableism.* New York: Routledge, 2014.

Wolbring, Gregor. "The Politics of Ableism." *Development* 51 (2008): 252–58.

Actor Network Theory

Actor Network Theory (ANT) is a method of sociological analysis that designates phenomena as actors or agents situated within networks of relations. It is a constructivist discourse in so far as it does not recognize any essential objects, qualities, or forces independent of the networks of relations in which they are situated. Furthermore, ANT does not endow priority to humans as social agents, but rather, attributes them equal status to nonhuman actors including objects, materials, and processes. ANT is most commonly associated with scholars Michel Callon, Bruno Latour, and John Law, who developed it in the early 1980s as an extension of their research in sociology and science studies.

ANT considers social, cultural, historical, and natural entities, or actors, as constituted through networks of interrelations. Its central claim is that there is no reality or phenomena external to these relations. For example, in *Aircraft Stories* (2002) Law gives an account of the British military aircraft TSR2 that moves beyond a direct description of military technology to a more comprehensive description of the networks comprising the social system of the "Euro-American World" after the Second World War. For Law, the TSR2 is not merely a plane but rather an object best understood as an actor positioned within, *and constituted by*, a complex set of network relationships (involving technology, culture, economics, weapons, telecommunications, and so on). It is "a fractionally coherent subject or object . . . that balances between plurality and singularity. It is more than one, but less than many."

Because in ANT there is no strict division between nature and culture, between facts and society, or objects and situations, all entities are considered to be actors inseparable from their relations to other actors; in short, an actor is nothing other than a constellation of relations. As Latour puts it in talking about microbes, "There are not only 'social' relations, relations between man and man. Society is not made up just of men, for everywhere microbes intervene and act." This is perhaps Latour's most infamous example, proposed in *The Pasteurization of France* (1988), where he argues that microbes are as much a product of networks of culture as they are those of science, leading to his claim that before Pasteur's revolution microbes did not exist, and yet following it, they had existed all along.

Since ANT emerged in the 1980s, its reception has been framed in part by the theoretical horizon of postmodernism, as well as the intellectual and cultural impact of emerging technologies like computing and telecommunications, that characterize the network society and post-structuralism. Law's description of his method as "material-semiotics" acknowledges this relation to post-structuralism by showing how semiotics conceived as a study of relations can also be applied to materials. Other significant intellectual coordinates for ANT include Michel Foucault's account of subject/object relations in the context of knowledge, truth, and power; accounts of the social construction of facts from the history of science such as Thomas Kuhn and Paul Feyerabend; and Michel Serres's accounts of quasi-objects as dependent upon their relations and context for their identity. ANT also shares some of the spirit of Gilles Deleuze's philosophy of immanence, "transcendental empiricism," in its dismissal of any essentialism concerning the identity of objects. Given these intellectual reference points, criticisms of ANT are similar to those aimed at other strands of postmodern thought, namely that it leads to a potentially amoral, depoliticized relativism in which the primacy of human values and objective facts are called into question. ANT's proponents might counter these critiques with Law's claim that ANT brings "less direct ways of knowing into being," and in doing so offer new ways of thinking about the world beyond conventional perspectives.

(*See also* Chapter 9, Rhetoric; Chapter 11, Cultural Studies; Chapter 23, Materialisms; Cybernetics; *and* Network Society)

Francis Halsall, *National College of Art and Design, Dublin (Ireland)* and *University of the Free State, Bloemfontaine (South Africa)*

Further Reading
Latour, Bruno. *Reassembling the Social: An Introduction to Actor-Network Theory.* Oxford: Oxford University Press, 2005.
Law, John. *Aircraft Stories.* London: Duke University Press, 2002.

Adorno, Theodor W.

As much an essayist and philosopher as he was a composer and sociologist, Theodor Adorno (1903–69) was one of the twentieth century's most intriguing and significant thinkers. A leading member of the so-called Frankfurt School, he was responsible, along with Max Horkheimer, Walter Benjamin, Erich Fromm, Herbert Marcuse, and others, for the creation and exemplification of critical theory, a sustained insight that shunned the unreflective and uncritical orientation of traditional theory by pursuing the unacknowledged presuppositions of concepts and theories that present themselves as exclusive means of providing wisdom and special access. The confidence and convictions traditional philosophy might once have bequeathed on a concept or syllogism Adorno instead settled at the foot of his own experience. Personally and professionally victimized by Nazi anti-Semitism, Adorno's leitmotif was the compromised and paradoxical situation of human subjectivity, which he took to be a remarkable historical achievement capable at once of ineluctably poignant aesthetic experience as well as seemingly unlimited self-destruction. Some of his most important work shows how the manner and forms of subjectivity are inextricably tethered to the domination of nature as well as of other human beings. His vigilance against kitsch, and what he and Horkheimer termed the "culture industry," has often led to the mischaracterization of Adorno as elitist. But his work successfully witnessed how the culture industry substitutes preformed ersatz stimulation for experience, in the aim to distract and forestall every experience that threatens to undermine the extorted consensus complicit with the status quo. The culture industry is itself but a symptom of the overarching tendency to transform reason into instrumental rationality—thus the topic of *Dialectic of Enlightenment,* coauthored with Horkheimer in 1944. The misunderstanding of Adorno's resistance to the seductions of Hollywood movies, as well as to his writings against certain forms of popular music, arises from the mistaken belief that Adorno was underwriting a hierarchy of cultural goods. He was instead merely acknowledging that certain works of art come into existence as strategic vehicles of manipulation rather than coming to be from a wish or inclination to evoke or disrupt experience.

Touchstones throughout his works include the utopianism of Ernst Bloch, the dialectics of Karl Marx and Georg Hegel, as well as the omnipresence of the Freudian unconscious. Adorno's extensive writings on aesthetics, including his late unfinished *Aesthetic Theory* (1970), arrange themselves nearly always from the point of view of what happens in human experience. His attention was drawn toward what remained incomplete, thwarted, or even deformed in human experience, best exemplified by his statement that the splinter in the eye is the best magnifying glass. Artworks, Adorno surmised, might sometimes flash with a runic residue of no longer visible features of what eludes subjectivity, but so too do artworks provide occasions whereby subjectivity might sidestep and momentarily overcome its own fractured identity. In this regard Adorno locates himself in the aesthetic tradition of Immanuel Kant and Friedrich Schiller, whose primary emphasis is how aesthetic experience serves at once both fully to evoke (beauty) and to efface (the sublime) subjectivity. Adorno's focus on the character of subjectivity dovetails neatly with the longstanding historical concern of aesthetic theory with the problem of how subjectivity comes into existence. His dialectical insistence on the primacy of the object—no doubt inspired as much by Walter Benjamin's treatments of childhood experience and the mimetic impulse (not to mention the apparent opacity of everyday objects) as well as by Adorno's own experience of music—was to turn toward the subjective share in every artifact no less than to turn toward the very objective character of subjective experience itself.

(*See also* Authenticity; Bourgeoisie; Chapter 4, Marxism; Chapter 12, Postmodernism; Critique; Cultural Critique; Culture; Enlightenment; Machine; Migration; *and* Negation)

Tom Huhn, *School of Visual Arts, New York City (United States)*

Further Reading

Adorno, Theodor W., and Max Horkheimer. *Dialectic of Enlightenment* [1944/1947]. Trans. John Cumming. New York: Herder & Herder, 1972.

Adorno, Theodor W. *Minima Moralia: Reflections from Damaged Life* [1951]. Trans. E. F. N. Jephcott. London: New Left Books, 1974.

Adorno, Theodor W. *Negative Dialectics* [1966]. Trans. E. B. Ashton. New York: Seabury Press, 1973.

Adorno, Theodor W. *Aesthetic Theory* [1970]. Eds. Gretel Adorno and Rolf

Tiedemann. Trans. Robert Hullot-Kentor. London: The Athlone Press, 1997.

Hullot-Kentor, R. *Things Beyond Resemblance: Collected Essays on Theodor W. Adorno*. New York: Columbia University Press, 2006.

Aesthetics

The history of aesthetics has at core a fundamental problem. Most aestheticians want to center their practice on giving an account of beauty because that seems an effective means of distinguishing values basic to the experience of art from those basic to other social practices. But what happens when beauty seems inadequate or even false as ground for those distinctive values? Many modernist artists and critics fear to talk about beauty because it ignores the radical qualities of shock or pain or just direct expressive intensities that ground their visions of how art works most fully affect audiences. And they suspect that talk of beauty really comes down to protection of class distinctions between those who are stuck with ordinary jobs and those with the freedom to cultivate their sensibilities.

Yet, if aesthetics cannot establish a single concrete end shared by the arts, the discipline turns to discourses shaped by social values. Aesthetics collapses into various versions of cultural theory, which in turn tends to reduce modes of presence and of power distinctive in individual works to various forms of statement (often despite claims to acknowledge how these works involve concrete sensuousness). These works become instances of cultural practices to be understood within the frameworks of contemporary critical languages.

Robert Pippin's title *After the Beautiful* (2014) succinctly evokes this dilemma. Pippin insists that Modernist art emphasizes how particular works see themselves as responding to deep problems of identity because they can no longer share constitutive ideals involving the production of beautiful objects. Instead this work seeks to develop modes of human self-knowledge that do not rely on the form of other cognitive claims but insist on correlating the conceptual with the sensuous. The task of philosophical aesthetics then becomes providing audience conditions by which it becomes possible to process these particular modes of intelligibility: we learn to see how knowledge can be amenable to the production of dense particulars.

Pippin is right that some works of art offer concrete images that do dramatize and sharpen our awareness of various features of the social world. Here we can speak of adapting to other modes of cognition. But a distinctive domain of aesthetics is necessary for preserving the sense that some works of art offer powerful challenges to any inquiry seeking affinities with modes of cognition and practical judgment. We need a philosophical practice capable of challenging the dominance of cognitive practices—not now in the name of beauty but in the name of the imagination, the productive force that is primarily responsible for how artworks make demands on audiences.

The clearest case involves how an understanding of aesthetic modes of presentation can simply overwhelm or beggar efforts at moral understanding. Othello is not just a murderous fool and Swan not simply one who succumbs to jealousy. These characters transform their limitations into sublime modes of performance where the details prove sufficiently compelling to resist all but aesthetic judgments about coherence and power. Similar challenges to the understanding occur on both small and grand scales. Aesthetics has stressed how imaginative works defamiliarize and shape new expressive modes of coherence, distinctive not for the understanding but for combinations of delicacy and density. And on a grand scale works like Dante's *Comedia* simply refuse to stand for judgments of truth and falsity. What matters becomes an intelligence so capacious and yet sensitive to nuance that it makes the domain of possibility itself present as something that must have a place in any serious mental life. Artists like Dante and Caravaggio and Beethoven typically establish conditions of regulated excess that one requires not just a sense of the limitations of concepts but of the limitations of any kind of discursive understanding.

(*See also* Adorno, Theodor W.; Affect; Chapter 4, Marxism; Chapter 9, Deconstruction; Chapter 11, Cultural Studies; Chapter 12, Postmodernism; Chapter 16, Pop Culture; Chapter 19, Media Studies; Chapter 20, Digital Humanities; Chapter 27, Antitheory; Cultural Critique; de Man, Paul; Figuration; Hegel, Georg W.; Kant, Immanuel; Literature; Marx, Karl; Modernism; New Criticism; Nietzsche, Friedrich; Poetics; Rancière, Jacques; Reception Theory; Reflexivity; Remixology; Systems Theory; *and* Taste)

Charles Altieri, *University of California, Berkeley (United States)*

Further Reading

Eldridge, Richard. *An Introduction to the Philosophy of Art*. Second ed. New York: Cambridge University Press, 2014.

Pippin, Robert. *After the Beautiful: Hegel and the Philosophy of Pictorial Modernism*. Chicago: University of Chicago Press, 2014.

Wollheim, Richard. *Art and its Objects*. New York: Cambridge University Press, 2015.

Affect

Some branches of affect theory (or affect studies) treat "affect" as a synonym for feeling or emotion, asking questions about the generation, circulation, and consequences of affect within and between texts and readers. The genre of the sentimental novel can serve as a useful example here, with its models of appropriate feeling and its explicit attempts to create feeling in readers. In some modes of writing—for example, the abolitionist novel—this translates into an attempt to emotionally move the reader, and thereby to more literally *move* the reader to take some sort of action. Other genres—horror, most obviously—are arguably affective first, at the level of forms, features, and effects (and, again, attempts to *move* the reader into a startled jump, for example).

Recently, affect theory has increasingly turned its attention to precognitive forces that are operating below and before anything as recognizable as a feeling or emotion, as well as to pre-personal forces that emerge from and circulate within culture and history, impressing feelings upon objects, texts, and people at all times. Sara Ahmed, for example, has written at length about the affects that become attached to the feminist body (killjoy, troublemaker), the queer body (unhappy, and source of unhappiness), and even domestic objects (the happy family photograph, the happy table).

To imagine affect as pre-personal, and as largely recognizable only in its effects on (or orientations of) a body, is to follow a line of thought one could trace backward from Brian Massumi to Gilles Deleuze, and Henri Bergson, and Baruch Spinoza. Its instability and related unpredictability creates anxiety for a wide range of thinkers, from those who still subscribe to a W. K. Wimsatt and Monroe Beardsley brand of New Criticism that critiques the "affective fallacy" of attending too closely to a text's (largely unrepeatable, immeasurable, and unverifiable) effects on readers, to a politically oriented brand of criticism that worries that Deleuzian strands of affect theory are good for little more than retroactive descriptions and claims of events as particularly affective or aligned with the philosophy of a particular affect theorist. (An affect theorist, to be fair, might emphasize the value of an affective receptivity and orientation that could prepare one to constructively harness emergent political opportunities, while avoiding a rigid, programmatic politics that interrupts flows and circulations.)

The most familiar brand of attention to affect is represented by studies of individual feelings and aesthetic effects, from, for example, Immanuel Kant's and Edmund Burke's descriptions of the beautiful and especially the sublime, to contemporary essays focused on joy and optimism, to more minor feelings, like irritation, envy, and anxiety. (These last, in particular, have been explored by Sianne Ngai, who has also examined the affective dimensions of judgments like "cute," "interesting," and "zany.")

Because studies of affect so often operate at various disciplinary intersections—literary and cultural studies, history, biology, cognitive neuroscience, philosophy, psychology— it is not uncommon to find citation of a figure like psychologist Silvan Tomkins at the center of discussions of affect in literature, film, or visual art. Tomkins's catalogs of biological affects remain canonical in the field.

(*See also* Chapter 26, Affect Studies; Emotions; *and* Neuroscience)

Paul Ardoin, *University of Texas, San Antonio (United States)*

Further Reading
Ahmed, Sara. *The Promise of Happiness.* Durham: Duke University Press, 2010.
Massumi, Brian. *Politics of Affect.* Cambridge: Polity Press, 2015.
Ngai, Sianne. *Ugly Feelings.* Cambridge: Harvard University Press, 2005.

Agamben, Giorgio

Giorgio Agamben (born 1942) is the most influential living philosopher in the Western world and a major influence on literary study around the world.

There are two distinct modes in which Agamben engages with literary texts. In the first mode, a given writer (such as Dante or Patrizia Cavalli), a given discipline (such as aesthetics or poetics) or a given literary figure (such as enjambment or ellipsis) is Agamben's topic and is treated in its own right and context. While these studies are innovative, they approach their object in an essentially conventional manner. In Agamben's second— more controversial—mode, he takes a given figure or idea from a literary work—such as Herman Melville's scrivener Bartleby or Keats's letters on poetic creation—as a "paradigm" through which to explore a notion from another domain, such as modal categories in Aristotle's metaphysics or the challenge of testifying to the horror of the Nazi concentration camps. In this second mode, Agamben's aim is not to present literary figures in their original context, but, instead, to use them to elucidate other contexts.

Agamben was born and educated in Rome where, in the mid-1960s, he became close to a number of prominent artistic figures, chief among which was Elsa Morante (about whom he was, many years later, to write) and which also included Pier Paolo Pasolini (in whose film *The Gospel of Saint Matthew* Agamben appears). At this time, Agamben was principally a poet and his publications from the period are primarily poetic (along with a few essays on literary questions). During this same period Agamben first attended Martin Heidegger's seminars in the south of France, hosted by the great French poet (and hero of the Resistance) René Char. These seminars were classical in form and content, with participants convening in the shade of a sycamore tree to discuss philosophy's oldest mysteries—beginning with the topic of the first seminar in 1966, the fragments of Heraclitus. For Agamben, the experience proved decisive. He described the seminars as much more than a simple forum "in which one learns things." They formed, instead, what he called a "constellation": a coming together of elements resulting in something truly unexpected. This unexpected thing was a turn away from poetry and to philosophy. As he would later remark, it was during those seminars that, for him, "philosophy became possible." While Agamben indeed ended his poetic career at this early stage, seen another way, he continued it by new means in his many and diverse reflections on poetic creation, and has often approvingly cited Ludwig Wittgenstein's claim that "philosophy should really only be done through poetry."

In the ensuing years Agamben was to go on to be an extraordinarily prolific writer, the author of more than thirty books and a huge number of essays on topics in philosophy, legal theory, religion, theology, ontology, linguistics, philology, political philosophy, dance, cinema, painting, theater, the philosophy of language, and the relation between literature and philosophy. Agamben has often remarked what is essential to him in a thinker is the "capacity for development" (the term is Feuerbach's) which their works possess. The three modern thinkers whose works Agamben has most developed are Michel Foucault, Heidegger, and Walter Benjamin. Agamben's interest in Foucault's notions of genealogy, archaeology, and paradigm are most visible in the nine books of the *Homo Sacer* series. Agamben's development of ideas and motifs from Benjamin (of whom he is a major editor, translator, and discoverer of hitherto lost manuscripts) and Heidegger is a more complex matter, beginning with Agamben's first book,

the work on aesthetics *The Man Without Content* (1970) and the crucial roles that Heidegger and Benjamin play therein. Agamben's development of Heideggerian notions is on most striking display in *The Use of Bodies* (2014). The development of notions that Benjamin did not live to more fully explore is best visible in Agamben's magisterial reading of Pauline messianism, *The Time That Remains* (2000).

(*See also* Bare Life; Biopolitics; Chapter 15, Biopower and Biopolitics; Exceptionalism, State of; *and* Political Theology)

Leland De la Durantaye, *Claremont McKenna College (United States)*

Further Reading
Agamben, Giorgio. *The Omnibus* Homo Sacer. Stanford: Stanford University Press, 2017.

Agency

Many entities in the universe move, but only certain entities act. The former obey laws of motion, and their behaviors are often predicted with great accuracy. The latter are "agents": not dumb bodies extended in time and space, but entities that can be praised and blamed, given credit and held responsible. In most cases, agents are said to be motivated by "beliefs," "hopes," "loves," "wishes," and other intentional states, a holistic set of terms that justify *why* they perform this-or-that action. "He opened the window," we say, "because he *wanted* to let in more air." But distinguishing motion from action, law-governed things from purposeful agents, is not yet to say how or when the distinction applies. Indeed, our culture is remarkably uncertain about which things count as agents and which do not. A tradition stemming from Rene Descartes would restrict agency to human beings, creatures whose intentional states are said to have a special inner house, the "mind," that propels the body into motion. But this picture has generated criticisms from across the philosophical spectrum. Philosophical naturalists, for instance, find such claims dubiously unscientific; human beings, they argue, are merely matter, hence explicable in the same causal terminologies as anything else. Many continental thinkers have likewise been unwilling to identify agency with human beings, and emphasized the ways that individuals are fashioned by history (Friedrich Nietzsche), language (Martin Heidegger), economics (Karl Marx), or the unconscious (Sigmund Freud). Such assaults on agency risk incoherence; a critic needs to explain how his or her own theory escapes the constraints that it describes. Yet these criticisms do remind us just how blurry the notion of "agency" is. Few people would say that rocks and planets—objects whose motions can be calculated in precise ways— think and act. But do animals? Do computers? It is not obviously metaphorical to say that a family or government "expresses" or "believes" something, nor that we are speaking fancifully when we say that a certain culture or subculture "wants" more power or "seeks" to have a "voice." And what of sentences, books, poems, statues, or musical pieces, which are also often said to articulate complex moods and states of mind, and in ways that inert matter could never convey on its own? Such uncertainty has given rise to a range of arcane-looking philosophical thought experiments: Hilary Putnam's brains in vats, John Searle's "Chinese rooms," Donald Davidson's "Swampman." But it also underlies some of the most widely circulating narratives in our culture. Stories of haunted houses, talking animals, cunning robots, ghosts, gods, and vengeful storms are intelligible precisely because agency seems so plausibly attributable beyond the individual human being. Perhaps the ability to make such ascriptions is biologically hardwired; children, after all, regularly speak to dolls and toy trucks. But specific ascriptions of agency are deeply cultural and historical. They reflect the values and beliefs of a given community at a given time, not only in the imaginative stories it tells but also in its characteristic assignments of moral and legal responsibility.

(*See also* Apparatus; Chapter 8, Rhetoric; Chapter 16, Pop Culture; Chapter 21, Late Capitalism; Chapter 22, Identity Studies; *and* Chapter 24, Posthumanism)

Robert Chodat, *Boston University (United States)*

Further Reading

Chodat, Robert. *Worldly Acts and Sentient Things: The Persistence of Agency from Stein to DeLillo.* Ithaca: Cornell University Press, 2008.

Sellars, Wilfrid. "Philosophy and the Scientific Image of Man." In *Science, Perception and Reality.* London: Routledge & Kegan Paul, 1963. 1–40.

Speight, Allen. *Hegel, Literature, and the Problem of Agency.* Cambridge: Cambridge University Press, 2001.

Wittgenstein, Ludwig. *Philosophical Investigations* [1953]. Rvsd. fourth ed. Trans. G. E. M. Anscombe, P. M. S. Hacker, and Joachim Schulte. Oxford: Blackwell, 2009.

Alienation

The concept of alienation is fundamental to Karl Marx's critique of capitalism, but it has acquired a number of other meanings as well. It is one of the few terms from Marxism to have entered into ordinary language where it often denotes vague feelings of malaise or meaninglessness. In Marx it has a more precise meaning derived from Hegel's philosophy. Alienation exists when our own activities or products become independent of us and act against us. Alienation can be experienced in many areas of life, including work and social and economic relations; one can also be alienated from oneself. The paradigm case for Marx is religion: although gods are our creation we experience them as independent and often hostile.

The main topic of Marx's account of alienation is the social and economic relations of capitalism. These relations take on a life of their own. The market becomes an independent power that threatens the well-being of those who create and maintain it. This is not the way we must or should relate to our own products or relations; we are capable of realizing ourselves through our work and in our social lives. Capitalism thwarts these possibilities, and that is the basis of Marx's criticism of it.

On Marx's view, alienation is a historically specific phenomenon, it can therefore be overcome. It came into being with the development of the dominance of commodity production and the market, and it can eventually be superseded. This will entail, says Marx in *Critique of the Gotha Programme* (1875), a radical social transformation to replace capitalism by a form of society that is no longer ruled over by the alien forces of the market but ruled by the "associated producers" and governed by the principle, "from each according to their abilities, to each according to their needs."

A very different conception of alienation is developed by Martin Heidegger in *Being and Time* (1927). He maintains that estrangement from ourselves, from others, and from our world is not a historical but an "ontological" condition, a form of inauthenticity that is an inescapable aspect of our very being. It is superficial to imagine that it can be overcome simply through social or economic changes.

Marx's concept is also the inspiration behind the "alienation effect" (*Verfremdungseffekt*), the modern theatrical technique, pioneered by Bertolt Brecht, in which the audience is deliberately hindered from identifying with the illusory world on stage so that it can reflect critically upon it.

Marx's notion of alienation has been hugely controversial, even among Marxists. The concept has been criticized and rejected for presupposing a "humanist" conception of the human subject. These criticisms have been made most influentially by the French structuralist philosopher, Louis Althusser, who attempted to expunge from Marxism all reference to Hegelian notions like alienation. However, others have defended the centrality of these ideas, and the concept of alienation remains central to much modern social and political thought.

(*See also* Althusser, Louis; Chapter 15, Biopower and Biopolitics; Chapter 18, Translation; Chapter 21, Late Capitalism; Chapter 26, Affect Studies; *and* Marx, Karl)

Sean Sayers, *University of Kent (United Kingdom)*

Further Reading

Brecht, Bertolt. *Brecht on Theatre.* Ed. and trans. John Willett. London: Methuen, 1964.

Marx, Karl. "Economic and Philosophical Manuscripts of 1844." In *Early Writings*. Harmondsworth: Penguin, 1975. 279–400.

Sayers, Sean. *Marx and Alienation: Essays on Hegelian Themes.* New York: Palgrave Macmillan, 2011.

Allochronic Discourse

A term coined and elaborated by Johannes Fabian, allochronism originally referred to practices in the field of anthropology, though it can be expanded very easily to apply to other cultural studies fields. Fabian first points out that a major flaw in Western anthropological studies is a "denial of coevalness," which he terms "allochronism," under which not only the European-studying subject observes his or her study objects, non-European others, in a different colonized space but that in this act of observation while both the ethnographer and his or her object exist in the same time, the ethnographer renders the object of study as if existing in another, past, time, thus stabilizing the present of Europe as the real time and plotting the objects of study in a past time. This happens even though the two participants in this exchange exist in the same serial time. This, thus, ends up offering the colonial cultures as ossified, static, and "primitive."

Allochronic discourse, thus, can be a kind of discourse that takes the European temporality as the present and contemporary and then posits people from the global periphery as those existing in a different, and unchanging, time. Note that this is pretty similar to Edward Said's concept of orientalism, which was also a discourse that rendered the non-European natives as inert, unchanging, and primitive. Any time a dominant culture offers its own time as the present and as the only "true" time, it also then must create objects that fall outside this normative time, and this normalization of European time as the "actual" time relies on the allochronic discourse. In cultural studies, this concept could be quite useful in discussing any cultural, gender, or race stereotypes as all readings of the other, in dominant Euro-American texts, will in one way or the other rely on allochronic discourse.

(*See also* Chapter 22, Identity Studies; Orientalism; *and* Said, Edward)

Masood Raja, *University of North Texas (United States)*

Further Reading
Fabian, Johannes. *Time and the Other: How Anthropology Makes its Object*. New York: Columbia University Press, 2006.

Alterity

Alterity is a term for "otherness" or for being "different from" something else. Alterity was a key concern in twentieth-century European philosophy and in the literary and cultural theory inspired by it. This entry discusses two understandings of alterity: *absolute* or *radical* alterity, and *human* alterity.

Absolute or *radical alterity* can be understood as a term for a cluster of epistemological, ontological, linguistic, and phenomenological considerations. Epistemologically, it refers to what is unfamiliar, what is unknown, to what defies comprehension. Linguistically, it refers to what cannot be directly expressed or articulated. Ontologically, it is a kind of an antithesis to the notion of *haecceity* in medieval philosophy, a term for "not-this-ness," for what is "other than" what is. Phenomenologically, it describes facets of our experience of world and self that confound our capacity to fully or directly experience them.

One of the great projects of twentieth-century European philosophy was to make sense of absolute alterity—a paradoxical project inasmuch as it involves trying to conceptualize the seemingly ungraspable. Thinkers such as Georges Bataille and Maurice Blanchot, as well as postwar existentialists, were fascinated by "limit experiences," such as pain, madness, and anxiety, which unsettle us by challenging customary ways of ordering reality, providing visceral, firsthand experiences of radical alterity.

Absolute alterity was also important to post-structuralism. The linguist, Ferdinand de Saussure, observed that meaning in symbolic systems is defined by difference—a sign's meaning is defined by its differences relative to other signs. This proposal led post-structuralists, such as Jacques Derrida and Jean Baudrillard, to champion the idea that all language is defined by something like radical alterity. Because meaning is never directly given, but made possible by what is unspoken or unwritten, there is a sense in which all linguistically dependent thought relies on sources or grounds it cannot convey. Here there is a similarity between absolute alterity and Derrida's notion of *différance*—his idea that the meanings of words and signs are produced by their *differences* but, consequently, that meaning is provisional and uncontainable, perpetually being *deferred*.

A second understanding of alterity is *human alterity*. Several figures in European philosophy developed theories of human intersubjectivity but grounded them in analyses of interpersonal interactions in which we are struck by other peoples' inaccessibility or foreignness, their otherness. Many concluded that alterity is central to human intersubjectivity. For example, Jean-Paul Sartre suggests that the privacy of others' minds compels us to acknowledge them as enigmatic—competing sources of interpretations of our world we cannot subsume or control. Others, such as Simone de Beauvoir, associate human alterity with groups who are assigned oppositional or secondary statuses in a community, such as women in Beauvoir's case, whose stigmatization as "other" may play a critical role in a hegemonic group's construction of its self-understanding.

It's worth noting that some philosophers in this tradition also held that human alterity and absolute alterity are interrelated, such that human alterity provides our most undiluted apprehension of absolute alterity. Emmanuel Levinas is the clearest example. Levinas flatly states in *Totality and Infinity* (1961) that "the absolutely other is the human other." Human

alterity on Levinas's view "concretizes" radical alterity—acknowledging other persons *as other*, as vulnerable in contradistinction to our experience of ourselves as efficacious subjects, compels us to recognize them as sources of ethical responsibility, hence as "concretizing" something infinite or transcendent, the absolutely other.

(*See also* Chapter 10, Feminism; Chapter 24, Posthumanism; Différance; *and* Other, The)

Joshua Shaw, *Penn State University (United States)*

Further Reading

Baudrillard, Jean, and Marc Guillaume. *Radical Alterity* [1994]. Trans. Ames Hodges. Cambridge: MIT Press, 2008.

Levinas, Emmanuel. *Alterity and Transcendence* [1995]. Trans. Michael B. Smith. New York: Columbia University Press, 1999.

Spivak, Gayatri. "Who Claims Alterity?" In *Remaking History*. Ed. Barbara Kruger and Phil Mariani. Washington: Bay Press, 1989. 269–92.

Althusser, Louis

Louis Althusser (1918–90) was a French Marxist philosopher and a major intellectual influence in France during the 1960s and 1970s. He has had a profound impact on the fields of literary and cultural theory, not only in France but also around the world.

In his innovative "return to Marx" Althusser stressed the *materiality* of texts, that is to say, their contradictory production and reproduction, which invariably generate multiple and conflicting readings. It is crucial, he insisted, to adopt a "protocol of reading" according to which one reads texts *symptomatically* by discerning the silences and recovering the marginal elements that have been historically excluded from, or passed over by, dominant interpretations.

For Althusser literature, art, and culture exist within ideology—as do all human activities—but they are never merely expressions of ideology. For example, in a letter to André Daspre on the nature of art Althusser insisted that "authentic" art allows something to be *recognized* about the ideologically laden world of "lived experience" by introducing into it an "internal distance." Yet an adequate scientific *knowledge* of how art operates would require going beyond spontaneous ideological notions of the artist as a "creator."

In a posthumously published work on *Philosophy for Non-Philosophers* (2017), Althusser argued for the primacy of social practices over their subsequent theorization and situated *aesthetic* practice in its complex articulation with other practices, for example, *scientific* practice, *ideological* practice, and *philosophical* practice. Although works of art exist concretely and are invested with sensuous form, they deal primarily with abstractions that tend to exceed their ideological appropriation. Two dangers facilitate such appropriation: (a) a vulgar materialist threat of art falling under the influence of ideology in order to "strengthen the social bond," as do sports, spectacles, and other forms of collective entertainment; and (b) an idealist threat of a "flight into art," which occurs when art is taken to uphold such ideologically laden values as "purity" and "beauty" that supposedly exist in "absolute autonomy" from social struggles. Just as the "flight into religion" in which imaginary solutions are proposed for real social problems, the "flight into art" suffers from "bad abstraction."

During his lifetime Althusser published two significant studies devoted to art and culture. In "The 'Picolo Teatro': Bertolazzi and Brecht" he advanced a materialist conception of theater and reworked Bertolt Brecht's theory of the "alienation-effect" to account for how the staging of a play could decenter both theatrical pace and time and the relationship between actors and spectators. In "Cremonini, Painter of the Abstract" he explored the "radical anti-humanism" evidenced in paintings by Italian artist Leonardo Cremonini, whose depiction of abstract relations between "things and their men" posed a revolutionary challenge to an aesthetic ideology rooted in subjectivities of creation and consumption.

Althusser's impact on literary and cultural theory has been apparent in such writers as Pierre Macherey, Terry Eagleton, Stuart Hall, Judith Butler, Michael Sprinker, and Warren Montag. An important but underappreciated influence of Althusser's writings has been in the fields of religion, theology, and Biblical criticism.

(*See also* Alienation; Apparatus; Assujettissement; Chapter 4, Marxism; Chapter 22, Identity Studies; Chapter 24, Posthumanism; Encounter; Ideology; *and* Interpellation)

Ted Stolze, *Cerritos College (United States)*

Further Reading

Althusser, Louis. "A Letter on Art in Reply to André Daspre." In *Lenin and Philosophy and Other Essays* [1968]. Trans. Ben Brewster. New York: Monthly Review Press, 2001. 151–55.

Althusser, Louis. "Cremonini, Painter of the Abstract." In *Lenin and Philosophy and Other Essays* [1968]. Trans. Ben Brewster. New York: Monthly Review Press, 2001. 157–66.

Althusser, Louis. "The 'Picolo Teatro': Bertolazzi and Brecht." In *For Marx* [1965]. Trans. Ben Brewster. New York: Verso, 2005. 129–51.

Montag, Warren. *Louis Althusser*. New York: Palgrave Macmillan, 2003.

American Structuralism

American Structuralism (or structural linguistics). Associated with Leonard Bloomfield, who was Sterling Professor of Linguistics at Yale, structural linguistics embraced ethnographic study. Bloomfield studied Germanic philology, Sanskrit, but perhaps most notably, languages spoken by American Indians. Bloomfield was a positivist and undertook the formal study of language independent of epistemology. He was concerned with uncovering fundamental syntactic structures within language in order to ascertain an early or proto state of development, as in the case of North American Indian languages.

(See also Chapter 2, Structuralism and Semiotics)

Herman Rapaport, *Wake Forest University (United States)*

Further Reading

Nöth Winfried. *Handbook of Semiotics.* Bloomington: Indiana University Press, 1990.

Anthropocene

From a rhetorical perspective, what we call the "anthropocene" has always been a literary fable—that supposedly geological era that we can't quite date and which testifies to a future reader, pretends to be that reader after man's disappearance, thus confirming his destructive scar in the sediment. It may, in the end, mark less an epochal hypothesis than the last fifteen years or so of the term's viral entry into interdisciplinary and critical discourses. So far as what the twenty-first century is likely to experience in an era of increasing climate chaos, it appears this period of "anthropocene talk" has burned itself up or served its role of distraction and has abruptly shifted to Phase 2—what one might call the *Trumpocene*. That shift corresponds roughly to a date, 2016 or so, when tipping points in the current ecocidal acceleration would essentially have passed, and been discretely acknowledged (in the laughable math of the "Paris" accords' façade). With this abrupt shift, the "anthropocene's" proleptic styles of warning and speculation that comprised the rhetoric of Phase 1—an "anthropocene talk" that, Jedediah Purdy notes, accomplished nothing and produced no "we" to correspond to it or act—becomes past tensed, irreversible, passing into irreversible accelerating mega-extractivism and extinction events. The unexpected character of Phase 2, for those expecting the Anthropocene imaginary to slowly shape world civilization, is that it takes the form in its signature American redaction of a cancellation of the "anthropocene" by fiat, a banning of mention of "climate change" (as "fake news"). Rather than accept the dismissal of "climate change" at face value or as serving fossil-fuel interests, it need also be read as a strategy fully aware of the ecocidal acceleration it chooses to advance. The early Trumpocene, forerunner to a normatization of triage, is about separating out winners from disposable losers as unfolds over the next generations. It comprises what amounts to a default imaginary "escape" strategy: the illusion of rescuing, halting, preserving, or managing climate chaos is replaced by an accelerated doubling down—designed to achieve escape velocity for a retooled few (a virtual species split). One would want to distinguish the Trumpocene's masking the former's logics from, say, Bernard Stiegler's concern with "escaping the Anthropocene" as a dead-end trap. When we decide the term "Anthropocene" will name a geological epoch, the assumption is that our heirs decades and centuries in the future will retain the term or name; however, one may speculate that they might regard it with mockery, consider the term applied, again, to the cohort or generations that couldn't stop talking about it, like a stutter, as they watched said tipping points pass on their watch. They might, these heirs looking back, consider the whole terminology a symptom, a rite of passage upon apprehending the scale of the extinction events and ecocide. Moreover, it is entirely likely that these heirs—the ones that control the archive, narratives, and data—will see themselves as and be different beings, gene-edited, hybridized, A.I. wired, perhaps adapted to different toxicities, and that what we call "Anthropos" will be looked back on as a product of the messy organic era of life, over-populated, mnemo-hacked, a lesser form which collectively might need retirement to up the odds of the hyper-elites' techno-evolution and (as the plan now appears) departure to Mars and so on, as Earth becomes uninhabitable.

(*See also* Chapter 6, Historicisms; Chapter 14, Ecocriticism; Chapter 24, Posthumanism; Critical Climate; *and* Environmental Humanities)

Tom Cohen, *University at Albany, SUNY*
(United States)

Further Reading

Cohen, Tom. *Telemorphosis: Theory in an Era of Climate Change*. Ann Arbor: Open Humanities Press, 2012. http://quod.lib.umich.edu/o/ohp/10539563.0001.001

Cohen, Tom, Claire Colebrook, and J. Hillis Miller. *Twilight of the Anthropocene Idols*. Ann Arbor: Open Humanities Press, 2016. http://www.openhumanitiespress.org/books/titles/twilight-of-the-anthropocene-idols/

Colebrook, Claire. *Death of the Post-Human: Essays on Extinction, Vol. 1*. Ann Arbor: Open Humanities Press, 2013. http://www.openhumanitiespress.org/books/titles/death-of-the-posthuman/

Ghosh, Amitav. *The Great Derangement: Climate Change and the Unthinkable*. Chicago: University of Chicago Press, 2016.

Stiegler, Bernard. *The Neganthropocene*. Ed. and trans. Daniel Ross. Ann Arbor: Open Humanities Press, 2018. http://www.openhumanitiespress.org/books/titles/the-neganthropocene/

Antihumanism

The roots of antihumanism lie in the strong negative reactions to the humanistic philosophies of the Enlightenment and to the French Revolution that these philosophies helped to inspire. The secular humanism of this time was based on the belief that humanity will achieve its full potential by discarding religious beliefs and traditional social customs, and developing democratic forms of government guided by human reason. Such a view assumes that human beings have both the power and the freedom to determine their own destiny. The French Encyclopedist Marquis de Condorcet (1743–94), for instance, believed that both morality and politics can be perfected by using mathematical models of collective decision-making, and that once these models are in place, human progress is assured. Such disregard for traditional values and social institutions provoked the wrath of reactionary thinkers such as Edmund Burke in England and Josephe de Maistre in France. They saw human beings as irremediably flawed and the elevation of human reason to divine status as a travesty of true religion. Both believed that only strong political authority could command the respect and obedience of an inherently unruly and irrational polity.

In the mid-nineteenth century, Max Stirner and Friedrich Nietzsche mount a similar attack on Enlightenment Humanism. Like Burke and de Maistre, they reject the narrative of human progress based on the perfection of human reason, and they distrust the culture of democracy, especially the shifting values of the emerging middle class, but unlike the earlier thinkers, they are avowed atheists who reject the authority of revealed religion and they question the legitimacy of traditional political institutions. Both charge that humanist ideals impose unwarranted restraints on the self-expression of exceptional people like themselves. Whereas humanism celebrates universal ideals, these philosophers value the virtues specific to the individual. For this reason, Stirner claims that by committing the individual to a shared set of values, humanism performs the same repressive function as the Christian religion. Nietzsche is similarly dismissive of the "herd mentality" of liberal reformers that represses the excellence of individuals in the interests of an imaginary collective good.

In the twentieth and twenty-first centuries, antihumanists have amplified the claims of their nineteenth-century predecessors. Among these, the French post-structuralists are perhaps the most-outspoken critics of humanism. Michel Foucault famously announces the end of the human era and predicts that in hindsight the concept of man will turn out to have been relatively unimportant. Louis Althusser, Roland Barthes, and Jacques Lacan, among others, express similar antihumanist sentiments. Like Nietzsche, these thinkers call into question humanist assumptions about the human subject. According to their arguments, human individuals are concatenations of diverse impulses and behaviors. They are not unified and autonomous agents with a predisposition to rational behavior. Also like Nietzsche and Stirner, modern antihumanists deny the existence of human nature; they deny the existence of a shared human essence that commits human beings to a common set of values. To the extent that reason does shape

human affairs, these antihumanists feel that it is likely to function as a force of repression rather than liberation. Typically, contemporary antihumanists see claims about a universal human nature, including appeals to human reason, as veiled attempts to impose Western culture's values on non-Western societies. Finally, and perhaps most importantly, antihumanists question the extent to which human beings, individually or collectively, are free to choose their own destiny. They believe that human choices are always constrained by language and culture, and that language and culture are the products of historical forces largely beyond human control.

In recent debates, however, the differences between humanists and antihumanists tend to be increasingly subtle. Many contemporary humanists, for instance, agree with antihumanists in rejecting the meliorist narrative of historical progress, and existential humanists, like Jean-Paul Sartre, also agree that there is no human nature that can guide us in making decisions about human values. Yet, humanists continue to differ most dramatically from their antihumanist critics in their optimistic faith in the human ability to change the world.

(*See also* Althusser, Louis; Barthes, Roland; Chapter 6, Historicisms; Chapter 24, Posthumanism; Enlightenment; Humanism; Lacan, Jacques; Nietzsche, Friedrich; *and* Posthumanism)

Allen R. Dunn, *University of Tennessee*
(United States)

Further Reading

Foucault, Michel. *The Order of Things: An Archaeology of the Human Sciences* [1966]. New York: Random House, 1970.

Norman, Richard. *On Humanism*. London: Routledge, 2004.

Sorper, Kate. *Humanism and Anti-Humanism*. London: Hutchinson, 1986.

Antitheory

A dozen or more antitheory factions have emerged in North America and the UK since the rise of theory during the 1970s. It's an odd phalanx. Among them are traditional literary critics; aesthetes; critical formalists; political conservatives; ethnic separatists; some literary stylisticians, philologists, and hermeneuticists; certain neopragmatists; champions of low and middlebrow literature; creative writers; defenders of common sense and plain style; plus some committed leftists. What most characterizes many of the antitheory factions as well as independent and maverick critics of contemporary theory are arguments calling for a return to the exclusive close reading of canonical literature, for clear writing of critical prose that avoids obscurity and jargon, and for settling disagreements through reasoned argumentation rather than statements of personal beliefs. Moreover, antitheorists often complain bitterly about contemporary theory's commitments to social constructionism (versus scientific truth and objectivity), to multiculturalism with its critical focus on race-class-gender analyses, and to ideology critique and the demystification of great literature. For their part, theorists refer to antitheorists as the "I love literature crowd." When tolerated at all by antitheorists, theory serves as a handmaiden to appreciation of literary texts. In no case should theory become autonomous, a separate field, or a new academic discipline (or subdiscipline). This is a consecration to be accorded above all and only to literature itself.

(*See also* Chapter 27, Antitheory; *and* Close Reading)

Vincent B. Leitch, *University of Oklahoma (United States)*

Further Reading

Holbo, John, ed. *Framing Theory's Empire.* West Lafayette: Parlor Press, 2007.

Leitch, Vincent B. "Antitheory." In *Literary Criticism in the Twenty-First Century: Theory Renaissance.* London: Bloomsbury, 2014. 11–32.

Patai, Daphne, and Will H. Corral, eds. *Theory's Empire: An Anthology of Dissent.* New York: Columbia University Press, 2005.

Apparatus

In his essay "What is an Apparatus?" (2009), Giorgio Agamben focuses exclusively on the genealogy of the concept in the work of Michel Foucault. He says, "The word *dispositif,* or 'apparatus' in English, is a decisive technical term in the strategy of Foucault's thought." But the term *apparatus* itself is most often associated with a germinal essay—"Ideology and Ideological State Apparatuses" (1970)—by Louis Althusser, a contemporary and theoretical rival of Foucault. As with all of Althusser's concepts, his understanding of apparatus is only meaningful in his overall theoretical problematic, which synthesizes his understanding of Lacanian psychoanalysis, structuralist linguistics, and Western Marxist political thought to answer what he sees as a fundamental question: how does the capitalist mode of production reproduce not only the forces of production—that is the raw materials, technology, and fixed capital of the factory—but also the subservience to the inherently unequal relations of production. Workers, managers, and functionaries are not only instilled with the appropriate skills to do their jobs, but also inclined to consent to the ruling ideology. For conventional economic theorists, the *homo economicus* of Adam Smith or Gary Becker is simply an aspect of the natural world to be exploited: it is human nature to truck and barter, to be the materially acquisitive, self-interested subjects of wage labor and capital. For Althusser, however, these subjects must be actively produced by the apparatuses of the state.

An apparatus is simultaneously the bureaucratic institutions of the state—the discourses, laws, and policies that instruct and regulate—as well as the material instantiation of those in architecture, buildings, and practices. The state here includes not only the official public state, but private institutions that function as state apparatuses. Althusser divides the state apparatus into the *repressive* and the *ideological*: the former operates predominantly through repression and coercion (as in the police, the prisons, the military, and the law); the latter, which is the most important part of his understanding, operates predominantly through ideology and consent (schools, churches, culture, communication, political parties, and, again, the law). The ideological apparatuses help legitimate the repressive apparatus as well as the totality of social relations; as he puts it, apparatuses interpellate concrete individuals as subjects. This means that, while individuals effectively choose to be good subjects—obedient and diligent students, workers, etc.—the apparatuses of the society make this position of subjectivity the most comfortable, convenient, and apparently successful, with the threat of social exclusion, prison, and death at the extreme opposite for those "bad subjects" who reject their interpellation by the apparatuses of the state.

While Foucault also adopts the concept of the apparatus, he is more fluid in his understanding of both its strategic function and its efficacy. Instead of beginning from the question of capitalist social relations, he considers a wider array of social institutions—prisons, mental hospitals, medical clinics—and discerns the way they operate as apparatuses, constituting subjects—inmates, patients—into their dominant discourses and thereby reproducing their power in and through the knowledge they produce about those subjects. At the same time, he argues that individuals have more ability to resist—often appropriating the very discourses through which they are constituted in the interests of their individual and collective agency.

In contrast, some of the most deterministic articulations of the apparatus can be found in film and media studies, in the writings of Jean-Louis Baudry, Christian Metz, and Laura Mulvey, which spawned debates in film journals like *Cahiers du Cinema* and *Screen*. Like Althusser, this controversial set of ideas is heavily influenced by Lacanian psychoanalysis, but these theories posit the physical relations between projector, screen, the darkened theater, and spectator in the conventional movie-going experience as the apparatuses interpellating the subject into the imaginary of the dominant ideology, robbing him (and especially her) of any possible agency. This rigidly structuralist understanding of the cinematic (and, by extension, media) apparatus was highly contested within audience-oriented Cultural Studies, which was grounded in empirical studies of active audiences and fan communities who were far more creative as readers and viewers. As these empirical studies were infused with post-structuralist, postmodernist, and feminist theories of language, experience, and metanarratives, the more Foucauldian understanding of the apparatus has become dominant within cultural theory.

(*See also* Agency; Althusser, Louis; Chapter 10, Feminism; Chapter 15, Biopower and Biopolitics; Chapter 21, Late Capitalism; Foucault, Michel; Ideology; *and* Subjectivity)

Sean Johnson Andrews, *Columbia College Chicago (United States)*

Further Reading

Althusser, Louis. *On the Reproduction of Capitalism: Ideology And Ideological State Apparatuses* [1995]. Trans. G. M. Goshgarian. New York: Verso. 2014.

Read, Jason. *The Micro-Politics of Capital: Marx and the Prehistory of the Present.*

Albany: State University of New York
Press, 2003.
Martel, James R. *The Misinterpellated Subject*.
Durham: Duke University Press, 2017.

Archi-Trace

The notion of the archi-trace, together with archi-writing and *différance*, is part of a constellation that makes up the Derridean critique of metaphysics and its attendant principle of *Being* as presence. While metaphysics of presence rests on the separation of speech and writing, whereby the latter is subordinated as an artificial notation of the former, deconstruction proposes that writing is interior to speech rather than its derivative. By revealing how *phoné*, or logocentrism, rests on the secondary nature of writing, deconstruction shows how the trace of writing, or archi-writing, is already present at the moment of its constitution. Indebted to Martin Heidegger's notion of *sous rature* ("under erasure") and Freud's analysis of the psychic apparatus as a system of writing which erases and retains itself, Derrida's notion of the trace brings the very notion of origin as presence into question. As an inscriptionality that is prior to any binary logic, the archi-trace, an originary moment of difference and deferral, is already inherent to the supposed presence of being.

As that from which a sign differs/defers, the trace is the absent part of the sign's presence, that is, the visible absence of presence. Because all signifiers viewed as *present* will necessarily contain traces of other absent signifiers, the signifier is neither wholly present nor wholly absent. Through the act of *différance*, a sign leaves behind a trace, which is whatever is left over after everything *present* has been accounted for. Graphic writing is but the representation of that archi-writing, the trace of its trace that marks the division of presence from itself. Language thus emerges as a trace-structure, effacing it at the same time as it presents its legibility. Archi-writing institutes origin as différance, as difference and deferral, and as such the origin is always displaced and delayed. Both temporalization and spacing then, this trace of a trace, or achi-trace, erases the myth of a present origin, because difference and deferral are already inscribed at the origin. This lack at the origin is the very condition of language, thought, and experience.

Because the trace cannot be reappropriated at any time as simple presence, the origin is not retrievable except as trace or repetition. This suspension of origin is foundational; it is a non-origin which is originary. The "originary" of originary repetition is always already crossed through by numerous traces and inscriptions. Repetition is thus labeled originary only to suspend and undermine the idea of an origin. This notion of the archi-trace as suspension of origin radically informs the idea of the archive. As a critique of locating things spatiotemporally, the archi-trace shows that the archive cannot be conflated with origin or *arché*. This does not mean that the origin has disappeared, but rather that it was never constituted except reciprocally by a non-origin, the trace, which thus becomes the origin of the origin. The notion of archi-trace thus acknowledges both the *arché* and its erasure or effacement through traces. When Derrida warns of the irresponsible desire to return to the origin in *Mal d'Archiv* (1995) it is this impossible retrieval of an origin untouched by the trace that is at stake. Ultimately, the very archived event is always already marked by the trace of its own inscription in the archive.

(*See also* Chapter 9, Deconstruction; Différance; Derrida, Jacques; Origin; Presence; *and* Writing)

Daniela Agostinho, *University of Copenhagen (Denmark)*

Further Reading

Derrida, Jacques. *Of Grammatology* [1967]. Trans. Gayatri Spivak. Baltimore: Johns Hopkins University Press, 1974.

Derrida, Jacques. "Freud and the Scene of Writing." In *Writing and Difference* [1967]. Trans. Alan Bass. London: Routledge and Kegan Paul, 1978.

Derrida, Jacques. *Archive Fever: A Freudian Impression* [1995]. Trans. Eric Prenowitz. Chicago: University of Chicago Press, 1996.

Archive (*See* Archi-trace)

Aristotelianism

Aristotelianism designates the philosophy of Aristotle and the schools of thought it influenced. Plato's most illustrious student, Aristotle has been variously understood as an heir of Platonism, as its critic (especially of Plato's Forms), or as both. Unlike his idealist mentor, Aristotle developed a dynamic way of thinking that describes the world in terms of activity. For Aristotle, matter is as important as form, while universals do not precede particulars but are derived from them. Thus, Aristotle reinstated natural philosophy—he is considered the founder of many life sciences such as biology, zoology, and botany—after its subordination in Plato's thought. Alienated by the academy's internal politics, and excluded from its leadership upon Plato's death, Aristotle founded his own school at Athens: the Lyceum. His disciples were known as the Peripatetics; they influenced Stoicism and Neoplatonism—the latter school having offered commentaries on both Plato and Aristotle.

Being considered the all-knowing man of his era, even today Aristotle's reputation as a philosopher rivals only that of his great mentor. That Thomas Aquinas referred to him as "The Philosopher," while Dante called him "the master" is indicative of the special status he commands in the history of philosophy. Indeed, the most seminal reception of Aristotle occurred during the Middle Ages, chiefly through the philosophical pursuits of Scholasticism and Thomism. This medieval reception is termed "the Recovery of Aristotle," and it fertilized the theology of the three monotheisms: Averroës and Avicenna, Aquinas, and Maimonides, all tried to synthesize Greek reason with religious revelation in the Islamic, Christian, and Jewish traditions, respectively, via commentaries on Aristotle. Apologetics about the existence of God relied on Aristotle's logic to enhance and legitimate further the element of belief.

Of particular interest to literary scholars is the fate of Aristotle's *Poetics*, the founding text of literary theory: it was forgotten until its rediscovery in the Renaissance, from which time onwards it continues to be influential. Notable in this context is also the Chicago school of rhetoric, which has revived Aristotelian rhetorical criticism. This school is referred to as Neo-Aristotelianism, and includes critics such as Richard McKeon and Wayne Booth.

While modern thought has revised the content of many of Aristotle's categories—having, for instance, discredited his *Physics*—and even set to undo basic aspects of his logic—the cancellation of the principles of identity and noncontradiction by dialectical philosophers like Georg Hegel, or the critique of causation and teleology from Friedrich Nietzsche to postmodernism are such examples—the logical foundations he had laid remain indispensable for the practice of philosophy. There is even the argument that beyond his emphasis on systematic reason, Aristotle was a proto-phenomenologist, interested in nature and the world as modalities of experience, and not as simply reified, measurable entities. It is this latter focus that has attracted phenomenologists such as Martin Heidegger to Aristotle's corpus as well.

The most important resurgence of Aristotle in recent times involves his contribution to ethics, which stresses the notions of character, habit, and virtue. While deontological ethics centers on obligation, and utilitarian on consequence, Aristotle's *eudaemonistic* ethics foregrounds the human being's capacity to work on its nature and build its character through cultivation of virtuous habits. Upon first glance, this looks like an outdated account of ethical life; yet it has become a growing field in contemporary ethics to the point that we now speak of a "eudaemonistic turn." Ethicists inspired by Aristotle include luminaries such as G. E. M. Anscombe, Bernard Williams, Philippa Foot, Julia Annas, Alasdair MacIntyre, and Martha Nussbaum.

(*See also* Chapter 1, Early Theory; Capacity; Formalism; Logic; Metaphysics; *and* Poetics)

Kalliopi Nikolopoulou, *University at Buffalo (United States)*

Further Reading

Chappell, Timothy, ed. *Values and Virtues: Aristotelianism in Contemporary Ethics.* Oxford: Oxford University Press, 2006.

Grant, Edward. *God and Reason in the Middle Ages*. Cambridge: Cambridge University Press, 2001.

Roochnick, David. *Retrieving Aristotle in an Age of Crisis*. Albany: State University of New York Press, 2013.

Assujettissement

Assujettissement, or subjectivation, describes how a subject is formed. It also describes what it means to be subject *to* certain things. In *Discipline and Punish* (1975), Michel Foucault considers a person subject to a disciplinary regime: overwhelmed by that regime's power, subjectivity means subjugation. Subjectivity is simply an outcome of that dominance, structured by it, an effect of that power. This emphasis is echoed by Louis Althusser: the subject is not independent of the forces that come to bear upon it. For Althusser, "ideology" is the force here. We are hailed by ideology, interpellated by it, receive its insinuations, norms, and biases as the price we pay to be regarded as subjects in whatever realm (e.g., the bourgeois state) that ideology holds sway. Yet, as Judith Butler observes, while these forces seem external, they penetrate "inside" the self, to the places where the subject consents to the power by which it is suborned. That "place" is the lodgment of the psyche. Subjectivation describes the incorporation of power, and names the place where power "lives"—power has a psychic life. Likewise, for Friedrich Nietzsche, Christian morality has a life only when the "soul" is invented as the receptacle for its dictates. Much depends, however, on how power is theorized, on the hypostases of the Law (the state, patriarchy, the Father). For Jacques Lacan, subjectivation describes the traumatic passage through the various stages described by psychoanalysis—up to and including our entry into the domain that assembles the symbolic figures of authority itself (a.k.a. the Father). The common theoretical point is that one receives subjectivity; it is something bestowed. What is granted thereby is the prerogative to regard oneself as a subject, but it also implies an enjoining to subjectivity by whatever has the force to do so—the Law, ideology, disciplinary regimes, normative morality. Is there any scope for subjective self-assertion? Even benignly ethical scenarios suggest not. For Emmanuel Levinas, the self becomes a "hostage" in order to respond responsibly to the Other.

"Response" is the keyword: the subject is bidden to respond, and awaits the occasion of interpellation in order to become a subject. In Butler's *Giving an Account of Oneself* (2005), and in Ricoeur's *Oneself as Another* (1995), the event of subjectivity occurs the moment one responds to the question "who are you?" One is called to account for oneself, and recount one's own story. In these scenarios, there is activity, but much passivity—perhaps too much. Contemporary theory has accordingly sought to refurbish a model of the initiative-taking, willful self. A more complete portrait of the subject balances the voluntary and the involuntary. The recent philosophical interest in habit, for example, poses an intriguing question: are habits entirely involuntary, or does the will play a role nonetheless? Other philosophical and theoretical enquiries concern the subject in love, subject to the enthrallment of love's sweet yoke, but not exactly deprived of will and initiative for all that. Then there is the subject in mourning, or before death. The complexities of these experiences—the sense of having to undergo an experience that structures one's very sense of self—are such that the masterful subject, enjoying a subjectivity secured by the repeated assertions "I think" and "I am," has been thoroughly dislodged, if not done to death. The death of a certain subject has been declared, prompting a new question: what comes after the subject?

(*See also* Chapter 15, Biopower and Biopolitics; Ideology; Interpellation; Other, The; Subject; *and* Subjectivity)

Brian O'Keeffe, *Barnard College*
(United States)

Further Reading

Butler, Judith. *Giving an Account of Oneself*. New York: Fordham University Press, 2005.

Butler, Judith. *The Psychic Life of Power: Theories in Subjection*. Stanford: Stanford University Press, 1997.

Foucault, Michel. *Discipline and Punish: The Birth of the Prison* [1975]. Trans. Alan Sheridan. New York: Vintage Books, 1995.

Ricoeur, Paul. *Oneself as Another* [1990]. Trans. Kathleen Blamey. Chicago: University of Chicago Press, 1995.

Authenticity

Authenticity is generally defined as sincerity or genuineness and refers to something that is factually true or in line with facts. It can describe people (a sincere friend) or objects (a real gold nugget). However, with the onset of modernity and the Industrial Revolution, philosophers such as Søren Kierkegaard and Friedrich Nietszche began to question the formerly solid foundations (traditional values and religious beliefs) of "existence" at a collective and individual level. Along with Sigmund Freud's development of ego psychology, in which the "authentic" self can never fully be known thanks to the realm of the unconscious, this questioning of the very ontological ground of existence would influence much philosophy in the twentieth and twenty-first century.

The philosopher Martin Heidegger, for instance, made authenticity the cornerstone of his major work *Being and Time* (1927), which argued that "Dasein" (human being) is the being whose being is always in question. To live authentically, one must be aware of this fact and recognize the inevitable horizon of death. In *Being and Nothingness* (1943), existentialist philosopher Jean-Paul Sartre provided a famous example of a waiter who is so good at "being" a waiter that he is essentially a zombie and acting inauthentically or in "bad faith." Authenticity, for Sartre, came from embracing the meaninglessness of existence, yet nevertheless freely choosing to act, thereby creating meaning.

The post-Second World War world, however, saw the rise of mass culture and mass man as capitalism birthed a whole slew of new commodities, most notably television. Walter Benjamin had already claimed that in an age of mechanical reproduction, erstwhile concepts of an "origin" or "authenticity" were problematic, and in *Dialectic of Enlightenment* (1944), fellow Frankfurt School thinkers Theodor Adorno and Max Horkheimer critiqued the emergence of what they called "the culture industry," which churned out programmatic, money-making cultural "products" for a captive, popular audience. The ideology of popular culture duped people, they argued, into living inauthentic lives and could easily lead to fascism.

An increasingly image-based and mediated post-1968 world lead Jean Baudrillard to assert, in *Simulacra and Simulation* (1981), that various media (television, computers, and virtual reality) create "reality." We supposedly lived in a "hyperreal" world of "simulation" where ideas of "the real" or "authenticity" made no sense anymore. Indeed, what is "authentic" if, as Fredric Jameson claims in *Postmodernism* (1991), nature itself had been completely colonized by culture and capital? Despair or cynicism seems inevitable. Some recent thinkers, however, have offered accounts of being that transcend the authentic/inauthentic binary. Judith Butler's concept of "performativity," for example, accounts for the ontological baselessness of being in a positive way. Sartre's waiter, for Butler, is not necessarily inauthentic but reveals the performative nature of being—that a set of embodied acts and habits will, in this case, make for "waiterness." Further, Giorgio Agamben's notion of "whatever singularities" in *The Coming Community* (1993) postulates a unique core to beings comprised of irreducible and unsignifiable difference—not the similarity or commonness that authenticity

depends upon. Authenticity, nonetheless, remains a problematic concept.

(*See also* Chapter 10, Feminism; Chapter 11, Cultural Studies; Origin; *and* Performativity)

Ralph Clare, *Boise State University (United States)*

Further Reading
Sloterdijk, Peter. *Critique of Cynical Reason.* Minneapolis: University of Minnesota Press, 1987.
Taylor, Charles. *The Ethics of Authenticity.* Cambridge: Harvard University Press, 1992.
Trilling, Lionel. *Sincerity and Authenticity.* Cambridge: Harvard University Press, 1972.

Author

A contested figure throughout literary and cultural history, the author has been variously seen as an embodied person, a textual construct, or a function of discourse; an individual genius, or a commercial entity operating within a market system; historically situated but also open to difference and interpretation. The large body of criticism surrounding the author-debate has focused on the dynamic relationship among writer, reader, work/text, and literary tradition, which has endowed the author-figure with varying degrees of agency and authority—from the romanticist notion of the author as an origin of meaning and source of originality to post-structuralist theories that have shifted the critical emphasis from author *to* reader *to* discourse. In "The Death of the Author" (1967), Roland Barthes sought to replace the sovereignty of the "Author-God" with that of the reader/critic, albeit one stripped of history, biology, and psychology. Similarly, in "What Is an Author?"

(1969), Michel Foucault conceived of the author-function as the "total effacement" of the writer's individual characteristics by the historically and culturally specific discourse. The author's demise—which can be traced to T. S. Eliot's famous reaction against personality in "Tradition and the Individual Talent" (1921) and explained in terms of the crisis of faith brought about by Friedrich Nietzsche's proclamation of the "death of God"—has come back to haunt deconstructive theory, making its project of dismantling of the metaphysical concepts of subjectivity and presence untenable. This is the very premise of Seán Burke's inquiry in *The Death and Return of the Author: Criticism and Subjectivity in Barthes, Foucault, and Derrida* (1992), which has been extremely influential in reconciling the biographical and deconstructive approaches to authorship. On this view, the author figures as both a creating subject—a product of a vast pool of formative influences—and a created subject—(re-)born in the act of reading, or even rewriting, as indicated by the recent spate of fictionalized biographies of historical writers. Never was Mark Twain's joke about the exaggerated rumors of the author's death taken more seriously than in the 1980s, during the identity politics phase of cultural critique centered on class, gender, sexuality, race, and ethnicity. The assumption was that if any of these identity categories loses its relevance, then the displacement of the writing subject's authority becomes a reenactment of oppression. Thus, from both a feminist and postcolonial perspective, to write out the author-figure's individuality is seen as politically disabling because it erases the historical particularities of the writing subject's experience. At the same time, however, the assumption that "X writes what he/she knows/feels" is extremely reductive, as it may lead readers to overlook aspects of technique, complexity, aesthetics, intellectual depth, etc.—in other words, the very means by which a writer translates life, in all its beauty and mystery, into a subjective representation. Regardless of how closely aligned writers and readers, intention and reception, texts and contexts may be, the author remains a variable of textual meaning—a valuable *actant*, to use Bruno Latour's term from Actor Network Theory—and therefore, an elemental tool of scholarship.

(*See also* Barthes, Roland; Chapter 2, Structuralism and Semiotics; Chapter 8, Rhetoric; Chapter 24, Posthumanism; *and* Foucault, Michel)

Laura Savu, *Columbia College, South Carolina (United States)*

Further Reading

Barthes, Roland. "The Death of the Author [1967]." Trans. Stephen Heath. *Image Music Text.* Ed. Stephen Heath. London: Fontana/Collins, 1977. 142–48.

Burke, Seán, ed. *Authorship: From Plato to the Postmodern.* Second ed. Edinburgh: Edinburgh University Press, 2000.

Burke, Seán. *The Death and Return of the Author: Criticism and Subjectivity in Barthes, Foucault, and Derrida.* Edinburgh: Edinburgh University Press, 1992.

Foucault, Michel. "What Is an Author? [1969]" Trans. Donald F. Bouchard. *Language, Counter-Memory, Practice.* Ed. Donald F. Bouchard. Oxford: Blackwell, 1977. 113–38.

Autonomy (*See* Heteronomy)

B

Badiou, Alain

Four different approaches might be taken to introduce the philosopher, Alain Badiou (born 1937). First, one might consider the crucial role that mathematics has played in the development of his thought. From his earliest philosophical work in the 1960s, he began to develop a theory of novelty through a material engagement with mathematical formalization. When "novelty" coalesced as "event" in his most significant work, *Being and Event* (1988), it was underwritten by a clear and precise response to developments in Set Theory: the crisis it occasioned in mathematics when first proposed by Georg Cantor, the paradoxes formulated by Gottlob Frege and Bertrand Russell, its resolution through axiomatization by Ernst Zermelo and Abraham Fraenkel, John von Neumann, and Kurt Gödel. Drawing on the language of Set Theory, Badiou would affirm four points of his ontology: situations are pure indifferent multiplicities, within these multiplicities there may emerge some rupturing element called an "event," such events are only to be discerned by the active fidelity of a "subject" attesting to its existence, and the truth produced by this combination of "event" and "subject" is generic, or, in other words, not circumscribed by a particular predicate, even if it is located in a particular situation. If *Being and Event* proposed an ontology based on Set Theory, its sequel, *Logics of Worlds* (2006), turned to Category Theory to develop a system of appearances, whereby the consequences of

events might be tracked as they manifested by the responses of subjects in situations (now recast as "worlds") point by point. Mathematics, often regarded as a synecdoche for Science by Badiou's commentators, is the productive operator for describing how newness enters into situations or worlds as a result of an impasse in their own internal logic (rather than from "the outside").

Why, it must be asked, is Badiou so interested in newness? The answer might be found in his commitment to emancipatory politics. His formative political experience came during the student uprisings of May 1968. Already a follower of Louis Althusser in the middle 1960s, he broke with Althusser to contribute to the development of French Maoism in the early 1970s, alongside Natacha Michel and Sylvain Lazarus. His political writings, often published as Sartrean *Circumstances*, try to respond philosophically to political happenings in the present. Equally, his artistic preference for Modernism promotes the importance of aesthetic newness. His early novels and plays may be political in their content, but, formally, they owe more to Samuel Beckett than to Bertolt Brecht. Newness is as likely to come from artistic innovation as political action. Finally, he finds an ethical commitment in recognizing otherness. This is not an ontological encounter with an Other, as for Emmanuel Levinas. Rather it is a matter of love: the recognition of a self-effacing otherness in both the Other and the Same when they come together in the formation of a Couple. Badiou is shaped by four realms of thought, which suture together his philosophy and, unsurprisingly, provide its staging grounds, its situations, its worlds, and its bodies: scientific results, political organizations, artistic works, and loving couples. For Badiou, the task of philosophy is not to claim truths: it is to trace them as they manifest through the recognition of events (scientific, political, artistic, loving) by active subjects.

(*See also* Event)

Arthur Rose, *Durham University*
(United Kingdom)

Further Reading
Badiou, Alain. *Being and Event* [1988].
    London: Continuum, 2006.
Badiou, Alain. *Logics of Worlds: Being and*
    Event II [2006]. London: Continuum, 2009.
Badiou, Alain. *Handbook of Inaesthetics*
    [1998]. Stanford: Stanford University
    Press, 2005.

Bakhtin, Mikhail

Mikhail Bakhtin (1895–1975), philosopher of language and phenomenologist of culture, has two lives: his obscure lived biography as autodidact, invalid, political exile, and eventually professor of literature at a provincial teachers' college, and then his posthumous life as globally famous twentieth-century Russian thinker.

Born into a banker's family, fluent in German since childhood, he grew up in Oryol, Vilnius, and Odessa. Between 1913 and 1918, he studied the classics at Odessa and Petrograd Universities, but received no academic degrees (poor health and the First World War were major factors). During the Civil War he took refuge in the western-Russian towns of Nevel and Vitebsk, where a circle coalesced that relocated to Leningrad in 1924. In 1929, soon after his first book (on Dostoevsky)

appeared, Bakhtin was arrested for illicit religious activity and exiled to Kazakhstan from 1930 to 1936. In 1938, after decades of worsening osteomyelitis, his right leg was amputated, which improved his health sufficiently that he could hold a full-time job at the Saransk Pedagogical Institute. In 1940 Bakhtin submitted his manuscript on Rabelais as a dissertation to the Gorky Institute of World Literature in Moscow. Its defense in 1946 was a scandal. Invited back to Saransk, Bakhtin chaired its world literature department until his retirement in 1961. Three young philologists from Moscow discovered him, became his enablers and disciples, and worked tirelessly to bring his writings into print.

In translation, Bakhtin's work became world famous out of sequence: first his carnival ideas (in the 1960s); then his theory of the novel (in the 1970s); finally in the 1990s, his early idealist-philosophical essays. During the "Bakhtin boom" of the 1980s–1990s, debates raged over the proportion of materialist Marxism to Christian existentialism in his thought. The six-volume Russian *Collected Works of Bakhtin* (1996–2011) explicates his sources and inspirations, very distant from the contexts to which his thought has been applied.

Five phases, or basic idea-clusters, mark Bakhtin's intellectual development. Common to them all is the distinction between *inside* ("I"/myself) and *outside* ("you"/others), and between *open* (laughing, unfinished, mobile: a personality) and *closed* (serious, completed, static: a thing). All human acts move between these two poles. In his first phase (Kantian essays of the 1920s) Bakhtin focuses on vision, space, responsibility, and value: what does your being outside me enable me to know and oblige me to do? In his second phase (beginning 1929), words move to the fore, with dialogism (an architectonics of utterances) and polyphony (an authorial stance granting equal validity to all voices) exemplified by Fyodor Dostoevsky, master of interaction and coexistence. The third and fourth phases, more inflected by Hegelian becoming, overlap in the 1930s. Expanding dialogism into heteroglossia, Bakhtin advances a theory of the origin of novels in the multiplicity of languages, traced historically through evolving chronotopes (time-space matrices). Analogous with the double-voiced word, Bakhtin develops through Rabelais the double-bodied image of carnival. The grotesque image and the polyphonic word are compatible concepts: both can be weakened (as Bakhtin's dark writings of 1943–46 testify) but not killed, made formless but never static, and both reside in Great (not Small) Time and Experience. In his fifth phase (the 1950s–1960s) Bakhtin experiments with a civic voice: questions of genre and, as he regained an audience, cultural commentary. His very survival, he insisted, had been carnival.

(*See also* Chapter 4, Marxism; *and* Dialogue)

Caryl Emerson, *Princeton University (United States)*

Further Reading

Brandist, Craig. *The Bakhtin Circle: Philosophy, Culture and Politics*. London: Pluto Press, 2002.
Erdinast-Vulcan, Daphna. *Between Philosophy and Literature: Bakhtin and the Question of the Subject*. Stanford: Stanford University Press, 2013.
Holquist, Michael. *Dialogism: Bakhtin and his World*. New York: Routledge, 1990.
Renfrew, Alastair. *Mikhail Bakhtin*. New York: Routledge, 2015.

Bare Life

Bare life is a key term in Italian philosopher Giorgio Agamben's political theory, particularly as it is developed in *Homo Sacer: Sovereign Power and Bare Life* (1995). Elaborating on Michel Foucault's explanation of the modern invention of biopolitics, where the life of individuals and of collectives becomes increasingly the focus of the state's political strategies, Agamben contends that sovereign power and the state have become more and more implicated in the management of life itself. In his view, the classical distinction between *zoe* and *bios*—between the mere or "bare" existence common to all living things (*zoe*), and qualified life (*bios*), or the way of life "proper to an individual or group"—is fundamental to Western politics from its inception. This distinction accounts, for example, for Aristotle's notion of man as *animal rationale,* a form of animal life capable of directing itself toward the "good life," with all the rights and duties proper to a member of the *polis* or political community.

In the modern period, when sovereign power is no longer grounded in a pre-given theology or conception of nature, "bare life," which had been peripheral to the construction of the political order, slowly becomes its veiled foundation. This happens in part through the way the logic of modern sovereignty exacerbates and rearticulates the distinction between *zoe* and *bios*. Agamben explores this by drawing on political philosopher Carl Schmitt's definition of the sovereign as "he who decides on the exception," which points to a paradox in the logic of modern sovereignty that allows the sovereign to be at once inside and outside the political order. By instituting the law, the sovereign is also the only element of the political order capable of suspending the law and deciding when an exceptional situation, such as a state of emergency, comes into being. In this suspension, however, the legal or political order does not dissolve; law remains in place without being applied. As a result, the distinction between bare life and the life of the citizen comes back into play.

It becomes, according to Agamben, the very object itself of the sovereign's decision on the exception, and as such defines who remains inside the political order, and who, excluded from this political order, is still subject to it while being deprived of any legal standing or protections. "Bare life" as a political concept is thus not simply a return to a Hobbesian state of nature, but is instead the result of the very constitution of the political order itself and of the sovereign's decision on the value or non-value of life. Claiming that the Nazi death camps constitute the logical extension of this relation between bare life and sovereign decision, Agamben argues that the creation of the camps—where prisoners were stripped of any political or civil rights and where they were completely exposed to the power of the sovereign's decision over the status of their lives—resulted from the normalization of a state of exception first instituted by the Nazi regime in 1933. While this may be the most extreme manifestation of the relation between sovereign power and bare life, Agamben argues in *State of Exception* (2003) that this relation continues to define modern politics, as evidenced most recently by the nonlegal status of those interned at the US detention center at Guantanamo Bay, and by the ongoing refugee crisis around the world.

(*See also* Agamben, Giorgio; Biopolitics; Chapter 15, Biopower and Biopolitics; *and* Exceptionalism, State of)

Kir Kuiken, *University at Albany, SUNY (United States)*

Further Reading

Agamben, Giorgio, *Homo Sacer: Sovereign Power and Bare Life* [1995]. Trans. Daniel Heller-Roazen. Stanford: Stanford University Press, 1998.

Agamben, Giorgio. *State of Exception* [2003]. Trans. Kevin Attrell. Chicago: University of Chicago Press, 2005.

Barthes, Roland

Along with historian/philosopher Michel Foucault, anthropologist Claude Lévi-Strauss, and psychoanalyst Jacques Lacan, Roland Barthes (1915–80) was a key exponent of the Parisian structuralism whose attention to language and formal analysis influenced literary and cultural theorists on both sides of the Atlantic during an era of grand theory between 1950 and 1980.

Barthes studied classics and philology in Paris before embarking on a career as a researcher, critic, and theorist characterized by an openness to methods adapted from linguistics, psychoanalysis, and social sciences. His first book, *Writing Degree Zero* (1953), responded to Jean-Paul Sartre's 1948 call in *What is Literature?* for the writer to reject a poetic attitude that isolated her/him from history in favor of a prose attitude that thrust her/him into the moment. Countering Sartre's poetry/prose distinction, Barthes advocated a morality of form he called *writing* (*écriture*) as a third term between language and style. Fifteen years later, the priority of text over authorial intention in Barthes's *On Racine* (1963) drew the ire of Sorbonne professor Raymond Picard. In the interim, the "little mythologies of the month" that Barthes wrote starting in 1953 drew on the writings of linguists Ferdinand de Saussure and A. J. Greimas to address topics ranging from wrestling and striptease to the Citroën DS sedan and Greta Garbo's face. *Mythologies* (1957) marked Barthes's initial foray into the study of the social life of signs known as semiology. Its light tone suited Barthes's goal to disclose (demystify) how mass media from advertising and the tabloid press to popular cinema suppressed historical struggles in favor of a timeless nature. Later writings on trips to Japan and China chronicled encounters with cultural signs and systems Barthes could only begin to grasp.

Barthes's commitment to formal analysis peaked and ebbed in *S/Z* (1970), in which he mobilized five codes—hermeneutic, proairetic, cultural, semantic, and symbolic—to produce a passage-by-passage reading of Balzac's 1830 novella, *Sarrasine*. Unexpected and thus all the more forceful was Barthes's claim that these codes might vary in kind and number from one reading to the next and from one text to another. *S/Z* marked Barthes's turn toward a consideration of the reading process he would cast starting in *The Pleasure of the Text* (1973) as a transition from Classical ("readerly") to modern ("writerly") practices. The publication of *Camera Lucida: Reflections on Photography* (1980) within months of his death marked a final phase of Barthes's evolution, inflected this time via Susan Sontag's *On Photography* (1978) and Sartre's *The Imagination* (1940). Among Barthes's lasting legacies were his paired notions of *spectrum* and *punctum*, with the latter understood as an emotional response to a detail that seemingly jumped out to touch the viewer.

Barthes's critical engagement with elite and mass cultures persists in writings by Michel de Certeau, Jean Baudrillard, Marc Augé, and the Situationist Guy Debord. Since Barthes's death, his later work has attracted attention in conjunction with notions of the neutral, gay writing, and the critiques of everyday life undertaken starting in 1947 by sociologist Henri Lefebvre.

(*See also* Author; Chapter 2, Structuralism and Semiotics; Chapter 3, Narrative and Narratology; Chapter 5, Post-structuralism; Erotic; Jouissance; Langage; *and* Structuralism)

Steven Ungar, *University of Iowa*
(United States)

Further Reading

Barthes, Roland. *Mythologies* [1957]. Trans. Annette Lavers. New York: Hill and Wang, 1972.

Barthes, Roland. *S/Z* [1970]. Trans. Richard Miller. New York: Hill and Wang, 1975.

Barthes, Roland. *Camera Lucida: Reflections on Photography* [1980]. Trans. Richard Howard. New York: Hill and Wang, 1981.

Rabaté, Jean-Michel. *Writing the Image after Roland Barthes*. Philadelphia: University of Pennsylvania Press, 1997.

Ungar, Steven. *Roland Barthes: The Professor of Desire*. Lincoln: University of Nebraska Press, 1983.

Base and Superstructure

As Ellen Meiksins Wood puts it in her essay on the aforementioned two terms, "The terms base and superstructure may be more trouble than they are worth." Karl Marx first uses the term in *A Contribution to a Critique of Political Economy* (1859), setting up a division between the economic relations between wage labor and capitalists as the economic "base" of society—using Georg Hegel's term of civil society, and the juridical, religious, social concepts that emerge out of the base as a reflection of the economic arrangements. The short paragraph below from *Contribution* clearly illustrates Marx's wish to unify social relations (the organization of capitalist economic production) with concomitant notions in the sphere of noneconomical cultural and political institutions:

In the social production of their existence, men inevitably enter into definite relations, which are independent of their will, namely [the] relations of production appropriate to a given stage in the development of their material forces of production. The totality of these relations of production constitutes the economic structure of society, the real foundation, on which arises a legal and political superstructure, and to which correspond definite *forms of social consciousness*.

Prior to writing *Contribution*, in *The Poverty of Philosophy* (1847), Marx argues for a deterministic relationship between the economic base and superstructure: a reading that would become "orthodoxy" for multiple generations of Marxists: "In acquiring new productive forces, men change their mode of production; and in changing their mode of production, in changing their way of earning a living, they change all their social relations. The handmill gives you society with a feudal lord; the steam mill society with an industrial capitalist."

Social relations of production thus determine the effective extent and character of superstructural forces inasmuch as the reach of superstructure can never undermine the economic base from which it springs. Questions of the determination of the superstructure by the base emerge almost as soon as the term is deployed, as sociologists and thinkers following Marx, such as Max Weber in *The Protestant Work Ethic and the Spirit of Capitalism* (1905), would attempt to analyze the power of the religious, legal, and political spheres' determination of production in order to prioritize either the economic base or the superstructure of ideas as determinant, with scholars generally favoring reading of the base as primary. After Marx's death, Friedrich Engels would intervene to correct this reading, arguing that base and superstructure work dialectically, codetermining each other, with the economic base only central in the final instance. Following Engels, Raymond Williams, Meiskins Wood (to name only but a few), base and superstructure become conceptually intermingled and provide the basis for the development and investigation of notions more related to subjective historical agency such as mediation, and determination, as well as having influenced classic Marxist research on ideology and relations of production, such as Louis Althusser's famous essay "Ideology and Ideological State Apparatuses (Notes towards an Investigation)."

(*See also* Chapter 4, Marxism; Chapter 22, Identity Studies; Cultural Materialism; Ideology; Marx, Karl; *and* Production)

Carlos M. Amador, *Michigan Technological University (United States)*

Further Reading

Harman, Chris. "Base and Superstructure." *International Socialism* 2.32 (1986): 3–44.

Meiksins Wood, Ellen. "The Separation of the Economic and the Political in Capitalism." *New Left Review* I/127 (May–June 1981).

Williams, Raymond. *Keywords: A Vocabulary of Culture and Society.* Third ed. Oxford University Press, 2015.

Bataille, Georges

Georges Bataille (1897–1962) is among the most influential twentieth-century critical thinkers, yet his work is at the same time often difficult and hard to categorize, for two reasons. The first is that his domains of interest are extremely diverse: his writings range from philosophy and ethnography to sociology, economy and cultural themes— sometimes in extended and "scholarly" formats, sometimes in much more personal and unorthodox texts—to literary criticism and art history, novels and erotic fiction, the last category being the one which gained the widest, albeit largely posthumous, readership. The second reason is that his thought often seeks to challenge received structures and categories of understanding, and to propose instead a "heterology" that would destabilize hierarchies, to grasp those phenomena that elude classification: the formless, excess, waste, violence, and otherness that constitute the sacred in society. This makes for a body of work that incorporates contradiction, paradox, and a measure of impossibility, without losing any of its solemnity or intimacy.

Leading an outwardly unremarkable life (spending much of his career as a librarian), reticent in demeanor, he was nevertheless at the thick of intellectual debates in mid-century France; themes of community and communication are central to his work. Bataille's thought is most conveniently approached in the context of French surrealism, though he was at first famously critical of its positions, deeming them steeped in an idealism which his notion of a "base materialism" explicitly opposed. Many have pictured him as exemplifying a "dissident surrealism" (especially in the journal *Documents* and his founding of intellectual circles such as the College of Sociology and Acéphale), undaunted by the limits to which surrealism aspired but could not access. Nevertheless, in the mid-1930s he joined the surrealists in the anti-fascist Contre-Attaque movement, and both parties acknowledged their mutual ground and complementarity of ideas. Championed after his death by French critics of the *Tel Quel* circle, Bataille's work has subsequently had a significant impact on Anglophone critical writing, particularly in the field of cultural theory as developed in the pages of *October*.

His editorship of *Documents* (1929–30) pitched critical writings on arts and society against diverse materials from popular culture and ethnography sources. It also hosted a "Critical Dictionary" of short, incisive texts

on key but unexpected questions, of which his "The Big Toe" and "Formless" are among the most celebrated. These confirmed Bataille's territory as the sacred, the base, and the transgressive—a transgression that has no meaning without the taboo it completes. His erotic novella *The Story of the Eye* (1928), first published anonymously, cements this view of a writer prepared to access the most challenging ideas head-on. It expressed in searing prose what later writings such as *Eroticism* (1957) explored in more scholarly terms, the contiguity between Eros and Thanatos at the heart of human interactions with others and the world. Other works—many completed later in life—deal in more measured scope with themes such as economy, sovereignty, sacrifice, inner experience, and mortality, however much their subject also remained the rending and impossible truth of human limits.

(*See also* Alterity; Chapter 9, Deconstruction; Erotic; *and* Sovereignty)

Krzysztof Fijalkowski, *Norwich University of the Arts (United Kingdom)*

Further Reading
Hewson, Mark, and Marcus Coelen, eds. *Georges Bataille: Key Concepts*. London: Routledge 2015.
Richardson, Michael. *Georges Bataille*. London: Routledge, 1994.
Surya, Michel. *Georges Bataille: An Intellectual Biography*. London: Verso, 2010.

Baudrillard, Jean

Jean Baudrillard (1929–2007) was a poet, pataphysician, translator, photographer, public intellectual, theoretician, enfant terrible, and personae non gratae of French philosophy, whose works had a major worldwide influence in academia and popular discourse. Across a seemingly heterogeneous oeuvre—of more than fifty books and numerous other publications from articles, poems, and songs, to interviews and photographs—that touched upon almost every discipline across the humanities and social sciences Baudrillard had one predominant concern: a theorization of the "object."

From Baudrillard's earliest theorizations of the "object system," and the general semiological process and logic for social integration in affluent consumer societies (e.g., *The System of Objects*, 1968) to his final essays on taking up the position of the object in the wake of mediatization, virtualization, and the disappearance of the subject to imagine a world without humans (e.g., *Why Hasn't Everything Already Disappeared?*, 2007), Baudrillard's oeuvre is a remarkably consistent treatise on the disappearance of the object and its appearance as image, sign, simulacra, simulation, hyperreality, integral reality. Through an inversion of perhaps the most famous of philosophical questions, Baudrillard asks, "Why is there nothing rather than something?" to simulate and challenge *the reality principle*: the systematic completion and overpowering of the world through technology and the elimination of all illusion and enigma.

More than an initiator of post-structuralism Baudrillard was one of the world's most fêted, influential, provocative, and divisive thinkers. Eschewing the restrictions and responsibilities of an academic career, Baudrillard was nevertheless serious, but it seems that Baudrillard's philosophy was not taken seriously enough during his lifetime. While more than ten years after his death Baudrillard's theoretical writings continue to inspire by matching and anticipating the form and direction of the state of the world (the world appears to be playing catch-up to Baudrillard's theorizations); they are also assuming more importance as it is increasingly realized that the later Baudrillard's

books were published the more interesting they are. Most research and opinion with regard to Baudrillard's ideas to date have either focused on his earliest works, or have incorrectly sought to restrict Baudrillard's importance to a particular epoch (as a philosopher of his times; the chief diagnostician of postmodernity) or decade (the fashionable philosopher of the 1980s when Baudrillard's work on simulation had a huge impact, especially in the art world), whereas the fact of the matter is that on the cusp of his death Baudrillard was signaling another development in his thinking by theorizing a situation where integral reality has become all-encompassing and hegemonic.

(*See also* Alterity; Authenticity; Chapter 2, Structuralism and Semiotics; Consumer Society; *and* Introduction: Theory in the New Millennium)

Richard G. Smith, *Swansea University (United Kingdom)*

Further Reading

Baudrillard, Jean. *Revenge of the Crystal: Selected Writings on the Modern Object and its Destiny, 1968-1983*. Sydney: Power Institute, 1990.

Baudrillard, Jean. *Carnival and Cannibal, or the Play of Global Antagonism*. London: Seagull, 2010.

Smith, Richard G. ed. *The Baudrillard Dictionary*. Edinburgh: Edinburgh University Press, 2010.

Smith, Richard G., and David B. Clarke, eds. *Jean Baudrillard: From Hyperreality to Disappearance, Uncollected Interviews*. Edinburgh: Edinburgh University Press, 2015.

Smith, Richard G., and David B. Clarke, eds. *Jean Baudrillard: The Disappearance of Culture, Uncollected Interviews*. Edinburgh: Edinburgh University Press, 2017.

Beauty (*See* Aesthetics; Kant, Immanuel; *and* Taste)

Beauvoir, Simone de

Beauvoir (1908–86) remains best known for her groundbreaking feminist work, *The Second Sex* (1949), her partnership with Jean-Paul Sartre in launching existentialism in the 1940s, and her novels and autobiographies, which corroborate her lifelong rejection of "an abstract voice." Throughout her life, Beauvoir insisted on being viewed as a writer rather than a philosopher, a position she famously conceded to Sartre.

Thanks, however, to indefatigable, non-hagiographic work by feminist scholars, Beauvoir's stock as an independent, distinctive thinker and cultural critic continues to rise. The discovery and publication of essays and letters dating back to her student days, and analysis of her work outside the glare of intellectual stardom that surrounded her and Sartre during their lifetimes, has demonstrated her philosophical and critical achievements despite her self-definition. They've also revealed her to hold positions at times in advance of her famous "primary" partner, and in some instances at odds with his.

Perhaps the foremost difference between Beauvoir and Sartre in their intellectual approaches to all matters was Beauvoir's never-abandoned "eyes wide open" reportorial commitment to the world around her. Sartre's taste for abstractions, in contrast, eventually drew him away from literature and accessible prose. In *The Ethics of Ambiguity*, Beauvoir wrote that "we must affirm the concrete and particular thickness of this world and the individual reality of our projects and ourselves." In her article, "New Heroes for Old," she declared, "The human condition is carnal." Much later, in *All Said and Done*, the last volume of her autobiography, she remarked that "knowing meant directing my awareness towards the world."

Beauvoir exerted her greatest influence on culture in three main areas: feminism, literature, and intellectual lifestyle.

Nearly seventy years after its publication, *The Second Sex* continues as a touchstone and interlocutor for every feminist thinker, whether sympathetic or opposed to Beauvoir's approach. Few disagree with Beauvoir's famous opening salvo that "a woman is not born, but rather becomes, a woman"—that is, a socially constructed one. Beauvoir is not just feminism's "mother of us all," but the great modern whistleblower who argued that men engineer the concept of "woman" and conventional feminine "gender" characteristics to position woman as the inferior "Other."

Whereas Sartre in his existentialism emphasized a kind of "absolute freedom" of every individual to project and construct a desired life, Beauvoir always stressed the real-world circumstances that constrained one's freedom to do so—for example, being a woman, black, Jewish, poor, old. At the same time, she shared with Sartre the aspiration for all people to seize freedom in the strongest way possible. The human species, she wrote in *The Second Sex*, "is forever in a state of becoming."

Some subsequent feminist thinkers reject Beauvoir's perceived harshness toward marriage and motherhood, while discerning positive elements in feminine characteristics Beauvoir largely saw as symptoms of gender oppression. Whereas Beauvoir believed the liberation of women required economic autonomy outside the home, which in turn would provide freedom to pursue lives and careers traditionally restricted to men, later feminists sometimes celebrate such characteristics as "caring for others" as marks of a separate, independent, and even superior morality.

Beauvoir's realist conception of literature, enriched by publication of previously neglected essays and articles, places her as a defender of *engage* notions of literature found more in Paris's publishing world than its postmodern university climes. In a famous 1964 public debate about literature, Beauvoir stated that "one of the essential functions of literature . . . is the overcoming of that isolation which is common to us all." She defined literature as "the privileged place of intersubjectivity" that gives us "the incommunicable," a "taste of another's life." Defending "committed literature' against what she viewed as the over-aestheticized, navel-and-language-gazing of the French "New Novel," she declared in her 1947 defense of the popularity of American novels in France that "the true mission of the writer" is "to describe in dramatic form the relationship of the individual to the world in which he stakes his freedom."

Finally, Beauvoir's cultural influence endures from the unconventional life she led with Sartre. Their rejection of conventional marriage and family, their devotion to smoking *Gitanes* and working in cafes, their openness to multiple romantic and sexual "secondary" liaisons, modeled a life that excited, challenged, and still affects writers, artists, and intellectuals. The key change after their deaths, fueled by freshly revealed information, has been recognition that Beauvoir as well as Sartre behaved dishonestly and disloyally, as the two treated secondary partners more shabbily than each other.

(*See also* Alterity; Chapter 10, Feminism; Existentialism; Feminist Theory; Gender; *and* Other, The)

Carlin Romano, *Ursinus College*
(United States)

Further Reading

Beauvoir, Simone de. *The Second Sex* [1949]. Trans. Constance Borde and Sheila Malovany-Chevallier. Alfred A. Knopf, 2010.

Mussett, Shannon M., and William S. Wilkerson, eds. *Beauvoir and Western Thought from Plato to Butler*. Albany: State University of New York Press, 2012.

Simons, Margaret A., and Sylvie Le Bon de Beauvoir, eds. *The Beauvoir Series*. Four vols. Urbana: University of Illinois Press, 2008.

Tidd, Ursula. *Simone de Beauvoir*. Islington: Reaktion Books, 2009.

Benjamin, Walter

Benjamin (1892–1940) was a German-Jewish literary writer, philosopher, and cultural critic whose work had a tremendous impact on art, literature, philosophy, and religion in the twentieth century. He studied philosophy at the University of Berlin and then the University of Bern, completing a dissertation on "Art Criticism and German Romanticism" in 1919. Benjamin struggled to become a professor, abandoning his habilitation dissertation that would qualify him for an academic position in 1925. This project was published as a book, *The Origin of German Tragic Drama*, in 1928.

Instead of academic texts, Benjamin wrote complex and original essays with literary, philosophical, political, and religious themes. These essays have become well known and influential in many disciplines and intellectual contexts. Benjamin was also working on a massive book, the *Arcades Project*, on the Paris arcades in the 1800s, that was unfinished when he died. Benjamin was friends with Theodor Adorno and Max Horkheimer of the Institute for Social Research at Frankfurt, and he was targeted by the Nazi regime when it assumed power in the 1930s. Benjamin fled to Paris before the outbreak of the Second World War, but when France surrendered he tried to get to Portugal through Spain to emigrate but was trapped by Spanish authorities at the Spanish border. Assuming he would be delivered to the Nazis, Benjamin committed suicide on September 25, 1940.

Hannah Arendt edited and introduced a selection of Benjamin's essays in 1968, called *Illuminations*, that included two of his most influential essays: "The Work of Art in an Age of Mechanical Reproduction," and "Theses on the Philosophy of History," which was the last essay Benjamin completed before he died. In 2003 Harvard University Press published four volumes of Benjamin's *Selected Writings*, translated from his *Gesammelte Schriften*, published in German in 1972.

His contributions are too wide and varied to do more than sketch, so I will briefly focus on two of his famous essays. In "The Work of Art in an Age of Mechanical Reproduction," Benjamin analyzes how our experience of art changes due to modern technology, including the camera and the cinema. The importance of a work of art lies in its purported authenticity, which is threatened by its technical reproduction. He says "that which withers in the age of mechanical reproduction is the aura of the work of art." This aura disappears, but invokes a desire to bring it back. Film induces a shock effect on the viewer, and this tears the spectator out of the context of the artwork as a cultural and social phenomenon and delivers over to the spectacle of mass formation. Fascism introduces aesthetics into political life to counter the loss of the aura from human experience, and film assists in this process. Fascism leads to war, which is the consummation of art for art's sake. The alternative, the politicization of art by communism, is not really developed in the essay, but provocatively mentioned at the end. This analysis remains significant today, with our media dominated culture and its constitution of a popular audience who depend on "infotainment."

Finally, in his "Theses on the Philosophy of History," Benjamin calls into question our ideas of modernity, referring to a painting by Paul Klee of the "Angel of History" who is blown forward by the storm that we call progress. In incisive paragraphs, Benjamin argues that universal history is a disaster, but a historical materialism inspired by Karl Marx possesses a "weak messianic power" to redeem the past from its lesson that might makes right. A historical materialist arrests the flow of linear historical time, taking "cognizance of it to blast a specific era out of the homogeneous course of history." The now-time as the empty but pregnant moment of the present becomes an opportunity to revolutionize history in a quasi-messianic way. This constructive formulation prefigures many later theories about history, politics, messianism, post-structuralism, and the event.

(*See also* Authenticity; Chapter 4, Marxism; Chapter 18, Translation; Homogenous, Empty Time; *and* Translation)

Clayton Crockett, *University of Central Arkansas (United States)*

Further Reading

Benjamin, Walter. *The Arcades Project* [1982]. Trans. Howard Eiland and Kevin McLaughlin. Cambridge: Harvard University Press, 1999.

Benjamin, Walter. *Illuminations: Essays and Reflections* [1955]. Ed. Hannah Arendt. New York: Schocken Books, 1968.

Benjamin, Walter. *Selected Writings*. Four vols. Multiple translators. Cambridge: Harvard University Press, 2003.

Binary Opposition

The concept of binary opposition was foregrounded in twentieth-century intellectual history by two separate theoretical developments: digital information processing and structural linguistics.

Digital information processing is based on discrete binary differences—0 or 1, *off* or *on*—and is the basis of modern computing. Digital computing machines were first imagined by Pascal and Leibniz in the eighteenth century. George Boole developed binary algebra in the nineteenth century, and John V. Atanasoff built the first electronic computer between 1939 and 1942. As modern computers and cinematic special effects show, the world is remarkably representable through a patient and complex use of binary differences.

The germ of structuralism is the belief that real patterns in nature and thought can be modeled as abstract structures. Linguistic structuralism applied that idea to cultural meanings. Contrary to referential models of meaning, Ferdinand Saussure reduced linguistic meaning to systems of internal semantic differences. Claude Lévi-Strauss maintained that cultures are built up from such differential relations into vast taxonomies that provide the fundamental maps of a culture.

Whereas digital information storage proved remarkably stable, differential structures of linguistic meaning proved less so for several reasons. First, differential semantics describes relations *between* selected traits. This privileges a context of relations over accurate reference to the objects so related. Such systems can be internally coherent, but unrepresentative of the world. Second, most semantic differences discriminate kinds, not particulars (e.g., gender, racial, religious, ethnic, species, etc.). But kinds are less homogeneous than a simple taxonomy of contrasts would indicate (the fallacy of stereotyping). Third, because semantic relations are systematic and interrelated, the meanings of elements are mutually influencing. Taxonomies separate into pigeon-holes, but meaning leaks across semantic units, often unnoticed. Thus, the binary-oppositional semantics oversimplifies the complexity of things and their relationships.

Semantic construction also constructs social privilege. Anthropologist David Bidney wrote that all cultures tend to identify their beliefs and preferences as natural law—whether by appeals to religion, history, or directly to nature—implying their natural superiority to others. In a patriarchal society, anything associated with maleness enjoys a halo effect. In a racist society, all things white take on a privilege. In a youth-centric culture, ageism seems natural. Such cultural distortion is overdetermined by psychological tendencies to stereotype, ruling-class tendencies to self-privilege, and cultural tendencies toward chauvinism. With the rise of feminism, minority studies, and postcolonial studies, cultural theorists exposed the naturalization of meaning by artificial schemes of difference in the service of political and social power. As the "deconstruction" of privileged binary oppositions showed their liability to alternative interpretations, such structures appeared less like secure semantic foundations than channels through which changing meanings flow, like river banks that might narrow, widen, or even split under pressure.

Deconstruction proved popular among social critics for unmasking the artificiality of social identity and authority. More analytically inclined philosophers of language, however, criticized preoccupation with semantic slippage, preferring to look beyond the syntax of difference to pragmatic and other formally theorizable aspects of signification and communication.

(*See also* Chapter 2, Structuralism and Semiotics; Chapter 5, Post-structuralism; Chapter 23, Materialisms; Chapter 24, Posthumanism; Culture Wars; Distinctive

Feature; Queer Theory; Structuralism; *and* Supplement)

Horace Fairlamb, *University of Houston-Victoria (United States)*

Further Reading

Derrida, Jacques. *A Derrida Reader*. New York: Columbia University Press, 1991.

Groden, Michael, and Martin Kreiswirth. *Contemporary Literary and Cultural Theory*. Baltimore: Johns Hopkins Press. 2012.

Searle, John R. "The World Turned Upside Down." *New York Review of Books* (October 27, 1983).

Biopolitics

Biopolitics designates a politics of life itself. In its most well-known formulation, in Michel Foucault's *The History of Sexuality, Volume 1* (1976), it indicates a modern condition in which "the life of the species is wagered on its own political strategies." Foucault describes a transition from a centralized form of power predicated on "the right to *take* life or *let* live"—a form of power associated with early modern European polities, generally symbolized in the figure of the monarch and characterized by spectacular instances of violent punishment—to a more decentralized and subtle "power to *foster* life or *disallow* it to the point of death." *Biopower*, as this latter form of power comes to be designated, includes the management of populations through demography, urban planning, public health, and other practices, as well as the control of bodies through disciplinary apparatuses, including schools and hospitals. Crucially, Foucault analyzes the power involved in biopolitics not as a repressive force but as a force that cultivates certain kinds of individuals, populations, and conducts.

Although Foucault offers the most canonical account, there are other theories of biopolitics that expand the term's purview. Giorgio Agamben, for instance, has popularized the association of biopower with the Roman concept of the *homo sacer* ("sacred man"), a figure that can be killed without ceremony in *Homo Sacer: Sovereign Power and Bare Life* (1995). For Agamben, biopolitics and sovereignty are coextensive, such that even the earliest forms of politics involve a sovereign decision regarding which forms of life are worthwhile and which without value. In this theory, biopolitics largely revolves around state-sanctioned killings. Achille Mbembe suggests that this aspect of biopolitics be specified as "necropolitics"; Mbembe elaborates that political and economic regimes such as the plantation system, colonialism, and chattel slavery exemplify necropolitics in their division of national peoples into races of more or less vulnerable peoples ("Necropolitics"). Mbembe's intervention has facilitated a productive collaboration between critical race theory, postcolonial theory, and biopolitics in the work of critics such as Jasbir Puar, Mel Chen, and Alexander Weheliye. In contrast, Marxist theorists, including Antonio Negri, Paolo Virno, Melinda Cooper, and Kaushik Sunder Rajan identify biopolitics with political struggles over labor power the embodied potentiality for work—or with the increasing penetration of biological life by capitalism. In *Empire* (2000), Michael Hardt and Antonio Negri make a polemical distinction between biopower, understood as the control of life by an increasingly global empire, and biopolitics, understood as an emancipatory force embodied by "the multitude." This distinction makes explicit what is only implicit in Foucault's account, namely, that biopolitics includes not only a power *over* life (necropolitics, control, etc.) but also a power *of* life (emancipation, resistance, etc.).

The diversity among theories of biopolitics suggests a distinction between biopolitics as phenomenon, on the one hand, and biopolitics as critical theory, on the other. As a phenomenon, biopolitics includes any number of practices or matters of social life, from reproductive rights to public policy regarding human cloning. Feminist theory grapples with biopolitics in its concerns for the politics surrounding women's bodies. Silvia Federici, for example, argues in *Caliban and the Witch: Women, the Body and Primitive Accumulation* (2004) that the transition into modernity depended on the institutionalization of new regulations affecting women, in particular, the control of women as a source of biological reproduction and household labor. Animal studies expands the focus of biopolitics to include interspecies relations, with scholars such as Jacques Derrida, Donna Haraway, and Cary Wolfe demonstrating how the idea of animality fundamentally structures politics.

As a critical discourse, biopolitics has a twofold genealogy. On the one hand, it can be traced back to nineteenth-century social Darwinism and eugenics—this uncritical strand of biopolitics operates on racist and Eurocentric presumptions. It can be seen at work in historical contexts that range from Nazi concentration camps to the forced sterilization of women of color by the US government. On the other hand, the critical discourse of biopolitics can also be traced back to the revolts and the communal living experiments of the 1960s, which renewed a sense of politics as the contestation of intimate matters or as ongoing struggles over what a body can do. It is this latter genealogy that constitutes the basis of what has been called the biopolitical turn in the humanities, or the increasing focus on biology and corporeality in connection with language, culture, and politics.

(*See also* Agamben, Giorgio; Bare Life; Capacity; Chapter 15, Biopower and Biopolitics; Chapter 23, Materialisms; Control; Cyborg; Foucault, Michel; Labor; *and* Thanatopolitics)

Christian P. Haines, *Dartmouth College (United States)*

Further Reading
Campbell, Timothy, and Adam Sitze, eds. *Biopolitics: A Reader*. Durham: Duke University Press, 2013.
Foucault, Michel. "Right of Death and Power Over Life." In *The History of Sexuality, Volume 1* [1976]. Trans. Robert Hurley. New York: Vintage Books, 1978. 133–59.
Puar, Jasbir. *Terrorist Assemblages: Homonationalism in Queer Times*. Durham: Duke University Press, 2004.

Biopower (*See* Biopolitics; *and* Thanatopolitics)

Biotechnology

A fifth of the global population's energy needs are satisfied by cheap, filling, and starch-heavy rice, a number rising to 50–70 percent in those developing nations that produce 95 percent of the world's rice. But rice offers scarce nutrients like proteins and iron, and—unlike carrots, kale, and sweet potatoes—no beta carotene (vitamin A). The resultant vitamin A deficiencies affect 250 million people worldwide and permanently blind up to half a million children each year.

So why shouldn't rice produce vitamin A? Rice grains already contain the raw ingredients of vitamin A (carbon, hydrogen, oxygen), but not the genetic codes needed to construct the complex enzymes that transform these precursors into the desired product. To rectify this, bioengineers led by Ingo Potrykus borrowed the DNA-editing capacity of infectious bacteria to transplant the enzyme-producing genes of daffodils and root-rot bacteria into the reproductive systems of rice flowers. The result: "golden rice," saffron grains glowing with precious retinol.

Golden rice, vaccine-secreting potatoes, and radiation-guzzling algae are fruits of *biotechnology*, the conjoined use of biological processes and scientific engineering to achieve human ends. In medicine, industry, and agriculture, biotechnology suggests science-fiction scenarios both monstrous and utopian. Microorganisms might produce fully renewable biofuels; doctors equipped with human genome maps might tailor treatment to the unique genetics of their patients. Scientists could combine viruses into weaponized "superbugs"; parents could use gene therapies to cure their "designer babies" of autism, ugliness, and homosexuality.

In 2013, Philippine protesters destroyed experimental plots of golden rice; in 2016, 107 Nobel laureates petitioned Greenpeace to drop its opposition to golden rice and other genetically modified crops. Many suspect that the humanitarian aims of the scientist conflict with the economic interests of the corporations who provide the large amounts of capital needed for biotechnological research. The potential to patent and market biological material seems to cement the triumph of industrial capitalism's empire over the natural world, and even our own bodies. In themselves, the multispecies hybrids produced by biotechnology inspire the uncanny shudder condensed in the term "Frankenfood." Yet they also threaten human and ecological diversity with standardization—why accept the messiness of your genome when you could perfect it? Biotechnology arouses anxieties over the rationalization and technologization of human life, as it sharpens the feeling that we lose something when we wrest control of our biological destiny from unassisted evolution.

But rice, after all, was always a genetically modified organism: thirteen thousand years ago, generations of gatherers in China, selecting the largest seeds from wild grasses, unconsciously transformed them, at the genomic level, into the domesticated rice we know today. Ancient biotechnology sparked human society, when Sumerians and Egyptians first used yeast to preserve beer, bread, and cheese. Louis Pasteur's research into the microbiology of yeast led to the development of industrial fermentation, food preservation, and vaccination. It's hard to find a human technology that *isn't* biotechnological; indoor plumbing, industrial smoke, and treadmills all affect, if not the molecular structure of the human genome, the way in which human DNA toggles protein generation to direct the growth and behavior of the individual body. And humans aren't alone in manipulating biological means to achieve their ends: just like early humans, bees cultivate bacteria and yeasts to ferment and safely store their pollen supplies.

The philosopher Jean-François Lyotard argues that "technology wasn't invented by us humans," but instead that humanity emerges from the technological processes—the simultaneous reading and rewriting of environmental information, which always returns to affect the editing organism—that already enabled biological evolution. Biotechnology, at first, seems easy to define: it's when technology finally penetrates biology. But maybe biotechnology instead reveals the deep complexity of the relations between technology, biology, human will, evolutionary processes, economic agendas, culture, agriculture, and other forms of present or future life.

(*See also* Chapter 24, Posthumanism; *and* Posthumanism)

Simon Porzak, *Columbia University (United States)*

Further Reading

Borém, Aluízio. *Understanding Biotechnology*. New Jersey: Prentice Hall, 2003.

Bud, Robert. *The Uses of Life: A History of Biotechnology*. Cambridge: Cambridge University Press, 1994.

Clark, Andy. *Natural-Born Cyborgs: Minds, Technologies, and the Future of Human Intelligence*. Oxford: Oxford University Press, 2003.

DeFries, Ruth. *The Big Ratchet: How Humanity Thrives in the Face of Natural Crisis: A Biography of an Ingenious Species*. New York: Basic Books, 2014.

Latour, Bruno. *The Pasteurization of France* [1984]. Trans. Alan Sheridan and John Law. Cambridge: Harvard University Press, 1988.

Blanchot, Maurice

Maurice Blanchot (1907–2003) belongs to the generation of French writers (Jean-Paul Sartre, Maurice Merleau-Ponty, Margeurite Duras, among others) who began to flourish during the Occupation, and who shaped French intellectual life for the next thirty or more years. In particular, Blanchot's critical essays and his own experimental writings helped to create a culture of radical innovation in both philosophy as well as literature (think of the baroque prose of Michel Foucault and Jacques Derrida, the French *Nouvelle Roman*, or the later paratactic works of Samuel Beckett).

Blanchot's starting point is arguably the French poet Stéphane Mallarmé's thesis that poetry is made of words but not of anything that we use words to produce—predications, concepts, descriptions, expressions of feeling. This was a thesis famously contested by Jean-Paul Sartre in *What is Literature?* (1948), in which he proposed that literature only comes into its own in the works of prose writers for whom language is an instrument for engaging the world in order to change it. Sartre's writings on this point are basically a polemic against Blanchot's essays from the 1940s, many of which are a critique of the propositional style philosophical thinking in which the existence of real things is annihilated and replaced by concepts. In "Literature and the Right to Death" (1949), Blanchot writes: "My hope [for the world of mere things] lies in the materiality of language, in the fact that words are things too, are a kind of nature. . . . Everything physical takes precedence: rhythm, weight, mass, shape, and then the paper on which one writes, the trail of ink, the book." If conceptual determination "dematerializes" the world, the task of literature is to rematerialize it, starting with itself, producing works outside all schemes of identity: "The work," Blanchot writes in "Literature and the Original Experience" (1955), "is eminently *what* it is made of."

As Mallarmé proposed, writing occupies space without taking up time. This is something like the regulating idea of Blanchot's *The Space of Literature* (1955)—and, indeed, of his later, increasingly fragmentary writings (e.g., *Awaiting Oblivion* [1962]). The temporality of writing is that of the *entretemps*—the "between"—in which the present recedes into a past that never was, and the future never arrives. In 1969 Blanchot collected a number of his essays under the title *The Infinite Conversation*, which begins with a meandering dialogue between two elderly interlocutors, one of whom "*has lost the power to express himself in a continuous manner.*" Much of what follows is an attempt to gain some purchase on this nonlinearity, as in "The Fragmentary Word," which canonizes "a new kind of arrangement . . . that does not compose but juxtaposes, that is to say, leaves each of the terms that come into relation *outside* one another."

Accordingly, two later works—*The Step Not Beyond* (1973) and *The Writing of the*

Disaster (1980)—are self-reflexive exercises in fragmentary writing, or perhaps one should say fragmentary thinking, in the style of paradoxical *pensées*: "While everything keeps going, nothing goes together."

Or again, one could consider as a closing conundrum: "Let us share eternity in order to make it transitory" (*The Writing of Disaster*).

(*See also* Alterity; Chapter 18, Translation; Nouveau Roman; *and* Novel)

Gerald L. Bruns, *The Univerity of Notre Dame (United States)*

Further Reading

Blanchot, Maurice. *The One Who Was Standing Apart from Me*. Trans. Lydia Davis. Barrytown: Station Hill Press, 1993.

Blanchot, Maurice. *Thomas the Obscure* [1941]. Trans. Robert Lamberton. Barrytown: Station Hill Press, 1973.

Holland, Michael, ed. *The Blanchot Reader*. London: Basil Blackwell, 1995.

Book Culture (*See* Print Culture)

Bourdieu, Pierre

Pierre Bourdieu (1930–2002) was a French sociologist whose research and theories of social relations and epistemic reflexivity have influenced inquiry in diverse disciplines across the social sciences and humanities. Bourdieu's work did much to challenge the theoretical and methodological assumptions underpinning academic disciplinary divides, constantly stressing the need to identify and question the tacit premises guiding any area of study. The work of analyzing the conditions that make social analysis possible and that shape its form is never complete, and this accounts in part for Bourdieu's insistence on the open-ended character of his theorizations. This open-endedness springs as

well, however, from Bourdieu's commitment to overcoming conceptions of theory and empirical investigation as separable parts of a research program. Empirical work is always informed by theorization, and theorization must always proceed from empirical data if social analysis is to increase in accuracy and to have purchase on social life itself. For the goals of socioanalysis, as Bourdieu conceives it, are not merely to describe reality, but to provide tools for denaturalizing social hierarchies and ways of seeing the world, thereby enhancing freedom and the ability to combat symbolic domination. As an endeavor that unfolds within social struggles, not outside or alongside them, social science in Bourdieu's view requires careful attention to its ethical and political implications, and constant vigilance against settling into dogmas or critical orthodoxies.

These deep commitments underpin Bourdieu's efforts to develop conceptual tools capable of accounting for the persistence of social hierarchies as well as processes of historical change and transformation. Intended to transcend divisions between structuralist and voluntarist conceptions of agency, and also between objectivist and subjectivist approaches to social knowledge, the concepts of *habitus* and its social correlate, *field*, are two such tools. Habitus is most easily described as a set of dispositions or schemes of perception that shape the way a subject (or *agent*) makes sense of and moves through the world. Developed through experience and conservative in practice (in that it disposes agents, through its anticipatory function, to seek out familiar situations in which they feel at home), the habitus is never rigidly determined, but instead remains open to revision through new experiences and contact with changing social forces. As history incorporated into the body and forgotten as history, habitus is not easily transformed—we cannot dispel it merely by becoming conscious of how it functions. Yet as history, rather than essence, habitus is open to transformation; habitus only exists in relation to the social *fields* to which it is attuned, fields which are themselves dynamic and constantly subject to redefinition. As spaces of conflict, social fields are structured through a process of questioning and contestation, as much as they themselves structure those questions. Recognizing and understanding this relational dynamism is key to effectively contesting the naturalization of historically produced categories, dispositions, and practices that the exercise of violence, particularly symbolic violence, involves.

The critical work of recalling the repressed, historical dimension of a symbolic order taken for granted as natural is a collective endeavor, carried out through mutual, dialogical contestation. This work cannot be accomplished by any one individual through a solipsistic operation of logic, but only through the mutual encounter of difference and close attention to particularity: the careful investigation of the specific ways naturalization takes on content differently in different times and spaces. In this lie the challenges but also the generative and emancipatory possibilities of a reflexive analytical practice.

(*See also* Class; Cultural Critique; Cultural Capital; Public Intellectual; Symbolic Agency; *and* Taste)

Nicole Simek, *Whitman College*
(United States)

Further Reading

Bourdieu, Pierre. *The Logic of Practice* [1980]. Trans. Richard Nice. Stanford: Stanford University Press, 1990.

Bourdieu, Pierre, and Loïc J. D. Wacquant. *An Invitation to Reflexive Sociology.* Chicago: University of Chicago Press, 1992.

Brown, Nicolas, and Imre Szeman. *Pierre Bourdieu: Fieldwork in Culture.* Lanham: Rowman & Littlefield Publishers, 2000.

Gorski, Philip S., ed. *Bourdieu and Historical Analysis.* Durham: Duke University Press, 2013.

Bourgeois

To quote Raymond Williams, "Bourgeois is a very difficult word to use in English." The term "bourgeois" predates its inclusion into the lexicon of Marxism and later critical theory by several hundred years. Initially signifying those residing within the walls of the medieval city that included guilds members, merchants, and artisans, it came to emerge as a distinct and legally enfranchised identity during the feudal period. The bourgeoisie in this early incarnation was a mediating or "middle" class in between the feudal peasant and the aristocratic classes. It quickly will become arguably the most significant term for the study of capitalism, easily as important as its generally accepted antipode, the *proletariat.* For Marx and Engels, the term comes to denote in *The Communist Manifesto* the social class with ownership over the means of production and the class that has remade the world in its image through the development of capitalist hegemony and a specifically *bourgeois* mode of cultural expression and civic engagement as the superstructure holding it in place. *Bourgeoisie,* then, signifies both those human subjects in control of the means of production and able to exploit billions to extract profit, and a *mode* of civic and collective being that subtends and reproduces the frame necessary for capitalist exploitation.

In other words, the term bourgeoisie defines the class with control over the social relations of production in their material and ideological manifestations. As the development of capitalism goes, so does historically the question of who particularly can claim membership in the bourgeoisie class. As the managerial and bureaucratic sections of the capitalist economy developed, scholars such as Theodor Adorno, Max Horkheimer, and Nicos Poulantzas researched the expansion of the definition of the bourgeoisie; they include questions about those who directly serve the development and maintenance of the capitalist regime, and how the cultural sphere necessary for justification developed.

For example, Franco Moretti signals the crucial intersection between the bourgeoisie as a social grouping and the expression of a particular self-consciousness of culture. The bourgeoisie and bourgeois culture stand in between and apart from the traditional antagonisms between wealthy nobility and the vassals or peasant classes. Initially, the bourgeoisie mediates between the upper and lower classes, but as capitalism develops, the class mediates social and cultural relations as a whole. As the commodification of culture expands, the bourgeoisie is defined by hegemony; bourgeois thought deepens their economic control over society and avoids or pacifies the contradictions and crises of capitalist society.

Scholars such as Erik Olin Wright, focus on how the bourgeoisie as a class intersects with the state as a political apparatus, exposing the tensions and convergences between capitalist production and political life. Thus the bourgeoisie is not framed as either fully independent from or totally dominating the state apparatus, which retains its capacity to affect economic relations—another political valence that adds to the bourgeoisie's prescriptive power.

(*See also* Chapter 4, Marxism; Chapter 11, Cultural Studies; Chapter 15, Biopower and Biopolitics; Chapter 19, Media Studies; Class; Epistolary Novel; Labor; Marx; Marxism; Political Unconscious; Public Sphere; Production; *and* Revolution)

Carlos M. Amador, *Michigan Technological University (United States)*

Further Reading
McCloskey, Deirdre N. *The Bourgeois Virtues: Ethics for an Age of Commerce.* Chicago: University of Chicago Press, 2007.
Moretti, Franco. *The Bourgeois: Between History and Literature.* New York: Verso, 2014.
Poulantzas, Nicos. *Classes in Contemporary Capitalism.* New York: Verso, 1978.
Wright, Erik Olin. *Understanding Class.* New York: Verso 2015.

Bourgeoisie (*See* Bourgeois)

Brain (*See* Neuroscience)

Butler, Judith

Judith Butler has been one of the most influential thinkers in the humanities and social sciences over the last thirty years. She is best known for her critique of the foundational assumptions that become routine in our thinking, indeed, so much so that they accrue the status of truths that require no justification. Butler's attention to "the given," or what conventionally goes unremarked, reveals a raft of political prejudices within the everyday beliefs that circulate in popular culture, and these prejudices are also at work in what counts as reason and logic in philosophical debate. The interdisciplinary breadth of Butler's interventions is comprehensive as a consequence, covering feminism, queer theory, cultural studies, literary theory, philosophy, ethics, political theory and legal studies. As Butler's output in monographs, edited volumes, and journal articles is prolific (thirteen single authored books alone), what follows is merely an analytical "taster," or brief example, of the style of structural analytics that drives her work.

One of her earliest and most popular books to this day is *Gender Trouble* (1990). Here, Butler unpacks how the difference between nature and culture, or what we conventionally understand as the sex/gender distinction, comes to justify a heteronormative set of values about how we should live our lives. According to Butler, all forms of cultural mediation are "worlding" because significance is produced within language and representation rather than from an unmediated reality whose truth is transparently available to us. The radical implications of Butler's "cultural constructionist" position is that culture becomes the productive engine of how our values and judgments are determined: meanings and behaviors are not prescribed but "performed" again and again, precisely because they are not fixed in nature. For Butler, ideas and concepts about how the world works actively "materialise" as what comes to matter, and they even shape how we perceive and experience the world around us. As these regimes of truth production are all-encompassing, it follows that what seems true, possible, or indeed, impossible, will be generated from within these invisible structures of meaning-making.

However, if everything is culture we might wonder what happens to nature, to the body, to what we regard as already determined, such as our sex. Butler responds to this question by explaining that what appears as nature, in all its manifestations, is nevertheless an interpreted nature that is necessarily represented and made sense of within cultural frames of reference. Hence, for Butler, what counts as nature is really culture in disguise because reality is always mediated. The importance of this maneuver is that all foundational "givens"—nature, the body, sex, truth, what counts as logic—are revealed as political determinations, more invented than prescribed, and therefore open to change and contestation.

(*See also* Assujettissement; Chapter 10, Feminism; Chapter 23, Materialisms; Gender; Interpellation; Performativity; Queer Theory; Resistance; *and* Sexuality)

Vicki Kirby, *The University of New South Wales, Sydney (Australia)*

Further Reading

Butler, Judith. *Gender Trouble: Feminism and the Subversion of Identity* [1990]. New York: Routledge, 2006.

Cheah, Pheng. "Mattering." *Diacritics* 26.1 (1996): 108–39.

Kirby, Vicki. *Judith Butler: Live Theory* London: Continuum, 2006.

C

Canguilhem, Georges

Georges Canguilhem (1904–95) was a French historian and a philosopher of the life sciences (primarily physiology and medicine). Canguilhem's lasting impact on philosophy, the history of science, and theory more broadly can be seen in four different ways.

First, as a teacher and president of the jury d'agrégation—an intensely competitive examination for prospective academics—in philosophy, Canguilhem enormously influenced many of the most famous French philosophers and intellectuals of the latter half of the twentieth century: Louis Althusser, Michel Foucault, Pierre Bourdieu, Jacques Derrida, Jacques Lacan, among others. For example, it was Canguilhem who sponsored Foucault's dissertation *Folie et Déraison: Histoire de la folie à l'âge classique*. Canguilhem's rigorous scholarship, teaching, and commitment to political freedom led Foucault and others to draw a link between a "heroic" political will to resist and what has been called the "philosophy of the concept," in contrast to the "philosophy of experience." The former, embodied in the wartime resistance of figures like Canguilhem, Jean Cavaillés, and Albert Lautmann, all philosophers of science or mathematics, seems all the more remarkable in contrast to, for example, Martin Heidegger's explicitly fascist phenomenological ontology, or its Sartrean variants.

Canguilhem's second major impact derives from his particular way of pursuing "the philosophy of the concept," of studying scientific reason in its dispersion into local rationalities. Along with Gaston Bachelard, he is the preeminent representative of French "historical epistemology." Where Bachelard, and followers like Foucault and Althusser, emphasized the discontinuities of scientific reason, those epochal breaks in rationality through which new objects and modes of knowing them emerge, Canguilhem's approach focused on concepts, rather than on complete theories or broader épistémes. Indeed, sometimes the basic concepts of a science are not found in its acknowledged "predecessors" but in problematics established in other disciplines entirely. Central to Canguilhem's thought here is the prima facie paradoxical notion of "scientific ideology," the extension of the ambitions of science, with methods and concepts often drawn from neighboring scientific fields, beyond legitimacy and into new domains. This approach to the history and philosophy of science remains influential in French universities and beyond (e.g., it deeply informs research programs in the history of science at the Max-Planck-Institut für Wissenschaftsgeschichte in Berlin and at several prominent American institutions).

Thirdly, Canguilhem's substantive claims have deeply shaped subsequent thinking about health, illness, normalcy, normativity, medicine, and healing, from the biological to the social sciences. In his landmark work, *The Normal and the Pathological* (1966), Canguilhem argues forcefully against the idea that pathological states can be understood as mere quantitative deviations from "normal" states, for example, some statistically average state of being. Rather, we need to view pathology, and corresponding notions of illness, from the point of view of the living organism that establishes its own "normal" relations with its environment. The healthy organism is flexible and adaptive in its relations to its milieu, while the unhealthy one is no longer able to cope; its norms of living have become stagnant and nonresponsive. To put this as a slogan: to live is to have a relation to normativity, and to be cured is to establish a new one. Thus, any science of illness is not the study of an objective state of affairs, if objectivity is construed as the absence of subjectivity or values.

Finally, in virtue of his starkly anti-reductionist stance in the philosophy of biology, refusing to cast living phenomena in purely mechanistic terms, one can place Canguilhem in a venerable tradition of vitalism in philosophical thought, from Friedrich Nietzsche through Henri Bergson and Gilles Deleuze. For all of these thinkers, human engagement with the world is an expression of "Life," an often impersonal force that sets its own values, faces its own problems, and devises its own solutions. While Canguilhem's version of vitalism might avoid more baldly metaphysical commitments, it is clear that he takes "Life" as an irreducible source of norms, even norms of truth and error. The life sciences, therefore, must be seen as a form of self-knowledge of an essentially evaluative kind. This emphasis on the centrality of the life sciences to philosophical knowledge thus locates Canguilhem, along with his contemporaries Raymond Ruyer and Gilbert Simondon, at the forefront of a peculiarly French "biophilosophy" in the 1960s. The legacies of vitalism and biophilosophy mark an exciting frontier for theoretical work in the present day.

(*See also* Chapter 15, Biopower and Biopolitics; *and* Vitalism)

Patrick Gamez, *Missouri University of Science & Technology (United States)*

Further Reading

Osborne, Thomas, and Nikolas Rose, eds. "Special Issue on Georges Canguilhem." *Economy and Society* 27.2/3 (1998).

Roudinesco, Elizabeth. *Philosophy in Turbulent Times: Canguilhem, Sartre, Foucault, Althusser, Deleuze, Derrida* [2005]. Trans. William McCuaig. New York: Columbia University Press, 2008.

Wolfe, Charles T. "Was Canguilhem a Biochauvinist? Goldstein, Canguilhem and the Project of Biophilosophy." In *Medicine and Society, New Perspectives in Continental Philosophy*. Ed. Dorian Meacham. Dordrecht: Springer 2015. 197–212.

Canon

The term *canon* derives from Catholic theology, where it designates a set of norms of conduct and belief, or a body of sacred texts defining those norms, and thus limning the fundamental tenets of the faith. When the discourse of aesthetics borrows the word and puts it to use, it is perhaps still largely a matter of faith. In this new usage, canon is taken to mean the set of texts or artifacts that define a given tradition. One can speak, for instance, of the canon of European classical music, or the canon of Italian Renaissance painting, or the canon of West African religious sculpture. In literary and philosophical studies, one may think of Robert Hutchins and Mortimer Adler's "Great Books" project (1952), which attempted to postulate a canon of Western thought in fifty-four volumes. More recently, Harold Bloom identifies twenty-six canonical writers from William Shakespeare to Samuel Beckett in his book *The Western Canon* (1994). In *Cultural Literacy: What Every American Needs to Know* (1987), E. D. Hirsch provides a lexicon intended to imbue its users with cultural fluency. Clearly enough, the idea of the canon hinges on consensus. It is legitimate to ask, however, *whose* consensus that may be, or *who* might be served by an appeal to the canon. While few people would deny that *Moby-Dick* is essential to the American literary tradition, or *Madame Bovary* to the French, the notion of the canon proves to be significantly slippery, the closer one inspects it. For the term is often invoked in an effort to define, circumscribe, and defend a given cultural territory, in ways that afford that territory an appearance of uniqueness, logic, and stability over time. It is undoubtedly reassuring to think about culture in that way, and to imagine it developing organically, programmatically, and indeed *inevitably* over the centuries, pointing straight toward the moment that we ourselves occupy. Yet, culture is a significantly mobile phenomenon, and efforts to seize it and codify it are most often doomed—or at the very least vexed—by that mobility. Culture is also patently plural: different kinds of people imagine culture in different ways. Those different conceptions of culture are sometimes mutually complementary, sometimes mutually refractory. It makes sense, then, to conceive the notion of the canon in relative rather than absolute terms, as a mobile, plural construct, one that necessarily shifts over time, place, constituency, and discursive demands. In that perspective, if it is sometimes useful to invoke the American literary canon, it is also crucial to recognize that certain other literary currents—Chicano literature, for instance, or feminist literature, or African American writing, or so-called popular fiction—call that canon dramatically into question, and moreover cohere into traditions and canons of their own. It must furthermore be acknowledged that this cultural competition is not exclusively a function of our own age, but that culture has always been agonistic in character, and unrelenting in its demand that we reconsider who we are, and imagine ourselves to be.

(*See also* Chapter 13, Race and Postcolonial Studies; Chapter 20, Digital Humanities; Chapter 22, Identity Studies; Chapter 27, Antitheory; Feminist Theory; Intertextuality; Multiculturalism; Neopragmatism; New Criticism; Revisionism; *and* Rights)

Warren Motte, *University of Colorado, Boulder (United States)*

Further Reading

Bloom, Harold. *The Western Canon: The Books and School of the Ages*. New York: Harcourt Brace, 1994.

Hirsch, E. D. *Cultural Literacy: What Every American Needs to Know*. Boston: Houghton Mifflin, 1987.

Hutchins, Robert, and Mortimer Adler. *The Great Books of the Western World*. Chicago: Encyclopaedia Britannica, 1952.

Capacity

The concept of *capacity* posits potentiality as a material reality. Aristotle offers one of the earliest and most often cited articulations of the concept in his *Metaphysics*, distinguishing between an action and its source: "'Potency' [*dynamis*: potentiality, capacity] means (I) a source of movement or change, which is in another thing than the thing moved or in the same thing *qua* other; e.g. the art of building is a potency which is not in the thing built." To speak of a particular capacity is not to speak of an act in motion but of that which enables the act in the first place: the capacity to design a building is not in the building but in the architect who can design other buildings. Particular capacities are therefore synonymous with subjective faculties, so that, for instance, one can articulate the faculty of speech as the capacity to enunciate a specific utterance by drawing on the resources of a language, or, in terms of Ferdinand de Saussure's linguistics, the faculty of speech is what allows a subject to transform *langue* (a linguistic system) into *parole* (a specific utterance or statement).

Capacity can, however, indicate a more general potentiality. Here, capacity is not a faculty tied to a specific range of actions but rather the energy that allows faculties to develop. It is a being's vitality, the potency that enables a creature to act in general. The social and political implications of this problem become clear in the Marxist formulation of the concept of labor power. Labor power is not this or that concrete instance of work but, as Karl Marx puts it in *Capital* (1867), "the aggregate of those mental and physical capabilities existing in the physical form, the living personality, of a human being, capabilities which he sets in motion whenever he produces a use-value of any kind." Capitalism depends on the commodification of labor power and labor conflicts tend to revolve around the contractual terms and/or material conditions under which this commodification occurs. Paolo Virno has suggested in *A Grammar of the Multitude* (2004) that such struggles over labor power over the "living body" of the worker as "tabernacle of *dynamis*, of mere potential"—constitute biopolitics, or a politics of life itself. Italian Autonomist Marxists of the 1970s and 1980s (e.g., Mario Tronti and Antonio Negri) theorize the refusal of labor as a reappropriation of living labor, that is, as a recuperation of the human potentiality buried in commodified labor power. This argument becomes even more significant in the contemporary context of neoliberalism in which corporations, schools, and other institutions frame individual capacities, skills, and talents as "human capital." The concept of human capital, as popularized by economist Gary Becker and critically elaborated on by Michel Foucault, among others, equates the realization of human potentiality

with making oneself marketable, or acting like an entrepreneur in all of one's affairs. One of the political questions that emerges from this situation is that of how one can articulate potentiality in terms irreducible to capitalist markets.

The affinity between the refusal of activity and the expression of potentiality is implicit in the very concept of capacity. Giorgio Agamben argues in "On Potentiality" that potentiality or capacity is defined not by the ability to do this or that but by the ability *not to*—by "impotentiality." Put differently, potentiality realizes itself not in the act but in the process of exhibiting its own irreducibility to the actual order of things. From this perspective, the feminist refusal to identify femininity with motherhood and queer theory's refusal to subsume sexuality under heteronormativity constitute recuperations of human capacity. In a similar fashion, the field of disability studies contests the reduction of capacity to normative intellectual and corporeal forms and, in doing so, expands the realm of human freedom.

(*See also* Chapter 26, Affect Studies; Disability; Cultural Capital; Desire; Drive; *and* Labor)

Christian P. Haines, *Dartmouth College (United States)*

Further Reading

Agamben, Giorgio. "On Potentiality." In *Potentialities: Collected Essays in Philosophy*. Ed. and trans. Daniel Heller-Roazen. Stanford: Stanford University Press, 1999. 177–85.

Aristotle. *Metaphysics*. In *The Basic Works of Aristotle*. Ed. Richard McKeon. New York: Modern Library, 2001. Book V, Chapter 12 and Book IX, Chapters 1–10.

Marx, Karl. *Capital* [1867]. Vol. 1. Trans. Ben Fowkes. New York: Penguin, 1976.

Capitalism

Capitalism refers to the economic system based on the privately owned production of goods and services sold for profit in competitive markets (rather than hereditary or state-ruled economies). The word itself came into use during the mid-nineteenth century when critics of the capitalist political economy such as Friedrich Engels and Karl Marx described the "means of production" whereby owners of capital could exploit workers to accumulate more capital for the ruling classes (although "capitalism" only appears two times in Volume 1 of Marx's *Das Kapital*). But the term "capitalists" was used earlier in the nineteenth century by some of the classical economists such as David Ricardo, and Marx used it more than 2,600 times in the three volumes of *Kapital*. Interestingly, in his founding book of classical economics, *The Wealth of Nations* (1776), Adam Smith never once used the words "capitalism" or "capitalist," although the word "capital" (as a reference to accumulated stock, reserves, and wealth) appears frequently. Indeed, "capital" (root word "capitale") goes back at least to the twelfth century, even though its use is rare until the late eighteenth century.

Capitalism has had many variations, each emphasizing a different historical or structural feature: mercantile capitalism, industrial capitalism, free market capitalism, monopoly capitalism, state-managed capitalism, welfare capitalism, neoliberal capitalism, late capitalism, transnational capitalism, financial capitalism, casino capitalism, etc. The common features of each version include the use of wage labor to produce surplus profits for the owners of capital who control all business decision-making; the competitive market pricing of goods and services; individual ownership of private property; and the further accumulation of capital through investment. All versions of capitalism stand in competitive contrast with any public or collective means for organizing production such as socialism or communism.

Despite all their differences, most historians accept that, following the collapse of feudalism, there have been roughly four main phases of capitalism over the last five hundred years. Feudalism consisted of the hereditary ownership of land used for agrarian modes of producing food and other necessities in self-contained manors that had little use for money or markets. The first transitional phase (1500–1800) of capitalism is often called "mercantilism" because a rising class of merchants gained control of economic exchanges in the expanded, global market system opened up for trade by European colonial conquests. By the late eighteenth century, the Industrial Age began as a new class of private capitalists gained control of mechanized factories. This second phase is often referred to as monopoly capitalism because privately owned corporations gained exclusive control of the production and exchange of goods. It corresponds to the rise of the British colonial empire, but it reached a breaking point following the First World War and the Great Depression. The emergence of state-managed capitalism characteristic of the North Atlantic welfare states began in the 1930s, but especially after the Second World War when democratic governments funded some human resources (social security, etc.) and international financial institutions such as the World Bank and the International Monetary Fund orchestrated global economic exchanges. This system produced the most expansive world economic growth ever recorded, but the expansion came to an end during the 1970s following the 1973 Arab oil embargo and the gradual undoing of welfare-state regulations; saturated markets and diminishing resources constrained endless accumulation. The latest, "neoliberal" version of capitalism emphasizes privatization of all resources, deregulated markets (but regulations against collective bargaining and worker unionization), the shrinking of the public sphere by various "austerity" policies calling for diminished governmental funding of health-care, education, and welfare.

In the twenty-first century, the "crisis of capitalism" has been characterized by intense conflict between the critics and supporters of capitalism. On the one hand, the critics have railed against escalating inequality and devastating forms of climate change that go hand in hand with the emphasis on private profit over public good. In contrast, the powerful "neoliberal" supporters stress the improved goods that depend on competitive markets, increased prosperity through economic growth, and the efficiency and flexibility of capitalism to respond dynamically to changing global economic and political conditions.

(*See also* Alienation; Chapter 4, Marxism; Chapter 12, Postmodernism; Chapter 21, Late Capitalism; Chapter 22, Identity Studies; Chapter 25, University Studies; Class; Labor; Marx, Karl; Neoliberalism; Print Capitalism; *and* Production)

David B. Downing, *Indiana University of Pennsylvania (United States)*

Further Reading
Fraser, Nancy. "Contradictions of Capital and Care." *New Left Review* 100 (2016): 99–117.
Harvey, David. *Seventeen Contradictions and the End of Capitalism*. New York: Oxford University Press, 2014.
Streek, Wolfgang. *How Will Capitalism End?: Essays on a Failing System*. London: Verso, 2016.

Cartesianism

Cartesianism is a rationalist philosophy based in the work of the seventeenth-century philosopher, René Descartes (1596–1650). Cartesianism proposes a deductive reasoning based on incontrovertibly "clear and distinct" ideas, and the analytic division of problems into smaller units, to be resolved in a rational progression from simplest to most complex. Inspired by the model of geometry, classic Cartesianism also draws a sharp distinction between mind and matter, viewing the latter in essentially mechanical and mathematical terms, while the former's validity is guaranteed by the existence of a benevolent God.

Descartes's intellectual trajectory was fundamentally motivated by the refutation of skepticism and concomitant search for an "unshakeable" principle of certainty that could serve as the basis from which to derive a properly scientific philosophy. Through a heuristic and hyperbolic exercise of doubt that effectively tests the limits of skepticism, Descartes locates this first principle in the ability to doubt literally everything except for the fact that one is engaged in the act of doubting. Doubting, understood as a form of thinking, or cogitation, in turn implies the existence of the agent or subjectivity doing the thinking, whence the self-evidentiary or "innate" truth of his most famous line, *cogito ergo sum*, "I think therefore I am."

Along the way to this fundamental insight, however, and then in his subsequent thinking, Descartes adumbrated various other propositions that became the hallmarks of Cartesianism as a form of rationalist idealism. The classic skeptical insistence on the unreliability of sensory perception, for example, not only contrasts with his claim for the epistemological superiority of mathematical formulas and innate ideas, but that distinction motivates a more radical separation between substance and thought, or mind and body. This dualism in turn creates its own set of new problems, including the exact nature of the relation between the two realms, that Cartesianism forever remains at pains to try to resolve (although Descartes himself comes close in his late *Passions of the Soul*). Moreover, the foundationalism of innate ideas, from which the features of reality are subsequently to be explained, tends to support a doctrinaire form of deductive reasoning whose failures (the attempt in Part V of the *Discourse on Method* to explain the circulation of the blood in terms of heat transfer) are as glaring as its successes (the invention of analytic geometry).

And while the reduction of perceived reality to mathematical and mechanical principles inaugurates the scientific revolution, the limitations of Cartesian rationalism were soon countered by the inductive approach of British empiricism; and then later by the Kantian critique of reason as presupposing *a priori* concepts of space and time; the Freudian notion of the unconscious which undermines the apparent autonomy of the conscious, cogitating subject; the Heideggerian overcoming of the Cartesian subject/object distinction through the ontologically prior concept of *Dasein* as Being-in-the-world; and a host of other modernist and postmodernist rejections of rationalism. Nonetheless, strong revivals of Cartesian thinking also appear in Husserlian phenomenology, Chomskyian linguistics, and many forms of structuralism. All of these, very different, approaches nonetheless reaffirm, with explicit reference to Descartes, the methodological value of abstract or universal concepts as the basis for strong forms of deductive analysis.

(*See also* Agency; Chapter 23, Materialisms; Chapter 24, Posthumanism; Chapter 26, Affect Studies; Intersubjectivity; Metaphysics; New Materialism; Objects; *and* Subjectivity)

Georges Van Den Abbeele, *University of California, Irvine (United States)*

Further Reading
Bordo, Susan. *The Flight to Objectivity: Essays on Cartesianism and Culture.* Albany: State University of New York Press, 1987.
Descartes, René. *Discourse on Method* [1637] *and Meditations on First Philosophy* [1641]. Trans. Donald Cress. Indianapolis: Hackett, 1998.
Frankfurt, Harry. *Demons, Dreamers, and Madmen: The Defense of Reason in Descartes's Meditations.* New York: Bobbs-Merrill, 1970.
Nancy, Jean-Luc. *Ego Sum: Corpus, Anima, Fabula.* Trans. Marie-Eve Morin. New York: Fordham University Press, 2016.

Castration

Castration is a foundational concept in psychoanalysis. Although as a structural concept it predates Sigmund Freud, it is Freud's body of work which first explores its psychic affects and ramifications with depth and controversy. Freud's theories of castration are most directly traced to his 1909 case study of Little Hans. For Freud, the fear of castration is a pivotal moment for both sexes. The anxiety surrounding its mythic occurrence and the aftermath determine childhood psychosexual development and mental health, particularly the potential presence of hysteria, in adulthood.

For Freud, the psychic reality of castration affects the sexes at different points in relationship to the Oedipal fantasy of doing away with the father so as to solely possess the mother. For boys, castration marks the prohibition against the maternal object, and initiates an aggressive relationship with the paternal figure. It is also the point at which the superego is formed by the boy's failure at fulfilling the fantasy and consequent internalization of such aggression against himself for the fantasy.

In girls, the encounter with castration is the trigger to begin the Oedipal fantasy. This point leads to much feminist criticism of Freud, as he is clear that, in his perspective, castration anxiety leads to desire of the "paternal penis" and penis envy. This literal reading is somewhat of an oversimplification of Freud's notion. Lacan's structuralism attempts to overcome that oversimplification. For, in Jacques Lacan's topological conceptualization, castration is severing of a subject from the maternal bond and the fantasy of the Imaginary. This initiation into symbolic castration produces awareness of lack. That knowledge of lack in the subject results in the refusal of jouissance or the understanding that the jouissance of the subject will always be mediated and will thus be the jouissance of the Other. If castration is disavowed, it is destined to return, as in Freud, as a fetish. The difference between Freud and Lacan over this return is that, for Freud, the fetish is something to be overcome as a mechanism for alleviating castration anxiety. For Lacan, the fetish as a representation of that anxiety is to be exploited as means to attain the jouissance of the subject.

For Lacan, like Freud, male castration occurs in totality, but, unlike Freud, it precedes the Oedipal fantasy and occurs via the acquisition of language. For women in Lacan's perspective, though, castration is not total. There is something that escapes. That escape means that, for Lacan, women cannot be categorized as such. Woman, as an individual entity, exists, but women, as a category subject to the law of the father given through

the act of castration, does not exist. Joan Copjec develops this idea by theorizing that castration, for a son, occurs at the will of the father, but for a daughter it occurs at her own will and is not a limiting prohibition, as it is for the son.

Melanie Klein broadens the target of castration and the ensuing anxiety, from a focus on the father to the mother as well, by asserting that any object from which an infant is taken, such as the breast, can stand for the phallic object. Klein also finds that castration, and the fear of it, can lead to extreme aggression in children, as a defense mechanism.

In the object relations theory of D. W. Winnicott, the transitional object appears as a substitute for both the breast after weaning and the castrated penis, providing a way for the child to gain back control.

Julie Kristeva's perspective, moving from Lacan, positions castration as being the symbolic move from the semiotic register of *la langue* to the discourse of logic or daily life.

(*See also* Chapter 7, Psychoanalytic Theory; Deferred Action; Desire; Jouissance; Primordial Discord; Psychoanalysis; *and* Žižek, Slavoj)

Gina Masucci MacKenzie, *Holy Family University (United States)*

Further Reading

Freud, Sigmund. *Inhibitions, Symptoms and Anxiety*. New York: W. W. Norton and Company, 1990.

Lacan, Jacques. *The Seminar of Jacques Lacan: The Ethics of Psychoanalysis* [1959–1960]. Trans. Jaques Alain Miller. New York: W. W. Norton and Company, 1997.

Civil Society

An ancient category of political philosophy, "civil society" describes an intermediate sphere of voluntary associations standing between the private strivings of self-serving individuals and the public concerns of society at large. It plays a mediating function, diffusing the impact of political power on economic life, on the one hand, and democratizing the state with the particularistic claims of local interests, on the other. Its recent rise to prominence is a result of the general attack on the welfare state that has characterized contemporary politics since Ronald Reagan and Margaret Thatcher.

It was Alexis de Tocqueville who observed Americans' propensity to organize themselves into spontaneous local associations to provide for community needs in the absence of a centralized government. Concerned that a passion for equality would threaten political liberty, he hoped that local power would blunt the centralizing thrust of democratic politics. President George H. W. Bush brought the concept to the center of American affairs with his suggestion that citizen voluntarism could generate "a thousand points of light" that would make up for the social welfare functions that were being abandoned by the government he headed. Seconded by Bill Clinton's bipartisan claim that "the era of big government is over," the term has come into general use to describe a broader arena of democratic activity that holds the state accountable to local interests by channeling private impulses into state activity.

But this understanding is only the latest in a long theoretical history. Greek and Roman thinkers began talking about "civil society" as part of a more general attempt to establish a geometry of human relations. Their tendency to privilege political matters drove them to think of "civility" as an orientation toward the common good and the requirements of effective citizenship rather than as a matter of domestic relations or good manners, a trend that culminated in the classical identification of civil society with the political commonwealth. At the same time, a recognition that life is lived in different spheres that have their own internal logic drove toward a more nuanced approach that made possible a recognition of social complexity and the limits of public life.

The classical understanding could not survive the development of powerful markets and states. Modernity meant that the private strivings of "economic man" were supplanting the public spirit of the aristocratic citizen. Thomas Hobbes, John Locke, and Adam Smith were equally sure that civil society was a sphere of self-interested activity with which the state should not interfere unless civic order was threatened. But if the self-serving activity of people in markets, rather than the general orientation given by political life, is the real glue of civil society, then capitalist social relations inevitably produce levels of economic inequality that threaten political order and stability. Hegel and Marx addressed this problem directly, and the latter's claim that civil society itself had to be democratized lay at the heart of his commitment to "real, human emancipation."

Liberalism developed a theory of civil society because it wanted to democratize the state. Marxism developed a theory of the state because it wanted to democratize civil society. The debate between these traditions has acquired renewed importance. Historic levels of economic inequality constitute a direct threat to political democracy. Orienting civil society toward state power is one of the central tasks facing contemporary democratic thought and action.

(*See also* Chapter 15 Biopower and Biopolitics; Chapter 22, Identity Studies; Critique; Neoliberalism; *and* Sovereignty)

John Ehrenberg, *Long Island University*
(United States)

Further Reading

Ehrenberg, John. *Civil Society: The Critical History of an Idea*. Second ed. New York: New York University Press, 2017.

McConnell, Grant. *Private Power and American Democracy*. New York: Knopf, 1966.

Tocqueville, Alexis de. *Democracy in America*. New York: Bantam Books, 2000.

Cixous, Hélène

Hélène Cixous (born 1937) is one of the most innovative writers in contemporary world literature, and an influential theorist, especially in the field of feminist and gender studies as well as, increasingly, in animal studies and in the arts. Cixous's writing defies any classification by genre, since it combines autobiographical and fictional narrative with philosophical reflection in a poetic mode. It exploits the richness and ambiguity of the French language in a most fruitful and original way, dialoguing with the greatest literary works of European culture, from the Bible, Montaigne, von Kleist and Stendhal, up until contemporary writers such as Bachmann, Bernhard, Lispector, or Tsvetaeva, among many others.

Born in Algeria, when it was a French colony, to a Sephardic Algerian father and an Ashkenazi German mother, Cixous's early experience of colonial domination and exclusion shaped her vision of the world. Her broad oeuvre (nearly 100 books) reflects the most tragic episodes of twentieth-century world history, but is also permeated with humor and tenderness.

Cixous's first novel (*Dedans*, Médicis prize, 1969) was followed by other "fictions" such as *Partie* (1976) or *The Book of Promethea* (1983), among many other highly poetic and complex texts, full of literary and mythical references. *OR. Les lettres de mon père* (1997) seemed to represent a turn in Cixous's oeuvre: certain images and themes (her childhood in Algeria, a reflection on Jewishness, the impact of dreams, etc.), already present in her world, stand out with more intensity in *The Day I Wasn't There* (2000) or *Reveries of the Wild Woman* (2000), or the books that focus on the narrator's mother, in order to "explore" old age and death, such as *Hemlock. Old Women in Bloom* (2008) or *Mother Homer is Dead* (2014). *Gare d'Osnabrück à Jérusalem* (2016) opens yet another new path, turning to her mother's side of the family, to those who died in concentration camps.

Her early text, "The Laugh of the Medusa" (1975), gained Cixous an international audience, since it departed from mainstream feminism of the time, in order to liberate women by embracing "sexual difference." Although this celebration of difference was judged "essentialist" by materialist feminists, this and other theoretical-fictional texts by Cixous such as "Tales of Sexual Difference" (1994) precede queer theory while insisting on the fluidity of gender/sexual positions.

Cixous is also a remarkable playwright, mostly for Ariane Mnouchkine's *Théâtre du Soleil*. Her plays, following ancient Greek and Shakespearian tradition, tackle major political issues, such as the independence of India (*The Indiade or India of Their Dreams*, 1987), the Khmer revolution in Cambodia (*The Terrible but Unfinished Story of Norodom Sihanouk, King of Cambodia*, 1985), and the scandal of HIV-contaminated blood in France (*The Perjured City*, 1994).

Cixous also led a brilliant academic career. After a Ph.D. on James Joyce, she became a professor of English literature and, in the aftermath of May 1968, she was a founder of the experimental Université de Vincennes (later University of Paris 8), where Michel Foucault, Gilles Deleuze, and other French thinkers taught. She also launched one of the first doctoral programs on women's studies in

Europe in the early seventies. Her personal and intellectual relationship with Jacques Derrida led to a series of crossed works, such as Derrida's *H.C. for Life, That Is to Say* (2000) or Cixous's *Portrait of Jacques Derrida as a Young Jewish Saint* (2001).

(*See also* Chapter 1, Early Theory; Chapter 10, Feminism; Jouissance; *and* Phallocentrism)

Marta Segarra, *CNRS (France)* and
Universitat de Barcelona (Spain)

Further Reading

Cixous, Hélène. *Three Steps on the Ladder of Writing*. Trans. Sarah Cornell and Susan Sellers. New York: Columbia University Press, 1993.

Cixous, Hélène. *The Hélène Cixous Reader*. Ed. Susan Sellers. London and New York: Routledge, 1994.

Cixous, Hélène. *The Portable Cixous*. Ed. Marta Segarra. New York: Columbia University Press, 2010.

Cixous, Hélène. *Stigmata: Escaping Texts*. New York: Routledge, 1998.

Class

Class can be defined as the social relationship between those who hold economic power in society and those who do not. The late-nineteenth and early-twentieth-century German sociologist Max Weber distinguished class (or economic power) from social power (or status) and political power (exercised through parties). But as Weber's predecessor Karl Marx argued, class under capitalism is not simply wealth or income either: rather, it is the distinction between those who control the means of economic production (whom Marx called the bourgeoisie) and those (the proletariat) who, lacking such control, can live only by selling their labor.

We can understand literary history in relationship to historical changes in the class structure. The Marxist literary critic Georg Lukács argued in the early twentieth century that the historical novels of Walter Scott provided allegorical depictions of the rise of the capitalist bourgeoisie from an older, aristocratic order. Since then a number of critics have argued that the eighteenth-century novel reflects the worldview of the rising middle class created by capitalism, reading works such as *Robinson Crusoe* (1719) and *Pamela* (1740) as typically middle-class tales of upward mobility grounded in individual virtue and effort. By the same token, we might also understand literary genres that emerged during earlier periods as reflecting different modes of economic production—relating the medieval romance, for instance, to the feudal system of land ownership.

Yet, while the novel is perhaps the preeminent genre of the capitalist era, its investment in subtle and complex representations of social relations can sometimes make it difficult to read in Marxist terms. For this reason literary critics have been drawn to other approaches to class, such as the French sociologist Pierre Bourdieu's analysis of how taste constitutes a form of symbolic capital in modern society. Such culturalist accounts can tell us much, although they have several dangers, including a tendency to falsely celebrate the power of symbolic capital over real capital—thereby both reinforcing right-wing criticism of "cultural elites" and obscuring phenomena like adjunctification. As critics of "neoliberalism" have argued, the idea that people are entrepreneurs of symbolic capital has both obscured the proletarianization of mental labor and extended the logic of economics into every aspect of life.

The ability to understand class as a relation has also been complicated by the late-twentieth-century rise of forms of identity politics organized around factors like race, gender, and sexuality. As Walter Benn Michaels has argued, the problem with treating class as a form of identity is that it transforms working-class poverty into something to be preserved and celebrated, rather than overcome. The debate between class politics and identity politics has recently moved into mainstream political circles, as the former have regained a role in public discourse they haven't had since the start of the Cold War. By setting class and identity politics in opposition, however, this debate obscures the complicated interrelations between the two in both real life (where, for instance, women of color are disproportionately represented in low-wage jobs) and literature.

(*See also* Bourgeois; Chapter 4, Marxism; Chapter 11, Cultural Studies; Chapter 22, Identity Studies; Cultural Studies; Hegemony; Identity Politics; Ideology; Intersectionality; Political Unconscious; Revolution; Subaltern; Symbolic Agency; *and* Whiteness)

Andrew Hoberek, *University of Missouri (United States)*

Further Reading

Benn Michaels, Walter. *The Trouble with Diversity: How We Learned to Love Identity and Ignore Inequality*. New York: Metropolitan, 2006.

Brown, Wendy. *Undoing the Demos: Neoliberalism's Stealth Revolution*. Cambridge: MIT Press, 2015.

Watt, Ian. *The Rise of the Novel: Studies in Defoe, Richardson and Fielding* [1957]. Berkeley: University of California Press, 2001.

Close Reading

Close reading is inseparable from the New Criticism, although it now implies the general practice of paying close attention to language when studying literature and other cultural texts. Under the influence of I. A. Richards and T. S. Eliot, the New Critics—who included Cleanth Brooks, John Crowe Ransom, Allen Tate, Robert Penn Warren, and William Wimsatt, among others—professionalized literary criticism and secured for it an institutional home in the American university during the 1940s and 1950s. New Critical close reading is both a pedagogy and a method of "practical criticism." It presupposes that the meaning of a literary text is evident in its language as opposed to external contexts such as biography, history, the author (i.e., the "intentional fallacy"), or the reader (i.e., the "affective fallacy"). The New Critics valued irony and paradox in literature and produced readings (often of lyric poems because of their pedagogical effectiveness) that demonstrated how a text possessed an internal order that resolved its tensions to form an organically unified whole. Such theoretical premises overlapped with a social-political vision where the autonomous work of art—a poem as an autotelic "verbal icon"—assuages the critic's desire for redemption from his modern alienation and the chaos of history. Yet, however we judge their politics, the New Critics saw close reading as democratic. It enabled students who lacked a privileged background (and therefore the necessary historical contexts) to devote an entire class to discussing how a poem's language conveys its meaning.

Not all mid-century Anglo-American scholars were New Critics though close reading distinctly shaped the direction of the postwar academy. Northrop Frye and Frank Kermode immediately contested New Critical orthodoxy while F. O. Matthiessen, R. P. Blackmur, and others borrowed from its teachings. Later scholars critiqued the New Critic's assumed dismissal of ideology, culture, and history.

The most significant challenge developed by extending the New Critic's own method of studying literature. Most prominently, Paul de Man's early work undermined a poem's organic unity by attending to, and failing to resolve, its irony. What he later called "rhetorical reading" may be described as an even more rigorous style of close reading that locates an irresolvable contradiction between language's figural and rhetorical dimensions. Because the meaning of a literary or cultural text emerges through its language, scholars coming-of-age after the New Critics continue to labor under their influence. Even if we refute their theoretical tenets, we must raise the philological question of where a text's language takes us: to an author, a cultural milieu, another literary text, a different context that lays claim to meaning, or maybe nowhere? Regardless of our answer, close reading requires that the critic avoid mere summary (i.e., the "heresy of paraphrase") and continually engage with the intransigence of language. To this end, close reading literature implicates us in a struggle for meaning that remains an ethical and political act.

(*See also* Antitheory; Chapter 2, Structuralism and Semiotics; Chapter 19, Media Studies; Chapter 26, Affect Studies; Chapter 27, Antitheory; Fish, Stanley; Formalism; *and* New Criticism)

Daniel Rosenberg Nutters, *Temple University (United States)*

Further Reading
Brower, Reuben A. "Reading in Slow Motion." *In Defense of Reading: A Readers Approach to Literary Criticism*. Ed. Reuben A. Brower and Richard Poirier. New York: E.P. Dutton & Co., 1962. 3–21.
Brower, Reuben A. *The Fields of Light* [1951]. Philadelphia: Paul Dry Books, Inc., 2013.
DuBois, Andrew, and Frank Lentricchia, eds. *Close-Reading: The Reader*. Durham: Duke University Press, 2003.

Colonialism

Scholars in broad interdisciplinary contexts have turned their attention to the study of colonialism and to its postcolonial, transcolonial, and transnational legacies. Historically, the term *colonialism* has been used to describe the global expansionist drive of European nation-states as continuations of earlier conquests, expeditions, explorations, and missionary drives that can be detected as early as the fifteenth century. The Congo Conference, convened in Berlin by German chancellor Otto von Bismarck in 1884–85, yielded a General Act that triggered what became known as the "Scramble for Africa," a reference to the significant intensification of external activity and presence on the African continent. In each individual case, the enterprise was motivated by economic opportunism as a logical outcome of the exercise of uneven power relations that resulted in the occupation and control over a foreign territory, while also establishing outlets for goods and services.

Broadly speaking, French colonialism could be distinguished by the fact that it was not predominantly mercantilist or trade-driven in nature, but rather augmented by entrenched control over foreign territories and concerted assimilationist efforts defined by the imperatives of enacting a civilizing mission. The French went so far as to coin the category of *evolved* subjects in order to categorize those colonized who had successfully internalized French cultural and social norms. Extensive recourse was made to colonial exhibitions as a way of enlisting public support and justification for the colonial project, and these operated alongside theories of scientific racial representation that helped shape the visual displays and diffusion of theories in "human zoos." Colonialism, one could safely say, was deeply impregnated in the fabric of Western European societies.

Powerful condemnation and critiques of colonialism have been launched by activists and intellectuals, notably in such influential works as Aimé Césaire's *Discourse on Colonialism* (1950) and Frantz Fanon's *Black Skin, White Masks* (1952), and more recently in Achille Mbembe's *Critique of Black Reason* (2013), a work that examines the foundations of the colonial apparatus "through which the European pretension of universal domination was made manifest. It was a form of constitutive power whose relationship to land, populations, and territory brought together the three logics of race, bureaucracy, and commerce." Several racial advocacy groups in European societies have emphasized transhistorical links with colonial-era representations and policies as a way of explaining lingering societal inequity.

Colonialism remains a controversial issue in contemporary European societies in which former colonial powers have struggled to look critically at their respective colonial histories and to accordingly address the tenuous relationship between the humanist ideals that served to justify the practice and the exploitative practice of colonization itself. Likewise, the connection between postcolonial-era immigration from the "global south" to former colonial centers remains an unresolved question, as do neocolonialist practices. More recently, critics and observers have employed the label "China Colonization," thereby establishing a link with various historical precursors, as a way of describing Chinese economic activity on the African continent.

(*See also* Capitalism; Chapter 13, Race and Postcolonial Studies; Creolization; Decolonization; Essentialism; Hybridity; Postcolonialism; Resistance; Revolution; Rights; Said, Edward; Spivak, Gayatri; Subaltern; Subjectivity; Transnational; *and* Whiteness)

Dominic Thomas, *University of California, Los Angeles (United States)*

Further Reading
Bancel, Nicolas, Pascal Blanchard, and Dominic Thomas, eds. *The Colonial Legacy in France: Fracture, Rupture, and Apartheid.* Bloomington: Indiana University Press, 2017.
Césaire, Aimé. *Discourse on Colonialism* [1950]. Trans. Joan Pinkham. New York: Monthly Review Press, 2000.
Fanon, Frantz. *Black Skin, White Masks* [1952]. Trans. Richard Philcox. New York: Grove Press, 2008.
Mbembe, Achille. *Critique of Black Reason* [2013]. Trans. Laurent Dubois. Durham: Duke University Press, 2017.

Community

Since the advent of the West, community has served as a quasi-free-floating signifier demarcating the desire to belong. No other kind of social relationship has appeared as more desirable yet dangerous, more attainable yet tenuous, or more present yet lost than community in modern thought. With the violent European colonization of most of the world, the appropriation and eventual conversion of everything including persons into property, and the generalized destruction of life in the wake of capitalism, *community* represents that which has been lost and must be rediscovered. This narrative of loss and recovery is articulated in the social contract aiming to establish a legalistic, civic, and democratic community, in the republican models that found the constitution in the *res publica*, in the communist goal of establishing a community on the basis of communal property, in the neoromantic calls for a return to a simpler and more naturalistic mode of living together, in cooperative calls for a utopian way of living within an integrated whole, even in nationalist movements hell-bent on forging a proper and thus autonomous people. For each, community represents that which has been lost and that which must be recovered. It is the past and the future, the horizon and the goal.

The communal signifier, however, is not freely floating without direction. In Western thought, at least two key axioms have shaped seemingly disparate articulations of community. First, community is conceived through the dispositif of the proper. That is, since community or the commons was gradually lost through the accumulation of private property, community can only be resurrected by converting private property into communal property. The divisiveness of the *idios kosmos,* the mass alienation experienced, can only be overcome by a collective movement that appropriates things, lands, beings, even identity, and then redistributes them communally. The *koinos kosmos* is a shared and common world. This formula is repeated across our political spectrum from far-right nationalist movements, liberal theories of civil rights, to leftist calls for collectivist modes of sharing economies. Resistance and change are formulated through the dialectic of alienation and appropriation.

Second, community is formulated as closed and exclusionary. It represents the desire to be united together as a com-unity. Again, this orientation has been repeated across the political spectrum. Whether articulated in the anti-colonial movements in the 1960s and 1970s seeking to establish a national identity, the totalitarian and fascist projects aimed at fusing a people together, even the fleeting and ephemeral communities formed during the heat of an action by an affinity group, community is realized only in the modality of uniting together. It matters little if the unity is produced by participants acting autonomously or by dominated subjects. It also matters little if the fusion is never achieved—it never is. The material basis of community is the gathering together process. Each part is divided up and propelled toward becoming a whole.

Near the end of the last decade a series of texts written by such theorists as Giorgio Agamben, Benedict Anderson, Zygmunt Bauman, Maurice Blanchot, Judith Butler, Roberto Esposito, Miranda Joseph, Alphonso Lingus, Jean-Luc Nancy, and others, sought to challenge the proprietary and unitary logic framing how community is conceived. None of them, however, calls for an abandonment of the desire to belong-together; rather, each argues that we need to radically reconceive belonging in our globalized world. This is as much an ontological problem as it is a political economy one. Community must be rearticulated so that it is no longer conceived through a division between the proper and the improper, *having* a share in a common property, and being-in-common must no longer be determined by the domination of having over being. Being-in-common must be experienced as a sharing that divides us up and shares us out in common. That which is included in this sharing and division extends beyond human life in our biopolitical order. Living in common though is not enough; we might take our cue from recent texts by Achille Mbembe and Jaspir Puar on the notion of *conviviality.*

(*See also* Alienation; Bare Life; Bataille, Georges; Chapter 9, Deconstruction; Chapter 11, Cultural Studies; Chapter 19, Media Studies; Chapter 21, Late Capitalism; Chapter 22, Identity Studies; Culture; Exceptionalist State; Fish, Stanley; Introduction, Theory in the New Millennium; *and* Print Capitalism)

Greg Bird, *Wilfrid Laurier University (Canada)*

Further Reading

Bird, Greg. *Containing Community: From Political Economy to Ontology in Agamben, Esposito, and Nancy.* Albany: State University of New York Press, 2016.

Delanty, Gerard. *Community.* Second ed. New York: Routledge, 2010.

Joseph, Miranda. *Against the Romance of Community.* Minneapolis: University of Minnesota Press, 2002.

Consensus

The term *consensus* comes from Latin where it means agreement or feeling together.

In Roman contract law, consensus is one of four types of contractual obligations. Consensual contracts required only the consent of the parties and no writing or ceremonial formalities. The notion of consensus also had a wider significance in the Roman humanist understanding of rhetoric. In this tradition, the goal of oratory is to forge an agreement among listeners and, by extension, the community at large. The search for consensus was underwritten by a philosophical belief, articulated by Aristotle and Cicero among others, that the opinions that people hold, especially in regard to normative rightness, contain within them an element of truth, which then requires further refinement. The successful orator can reach consensus by appealing to, and elaborating, this preexisting knowledge of truth. In this tradition, the *consensus omnium* (or *consensus gentium*), the consensus of all men, or later, the *consensus fidelium*, the consensus of all believers, may serve as evidence of the truth of the beliefs.

It is important to emphasize that in this tradition consensus is seen as the outcome of a process managed by a skillful orator. This process dimension played an important role in Roman political philosophy. According to Cicero, a republic is constituted by a consensus on the law (*iuris consensu*). The search for such a consensus is understood as important for resolving civic conflicts and is associated with toleration and good will.

Modern usages of the term retain elements of the voluntarist usage in contract law and the process-oriented elements of the humanist tradition without necessarily staying committed to the entire worldview.

In many contexts, consensus refers to a method of reaching agreement not through voting. Sometimes it is distinguished from *unanimity* in that it does not require expressed confirmation but no objection is sufficient. Consensus is widely used as a method of reaching agreement in international organizations and international treatises. Some aboriginal communities use consensus circles to determine sentencing in criminal procedure as a way to restore justice and heal the community.

With the post-metaphysical turn in political philosophy, there is an interest in the idea that consensus can serve as a standard of democratic legitimacy and even as an indication of truth. The idea is that if, under certain conditions and following a certain process, an agreement is reached then this agreement is the indication of the legitimacy of the decision. In the 1990s, the philosopher John Rawls suggested that a constitutional consensus over liberal principles is possible even among people who hold non-liberal worldviews. Some pragmatists, including Jürgen Habermas in his early work, suggested that the meaning of the concept of truth has to be understood as a consensus among inquirers.

There is also a strand of thought that is suspicious of the idea of consensus. Wide agreement is viewed as an indication of groupthink or collective myopia. Rhetorical appeals to consensus are seen as attempts to gloss over and erase disagreement and dissent. In the late 1950s, the sociologist Ralf Dahrendorf suggested a distinction between consensus and conflict theories of society. Consensus theories assume utopian and fictional consensus on social values and interpreted departure from the consensus as deviance. In the 1960s, Thomas Kuhn suggested that a mature science is marked by consensus on paradigmatic exemplars, but such consensus is bound to be replaced by another one. In the 1990s, John Williams's term *Washington Consensus* became popular as a way to describe the shared beliefs in neoliberal economic principles among policymakers in Washington, particularly in regard to development policies.

(*See also* Canon; Chapter 13, Race and Postcolonial Studies; Chapter 22, Identity Studies; *and* Habermas, Jürgen)

Amit Ron, *Arizona State University (United States)*

Further Reading

Dahrendorf, Ralph. *Class and Class Conflict in Industrial Society.* Stanford: Stanford University Press, 1959.

Rawls, John. "The Idea of an Overlapping Consensus." *Oxford Journal of Legal Studies* 7.1 (1987): 1–25.

Remer, Gary. *Humanism and the Rhetoric of Toleration.* University Park: Penn State University Press, 2008.

Consumer Society

The conception of the "consumer society" materialized during the twentieth-century "long boom" in the postwar capitalist world-system. This period of economic expansion, bookended by the end of the Second World War and the monetary crises of the early 1970s, witnessed increasing productivity rates in the advanced capitalist economies of the Global North in general and the United States in particular. The relative economic prosperity afforded by high industrial productivity witnessed the mass production and increased consumption of non-subsistence commodities across class strata. Early critics of consumerism, such as John Kenneth Galbraith, Vance Packard, and Herbert Marcuse, attempted to situate the social-psychological implications of generating consumer demand through increased advertising, marketing, branding, and the symbolic production of promotional culture. In *The Affluent Society* (1958), Galbraith famously outlined "the dependence effect" by stressing the mutually constitutive interrelation between "outlays for the manufacturing of a product" and "outlays for the manufacturing of demand for the product." As the creation of commodities within the capitalist mode of production is aimed explicitly at exchange within impersonal markets, the early critics of consumer society expanded the attendant alienation of social relations within commodity production to the realm of commodity consumption. In Marcuse's *One-Dimensional Man* (1964), the standardized rationalization inherent in Fordist exchange relations subjectivizes the individuals of the advanced capitalist economies precisely as consumers—they can only reproduce their social existence through commodities. As a result of the increasing commodification of everyday life, the agency of the individual subject is flattened and the dehumanized consumer understands their social reproduction only through the mediation by market logics and the passive consumption of mass-produced commodities.

The notion that consumerist desire develops from a mode of ostentatious exhibition aimed at signifying class affiliation through the acquisition of luxury commodities at the turn of the twentieth century (Thorstein Veblen's "conspicuous consumption"), to its generalization as ideologically mediating the entire affective experience of a society obligated to consume, overlooks the historical specificity of the consumer society's ascendance as a direct result of capital's own restructuring throughout the twentieth century. When, in *The Consumer Society* (1970), Jean Baudrillard privileges the sphere of consumption over that of production and claims "we are at the point where consumption is laying hold of the whole of life," he erroneously attributes a level of autonomy to the symbolic that obscures structural shifts at the level of the real economy. Against privileging the growth of consumption as the driver of capitalist development, twenty-first-century consumer societies must be understood as a symptomatic manifestation of capital's *longue durée* crisis of accumulation due to overproduction. Consumption is merely one component of capital's more general circulation. Within today's context of a truly integrated world market, developing and newly industrialized countries are inextricably linked to the consumer societies of the deindustrializing advanced capitalist economies through commodity supply chains, globalized capital flows, and the systems of what David Harvey calls "accumulation by dispossession": debt encumbrance, deregulation of trade barriers, privatization of public resources, and structural adjustment policies.

(*See also* Baudrillard, Jean; Chapter 11, Cultural Studies; Chapter 12, Postmodernism; Chapter 19, Media Studies; Chapter 21, Late Capitalism; *and* Chapter 24, Posthumanism)

Alden Sajor Wood, *University of California, Irvine (United States)*

Further Reading

Arvidsson, Adam. *Brands: Meaning and Value in Media Culture*. New York: Routledge, 2006.

Baudrillard, Jean. *The Consumer Society: Myths and Structures*. Thousand Oaks: Sage Publications, 1998.

Galbraith, John Kenneth. *The Affluent Society* [1958]. New York: Mariner Books, 1998.

Contradiction (*See* Negation)

Control

The concept of *control* largely derives from a short essay that Gilles Deleuze published late in his life. Having broached the subject in an interview, Deleuze wrote the "Postscript on Control Society" (1991) to elaborate the principles of a new regime of power in the aftermath of Michel Foucault's disciplinary societies. Set amid the dismantling of the welfare state, control describes the metamorphosis of power from an analogical and institutional expression ("the factory is a prison") to a digital and dispersive one. Far from concentrating power (in a sovereign) or distributing it (across institutions), control disseminates power into the most capillary and micropolitical of instances.

For Deleuze, control designates an episteme, a political economy, and a biopolitics—with the proviso that, in the digital age, these very categories (roughly, language, labor, and life) are themselves transformed. The molds of discipline, which aggregated masses and individuated subjects, give way to the smooth space of a digital domain on which we perpetually glide, "moving among a continuous range of different orbits." "*Surfing* has taken over from all the old *sports*," Deleuze writes, and the subsequent coinage—"surfing the internet"—all but confirms the nature of control. The instruments of continuous tracking are woven into the fabric of space as well as cyberspace: phone and cars are equipped with GPS, purchases and internet histories are recorded, and workers are now voluntarily implanted with digital chips. "We don't have to stray into science fiction to find a control mechanism that can fix the position of any element at any given moment."

Nevertheless, Deleuze insists that "information technology and computers" cannot account for control ("machines don't explain anything"). Rather, digital technology ought to be grasped in relation to a "mutation of capitalism." Consider once more disciplinary societies, which flourished in the age of industrialization and made the factory a site of production for goods as well as subjects. Centralized, concentrative, and proprietorial, this model of capitalism succeeded in the marketplace by "reducing costs" and "specializing production." By contrast, in Deleuze's post-Fordist account of control, manufacturing is outsourced, factories give way to businesses, and production is replaced by marketing and sales ("Marketing is now the instrument of social control"). For all that, the "Postscript" never uses the term *neoliberalism* (ironically, Deleuze seems to have been unfamiliar with Foucault's lectures on the subject in *The Birth of Biopolitics* (1978), the book to which the "Postscript" ought, by rights, to have been addressed).

Perhaps this explains why Deleuze, despite stressing capitalism, does not anticipate the degree to which surveillance, data harvesting, and algorithmic processing have been commercialized, marketed, and incentivized. Today, control society relies on our freedom to choose, the exercise of which yields the metadata whereby we are figured in a "grid of intelligibility." The disciplinary molds dissolve into the fluid modulation of spaces; likewise, the unit of the individual becomes the "dividual"—the variable code, the aggregate of "transactions," on which countless algorithms invisibly operate. Doubtless, this is why the challenge of resisting control remains so daunting.

(*See also* Biopolitics; Chapter 15, Biopower and Biopolitics; Cybernetics; Deleuze, Gilles; Multitude; Negri, Antonio; Network Society; *and* Systems Theory)

Gregory Flaxman, *University of North Carolina, Chapel Hill (United States)*

Further Reading
Beckman, Frida, ed. *Control Culture: Foucault and Deleuze after Discipline.* Edinburgh: Edinburgh University Press, 2018.
Foucault, Michel. *The Birth of Biopolitics: Lectures at the College of France, 1978-1979.* Eds. Michael Senellart. Trans. Graham Burchell. Basingstoke: Palgrave Macmillan, 2008.
Galloway, Alexander. *Protocol: How Control Exists after Decentralization.* Boston: MIT Press, 2004.

Control Society (*See* Control)

Creolization

The term *Creole*, from the Spanish and the Portuguese *criar* ("to create," "to grow," "to feed," "to raise") emerged on the slave plantation in the 1600s. Creole quickly began to refer to humans, animals, and plants of African, Asian, or European provenance born and raised in the New World in contrast both with indigenous and with recently arrived populations and species. Creole subsequently became synonymous albeit not equivalent to métis, mestizo, mixed-race, and hybrid. The linguistic formations based on a predominantly European lexicon, but altered enough by African syntax to fashion new languages, were called Creoles. The massive and speedy encounters between indigenous, European, African, Asian, and Middle Eastern people in the Caribbean were necessary conditions to the birth of such composite forms. Zones of creolization extend beyond the Caribbean to include, among others, Brazil, the Guianas, Mexico, Louisiana, and the coasts of Africa both on their Atlantic and Indian Ocean shores marked by intensive cultural encounters.

Creolization, the process of becoming mixed or composite in a new site, derives from this multiplicity of human, historical, geographical and cultural groundings. The term "creolization" makes its first appearance in the English language in the 1880s in the New Orleans and West Indian works by Greek-Irish writer Lafcadio Hearn. While often associated with hybridity and *métissage*, creolization departs from these concepts since it is grounded in linguistics rather than in biology and ethnicity. Creolization is closer to the concept of *transculturalism*, developed by Cuban essayist Fernando Ortiz (1940) after José Marti's "Nuestra America" (1881) referring to the process of future-forward cultures intermingling. In addition, while *métissage* can lead to fixed products, the unpredictable process of creolization generates forms that supersede the sum of their original elements.

In the 1980s, Anglophone and Francophone Caribbean writers Barbadian Kamau Brathwaite, Guyanese Wilson Harris, and Martinican Edouard Glissant championed each in their own way the theory of creolization. For Brathwaite, creolization constitutes a restorative cross-cultural force leading to national and cultural healing and opposing the gaps and interruptions caused by the immense disruption of the slave trade and colonialism. Creolization or the implementation of "cross-cultural imagination" for Harris, also responds to the traumas of the past through the embrace of indigenous and imported myths. Glissant's *Créolisation*, in tandem with his notion of *Antillanité* or Caribbeanness, provides a model to understand the French overseas department of Martinique in its Caribbean cultural and geographical surrounding departing from a primary association with Africa advocated in Aimé Césaire's Negritude, and from the stifling cultural and political assimilation with the French neocolonial nation.

Paradoxically, the model of creolization, theoretically based on the rejection of pure categories and processual openness, has in practice occasionally excluded more established categories. Brathwaite, for instance, considers East Indians as being incompatible with the construction of creolized Caribbean national models. In 1989, novelists Raphaël Confiant and Patrick Chamoiseau, and Creole linguist Jean Bernabé published *Éloge de la Créolité / In Praise of Creoleness*, proclaiming themselves neither European, nor African, nor Asian, but Creoles. The manifesto caused the ire of critics such as Guadeloupean novelist Maryse Condé who denounced the exclusion of Africanness, and of women writers, in the Martinican writers' statement. Créolité, however, while often associated with creolization, cannot be confused with it. While Créolité refers to a product, creolization is a process. In Glissant's thought creolization is often used interchangeably with *Relation*, the process of linking, relating, and relaying in an infinite network in which no component can be elected as central. While initially tied to the cultural, geographical, and political experience of Martinique, Glissantian creolization is a philosophical concept that can function away from plantation zones. Jazz, Ajiaco, gumbo, and other musical and culinary productions yet to come, based on variations on many themes, improvisation, and unpredictability best exemplify the infinite potentialities and beautiful chaos of creolization.

(*See also* Chapter 13, Race and Postcolonial Studies; Chapter 17, Comparativisms; Chapter 18, Translation; *and* Hybridity)

Valérie Loichot, *Emory University (United States)*

Further Reading

Bernabé, Jean, Patrick Chamoiseau, and Raphaël Confiant. *Éloge de la créolité / In Praise of Creoleness*. Paris: Gallimard, 1989.

Brathwaite, Kamau. *The Development of Creole Society in Jamaica, 1770–1820*. Oxford: Clarendon, 1971.

Condé, Maryse, and Madeleine Cotten-et-Hage, eds. "Penser la Créolité." Paris: Karthala, 1995.

Glissant, Edouard. *Caribbean Discourse: Selected Essays* [1981]. Trans. J. Michael Dash. Charlottesville: University Press of Virginia, 1989.

Glissant, Edouard. *Poetics of Relation* [1990]. Trans. Betsy Wing. Ann Arbor: University of Michigan Press, 1997.

Critical Climate

Critical climate names the branch of critical thinking that deals with climate change and, increasingly, the Anthropocene. Its inception can be traced to the 2005 formation of the Institute of Critical Climate Change (IC³) at SUNY, Albany by Tom Cohen. This led to Cohen's *Telemorphosis* (2012) and coincided with special issues on climate change in prominent literary theory journals, such as *Diacritics* (2013), which termed it "climate change criticism," and *symplokē* (2013), which introduced it as "critical climate." These publications helped to establish the range of prominent thinkers in the field, including Timothy Clark, Claire Colebrook, Timothy Morton, and Karen Pinkus.

The designation of "critical climate" helpfully collapses several concerns at once: it punningly conjures up climate as both meteorological condition and prevailing cultural mood, and thus reflects how climate change is at once an environmental phenomenon and a social, political, and even existential problem. This correlates to two categories of critical climate analysis, which, though not discrete, helpfully indicate the ways in which critical climate has tended to frame itself.

First, there occur critical analyses of climate change, in terms of, for example, its constructedness (drawing on, among other things, science and technology studies) and its unrepresentability (as an expression of the postmodern condition *par excellence*). That is, critical climate applies literary and critical theory to climate change. It becomes, in other words, a kind of "climate change studies" alongside disability studies, trauma studies, and so on. Critical climate in this mode has been clearly distinguishable from ecocriticism, which has conventionally eschewed (and, early in its history, actively disdained) theory in favor of more traditional literary-critical modes of author scholarship and close reading in order to foreground more overtly "nature"-oriented genres and texts.

Secondly and more profoundly, critical climate understands climate change to be a radical challenge to the foundations and horizons of human thought and expression. That is, climate change deconstructs existing conceptualizations of ontology, undoing old notions of humans' relationship with spatiality, temporality, and ecology. This has become more acute, urgent, and discernible, as not just the idea of the Anthropocene but its implications take hold. The questions that critical climate now seeks to answer hinge not on what climate change might be or what it might do to the human condition, but on the very status, idea, and relevance of human *being* at such a point in the Earth's history. That is, how to construe space, time, and species, given the identification of humanity as a geological agent capable of destroying the biosphere and enacting millennial timescale events? With this more urgent set of questions, critical climate and ecocriticism are converging, as recent ecocritical investigations have explored the permeability of human-nonhuman boundaries and the interconnectedness of human with nonhuman agency. Indeed, such questions constitute something of a watershed for the project of literary and critical theory, for it may be the insights of theory that offer the best chance of understanding the inherently unstable category of Anthropos in the Anthropocene.

(*See also* Anthropocene; Environmental Humanities; Object-Oriented Ontology; Speculative Realism; *and* Subjectivity)

Adeline Johns-Putra, *University of Surrey (United Kingdom)*

Further Reading

Cohen, Tom, ed. *Telemorphosis: Essays in Critical Climate Change*. Ann Arbor: Open Humanities Press, 2012.

Johns-Putra, Adeline, ed. *Critical Climate*. Special issue. *symplokē* 21.1–2 (2013): 1–238.

Pinkus, Karen, ed. *Climate Change Criticism*. Special issue. *Diacritics* 41.3 (2013): 1–113.

Critique

In the preface to the 1788 edition of the *Critique of Practical Reason*, Kant confidently declares "Ours is the age of critique, to which everything must be subjected. Religion and legislation may wish to avoid this by virtue of their holiness and regality. But in so doing, they bring justified suspicion upon themselves, and must forego any claims they may have had to the respect that reason concedes only to those that can pass the test of free and open examination." The connections Kant makes between critique, reason, and open examination offer a very good introduction to the concept of *critique*. In *The Structural Transformation of the Public Sphere* (1962), Jürgen Habermas broadly follows Kant in suggesting that while isolated individuals will surely struggle to achieve reflexive lucidity about their ethical duties and political obligations, a critical public can achieve such lucidity through open debate and a vigorous exchange of informed and in, many cases, opposed opinions. There is thus a clearly discernible but nonetheless complex line of thinking about critique that runs from Kant and Theodor W. Adorno to Habermas and more contemporary thinkers. It is a line of thinking that convincingly shows that there is a historically conditioned (not absolute or metaphysical) discrepancy between the self-understanding and official public presentation of institutions such as the family, civil society, and the state, and the actual functioning of those institutions in practice. The allusion to these three specific institutions is not casual. In the *Philosophy of Right* (1821), Hegel maintains that the modern state is a historically new and extraordinarily supple form of political authority. He claims that the *unmediated unity* between humanity and nature in the family, based on natural ties of emotion and affect, experiences rupture in the *mediated disunity* citizens experience in their various contractual and instrumentally rational pursuits in civil society. Mediated disunity is transcended in the *mediated unity* between humanity and nature institutionalized in the modern state. In the state, Hegel thinks, our understanding of ethical responsibility and political obligation is raised from the level of instinct and affect nurtured in the family to rational acceptance of the claims of post-feudal authority made on us by modern law, as opposed to tradition, custom, and command. Key in this regard is his thesis that the transition from unmediated unity in the family to mediated unity in the state is only possible because of the challenges to reason and critique posed by the mediated disunity we experience in the civil sphere of utilitarian calculation. Hegel suggests that people sense that their ability to act instrumentally depends on a more substantive foundation provided by the state. In his view, the modern state manages to integrate human beings on a consensual basis precisely because it allows them to be both autonomous individuals in civil society with highly divergent life projects, and mature citizens in the modern state with a common aim. The implication is that the antagonisms of civil society cannot be ignored or wished away. But the rationally grounded hope persists that they might be transcended in the right form of state. This idea clearly animates the young Marx's reading of the *Philosophy of Right*.

Critique from Adorno and Habermas and beyond to more recent thinkers challenges the theory of consensual integration defended by Hegel, without, however, abandoning Hegel's fundamental insight that a valid contract *presupposes* a valid state that makes contractual exchange valid in the first place. The idea and practice of the modern state both presuppose the mediated unity of humanity and nature in a political community of equal citizens, and, such thinking also regards the process of integration to result in mediated unity between law and authority. Critique attempts to address this tautology in dialectical terms. Critique and dialectics are thus closely connected. The question remains, however: what kind of dialectics?

In conclusion, it is important to return to the point about the historically conditioned discrepancy between the self-understanding and official public presentation of institutions such as the family, civil society, and the state, and the actual functioning of those institutions in daily practice. Critique demands that this discrepancy be addressed, without, however, seeking flight into a world of a perfect harmony between our conceptual understanding of reality and reality itself. Kant signals that this discrepancy has to do with what he considers to be the factual distinction between the objects of our knowledge and experience, and the forms in which knowledge and experience achieve objective validity in concepts. If Kant tends anthropologically to naturalize the difference between knowledge and the forms in which our knowledge becomes conceptually intelligible, dialectical critique interrogates the sociohistorical and institutional conditions under which these discrepancies and differences might be reconciled, without synthesizing them in an authoritarian fusion. Here one glances, however fleetingly, what the right form of state might look like in actual institutional terms. Adorno aptly summarizes the matter by declaring "critique of epistemology is critique of society and vice versa." In qualified departure from the Hegelian model of mediated unity, and in opposition to Martin Heidegger's insistence on the non-mediated nonidentity of thought and being, Theodor W. Adorno develops the concept of *mediated nonidentity*. In so doing, he outlines a critique of reality that remains firmly anchored in a vision of what reality might and could be, and in fact already is, however inchoately.

(*See also* Adorno, Theodor; Chapter 4, Marxism; Chapter 9, Deconstruction; Chapter 10, Feminism; Chapter 13, Race and Postcolonial Studies; Chapter 19, Media Studies; Chapter 26, Affect Studies; Chapter 27, Antitheory; Cultural Critique; Dialectic; Habermas, Jürgen; Hegel, Georg; Ideology; Kant, Immanuel; Marx, Karl; Postcritique; Surface Reading; *and* Žižek, Slavoj)

Darrow Schecter, *University of Sussex*
(United Kingdom)

Further Reading

Held, David. *Introduction to Critical Theory: Horkheimer to Habermas*. Berkeley: University of California Press, 1980.

Jarvis, Simon. *Adorno: A Critical Introduction*. Cambridge: Polity, 1998.

Schecter, Darrow. *Critical Theory and Sociological Theory*. Manchester: Manchester University Press, forthcoming.

Cultural Capital

Political economy's vision of a world of perfect competition and equal opportunity has always been at odds with the logic of capital itself, whose unequal accumulation and distribution sustains the "immanent regularities" of modern social structures, or the mechanisms that guarantee their reproduction. French sociologist Pierre Bourdieu extended this Marxian insight into the realm of symbolic exchange, arguing for the importance of social and cultural capital in perpetuating social stratification. Initially, "cultural capital" was used to account for class disparities in scholastic achievement, denoting a fluency in the codes of "legitimate" culture that is transmitted by inheritance and valorized by the educational system, conferring an unfair advantage on students from privileged backgrounds. The concept punctures the illusion of a neutral meritocracy that rewards "innate" abilities or aptitudes; at the same time, it demystifies the very forms of cultural production to which such "natural" talents are applied, collapsing the bourgeois ideology of the aesthetic as a "disinterested" realm uncontaminated by commerce, and exposing the ultimately material underpinnings of "high" culture in its putative transcendence.

Cultural capital is differentiated into three types: embodied (incorporated and cultivated within the self as a set of "durable dispositions"); objectified (as the tangible artifacts of cultural production); and institutionalized (in the form of academic degrees or similarly "objective" certifications). The first sense is extensively developed in Bourdieu's landmark work *Distinction* (1979), which examines cultural capital as manifested in the phenomenon of "taste": here it functions through the cultivation of various "dispositions" or "life-styles" that reinforce social boundaries and confer the power to exclude as well as dominate. Consistent with the educational system and "legitimate" culture alike, taste conceals its own material origins, perpetuating a fundamental "misrecognition" that accounts in large part for its symbolic efficacy.

The concept has been questioned for its relative silence on other "embodied" markers like race and gender, and on forms of cultural capital unrecognized by the dominant culture but still demonstrably of value in specific social environments. Its demarcation of "high" from mass culture also poses theoretical and methodological problems, even as it works to demystify the former: numerous empirical studies have refuted the centrality of what Bourdieu considers "elite cultural practices" to social reproduction, and the distinction is at any rate much harder to make in today's more densely mediated contexts. These shortcomings have by no means proven fatal to the concept, which remains a reference point in the humanities and social sciences. The neoliberal insistence on the capacity of the individual to invent and reinvent himself without limitations, despite increasingly insurmountable barriers to such self-actualization, ignores the extent to which capital in any of its forms predisposes some individuals more than others to success. In this context it is still a central task of these disciplines to discern the changing contours of cultural capital and emphasize its place in the reproduction of social hierarchies.

(*See also* Bourdieu, Pierre; Chapter 4, Marxism; Chapter 11, Cultural Studies; Chapter 17, Comparativisms; Chapter 19, Media Studies; *and* Taste)

Liane Tanguay, *University of Houston-Victoria (United States)*

Further Reading

Bourdieu, Pierre. *Distinction: A Social Critique of the Judgement of Taste* [1979]. Trans. Richard Nice. Cambridge: Harvard University Press, 1984.

Bourdieu, Pierre. "The Forms of Capital." In *Handbook of Theory and Research for the Sociology of Education*. Ed. John G. Richardson. New York: Greenwood Publishing Group, 1986. 241–58.

Cultural Critique

In the modern period, Immanuel Kant's *Critique of Judgement* (1790) marks the first major philosophical contribution to the idea that the aesthetic experience may be in some sort of opposition to everyday modes of experience, ways of thinking, and communicating. Kant's concept of "reflective judgment" was later described by Jean-François Lyotard as the "nerve of critical thought." Romanticism put Kant's philosophy into cultural practice, extending art to new everyday contents, experimenting with strange modes of presentation that would later be developed in more explicitly political inflections as defamiliarization (Bertolt Brecht), celebrating the value of the individual, merging with national liberation struggles, and protesting against the commodification of life and the industrialization of work that capitalism brought. Romanticism was the first political art movement of the modern era.

Yet the capacity of culture for critique of dominant social, political, and economic forces was very rapidly called into question by the extent to which cultural production was integrated into the social order. On the one hand, cultural production was industrialized; the "mass media" came under the formal control of large-scale capital that organized cultural work as closely as possible along the lines of the factory. Theodor Adorno warned against the conformity of the mind that the "culture industry" could produce and perhaps just as prophetically admonished intellectuals for the "tone of ironic toleration" they adopted in relation to it. Yet, artisanal modes of work persisted within the mass media because as Hans Magnus Enzensberger remarked in his essay "The Industrialisation of the Mind" (1962), while it can absorb anything, its weak point is that "it thrives on stuff which it cannot manufacture by itself." Even so, confronted by mass culture, cultural critique was often seen as best preserved in the specialized world of artistic movements, such as the various strands of modernism. Here though, while a greater distance from the power of commodification and the need to make a quick profit could be achieved, culture risked succumbing to the class stratification of art institutions, cultural knowledge, and minority audiences, as Bourdieu's work has shown.

Critique through culture requires that cultural practices and forms revivify themselves against institutional capture, whether by the culture industry or as Peter Bürger suggested in the case of the avant-garde, the art institutions. Cultural critique activates culture's capillary relationship with the social. Raymond Williams's notion of "structures of feeling" shows how cultural products have an extraordinary sensitivity to a broader hinterland of meanings and perspectives that official discourses are blind to. Reflective judgment need not mean bourgeois tranquility and complacency but opposition to the colonization of our communicative capacities by capitalist instrumentalism as for example in the work of Jürgen Habermas. Cultural critique brings us into contact with an array of Others that our impoverished public sphere has denigrated or repressed. It has a utopian charge prefiguring social transformation, as Fredric Jameson has found in popular film and literary modernism. Cultural critique is therefore fed by political critique and in the contemporary era, as with romanticism, anti-colonial and anti-imperialist struggles, out of which unequivocally great art and critique has emerged.

(*See also* Adorno, Theodor; Chapter 2, Structuralism and Semiotics; Chapter 4, Marxism; Chapter 27, Antitheory; Critique; Habermas, Jürgen; Kant, Immanuel; Marx, Karl; and Postcritique)

Michael Wayne, *Brunel University London (United Kingdom)*

Further Reading

Bloch, Ernst, Georg Lukács, Bertolt Brecht, Walter Benjamin, and Theodor Adorno. *Aesthetics and Politics* [1977]. Trans. Rodney Livingstone. London: Verso, 2007.

Eagleton, Terry. *The Idea of Culture*. London: Blackwell, 2000.

Wayne, Michael. *Red Kant: Aesthetics, Marxism and the Third Critique*. London: Bloomsbury, 2016.

Cultural Materialism

Cultural materialism stresses the materiality of cultural production, and thus its irreducibility to the economic "base" as one of its merely "superstructural" manifestations. It thus evades the disabling dualisms produced by "vulgar" Marxism's strict dichotomy between the "foundational" (base) and the "epiphenomenal" (superstructure) as well as the charge of "economic determinism" that such reductivism legitimately invites. Indeed, for cultural materialism, grounded in Raymond Williams's scrupulous reading of Marx's and Engels's key works, any serious engagement with cultural production had to conceive it as a form of material practice carried out in social and historical contexts by human agents, rather than a passive reflection of a fixed economic "infrastructure." Thus culture does not "reflect" relations of production, since it *is* production, and historical materialism, derived from Marxist political economy, must allow for the theorization of its "specificities."

Cultural materialism thus not only refutes the charge of reductivism but complicates the question of determinism itself, replacing mechanistic causality with a more nuanced understanding of "determination" as entailing the dynamic interaction of "pressures" and "limits" whose influence is observable within the sphere of culture. In this model, cultural production is irreducibly social and therefore enmeshed in, without being fully subordinate to, relations of production. In fact, Williams's own emphasis was on indeterminacy or "multiaccentuality," a term drawn from V. N. Volosinov's *Marxism and the Philosophy of Language* (1929). Strikingly, Williams's argument was that the difficulty with mainstream Marxism is not that it is "too" materialist (as critics claim) but rather that, by relegating "culture" to some abstract, intangible, and predetermined realm, it is not "materialist enough." It follows that as a form of material practice, cultural production forms a terrain of contestation in the struggle between capital and labor that may be "won," in specific instances, by one side or the other but that is never merely passive or reflective.

Unlike much of the "New Materialism," which retains some of its categories under a different rubric but without always granting it due credit, cultural materialism retains a place for agency in a world created, as Marx and Engels themselves insisted, by human beings. Rather than a focus on "affect," as the newer materialisms insist, or on the obdurate resistance of the material to the symbolic order, the concept of the "structure of feeling"—a central term in the cultural materialist lexicon—emphasizes a dimension of lived experience that is, like capitalism itself, inherently contradictory, but through which affective tensions can make manifest, if only obliquely, the possibility that things might always be otherwise.

Cultural materialism became a foundational concept in cultural studies—a discipline whose virtually unimpeded institutionalization, as Stuart Hall anxiously surmised, might neutralize its critical force. Nonetheless, as neoliberal logics insinuate themselves ever more completely into the warp and woof of linguistic and cultural production as well as the affective investments they enjoin, cultural materialism and its priorities may now be more relevant than ever.

(*See also* Agency; Base and Superstructure; Chapter 4, Marxism; Chapter 11, Cultural Studies; *and* Williams, Raymond)

Liane Tanguay, *University of Houston-Victoria (United States)*

Further Reading
Williams, Raymond. *Marxism and Literature*. New York: Oxford University Press, 1977.

Cultural Studies

Cultural Studies was established as a discipline at Birmingham University's Centre for Contemporary Cultural Studies in the 1960s and flourished under Stuart Hall's leadership from 1969. Its starting point is a broad, "anthropological" definition of culture as what Raymond Williams called "the relationships between elements in a whole way of life" and the patterns formed by those relationships; this way of formulating the concept seemed to radically disable the normative value systems that underpin traditional aesthetics. Yet, as many later critics have argued, this critical move remained incomplete, and in many ways Williams's work remained hostage to older accounts of culture, from Johann Gottfried Herder to F. R. Leavis, that see cultures (in the plural) as particularized expressions of the coherence of organic communities.

At the same time, Williams's broadening of the concept of culture to include the practices and institutions of everyday life opened up a rather different set of questions about how the economic and political spheres of successive English social formations are culturally embedded; how the "way of life" coincides with its cultural expression. For Stuart Hall, by contrast, the central question is much more urgently political: how is the political domination of one class secured culturally—and, more directly, how is the hegemony of the British ruling class secured by means of those cultural forms that the "popular" classes have made their own?

Popular culture—the tabloid press, television and the movies, talkback radio, popular music, sport, the world of consumer goods, shared cultures of talk and recreation and dress—is one of the crucial domains in which this struggle of values is negotiated; in the contest between what Hall calls "the power bloc" and "the people," popular culture is not expressive either of a popular will or of ruling-class values but is, rather, the *ground* on which a tension, negotiation, and accommodation of values take place, and thus on which popular values may be articulated to the political interests of the dominant class.

At the heart of the cultural studies project in its early phases is a conception of cultural practices as ways of dealing actively and often subversively with texts and institutions; members of a culture are not "cultural dupes" but seek to shape texts and institutions to their own ends in ways that embody values that may differ from those of the dominant culture. And if popular culture is a site of struggle rather than an expression of fixed class values, then it follows that it has no inherent meaning or value. The meaning of a cultural form or institution or event is given rather by the fields of practice and value with which it is articulated at any one moment in time.

What is distinctive about the project of cultural studies is its politically driven engagement with the "ordinary" cultural forms of the present, together with a methodological commitment to understanding the social relations with which those forms are articulated and which give them their historically particular value. It explores the social life of cultural forms: their use by ordinary people in the construction of everyday life.

(*See also* Chapter 11, Cultural Studies; Chapter 16, Pop Culture; Chapter 19, Media Studies; Chapter 27, Antitheory; Culture; Hall, Stuart; Pop Culture; *and* Williams, Raymond)

John Frow, *University of Sydney (Australia)*

Further Reading

Grossberg, Lawrence. *Cultural Studies in the Future Tense*. Durham: Duke University Press, 2010.

Turner, Graeme. *British Cultural Studies: An Introduction* [1990]. London: Routledge, 1996.

Culture

In his book *Keywords* (1976), Raymond Williams calls *culture*, "one of the two or three most complicated words in the English language." When Williams's working-class students (c. 1968) talked of culture, they usually meant something along the lines of what E. D. Hirsch and the conservative side of the US "culture wars" meant by the term. In his 1987 manifesto/book *Cultural Literacy*, cataloging the references "every American should know," Hirsch says parents and teachers should educate their children and students on this culture since it forms what Pierre Bourdieu had recently called "cultural capital." A utilitarian, Hirsch is often read through an elitist lens, colored in part by the near contemporaneous publication of Allan Bloom's *The Closing of the American Mind* (1987), which made this argument for the importance of culture as "high culture" more polemically. Bloom's reading of culture is nearly identical to that of Matthew Arnold, who describes culture as "sweetness and light" or "the best that has been thought and said" and is a frequent touchstone for the definition of culture as "high culture."

In contrast, for many people today, culture means popular culture, by which they mean the books, TV programs, magazines, movies, video games, and now social media that circulate widely. In other words, the products of what Adorno and Horkheimer termed, "The Culture Industry." Williams, Richard Hoggart, and others in the field of cultural studies intervened by asking scholars to take this kind of culture seriously: to think of these as culture and study them with the earnestness of the "high culture" Arnold lauded.

But at an everyday level, Hoggart, Williams, and Hirsch—whose list also included the southern dance The Charleston—converge in their conception of culture as something "common" in that it was the substance of a "community," widely produced and shared as part of a "whole way of life."

E. P. Thompson, on the other hand, argued it should be understood as a "whole way of struggle," noting that the materials valorized by the hegemonic order would likely be the culture of the victors. Other scholars like Paul Gilroy, Francis Mulhern, and Nick Couldry criticized Williams for his provincial, nearly racist understanding that culture was the product of "long experience" rather than legal citizenship alone. Yet, Williams's description of the experience of culture was not necessarily an endorsement, but an attempt to understand what he calls a particular structure of feeling. The defensive, nay "conservative," concept of culture both he and Thompson describe is a response to a global fragmentation of the ideology of the community and/as nation-state— an ideology that, as Williams himself notes, was long bound up with the nineteenth century strain of the concept, as found in Herder and elsewhere.

In his book, *Culture in the Age of Three Worlds* (2004), Michael Denning says culture as a concept emerges only under capitalism. In the modernist era, culture "named those places where the commodity did not yet rule." This helps explain the contradiction of using the word "culture" to describe the profane elements of the everyday life of both the metropolitan working classes and the peripheral precapitalist societies of early anthropologists, as well as the "arts, leisure, and unproductive luxury consumption" of the metropolitan elites. In contrast, "the postmodern concept of culture was the result of the generalization of the commodity form throughout the realm the modernists had called culture. . . . Far from marking the places outside capital's empire, culture was itself an economic realm, encompassing the mass media, advertising, and the production and distribution of knowledge."

The postmodern collapse of culture and capital, local and the global, continues apace,

particularly with the rise of what José Van Dijck calls "the culture of connectivity," where our very sociality and interpersonal relationships are commodified by corporate platforms like Google and Facebook. George Yudice documents the ways the authentically lived, "long experience" of culture in the developing world has often been replaced by an outward-facing notion of "culture as a resource," where the performance of local culture is crafted to fit with the preconceptions of global tourists. Resistance to so-called cultural appropriation reinstates new forms of essentialist identity, arguing over who has the right to its profitable exploitation and, in some cases, ownership by emergent forms of intellectual property. And the rise of populist movements, from the left, right, Christian, Hindu, and Muslim, have attempted to reinstate cultural nationalisms even in the face of this collapse. Williams said culture was a noun of process: the process continues.

(*See also* Chapter 11, Cultural Studies; Chapter 13, Race and Postcolonial Studies; Chapter 16, Pop Culture; Chapter 22, Identity Studies; Culture; Hall, Stuart; Pop Culture; *and* Williams, Raymond)

Sean Johnson Andrews, *Columbia College Chicago (United States)*

Further Reading

Adorno, Theodor W. *The Culture Industry: Selected Essays on Mass Culture*. Second ed. New York: Routledge, 2001.

Denning, Michael. *Culture in the Age of Three Worlds*. New York: Verso, 2004.

Williams, Raymond. *Resources of Hope: Culture, Democracy, Socialism*. Ed. Robin Gable. New York: Verso, 1989.

Yudice, George. *The Expediency of Culture: Uses of Culture in the Global Era*. Durham: Duke University Press, 2003.

Culture Industry (*See* Adorno, Theodor W.;
Authenticity; Chapter 4, Marxism; Cultural
Critique; Culture; Seriality; Surveillance;
and Symbolic Agency)

Culture Wars

In 1992, at the Republican National Convention, defeated presidential candidate, Patrick
J. Buchanan, offered a rousing speech urging
the three million Americans who voted for
him to support and vote in November for the
nominee, George H. W. Bush against eventual winner, William J. Clinton. The election,
Buchanan explained,

> is about what we stand for as Americans.
> There is a religious war going on in our
> country for the soul of America. It is a cultural war, as critical to the kind of nation we
> will one day be as was the Cold War itself.

Battling for the soul of America were—and
are—the Republican Party and the Democrat Party, and the lines dividing the two
parties and the nation were then—as now—
seemingly clear: against or in favor of a
woman's right to an abortion; of equal rights
and treatment of women, racial minorities, and homosexuals; of the preservation
of the environment; of immigration, multiculturalism, and affirmative action; of a
globalized economy; of nationalism, patriotism, and the military; of secularization in
social institutions.

But as with many historical designations,
the "culture wars" is at once helpful and problematic, because the "culture wars" oversimplifies what it aims to encompass, reducing
complicated issues and alliances to binary
oppositions, for and against. In fact, in the
1980s and 1990s, conflict emerged within the
warring parties, and sometimes, if rarely, partisans of the Left and the Right joined forces,
making strange bedfellows. The most striking

example of the latter was the alliance in
debates about pornography between religious
conservatives, including attorney general of
the United States, Edwin Meese, and anti-pornography feminists, such as Andrea Dworkin
and Catharine Mackinnon. Examples of the
former are numerous and indeed constitutive
of the warring parties and of the war itself:
extremists on both sides fuel the anger of the
other, and sometimes alienate moderates, too.
On the Left, Leonard Jeffries, Jr., unhappy
with black and white liberals' promotion of
race as a social construction, offered a version of Afrocentrism that excoriated whites as
irredeemable, peoples who stole everything,
including ideas, from Africa. Too, the Left's
new focus on culture and identity loosened
a prior focus on economic protectionism,
resulting in a slow embrace of free trade and
neoliberalism. On the Right, neoconservatives upended traditional conservative thought
and policy; neoconservatives also gave intellectual ballast to conservative attacks on the
counterculture; at the same time, populist conservatives and religious conservatives gained
traction via Pat Buchanan's fiery rhetoric.
Further, that the neoconservatives were former liberal intellectuals, many of them Jewish, such as Daniel Bell, Irving Kristol, and
Norman Podhoretz, who moved to the Right
during the 1960s and 1970s, demonstrates the
flux and the galvanizing intensity of social
change during the period and throughout the
decades following. Such moves demonstrate
that Left and Right shift and realign through
time, thus making the "culture wars" less
a curious anomaly than a constant of social
and political life that erupts occasionally into
heightened importance.

(*See also* Chapter 25, University Studies;
Chapter 27, Antitheory; *and* Culture)

Sharon O'Dair, *University of Alabama*
(United States)

Further Reading

Hunter, James Davison. *Culture Wars: The Struggle to Define America*. New York: Basic Books, 1991.

Williams, Rhys H., ed. *Cultural Wars in American Politics: Critical Reviews of a Popular Myth*. New York: Routledge, 1997.

Cyberculture

The term *cyberculture* encompasses a diverse array of cultural formations and social interactions around digital communications technologies. Cyberculture includes an ever-expanding range of theoretical perspectives, subcultures, and discourse communities. Because of the ubiquity of networked communications technologies, cyberculture studies have intersections with almost every discipline of critical and cultural theory, which now must contend with the fact that digital technologies directly or indirectly affect almost every facet of human existence. Theorists of cyberculture seek to understand and track the influence of such intersections of humanity with digital technologies across a variety of technological, philosophical, sociological, psychological, and cultural registers.

The earliest beginnings of what would later become cyberculture coincide with the development of networked computers and communications technologies. While cyberculture, generally speaking, can be traced to the beginnings of modern digital computing in the 1940s, scholars generally situate the origins of contemporary cyberculture with the explosive growth of personal computing in the 1970s and 1980s. This period of technological growth connected cyberculture with the ideals of personal liberty and individualism coming out of cultural movements in the 1960s, joining these ideals from the 1960s to the proliferation of the personal computer.

As computers made their way into homes, networked computing reached a price point where it became easily available to consumers, and in the 1990s, the public became largely aware of cyberculture, as the World Wide Web became a household technology.

The web represents one well-known facet of the deterritorialized terrain of *cyberspace*, a term coined in William Gibson's science-fiction classic, *Neuromancer* (1984), referring to the vast communications networks of the internet as well as related technologies that mediate human-computer interaction. Since Gibson's use, the term has left science fiction and now connotes any application or process that includes computers and communications networks, including the internet, mobile device apps, virtual reality, augmented reality, and innumerable other intersections of human consciousness with computational technologies.

The pivotal figure of cyberspace is the *cyborg*, a hybrid of technology and human that exceeds the potentialities of both. Cyborgs can be material, literally human beings enhanced by the implantation or augmentation of the human body with technology, but they are also considered to be virtual beings, advanced by the access to vast digital databases of knowledge and algorithmic search engines. Many theorists of cyberculture argue that everyone living on the planet who has contact with digital computing and interconnected communications technology is already a cyborg.

Cyberculture and its key figure, the cyborg, have long been configured as potentially liberatory spaces and identities, in line with feminist philosophy that informs much of the writing on cyborgs and hybrid technological subjectivities. In postmillennial moment, as cyberspace is increasingly dominated by international corporations and panoptic technologies that report on every interaction, the liberatory potentialities of cyberculture become increasingly difficult to argue, as almost all behavior on the networks is quantified and turned against the user in the form of targeted advertising and manipulative technological interactivity.

(*See also* Chapter 20, Digital Humanities; *and* Cyborg)

Jeffrey A. Sartain, *University of Houston-Victoria (United States)*

Further Reading

Bell, David. *An Introduction to Cybercultures*. New York: Routledge, 2001.

Haraway, Donna. *Simians, Cyborgs, and Women: The Reinvention of Nature*. Second ed. London: Free Association Books, 1996.

Johnson, Annemarie, and Darren Tofts. *Prefiguring Cybercultures: An Intellectual History*. Cambridge: MIT Press, 2004.

Kennedy, Barbara M., and David Bell. *The Cybercultures Reader*. Second ed. New York: Routledge, 2007.

Turner, Fred. *From Counterculture to Cyberculture: Stewart Brand, the Whole Earth Network, and the Rise of Digital Utopianism*. Chicago: University of Chicago Press, 2008.

Cybernetics

Though the term now seems synonymous with computer culture, virtual reality, and robotics, *cybernetics* is important to cultural theory in ways that are both more precise and more wide-ranging than its common uses might suggest. Cybernetics' pioneering study of self-controlling mechanisms influenced several post-structuralist thinkers, including Jacques Lacan, Jacques Derrida, and Michel Foucault. It coincided with these figures' critiques of Western, humanistic subjectivity, and it offered models for how agency, language, and learning could arise through purely mechanistic, decentered, and nonrational systems.

Cybernetics was born in the immediate post–Second World War period. Named by Norbert Wiener, a mathematician, philosopher, and engineer, cybernetics was conceived of as the interdisciplinary study of "control and communication in animal and machine," as Wiener wrote. A central concept was that of the circular, causal system—a system that, solely through the interrelationships of its components, can act, absorb information from the environment, change itself because of that information, absorb more information, and act again. For cybernetics, information is the force that allows for control and action. Yet information is to some extent contentless. It is defined in mathematical, statistical terms— for instance, as the distributions of 1s and 0s in computer code, the difference between a transistor's "on" or "off" state, or significant statistical deviations from random noise.

As Wiener's reference to "animal and machine" suggests, cybernetics views all information-exchanging systems equally, whether those systems are living or nonliving, large or small scale. The components that absorb and react to inputs can be transistors, neurons, groups of cells; they can also be whole machines or entire human beings. All of these components act in similar ways according to the cyberneticians. They self-organize according to recursive patterns of inputs and outputs, with those patterns, inputs, and outputs able to be represented diagrammatically or mathematically. One major implication of this position is that the difference between "mind" and "machine" is no difference at all. Thus, cognitive science, which has its roots in cybernetics, began from the position that the mind is structured like a machine, while the science of artificial intelligence is similarly indebted to the cybernetic principle that machines can act identically to minds.

During the period of its greatest activity, from the mid-1940s to the mid-1970s, cybernetics elaborated a philosophical position that was similar in its antihumanism to the ideas of Derrida, Lacan, Deleuze and Guattari, and other post-structuralists. Indeed, as Lydia Liu and Céline Lafontaine have shown, prominent French post-structuralists had contacts with scientists, engineers, mathematicians, and philosophers associated with the cybernetic movement, and they make use of concepts borrowed from cyberneticians. Like post-structuralism, cybernetics rejects the specialness of humanity and any notion that subjectivity has metaphysical properties. Human selves, along with human cultures, can be understood as made up of systemic elements that take on different states based on inputs or changes in other parts of the system. These changes constitute information, which itself is nothing but difference from statistical noise. The cybernetic universe thus appears somewhat like a system of differences with no positive values, to use a formulation important to structuralist linguistics.

Cybernetics' influence on contemporary culture is obvious, as it is a source of content in philosophy as well as literature and film, with countless works drawing on cybernetic visions of self-regulating computer networks, robots, and devices. Its effect on contemporary literary criticism is most clearly felt in cognitive criticism, as cognitive science was originally an outgrowth of cybernetics' conceptualization of the mind as an information-processing machine. Yet, with its antihumanistic rejection of metaphysics, its envisioning of the primacy of dispersed, decentered systems, and its equivalence of the living and nonliving, it has deep affinities with important trends in critical theory, including actor network theory, thing theory,

and ecocriticism, as well as several other strains of post-structuralist thought.

(*See also* Affect; Chapter 9, Deconstruction; Chapter 22, Identity Studies; Chapter 26, Affect Studies; Cyborg; *and* Machine)

Amanpal Garcha, *Ohio State University* *(United States)*

Further Reading

Boden, Margaret. *Mind as Machine: A History of Cognitive Science*. Oxford: Oxford University Press, 2006.

Dupuy, Jean-Pierre. *The Mechanization of the Mind: On the Origins of Cognitive Science*. Princeton: Princeton University Press, 2000.

Lafontaine, Céline. "The Cybernetic Matrix of 'French Theory.'" *Theory, Culture & Society* 24.5 (2007): 27–46.

Liu, Lydia H. "The Cybernetic Unconscious: Rethinking Lacan, Poe, and French Theory." *Critical Inquiry* 36 (2010): 288–320.

Cyborg

The first use of the term "cyborg" in its critical and theoretical sense occurs in Donna J. Haraway's article "A Manifesto for Cyborgs: Science, Technology, and Socialist-Feminism in the Late Twentieth Century" (1985). As Haraway explains by way of the word's etymology, "A cyborg is a cybernetic organism, a hybrid of machine and organism, a creature of social reality as well as a creature of fiction" that enables critical challenges to the orthodoxies of disciplinary thinking, the social, cultural, and ideological situation of women, and the rift between intellectual life and political action. This essay first appeared in the US quarterly journal *Socialist Review*; it was subsequently reprinted in Haraway's *Simians, Cyborgs, and Women: The Reinvention of Nature* (1991), a book in which she links the concept of the cyborg to others informing her research across the disciplines of biology, literature, women's studies, and politics. The essay has also featured in numerous anthologies since the early 1990s, constituting a foundational text in a wide-ranging theoretical field.

Before its critical usage, cyborg was a term in science and, soon after, science fiction. It was coined in 1960 by medical researchers Manfred E. Clynes and Nathan S. Kline, who proposed that future astronautics would entail altering humans through technology to function in space for extended periods. Drawing on the original sense of the word "cybernetic," itself a neologism first used in 1948 by computing pioneer Norbert Wiener to designate the technological control of any system, Clynes and Kline defined cyborgs as "self-regulating man-machine systems." Through computer control, for example, a device could oxygenate the human body and replace respiration, obviating the need to transport an atmosphere. The idea of technologically enhanced humans was then fictionalized in movies such as *Cyborg 2087* (1966) and TV shows such as *Lost in Space* (1965–68). Science-fiction writers of the so-called New Wave of the 1960s and 1970s, among them Philip K. Dick and Samuel R. Delany, raised philosophical questions of how interactions with technology alter the notion of the human: their fiction speculates on how machines affect genetic composition, mental experience, and social organization. Dick constructed plots around the generation of alternate realities, suggesting that no part of the human world remains untouched in the age of all-encompassing technology.

Aligning her work with this genealogy, Haraway credits as sources the work of Delany and other feminist science-fiction writers, namely Anne McCaffrey, Joanna Russ, James Tiptree Jr. (Alice Bradley Sheldon), Vonda McIntire, and Octavia Butler, all of whom have challenged the binarity of gender. Haraway notes Butler's *Xenogenesis* series, in which an extraterrestrial race offers humans genetic modifications that free them from the constraints of gender, sexuality, race, and social stratification. Haraway, a trained biologist, shows a special interest in criticizing the tendency in feminism to distrust technology; she instead examines it for transformative potential. At the same time as Haraway's essay first appeared, the science-fiction genre of cyberpunk emerged, especially in the work of William Gibson, Bruce Sterling, and Pat Cadigan. Gibson's novel *Neuromancer* (1984), which introduced the word "cyberspace," presents a fully simulated world with both utopian and dystopian aspects. Closely related to cyberpunk, and similarly stemming from New Wave science fiction, is what critics have termed "cyborg cinema," whose staples are human-machine hybrids and artificial realities. In movies such as James Cameron's *The Terminator* (1984, with sequels in 1991, 2003, 2015, and a TV series in 2008–09), David Cronenberg's *Videodrome* (1983) and *eXistenZ* (1999), and the Wachowski sisters' *The Matrix* (1999, with two sequels in 2003), the dystopian aspects of cyborg technology tend to reign, confronted by a hero who may or may not succeed at mastering its transformative capacities.

These currents in science-fiction literature and cinema have attracted the attention of critics building not only on Haraway's idea of the cyborg but also on the "biopolitics" of Michel Foucault and concepts formulated by Gilles Deleuze and Félix Guattari such as the "body without organs." In light of interactions between human bodies and their natural, social, political, and technological environments, investigations in this vein have questioned the idea of the human being as autonomous moral and epistemological agent, prevalent in Western thought since the eighteenth century. Several scholars, most prominently N. Katherine Hayles, Scott Bukatman, and Rosi Braidotti, have offered syntheses of these lines of inquiry, elaborating "posthumanism" as a major outgrowth of cyborg thinking.

(*See also* Chapter 22, Identity Studies; Chapter 24, Posthumanism; Cyberculture; Haraway, Donna; Machine; *and* Transhumanism)

Hassan Melehy, *University of North Carolina, Chapel Hill (United States)*

Further Reading

Bukatman, Scott. *Terminal Identity: The Virtual Subject in Postmodern Science Fiction.* Durham: Duke University Press, 1993.

Haraway, Donna J. *Manifestly Haraway.* Minneapolis: University of Minnesota Press, 2016.

Hayles, N. Katherine. *How We Became Posthuman: Virtual Bodies in Cybernetics, Literature, and Informatics.* Chicago: University of Chicago Press, 1999.

D

Debt

Since the economic crash of 2008, debt has become a major topic for literary and cultural theorists. At the university level, it has become a topic of interest because of rising student debt, which has increased fifteenfold in the United States since 1980, and 84 percent since 2008, with total student debt in the United States currently set at $1.2 trillion. However, rising levels of debt are not only a university problem, but also societal and global concerns. At the national level, 75 percent of people in the United States have some form of debt, and the gross debt worldwide, that is the combined debt of public and private liabilities, has been set at $152 trillion dollars, with the International Monetary Fund reporting that global debt had reached 225 percent of world gross domestic product.

Andrew Ross has termed the kind of society resulting from the recent economic crash and our ubiquitous debt a "creditocracy," a society where everyone is up to their neck in debt that cannot be repaid, and Jeffrey R. Di Leo, Peter Hitchcock, and Sophia McClennen argue that we are now living in the "debt age," an age where debt is not simply an external hindrance, but rather defines the very nature of man. Whereas philosophers from Adam Smith through Friedrich Nietzsche and Michel Foucault have convinced generations of thinkers to consider man in general as *homo economicus,* the rise of the debt age has resulted in a new type of man, *homo debitor,*

a designation coined by Maurizio Lazzarato in *The Making of Indebted Man* (2012). In this work as well as work by Ross, Michael Hardt and Antonio Negri, Richard Dienst, and David Graeber, debt is shown to be an internal dynamic of neoliberalism. As such, much of the critique of debt is also a critique of neoliberalism. One of the more controversial versions of this critique comes from Graeber, who in *Debt: The First 5,000 Years,* argues "paying one's debts is not the essence of morality." Graeber, like many commentators on the debt age, struggles to find a principled way to resist debt. His own solution involves both exposing the principle of repaying our debts as a "flagrant lie" and seeking an alternate economy not founded upon bourgeois ideologies of exchange.

Nevertheless, the global debt resistance movement by and large follows broadly established moral principles. The burden here though is not just on the debtor, but also on the creditor. For example, creditors who provide loans to people who clearly cannot pay back these loans should be held accountable for their predatory behavior. However, when it is determined that such loans have been afforded, mercy needs to be meted out with justice in remediating this predatory debt.

Much recent work on debt explores the ways that contemporary literature and culture have responded to rising debt and the economic collapse of 2008. Work here varies though as to whether there is a moral obligation to repay debt. Other work examines the variety of connections debt has with other areas of theoretical interest such as human rights, materialism, education, labor, democracy, pedagogy, youth, financial literacy, citizenship, and even, zombies. The common thread in most of this work though is that the debt age is one to be resisted and overcome—rather than embraced and intensified.

(*See also* Chapter 25, University Studies; Finance; Neoliberalism; Political Economy; *and* University)

Jeffrey R. Di Leo, *University of Houston-Victoria (United States)*

Further Reading

Di Leo, Jeffrey R., Peter Hitchcock, and Sophia McClennen, eds. *The Debt Age.* New York: Routledge, 2018.

Graeber, David. *Debt: The First Five Thousand Years.* New York: Melville House, 2011.

Lazzarato, Maurizio. *The Making of Indebted Man* [2011]. Trans. Joshua David Gordon. New York: Semiotext(e), 2012.

Ross, Andrew. *Creditocracy and the Case for Debt Refusal.* New York: OR Books, 2013.

Decolonization

Decolonization is associated commonly with the political end of modern imperialism in Africa, Asia, the Middle East, the Pacific, and certain territories of the Americas during the three decades after the Second World War. In the period from 1944 to 1975, says Aijaz Ahmed in *In Theory* (1991), anti-colonial resistance movements produced "the unstoppable dynamic of decolonizations" that brought down colonial regimes, from the "dissolution of the British Indian Empire in 1947" through "the independence of Ghana in 1957 and the decolonization of Algeria in 1962."

A contradictory process and transformative period in world history, decolonization marks the wholesale collapse of colonial regimes and the transfer of power to postcolonial nation-states, as well as the formation of the Third World and the strategic reordering of global politics in terms of the emerging Cold War rivalry between the United States and the Soviet Union. The United Nations General Assembly confirmed the discursive hegemony of decolonization when it adopted Resolution 1514 (XV) of December 14, 1960, "on the Granting of Independence to Colonial Countries and Peoples." Nevertheless, in the context of the Cold War, Western European powers and the United States sought to roll back, undermine, or contain anti-colonial revolutionary movements led by socialists and communists, as was the case in Indochina, where the Viet Minh defeat of the French colonial army in 1954 was followed by the US war in Vietnam (1955–75).

In some regions, a strategic decolonization allowed the colonial authority to withdraw, yet retain significant influence, for instance in Senegal, which achieved nominal independence from France through a transfer of power agreement in 1960. Elsewhere, anti-colonial movements fought wars of independence against colonial regimes. The Algerian National Liberation Front struggled against French rule (1954–62) and the Mozambique Liberation Front battled an entrenched Portuguese colonialism (1964–75). For Frantz Fanon, author of *The Wretched of the Earth*, "Decolonization is always a violent phenomenon." In other regions, such as the Indian subcontinent, Palestine, Yemen, and Indochina, territorial partition, military occupation and/or protracted regional conflict disrupted or permanently deferred decolonization. As Fredric Jameson observes in "Periodizing the '60s" (1984), "Decolonization historically went hand in hand with neo-colonialism."

Despite the importance of territorial decolonization, countering the profound effects of colonialism demands persistent opposition to the neocolonial relation grounded in the languages, legacies, and laws of empire. In *Decolonising the Mind* (1986), Ngũgĩ wa Thiong'o asserts that "my writing in Gĩkũyũ language, a Kenyan language, an African language, is part and parcel of the anti-imperialist struggles of Kenyan and African peoples. . . . I want (Kenyans) to transcend colonial alienation." Similarly, Barbara Harlow points out in *Resistance Literature* (1987) that opposition to colonialism and imperialism is also a struggle over the historical and cultural record." Transcending colonial alienation and struggling over the historical and cultural record evoke the intellectual work often associated with the concept of *decoloniality*. For Walter D. Mignolo and Arturo Escobar in *Globalization and the Decolonial Option* (2010), decoloniality proposes a fundamental epistemological break with colonial forms of knowledge in contrast with the political framework of decolonization.

(*See also* Chapter 10, Feminism; *and* Chapter 13, Race and Postcolonial Studies)

Salah D. Hassan, *Michigan State University (United States)*

Further Reading

Ahmed, Aijaz. *In Theory: Classes, Nations, Literatures*. New York: Verso, 1991.

Fanon, Frantz. *The Wretched of the Earth* [1961]. Trans. Constance Farrington. New York: Grove Press, 1963.

Harlow, Barbara. *Resistance Literature*. New York: Methuen Press, 1987.

Jameson, Fredric. "Periodizing the '60s." *Social Text* 9/10 (1984): 178–209.

Mignolo, Walter D., and Arturo Escobar, eds. *Globalization and the Decolonial Option*. London: Routledge, 2010.

Ngũgĩ wa Thiong'o. *Decolonising the Mind: The Politics of Language in African Literature*. Nairobi: East African Educational Publishers, 1986.

Deconstruction

In "Letter to a Japanese Friend," Jacques Derrida discusses the problem of translating the term *deconstruction*. The translatability of this word raises questions of the stability of its meaning or definition across languages and idioms. Since deconstruction, as a "good" old French word, is also Derrida's novel adaptation of Martin Heidegger's German term *Destruktion*, the word is embroiled in translational issues from the outset. Deconstruction endures the limits of translatability—its various border-crossings are always marked by an untranslatable remainder—and yet it is always "in" translation, calling for translation, without "pure" origin. For Derrida, such problems do not merely affect the possibility of deconstruction's definition, but they are therefore at stake in the very movement or operation of deconstruction. When we recall Derrida's suggestion that the secondarization of writing in relation to speech is constitutive of metaphysics itself, which valorizes the spoken word as the self-expression of living presence, it is unsurprising that a deconstruction of the metaphysical tradition (that which determines being *as* presence) cannot but deeply question the possibility of a pure "word" that is beyond translation and never in need it. Translation is not, therefore, a problem that deconstruction may overcome or dominate, but is instead one it must affirm.

The French sense of the term implies formal, mechanical or architectural disassemblage. However, Derrida reminds us that deconstruction does not restrict itself to the critical analysis of structures or systems.

Rather, the deconstructive thinking of *dif-férance*, trace, supplement, arche-writing, etc., remains highly receptive to an asystematic reserve, a non-present remainder or heterogeneous other which exceeds all structures and systems even while making them possible. Deconstruction is thus not, as might be supposed, negative, nihilistic, or destructive, but instead it affirms an inappropriable difference as that which may yet come to transform whatever we inherit. Alongside the question of translatability that affects the word from the outset, the constitutive importance of this asystematic reserve for deconstruction means that it cannot be expressed in terms of a simple self-identity or, therefore, be taken as anything more than an improper term or "nickname." For similar reasons, deconstruction—precisely in its rigorous attention to the asystematic supplement of all systems, structures, or methodologies—is not to be confused with a plain *method* or *system* of inquiry. Nor may deconstruction be properly called a form of *analysis* or *critique*, since "analysis" typically aims to uncover an essential ground, basis, or root, while "critique" implies a standpoint of stable, critical distance from which the "object" may be properly identified and evaluated as such. By way of its thinking of the supplement, trace, dissemination, *différance*, arche-writing, and so on, deconstruction questions both the unity and self-identity of a "ground" and, relatedly, the possibility of a secure extraterritorial (subject) position. Thus, deconstruction isn't reducible to the idea of an *act* or intention in view of an "object," since deconstruction questions the very *grounds* of both subject and object. It is already at work in the play of *différance* that both constitutes and exceeds such "grounds" operating as the basis of every system, structure, form, or identity. In seeking to affirm a radically heterogeneous and inappropriable other, deconstruction is,

too, at the limits of philosophy. It therefore puts at issue the third-person present indicative and the predicative or propositional form of language: another reason why the question of its own definition is also the question of definition in general.

(*See also* Archi-trace; Chapter 1, Early Theory; Chapter 5, Poststructuralism; Chapter 9, Deconstruction; Chapter 27, Antitheory; Critique; Derrida, Jacques; de Man, Paul; Différance; Event; Metaphysics; Origin; Presence; Spivak, Gayatri; Supplement; *and* Writing)

Simon Morgan Wortham, *Kingston University (United Kingdom)*

Further Reading

Bennington, Geoffrey, and Jacques Derrida. *Jacques Derrida*. Trans. Geoffrey Bennington. Chicago: University of Chicago Press, 1992.

Derrida, Jacques. "Letter to a Japanese Friend." In *Psyche: Inventions of the Other, Volume II* [2003]. Eds. Peggy Kamuf and Elizabeth Rottenberg. Stanford: Stanford University Press, 2008.

Derrida, Jacques. *Positions* [1972]. Trans. Alan Bass. Chicago: University of Chicago Press, 1981.

Deferred Action

Deferred Action (Nachträglichkeit) is a somewhat illusive term in the history of psychoanalysis. Sigmund Freud coins it, but does not clearly define it in any of his works. Jacques Lacan makes great use of the term, to both define it, à la his reading of Freud's work, and to use it to develop his own. The term itself is only defined precisely by Laplanche and Pontalis in their 1967 work, to which psychoanalysis really owes its understanding.

Freud's basic concept of deferred action is that the unconscious revises a past event, of which the subject had little understanding at the time, once the subject has gained understanding that enlightens that past event with psychic importance. The unconscious after the fact dreams the origin of a current situation. There is some indication that deferred action can also be taken in the form of revision when an event is too traumatic to be incorporated and is acted upon so as to be manageable for the ego. Such action through revision happens in a process akin to dream work, wherein a contemporary event becomes like a day's residue, providing the visuals through which repressed material returns. It is, as Lacan helps readers to understand, linked to psychosexual development as a subject experiences an event which later takes on traumatic force as the infant matures, hence the original action taken in that experience is deferred. A perfect example of this complex notion in Freud is that of the deferred guilt, self-punishment, and adoption of a defensive inhibition long after the fact, as in the original primal scenario of the murdered father and the sons establishing the law after the fact that both elevates the father into a god and makes expressions of sexuality toward females of the tribe taboo. The subsequent maintenance of the incest taboo would then be an instance of deferred action, an internalized, revisionary respect for the traumatically violated law.

Freud theorizes, and Lacan defends and expands, this explanation of deferred action, using the case of *The Wolf Man* (1904). In *The Wolf Man*, the infant witnesses the primal scene, but is unable to process it until it recurs in his dream at age four, at a time at which he is ready to link his memory to his Oedipal fantasies. Lacan uses this basis to attribute three processes to deferred action. For Lacan, deferred action gives credibility to the injunction against masturbation at the moment

of Oedipal crisis and the recognition of the difference between the anatomical sexes. He claims that it is only through deferred action in the Oedipal cycle that female genitalia become significant because before the imagined castration, there is no perception of anatomical difference.

Also, in the *Écrits*, apropos of the Wolf Man case, Lacan points out that the material which comprises the Real is that which is excluded from "primordial symbolization." For the Wolf Man, this is his witnessing of the primal scene which he misunderstands and defers. For Lacan the deferred action contains material that is extra, or that escapes the Symbolic. If such material is that which escapes representation by disavowal, it becomes part of the Real, making deferred action a necessary part of the journey to self-nomination.

(*See also* Chapter 7, Psychoanalytic Theory; Freud, Sigmund; Lacan, Jacques; Oedipus Complex; *and* Psychoanalysis)

Gina Masucci MacKenzie, *Holy Family University (United States)*

Further Reading
Freud, Sigmund. *The Wolfman and Other Cases*. Trans. Louise Adey Huish. New York: Penguin Classics, 2003.
Lacan, Jacques. *Écrits* [1966]. Trans. Bruce Fink. New York: Norton, 2007.

Deleuze, Gilles

Gilles Deleuze (1925–95) was a French philosopher who addressed a wide range of subjects in his many books, which include four influential works coauthored with Félix Guattari (*Anti-Oedipus* [1972], *Kafka: Toward a Minor Literature* [1975], *A Thousand Plateaus* [1980] and *What is Philosophy?* [1991]). His primary literary studies are *Proust and Signs* (1964; rev. 1970 and 1976), *Masochism: Coldness and Cruelty* (1967), *Kafka* (1975) and *Essays Critical and Clinical* (1993). Perhaps his best-known literary concept is that of minor literature, which he developed with Guattari in *Kafka*. Not to be confused with minority literature, minor literature entails a minor usage of language, one that may be found among ethnic minorities but also among other groups. In minor literature, Deleuze and Guattari bring together the modernist projects of politically engaged literature and avant-garde formal experimentation. Minor literature is immediately social and political; it engages and enunciates a collective voice; and it "deterritorializes" language. Minor writers deterritorialize language by discovering a foreign language within their own language, by making language stutter. In Kafka's works, Deleuze and Guattari find a minor usage of German, an ascetic reduction of vocabulary that lends a strangeness to the language. In *The Trial* that minor usage is deployed in a critical mapping of the machinery of the Austro-Hungarian legal bureaucracy, with the ultimate goal of disclosing both the diabolical powers of the future (fascism, Stalinism, American capitalism) and the possibilities for revolutionary transformation immanent within that bureaucracy.

Deleuze's main contributions to film theory are *Cinema 1: The Movement-Image* (1983) and *Cinema 2: The Time-Image* (1985). Combining concepts from Bergson and Peirce, Deleuze develops a taxonomy of cinematic images and signs that distinguishes a classic cinema of movement-images from a modern cinema of time-images. Eschewing a narrative-based approach to film, Deleuze argues that narrative is a secondary product of the shaping of images, which are immanent within an unformed signaletic matter imbued with various modulations—sensory (visual and sonic), kinetic, intensive, affective,

rhythmic, tonal, and verbal. The classic cinema's movement-images are regulated by the sensory-motor schema, which assures that all images may be assimilated within the coordinates of common sense space and time. The modern cinema's time-images, by contrast, disrupt the sensory-motor schema and present images of different kinds of time, including crystal-images, which consist of mirror reflections of virtual and actual images that oscillate within an infinitesimal time; sheets of the past, in which various memory spaces coexist in a virtual past; and peaks of the present, in which contradictory present moments circulate without temporal prioritization.

Deleuze's most discussed contribution to cultural theory is the concept of control societies, which he sees as the successors to Foucault's disciplinary societies. In control societies, power relations are no longer site-specific, but thoroughly dispersed across society and immanent within social organization. Power operates via constant controlling modulations of a seamless continuum of matter and information, such that the primary means of transforming the social is to create vacuoles of noncommunication in which something new may emerge.

(*See also* Affect; Chapter 15, Biopower and Biopolitics; Chapter 24, Posthumanism; Chapter 26, Affect Studies; Control; Diagram; Event; Force; Machine; Oedipus Complex; Origin; Repetition; Resistance; Subjectivity; Symbolic Agency; *and* Vitalism)

Ronald Bogue, *University of Georgia (United States)*

Further Reading

Buchanan, Ian, and John Marks, eds. *Deleuze and Literature*. Edinburgh: Edinburgh University Press, 2000.

Deleuze, Gilles, and Félix Guattari. *Kafka: Toward a Minor Literature* [1975].

Trans. Dana Polan. Minneapolis: University of Minnesota Press, 1986.

Deleuze, Gilles. *Cinema 1: The Movement-Image* [1983]. Trans. Hugh Tomlinson and Barbara Habberjam. Minneapolis: University of Minnesota Press, 1986.

Deleuze, Gilles. *Cinema 2: The Time-Image* [1985]. Trans. Hugh Tomlinson and Barbara Habberjam. Minneapolis: University of Minnesota Press, 1989.

De Man, Paul

Paul de Man (1919–83), was a prominent literary critic and theorist, publishing actively from the late 1950s to the early 1980s, while he taught at Cornell, Johns Hopkins, and Yale where he finished his career. He was the foremost practitioner in North America of what came to be called, after Derrida, deconstruction. He preferred to think of what he did, eventually, as "rhetorical reading," a practice of reading literary and nonliterary texts with attention to how they worked, including a focus on the complexities, tensions, and aporias at work in their performance. This entailed granting priority to poetics rather than hermeneutics, with critical-linguistic analysis being in the late work the indispensable starting point for ideological analysis.

His early work, much indebted to philosophical phenomenology, considered the ontological status of the literary work and tended to find it less mystified than most philosophical and critical texts, the latter marked by a kind of constitutive blindness to their own operations. Literature, at least, was conscious of its own status as fiction and thus a privileged medium of insight, indeed the only form of language free from the fallacy of unmediated expression.

Later work, roughly from "The Rhetoric of Temporality" (1968) on, zeroed in on the classical concerns of figures of speech and strategies of persuasion, with an eye to how such elements of language complicated claims for the referential, organic, or totalizing character of works of literature. These protocols were supplemented by drawing powerfully on J. L. Austin's theory of speech acts, especially performatives, which exceed and stand apart from the regime of representation, conceived of as language representing the world outside it. Rhetoric was also treated in relation to grammar and, to a lesser extent, logic, often to highlight tensions or undecidable relations between the first two. "The Rhetoric of Temporality" also argued for the historical and theoretical pertinence of allegory, a preoccupation which would inform the next sequence of his career, focusing on readings of Jean-Jacques Rousseau and Friedrich Nietzsche.

Work in the late, last phase went under the rubric of "aesthetic ideology," via readings of Kant, Hegel, and more. The essays were less demystifying of Kant or Hegel than of their readers (starting with Friedrich Schiller) who had a commitment to the unassailable value of the aesthetic often conceived of as transcending ideological limits and even somehow serving to resolve social problems. De Man appealed repeatedly to the idea and fact of materiality as a force at the level of the letter or signifier that disrupts and undermines the authority of aesthetic-ideological programs in which it is enlisted and more generally complicates any easy passage between phenomenality and cognition.

De Man's reputation was undermined posthumously by the revelation, in 1987, of collaborationist writings in the early years of the war after his native Belgium was occupied by the Nazis. This undeniable collaboration coexisted with some evidence of resistance to the occupying forces, in publishing efforts and sheltering Jews, and it followed some markedly anti-fascist, non-fascist editorial work in the prewar years. The fact of collaboration remained a dominant feature of his posthumous reputation, though critical work responding positively to his writing persists in literary criticism and several other fields.

(*See also* Chapter 8, Rhetoric; Chapter 9, Deconstruction; Chapter 14, Ecocriticism; Close Reading; Ethical Criticism; *and* Kant, Immanuel)

Ian Balfour, *York University (Canada)*

Further Reading
de Man, Paul. *Blindness and Insight.* Second ed. Minneapolis: University of Minnesota Press, 1983.
de Man, Paul. *Allegories of Reading.* New Haven: Yale University Press, 1979.
McQuillan, Martin. *Paul de Man.* New York: Routledge, 2001.
Redfield, Marc, ed. *Legacies of Paul de Man.* New York: Fordham University Press, 2007.
Waters, Lindsay, and Wlad Godzich. *Reading de Man Reading.* Minneapolis: University of Minnesota Press, 1989.

Democracy

In *The Public and Its Problems* (1927), John Dewey described democracy—from the Greek *demokratīa*—as "a word of many meanings," and, indeed, democracy has historically been open to many interpretations and political actualizations. To name just a few: liberal democracy, deliberative democracy, managed democracy, democratic centralism, federalist democracy, democratic socialism, radical democracy, local democracy, direct democracy, constitutional democratic monarchy, theocratic democracy, corporate democracy, dollarocracy, sociocracy, inclusive democracy, authoritarian democracy, beautiful democracy, representative democracy, digital democracy, hipster democracy, Christian democracy, party-state democracy, democratic anarchism, and so on. Of course, this list, with its apparently endless inventional possibilities, is profoundly misleading. Democracy today is less creative, and more fixed, than it was when Dewey was writing in the 1920s. One of neoliberalism's greatest triumphs has been to define democracy as a retail transaction. Neoliberalism has almost completely captured democracy with its rhetoric of the market, making democracy just another thing we do as consumers with our wallets. Today's failure of democracy is a failure of imagination and rhetoric.

There is a radical tradition of democracy that is much older than neoliberal democracy and that, in fact, is antithetical to neoliberalism and the reign of the market. The English word *democracy* is derived from the classical Greek *demokratīa*, which means "the power of the citizens": a compound of *demos*, the citizens of the polis, and *kratos*, power, sovereignty, rule. In the classical world, democracy was invested in empowering the group of citizens who had the least power to control their destinies and the smallest say in politics: the poor. Democracy seeks to empower the most vulnerable groups in society to resist oppression. In contemporary moments of resistance to neoliberalism, democracy retains a hint of this ancient meaning. The trouble for democratic activists today is to forge horizontal relationships between oppressed groups who have little else in common other than that neoliberalism has failed them and made their lives expendable. Here we can learn from Dewey, who taught that democracy is at bottom a practice of communication and deliberation. Deliberation is foundational to democracy because it is through talking with our fellow citizens who understand what goods we hold in common and how we might work together to protect those common goods.

Some democratic theorists—especially those scarred by the social justice movements of the late 1960s and early 1970s, after which they began to believe that the cure for democracy is actually *less* democracy—view deliberation as a replacement for, and an antidote to, activism. I do not. Deliberation and activism are the systole and diastole of democracy. Having talked and argued and laughed and cried and prayed and chanted and jammed with our fellows, then we organize and take to the streets to collectively resist neoliberalism and ensure that everyone has the goods necessary to live, to thrive, and to flourish. Americans practice democracy every time they band together to resist oppression and defend the common good. Democracy is a verb, not a noun.

(*See also* Chapter 9, Deconstruction; Chapter 21, Late Capitalism; Chapter 22, Identity Studies; Civil Society; Free Market; Identity Politics; Neoliberalism; Neopragmatism; Object-Oriented-Ontology; Rhetoric; *and* Rorty, Richard)

Jeremy David Engels, *Penn State University (United States)*

Further Reading

Brown, Wendy. *Undoing the Demos: Neoliberalism's Stealth Revolution*. New York: Zone, 2015.

Engels, Jeremy. *The Art of Gratitude*. Albany: State University of New York Press, 2018.

Gilbert, Jeremy. *Common Ground: Democracy and Collectivity in an Age of Individualism*. London: Pluto Press, 2014.

Derrida, Jacques

Born in 1930 in French Algeria, as a child Jacques Derrida was expelled from school by Algerian administrators keen to impose anti-Semitic quotas demanded by the Vichy government, but nonetheless he lacked enthusiasm for alternative Jewish schooling. Something of an outsider, as a student at the Ecole Normale in Paris during the early 1950s Derrida chose to work on the problem of genesis in Husserl, writing a paper which, he tells us in the interview "Politics and Friendship," Louis Althusser was unwilling to evaluate since it seemed to him too difficult, obscure, and innovative for the aggregation. Indeed, Michel Foucault assessed it as either an A+ or an F. Derrida thought this episode gave a fair impression of his relationship to academic authority, not merely in terms of the examination committees of the time, since his approach to Husserl—and philosophy—was markedly different from that of Jean-Paul Sartre, Maurice Merleau-Ponty, French Marxism, or other more dominant intellectual positions in Paris. Between 1956 and 1957, Derrida spent a year at Harvard University, after which he completed his military service as a teacher in civilian clothes, before returning to Paris in 1960. For four years he served as a teaching assistant at the Sorbonne, during which time his introduction to Husserl's *The Origin of Geometry* was published. Soon afterward, he returned to the Ecole Normale to teach, at the invitation of Jean Hyppolite and Louis Althusser. Derrida taught for many years as an agrégé-répétiteur at the Ecole Normale, and himself noted the divisive nature of the role which marked his connection to the institution, repeating and reproducing officially sanctioned knowledge while at the same time introducing, like contraband, ideas and propositions that sat uneasily with the general agrégation, and even undermined it. In 1966, Derrida lectured abroad for the first time, returning to the United States to participate in the famous Johns Hopkins conference in Baltimore, at which he delivered his paper, "Structure, Sign, and Play in the Discourse of the Human Sciences"—a lecture concerning the deconstructibility of dominant structuralist ideas and assumptions that was to dramatically elevate Derrida's reputation internationally, ushering in a lifelong period of worldwide travel in response to a burgeoning number of academic invitations. In 1967, three major texts by Derrida appeared: *Of Grammatology*, *Voice and Phenomenon*, and *Writing and Difference*, which have come to be known as seminal works outlining the possibilities of a deconstruction of the metaphysics of presence, making possible a rigorous exposure of the effects of logocentrism and phonocentrism in the Western canon and tradition, as well as bringing together Derrida's critical readings of structuralism and linguisticism as key trends in modern thought. From the late sixties onward, Derrida also undertook regular teaching obligations at numerous US institutions. From the 1980s onward he was to receive a significant number of honorary doctorates from universities in the United States, Britain, Europe, and beyond, including the one awarded him by Cambridge University in 1992, after the well-known fiasco involving a letter of opposition written by academic colleagues dismissive of Derrida's work. Working imaginatively across and between literary and philosophical texts, and a celebrated reader not only of Husserl, but of Friedrich Nietzsche, Sigmund Freud, Martin Heidegger, Georg W. F. Hegel, Immanuel Kant, Emmanuel Levinas, Karl Marx, and many others, Derrida's writings on a multitude of topics including friendship and politics, hospitality, forgiveness, specters, Europe, the university institution, the archive, fiction and testimony, sovereignty and animality, and the death penalty have bequeathed a rich legacy to contemporary critical thought. Jacques Derrida died in 2004.

(*See also* Alterity; Archi-trace; Chapter 1, Early Theory; Chapter 5, Poststructuralism; Chapter 9, Deconstruction; Chapter 18, Translation; Chapter 24, Posthumanism; Chapter 25, University Studies; Critique; Deconstruction; Différance; Dissemination; Event; Force; Husserl, Edmund; Law; Metaphysics; Origin; Other, The; Platonism; Presence; Repetition; Self; Sovereignty; Spivak, Gayatri; Subjectivity; Supplement; Text; Translation; *and* Writing)

Simon Morgan Wortham, *Kingston University (United Kingdom)*

Further Reading

Derrida, Jacques. *Writing and Difference* [1967]. Trans. Alan Bass. London: Routledge and Kegan Paul, 1978.

Derrida, Jacques. *A Derrida Reader: Between the Blinds*. Ed. Peggy Kamuf. New York: Columbia University Press, 1991.

Peeters, Benoît. *Derrida: A Biography* [2010]. Trans. Andrew Brown. Malden: Polity Press, 2013.

Wortham, Simon Morgan. *The Derrida Dictionary*. London: Continuum, 2010.

Descriptive Turn (*See* Surface Reading)

Desire

Desire as a theoretical concept is primarily associated with psychoanalytic criticism developed from the work of Sigmund Freud and Jacques Lacan. Plato, in the *Republic*, is the first philosopher to articulate the concept of desire in a systematic way and anticipates some of the major discoveries of psychoanalysis. He has Socrates state that we all contain unnecessary and often lawless desires that are kept under control by convention and reason; when the rational mind is asleep, the wild unruly part causes a person to act as if he or she were totally lacking in moral principle. In *The Symposium*, Plato records Aristophane's comic perspective on sexual desire. In this myth, human beings were originally double the size and grew to threaten the Gods. They were cut in half by Zeus and have since desired to become whole again, finding temporary satisfaction only through their sexuality.

Kant situates desire as the capacity for action. The subject begins with a representation of an ideal and desire stimulates him or her to bring this state of affairs into existence. For Kant, a person is only praiseworthy if he or she is motivated by duty and not from desire. This sounds like cognition and feeling are opposed to one another but Kant argues that moral action requires the existence of the feeling of respect for the moral law, which is caused by our consciousness of the demands of the moral law.

For Freud, desire emerges from the unconscious and can be discovered through the interpretation of dreams, jokes, and slips-of-the-tongue. Freud posits that dreams are primarily wish-fulfillment and expressions of repressed desire. Through a series of complexes, beginning with the Oedipal complex, the infant learns to channel desire along socially acceptable pathways. The wild desires that Plato had hoped to keep in check with reason are revealed to have been central to the subject all along.

Like Aristophane's myth, desire for Lacan is predicated upon an originary lack. In the *Écrits*, he explains that the formation of the subject is inaugurated by the mirror stage that catalyzes a series of alienating identifications. When the infant first encounters his or her image in the mirror, they greet it with jubilation and excitement. The image appears as a *gestalt* or a unified whole that contrasts the myriad desires that the infant feels are animating them. In an echo of Kant, the external symbolization of the ego's mental permanence causes the infant to perceive him or herself as a subject of lack and to aggressively attempt to take the place of the *gestalt*. The mirror stage is the point of transition from the pre-linguistic sense of plentitude and satisfaction, dubbed the Imaginary, to the Symbolic order, which is language and the entire realm of culture conceived as a linguistic system. Upon entry into the Symbolic, the subject replaces direct interaction with the world with signifiers—Lacan claims that the word "murders" the thing—and this is a "castration" or lack that cannot be fulfilled, resulting in desire as a relentless search for satisfaction and catalyst for change.

(*See also* Chapter 7, Psychoanalytic Theory; Diagram; Drive; Fantasy; Jouissance; Lacan, Jacques; Libidinal; object petit a; Other, The; Phallocentrism; Sexuality; Subject; Sublimation; *and* Psychoanalysis)

Graham J. Matthews, *Nanyang Technological University (Singapore)*

Further Reading

Freud, Sigmund. *The Interpretation of Dreams* [1899]. *The Standard Edition of the Complete Psychological Works,* vol. IV. Trans. James Strachey. London: Vintage, 2001.

Lacan, Jacques. *Écrits* [1966]. Trans. Bruce Fink. New York: Norton, 2007.

Plato, *Republic*. Trans. Robin Waterfield. Oxford: Oxford University Press, 2008.

Diachronic (*See* Synchronic and Diachronic)

Diagram

The diagram is a concept that features in the semiotic theory of Gilles Deleuze and Félix Guattari. The concept appeared initially in Guattari's sole-authored work of the 1970s and was developed in their collaborative opus *A Thousand Plateaus* (1980). Deleuze also used it in his books on the painter Francis Bacon and philosopher Michel Foucault published in the 1980s. While the precise meaning of the concept changed throughout its various deployments, it can be defined in broad terms as a nonrepresentational semiotic framework capable of grasping the self-expressivity of dynamic matter. A diagram thus defined is not a drawing or geometric figure intended to represent already formed objects, ideas, or states of affairs but a mental map of the processes by which material reality is formed and transformed by the forces operating within it. The chief advantage of "diagrammaticism" (as Deleuze and Guattari call it) over other semiotic frameworks is its capacity to account for "asignifying signs," that is, semiotic effects that elude established sign systems. In *A Thousand Plateaus*, diagramming is defined as extracting asignifying signs or "traits" from existing semiotic regimes in order to "deterritorialise" or push those regimes toward new possibilities.

Guattari adapted the diagram from the American pragmatist philosopher Charles Sander Peirce's use of the term. Guattari, a psychoanalyst and revolutionary activist, was responding to what he perceived as the political shortcomings of Lacan's structuralist reinterpretation of Freud, which was heavily critiqued in Deleuze and Guattari's incendiary *Anti-Oedipus* (1972). For Deleuze and Guattari, structuralism remains within a representationalist account of language, even when the autonomy of the signifier is granted at the expense of the signified. Lacan linked the disappearance of the signified to a lost or inaccessible object of desire, and thus defined desire as lack. This idea is a principal target of Deleuze and Guattari's critique of psychoanalysis because, they claim, it contains subjectivity within linguistic structures and reduces desire to the status of fantasy or ideological image. The diagram thus emerges from a politically motivated attempt to escape linguistic reductionism and restore to the theory of desire a properly materialist basis.

One of the main inspirations Guattari took from Peirce was the idea that diagrams do not just illustrate already formed thoughts but may be used to guide thought toward conclusions. Diagrams, then, can be regarded as pragmatic constructions, machines for producing thought. Indeed, the diagram is often described as an "abstract machine." The emphasis on abstraction may appear to contradict Deleuze and Guattari's avowed materialism, but abstraction here means extracting from substantial reality the power relations or lines of force involved in its composition. Deleuze argues that Bacon's paintings do not depict bodies so much as the forces that act upon them. Bacon's achievement was to render these forces visible using unorthodox techniques such as scrubbing the canvas, such scrubbed zones constituting painterly diagrams. Deleuze emphasizes how Foucault describes Jeremy Bentham's famous "panopticon"—his architectural model for institutional buildings—as a diagram of modern disciplinary power conceived as an abstract force immanent to society as a whole.

(*See also* Chapter 5, Poststructuralism; Chapter 15, Biopower and Biopolitics; Deleuze, Gilles; *and* Peirce, Charles Sanders)

Aidan Tynan, *Cardiff University (United Kingdom)*

Further Reading

Watson, Janell. *Guattari's Diagrammatic Thought: Writing between Lacan and Deleuze.* London: Continuum, 2009.

Zdebik, Jakub. *Deleuze and the Diagram: Aesthetic Threads in Visual Organization.* London: Continuum, 2012.

Dialectic

Dialectic (from the Greek *dialektikē*) is an ancient discipline whose ideas and practices persisted in the Middle Ages and modernity alike, chiefly in philosophy and critical theory. While Immanuel Kant had used the term "dialectic" in his three critiques, it is in Georg W. F. Hegel's name that one usually speaks of "the" dialectic. Hegel renewed the dialectic after the discipline itself experienced considerable derision in early modernity. For him, as for Plotinus, Proclus, and medieval philosophers, dialectic is the means by which we come to know the world and its processes, and it's the way in which we can describe our own operations of knowing. It's also, more controversially, the basic law of all phenomena—natural or cultural. While the dialectic includes many logical forms and techniques, its central mechanism is the categories of identity and difference. The identity of any given thing is bound up with its difference from the identities of other things: hence, identity in difference. In the same way, then, there is no pure identity for Hegel, there is no pure "synthesis" or "resolution," two terms commonly used in conversations about the Hegelian dialectic. Hegel says in the *Science of Logic* (1812–16) that the task of "grasping opposites in their unity, or the positive in the negative" is "the most important aspect of dialectic." This is true, for Friedrich Engels spoke in *Dialectics of Nature* (1883) of "separation and opposition . . . only within . . . mutual connection and union," and vice versa, and Vladimir Lenin discussed the "unity of opposites" in his *Philosophical Notebooks* (1913). The point is that there's always a contradiction or "difference" in any synthesis or unity. Everything is dialectical—an identity in difference. Or as Hegel emphasizes in his *Science of Logic*, "*Identity is something different.*" Likewise, everything has its other. Even observers have a stake in the dialectical process in the way subjects come to know initially strange objects, processes, and events; and—on the flipside—the way world spirit (Weltgeist) comes to realize and know itself in events and phenomena. "Becoming" and "movement" are central to the dialectic and dialectical thinking—with the idea being that everything is in a state of continual becoming and dissolution (auflösung). The very famous Hegelian term, *aufhebung*, which has long been translated as "sublation," is an important feature of the dialectic in the way it means two things at once, as if to bundle opposition into a single word, an identity in difference: "The German '*aufheben*' . . . has a twofold meaning in the language: it equally means '*to keep*,' 'to "preserve,"' and 'to cause to cease,' '*to put an end to.*' . . . It must strike one as remarkable that a language has come to use one and the same word for two opposite meanings," writes Hegel in *Science of Logic*. For all of these reasons, one should never summarize the dialectic by the clichéd "thesis, antithesis, and synthesis," even if the mighty Marx experimented (granted, polemically) with this triad in the *Poverty of Philosophy* (1847)—chiefly because this is Kant's idea, not Hegel's, but also because there can be no genuine synthesis when contradiction of some kind always remains and was already in place in the identity of the very "thesis" itself, without the need to export in from the outside some pat and arbitrary "antithesis."

As a close reader of Hegel, Marx was fairly sparing in his use of the term dialectic; generally, he means to describe his dialectical "method" of exposition and analysis, as he does in *Capital* (1867) as well as indicate the way history moves from crisis to crisis constituted by "opposed" forces, which others (including his coauthor Engels) would call a "dialectical" point of view. Today, the term "dialectical" is generalized in theory, usually meaning the interplay between two entities or the processes of becoming and decay. In many ways, this general way of naming originates in Hegel and Marx themselves, and is continued by Fredric Jameson and Slavoj Žižek, who all use the word "dialectic" in a broad and various fashion. All traditions focused on "the negative" and of course negative dialectics themselves (as in Theodor Adorno) are, despite statements to the contrary, indebted to Hegel.

(*See also* Adorno, Theodor; Chapter 4, Marxism; Hegel, Georg W. F.; Jameson, Fredric; Negation; *and* Žižek, Slavoj)

Andrew Cole, *Princeton University (United States)*

Further Reading

Cole, Andrew. *The Birth of Theory*. Chicago: University of Chicago Press, 2014.

Engels, Friedrich. *Dialectics of Nature* [1883]. Vol. 25. *The Collected Works of Karl Marx and Frederick Engels*. 50 vols. New York: International Publishers, 1975–2005.

Hegel, G. W. F. *Science of Logic* [1812-16]. Ed. and trans. George di Giovanni. Cambridge: Cambridge University Press, 2010.

Jameson, Fredric. *Valences of the Dialectic*. New York: Verso, 2009.

Lenin, Vladimir. "Conspectus of Hegel's Book the *Science of Logic*." Vol. 38. *Collected Works*. 45 vols. Moscow: Progress Publishers, 1972. 85–237.

Marx, Karl. *Capital: A Critique of Political Economy* [1867]. Vol. 1. Trans. Ben Fowkes. New York: Vintage, 1977.

Dialogue

The idea of dialogue (from Greek *dialegeisthai*, "converse") has exerted a strong effect on Western consciousness, due largely to the influence of the philosophical dialogues of Plato and to a lesser extent those of Xenophon. The genre of the dialogue was unknown in the time of Plato and does not seem to have had a name. In referring to popular educational tools Plato's contemporary Isocrates refers to "so-called . . . dialogues" in his *Panegyricus,* as if the term were not exactly current. In the *Poetics*, Aristotle refers only to works he calls *Socratikoi logoi*, "Socratic speeches," by which he may refer to other authors, in addition to Plato. By the first century the situation has changed. Cicero refers to his *Academica* as a *dialogus,* and by the time of Diogenes Laertius in the third century CE the term is standard for referring to the philosophical dialogue.

In Plato, Socrates is portrayed as engaging in philosophical conversations with contemporaries on a wide variety of topics. Although he usually takes the lead in these conversations, he asks his interlocutor to join him in a common search for truth. Socrates does not lecture, nor does Plato explain his reasons for structuring the dialogues as he does. Thus, the dialogues are different from philosophical treatises in which an author takes responsibility for a distinct point of view. As a result, the dialogues present significant interpretive challenges and resist attempts at easy summary. Despite this aspect of the dialogue form, Plato has had many imitators, from Cicero and Tacitus in the Roman world to the dialogues of eighteenth-century philosophers George Berkeley and David Hume and beyond.

The idea of dialogue has continued to exert an important effect on literary studies, particularly those inspired by the work of the Russian philosopher Mikhail Bakhtin. Bakhtin uses dialogue as a metaphor for describing the way literary texts and the fictive worlds they represent interact with the wider world of literary and non-literary discourses. For him the essential feature of *dialogism* is its ability to represent reality as unfolding (not static), characterized by what he calls *heteroglossia*: the texts, words, opinions, and expectations of others. These divergent voices participate in a continuous dialogue with the utterances produced by individual speakers and writers. Just as a discussion can never be said to be complete, since there always exists the possibility of a further response, so a text and the *heteroglossia* it responds to is always incomplete, subject to reevaluation with the emergence of new linguistic conditions. Dialogism, then, describes this progressive creation and recreation of meaning.

As a phenomenon associated with literary history, dialogism is useful for thinking about the way different genres ignore or incorporate *heteroglossia*. Epic, as Bakhtin understands it, tries to restrict the free play of language by ignoring the existence of other genres and maintaining a strong stylistic homogeneity. The result is an artifact that appears to be static and unchanging, that is, non-dialogic. The novel, by contrast, cultivates a diverse dialogism by employing stylistic diversity and incorporating within itself diverse material: narration, dialogue, songs, letters, sub-literary documents, etc.

The most important texts for understanding Bakhtin's ideas about dialogism are *Problems of Dostoevsky's Poetics*, originally written in the 1920s but later revised and expanded, and *The Dialogic Imagination*, a series of related essays written in the 1930s and 1940s.

(*See also* Bakhtin, Mikhail; Chapter 1, Early Theory; Chapter 18, Translation; Chapter 20, Digital Humanities; Intertextuality; Kristeva, Julia; *and* Platonism)

Charles Platter, *University of Georgia (United States)*

Further Reading

Bakhtin, Mikhail. *Problems of Dostoevsky's Poetics*. Ed. and trans. Caryl Emerson. Minneapolis: University of Minnesota Press, 1984.

Bakhtin, Mikhail. *The Dialogic Imagination: Four Essays*. Trans. Caryl Emerson and Michael Holquist. Ed. Michael Holquist. Austin: University of Texas, 1981.

Diaspora

Diaspora is an ancient term that has gained new currency in our contemporary moment. Since its revival by theorists such as James Clifford and Paul Gilroy in the 1990s, the diaspora concept has become ubiquitous across the disciplines, emerging as a central category of analysis in both the humanities and the social sciences. Deriving from the Greek term *diaspeirein* (to disperse or scatter), diaspora originally designated the expulsion of the Jews from the Kingdom of Judah after its conquest by the Babylonians in 586 BCE. Since the 1960s, the vocabulary of diaspora has resonated powerfully in the context of the Middle Passage and African slavery. Also traditionally associated with the Armenian genocide of 1915–1916, over the last several decades the term has circulated widely beyond these three "classic" diasporas. In what Rogers Brubaker calls "the diaspora diaspora," it has come to designate an ever-expanding array of historical and cultural experiences, leading to such neologisms as "labour diasporas," "imperial diasporas," "queer diasporas," and so forth.

The emergence of diaspora theory in the early 1990s reflected a larger shift in cultural theory away from an understanding of culture as geographically bounded. Accordingly, such discussions recast diaspora, not as a tragic condition of inauthenticity, but as an alternative space of belonging. At the same time, this body of theory can be understood as a response to the problem of definition resulting from the term's proliferation. The apparently limitless plasticity of a term whose original definition was quite narrow led to competing definitions as well as anxieties regarding the dilution of its meaning. In 1991, in the inaugural issue of the journal *Diaspora*, William Safran proposed a typological model that derives six characteristic features of diaspora from the "ideal type" of the Jewish experience of *galut* (exile). In response, in his seminal essay "Diasporas," Clifford argued against a fixed set of definitional criteria in favor of a relational approach that identifies areas of both overlap and divergence between diasporism and nationalism as well as indigeneity. Subsequent diaspora theory similarly has been characterized by a split between positivisitic and culturalist models. While positivistic approaches focus on the empiricist study of human displacement and on establishing taxonomies, culturalist approaches are concerned with the ongoing and dynamic processes through which diasporic subjectivities are formed and performed.

Literary and cultural studies tend to favor the latter model, approaching diaspora less as an object of study requiring taxonomic classification than as a set of cultural, aesthetic, and discursive practices. Diaspora theory offers literary scholars a lens through which to open up the study of literature to transnational and global perspectives, thereby unsettling the methodological nationalism of the discipline. Addressing contemporary experiences of migration and displacement associated with decolonization and globalization, diaspora, with its ancient pedigree, simultaneously provides a salutary reminder of the deep history of these phenomena. Moreover, because of what Gilroy calls the "intercultural history of the diaspora concept"—the way in which it has travelled back and forth between different cultural traditions—the diaspora framework encourages a comparative, cross-cultural mode of reading that is particularly apposite to our increasingly interconnected world.

(*See also* Chapter 17, Comparatisms)

Sarah Phillips Casteel, *Carleton University* (Canada)

Further Reading
Braziel, Jana Evans, and Anita Mannur, eds. *Theorizing Diaspora*. Malden: Blackwell, 2003.
Clifford, James. "Diasporas." *Cultural Anthropology* 9.3 (1994): 302–44.
Hirsch, Marianne, and Nancy K. Miller, eds. *Rites of Return: Diaspora Poetics and the Politics of Memory*. New York: Columbia University Press, 2011.

Différance

A term coined by Jacques Derrida, *différance* conjures the sense of differing and deferral, spacing and temporalization, implied by the French word *différence*. As homophones, however, the difference of these two terms cannot be captured by the spoken word. If *différance* means to say something (and we should question whether it "means-to-say" anything at all, in the sense of an expressed intention), this cannot therefore become fully manifest in speech. Instead, as Derrida wryly observes, *différance* unavoidably calls for a certain recourse to writing, in order to elaborate the difference (*différance*) at the origin of *différence*. Since the metaphysics of presence grants priority to speech as a means of full expression, *différance* thus marks the limit of logo-phonocentric thought.

For Saussure, the relation of the signifier to the signified is arbitrary and relational. Language is therefore construed by him as a system of differences. But, asks Derrida in his essay "*Différance*," what produces and maintains these differences, what gives possibility to the play of differing and deferring which allows signification to take place? To make such a force *signify* would be to include and present it as an element in the system which it supposedly renders possible. *Différance* is thus the non-signifying difference that traverses every mark, the unpresentable and unsystematizable remainder which at once constitutes and exceeds the mark's very possibility. (Derrida's affirmation of an originary *différance* answers those who would seek to reduce deconstruction to a mere linguisticism or crude textualism.)

While it makes conceptuality and nameability possible, *différance* cannot therefore be made to signify as a proper name, term, or concept. If it is the play of *différance* that produces and maintains those systems of opposition (signifier/signified, speech/writing, presence/absence, nature/culture, etc.) that define the metaphysical tradition inherited by Saussure, *différance* is nonetheless not a master word, nor is it a stable heading. (Derrida includes *différance* in an unmasterable chain or untitleable series that also includes the trace, the supplement, the remainder, writing, dissemination, pharmakon, cinder, etc.) Nor is *différance* reducible to a positive or negative term falling on one or other side of any given opposition. Hence, *différance* is not to be construed either in terms of an original presence or a transcending absence. It cannot be thought to rise above the field of differences in which it is at play, anymore than it might be "properly" included within the signifying system that endeavors to reduce and contain *différance* or name it otherwise. Since *différance* belongs properly to neither side of the opposition that it marks, Derrida is frequently given to correct the misperception that *différance* allows him merely to reverse the order of priority that puts speech before writing. Instead, *différance* calls us to rethink the relations of speech and writing in their classical sense, giving rise to an enlarged and transformed

sense of writing which puts in question the metaphysics of presence.

Différance is a term that comes into play wherever Derrida reflects upon the deconstructible relations which both limit and maintain the philosophy, history, culture, and politics of the Western tradition, a tradition constituted in terms of its metaphysical determination of being as presence.

(*See also* Alterity; Archi-trace; Chapter 5, Poststructuralism; Chapter 9, Deconstruction; *and* Dissemination)

Simon Morgan Wortham, *Kingston University (United Kingdom)*

Further Reading

Bennington, Geoffrey, and Jacques Derrida. *Jacques Derrida*. Trans. Geoffrey Bennington. Chicago: University of Chicago Press, 1992.

Derrida, Jacques. "*Différance*." *Margins of Philosophy* [1972]. Trans. Alan Bass. Chicago: University of Chicago Press, 1982.

Derrida, Jacques. *A Derrida Reader*. Ed. Peggy Kamuf. New York: Columbia University Press, 1991.

Digital Humanities

The term *digital humanities* can refer to a large body of theoretical concerns and methodological approaches across multiple disciplines in the humanities. Even within literary and cultural studies, digital humanities can still refer to the following and more: (1) A set of tools for digital reading, the collection and visualization of "big data," and other quantitative approaches to large bodies of literary works. This sometimes polarizing set of approaches has seen recent popularization by figures like Matthew L. Jockers and especially "distant reading" proponent Franco Moretti, but it has a longer tradition under labels like "Humanities Computing," and it sometimes resembles tools as traditional as the concordance; (2) A call for serious scholarly attention to the particular forms and contexts of "born digital" texts, including, for a few examples, video games; webcomics; blogs; hypertext poetry; online fan fiction; "tweets," "yaks," and other social media posts; and even lines of computer code (through the lens of critical code studies). Here, digital humanities work in literary studies comes into frequent contact with work in new media studies and comparative media studies. Therefore, N. Katherine Hayles and Jessica Pressman, among others, have suggested that those in literary studies might be wise to turn toward approaches that acknowledge and attend to "comparative textual media" (or "transmedia" forms of storytelling that interweave the narrative threads of, for example, a television show and a smartphone app); (3) A renewed focus on materiality and production, alongside attention to the various complications that the digital era presents for these. We might imagine here a continuation (or exacerbation) of, say, Walter Benjamin's commentary on the mechanically reproduced work of art, or Marshall McLuhan's attention to the relationship between medium and message, or Benedict Anderson's arguments connecting print capitalism to the formation of imagined communities. Along these lines, we might imagine the various ramifications of digital production and distribution for commerce, text, art, identity, and more; (4) New questions about the impact of digital texts and networks on other "real world" issues, texts, readers, and users. We might file here an attention to such hybrids as "augmented reality," as well as conversations in critical theory about becoming "posthuman"; (5) The development and deployment of new tools for the preservation and archiving of texts, from digital genetic archives of texts by single authors, to networked archives that allow linking of texts to various other texts and contexts, to conversations about archiving practices for newer forms of genesis and composition (how and whether to uncover and preserve earlier drafts of a novel composed in a Microsoft Word document, for example); (6) Critical self-examinations of the field of digital humanities itself, including, for example, through the lenses of race, gender, sexuality, and class. Thinkers like, say, Moya Bailey ask questions about the brands of access and power that act to shape the field of digital humanities itself; (7) Attention to the reasons for and ramifications of an increasing turn toward digital modes of sharing research, from blog posts and tweets that operate outside of the realm of traditional peer review, to open access journals and monographs; and (8) The role for digital tools and methods in the classroom, from student projects creating literary Google maps and word clouds (for two examples) to larger-scale laboratory approaches to pedagogy.

(*See also* Chapter 20, Digital Humanities; Cyberculture; Electronic Literature; Mediation; *and* Remixology)

Paul Ardoin, *University of Texas, San Antonio (United States)*

Further Reading

Bailey, Moya. "#transform(ing)DH Writing and Research: An Autoethnography of Digital Humanities and Feminist Ethics." *DHQ: Digital Humanities Quarterly* 9.2 (2015).

Hayles, N. Katherine, and Jessica Pressman, eds. *Comparative Textual Media: Transforming the Humanities in the Postprint Era*. Minneapolis: University of Minnesota Press, 2013.

Moretti, Franco. *Graphs, Maps, Trees: Abstract Models for a Literary History*. London: Verso, 2005.

Disability

Disability is not a rare occurrence: nearly one-fifth of any given population has a disability. Given the prevalence of impairment, one might ask why literary forms rarely concern themselves with disabled characters or themes. And when disability does appear in literary works, the portrayals and perspectives are often limited, stereotypical, and viewed from an ableist perspective.

Disability studies (or critical disability studies) aims to correct that tendency; seeing bodily or mental impairment as part of human diversity, the field seeks to place disability within current discussions of identity in literature and media. One of the central insights of disability studies is that there are impairments and there is disability. The latter tends to arise when accommodations are not made for the former. So a wheelchair user is only disabled when confronted with stairs without ramps or elevators; a deaf person is only disabled when sign language interpreters are not present. In other words, it is the social/political surround that creates the disabling environment not the individual with an impairment.

If disability is a political formation, disability studies attempts to unpack the complex biocultural and biopolitical forces that are involved in ableism. Working along with the initial insights of disability activists, scholars have arrived at certain repeated scenarios in narrative. As with the coquettish woman or the hypersexualized African American, readers and viewers have come to expect the innocent, sexless disabled person, on the one hand, or the bitter revenging cripple, on the other.

In addition to analyzing works by nondisabled people, disability studies promotes work by artists, writers, poets, and filmmakers with disabilities. Many of those works present disability as a lived experience without romance, denigration, or misconceptions. Often the work of disabled creators are ignored by general readers and critics, and disabled actors most often do not play disabled roles and are not cast to play "normal" people. Thus the entire enterprise of representation is decidedly tilted toward misrepresentations of the disability experience and disability activism.

(*See also* Ableism; Capacity; Chapter 11, Cultural Studies; Chapter 19, Media Studies; *and* Reading)

Lennard Davis, *University of Illinois at Chicago (United States)*

Further Reading
Davidson, Michael. *Concerto for the Left Hand: Disability and the Defamiliar Body.* Ann Arbor: University of Michigan Press, 2008.
Davis, Lennard J., ed. *The Disability Studies Reader.* Fifth ed. New York: Routledge, 2017.
Davis, Lennard J., ed. *Beginning with Disability: A Primer.* New York: Routledge, 2017.
Seibers, Tobin. *Disability Aesthetics.* Ann Arbor: University of Michigan Press, 2010.
Thomson, Rosemarie Garland. *Extraordinary Bodies: Figuring Physical Disability in American Culture and Literature.* New York: Columbia University Press, 1996.

Disablism (*See* Ableism)

Disciplinary Society

Disciplinary society is a concept formulated by Michel Foucault to refer to an historical period organized around a form of power that emerged in Western Europe around the seventeenth century and which is based on a rigid, meticulous, yet largely internalized control of the body, its habits, and movements. Though this concept was prefigured by thinkers such as Max Weber, Marcel Mauss, and Norbert Elias, Foucault's understanding of discipline is original and has proved highly influential in the fields of history, sociology, anthropology, critical theory, and cultural studies.

In *Discipline and Punish: The Birth of the Prison* (1975), Foucault cites the drill tactics used in early modern armies and the physical effects they sought to achieve—upright posture, responsiveness to orders, and coordinated action—as a significant step in the development of a disciplinary power aimed at producing "docile bodies." According to Foucault, disciplinary power was further characterized by the following: (1) The "power of the Norm," that is, the regulation of bodily conduct in terms of generic standards (such as health norms or standardized production processes) that establish principles of social homogeneity while measuring and ranking individuals in terms of their deviation from these models; (2) Surveillance, that is, the fact—and the awareness of the fact—that one's conduct is being observed (which entailed a new form of institutional architecture focused on making individuals visible, best epitomized by Jeremy Bentham's Panopticon, a prison in which all inmates can be observed from a central surveillance tower); and (3) New forms of science and knowledge (such as pedagogy and criminology), which, in their aspiration to understand human conduct, are inseparable from disciplinary power itself (thus illustrating Foucault's important concept of "power-knowledge").

Though Foucault introduced the concept of disciplinary power in his study of the history of prisons, he maintained that discipline was an example of a broader "political technology" that became pervasive at a particular historical juncture and that exists independently (at least in principle) of any specific political regime or economic system. At a theoretical level, discipline was, moreover, crucial for the development of Foucault's innovative understanding of power as a phenomenon that is creative (rather than purely repressive), decentralized and "microphysical" (rather than emanating from the state), and relational (rather than a quality that can be possessed).

Though Foucault returned to the concept of discipline in *The History of Sexuality: An Introduction* (1976), he partially qualified his earlier position: rather than suggesting that discipline is the modern form of power par excellence, he now claimed that discipline often coincided with and, in some instances, was succeeded by what he called "biopower," a power technology aimed at large collectivities (notably "populations") that strives to maximize their wealth, health, and fertility. Discipline's surveillance of individual bodily conduct and biopower's regulation of aggregate vitality constitute, for Foucault, the alternative (and often overlapping) poles of the modern experience of power.

Foucault's concept of discipline is noteworthy for bringing greater scholarly recognition to the ways in which the body, its organization, and conduct have frequently been the targets of power systems—of what Foucault called a "political anatomy"—not least in seemingly apolitical institutions, such as schools and hospitals.

(*See also* Biopolitics; Chapter 5, Poststructuralism; Chapter 15, Biopower and Biopolitics; Discipline; Foucault, Michel; Power-Knowledge; *and* Surveillance)

Michael C. Behrent, *Appalachian State University (United States)*

Further Reading

Deleuze, Gilles. *Foucault* [1986]. Trans. Sean Hand. New York: Bloomsbury Academic, 2013.

Foucault, Michel. *Discipline and Punish: The Birth of the Prison* [1975].

Trans. Alan Sheridan. New York: Vintage Books, 1977.

Foucault, Michel. *The History of Sexuality, Volume I: An Introduction* [1976]. Trans. Robert Hurley. New York: Vintage Books, 1978.

Discipline

There are two uses of the word "discipline" in Foucault's writings. The archaeological use is found in Foucault's December 2, 1970 inaugural lecture at the *Collège de France* (*L'ordre du discours*, 1971, published in English as "The Discourse on Language," appended to *The Archaeology of Knowledge*, 1972). The genealogical use, and the more common use of the term, is found in *Discipline and Punish* (1975) and *The History of Sexuality, Volume 1* (1976).

In the inaugural lecture, Foucault presents "discipline" as one of three "internal rules" that governs discourse, along with commentary and the author. Disciplines are "groups of objects, methods, their corpus of propositions considered to be true, the interplay of rules and definitions, of techniques and tools." Foucault is clear that a discipline is not "the sum total of all the truths that may be uttered concerning something," for only truths that come about in coherence with the rules, definitions, methods, etc. count in the discipline. A statement might be "true" insofar as it corresponds to the matter being discussed, but without the methodology or adherence to disciplinary rules, the statement is not "in the true" (*dans le vrai*). New truths are only admitted by following disciplinary procedures; otherwise, they are merely conjectures.

In the genealogical works, "discipline" takes on a different sense. In *The History of Sexuality*, discipline is described as the technique of biopower that creates individ-

ualized bodies in comparison to the regulation of populations. Discipline is "centered on the body as a machine: its disciplining, the optimization of its capabilities, the extortion of its forces, the parallel increase of its usefulness and its docility, [and] its integration into systems of efficient and economic controls." These disciplinary techniques are described in more detail in *Discipline and Punish*.

Discipline and Punish discusses discipline in terms of three aspects: docile bodies, correct training, and panopticism. To create docile bodies, individual people have to be spatially and temporally arranged and managed. In so doing, one can maximize the efficiency of the use of individual bodies, mechanizing activities so that humans and the machines they use can become one unified activity. The word *dressage* is used by Foucault to focus on the similarity to training horses. In addition, the smallest of motions and moments were monitored, judged, and surveilled. Inefficient behavior was punished or otherwise "corrected" in order to improve the efficiency of the underperforming. The examination serves as the culmination of the evaluative process, turning everyone into a performance record. In order for surveillance to at least seem omnipresent, panoptic technologies were created to give all individuals the sense of being watched, judged, and evaluated at all times, which improved overall behavior and performance.

Both senses of "discipline" suggest that there is a procedural threshold that must be cleared for a statement or an individual to be "acceptable" in a given arrangement of power. Discipline is just one of the many ways that power operates in the realms of discourse and subjectivity.

(*See also* Biopolitics; Chapter 5, Poststructuralism; Chapter 15, Biopower and Biopolitics; Chapter 22, Identity Studies; Disciplinary

Society; Foucault, Michel; Power-Knowledge; Subjectivity; *and* Surveillance)

Brad Elliott Stone, *Loyola Marymount University (United States)*

Further Reading

Foucault, Michel. *Discipline and Punish: The Birth of the Prison* [1975]. Trans. Alan Sheridan. New York: Vintage Books, 1977.

Foucault, Michel. *The History of Sexuality, Volume I: An Introduction* [1976]. Trans. Robert Hurley. New York: Vintage Books, 1978.

Foucault, Michel. "The Discourse on Language [1971]." In *The Archeology of Knowledge* [1969] *and The Discourse on Language* [1971]. Trans. A. M. Sheridan Smith. New York: Pantheon Books, 1972. 215–38.

Discourse (*See* Chapter 3, Narrative and Narratology; Discipline; *and* Discursive Formation)

Discursive Formation

There is no simple explanation of the concept of "discursive formation." Its sense depends on the role it plays in Foucault's project of an "archaeology of knowledge," though it bears resemblances to the concept of an *episteme* as employed in *The Order of Things* (1966). The archaeology of knowledge is a methodological innovation in history, or historiography, reflecting and responding to changes in the discipline, in France and elsewhere, in the 1950s and 1960s. While Foucault acknowledges the fruitfulness of shifts in historiography to, for example, accepting a variety of levels of analysis, the emergence of the *longue durée*, etc., traditional approaches to intellectual history—the history of science, or literature, or ideas, or philosophy of history—still take for granted the unity of their objects: for example, an author or set of authors, an oeuvre, a tradition, a scientific theory or set of theories. The archaeological approach, on the other hand, does not.

The archaeology of knowledge, rather, aims to investigate discourse. In philosophy, the "discursive" is often contrasted to the "intuitive" or "affective." It denotes finite thought about determinate, given content. Kant's great philosophical project in the *Critique of Pure Reason* (1781) was to interrogate the conditions of the possibility of experience, which took the form of explicating finite, discursive human understanding as applied to sensible intuitions. This provided human beings with coherent *objects* of experience, unified by the cognitive faculties of the knowing subject, providing content to our discourse. The archaeology of knowledge is, in some sense, a Kantian project. It aims at uncovering the source of the *unity* of the types of discourse, or discursive formations—for example, economic discourse, biological discourse, psychiatric discourse—one seeks to investigate archaeologically. However, it is a distinctly antihumanist, anti-subjective, and historicist project.

Where traditional histories find the unity of discourse in objects (e.g., the "regional ontologies" of phenomenology), concepts (e.g., Georges Canguilhem's history of science), or themes (e.g. the history of ideas), discursive formations are those areas of linguistic performance that share a set of rules and structures that make possible the formation and transformation of objects, concepts, strategies, and subject positions (or "enunciative functions"). The hypothesis, and hope, of the archaeology of knowledge is that by investigating discursive formations one can account for these unities, these forms or styles of thought, without appeal to anything beyond discourse. By establishing the structures and "rules of transformation" of discursive formations, one might establish a history of thought beyond the human.

Critics of Foucault have claimed that the concept of a discursive formation, and the archaeological project into which it fits, is far too linguistic, without paying attention to the material dimensions of history, which shape the objects of our concern, and hence our discourses. But this ignores the fact that Foucault's method of analyzing discursive formations is in terms of the relations of *statements*, a peculiar and unique form of linguistic entity, superficially resembling speech acts, but explicitly capable of including material objects and artifacts. The analysis of discursive formations will be a matter of tracing how statements are related to, and transform, each other.

Though the concept of a discursive formation had a brief career in Foucault's writing, it remains a promising tool for those interested in investigating the history of thought without recourse to either reductive materialism or transcendental subjectivity.

(*See also* Canguilhem, Georges; Chapter 5, Post-structuralism; Chapter 6, Historicisms; Episteme; Foucault, Michel; *and* Kant, Immanuel)

Patrick Gamez, *Missouri University of Science & Technology (United States)*

Further Reading

Gutting, Gary. *Michel Foucault's Archaeology of Scientific Reason.* New York: Cambridge University Press, 1989.

Webb, David. *Foucault's Archaeology: Science and Transformation.* Edinburgh: Edinburgh University Press, 2013.

Dispositif (*See* Apparatus)

Dissemination

While the notion of *dissemination* is often put to work performatively in the earlier work of Jacques Derrida in particular, the 1972 volume of the same name by him includes several texts that shed light on this term. The preface, "Outwork," announces: "This (therefore) will not have been a book." Less still will *Dissemination* constitute a collection constituted by thematic coherence or consistency. Instead, the writing found here serves to disorganize the always *instituted* unity of the book, both in its concept and form, in the process disturbing the supposed integrity of a philosophical discourse which imagines itself possessed of the resources to control *as its own* the relation to an "outside." Thus, the movement of *différance* underway in these texts puts into question the synthetic or dialectical process by means of which philosophy hopes to incorporate, resolve, transcend, and master *without remainder* all differences found at its margins. Indeed, this aspiration on the part of philosophy to direct its own self-completion should render the act of prefacing inessential. Philosophy should have no lasting need of some preliminary or preparatory discourse. Since philosophy itself names the transcendence of thought over language, concept over word, truth and presence over writing and difference, philosophy "proper" should be able either to incorporate or to exclude and secondarize all that is merely *prefatory*. Yet since the metaphysical tradition seems bound to configure the arrival of philosophical truth in terms of overcoming philosophy's "outside" or "other"—a procedure upon which philosophy itself finally depends—such activity should be construed as *bordering* on philosophy without being properly philosophical. Neither the moment of philosophy itself, however, nor separable from the process of philosophy's self-completion, it is typically driven into philosophical prefaces as an inessential outwork, functioning nonetheless as the disseminal requisite of philosophy.

This, too, is the relation of "Outwork" to *Dissemination* as a "whole," to that which "(therefore) will not have been a book."

"Outwork"—indeed, the "prefatory" in general—is thus something like the *pharmakon* treated in "Plato's Pharmacy": at once medicine and poison, a supplement that may be both remedial and toxic. Meanwhile, Derrida's treatment of Philippe Sollers's *Numbers* demonstrates a degree of textual and typographical complexity and experimentation with citational practice that paves the way for 1974's *Glas*. Similarly, "The Double Session" opens with Mallarmé's short prose work *Mimique* inset into a passage from Plato's *Philebus*. This inaugurates anew the encounter between a metaphysics of "truth" and the issue of the poetic with which Platonism classically deals by way of censure. Mimesis has helped to order philosophy's typically pejorative attitude to poetry or literature. For Derrida, however, Mallarmé's text helps name the slender veil between the two: the hymen. This hymen not only divides and connects Plato and Mallarmé, as exemplary figures in the age-old confrontation between philosophy and the arts, but asks for its deconstructibility to be read back into the entire field of conceptual distinctions on which mimetic discourse—and its rejection—is classically founded, those that determine our understanding of the relationship between original and copy, signified and signifier, referent and sign, literature and truth. These texts by Derrida, then, not only characterize the workings of dissemination from a deconstructive point of view, but are themselves disseminal in practice.

(*See also* Chapter 5, Post-structuralism; Chapter 9, Deconstruction; Derrida, Jacques; Différance; *and* Other, The)

Simon Morgan Wortham, *Kingston University (United Kingdom)*

Further Reading

Bennington, Geoffrey, and Jacques Derrida. *Jacques Derrida*. Trans. Geoffrey Bennington. Chicago: University of Chicago Press, 1992.

Derrida, Jacques. *Dissemination* [1972]. Trans. Barbara Johnson. Chicago: University of Chicago Press, 1981.

Derrida, Jacques. *Glas* [1974]. Trans John P. Leavey and Richard Rand. Lincoln: University of Nebraska Press, 1986.

Distant Reading (*See* Digital Humanities; *and* Surface Reading)

Distinctive Feature

A linguistic term, the *distinctive feature* represents a value expressed by a binary opposition. Winfried Nöth notes that Nicolai Trubetzkoy uncovered language as atomic structure, which he saw as material structure that in terms of phonology concerns linguistic sounds as functional elements. Whereas there are an unlimited amount of phonetic differences across languages, phonology factors these differences down into a small number of oppositions. Phonemes are classes of sounds whose substitutability contributes to differences of meaning. Roman Jakobson is credited with categorizing features of phonemic differences in terms of binary oppositions (+/-) that are universal and as such apply to all languages. There are only a very limited number of such oppositions in any given language—a code, as it were—that gets operationalized when sounds are concatenated.

(*See also* Binary Opposition; *and* Chapter 2, Structuralism and Semiotics)

Herman Rapaport, *Wake Forest University (United States)*

Further Reading

Jakobson, Roman. *On Language*. Cambridge: Harvard University Press, 1990.

Nöth, Winfried. *Handbook of Semiotics*. Bloomington: Indiana University Press, 1990.

Diversity (*See* Class; *and* Multiculturalism)

Double Consciousness

The term "double consciousness" was conceived by W. E. B. Du Bois in *The Souls of Black Folk* (1903) to characterize the contradictory dilemma of the African American being both American and black, where being black is considered other and therefore is denigrated by the mainstream US society. Du Bois was fully aware that the US norm, which does not provide the African American with true self-consciousness, teaches the African American to hate and therefore to reject his black/Negro self. "It is a peculiar sensation, this double consciousness, this sensation of always looking at one's self through the eyes of others." Viewing double consciousness as a "gift" of "second-sense" and rejecting the binary logic of subordination and domination, Du Bois constructs African American subjectivity to be not either American or black but to be both American and black, "two unreconciled strivings," "two warring ideals," accepting as permanent the tension and the contradiction between the two *equal* terms. In deciding to accept/embrace and study the history and existence of the black self, Du Bois becomes one of the first scholars of African American studies. But throughout the twentieth century many African American historians, critics, intellectuals and scholars focused on the "longing . . . to merge [the] double self into a better and truer self," totally ignoring Du Bois's desire not to "Africanize America" or to "bleach [the] Negro soul in a flood of white Americanism." As modernists, these intellectuals and scholars did not define double consciousness as a third hybrid space but as a conflict to be resolved.

But with developments in postmodern and post-structural notions of subjectivity, where the subject is constituted not as whole and unified but as plural and multiple, the term "double consciousness" is reconfigured, especially for Africans-Americans, other people of color, and women who live in societies where their uniquely different self is othered and repressed and their normative American self is accented. This reconfiguration influenced the cultural and political psychology of people of color and women throughout the Western Hemisphere. The Du Boisian subject is complicated, mobile, plural, and open. As a subject with multiple, shifting identifications, the Du Boisian subject travels between the two or three categories, thinking his or her differences from other Americans and accepting his or her equality to them, with the conflict and tension keeping him or her healthy, stimulated, progressive, and alive. The Du Boisian double consciousness has an alien and critical perspective, one that can alter its focus as it moves between the two or three categories, seeing the gaps in all categories. This means that in the experience of instability and hybridity, the Du Boisian subject comes to know, embrace, and empathize with and to be critical of all spaces. In short, the subject learns to empathize with and to know the Other. Du Bois's notion of double consciousness paves the way for other hybrid or multiple western/American subjects to name themselves. More importantly, with this notion, he is de-territorializing the mainstream American regime of power/knowledge that defines the black/Other in devalued terms and is re-territorializing the black/Other not as Other but instead as something positive, as something that is different from the norm but equal to it in value.

(*See also* Chapter 13, Race and Postcolonial Studies; Chapter 22, Identity Studies; Hybridity; Other, The; Self; Subject; *and* Subjectivity)

W. Lawrence Hogue, *University of Houston (United States)*

Further Reading

Beal, Frances M. *Double Jeopardy: To Be Black and Female*. New York: Third World Women's Alliance, 1969.

Du Bois, W. E. Burghardt. *The Souls Black Folk: Essays and Sketches* [1903]. Eighth ed. Chicago: A. C. McClurg, 1909.

Hogue, W. Lawrence. *Postmodernism, Traditional Cultural Forms, and African American Narratives*. Albany: State University of New York Press, 2013.

Lewis, David Levering. *W. E. B. Du Bois: A Biography of a Race, 1868-1919*. New York: Henry Holt and Company, 1993.

Wright, Michelle M. *Becoming Black: Creating Identity in the African Diaspora*. Durham: Duke University Press, 2004.

Drive

Drive is a psychoanalytic concept used to approach the fundamental animating forces in the psyche. Drives (*Trieben*) should be distinguished from instinct (*Instinkt*), which refers to the inherent inclination of a living organism in response to stimuli. Drives, by contrast, are psychical representations of these forces; hence drive, for Sigmund Freud, is a "frontier-concept between the physical and the mental."

For Freud, the drives manifest as constant, relentless pressure arising from within the individual, from which "no actions of flight" can be taken. Drives operate according to the laws of the pleasure principle: the instinctual seeking of release from the ever-building tension of primal psychic forces. However, because the pleasure principle often comes into conflict with the reality principle—the dictates of an external world that resist the lawless push toward satisfaction—drives are subjected to repression, which cuts them off—at least temporarily—from the possibility of gratification.

Freud's concept of *Trieb* underwent several revisions throughout his career—revisions with significant implications for the development of post-Freudian psychoanalysis. Freud initially posited a duality between drives of libido and the ego—the former understood as primal sexual impulses and the latter as a drive toward self-preservation. Later—beginning with *Beyond the Pleasure Principle* (1920)—Freud posited a second duality between Eros and the death drive (*Todestrieb*). Whereas Eros is an impulse toward change and development, the death drive is a force pulling the organism back toward death—a "return to the peace of the inorganic world."

The questions dividing post-Freudian psychoanalysis relate not only to the character of the drives but to their direction and their objects. Do the drives merely contact external reality, as an arrow makes contact with a target? Or are the drives unformed *without* external reality, as an arrow is inseparable from the wood from which it is carved? According to the object relations approach of Melanie Klein, W. Ronald Fairbairn and D. W. Winnicott, drives are inherently object-seeking rather than satisfaction-seeking. For Klein, there is no drive that "does not involve objects." Fairbairn went even further in redefining the drives as "strategies of relating to objects." Winnicott added a developmental component by arguing that drive impulses imply a "capacity for total experience . . . the rider must ride the horse, not be run away with." In other words, drives point toward development and enrichment of the self and its relational capacity, not toward the satisfaction of asocial desires.

For Jacques Lacan, by contrast, the concept of drive obliterates the idea of social relation. The "preaching" and "therapeutics" of those who ascribe developmental force to drive amount to "a "political segregation of anomalies." Drive, for Lacan, is characterized above all by its impossibility. Drives are quanta of energy that are only given direction by a gap or lack between this energy and fantasies of its satisfaction. Drive "divides the subject and desire," and desire subsists because it misrecognizes this division as being caused by an object that it then pursues. Desire always "comes from the Other," and the pursuit of desire is thereby inherently futile. The concept of drive in Lacan retains a coloration of lawlessness and excess insofar as it emphasizes the lack that drive necessarily creates within the subject—a lack covered over but never adequately resolved by fantasy and desire.

(*See also* Chapter 2, Structuralism and Semiotics; Chapter 7, Psychoanalytic Theory; Fantasy; Freud, Sigmund; Lacan, Jacques; Libindinal; Other, The; Psychoanalysis; Sublimation; *and* Uncanny, The)

David W. McIvor, *Colorado State University (United States)*

Further Reading

Freud, Sigmund. *On the History of the Psycho-Analytic Movement, Papers on Metapsychology and Other Works. The Standard Edition of the Complete Psychological Works of Sigmund Freud.* Volume XIV [1914-1916]. London: Vintage Classics, 2001.

Lacan, Jacques. *The Seminar of Jacques Lacan: The Four Fundamental Concepts of Psychoanalysis, Vol. XI [1954-1955].* Ed. Miller, Jacques-Alain. Trans. Alan Sheridan. New York: W.W. Norton & Company, 1998.

Winnicott, D. W. *Playing and Reality.* London: Routledge, 2002.

E

Eco, Umberto

Umberto Eco (1932–2016)—Italian novelist, philosopher, semiotician, and critic— exercised a powerful cultural influence over multiple fields in the late twentieth and early twenty-first century.

He began his prolific career—nearly forty books—with the publication of his revised dissertation, *The Aesthetics of Thomas Aquinas* (1956). Eco said later that he wrote it in a "spirit of adherence" to Aquinas's Christian world, a mindset he quickly abandoned. The apostasy came as Eco entered the nonacademic world, working as a cultural editor for Italian television (RAI) and, for sixteen years, as senior nonfiction editor at the Italian publisher Bompiani.

Becoming a leading figure in Gruppo 63, an avant-garde movement of Italian intellectuals and artists, Eco turned his attention to modern and contemporary art and culture. Soon he started writing about groundbreaking authors such as Joyce and Borges, and a rich array of pop-cultural icons, among them the Italian game-show host Mike Bongiorno, James Bond, Donald Duck, Charlie Brown, and the Beatles. At the same time, complex thinkers about language such as the American pragmatist Charles S. Peirce and Swiss philosopher Ferdinand de Saussure began to fascinate him. The combined influence pointed Eco toward the then still esoteric subject of semiotics, the study of signs.

Eco included pop-cultural material in his analysis of semiotics even as he approached the subject with scholarly and philosophical rigor. For him, culture equaled a system of communication, and every cultural act or event comprised signs that required contextual decoding. Through both his scholarly and journalistic writing about the interpretation of art and popular culture icons (*The Open Work*, 1962; *Apocalittici e integrati*, 1977), and his effort to give semiotics a theoretical architecture (*A Theory of Semiotics*, 1976), Eco achieved his first great impact on modern culture. He broke out semiotics to a wider intellectual public, becoming the international thinker most associated with the subject. He also established the University of Bologna, where he became a distinguished professor, as a world center for studying the subject.

Even that influence paled before his impact on the international literary world with his first novel, *The Name of the Rose* (1980), a global best seller. Cerebrally dazzling and carefully plotted, a mix of detective novel, scholarly arabesque, philosophical meditation, and apotheosis of humor as the ultimate sword against intellectual pomposity, *The Name of the Rose* established a new genre of intellectually challenging "who-dun-it." It convinced almost every living, breathing humanist that he or she had an Umberto Eco novel inside fighting to break out.

Although Eco continued to publish erudite, complex novels such as *Foucault's Pendulum* (1988), *The Island of the Day Before* (1995), and *The Mysterious Flame of Queen Loana* (2005)—none of which equaled the commercial success of *The Name of the Rose*—literary observers today credit him with clearing a path for erudite, sophisticated large fictions that combine learning and scholarship with airport-read suspense. He opened the way for writers as different—and as differently received in the literary world—as Dan Brown and Richard Powers.

A third major influence, stemming from Eco's cultural criticism and philosophical work, came in his contribution to the demolition of academic resistance to pop culture. Following in the footsteps of Roland Barthes in Europe and much like Susan Sontag in the United States, Eco applied his wry, erudite prose and critical eye to the entertainment world, suggesting that popular culture embodied serious semiotic messages to which intellectuals must attend. By the end of his life, ironically, Eco came to feel that the pendulum of critical attention had perhaps swung too far toward pop culture—he bemoaned the ignorance on the part of twenty-first-century students of elite artists such as Luciano Berio and Jean-Luc Godard.

Finally, one cannot underestimate Eco's sway over the culture of Italy, his own country. For decades, through his regular *L'Espresso* column, "La Bustina di Minerva," and his endless publication of critical nonfiction books, Eco served as a kind of high cultural commissar of the nation, providing Italians with a good-natured, humorous, but at times highly contentious vision of how to think about contemporary Italian life.

(*See also* Chapter 2, Structuralism and Semiotics; Chapter 19, Media Studies; Peirce, Charles Sanders; Semiotics; Sign; Text; *and* Translation)

Carlin Romano, *Ursinus College*
(United States)

Further Reading
Beardsworth, Sara G., and Randall E. Auxier, eds. *The Philosophy of Umberto Eco.* Chicago: Open Court, 2017.

Eco, Umberto. *The Name of the Rose*. Trans. William Weaver. New York: Mariner Books, 1981.
Eco, Umberto. *The Open Work*. Trans. Anna Cancogni. Cambridge: Harvard University Press, 1989.
Merrell, Douglass. *Umberto Eco, The Da Vinci Code, and the Intellectual in the Age of Popular Culture.* New York: Palgrave Macmillan, 2017.

Electracy

Electracy is to digital technology what literacy is to alphabetic writing. Gregory Ulmer introduced the term to update "secondary orality" used by Walter Ong to distinguish electronic culture from oral and literate civilizations. "Electracy" is a portmanteau combining "electricity" and "trace," the latter referencing Jacques Derrida's grammatology replacing semiotic signs with relational *différance* as the basis of signification. Electracy subordinates the catachresis "digital literacy" within the frame of "apparatus" (*dispositif*), to indicate that technology is one dimension of a three-dimensional matrix, including institution formation and individual and collective identity behaviors. Apparatus theory (developed by the Tel Quel group, 1960–82) opposes technological determinism by defining literacy and electracy as invented, partly technological and partly ideological desiring machines. Computing as apparatus, for example, is understood as the meeting of Aristotle's truth tables and Leibniz's binary numbers in Tesla's logic gate. Electracy emerged out of literacy beginning with the Industrial Revolution. Immanuel Kant's promotion of aesthetics (Pleasure-Pain) to equal status with the faculties of pure and practical reason provided the metaphysical framework for the new epoch.

Concerned with the history and theory of writing from Paleolithic origins to the present across all writing systems, grammatology identifies opportunities for inventing electracy by analogy with the emergence of literacy out of orality in Classical Greece. Western literacy includes not only alphabetic writing, but also the first school (Plato's Academy, 387 BCE), within which was invented the operating metaphysics eventually transforming civilization from the religious worldview of orality to the scientific worldview of literacy. Vanguard artists of the bohemian cabaret scene in nineteenth-century Paris are electrate "Presocratics," creating Dadaism as the logic of software. The identity behaviors of individual selfhood and the democratic polis are literate inventions, matched in electracy with branding and social media supporting globalized commodification. Electracy does not replace the institutions of orality and literacy but supplements and displaces them with a new order in every dimension, as in this list comparing literacy/electracy: science/entertainment; state/corporation; citizen/tourist; knowledge/fantasy; reason/appetite; true-false/attraction-repulsion. The "Plato" of electracy is Walt Disney—Theme Park is our School, Mickey Mouse our Socrates, Animation our Dialogue, Caricature our Categories—augmenting visceral experience.

(*See also* Apparatus; Archi-trace; Différance; *and* Digital Humanities)

Gregory L. Ulmer, *University of Florida (United States)*

Further Reading

Derrida, Jacques. *Of Grammatology* [1967]. Trans. Gayatri Spivak. Baltimore: Johns Hopkins University Press, 1974.

Ong, Walter J. *Orality and Literacy: The Technologizing of the Word.* New York: Methuen, 1982.

Stiegler, Bernard. *Technics and Time, 3: Cinematic Time and the Question of Malaise.* Trans. Stephen Barker. Stanford: Stanford University Press, 2011.

Ulmer, Gregory L. *Internet Invention: From Literacy to Electracy.* New York: Longman, 2003.

Electronic Literature

Electronic literature is a field of creative practice, academic research, and pedagogy focused on new forms and genres of writing that explore the specific capabilities of the computer and network—literature that would not be possible without the contemporary digital context. Although some forms of electronic literature, such as poetry generators, have histories that stretch back to the 1950s, until the late 1990s—outside of a few outliers like Robert Coover's digital writing workshops at Brown University and the hypertext publisher Eastgate Systems—there were very few academic or cultural homes for literary experimentation in digital media. But with the arrival of the World Wide Web and its swift public adoption, interests grew in the potentialites of networked and programmable literature. The arrival of the nonprofit Electronic Literature Organization (ELO) in 1999 provided an interdisciplinary institutional umbrella for researchers and authors of diverse literary experiences made for digital media and has been the center of an international network focused on these practices, for example by publishing three volumes of the *Electronic Literature Collection* and through regular conferences in the United States, Canada, and Europe. In 2004, an ELO committee attempted to establish a definition that would be applicable to the forms of literary practice that were its central focus. The result defined works of electronic literature as those with "important literary aspects that take advantage of the capabilities and contexts provided by the stand-alone or networked computer." The committee also produced a list of exemplary forms including hypertext fiction and poetry, kinetic poetry, computer art installations with literary aspects, conversational characters, interactive fiction, novels that take the form of emails, SMS messages, or blogs, poems, and stories that are generated by computers, collaborative writing projects that allow readers to contribute to the text of a work, and literary performances online that develop new ways of writing. Electronic literature is a fundamentally experimental literature: the writers and artists producing these works are centrally concerned with narrative forms and poetic practices that emerge from the culture's engagement with the digital. The genres of electronic literature are fluid and responsive to changes in the technological environment itself—when the web was new in the 1990s, authors were most often developing hypertext that explored the nature of the network and the poetics of linked interactive narratives, while during the 2000s many authors explored the capabilities of animation software such as Flash to enable kinetic poetry, while in the present many authors are exploring the use of location, ubiquitous computing, and virtual reality in the production of new literary experiences. Many of the forms of practice in electronic literature have strong affiliations with twentieth-century avant-garde movements, such as the Futurists, Lettrists, Surrealists, the Oulipo, Language poets, and postmodernism. While it emerges from a literary context, the venues and contexts of electronic literature are modeled less on those of print culture than on the contexts of arts practice. While there are online journals and anthologies dedicated to digital literature, work is as often published through museum and library exhibitions and performances, as well as online.

(*See also* Chapter 20, Digital Humanities; Digital Humanities; *and* Literature)

Scott Rettberg, *University of Bergen (Norway)*

Further Reading

The Electronic Literature Collection. Vols. 1–3. http://collection.eliterature.org

The ELMCIP Electronic Literature Knowledge Base. http://elmcip.net/knowledge-base

Rettberg, Scott. "Electronic Literature as Digital Humanities." In *A New Companion to the Digital Humanities*. Eds. Ray Siemens, Susan Schrieberman, and John Unsworth. Oxford: Blackwell, 2016. 127–36.

Emotions

At once intensely personal and surprisingly conventional, emotions draw us into fundamental questions about where to draw boundaries among ourselves, other people, and things in the world. Consider, for example, the ambiguity in the very notion of having a passion. Passion, from the Latin *passio* ("suffering"), quite literally means to suffer. Feeling passion *for* something is to suffer *from* it. Who or what, then, is having *this* feeling?

Having an emotion would seem to imply having a body one can not only feel but also understand. However, the tradition of Freudian psychoanalytic criticism, rooted in a practical model of therapeutic exchange, has long questioned the immediacy of our emotional experiences as they are refracted not just within the competing aspects of individual psychology but also a history of cultural prohibitions and repressions that shape our self-descriptions. Sigmund Freud's *Civilizations and its Discontents* (1930) analyzes how civilizing institutions repress desire and how emotional norms are consolidated through cultural practices. Studying cultural production, historical materialist, and sociological thinkers influenced by psychoanalysis have tracked how emotional representations reinforce moral, political, and economic imperatives around personality, productivity, or social relations. In *Black Skin, White Mask* (1952), Franz Fanon uses Freudian techniques to analyze colonial contexts in which emotions present as tensions between the "epidermal" projections of colonial power and the experience of being a racialized colonial subject.

Building off these critiques, Rei Terada defined emotions in *Feeling in Theory: Emotion After the "Death of the Subject"* (2001) as highly mediated "ideas" rooted in a Cartesian model of subjectivity: "I think [I am angry, happy, sad] and therefore I am." Terada's work is part of a broader interdisciplinary cluster of "affect theory" that opposes the differential force of feeling to stable emotional "concepts." Complex experiences like sentimentality or nostalgia, for example, involve both emotions and affects, in the sense that one is not only feeling empathetic or untimely but also encoding these feelings through ideologies or conventions of identity or authenticity. Maintaining the difference between emotions and affects is particularly important to reflexive critical paradigms (post-structuralism, posthumanism, postcolonialism) that treat "feeling" as a site of internal dissonance to ethical norms, concepts of being human, citizenship, or racial formation.

In the diverse traditions of vitalism, phenomenology, existentialism, and pragmatism, emotions have long been thought as material agents or forces in the social drama of subjects and objects shaping each other. In his pivotal article "What is an Emotion?" (1884), William James argued that emotions are embodiments of shifts in consciousness. One cannot conceive of feeling without the concomitant physical changes they bring about in both a person and the social relations we articulate with, or to, others. James has also been adapted by philosophers working in an Aristotelian tradition of ethics and value theory to make arguments for emotions as forms of moral intelligence we use to evaluate actions or situations. Conversely, materialist thinkers have sought to account for the roles emotions play in either sustaining or altering our institutions, political orders, or economies (in which moralities are constructed). In *The Long Revolution* (1961), Raymond Williams further developed the concept of "structures of feeling" in order to account for how feelings intersect with structures and historical processes. Williams's work is consonant with theorists of everyday life who see emotional experience as an embodied limit, however minimal or transient, to the totalizing exploitation of labor, imagination, or erotic life. Theories and histories of "reception" in cultural studies and aesthetics by thinkers like Herbert Marcuse or Stuart Hall see emotional experience as a critical agency in reader responses to dominant (or oppressive) paradigms of communication.

The burgeoning field of "histories of emotion" treats emotions as contested historical objects. In *Doing Emotions History* (2013), Susan Matt and Peter N. Stearns give the example of how changing relationships to "love" has paralleled the legal, political, and geographical history of marriage. Only recently could the fickle complexities of "love" be considered a valid basis for such a contract. Work in histories of emotions intersects with recent work in cognitive neuroscience to map the neurological roots of our emotional ideas and behaviors, raising further questions about what it means to have an emotion and express it to others.

(*See also* Affect; Chapter 3, Narrative and Narratology; Chapter 26, Affect Studies; Material Culture; Neuroscience; Terror; *and* Trauma)

Christopher Patrick Miller, *University of California, Berkeley (United States)*

Further Reading

Adorno, Theodor W., Else Frenkel-Brunswik, Daniel J. Levinson, and R. Nevitt Sanford. *The Authoritarian Personality*, vols. One and Two. New York: Norton, 1950 & 1969.

Ahmed, Sarah. *Cultural Politics of Emotions*. New York: Routledge, 2015.

James, William. *Psychology, Briefer Course* [1920]. Cambridge: Harvard University Press, 1984.

Matt, Susan J., and Peter N. Stearns, eds. *Doing Emotions History*. Champaign: University of Illinois Press, 2013.

Nussbaum, Martha. *Upheavals in Thought: The Intelligence of Emotions*. Oxford: Oxford University Press, 2003.

Empty Homogeneous Time (*See*
Homogenous, Empty Time)

Encounter

The philosophical concept of encounter is central to the later writings (1978–87) of Louis Althusser, which have been collected and published posthumously as *Philosophy of the Encounter* (2006). The years of the "late Althusser" represent a time of personal, political, and philosophical turmoil, and recent scholarship has produced healthy debate as to whether his work on "the materialism of the encounter" signifies a major break from the central tenets of Althusserian thought found in *Reading Capital* (1965) and *For Marx* (1965). The term itself is most directly

addressed in "The Underground Current of the Materialism of the Encounter" (1982–83) collected in *Philosophy of the Encounter.*

Derived from Epicurus, by way of Lucretius, *encounter* refers to the "clinamen" or "infinitesimal swerve" that caused the universe's material (previously free-falling through space as isolated atoms) to pile up on itself. Thus, the "almost negligible" movement of a single atom resulted in an *"encounter* with the atom next to it, and, from encounter to encounter," induced "the birth of a world." Encounter, though, is only the founding premise for a much larger theoretical reconceptualization, which Althusser calls "aleatory materialism." In a series of encounters with figures in the history of philosophy—running the gamut from Democritus, Epicurus, Machiavelli, Spinoza, Hobbes, Jean-Jacques Rousseau, Montesquieu, Karl Marx, Martin Heidegger, and Ludwig Wittgenstein—"Underground Current" mounts evidence for establishing a philosophy (and thus a politics) for a world that is both necessary and contingent, founded on the principles of causation while jettisoning the idealism of teleology.

Certainly, one could argue that Althusser's coining of the term is, in itself, a somewhat aleatory performance, an accomplished fact of the larger theoretical milieu of France in the late 1970s. G. M. Goshgarian has noted that the consequences of Althusser's late revelation were already anticipated in Gilles Deleuze and Felix Guattari's *Anti-Oedipus* (1972), for "the heart of [aleatory materialism] is the Deleuzian-Althusserian claim that capitalism might not have happened. The stake of it is the idea that communism might never happen." The philosophical significance, it must be added, is that everything that exists in the world of "accomplished facts" has the capacity to be otherwise. Such provisional materialism can be (must be?) both determined by material conditions and at the same time be in "opposition to any idealism of consciousness or reason." While it is difficult to tell whether Althusser's nascent philosophy of the encounter ultimately escapes its own critique of rationalist materialism (*a la* Marx, Engels and Lenin) to become, itself, more than "a disguised form of idealism," the fundamental incoherence that Althusser isolates in his later work is palpable in recent attempts to think through/within the paradox of traditional Marxist thought. To cite a salient example from *Specters of Marx* (1993), when Derrida calls for a "new thinking or a new experience of the event and of another logic" aimed at undoing the "sleight-of-hand trick between . . . historical empiricity and teleological transcendentality," he also invokes the spirit of Althusser's philosophy of the encounter.

(*See also* Althusser, Louis; *and* Chapter 26, Affect Studies)

Joel P. Sodano, *Keele University*
(United Kingdom)

Further Reading

Althusser, Louis. *Philosophy of the Encounter: Later Writings, 1978-87*. Eds. François Matheron and Oliver Corpet. Trans. and intro. G. M. Goshgarian. New York: Verso, 2006.

Diefenbach, Katja, Sara R. Farris, Gal Kirn, and Peter Thomas, eds. *Encountering Althusser: Politics and Materialism in Contemporary Radical Thought*. New York: Bloomsbury, 2013.

Montag, Warren. *Louis Althusser*. New York: Palgrave Macmillan, 2003.

Enlightenment

The term "enlightenment" is famously defined by Immanuel Kant: it is "man's emergence from his self-incurred immaturity." He elaborated on that phrase by suggesting that, rather than depend upon traditions and institutions to do his thinking for him, the enlightened man was to think for himself with the exercise of his own reason. Kant showed how reason operated through the use of concepts and ideas; he also argued that the independent use of the mind was political, since the use of our internal faculties to understand and act in the world constitutes our freedom.

Kant provides only one instance of a whole range of diverse thinkers that—in one way or another—emphasized the value of reason and/or understanding, independent thought, and political self-determination. Although the movement is usually considered to be an eighteenth-century European phenomenon, many historians think of early modern writers like Francis Bacon or Hugo Grotius as precursors to the age of enlightenment. Bacon, for instance, emphasized the importance of scientific learning, and imagined an ideal Christian commonwealth guided by rational principles of government. The increasingly more secularized perspective of later philosophers, however, more clearly distinguishes their work as "enlightened" insofar as they stress the conceptual and political architecture of our world as distinctively human-made and capable of improvement through empirical observation and modified action. John Locke showed how our ideas derive from sensations; philosophers from Baron Holbach to Joseph Priestley made scientific inquiry into the basis for understanding and changing social institutions. David Hume, somewhat more modestly, showed how such sensations are ultimately synthesized as social custom; custom in Hume and "moral sentiment" in Adam Smith, furthermore, became a way for enlightenment thinkers to develop a solution to how individual agents with knowledge, property, and power could become peaceable citizens of a polity. Jean-Jacques Rousseau, who also looked back to Thomas Hobbes's *Leviathan*, developed the idea of self-determining agency into a full-blown theory of social contract that joined individuals and collectives together as a transparent sovereign power. Differences among such thinkers abound: Denis Diderot was an atheist, while Mary Wollstonecraft was a Unitarian; Jeremy Bentham was a celebrated political reformer, while William Godwin was (and still is) often considered an anarchist. Intellectual historians from Peter Gay to Roy Porter, moreover, have emphasized complications involved in any attempt to arrive at uniform ideas of enlightenment rationality; such ideas appear to avoid considerations of the body, sexuality, humor, and irrational beliefs. Despite such variations and complications, the enlightenment often served as a stable focal point for critical schools throughout the twentieth and twenty-first centuries, which articulated their claims in a vivid contrast with enlightened principles. Max Horkheimer and Theodor Adorno directly linked enlightened reason with the rise of capitalism, which they strenuously opposed. Jacques Derrida accused philosophers from Rousseau to Kant of inflexible aesthetic principles that his own theories attempted to complicate and "deconstruct." Still other theorists, however, have appropriated and adjusted enlightenment thinking toward more aesthetically and politically progressive purposes. Jacques Lacan famously claimed that pleasure was the unacknowledged principle of Kantian reason, a point that Slavoj Žižek has explained and endorsed. Jurgen Habermas, John Rawls, and Michael Warner—among others—locate liberal, even radical, potentials in enlightened ideals of reason and publicity.

(*See also* Adorno, Theodor W.; Antihumanism; Chapter 4, Marxism; Chapter 22, Identity Studies; Habermas, Jürgen; Humanism; Idealism; Kant, Immanuel; *and* Nietzsche, Friedrich)

Mark Canuel, *University of Illinois, Chicago (United States)*

Further Reading

Foucault, Michel. "What is Enlightenment?" In *The Foucault Reader*. Ed. Paul Rabinow. New York: Pantheon, 1984. 32–50.

Horkheimer, Max, and Theodor W. Adorno. *Dialectic of Enlightenment* [1944/1947]. Trans. Edmund Jephcott. Stanford: Stanford University Press, 2007.

Kant, Immanuel. "An Answer to the Question: 'What is Enlightenment? [1784]'" In *Kant's Political Writings*. Ed. Hans Reiss. Cambridge: Cambridge University Press, 1970. 54–60.

Environmental Humanities

The environmental humanities have emerged as a new interdisciplinary matrix of environmentally oriented research fields in the humanities and social sciences since approximately 2005. Ecocriticism (the environmentally inflected subfield of literary studies), environmental history, and environmental philosophy constitute the core areas in this matrix, which also includes environmental anthropology, cultural geography, gender studies, political science, and religious studies, among others. The environmental humanities emerged amid a wave of attempts to forge new connections between humanistic research and the public sphere, and the recognition that the sciences and technology alone are insufficient in solving current ecological problems. The field has achieved particular visibility and institutionalization in Australia, Canada, Western Europe, and the United States.

Conceptually, the environmental humanities have focused on the Anthropocene and its relation to humanism, posthumanism, and multispecies theory; on the tension-fraught intersection between the study of global ecological change and research on cultural difference, socioeconomic inequality, environmental justice and injustice, and geopolitical power struggles; and on the role that narratives of decline, progress, and change play in current accounts of ecological pasts and futures.

The Anthropocene, proposed in 2000 by the scientists Paul Crutzen and Eugene Stoermer, hypothesizes that humans have changed the biological and geological structures of Earth so much that their impact will be visible in geological strata. This exclusive focus on human agency, often interpreted as a story of degradation and destruction, sometimes complements and sometimes conflicts with environmental humanists' investigation of human activities as part of a complex field of cooperation and conflict with nonhuman species; with events such as droughts, floods, fires, and earthquakes; and with long-term processes of climatological and geological change. From Bruno Latour's actor network theory to the recent wave of posthumanisms, new materialisms, and varieties of multispecies theory, social scientists and humanists have foregrounded networks of agency and exchange that include but are not limited to humans, and have questioned the centrality and exceptionality of the liberal human subject.

Environmental humanists typically foreground that different human populations contribute unequally to ecological problems such as toxification, resource depletion, and climate change, and that they benefit and suffer unequally from their consequences. Advocates for environmental justice and political ecologists have highlighted the disproportionate exposure of the poor and communities in the developing world to water and air pollution, hazardous waste, unsafe buildings and work places, and the consequences of climate change. In some cases, this unequal exposure has roots in colonial and postcolonial structures of economic and political oppression. In this view, ecological degradation and social oppression are historically intertwined and should be studied in conjunction with inequalities of gender, race, and class as well as with cultural histories that condition different responses to environmental crises.

In addressing these issues, environmental humanists foreground the narratives, metaphors, and textual and visual strategies that convey stories of environmental change and shape particular communities' perceptions and responses to them. A narrative of environmental decline under the impact of modern society has functioned as a powerful tool of political resistance to dominant narratives of progress in Europe and North America, for example, but it has also been criticized for offering few optimistic visions of a better future. Wilderness, pastoral, apocalypse, and conversion narratives have played important roles in environmental rhetoric, as have images such as oil-covered seabirds and polar bears on melting ice floes. The environmental humanities seek to analyze and understand such strategies in different cultural contexts and to foster the creation of new narratives and images.

(*See also* Anthropocene; Chapter 14, Ecocriticism; *and* Critical Climate)

Ursula K. Heise, *University of California, Los Angeles (United States)*

Further Reading
Emmett, Robert S., and David E. Nye. *The Environmental Humanities: A Critical Introduction.* Cambridge: MIT Press, 2017.

Heise, Ursula K., Jon Christensen, and
Michelle Niemann, eds. *The Routledge
Companion to the Environmental Human-
ities*. Oxon: Routledge, 2017.

Oppermann, Serpil, and Serenella Iovino,
eds. *Environmental Humanities: Voices
from the Anthropocene*. London: Rowman
& Littlefield, 2017.

Episteme

The ancient Greek word *epistêmê* referred to "knowledge," but the term *episteme* has gained significance in literary and cultural theory based on the special meaning given to it by Michel Foucault in *The Order of Things: An Archaeology of the Human Sciences* (1966) and *The Archaeology of Knowledge* (1969). Foucault defines "episteme" in *Archaeology* as "the total set of relations that unite, at a given period, the discursive practices that give rise to epistemological figures, practices, and possibly formalized systems." The episteme is thus the precondition for knowledge or for science at a particular historical moment, and this episteme governs the ways in which competing forms of knowledge or epistemic discourses achieve dominance or are subordinated. Indeed, what will count as knowledge or science, as well as what will count as legitimate scientific practice or theory, will depend on the episteme of that particular discursive formation. The episteme is thus somewhat like the vaguer idea of the *Weltanschauung* or "worldview," but more precisely understood as the "totality of relations" between sciences as these can be discovered through the manner of writing or speaking about them.

In *The Order of Things*, Foucault demonstrates how the episteme of the Renaissance gave way to a Classical (i.e., seventeenth- and eighteenth-century) episteme by showing how an entire array of "sciences," which

today would appear primitive and mystical, were suddenly replaced by other, newer visions based not merely on the accumulation of more knowledge, but on an entirely different epistemological framework within which they take on the character of a systematic science or discursive formation. So, for example, the principles of similitude and resemblance, which in the sixteenth century dictated that, say, ailments of the human body could be cured by plants that resembled or had some other affinity with the body part, suddenly ceased to underlie scientific discourse a hundred years later. This earlier episteme is replaced by another, for which representation, order, and identity demand a strict categorization and taxonomy. Foucault shows how this epistemic break, a concept borrowed from Gaston Bachelard, does not just emend and augment what had previously been understood to be "true," but transforms the conditions for the possibility of knowledge in the new epistemic formation. In other words, Foucault insists, our knowledge does not develop according to some progressive history of science in which we gradually learn more and more about a subject, but rather it is subject to nonlinear movements, false starts, and radical breaks that separate incommensurable fields of knowledge. For this reason, Foucault's notion of the episteme is sometimes likened to the "paradigm" of Thomas Kuhn, who argued that scientific revolutions were not based on the accumulation of knowledge but on paradigm shifts, in which the whole way of looking at the scientific field itself abruptly changed.

Foucault spends much of *The Order of Things* examining the Classical episteme, demonstrating how the "discursive regularities" of its epoch are replaced by those of a more humanistic modern episteme, such that general grammar gives way to linguistics, analysis of wealth to political economy, and natural history to biology, for example. In showing how the Classical episteme emerged, functions, and then disappeared, Foucault suggests in *The Order of Things* that our own systems of knowledge in which we are so confident may themselves evanesce, "like a face drawn in sand at the edge of the sea."

(*See also* Chapter 5, Post-structuralism; Discursive Formation; *and* Foucault, Michel)

Robert T. Tally Jr., *Texas State University (United States)*

Further Reading

Foucault, Michel. *The Archaeology of Knowledge* [1969]. Trans. A. M. Sheridan Smith. New York: Pantheon, 1972.

Foucault, Michel. *The Order of Things: An Archaeology of the Human Sciences* [1966]. Trans. anon. New York: Vintage, 1970.

Kuhn, Thomas. *The Structure of Scientific Revolutions*. Chicago: University of Chicago Press, 1962.

Epistolary Novel

The *epistolary novel* is a fictional narrative told through a series of letters or journal entries written by the characters. This form of the novel appeared in the eighteenth century. One of early British novelists, Samuel Richardson, is believed to be the founder of this novel form, which by the eighteenth- and early nineteenth centuries was widely accepted. Richardson's work *Pamela; Or, Virtue Rewarded* (1740) was one of the early forms of the novel and an important work discussed for its epistolary form. The story of *Pamela* is told through the letters that a young servant girl writes to her parents, as well as the journal diaries she keeps when her master fails to seduce, and then kidnaps her.

The epistolary form is identified as a key feature of the novel in Ian Watt's theory of formal realism in *The Rise of the Novel*. The epistolary form is distinctive for its account to reality by presenting firsthand experience in the letters or journals. Richardson's originality is credited in this form in that it offers "particularity of description," as well as the novel's interest in truth claims. The story told by the epistolary form seems to be truer because the author appears to be in a relatively objective position, as an editor of the letters or journal entries, rather than intervening in the story from the author's subjective view. This narrative technique is marked for its presentation of one's private world that is later categorized as a kind of "psychological novel." The psychological novel, often regarded as a delineation of modern subjectivity, works to reflect how a bourgeois individual is formed.

Moreover, the psychological novel is mentioned when we consider the social function of the novel. When Jurgen Habermas articulates his definition of modernity, which presupposes the establishment of a public sphere, the epistolary form of the psychological novel is noted for mediating the privatized individuals to a reality in the form of "trans-temporal continuity." The letter form presents one's private experience in a public way, and readers are encouraged to engage with the reality as the novel presents, and learn the morals (especially getting the right kind of judgment on truth, rationality, and virtue). The novel functions as a model that demonstrates an ideal of bourgeois subjectivity cultivated by a literary culture, grounded in the circulation of the novel.

Samuel Johnson, one of the early literary critics of the eighteenth century, defines the novel with this didactic mission of delivering the probable kind of reality and moral truth. Besides Richardson's *Pamela*, and his later work *Clarissa* (1749), Tobias Smollett's

Humphry Clinker (1771) and Fanny Burney's *Evelina* (1778) are other notable early examples of the epistolary novel in the eighteenth century, which were writing at the same time the modern novel was invented in the formal realist mode.

(*See also* Chapter 22, Identity Studies; Habermas, Jürgen; Hegel, Georg W.; Literature; Nouveau Roman; Novel; Public Sphere; *and* Subjectivity)

Szu-Ying Chen, *University at Albany, SUNY*
(United States)

Further Reading

Habermas, Jürgen. *The Structural Transformation of the Public Sphere: An Inquiry into a Category of Bourgeois Society* [1962]. Trans. Thomas Burger and Frederick Lawrence. Cambridge: MIT Press, 1989.

Watt, Ian. *The Rise of the Novel* [1957]. Berkeley: University California Press, 2001.

Erotic

The erotic is often associated to representations of sexuality or instances when writing might arouse readers. However, in literary theory the erotic focuses on a different form of eroticism, one that has less to do with the sexual act than with a sensual approach to the materials that create texts—language, sounds, orthography, and page design. Examining the erotic uses of these materials, says Susan Sontag in "Against Interpretation" (1966), allows readers to discover the "pure, untranslatable, sensuous immediacy" of writing. As Sontag points out in her essay, readers tend to focus on the content of literary works instead of taking into account the sensory and sensuous experiences that their form triggers. She states, "In place of a hermeneutics we need

an erotics of art." Her statement condemns literary critics' assault on sensuality, as, for her, repression of desire and sensations in the critical sphere is illogical and fruitless. Instead, she calls for a perspective that gives justice to the importance of pleasure in analytical readings of art. Yet, her erotics of language is less devoted to sexual arousal than it is invested in a form of intellectual ecstasy. What literary eroticism shares with the sexual experience is a form of excess. Indeed, the erotic, in sexuality, exceeds mere reproductive goals. Likewise, textual bliss surpasses any use of language for a specific end. This excess implies that literary works do not just attempt to communicate a message but include an excess of unassimilable materials that cannot be contained within a traditional production of meaning (e.g. ambiguity, sound play, repetition, visual arrangements, etc.). This moment is associated to a loss of control from readers because they cannot rely on the habits and strategies that they depend on for conventional modes of communication. To qualify such experiences, Roland Barthes coins the term *jouissance*, a form of acute bliss that, instead of confirming interpretive and social norms, relies on an interaction of codes through illogicality, incongruity, repetition, and a mix of languages. For Barthes in *The Pleasure of the Text* (1973), these radical textual practices violate stability and lead the reader to access bliss, a state that unsettles the self. Georges Bataille comments in *Eroticism* on this challenge of the self, noting that, during the sexual act, two beings interact intimately, thereby losing their discontinuity. For him, disruption and dissolution of the subject are inherently erotic. Discontinuity implies a fusion of bodies during sexuality and a fusion of the reader and the artistic medium. An erotic experience of literature, much like the discontinuous experience of sexuality, invites readers, in their loss of control of habitual reading strategies and straightforward access to information, to become one with the text.

(*See also* Barthes, Roland; Bataille, Georges; Chapter 7, Psychoanalytic Theory; Chapter 18, Translation; Phallocentrism; *and* Sexuality)

Flore Chevaillier, *Texas State University* *(United States)*

Further Reading

Barthes, Roland. *The Pleasure of the Text* [1973]. Trans. Richard Miller. New York: Hill and Wang, 1975.

Bataille, Georges. *Eroticism: Death & Sensuality* [1957]. Trans. Mary Dalwood. London and New York: Marion Boyars, 1987.

Chevaillier, Flore. *The Body of Writing: An Erotics of Contemporary American Fiction*. Columbus: Ohio State University Press, 2013.

Sontag, Susan. "Against Interpretation." In *Against Interpretation and Other Essays*. New York: Farrar, Strauss and Giroux, 1966. 4–14.

Essentialism

Essentialism as a literary-critical term derives from post-structuralist theory's insistence that philosophical efforts to identify an essence, what make something what it is, both foster and build on linguistically mediated cultural stereotyping, thus mystifying by naturalizing invidious evaluations and hierarchies. Philosophically, critique of essentialism is integral to the anti-metaphysical tradition running from Friedrich Nietzsche to Martin Heidegger to Jean-Paul Sartre to Jacques Derrida; politically, it is understood to contest coercive, oppressive social norms and prejudices. Anti-essentialist literary criticism endeavors to identify representational techniques that essentialize—as in presenting marriage as a happy plot resolution for female protagonists, portraying "good" dark-skinned colonial natives as loyal servants, etc. While resistant or unmasking readings critique essentialist rhetoric within literary texts, appreciative ones identify and valorize within texts, or parts thereof, internal or implicit contestation of essentialist thought.

Critiquing essentialism, however, has proved easier than articulating philosophically coherent and politically palpable alternatives. If conceptual and evaluative thought are taken to be in their essence complicit with essentialism, then anti-essentialist critique might well issue in a slack relativism that makes the moral-political energy animating it unaccountable on its own terms. Such a charge was leveled by a number of studies of post-structuralist theory around 1990—by Peter Dews, Charles Taylor, John McGowan, among others. To address the issue in relation to postcolonial theory, Gayatri Chakravorty Spivak introduced the term "strategic essentialism," by which she meant the use of essentialism as a rhetorical ploy by oppressed or marginalized groups to advance progressive agendas. The idea that essentialism might be employed "strategically," that is, sophistically, without one actually buying into claims made to achieve desirable political-moral ends, was embraced within some feminist and queer theory discourse, but Spivak herself later repudiated the notion—arguing that "strategic" use of essentialism need not be limited to oppressed groups and progressive agendas, and that the use of a rhetoric slips easily into believing it.

More broadly, anti-essentialist dismissal of claims to intrinsic identity or constitutive attributes can have sobering non-progressive consequences, as in right-wing assertions that being gay is merely a lifestyle choice. Further complicating matters is the easy confusion of critique of essentialism with rejection of all claims to universalism, both ethical universalism and descriptive or categorical universalism. Chinua Achebe and Kwame Anthony Appiah reject relativizing of ethics as a reprise of colonialist thinking, in which the native is seen as fundamentally unlike Europeans, so that no shared standard or value may be expected. Descriptive or categorical universalism, as first used in linguistics, denotes invariant or prevalently recurrent patterns among geographically and historically separated groups. Explorations in neurocognitive science of the impress of bodily experience on species-wide patterns of categorization and conceptualization, for example, presents good evidence of universalism in this sense—as George Lakoff and Mark Johnson argue. Building on such work, Patrick Colm Hogan develops the notion of "literary universals," as in the recurrence of romantic, heroic, and sacrificial plot prototypes in a wide range of disparate cultures. Hogan's work highlights how the non-conflation of universalism and essentialism is central to cognitive literary theory and criticism. More generally, the adequacy of the practice of criticism as critique, largely honed to contest essentialism, has been searchingly questioned by Rita Felski, Bruno Latour, and others.

(*See also* Chapter 10, Feminism; Chapter 12, Postmodernism; Chapter 22, Identity Studies; Identity Politics; Patriarchy; *and* Spivak, Gayatri)

Donald R. Wehrs, *Auburn University (United States)*

Further Reading

Felski, Rita. *The Limits of Critique*. Chicago: University of Chicago Press, 2015.
Fetterley, Judith. *The Resisting Reader: A Feminist Approach to American Fiction*. Bloomington: University of Indiana Press, 1978.
Hogan, Patrick Colm. *The Mind and Its Stories: Narrative Universals and Human Emotion*. Cambridge: Cambridge University Press, 2003.
Spivak, Gayatri Chakravorty. *In Other Words: Essays in Cultural Politics*. London: Methuen, 1987.
Spivak, Gayatri Chakravorty. *Other Asias*. Malden: Blackwell, 2008.

Ethical Criticism

Ethical criticism was long thought of as moralistic, as heir to Victorian preoccupations with whether a work's tendencies were "improving" or its author respectable. Reaction against moralistic thought, hardened by post-First World War disillusionment, tended to make ethics, at best, a veiled subtext in formalist and historicist criticism. The Holocaust and the cultural upheavals of the 1960s and 1970s undermined conflation of the ethical with the moralistic, but also subsumed ethics into a politics of liberation. Thus in Roland Barthes, the reader was to be emancipated from writerly texts, in Michel Foucault from discursively naturalized conceptualization and power relations, in Jacques Derrida and Paul de Man from coercive logocentric hermeneutics, and in Jacques Lacan, Louis Althusser, and others from identification with repressive/hegemonic subject positions. 1980s criticism further absorbed ethics into politics by employing post-structuralist reading practices to expose, redress, or champion resistance to wrongs done to those disadvantaged, marginalized, or silenced on the basis of gender, race, class, colonial history, culture, sexual orientation/identity, disability, or other criteria.

Contemporary ethical criticism began to emerge around 1990, fueled in part by concerns that post-structuralist methodological skepticism tended to make liberation from metaphysical-political dogmatism contingent upon a dubious moral relativism ultimately antithetical to progressive values and commitments. The 1987 discovery of Paul de Man's collaborationist wartime journalism reinforced such concerns, addressed directly or obliquely not only by pioneering ethical literary criticism by Stanley Cavell, Wayne Booth, Tobin Siebers, and Geoffrey Galt Harpham, but also by the 1980s revival by Alasdair MacIntyre, Charles Taylor, Martha Nussbaum, and others of Neo-Aristotelian moral philosophy. Concurrently, the very conception of ethics was radically transformed by belated reception of Emmanuel Levinas's writing. Levinas, a French-Lithuanian philosopher, religious thinker, and Holocaust survivor, located the ethical not in perception of (true) reality, nor in pursuit of autonomy, nor in liberation from conformity or oppressive naturalizations, but in encountering an Other whose presence, claims, and needs put in question the ego's assertion of its own privilege and priority. The trauma of this encounter, Levinas argued, grounds both human sociality and linguistic-cultural signification. Cavell argues similarly that imperatives of ethical acknowledgment are uncompromised by epistemic skepticism. Ethical criticism highlights how literary discourse may work to elicit acknowledgment and expose egoism's violence, thus bringing home to readers subjectivity's rootedness in responsibility to and for the Other. Ethics so understood becomes the enabling condition for critiques of unjust social structures and totalizing conceptualities.

Ethical criticism has further been energized by research in neurocognitive science and affect studies. Levinas treats ethical consciousness as a "pre-original" constituent of consciousness, leading some to think his account dependent on his religious convictions. But the 1990s discovery of "mirror neurons" that, triggered by observing or imagining another's bodily experience, spontaneously "mirror" neurocognitive-affective sensations felt in undergoing the perceived experience places phenomenology of ethical consciousness within a biological-evolutionary context. Indeed, recent evolutionary theory insists that affective-ethical sociality, dependent on but enlarging neural mirroring, *precedes* modern humans' neurophysiological constitution. Such work provides ethical criticism a deep historical, materialistic, species-wide, and transcultural basis.

(*See also* Aristotelianism; Chapter 8, Rhetoric; Kant, Immanuel; Levinas, Emmanuel; Neuroscience; Other, The; *and* Subjectivism)

Donald R. Wehrs, *Auburn University (United States)*

Further Reading

Booth, Wayne. *The Company We Keep: An Ethics of Fiction*. Berkeley: University of California Press, 1988.

Harpham, Geoffrey Galt. *Getting It Right: Language, Literature, and Ethics*. Chicago: University of Chicago Press, 1992.

Shankman, Steven. *Other Others: Levinas, Literature, Transcultural Studies*. Albany: SUNY, 2010.

Wehrs, Donald R., ed. *Levinas and Twentieth-Century Literature: Ethics and the Reconstruction of Subjectivity*. Newark: University of Delaware Press, 2013.

Ethnicity

Kinships or group solidarities with common languages and cultures have been present in every historical period and on every continent. But, identifying these groups ethnically in the United States first appeared in 1941 in *The Social Life of a Modern Community* by W. Lloyd Warner and Paul S. Lunt, with the use of the term becoming in vogue in the 1970s. An *ethnic group* was typically defined as a social group who shared a common and distinctive cultural heritage, religion, nationality, customs, and/or language. Race was a dominant feature, but it was only one of the dimensions of the larger cultural and historical phenomenon of ethnicity. With its unique features and characteristics, an ethnic group was considered natural, stable, relatively fixed, or, at least, known as a self-evident category. It was separate from other ethnic groups and was considered authentic. An individual was classified as belonging to a specific ethnic group if she considered herself or was considered by a community as a member of the group, and if she participated in the activities of the group. Since the United States historically has been an immigrant country, immigrants to the United States usually end up in ethnic communities, populated by people from their own country. The existence of many of these ethnic communities was reinforced by either de jure segregation or de facto segregation. The Chinatowns of the 1880s were continually repopulated with working-class immigrants from China, Hong Kong, and Taiwan in the 1950s, 1970s, and 1990s because they possessed familiar language, customs, and cultural heritage. And until US suburbanization after the Second World War, ethnic European immigrants from Ireland and Italy settled in established ethnic Italian and Irish communities in New York, Boston, Chicago, and San Francisco because they shared a cultural heritage or religion with these communities. With increased immigration and globalization at the end of the twentieth century and the beginning of the twenty-first century, ethnic communities have continued to develop throughout the Western Hemisphere for the same reasons.

But with developments in modern linguistics, the post-structural works of Michel Foucault, Michel de Certeau, Hayden White, and the anthropological and historical works of James Clifford, Michael Fischer, Ernest Gellner, and Benedict Anderson, we now define ethnicity differently. As Foucault and others interrogated ready-made, unexamined syntheses, exposing them as constructions or inventions of bodies of knowledge that permit and exclude, we have had to look at ethnicity not as an essential category but as a cultural invention. We have had to accept the undeniable fact that ethnic groups are a part of a historical process that is continually becoming, as these various groups interact and intermix with each other. And in this dynamic interaction, ethnic groups incorporate outside signals, behaviors, foods, customs, and languages from other ethnic or kinship groups. Thus, we now know, then, that ethnicity is not a thing but a process. American categories of "American Indian" and "white," "black" and "American Indian" or "Irish" and "Anglo" are inadequate to describe a highly miscegenated, poly-ethnic culture in the United States and increasingly in Europe.

(*See also* Chapter 11, Cultural Studies; Chapter 13, Race and Postcolonial Studies; Hybridity; Minority; Postcolonialism; *and* Race)

W. Lawrence Hogue, *University of Houston (United States)*

Further Reading
Cornell, Stephen, and Douglas Hartmann. *Ethnicity and Race: Making Identities in a Changing World.* Second ed. Thousand Oaks: Pine Forge Press, 2007.

Hutchinson, John, and Anthony D. Smith, eds. *Ethnicity*. Oxford: Oxford University Press, 1996.

Sollors, Werner. *The Invention of Ethnicity*. New York: Oxford University Press, 1989.

Warner, W. Lloyd, and Paul S. Lunt. *The Social Life of a Modern Community*. Volume 1, Yankee City Series. New Haven: Yale University Press, 1941.

Eurocentrism

Predating the rise of postcolonial socioeconomic and literary-cultural analysis, with which the *word* as such entered the vocabulary of "critique" and spread across the humanities, the *concept* of *Eurocentrism* has a longer and multifaceted history inside and outside European tradition. For one thing, the term's birth and dissemination speak to this tradition's capacity to distance itself from its own self-centered take on the world, that is, from viewing itself and others through lenses crafted exclusively in its cultural workshop. In response to modern-era crises and ensuing paradigm shifts within and without the continent, more and more European and non-European scholars have come to grips with the actual intellectual optics of such lenses, whose workings and effects have run a whole gamut from "soft" to "hard," viz., from benign subjectivity of perception and ill-informed asseverations to arrogant bias and allegations of superiority, "exceptionalism," and the like. Thus, it has become clear that inevitably "perspectival" lenses can easily turn into distorting prisms, and, further, that obtaining distortions can, directly or indirectly, do the bidding of political agendas of imperialist-hegemonic nature. Put otherwise, culturocentrism in European form activates modalities of seeing and knowing (cognitive maps) that, on closer inspection, prove constructed or given in advance by apriorisms—notions, assumptions, biases, reading models, entire epistemologies—that render the encounter with the territory or the knowledge object a pretext for the knowing subject's self-affirmation.

In this sense, Eurocentrism can be and has been an intellectual narcissism. But culturocentrism is in no way a European "invention" or monopoly. Nor are all European mappings of world territories and knowledge domains—including of its own—culturocentric, for understanding is never strictly determined by one's background or location. Simply put, cultural gazing need not be, in Europe and elsewhere, navel-gazing. Vice versa, the idea that the world outside yours converges or is centered on your own world, the notion that you are somehow the familiar world's *omphalos* ("navel" in Ancient Greek) are myths shared by European and non-European cultures alike. Recent centuries, however, have witnessed a disproportionate number of large-scale attempts to center the world intellectually, economically, and politically in and around Europe and European modes of world cartography, with modern geography, its coordinates, and spatial-temporal measurements a literal case in point. That is to say, while Eurocentrism is just one of existing or imaginable culturocentrisms, not all culturocentrisms are the same. Afrocentrism, for example, has been a critical, anti-colonial reaction against Eurocentrism in its most egregious forms, for indeed, a cultural discourse recentered around an African "worldview" or "mindset" that works to decenter a "European" or "Europe-centered" understanding of "Africa" can be empowering and fruitful. The scare quotes in the previous sentence mean to underscore one of the problems—and the main provocation—surrounding today Orientalism and its less talked-about correlative Occidentalism, arguably special instantiations or subsets of the "centrisms" swirling around the debates on European cultural bias, "provincialism," "parochialism," and so forth. These discussions have been plagued by misinformed or hasty blanket statements and presuppositions about what constitutes "Europe" and "European" as much as they have been marred by under-researched, presumptuous, self-interested, simplifying, homogenizing, and blatantly racist pronouncements on African and Asian cultures.

(*See also* Chapter 13, Race and Postcolonial Studies; *and* Hybridity)

Christian Moraru, *University of North Carolina, Greensboro (United States)*

Further Reading

Amin, Samir. *Eurocentrism: Modernity, Religion, and Democracy: A Critique of Eurocentrism and Culturalism.* Trans. Russell Moore and James Membrez. Second ed. New York: Monthly Review Press, 2010.

Ismail, Qadri. *Culture and Eurocentrism.* Lanham: Rowman and Littlefield, 2015.

Shohat, Ella, and Robert Stam. *Unthinking Eurocentrism: Multiculturalism and the Media.* Second ed. Abingdon: Routledge, 2014.

Event

The idea of the event emerges with the thought of Martin Heidegger. In his posthumously published *Contributions to Philosophy* (1936–38), Heidegger develops the idea of the *Ereignis*, which is usually translated as an event of appropriation. For Heidegger, the *Ereignis* is an event of Being revealing itself to beings in a new way. The original event of Being was given to the pre-Socratic Greeks, but this thinking that shaped Western philosophy has exhausted itself, and we must open ourselves up to a new Event of Being that can only come without our own willful grasping.

The later Heidegger's conception of the Event influences French philosophers like Jacques Derrida, Gilles Deleuze, and Alain Badiou. For Derrida, the notion of event is how he critiques the limits of structuralism as it was understood in France in the 1960s. In his essay, "Structure, Sign, and Play in the Discourse of the Human Sciences (1966)," Derrida declares "Perhaps something has occurred in the history of the concept of structure that could be called an 'event,' if this loaded word did not entail a meaning which it is precisely the function of structural—or structurality—thought to reduce or to suspect." An event is that which ruins any perfect or complete structure, as well as what makes it possible for a structure to exist in the first place. For Derrida, the event is essential for understanding his theory and practice of deconstruction. Deconstruction concerns what happens, by appreciating that the conditions for anything to occur are at the same time conditions of impossibility for anything to fully occur and exhaust itself.

For Gilles Deleuze, the event is not simply what happens; it is what is going on inside what happens. In *The Logic of Sense* (1969), Deleuze says that an event is a kind of singularity that fundamentally transforms what is going on. The event occurs along the surface of sense, or language, but language also participates in the depths of the body and its own incorporeal nonsense. The event is a complex concept that refers to the affect that takes place in any experience. For example, one can exhaustively describe a song, but the impact it can make for a person in a particular situation can be transformative.

Finally, Alain Badiou in his book *Being and Event* (1988) thinks the event as a radical break from being or ontology. Being is understood in terms of mathematical set theory, and it adequately describes a situation in a way that proscribes an event, even as it can constitute an eventual site where an event may irrupt. The event is technically an unpredictable and undecidable occurrence in terms of ontology, but it radically transforms a situation, and a person becomes a subject out of fidelity to an event. There are events of love, of science, of politics, and art. These ideas of the event have proven influential in many discourses, including literary and cultural theory.

(*See also* Badiou, Alain; Deleuze, Gilles; Derrida, Jacques; and Heidegger, Martin)

Clayton Crockett, *University of Central Arkansas (United States)*

Further Reading

Badiou, Alain. *Being and Event* [1988]. Trans. Oliver Feltham. London: Continuum, 2005.

Derrida, Jacques. "Structure, Sign, and Play in the Discourse of the Human Sciences [1966]." In *Writing and Difference* [1967]. Trans. Alan Bass. Chicago: University of Chicago Press, 1978.

Deleuze, Gilles. *The Logic of Sense* [1969]. Trans. Mark Lester with Charles Stivale. Ed. Constantin V. Boundas. New York: Columbia University Press, 1990.

Exception, State of (*See* Agamben, Giorgio; Exceptionalist State; Bare Life; Biopolitics; *and* Sovereignty)

Exceptionalist State

In his very influential books *Homo Sacer* (1995) and *The State of Exception* (2003), Giorgio Agamben meditates on the normalization of the state of exception in Western modernity, in which the law is abrogated by the sovereign in order to preserve it, and human life (*bios*) is reduced to bare life (*zoé*): life that can be killed without the killing being called murder. In his genealogy of the state of exception, Agamben locates its genealogical origins in ancient Rome and overdetermines European history. Agamben's genealogy of the normalization of the state of exception constitutes a major contribution to the theoretical diagnosis of the contradictions inhering in Western (democratic) capitalist modernity and its nation-state system. But I would like to suggest that in restricting his genealogy to Europe, or rather, in including the United States as a subset of the European nation-states, Agamben fails to adequately perceive that the major player in the inexorable momentum that is reducing human life to bare life in the post–Second World War world is the United States. I want to suggest that the United States' unique notion of the nation-state contains within its onto-cultural structure the entire dehumanizing potential of the state of exception. I am referring to the nation's understanding of itself as an *exceptionalist state* in the sense of the term that has determined the American national identity from its founding, when the "divinely elected" Puritans undertook their "errand in the wilderness" of the "New World": American exceptionalism, an ethos which, in perceiving itself as superior to other peoples, also perceives its relationship to the rest of the world in terms of the logic of the Friend/foe binary.

More historically specific, the exceptionalist ethos of the American state became one with the state exception when, in pursuit of its divinely ordained errand in the wilderness, the Puritans confronted the paradox that their very civilizing mission ("betterment" in the language of the later American pioneers), in inevitably producing comfort, also produced a "back sliding" that threatened to dissipate the essential energy and unity of their covenantal community. In the face of this intrinsic recidivism, the Massachusetts Bay Colony Puritans, as Sacvan Bercovitch has famously observed, inaugurated the tradition of the "American jeremiad." This was the perennial ritual that reminded the backsliding covenantal community of its divinely ordained errand to rationalize the "New World" wilderness by way of perpetually producing anxiety in its members.

More specifically, the ritual of the American jeremiad rendered the original threat posed by the nomadic "savages" to the founding Puritan covenant a perennial condition: the need for an enemy or, alternatively, a threatening frontier that, in provoking anxiety, would always already reenergize and reunite the always flagging covenantal community in behalf of its divinely (later, after the establishment of the United States, History) ordained "civilizing" vocation. This explains the United States' perennial obsession with the idea of the frontier. I am not only referring to the systematic and brutal westward removal of the native Americans beyond one frontier to the next and their eventual confinement to enclosed reservations or, for all intents and purpose, interment in concentration camps. I am also referring to the United States' perennial anxiety over the waning of the western frontier, as the history of American culture hegemonized by Frederick Jackson Turner at the time of the official closing of the American frontier at the end of the nineteenth century, testifies.

Once this ideological structure of the original (ontological) myth of American exceptionalism is recognized, its disastrous historical, cultural, and political consequences that have been effaced by the materialist achievements of progress become remarkably visible. It not only goes far to explain the "New Frontier" of the John F. Kennedy administration at the beginning of the 1960s—the doctrine that extended the western frontier beyond the coast of California into the Pacific, an imperial initiative that eventually bore witness to the wholesale forced removal of South Vietnamese villagers from their ancestral homes into the dehumanizing internment camps that the American government cultural army in Saigon called "New Life Hamlets." Equally horrific, this American exceptionalist ethos goes far to explain the United States' declaration of its "war against terror" in the wake of the bombing of the World Trade Center and the Pentagon by Al Qaeda, in which, according to the Friend/enemy logic of American exceptionalism, the frontier became the unlocalized norm—and the state of exception the rule.

In this late or liminal dispensation, the binary (Friend/foe) logic of belonging intrinsic to the exceptionalist state (what the founding Puritans called "the covenantal community of saints") has gone extremely far in the name of its exceptional greatness to render the state of exception the rule and the concentration camp its (bio)political paradigm, in which, as Giorgio Agamben testifies, human life has becomes bare life, life that can be killed with impunity. One cannot help but hear the ominous echoes of this relationship between the American exceptionalism state and the normalized state of exception in the motto inscribed in the red baseball cap the elected president of the United States, Donald Trump, wears where he goes "Make America great again," only this time, to adapt Karl Marx, as dangerous farce.

(*See also* Agamben, Giorgio; Bare Life; Biopolitics; Sovereignty; *and* Terror)

William Spanos, *Binghamton University (United States)*

Further Reading

Agamben, Giorgio. *State of Exception* [2003]. Trans. Kevin Attrell. Chicago: University of Chicago Press, 2005.

Benjamin, Walter. "Critique of Violence [1921]." In *Reflections: Essays, Apho-*

risms, Autobiographical Writings. Ed. Peter Demetz. New York: Harcourt Brace Jovanovich 1978.

Spanos, William V. *The Exceptionalist State and the State of Exception: Herman Melville's Billy Budd, Sailor*. Baltimore: Johns Hopkins University Press, 2011.

Existentialism

Existentialism is the name given to certain philosophical, literary, and general cultural tendencies that saw their heyday in the immediate post-Second World War years, beginning in Paris and radiating out from there. The three names most closely associated with it at the time were those of Jean-Paul Sartre, Simone de Beauvoir, and Albert Camus, all of them philosophers who were also successful essayists and novelists. However, other writers—notably Gabriel Marcel and the exiled Russian author Leon Shestov (whose *Kierkegaard and the Existential Philosophy* was published in French in 1936)—had already begun using the term well before Sartre and Beauvoir were persuaded to accept this label that was, as it were, thrust upon them; and Camus insisted, even though historians have generally disregarded this, that he was an "absurdist," rather than an existentialist, thinker. Moreover, as Shestov's title reference to the early-nineteenth-century Danish figure, Søren Kierkegaard, makes evident, there is widespread agreement that existentialism's antecedents extend back at least into that century (with, among others, Friedrich Nietzsche, Fyodor Dostoevsky, and, in the early twentieth century, Franz Kafka being widely regarded as proto-existentialists) and perhaps even much earlier (the name of Blaise Pascal being most often invoked in this context).

Among the common characteristics of existentialist thought, besides its obvious interdisciplinarity, are an emphasis on our freedom and on the anxiety that it can occasion, a downgrading of worldviews that take the "human essence" to be fixed and stable, a questioning of traditional doctrines of ethics and theology, and, in short, an orientation toward unconventionality and openness. Whereas it is usual to distinguish sharply between theistic and non-theistic existentialists, some of the most prominent among the latter retained strong quasi-religious influences in appealing to one or another form of transcendence—as for instance Martin Heidegger, a lover of poetry though not a literary figure, in his call for a return to the question of "Being." Sartrean existentialism, in particular, came to be associated with sociopolitical commitment, *engagement*, as a consequence of his advocacy of it in a long, much-debated essay, "What Is Literature?" (1948). His colleague Beauvoir defended the value of the literary novel as a *genre*.

Existentialism's literary and cultural influences—some disputed, most not—have been very wide-ranging. Richard Wright was self-identified as an existentialist, but many other authors and playwrights, such as Jack Kerouac, Harold Pinter, Edward Albee, Eugene Ionesco, Samuel Beckett, and Jean Genet have also been associated to one degree or another with the movement. Cinema, from the Nouvelle Vague to Ingmar Bergman to Woody Allen; painting, from Giacometti to Jackson Pollock (similarly self-identified as an existentialist) and numerous others; music—Sartre himself was something of a jazz connoisseur; theology, including Karl Barth and Paul Tillich; psychiatry (R. D. Laing, Ludwig Binswanger, Medard Boss, Rollo May); and no doubt many other fields were strongly indebted to existentialism for their twentieth-century configurations. Although now hardly the popular fad that it was in the late 1940s, existentialism has permanently altered cultural landscapes worldwide.

(*See also* Beauvoir, Simone de; Bakhtin, Mikhail; Chapter 1, Early Theory; Chapter 24, Posthumanism; Humanism; Heidegger, Martin; Literature as Philosophy; Nietzsche, Friedrich; Rorty, Richard; *and* White, Hayden)

William McBride, *Purdue University*
(United States)

Further Reading
Crowell, Stephen, ed. *The Cambridge Companion to Existentialism*. Cambridge: Cambridge University Press, 2012.
Sartre, Jean-Paul. *Existentialism Is a Humanism* [1996]. Trans. C. Macomber. New Haven: Yale University Press, 2007.
Wartenberg, Thomas E. *Existentialism: A Beginner's Guide*. Oxford: Oneworld, 2008.

F

Fantasy

One of the most important epistemological contributions of psychoanalysis was to prioritize *psychical reality*—that is, *the role of fantasy*—as underlying all psychological life. This assertion sets psychoanalysis apart from the natural sciences. Whereas a biological instinct can be said to have a *natural* object, this does not hold for human sexuality (for the Freudian concept of *the drive*), which is defined by its relation to a *psychical* object, that is, to an object formed and elaborated by fantasy.

For psychoanalysis there can be no unproblematic recourse to a merely "objective" reality once the foundational role of unconscious desire has been recognized. Questions of origin, otherness, identity, difference, sexuality, and enjoyment (*jouissance*) are always mediated by fantasy. Hence Jean Laplanche and Jean-Bertrand Pontalis state in "Fantasy and the Origins of Sexuality" (1968) that fantasy is "the fundamental object of psychoanalysis." It is thus erroneous to oppose "reality" and fantasy, to imply that fantasy is an add-on, a distortion, a fanciful distraction or obstruction to seeing the world "as it really is." Fantasy is rather, as Slavoj Žižek stresses in *The Plague of Fantasies* (1997), the very frame that guarantees our access to reality; to do away with fantasy would not result in an objective view of the world "as it actually is"—it would mean we *cease to have access to reality at all.*

Sigmund Freud used the notion of fantasy to describe a scene—the famous "Other scene" of the unconscious—in which repressed desires are played out. This staging is disguised, subject to the primary process (operations of displacement, condensation, symbolization, inversion, etc.). Fantasy scenarios are also thus subject to multiple transformations. Freud's analysis of the fantasy "A Child is being Beaten" (1919), for instance, yields two earlier phases of the fantasy ("My father is beating a child I hate" and "I am being beaten by my father") both of which disguise an incestuous desire for the father. This desire has been reformulated: not only has an original position of agency (the desiring child) been replaced by a position of subordination (being beaten) but the incestuous wish has been reversed into one of punishment. The example also shows how the desiring subject cannot be allocated one position in a given fantasy, but can be identified variously as: agent/recipient or audience of the fantasied scene.

Laplanche and Pontalis provide an overview of the different types of fantasy described in Freud's work. Fantasy, they argue, is intricately connected to speculations of origin, and we can thus identify a series of different origin fantasies: of human beings ("*Menschenkinder*"), of the individual (the primal scene), of sexuality (seduction), and of the difference between the sexes (castration).

(*See also* Castration; Chapter 7, Psychoanalytic Theory; Drive; Jouissance; Freud,

Sigmund; Libidinal; objet petit a; Origin; Other, The; Primordial Discord; Psychoanalysis; Sexuality; *and* Žižek, Slavoj)

Derek Hook, *Duquesne University (United States)*

Further Reading

Freud, Sigmund. "'A Child is being Beaten': A Contribution to the Study of the Origin of Sexual Perversions [1919]." In *The Standard Edition of the Complete Psychological Works of Sigmund Freud.* Volume XVII. Trans. J. Strachey. London: Hogarth, 1966–74. 175–204.

Laplanche, Jean, and Jean-Bertrand Pontalis. "Fantasy and the Origins of Sexuality." *International Journal of Psychoanalysis* 49.1 (1968): 1–18.

Žižek, Slavoj. *The Plague of Fantasies.* London: Routledge, 1997.

Feminist Materialism

In a broad sense, feminist materialism (or materialist feminism) can be understood as a feminist retheorization of historical materialism. During the second wave, feminist thinkers reflected upon the oppressive properties of capitalist infrastructures. While Marxist ideology could provide a framework for identifying the subjugated positions of women within the market, theorists also wanted to communicate the implications of race, ethnicity, nationality, and sexuality as facets of women's oppression. All of these factors are reflected in the material realities of women's lives, but Western feminists prior to this turn seemed to study abstract properties of oppression such as desire and demand. Marxism itself lacked a gendered rhetoric through which notions of class, production, labor, and wealth could be articulated. Conversely, feminist theory was inadequately oriented with materialism and

lacked sufficient historical framing. Cultural theorist Teresa Ebert warned against reducing Marxist feminist ideas to mere questions of epistemology or confining them to texts, and thus the need for a revised theory of materialism with postmodernism in mind arose.

The term "feminist materialism" was coined by French feminist sociologist Christine Delphy in her efforts to locate the basis of women's oppression within material reality, rather than within ideology. Delphy identified patriarchal models of production via the family and the default position of married women as contracted childbearers as the key constituents of material oppression. In both instances, women's labor is appropriated by men and divorced from women on the market. Delphy's assertion signaled a shift from Marxist feminist efforts to fight for women's wages in the workplace and instead suggested that the domestic sphere was the location of greatest oppression. British feminist theorists Anette Kuhn, Anne Marie Wolpe, Michèle Barrett, and Mary McIntosh also adopted the term in order to signal the deficiency of Marxism in articulating a gendered politics of labor and class. Later scholars like Rosemary Hennessy and Chrys Ingraham extrapolated upon this concept and maintained that emergent modes of feminism needed to join class politics with the positionality of women since capitalism is predicated upon hierarchical class structure. Through historical materialism, systems of oppression could be traced and thereby corrected in the hopes of attaining social transformation. Feminist materialism served as a catalyst for the critique of empiricism and postmodern ideas of subjecthood outside of the realm of art and literature. Since this concept was explored by feminists well into the third wave, feminist materialism allowed for the consideration of topics like queerness and prostitution that had been previously neglected by Marxist feminists.

(*See also* Chapter 4, Marxism; Chapter 10, Feminism; Chapter 23, Materialisms; Feminist Theory; Marxism; *and* Materialism)

Rita Mookerjee, *Florida State University (United States)*

Further Reading

Delphy, Christine. "For a Feminist Materialism." In *Materialist Feminism: A Reader in Class, Difference, and Women's Lives.* First ed. Ed. Rosemary Hennessey and Chrys Ingraham. New York: Routledge, 1997. 59–65.

Hennessey, Rosemary. *Materialist Feminism and the Politics of Discourse.* New York: Routledge, 1992.

Kuhn, Annette, and Ann Marie Wolpe. "Feminism and Materialism [1978]." In *Materialist Feminism: A Reader in Class, Difference, and Women's Lives.* Ed. Rosemary Hennessey and Chrys Ingraham. New York: Routledge, 1997. 83–88.

Feminist Narratology (*See* Chapter 3, Narrative and Narratology)

Feminist Theory

Though colorful bumper stickers often tell you that "Feminism is the Radical Idea that Women are Equal Too," feminism has a much more historically, geographically, and intellectually varied repertory of ideas. Though feminism may have entered literary studies in the role of discerning and embarrassing "images of" sexism and patriarchy within the canonical traditions of literature, or to find "images of" "strong women" as "role models," this method is too limited to account for the wide-ranging inquiry that falls under the feminist label. Not just about a liberal call to equality, not even just about a multicultural call to recognition and inclusion, feminism has taken, for example, leftist and Marxist forms, with a variation insisting on pay for the unpaid sectors of the reproductive economy, and another variation analyzing the development of social structures through the exchange of women, and another variation interested in the commercialization of femininity in popular culture and the media. What is important to remember about feminist theory is that it is integrally linked to activism, that is, to producing a vision of a future that is better for all women everywhere and then acting to actualize that vision.

A mid-twentieth-century version of feminism in literary studies challenged the white male canon, retrieving texts written by, for, and about women that had been lost, gone out of print, or gone unnoticed. In a very real sense, such feminist retrieval set the critical world awry by exposing the limits of critical practice and questioning how value is assumed to reside in certain texts when value is, really, an historical production and an effect of power. This recovery process brought up a skepticism about what was guiding the collection of objects retrieved. Could an experience of "woman" be identified and defined? What made the text identifiable as a "woman's" text? Was the "woman's" text producing a norm or a singular manifestation of what it meant to be a woman, or was it mirroring a transhistorical and transcultural reality? Could it be accused of paranoically keeping a lid on something that was inherently slippery, multiple, and elusive?

What most often falls under the umbrella of "feminist theory" in its contemporary literary and critical appearances is therefore a body of writing for the most part concerned with language and subjectivity. One of the central questions is, what does "woman" mean? Can "woman" only be defined in opposition to something else? Is "woman" just a cultural convention? How does "woman" come to be? Is "woman" a designation of a body?

If so, is that body coherent? Does that body always have the same appearance and the same meaning, and does it always fit with that term, in all ways? Does the "female" of the body restrict, enhance, or direct desire? How can we account for the differences between, on the one hand, the abstraction of the word "woman" with its universalizing tendencies, and, on the other, particular, concrete lives? Is "woman" a place in society? A way of knowing? A type of work? A particular sensation? A body part? A type of action? A cultural formation? An institution? An experience? A love object? A sex? A sense of the future? Do I know it when I see it? Does it always feel the same way? What is the relationship between "woman" and "human"? Between "woman" and "culture"? What does it mean to say "I" am a "woman"? Does the "I" need a gender in order to have language at all? What does it mean for a "woman"—who historically has a negative relationship with the knowing subject—to read, to write, or to claim a legacy as "author" from a tradition that assumed that function as male? Such questions have inflections in post-structuralism, psychoanalysis, postcolonialism, structural linguistics, deconstruction, Marxism, critical race theory, queer theory, and phenomenology.

(*See also* Beauvoir, Simone de; Butler, Judith; Chapter 1, Early Theory; Chapter 10, Feminism; Chapter 27, Antitheory; Cixous, Hélène; Feminist Materialism; Gender; Haraway, Donna; Intersectionality; Irigaray, Luce; Kristeva, Julia; New Materialisms; Patriarchy; Performativity; *and* Sexuality)

Robin Truth Goodman, *Florida State University (United States)*

Further Reading

Beauvoir, Simone de. *The Second Sex* [1949]. Trans. H. M. Parshley. New York: Knopf, 1953.

Butler, Judith. *Gender Trouble: Feminism and the Subversion of Identity.* New York: Routledge, 1990.

Goodman, Robin Truth, ed. *Literature and the Development of Feminist Theory.* Cambridge: Cambridge University Press, 2015.

Hemmings, Clare. *Why Stories Matter: The Political Grammar of Feminist Theory.* Durham: Duke University Press, 2011.

Fetish (*See* Castration)

Figuration

The term *figuration* denotes the act of representation through "figures," in other words, a way of according shape or form to something in a given representational medium. In different branches of aesthetics, the word can mean different things. In painting, for instance, figuration is often taken to mean the representation of the real, rather than the imagined. Art that is recognizably derived from objects in the real world can be thought of as guided by the principles of figuration. In music, the term can refer to effects of ornamentation or embellishment; it can sometimes also denote the use of repetitive patterns in a musical composition. In rhetoric, it can mean the gesture of representing symbolically in a systematic fashion, as in allegory. In literature, figuration is generally used to describe representational norms that are mimetic in character, that is, norms that attempt to present objects and phenomena in the real world with as much verisimilitude as possible. It should be understood, of course, that the protocols of mimesis and the idea of verisimilitude that subtends those protocols vary from culture to culture and period to period, and that what may seem like a very faithful representation of reality to one group of readers may not seem particularly faithful to another group. That being said, however, figuration can be seen as a principle that has played a crucial role in the history of art and literature, sometimes occupying the center of the stage, sometimes the background, depending upon the dominant aesthetic of the moment. The distinguished comparatist Erich Auerbach proposed a diachronic, historical account of figuration in his book *Mimesis: The Representation of Reality in Western Literature*, which first appeared in German in 1946. Therein, he traced the impulse toward figuration from ancient texts like *The Odyssey* and *Genesis* through high modernist writers such as Marcel Proust and Virginia Woolf. The French theorist Gérard Genette has worked on the notion of figuration in a more synchronic manner throughout his career, focusing upon the "figures" that literature relies upon in order to come to terms with the world. Genette has proposed extended analyses of figures such as metaphor, metonymy, and metalepsis; and he has also turned his attention to techniques of narrative representation like voice, duration, and order. Whatever approach one may take to the idea, it is undoubtedly useful to think of figuration as a matter of transformation, or translation. For if we perceive the world in a crude, largely unmediated way, we *understand* the world through a set of representational norms, organizing our experience into a story that makes sense to us. Though we may accept that the world and its phenomena have no particular shape, it is reassuring to imagine that our experience of the world assumes certain shapes, shapes that we can recognize and transmit to others. In that perspective, figuration may be seen as a key feature of cognition, one that enables us to navigate the labyrinth of the real with some sense of direction.

(*See also* Chapter 3, Narrative and Narratology; *and* Chapter 8, Rhetoric)

Warren Motte, *University of Colorado, Boulder (United States)*

Further Reading

Auerbach, Erich. *Mimesis: The Representation of Reality in Western Literature* [1946]. Trans. Willard Trask. Princeton: Princeton University Press, 1953.

Genette, Gérard. *Narrative Discourse: An Essay in Method*. Trans. Jane Lewin. Ithaca: Cornell University Press, 1980.

Finance

In the Middle Ages, the term "finance" originally meant the process of putting an end (hence the prefix *fin-*) to a debt or obligation. In the eighteenth century, its meaning shifted to the current usage, indicating: (as verb) to provide monetary support for an enterprise, individual, government, or establishment; or (as noun) the money used for such purposes. Within contemporary academic discussions of literature and culture, however, it tends to be used as a modifier, delineating a specific kind of capital. In Marxist terms, *finance* capital is that which does not reproduce itself by passing through the commodity form (M-C-M') but grows, rather, directly (M-M') as it is loaned out, at interest, to other capitalists. Karl Marx also refers to it as "fictitious money," because it does not participate in the valorization process embodied in labor, though he stresses that it cannot be separated from "productive" capital; the two are mutually dependent.

While finance capital has dominated economic accumulation many times over the history of capitalism—inevitably cut short by a massive economic constriction—we are now experiencing a finance cycle that is historically unprecedented, both in duration (from the 1970s into the present) and in volume. Historically, imperial powers often saw rapid expansion of the finance sector shortly before their collapse; some scholars believe the current era of financialization heralds the end of a world order in which the United States has functioned as global hegemon. And because finance traffics less in commodities than in debts to be repaid in future time, its growing dominance over markets is inseparable from a growing field of indebtedness, on the part of governments, industries, and individuals. Austerity measures have become the norm as states struggle to repay creditors, while corporations often find the need to pay off shareholders triumphs over the long-term health of their companies.

These trends have generated new scholarship in literary and cultural studies in the burgeoning fields of debt studies and critical finance studies. These new areas focus on how financialization and debt are becoming new modes of governing and controlling subjectivities, demanding individuals to think of themselves primarily as "human capital," entrepreneurs of their own lives. Scholars also show that organized resistance is more difficult when finance dominates wealth accumulation; strikes are the obvious tool of workers in a manufacturing system because they deprive industrialists of the labor needed to generate profit. When the majority of wealth arises from interest paid servicing debt, resistance may depend on the solidarity of *debtors,* on creative ways to interrupt the debt/finance cycle. And while scholars, activists, and indebted governments struggle to find means of resistance, financial officials are equally creative in discovering new means to profit from payment. Thus, while "finance" originally began as a word to indicate the end of a debt, it has now come to mean its exact opposite; the process of perpetuating debt forever.

(*See also* Chapter 12, Postmodernism; Chapter 21, Late Capitalism; Capitalism; Debt; Neoliberalism; *and* Political Economy)

Marcia Klotz, *University of Arizona*
(United States)

Further Reading

Arrighi, Giovanni. *The Long Twentieth Century: Money, Power, and the Origins of our Times*. New York: Verso, 1994.

Ho, Karen. *Liquidated: An Ethnography of Wall Street*. Durham: Duke University Press, 2009.

Krippner, Greta R. "The Financialization of the American Economy." *Socio-Economic Review* 3.2 (2005): 173–208.

Fish, Stanley

Stanley Fish loomed large throughout the heyday of North American literary theory. His impact remains palpable today. He created a hinge where a native tradition of close reading opened onto a new edifice of structuralism and post-structuralism newly arrived from the Continent. His spectacular renovations of Anglo-American rhetorical criticism helped dislodge formalist, Christian-agrarian New Criticism. By shifting the emphasis of literary criticism away from the bare text and toward the subjectivity of the reader, he fashioned what was known as reader-response theory. Heightened attention to the reader became a dominant intellectual force during the crucial first decade of the American literary theory revolution. That Fish had a special genius for imagining readers' reactions, was proven every time he addressed a group. His spellbound audience tended to sit up straighter and at moments seemed about to rise. It was like watching St. Patrick lure the snakes out of Ireland. It was this combination of intellectual power, rhetorical skill, and personal charisma that made Fish great.

At present, Fish is Professor of Humanities and Law at Florida International University and Floersheimer Distinguished Visiting Professor at the Benjamin Cardozo School of Law. He has taught at Berkeley, Hopkins, Duke, and the University of Illinois, Chicago.

Moving between scholarship and administration, he rebuilt average English departments into global engines of literary theory. Simultaneously, he embarked on his second act as a prominent legal theorist. Along the way, he became director of the Duke University Press and built its reputation as a theory press.

To date, Fish has written fifteen books, most recently *Versions of AntiHumanism: Milton and Others (2012), How to Write a Sentence* (2011), *Save the World on Your Own Time (2008), The Fugitive in Flight* (2011; about a TV show), and *Versions of Academic Freedom: From Professionalism to Revolution* (2014). In his spare time he wrote a biweekly column for the New York Times. His column, "Timely Topics," ran from 2008 to 2013 and included a variety of topics from "An Ontology of Plagiarism" to "Sharia Law" to "Max the Plumber" to "Antaeus and the Tea Party" to "Race to the Top of What? Obama on Education." Fish was a walking *discordia concors*, for even while he maintained his preeminence as a legal theorist and dean of Milton studies, he also built a wide popular following outside academia, finding his fans among people for whom Milton was just a man's first name.

Inarguably a brilliant thinker, philosopher, critic, speaker, and debater, Stanley Fish simultaneously wrote for law reviews and taught in law schools, invented or cofounded reader-response theory and anti-foundationalism, invented new objects of study—"professionalism," "interpretive communities," "self-consuming artifacts"— sustained his popular column in the US newspaper of record, and assembled superstar English departments. The question is how did he do it?

His deep beliefs account for his enduring impact. Consistency was a factor. Just as he fought for the right to professionalize literary studies in 1980, he is today pressing for academic freedom, virtually the same rights

under a different rubric. His dominance in Milton studies can be explained partly by his profound understanding of Milton's commitments, which caused the greatest English epic poet to table his raging poetic ambitions while he threw himself into the thankless task of writing political pamphlets. It's plain that Fish was attracted to this strange convergence of literary genius and political engagement; in fact, his own later career in a sense reiterates Milton's.

Yet, overall, Fish has remained a humble essayist, never attempting a magnum opus that would systematically collect and unify his thought. Perhaps it cannot be unified. He has generally seized upon a problem or entered an ongoing debate, confronted the leaders in the field, corrected what he felt were mistakes, and then simply stopped. At times this counterpunching method leads him into contradictory positions. In his recent book on academic freedoms, he cautions professors to leave their politics outside the classroom and "save the world on your own time!" But he is better known for taking the opposite position and dismissing clear-cut stark binaries, such as politics versus the classroom. He has in fact made a career of proving that supposedly eternal boundaries are provisional and negotiable. But if these and Fish's other positions occasionally seem inconsistent, he is untroubled by it. He is a neopragmatist, for whom ideas may contradict each other so long as they are valid in their local contexts. Fish has been a unique figure, a counterpuncher and pamphleteer in a world of system builders and keepers of the faiths. While he relishes the position of an outlier, his ideas have had extensive mainstream acceptance. Rhetoric and pragmatism had a modest presence in intellectual life before Stanley Fish came along; after him, these ideas will never be marginal again.

(*See also* Chapter 8, Rhetoric; Close Reading; Introduction, Theory in the New

Millennium; Neopragmatism; Reading; Text; *and* University)

Harold Aram Veeser, *City College of New York (United States)*

Further Reading

Mailloux, Steven. *Interpretive Conventions: The Reader in the Study of American Fiction*. Ithaca: Cornell University Press, 1982.

Olson, Gary A. *Stanley Fish: America's Enfant Terrible: The Authorized Biography*. Carbondale: Southern Illinois University Press, 2016.

Robertson, Michael. *Stanley Fish on Philosophy, Politics, and Law: How Fish Works*. Cambridge: Cambridge University Press. 2014.

Veeser, H. Aram. *The Stanley Fish Reader*. London: Blackwell. 1999.

Force

The concept of *force* features heavily in Gilles Deleuze's influential reading of Friedrich Nietzsche in *Nietzsche and Philosophy* (1962). Deleuze characterizes Nietzsche as a symptomatologist for whom all bodies and all phenomena are assessed in terms of relationships between forces. Nietzsche thus diagnosed the spiritual illnesses of bad conscience and *ressentiment* (embodied in morality, religion and culture more generally) as symptoms of reactive, negative, or life-denying forces triumphing over active, positive, or life-affirming ones. Forces, however, only exist in dynamic relationship with one another: every force takes another force as its object. Every relationship between forces thus constitutes a difference, and this differential element is never eliminated, even in the most life-denying phenomena. What this means is that there is always a becoming-active of

reactive forces and a becoming-reactive of active ones. This understanding of force as dynamic and differential allows Deleuze to extract from Nietzsche's thought an ontology of becoming. In addition, Deleuze distinguishes force from Nietzsche's much misunderstood concept of the will to power by stating that the latter is the differential element between forces, that which synthesizes and determines the difference between them. The will to power is what allows forces to confront one another as determinate degrees of power, but also what prevents a final triumph of one force over another. Hence, even the weakest, most reactive force is a manifestation of the will to power and thus indicates a becoming-active. In this way, according to Deleuze, Nietzsche's ethico-political critique is inextricable from his ontology, which constitutes a "superior empiricism."

Deleuze's account of force in Nietzsche laid the groundwork for the metaphysics of becoming, the virtual, and difference that he established in his subsequent works. His major philosophical treatise *Difference and Repetition* (1968) developed an ontology of differential relations intended to break with conceptualizations of difference as the negative of, and thus as subordinate to, identity. Difference in its positive and autonomous form is described by Deleuze in terms of forces or dynamisms that escape the logic of representational thinking. In Deleuze and Guattari's *Anti-Oedipus* (1972) and *A Thousand Plateaus* (1980), an ethico-political critique of culture is combined with a materialist ontology in which the arts and sciences are seen to provide maps of forces that escape the established power structures of the State and subjectivity.

Force also appears prominently in Derrida's work in texts such as "Force and Signification" (1963) and "Force of Law: The 'Mystical Foundation of Authority'"

(1990), as a means of thinking the relationship between theology and violence. In the earlier text, force is used to demonstrate the limits of structuralism, while in the latter it suggests the groundlessness of the violence by which laws are established. Whereas in Deleuze force features as part of a metaphysics of becoming, for Derrida it is precisely the dynamic and temporal element that metaphysics—as metaphysics of presence—cannot account for.

(*See also* Chapter 26, Affect Studies; Deleuze, Gilles; Derrida, Jacques; Law; *and* Violence)

Aidan Tynan, *Cardiff University (United Kingdom)*

Further Reading
Connors, Clare. *Force from Nietzsche to Derrida*. London: Legenda, 2010.
Deleuze, Gilles. *Nietzsche and Philosophy* [1962]. Trans. Hugh Tomlinson. New York: Columbia University Press, 1983.
Derrida, Jacques. "Force and Signification." In *Writing and Difference* [1967]. Trans. A. Bass. Chicago: University of Chicago Press, 1978.

Formalism

Critical methods described as "formalism" have had little in common. At the inception of theoretical reflection on literature in the Western tradition, traceable roughly to Aristotle's *Poetics*, the varieties of literary form were understood as comparable to those found in the natural world. Genres for Aristotle were rather like animal species, and the various literary devices had their own distinct place in a typology organized from big (genre) to small (minute phonetic differences).

More recently, there are three critical movements that, rightly or wrongly, have been taken as emblematic of a formalist approach to literature. There are many differences between them, but they share a sensitivity to the subtle modulations of rhythm, semantics, and syntax at the level of the literary line. This does not mean that these methodologies have neglected questions of history or context, but they have tended to place an emphasis on how literature can create its own fictional worlds through the precise manipulation of figural language.

The first movement is "Russian Formalism," comprising the work of Vladimir Propp, Viktor Shklovsky, Roman Jakobson, Boris Eichenbaum and others, stretching from the 1910s to the 1930s. There is no unifying philosophy across these diverse texts, but there are some constants: a rejection of psychological or biographical approaches to literature; an emphasis on what makes literature a distinctive use of language; and a commitment to a "scientific" approach, one that attempts to define literature's specific properties and capacities as distinct from those to be found in other domains.

The second is the "New Criticism," a term associated variously with the practical criticism of I. A. Richards, with William Empson, with T. S. Eliot, and with US literary critics such as John Crowe Ransom and Cleanth Brooks. The New Critics emphasized close reading, which involves the bracketing of questions of authorial intention and cultural context in favor of an exacting attention to meter, character, plot and imagery, as well as paradox and irony. New Criticism offered a portable and teachable method of literary study that found favor in high school English, and became the dominant mode of English instruction in British and American Universities from the 1950s to the early 1970s.

The third movement is structuralism, a school of thought that traces its roots in part to Russian Formalism. A dominant trend in mid-century France, structuralism sought to locate the impersonal structures or forms that give rise to society, the psyche, and to cultural phenomena of all kinds. Structuralist literary critics such as Roland Barthes employed the tools of linguistics to analyze the conceptual oppositions that structure human thought and experience. This approach was eventually criticized by critics such as Jacques Derrida for its inattention to the instabilities of language, but its influence persists in approaches such as semiotics and deconstruction, where an emphasis on the centrality of language to human experience is also to be found.

In the 1980s and 1990s, formalist methods fell out of favor. Critics instead preferred to highlight the historical and contextual factors that influence literary texts. Nonetheless, most critics still employ close reading as a central part of their work, and Marxist historicists such as Fredric Jameson have proposed analyzing form as a means of insight into history and politics. It may be this Marxist politics of form, one that began with the work of Marxist critics of the 1930s, 1940s and 1950s such as Georg Lukács and Theodor Adorno, that remains the most fertile arena of formalist analysis today.

(*See also* Chapter 6, Historicism; Chapter 14, Ecocriticism; Chapter 27, Antitheory; Close Reading; Genre; Husserl, Edmund; Kant, Immanuel; New Criticism; Political Unconscious; Russian Formalism; *and* Structuralism)

Tom Eyers, *Duquesne University (United States)*

Further Reading

Jameson, Fredric. *The Political Unconscious: Narrative as a Socially Symbolic Act.* Ithaca: Cornell University Press, 1982.

Leighton, Angela. *On Form: Poetry, Aestheticism, and the Legacy of a Word.* Oxford: Oxford University Press, 2007.

Wellek, René, and Austin Warren. *Theory of Literature* [1948]. Orlando: Harvest Books 1984.

Foucault, Michel

In 1980 the first cases of AIDS were reported. In 1982, the disease was named. By the spring of 1983, Michel Foucault (1926–84) was symptomatic and more than likely had a definitive diagnosis by the end of the year. In June 1984, he died at the age of fifty-seven, shortly after correcting the proofs of volumes two and three of the *History of Sexuality,* cutting short the life of one of the most remarkable philosophers of the last half of the early twentieth century.

In the early 1980s, Foucault's work had turned from a direct engagement with modernity and its immediate genealogy in works like *Madness and Civilization* (1964), *The Order of Things* (1966), and *Discipline and Punish* (1975), to an engagement with the texts of antiquity. While volumes two and three of *History of Sexuality*, ostensibly continued the work of volume one, as every commentator observed, they were very different. The final volumes of the *History of Sexuality*, far from retelling the history of a golden age of sexual freedom, as has sometimes been alleged, in fact, pay special attention to the formation of the subject in the ancient world, and specifically to the techniques used to fashion a self capable of recognizing its own desire, monitoring that desire, and shaping it in ways that allow the subject to wield power over itself and others. Such a subject is one who plumbs himself as the locus of a truth that lies hidden. This is the origin of the modern confessing subject but also of the philosopher as truth-teller, as someone empowered to speak the truth to power. Foucault in these volumes and his final lectures at the Collège de France is writing a history of the power of truth, a history of the "will to know." He is seeking to define the philosophical life that he has been living for more than fifty years even as it visibly draws to its close.

For Foucault, even in his most engaged work on the origins of the prison or the asylum, the task of the philosopher was never political in the narrow sense. It was not his job to tell people who to vote for, what tax plan to adopt, or even what laws should or should not regulate sexual conduct, although he like anyone else had opinions on these topics, but those opinions were not per se philosophical. The philosopher for Foucault rather stands as an index of truth in relation to the political, as someone who is willing to take personal risks to speak the truth regardless of party or program, as someone who has formed him or herself in the commitment to that truth, not simply as a profession but as a mode of life. The philosopher *d'après* Foucault, in forming him or herself as a truth-teller, creates spaces of resistance, not by telling people what they should believe, nor by enforcing ideological or party discipline, but by allowing subjugated forms of knowledge to come to the fore, by problematizing the space in which government seeks to inscribe individuals (especially the marginalized), and by making possible new forms of experience whose truth has yet to be imagined. His work from its beginning to his final lectures was concerned with juncture between the "will to know" and the exercise of power, and the ways in which that juncture was inscribed in our bodies and on the contours of our souls.

(*See also* Author; Assujettissement; Biopolitics; Chapter 1, Early Theory; Chapter 5, Post-Structuralism; Chapter 6, Historicisms; Chapter 9, Deconstruction; Chapter 15, Biopower and Biopolitics; Chapter 24, Posthumanism; Control; Disciplinary Society; Discipline; Discursive Formation; Episteme; Knowledge-Power; Sexuality; Subject; *and* Surveillance)

Paul Allen Miller, *University of South Carolina (United States)*

Further Reading
Eribon, Didier. *Michel Foucault et ses contemporains*. Paris: Fayard, 1994.
Gutting, Gary, ed. *The Cambridge Companion to Foucault*. Cambridge: Cambridge University Press, 1994.
Halperin, David M. *Saint Foucault: Towards a Gay Hagiography*. Oxford: Oxford University Press, 1995.
Larmour, David H. J., Paul Allen Miller, and Charles Platter, eds. *Rethinking Sexuality: Foucault and Classical Antiquity*. Princeton: Princeton University Press, 1998.
Macey, David. *The Lives of Michel Foucault*. New York: Pantheon, 1993.
Miller, Paul Allen. *Postmodern Spiritual Practices: The Construction of the Subject and the Reception of Plato in Lacan, Derrida, and Foucault*. Columbus: Ohio State University Press, 2007.

Free Market

Even from the historically distanced perspective of classical antiquity, the dual notion of the Greek *agora* as both a "public assembly" and a "marketplace" already expressed the contradiction at the core of the market's mediation of social relations. Lauded as the space that facilitated both the exchange of material goods and the politics of the citizenry, the *agora* occupies a site in the Western cultural imaginary as the precursor for both liberal democracy and market-based exchange relations. Yet, uncritical assessments of the *agora* overlook the inherent inequalities embedded into its "free" space of social exchange, such as the trading of slaves alongside material goods and the exclusion of women, resident aliens, and slaves from the participatory democracy of the *polis*. In an analogous manner, contemporary ideological justifications for "free market" economic policies often occlude material disparities—such as the exploitation of surplus labor indicated by Marx—that still structure deregulated approaches to capitalist exchange relations.

In *World-Systems Analysis: An Introduction* (2004), Immanuel Wallerstein argues that a free market must, in theory, have "multiple sellers, multiple buyers, perfect information (all sellers and buyers know everything about price variations), and no political constraints on the operation of the market" and then critically concludes that "few markets, real or virtual, have ever met this definition." Left to its own devices, such a market would ostensibly self-regulate, as supply and demand would reach a point of natural equilibrium. The theoretical impetus for the free market first emerges most cogently in Adam Smith's critique of the Mercantilist enactment of substantial trade tariffs and his building upon the laissez-faire tradition of the Physiocrats in *The Wealth of Nations* (1776), the text that ushers in the era of classical political economy. Smith views the individual's rational self-interest as the motivating agent promoting the more expansive interests of society at large. Taken in aggregate, this political economy of individuals acting out of their own self-interest structures Smith's well-known metaphor of the "invisible hand" as the social mechanism which "naturally" self-regulates competitive free market exchange relations and tends toward maximum efficiency. In *Law, Legislation and Liberty, Volume 1* (1973), Friedrich Hayek expands on Smith's "invisible hand" by framing the free market as a "spontaneous order" that "arises from each element balancing all the various factors operating on it and by adjusting all its various actions to each other, a balance which will be destroyed if some of the actions are determined by another agency on the basis of different knowledge and in the service of different ends." Such Hayekian markets, spontaneously ordered and entirely unmarred by government intervention, information asymmetry, and monopolized market power, have never truly existed. Yet idealized free market rhetoric nonetheless has significant ideological, political, and material implications for the capitalist world-system insofar as neoliberal economic policy has been used to justify attacks on organized labor, the privatization of the social commons, the commodification of aesthetic and cultural production, the dismantling of the welfare state, and the untenable development of capital accumulation.

(*See also* Capitalism; Chapter 15, Biopower and Biopolitics; Consumer Society; Democracy; Neoliberalism; *and* Public Sphere)

Alden Sajor Wood, *University of California, Irvine (United States)*

Further Reading

Hayek, Friedrich A. *The Road to Serfdom* [1944]. Chicago: University of Chicago Press, 2007.

Polanyi, Karl. *The Great Transformation* [1944]. Boston: Beacon Press, 2001.

Smith, Adam. *The Wealth of Nations* [1776]. New York: Bantam Classics, 2003.

Freud, Sigmund

Sigmund Freud (1856–1939), the father of psychoanalysis, was born Sigismund Schlomo Freud on May 6, 1856 in Moravia. He was raised in the Jewish ghetto of Vienna as the favored son of a family with two much older half-brothers, two younger brothers (one who died in infancy) and five sisters. As a boy Freud studied obsessively, which lead to his acceptance to the University of Vienna. While he hoped to become a scientific researcher, caps on the number of Jews in the field led him to practice medicine instead.

Early in his medical career, Freud went to France to study hysteria with Jean-Marie Charcot, whose innovative practices led Freud to an understanding of the mind that he would develop into his theory of the unconscious. Back in Vienna, he worked with Josef Breuer with whom he published *Studies in Hysteria* in 1895. In this first of his great works, Freud makes the connections between the verbalization of symptoms and their disappearance, a technique soon to be known as "the talking cure," which revolutionized psychoanalysis and the entire field of mental health in the twentieth century. For this innovation alone Freud earned his fame and importance in the histories of medicine and thought.

As Freud's work with hysteria was taking shape and becoming his growing passion, Freud met Martha Bernays, a friend of his sister, who he courted long-distance for several years before marrying. Together, they had six children in eight years, the youngest, Anna, who went on to be a famous psychoanalyst herself. During their courtship and early marriage, Freud also engaged in the first major controversy of his career, advocating the use of cocaine's medicinal purposes. While Freud eventually stopped championing cocaine and no longer used it himself, his affinity for controversy grew as he developed theories of dream work, sublimation, infantile sexuality, the libido, the unconscious, repression, the Oedipal Complex, and transference.

The thread connecting all of his theories is the biological fact that human beings begin life as helpless infants unlike other species and so need the socialization that they experience as a confining burden blocking the fulfillment of their desires. For Freud, this radical ambivalence, however ameliorated by rational practices and everyday experiences, is never abolished, except in fantasy and dream, and then momentarily and ultimately unsatisfactorily. Whether such inbred discontent leads to apocalyptic resentment, tragic self-destruction, or merely normal misery, is largely up to the individual subject to determine. For instance, in 1938, Freud and Martha were forced to flee Vienna and the Nazi regime. They relocated to London, where Freud died on September 9, 1939 after requesting a lethal dose of morphine to end his long and painful struggle with oral cancer.

His legacy is immeasurable. Freud's work has influenced medicine, psychology, philosophy, literary theory, and popular culture. Along with Charles Darwin, his concepts changed the ways in which people perceived themselves in relation to the massively changing world of the first part of the twentieth century. It can be easily argued that his theories encapsulate the modern era. His focus on the role of sex and sexuality in the development and daily life of each individual from infancy onward flouted Victorian norms and decorum. It opened conversation in both personal and scientific spheres, paving the way for the social changes of the sexual revolution and scientific studies like those of Masters and Johnson and Alfred Kinsey. Freud's work on sexuality and its subsequent central place in psychoanalytic studies have also made possible free discussion and greater acceptance of the LGBTQ community. His work on sexuality is not without its controversy. Freud's work, especially on the development of the Oedipal Complex and related penis envy, contribute to the idea of his misogyny. While there is some credibility to that claim, it does not outweigh his importance and is symptomatic of his time.

His focus on the unconscious as the seat of the Ego, the Superego, and the Id, three agencies or active modes of the psyche that influenced

Lacan's three psychic registers of the Imaginary, the Symbolic, and the Real, respectively. Freud's work contributed to "the death of god" controversy, which negated any external god figure, thereby reinforcing the already prevalent Modernist questioning of formal religion. This contest between religion and reason (and science) continues unabated, along lines of research and critique laid down by Freud.

(*See also* Castration; Chapter 7, Psychoanalytic Theory; Deferred Action; Drive; Fantasy; Hysteria; Libidinal; Mourning; Oedipus Complex; Phallocentrism; Primordial Discord; Psychoanalysis; Sublimation; Symptom; Uncanny; *and* Unconscious, The)

Gina Masucci MacKenzie, *Holy Family University (United States)*

Further Reading

Erwin, Edward, ed. *The Freud Encyclopedia.* New York: Routledge, 2002.

Gay, Peter, ed. *The Freud Reader.* New York: W. W. Norton and Company, 1989.

G

Gadamer, Hans-Georg

Hans-Georg Gadamer (1900–2002) is usually regarded as the founder of philosophical hermeneutics, as presented in his major work *Truth and Method* in 1960. This work is an original synthesis and reformulation of selected views taken from Wilhelm Dilthey, Edmund Husserl, and his teacher Martin Heidegger, with a focus on interpretation. Like Dilthey, Gadamer wants to give legitimacy to the interpretive character of the human sciences—the question of "truth"—against the stifling power of the natural sciences of his time—the question of "method." From Husserl, Gadamer takes up the key notions of consciousness as lived experience (*Erlebnis*) and consciousness as always operating within horizons and thus enduring in time, but broadens these views to the dimension of history: consciousness is historically sedimented or "exposed to the effects of history" (*wirkungsgeschichtliches Bewusstsein*).

Going beyond Dilthey's psychological enterprise, Gadamer follows Heidegger and considers that the world is articulated in a "dimension of language" (*Sprachlichkeit*): the world itself and its objects have been entangled in a discursive dimension that has given them a meaningfulness and intelligibility that go beyond their physical properties. In a provocative expression, Gadamer claims in *Truth and Method* that "being that can be understood is language."

The central concept of philosophical hermeneutics is also from Heideggerean provenance: "Understanding" is a fundamental character of human beings—an existential of Dasein. Human beings are those who "understand" their surroundings and, in those surroundings, understand themselves. Interpretation, thus, goes far beyond the interpretation of texts, as in the traditional romantic hermeneutics founded by Friedrich Schleiermacher. Interpretation pertains to the ontological structure of human existence. Because both the objects to be interpreted as well as the interpreters themselves are historically situated and carry their historical and cultural backgrounds with them, interpretation takes the form of a "fusion of horizons": interpreters come to the text with their questions and concerns, just as the text offers resistance as a cultural entity with its own specific background. Gadamer speaks of the "event" of interpretation as something that happens both to interpreters and to texts.

Because of its event-character, interpretation is a form of "play," which is a central concept of *Truth and Method,* as opposed to a mastery of the text. Gadamer appeals to Plato's notion of "dialogue" in order to describe the back-and-forth process of "question and answer" that takes place between readers—who can be transformed by the text, exposed to a "claim" that comes from the text—and texts—which can gain a new life in being questioned from new perspectives and "applied" to new problems and issues.

Instead of being a transitive and progressive enterprise of "understanding better" (as it was for Schleiermacher), interpretation thrives on difference: "We understand in a different way if we understand at all."

Besides being a theoretician, Gadamer was also a master interpreter—his interpretations of ancient Greek philosophy remain one of his most significant achievements—as well as a skilled and sought-after debater about the many intellectual issues in the twentieth century with major figures including Emilio Betti, E. D. Hirsch, Karl Otto Apel and Jürgen Habermas, Jacques Derrida, and Donald Davidson.

(*See also* Chapter 6, Historicisms; Chapter 18, Translation; Heidegger, Martin; Hermeneutics; Husserl, Edmund; Interpretation; Presence; *and* Tradition)

Pol Vandevelde, *Marquette University (United States)*

Further Reading
Gadamer, Hans-Georg. *Truth and Method* [1960]. Second ed. Trans. rvsd. Joel Weinsheimer and Donald G. Marshall. London: Continuum, 1998.
Gadamer, Hans-Georg. *Hermeneutics between History and Philosophy*. Ed. and trans. Pol Vandevelde and Arun Iyer. London: Bloomsbury, 2016.
Grandin, Jean. *Hans-Georg Gadamer: A Biography*. New Haven: Yale University Press, 2003.
Vandevelde, Pol. *The Task of the Interpreter: Text, Meaning, and Negotiation*. Pittsburgh: University of Pittsburgh Press, 2005.

Gender

Gender is a social construct that does not necessarily align with biological sex. As theorists of the twentieth and twenty-first centuries have demonstrated, gender is a fluid spectrum that ranges from feminine to masculine and is thus inclusive of many variations of gender identity, including identities that subvert the very idea of a two-gendered system (such as nonbinary or genderqueer). Seen in this way, gender is dynamic, rather than static. In *The Second Sex* (1949), Simone de Beauvoir famously declared that women become women, rather than being born women, a non-essentialist statement which can be expanded to all gender identities. We are not born into or as a gender but instead are continually in the process of becoming.

For post-structuralist feminist Judith Butler, the becoming of gender identity is what she terms *performative*. As she explains in *Gender Trouble* (1990), gender is a matrix of habits—iterative acts and gestures. These repetitions (ways of walking, speaking, dressing) gain meaning in the social sphere according to consensus on what it looks like to be masculine or feminine, rather than based on some sort of inherent meaning. Notably, Butler does not mean that gender is performed or is a performance. To think of gender as performed implies an essential identity. For example, the actor in a play performs a character. She puts on a costume and "gets into character" by trying to speak and think and gesture like the character she performs, but after the standing ovation, when the curtain falls and the lights go out, she takes her costume off, steps out of character, becomes once again herself. Thus, if we think of gender as *performed*, we assume some stable identity behind the costume or the mask, the "true" identity of the actor (the "inner" biological sex hidden beneath the "outer" performed gender). And yet, such an "inner" or "natural" self does not exist, according to Butler, who further argues that sex is also performative. Expanding on the work of Foucault in her 1993 *Bodies that Matter*, Butler explains how the idea of biological sex is itself a norming or regulatory standard, which does not erase the materiality of the body but conceives of the body as constituted or produced through power. What was assumed to be "natural" (sexual difference based upon biological sex) turns out to have always been "cultural."

Nevertheless, the social assumption that gender should correspond to sex means that gender is constantly policed through various institutions including the family, state, school, and church and reinforced through gendered social systems like language. In the family, for example, gender roles may determine the distribution of labor practices and household duties. In the realm of education, assumptions about who is "naturally" better at math and science reinforce gender norms that then produce effects in the workforce. Ideas about gender significantly impact daily life through these types of social norms, but they also affect official policy-making, where competing understandings of gender inform current debates regarding public restroom use, military service, health insurance coverage, and even fitness for elected office.

(*See also* Beauvoir, Simone de; Butler, Judith; Chapter 2, Structuralism and Semiotics; Chapter 10, Feminism; Cixous, Hélène; Chapter 23, Materialisms; Feminist Theory; Intersectionality; Patriarchy; Performativity; Queer Theory; *and* Sexuality)

Laci Mattison, *Florida Gulf Coast University* *(United States)*

Further Reading

Beauvoir, Simone de. *The Second Sex* [1949]. Trans. Constance Borde and Sheila Malovany-Chevallier. New York: Vintage Books, 2010.

Butler, Judith. *Gender Trouble: Feminism and the Subversion of Identity*. New York: Routledge, 1990.

Goodman, Robin Truth. *Gender Work: Feminism after Neoliberalism*. New York: Palgrave, 2013.

Genre

In the ordinary acceptance of the term, which is also that of most literary theory since Aristotle, *genre* is understood taxonomically, as a classification device with relatively fixed features; texts "belong" to more or less stable kinds. At the same time, we ordinarily distinguish between "genre" texts (science fiction novels or heist movies, for example) and texts that escape genre (many literary texts, for example). Genre is a kind of law, and since the romantic period we tend to admire those texts that seem to escape the law of genre.

The first problem with this understanding is that it is either reductive (texts are no more than instances of a genre) or else it posits that texts transcend the conventional framings of a literary system and a culture; it is either prescriptive, or it assumes that literary texts are lawless works of genius. The second problem is that, on both these assumptions, it misses the cognitive and social force of formal structures.

One way of thinking rather differently about genre would be to understand it as a structure that mediates between texts and the situations in which and upon which they operate, embodying at once a framework of expectations and possible strategic responses to it. In Carolyn Miller's words, genres are "typified rhetorical actions based in recurrent situations"; they acquire meaning from the kinds of situation they typically relate to, and texts respond pragmatically to those embedded meanings.

Texts are thus not instantiations of a genre, and they are not to be situated "in" a genre; rather, any text has a more or less complex relationship to one or more genres, which may be one of simple repetition but is more usually one of slight or significant transformation. All texts are informed by generic frameworks; any text may be read through more than one generic frame; many texts participate in multiple genres.

Structurally, genres are composed of thematic, formal, and rhetorical dimensions, which are differently weighted for different genres; that is, they have a typical kind of subject matter, particular kinds of formal structure (prose or verse, long or short, "high" or "low" decorum, and so on), and they set up a characteristic kind of relation between speaker and hearer, author and reader. If we can assume that each of these three dimensions has a constitutive role in the make up of genre, and that there is no genre whose properties are not codified (but differently weighted) in each dimension, we can then distinguish genre from organizations of discourse which are *more* general (e.g., from mode, style, speech variety, or discursive formation) and *less* general (e.g., speech acts or thematically defined subgenres).

A central implication of the understanding of genre as a structure of embedded meanings to which texts respond is that, far from being merely "stylistic" devices, genres create effects of reality and truth which are central to the different ways the world is understood. The realities in and among which we live are not transparently conveyed to us but are mediated by systems of representation: by talk, by writing, by acting (in all senses of the word), by images, even by sound. Being is never detached from the forms and occasions of its enunciation, and is thus no more singular than the multiplicity of genres that articulate it.

(*See also* Chapter 6, Historicisms; Chapter 19, Media Studies; Chapter 20, Digital Humanities; Dialogue; Formalism; Liminality; Novel; *and* Text)

John Frow, *University of Sydney (Australia)*

Further Reading
Duff, David, ed. *Modern Genre Theory*. Harlow: Longman, 2000.
Frow, John. *Genre*. Second ed. London: Routledge, 2015.
Todorov, Tzvetan. *Genres in Discourse* [1978]. Trans. Catherine Porter. Cambridge: Cambridge University Press, 1990.

Global Media

The origin of the current debates and theories in global media can be traced to Herbert Schiller's cultural/media imperialism thesis. Writing in the critical political economy tradition Schiller contended that media content worldwide was heavily influenced by the United States. The US policy of free flow of information went together with US hegemony and imperial domination. Situating his argument within the political context of the Cold War, Schiller highlighted that national and individual needs went hand in hand with private business objectives. Tom McPhail redefined this imperialist domination in terms of technology and infrastructure. He used the term *Electronic Colonialism* to refer to the dependency relationship created by foreign communication hardware, software, and engineers. This dependence, he argued, creates a different set of protocols, values, and expectations that influence the local or national cultures and socialization processes. Ogan saw this electronic dependency as a process whereby the West exploits third-world markets for profits. John Tomlinson refuted these claims and argued that globalization far from destroying cultural identity creates and proliferates a modern identity. The imperialism dominance thesis was also refuted by active audience theorists Ien Ang and John Fiske, who argued that media consumers in the third world were not cultural dupes incapable of diverse interpretations. Additionally, the audiences did not just interpret content in different ways they preferred different content. Joseph Straubhaar's analysis of Brazilian media preferences highlighted the fact that viewers preferred media content that was more proximate to their own culture. Jan Ekecrantz pointed out that most of the studies within the dependency and imperialism framework ignored the socioeconomic difference among countries, global power relationships and differences in systems of government within the so-called dependent nations. The effort to think about countries as a diverse set of socioeconomic orders, with different forms of government and equally diverse media systems came about almost a decade later.

The cultural turn in globalization and global media theory came with Ronald Robertson, George Ritzer and Arjun Appadurai. Cultural theories usually follow three arguments: (1) homogenization of the world; (2) heterogenization of the world; and (3) Hybridization of the world. Ritzer popularized the term *McDonalization*, as an example of global homogenization. Appadurai's thesis on the global cultural economy applied a different take; he saw a constant tension between cultural homogenization and heterogenization. His "scapes" and the flows between those "scapes" create transnational cultural spaces that are new, syncretic, and not tied to "nation states." Hence these spaces are disjunctive by creating a disjuncture between culture and politics as well as the economy. Similar debates about media-led cultural homogenization and heterogenization have shaped up global media theory.

In the current global "mediascape," British theorist David Morley alerts us to contemporary issues of media power. Although, there are many forms of media counterflows today, why does media from only a select few nations get "reinterpreted" and "globalized"? As we rethink questions of media power and audience reception, the answer is not a resurgence of imperialism, but it isn't unbridled audience freedom either.

(*See also* Chapter 19, Media Studies; Globalization; *and* Hybridity)

Swapnil Rai, *Brown University (United States)*

Further Reading

Ang, Ien. *Watching Dallas: Soap Opera and the Melodramatic Imagination.* London: Methuen, 1985.

Boyd-Barrett, Oliver. "Media Imperialism: Towards an International Framework for the Analysis of Media Systems." In *Mass Communication and Society.* Eds. James Curran and Michael Gurevitch. London: Edward Arnold, 1977. 116–35.

Dorfman, Ariel, and Armand Mattelart. *How to Read Donald Duck: Imperialist Ideology in the Disney Comic.* New York: International General, 1984.

Schiller, Herbert. *Mass Communication and American Empire.* New York: August M. Kelley, 1969.

Straubhaar, Joseph. "Beyond Media Imperialism: Asymmetrical Interdependence and Cultural Proximity." *Critical Studies in Mass Communication* 8 (1991): 39–59.

Globalization

Driven by a host of techno-economic, political, and cultural forces, globalization is the multifaceted, pluricentric, nonlinear, and oftentimes contradictory process through which the world's places, cultures, and communities become more and more interconnected. Unevenly affecting the planet's regions and various chapters in the story of humanity, this process is, for some, nonetheless coextensive with world history and therefore traceable back to the intercontinental human migrations of prehistoric times. This is the extreme version of the *longue durée* view of the phenomenon. In its milder forms, this genealogy sees globalization as coeval with and basically triggered by developments set in motion in Western Europe with the Venetian Polo family's travels, then with Portugal's Henry the Seafarer, and culminating in "discoveries" and explorations of "new worlds" by Christopher Columbus and Vasco da Gama. While most historians tend to privilege the European empires-originated overtures, expeditions, and conquests as they point to the early Renaissance as the dawn of "actual" globalization, postcolonial scholars have proposed alternate models. For a large group of critics belonging to the former category, the fifteenth-century onset of European modernity coincides with and actually sets off globalization. This has happened, they maintain, according to a chronology that either roughly follows Immanuel Wallerstein's periodization of his world-system or emphasizes the increasing differentiations of globalization stages within or even *after* modern history, with more recent milestones such as the Industrial Revolution, the end of the Second World War, or the 1989–1992 interval as watershed world events that have brought about epoch-making qualitative adjustments to an otherwise age-old evolution.

Having witnessed the fall of the Berlin Wall, the collapse of the Soviet Union, the birth of the Internet and related communication technologies, as well as the consolidation of world markets, transnational corporations, nongovernmental organizations, supranational media sociality, and international networks of finance, digital knowledge exchange, crime, and terror sometimes at the expense of statal actors, national sovereignties, and political borders, the early years of the post-Cold War era brought about not only unprecedented intensities and extensities of globalization that rendered the world more global than ever before but also a sharp increase in the collective awareness of the world's ongoing globalization. "Late," "accelerated," or "contemporary," post-1989 globalization is, as various critics have pointed out, also "strong" because it is demonstrably much better marked than ever before in people's lives as well as in public consciousness. More "compressed" spatially and temporally, more transcultural, more "creolized" and eclectic linguistically, aesthetically, and otherwise, the late global world is arguably unique *and* pressures us to think this uniqueness through. The feedback loop provided by various discourses *on* globalization adds another layer *to* globalization and indexes the rise of *globalism*, namely, that aspect or upshot of globalization that speaks to the emergence of a culture that appears to be both symptomatic of our moment in globalization history and to work as an engine of ongoing globalization. At the same time, it is clearer now than three decades ago that globalization is not a "myth" but as real as it can be, even though it is not solely a financial, commercial, communicational, or leisure industry reality but also, in some quarters at least, a political *project* in world governance or, as mentioned above, discourse, talk about the global; that it can be both an ideal to some and a nightmare to others; that it can be approached descriptively and prescriptively; that it has homogenizing, rationalizing, and other worrisome tendencies poised to extend older hegemonies and imperialisms, which tend to construct the world as an ominous totality, but it can also be managed and critically *reconstructed* according to theoretical platforms where the ethically, politically, and ecologically responsible paradigms of "earth," "world," and "planet" may and perhaps should supplant the economistic-corporatist-militarist rhetoric of the "globe" and its cognate anthropocentrist rationalizations.

(See also Chapter 12, Postmodernism; Chapter 13, Race and Postcolonial Studies; Chapter 22, Identity Studies; Global Media; Hybridity; Negri, Antonio; Planetary Criticism; *and* Transnational)

Christian Moraru, *University of North Carolina, Greensboro (United States)*

Further Reading

Appadurai, Arjun. *Modernity at Large: Cultural Dimensions of Globalization.* Minneapolis: University of Minnesota Press, 1999.

Moraru, Christian. *Cosmodernism: American Narrative, Late Globalization, and the New Cultural Imaginary.* Ann Arbor: University of Michigan Press, 2011.

Moraru, Christian. *Reading for the Planet: Toward a Geomethodology.* Ann Arbor: University of Michigan Press, 2015.

Greimasian Semiotic Square (*See* Semiotic Square)

H

Habermas, Jürgen

The German philosopher and social theorist Jürgen Habermas (born 1929) was, in his early career, associated with the neo-Marxist Frankfurt School, albeit that his political philosophy has developed a more liberal outlook since the 1990s. While his work is extremely wide-ranging in its scope and implications, at its core lie commitments to the role of public discourse and consensus formation in political life, and to what he has called the project of modernity—that is to say, a defense of the European Enlightenment's goal of pursuing truth through rational inquiry. This position has at once put him at odds with postmodernist thinkers such as Jean-François Lyotard, but also drawn him into constructive debates with the likes of Hans-Georg Gadamer, Jacques Derrida, and Richard Rorty.

Habermas's first work to bring widespread recognition was a historical study of the development of the public sphere, the social institutions (such as journalism and the coffee house) through which debate within the European bourgeoisie was channeled, and political opinion formed, from the seventeenth century onwards. This work already gives Habermas a model of the importance of free, open, and rational debate in forming political opinion and in exerting pressure in the formation of government policy. Crucially, the study concludes by documenting the decline of such debate in the twentieth century, as political processes, molded by advertising and public relations, become merely the aggregation of isolated individual opinions, as opposed to genuine processes of sharing, influence, and criticism.

Habermas's mature work centers around his theory of communicative action. In a grand summation of the traditions of social theory, he puts forward an analysis of how societies develop and are sustained. At the core of this process lies the ability that all competent social agents have to communicate with each other, and thereby to negotiate a shared understanding of their cultural and physical environment, and thus coordinate their actions within that environment. Habermas argues that, underpinning everyday interaction, there is a counterfactual presupposition of an ideal of free and open communication, whereby any participant is free to challenge the truth of what their interlocutor is saying and their right to say it. In practice, Habermas is fully aware that actual communication is distorted by imbalances of power and lack of information, systematically excluding repressed individuals and groups from debate (and thus full social participation). He thus develops an ethics, a theory of justice, and a theory of law, that outline ideal processes of social interaction that could bring about a good and just society, but crucially as critical tools, allowing the actual injustices of actual interaction to be identified and challenged.

Habermas's most recent work, motivated in large part as a reaction to September 11, 2001, has focused on the role of religion in contemporary "post-secular" society, and thus on how substantial beliefs or worldviews might influence, for good or ill, democratic political processes. Habermas's work, on the public sphere, communication, and postsecular society thereby continues to have relevance, not least as new, digital forms of communication pose new opportunities for inclusion in political debate, and new forms of exclusion.

(*See also* Chapter 10, Feminism; Chapter 22, Identity Studies; Consensus; Critique; Cultural Critique; Enlightenment; Kant, Immanuel; Neopragmatism; Public Sphere; *and* Rorty, Richard)

Andrew Edgar, *Cardiff University (United Kingdom)*

Further Reading

Edgar, Andrew. *The Philosophy of Habermas*. Chesham: Acumen, 2005.

Habermas, Jürgen. *The Philosophical Discourse of Modernity: Twelve Lectures* [1985]. Trans. F. G. Lawrence. Cambridge: MIT Press, 1988.

Rasmussen, David, and Swindal, James, eds. *Jürgen Habermas*. London: Sage, 2002.

Hall, Stuart

Born into the Jamaican "brown middle-class," Stuart Hall (1932–2014) came to England in the 1950s, quickly immersing himself in the emerging intellectual milieu of the British "New Left." As the founding editor of the seminal "New Left Review," Hall's early essays already expressed many of the interests that would come to characterize his later work: a concern to understand the changing class dynamics of advanced capitalist societies; a close attention to the emerging world of consumerism and mass-mediated commercial culture; a commitment to an anti-imperialist, democratic, and libertarian socialism.

Hired by Richard Hoggart at the University of Birmingham's Centre for Contemporary Cultural Studies, in the early 1960s Hall took over as director of the center after a few years, establishing it as a unique location in the English-speaking world for the kind of critical, interdisciplinary scholarship that would come to characterize the best of the cultural studies tradition. While Raymond Williams was the key intellectual influence on the early work of the center, a number of other currents shaping the international radical left would soon converge there. The growing interest in "Western Marxism"— which saw translations of Antonio Gramsci, Georg Lukács, Valentin Volosinov, etc. become increasingly available—was a key factor, as was the development of structuralism in France. Above all, the influence of Louis Althusser, who synthesized both of these currents with Lacanian psychoanalysis became fundamental to Hall's thinking and the work of the center in the early 1970s; although ultimately it would be Gramsci more than Althusser who would prove to be Hall's lifelong theoretical lodestar.

Hall played a key role in transmitting many of these ideas to an Anglophone audience over the course of the 1970s, particularly through a series of hugely influential expository essays setting out the analytical methods which were being developed at the center, amounting to a form of sophisticated ideology critique which could incorporate ethnography, political economy, historical analysis, and close textual reading into a powerful synthesis. The ultimate vindication of this method was the book published by Hall and several colleagues in 1978. *Policing the Crisis* analyzed a moral panic around "mugging" in the British press of the mid-1970s, and diagnosed it as a symptom of the crisis of the postwar social consensus and the emergence of a new form of right-wing politics, combining authoritarianism and coded racism with hostility to unions and the welfare state. Hall and his colleagues had successfully predicted the emergence of the New Right.

Hall's acuity as a political analyst led to his involvement with the highly influential political magazine *Marxism Today* in the 1980s, where he coined the term "Thatcherism" and came to be widely recognized as the most important intellectual on the British Left. During this time he moved from Birmingham to the Open University, bringing "Birmingham" cultural studies into the heart of its syllabuses in the humanities and social sciences, from where Hall's influence would spread across the English-speaking world.

While his health failed him in the 1990s and subsequently, Hall remained a figure of immense importance, helping to popularize postcolonial theory and various strands of engaged post-structuralism within media studies, literary studies, history and sociology. An iconic figure to a new generation of young black British artists, he became heavily involved with the creation and management of institutions committed to multiculturalism in the visual arts, as well as remaining a powerful and influential commentator on the British Left until his death in 2014.

(*See also* Althusser, Louis; Chapter 11, Cultural Studies; Chapter 16, Pop Culture; Chapter 19, Media Studies; Cultural Materialism; Cultural Studies; Hegemony; Pop Culture; Reception Theory; Resistance; *and* Williams, Raymond)

Jeremy Gilbert, *University of East London (United Kingdom)*

Further Reading

Chen, Kuan-Hsing, ed. *Stuart Hall: Critical Dialogue in Cultural Studies*. New York: Routledge, 1996.

Hall, Stuart. *Cultural Studies 1983*. Eds. Lawrence Grossberg and Jennifer Slack. Durham: Duke University Press, 2016.

Hall, Stuart. *Selected Political Writings: The Great Moving Right Show and Other Essays*. Eds. Sally Davison, David Featherstone, Michael Rustin, and Bill Schwarz. Durham: Duke University Press, 2017.

Hall, Stuart, Brian Roberts, John Clarke, Tony Jefferson, and Chas Critcher. *Policing the Crisis: Mugging, the State, and Law and Order*. New York: Macmillan, 1978.

Haraway, Donna Jeanne

Distinguished Professor Emerita in the History of Consciousness program at the University of California, Santa Cruz, Donna Haraway has profoundly influenced critical theory, feminist science studies, and human-animal studies. *Simians, Cyborgs, and Women* (1991) exposed how cultural discourses shape supposedly neutral scientific research. Science, then, is another powerful form of myth-making tending to support sexism, racism, and heteronormativity. In *Modest_Witness* (1997), Haraway continued the challenge to scientific authority with her analysis of the figure of the scientist as a "modest witness" that claims to transcend the biases of his material embodiment (as white, male, middle-class, heterosexual) and achieve objectivity. This figure not only treats the objects of knowledge as nonactors, but also tacitly excludes from authority any bodies (women, people of color, nonhuman animals) assumed to be unable to see past their own biased embodiment. As *all* viewpoints are necessarily limited, knowledge claims should not claim unquestioned authority, giving way instead to the recognition of a "radical multiplicity of local knowledges," as she says in *Simians,* while maintaining a "no-non-sense commitment to faithful accounts of a 'real' world."

Even as her approaches and foci have evolved, Haraway's aims have remained remarkably consistent: to construct alternatives to the harmful discourses that organize our ways of being and relating. She has considered a number of visions of a subject that embraces the boundary-blurring inter-dependency across "tri-part" ecologies of "humans, critters other than humans, and technologies," beginning with the cyborg. A "split and contradictory self," she writes in *Simians,* the cyborg can achieve "affinity" without claiming an organic wholeness, insularity, or purity. In *Modest_Witness,* Haraway proposed the vampire as a figure that embraces "pollution," "mak[ing] categories travel." Haraway's more recent work in *When Species Meet,* particularly impacting human-animal studies, offers the idea of "companion species," "queer messmates in mortal play" where the smallest unit of study is two beings in relationship. The idea that species co-constitute each other is neither a rosy view of interspecies symbiosis nor an ominous portent of eternal struggle; species co-constitute each other for better or worse. Yet, by avoiding clear ethical line-drawing (as to meat-eating, dog breeding, and animal experimentation, for example), her work has drawn the criticism of feminist animal studies scholar Carol J. Adams, among others, for falling short of the call to radical action expected of a "manifesto."

Haraway's latest book, *Staying with the Trouble* (2016), urges us to be more attentive and open to developing positive practices of co-constitution. Her choice of Chthulucene (rather than Anthropocene) as a name for the present age posits all beings as actors in a tangled web, each affecting the other, rather than focusing on one group (humans) dom-inating others (nonhuman animals). Seeking to "ret[ie] some of the knots in ordinary mul-tispecies living on earth," she considers in *When Species Meet* how even prosaic multi-species encounters, such as between a human and dog, could be taken "seriously" for how they might "dra[w] us into the world, make us care, and ope[n] up political imaginations and commitments."

(*See also* Biopolitics; Chapter 10, Feminism; Chapter 22, Identity Studies; Chapter 24, Posthumanism; Cyberculture; Cyborg; Feminist Theory; Machine; *and* Posthumanism)

Keridiana Chez, *Borough of Manhattan Community College, City University of New York (United States)*

Further Reading
Haraway, Donna J. *Simians, Cyborgs, and Women: The Reinvention of Nature.* New York: Routledge, 1991.
Haraway, Donna J. *Modest_Witness@Second_Millennium.FemaleMan©_Meets_OncoMouse™.* New York: Routledge, 1997.
Haraway, Donna J. *When Species Meet.* Minneapolis: University of Minnesota Press, 2008.

Hegel, Georg Wilhelm Friedrich

Hegel's (1770–1831) work is philosophically important in the history of literary, aesthetic, and cultural theory in a number of ways. On a theoretical level, his contextualization of these topics within a broader understanding of Spirit or *Geist* (with the implicit appeals to history and sociality that this involves) opened up new avenues of literary analysis for later thinkers in the nineteenth and twentieth centuries, as did the particular dialectical tools that he came to employ, most strikingly perhaps in his construal of conflict as at the heart of tragedy.

Coming of philosophical age in the remarkably fertile literary period that followed the publication of Immanuel Kant's 1781 *Critique of Pure Reason*, Hegel was able to draw not only on the rich classical background available in German education at the time but also on the explosion of literary efforts among such figures as the early romantics. As a roommate of Friedrich Schelling and Friedrich Hölderlin studying theology at Tübingen, Hegel's earliest engagement with classical texts was direct; although his early translations of key texts such as Sophocles's *Antigone*, unlike Hölderlin's later remarkable ones, have not survived, the immediacy of his engagement in the details of the Greek is evident in what he writes later on. Hegel's readings of key literary texts have remained touchstones for later readers—perhaps most prominently his interpretation of Sophocles's *Antigone*, which has informed a wide range of commentary from Johann Jakob Bachofen to Jacques Lacan to Judith Butler, but also his readings of the work of such contemporaries as Johann Wolfgang von Goethe, Friedrich Schiller, Friedrich Heinrich Jacobi, Novalis and the Schlegels.

On a practical level, Hegel himself must also count—at least certainly in his early *Phenomenology of Spirit* (1807)—as among those philosophers such as Plato, Friedrich Nietzsche, and Søren Kierkegaard whose writing compels literary as well as conceptual analysis. The distinctive literary shape of the *Phenomenology of Spirit* has been characterized by Josiah Royce and others as a form of *Bildungsroman*, but Hegel's appropriation of literary modes in that text is much more complex and carefully contextualized, making use of the genres of tragedy and comedy as well and drawing on works as diverse as Denis Diderot's *Rameau's Nephew* and Friedrich Schlegel's *Lucinde*.

In his later aesthetic theory, articulated over a series of lectures when he was a professor in Berlin, Hegel situates literature within an account of what he termed the *Ideal* (the embodiment of the Idea in a particular shape or form) and in the historical emergence of conceptually different forms of art (his famous account of the symbolic, classical, and romantic modes). In the lectures, Hegel also develops in great detail the five individual arts that had become canonical by the time of Charles Batteux—that is, architecture, sculpture, painting, music, and poetry, with poetry holding the status of the "highest" art and with the epic, lyric, and dramatic genres explored in that order. Although Hegel did not develop an explicit theory of the emerging genre of the novel, his engagement with several key (primarily epistolary) novels of the period is important to note and may be fruitfully compared to the later theories of figures such as Georg Lukács and Mikhail Bakhtin.

(*See also* Alienation; Chapter 4, Marxism; Chapter 9, Deconstruction; Civil Society; Critique; Dialectic; Heteronomy; Idealism; Marx, Karl; Negation; Other, The; Political Unconscious; Repetition; *and* Subjectivism)

C. Allen Speight, *Boston University (United States)*

Further Reading

Gellrich, Michelle. *Tragedy and Theory: The Problem of Conflict since Aristotle*. Princeton: Princeton University Press, 1988.

Rutter, Benjamin. *Hegel on the Modern Arts*. Cambridge: Cambridge University Press, 2010.

Speight, Allen. *Hegel, Literature and the Problem of Agency*. Cambridge: Cambridge University Press, 2001.

Hegemony

In literary and cultural studies *hegemony* refers to the struggle over culture by different classes and cultural groups. The concept was developed by Italian Marxist philosopher Antonio Gramsci who emphasized that in order for a class to maintain its dominance it must educate other classes to its common sense. For Gramsci the dominant group's hold over civil society is always tentative and requires the cultural knowledge-making work of permanent persuaders who he termed "traditional intellectuals." Gramsci encouraged the possibility of radical change through the culture-transforming knowledge-making practices of "organic intellectuals," who, by making a new common sense could create the conditions for a revolution from below.

Gramsci's conception of hegemony was taken up in literary and cultural studies most notably by Raymond Williams and Stuart Hall. Ernesto Laclau and Chantal Mouffe led a number of scholars in developing a political theory of radical democracy. Subsequent theorists expanded Gramsci's class-based and political-party based conception of hegemony in the later twentieth century. Hall's scholarship as well as Laclau and Mouffe's significantly expanded the contemporary conception of hegemony by drawing on structuralism, post-structuralism, deconstruction, and pragmatism. In the expanded conception of hegemony a multiplicity of cultural groups including races, ethnicities, genders, and sexes in addition to classes vie for hegemonic dominance. Recent theories of hegemony have difference at their center. They recognize that the subject, the society, language and culture are constituted by difference and antagonism. Contemporary theories of hegemony largely share a view of a constructed nonessential subject and a constructed nonessential society.

Gramsci placed great emphasis on the centrality of education to politics and culture. Political struggle involves educating others to the language, assumptions, and ideologies of one's class and cultural groups. The recog-

nition of the constructedness of the self and society in contemporary theories of hegemony means that signifying practices are educative in that they affirm or contest existing sets of meanings, broader public discourses. Meaning-making practices such as cultural work and the activities of everyday life are implicated in forging culture, reworking shared meanings and social relations, and creating subject positions and identifications for others. Hegemony theory suggests that cultural work is not marginal to power and politics but rather is at the center of it. It provides an antidote to economistic perspectives that comprehend the self and society and culture as a reflection or effect of material relations of production. It also provides an antidote to conservative theories of culture that treat culture as an inheritance of the best and the brightest that ought to be transmitted as dogma. Hegemony theory recognizes cultural politics—that is, signs and meanings are contested, dynamic, and in play and that the meaning-making practices that people do matter politically and socially. It also recognizes that people can hold cultural views that may not correspond to the social location of the subject. Approaches to education, journalism, and other cultural production that deny the contested and political dimension of culture play a conservative role of attempting to maintain the culture of ruling groups while denying that class- and group-specific cultural forms are specific and particular. Ruling groups universalize and impose ruling culture while denying cultural politics. Subordinate groups cultivate new organic intellectuals who can articulate a new emancipatory common sense, culture, civil society, and consciousness.

(*See also* Chapter 4, Marxism; Chapter 11, Cultural Studies; *and* Chapter 27, Antitheory)

Kenneth J. Saltman, *University of Masssachusetts, Dartmouth (United States)*

Further Reading

Giroux, Henry. *Teachers as Intellectuals: Toward a Critical Pedagogy of Learning.* New York: Praeger, 1988.

Gramsci, Antonio. *Selections from the Prison Notebooks.* New York: International Publishers, 1971.

Hall, Stuart. *Cultural Studies 1983.* Durham: Duke University Press, 2017.

Laclau, Ernesto, and Chantal Mouffe. *Hegemony and Socialist Strategy.* London: Verso, 1989.

Mouffe, Chantal. *Agonistics: Thinking the World Politically.* Brooklyn: Verso, 2013.

Williams, Raymond. *Marxism and Literature.* Oxford: Oxford University Press, 1977.

Heidegger, Martin

Martin Heidegger (1888–1976), one of the most prominent philosophers of the modern age, was and remains a very controversial figure. On the one hand, he inaugurated the postmodern era by means of his *Destruktion* (de-structuration) of the traditional ontological structure that, in thinking being metaphysically (meta ta physika: above or beyond or after things as they exist), reduced their radical temporality to a graspable spatial form or structure. On the other hand, he has been insistently, and in an increasing way, accused of being a Nazi sympathizer and a determined anti-Semite.

In this entry, I will bracket the question of Heidegger's alleged Nazism and his anti-Semitism by way of suggesting that those who insist on making these charges categorically are, in fact, ideologically committed to the preservation of that humanist-liberal tradition that Heidegger—and his more radical postmodern heirs: Jacques Derrida, Jean-François Lyotard, Michel Foucault, and more recently Giorgio Agamben and Alain Badiou—has

shown, by way of his persuasive ontological critique of the Western (onto-theo-logical) philosophical tradition, leads inexorably to the dehumanization of humanity in the modern era.

Heidegger, as opposed to traditionalist humanist historians, and like all those who followed him, was an engaged thinker who understood his vocation as that of writing a history of the present historical occasion. But in order to accomplish this project, it was necessary to undertake a de-structive genealogy (*Wiederholen*: repetition, as Heidegger called this initiative), which, with the present historical condition as a forestructure put at risk, returns to the past to retrieve for the present the beginning in all its open potentiality.

What Heidegger disclosed by way of this destructive genealogical repetition is that (1) Western history, which he called the "onto-theological tradition," has always been a metaphysical tradition that has thought being metaphysically: from after or above or beyond things as they are, and, in thus privileging the panoptic eye over the other human senses, spatializes (reifies or structures) the irreparable temporal dynamics of being to render its original potential a comprehendable (take holdable) object. His genealogy also disclosed (2) that this Western onto-theo-logical tradition had its origin, not in ancient Greece, as virtually all histories of Western civilization affirm, but in Rome, when the agents of the Roman imperial project, anxious about the influence of the errancy of Greek thinking, reduced its radically temporal notion of truth—a-letheia: the never-ending process, as the hyphen suggests, of un-concealing and concealing—to veritas, the adequation of mind and thing; that is, to a final correctness. It was a reductive reification that, in the name of humanism (homo humanus) would enable the colonization of the barbarian creatures of the peripheral "terra incognita" by way of conquering, domesticating, and integrating their wildness into the central City.

As noted, Heidegger called this history of Western philosophy the "onto-theo-logical tradition" to point to the continuity of its three apparently different phases—the onto-logical, the theo-logical, and the anthropo-logical: Roman, medieval, and modern—all three of which, despite these differences, were subsumed by a higher, transcendental Logos (or presiding Center). But for the sake of brevity—and to underscore Heidegger's abiding concern for the present historical occasion, further commentary will be limited to modernity: the era of Anthropo-logos.

Heidegger's genealogy discloses that the origin of the present, anthropological, phase of the Western tradition lies in the fulfillment in the Renaissance of the logic of the kind of Humanism introduced by the Romans in antiquity by way of the truth of veritas and the "erudition et institutio in bones artes" (education and training in good conduct). Unlike that of the pre-Socratic Greeks, whose a-le-theia implied a notion of the human that was devoid of identity, it was a *humanism*, that is, one that, in privileging the anthropologos, also privileged a mode of thinking Heidegger appropriately called "enframing." In the modern era, this structuring mode of thinking (techne) became technology, which, in turn, transformed the otherwise irreparable temporality of being into what Heidegger appropriately called the "Age of the World Picture": a spatialized structure that could be seen and grasped all at once.

Under this totalized enframing dispensation, modern man, the lord over all he surveys, as Heidegger ominously observes in his great essay, "The Question Concerning Technology," has reduced all the temporal phenomena—the be-ing—of being, to Bestand: standing or, to point to the radicalness of this modern condition, disposable, reserve. And in the process, man himself is threatened to be reduced to disposable reserve.

It is this Heideggerian diagnosis of technological modernity understood as the "Age of the World Picture," that, in the face of the mounting demand by traditionalist liberal humanists for the categorical dismissal of Heidegger's intervention as essentially reactionary, has sustained the attention of radical worldly contemporary thinkers such as Agamben, Badiou, Slavoj Žižek, Judith Butler, and others, who are profoundly concerned about the dehumanizing consequences of the structure of the modern world at large assumed by the dominant technological capitalist culture. This concern is especially evident, for example, in the thinking of Agamben, who put the modern dehumanizing momentum diagnosed by Heidegger as "disposable reserve" more radically. Following Michel Foucault's account of the biopoliticization of modern human, he diagnosed the dehumanizing dynamics of modern as the reduction of human life (bios) to "bare life" (zoe, nuda vida): life that can killed without the killing being called murder.

This is not to say, as traditionalist humanists invariably do, that Heidegger and those recent radically world-oriented thinkers he has influenced, are antihumanists. It is to suggest, rather, that he and they, if far more radically, look forward, by way of this genealogical retrieval of the beginnings of the West, to a coming polis composed of humans, true to their irreparable condition as finite ex-sistent in-sistents, who are non-identitarian identities—"whatever" beings, in what I take to be Agamben's translation of Heidegger's "Da-sein," thrown being there. Or to put this retrieved understanding of the humanness of a humanity that has been divested of a historically imposed identity, in the resonant paradoxical language that the late Edward Said coined in the context of the Palestine question, it is a "non-humanist humanism," a non-identitarian humanism that enables the perception of a coming human community in which the "'complete consort danc[es] together' contrapuntally."

(*See also* Agamben, Giorgio; Alienation; Archi-Writing; Authenticity; Cartesianism; Chapter 1, Early Theory; Chapter 5, Poststructuralism; Chapter 8, Rhetoric; Chapter 9, Deconstruction; Critique; Deconstruction; Derrida, Jacques; Event; Existentialism; Gadamer, Hans-Georg; Hermeneutics; Humanism; Husserl, Edmund; Intersubjectivity; Levinas, Emmanuel; Linguistic Turn; Metaphysics; Nancy, Jean-Luc; Object-Oriented Ontology; Objects; Origin; Phenomenology; Presence; Repetition; Subject; Subjectivity; Worldiness; *and* Worldhood)

William Spanos, *Binghamton University (United States)*

Further Reading

Gadamer, Hans-Georg. *Truth and Method* [1960]. Trans. W. Glen Doeopel. London: Continuum, 2004.

Heidegger, Martin. *Parmenides* [1942-43]. Trans. Andre Schuwer and Richard Rojcewicz. Bloomington: Indiana University Press, 1992.

Spanos, William V. *Heidegger and Criticism: Retrieving the Cultural Politics of Destruction*. Minneapolis: University of Minnesota Press, 1993.

Hemisphere (*See* Chapter 17, Comparatisms; *and* Transnational)

Hermeneutics

Although hermeneutics only appeared in modernity as the "art" or "technique" of establishing and interpreting texts or documents, it had existed previously in different forms and, as in many disciplines, it shaped itself by reformulating its previous incarnations. The need for a method of interpretation is motivated by the dual aspect of what is said or written: besides the meaning expressed by words and sentences, there is a possible sense that those sentences "make" or do not make to readers. In one of its first incarnations in ancient Greece—but there are instances in the Hindu tradition as well—the art of interpretation took the form of an allegorization, which is, on the one hand, a creative transfer of what is described, for example in Homer's *Iliad* and *Odyssey*, to the life of readers or listeners, and, on the other, a free "application" of what then become models and virtues.

The same kind of interest in "application" motivated the medieval "exegesis" of the biblical writings. A particular story in the Bible has a patent, "literal" meaning, but this meaning may carry an "allegorical" sense, revealing what is to be believed, or a "moral" sense, telling readers how to live, or even an "anagogical" sense of what is prophesized to come. In both its ancient and medieval forms, allegorization is a creative application as a forward-looking transfer from a sense whose intention is not in question—texts are variegated "expressions" of antecedent intentions—to the life of readers or listeners where the sense remains alive.

It is only with Reformation and the subsequent arising of philology that a "critical" component enters hermeneutics, which now calls itself such, as a specific discipline of interpreting but also of establishing the correct texts. Interpretation is no longer a creative transfer and free application not strictly bound by the text, as in allegory. Interpretation starts with the text and retrospectively "reconstructs" the true meaning it conveys in order to "understand better" (the motto of Schleiermacher's romantic hermeneutics) by unveiling deposited meanings that may exceed what historical writers meant.

On this basis, Wilhelm Dilthey could show that "understanding" is the specific activity—the methodology—of the human and social sciences, and defend them against the encroachment of the ever-expanding natural sciences, all dedicated to "explanation." By contrast with Dilthey's defensive and methodological views, Martin Heidegger's hermeneutics is assertive—understanding is a structural component of human existence—and ontological—human beings are those who interpret themselves and the world around them. Hans-Georg Gadamer combined Dilthey's and Heidegger's views into a "philosophical hermeneutics." Instead of a free transfer from meaning to life (allegory) or a critical "understanding better" (Schleiermacher), interpretation is an "appropriation" of past sources in a "fusion of horizons" between text and reader so that past texts remain alive, speaking to us, and we remain vulnerable to their questioning, unsettled in our present.

Hermeneutics has also been influential in the movements it stimulated (Paul Ricoeur's theory of narratives) and the reactions it elicited: structuralism (Claude Lévi-Strauss), postmodernism (Jean-François Lyotard), deconstructionism (Paul de Man, Jacques Derrida), or archaeology (Michel Foucault).

(*See also* Chapter 8, Rhetoric; Chapter 18, Translation; Chapter 19, Media Studies; Chapter 24, Posthumanism; Chapter 27, Antitheory; Gadamer, Hans-Georg; *and* Reading)

Pol Vandevelde, *Marquette University*
(United States)

Further Reading

De Lubac, Henri. *Medieval Exegesis: The Four Senses of Scripture* [1959-64]. Three vols. Trans. Mark Sebanc. Grand Rapids: Eerdmans, 1998.

Gadamer, Hans-Georg. *Truth and Method* [1960]. 2nd ed. Trans. revised by Joel Weinsheimer and Donald G. Marshall. London: Continuum, 1998.

Vandevelde, Pol. *The Task of the Interpreter: Text, Meaning, and Negotiation*. Pittsburgh: University of Pittsburgh Press, 2005.

Heteroglossia (*See* Dialogue)

Heteronomy

Heteronomy is a term from Kantian philosophy that appears most prominently in his *Groundwork of the Metaphysic of Morals* (1785). In contrast to Kant's desire for a self-legislating autonomous subject, the ground for any theory of universal morality, heteronomy, the inverse of autonomy, refers to a rational being who is subject to external laws. In the *Groundwork*, for example, Kant argues that past philosophical attempts to discover a "supreme principle of duty" are "conditioned" and therefore unable to "serve as a moral law." The heteronomous subject is thus unable to become "independent of determination by causes in the sensible world." Kant describes those dependencies as "interests" and they can be both empirical, such as "*personal happiness*," and rational, for instance the "ontological concept of *perfection*."

Kant's *Critique of Judgment* (1790) is the text that continues to exert the most influence in literary-critical circles. Its distinction between beauty and the sublime and its definition of genius buttress arguments for the autonomy of art. Yet, the espousal of autonomy in the realm of ethics is equally evident in the work of scholars—for example, the mid-century New Critics—who write from a humanist political orientation. As a result, the critical legacy of heteronomy might be understood in terms of an antihumanist tradition: what is better known as the emergence of philosophical determinism. Even though Hegel, Kant's great successor, equally values autonomy, his theory of the human subject posits that self-consciousness is conditioned on history and otherness (i.e., recognition). Hegelian thinking would assume that heteronomy is the condition for achieving autonomy in history. We can see Hegel's emphasis on contingent selfhood in Karl Marx, Friedrich Nietzsche, and Sigmund Freud, where subjectivity is determined by material conditions, the will, or sexual development. Despite being labeled as determinists, however, Nietzsche and others remain committed to many humanistic principles such as freedom. Even Michel Foucault, the most important postwar thinker of social constructivism, searched for human agency by analyzing Greek practices of self-making and by theorizing a hermeneutics of the subject. It would be mistaken to see a simple dichotomy between autonomy and heteronomy in the history of literature and criticism. Instead, we should think of the terms as complementary, the necessary dialectic (represented by Kant and Hegel respectively) within which the artist and critic labors.

(*See also* Kant, Immanuel; *and* Subject)

Daniel Rosenberg Nutters, *Temple University (United States)*

Further Reading

Guyer, Paul, ed. *The Cambridge Companion to Kant and Modern Philosophy*. New York: Cambridge University Press, 2006.

Kant, Immanuel. *Groundwork of the Metaphysic of Morals* [1785]. Trans. H. J. Paton. New York: Harper Torchbooks, 1964.

Homogeneous, Empty Time

Most directly attributed to Walter Benjamin in his essay "On the Concept of History" (1940) (also known as "Theses on the Philosophy of History"), the phrase "homogeneous, empty time" (*eine homogene und leere Zeit*) echoes Henri Bergson's earlier discussion of "homogeneous time" (*le temps homogène*) in *Time and Free Will* (1889). For both Bergson and Benjamin, the widespread perception of time as fungible and devoid of intrinsic value characterizes the experience of modernity. This temporal homogeneity appears to link together the experiences of individuals in the present and also to extend that modern monoculture into the future. For both Bergson and Benjamin, homogeneous time is not objectively real, but rather a form of false consciousness in which individuals are unable to perceive time's true richness, variety, and significance. In philosophical terms, Bergson critiques the concept of homogeneous time as a Kantian error that conflates time with space. Bergson argues that the notion of homogeneous time presumes a mechanistic causality that masks the freedom inherent in "duration," his term for time decoupled from misleading spatial analogies. In a more directly political critique, Benjamin identifies homogeneous, empty time with "progress" and "historicism," in the ideological sense associated with bourgeois liberalism. Benjamin's concept of "Jetztzeit," or "now-time," signifies a contrasting and more real presence of revolutionary energy, the possibility of explosion within any moment. In "Paralipomena to 'On the Concept of History'" Benjamin comments, "A conception of history that has liberated itself from the schema of progression within an empty and homogeneous time would finally unleash the destructive energies of historical materialism which have been held back for so long."

Benjamin's phrase "homogeneous, empty time" has been influentially adopted and critiqued by Benedict Anderson and Homi Bhabha. In *Imagined Communities* (1991), Anderson argues that homogeneous, empty time is the time of the modern nation. The common temporal experience of modernity, promulgated by artifacts of modern print culture such as newspapers and almanacs, enables individuals spread across geographical space to create a shared narrative identity as a national collectivity. In his influential essay "Dissemination," Bhabha critiques Anderson's theory from a postcolonial point of view, arguing that the time of the modern nation is "split" into "pedagogical" and "performative" modes, a "ghostly simultaneity of a temporality of doubling." Bhabha looks to Benjamin's essay "The Storyteller" to locate a "strange temporality" or "alienated time" in the act of narration, a time that destabilizes the apparent homogeneity of modern temporal experience and opens up possibilities for revolutionary change.

(*See also* Benjamin, Walter; *and* Print Capitalism)

Thomas Allen, *University of Ottawa (Canada)*

Further Reading

Anderson, Benedict. *Imagined Communities: Reflections on the Origin and Spread of Nationalism.* Rvsd. ed. London: Verso, 1991.

Benjamin, Walter. "On the Concept of History." Trans. Harry Zohn. *Selected Writings, Volume 4: 1938-1940.* Ed. Howard Eiland and Michael W. Jennings. Cambridge: The Belknap Press of Harvard University Press, 2003. 389–400.

Benjamin, Walter. "Paralipomena to 'On the Concept of History.'" Trans. Edmund Jephcott and Howard Eiland. *Selected Writings, Volume 4: 1938-1940.* Cambridge: The Belknap Press of Harvard University Press, 2003. 401–11.

Bergson, Henri. *Time and Free Will: An Essay on the Immediate Data of Consciousness* [1889]. Trans. H. L. Pogson. Mineola: Dover, 2001.

Bhabha, Homi. *The Location of Culture.* London: Routledge, 1994.

Humanimal

A foundational tenet of Western humanism, the human-animal divide refers to the idea that humans and animals are completely disparate—ontologically, biologically, intellectually, spiritually, and culturally—for the purposes of apportioning value, rights, and privileges. For the most part, we have defined the category of the human through the ongoing exclusion of the (inferior) animal, consigning the latter to a category of critical lack (of reason, language, souls). The human-animal divide is often described as a "boundary," indicating the maintenance of a frontier between the two polar categories of the human self and the devalued nonhuman animal Other, which has historically justified the human exploitation of animals. In turn, this speciesism grounds human-on-human oppression, in that the attribution of the same incapacities onto select groups of humans has historically legitimized racism, sexism, classism, and discrimination against people with disabilities. While its precise definition varies depending on context, the neologism "humanimal" at a minimum signals an intent to challenge this material and/or discursive separation of humans and other animals.

In technoscientific research, "humanimal" may refer to the development of genetically engineered chimeras, such as attempts to implant animal embryos injected with human stem cells into the wombs of sheep and pigs in the hopes of growing transplant organs for human use. In the arts, "humanimal" describes representations of bodies that are visually identifiable as part human, part nonhuman animal: skin that seamlessly fuses with pelt or a deer's head that sits on the shoulders of a human body. Such figures may fascinate or even terrify as they transgress the human-animal divide that Western thought takes so firmly as a given. By embracing hybridization, these chimerical bodies confound the species divide to some degree, but may also sustain it to the extent that they suggest that humans and other animals were already distinctly separable and separate before their willful hybridization.

The posthumanities deployment of the term does not concern the production of chimeras per se, but rather seeks to complicate, or even dismantle, the apparatuses of the human-animal divide. Some use "humanimal" to posit that the human-animal divide is blurred, shifting, and unstable. The divide is also often described as a "gulf," suggesting that there exists a wide swath of space—an indeterminate zone—within which a range of discursive hybridizations has always already occurred, and "humanimal" may refer to these varied and evolving interfaces. To Carrie Packwood Freeman, for example, the term "humanimal" could serve as an alternative way to refer to humans that reminds us we are also animals by the terms of our own taxonomies. Or, as in Kalpana Rahita Seshadri's variation, "humAnimal" may mark out the categories (and a zone between them) that should be perpetually exposed and deconstructed.

(*See also* Chapter 24, Posthumanism; *and* Posthumanism)

Keridiana Chez, *Borough of Manhattan Community College, City University of New York (United States)*

Further Reading

Agamben, Giorgio. *The Open: Man and Animal* [2002]. Trans. Kevin Attell. Stanford: Stanford University Press, 2004.

Derrida, Jacques. *The Animal That Therefore I Am* [2006]. Ed. Marie-Louise Mallet. Trans. David Wills. New York: Fordham University Press, 2008.

Freeman, Carrie Packwood. "Embracing Humanimality: Deconstructing the Human/Animal Dichotomy." In *Arguments About Animal Ethics*. Eds. G. Goodale and J. E. Black. Lanham: Lexington Books, 2010. 11–30.

Haraway, Donna J. *When Species Meet*. Minneapolis: University of Minnesota Press, 2007.

Humanism

Humanism is a term with several different meanings, not all of which can be fit into a single coherent concept. The word itself comes from classical Roman culture where *humanitas* referred to both a broad education in humanities subjects such as literature, rhetoric, history, and politics and to a commitment to humane values. This implies that those educated in the humanities will respond humanely with empathy and understanding to the suffering of those around them. Such assumptions, of course, persist to this day in the notion that a humanities education can and should make students more morally and politically sensitive to the sufferings of various disadvantaged groups.

The term acquires a second dimension of meaning in the work of the Renaissance Humanists such as Marsilo Ficino (1433–99) and Pico della Mirandola (1463–94) in Italy, Erasmus (1466–1538) in Holland and Thomas More (1478–1535) in England. Like the Roman advocates of *humanitas*, these humanists argued for the importance of a broad reading in classical literatures, including Greek. In such a curriculum, they found the antidote to what they saw as the claustrophobic narrowness of medieval scholasticism. They rejected the monastic culture that supported the scholastic tradition and insisted that scholars should engage the world, that their knowledge should be useful. This belief in worldly engagement was supported by the Renaissance Humanists' conviction that humanity has the freedom and the power to shape its own destiny in new and unprecedented ways. This faith in the power of human agency was especially evident in these humanists' attitudes toward politics. More interested in political practice than theological foundations of the state, they believed that the historical record makes it possible to study and understand human behavior like any other natural phenomenon and that by better understanding human behavior, the humanist scholar could make substantial practical recommendations for improving governing institutions. Such beliefs gave rise to very different works including Machiavelli's *The Prince* (1532), an instruction manual for tyrants, and Thomas More's *Utopia* (1516), a speculative fiction about a society that is administered in a purely rational way so that it avoids the evils that plagued the Europe of More's time.

Humanists of the early modern period are all Christians; indeed, Thomas More was famously martyred for upholding the authority of the Roman Catholic Church in its dispute with King Henry VIII over the king's divorce. However, most humanists of this time were impatient with the disputes over dogma that divided the Christian Church, and some were syncretists who believed that all religions are revelations of the same basic truths. Leonardo Bruni (1370–1444), for instance, argues that Plato's philosophy does not differ in its essential message from the Christianity that follows it. With the Enlightenment and French Revolution, however, there emerge various secular humanisms that add a third dimension to the term. These secular humanisms deny the authority of revealed religion and insist that all values are human values. Many of these secular humanists, Nicolas de Condorcet and Auguste Comte, for example, argue that

human history reveals the triumph of human reason as it discredits the superstitions of religious thinking. Such secular humanisms provoke a strong antihumanist response from those who are offended by the glorification of what they see as a very flawed human nature.

The wars and genocides of the twentieth century have challenged these meliorist views of history, but not eliminated them. Although many contemporary humanists reject narratives of human progress, they continue to insist that all values have a human origin and reject claims that either God or nature sets the standard for good and fulfilling human lives. An exchange between Jean-Paul Sartre and Martin Heidegger defines the contemporary debate about humanism. In *Existentialism as Humanism* (1946), Sartre rejects the narrative of human progress, but he argues that human freedom is absolute and insists that all values are human creations and cannot be validated with appeals to superhuman powers. In "Letter on Humanism" (1947), Heidegger expresses a distrust of this appeal to an unrestrained human freedom. He argues that true freedom is found by questioning the world (Being) rather than by imposing a human will upon it.

(*See also* Antihumanism; Chapter 22, Identity Studies; Chapter 24, Posthumanism; Heidegger, Martin; Platonism; *and* Transhumanism)

Allen R. Dunn, *University of Tennessee (United States)*

Further Reading

Law, Stephen. *Humanism: A Very Short Introduction*. Oxford: Oxford University Press, 2011.

Norman, Richard. *On Humanism*. London: Routledge, 2004.

Said, Edward. *Humanism and Democratic Criticism*. New York: Columbia University Press, 2004.

Husserl, Edmund

Edmund Husserl (1859–1938) was originally trained as a mathematician, then turned to philosophy of mathematics and eventually became the inventor of the philosophical movement known as *phenomenology*. Husserl was Martin Heidegger's teacher and mentor until the publication of *Being and Time* in 1927; Husserl fled from Nazi Germany in 1936. Three of Jacques Derrida's first book-length manuscripts are devoted to Husserl's thought.

Husserl's philosophy, at its core, combines two tendencies that may seem opposed, but that structure makes it fertile ground for literary theory and criticism. On one side, meanings, particularly those found in linguistic expressions, are deemed independent by Husserl. Meanings are, if not objects, then "objectivities," and thus can be approached and treated on their own terms. Husserl's embrace of meaning's objectivity joins up with parallel construals of meaning in formalism and structuralism, though for him language remains secondary. Instead, everything that can be said to be, including meaning, for Husserl, is rooted in intentional acts and lived experiences. A life of understanding, with a temporality specific to it, lies over against everything objective, including meaning.

From Husserlian phenomenology three strands of criticism sprang. A first focuses on the experiencing of literary texts. A second attends to the relative independence and autonomy of meanings. A third takes up both vectors and conceives them afresh—an approach often in more direct contact with Husserl's project than the first two.

The first, reader-response criticism, looks to the act of reading for the critic's object rather than to the author's intention or to the linguistic structures that the work embodies. Only in the reader's experience of a text—in going through it, making connections across it, as well as actualizing it in imagination (giving Hamlet a certain color of hair or Emma a specific smile)—does a story, play, or poem finally exist.

Though shaped by other influences, the New Criticism of the postwar era is the best-known movement affiliated with Husserl's avowal of meaning's autonomy. Rene Wellek, a prominent New Critic, took up a version of Husserl's work to explain the status of literary form in this criticism, an analysis on which Cleanth Brooks and other New Critics relied.

Wellek's version of Husserl's thought originated in one of Husserl's early students, Roman Ingarden. Ingarden himself falls into the third camp of theorists. An important philosopher in his own right, Ingarden plied both sides of Husserl's thinking and was intimately familiar with his teachings. Ingarden's study of first, the ontology, and then, the cognition, of the literary work, in two separate volumes, disclosed the complex structure of a literary text, while also attending to the acts that "concretized" it, acts which, Ingarden claimed, brought its otherwise empty, formal meaning structures to life. Reader-response criticism descends from this aspect of Ingarden's thought.

The third camp is very wide-ranging; it stretches from E. D. Hirsch to Derrida. Hirsch argues for authorial intention as the sole secure reference point for interpreting and evaluating literary works, by way of Husserl's model of intentional consciousness. Derrida took up considerations he first found in Husserl concerning writing's role in the transcendental constitution of scientific and mathematical objects to deconstruct the conceptuality pertaining to language and the work.

Finally, critics today turn to Husserl on these, and still more, accounts: when treating topics like empathy or ecology in literary contexts; in interpreting narrative innovations in Modernist authors such as Samuel Beckett or Virginia Woolf; or when approaching late-nineteenth- and early-twentieth-century literature in historical contexts, with an eye to the various movements initiated by Husserl's writings, as well as related ones, such as those associated with William James.

(*See also* Chapter 9, Deconstruction; Derrida, Jacques; Gadamer, Hans-Georg; Objects; Phenomenology; Reading; *and* Subjectivity)

Joshua Kates, *Indiana University (United States)*

Further Reading

Ahmed, Sara. *Queer Phenomenology: Orientations, Objects, Others*. Durham: Duke University Press, 2006.

Maude, Ulrika, and Matthew Feldman, eds. *Beckett and Phenomenology*. London: Continuum, 2009.

Poulet, Georges. "A Phenomenology of Reading." *New Literary History* 1 (1969): 53–68.

Hybridity

Following older themes of syncretism in anthropology and creolization in linguistics, hybridity has increasingly become a prominent theme in cultural and postcolonial studies. On the micro level, hybridization has been associated with the study of the breaking up of racial, national, linguistic, or other identity binaries, as well as revealing connectors and influences across "national" borders, in the process refuting the "boundedness" and "essentialism" of the modern episteme. The complexity of individuals' identities and their own personal route has hence been highlighted. On the macro level, hybridity is seen as a way to analyze the impact of globalization, sometimes with direct connection with the "reactive nationalisms or ethnicities" in the Balkans and Africa. The common starting point of all of these approaches is the focus on the wide register of multiple identity, crossover, pick-n-mix, boundary-crossing experiences and styles.

Hybridity studies have a specific connection with racial studies that cannot be denied. More precisely, it is the Eurocentrically articulated theory of race which determines the modern intelligibility of hybridity. Hybridity, according to Joshua Lund in *The Impure Imagination* (2006), is generally understood as the "impurification of standard or canonized forms." Hence, for Lund, hybridology needs to be linked to considerations of the "coloniality of power," which is not currently done in the common work on creolization and *mestizaje*. This is what brings certain authors to say that hybridity is more than just another form of syncretism. Finally, hybridity is inherently linked with the work of Homi Bhabha, for whom hybridity, in *The Location of Culture* (1994), is a third space, "a difference 'within,' an 'in-between' reality." It is a space of translation, "where the construction of a political object that is new, *neither the one nor the other*, properly alienates our political expectations, and changes, as it must, the very forms of our recognition of the moment of politics." For Bhabha, hybridity is not necessarily a third term that resolves the tension between two cultures, but rather holds the tension of the opposition and explores the spaces in-between fixed identities through their continuous reiterations.

Migrating from the cultural and postcolonial fields, hybridity considerations have now permeated many disciplines, including peace and conflict studies, international development, and law. However, the hybridity lens has not gone unchallenged. Jan Nederveen Pieterse rightly points out that the most conspicuous shortcoming of the hybridity literature is that it is seen as the triumph of neoliberal multiculturalism, which leads some hybridity scholars to skip over questions of power and inequality. There is indeed a form of vacuousness in the general "hybridist post-national talk," as Gayatri Spivak terms it in *A Critique of Postcolonial Reason* (1999), reproducing in certain instances discourses of globalization and cosmopolitanianism while celebrating the "creolization" of the world. This is why we agree with Marwan Kraidy that it is essential to situate every analysis of hybridity in a specific context where the conditions that shape hybridity(ies) are addressed in order to make salient the violent hierarchies and the hegemonically constructed identities by dominant societal actors.

(*See also* Chapter 11, Cultural Studies; Chapter 13, Race and Postcolonial Studies; Chapter 14, Ecocriticism; Chapter 17, Comparativisms; Chapter 19, Media Studies; Chapter 22, Identity Studies; Chapter 24, Posthumanisms; Creolization; *and* Double Consciousness)

Nicolas Lemay-Hébert, *University of Birmingham (United Kingdom)*
Rosa Freedman, *University of Reading (United Kingdom)*

Further Reading

Kraidy, Marwan. *Hybridity, or the Cultural Logic of Globalization*. Philadelphia: Temple University Press, 2012.

Lemay-Hébert, Nicolas, and Rosa Freedman. "Critical Hybridity: Exploring Cultural, Legal and Political Pluralism." In *Hybridity: Law, Culture and Development*. Eds. Nicolas Lemay-Hébert and Rosa Freedman. London: Routledge, 2017. 3–14.

Hyperobject

Hyperobject is a term in ecological philosophy that was first coined by Timothy Morton

in his 2010 book *The Ecological Thought* and developed further in his 2013 book bearing the same name. The term hyperobject can be situated at the intersection of post- or antihumanism, object-oriented philosophy, and the environmental humanities. Having emerged early in the twenty-first-century, hyperobject is Morton's way of describing large-scale, planet-wide "objects" like global warming or radioactive plutonium. As hyperobjects are considered to be "massively distributed in space and time," their magnitude renders them largely invisible to the naked human eye. Global warming, to use Morton's favorite example, cannot be seen or identified as such. Instead, hyperobjects force us to acknowledge that their large-scale cumulative effects have multiple and varied causes that are distributed widely across space and time and at scales that far exceed human comprehension.

The prepositional force of the prefix *hyper* suggests that the substantive it modifies—"object"—carries with it a distinctive sense of excess or going beyond measure. Hyperobjects are indeed excessive—they are so large we cannot even see them or measure them directly—while the definition of "object" that the prefix modifies can also be considered to participate in a kind of rhetorical hyperactivity or excess. To that end, the conceptual legibility of the noun "object" in hyperobject must be understood as referring to the eccentric definition of "object" that has been put forth by object-oriented philosophy, a crypto-obscurantist system of thought first developed by the popular writer Graham Harman in 1999. Uniting object-oriented philosophy and Morton's ecological notion of hyperobjects is the wish to "decenter" the human from philosophy and nature.

Hyperobjects help to shine critical light on the idea that "all entities whatsoever are interconnected in an interobjective system" that Morton describes as "the mesh." Trapped within this mesh are objects both real and imagined. Morton borrows heavily from object-oriented philosophy when he describes everything as an object: global warming, concrete, a coffee cup, and the tooth fairy would all be objects on equal ontological footing because, in this system, they are all said to be "totally incapable of being objectified" as such. The rhetorical force of this listicle derives its philosophical punch from a post- or antihumanist desire to demonstrate how human cognition or existence is "less privileged" than the last four hundred years of philosophy has incorrectly imagined it to be. Too much thinking about thought has come at the expense of contemplating the wondrousness of objects. Considering everything to be an actant or object on a flat ontological ground or mesh helps to redefine dead, inert matter as being just as alive as human existence. As the *Oxford English Dictionary* notes in its entry on "hyper," since the seventeenth century the prefix has come to operate as "a kind of living element, freely prefixed to adjectives and substantives." Theorizing hyperobjects as things that escape direct human perception has the effect of lending them a quasi-vitalistic or pseudo-spiritual quality. Even though hyperobjects cannot be experienced directly, we know they are there.

Morton's hyperobjects can be considered alive and ontologically ubiquitous in their philosophical and historical-etymological senses. The ability of hyperobjects to trap us in a planetary-wide mesh of aliveness, coupled with the term's rapid rise in popularity outside of specialist academic discourses, resonates equally well with the *OED*'s definition of "hyper" in its adjectival form as denoting "excitable or highly-strung." Tracing this particular usage to the mid-twentieth century, Morton's deployment of "hyper" is inseparable from its historical development as slang or vernacular. In this sense, considering everything to be interconnected within a hyperobject is less an empirical claim about the world than it is an aesthetic "tuning to the object." The imperative that we "tune" ourselves to objects in general and hyperobjects in particular is best viewed as an argument in favor of "returning to sentimentalism or sensationalism." Because hyperobjects are ubiquitous, they are able to be perceived, however obliquely, by everyone. Hyperobjects, then, are most valuable because they help us retune or resituate aesthetic taste or judgment within an eccentrically populist, though by no means limited to the human, register.

(*See also* Antihumanism; Chapter 23, Materialisms; Environmental Humanities; Object-Oriented Ontology; *and* Posthumanism)

Michael Miller, *Rice University (United States)*

Further Reading
Ghosh, Amitav. *The Great Derangement: Climate Change and the Unthinkable.* Chicago: University of Chicago Press, 2016.
Heise, Ursula K. *Imagining Extinction: The Cultural Meanings of Endangered Species.* Chicago: University of Chicago Press, 2016.
Morton, Timothy. *Hyperobjects: Philosophy and Ecology after the End of the World.* Minneapolis: University of Minnesota Press, 2013.
Nixon, Rob. *Slow Violence and the Environmentalism of the Poor.* Cambridge: Harvard University Press, 2013.

Hysteria

Hysteria is a condition in which the sufferer complains of often vague or unlocalized symptoms that have no organic cause, or that migrate from one part of the body or one neurophysiological system to another. It may also take the form of motor difficulties, paralyzes, mutism, or trance-like states in which the hysteric adopts another personality or speaks another language. Hysteria is often considered as a woman's complaint, and for thousands of years medical wisdom held that hysteria (from the Greek *hystera*, "uterus") had something to do with the particularities of female sexuality. In ancient Egyptian and Greek medicine, the mobile symptoms characteristic of hysteria were attributed to the perambulations of a "wandering womb," a uterus that had somehow detached itself from the genital zone and become lodged in another part of the body. Ancient treatments for hysteria relied upon scent therapy, thought to induce the uterus to return to its correct position by placing good smells under the genitals. With the advent of the industrial age, hysteria was often treated either with hydrotherapy (high-pressure blasts of water directed at the abdomen) or with manual or mechanical massage of the genitals to provoke "hysterical paroxysm," or what today would be called orgasm. Both treatments supposed that the womb was "congested" and needed to discharge, and the operation was performed as clinically as if the doctor were draining an abscess.

Modern discussions of hysteria are indebted to Sigmund Freud, the father of psychoanalysis, who first worked with hysterics while completing his medical residency in Paris. There he worked under the supervision of Jean-Martin Charcot, who confided to Freud his belief that hysteria had a sexual etiology. Freud adopted Charcot's hypothesis, but developed it in a particular direction by conceiving sexuality in mental rather than physiological terms. He maintained that hysteria was neither an organic illness

nor the result of an overactive or frustrated sexual appetite, but rather a specific manifestation of the psychic structure of neurosis. Advancing that "a neurotic's symptoms represent his sex life," Freud argued that the hysteric's symptoms attest to the presence of an unconscious body whose sexuality cannot be reduced to biology, a body distinct from the organism. The symptom reveals that this body is superimposed on the organism in the form of erogenous zones: neurophysiological systems, organs, orifices, or limbs that are overwritten by an unconscious fantasy and made to function according to its logic. For Freud's successor Jacques Lacan, hysteria is precious to psychoanalysis because it reveals so well the *corps morcelé* or fragmented body that defines the psychic anatomy of every human being.

Freud maintains that the cause of all neurosis, including hysteria, is the incompatibility between the ego and some wish or idea that it cannot avow. The specificity of hysteria is that the repressed ideational content finds expression in a bodily symptom, through a process that Freud calls "somatic conversion." In his *Studies in Hysteria* (1895), Freud claims that the hysteric "suffers mainly from reminiscences," since repressed ideas "take [their] revenge . . . by becoming pathogenic," inscribing themselves in the body when they are rejected from consciousness. The mechanism that produces hysteria therefore represents, on the one hand, an "act of moral cowardice," and, on the other, a "defensive measure which is at the disposal of the ego." This is because the subject is no longer conscious of the unacceptable idea or unwelcome desire in its "converted" or somatic form, and therefore not obliged to confront or take responsibility for it.

The psychoanalytic treatment of hysteria constrains the patient to find words for what is inscribed in the body, allowing it to obtain conscious expression so that she can confront and take responsibility for the repressed thoughts. This implies that the symptom is a form of unconscious speech, a way of expressing what the patient is unable or unwilling to put into words. It must be translated into language over the course of the treatment, so that it can become an object of conscious knowledge. In the case of Elisabeth von R., a young woman suffering from debilitating leg pains and difficulty standing or walking, Freud uses the painful stimulation of this erogenous zone to call up memories and associations that allow the patient to evoke for the first time something that has never been represented. These associations take the form of idiomatic expressions that relate the patient's psychic state to her motor difficulties. Elisabeth admits that she is unable to "stand alone" or "take a single step forward" in her life, and recalls a traumatic memory in which she "stood stock still as though rooted to the ground," In this way, writes Freud, "her painful legs began to 'join in the conversation,'" furnishing an answer to the analyst's queries there where the conscious memories of the patient were unable to.

(*See also* Castration; Chapter 7, Psychoanalytic Theory; Freud, Sigmund; Libidinal; Oedipus Complex; *and* Trauma)

Tracy McNulty, *Cornell University (United States)*

Further Reading

Breuer, Josef, and Sigmund Freud. *Studies on Hysteria* [1895]. New York: Basic Books, 2000.

Certeau, Michel de. *The Possession at Loudun* [1970]. Trans. Michael B. Smith. Chicago: University of Chicago Press, 1996.

David-Ménard, Monique. *Hysteria from Freud to Lacan: Body and Language in Psychoanalysis*. Ithaca: Cornell University Press, 1989.

Freud, Sigmund. *Dora: An Analysis of a Case of Hysteria* [1905]. New York: Simon & Schuster, 1997.

Kahane, Claire, and Charles Bernheimer, eds. *In Dora's Case: Freud-Hysteria-Feminism*. New York: Columbia University Press, 1990.

Lacan, Jacques. "The Mirror Stage." In *Écrits* [1966]. Trans. Bruce Fink. New York: W. W. Norton & Co, 2007. 75–81.

I

Idealism

In the broadly philosophical use, "idealism" refers to the metaphysical view that reality is subject-dependent. In contrast to materialism, idealism holds that there is no reality independent of mind, or at least that the contents of mental representation (ideas, sensations, perceptions) are in some sense more real than the external, material world. Early versions of this view can be found in Plato's theory of forms, the pantheism of Spinoza, and Cartesian rationalism. More systematic accounts of idealism, however, emerged within—and indeed, on either side of—the more familiar epistemological debates of the eighteenth century between rationalism and empiricism. Thus, rationalists such as Gottfried Leibniz and Christian Wolff could claim idealism as a doctrine of metaphysical ontology while George Berkeley rallied early empiricists around the famous idealist dictum: *esse est percipi* ("to be is to be perceived"). More significantly, Immanuel Kant attempts to reconcile the rationalist-empiricist schism by replacing the "dogmatic" idealism of his predecessors with what he called "transcendental" idealism, a distinctly epistemic form of idealism premised on the distinction between the *appearance* of things and *things as they are in themselves*. Kant famously characterized objects of experience as "empirically real," and therefore knowable, yet "transcendentally ideal," meaning that we can have no epistemic access to them beyond the limits of experience. The impact of Kant's philosophy is felt well into the nineteenth century, as the most (and last) philosophically robust form of idealism, namely, German idealism, begins to take shape around three central figures: G. W. F. Hegel, J. G. Fichte, and F. W. J. Schelling. Though formulated as a collective response to the unresolved tensions of Kantian philosophy (particularly the relation between self and world), ultimately each thinker cultivates a competing brand of German idealism, among which the young Hegel's would prove the most influential. The distinctive feature of Hegelian idealism is the proposition that autonomous selfhood is achieved intersubjectively, through the making and testing of identity claims in relation to other rational beings. Hegel emphasizes the sociality of reason over Fichte's "subjective" idealism, which posits the self as the normative source of an external world, as well as Schelling's "objective" philosophy, which posits the mind as identical to nature. But he leverages it more forcefully against the later manifestations of idealism in German romanticism, which he accused of fostering a radical form of subjectivism. Held together by a loose contingency of poet/philosophers, including Friedrich Hölderlin, Novalis, and the brothers Friedrich and August Wilhelm Schlegel, German romanticism challenged the Enlightenment's faith in the sovereignty of reason by appealing to the moral and epistemic virtues of beauty, particularly as found in modern (i.e., *romantic*) poetry. The far-reaching legacy of romanticism can be measured by the extent to which its signature philosophical and aesthetic devices—the use of irony, ambiguity, textual fragmentation, etc.—have been adapted to post-structuralist literary and cultural theory. Still, credit for the lasting impact of idealism is due principally to Marx, who famously "turned Hegel on his head" in pursuit of an economic, or *material*, analysis of culture while preserving the dialectical method of Hegelian critique that would prove useful for generations of Marxist theorists.

(*See also* Chapter 22, Identity Studies; Kant, Immanuel; *and* Žižek, Slavoj)

Jason Miller, *Warren Wilson College*
(United States)

Further Reading

Henrich, Dieter. *Between Kant and Hegel: Lectures on German Idealism.* Cambridge: Harvard University Press, 2008.

Pinkard, Terry. *German Philosophy 1760-1860.* Cambridge: Cambridge University Press, 2002.

Rush, Fred. *Irony and Idealism.* Oxford: Oxford University Press, 2016.

Identity Politics

Out of the political and cultural upheavals of the late 1960s and early 1970s arose a number of emancipatory movements—including Women's Liberation, Black Power, Gay Liberation, Native American Rights, Chicano Rights, and the decolonizing efforts of former European colonies—that sought to establish equality and social justice for historically marginalized and oppressed peoples in the United States and the world over. In many ways an extension of the Civil Rights Era, these movements based their politics upon a group's shared sexual, gender, racial, ethnic, or national identity (later iterations include disability, age, and religion, among others). This strategy eventually came to be known as identity politics.

While identity politics' goals are to confront minority stereotypes, promote equality, and extend civil and human rights to those who have long been denied them, significant theoretical issues regarding the nature of subjectivity, identity, and universalism underlie such a politics. A primary example is the social constructivism versus essentialism debate. Identity politics was formed amid the heyday of postmodernist thought, which radically decentered the notion of a stable and autonomous subjectivity or self, yet it has often had to rely on strong or weak forms of essentialism in making its case for a cohesive group identity. A marginalized group, for example, may band together and claim or create a subject position or identity that fosters a strong sense of self-worth among its members, helps them to withstand hegemonic discrimination, and grants them the political representation and means to redress it. Yet this risks "essentializing" identity by assuming that there is an unchanging, preexisting essence to subjectivities, which can ultimately bolster or lead to further prejudicial treatment. Furthermore is the issue of a politics founded on "difference" instead of "universal" sameness—that is, how might a truly "multicultural" society thrive if its various groups' essential differences cannot be overcome and a common ground established between them? In short, the challenges of identity politics encapsulate the very challenge of liberal democracy itself as a viable form of government.

Accordingly, those on both the political Right and Left have criticized identity politics. The Right believes it limits personal freedoms and has thus fought to end Affirmative Action, overturn *Roe v. Wade* (1973), and precipitated the so-called Culture Wars of the 1990s. In turn, some on the Left have argued that identity politics hampers its ability to form a broad, progressive coalition and that it does not adequately account for issues of class or income inequality that affect all people, yet disproportionately affect minorities.

Nevertheless, identity politics' activism remains strong, as evidenced in the passing of the American with Disabilities Act (1990), the formation of Black Lives Matter, the legalization of gay marriage, the movement for trans-rights, and in the continuing battles fought over immigration. While identity politics has clearly been successful in enacting real social, cultural, and political change, it must continue to be wary of the theoretical issues outlined above as it adapts to confront new forms of oppression in an always-changing political landscape.

(*See also* Chapter 10, Feminism; Chapter 22, Identity Studies; Class; Intersectionality; *and* Whiteness)

Ralph Clare, *Boise State University (United States)*

Further Reading

Alcoff, Linda Martín, Michael Hames-García, Satya P. Monanty, and Paul M. L. Moya, eds. *Identity Politics Reconsidered.* New York: Palgrave Macmillan, 2006.

Gitlin, Todd. *The Twilight of Common Dreams: Why America is Wracked by Culture Wars.* New York: Metropolitan Books, 1995.

Taylor, Charles, and Amy Gutmann. *Multiculturalism: Examining the Politics of Recognition.* Princeton: Princeton University Press, 1994.

Ideology

There are two definitions of *ideology* that are important in literary and cultural theory, and both of these derive from Marxism. In the less frequently used of these two meanings, ideology is a neutral term for a system of beliefs held by a group, especially regarding political questions or having political significance. In Marxism, ideology in this sense is often associated with a particular social class. One can therefore speak of "socialist ideology," "proletarian ideology," or "American ideology" without any positive or negative implication.

The second sense of ideology is more common and more difficult: ideology here is a system of ideas that both serves and masks the interests of a group, usually a social class. It derives specifically from Marx and Engels in *The German Ideology* (1846), where they hold that "the ruling ideas are nothing more that the ideal expression of the dominant material relationships, the dominant material relationships grasped as ideas." Thus the ruling ideas of any given period are the ideas that serve the interests of the ruling class but are understood by most people simply as "common sense" or "the truth." Since these ideas must distort reality in order to make a particular class's interests appear as if they were human interests, ideology implies systematic distortion: "In all ideology men and their circumstances appear upside down as in a *camera obscura.*" In this sense, ideology is false consciousness, a fundamental misunderstanding of reality, but one which can be corrected by making people aware of the distortion, the project of the "critique of ideology."

Paul Ricoeur has classified this sense of ideology as entailing a "hermeneutics of suspicion," because the overt meanings of the ideas in question must be reinterpreted to reveal the covert class interests they serve. Ricoeur also classifies psychoanalysis as a hermeneutics of suspicion in which surface meanings are reinterpreted as reflections of unconscious desires. Interestingly, the work of Louis Althusser brought these two systems together. He defined ideology as "the imaginary relationship of individuals to their real conditions of existence," and he located the seat of this imaginary relationship in the unconscious. As a result, in Althusser's conception, ideology is extraordinarily tenacious, since human beings have no direct access to the unconscious. Moreover, where Marx and Engels were mainly concerned with the content of ideas, Althusser shifted the focus to the institutions that perpetuate those ideas, which he called the "ideological state apparatus," including entities such as the church which we normally don't think of as part of the state. Like Althusser, Slavoj Žižek was also influenced by French psychoanalyst, Jacques Lacan, but Žižek locates ideology's tenacity not in the structure of the individual's mind, but in habits of mind under late capitalism. He asserts in *Mapping Ideology* (1994) that "the traditional critique of ideology no longer works" because false consciousness has been replaced by cynical consciousness in which "one is well aware of a particular interest hidden behind an ideological universality, but still one does not renounce it." This theory, however, has not prevented Žižek himself from doing critique of ideology, which is in fact what the theory itself is doing: interpreting the disguised motive behind the failure of other critique.

(*See also* Althusser, Louis; Apparatus; Assujettissement; Chapter 4, Marxism; Chapter 19, Media Studies; Chapter 21, Late Capitalism; Chapter 22, Identity Studies; Chapter 24, Posthumanism; Chapter 27, Antitheory; Interpellation; Marx, Karl; *and* Žižek, Slavoj)

David R. Shumway, *Carnegie Mellon University (United States)*

Further Reading
Kavanagh, James. H. "Ideology." In *Critical Terms for Literary Study*. Second ed. Ed. Frank Lentricchia and Thomas McLaughlin. Chicago: University of Chicago Press, 1995. 306–20.
Williams, Raymond. "Ideology." In *Marxism and Literature*. Ed. Raymond Williams. Oxford: Oxford University Press, 1977. 55–71.
Žižek, Slavoj, ed. *Mapping Ideology.* London: Verso, 1994.

Infrastructure

Infrastructures are systems that enable movement—roads move people and goods, pipes move water, sewers move waste. Infrastructure makes the work of other things possible. Energy infrastructures ensure the reader of this handbook has light to read the physical book or a running computer to read the electronic version. The definition of infrastructure does not need to be limited to pipes, roads, and wires. Infrastructures can encompass vast interdependent networks of materials, people, and nature to enable the functioning of modern life.

Infrastructures are commonly a banal part of everyday life. When infrastructures are working properly, we rarely take note of them. They become part of the background, enabling other kinds of work. Susan Leigh Star in "The Ethnography of Infrastructure" (1999) writes that infrastructures are invisible, until they break down, that is. It is easy to take infrastructure for granted, to assume it is stable. Yet, infrastructures are never given. They are always becoming, always a work in progress. We are not aware of these processes because much of infrastructure is black-boxed, obscured from our view. We benefit from water coming out of the faucet, but we rarely stop to think about all of the processes that delivered the water. Even if we did stop to consider these systems, they remain unknown to all but the people who work to maintain them, people whose work often remains out of sight of users. Yet, infrastructure is not stable for all equally. As Stephen Graham and Simon Marvin argue in *Splintering Urbanism* (2001), increasingly, some areas enjoy better infrastructure, both globally and within particular cities. Residents of both Hanoi, Vietnam and Flint, Michigan (among many other places) do not take potable water for granted. Dennis Rodgers and Bruce O'Neill, in "Infrastructural Violence" (2012), describe conditions when infrastructure harms through its lack or its direct impact. Passive infrastructural violence occurs from infrastructure's limitations, even if there is no clear intent that can be attributed to a particular actor. Lack of access to water is one example of passive infrastructural violence. Active infrastructural violence occurs when there is a clear intent to do harm through infrastructural systems. In this case, infrastructure has been designed to be violent. Examples include infrastructures of warfare or infrastructures otherwise designed to keep populations under control, such as violent policing of vulnerable populations.

Social scientists and humanities scholars ask different kinds of questions regarding infrastructure than the engineers who seek to ensure they work effectively. Whereas a transportation engineer might ask how to design a road to move vehicles efficiently, an anthropologist studying road infrastructure might ask how the design of a road impacts a commuter's bodily experience of the road, how the construction of a new road is affecting the surrounding neighborhood, or how the policymakers are making decisions about where to construct the road. A literary scholar might analyze how an author utilizes fictional strategies to elucidate how daily life is shaped by infrastructure and our dependency on it in order to interrogate issues around access and rights, as Michael Rubenstein, Bruce Robbins, and Sophia Beal do in their 2015 special issue

of *Modern Fiction Studies* on "Infrastructuralism." These questions pertain to, in the words of Brian Larkin (2013), the "politics and poetics of infrastructure" and are a vital component of understanding the contemporary human condition.

(*See also* Chapter 9, Deconstruction; Chapter 20, Digital Humanities; Cultural Materialism; Global Media; *and* Machine)

Jessica Lockrem, *Rice University (United States)*

Further Reading

Howe, Cymene, Jessica Lockrem, Hannah Appel, Edward Hackett, Dominic Boyer, Randal Hall, Akhil Gupta, Elizabeth Rodwell, Andrea Ballestero, Trevor Durbin, Farès el-Dahdah, Elizabeth Long, and Cyrus Mody. "Paradoxical Infrastructures: Ruins, Retrofit, and Risk." *Science, Technology & Human Values* 41.3 (2016): 547–65.

Larkin, Brian. "The Politics and Poetics of Infrastructure." *Annual Review of Anthropology* 42 (2013): 327–43.

Rubenstein, Michael, Bruce Robbins, and Sophia Beal. "Infrastructuralism: An Introduction." *MFS Modern Fiction Studies* 61.4 (2015): 575–86.

Interpellation

Interpellation is a concept introduced by the French Marxist structuralist theorist, Louis Althusser, first in the essay, "Three Notes on the Theory of Discourses" (1966), and then more famously in his "Ideology and Ideological State Apparatuses" (1970), itself an extract from his unfinished, posthumously published book, *On the Reproduction of Capitalism* (1995). Derived in part from Jacques Lacan's notion of the "mirror stage," *interpellation* refers to the process by which ideology constitutes individuals as subjects in a way that ensures the reproduction of any particular historical and social situation. Because in Althusser's formulation there is "no outside" of ideology (except in the special condition of "scientific" knowledge), all individuals are subject to interpellation by the various mechanisms of what he names "Ideological State Apparatuses" (ISAs) (family, church, school, media, and so forth).

Althusser maintains, "All ideology hails or interpellates concrete individuals as concrete subjects." He illustrates this process through a scene of "the most commonplace everyday police (or other) hailing: 'Hey, you there!'" In the moment the individual responds to this hail, "he becomes a *subject.* Why? Because he has recognized that the hail was 'really' addressed to him, and that 'it was *really him* who was hailed' (and not someone else)." Althusser stresses that such a sequential narrative should be understood only as a figure: because the "individual is always-already [*toujours-déjà*] a subject, even before he is born," the process of hailing and the existence of "are one and the same thing." Enmeshed in a "system of interpellation as subjects," Althusser concludes, "the subjects 'work,' they 'work by themselves' in the vast majority of cases, with the exception of the 'bad subjects' who on occasion provoke the intervention of one of the detachments of the (Repressive) State Apparatus. . . . the individual *is interpellated as a (free) subject in order that he shall submit freely to the commandments of the Subject, i.e., in order that he shall (freely) accept his subjection.*"

While the notion of interpellation has been a central and much debated aspect of Marxist critical theory since the essay's original publication—as evident in the essays in the Slavoj Žižek edited collection, *Mapping Ideology* (1994)—it also became in the 1990s an increasingly important concern in queer theory, thanks in a large part to Judith Butler's work on the performative dimensions of subject formation. In her landmark essay, "Gender is Burning" (1993), Butler opens by raising the question of "the range of *disobedience* that such an interpellating law might produce." Butler underscores in *The Psychic Life of Power* (1997) the "risk of a certain *misrecognition*" always haunting interpellation: "The one who is hailed may fail to hear, misread the call, turn the other way, answer to another name, insist on not being addressed in that way." Butler further argues that because interpellation is a process continuously reproduced and enacted through the repetition of social rituals and "cannot be linguistically guaranteed without [the subject's] passionate attachment to the law," a possibility exists that it may fail, opening up "the path toward a more open, even more ethical, kind of being, one of or for the future."

More recently, Warren Montag has restored the Spinozist dimensions of Althusser's formulation in order to argue that "recognition cannot be an act of consciousness but must be immanent in the actions of the body. . . . The interpellation is not merely a matter of recognition, except insofar as this recognition arrives fully embodied and fully armed." The full realization of this aspect of Althusser's intervention, Montag further demonstrates, occurs in the work of Michel Foucault and his notion of discipline.

(*See also* Althusser, Louis; Apparatus; Assujettissement; Butler, Judith; Chapter 22, Identity Studies; Chapter 24, Posthumanism; *and* Žižek, Slavoj)

Phillip E. Wegner, *University of Florida (United States)*

Further Reading
Althusser, Louis. *On the Reproduction of Capitalism: Ideology and Ideological*

State Apparatuses [1995]. Trans.
G. M. Goshgarian. New York: Verso, 2014.

Butler, Judith. *The Psychic Life of Power:
Theories in Subjection*. Stanford: Stanford
University Press, 1997.

Montag, Warren. *Althusser and His Contemporaries: Philosophy's Perpetual War*.
Durham: Duke University Press, 2013.

Interpretation

Interpretation is the methodologically
grounded process through which critics determine the meaning of a literary text or any other
cultural document. It is necessary to interpret
whenever understanding fails to materialize
by itself, that is, when the meaning is not
self-evident. This is typically the case when
historical or cultural distance has rendered the
text opaque, yet it also applies where the complexities of content or style present an obstacle to immediate understanding.

There are many different forms of interpretation, most agree that a convincing interpretation is one that is able to account as
exhaustively as possible for as many textual
elements as possible; failing to achieve such
depth and scope is a mark of both under- and
overinterpretation where the critic draws
either insufficient or excessive conclusions
based on inadequate textual evidence. This
idea amounts to a coherence criterion of interpretive validity and originates in hermeneutics, a discipline with both ancient roots and
modern extensions that analyze the nature of
understanding and interpretation. The concept of the "hermeneutic circle" is crucial in
this regard. In its original version, this concept describes the process of interpretation
as a potentially unending back-and-forth
between the constituent parts and the text
as a whole. However, the hermeneutic circle
also suggests that the aim of interpretation is
a near-perfect integration of analytical obser-

vations within a holistic understanding of the
text. Additionally, it expresses the view that
meaning is context-dependent and that interpretation always requires us to see the object
as part of a larger contextual whole.

Critics have argued that the principle of
coherence presupposes a classicist ideal of
harmony and formal integration, and that
hermeneutics is therefore aesthetically and
politically conservative. In this view, a hermeneutic approach is unable to account appropriately for texts that fail to display the desired
internal coherence—Modernist poetry, for
example, with its emphasis on ambiguity and
semantic multiplicity. This criticism has a
point in relation to some forms of hermeneutic practice that "normalize" texts by ignoring
elements that do not conform to the overall
meaning as identified by the critic. However,
hermeneutic theories of interpretation have
long stressed the need to recognize, rather
than explain away or assimilate, the ironi-
cal, polysemic or outright incomprehensible
aspects of a text. Accordingly, it is a key challenge for any interpretation to gain an understanding of the whole without eradicating the
singularity of the parts.

Other lines of criticism highlight how
interpretation neglects non-semantic aspects
of the text, risks doubling and ultimately
replacing its object, and sometimes becomes
a sterile academic exercise in producing new
"readings" of canonical texts. These concerns have lent credence to the view that
interpretation is old-fashioned or even obsolete. However, the increasing globalization
of the literary field, epitomized by the rise
of world literature studies, and the reorientation of cultural literacy toward visual and
digital forms have arguably intensified the
problem of understanding when engaging
with cultural documents from other countries
or historical periods. In this situation, interpretation becomes relevant again as a way of

establishing meaning and thereby mediating between different cultural horizons.

(*See also* Chapter 7, Psychoanalytic Theory; Chapter 18, Translation; Chapter 19, Media Studies; Eco, Umberto; Gadamer, Hans-Georg; Hermeneutics; Psychoanalysis; *and* Ricoeur, Paul)

Jesper Gulddal, *University of Newcastle (Australia)*

Further Reading

Eco, Umberto. *Interpretation and Overinterpretation*, with Richard Rorty, Jonathan Culler, and Christine Brooke-Rose. Ed. Stefan Collini. Cambridge: Cambridge University Press, 1992.

Gulddal, Jesper. "Interpretation." In *Literature: An Introduction to Theory and Analysis*. Ed. Mads Rosendahl Thomsen, Lasse Home Kjældgaard, Lis Møller, Dan Ringgaard, Lilian Munk Rösing, and Peter Simonsen. London: Bloomsbury, 2017. 15–26.

Zimmerman, Jens. *Hermeneutics: A Very Short Introduction*. Oxford: Oxford University Press, 2015.

Intersectionality

Kimberlé Crenshaw, distinguished UCLA professor of law, is widely credited with coining the term *intersectionality* in an influential 1989 article on the invisibility in US antidiscrimination law of black women's experiences, which she conceptualized as uniquely shaped by the "intersection" of race and gender oppressions. Intersectionality has since become an umbrella term for a broad array of critical theory and praxis addressing complex nexuses of race-gender-class identities and inequalities. As such, it has attracted passionate, yet highly generative debates that expanded Crenshaw's original arguments about simultaneous race and gender oppressions (and hence identities) for black women, to the idea of multiple "axes" of social difference and institutional discrimination including categories like class, sexuality, and age. In the early 2000s, the term was taken up with renewed interest by scholars across the humanities and social sciences, largely in the Global North. Meanwhile, Crenshaw spearheaded efforts among international antiracism activists to bring "intersectional" frameworks to United Nations human rights law. In the 2010s, intersectionality went viral as a new generation of activists, responding to digitally mediated social movements like Black Lives Matter, adopted and debated the term. At a time of political ferment in the United States and Europe especially, some have dubbed this new round of online debates "the intersectionality wars."

The relative mainstreaming of the term has led to a bewildering variety of definitions, applications, and critiques in and outside the academy. This has created new dilemmas for proponents who insist that intersectional approaches must preserve their historically close ties to genealogies of African American feminist thought that emerged within anti-racist struggles since the nineteenth century (Crenshaw herself found inspiration in Sojourner Truth's 1851 speech "Ain't I a Woman?" and the 1977 Combahee River Collective Statement is a common touchstone). Fending off the superficial sloganeering of some critics and online activists alike, and wary of losing hard-won ground in the academy to white theorists' appropriations, proponents can be skeptical of integrating intersectionality theory with historically dominant Western social thought and methods. Any application or critique of intersectionality is thus bound up with race politics in the United States, even as intersectionality theorists encounter other, non-Western geneologies of subaltern thought like postcolonial studies.

Debates about the epistemological or ontological premises of intersectional approaches are fundamentally shaped by ongoing tensions between academic and activist praxis. Black feminist theorists like Crenshaw all along refused discrete boundaries between the two, critiquing the methodological assumptions of their own disciplines that they said undergirded the dynamics of privilege, and insisting that intersectional theories contribute to concrete efforts to empower women of color. The crux of the debates centers on the status of "identity politics": the nature of the human subject and its relationship to collective identity, action and institutions. Critics decry the "divisive" infinite regress of identity categories listed in intersectional approaches or argue that theorists are limited by their notion of a segmentable liberal subject seeking legal rights and protection, which takes them onto shared grounds with the biopolitics of nation-states. Meanwhile, proponents dismiss superficial identity politics focusing on individual subjects. They argue instead that intersectionality all along has called for a paradigm shift to conceptualizing fundamentally relational subjects caught up in "interlocking systems of power," in which categories of difference like race, gender, and class are "mutually constituted" in practice. Only such an approach, they say, can render visible the unique identity dilemmas and oppressions of multiply disadvantaged people and thereby inform activist efforts to expand their rights and benefits in national and international contexts.

(*See also* Chapter 13, Race and Postcolonial Studies; Chapter 22, Identity Studies; *and* Minority)

Charlene Makley, *Reed College*
(United States)

Further Reading

Collins, Patricia Hill, and Sirma Bilge. *Intersectionality (Key Concepts)*. New York: Polity, 2016.

Crenshaw, Kimberlé. *On Intersectionality: Essential Writings*. New York: The New Press, 2017.

Nash, Jennifer. "Intersectionality and Its Discontents." *American Quarterly* 69.1 (2017): 117–29.

Patil, Vrushali. "From Patriarchy to Intersectionality: A Transnational Feminist Assessment of How Far We've Really Come." *Signs* 384 (2013): 847–67.

Intersubjectivity

This expression is misleading insofar as it suggests originally isolated subjects (or selves) who manage to communicate with one another. For most sign theorists, the isolated subject (or Cartesian ego) is a theoretical fiction. In the language of Martin Heidegger, we are "always already" *with* others. Such theorists challenge precisely the presupposition of a self cut off from the world, thus from other selves. This term avoids being misleading insofar as it implies this challenge.

While thinkers throughout history have hardly neglected the social dimension of human existence, they have given it greater priority in recent decades. By means of his method of systematic, universal, and hyperbolic doubt, René Descartes claimed to have triumphed decisively over skepticism. But the "I" who proclaims this victory is a solitary, disembodied, and unsituated self (a consciousness enclosed within itself, bereft of its body as well as relationships with other human beings and indeed the physical world). By the end of his *Meditations* (1641), however, the "I" has recovered both its own body and the physical world. Though not often noted, Descartes nowhere in this work even attempts to prove the existence of other minds, with the exception of his arguments for the divine mind. The reality of other human minds is left unproven and indeed obscure. What is dramatically true of Descartes's project is no less true of other early modern thinkers, including ones from the empiricist tradition. The connection between mind (or consciousness) and world has been attenuated or even severed. Thinkers set for themselves the task of forging a connection between their ideas, conceived as representations of reality outside of their minds, and these realities. As a result, the problem of skepticism takes hold and continually reasserts itself. From Descartes to Kant and beyond, thinkers felt the necessity to prove the existence of the world.

In the *Critique of Pure Reason* (1781), Immanuel Kant wrote, "It still remains a scandal to philosophy and to human reason in general that the existence of things outside us . . . must be accepted merely on *faith*," rather than as the result of a proof. But Martin Heidegger would counter this claim in *Being and Time* (1927) by asserting that the "'scandal of philosophy' does not consist in the fact that the proof is still lacking up to now, but *in the fact that such proofs are expected and attempted again and again.*" Nothing could be more certain than the existence of other beings, especially other communicative and responsive beings. From a semiotic perspective shared by countless theorists, the problem of other minds and that of the external world tend to be viewed as pseudo-problems, not worthy of our attention.

Charles S. Peirce insists, "We have to set out upon our intellectual travels from the home where we already find ourselves. . . . It is not inside our skulls . . . but out in the open. It is the external world that we directly observe." There is of course divergence among semioticians. Certainly, not every sign theorist agrees with Peirce on this point.

Some are indeed working within a modernist framework. They are in effect beginning with the isolated subject. Others, however, are "deconstructing" this framework. As Peirce, Ludwig Wittgenstein, and Heidegger do, they insist upon intersubjectivity as primordial. The social, embodied, and situated self cannot but take itself to be one self among countless others. *Intersubjectivity* names both this primordial condition and the formal recognition of this condition.

(*See also* Alterity; Beavoir, Simone de; Cartesianism; Chapter 19, Media Studies; Chapter 22, Identity Studies; Heidegger, Martin; Kant, Immanuel; *and* Peirce, Charles Sanders)

Vincent Colapietro, *Pennsylvania State University (United States)*

Further Reading

Glendinning, Simon. *Being with Others: Heidegger, Derrida, Wittgenstein*. London: Routledge, 1998.

Heidegger, Martin. *Being and Time* [1927]. Trans. Joan Stambaugh. Rvsd. Dennis J. Schmidt. Albany: SUNY: Press, 2010.

Peirce, Charles S. "Man's Glassy Essence" and "The Law of Mind." In *The Essential Peirce*, vol. 1. Ed. Nathan Houser and Christian Kloesel. Bloomington: Indiana University Press, 1992. 312–51.

Schutz, Alfred. *The Structures of the Life-World*. Evanston: Northwestern University Press, 1973.

Intertextuality

Before *intertextuality* is a theory of text, it is a general idea about language. Mikhail Bakhtin formalized the claim that texts are dialogic, made up of relations between texts. This construction of literature, which is shared by Claude Lévi-Strauss's linguistic anthropology and Roland Barthes's cultural semiology, denies the unity and autonomy of writing, extending to all literature the character of folk tales, religious texts, and oral narratives that emerge over time. For example, in 2016 the rock band Led Zeppelin successfully defended "Stairway to Heaven" in court from a charge of plagiarism because it showed its chord progression derived not from the plaintiff's composition but from the baroque basso lament.

In the 1960s Julia Kristeva developed intertextuality as a method for reading. For Kristeva, psychological and ideological conflicts associated with one text help shape another text when an aspect or element of one text appears in the other. Unlike theories of influence, which make literary relations discrete, for Kristeva the conflicts of texts reflect cultural struggles. For this reason, using the term to describe allusion, parody, or quotation misses the main point of intertextual theory. For example, although Victor Burgin's book of photographs, *Some Cities*, quotes from Italo Calvino's *Invisible Cities* at the end, what makes Calvino Burgin's intertext, his invisible city, is their contest over allegorical space. The quotation affirms, but is incidental to, their relation. Quoting a text does not make it an agent in the new text. Although LucasArts' video game *Day of the Tentacle* (1993) quotes from Star Wars ("you're my only hope"), this is arguably no more than a lazy joke in the game. Then again, an intertextual reading might show its significance to alternate logics of Tentacle.

For Michael Riffaterre, intertexts can make sense of apparently arbitrary literary constructions. The word "glazed" in the line "glazed with rain / water" in W. C. Williams's "XXII" ("The Red Wheelbarrow") brings a craft-aesthetic register to the poem's idea of nature. In Jimmy Webb's song "Watermark" (1977), the line "How delicate the tracery of her fine lines" might show Webb's intertext to be Marcel Proust's "delicate tracery of reddening leaves," from the end of *Swann's Way* (in Moncrieff's ubiquitous translation): Marcel's nostalgia for Mme. Swann would then generate the logic of Webb's song.

Intertextuality democratizes the canon: any text can be an intertext, and no text has no intertext, in principle. The musical signature of "The Ballad of Sidewinder and the Cherokee" from the TV series *Daniel Boone* (season 4 episode 1, 1967) appears in Mark Knopfler's "Speedway at Nazareth"; both see America as reckless but steadfast, and draw on the cultural archive of English ballad meter. In practice intertextual readings are drawn to passages that orient the text or determine its meanings, so the frame of reference for intertextual study, though flexible and changing, tends to single out literary objects that, as Riffaterre says, are common knowledge.

(*See also* Bakhtin, Mikhail; Barthes, Roland; Canon; Kristeva, Julia; *and* Text)

Eyal Amiran, *University of California, Irvine (United States)*

Further Reading

Kristeva, Julia. *Sèméiotikè: Recherches pour une sémanalyse.* Paris: Seuil, 1969.

Morgan, Thaïs. "The Space of Intertextuality." In *Intertextuality and Contemporary American Fiction.* Ed. O'Donnell, Patrick, and Robert Con Davis. Baltimore: Johns Hopkins University Press, 1989. 239–79.

Riffaterre, Michael. *Semiotics of Poetry.* Bloomington: Indiana University Press, 1978.

Irigaray, Luce

Luce Irigaray (1932-) is a French feminist philosopher, linguist, and psychoanalyst. Born in Belgium and educated at Louvain and the University of Paris, she has been the director of research in philosophy at the Centre National de la Recherche Scientifique de Paris since 1964. Irigaray is known for her opposition to the cultural and intellectual negation of woman in the form of "an/other woman," that is, woman taken to be an other of the *same*, which is "man," or "mankind," rather than an/other subject, irreducible but sharing equivalent dignity. She argues that in life, language, and philosophy, women have been women only in relation to a system of oppositions made by men. These oppositions, such as virginal/deflowered, pure/impure, innocent/experienced displace women from situating themselves in their own terms. Irigaray suggests that women could characterize themselves in a language that expresses fluidity rather than the language of solids, which is static, homogeneous, and unchanging. She refers to this alternative as *sexual difference* and calls it the issue of our time. In her early book, *Speculum: Of the Other Woman* (1985), Irigaray examines some of the key scientific and psychoanalytic theories of woman defined by the lack of male characteristics, and she reformulates Plato's philosophy, especially the division into *intelligible and sensible* from the point of view of fluid thinking, existing, and writing. In *The Ethics of Sexual Difference* (1993), she goes on to rewrite the philosophy of several major Western philosophers—Plato, Aristotle, René Descartes, Spinoza, Maurice Merleau-Ponty, and Emmanuel Levinas—as if they had been women. Elsewhere, she addresses Friedrich Nietzsche, Martin Heidegger and pre-Socratic philosophers. Intrinsic to all of her work is the idea that the representation and control of women's bodies has been the philosophical and political foundation of Western thinking and that when this hidden ground is brought to light, the "two" of sexual difference can enter language. Sexual difference thus calls for a revolution in thought and ethics, a rein-

terpretation of the subject and language, the world, the cosmic, the microcosm, and macrocosm. Specifically, Irigaray posits a model of a formal language that corresponds to her description of the woman who does not speak like or the same as the one (in metaphor using similarity or likeness) but speaks fluid (using metonymy or association), and so also considers the Imaginary meaning of logical structures as articulated by the science of psychoanalysis. If language is no longer based on the neutral one, then the demand for social and political "equality" must also be rethought. This is a second aspect of sexual difference. Specifically, Irigaray calls for the creation and utilization of a "double universal," which would set forth the conditions that allow for the emergence of a distinct feminine culture in language, social roles, and law. This includes laws that do not overlook women's existence, including their bodies and modes of speaking, by accounting for them as simply not-male or as neutral. The universal has been thought as one, however, Irigaray maintains, this one does not exist and by reformulating formal language systems—mathematical, logical, physical, psychoanalytic, social, legal—we can think that human nature, the universal one, is at least two.

(*See also* Chapter 1, Early Theory; Psychoanalysis; *and* Subjectivity)

Dorothea Olkowski, *University of Colorado, Colorado Springs (United States)*

Further Reading

Irigaray, Luce. *Je Tu Nous: Towards a Culture of Difference* [1990]. Trans. Alison Martin. New York: Routledge, 1993.

Whitford, Margaret. *Luce Irigaray: Philosophy in the Feminine*. New York: Routledge, 1991.

Whitford, Margaret, ed. *The Irigaray Reader*. Malden: Blackwell, 1991.

Irony

Irony has had many guises: it has been a keystone of poetics, a paradigm of criticism, a mode of consciousness, a philosophical stance vis-à-vis the universe, an informing principle of personality, and a way of life. There is situational irony, cosmic irony, the irony of fate. The historically influential romantic view of irony as the perception and transcendence of the epistemological, ethical, or experiential paradox of appearance versus reality morphed to appear in such diverse critical places as Marxist theory and deconstructive aesthetics. In its semantic doubleness, irony centrally informed New Criticism, queer theory, and even neopragmatism.

At its literary and cultural core, however, is the sense of irony as a communicative process, not a static rhetorical tool to be deployed; it comes into being in the relations between meanings, between people and utterances, between intentions and interpretations. As a discursive practice or strategy, it always involves relations of power based in relations of communication: one says one thing (that one doesn't really mean) and expects one's interlocutor to understand not only what is actually meant but also one's attitude toward it. Unlike metaphor, which also requires such supplementing of meaning, irony has an evaluative edge and manages to provoke affective responses in those who "get" it and those who don't, as well as in its targets and what some consider its victims. That said, irony is trans-ideological in that it can and does function tactically in the service of a wide range of political positions, legitimating or undercutting a wide variety of interests. Irony's critical edge can cut both/all ways, just as its multivocal instability makes it suspect and risky. Irony's edge (or affective charge) cannot be separated from its politics of use, given the range of response it provokes—from anger to delight—and the various degrees of motivation and proximity it implies—from distanced detachment to passionate engagement.

Irony isn't irony until it is interpreted as such, at least by the intending ironist if not the intended receiver. Someone attributes irony; someone makes irony "happen," and it happens within a communicative situation where a shared discursive community provides the broader context for both its deployment and attribution. This is why irony is inclusionary as well as exclusionary. In semantic terms, irony exists in the space between (and including) the said and the unsaid. Ironic meaning is therefore inclusive (i.e., both/and, not antiphrastic), as well as relational. The ironist intends to set up an ironic relation between the said and the unsaid, but may not always succeed in communicating that intention or that relation. The interpreter of the irony makes (or infers) semantic meaning in addition to what is stated, together with an evaluative attitude toward both the said and unsaid. This is triggered and then directed by conflictual evidence or by contextual signals or textual markers that are agreed upon in a discursive community. Irony always happens in a context—and therein lies both its risk and its appeal.

(*See also* Chapter 8, Rhetoric; Chapter 12, Postmodernism; Close Reading; Formalism; Idealism; New Criticism; Trope; *and* White, Hayden)

Linda Hutcheon, *University of Toronto (Canada)*

Further Reading
Booth, Wayne. *A Rhetoric of Irony*. Chicago: University of Chicago Press, 1974.
Colebrook, Claire. *Irony*. London: Routledge, 2004.
Hutcheon, Linda. *Irony's Edge: The Theory and Politics of Irony*. London: Routledge, 1995.

J

Jameson, Fredric

Fredric Jameson (born 1934) is the leading Marxist literary and cultural critic in the United States and, arguably, in the English-speaking world in the late twentieth- and early twenty-first centuries. In a career that spans more than sixty years, Jameson has produced some twenty-five books and hundreds of essays in which he has demonstrated the versatility and power of Marxist criticism in analyzing and evaluating an enormous range of cultural phenomena, from literary texts to architecture, art history, cinema, economic formations, psychology, social theory, urban studies, and utopianism, to mention but a few.

In his early work, Jameson introduced a number of important twentieth-century European Marxist theorists to American audiences. Jameson's earliest writings on Sartre in the 1950s critically assessed France's leading intellectual at the very moment when Sartrean existentialism would become an influential presence in American literature and philosophy. During the 1960s and culminating in his *Marxism and Form* (1971), Jameson was among the first in the United States to write about such thinkers as Adorno, Benjamin, Bloch, and Lukács, often before their works had been translated into English. Then, as a scholar of French and German culture so attuned to twentieth-century European thought, Jameson was ideally positioned to recognize and respond to the explosion of

theory in the 1970s. In *The Prison-House of Language* (1972) and *The Political Unconscious* (1981), he deftly articulated such topics as the linguistic turn in literature and philosophy, the concepts of desire and national allegory, and the problems of interpretation and transcoding in a decade when continental theory was beginning to transform literary studies in the English-speaking world. Jameson's essays of the 1970s and early 1980s gave insight into the ostensibly strange, new ideas associated with structuralism, post-structuralism, psychoanalysis, semiotics, and critical theory. *The Political Unconscious* remains one of the most influential works of Marxist literary criticism today.

Unexpectedly intervening in the postmodernism debates in the 1980s, Jameson immediately became the central theorist of this famously decentered cultural phenomenon, and his books and essays of this era addressed the postmodern in art, architecture, cinema, literature, philosophy, politics, social theory, and urban studies, to name just a few of the areas. His *Postmodernism, or, the Cultural Logic of Late Capitalism* (1991), which incorporated his famous 1984 essay of that name as its first chapter, helped to reorient the postmodernism debates; moreover, Jameson demonstrated the power of Marxist theoretical practice to make sense of the system underlying the discrete and seemingly unrelated phenomena. By the early 1990s, Jameson had become an unavoidable theorist and critic for anyone engaged in contemporary literary and cultural studies, broadly conceived. Grounding the seemingly groundless postmodernism in the material condition of a postcolonial and post-Cold War epoch of globalization, as well as in the economics of postindustrial capital and financialization, Jameson's work helped to redefine the millennial moment.

Jameson's lifelong commitment to utopian thought and dialectical criticism has found more systematic expression in such books as *Archaeologies of the Future* (2009) and *Valences of the Dialectic* (2009), and he has continued to work on a major, six-volume project titled "The Poetics of Social Forms," the trajectory of which ultimately covers myth, allegory, romance, realism, modernism, postmodernism, and beyond. Given Jameson's prodigious breadth of interests and expertise, as well as his insistence upon understanding the logic of the social and historical situation, it is perhaps appropriate that his work remains both powerfully influential and yet incomplete, awaiting the ruses of history to ultimately determine their significance.

(*See also* Authenticity; Chapter 4, Marxism; Chapter 6, Historicisms; Chapter 10, Feminism; Chapter 12, Postmodernism; Chapter 22, Identity Studies; Chapter 26, Affect Studies; Dialectic; Formalism; Political Unconscious; Postmodernism; Production; Revolution; Semiotic Square; Subject; *and* Surface Reading)

Robert T. Tally Jr., *Texas State University (United States)*

Further Reading

Jameson, Fredric. *The Political Unconscious: Narrative as a Socially Symbolic Act.* Ithaca: Cornell University Press, 1981.

Jameson, Fredric. *Postmodernism, or, the Cultural Logic of Late Capitalism.* Durham: Duke University Press, 1991.

Tally, Robert T., Jr. *Fredric Jameson: The Project of Dialectical Criticism.* London: Pluto Press, 2014.

Wegner, Phillip E. *Periodizing Jameson: Dialectics, the University, and the Desire for Narrative.* Evanston: Northwestern University Press, 2014.

Jouissance

The concept of *jouissance* (usually translated as "enjoyment" rather than "pleasure") emerges in Jacques Lacan's thought in relation to a complication or failure of the paternal function. In Lacan's revision of Sigmund Freud's Oedipal theory, the symbolic father mediates between mother and child, allowing the desire of the mother to be established and symbolized beyond the child, and thereby providing room for the emergence of the child's own desire, beyond incestuous jouissance. Object-constancy, the formation of the ego, and the child's access to language depend on this symbolic mediation of "reality," organized by the pleasure principle and representation. Accordingly, in a famous formulation in "The Subversion of the Subject," Lacan writes, "Castration means that Jouissance must be refused so that it can be reached on the inverted ladder of the law of desire." Rather than an actual father who prohibits, as in Freud, then, it is the signifier, and even the discourse of the mother, that serves as a protection against maternal jouissance. Around 1960, however, the symbolic law appears to be increasingly unstable. The operation of the symbolic, far from eliminating jouissance, seems to produce a surplus jouissance, an excessive, superegoic jouissance that contradicts pleasure and appears in certain formations of the "voice" and "gaze," those formations of the "object a" that arise in Lacan's conceptual arsenal alongside jouissance, marking the complex scaffolding that surrounds these fissures in the symbolic law. These developments were explored in literary criticism by many, perhaps most famously by Roland Barthes in *The Pleasure of the Text* (1973).

In the *Ethics of Psychoanalysis* seminar (1960), Lacan develops this problem through an analysis of Marquis de Sade, claiming that law and transgression are not opposites, but mutually constitutive (like "civilization" and its "discontents"). Jouissance, which was initially a primordial, pre-symbolic enjoyment that could be transcended through the symbolic order, is now a surplus effect of the symbolic itself. The concept of jouissance proliferates as a result: the "jouissance of the subject," initially understood as the "enjoyment" contained in the symptom, which the subject is unable to relinquish and which compromises desire, is now set alongside the "jouissance of the Other," understood as a feature of a symbolic Other that malfunctions and appears to demand the subject's suffering. In his accounts of perversion and psychosis, Lacan speaks of a "père-version," a "turning toward the father" in this sadistic form, such that the subject becomes the instrument of the Other's enjoyment. In his "Names of the Father" seminar (1963), where the name of the father is pluralized in response to this problem, Lacan writes: "The *a*, the object, falls. That fall is primal. The diversity of forms taken by that object of the fall ought to be related to the manner in which the desire of the Other is apprehended by the subject." If the desire of the Other is misapprehended or distorted, as in cases of paranoia or psychosis, the subject becomes the instrument of the Other's jouissance, prey to the intrusive gaze or voice that speaks "in" the subject, or persecutes from outside. In the same seminar, in his analysis of Caravaggio's painting, *The Sacrifice of Isaac*, Lacan

explores the relationship between Abraham and God, and the former's experience of being "called" to sacrifice his only son, a sacrifice the Other finally refuses. One other development, highly significant for feminist theory and gender studies, is the concept of "feminine Jouissance" (sometimes called "the other jouissance"), which Lacan developed in his 1972–73 seminar *Encore*, where Lacan proposed an alternative to the normal "phallic" relation to the law, and therefore a different "feminine" relation to language. This development was explored by French feminist thought, including Hélène Cixous in "The Laugh of the Medusa" (1976).

(*See also* Barthes, Roland; Castration; Chapter 1, Early Theory; Chapter 7, Psychoanalytic Theory; Erotic; Freud, Sigmund; Libidinal; Oedipus Complex; Psychoanalysis; Symptom; *and* Žižek, Slavoj)

Charles Shepherdson, *University at Albany (United States)*

Further Reading

Braunstein, Néstor A. "Desire and Jouissance in the Teachings of Lacan." In *The Cambridge Companion to Lacan*. Ed. Jean-Michel Rabaté. Cambridge: Cambridge University Press, 2003. 102–15.

Copjec, Joan. "Sex and the Euthanasia of Reason." In *Supposing the Subject*. Ed. Joan Copjec. London: Verso, 1994. 16–44.

Evans, Dylan. "From Kantian Ethics to Mystical Experience: An Exploration of Jouissance." In *Key Concepts of Lacanian Psychoanalysis*. Ed. Dany Nobus. New York: Other Press, 1999. 1–28.

Žižek, Slavoj. "Why Are There Always Two Fathers?" In *Enjoy Your Symptom: Jacques Lacan in Hollywood and Out*. New York: Routledge, 1992. 149–94.

K

Kant, Immanuel

Kant's writing has cast a long shadow on critical theory from the eighteenth century to the present day. It took very little time for his work to be known in translation to writers of literature and criticism across Europe, and—even in the present day—his name has often been attached to the term "formalism" as if he were primarily responsible for it.

Kant's work as a whole ranges over many subjects from epistemology and ethics to anthropology and aesthetics. He considered his work to have furthered what he called a "Copernican Revolution" in which representations furnish us with our notions of objects, as opposed to the empiricist tradition that had attempted to argue the reverse. Deeply indebted to the empiricists, Kant redescribed David Hume's account of the role of custom and convention in our understanding of objects by claiming that our accounts of objects require *a priori* concepts. Our ethical approach to the world, moreover, is also located not in imitable models for action but rather in the free use of our reason: to act ethically is to act freely. Kant's ethics yield a political point: the ideal "enlightened" political structure is one in which our freely dissenting ideas can engage in the process of government. Political theorists from John Rawls to Jurgen Habermas have turned to Kant's work as inspiration in their own understanding of the norms and structures required for the achievement of just institutions.

For a long line of literary critics and cultural theorists, it is Kant's aesthetic theory that has proved the most influential. Explored in his *Critique of Judgment* (1790), the experiences of the sublime and the beautiful constitute two different noncognitive experiences of the world: to experience beauty is to experience a "purposiveness" in objects that is so generalized as to detach itself from epistemological demands; to experience the sublime—which is in us rather than in objects—is to experience (as we assert unity amid magnitude or power against physical might) a more radical interiority. The sublime exposes internal freedom even while it still allows us to communicate our experience to others. The two experiences are divided into two separate "analytics" in this treatise; but even while they appear to be in many ways distinct, the convergence and overlap is striking, in part because the discussion of beautiful art appears under the sublime. Poetry, moreover (in Kant's celebrated reading of a poem by Frederick the Great), is described in terms that echo both the sublime and the beautiful. Put together, the sublime and beautiful perhaps seek to describe an orientation toward aesthetic observation that claims minimal convergence amid dissent and disagreement.

Critics and theorists have debated Kant's legacy and, in doing so, offered quite different versions of it. Horkheimer and Adorno associated Kantian aesthetics and ethics with abstraction and an indifference to human particularity. American New Critics were more enthusiastic about the way that Kant (and English writers such as Samuel Taylor Coleridge) offered a way of reading aesthetic objects as internally purposive. But deconstructionist critics such as Paul de Man showed how Kantian accounts of unity were just as material and contingent as the objects they sought to contain. More lately, Kantian aesthetics has been reevaluated (by Frances Ferguson, for example) to stress aspects of form that are more compatible with materialism and historicism than many theorists have previously claimed.

(*See also* Adorno, Theodor W.; Bakhtin, Mikhail; Critique; Cultural Critique; de Man, Paul; Desire; Discursive Formation; Enlightenment; Heteronomy; Idealism; Intersubjectivity; Marx, Karl; Metaphysics; Nancy, Jean-Luc; New Criticism; Objects; Ontology; Scientific Method; Social Constructionism; Subject; *and* Subjectivity)

Mark Canuel, *University of Illinois, Chicago (United States)*

Further Reading

Coleridge, Samuel Taylor. *Biographia Literaria* [1817]. Ed. James Engell and W. Jackson Bate. Two vols. Princeton: Princeton University Press, 1983.

Ferguson, Frances. *Solitude and the Sublime: Romanticism and the Aesthetics of Individuation*. London: Routledge, 1992.

Kant, Immanuel. *Critique of Judgment* [1790]. Trans. J. H. Bernard. London: Macmillan, 1914.

Kristeva, Julia

In a career that has spanned six decades, Julia Kristeva (born 1941) has distinguished herself as one of the most influential French theorists and public intellectuals of the last half-century. Radically engaging linguistics, philosophy, psychoanalysis, feminism, religion, and literature, Kristeva's work is "superdisciplinary," as rigorous as it is eclectic. Kristeva emigrated to Paris from Bulgaria in 1965 to study with Roland Barthes and Claude Lévi-Strauss, among others, establishing herself as a formidable thinker from the start. Fluent in Russian, Kristeva brought Mikhail Bakhtin's work to a Western European audience; it was in Barthes's seminar that she first presented Bakhtin's concept of intertextuality, of the literary text as dynamic and heterogeneous, and dialogic. Kristeva "confront[s] language at the point where it undoes itself," whether in literature, religious practices, or the extremes of psychic states informing her earliest work, where she began laying the groundwork for the engagement between semiotics and psychoanalysis she calls "sémanalyse."

In *Revolution in Poetic Language* (1974), she rejects as "necrophiliacs" linguists who "persist in seeking the truth of language by formalizing utterances that hang in midair." Signification is a dynamic process, not a static object, an expression of an embodied subject, a "speaking subject." Kristeva's theory of subject formation diverges crucially from Jacques Lacan's by seeing its stirrings at the first moments of literal separation from the (m)other, at birth. Signification is written on and by the body, from the beginning. Kristeva gives various names—the semiotic, "*signifiance*"—to this prelinguistic stage of "primary narcissism" that is nevertheless full of meaning. She most powerfully traces its force in the trio of books that coincide with her career as a practicing psychoanalyst: *Powers of Horror* (1980), *Tales of Love* (1983), and *Black Sun* (1989). These books concern themselves equally with the acute experience of the subject-in-crisis and the larger social systems that engage the "borderline discourses" of abjection, passion, depression, and grief. *Powers of Horror:*

An Essay on Abjection, which defines the "abject" as a near-death experience that thrusts the subject to the limits of language, meaning, and being as such, is her most widely read book.

Kristeva's subsequent work took a more overtly political turn, but remained partial to those whose crises thrust them to the margins in one form or another. In the 1990s she turned her psychoanalytic emphasis to the fractured otherness of subjectivity to the rise of European nationalist tensions, anxiety over refugees, and the postcolonial subject; more recently, to the truth and reconciliation commissions in South Africa. Her most recent works—*This Incredible Need to Believe* (2009), *Hatred and Forgiveness* (2010), and *The Severed Head* (2012)—affirm these chief concerns persist. Kristeva's interest in religion, the morbidity of Western art, and the often ecstatic, poetical style of her writing may mislead readers that her metapsychological meditations are devotional, but she eschews such beliefs, even while she marvels at the sublime possibilities of literature or the rich implications of religious ideologies. Both are part of her lifelong effort "to take transcendence seriously and to track down its premises into the most hidden recesses of language. My prejudice is that of believing that God is analyzable. Infinitely."

(*See also* Castration; Chapter 1, Early Theory; Chapter 2, Structuralism and Semiotics; Chapter 10, Feminism; Intertextuality; Libidinal; Liminality; object petit a; Other, The; Primordial Discord; Semiotics; *and* Symptom)

Megan Becker-Leckrone, *University of Nevada, Las Vegas (United States)*

Further Reading

Kristeva, Julia. *The Kristeva Reader*. Ed. Toril Moi. Oxford: Basil Blackwell, 1986.

Kristeva, Julia. *Powers of Horror: An Essay on Abjection* [1980]. Trans. Léon Roudiez. New York: Columbia University Press, 1982.

L

Labor

Labor, as Karl Marx writes in *Economic and Philosophical Manuscripts of 1844*, is the "life-activity" which characterizes humanity as a "species-being." Such an abstract notion of labor as productive life activity in general, irrespective of the specific types of labor engaged in or the concrete use-values produced, was central to the classical political economy of Adam Smith and David Ricardo in which labor was taken to be the "source of value." Marx in his critique of classical economics in *Grundrisse* (1858), explains how the abstract concept of labor that "economics places at the head of its discussion [as] valid in all forms of society" is itself a reflection of the practical commodification of labor in capitalist society in particular, in which "individuals can with ease transfer from one labor to another, and where the specific kind is a matter of chance for them." By historicizing the concept in *Capital, Volume 1* (1867), Marx produces a more concrete understanding that what the capitalist purchases from the worker is not labor, but labor power—the capacity of workers to produce value in excess of the wages they receive during the "working day." Marx's labor theory of value pushes the concept of labor beyond the limits of bourgeois economics and makes it a "ruthless critique" of "ideology": the modes of sense making that mystify labor's transformative agency by restricting it to producing profit.

Labor is a controversial term in the dominant "post-al"—as Mas'ud Zavarzadeh puts it—cultural theory, which claims that in post-industrial/postmodern/post-Fordist societies the primary source of value is no longer labor power at the point of production but "knowledge." Peter Drucker's "knowledge work" and such related terms as Maurizio Lazzarato's "immaterial labor," Pierre Bourdieu's "cultural capital," Slavoj Žižek's "general intellect," and the like, represent the dominance of neoliberal economics in cultural studies since the 1970s. In Michel Foucault's lectures on "biopolitics" at Collège de France in 1978–79, for example, he seems to agree with the neoliberal views of those he is annotating when he says "labor is not a commodity reduced by abstraction to labor power and the time [during] which it is used," but rather "a machine that produces" consumer enjoyment for the worker. In this vein, theories of "cognitive capitalism" suggest that controlling post-class, post-labor information flows has replaced wage-labor exploitation, thereby abolishing "any measure of the working day," following Michael Hardt and Antonio Negri in *Empire* (2000) and ushering in the "Communism of Capital," following Paulo Virno in *A Grammar of the Multitude* (2004). Similarly, foregoing Marx's crucial distinction in *Theories of Surplus Value* (1863) between productive and unproductive labor that explains the source of surplus value, theoretical movements such as Accelerationism, according to Nick Srnicek and Alex Williams in *Inventing the Future* (2015), call for the "end of work" from within capitalism through automation.

Whether it is material or immaterial, however, labor is "only the manifestation of a force of nature" (Marx) that in its generality hides the concrete surplus-labor time expended and absorbed as capital in production for profit (surplus value). Labor remains the material "outside" of ideology because it is the exploitation of wage labor by capital that drives society into antagonistic class struggles over the surplus. As such, Marx's labor theory of value remains central, contends Teresa Ebert in *The Task of Cultural Critique* (2009), if cultural theory is to become not yet another "interpretation" of capital and its spectral concrete, but a force for social transformation.

(*See also* Capacity; Capitalism; Chapter 4, Marxism; Chapter 22, Identity Studies; Feminist Materialism; Marx, Karl; Multitude; Post-Fordism; Private Property; Production; *and* Professor)

Stephen Tumino, *Fordham University*
(United States)

Further Reading

Ebert, Teresa, and Mas'ud Zavarzadeh. "The Digital Metaphysics of Cognitive Capitalism: Abandoning Dialectics, the North Atlantic Left Invents a Spontaneous Communism within Capitalism." *International Critical Thought* 4.4 (2014): 397–417.

Tumino, Stephen. *Cultural Theory after the Contemporary*. New York: Palgrave Macmillan, 2011.

Wilkie, Rob. *The Digital Condition: Class and Culture in the Information Network*. New York: Fordham University Press, 2011.

Lacan, Jacques

Jacques Lacan (1901–81) was a French psychoanalyst who made major intellectual contributions to the fields of psychoanalysis, post-structuralism, cultural studies, and literary and film theory. Lacan founded the *École freudienne* in 1964 and gave regular seminars in Paris for over thirty years.

Although Lacan was a self-professed Freudian whose stated purpose was to "return to Freud," his work for many radically alters Freudian psychoanalysis. Lacan's major revision of Freud was to apply Saussurian linguistics to an understanding of the unconscious. Noting that many Freudian principles were linguistic in nature, he famously stated that the unconscious was structured like language, and as a result of that structure the unconscious was subject to the same problems of representation that Saussure and, later, Jacques Derrida found in language.

At the center of Lacan's reconceptualization of Freud is his version of psychosexual development. According to Lacan, three orders constitute the human psyche. The Imaginary Order is the state in which an infant identifies itself as an entity unified with its surroundings and its biological dependence on the mother, who meets those biological and instinctual needs. This order exists in the preverbal. In the Imaginary, the subject will ultimately enter into the Mirror Stage, a moment of recognition that the self is indeed separate from the mother; the source of pleasure (biological needs being met) is outside of the self, and the subject begins to project its own sense of self. The subject then moves into the Symbolic Order; this order Lacan identifies with the Law of the Father and emerges with the acquisition of language, characterized by rules and constructs. The subject then only interacts with the world through various forms of representation and structures of meaning. The subject in the Symbolic is a fragmented self who desires the undivided self of the Imaginary but is left with only illusory representations of wholeness in others (*objet petit a*) that the subject mistakes for the ultimate Other. Desire for the Other is never truly attainable, and the lack that results persists within the Symbolic. Finally, Lacan identifies the Real, the order that is beyond the self-projection of the Imaginary, beyond the structure and representation of the Symbolic, and is accessible only in fleeting moments of joy and terror he calls *jouissance*. Human existence is therefore defined by a self-identity that rests between the isolation and fragmentation of the Symbolic and the desire for the Imaginary self, which is further distanced from the Real.

Lacan's understanding of psychical development has led to key principles in contemporary theory and cultural studies. How subjects view and perceive the world is dictated by both ideal self-projection and the limitations of structural systems, which is manifested first in language but ultimately in all ideologies that govern interaction with the world. *How* subjects desire becomes more important that what they desire. How subjects attempt to eliminate the state of emptiness and lack that persists in Symbolic existence is directly tied to how they interact with ideologies, how they interact with those others that become sources of self-identification. They project their ideal self onto the world and the world projects itself back to them. However, simultaneously the pressures of the Real are always felt, drawing subjects to the unimpeded possibilities of the sublime.

(*See also* Castration; Chapter 1, Early Theory; Chapter 2, Structuralism and Semiotics; Chapter 5, Poststructuralism; Chapter 7, Psychoanalytic Theory; Chapter 22, Identity Studies; Deferred Action; Desire; Drive; Jouissance; Libidinal; Mirror Stage; objet petit a; Other, The; Phallocentrism; Primordial Discord; Psychoanalysis; Repetition; Sublimation; Symptom; Trauma; Unconscious; *and* Žižek, Slavoj)

Jacob Blevins, *Sam Houston State University*
(United States)

Further Reading

Fink, Bruce. *A Clinical Introduction to Lacanian Psychoanalysis: Theory and Technique*. Cambridge: Harvard University Press, 1999.

Lacan, Jacques. *Écrits* [1966]. Trans. Bruce Fink. New York: Norton, 2007.

Lacan, Jacques. *The Four Fundamental Concepts of Psycho-Analysis, 1954-1955*. Ed. Jacques-Alain Miller. Trans. Alan Sheridan. New York: Norton, 1978.

Žižek, Slavoj. *How to Read Lacan*. New York: Norton, 2007.

Langage (fr.)

Language is the sense of a social institution, a system of values, an abstract signifying structure governed by rules. According to Roland Barthes in *Elements of Semiology* (1964), "Saussure started from the multiform and heterogeneous nature of language, which appears at first sight as an unclassifiable reality, the unity of which cannot be brought to light, since it partakes at the same time of the physical, the physiological, the mental, the individual, and the social." This heterogeneity disappears, Barthes claims, when a social object is extracted; language thus is "the systematized set of conventions necessary to communication, indifferent to the material of the signals which compose it, and which is a language (*langue*); as opposed to which speech (*parole*) covers the purely individual part of language (phonation, application of the rules and contingent combinations of signs)." *Langage* is a medium, the stuff or matter we use in order to communicate. However this stuff isn't intelligible until a social object is introduced, whether in the person of someone who communicates with *langage* or in the form of a systematized set of rules that indicate how *langage* is to be performed, for example, in a court of law, at a social gathering, at a business meeting, etc.

(*See also* Chapter 2, Structuralism and Semiotics; Langue; Parole; *and* Saussure, Ferdinand de)

Herman Rapaport, *Wake Forest University*
(United States)

Further Reading

Barthes, Roland. *Elements of Semiology* [1964]. Trans. Annette Lavers and Colin Smith. New York: Hill and Wang, 1973.

Saussure, Ferdinand de. *Course in General Linguistics* [1916]. Eds. Charles Bally and Albert Sechehaye. Trans. Roy Harris. Chicago: Open Court, 1998.

Langue (fr.)

The tongue derived from *langage*. *Langue* may be a dialect, a style, an idiosyncratic way of speaking. It is what the individual or the group selects out of *langage*. Langue may be the consequence of socio-linguistic relations wherein certain groups adopt linguistic practices that diverge from the standard language in order to assert a specific social identity. But langue also pertains to the individual's style of language use, which often betrays one's level of education, creativity, or inherent verbal acuity. *Langue* may also reflect something about a person's psychology or general attitude.

(*See also* Capacity; Chapter 2, Structuralism and Semiotics; Langage; Parole; *and* Saussure, Ferdinand de)

Herman Rapaport, *Wake Forest University*
(United States)

Further Reading

Barthes, Roland. *Elements of Semiology* [1964]. Trans. Annette Lavers and Colin Smith. New York: Hill and Wang, 1973.

Jameson, Fredric. *The Prisonhouse of Language*. Princeton: Princeton University Press, 1975.

Saussure, Ferdinand de. *Course in General Linguistics* [1916]. Eds. Charles Bally and Albert Sechehaye. Trans. Roy Harris. Chicago: Open Court, 1998.

Law

What the word "law" means is apparently so obvious and so universally known as hardly to need an entry in this book. However, as soon as you start jumping up and down on this seemingly solid board, that is, interrogate the word "law," the board vibrates. It may even break, dropping you into an abyss of verbal and conceptual problems.

The word "law" is used in a large number of not entirely compatible everyday idioms in English, each with its own context and nuance: "make the law," "enforce the law," "repeal the law," "rule of law," "law and order," "lawful," "law-abiding citizen," "traffic laws," "break the law," "against the law," "delays of law," "unlawful," "lawyer," "lawman," "law offices," "court of law," "law jargon," "Biblical law," "Sharia or Islamic law," and so on, more or less ad infinitum. We use the word "law" all the time without thinking much about what we mean by the word.

I do not have space here to comment on the words for "law" in various European romance languages going back to Latin, except to say that they tend to preserve the initial "l" sound: lex, legge, loi, law. The German word for "law," "Gesetz," has a different valence, suggesting something set in place, whether by human legislation or by divine authority, as in Franz Kafka's marvelous parable, "Vor dem Gesetz" (1915; "Before the Law").

The presumed source of a given law's enunciation and authority establishes a crucial distinction among laws. The enunciation of any law is what J. L. Austin calls a "speech act," that is, a "performative" statement: "I declare this is the law." Human laws are promulgated by legislative bodies that are secular, even though the legislators may have sworn on the Bible an oath of office. The authority of such laws comes from the governing body that "passed" them. Nevertheless, a vague divine sanction may remain somewhere in the background, as in the implicit assumption that legislative bodies in the United States are Christian. In spite of our prized separation of church and state, the United States Congress fifty years ago added the phrase "under God" to our "Pledge of Allegiance." We are now "one nation under God, indivisible, with liberty and justice for all."

Nevertheless, we distinguish fundamentally between human law and divine law. Examples of the latter are Moses in *Exodus* descending from Mt. Sinai bearing the Ten Commandments inscribed by God on the "Tablets of the Law," or Jesus's statement in the Christian New Testament in *Matthew*: "Think not that I am come to destroy the law, or the prophets: I am come not to destroy, but to fulfill."

Jacques Derrida's "Force de loi" (1990; "Force of Law") is subtitled "The 'Mystical Foundation of Authority.'" This essay develops a crucial distinction between "law" and "justice." A lot of unjust human laws have been passed and then enforced by civil authorities, whereas justice is always quasi-divine and extremely difficult to identify in a given case. Though laws are particular, in the sense of being instituted within a given history and culture, they are universal in the sense that "everyone is equal before the law" and in the sense that laws are general rather than specific. They do not take into account the singularity of each special case. Laws are immanent, this-worldly. Justice, however, is transcendent and ineffable. Just to apply the laws is by no means necessarily to be just. "A decision," says Derrida, "that didn't go through the ordeal of the undecidable would not be a free decision, it would only be the programmable application or unfolding of a calculable process. It might perhaps be legal; it would not be just."

I conclude by observing that scarcely a single novel exists that does not in some way dramatize details about law in a specific country at a specific time. Most novels include lawyers among their characters. One example among almost innumerable ones is Anthony Trollope's admirable *Doctor Thorne* (1858). Its most memorable lawyer characters are Mr. Gazebee and Mr. Bideawhile. Like so many of Trollope's novels, *Doctor Thorne* turns on questions of marriage and inheritance. The novel is about the passing on of rank, money, and property by way of new marriage alliances. In this case, the big question, necessarily decided in the end by the lawyers, is whether the illegitimate Mary Thorne is nevertheless the heiress of an enormous fortune left to his eldest grand-daughter by the one-time stone mason, Roger Scatcherd, now Sir Roger. The legal authorities declare Mary the lawful (and just) heiress, and so the novel ends happily.

(*See also* Force; *and* Sovereignty)

J. Hillis Miller, *University of California, Irvine (United States)*

Further Reading

Derrida, Jacques. "Force of Law: The 'Mystical Foundation of Authority' [1990]." In *Deconstruction and the Possibility of Justice*. Eds. Drucilla Cornell, Michel Rosenfeld, and David Gray Carlson. Trans. Mary Quaintance. New York: Routledge, 1992. 3–67.

Posner, Richard. *Law and Literature*. Third ed. Cambridge: Harvard University Press, 2009.

Levinas, Emmanuel

Emmanuel Levinas (1906–95) was born in Kaunas, Lithuania, went in 1924 to study philosophy at the University of Strasbourg, including a year at the University of Freiburg taking classes with Edmund Husserl and Martin Heidegger, completed his first doctorate in 1930, married, became a French citizen, moved to Paris to work at the Alliance Israelite, was drafted and spent the duration of the Second World War in a German prisoner-of-war camp for Jewish prisoners, returned to Paris after the war, and was eventually appointed professor of philosophy successively at the universities of Poitier (1961), Paris-Nanterre (1967), and Paris-Sorbonne (1973). Not only distinguished as a first rank phenomenologist, over fifty years he developed—especially in *Totality and Infinity* (1961) and *Otherwise than Being or Beyond Essence* (1974)—an original and fundamental ethics of alterity. Early critic of the regnant "philosophy of presence" in its epistemological (Parmenides to Edmund Husserl and positivism) and aesthetic (Freidrich W. J. Schelling to Martin Heidegger and Gilles Deleuze) forms, Levinas discovered the source of intelligibility in the irreducible ethical transcendence of moral responsibility to and for each other person, all the way to the political demand for social justice for all others. Ethics so conceived is at once singularity and society, language and expression, humanism and "adult" religion. While his primary antagonist Heidegger never deigned to respond to Levinas's radical criticisms of ontology or his prioritization of ethics, Jacques Derrida, despite having borrowed from Levinas both the critique of presence and the notion of the "trace," first attacked Levinas's ethics in 1967. Starting in December 1988 Derrida attempted also to embrace it, though never repudiating his own antithetical "deconstructive" amalgam of Heidegger and Ferdinand de Saussure. The great importance of Levinas's ethics for literary and cultural theory lies in its demand that literature and culture find their proper orientation not simply within the semiotic and semantic reverberations of differential or postmodernist analyses, but further and more profoundly according to the imperative vectors of the ethical responsibilities of interpersonal morality and social justice. Concretely this means that literary and cultural criticism is at once an internal moment of literature and cultures *and* inescapably a link to the broader horizons of art history and social history. Art historical criticism and social-political-historical criticism, therefore, are not luxuries or distractions exterior to literature and culture but radical and inexorable elements of its very constitution, inextricable lines of significance—signification and obligation—that locate and orient the aesthetic within the ethical inspiration of the human. In "Reality and its Shadow" (1947), Levinas underscores the need for criticism to counter the tendency of all art—hence literature and culture—to close in upon itself, to coagulate into a "said," "self-presence," "idolatry," at the expense of the dynamism and height of "saying," "diachrony," not by affirming, as did the surrealists, a wild rebellion, which in its contingency still remains bound to ontology, but more radically by upholding the ruptures of ethical deterritorialization which irrecoverably break with the inevitable closure of text into textuality.

(*See also* Alterity; Assujettissement; Chapter 9, Deconstruction; Ethical Criticism; *and* Other, The)

Richard A. Cohen, *University at Buffalo (United States)*

Further Reading

Cohen, Richard A. "Levinas on Art and Aesthetics: Getting 'Reality and its Shadow' Right." *Levinas Studies*, vol. 11. Eds. Richard A. Cohen and Jolanta Saldukaityte. Pittsburgh: Duquesne University Press, 2017. 149–94.

Levinas, Emmanuel. "Meaning and Sense." Trans. Alphonso Lingis. *Emmanuel Levinas: Collected Philosophical Papers*. Ed. Alphonso Lingis. Dordrecht: Martinus Nijhoff Publishers, 1987. 75–107.

Levinas, Emmanuel, "Reality and Its Shadow." In *The Levinas Reader*. Ed. Sean Hand. Trans. Alphonso Lingis. Oxford: Basil Blackwell, 1989. 129–43.

Lévi-Strauss, Claude

French anthropologist Claude Lévi-Strauss (1908–2009), as a presence, and his works, as classics, studded the last half of twentieth century's intellectual history in the West. Born in Brussels of French Jewish parents, he was affiliated with the University of Paris and the College of France, first studying philosophy and law from 1927 to 1932, later receiving a doctorate in anthropology in 1948.

Before that doctorate, in Brazil between 1935 and 1938, Lévi-Strauss made several field trips to visit tribes in the Amazon, this experience reflected in his ethnographic and theoretical treatises. Back in Paris from Brazil at the outset of the Second World War, he chose to relocate in 1941 to the New School for Social Research in New York City, where he met innumerable European expatriates including Roman Jakobson and American intellectuals such as Franz Boas. In 1942 Lévi-Strauss was present at the luncheon where Boas died, noting that it was the close of an era.

Stimulated by structuralism generally and Ferdinand de Saussure's linguistics particularly, Lévi-Strauss generalized a methodology for eliciting universal principles underlying systems of marriage alliance. One such principle is reciprocity, fed by exchange/circulation/communication, whereby the process has value beyond what is exchanged. Restricted and generalized exchange not only elucidate the circulation of goods, women, and words, but further help explain the incest taboo, in that incest itself would preclude expanding systems of reciprocity. Lévi-Strauss also isolated fundamental themes constituting all creation myths, introducing the concept of "mytheme" as a unit of universal meaning applicable to all such myths, overriding superficial cross-cultural variation.

Lévi-Strauss's structuralist approach anticipated information theory, cybernetics, chaos theory, and cognitive science. His monographs fueled and grounded twentieth-century structuralist anthropology. Initially published in French, and sometimes best known by their French titles, Lévi-Strauss's first major works, including *The Elemental Structures of Kinship* (1949), *Tristes Tropiques* (1955), *The Savage Mind* (1962), and *Totemism* (1962), focused on kinship and marriage rules in small-scale societies. He went on, in later works, such as *Totemism* (1962), his *Mythologiques* tetralogy (1964–71), and his two volumes of *Structural Anthropology* (1958 & 1973) to concentrate on belief systems embodied in myths. In several overlapping realms, his aim was the same—to reveal the consistent and logical relations underlying cultural systems, rendering coherent the opaque and seemingly arbitrary practices and beliefs of culture: "Structuralism is the search for hidden harmonies." Nor did Lévi-Strauss neglect Western society's aesthetics and contemporary ecological predicaments, evidenced by works such as *Look, Listen, Read* (1993) and "Structuralism and Ecology" (1973).

Lévi-Strauss's work was structural in its synchronic bias, and in its dissatisfaction with temporal explanations of similarities. History is relevant, but not because it is prior and certainly not because of claims to authenticity. He abduced universal principles inherent in the mind, finding congruent transformational logics through techniques of analogy, homology, inversion, symmetry, redundancy. Lévi-Strauss demonstrated that human cognition is fundamentally universal, generating the symbolic processes that underlie culture, linked via languaging and bricolage, and elucidated by enduring frameworks of structuralist methodologies. His death as centenarian likewise evoked the refrain: "The end of an era."

(*See also* Binary Opposition; Chapter 2, Structuralism and Semiotics; Chapter 5, Poststructuralism; Material Culture; Semiotics; Sign; *and* Structuralism)

Myrdene Anderson, *Purdue University* *(United States)*

Further Reading

de Josselin de Jong, Jan Petrus Benjamin. *Lévi-Strauss's Theory on Kinship and Marriage*. Leiden: E. J. Brill, 1952.

Hénaff, Marcel. *Claude Lévi-Strauss and the Making of Structural Anthropology* [1991]. Trans. Mary Baker. Minneapolis: University of Minnesota Press, 1998.

Jenkins, Alan. *The Social Theory of Claude Lévi-Strauss*. New York: Palgrave Macmillan, 1979.

Leach, Edmund. *Lévi-Strauss*. London: Viking, 1970.

Rossi, Ino, ed. *The Unconscious in Culture: The Structuralism of Claude Lévi-Strauss in Perspective*. New York: E. P. Dutton, 1974.

Libidinal

Libidinal energy, more often referred to as libido, is the anxiety organized around and toward a point of erotogenic focus. For Sigmund Freud, libidinal energy is part of a subject from birth and progresses through stages: oral, anal, latent and genital. Any interference with a developmental stage can lead to an arrested progress through the phases, hysteria or neurosis. The first two stages, worked through in childhood, introduced the public to infantile sexuality, one of the most controversial parts of Freudian theory.

In his earlier work Freud theorizes two drives: sex or life (ego) and death or nirvana principle. As his work progresses, the drives merge into one, the death drive, as the life drive splits into ego and superego energies, with the latter being self-destructive, hence linking together the libido and the end of the life. Lacan uses this death drive in a metaphoric fashion, making literal death into the death of the subject in the Symbolic, and using the libido as the force that pushes and either locks the subject into his subjectivity or frees that subject, depending on the direction of the libidinal focus. Coming from Freudian theory, Jacques Lacan links anxiety and the libido, making anxiety the signal of the libidinal relationship between the subject and the partial object of his desire. That object, as the marker of the place where anxiety arises is also the nodal point, from which a subject can experience jouissance, either of the object through the Other, or through disavowal leading to an experience of the Real.

The failure of the libido in the Symbolic leads to Lacan's famous claim, "There is no sexual relationship" indicating that the libido of each subject operates like tectonic plates, causing friction against each other, but essentially, missing a true connection—because the libido always misses its mark, even ever so slightly. As Ellie Ragland asserts based on Lacan's work, the libidinal energy takes the form of montage at odds with normative logically consecutive behavior. Think explosive versus mechanical action.

Melanie Klein furthers the notion of the libido existing outside the norm by linking libidinal energy and aggressive tendencies. She explains that, in children, libidinal energy manifests as the violent desire to expunge and defile the mother's body rather than lose that body to another or recognize the mother's "castrated" physicality. The phallic mother is the earliest fantasy formation in Freud, Klein, Lacan, and Julia Kristeva.

Such defilement leads to the Kristevian concept of abjection that closes the loop of Lacan and Klein, making the libidinal aggression of Klein the mechanism for abjection that leads to the Real. For Kristeva, abjection has no object, which means it is also an expulsion of libido, granting a subject potential access to a Real experience.

(*See also* Chapter 7, Psychoanalytic Theory; Drive; Freud, Sigmund; Lacan, Jacques; Mirror Stage; Primordial Discord; *and* Psychoanalysis)

Gina Masucci MacKenzie, *Holy Family University (United States)*

Further Reading

Freud, Sigmund. *Three Essays on the Theory of Sexuality* [1905]. Trans. James Strachey. New York: Basic Books, 2000.

Kristeva, Julia. *Powers of Horror: An Essay on Abjection* [1980]. Trans. Leon S. Roudiez. New York: Columbia University Press, 1982.

Ragland, Ellie. *The Logic of Sexuation: From Aristotle to Lacan*. Albany: State University of New York, 2004.

Liminality

Anthropologists analyze rites of passage as consisting of three phases: *pre-liminal* (separation from the familiar world), *liminal* (a threshold-period of tests and trials in an unfamiliar environment) and *post-liminal* (return to the ordinary world under changed conditions). While the first and last concern *states* the middle phase is qualitatively different: it is *dynamic* and involves processes. In the liminal phase, which Victor Turner defined as "a

place that is not a place, and a time that is not a time," status and identity are subverted or annulled (or, conversely, magnified). Lying outside structure and hierarchy, the threshold (Latin *limen*) flaunts categories and appears dangerous or terrifying; but precisely *qua* unstructured, it may also be seen as a source of liberation or transcendence. Being transformative, liminal sites partake of ambivalent or contradictory traits: they connote both promise and risk, harmony and pollution, intensity and deprivation.

The concept entered critical studies in the 1980s, partly due to its narratological potential. Liminal sites include the Forest of Adventure, the haunted castle, the labyrinth, Prospero's island, outer space, dystopia. But the ambiguous *limen* may be the Other side or a gateway to the Other: the city of Troy *and* the sea of trials which returning Odysseus must navigate, the wardrobe *and* the realm of Narnia "behind" it. An experiential, relativistic concept, liminality is not an intrinsic feature of certain spaces but a value assigned to whatever at some point is deemed alien, interjacent, parenthetical.

"Liminality" identifies the condition of those who walk the boundary (the frontiersman) or the interstice (Ralph Ellison's "invisible man"). Traditional heroes are denizens of the border, but so are their adversaries (Beowulf crosses the sea to slay Grendel, but Grendel is a "wanderer of the marches"). Because threshold entities partake of two or more states, many types are *inflected* characters whose ontological ambiguity renders them threatening yet sympathetic (the Loathly Lady, the trickster, Jekyll/Hyde), powerful yet vulnerable (the double-identity superhero).

Formally, such narrative strategies as iteration, phasing, or formulaic diction help generate liminal environments in ballad, folktale, or gothic novel. It is also useful to "think liminal" when confronting an unstable text shaped by a plurality of forms (the folk-tale-*type*, the *multiform* in oral epic, the three versions of *Hamlet*), genres where two poetics meet (visual poetry), or the undecidability between the two readings of Henry James's *The Turn of the Screw* (1898).

As a theoretical tool, liminality interests the analysis of textual borders (Gérard Genette's *paratexts*) and textual relations (Julia Kristeva's *intertextuality*, Jacques Derrida's *trace*), or the study of genre formation (Roman Jakobson's *transitional genres*). These and other notions—Michel Foucault's *heterotopia* ("a place outside all places"), Kristeva's *abjection* (the horror of borders), Mikhail Bakhtin's *heteroglossia* (an irreducible plurality of voices), Homi Bhabha's *third space* or the *post-* of postmodernism, post-structuralism or postcolonial studies—are configuring a critical paradigm which views cultural systems as active sites of mediation, conflict, or transition and looks anew at the in-between, the composite and the unstable. Instead of charting discrete "states," then, a Gestalt shift allows the liminalist cartographer to reappraise the literary field as a *dynamic* map of intersections.

(*See also* Chapter 17, Comparativisms; Genre; Kristeva, Julia; *and* Worldhood)

Manuel Aguirre, *Universidad Autónoma de Madrid (Spain)*

Further Reading

Aguirre, Manuel, Roberta Quance, and Philip Sutton. *Margins and Thresholds: An Enquiry into the Concept of Liminality in Text Studies*. Madrid: The Gateway Press, 2000.

Jakobson, Roman. "The Dominant" [1935]. In *Roman Jakobson: Language in Literature*. Eds. Krystyna Pomorska and Stephen Rudy. Cambridge: The Belknap Press 1996. 41–46.

Turner, Victor. *The Ritual Process: Structure and Anti-Structure* [1969]. New York: Aldyne de Gruyter, 1995.

Linguistic Turn

Privileging the philosophy of language over philosophical anthropology ("man"). The linguistic turn occurred during the 1950s and 1960s in France. It occurred, as well, in the philosophy of Martin Heidegger. The linguistic turn speaks to the conviction that man is the effect of language and not the other way around. In France this harkened back to Marx's view that the social subject is an effect of the economic system in which he or she is cast. In the early nineteenth century, Johann Gottlieb Fichte, in *Addresses to the German People* (1808), argued that a national people are the effect of the language they speak in common. Heidegger developed this sort of thinking by means of saying enigmatically that language is the shepherd of being. Language indicates being in a way that reveals to us our proper relationship to it. Heidegger sometimes deferred to the intermediary of the poet who has the capacity to receive this shepherding of language as determinative for us as historical social subjects. Ludwig Wittgenstein's emphasis upon ordinary language in his many writings also points to a major concern with the priority of language as a performative rule-based system that we enact. What we can say and do is restricted by whatever language game we are playing. In critical theory, the advent of the New Criticism also posited a concern with language as more primary or foundational than, say, biography or historical context, which were always the critical mainstays of literary historicism. The emergence of linguistics in the 1960s and 1970s as a foundational field for critical analysis also marked a linguistic turn as did the pivot to language-centered work in conceptual art. In general, the linguistic turn has been seen as anti-Cartesian in terms of a decentering of the subject. Lacanian psychoanalysis presupposes such a turn as foundational to a revision of Freud.

(*See also* Chapter 2, Structuralism and Semiotics; Chapter 10, Feminism; Chapter 12, Postmodernism; Chapter 23, Materialism; Chapter 26, Affect Studies; Heidegger, Martin; Jameson, Fredric; *and* Text)

Herman Rapaport, *Wake Forest University (United States)*

Further Reading
Jameson, Fredric. *The Prisonhouse of Language*. Princeton: Princeton University Press, 1975.

Literature

Writing is a form of human interactive and expressive practice and, as such, is as much a part of our natural history as pointing, laughing, and yawning, even though different groups do it differently. Literature, or the aestheticization of writing, differs from this practice in abstracting it from the specific contexts in which it occurs naturally, raising the question of what gives writing its significance in *any* context. Why recount actions that, being fictional, have no effect on anyone else's actions? What moves someone to express emotions she does not presently feel? That we do not perpetually raise such questions is no evidence we can answer them. On the contrary, the dependence of literature on convention, on forms of interaction and expression in which humans engage without knowing why, suggests that there is no answer, or not unless literature is an answer. This silence on the question of its significance has tempted thinkers from Plato and Hamlet to Sigmund Freud and Martha Nussbaum to seek an ethical or political explanation for aesthetic writing or, finding none, to attribute it to economic, psychological, or other causes. However, literature's significance differs from the significance of writing in specific contexts, not as an aimless diversion differs from a practical task, but as knowledge we repress differs from information we lack. That is, it is a significance with which, being literate, we could hardly be more familiar but which, for just that reason, seems difficult to recognize. Writing feels perfectly natural, raising few questions, until it feels artificial, at which point it raises questions to no end.

Literature's answer to them materializes only where its silence, instead of a lack of information, leaves nothing more to say. Such an answer takes the form of exposed connections. Something that in specific contexts *necessarily* goes without saying—a background of possibility in relation to which any word acquires its value and impact—materializes in aesthetic writing, making our connection with it into an issue. It is as though literature reenacted the scene of our earliest acculturation, in which society's possibilities are staked in the infant's response to the voices, facial expressions, and gestures around her. This background has been called by many names: imagination, the Absolute or Ideal, subjectivity, culture, being, the Chora or Real or unconscious. Ludwig Wittgenstein calls it "grammar," a term invoking a word's connection, not just with other words, but with contexts of use, characteristic inflections, bodily reactions, and much more. Although establishing the limits of understanding, such a background is neither more nor less fixed than individual tastes, and despite its necessity for literary creation, it preexists creation neither more nor less than love preexists the beloved. Therefore, if we ask what gives writing its significance in *any* context, citing this background is as uninformative as saying the words *feel* right. On the contrary, the only informative response is to recognize our personal and collective history in which this form of interactive and expressive practice has developed naturally, and if that answer feels lacking, then perhaps we do not recognize how hard we are working to repress it.

(*See also* Aesthetics; Novel; *and* Writing)

R. M. Berry, *Florida State University*
(United States)

Further Reading
Cavell, Stanley. "Aesthetic Problems of Modern Philosophy." In *Must We Mean What We Say?* Updated ed. Cambridge: Cambridge University Press, 2002. 68–90.
Gibson, John. *Fiction and the Weave of Life.* New York: Oxford University Press, 2007.
Schalkwyk, David. "Fiction as 'Grammatical' Investigation: A Wittgensteinian Account." *The Journal of Aesthetics and Art Criticism* 53.3 (1995): 287–98.

Literature as Philosophy

The field of philosophy as practiced in the Western tradition covers such areas as ethics, social and political philosophy, epistemology, metaphysics and logic. Philosophy is also used to examine the first principles and structure of other disciplines. In this case we use the preposition "of" as in: philosophy of art (aesthetics) and philosophy of science, etc. In these cases the methodology is largely expressed via deductive logical arguments that we have termed *direct discourse philosophy*. This sort of philosophy is most effective when the explanadum is subject to externalist intersubjective empirical justification. Disagreements about the truth of particular premises can be determined via measurement to which all can agree. If someone disagrees that the boiling point of water at sea level is 100 degrees centigrade, then he can go out

and measure it in a public setting. When one gathers premises that can be factually determined, along with other commonly agreed-to-maxims and combine them according to a system of formal logic, then the resulting conclusion will be indubitably demonstrable. That sounds pretty good. Whenever it is possible to use direct discourse arguments, one should do so.

The problem is that there are many points of contention that are not amenable to direct discourse presentations. For these, *indirect discourse philosophy* is called for. Indirect discourse philosophy comes in two forms. The first form employs a logical presentation that follows from the acceptance of an hypothesis. If one can generate a contradiction from what follows logically from the hypothesis it is assumed that such a contradiction reveals a deep incoherence in the hypothesis itself. For example, in Plato's *Republic,* the speaker, Socrates, examines Thrasymachus's hypothesis "Justice is the rule of the strongest." In five different instances Socrates shows how the acceptance of this hypothesis leads to a contradiction and thus ought to be rejected. This form of indirect discourse is commonly referred to as reductio ad absurdum. It is often connected with internalist epistemological investigation into the origins of coherence or its absence.

The second form of *indirect discourse philosophy* is one in which there is no straightforward way to create a deductive or inductive string of propositions that can be used to solve the point of contention. This is because the critical points cannot be set out and verified through externalist or internalist epistemology. Examples can include such topics as: Can a good person overcome an evil one? Can mercy turn the heart of a human soul? What are the limits of human endurance? And so on. This sort of approach we call *fictive narrative philosophy.* In fictive narrative philosophy, rather than relying on a narrow series of propositions and facts to make a point or establish a claim, it relies upon the dramatization of philosophical questions by reinserting an audience in the historically and emotionally textured experience from which the questions being considered arise, the result being connections that resonate with readers. The vehicle of this presentation is a story that delivers specificity and significant details that vividly exhibit the assumptions of questions in such a way that readers are made to imaginatively, critically, and emotionally live the exploration of ideas.

A many-splendored example of this approach is Ralph Ellison's *Invisible Man* (1952), a work that probes questions of appearance versus reality, social invisibility, the polymorphous character of human seeing, the integrative process of human imagination, the fluidity of the self, and the issue of how shall we live authentically. Another example is the philosopher Jean-Paul Sartre's play "No Exit" (1944). In that work three characters find themselves brought by a mysterious valet to a room that is hell. At first they deny their guilt that led to their doom, but then one of them, Inez, demands that they stop the deception. They discover that their inability to interact with others authentically is the cause of their failures. This includes the cell in which they are presently imprisoned—but it is a captivity of their own making. Thus, Sartre is able to *show* his vision of a communitarian political philosophy in the background of existentialism. A final example that operates differently from the other two is Iris Murdoch's *An Accidental Man* (1971). In this novel, Murdoch explores the groundwork of obligation. The most explicit nod to the history of philosophy occurs when Ludwig Leferrier must choose whether to stay in Britain and make use of his dual citizenship to avoid the Vietnam draft or go back home to fight for America. Ludwig's

father brings up Socrates's argument from the *Crito* in an effort to get his son to come home and "do his duty." This is one of two plot lines that shows through daily living how and why individual responsibility arises. By commenting directly to Plato (in one of the two stories) Murdoch effectively brings her plot to counterpoint direct discourse philosophy. And the narrative proves to be the more compelling. Fictive narrative philosophy is powerful, even total, as an experience, in its mode of presentation and uniquely addresses itself to some of the most complex questions concerning human existence.

Together, these three modes constitute the field of philosophy parsed according to its presentational modes.

(*See also* Existentialism)

Michael Boylan, *Marymount University (United States)*
Charles Johnson, *University of Washington (United States)*

Further Reading

Boylan, Michael, and Charles Johnson. *Philosophy: An Innovative Introduction— Fictive Narrative, Primary Texts, and Responsive Writing.* Boulder: Westview, 2010.

Boylan, Michael. "On the Road with Charles Johnson." *The Pluralist* 12.1 (2017): 38–49.

Johnson, Charles. "The Truth-Telling Power of Fiction." In *The Way of the Writer: Reflections on the Art and Craft of Storytelling.* New York: Scribner, 2016. 213–25.

Logic

Logic, a branch of philosophy that concerns itself with the forms of thought and the nature of valid inference, was developed in ancient times and continues to be a subject of study in its own right and an influence on other philosophical fields, particularly analytic philosophy. For readers of European literature, the logical tradition initiated by Aristotle has a dual relevance. On the one hand, knowledge of key logical concepts and thinkers can help us to understand specific literary texts in relation to their historical intellectual context. On the other, logical accounts of the structures of thought and their relation to language can be used to study the workings of literature generally.

Formal logic as a discipline originated with Aristotle, whose *Organon* established a system of deductive inference. At its center is the syllogism, a form of reasoning in which a general statement (the major premise) is combined with a specific statement (the minor premise) to yield a conclusion. For example, knowing that all men are mortal, and that Socrates is a man, we may conclude that Socrates is mortal. Aristotle's concept of logic is called a *term-logic* because it focuses on the relations of terms such as "man" and "mortal"; the second major classical theorist, the stoic Chrysippus, developed a logical system concerned with the relations of propositions rather than terms. Aristotle's theory of the syllogism would dominate medieval logic, beginning with the writings of Boethius, who translated Aristotle and wrote extensively on the syllogism. The *logica nova* of the later Middle Ages would, however, subsume Aristotelian logic within a larger account of modal logic, in which the premises are qualified, as in "men are usually mortal," "it is obligatory that men be mortal," or "it is believed that men are mortal."

After reaching a high point in the fourteenth century, formal logic would suffer relative neglect until the nineteenth century, when George Boole revitalized it by developing mathematical or symbolic logic. Building

on George Peacock's argument for the formal character of symbolic algebra—its meaningfulness regardless of its "content," or the objects on which it operated—Boole devised an algebraic system for solving syllogisms. Such a system, as he and his peers quickly recognized, was more capacious and reliable than Aristotle's, which was couched in ordinary language. This use of mathematics to expand upon the capacities of logic would, in turn, lead to *logicism*, a theory, first fully articulated by Gottlob Frege, that the axioms of mathematics could be deduced from a set of fundamental logical axioms, such that mathematics could be shown to be a subsidiary of logic. Bertrand Russell sought to provide just such a set of logical foundations for mathematics, and to preserve them from paradox. Kurt Gödel's incompleteness theorem, however, proved that any set of axioms and inference rules intended to encapsulate mathematics must either be inconsistent or incomplete. Work in symbolic logic would influence analytic philosophers such as Ludwig Wittgenstein, who typically regard the object of philosophy as the logical clarification of thought and the language in which it is cast.

Even in this cursory history of logic one can perceive its implications for both writers and critics of literature: because it concerns itself with the forms of thought and the relation of thought to language, logic is relevant both to the subjects and the modes of literary writing. More generally, it provides models for thinking about what we know and how we know it. It explores induction and deduction, pragmatism and belief; it examines analogy, probability, and coherence as warrants for knowledge; and it raises the question of the role of fiction and the function of counterfactuals and even vagueness in human speech and thought. Within English literary studies, scholars have perhaps devoted the most attention to twentieth-century logic, especially that of Wittgenstein. Because they focus on the social uses of language rather than its referential function, Wittgenstein's later writings have proven particularly fruitful for critics of twentieth-century literature. Earlier forms of logic have, however, also figured importantly in literature and literary criticism: Chaucer, for instance, was well-versed in Boethian philosophy, and Victorian novelists from Lewis Carroll to George Eliot commented on the powers and limitations of logical language.

(*See also* Binary Opposition; Chapter 2, Structuralism and Semiotics; Chapter 9, Deconstruction; *and* Peirce, Charles Sanders)

Andrea Henderson, *University of California, Irvine (United States)*

Further Reading

Bochenski, I. M. *A History of Formal Logic.* Trans. Ivo Thomas. South Bend: University of Notre Dame Press, 1961.

Gibson, John, and Wolfgang Huemer, eds. *The Literary Wittgenstein.* London: Routledge, 2004.

Lynch, Kathryn. *Chaucer's Philosophical Visions.* Cambridge: D.S. Brewer, 2000.

Logocentrism (*See* Derrida, Jacques; *and* Platonism)

Lyotard, Jean-François

Jean-François Lyotard (1924–98) is one of the most important, but complex, French thinkers of the twentieth century. Known principally as a philosopher in France, his reception and legacy elsewhere is bound up in cultural theory with an important impact on literature and the social sciences.

What is often overlooked is the early political commitment Lyotard demonstrated as an active member of the heretical Marxist group Socialisme ou Barbarie, heretical in its divergence from the dictates of the French Communist Party and the Soviet Union. For ten years (1954–64) Lyotard was an active member of Socialisme ou Barbarie, writing in the eponymous journal on the situation in Algeria at the time of the struggle for independence, highlighting and analyzing the economic and political inequalities at the heart of the "Algerians' war."

Undoubtedly, Algeria, where Lyotard had taught in 1950–1952, was central to his political awakening. It was also fundamental to his later work on the irreconcilable differences, named *differends*, which cannot be resolved without injustice, explored in his major philosophical work of 1983, *The Differend*.

Confounding conventional expectations, this major publication—the result of at least a decade's work—was far from monumental in scale: it is deceptively svelte. The pared back paragraphs run to less than two hundred pages in the English translation (1988), yet its "phrases in dispute" (as the English subtitle indicates) weave a powerful analysis of language, politics, and unquestioned assumptions. It is this latter idea of confronting expectations and questioning presuppositions that is, perhaps, the one guiding thread through Lyotard's thought. It is one that also leads to ruptures, breaks, and a sense of disjuncture as the style and approach taken by Lyotard, to both his writing and thought, seem to change with each publication and project.

As a result of this there is a resistance by Lyotard to the presentation of his work as a body. It is certainly not one that progresses to a conclusion or methodological statement; yet this has also led to the fragmentation of his ideas through the attention given by others to isolated events. This is the case with his most popular work *The Postmodern Condition* (1979) that, some have argued, was a comparatively minor piece written as part of the development of ideas relating to *The Differend*, yet which received global attention.

It is important to state that while Lyotard's writings have had a fundamental role in the debates around postmodernism, his understanding is often at odds with the perceived celebration of eclecticism. His famous dictum "incredulity toward metanarratives" was a reflection on the changing attitudes he saw in industrially developed societies in the late 1970s, not an invitation to develop "post-truths" as some now seem to suggest.

The arts, especially contemporary painting, had a profound importance for Lyotard: his engagement with art and contemporary artists is sustained and central to his work—from his first major book *Discourse, Figure* (1971), translated in 2011, to the writings on more than thirty contemporary artists (now collected in six volumes) and the major exhibition he cocurated at the Pompidou Centre, Paris in 1985, *Les Immatériaux*. In art and literature Lyotard felt a resistance to the dominant voices he had termed "discourse," attending to the silent voices which struggle to make themselves heard yet to which we are obligated to listen.

(*See also* Biotechnology; Chapter 12, Postmodernism; *and* Semiotic Square)

Kiff Bamford, *Leeds Beckett University (United Kingdom)*

Further Reading

Bamford, Kiff. *Jean-François Lyotard: Critical Lives*. London: Reaktion, 2017.

Crome, Keith, and James Williams, eds. *The Lyotard Reader and Guide*. Edinburgh: Edinburgh University Press, 2006.

Lyotard, Jean-François. *The Differend: Phrases in Dispute* [1983]. Trans. Georges Van Den Abbeele. Minneapolis: University of Minnesota Press, 1988.

M

Machine

Cultural theory has worked with machines as both its object of analysis and its conditioning infrastructure. While theory articulates culture through machines, machines are also the infrastructure which enable writing, perceiving, and analysis. Indeed, even writing itself has fundamentally changed in the age of technical media as Friedrich Kittler argued relying on Friedrich Nietzsche's thoughts sitting in front of the typewriter. But, besides writing, audiovisual and computational machines have also made their impact on the modalities and focus of theory.

The past 150 to 200 years of technological culture is also the history of theories of machines and technology. Paper machines preceded electronic logistics and rationalization, and formed an early part of the organization of colonial empires and information systems such as libraries. The centrality of thermodynamic machines grounds the industrial regime while the machine also enters the literary and visual narratives that depict this world. The age of the fossil-fuel machine has had its later repercussions in the awareness of the Anthropocene and twenty-first century climate change. Recalling the violent history of technology, many twentieth-century machines are ones that tear bodies apart. From the human suffering in factories to the technological battlefields, violence is central to understanding the transformation of cultures by machines.

The machine is one key conceptual term that has migrated from designating a simple tool to being a term for a whole-world system: a mega-machine as Lewis Mumford articulated it in the 1930s. By that period it had become a key part of theoretical discourse, with theorists such as Mumford, Walter Benjamin, and Theodor Adorno arguing that machines express the rational world order. But it was also emphasized to look at what unfolds in this worlding when machines do not function, as Martin Heidegger famously put it. Also Paul Virilio added important notes about the question of technological accidents. At the same time, dysfunctional, useless, and irrational machines have been a key part of the avant-garde aesthetic response to technological culture.

The megamachines of current culture are complex infrastructural systems that are increasingly invisible data environments. One of the crucial questions that theorists have had to face is how to address planetary-scale complex systems. While the machine has become an infrastructural part of conceptual work in cultural theory, machines have increasingly also disappeared from hand-graspable tools to a more invisible sort of data infrastructure for cultural reality.

Since the middle of the twentieth century, cultural and literary theory has gradually had to face the dilemma of mathematical computing machines. In this sense, Alan Turing, the mathematician behind the model of the Turing Machine, is to be included as part of the canon of thinkers central to contemporary concerns about machines. Information theory and cybernetics has had massive influence on contemporary concerns with the machine. Donna Haraway's early influential note about the cyborg included an awareness of the complexity of the machine as radically changing notions of the subject: "We are all chimeras, theorized and fabricated hybrids of machine and organism."

While the debate about technological determinism has been one central and recurring part of this story and outlining differences between certain strands of media theory (Marshall McLuhan) and cultural studies (Raymond Williams), it is also important to note other sorts of positions that emerged outside this binary. Gilles Deleuze and Félix Guattari shift machines from being merely technical to reminding us that all machines are first social: they function to produce and organize subjectivities and desire. Many theorists such as Rosi Braidotti have effectively continued to develop this machinic ontology in the context of contemporary culture, gender, and biopolitics.

(*See also* Adorno, Theodor; Benjamin, Walter; Chapter 15, Biopower and Biopolitics; Chapter 20, Digital Humanities; Chapter 22, Identity Studies; Chapter 24, Posthumanism; Control; Cybernetics; Cyborg; Deleuze, Gilles; Diagram; Discipline; Haraway, Donna; Labor; Systems Theory; *and* Transhumanism)

Jussi Parikka, *Winchester School of Art, University of Southampton (United Kingdom)*

Further Reading

Hayles, N. Katherine. *How We Became Post-human: Virtual Bodies in Cybernetics, Literature and Informatics*. Chicago: The University of Chicago Press, 1999.

Kittler, Friedrich A. *Gramophone, Film, Typewriter* [1986]. Trans. Geoffrey Winthrop-Young. Stanford: Stanford University Press, 1999.

Raunig, Gerald. *A Thousand Machines* [2010]. Trans. Aileen Derieg. Los Angeles: Semiotext(e), 2010.

Market (*See* Free Market)

Marx, Karl

Karl Marx (1818–83) is not an obvious choice for inclusion in a volume devoted to literary and cultural theory. Marx is, of course, better known for his contributions to three primary fields: philosophy, politics, and, especially, political economy. In other words, Marx distinguished himself, often working collaboratively with his friend and benefactor, son of Manchester factory owner, Friedrich Engels, and author of *The Condition of the Working Class In England* (1845), by confronting dominant perspectives in these fields. He questioned the Idealist premises of Hegelian philosophy, the inherently moral as opposed to historical grounding of utopian socialism and the ahistorical, "Crusonade" assumptions of the political economy of figures such as Adam Smith, David Ricardo, James Mill, Jeremy Bentham, William Petty, and others. Marx's central idea was "critique" (*Kritik*), a word that was included in many of his most famous works, from the "Contribution to the Critique of Hegel's *Philosophy of Right*" (1844) to *Capital: The Critique of Political Economy* (1867). While Kant had held that the role of critique was to delimit the very topos of reason and judgment, for Marx, as for Hegel before him, critique entailed the operation of *Aufhebung* or the simultaneous cancelling *and* preserving of the aspects of the object of critique. Critique was, as Marx explained in the critique of his Idealist predecessor, the process of "rescuing the rational kernel from the mystified shell." Through critique, Marx drew out the dynamic potential of the otherwise ahistorical categories of bourgeois political economy. Here he made his fundamental contribution to social theory: the discovery that capital was nothing other than a social relation comprised of "self-valorizing value" based on the extraction of surplus-labor time from the worker.

But how could Marx be said to contribute to *cultural* and *literary* theory if his significant contribution was to the critique of the categories of political economy? Marx contributed to the field of literary and cultural theory in at least four ways. The first is that Marx was profoundly interested in questions of the politics of art, for example, having participated in the so-called Sickingen debate in 1859 with Engels and Lassalle over the nature of the sort of literature the fledgling socialist movement ought to encourage in the service of building of an emancipated society. Secondly, Marx was himself deeply concerned with matters that emerge within the traditional discipline of aesthetics and indeed planned to write a treatise on philosophical aesthetics though he never completed it. Thirdly, Marx's work has proven widely influential for generations of literary and cultural theorists from Georg Lukács, Antonio Gramsci, Theodor W. Adorno, Walter Benjamin, Ernst Bloch, Louis Althusser, and, more recently, Raymond Williams, William Hogarth, Fredric Jameson, and Terry Eagleton. Fourthly, Marx's work is littered with allusions to and direct citations of the great poets such as Ovid, Dante, Shakespeare, Johann Wolfgang von Goethe, and other writers comprising the classical literary canon. So powerful is this dimension that particular interpreters have argued that Marx's magnum opus, namely, *Capital, Volume I* can be read as descent into Dante's *Inferno*.

Overall, Marx brings together a "historical materialist" philosophical commitment to the central importance of sensuous experience with an interest in traditional aesthetics. In texts as diverse as the *Economic and Philosophical Manuscripts of 1844*, *The Communist Manifesto* (1848), and *The Eighteenth Brumaire of Louis Bonaparte* (1852), Marx shows their profound interconnection. Attention to the "aesthetic" dimension of Marx, shows him to be a much more complex and sophisticated thinker than he is often portrayed to be by his putative disciples with a simplistic mechanical conception of a political, legal, ideological (broadly "cultural") superstructure resting on an "economic" base.

(*See also* Alienation; Base and Superstructure; Bourgeois; Capitalism; Chapter 4, Marxism; Class; Dialectic; Ideology; Labor; Marxism; Negation; Production; *and* Revolution)

Samir Gandesha, *Simon Fraser University (Canada)*

Further Reading

Gandesha, Samir, and Johan Hartle, eds. *Aesthetic Marx*. London: Bloomsbury, 2017.

Roberts, William Clare. *Marx's Inferno: The Political Theory of Capital*. Princeton: Princeton University Press, 2017.

Rose, Margaret A. *Marx's Lost Aesthetic: Karl Marx and the Visual Arts*. Cambridge: Cambridge University Press, 1988.

Marxist Theory

Marxism is dedicated to both a critique of political economy in general and to an analysis of social transformation in particular. While it is true that much of Karl Marx's own writing focused on a specific understanding of capital and capitalism, often historically and spatially bound by the industrial economy of nineteenth-century England, the rigors of his dialectical method reveal their force in the way they can be applied to other moments and spaces of political and economic activity. This sense of class struggle across history has proved to be a vital impetus for Marxist theory up to the present.

On one level, Marxist theory is really only an ongoing attempt to produce a Marxism adequate to the moving contradictions of its object—capitalism as such. On another level, Marxist theory is interested in a radical creativity, one that, in the subsumption of capitalism and its class relations, would render Marxism itself superfluous. Although there is no space here to explore the depth and vibrancy of such concerns, one can at least indicate a certain tension, if not antinomy, between such claims. The classical Marxism of Marx and Engels themselves cleaved to a critique of political economy as a set of first principles, on commodification, on value, on accumulation, on credit, on profit, on labor, on the working day, and so on. By beginning with the means of production and the exploitative relations that attend them, this Marxism elaborated the complex lineaments of a mode of production in general, one whose concrete processes helped determine the terms of social struggle and revolution. Yet the more one pursued elements of the critique according to their concrete reality after Marx, the more Marxist theory itself had to explain both its own shortfall in meeting its classical expression, and the limits of the original model proposed. The paradox of Marxian dialectics is that the truth of social reality it reveals in situ simultaneously produces an insufficiency as a universal condition (or, rather, the insufficiency is constitutive of its "bounded" universality). This is why classical Marxism inexorably begets variegations of post-Marxism, or Marxism beside itself.

The philosophical and political components of Marxist theory since Marx trace several specific histories. The Marxism of Vladimir Lenin's *State and Revolution* (1917), for instance, does not limn easily with Leon Trotsky's *History of the Russian Revolution* (1930), or even Louis Althusser's Leninist inclinations in *Lenin and Philosophy and Other Essays* (1968). The psychoanalytic Marxism to be gleaned from Lacan's conception of the subject (*Four Fundamental Principles* [1954-1955], etc.) does not adequately describe the subject for Foucauldian discourse theory, even though the institutional critique in the latter has clear genealogical links to a Marxist anti-capitalist approach to socioeconomic structure. The rich and radical traditions of Marxist feminism, black Marxism, and anti-imperialism redolent in thinkers like Alexandra Kollontai, Rosa Luxemburg, Silvia Federici, Frantz Fanon, Cedric Robinson, and Angela Davis have struggled mightily with the economism, sexism, and racism of Marxist orthodoxy, and have revolutionized revolutionary theory in the process. One of the main lessons of Marxist theory is not that it is frozen in its historical opposition to class hierarchies and oppression but that it is a dynamic catalyst in thinking beyond the dead ends of the present.

(*See also* Adorno, Theodor; Alienation; Althusser, Louis; Bakhtin, Mikhail; Base and Superstructure; Benjamin, Walter; Bourgeois; Capitalism; Chapter 4, Marxism; Civil Society; Class; Critique; Cultural Capital; Cultural Critique; Cultural Materialism; Dialectic; Feminist Materialism; Hall, Stuart; Hegemony; Ideology; Jameson, Fredric; Labor; Marx, Karl; Material Culture; Materialism; Negation; Negri, Antonio; Political Unconscious; Postcolonialism; Production (and Reproduction); Revolution; Spivak, Gayatri; Subaltern; *and* Williams, Raymond)

Peter Hitchcock, *City University of New York (United States)*

Further Reading

Davis, Angela Y. *Freedom Is a Constant Struggle: Ferguson, Palestine, and the Foundations of a Movement.* New York: Haymarket Books, 2015.

Fanon, Frantz. *The Wretched of the Earth* [1961]. Trans. Richard Philcox. New York: Grove Press, 2005.

Federici, Silvia. *Revolution at Point Zero.* New York: PM Press, 2012.

Kollontai, Alexandra. *Sexual Relations and the Class Struggle: Love and the New Morality.* Bristol: Falling Wall Press, 1972.

Marx, Karl. *Capital* [1867; 1885; 1894]. Three Vols. Trans. David Fernbach. New York: Penguin, 1993.

Robinson, Cedric. *Black Marxism.* Chapel Hill: University of North Carolina Press, 2000.

Material Culture

Material culture is the interdisciplinary study of the role "objects" play in the circuits of production and consumption of "culture." The term is in broad use in disciplines from literary studies, anthropology, archaeology, philosophy, history, psychology, and others; the objects of material culture studies range from food, furniture, books, cars, clothing, and hair care products, to rocks, trees, textiles, and so on. Material culture studies open up understandings of the panoply of objects produced by human intervention and creation, including (but not limited to) analyses of the political and social impact of objects in the world; the specific function of objects within communities of all scales; and the specific roles of objects in ritual and religious contexts.

Some of the earliest material culture studies developed in anthropology and archaeology, specifically elucidating the roles objects and production took in non-Western cultures.

The early to mid-twentieth century would witness an explosion of works that would mark the field's contours, such as Marcel Mauss's *The Gift* (1923–24), Claude Lévi-Strauss *The Raw and The Cooked* (1964), and Mary Douglas's *Purity and Danger* (1966). In 1949, Leslie White's *The Science of Culture* defined the field's early methodological parameters, especially the necessity for examining cultural evolution at least partially through the development and use of objects across social functions.

In the 1980s, arguably beginning with museum studies and art history, material culture studies takes on a more interdisciplinary and politicized configuration, incorporating insights from Marxism, post-structuralism, and radical anthropology. This work critiqued material objects and processes of commodification, industrial control, and institutional politics. Anthropologists Arjun Appadurai's *The Social Life of Things* (1986) and Daniel Miller's *Materiality* (2005) exemplify this interdisciplinary shift, anthologizing work on material objects that cross ethnographic work with studies of racialization, political economy, subaltern studies, and community policy.

Subsequently, feminism, queer theory, and gender studies have developed robust work on material objects and social activity. Maureen Daly Goggin and Beth Tobin Fowkes produced the well-regarded collection *Women and Things, 1750-1950* (2011).

In American literature, Bill Brown's *A Sense of Things* (2003) developed a seminal analysis of the role nineteenth-century literature played in accounting for the transformative role of commodity production and objects in the young United States; Brown opened spaces for further literary research on materiality and cultural expression. In a more holistic vein, emphasizing the role of decommodification, storage, and nostalgia for objects. Maurizia Boscagli's *Stuff Theory* (2014) models material culture as a network of emotional and poetics concerns influenced as much by human desire as by the role of commodification and capitalist production.

Given its interdisciplinary nature, material culture studies is best understood as emphasizing specific problematics associated with objects of culture within established disciplinary configurations, especially the complexity of human *making* and *consuming*—practices that define our species as *homo faber* as well as *homo sapiens*.

(*See also* Chapter 4, Marxism; Chapter 23, Materialisms; Culture; Objects; *and* Thing Theory)

Carlos M. Amador, *Michigan Technological University (United States)*

Further Reading

Boscagli, Maurizia. *Stuff Theory: Everyday Objects, Radical Materialism*. New York: Bloomsbury, 2014.

Donald, Moira, and Linda Hurcombe, eds. *Gender and Material Culture in Historical Perspective*. New York: Palgrave, 2010.

Goggin, Maureen Daly, and Beth Fowkes Tobin. *Women and Material Culture*. Three vols. New York: Ashgate, 2010.

Salazar-Porzio, Margaret, Joan Troyano, and Lauren Safranek, eds. *Many Voices, One Nation: Material Culture Reflections on Race and Migration in the United States*. Washington: Smithsonian Institution Scholarly Press, 2017.

Tilley, Chris, Webb Keane, Susanne Küchler, Mike Rowlands, and Patricia Spyer, eds. *Handbook of Material Culture*. Thousand Oaks: Sage, 2013.

Materialism

Materialism is a key concept in both critical theory and philosophy. Like many key concepts, its meanings are not only multiple but sometimes contradictory. There are many versions of materialism employed by disparate branches of critical theory from Marxism, feminism, and psychoanalysis to phenomenology, ontology, and the emergent approaches grouped under the banners new materialism and speculative realism. While materialisms differ, they all tend to be posited in opposition to idealism, the doctrine that ideas are the prime motive force in the universe. Materialisms, in contrast, see the material as such a force. An initial distinction can be made between materialism as an account of matter and materialism as an account of systemic constraint and possibility. The former account is central to much continental philosophy from Pre-Socratics and Aristotle through Martin Heidegger to contemporary new materialist and speculative realist accounts of matter as vibrant, dynamic, agentic, and/or as intertwined with yet in excess of human consciousness. The account of materialism as systemic constraint and possibility is most prominently associated with Marxist theory, but can also be aligned with psychoanalysis structuralism, and post-structuralism. Within such a framework the focus is much less on the individual manifestation of materiality and more on various societal structures, such as the political economy in Marxism, the symbolic in Lacanian psychoanalysis, and structure itself in structuralism.

The version of materialism that emphasizes individual instantiations of matter can take a number of forms, from positing matter as dynamic, contingent, and/or agential to structured, necessary, and/or recalcitrant. Most versions of this form of materialism are ontological. Given that they usually posit matter as at least partially distinct from the perceiving and experiencing subject, they necessarily posit ontological questions of the being of matter and not just its apprehension or manipulation by a human subject. The speculative realist work associated with thinkers such as Quentin Meillassoux, Ray Brassier, Isabella Stengers, and object-oriented ontologists such as Graham Harman and Levi Bryant pushes beyond what Meillassoux describes as "correlationism" or the post-Kantian doctrine that argues that human's only have access to that which correlates with their thought and not to things in-themselves. In other words, speculative realists posit aspects of materiality that exceed direct human apprehension. Their work is thus ontological in a strong sense. Those working under the banner of new materialism, such as Stacy Alaimo, Karen Barad, Sara Ahmed, Bruno Latour, and Samantha Frost, rather than positing that which exceeds subjective apprehension tend to undo or deconstruct the subject/object oppositions, articulating instead a more delimited ontology that is organized around the intermixing of subjective and material properties. The version of materialism that understands it as systemic constraint and possibility is less interested in the individual manifestation of matter and more concerned with the way in which systems of economic, psychic, or linguistic organization produce structures that both enable and inhibit political-economic and sociopolitical change. It is also interested in various dynamics of de-materialization and re-materialization as produced by the interaction of humans with language and/or the material world.

(*See also* Chapter 4, Marxism; Chapter 8, Rhetoric; Chapter 10, Feminism; Chapter 11, Cultural Studies; Chapter 14, Ecocriticism; Chapter 22, Identity Studies; Chapter 23, Materialisms; Chapter 26, Affect Studies; Cultural Materialism; Encounter; Feminist Materialism; New Materialism; Speculative Realism; *and* Thing Theory)

Christopher Breu, *Illinois State University (United States)*

Further Reading

Coole, Diana, and Samantha Frost, eds. *New Materialisms: Ontology, Agency, and Politics*. Durham: Duke University Press, 2010.

Gratton, Peter. *Speculative Realism: Problems and Prospects*. New York: Bloomsbury, 2014.

Harvey, David. *The Limits to Capital*. Updated ed. London: Verso, 2007.

Media Ecology

Media ecology represents an interdisciplinary theory of media studies that considers how communication media shapes the way we think, feel, and understand our world. Although its adherents might suggest that it has a longer historical trajectory, the roots of media ecology are typically linked to early- and mid-twentieth-century Canadian scholars, Harold Innis and Marshall McLuhan. Other prominent scholars associated with the media ecology tradition include Eric Havelock, Susanne Langer, Neil Postman, Jacques Ellul, Walter Ong, Lewis Mumford, Elizabeth Eisenstein, and Edmund Carpenter.

The theory situates media within a broader communication environment to discern how these technologies structure the formal and informal parameters of communicative possibility and how our senses experience this possibility. With its emphasis on the ecology metaphor, media ecology theory reflects on the media-communication relationship within a symbolic environment. Media ecologists aim to make the invisible symbolic environment visible by moving us to attend to how our media both constitute and are constituted by it. As such, media do not merely deliver content. Instead, per McLuhan's famous dictum, "The medium is the message," media are as important, if not more important, than their content as they allow and mitigate what can and cannot be communicated and thereby subtly shape our symbolic environment.

Media ecology theory tends to define media technologies broadly. Certainly, McLuhan's, *Understanding Media* (1964), features chapters on conventional media like writing, the photograph, telegraph, typewriter, film, and radio. However, McLuhan also considers technologies that would not fit into a general understanding of media. These include the wheel, electric light, numbers, clothing, games, and cars as forms of communication technology as well. Similarly, Lewis Mumford's, *Technics and Civilization* (1963), addresses how technologies like the clock change humanity's relation to space and time. Media ecology theorists will then address these technologies for the way they influence culture, society, and thought. For example, in his *Amusing Ourselves to Death* (1985), Postman considers eyeglasses not only as an innovative technology that allow people to see more clearly, but also as that which moves them to reconsider the irreversibility of physical decline for the first time in history. As part of their analysis, some media ecologists consider the morality of the changes wrought by new media technologies. Postman encourages us to carefully evaluate what is given and what is taken away as we adopt and integrate new media technologies into our symbolic environments.

Given the powerful role media ecology attributes to communication technology, some critics would suggest that the theory represents an untenable technological determinist perspective on media's impact on culture and society. Other critics would take media ecology to task for presenting a theory that can neither be proven nor denied. However, media ecology's value lies in its presentation of a far-reaching alternative to more narrowly focused, empirically-oriented media effects theories.

(*See also* Chapter 19, Media Studies)

Andrew Baerg, *University of Houston, Victoria (United States)*

Further Reading

McLuhan, Marshall. *Understanding Media: The Extensions of Man*. New York: Signet Books, 1964.

Mumford, Lewis. *Technics and Civilization*. New York: Harcourt & Brace, 1963.

Postman, Neil. *Amusing Ourselves to Death*. New York: Penguin, 1985.

Media Effects

Up until the mid-twentieth century, media effects were understood through the metaphor of the hypodermic needle. Media would presumably present a direct message that would be uniformly internalized by audiences experiencing it. In 1940, this uniform direct effects theory was challenged by Columbia researcher, Paul Lazarsfeld, and his two-step flow theory of media effects. Lazarsfeld posited that media effects were not as direct as had been presumed and asserted that these effects were filtered through other intermediaries like influential family and friends. In Lazarsfeld's two-step flow theory, a media message came to a group of opinion leaders who would then interpret and relay the message to others in a community.

Following Lazarsfeld, other media effects theories arose. One of the more prominent effects theories has been Uses and Gratifications theory. Uses and Gratifications theory originated with Elihu Katz in 1959. The theory asserts that media audiences make active choices in their media consumption. People make these choices to use media for meeting specific needs and to gratify specific desires, hence the theory's Uses and Gratifications moniker. By contrast to more top down understandings of media effects, Uses and Gratifications shifts the effects question by acknowledging that audiences have different desires, motivations, and objectives in their media use. The theory also departs from the uniform effects model by assuming that people can accurately communicate their motivations for their media use.

Another prominent perspective on media effects has come from Cultivation Theory. Cultivation Theory derives from the 1972 work of George Gerbner. Gerbner noted the way that broadcast media, particularly television, had become the foremost narrative agent in the culture. Gerbner promoted extensive content analysis of television, surveyed audiences about their social realities, and then compared the difference between light and heavy television users with respect to issues like violence. Gerbner theorized that the heaviest users would undergo mainstreaming, that is, develop a common perception of the world. As Gerbner and his fellow researchers developed the theory, they proposed a new measure of effects called the Mean World Index. This index reported the degree of audience agreement with statements about others' selfishness, trust in other people, and the golden rule. The heaviest television viewers typically scored highest on the Mean World Index.

A third theoretical framework for understanding media effects has been Agenda Setting theory. Agenda Setting theory was developed by Maxwell McCombs and Donald Shaw in 1972. Agenda Setting theory considers the nature of the media agenda, the pattern of topics the media present to the public, and the nature of the public agenda, issues that surveys reveal to be important to the public. If the media make a topic salient, the theory asserts that the public will consider that topic important as well. Agenda Setting theory thereby initially argued that the media do not tell the public what to think, but what to think about. Subsequent refining of the theory has argued for media framing as part of agenda setting. Framing theory argues that the media emphasize certain attributes at the expense of others resulting in the media prodding audiences on how to think about important issues.

Given the mid- to late-twentieth-century context in which they arose, media effects theories may need to be refined or new theories developed to measure and assess a new media context. However, uses and gratifications, cultivation theory, and agenda setting theory still provide a useful foundation from which to work on the subject.

(*See also* Chapter 19, Media Studies)

Andrew Baerg, *University of Houston-Victoria (United States)*

Further Reading
Gerbner, George. "Cultivation Analysis: An Overview." *Mass Communication & Society* 1 (1998): 175–94.
Katz, Elihu, and Lazarsfeld, Paul. *Personal Influence: The Part Played by People in the Flow of Mass Communications* [1955]. New York: Routledge, 20005.
McCombs, Maxwell, and Shaw, Donald. "The Agenda-setting Function of Mass Media." *Public Opinion Quarterly* 36.2 (1972): 176–87.

Mediation

Mediation is the process by which messages are represented and communicated. On the formal level, mediation requires some physical material to embody the process of representation and communication. The definition of mediation is therefore connected with the question of the nature and importance of the medium. Mediation also requires techniques for encoding and interpreting messages, and these techniques are defined (at least in part) by cultural contexts.

There has been a decades-long debate on the role that the medium as a material technology plays in the process of mediation. Those who ascribe a central role to the so-called affordances of the material medium are often accused of *technological determinism*. Marshall McLuhan is often regarded as the classic technological determinist for his argument that the "medium is the message." His view that each medium changes or extends the "human sensorium," has generally been rejected by cultural studies and literary theorists, but McLuhan remains influential in popular discourse about media, particularly the new technologies of digital media.

The process of mediation has been extensively studied from technical, aesthetic, philosophical, cultural, and literary-critical perspectives. Each perspective with its associated discipline focuses on certain aspects of the process. Communication studies integrates the social sciences with the humanities in its approach, emphasizing the process of and audience for mediation. Semiotics, the study of signs, examines mediation as a process of signification abstracted from any material medium. Media studies, on the other hand, focuses on the materiality and history of each medium and its interaction with other cultural elements. For example, a researcher in media studies might examine the archaeology of early cinema or the technical and economic development of the World Wide Web in the 1990s. Cultural studies focuses on the ways in which messages as cultural texts are determined by such factors as economic class, ideology, race, and gender, contending that the messages are encoded with values of the dominant institutions in a society and then received and decoded by an audience that may only partly share those values. Cultural

studies is particularly interested in the way which audiences may creatively appropriate the messages they receive from such media sources as film and television.

Literary-critical studies is concerned primarily with texts themselves as products of mediation. In its analysis, however, it may draw on any of the other disciplines mentioned and therefore on any of the phases of mediation from production to reception. It has its own version of media archaeology in the traditional discipline of bibliography (the study of printing and other forms of book production). The new discipline of digital humanities (a hybrid of media studies and literary studies) is concerned with process as well as product. In recent decades, cultural studies has strongly influenced literary-critical studies, and one effect of that influence has been to broaden the kind of media forms considered worthy of cultural and aesthetic analysis, including graphic novels, posters, magazines as well as television, film, and now even social media and videogames.

(*See also* Chapter 2, Structuralism and Semiotics; Chapter 11, Cultural Studies; Chapter 19, Media Studies; Chapter 20, Digital Humanities; Cultural Studies; Eco, Umberto; *and* Semiotics)

Jay David Bolter, *Georgia Institute of Technology (United States)*

Further Reading

Eco, Umberto. *A Theory of Semiotics.* Bloomington: University of Indiana Press, 1976.

McLuhan, Marshall. *Understanding Media: The Extensions of Man*. New York: New American Library Inc., 1964.

Sturken, Marita, and Lisa Cartwright. *Practices of Looking: An Introduction to Visual Culture*. Second ed. New York: Oxford University Press, 2009.

Memory

From Plato's wax tablet to Sigmund Freud's mystic writing pad, individual memory is often figured through the idea of stored, permanent impressions. Frederic Bartlett, by contrast, viewed memory as changeable and its retrieval as creative. To demonstrate this, he used an experiment involving research subjects reading a story, *The War of the Ghosts*, and then recalling it at varied intervals afterward. The narrative was Bartlett's adaptation of a translation of a Kathlamet Chinook tale told to Franz Boas by Charles Cultee in 1891 and again in 1894. The story was retold so Boas, who was seeking to preserve aspects of Chinook oral culture from perceived oblivion, could test Cultee's linguistic memory. Bartlett, also employing repetition, found that when recollecting the tale, his subjects tended to abbreviate and embellish it, forgetting aspects and inventing others, thereby demonstrating that memory is reconstructed, malleable. In *Remembering* (1932), Bartlett's overview of *The War of the Ghosts* is selective. He refers to it as a North American folktale rather than a story of the Kathlamet, a then distinct First Nations people of the Pacific Northwest. This lack of specificity runs against Boas's project to preserve manifestations of Kathlamet culture beyond what he believed would be the people's living memory, to safeguard cultural memory.

As a concept cultural memory postdates Boas's actions, evolving from Maurice Halbwachs's theory of collective memory, the idea that individual memory depends upon social frameworks. Halbwachs died at Buchenwald, leaving a major work, *La mémoire collective* (1950), unfinished. The Holocaust has significantly influenced understanding of memory. Charlotte Delbo, a survivor of Auschwitz and Ravensbrück, distinguished between the intellectual memory (cognitions) and the deep memory (physical sensations) of her experiences. Michael Rothberg's idea of multidirectional memory (a dynamic, politically engaged alternative to the conservativeness and competitiveness of collective memory) and Marianne Hirsch's conception of postmemory (a form of retrospective memory assumed by surrogates on behalf of those with direct experience of an event) are both indebted to Holocaust research. Richard Crownshaw, a key exponent of the notion of transcultural memory (memory that travels through and across cultures), also works in Holocaust Studies.

The War of the Ghosts can be interpreted as transcultural remembrance, Kathlamet collective memory traveling to Cambridge via New York, transformed by this process yet nonetheless preserved. Traces of imperialism, however, taint this transcultural memory. Bartlett's decision to use a performance of memory appropriated from a culture other than his own to engage in a conflict over the nature of memory is deeply problematic. His footnote (p. 64, fn3) referencing Boas's *Kathlamet Texts* (1901) in *Remembering* gives page numbers 184–85, which fall across Cultee's 1891 and 1894 versions of *The War of the Ghosts*, conforming to neither. This memory slip gestures toward the more troubling forgetting of Cultee himself: Bartlett mentions only Boas. *Kathlamet Texts* also involves a deprivation of voice. It is fronted by a black and white photograph of Mrs. Wilson, a Kathlamet woman shown in side-view and front-view, cataloged, silently burdened with memorializing her people. These violent impositions and omissions demonstrate the necessity of attending to the politics of memory. In this context, Dell Hymes's exposition of how the repeat performances Cultee gives of tales that embody Kathlamet collective memory are inflected by Cultee's artistry and personality, as they manifest through performative variations, assumes considerable importance.

(*See also* Chapter 9, Deconstruction; Trauma; *and* Writing)

Nicholas Chare, *Université de Montréal (Canada)*

Further Reading

Chare, Nicholas, and Dominic Williams. "Questions of Filiation: From the Scrolls of Auschwitz to *Son of Saul.*" *Mémoires en jeu/Memories at stake* 2 (2016): 63–72.

Erll, Astrid. *Memory in Culture* [2005]. Trans. Sara B. Young. Houndmills: Palgrave Macmillan, 2011.

Radstone, Susannah. "Memory Studies: *For* and *Against.*" *Memory Studies* 1.1 (2008): 31–39.

Metaphysics

Metaphysics is a branch of philosophy whose object of study has changed from the ancient world to the present. "Metaphysics" was coined by an editor of Aristotle in first century CE as an umbrella term to encompass the works of the philosopher that most likely were to be studied after his treatise on nature (*Physics*). While the *Physics* addressed the changing world, the *meta ta physika* (*Metaphysics*) dealt with what remains unchanging in reality.

Thus, in ancient and medieval philosophy, metaphysics referred to the philosophical study of the unchanging nature of things, investigating their being and substance (what later fell under ontology), and first causes. The requirement of immutability for the object of its inquiry originally united ancient and medieval metaphysics, but this requirement is no more applicable. Modern thought, at least since the seventeenth century, has added to the pursuit of metaphysics questions that were earlier categorized under the physical, mutable world: the dualism of mind and body (as elaborated, for instance, by Descartes); space and time (the transcendental categories developed by Kant in an attempt to rescue metaphysics from empirical skepticism); the binary of determinism and free will that underlies ethical thought (for instance, Friedrich Nietzsche's double reception in Anglophone and continental traditions as a naturalist and as an anti-naturalist, respectively, refers to the disagreement in interpreting his leanings along this binary).

Despite the fact that metaphysics lacks now the strict unity of its object of inquiry (thus also of its method), or perhaps because of this inherent disarray, it has undergone some of the most pointed interrogation, and even condemnation, than any other branch of philosophical inquiry. Some scholars, such as Herbert De Vriese and others, have recently argued that this virulent critique started not from inside philosophy itself, but was a result of a larger cultural shift in the nineteenth century, during which any lofty idealism was displaced by modernity's immanent, materialist concerns. Modernity's revolutions and cultural breaks with the past are all read in tandem with this abandonment of metaphysics. Presently, while analytic philosophers have raised doubts about the viability of metaphysics, since its questions are no more tightly conjoined—or worse—may never be satisfactorily answered, postmodern theorists have denounced metaphysics both historically and thematically: metaphysics, from Plato onwards, is blamed for the direction not only of philosophy, but of politics and Western culture as such.

This postmodern line of thought can be traced back to Nietzsche, and continues in the vein of Martin Heidegger, who famously saw in Plato the forgetting of Being. It is pervasive in the works of Theodor Adorno, Maurice Blanchot, Jacques Derrida, and Giorgio Agamben, among others, who all attribute the historical and political violence of modernity to metaphysics while eliding the specific, epochal distinction that obtains between antique metaphysics and its refashioning in the Western, systematic philosophical tradition from Leibniz onward. For the above thinkers, metaphysics appears as a sufficiently unified endeavor to warrant such a wholesale assault. Though these critics claim different philosophical affinities and lineages, they are linked by their common concern "to overcome" metaphysics at the same time as some of them concede that this overcoming is not necessarily a denial of the metaphysical tradition. To the contrary, there is even an understanding that the horizon of metaphysics cannot be surpassed in a terminal and definitive manner, but only through micro-gestures that adjust the metaphysical categories temporarily.

(*See also* Agamben, Giorgio; Archi-Trace; Aristotelianism; Chapter 1, Early Theory; Chapter 9, Deconstruction; Chapter 23, Materialisms; Capacity; Cartesianism; Deconstruction; Différance; Dissemination; Force; Heidegger, Martin; Nancy, Jean-Luc; Object-Oriented Ontology; Objects; Ontology; *and* Speculative Realism)

Kalliopi Nikolopoulou, *University at Buffalo (United States)*

Further Reading

De Vriese, Herbert, Geert Van Eekert, Guido Vanheeswijck, and Koenraad Verrycken, eds. *1830–1848: The End of Metaphysics as a Transformation of Culture*. Leuven: Peeters Publishers, 2004.

Mounce, Howard O. *Metaphysics and the End of Philosophy*. London: Continuum, 2008.

Mumford, Steven. *Metaphysics: A Very Short Introduction*. Oxford: Oxford University Press, 2012.

Migration

Migration arguably began with history. Settlements in newly found territories prompted people to migrate for betterment in their economic and political condition. By the same token, people also migrated from one part of the region to another to avoid persecution, as shown in Langston Hughes's poem, "Migration" (1947). In this poem, originally published in 1923 under the title "The Little Frightened Child," Hughes talks about a black boy who moves to the North of the United States to escape racism in the South, only to find the white kids in the north taunting him for his skin color. However, mass migration as a result of war, famine, and unequal distribution of labor and economic opportunities is a modern phenomenon—at least in terms of scale. The twentieth and the first decade of the twenty-first century witnessed global migration of people on a scale unseen in previous history. Animals and birds have witnessed similar migration due to a loss of their habitat owing to human activities.

Twentieth-century literature has captured this crisis of mass migration in various works. In fact, one could argue that migration has occupied a center stage in the second half of twentieth-century literary history with such works as Salman Rushdie's *The Satanic Verses* (1988), V. S. Naipaul's *A House for Mr. Biswas* (1961), Bharati Mukherjee's *Jasmine* (1989), Amy Tan's *The Joy Luck Club* (1993), Jamaica Kincaid's *Lucy* (1990), J. M. Coetzee's *Waiting for the Barbarians* (1980), and Jhumpa Lahiri's *Interpreter of Maladies* (1999), to name only a few works. In Mukherjee's *Jasmine*, the protagonist arrives in the United States from India looking for economic opportunity, but also to avoid tradition's persecution of her as a young widow. All this happens while she is on fake immigration documents, which further complicates her life, on top of being raped by her smuggler upon her arrival in her new "home." In Coetzee's *Waiting for the Barbarians*, migration becomes part of people's everyday life, thanks to the stewards of Empire, who resort to brutal methods of interrogation to weed out the so-called barbarians, who are only everyday folks making their living by herding and moving from place to place to avoid extreme seasonal weathers. Perhaps, the best literary representation of migration happens in Rushdie's *The Satanic Verses*. The novel became controversial for religious reasons, but the main topic it is concerned with is not religion but migration. Set in the England of the 1980s, the novel shows the predicament of Mr. Saladin Chamcha, a Briton of Indian descent, who is mistaken for an illegal immigrant by the immigration officials once his plane explodes in mid-air, and he, along with a fellow compatriot, Gibreel Farishta, is washed up on a beach near the English Channel.

Literary representation of migration finds theoretical grounding in works such as Theodor Adorno's *Minima Moralia* (1951), Lisa Lowe's *Immigrant Acts* (1996), Paul Gilroy's *The Black Atlantic* (1993), and Edward Said's *Culture and Imperialism* (1993), among many others. Adorno's *Minima Moralia*, which was influential on many later theoretical works including those of Said's, is a collection of loosely connected essays in terms of a topic. However, the undercurrent in each essay is loss, and the accompanying opportunity because of migration. Said's *Culture and Imperialism* is a critical analysis of classic literary texts such as Rudyard Kipling's *Kim* (1901) and their complicity with imperialism's havocs at a global scale, which, Said argues, result in mass migration of people and animals.

(*See also* Chapter 17, Comparativisms; Colonialism; Diaspora; Globalization; *and* Said, Edward)

Ubaraj Katawal, *Valdosta State University*
(United States)

Further Readings

Adorno, Theodor. *Minima Moralia: Reflections on a Damaged Life* [1951]. Trans. E. F. N. Jephcott. New York: Verso, 2005.

James, C. L. R. *Mariners, Renegades & Castaways: The Story of Herman Melville and the World We Live In*. Lebanon: University Press of New England, 2001.

Said, Edward. *Culture and Imperialism*. New York: Vintage, 1993.

Mimesis (*See* Figuration; *and* Ricoeur, Paul)

Minority

Since the 1970s, the various civil rights movements successfully changed the trajectory of people of color's social and intellectual history in the United States, allowing people of color to find critical voices beyond the dominant American narrative. As a consequence, literary and cultural critics and theorists of color made an intervention into the reading of mainstream literary and cultural productions such as films, television shows, and the literatures of people of color, reconfiguring history and subjectivity. Among these critics and theorists are traditional critics, nationalist critics, feminist and womanist critics, intersectional critics, postcolonial critics, Afrocentric and black aesthetic critics, Omni-American critics, trickster theorists, deconstructionists, Marxist critics, and cultural critics.

The aim of most of these literary and cultural theorists and critics of color is to de-territorialize long-standing stereotypes and devalued images and representations of American Indians, African-Americans, Asian-Americans and Hispanics such as Fu Manchu, Charlie Chan, Hop Sing, evil Japanese soldier, lotus blossom or dragon lady, noble savage, the lazy primitive black, Aunt Jemima, warrior, the alcoholic, which historically have been culturally embedded in the social fabric of American society. Instead, their aim is to use traditional and indigenous cultural forms such as the blues, jazz, working-class Mexican American and African American cultures, African belief systems and religions, and Asian-American, Chicano/a and Native American folklore, myths, legends, trickster figures, and historical figures like Pocahontas, Hua Mulan, la Malinche and La Llorona to intervene and disrupt or decode the majority language, along with their own racial/ethnic literatures, and their devaluation and stereotyping of people of color. They want to re-territorialize the reading of mainstream cultural productions and these literatures, giving complex, humane, and, at times, hybrid and varied portraits of people of color. Ultimately, they want to produce people of color who can construct themselves as subjects capable of investing in desire and projecting themselves into the future. This entails paying attention to the repressed, excluded and/or subordinated history, culture and social milieu of people of color. It also means accepting the fact that Americans have different definitions of life. Afrocentrists, Womanist and nationalist critics and theorists such as Addison Gayle, Larry Neal, Barbara Christian, Alice Walker, Elaine Kim, Roberta Fernandez, Rodolfo Acuna, Simon Ortiz, Robert Allen Warrior, Jace Weaver, and Craig Womack, want to read the literature in terms of the wholeness of the culture and history of the past, as a form of resistance to the mainstream's devaluation of their respective ethnic/racial group. Cultural critics like bell hooks, Cornel West, Jeff Yang, Jeff Chang, Viet Thanh Nguyen, Alicia Gaspar de Alba, and others use feminism, queer theory, Marxism, and deconstruction to reexamine and reposition racist and sexist portrayals of African-Americans, Asian-Americans and Chicanos/as in mainstream and ethnic/racial cultural and literary productions. Literary theorists such as Gerald Vizenor, later Houston Baker, W. Lawrence Hogue, Gloria Anzaldua, Fred Moten, and others use high theory to deconstruct devalued representations of people of color, advocating heterogeneity and differences. Feminists and Critical Race theorists such as Rafael Perez-Torres, Patricia Hill Collins, Kimberle Williams Crenshaw, and others use intersectionality to examine multiple/overlapping identities, including race, sex, class, gender, and sexual orientation. Breaking away from and complicating Western modernity and cultural nationalism, theorists of color such as Albert Murray, Gerald Vizenor, Gloria Anzaldua, David Treuer, Jose David Saldivar, Eric Liu, Sau-Ling Wong, Rey Chow, and Lisa Lowe accent the hybrid, Omni-American, diasporic, transnational nature of people of color in American society.

What many literary and cultural critics and theorists of color do is create links between the traditional cultural past and mainstream capitalist culture, fertilizing/enriching both. More importantly, they revisit the past not as a romantic retreat but as a way to challenge stereotypes and to redescribe, expand, and complicate the representation of people of color in a contemporary setting.

(*See also* Chapter 13, Race and Postcolonial Studies; Chapter 22, Identity Studies; Identity Politics; Multiculturalism; *and* Rights)

W. Lawrence Hogue, *University of Houston (United States)*

Further Reading

Acuna, Rodolph. *Occupied America: A History of Chicanos*. Eighth ed. New York: Pearson Publishing, 2014.

Crenshaw, Kimberle, and Neil Gotanda, eds. *Critical Race Theory: The Key Writings that Formed the Movement*. New York: The New Press, 1996.

Murray, Albert. *The Omni-Americans: Some Alternatives to the Folklore of White Supremacy*. New York: Vintage Books, 1983.

Vizenor, Gerald. *Manifest Manners: Narrative on Postindian Survivance*. Lincoln: University of Nebraska Press, 1999.

Mirror Stage

In his 1949 essay "The Mirror Stage as Formative of the I Function as Revealed in Psychoanalytic Experience," Jacques Lacan speculates about that signal event in which the human infant is propped up in front of a reflective surface and prompted by its betters to identify with what it sees. Lacan argues that, prior to this event, the infant lacks (or is as yet unburdened by) any coherent sense of identity; upon the moment of the mirror stage, the young one leans in toward its own idealized reflection and psychically sets out on a path of morphological mimicry that allows (or compels) it to start getting its act together and function as an "I" in the larger socio-symbolic order.

On Lacan's view, this self-inaugurating spectacle—a disciplinary cultural intervention always implicated in the regnant protocols of libidinal normalization—is shot through with ambiguity and ambivalence. For the outside image the infant takes in represents both itself and something *other*, an unfamiliar thing. Presenting the "I" to itself *as* an other, the mirror gives back the infant's *own* body as *some*body *else*, somebody *better*, superior in that the apparently free-standing figure singled out *by* the betters ("*there* you are," they say, "*there's* our darling little one") seems to hang together seamlessly, in a unified and autonomous way that trumps the real beholder's experiential dehiscence, agential incompetence, and suckling dependence. Self-estranged at the get-go of subjectivity, the upstart ego only ever begins to comprehend itself "extimately," in an unhappily ecstatic *mis*recognition, psychically registering if not actually becoming the very discrepancy between the sharper image of idealized coherence and corporeal wholeness that it *sees* and the abjectly mess-making, perceptually fragmented body that it *is*.

We might map the dynamics of this orthopedic encounter onto Freud's famous slogan *Wo Es war, soll Ich werden*—where id was, there ego must be, or, where it (*das Es*) was, there I (*das Ich*) must come into being. But we should note the counterintuitive coordinates, the weirdly inverted where's and there's, of this ego-boosting cartography. If we apply our everyday understanding of the difference between an "I" and an "it" to the scene of the prelinguistic human situated before a mirror, we would normally place "child" on the "personological" side of the I/self/subject and "mirror" on the "material" side of the it/thing/object. In the mirror scenario, however, these "sides" are arguably reversed: the real living body of the child is the speechless "it," while the ego or "I" initially "resides" in a manufactured contraption of deadwood and glass. Paradoxically, the living infant exits the organically *real* and begins to enter that montage of the *imaginary* and *symbolic* that Lacan calls human reality by virtue of a formally *mortifying* experience: at the spectacular moment of the mirror stage, a *specter* of humanity, launched from the "dead" side of the mirror's surface, enters and inhabits/inhibits the dumb vitality of the infant, so that in a sense it's from the subjective position of the mirror image that the Freudian slogan is articulated: where "it," that stupid, merely living body on *that* side *was*, there "I," the culturally endorsed, symbolically validated, and appropriately gendered form of personhood must be established, must move in, take over, plant the socio-symbolic's self-colonizing flag.

Of course, there's next to nothing natural about this "planting." Like everything else in human reality, the mirror in question is always ever artifice, an anthropogenetic product of labor, while the word "stage" in Lacan's phrase points less to some phase of biological development than to the subjective performance of political theater. Back behind the mirror (offstage, as it were) an endless panoply of socially produced images—pretty pictures of ideal comportment and compliant identity—lies in wait, ready to capture any fledgling human subject's eye. Stationed at what Lacan calls the threshold of the visible world, the mirror stage is our initial imaginary gateway to the ongoing operations of normativity that help put the "I" in ideology and keep ideology in the "I."

(*See also* Castration; Chapter 1, Early Theory; Chapter 7, Psychoanalytic Theory; Chapter 22, Identity Studies; Desire; Interpellation; Lacan, Jacques; Other, The; Primordial Discord; *and* Psychoanalysis)

Calvin Thomas, *Georgia State University (United States)*

Further Reading

Althusser, Louis. "Ideology and the Ideological State Apparatus [1970]." In *Lenin and Philosophy and Other Essays*. Trans. Ben Brewster. New York: Monthly Review Press, 1971. 121–76.

Lacan, Jacques. "The Mirror Stage as Formative of the I Function as Revealed in Psychoanalytic Experience [1949]." In *Écrits: A Selection*. Trans. Bruce Fink. New York: Norton, 2002. 3–9.

Nobus, Dany. "Life and Death in the Glass: A New Look at the Mirror Stage." In *Key Concepts of Lacanian Psychoanalysis*. Ed. Dany Nobus. New York: Other Press, 1998. 101–38.

Thomas, Calvin. "Lesson Five: You are not yourself—or, I (think, therefore I) is an other." In *Ten Lessons in Theory: An Introduction to Theoretical Writing*. New York: Bloomsbury, 2013. 88–121.

Modernism

Modernism can be understood as a historical period, cultural style, or aesthetic achievement. Although each of these interpretations implies some version of the other two, only modernism's aesthetic achievement has the potential to absorb us as deeply as it did the modernists themselves. This achievement consists of various artistic solutions to a problem experienced with increasing urgency during the late nineteenth and early twentieth centuries and, in some quarters, still today. This problem is the breakdown of aesthetic tradition, where that means that access to art, or to its past achievements, is no longer mediated by even the most admired work of the previous generation. It is to such a disruption that Virginia Woolf refers when saying that for "the men and women who began writing novels in 1910 or thereabouts . . . there was no English novelist living from whom they could learn their business." Although similar breaks characterize romanticism and impressionism and represent a normal feature of historical modernity, modernism's break seems unprecedentedly fundamental. For Joyce, Stravinsky, or Picasso, producing art required something more than a new sophistication of technique, a democratized idiom, or a less parochial subject matter. It was as though the arts, at least as represented by the work of recent generations, had become confused with extraneous demands and expectations. Between contemporary artists and what still made art's past achievements absorbing, a set of arbitrary requirements had interposed itself.

Modernism's solution to this problem was to make the work of art into a discovery of what art is. More than a century after the earliest modernist paintings and poems, this achievement remains poorly understood. Two aspects seem particularly challenging. First, when satisfying, the modernist's work is determinedly negative. That is, it represents the solution to a problem of knowledge that presupposes no ignorance of art. The point of negating art's traditional interests is to remove obstacles to discovering what no one familiar with the arts seriously doubts. When the human figure is eliminated from sculpture and painting, when tonality is deferred indefinitely in music, or when chronology ceases to unify narration, we experience the constitutive role of conditions we previously experienced as inert. It is the *significance* of these givens that has become difficult to see. The modernist work lays bare, not facts, but actions. And, second, these actions are no one's if not our own. The breakdown of aesthetic tradition is synonymous with a break in the bond between artist and audience. Even recognizing the image of itself in a work, the audience experiences that work as another's. The aim of the modernist's negations is to obviate this denial. When painting acknowledges the constitutive function of its support, when music discloses the event of succession in discrete sounds, and when poetry enables us to hear everyday words mean, we experience as intentional what previously seemed given. That art can always be other than it is just means for the modernist that art is only if artist and audience want it to be. Aesthetic tradition ends where our responsibility for the world begins.

(*See also* Chapter 9, Deconstruction; Chapter 12, Postmodernism; Deconstruction; *and* Postmodernism)

R. M. Berry, *Florida State University (United States)*

Further Reading

Cavell, Stanley. *Must We Mean What We Say?* Updated ed. Cambridge: Cambridge University Press, 2002.

Fried, Michael. *Art and Objecthood.* Chicago: University of Chicago Press, 1998.

Stein, Gertrude. "Composition as Explanation [1926]." *Selected Works of Gertrude Stein.* New York: Random House, 1990. 511–23.

Mourning

We say that human beings enter mourning when we have sustained a profound loss that throws us out of the quotidian and into a condition of grief and struggle with what Hamlet spoke of as the "dread"-inducing "undiscover'd country from whose bourn no traveller returns." Western cultural rituals of mourning in recent centuries have prioritized a return of the alienated individual back to the security of the collective. Lexically as well as culturally, the idea of *mourning* bridges the individual and the social. That may be because in taking us away from our communal concerns, deep grief may inaugurate a counter-social impulse, as the discussion of Sophocles's *Antigone* below elaborates.

Recent centuries have seen a deep concern with *normal* or *healthy* mourning. Sigmund Freud's designation of healthy mourning in contrast to pathological melancholia codified in a psychoanalytic register an existing cultural assumption that Philippe Ariès identifies with modern Western culture's reassessment of human destiny and meaning.

In aesthetic expression, *mourning* has been taken up most notably in elegiac registers from ancient times to the present and across geographic divisions. The elegiac genre has ancient roots, which are interestingly not limited to the topic of grief.

Elegiac lamentation often plays out the tension between the presence of the lost one and her/his/its absence through a set of genre conventions that have remained dynamic for centuries, including apostrophe and repetition. Very often, elegiac productions raise the question of whether solace is possible and what it might look like.

A "work of mourning" may effectively conserve social normativity or, by contrast, may be or seem to be disruptive. The normalizing push for social cohesiveness in US culture following the attacks of September 11, 2001 resulted in an atmosphere intensely hostile to any critique of US foreign policy. Likewise, Creon in Sophocles's ancient play *Antigone* seeks to manage his state by controlling the conditions for mourning the war dead, particularly his treasonous nephew Polyneices. Antigone transgresses state dictate by performing burial rituals for her brother Polyneices, claiming the primacy of divine law over civic authority. For Georg W. F. Hegel, Jacques Derrida, and Judith Butler, among others, the play's staging of a conflict between natural law and civil law reflects the ways in which the chasm opened by death's "undiscover'd country" may induce conditions of grief and mourning disruptive to the social order and even the nation-state itself.

In our contemporary world, there are many such cultural loci of intense conflict between individual and collective works of (signifying) mourning, including innumerable cases in which social mores or authoritative decrees have sought to manage individual or collective works of mourning and the management of dead bodies. In recent decades, US culture in particular has sought to manage the visibility and burial of the bodies of soldiers, victims of torture, persons of color shot by police officers, and many others.

Mourning must be understood as a cultural mode that integrates a negotiation between the unknowability of death's "undiscover'd country" and the perhaps normalizing demands of communal life within a literal or figurative polis on the other.

(*See also* Chapter 7, Psychoanalytic Theory; *and* Freud, Sigmund)

Ashley Byock, *Edgewood College (United States)*

Further Reading

Ariès, Philippe. *The Hour of Our Death* [1977]. Trans. Helen Weaver. New York: Alfred A. Knopf, Inc., 1981.

Eng, David L., and David Kazanjian. *Loss: The Politics of Mourning*. Berkeley: University of California Press, 2003.

Freud, Sigmund. "Mourning and Melancholia." In *The Standard Edition of the Complete Psychological Works of Sigmund Freud*. Volume XIV [1914-1916]. Ed. and trans. James Strachey. London: Hogarth Press, 1917.

Multiculturalism

Popularized in both literary studies and political discourse from the 1960s to the 1990s, multiculturalism signals attention to cultural diversity within a national imaginary and polity. In literary and cultural studies terms, multiculturalism broadens the range of contributors to include those identified by racial, ethnic, religious, linguistic, sexual, and gendered (and, to a lesser extent, socioeconomic) diversity as opposed to traditional literary canons in European and now democratic, settler colonial states which favor white, male, Christian authors. More radically, multiculturalism may challenge the very notion of canonicity to expose the ways in which it has historically served to marginalize or to silence already disempowered voices. In terms of state policy, demonstrated in legislation such as the Canadian Multiculturalism Act (1985), multiculturalism bolsters liberal pluralism by investing state resources in the recognition of and support for selected minority or marginalized communities. Political multiculturalism articulates an alternative to policies that promote assimilation, on the one hand, or xenophobic nationalism, on the other; however, it may also be a form of diversity management in service of hegemonic state interests. Whether literary or political, multiculturalism is tied to what Charles Taylor has described as "the politics of recognition" based upon categories of identity.

Multiculturalism's proponents emphasize the critical necessity of interrogating the terms and conditions of national belonging, of recognizing an individual's right to cultural identity, and of broadening the definition of diversity beyond its familiar association with race to include other markers of identity. Critics turn to these same elements to underscore multiculturalism's limitations in advancing robust, democratic perspectives and policies. First, multiculturalism complicates but does not fundamentally contest the key components of liberalism: the individual, the state, and the concepts of individual freedom and choice which capital markets easily co-opt. Multicultural perspectives emerge against the backdrop of the nation-state, and that emergence often depends upon a quasi-essentialist reading of identity (personal and national) as well as an assumption that a given author or text represents the culture in question. Thus, to read from or about a particular multicultural perspective may paradoxically render cultural specificity legible in ways that have otherwise been foreclosed even as it runs the risk of mythologizing the identity at hand and/or reducing the author or text to a fixture of narrowly defined otherness. To read from or about an Asian-American perspective, for example, may presume that there is such an identity as Asian-American that is authentic, stable, and representable and that the text, whatever else it may be doing, reflects that perspective. Alternatively, such a reading—when grounded in historical context, cultural production arising from that context, and material, lived experience—may reveal patterns of shared experience that have been subsumed by dominant narratives as well as the ways culture as a dynamic force manifests in imaginative, literary expression.

Second, multiculturalism's fraught relationship with anti-racist and Marxist critical discourses and its rootedness in the political and literary imagination of the state limit its emancipatory capacity. When multiculturalism substitutes for critical race studies, for example, it runs the risk of erasing the underpinnings of structural racism in favor of a focus on racialized cultural expressions. In such instances, acknowledging diversity, especially through various forms of cultural commodification, can obscure anti-racist politics. Because the immediate context of any given multicultural approach is the nation-state, critics hailing from postcolonial, feminist, and Marxist studies argue, respectively, that it can leave structures of domination intact (e.g., seeking tolerance as opposed to a redistribution of rights and resources), ignore schisms and hierarchies within cultural groups, and miss potential alliances among those rendered disposable by transnational capitalism.

To the extent that multiculturalism addresses cultural expression as dynamic and as historically, politically, and economically grounded, it provides a lens onto the significance of cultural belonging in relation to institutions of the state as well as of cultural production.

(*See also* Chapter 22, Identity Studies; Chapter 27, Antitheory; Culture Wars; *and* Identity Politics)

Alexandra S. Moore, *Binghamton University (United States)*

Further Reading

Benhabib, Seyla. *The Claims of Culture: Equality and Diversity in the Global Era.* Princeton: Princeton University Press, 2002.

Fraser, Nancy, and Axel Honneth. *Redistribution or Recognition? A Political-Philosophical Exchange.* New York: Verso, 2003.

Gordon, Avery F., and Christopher Newfield, eds. *Mapping Multiculturalism.* Minneapolis: University of Minnesota Press, 1996.

Taylor, Charles. *Multiculturalism: Examining the Politics of Recognition.* Ed. Amy Gutmann. Princeton: Princeton University Press, 1994.

Multitude

In classical political theory, the term *multitude* typically refers to a collectivity that is not unified under the auspices of "the people." Whereas "the people" are identifiable, numerable (e.g., they can be counted in a census) and manageable through apparatuses of social control (prisons, schools, hospitals, etc.), the multitude, like a mob or rabble, cannot so easily be identified, numbered, or controlled. The authority of the state is, in principle, justified by appeal to the will of the people but threatened by the unruly, resistant will of the multitude.

Historically, political thinkers have frequently interpreted such characteristics of the multitude as indicating that it cannot rule itself and therefore must be contained, tamed, and ruled. One exception is the Enlightenment philosopher Baruch Spinoza. Spinoza found in the multitude a potential for political praxis and collective association that preserves rather than effaces multiplicity and difference. Spinoza's multitude has proved useful to many contemporary Marxist theorists seeking models for mobilizing widespread opposition to global capitalism while also preserving and valuing the distinctiveness of separate oppositional groups and individuals.

Thus, the multitude is in many ways today's successor to the classical Marxist notion of the proletariat. Michael Hardt and Antonio Negri outline a number of historical transitions from the modern proletariat to the postmodern multitude. As capitalism has transformed from industrial capitalism predicated on national markets to global neoliberal capitalism founded on international free trade, privatization, and deregulation, the nature of labor has likewise shifted. Postmodern production, in Hardt and Negri's terms, is "immaterial"—that is, capitalism exploits not just labor power but "general intellect" (Marx's term for everything humans are capable of): workers still produce durable goods, of course, but increasingly, they also produce care (think nurses or childcare workers), services (fast-food workers, Uber drivers), knowledge and information (Google, patents on genetic code), social relations (Facebook, crowdsourcing), and so forth. The structure of capitalist production has shifted from a sequential and hierarchically organized assembly-line model to a highly dispersed network model of semi-autonomous productive agents. Notwithstanding the many negative effects these changes have on workers (leisure time is dissolving, jobs are increasingly precarious, etc.). Hardt and Negri claim that the regime of immaterial production also provides novel opportunities for resistance and revolt. Just as industrial capitalism unwittingly created conditions for organized labor and large-scale resistance by bringing formerly dispersed workers together under the factory roof, post-industrial capitalism's reliance on communication and social networks has opened up avenues for opposition by the multitude.

The multitude, like a photographic negative of post-industrial capitalism, functions by coordinating political agents (activists, affinity groups, community groups, etc.) in a horizontal relation of collaboration, as opposed to the hierarchical party structures that opposed industrial capitalism. Movements such as WTO protests beginning in Seattle in 1999, the Arab Spring, the Occupy Movement, Black Lives Matter, and others are organized horizontally as coalitions, not vertically like a traditional political party or a revolutionary vanguard. Current emphasis on intersectional identities likewise acknowledges the need for decentering power and recognizing the coexistence of plural differences instead of ranking one dimension of identity above others, while the model of allyship similarly guards against dangers of unifying disparate identities under a single, privileged identity.

For many political and social movements, then—including the "movement of movements" against global capitalism—the multitude provides a useful way of coordinating diverse forms of opposition. Far from being a fatal liability, the impossibility of numbering or demarcating the multitude or subsuming differences under a single identity stands, for adherents, as its greatest strength.

(*See also* Biopolitics; Capacity; Chapter 15, Biopower and Biopolitics; Chapter 22, Identity Studies; Labor; *and* Negri, Antonio)

James Liner, *University of Washington Tacoma (United States)*

Further Reading

Hardt, Michael, and Antonio Negri. *Empire.* Cambridge: Harvard University Press, 2000.

Hardt, Michael, and Antonio Negri. *Multitude: War and Democracy in the Age of Empire.* New York: Penguin, 2004.

Virno, Paolo. *A Grammar of the Multitude: For an Analysis of Contemporary Forms of Life.* Trans. Isabella Bertoletti, James Cascaito, and Andrea Casson. Los Angeles: Semiotext(e), 2004.

N

Nachträglichkeit (See *Deferred Action*)

Nancy, Jean-Luc

Jean-Luc Nancy (born 1940) began his career in the 1970s and has been a prolific thinker and writer publishing more than ninety works over a period spanning nearly five decades. His thinking can be situated in the wake of deconstruction (he was a close friend of Jacques Derrida) but more broadly can be placed within the trajectory opened up by the legacies of speculative idealism, romanticism, phenomenology, and existential phenomenology. Most often associated with his fundamental reworking of Heideggerian thought, Nancy in fact engages quite extensively with a broad range of canonical European philosophy. Key thinkers include, beyond Martin Heidegger, René Descartes, Emmanuel Kant, G. W. F. Hegel, and Friedrich Nietzsche, as well as, more implicitly, important figures in French phenomenology such as Maurice Merleau-Ponty. Nancy's thinking needs, first and foremost, to be understood in the context of attempts to overturn, overcome, or otherwise deconstruct the tradition of metaphysics within Western thought, a gesture principally associated with Nietzsche, Heidegger, and Derrida respectively. Nancy has consistently sought to elaborate ways in which the multiplicity of existence can be thought in all its dimensions in the absence of any founding essence, substance, or of any overarching principle,

either transcendent or immanent, which would ground that multiplicity in a horizon of unity or totality. Yet he has done so via a strikingly diverse series of commentaries, thought experiments, and philosophical gestures which themselves defy unification into a consistent whole or system. These include anti-foundationalist readings of Kant and Descartes in the 1970s and 1980s, readings that further elaborate the Heideggerian destruction of modern philosophical subjectivity, as well as the rethinking of community and of the political in the early to mid-1980s. This period also sees the emergence of Nancy's first elaboration of an ontology of coexistence in the absence of any shared identity or essence in the same period. These early deconstructive commentaries and attempts to rethink community as coexistence are further developed in the mature phase of Nancy's philosophy which runs roughly from the late 1980s to the present day. In the 1990s his thinking of shared finitude, of the sense of the world, and of being in the singular plural, all articulate an understanding of existence thought in the absence of any foundation or ground. It is in this context that Nancy comes to think sense, understood as a material and yet in some way meaningful, relation of contact and simultaneous separation of singular existents, as the very foundationless "stuff" or being of being itself. Nancy's vision is one of a relational universe where entities and things, both human and nonhuman, organic and inorganic, are constituted and come to presence as such only in their material spacing and reciprocal touching (in distance) each with the other. This relational vision of singular plural being opens onto a broad range of engagement with questions of embodiment, world disclosure, politics, justice, art and the visual arts, Christianity, and also with poetry and the relation of philosophy to literature and to the aesthetic in general.

(*See also* Presence; *and* Worldiness)

Ian James, *Cambridge University (United Kingdom)*

Further Reading

James, Ian. *The Fragmentary Demand.* Stanford: Stanford University Press, 2006.

Morin, Marie-Eve. *Jean-Luc Nancy.* Cambridge: Polity, 2012.

Nancy, Jean-Luc (with Jean-Christophe Bailly). *The Compearance* [1991]. Trans. Tracy B. Strong. Newbury Park: Sage, 1992.

Nancy, Jean-Luc. *Corpus* [1992]. Trans. R. A. Rand. New York: Fordham University Press, 2008.

Nancy, Jean-Luc. *The Sense of the World* [1993]. Trans. Jeffrey S. Librett. Minneapolis: University of Minnesota Press, 1997.

Negation

In the Hegelian and Marxist critical traditions, contradiction refers to the way in which seemingly static identities can be shown to contain their own negations, thus revealing the more dynamic or fluid condition of reality. In Hegel's dialectical thought, the identity of concept is shown to be related to its opposite through the principle of contradiction or negation, which then leads to the overcoming, cancelling, and preserving (in German, the term *Aufhebung* embraces all these meanings)

of each in a higher unity. This is sometimes envisioned as a triadic structure, in which the thesis is countered by its antithesis, a contradiction leading to a synthesis (which in turn may form the thesis of another set of relations, ad infinitum). Hence "Being" is shown to include "Non-Being," for example, which can be overcome, preserved, and canceled in the notion of "Becoming." A given concept contains its opposite (e.g., inner/outer, universality/particularity, quality/quantity), which reveals the degree to which the categories themselves are unstable or dynamic. For Hegel, only what is whole is true, so the *totality*, which includes those elements or moments that have been overcome, is crucial to understanding anything and everything.

From this Hegelian point of departure, various Marxist traditions have affirmed that contradiction lies at the heart of social formations or of existence itself. Mao Zedong, following Lenin, asserted "contradiction is present in all processes of objectively existing things and of subjective thought and permeates all these processes from beginning to end." Marxists have identified fundamental contradictions within the capitalist mode of production—for example, the vast productive power has produced, simultaneously, enormous wealth and extreme poverty and immiseration—which logically ought to lead to a revolutionary overcoming of this condition through the institution of socialism. Contradiction or negation also serves as a critical purpose in demonstrating the falseness of oversimplified visions of the social order, as may be seen in the critical theory of Theodor Adorno and the Frankfurt School, which generally insisted upon *negation* as a necessary philosophical and political act.

(*See also* Adorno, Theodor; Chapter 4, Marxism; Hegel, Georg W. F.; *and* Semiotic Square)

Robert T. Tally Jr., *Texas State University (United States)*

Further Reading

Adorno, Theodor W. *Negative Dialectics*
[1966]. Trans. E. B. Ashton. London:
Continuum, 2007.

Althusser, Louis. "Contradiction and Overdetermination." *For Marx* [1965]. Trans.
Ben Brewster. London: Verso, 2005.

Spencer, Lloyd. *Hegel for Beginners*.
Cambridge: Icon Books, 1996.

Zedong, Mao. *On Contradiction* [1937].
Peking: Foreign Languages Press, 1967.

Negri, Antonio

With his first collaboration with American literary theorist Michael Hardt—*Empire* in 2000—Antonio Negri (born 1933) burst into prominence in the English-speaking world, as one of the most original, important, and controversial theorists of *globalization*: a term holding currency and attention around the turn of the millennium. With the subsequent volumes *Multitude* and *Commonwealth*, Hardt's and Negri's trilogy transcended the boundaries of academic publishing, their work being reviewed and discussed in *The New York Times*, the *Los Angeles Review of Books*, the *Wall Street Journal*, the *London Review of Books*, the *Guardian*, the *Independent*, in addition to myriad journals across multiple academic disciplines. While these collaborations with Hardt turned Negri into an internationally recognized intellectual, he has been well known in both academic and activist circles since the 1960s. A central figure in the development of the Italian New Left in the sixties and seventies, Negri gained notoriety for his arrest—along with thousands of Italian activists and intellectuals—in 1979 on multiple charges of alleged involvement with the Red Brigades—this was followed by a four-year incarceration awaiting trial, flight to France in 1984, where he lived in exile until returning to Italy, and imprisonment, in

1997, which ended only after he gained full release in 2003.

Negri's early work within the Italian New Left has profoundly influenced the development of post-Marxist social/political and cultural theory. The *INL*'s *operaismo*—workerism—movement of the sixties was grounded in a "reversal of perspective" (first explicitly articulated by Mario Tronti) that read the development of late capital as being driven not by the control exerted by capitalist managerial apparatuses, but by the struggle of workers against the imposition of work. Negri expanded this reversal to the level of the entire cultural sphere beginning in the early-1970s, moving beyond analyzing the struggles of "mass workers" in industrial complexes, to those of the "social worker" extending beyond factories to include all realms of culture and social life—students, feminists, immigrants, squatters, and others—and all struggles against social control. This same expansion of the reversal of perspective led Negri and his collaborators in the nineties, and beyond, to analyze social life in terms of the struggles of a now globalized "multitude" (a term borrowed from Spinoza) against the force of "empire" seeking to impose order upon, and limit the productive power of, the multitude, again, across all social, political, economic, and cultural spheres; struggles for, and on behalf of the "common," or the ensemble of all things—material objects, information, discourses, relationships, affects—that emerge within, and are constituted by, and necessary to, social life.

The many references to literary figures and tropes in Negri's work expands with his collaboration with literary theorist Hardt, and reaches fruition in three plays written and performed between 2004 and 2006, and collected in *Trilogy of Resistance*. In them, Negri gives literary expression to the central themes of the production of new social subjects, and the relationship between revolutionary subjectivity, and power and violence—themes central to his work over the past five decades.

(*See also* Biopolitics; Capacity; Chapter 15, Biopower and Biopolitics; Chapter 26, Affect Studies; Globalization; Labor; Multitude; *and* Sovereignty)

Pierre Lamarche, *Utah Valley University (United States)*

Further Reading

Casarino, Cesare, and Antonio Negri. *In Praise of the Common: A Conversation on Philosophy and Politics.* Minneapolis: University of Minnesota Press, 2008.

Lamarche, Pierre, Max Rosenkrantz, and David Sherman, eds. *Reading Negri: Marxism in the Age of Empire.* Chicago: Open Court, 2011.

Murphy, Timothy S. *Antonio Negri.* Cambridge: Polity Press, 2012.

Negri, Antonio. *Marx and Foucault.* Trans. Ed Emery. Cambridge: Polity Press, 2017.

Negritude

Often associated with the works of Aimé Césaire, Léopold Sédar Senghor, and Léon Damas, Negritude is a literary, intellectual, and cultural movement that flourished in France in the 1950s. The movement found a candid expression with the publication of Senghor's *Anthologie de la nouvelle poesie négre et malgache de langue française* in 1948, which also featured Jean-Paul Sartre's essay "Orphée noir." Negritude gives continuation to Harlem Renaissance's valorization of distinct Black national and cultural identity. In fact, Langston Hughes and Richard Wright were big role models for the French writers and intellectuals to shape their own artistic and intellectual career. The Bandung Conference of 1955 provided more inspiration to the French Black poets and writers in their pursuit of Black national and cultural identity, leading them to hold the First Congress of Negro Writers and Artists in Paris in 1956. Needless-to-say, Negritude is an important moment in Black cultural history.

In the face of Western onslaught on people of African descent, the Black poets, writers, and intellectuals from around the world tried to find a voice that, unlike the European degradation and dehumanization of Africa, depicted Africa and its people possessing spirituality, human compassion, and dignified subjectivity. Despite Western capitalist objectification of Africa and its people, Negritude emphasized Africa's historical and cultural uniqueness in the world, a uniqueness that does not always lend itself to easy translation. In his poem "Congo," for example, Senghor presents Africa as a loving woman, who, like the mighty Congo River, is full of life force. Africa here is mother of all creatures, and a lover to those that seek cure to their ailing bodies and souls. To suggest Africa's untranslatable aspect, Senghor uses words in their original African forms such as guimm, koras, balaphon, Koyaté, Saô, ouzougou, and gongo. Even though the phrase associated with the West appears only once throughout the poem ("the White Man's soapy tunes"), the poem foregrounds Africa's vitality and sustaining power in the backdrop of Europe's implacable thirst for Africa's resources.

Senghor's poem has its literary precedence in such earlier works of Black writers and intellectuals as Langston Hughes's "The Negro Speaks of Rivers (1921)." Composed in the early 1920s, Hughes's poem celebrates rivers, and the earth. The speaker compares his body with the body of the earth, and claims that he has known the rivers. This knowledge comes to the speaker, however, not through the Enlightenment with observation and classification, but through bodily feeling. By comparing his soul with ancient rivers such as the Nile, the Euphrates, and the Mississippi, the speaker in Hughes's poem suggests that as long as these rivers flow Black people will live, too. By extension, despite the suffering that the rivers—read nature at large—have faced from capitalist commodification, they have maintained their flow, strength, and vastness. By evoking the rivers' indomitable presence despite civilizations' ravages, the speaker suggests the suffering of the Black folk in the Southern United States, and believes that racial injustices that Black people have faced in the United States and around the world will not destroy their souls, which have grown "deep like the rivers."

(*See also* Chapter 13, Race and Postcolonial Studies; *and* Creolization)

Ubaraj Katawal, *Valdosta State University* *(United States)*

Further Reading

Irele, F. Abiola. *The Negritude Moment: Explorations in Francophone African and Caribbean Literature and Thought*. Trenton: Africa World Press, 2011.

Jack, Belinda Elizabeth. *Negritude and Literary Criticism: The History and Theory of "Negro-African" Literature in French*. Westport: Greenwood Press, 1996.

Senghor, Léopold Sédar. *The Collected Poems*. Charlottesville: University Press of Virginia, 1991.

Neoliberalism

Neoliberalism, the doctrine that market exchange is an ethic in itself, is a broadly used term that refers to an economic and political project that rose to prominence in the 1980s and continues to the present.

Use of the term though can be confusing because it was coined in post-First World War Germany by the Freiburg School; is sometimes associated with Friedrich Hayek, Lionel Robbins, and the 1930s London School of Economics; is at other times associated with the work of Milton Friedman and the emergence of the Chicago School of economics in the 1960s; and is at still other times associated with the *neoliberalismo* of Latin American pro-market economists of the 1970s. Some even trace the foundations of neoliberalism to eighteenth-century thought—alternately, to the French Physiocrat's laissez-faire economics (fl. 1756–88), to the classical (laissez-faire and free market) economics of Scottish philosopher Adam Smith, or even to the social and political philosophy of British utilitarian Jeremy Bentham. Critics of the term sometimes point to its contested genealogy as evidence for dismissing it wholesale.

The so-called golden age of controlled capitalism (1945–75) preceded the emergence of the neoliberal project. It was inspired by the economic and political thought of John Maynard Keynes who advocated for the market but not the free market. Keynes believed that public spending by the government should be increased during economic recessions to spur growth, and decreased during periods of growth to keep inflation down. This project was scrapped during the first wave of neoliberalism in the 1980s by US president Ronald Reagan (1981–88) and British prime minister Margaret Thatcher (1979–90), both of whom shared the neoliberal belief that government is inefficient and strove to end the Keynesian era of "big government." The second wave of neoliberalism in the 1990s was forwarded by the market globalism of US president William "Bill" Clinton (1993–2001) and the Third Way of British prime minister Tony Blair (1997–2007), both of whom continued the neoconservative hyper-patriotism, militarism, neglect of the environment, and rejection of multiculturalism of first-wave neoliberalism. Also, both waves were marked by increasing privatization, strengthening of private property rights, market deregulation, corporate mergers and takeovers, and decreasing state intervention and support for social provisions and public goods.

The ideology of neoliberalism champions consumerism, global trading, and international free markets all aimed at producing a better world. Neoliberal governance advocates individualism (or radical self-interest), competition, decentralization, strategic plans, cost-benefit analyses, outcomes management, and performance-based funding. Its proponents believe that the world is structured by equations—and that it is everyone's job to maximize their economic, social, and political positions through mastery of these equations. Also, its proponents believe that everything is part of a market, and if it is not, "such as land, water, education, health care, social security, and environmental pollution," as David Harvey points out in *A Brief History of Neoliberalism* (2005), then these markets must be created, by the state, if necessary. Moreover, the neoliberal project argues that public value is *determined* by the market. The promise of neoliberalism, says Maurizio Lazzarato in *The Making of the Indebted Man* (2012), was that it would allow everyone the opportunity to be a shareholder, an owner, and an entrepreneur. But for Lazzarato, however, neoliberalism's "entrepreneurial man" soon gave way to the "indebted man," who now dominates the global economic landscape.

Since the late 1970s, there has been a wide-ranging critique of neoliberalism. In his 1978–79 lectures at the Collège de France, Michel Foucault explains how "neo-liberals," at least in the United States anyway, "try to apply economic analysis to a series of objects, to domains of behavior or conduct which were not market forms of behavior

or conduct; they attempt to apply economic analysis to marriage, the education of children, and criminality, for example." Henry Giroux, one of the most-outspoken critics of the neoliberal project, describes it in *The Terror of Neoliberalism* (2004) as "an ideology and politics buoyed by the spirit of a market fundamentalism that subordinates the art of democratic politics to the rapacious laws of a market economy that expands its reach to include all aspects of social life within the dictates and values of market-driven society." And William Davies describes it in *The Happiness Industry* (2015) as a "depressive-competitive disorder" that "arises because the injunction to achieve a higher utility score—be that measured in money or physical symptoms—becomes privatized." For him, the authority in neoliberalism "consists simply in measuring, rating, comparing and contrasting the strong and the weak without judgment, showing the weak how much stronger they might be, and confirming to the strong that they are winning, at least for the time being."

The eviscerating consequences of the neoliberal imperatives for corporate managerialism, instrumentalism, rationalization, and austerity in social, political, and educational policy and practice have been widely discussed. Harvey's *Brief History* surveys its economic and political dangers, while Giroux's *The Terror of Neoliberalism* links it to the rise of authoritarianism, militarism, and the eclipse of democracy and democratic values. Others, like Jeffrey R. Di Leo in *Higher Education under Late Capitalism* (2017), show how academic identity has been recalibrated by the neoliberal project, and in *Corporate Humanities in Higher Education* (2014) how the humanities have been reshaped by it. There is also a growing body of work that explores its implications for contemporary culture and literature, with David Harvey's *The Condition of Postmodernity* (1989) providing a fine starting point for the cultural consequences of neoliberalism. In short, neoliberalism is a broad door through which a dominant economic and political project has entered into the study of literature and culture.

(*See also* Biopolitics; Capacity; Capitalism; Chapter 11, Cultural Studies; Chapter 13, Race and Postcolonial Studies; Chapter 15, Biopower and Biopolitics; Chapter 19, Media Studies; Chapter 21, Late Capitalism; Chapter 25, University Studies; Class; Control; Debt; Democracy; Free Market; Labor; Postmodernism; Surveillance; Terror; Thanatopolitics; *and* University)

Jeffrey R. Di Leo, *University of Houston-Victoria (United States)*

Further Reading

Di Leo, Jeffrey R. *Higher Education under Late Capitalism: Identity, Conduct, and the Neoliberal Condition.* New York: Palgrave Macmillan, 2017.

Giroux, Henry. *The Terror of Neoliberalism: Authoritarianism and the Eclipse of Democracy.* Boulder: Paradigm, 2004.

Harvey, David. *A Brief History of Neoliberalism.* New York: Oxford University Press, 2005.

Huehls, Mitchum, and Rachel Greenwald Smith, eds. *Neoliberalism and Contemporary Literary Culture.* Baltimore: Johns Hopkins University Press, 2017.

Lazzarato, Maurizio. *The Making of the Indebted Man: An Essay on the Neoliberal Condition* [2011]. Trans. Joshua David Gordon. Los Angeles: Semiotext(e), 2012.

Neopragmatism

Neopragmatism names the revival of interest in the American pragmatist philosophy originally associated with Charles Sanders Peirce, William James, and John Dewey (active from 1870 to 1940). Its most prominent figure was Richard Rorty whose 1979 book, *Philosophy and the Mirror of Nature*, introduced Dewey (especially) to literary theorists by placing him in the company of Martin Heidegger and Ludwig Wittgenstein, while repudiating the Anglo-American philosophical tradition to which Rorty had previously been a prominent contributor. Rorty's apostasy made him a pariah for most philosophers—and a hero to the "theorists." In literary studies, Stanley Fish and Barbara Herrnstein Smith were the most noteworthy figures to adopt pragmatist themes that placed them, like Rorty, in dialogue, even if often at odds, with French thinkers like Derrida. By the early 2000s, when other famous philosophers, notably Hilary Putnam and Robert Brandom, followed Rorty's lead, even philosophy departments began to engage with neopragmatist themes.

Neopragmatism's closest affinity with postmodern theory resides in its anti-foundational anti-realism. We have no unmediated access to a mind-independent reality—and every piece of knowledge is produced in the motivated interaction of humans with the nonhuman. The narrative of those interactions over time constitutes history, while our current set of beliefs about the world constitutes culture. We have no way to locate a ground or foundation that would prove the truth of those beliefs. In the classic pragmatist formulation: "Truth is what is good in the way of belief." That is, truth is what works in current circumstances to get one the results aimed for. All our beliefs are fallible, open to revision when they prove inadequate to the situations in which they are deployed.

Neopragmatism also demotes reason. For Rorty (following James), our convictions (generated by temperament or received from our culture) come first and our reasons for holding them second. Plus Rorty is skeptical that reasoned argument changes minds very often. Symbols and stories are much more effective. He often refused to engage his critics on their grounds, preferring instead to offer an alternative vision. Let's stop talking in this way (about foundations and transcendental conditions), he would suggest, and start talking in terms of local influences and specific goals.

The most important goal is the preservation and enhancement of democracy (where Rorty is most indebted to Dewey). The commitment to democracy should take priority over any allegiance to philosophy. There is no philosophical justification for democracy. Rather, it should be understood as the political form that has evolved in certain places in the world—and has proved an imperfect, but fairly effective, way to substitute contentious debate and elections for more directly violent means to handle the distribution of power and resources. Rorty admits his view is "ethnocentric" insofar as it affirms the political form his society has adopted—and that he has no culture-independent reasons to offer for why another society should adopt the same form.

Rorty couples his democratic allegiance with a version of liberalism that, unlike the views of Kant and Habermas, does not rely on universalist foundations. Rather, liberalism, for him, expresses the desire to extend the benefits of material prosperity and protection against violence and humiliation to as many people as possible. The hardest ethical project is to overcome the tendency of people to care only for those in a fairly narrow circle (of family or ethnicity or other such groupings). Liberalism is sentiment based—and the goal is to increase the numbers of people with whom one can sympathize.

In literary studies, Smith aligned pragmatism's insistence that all value judgments are contextual with the ongoing assault on the canon that emerged alongside the rise of feminist and black studies' approaches to literature. Fish—and his Johns Hopkins's colleagues Walter Benn Michaels and Steven Knapp—pushed back against the metaphysical and transcendental proclivities of French theory by insisting that "theory" in no way influences practice. Thus, for example, they argue that Saussure's theoretical account on the "sign" holds no consequences for the way any reader understands a literary text. Such understandings are always the product of the immediate interaction of reader with text within a contingent set of cultural expectations. Of course, this description of reading is, itself, a general theoretical account. The claims of the neopragmatist literary critics and a set of counter-arguments from skeptics are collected in the influential volume, *Against Theory* (1985).

(*See also* Antitheory; Chapter 8, Rhetoric; Chapter 27, Antitheory; Fish, Stanley; Rhetoric; *and* Rorty, Richard)

John McGowan, *University of North Carolina, Chapel Hill (United States)*

Further Reading

Herrnstein Smith, Barbara. *Contingencies of Value: Alternative Perspectives for Critical Theory*. Cambridge: Harvard University Press, 1988.

Mitchell, W. J. T., ed. *Against Theory: Literary Studies and the New Pragmatism*. Chicago: University of Chicago Press, 1985.

Rorty, Richard. *Consequences of Pragmatism (Essays: 1972-1980)*. Minneapolis: University of Minnesota Press, 1982.

Network Society

Network Society refers to those forms of social order that emerged in the last third of the twentieth century. It is characterized by the historical and cultural impact of electronic technologies including the New Media of telecommunication and computation systems and the subsequent primacy of information as a metaphor for communication and organization. These technologies form the horizon for particular configurations of social systems that were established in modernity including economy, law, and the nation-state. It is most commonly associated with Manuel Castells' use of the term in his *The Rise of the Network Society* (1996), the first volume in his trilogy: *The Information Age: Economy, Society and Culture*.

Network has two, interrelated, definitions. The verb to network means to form connections such as engineering relations between elements in a system of communication or in a social context, to develop interpersonal relationships according to shared interests. The noun network refers to a form of organization involving a set of interconnected nodes (points of connection) within which information flows. The identity of a node will depend upon the conditions of the network within which it is situated; for example it might be a person, building, or an internet protocol address. This definition is, by necessity, abstract as it can be applied to a wide variety of phenomena including economies, political organizations, telecommunication systems and so forth. Networks are understood to be: interconnected; decentralized; dynamic (i.e., flexible and nonlinear) and unbounded. The internet exemplifies these qualities; it is, undoubtedly the dominant network of the contemporary moment.

In terms of production and economics the post-Fordist and post-industrial practices that emerged since the 1960s are best described as network processes. For instance the postwar phenomena of containerization, in which standardized shipping containers are transported between a network of shipping, roads, and trains radically changed the nature of trade in a global system that transcended nation-states. Technologies including mechanized production and computing brought mass-scale changes in labor and employment. The collapse of the Bretton Woods System of international economic management in the early 1970s, along with the American abandonment of the gold standard heralded the subsequent market fundamentalism of neoliberalism and its logic of deregulation and privatization in economic networks underwritten by the logic of speculation. It is no coincidence that this occurred alongside the military-industrial complex's development of telecommunication and computing networks including the internet (and its predecessor Arpanet) and the World Wide Web (in the early 1990s) that facilitated the rapid and massive exchange of information across networks of communication and control.

In this sense Network Society describes the conditions and cultures of late capitalism. Fredric Jameson argues that these conditions are synonymous with both postmodernity and the emergence of "the world system" in which the power of nation-states is effaced by global networks of capital and communication where information becomes the primary unit of capitalist exchange. In such cultures power no longer operates according to a disciplinary logic (as Michel Foucault observed of modernity) but rather *control* where power is distributed across networks (as Gilles Deleuze claimed in his famous "postscript" essay). Subjectivity is similarly understood to be both distributed across different communicative networks and also mediated by them; in other words human identity does not exist a priori but is in fact constituted by those different networks within which it is situated (such as social media). Hence, the conditions of the Network Society present radical challenges to the account of autonomous and rational humanity that emerges in the European Enlightenment. As in other accounts of the conditions of subjectivity in late capitalism, such as posthumanism and The Anthropocene, humans are identified as enmeshed within and reliant upon existing economic, technological, and ecological networks that are beyond their control. The Network Society thus points to a political imperative for forms of cultural production to mimic its effects, map its operations and reveal its conditions in order to open it up for critique and the proposal of alternatives.

(*See also* Actor Network Theory; Chapter 20, Digital Humanities; Cyberculture; Cybernetics; Deleuze, Gilles; Jameson, Fredric; Postmodernism; *and* Systems Theory)

Francis Halsall, *National College of Art and Design, Dublin (Ireland)* and *University of the Free State, Bloemfontaine (South Africa)*

Further Reading
Castells, Manuel. *The Rise of the Network Society*. Second ed. Oxford: Blackwell Publishing, 2000.
Galloway, Alexander R., and Eugene Thacker. *The Exploit*. Minneapolis: University of Minnesota Press, 2007.
Jagoda, Patrick. *Network Aesthetics*. Chicago: The University of Chicago Press, 2016.

Neurohumanities (*See* Neuroscience)

Neuroscience

In recent decades, brain research has advanced enormously, due principally to the development of noninvasive procedures for the study of brain function. This advance has inspired researchers in fields outside neuroscience—such as literary and film studies—to focus more on the brain, usually by drawing on findings and theories from neuroscientific researchers. This work in "neurohumanities" may be broadly divided into three orientations: empirical, historicist, and what we might term "integrationist."

"Empirical" neurohumanities work recruits the methods of neuroscience and related fields to the study of literature and film. For example, some researchers have undertaken to study what brain scans reveal when people read novels by Jane Austen. The empirical approach has been developed most extensively in film study.

Historicist neurohumanities may or may not attend to recent research in neuroscience. It is often focused on the "materialist" ideas of earlier historical periods and the ways in which understandings of the brain (and related psycho-physical objects, such as humors) affected representations of human cognition or emotion, particularly in literature. At the same time, historicists have raised some of the strongest criticisms of the recent enthusiasm for neuroscience. In particular, historicists have often been concerned that humanists accept the highly interpretive claims of brain researchers as if they were simply established facts.

The strongest influence of neuroscience on the humanities may be found in the third category. This work is "integrationist" in the sense that it brings together neuroscientific research with ideas from other fields to produce more encompassing accounts of literary production, literary structure, or literary reception and response. The most obvious group of this sort comprises cognitive literary and film critics. Cognitive critics combine neurological research with behavioral, linguistic, anthropological, or other forms of disciplinary study to examine particular topics in the humanities. For example, literary cognitivists interested in conceptual metaphor may draw on linguistic analyses along with functional MRI studies of brain activation in response to standard or novel metaphors.

In recent years, emotion has become an important topic in neuroscience and in the humanities. Work in the latter area may be roughly divided into two broad, integrationist tendencies. One sets out to follow neuroscientific and related research systematically. Writers of this orientation examine literature or film in relation to the basic structure of emotion episodes, the interconnection between emotion and varieties of memory, or other topics in "affective science." The second orientation, often referred to as "affect theory," tends to be more selective in its use of neuroscience. Affect theorists take up elements of mainstream, post-structuralist literary and film theory, often combining these with findings from neuroscience that promise to contribute to larger—often social and political—purposes.

Despite pockets of skepticism, neuroscientific work has established itself firmly within literary and film study. It seems unlikely that there will be widespread conversion from humanities to neurohumanities. But it also seems unlikely that attention to neuroscience will disappear. Indeed, it is likely to grow as one important contributor to cultural study generally.

(*See also* Affect; Chapter 26, Affect Studies; Emotions; Ethical Criticism; Materialism; Memory; Systems Theory; *and* Trauma)

Patrick Colm Hogan, *University of Connecticut (United States)*

Further Reading

Hogan, Patrick Colm. "Literary Aesthetics: Beauty, the Brain, and *Mrs. Dalloway*." In Patrick Colm Hogan, *Beauty and Sublimity: A Cognitive Aesthetics of Literature and the Arts*. Cambridge: Cambridge University Press, 2016. 19–45.

Phillips, Natalie M. "Literary Neuroscience and History of Mind: An Interdisciplinary fMRI Study of Attention and Jane Austen." In *The Oxford Handbook of Cognitive Literary Studies*. Ed. Lisa Zunshine. Oxford: Oxford University Press, 2015. 55–81.

New Criticism

New Criticism was an American mid-twentieth-century method of close reading that had its origins in the Fugitive poets at Vanderbilt University during the early 1920s. In the pages of the short-lived little magazine, *The Fugitive*, such writers as John Crowe Ransom, Donald Davidson, Robert Penn Warren, and Allen Tate engaged T. S. Eliot's modernist poetry and criticism in an attempt to create a modern southern literature. After *The Fugitive*'s run ended, these same poets returned to Nashville in the late 1920s to help form the Southern Agrarians, best known for their first forum, *I'll Take My Stand* (1930), a conservative and segregationist collection of essays that argues for the South as the last best hope for the European tradition of the educated gentleman farmer. Although beginning with a critique of alienated labor in northern industrial society that sounds almost Marxian, the Agrarians were staunchly anti-Communist. Cleanth Brooks, a key disseminator of New Criticism, attended Vanderbilt from 1924 to 1928 and contributed to the second Agrarian forum, *Who Owns America?* (1936).

Although their political vision failed, the Agrarians became tenured conservatives at liberal arts colleges and edited several preeminent literary reviews, including the *Southern Review* (Brooks and Warren, 1935–42); the *Kenyon Review* (Ransom, 1939–59), and the *Sewanee Review* (Andrew Lytle, 1943–44 and 1961–73; Tate, 1945–46). Ransom was the son of a Methodist minister, as was Brooks. To a certain extent, these foundational figures of New Criticism exchange the inerrancy of the biblical word for that of the poetic word. Irony, ambiguity, and metaphor are the holy trinity of New Critical reading. The critic carefully reads a literary work to see how the apparent tensions of these tropes resolve into the work's organic unity. Organic unity is New Criticism's god-term, one pointing to the way that the method subscribes to Kantian transcendental aesthetics. In focusing on the literary work as a site of aesthetic judgment, New Criticism attempted to remove literature not only from social and historicist contexts but also from any sense of literature as a communicative act. Toward that end, New Criticism brackets the author and the reader in two famous essays by W. K. Wimsatt and Monroe Beardsley: "The Intentional Fallacy" (1946), which argues that authors' intentions for their writing are irrelevant to aesthetic judgment, and "The Affective Fallacy" (1949), which argues that an individual reader's emotional response is equally irrelevant to understanding a work of literature.

One effect of New Critical practice was a narrowing of the canon. At the turn of the twentieth century, literary history was fairly broad, but New Critics, following Eliot's "Tradition and the Individual Talent" (1919), believed that only a few new works of literature deserved close consideration because they alone engaged the great works from the past. By mid-century, the anthology of American literature that most colleges used was *Sixteen American Authors*. All of these authors were white. Although Frank Lentricchia identified New Criticism as moribund as early as 1957, this method of close reading remained entrenched into the mid-1970s.

(*See also* Chapter 2, Structuralism and Semiotics; Chapter 6, Historicisms; Chapter 8, Rhetoric; Chapter 14, Ecocriticism;

Chapter 27, Antitheory; Close Reading; Formalism; Husserl, Edmund; Irony; *and* Text)

John N. Duvall, *Purdue University (United States)*

Further Reading

Brooks, Cleanth. *The Well Wrought Urn: Studies in the Structure of Poetry*. New York: Reynal & Hitchcock, 1947.

Duvall, John N. "New Criticism's Major Journals." In *The Oxford Cultural History of Modernist Magazines*. Vol. 2 North America, 1894–1960. Ed. Peter Brooker and Andrew Thacker. Oxford: Oxford University Press, 2012. 928–44.

Leitch, Vincent L. "The 'New Criticism.'" In *American Literary Criticism from the 30s to the 80s*. New York: Columbia University Press, 1988. 24–59.

Lentricchia, Frank. *After the New Criticism*. Chicago: University of Chicago Press, 1981.

North, Joseph. "The Critical Revolution Turns Right." In *Literary Criticism: A Concise Political History*. Cambridge: Harvard University Press, 2017. 21–55.

Ransom, John Crowe. *The New Criticism*. Norfolk: New Directions, 1941.

New Historicism (*See* Chapter 6, Historicisms)

New Materialisms

"New materialisms" designates a group of theoretical approaches that developed as a reaction to the structuralist and poststructuralist turn away from metaphysics toward language and culture. Emerging within feminist theory in the 1990s, new materialisms sought to address the lacuna in these discourses around embodied practices and the experience of bodies as material things. In light of scientific and technological advances that increasingly question the boundaries between the vital and the inert, and pressing geopolitical and ecological realities, new materialisms have grown to encompass a diverse set of critical injunctions into cultural and literary theory. These new materialisms are united by a common emphasis on how both animate and inanimate objects exert real and felt forces.

Challenging René Descartes's ontological dualism and Immanuel Kant's suspicion of our ability to know "things in and of themselves," new materialisms are not so much a rejection of earlier theories as a reframing of them to account for the materiality of objects. Bringing "thingness" to the fore, they confront philosophical traditions like Karl Marx's theory of the commodity fetish and deconstructivist and postmodern theories of the immaterial. As an alternative to simple binaries, new materialisms present materiality as part of dynamic processes of becoming and unbecoming. The emphasis on process over stasis often associates new materialisms with new vitalism and builds on the radical empiricism of Gilles Deleuze and Félix Guattari, an approach popularized by Jane Bennett's notion of "vibrant matter."

What makes new materialisms *new*—and not simply a return to earlier materialist theories—is the ways in which they incorporate post-structuralist models of contingent being into reappraisals of materiality. Informed by a fresh understanding of materiality as lively, new materialisms have developed in conversation with other philosophical and cultural discourses, including Speculative Realism, Object Oriented Ontology (OOO), and Posthumanism. While many of the scholars working in these fields overlap, and their intellectual contributions align, what distinguishes new materialisms is the ways in which they blur distinctions between subject and object; all things, human or otherwise, are material.

It is difficult to account for all of the new materialists and their various critical interventions. Two anthologies, however, helped formalize new materialisms as a distinct theoretical field: Stacy Alaimo and Susan Hekman's *Material Feminisms* (2008) and Diana Coole and Samantha Frost's *New Materialisms* (2010). Both posit new materialisms as a theoretical approach able to address global political, economic, and ecological crises. Displacing humans as primary actors or agents, new materialisms move from the microscopic to the cosmic, following the flux and flow of materials to propose more synthetic models of being as an antidote to stagnant social and political theories. As Jane Bennett (2010) writes, "Why advocate the vitality of matter? Because my hunch is that the image of dead or thoroughly instrumentalized matter feeds human hubris and our earth-destroying fantasies of conquest and consumption."

(*See also* Cartesianism; Chapter 23, Materialisms; Encounter; Feminist Materialism; Hyperobject; Kant, Immanuel; Materialism; Objects; Object Oriented Ontology; Posthumanism; Speculative Realism; *and* Thing Theory)

Padma D. Maitland, *University of California, Berkeley (United States)*

Further Reading

Bennett, Jane. *Vibrant Matter: A Political Ecology of Things*. Durham: Duke University Press, 2009.

Coole, Diana, and Samantha Frost, eds. *New Materialisms: Ontology, Agency, and Politics*. Durham: Duke University Press Books, 2010.

Van der Tuin, Iris, and Rick Dolphijn. *New Materialism: Interviews & Cartographies*. Ann Arbor: Open Humanities Press, 2012.

New Novel, The (*See* Nouveau Roman)

Nietzsche, Friedrich

Friedrich Wilhelm Nietzsche was born on October 15, 1844 in the Saxon village of Röcken (Germany). In 1869 he was appointed to the Chair in Classical Philology at the University of Basel (Switzerland). While posted at Basel, he published a number of books and essays, including *The Birth of Tragedy from the Spirit of Music* (1872), the four *Untimely Meditations* (1873–76), and *Human, All-Too-Human* (1878). Citing poor health, he resigned his University appointment in 1879.

Nietzsche spent the next ten years in search of climatic and atmospheric conditions conducive to his work. In this period, he published *Daybreak* (1881), *The Gay Science* (1882), *Thus Spoke Zarathustra* (1883–85), *Beyond Good and Evil* (1886), *On the Genealogy of Morality* (1887), and various new prefaces, appendices, poems, and other materials. In 1888, his final year of sanity, he wrote *The Case of Wagner, Twilight of the Idols, The Antichrist, Nietzsche contra Wagner*, and *Ecce Homo*. In January of 1889, he suffered a debilitating psychological and physical breakdown, which brought his writing career to an abrupt end. Nietzsche died on August 25, 1900.

Nietzsche's books and ideas have shaped the dominant trends of twentieth- and twenty-first century thought. To this day, he is acknowledged as a figure of influence in the fields of philosophy, psychology, psychoanalysis, classics, theology, history, anthropology, rhetoric, aesthetics, theology, political theory, and cultural criticism. Although his sphere of influence remains both extensive and diverse, the following influences are particularly noteworthy.

Nietzsche's first book, *The Birth of Tragedy*, is widely read and cited, especially for its influential pairing of Dionysus and Apollo as the patron deities of Attic tragedy and as the twin impulses responsible for the rise and health of a genuinely "tragic" culture. He later developed the psychological insights that informed *The Birth of Tragedy* to support his pioneering research in the field of depth psychology. Locating the source of human agency in the pre-reflective operation of unconscious drives and impulses, he proposed to treat (and explain) human psychology as a complex instance of animal psychology. His speculative account of the rise (and costs) of human civilization was later taken up by Sigmund Freud, who installed a similar hypothesis at the center of *Civilization and Its Discontents* (1930).

Nietzsche is also well known for his insistence on the personal, expressive, and subjective dimensions of philosophy. Pronouncing every great philosophy an "involuntary memoir and confession" of its author, he sought to isolate the "prejudices" that motivate seemingly impersonal (or objective) philosophical positions. His influence in this respect is particularly evident on the development of the philosophical and literary traditions associated with *existentialism*, which are variously concerned to produce an affirmative, authentic response to the crises of meaning and value that have emerged in the aftermath of the "death of God."

Nietzsche is also widely cited for his seminal contributions to the "hermeneutics of suspicion," which spurred the development of literary, aesthetic, political, religious, and cultural criticism in the twentieth- and twenty-first centuries. Inspired by Nietzsche's daring regimen of self-directed "experimentation," his readers have challenged orthodoxies across a wide range of cultural endeavors, including philosophy, science, history, literature, religion, art, psychoanalysis, politics, and law. A regimen of elevated suspicion is needed, he insisted, inasmuch as we "late moderns" have become unwittingly entangled in tasks and projects that are likely to exacerbate (rather than relieve) our experiences of anxiety and alienation. While diligently pursuing what we have faithfully identified as our own best interests, he warned, we inadvertently may accelerate our own demise.

Finally, Nietzsche remains influential for his bristling diagnosis of the *décadence* of European modernity. Rejecting the familiar Enlightenment narratives of growth, progress, and maturation, he exposed the leading institutions of European modernity as abject failures. Lamenting the ongoing disintegration of a distinctly European culture, he warned of the rise of squabbling nation-states bent on imperial expansion and colonial exploitation. If Europe is to return to its accustomed position of global dominance, he advised, a new European order would need to be forged.

(*See also* Anti-Humanism; Chapter 5, Poststructuralism; Chapter 23, Materialisms; Force; Platonism; Repetition; Subject; *and* Vitalism)

Daniel Conway, *Texas A&M University*
(United States)

Further Reading
Nietzsche, Friedrich. *The Birth of Tragedy* [1872] and *The Case of Wagner* [1888]. Trans. Walter Kaufmann. New York: Random House/Vintage Books, 1967.
Nietzsche, Friedrich. *Beyond Good and Evil: Prelude to a Philosophy of the Future* [1886]. Trans. Walter Kaufmann. New York: Random House/Vintage Books, 1989.
Nietzsche, Friedrich. *On the Genealogy of Morals* [1887] and *Ecce Homo* [1888]. Trans. Walter Kaufmann and R. J. Hollingdale. New York: Random House/Vintage Books, 1989.

Normativity

Normativity concerns the normative character of a situation or a practice. The normative character of a situation or a practice, in turn, concerns the norms that are operative in that situation or practice. Those norms, in further turn, are the rightness and wrongness, goodness and badness, or betterness and worseness, of aspects of those situations and practices.

Practices have their own norms. These are ways of going about the practices that are right or wrong, good or bad, and better or worse. Those norms can be divided into two types: rules and non-rule norms. Rules are constitutive of a practice. To violate a rule is to run afoul of some defining aspect of the practice. In chess, to move a piece in a way that is not allowed is a violation of a rule. By contrast, non-rule norms prescribe ways of going about a practice that are better or worse. To return to chess, it is generally better to make sure one's king is protected rather than to leave it exposed, although leaving a king exposed does not violate the rules of chess.

The normative character of a situation, by contrast with the normative character of a practice, is decided by judgment. Situations, as such, do not come with their own norms; they just are what they are (although what they are can be a matter of dispute). However, they can be normatively judged as right or wrong, good or bad, and better or worse. This happens through one or another practices of judgment: philosophical, literary, political, and so on. The judging practice contains norms of judgment that are then applied to the situation being judged. These norms of judgment are part of the judging practice. For instance, a practice of political critique can judge a situation to be unfair or inegalitarian or just.

Just as practices can be engaged for normative judgment on situations, so can practices be engaged for normative judgment on other practices, thus treating them as situations. One way to read Michel Foucault's famous history of the prisons, *Discipline and Punish* (1975), is as involving a political judgment of the wrongness of psychological practice on the basis of a practice of genealogically tracing its emergence and its effects.

There is an important confusion, one that has bearing on critical theory, that should be avoided when thinking about normativity. Normativity is often confused with the idea of the normal. The normal has at least two meanings. There is statistical normality, which is not normative; and there is normality as it appears in psychological practice, which is normative. The latter prescribes better and worse ways of being or acting. Any critique of normality as oppressive is itself a normative critique. In fact, any critique at all is normative: it involves norms. To attempt to abandon normativity is a self-defeating enterprise. We do not escape norms; we can only ask which norms are better and worse, and we must do so from within a particular normative space.

(*See also* Ableism; Canguilhem, Georges; Chapter 15, Biopower and Biopolitics; Chapter 22, Identity Studies; Chapter 26, Affect Studies; Disability; Foucault, Michel; Mirror Stage; Sexuality; *and* Social Constructionism)

Todd May, *Clemson University* *(United States)*

Further Reading
Lance, Mark, and Jonathan Hawthorne. *The Grammar of Meaning: Normativity and Semantic Discourse*. Cambridge: Cambridge University Press, 2008.
May, Todd. *Our Practices, Our Selves*. State College: Penn State Press, 2001.

Nouveau Roman

The new novel (or *nouveau roman* in French) designates a group of writers, among who figure Nathalie Sarraute, Alain Robbe-Grillet, Michel Butor, Marguerite Duras, Claude Simon, Robert Pinget, and Claude Mauriac. They were loosely affiliated in the first instance by circumstance: they all launched their careers in the 1950s, and they found a home at the Éditions de Minuit, a small publishing house that had been established during the Occupation as a clandestine press. Yet it gradually became clear that certain attitudes toward literature and its conventions served to affiliate them as well, in particular the sense that traditional forms (and most especially the novel) were exhausted, and consequently insufficient to the expressive needs of postwar France. Some individuals took it upon themselves to theorize those positions, notably Sarraute, in *The Age of Suspicion* (1956) and Robbe-Grillet, in *For a New Novel* (1963). The chief features of those works articulate a program that is reactive in character, and which puts into action the most fundamental gesture of the avant-garde, the will to sweep away the old in order to make space for the new. Thus, the new novel sought to do away with "plot" as conventionally conceived, putting in its place a less linear, more fragmented narrative, one better suited to a post-nuclear, post-Holocaust world where everything was suddenly open to question. The new novel would likewise eschew character "psychology"; it would not automatically promote the human subject as the privileged object of investigation, focusing instead on the phenomenological world, the world of *things*; it would jettison the notion of linear time in favor of a less chronological, more subjective perception of time; it would not seek primarily to bring order into the world, rather, it would attempt to limn the disorder of life as we live it. Inevitably, some new novelists followed that program more closely than others—and even among the theoreticians it proved true. Sarraute's *Tropisms* (first published in 1939, when people in France had other things on their minds, then republished in 1957 to very considerable acclaim) is perhaps the purest and most radical expression of the new novel. Robbe-Grillet's *Jealousy* (1957), often adduced as the quintessential new novel, is not as faithful to the program that its own author enunciates, however: it clearly has a "psychological" dimension, for one thing; for another, it wagers upon intrigue (even if that intrigue is not as sharply focused as it may be in more traditional fiction). Despite that variation, the new novel clearly possessed enough critical mass—and enough intellectual heft—to impose itself on the French cultural horizon for a decade and more. It served most certainly as a useful and tonic corrective to a practice of fiction that had grown stale. But its appeal was limited, largely restricted to a sophisticated, cultivated audience. In that perspective, its experiments were neither generalizable nor sustainable. As to its legacy, it can be argued that the new novel itself cried out for correction, and indeed in the French novel from the late 1970s onward one witnesses a circumspect but nevertheless patent return to the principle of narrativity.

(*See also* Chapter 2, Structuralism and Semiotics; Novel; *and* Postmodernism)

Warren Motte, *University of Colorado, Boulder (United States)*

Further Reading

Heath, Stephen. *The Nouveau Roman: A Study in the Practice of Writing*. Philadelphia: Temple University Press, 1972.

Robbe-Grillet, Alain. *For a New Novel* [1963]. Trans. Richard Howard. New York: Grove, 1965.

Sarraute, Nathalie. *The Age of Suspicion: Essays on the Novel* [1956]. Trans. Maria Jolas. New York, Braziller, 1963.

Sturrock, John. *The French New Novel*. Oxford: Oxford University Press, 1969.

Novel

While the history of the novel is eminently traceable, the "life-form" itself eludes its historical record and the theoretical injunctions invoked on its behalf. Scholars of the novel (perhaps most influentially Ian Watt, Peter Brooks, and Michael McKeon) tend to presuppose an historical development of the novel. Whether it takes its point of departure from oral traditions of the antique world, from Greek and Roman romances, from sixteenth-century pamphleteering, or from the eighteenth-century French *nouvelle*, into modernity, scholars assume that the novel expresses a relatively unproblematic continuity of narrative imagination, staged within the framework of social-temporal conditions.

The actual historical production of texts that may be gathered within the precincts of the officially sanctioned genre (and its obligatory studies) stands however, in contrast with the idea that the novel is a developing and genetically enduring literary form. In the spirit of Henry James's famous characterization of the novel as a "loose, baggy monster," it might be more accurate to say that the novel is a font of imaginative variations on the human capacity for storytelling. Cervantes' *Don Quixote*, (1605) so commonly cited as the beginning of a historical tradition of novel writing, insists, in its celebrated "Preface," upon voicing the conditions for reading it as integral to the act of its being written. Thus are the conditions for the novel rendered novelistic, continuous with the narration of narrative. Such kindred texts as the anonymously authored *Lazarillo de Tormes* (1554), Thomas Nashe's *The Unfortunate Traveler* (1594), Fielding's *Tom Jones* (1749), and Sterne's *Tristram Shandy* (1759) share an irresistible reflex for reflecting upon the conditions of their own existence.

Strikingly, this reflex is a hallmark of the most stridently anti-novelistic novels of the twentieth century, written against the grain of any conceivable history of the novel. I am thinking specifically of the "novels" of Maurice Blanchot. Blanchot invoked the French term *récit* in order to hold his "novels" to account for themselves. It is not the end of storytelling that the *recit* takes responsibility for, but the burden of knowing how capacious the mind of the story teller is, that is, that any formally discrete story is an injustice to storytelling.

So, contrary to an abiding assumption that the history of the novel is the record of a persisting form, it might be more correct to follow Bakhtin's lead. If we reach back to Menippean satire instead of Greek or Roman romance for the origins of the novel, we might come to an understanding that the novel is irreverently agnostic toward formally instantiated genre boundaries. It makes more sense to say that the novel is instantiated wherever point of view is contestable within a narrative perspective. This is not exactly to say that we should treat Flaubertian irony as the paradigmatic achievement of the novel, by virtue of the Menippean self-disruptions

the author enacts in texts such as *Bouvard et Pecouchet* (1881). But we might say that Flaubert's text is a relevant cautionary tale. It is buttressed by Georg Lukács' insistence upon the novel's trajectory of disintegration in *Theory of the Novel* (1914–15). We ought to resist seeing the novel as paradigmatic for human aspirations to ethical, political, epistemological, or sociological truths and totalities. This is even more importantly a hedge against the temptation to conflate the human knowledge that is purveyed novelistically with the concept of human character per se. In this context, the most we should say is that the novel is an *act* without which character cannot subsist in the realms of ethics, politics, and social identity.

(*See also* Chapter 4, Marxism; Chapter 22, Identity Studies; Bahktin, Mikhail; Epitolary Novel; Genre; Literature; *and* Nouveau Roman)

Alan Singer, *Temple University*
(United States)

Further Reading

Caserio, Robert L. *Plot, Story and the Novel: From Dickens and Poe to the Modern Period.* Princeton: Princeton University Press, 1979.

Mazzoni, Guido. *Theory of the Novel.* Trans. Zakiya Hanafi. Cambridge: Harvard University Press, 2017.

Schmidt, Michael. *The Novel: A Biography.* Cambridge: Belknap Press, 2014.

O

Object-oriented Ontology

Object-oriented ontology is a school of thought designed to chart a middle path between the Scylla of scientific naturalism and the Charybdis of social relativism, twin discourses in contemporary theory that reject the category of the object by either reduction or dissolution. For philosophers like Graham Harman, Ian Bogost, Levi Bryant, and Timothy Morton, objects can neither be reduced downward to their subatomic components or structures nor dissolved upward into socially constructed effects of ideology, human consciousness, or institutions. Indebted to "speculative realism" and Bruno Latour's groundbreaking philosophical-sociological work, OOO (its common abbreviation) rejects correlationist accounts of things—the assumption that objects exist only for a subject, in relation *to* a grounding subject—while also allowing the fundamental order of existence (which it aims to elucidate) to accommodate various scales and assemblages without prescribing a transcendental metaphysical hierarchy. To this latter end, object-oriented ontologists often describe reality as a world of objects strung together in a "Latourian litany" (as Bogost calls it), where things from various fields and scales share the same ontological status: wheat, dentists, granite, muskrats, iPhones, and the United Nations, to name one such possible constellation.

One rhetorical effect of such litanies is to draw attention to the way OOO breaks long-standing anthropocentric assumptions about the world of objects. One of the movement's founding texts, Harman's *Tool-Being* (2002), articulates its distinction from phenomenological approaches like Martin Heidegger's. Harman argues that Heidegger's master distinction between objects present-at-hand and ready-to-hand extends beyond human projects and significations to all object-object relations. All objects have a hidden reserve that withdraws as certain properties are activated in causal interactions; in other words, there is no single set of properties that can exhaust an object's sensual profile or explain its emergent powers. Generally, OOO describes the way objects mediate one another's properties—the way they *translate* those properties without ever directly accessing the thing-in-itself—while retaining some level of ontological and operational consistency.

From a few general ontological principles, OOO practitioners spin off in a variety of directions, particularly regarding the philosophical movement's normative implications. Recently, Harman and Morton distinguished object-oriented readings from other theoretical schools like New Historicism and Deconstruction on the basis of the literary object's recalcitrance to complete absorption by historical context or its various cultural causes. And what an object-oriented politics is or might be is a matter of continued debate. Morton's term "hyperobject," referring to objects that act on a nonlocal scale beyond human comprehension, has motivated an analysis of climate that lends OOO an ethical dimension: he argues that the exigency of global warming demands that we reckon with objects inarticulable from the perspective of an anthropocentric worldview and metaphysics. More generally, OOO is often used to theorize democracy anew, projecting new collectives that include those objects typically ignored as agents in our political projects. A movement born as much in the blogosphere as in traditional academic outlets, OOO itself practices a radically democratic form of inquiry, one wholly in line with its intellectual assumptions.

(*See also* Chapter 23, Materialisms; Democracy; Hyperobject; Materialisms; New Materialism; Objects; Speculative Realism; *and* Thing Theory)

Zachary Tavlin, *School of the Art Institute of Chicago (United States)*

Further Reading

Bryant, Levi R. *The Democracy of Objects*. London: Open Humanities Press, 2011.

Harman, Graham. *Tool-Being: Heidegger and the Metaphysics of Objects*. Chicago: Open Court, 2002.

Morton, Timothy. *Hyperobjects: Philosophy and Ecology after the End of the World*. Minneapolis: University of Minnesota Press, 2013.

Objects

The status of objects in the history of Western thought is not easy to summarize. Even a brief catalogue of the tradition's greatest hits shows the wide historical variation in defining something as seemingly brute as "object," *objectum*, *Gegenstand*. Aristotle's hylomorphic theory of bodies as compounds of matter and form was translated, in medieval Scholastic thought, into a conception of objects as representations set over against knowing subjects. Modern philosophy was born from Descartes's distinction between two types of substance: *res cogitans* (thinking thing) and *res extensa* (extended thing), which led to the British empiricist division between an object's primary and secondary qualities (the former contained within the object itself, the latter in the way it affects the sensorium of a particular observer). From Kant's Copernican Revolution through the German Idealists to Marx, the modern subject-object distinction was reformed in a variety of ways: made transcendental, sublated into the labor of the Concept or of human beings. And at the turn of the twentieth century, phenomenology found a new way back "to the things themselves" (as Husserl famously urged), wherein objects were encountered intentionally, appearing within the structure(s) of experience as the correlates of first-person perceptions.

Arguably, contemporary object theory—which falls under the heading "object-oriented ontology," or OOO—can be traced back (as prehistory) to Martin Heidegger's critique of his teacher Husserl. Heidegger breaks with early phenomenology's notion of intentional objects as one-sided sensuous profiles in favor of worldly objects revealed in various ways depending upon the uses to which they are put by human beings. One of OOO's founding texts, Graham Harman's *Tool-Being*, begins with—while also articulating its departure from—Heidegger's analysis of objects as human equipment or gear (*Zeug*). Harman argues that Heidegger's master distinction between objects present-at-hand (*Vorhand*) and items of gear ready-to-hand (*Zuhand*) extends beyond human projects and significations to all object-object relations. All objects have a hidden reserve that withdraws as certain properties are activated in causal interactions; there is no single set of properties that can exhaust an object's sensual profile or explain its emergent powers. Generally, OOO describes the way objects mediate one another's properties—the way they *translate* those properties without ever directly accessing the thing-in-itself—while retaining some level of ontological and operational consistency.

From this perspective, even the lowly stone—which Heidegger said was "worldless" and which the tradition has used over and over as an example of dumb matter—engages in a dance every bit as intricate as a ballerina, a whippoorwill, a Beethoven record, or a military convoy. And yet object-oriented ontologists do develop their own explanatory categories of object types. From Harman's "quadruple object" to Timothy Morton's "hyperobjects" (which exist at a scale beyond human comprehension) and Levi Bryant's "onto-cartography" (which differentiates between dark, dim, bright, and rogue objects), philosophers and theorists are still at work cataloging things according to the ways they relate to surrounding object ecologies. They continue to show us just how *worldly* objects truly are, whether we are around to notice them or not.

(*See also* Chapter 23, Materialisms; Cartesianism; Democracy; Heidegger, Martin; Husserl, Edumund; Hyperobject; Materialisms; New Materialism; Objects; Phenomenology; Speculative Realism; Thing Theory; *and* Worldiness)

Zachary Tavlin, *School of the Art Institute of Chicago (United States)*

Further Reading

Bryant, Levi R. *The Democracy of Objects*. London: Open Humanities Press, 2011.
Harman, Graham. *Tool-Being: Heidegger and the Metaphysics of Objects*. Chicago: Open Court, 2002.
Morton, Timothy. *Hyperobjects: Philosophy and Ecology after the End of the World*. Minneapolis: University of Minnesota Press, 2013.

objet petit a

In Lacanian psychoanalysis, notions of the Other and the Other's interaction with desire are key in how Jacques Lacan views the mechanisms of the unconscious and the Symbolic place of subjectivity. While Lacan views the Other (the "big" other) as the ultimate unattainable desire, existing not in an object but in the very corners of Symbolic representation itself, the *objet petit a* represents the object, the "other" on which subjects fix their projection of that desire.

Lacan asserts that desire for the Other is the desire for wholeness itself. According to Lacan, once subjects enter into the Symbolic system of language and other structural systems of meaning, wholeness is lost and subjectivity becomes forever fragmented. The result is the subject sublimating desire for the Other with desire for the *objet petit a*; these objects are essentially placeholders, things on which the subject fixes his/her gaze as if it is the actual obtainable object of desire, a desire that if realized can bring back the state of wholeness, can alleviate symptoms of anxiety. Lacan adopts Freud's principle of sublimation; however, Lacan also brings a post-structuralist understanding of empty signification and deferred meaning: the *objet petit a* has no meaning in itself (it can be desired by some but not others) and will finally force the subject to another object, and then to another, and so on. Frequently, the *objet petit a* is characterized as the unattainable object of desire; more precisely, all *objects* are unattainable sources of desire because they are not the true source of desire. The true desire for the subject is the desire for wholeness itself, a wholeness that is impossible in the Symbolic Order of language and deferred signification, and no object, no "other," can restore it.

Subsequent thinkers take up Lacan's *objet petit a* in various ways. Slovenian philosopher, Slavoj Žižek, invokes Lacan's *objet petit a* in his discussions of fantasy. In simple terms, once desire is fixated onto the object, the subject slides into a state of fantasy and wish-fulfillment. Žižek, however, goes further by stressing that the nature of the fixation and the fantasy is dictated by what other subjects want and expect from the subject. For Žižek, there is a distinct intersubjective nature to fantasy, thus to the nature of the *objet petit a*. Julia Kristeva, French feminist and psychoanalyst, uses the *objet petit a* to contrast her notions of the abject, the horrors of the Real that extend beyond articulation and Symbolic representation; the *objet petit a* is an illusory source of pleasure firmly set in the systems of culture and language while the abject is the sublime reality that exists beyond all structure.

(*See also* Chapter 7, Psychoanalytic Theory; Desire; Fantasy; Freud, Sigmund; Kristeva, Julia; Lacan, Jacques; Libidinal; Other, The; Psychoanalysis; Subjectivity; Sublimation; Unconscious; *and* Žižek, Slavoj)

Jacob Blevins, *Sam Houston State University (United States)*

Further Reading

Kristeva, Julia. *Powers of Horror: An Essay on Abjection* [1980]. Trans. Léon Roudiez. New York: Columbia University Press, 1982.

Lacan, Jacques. *The Four Fundamental Concepts of Psycho-Analysis* [1954–55]. Ed. Jacques-Alain Miller. Trans. Alan Sheridan. New York: Norton, 1978.

Žižek, Slavoj. *Plague of Fantasies*. Verso: London, 1997.

Oedipus Complex

The Oedipus complex is among Sigmund Freud's most famous concepts, and it lies at the heart of his theory of psychological development. The term comes from the ancient Greek myth of the King of Thebes, best known from the play "Oedipus the King" by Sophocles; as a result of multiple acts of hubris on the part of different characters, Oedipus unwittingly murdered his father and married his mother. Freud saw in this myth an element of primal desire on the part of the male for his mother and to see the father as a rival. A female version of this was later referred as the "Electra Complex," although Freud did not use the term.

Although he first used the term *Oedipus Complex* only in 1910 (in a study titled "A Special Type of Object Choice in Men"), Freud had developed his theory of the Oedipus complex over many years, and he went on to refine it throughout his later career. Freud had early in his career hit upon the notion of infantile sexuality, and although he abandoned a dubious early hypothesis (known as the "seduction theory," which posited as the "aetiology of hysteria" an early childhood seduction or molestation), Freud became convinced that a desire for something like seduction was part of childhood development, even a necessary stage of normal development. In "Analysis of a Phobia in a Five-year-old Boy (1909)," better known as "Little Hans," Freud connected the child's fear of horses with his unconscious sexual longing for his mother and subsequent fear that his father would castrate him in retaliation. Based on his own memories, reports from other adults, and here confirmed (it seemed) in the experience of a child, Freud asserted that this Oedipal stage, taking place roughly between the ages of three and six, was a normal part of childhood psychological development. However, if the complex is left somehow unresolved, this Oedipal conflict can lead to neuroses.

The Oedipal complex, defined as it is by reference to world literature, has been very influential in literary studies, and it is central to a lot of psychoanalytic literary criticism. Freud's friend and champion Ernest Jones wrote one of the first works of Freudian criticism in connecting the protagonist's malady in Shakespeare's *Hamlet* to an Oedipal conflict. Critics have found the Oedipal conflict to lie at the heart of numerous stories, particularly those involving family dramas. Harold Bloom, in *The Anxiety of Influence* (1973), applied this notion to literary history, arguing that various poets stood in relation to their celebrated forebears as children to fathers, thus requiring that they somehow kill the father (through unconscious misreading) to establish themselves. Others, perhaps most famously the French theorists Gilles Deleuze and Félix Guattari in *Anti-Oedipus* (1972), have vigorously criticized the Oedipus complex for its focus on fear and lack.

(*See also* Chapter 7, Psychoanalytic Theory; Deferred Action; Deleuze, Gilles; Freud, Sigmund; Psychoanalysis; *and* Sublimation)

Robert T. Tally Jr., *Texas State University*
(United States)

Further Reading

Deleuze, Gilles, and Félix Guattari. *Anti-Oedipus* [1972]. Trans. Robert Hurley. Minneapolis: University of Minnesota Press, 1980.

Freud, Sigmund. "Analysis of a Phobia in a Five-year-old Boy" [1909]. *The "Wolfman" and Other Cases*. Trans. Louise Adey Huish. New York: Penguin, 2003. 1–122.

Freud, Sigmund. "A Special Type of Object Choice Made by Men" [1910]. *Sexuality and the Psychology of Love*. Ed. Philip Rieff. New York: Simon & Schuster, 1963. 38–48.

Jones, Ernest. *Hamlet and Oedipus* [1919]. New York: W. W. Norton, 1976.

Ontology

Ontology is the study of being, existence, or reality; its nature and internal relations. In India, ontological speculation began with Vedic philosophy (circa mid-first millennium BCE). In the West, it began with Pre-Socratic philosophers (late mid-first millennium BCE). Western models included monism (Parmenides), process (Heraclitus), pluralism (Anaxagoras), and atomism (Democritus). For mainstream Greek metaphysics ("first philosophy"), ontology was considered the foundation for all of philosophy because it established the basic distinctions by which all things are to be understood: being versus becoming; appearance versus reality, monism versus pluralism; naturalism versus supernaturalism; universals versus particulars; substances and essences versus accidents; determinism versus indeterminism; idealism versus materialism; and so forth. Most subsequent ontological debates have adopted these terms, refining them and debating which is more fundamental and perhaps constitutive of its other.

In the classical period, Western ontology profoundly shaped epistemology. In the Greek view, essential Being involved such traits as necessity, coherence, persistence, stability, and transparency to the mind, all of which seemed to follow from the epistemic distinction between appearance and reality: surely reality would be epistemically more reliable, substantial, essential, and persistent than mere appearance. Thus, the most general features of reality would ground knowledge evidentially, or even with necessity. Not surprisingly, then, the Christianizing of Greek metaphysics in medieval culture became entangled in theological arguments about God's necessary features, as in the case of Anselm's Ontological Argument, one of the cornerstones of natural theology. Only in the modern period did the epistemic vulnerability of ontic generality (and thus metaphysics) become evident, rendering even concepts such as space and time subject to dispute and counterintuitive empirical evidence.

The credibility of ontological speculation declined after David Hume's empiricism cast doubt on metaphysical necessity. Immanuel Kant too jettisoned much metaphysics as undecidable, though he reconstructed epistemic necessity as a feature of reason itself. The work of Hume and Kant resulted in a division between positivist attacks on metaphysics per se and a number of post-empirical approaches by metaphysicians and ontologists.

In the shadow of Kant, Edmund Husserl's phenomenology began by "bracketing" the ultimate reality of the contents of experience to analyze out its necessary, or at least general, features. Thus, the structure of transcendental subjectivity became a kind of stand-in for classical ontology.

In a more traditional vein, Charles S. Peirce and Alfred N. Whitehead gave empiricism its due while generalizing the conceptual presuppositions of science and experience, extrapolating to science's and nature's most general features, including their evolutionary character. Thus, "process" philosophy and its wide influence expanded modern ontological attention from timeless Being to concrete Becoming.

Theorists of a more objectivist bent have adopted a more traditional orientation toward objects. In reaction to the subjectivist presuppositions of Kant and phenomenology, OOO looks toward a reality underlying our perception of objects, holding that the object's reality exceeds the perception. In the philosophy of science, causal structuralism aims for a similarly observer-independent objectivity.

Contemporary post-empirical ontologies have diversified into a variety of modalities, including perspectives on language, subjectivity, embodiment, biology, environmentalism, and other recent scientific and philosophical developments.

(*See also* Badiou, Alain; Chapter 22, Identity Studies; Event; Husserl, Edmund; Kant, Immanuel; Materialism; Metaphysics; Object-Oriented Ontology; Speculative Realism; *and* Žižek, Slavoj)

Horace Fairlamb, *University of Houston-Victoria (United States)*

Further Reading
Copleston, Frederick. *A History of Philosophy*. Books 1–3. New York: Image, 1985.
Kenny, Anthony. *A New History of Western Philosophy*. Oxford: Oxford University Press, 2012.

Orientalism

Orientalism or modern orientalism (there are various forms of orientalism involving the study of language, text, and fashion dating back to the sixteenth century) declared its emphatic advent in the eighteenth century through departures from the traditional strangleholds of theological and biblical studies, the view of the Middle East and Judeo-Christian *weltanschauung* (courtesy Voltaire, Louis-Mathieu Langle, Francois Volney, and others). Under such changing denominations (ever since the first conference of orientalism in Paris in 1873) that brought politics, religion, strategies of location, and thought into play, Edward Said (in his 1978 book *Orientalism*), within the tradition initiated by Franz Fanon, Aime Cesaire, Anwar

Abdel Malek, Abdullah Laroui and others, based his ideas on the epistemological and ontological distinctions made between the "Orient" and the "Occident." As a "style of thought" and a product of "imaginative geography," orientalism became a discourse informed by what Said calls "strategic location" and "strategic position," authorizing its own validity, repeating its own racist and fictional stereotypes, intensifying its pedagogical relevance by being a "textual project" and building an epistemological settlement around the "us-them" syndrome that was difficult to unsettle.

Informed by Foucaldian critique, orientalism, however, homogenized the Enlightenment and did not take the complexities of history adequately into account resulting in becoming a victim of the binary that it ironically sought to demonstrate and expose. The "Orient" as opposed to Said's predominant focus on the Arab world, encompasses the Central, North and South-east Asia, India, China, Tibet, and others. Orientalism comes to be rethought as an engagement not merely in imperialist lust and missionary zeal but in thoughts both metaphysical and cultural that called for a cross traffic of interest. It cannot be the staid binary of superior-inferior, history-ahistorical, enlightened-uneducated; rather, at certain levels, it helped flourish a negotiatory growth that ushered its own harvests on either ends. Orientalist interests were not merely territorial and hegemonic; it was theological and directed towards some forms of self-enlightenment and self-endowment that, in a way, makes it dialectical in principle and praxis.

Orientalism is much more complicated, conceptually and praxially, than Said's *Orientalism* would have us believe. It is an entangled phenomenon—"overlapping territories" in multiple histories, languages, narratives, events, and cultural-religious specificities and conflicts. Outside its Manichean limitations, orientalism today has a decisive link with politics, economy, and our humanistic thinking. It has repremised our engagements around violence and the processes of othering much beyond what Said's *Orientalism* suggested or demonstrated. A mere writing about the representational politics fails to note the claims and figurations from the non-European side of the discourse. So in our current debates on the orientalist divide between Islam and Christianity, the contributions of the post-orientalists—William Chittick, John Esposito, Barbara Metcalf, Lois Beck, and Michael Gilsenan—are remarkable. Post-orientalism moves out of the traditional view of understanding a religion into the realm of a fuller appreciation that includes a more perspicuous critique of the complexities and valence of the religion in question and the loaded connection that religion has with orientalism as a style and strategy of thought and attitude. We are, thus, in the forefront of a "new orientalism"; in counter-orientalist and post-orientalist forms it has, thus, built its own postliterary.

(*See also* Allochronic Discourse; Binary Opposition; Chapter 13, Race and Postcolonial Studies; Comparativisms; Eurocentrism; Philology; Said, Edward; *and* Spivak, Gayatri)

Ranjan Ghosh, *University of North Bengal (India)*

Further Reading

App, Urs. *The Birth of Orientalism*. Philadelphia: University of Pennsylvania Press, 2010.

Dabashi, Hamid. *Post-Knowledge and Power in Time of Terror*. New Brunswick: Transaction Publishers, 2009.

Elmarsafy, Ziad, Anna Bernard, and David Attwell, eds. *Debating Orientalism*. New York: Palgrave Macmillan, 2013.

Macfie, A. L., *Orientalism: A Reader.*
New York: New York University Press,
2000.
Turner, Bryan S. *Orientalism: Postmodernism and Globalism*. New York: Routledge,
1994.

Origin

In *Beginnings: Intention and Method* (1985),
Edward Said distinguishes between origins
and beginnings as follows: origins are mythical, divine, and sacred. Origin, or origination, is the prerogative of a God. Humans
only begin. We begin at a point in time, but
a God stands outside time, before time, creating *ex nihilo*, by *fiat*. Beginnings imply a
secular temporality, a continuum of historical time into which each beginning is slot-
ted. Each beginning necessarily relates to
the prior time of everything that has gone
before—we cannot get back before time,
to anachrony, and stage an unprecedented
moment of utter origination. Writers, as Said
shows, know beginning's agony (how to do
something different?) and suffer the agony
of influence—the intimidation of preeminent
precursors, the pressure of literary conventions enforcing repetition of the same thing.
From that agony emerge terms that surely
matter more than "origin," when the task is
to think about human activity, namely "difference" and "repetition," precisely. Certain
philosophers agree: Søren Kierkegaard's
Repetition (1843), for instance, strongly
argues that repetition should be the key topic
for philosophical enquiry. In *Difference and
Repetition* (1968), Gilles Deleuze argues
that repetition induces and produces difference. Repetition is indeed productive, just as
beginnings are for Said. Nonetheless, repetition has already begun, just as history has
already begun. Hence the a-temporal origin
is lost to "myth" or the "divine"—designa-

tions of inaccessibility. Origin, as a topic for
theoretical enquiry, seems to be a nonstarter.
But there are those who are more confident
with origins. Consider Martin Heidegger's
"The Origin of the Work of Art (1950)." The
artist is the origin of the artwork, but the real
question is whether particular artworks reveal
the essence of "art" as such. This is the other
origin we must explore. Often, however, the
(archaeological) inspection of art's origins
comes with a warning: leave origins alone. In
Henry James's "Last of the Valerii (1874),"
the statue of a Roman goddess is dug up, but
alas, she turns out to be Greek. James warns
against fetishizing the origins of one's own
culture. And perhaps the origins of Western
art are best left buried with the Greeks. His
European protagonist becomes the last of his
line because he favors not the future, but a
chimerical past (he neglects his American
wife for the statue). Fascination with origins
leads to sterile archaism—and also insanity.
In "The Unknown Masterpiece (1831)," Balzac's mad painter finds a beautiful woman to
be his model. He paints her, seeking to reveal
the origin of beauty and art. The masterpiece
is a smeared canvas. She, nakedly exposed,
sobs in a corner. Many artists conflate origins
with the female body. Courbet's *L'Origine
du Monde* (1866) makes this explicit. We
(men) desire to *see* the origin. Courbet adds
Woman to the list of candidates responsible
for the origin of the world: God, the Word,
Man. The fascination with origins is theological, anthropological, linguistic, archaeological. It is also philosophical: the term here
is *arche* (origin, first things). It is a matter
of getting back to origins, but also of starting: we start in order to continue thinking
(philosophy's preeminent exercise) and to
continue conceiving the world after chaos,
after time's first instant. Begin, therefore, at
the beginning. Beginning demystifies Said's
mythical and divine idea of origin, ensuring

that first things aren't last things—ensuring that human thought and history may carry on endlessly.

(*See also* Archi-trace; Chapter 9, Deconstruction; Deleuze, Gilles; Heidegger, Martin; Repetition; *and* Said, Edward)

Brian O'Keeffe, *Barnard College*
(United States)

Further Reading

Deleuze, Gilles. *Difference and Repetition* [1968]. Trans. Paul Patton. New York: Columbia University Press, 1993.

Heidegger, Martin. "The Origin of the Work of Art [1950]." Trans. Albert Hofstadter. *Poetry, Language, Thought.* New York: HarperCollins Perennial, 2001.

Kierkegaard, Søren. *Fear and Trembling* [1843]; *Repetition* [1843]. Trans. Howard and Edna Hong. Princeton: Princeton University Press, 1983.

Said, Edward. *Beginnings: Intention and Method.* New York: Columbia University Press, 1985.

Other, The

The concept of the "Other" has become prevalent in contemporary literary and cultural theory. Essentially, the "Other" refers to alterity, the identification of difference in others and the subsequent reaffirmation of sameness and the self. Although this element of difference is common in most uses of the term in today's critical discourse, the "Other" as critical idiom is varied and nuanced. There are two primary approaches to the Other: the first sees the Other as the result of a subversive cultural framework that structures and defines both self and other; the second sees the Other as an internal component of subjectivity that transcends structure altogether.

The initial use of the concept in philosophical discourse was by Georg W. F. Hegel, who identified a conflict arising from a consciousness of the self and the recognition of a consciousness in an Other. That Hegelian principle was followed by later thinkers such as Edmund Husserl and Jean-Paul Sartre, both of whom saw the Other as a guiding force of intersubjective relations. Jacques Derrida and Emmanuel Levinas apply ethical considerations to the emergence of otherness. Levinas sees the Other as an infinite and absolute presence (even represented and manifesting itself in godhead) while Derrida questions the very stability of the term. The implications in Derrida's and Levinas's dialogue over the nature of the Other are ultimately ethical. Levinas's Other suggests a kind of Kantian absolute ethics while Derrida's suggests a more tenuous relative ethics that arises from our sense of alterity. The Other as an indicator of gender marginalization is the focus of feminist theorists such as Simone de Beauvoir, Julia Kristeva, and Judith Butler. Ethnic marginalization of the Other was the basis of Edward Said's work on postcolonialism. The work of Said has laid the groundwork for examining how national and cultural ideologies impact the way we marginalize others while simultaneously validating our own identity. Though postcolonialism focuses on ethnic and cultural Others, the approach has implications for the subversion of women, gays/lesbians, and any other "group" that is viewed as outside the norm.

Although the Other is often connected to these kinds of external presences, psychoanalysis treats the Other as a component of internal desire and self-projection. The concept of the O/other is crucial in the theories of Jacques Lacan. Lacan differentiates between the "Other" and "other" (the *objet petit a*). Lacan's Other (the big O other) is characterized as an unattainable source of desire for wholeness, a kind of transcendental signifier for the manifestation of desire. The Other is situated both behind the limitations of representation (of language for example) and within the inarticulable realm of the Lacanian Real. Lacan's *objet petit a* is the other the subject mistakes for the Other; it manifests itself out of our own self-projection, our own self-reflective gaze. The other for Lacan is fantasy, existing only as a placeholder for our lack of Other. Although the subject's engagement with the O/other is rooted in an internal process of subjectivity, the displacement of desire to external markers (through the *objet petit a*) within the fragmented Symbolic lays a foundation for identifying the other outside of the self. Žižek's post-Lacanian use of the term shows othering as a function within ideological constructs. For Žižek, ideology becomes the structure through which the Lacanian Other emerges.

(*See also* Assujettissement; Castration; Chapter 7, Psychoanalytic Theory; Drive; Jouissance; Lacan, Jacques; Libidinal; Liminality; objet petit a; Phallocentrism; Primordial Discord; *and* Symptom)

Jacob Blevins, *Sam Houston State University* *(United States)*

Further Reading
Beauvoir, Simone de. *The Second Sex* [1949]. New York: Alfred Knopf, 1953.
Lacan, Jacques. *The Four Fundamental Concepts of Psycho-Analysis, 1954-1955.* Ed. Jacques-Alain Miller. Trans. Alan Sheridan. New York: Norton, 1978.
Miller, J. Hillis. *Others*. Princeton: Princeton University Press, 2001.
Said, Edward W. *Orientalism*. New York: Pantheon, 1978.
Shankman, Steven. *Other Others: Levinas, Literature, Transcultural Studies*. Albany: State University of New York Press, 2010.

Otherness (*See* Alterity)

Overdetermination

In psychoanalytic theory, overdetermination refers to the notion that a given effect may have multiple causes. As early as *Studies in Hysteria* (1895), co-authored with Josef Breuer, Sigmund Freud had noted that a given symptom may be "overdetermined" (in German, *überdeterminiert*), meaning that it may have more than one cause. Similarly, in *The Interpretation of Dreams* (1900), Freud maintains that elements of a dream are themselves always overdetermined, such that multiple meanings are always possible, if not indeed inevitable, when interpreting them. Freud employs the vivid metaphor of "a factory of thoughts," quoting Johann Wolfgang von Goethe's image of a loom weaving together materials in "infinite combination," to show how "each of the elements in the dream's content turn out to have been overdetermined" or "to have been represented in the dream-thoughts many times over." Borrowing from Freud but applying the term to social theory, the Marxist philosopher Louis Althusser employed *overdetermination* to show how historical events, such as the Russian Revolution, were made possible and influenced by a wide range of different, sometimes conflicting factors, such that one could not simply explain their emergence based on a single cause or even set of causes (e.g., by recourse to economics alone). This then becomes a principle for approaching history as a whole, in addition to psychology.

Freud's concept of overdetermination has evocative ramifications for literary criticism, both psychoanalytic and other varieties, as it insists upon the interpreter's being open to multiple meanings in a given text. Furthermore, the concept of overdetermination emphasizes that any given feature or effect has multiple origins, causes, or influences, which lead the critical readers to be attuned to many different possible ways of seeing the text and its elements in the context of a dynamic and complex field of meaning. Overdetermination implies polysemy, and the interpretation of texts thus moves beyond the simpler search for the text's meaning, into a more active exploration of potential meanings. A symbol, for example, may be overdetermined, thus symbolizing more than one thing, and interpretation is therefore not a simple act of detection, in which one discovers the corresponding meaning of a given symbol, but a ranging search of possible significance and referents. In *Moby-Dick*, for example, Herman Melville extrapolates upon the possible symbolic meanings of the white whale, refusing to limit himself to a single "correct" answer. The whale is, in that sense, also overdetermined.

(*See also* Althusser, Louis; Chapter 7, Psychoanalytic Theory; Freud, Sigmund; *and* Psychoanalysis)

Robert T. Tally Jr., *Texas State University (United States)*

Further Reading

Althusser, Louis. "Contradiction and Overdetermination." In *For Marx* [1965]. Trans. Ben Brewster. London: Verso, 2005. 87–128.

Freud, Sigmund. *The Interpretation of Dreams* [1900]. Trans. James Strachey. New York: Basic Books, 2010.

Ricoeur, Paul. *Freud and Philosophy: An Essay on Interpretation*. Trans. Denis Savage. New Haven: Yale University Press, 1970.

P

Parole (fr.)

Speech. This is an improvised, combinative activity, the expression of personal thoughts and attitudes. *Parole* is how the individual performs language as both *langage* and *langue*. *Parole* is often viewed as individual, not collective. Roland Barthes has identified speech with idiolect, the set of individual habits of speech at a given instant. However, Barthes wonders if when we speak to one another, do we speak in our own language or in the other's language, say, in terms of vocabulary, idiomatic usages, syntax, and so forth? In fact we do both. Jacques Derrida has said in an essay on monolinguism that even if we speak but one language, it really isn't ours. This problematizes speech because it's not entirely a black and white issue as to who or what is speaking. If I speak a language that isn't mine (which is everyone's condition) am I inherently alienated from everything I say? The style of a writer derives from tradition and community, not necessarily from himself or herself. Yet we recognize the voice of a particular poet as *parole*, never mind that it is pervaded by speaking that is traditional or social. Mikhail Bakhtin's conceptions of *polyglossia* and *heteroglossia* look at *parole* from the point of view of pluralization and intersectionality respectively with respect to language as a multiplicity of different language formations relating to socio-linguistic differences that are appropriated by us into our *parole*.

(*See also* Bakhtin, Mikhail; Chapter 2, Structuralism and Semiotics; Langage; Langue; Saussure, Ferdinand de; *and* Sign)

Herman Rapaport, *Wake Forest University (United States)*

Further Reading

Bakhtin, Mikhail. *The Dialogic Imagination: Four Essays*. Ed. Michael Holquist. Trans. Caryl Emerson and Michael Holquist. Austin: University of Texas, 1981.

Saussure, Ferdinand de. *Course in General Linguistics* [1916]. Eds. Charles Bally and Albert Sechehaye. Trans. Roy Harris. Chicago: Open Court, 1998.

Patriarchy

Patriarchy is a system of domination in many cultures that systematically benefits men through the disenfranchisement of women. Historically, patriarchy has been maintained through legal policies and social practices, including, for example, male control over household budgets, property ownership, and inheritance laws. The term is derived from the image of the patriarchal family, in which the patriarch (typically the father) is the "head of the household" and the mother and children obey him. Patriarchy, however, is not limited to family life or the private sphere but rather is a pervasive, hierarchical system of oppression that touches all aspects of life, including social, cultural, political, economic, and religious.

Theories of patriarchy grew out of the radical feminism of the late 1960s. In her *Sexual Politics* (1970), Kate Millett put forth a theory of patriarchy that identified three institutions of interconnected patriarchal power—state, society, and family—that overlap and support each other. Children, for instance, are educated into patriarchy through family life and carry this ideology with them into social interactions. This kind of family indoctrination often occurs in sync with social institutions such as education and religion. Sylvia Walby, in *Theorizing Patriarchy* (1990), expands Millett's three-pronged theory of patriarchy into six: the state, paid work, culture, housework, sexuality, and violence. Walby also argues that patriarchy takes two forms: public and private.

Two major schools of feminism—Marxist feminism and radical feminism—follow competing theorizations of patriarchy, differing in their understanding of its relationship to capitalism. For Marxist feminists, patriarchy is employed within the materialist modes of production (including reproduction as the repopulation of the proletariat). From this perspective, gender constitutes one subset of class. For radical feminists, on the other hand, patriarchy is the main system of domination and is distinct from capitalism but operates in conjunction with it. Through her historicizing of patriarchy, Gerda Lerner shows, contrary to Marxist points of view, that patriarchy does not grow out of capitalism but was already present in precapitalist societies, such as those described by Claude Lévi-Strauss, in which men controlled women's sexuality, and female bodies were exchanged in marriage to strengthen male ties.

Among feminists, the concept of patriarchy is not without critique. Scholars such as Lerner, in *The Creation of Patriarchy* (1986), and Judith Bennett, in *History Matters:*

Patriarchy and the Challenge of Feminism (2006), have challenged the ahistorical way in which feminists have employed the term. Patriarchy is also the central concept for a majority-white feminist movement, in which differences of race and ethnicity have been overlooked. However, the manifestations of patriarchy for Western white women cannot be so easily applied to all situations. As bell hooks argues, for example, the dynamics of the family for African-Americans is not one of total domination of women, since it also operates as a mode of resistance against racism.

For some, patriarchy relies on essentialist notions of gender, while for others masculine power, rather than biological males, creates and enforces patriarchal power. Nevertheless, patriarchy remains a significant concept for understanding the position of women in the twenty-first century, with their inheritance of rape culture, the gendered pay-gap, and debates over a women's right to make decisions about her own body. Intersectional attention to history, race, sexuality, culture, nationality, and ethnicity can only enrich discussions of how patriarchy is both pervasive and varied.

(*See also* Chapter 1, Early Theory; Chapter 10, Feminism; Chapter 14, Ecocriticism; Chapter 22, Identity Studies; Feminist Materialism; Feminist Theory; Phallocentrism; *and* Primordial Discord)

Laci Mattison, *Florida Gulf Coast University (United States)*

Further Reading

Lerner, Gerda. *The Creation of Patriarchy*. Oxford: Oxford University Press, 1986.

Millett, Kate. *Sexual Politics* [1970]. New York: Columbia University Press, 2016.

Walby, Sylvia. *Theorizing Patriarchy*. London: Basil Blackwell, 1990.

Peirce, Charles Sanders

C. S. Peirce's (1839–1914) interest in logic very early led him to the study of signs. While still quite young, he redefined logic as the theory of inquiry and, in doing so, felt compelled to inaugurate *semeiotic* (his preferred spelling for the study of signs). For "the woof and warp of all thought and all research is symbols, and the life of thought and science [or inquiry] is the life inherent in symbols." Later in life, he characterized his efforts to inaugurate this study by confessing: "I am, as far as I know, a pioneer, or rather a backwoodsman, in the work of clearing and opening up what I call *semiotic*, that is, the doctrine of the essential nature and fundamental varieties of possible semiosis; and I find the field too vast, the labor too great, for a first-comer."

Opening this field of inquiry required him to craft a truly comprehensive or general conception of "sign." In both the classical definition and the Saussurean, a sign is depicted as a dyadic or two-term relationship. In contrast, Peirce takes the term to designate an irreducibly triadic relationship. Just as any act of giving involves three functionally distinct components (a giver, a gift, and a recipient), so any instance of semiosis or sign-action involves an object, a sign, and an interpretant. "A gives B to C" is an act in which there is an essential and thus irreducible link between divestiture (A's giving) and acquisition (C's coming into possession of B). So too "S signifies O for I" is a process in which the link between an object and its representations is itself essentially linked to that between a sign and its interpretant(s). For there to be significance, there needs to be uptake (the sign must be taken up and carried forward). Moreover, then, semiosis is dynamic. The relationships among these components are not static or inert: they are rather dynamic and indeed generative (objects generate signs to represent them and, in turn, signs generate interpretants to elaborate their meaning). Hence, it is somewhat misleading to speak of Peirce's theory of signs, since what he is undertaking is an investigation of sign-activity or -process, or -function (in a word, *semiosis*). The interpretant is not to be confused with an interpreter. It is the "proper significate effect" of a sign (the effect of a sign bearing upon the question of meaning). In many (if not most) cases, a sign generates a sequence or series of interpretants, not a single significate effect. Finally, semiosis is, in its more complex forms, an open-ended process. Think here of the investigation of energy or the interpretation of the *Iliad*. Such an investigation or interpretation can be a process in which a provisional closure is more than an arbitrary interruption (e.g., a law governing the convertibility of mass and energy might be discovered and bring inquiry *in this regard* to a close, or the interpretation of a passage in an epic might in some respect be definitively offered). What Peirce says about science (it is "*essentially* incomplete") however might also be said of other semiotic practices. In other words, they are inherently open-ended.

Umberto Eco suggested, "Semiotics is in principle the discipline studying everything which can be used in order to lie." We might characterize Peirce's semeiotic as the discipline studying everything about which we might be mistaken. This shifts the focus from the utterer to the interpreter of signs, also from intentional deceit to unwitting error. One of the most basic distinctions in his theory is that between the immediate and the dynamical object of any sign-process. The immediate object is the object as it is portrayed or represented by a sign, whereas the dynamical object is the object as it is apart from this representation. The crucial point here is that the dynamical object has, given enough time, energy, and ingenuity on the part of inquirers, the efficacy to act as an experiential corrective to any given representation. The point of a scientific experiment is to expose our representations of reality to the dynamical efficacy of experiential reality (i.e., reality as it discloses itself in experience), for such exposure can show the respects in which our hypotheses are mistaken. One of Peirce's most important doctrines (his doctrine of fallibilism) is, consequently, woven into the fabric of one of his most important contributions (his inauguration of semeiotic).

Would it not be scientifically beneficial, Peirce asks, "for those who have both a talent and a passion for eliciting the truth about such matters, to institute a cooperative cenoscopic [or philosophical] attack upon the problems of the nature, properties, and varieties of Signs, in the spirit of twentieth-century science?" He was thoroughly convinced of the benefits to be derived from addressing these problems in a systematic, painstaking, and sustained manner.

There is, however, a tension at the heart of Peirce's endeavor to elaborate a comprehensive theory of signs. On the one hand, his principal purpose was to provide resources for renovating logic, by making this ancient discipline into a normative theory of objective inquiry (a theory showing in minute detail how an inquiry *ought* to be conducted). On the other hand, Peirce was inherently fascinated in the countless forms of signs and the various purposes made possible by their boundless proliferation. This fascination led him far beyond an exclusive or narrow focus on the signs and symbols on which the work of scientists depends. The applicability of his semeiotic to fields such as linguistics, poetics, psychology, literary criticism, and historical narration (to name but a handful) is indicative of the fecundity of his theory. His definitions, distinctions, and classifications of signs have proven to do what they were

designed to accomplish—to inspire and direct the ongoing exploration of a vast terrain, far too vast for any single explorer. This tradition of inquiry is itself an exemplification of semiosis in Peirce's sense, for it is an open-ended process in which important discoveries serve to propel research forward.

(*See also* Chapter 2, Structuralism and Semiotics; Deleuze, Gilles; Diagram; Eco, Umberto; Intersubjectivity; Ontology; Scientific Method; Self; Semiotics; Sign; *and* Social Constructionism)

Vincent Colapietro, *Pennsylvania State University (United States)*

Further Reading

Fisch, Max H. *Peirce, Semeiotic, and Pragmatism.* Bloomington: Indiana University Press, 1986.

Liszka, James. *A General Introduction to the Semiotic of Charles Sanders Peirce.* Bloomington: Indiana University Press, 1996.

Savan, David. *An Introduction to C. S. Peirce's Full System of Semeiotic.* Toronto: Toronto Semiotic Circle, 1987–88.

Short, T. L. *Peirce's Theory of Signs.* Cambridge: Cambridge University Press, 2007.

Performativity

Performativity is a concept that comes from Gender and Queer Studies and particularly the work of Judith Butler. Building upon feminist theory, which demonstrated that gender is not reducible to biological sex, Butler argues that gender is socially constructed and performative. Gender, then, is not an "essential" or innate part of a person. Instead, gender is performed, often unconsciously, through a series of repeated conventional actions and behaviors that are culturally and historically conditioned (such as by language, religion, tradition, etc.) but actually have no natural origin outside of any such context. In short, gender is all nurture (social), not nature (innate), and is therefore much more fluid than it appears.

However, it is crucial to distinguish between performativity and performance. Butler is not exactly saying that we perform gender roles the way an actor plays a part. This would suggest that gender roles are stable and natural for all people and that these roles can, on occasion, be performed differently and, therefore, inauthentically. A woman "acting like a man" could thus be considered unnatural; whereas Butler is saying that even a man "acting like a man" is performative, not natural. Combining Michel Foucault's concept of discourse (that discourse/language "produces" its own subject of knowledge, not vice versa), J. L. Austin's work on performative utterances (speech as doing/enacting, such as a wedding oath, "I do."), and notions of lived experience by French phenomenologists, Butler is able to reverse the normative understanding of gender. For Butler, therefore, one "does" gender. Gender is an *embodied* act. Performing gender brings it into material being at an individual and collective level, both socially and historically. When a performance ends, we return to "reality," but performativity means that our "reality" is what we enact or repeat without beginning or end. Effect is actually cause, act(tion) its own originless origin. Hence, gender is enacted or performed. Being originless, gender is thus both a set of received yet open possibilities that bodies can (re)produce in creative ways.

Theorists have also extended the notion of performativity to race and ethnicity, arguing that both are social constructs and performed in various contexts. For instance, the long history of racial passing in America—in which members of a marginalized group who visibly resemble the dominant group "pass" as members of this group to avoid prejudice or harm—reveals not only the arbitrary social and legal construction of race but also how it is performed in ways that coincide with received cultural perceptions of how people "naturally" are. The performative nature of race, then, suggests that its supposed ontological basis in "blood" or physical traits is not natural. Science has shown, for instance, that race does not exist at the cellular level. Nevertheless, race, similar to gender, is inscribed upon bodies through a long history of racialized discourse. However, marginalized peoples' struggles to achieve equality and to combat cultural appropriation (including racial passing by the dominant group), risks essentializing race and thus reinscribing the dominant culture's racial logic that it means to challenge.

(*See also* Authenticity; Butler, Judith; Chapter 9, Deconstruction; Chapter 23, Materialisms; Chapter 26, Affect Studies; Feminist Theory; Gender; Queer Theory; Repetition; *and* Subjectivity)

Ralph Clare, *Boise State University (United States)*

Further Reading

Butler, Judith. *Gender Trouble: Feminism and the Subversion of Identity*. New York: Routledge, 1990.

Ehlers, Nadine. *Racial Imperatives: Discipline, Performativity, and Struggles Against Subjection*. Bloomington: Indiana University Press, 2012.

Hall, Donald E., and Annamarie Jagose, eds. *The Routledge Queer Studies Reader*. New York: Routledge, 2012.

Persuasion

Persuasion is the strategic use of signification with the intent to incite action in audiences.

The practice of persuasion is as old as human communication. However, the art (*technê*) of verbal persuasion, or the theory of *rhetoric*, did not emerge until the sixth and fifth centuries BCE in the fertile context of democratic institutions, especially politics and law. In that context, when truth was apparent, as it was perceived to be in scientific demonstration, there was no need to persuade. Persuasion became critical when truth was unavailable or obscure and only probability remained in view. Since politics regards the efficacy of future actions, truth was unavailable and persuasion led citizens toward the best (probable) plan. Since law regards the likelihood of past actions, truth was obscure and persuasion led judges and juries toward the most reasonable (probable) verdicts.

Persuasion is ancient, but it is also modern. The institutions in which persuasion emerged (politics and law) and the media in which persuasion was enacted (verbal language) have more recently expanded in number and scope. Since the 1960s, postmodernism, post-structuralism, and deconstruction have thrown all institutions and their legitimating grand narratives into an epistemological crisis, turning even literary, philosophical, and scientific knowledge toward probability. Thus, while persuasion fulfilled a specific and limited role in ancient public society, it has become ubiquitous in modern (or postmodern) public society.

Literature persuades, not because it represents cultural values or universal structures, but because it reveals contextual strategies for acting in the drama of life's varied and uncertain situations. Philosophy persuades, not because it identifies certain realities or metaphysical truths, but because the tone and structure of its language seduce audiences into the conviction that philosophy represents reality and truth. Science persuades, not because it identifies indisputable facts, but because it uses the ruse of the scientific method to represent facts as beyond dispute.

While persuasion was a verbal art throughout the history of rhetoric, modern persuasion is an art of signifying in whatever medium communicates a message most effectively. Cultural actors still use language as a primary medium for persuasion, but more recently persuasions has been recognized and practiced in aural, tactile, and visual media. Register (or spoken verbal style) persuades, not because it is constant and inevitable, but because it is strategic and intentional. Clothing does not persuade because it represents true symbols of biological identities, but because it reflects the performance of situated identities requiring ideological responses from audiences. Architecture persuades, not because it represents universal beauty or idealized function, but because it leads its audiences along a visual path in which space signifies cultural values and ideological beliefs without any need for words.

Acting, seducing, representing, performing, responding, and signifying: these are the strategic activities associated with persuasion in our present time, so different from the ethos, pathos, and logos associated with persuasion in the ancient world. Nevertheless, despite its mutations over time, persuasion remains a vital and productive key term for understanding and critiquing contemporary literary and cultural theory.

(*See also* Chapter 8, Rhetoric; de Man, Paul; *and* Rhetoric)

Bruce McComiskey, *University of Alabama at Birmingham (United States)*

Further Reading
Booth, Wayne C. *The Rhetoric of Fiction*. Chicago: University of Chicago Press, 1961.

Gries, Laurie. *Still Life with Rhetoric: A New Materialist Approach for Visual Rhetoric*. Logan: Utah State University Press, 2015.

Rosteck, Thomas, ed. *At the Intersection: Cultural Studies and Rhetorical Studies*. New York: Guilford, 1999.

Phallocentrism

Understanding phallocentrism and its significance for twentieth-century feminists requires a nuanced understanding of what a "phallus" is in philosophical and psychoanalytic terms. For Sigmund Freud, female psychosexual development occurs through a desire for what they come to realize they lack—the penis—hence developing what he terms "penis envy" during the "phallic stage."

Freud's descriptions of sexual difference are first critiqued in the 1920s and 1930s by psychoanalysts Ernest Jones, Karen Horney, and Melanie Klein. Responding to Freud, they put forward theories of female sexual development that are not formulated around penis envy. Horney disputes Freud's idea that females feel a "lack" based on their genitals. She argues that girls and women have always been measured by masculine standards within a social order that privileges the penis. Similarly, Jones notes that "there is a healthy suspicion growing that men analysts have been led to adopt an unduly phallo-centric view of the problems in question [understanding female development], the importance of the female organs being correspondingly underestimated." Hence phallocentrism comes to stand for a way of viewing female psychosexual development that is centered around a veneration of the penis and male desire. Eventually, for feminist theorists, the phallus becomes a signifier of patriarchy, a political, social and cultural order in which men hold the balance of power.

Jacques Lacan abstracts Freud's idea of penis envy and lack by defining the phallus as a signifier of desire. Lacan believes that subjects enter into language (what he calls the "symbolic order") through the infant's desire to be/to have the mother's ultimate object of desire. He describes the father figure in Western culture as blocking that taboo desire. For Lacan, the phallus is not the biological organ. Instead it signifies that which is inaccessible to men and women alike—possessing the unobtainable object of one's love, or, being the locus of the other's desire, a subject who can provide exactly what the other desires of it.

In the 1970s, Luce Irigaray is critical of the "phallocratic order" for the way in which it defines female sexuality in relation to a privileged masculine desire and thus fails to recognize the plurality of female desire and erotic pleasure. She writes:

> In Freud, sexual pleasure boils down to being plus or minus one sex organ: the penis. And sexual "otherness" comes down to "not having it." Thus, woman's lack of penis and her envy of the penis ensure the function of the negative . . . in what could be called a phallocentric—or phallotropic-dialectic.

Irigaray is troubled that Lacan expands the concept of female penis envy by arguing that it also plays a role in the structural dimension (language) through his theory of the phallus as signifier.

Jacqueline Rose and others have defended Freud and Lacan's focus on the phallus in the development of female sexuality by noting that they are describing a psycho-social-sexual phenomenon rather than championing it. For Irigaray and other feminists such as Hélène Cixous, Freud doesn't take into account the historical determinants of his observations of female sexuality so the phallocentric order he describes often comes across as natural and fixed. Rose has qualified her defense of Lacan stating that there is "no question of denying here that Lacan was implicated in the phallocentrism he described."

(*See also* Chapter 7, Psychoanalytic Theory; Cixous, Hélène; Freud, Sigmund; Irigaray, Luce; *and* Lacan, Jacques)

Lara Stevens, *University of Melbourne* (Australia)

Further Reading
Cixous, Hélène. "Sorties: Out and Out: attacks/ways out/forays." In *Newly Born Woman* [1975]. Hélène Cixous and Catherine Clément. Trans. B. Wing. Manchester: Manchester University Press, 1986. 69–73, 78–86, 131.
Irigaray, Luce. *Speculum of the Other Woman* [1974]. Trans. Gillian C. Gill. Ithaca: Cornell University Press, 1985.
Irigaray, Luce. *This Sex Which Is Not One* [1977]. Trans. Catherine Porter with Carolyn Burke. Ithaca: Cornell University Press, 1985.
Rose, Jacqueline. *Sexuality in the Field of Vision*. New York: Verso, 2005.

Phenomenology

Phenomenology emerged at the beginning of the twentieth century. Philosophers firmly affiliated with this movement are Edmund Husserl, Martin Heidegger, and Maurice Merleau-Ponty. This list can be expanded by the names of other philosophers who were critical of certain aspects of phenomenology, but can arguably still be understood as phenomenologists since they built on and transformed the phenomenological project: Jean-Paul Sartre, Emmanuel Levinas, Jacques Derrida, to name just the most famous ones. When founding phenomenology, Husserl conceived of it as an open-ended approach that would continue to attend to further regions of phenomena as well as advance its method.

A preliminary definition of phenomenology could be given by stating that it focuses on "how" something appears to me rather than "what" it is. The focus on "how" objects appear or are given to us means that phenomenology comes to examine "ways" or "modes" of "givenness." If we examine "how" a spatiotemporal object is given to us, it turns out that it is given in "horizons," or through its connections and references to other objects. Husserl calls such horizons "worlds," thus leading us to arguably the most central concept in phenomenology, and the one that is most potent for literature and culture.

"World" is at the same time a difficult concept because we take world for granted to the extent that it becomes challenging to make it a concept as such. We can receive help from two domains: the domain of literature, and that of culture or the alien. Literature can open up worlds for us that are fictional, yet that still alert us to the significance of worlds. More precisely, the world that is opened up is always a cultural world of some sorts, and Husserl introduces the concept of the "alien" to conceptualize cultural worlds.

In *The Crisis of European Sciences and Transcendental Phenomenology*, Husserl calls alienness a "fundamental category of all historicity." The concept of the alien world allows developing a response to the question as to what an alien object is: the special feature of an alien object is that it is not only an object unfamiliar and incomprehensible to us, but an object that seems to belong to a context alien to us. Thereby, it makes us aware of the significance of world which otherwise remains hidden due to the familiarity of our home context.

Translation in the widest sense emerges as a central topic for such phenomenological explorations of culture. From a phenomenological perspective, language emerges as a world in which we learn to dwell (rather than a body of words to be accumulated). Translation thus has to negotiate between these worlds; the translator emerges in this process as a guide who bears ethical responsibilities rather than just striving for correctness or fluency. Furthermore, it turns out that there is translation within one and the same language as well as between linguistic and nonlinguistic languages, such as gestures or artistic expressions.

(*See also* Chapter 2, Narrative and Narratology; Chapter 8, Rhetoric; Chapter 9, Deconstruction; Chapter 23, Materialisms; Chapter 26, Affect Studies; Derrida, Jacques; Heidegger, Martin; Husserl, Edmund; Levinas, Emmanuel; Social Constructionism; *and* Translation)

Alexander Kozin, *University of Sussex (United Kingdom)*
Tanja Staehler, *University of Sussex (United Kingdom)*

Further Reading

Heidegger, Martin. *Being and Time* [1927]. Trans. Joan Stambaugh. Rvsd. Dennis J. Schmidt. Albany: SUNY: Press, 2010.

Husserl, Edmund. *The Crisis of European Sciences and Transcendental Phenomenology* [1954]. Trans. David Carr. Evanston: Northwestern University Press, 1970.

Lewis, Michael, and Tanja Staehler. *Phenomenology: An Introduction*. London: Continuum, 2010.

Merleau-Ponty, Maurice. *Phenomenology of Perception* [1945]. Trans. Donald A. Landes. London: Routledge, 2013.

Philology

Western philology was born when Akkadian-speaking scholars preserved the dying Sumerian language; or when the Homeric authors' songs were first written down; or when stage actors first emerged from the Greek chorus; or in the libraries of Alexandria or Baghdad; or in Renaissance humanism, or Napoleonic imperialism, or Prussian *Wissenschaft*, or even in the late-twentieth-century philosophical mode once called "deconstruction." Globally eastern and southern genealogies of philology are every bit as contested. Love of learning (philology in the etymological sense) often exceeds the collation of words (philology in the practical sense), which may explain the incompatible claims on philology made by the stuffiest scholars and radical intellectuals alike. They may not be incompatible at all, if we recognize that the transfixture of words in dictionaries, concordances, and other incunabula embraces the passage of time while resisting it: that is, if we recognize that the labor of scholarship entails irony, rather than naïveté, in knowing its own futility. Less commendably, philology has lent its hand to ethnonationalist campaigns against linguistic impurity and linguistic obfuscations or normalizations of dominion and plunder, in the suppression of Welsh, Scots, Irish, aboriginal North American, Australian, and Hawaiian languages, Basque, Catalan, Galician, Ukrainian, Polish, Lithuanian, Belarusian, Korean, Ryukyuan languages, and Kurdish, to name a very few. Revisionist conceptions of philology have more often complained of complicity (often the most liberal complicity) with empire than of traditionalism as such: the "return to philology" performed by a figure like Edward W. Said is neither an endorsement nor a rejection of paleography, codicology, diplomatics, *Wortphilologie*, or textual criticism more generally, but a critique of such practices' historical Orientalism, understood not as a conspiracy but as an inflection or episteme. It is not a matter of resignation to history, but of insisting that the best of philology (its humaneness and worldliness, its synthetic ambition) be actively separated from its worst (its technocratic inclinations, its analytic positivism, its racism). The apparent dilemma of philology is shadowed by the apparent dilemma of the state and the law, other assemblages of disciplinary practices that in ordering life in indispensable ways, the most fundamental of which no sane person could repudiate, nevertheless also narrow life and damage it, in ways it would be insane to deny. Literary scholars, the principal heirs of what was once called philology, may endure this contradiction with special intensity, given their role as custodians of state culture whose assistance in propping up empire is no longer needed. Some have proposed a new role for philology in the culturalization of the techno-sciences whose authority decisively displaced those of religion and nation in the era of decolonization—and which are no less susceptible to authoritarian canalization. It remains to be seen if this is a mission that matters.

(*See also* Chapter 1, Early Theory; Chapter 27, Antitheory; Hermeneutics; *and* Nietzsche, Friedrich)

Brian Lennon, *Penn State University (United States)*

Further Reading

Hamilton, John T. *Security: Politics, Humanity, and the Philology of Care*. Princeton: Princeton University Press, 2013.

Lennon, Brian. *Passwords: Philology, Security, Authentication*. Cambridge: Harvard University Press, 2018.

Pollock, Sheldon, and Benjamin A. Elman, ed. *World Philology*. Cambridge: Harvard University Press, 2015.

Turner, James. *Philology: The Forgotten Origins of the Modern Humanities*. Princeton: Princeton University Press, 2015.

Philosophy, Literature as (*See* Literature as Philosophy)

Planetary Criticism

Planetary studies in general and planetary literary-cultural criticism in particular come to the fore around the dawn of the twenty-first century, initially as a subcategory of and critical reaction to global studies. Complete with its own methodology, terminology, and foci, this interdisciplinary field has left its imprint on various areas of teaching and research, so much so that scholars have been talking about a "planetary turn" in the humanities. The turn itself is marked, rather ambiguously, by this multidisciplinarity. For, occurring dialectically by virtue of an evolutionary dynamic both symbiotic and adversarial, the shift has triggered moves away from certain disciplines and approaches as well as paradigm readjustments inside them. Accordingly, its transdisciplinary sweep has affected, besides global studies, work done in world-systems analysis, postcolonialism, transnationalism and postnationalism, cosmopolitanism, communications, ecocriticism, human rights, philosophy of Deleuzian-Guattarian inspiration, and World Literature, to list but a few. Pivotal to the complex realignments obtaining inside and across these knowledge domains is the notion that mainstream discourses struggling to come to grips with "globalization" provide just one way of viewing our incrementally integrated or "worlded" world and only one modality of articulating the relationship between culture and this world. As opposed to "globe," "globalization," and the rest of the global family, "planet," "planetarization," "planetarism," and "planetarity" seek, then, to supply another *worlding narrative*, another way of understanding and reading the increasingly world-systemic assemblage that, in the new techno-communicational and sociocultural environment of the post-Cold War late-global era, is weaving together national economies, as well as collective and individual, human and nonhuman, animate and inanimate, manufactured and natural actors, objects, sites, and phenomena.

Most globalization critics have summed up this integrative process as *totalization*. The globe, they have argued, sets the world up as a largely corporate arena of smooth capital flows, outsourcing, offshoring, and the like. Further, as globe, the world is neither an open biocultural system nor our natural environment/ground (the "earth") nor our cosmic address ("Earth"), but a mundane whole that flaunts an ominous *totality*. The global world purports to be a well-rounded, integrated existentially, and politically definitive closed system, a teleology enforced from a few hubs of power by feedback loops, symmetries, parallels, and exchange procedures across a web of links progressively overlapping with the world itself. The world worlds into globe, "goes global," we are told, once the infinite and multitudinous potentiality of worldly ontology has been repurposed materially and conceptually as domains of the one, the homogeneous, the circular, the repetitive, and the selfsame. Subject to lucrative, profit-taking calculations and rationalizations, the world as globe is reduced ontologically, and so it cannot function as an endless space of qualitative leaps and true progress, as a playground of being anymore. This ontological reduction has left its imprint on the entire critical model of globality.

"Planet" and its paradigm set out to offer an *alternative* to this world picture. Both descriptive and prescriptive, a concept as analytic as it is ethical, planet is for planetary critics not an accomplished oneness, a structured, coherently administered, and measured geopolitical totality. Therefore,

this system is characterized, both geoculturally and epistemologically, by multiplicity, open-endedness, and sociocultural and political potentialities. Neither an attained finitude nor a teleology, the planet is a soft system: young, evolving and expanding, a world but hardly *the* world. In brief, the planet is an incommensurability but not a globality. Ontologically (in terms of what it is) and philosophically (how planetary critics view it), the planet is not coextensive with our existential and cognitional gamut as humans, with all we can be and envisage, much as it encompasses a world vaster than the human, the anthropocene, and the animate. As spatial extension and ontological complexity, this concept has of late provided both the interpretive unit and the basic reading method for a criticism more and more interested in "reading for the planet," that is, in examining its object—books, movies, high-brow and low-brow artifacts, and entire traditions—as part of ensembles bigger than the nation-state and privileged by methodological nationalism.

(*See also* Chapter 4, Marxism; Chapter 14, Ecocriticism; Globalization; Hyperobject; Spivak, Gayatri; *and* Worldiness)

Christian Moraru, *University of North Carolina, Greensboro (United States)*

Further Reading

Elias, Amy J., and Christian Moraru, eds. *The Planetary Turn: Relationality and Geoaesthetics in the Twenty-first Century*. Evanston, IL: Northwestern University Press, 2015.

Moraru, Christian. *Reading for the Planet: Toward a Geomethodology*. Ann Arbor, MI: University of Michigan Press, 2015.

Spivak, Gayatri Chakravorty. *Death of a Discipline*. New York: Columbia University Press, 2003.

Platonism

Platonism refers both to Plato's philosophy and to schools of thought that derive or are influenced by Plato's core principles—namely, his idealist view of the world, which relied on the distinction between empirical reality and the ideal realm of Forms. For Plato, empirical reality is subject to time and corruption; its phenomena are perceptible but not intelligible. In contrast, the Forms are immutable; though imperceptible, they are intelligible. The philosopher should be devoted to the contemplation of the Forms, which alone provide the guidelines for an ethics that surpasses the logic of "might makes right." Plato founded his Academy in Athens, and it functioned as a school until its closure by Emperor Justinian in 529 CE.

The most important Platonism of late antiquity was Neoplatonism (third to sixth century CE), which fused Peripatetic and Stoic elements of Middle Platonism (first century BCE to third century CE) with mysticism. Its central figure was Plotinus, while other representative thinkers were Porphyry, Iamblichus, Proclus, and Hypatia.

Platonism influenced the Church Fathers, both Eastern and Western: in particular, Basil the Great and Gregory of Nazianzus for the East, and Augustine for the West. In the Middle Ages, Thomas Aquinas retained Platonic notions, even though Aristotle was the major pre-Christian source for the theology at the time. Later, during the Renaissance, Neoplatonism returned to inform Renaissance humanism, with Marsilio Ficino as its founder.

It is an understatement that Plato and Platonism have been at the foundations of Western philosophy, whether as inspiring forces or objects of critique. Platonism has been revivified through a twentieth-century debate concerning the very status of Plato's dialogues as a complete or deliberately incomplete expression of his system: on one side, the esotericists (represented by the Tübingen school, though there are variants of esotericism inside and outside this school) argue that the true Platonic doctrine remains unwritten and was spoken only to select students; on the other, the anti-esotericists reject this and interpret Plato through the extant corpus. Leo Strauss, an esotericist (not of the Tübingen persuasion), was an important Platonist in the United States, noted for his political—if also controversial—interpretations of Plato.

As mentioned above, Platonism is not only a font of philosophical inspiration, but also a target of critique. Most interesting for literary scholars are the criticisms launched by Friedrich Nietzsche, who expresses his distaste for Plato in terms similar to his distaste for Christianity. Nietzsche attacks Plato's ethereal Ideas for being as life-denying as the Christian promise of a remote, salvific world. After Nietzsche, Platonism became the target of postmodern critics, among them Jacques Derrida, for whom it is synonymous with metaphysical logocentrism. Despite these critical blows, the ethico-political questions Platonism inaugurated remain fresh and relevant even to some post-structuralists such as Alain Badiou, who affirms Plato as a major influence.

In addition to the continental-philosophical history of Platonism, "platonism" (often with lower-case "p") also applies to analytic strains of philosophy, which—although they do not embrace the entirety of Plato's philosophy—share the main concern with the foundations of logic, and posit the existence of abstract objects and mathematical truths as ontologically independent of our conceptual or linguistic constructions. Figures loosely gathering around this modern Platonism include Edmund Husserl, Bertrand Russell, Kurt Gödel, Gottlob Frege, W. V. O. Quine, and Hilary Putnam.

(*See also* Aristotelianism; Badiou, Alain; Chapter 1, Early Theory; Chapter 9, Deconstruction; Derrida, Jacques; Desire; Dialogue; Dissemination; Humanism; Husserl, Edmund; Idealism; Irigaray, Luce; Metaphysics; Nietzsche, Friedrich; Signifier and Signified; Sophist; *and* Writing)

Kalliopi Nikolopoulou, *University at Buffalo*
(United States)

Further Reading

Corrigan, Kevin, and John D. Turner, eds. *Platonisms: Ancient, Modern, and Postmodern*. Boston: E. J. Brill, 2007.

Moravcsik, Julius. *Plato and Platonism: Plato's Conception of Appearance and Reality in Ontology, Epistemology, and Ethics, and Its Modern Echoes*. Oxford: Wiley-Blackwell, 1992.

Zuckert, Catherine H. *Plato's Philosophers: The Coherence of the Dialogues*. Chicago: University of Chicago Press, 2009.

Pluralism

Pluralism is the state of multiple systems of belief, viewpoints, ideologies, perspectives, political parties coexisting. In literary and cultural spheres, the concept of pluralism is often applied to models of reading, criticism, teaching, and analysis that refuse explicitly to privilege one particular analytic framework over another.

Activists and cultural critics on the Left have pointed out that while pluralism may prima facie seem like a good idea, and may appear to be value-free, it is a central tenet of liberalism and is founded on liberal and neoliberal conceptualizations of the subject and the nation-state that, as Ellen Rooney has argued, erase difference in the service of promoting the endlessly persuadable "reasonable man." Critiques of pluralism complain that celebrations of pluralism evacuate the responsibility for making ethical choices among competing (and often incompatible) ideologies which are all presented as equally valuable, and that pluralism's supposed neutrality masks the materiality of historically and socially determined power relations that preclude the equal coexistence of multiple positionalities at any given time in any given space. For example, the uncritical advocacy of "free speech" by conservatives and liberals is viewed by some critics of pluralism as naïve in its inattention to context and its assumptions that all subjects have equal access to speech and that all subjects' speech utterances carry equal force (i.e., that all speech is equally "free"). For these critics, then, pluralism entrenches the status quo, since existing power relations are merely reproduced by a state (or other) apparatus that legitimates itself precisely by invoking the ideology of pluralism via a claim to welcome diverse (oppositional) viewpoints. Conservative reactions against #BlackLivesMatter in the United States (and elsewhere) in the 2010s offer one demonstration of this effect: under the mantle of pluralism (all lives should be equally valued), conservatives insist that "All Lives Matter," an insistence that effectively seeks to restore the status quo ante that also claimed that "all lives matter."

In literary studies, pluralism often takes the form of literary traditions, literary sub-specialties, or "schools" of critical theory that are presented (in anthologies, textbooks, and college classrooms) as peaceably coexisting or competing equally for the critic's favor, a model that has been scathingly dismissed as a "cafeteria counter" understanding of literary and cultural studies. The reader/critic/student is invited to choose from the smorgasbord on offer, as if all options are equally significant, as if all choices are equally (in)consequential, without any sense of how the options work with/against each other. Moreover, the array of options gives subjects a false sense of choice; in fact, choice is severely limited. Rooney points out the irony of pluralism being able to tolerate any ideology as long as it isn't anti-pluralist. Under capitalism, pluralism's political analog, consumer options do not include non-participation in capitalism.

Some critics have condemned postmodernism and post-structuralism for promoting an "anything goes" pluralism to the extent that either or both epistemologies refuse grand narratives, undermine canonical distinctions between high and low art, and reject universal truths as lacking historical and cultural specificity. Postmodernists and post-structuralists might respond that to recognize that values are historically and culturally conditioned is not necessarily to demur on making aesthetic, ethical, and political judgments, but rather to own the contingency of these judgments.

(*See also* Chapter 27, Antitheory; Culture Wars; *and* Multiculturalism)

Ian Barnard, *Chapman University (United States)*

Further Reading

Graff, Gerald. *Beyond the Culture Wars: How Teaching the Conflicts Can Revitalize American Education*. New York: Norton, 1992.

Rooney, Ellen. *Seductive Reasoning: Pluralism as the Problematic of Contemporary Literary Theory*. Ithaca: Cornell University Press, 1989.

Taylor, Keeanga-Yamahtta. *From #BlackLivesMatter to Black Liberation*. Chicago: Haymarket Books, 2016.

Poetics

Poetics suggests both reflections on the art of making a literary work as well as fundamental principles of literary construction (poesis). *Poetics* is frequently applied to any cultural activity, from the poetics of everyday life (as in Michel DeCerteau's *Ars de faire* or art of doing, usually translated as *The Practice of Everyday Life,* 1980) to Eduardo Glissant's *Poetics of Relation* (1990; creolization, errantry, exile, and multiplicity) to Christian Bök's "the poetics of an imaginary science," referring to Alfred Jarry's pataphysics, to—well—why not?, the poetics of fly fishing or kite flying. Cognitive linguist George Lakoff explores the "poetics of mind" (Raymond W. Gibbs's term), that is, the language-bound metaphoricity of perception. Poetics precedes theory, at least historically, with Aristotle's *Poetics* (fourth century BCE) being the inaugural work in the West. But Aristotle's defining treatise is bracketed by two works that extoll flux in contrast to Aristotle's measured (and potentially normative) precepts. Heraklitus (sixth century BCE), known to us only in fragments, has come to stand for a poetics of process and change. Lucretius swerves from Aristotle's precepts with perhaps the signal work of poetics in the Western canon, *De Rerum Naturum* (Of Things' Nature), a cosmology of world-making by atoms colliding in space, with no underlying principal or meaning. Lucretius wrote in verse and his verse remains a challenge to the prose of theory, which has, in the last half-century, replaced poetics as the governing discourse of literary and cultural studies. Since the revolutions of the word in the first part of the twentieth century, poetics has been associated with collectivist literary movements as well as with the formal innovations of individual poets. While manifestos typically put forward a specific program, poetics is more often associated with aesthetic reflection of individuals. In the present, poetics can be distinguished from theory or philosophy by its provisional nature and its contextual specificity. Poetics is an actor in a contested field, making cases for preferred poetic practices, not an arbiter of arguments or scientific knowledge. In de Certeau's sense, poetics is a tactic, not a theory or a strategy. As a result, poetics makes strange bedfellows, since its allegiances are to the aesthetic not the moral. This has given poetics a renewed urgency in our time. *Poetics is not a moral compass but a mortal rumpus.* Within the space of contemporary verse culture, *poetics* has come to be contrasted with *craft*. The Fenza Doctrine, named after D. W. Fenza, the long-time head of the influential Association of [Creative] Writing Programs, rejects the philosophical and ideological orientation of poetics, advocating a normative poetics that articulates itself as pedagogically friendly dogma. For this reason, university Ph.D. "poetics programs," offer a different approach than M.F.A creative writing programs, though in the past decade several M.F.A. programs have adopted a more "poetics"-friendly orientation. To adapt a precept of Robert Creeley's: Poetics is never more than the extension of poetry, just as poetry is never more than the extension of poetics.

(*See also* Aristotelianism; Chapter 3, Narrative and Narratology; Chapter 4, Marxism; Chapter 8, Rhetoric; Chapter 13, Race and Postcolonial Studies; de Man, Paul; Dialogue; Formalism; *and* Irony)

Charles Bernstein, *University of Pennsylvania (United States)*

Further Reading
Bernstein, Charles. *A Poetics.* Cambridge: Harvard University Press, 1992.

Political Economy

Before there was "economics," the field of inquiry concerning trade and banking practices, labor, the taxation policies of the nation-state, financial speculation, and debt was known as "political economy." In the eighteenth and nineteenth centuries, political economy was considered an offshoot of moral philosophy (in fact Adam Smith was professor of moral philosophy at the University of Glasgow from 1752 to 1764), but at the end of the nineteenth century the increasing relative prestige of the natural sciences led economists to prefer the term "economics," as in Alfred Marshall's influential *The Principles of Economics* (1890). The continuing trend toward privileging the natural-scientific or mathematical (i.e., econometric) aspects of economic theory has led to disciplinary clarity, but critics such as Karl Polanyi in *The Great Transformation* (1944) argue that economics has also lost touch with domains of thought that used to be considered relevant to political economy, such as historical, moral, anthropological, or ecological considerations. More particularly, removing the word "political" reflects an unspoken but highly influential assumption that markets can exist spontaneously in society without support from governments or other political organizations.

Though economic thought in the West goes back at least to Aristotle, political economy as a discipline is usually considered to start with Adam Smith's fusion of practical economic advice with a theoretical disciplinary overview in his *The Wealth of Nations* (1776), a volume that defends free trade (laissez-faire) against mercantilism and colonialism, and uses the metaphor of an "invisible hand" to reconcile moral strictures against selfish behavior with the merchant's traditionally-scorned search for profit. The "invisible hand" provides an image of a prosperous economy in which virtuous social order is paradoxically improved when regulators refrain from intervening in merchants' choices. Smith's vision of a self-organizing economy inspired many other political economists including Thomas Malthus, who argued that overpopulation might lead to extinction (a theory that influenced Darwin); David Ricardo, known for his theory of national "comparative advantage" in trade and for his grim vision of renters progressively driven to less productive land (a theory that influenced Marx); James Mill, who combined economic inquiry with Jeremy Bentham's utilitarian principle of "the greatest good for the greatest number"; and Nassau Senior, who argued against regulating factories. Mill's son John Stuart Mill reconsidered the legacy of utilitarianism in his definitive *Principles of Political Economy* (1848), which contained some socialist passages.

Though Adam Smith's work antedates most of the British industrial revolution, the work of political economists was increasingly pressed into political service in the interests of the rising capitalist class. The Whig-Radical coalition that came to power in 1832 combined political economy with utilitarianism to pursue rational reform, whose excesses were attacked by Charles Dickens. Meanwhile Henry Carey in America and Friedrich List in Germany reacted against British laissez-faire with their own theories of national protectionism. Political economy is sometimes known as "classical economic theory," as opposed to "neoclassical economics," which replaced the classical "labor theory of value" with marginal utility theory (based on consumer demand) in the late nineteenth century.

(*See also* Base and Superstructure; Capitalism; Chapter 4, Marxism; Chapter 15, Biopower and Biopolitics; Chapter 19, Media Studies; Community; Control; Cultural Capital; Cultural Materialism; Finance; Free Market; Labor; Marx, Karl; *and* Neoliberalism)

Eleanor Courtemanche, *University of Illinois at Urbana-Champaign (United States)*

Further Reading

Courtemanche, Eleanor. *The "Invisible Hand" and British Fiction 1818-1860: Adam Smith, Political Economy, and the Genre of Realism*. Basingstoke: Palgrave Macmillan, 2011.

Dickens, Charles. *Hard Times* [1854]. Ed. Kate Flint. Harmondsworth: Penguin, 2003.

Polanyi, Karl. *The Great Transformation: The Political and Economic Origins of Our Time* [1944]. Boston: Beacon Press, 2001.

Political Theology

Political theology is a philosophical concept that traces its origin to the work of Carl Schmitt. Schmitt published *Political Theology: Four Chapters on the Concept of Sovereignty* in 1922. Here he claims that all political concepts of the modern state are secularized theological concepts. Although he later became a supporter of the Nazis and was marginalized, his ideas have become more influential in recent decades, partly because of the return of religious extremism. For Schmitt, political theology helps explain the concept of sovereignty, where power works in a personal decisionist way rather than in terms of formal legal procedures. The sovereign has the power to decide what constitutes an exception to any norm or law.

Giorgio Agamben revived interest in political theology in the 1990s with his important book *Homo Sacer: Biopower and Bare Life* (1995). Agamben develops a genealogy of the entanglement of religious and political ideas from Greek and Roman antiquity to the present, including important elements of Christianity. He combines Schmitt's insights with Michel Foucault's reflections on biopower. The *homo sacer*, or sacred man, is the person who cannot be sacrificed but can be killed, and this Roman idea is expanded in contemporary society to include virtually everyone. We are all practically *homo sacer*, because nothing is sacred and we are all exposed to death, most intensely in concentration camps. In his follow-up *State of Exception* (2003), Agamben shows how Schmitt's ideas about the exception continue to inform global political situations, including the state of emergency in the wake of the September 11, 2001, terror attacks.

In more conventional theological works, Latin American liberation theologians like Gustavo Gutiérrez, Leonardo Boff, and Juan Luis Segundo argue that Jesus as suffering and crucified Christ means that God has a preferential option for the poor and oppressed. They appropriate Marxist analyses into Christian theology in important and controversial ways. German theologians like J. B. Metz and Jürgen Moltmann, inspired by the utopian philosophy of Ernst Bloch, have also argued that Christian conceptions of liberation and a God who suffers with the people give Christian theology a distinctive leftist political edge.

In the twenty-first century, a new focus on political theology has emerged in the context of radical and postmodern theologies influenced by the death of God. Political theology is a way to name the interrelation and interdependence of religious and political ideas, practices and analyses in what is sometimes called a postsecular or postsecularist world. In a postmodern world dominated by neoliberal capitalism, the resurgence of religion in various forms indicates a breakdown of modern liberalism, with its insistence on a clear and consistent distinction between a private sphere of religious freedom and a public sphere of nonreligious reason. Modern secularism is a premise of classical liberalism, but as liberalism is falling apart, secularism is being challenged along with it. We need tools

to understand what is going on with religion and politics today, and the discourse of political theology is one way to do that.

(*See also* Agamben, Giorgio; Bare Life; Chapter 8, Rhetoric; Chapter 15, Biopower and Biopolitics; *and* Exceptionalist State)

Clayton Crockett, *University of Central Arkansas (United States)*

Further Reading

Agamben, Giorgio, *Homo Sacer: Sovereign Power and Bare Life* [1995]. Trans. Daniel Heller-Roazen. Stanford: Stanford University Press, 1998.

Crockett, Clayton. *Radical Political Theology: Religion and Politics After Liberalism*. Columbia: Columbia University Press, 2011.

Schmitt, Carl. *Political Theology: Four Chapters on the Concept of Sovereignty* [1922]. Trans. George Schwab. Chicago: University of Chicago Press, 2005.

Political Unconscious

The political unconscious refers to the idea that works of art necessarily bear political content that is not immediately manifest. It was first theorized by Fredric Jameson in his 1981 treatise *The Political Unconscious: Narrative as a Socially Symbolic Act*, the most influential work of Marxist literary theory in the Anglophone context since the Frankfurt school. The two halves of the title seem to present an ambivalence: in order for something to be an act in any meaningful sense, it has to be conscious. Jameson's hermeneutic method, however, discerns three distinct horizons, and the "socially symbolic act" refers only to the first. On a first approach, the literary work is an intervention into a particular historical situation—understood immediately as a lived impasse or aporia and redescribed by criticism as a social contradiction—that the work of art seeks to resolve. The second horizon is that of social class, not understood sociologically as a categorizing concept, but as the fundamental antagonism that organizes capitalist societies: the literary work is unavoidably caught up in the ideological conflict between the "irreconcilable demands and positions of antagonistic classes." The third horizon is history itself, not in the sense of a sequence of punctual events, but in terms of the great historical crises and revolutions in a society's mode of production. This final horizon is registered primarily not in content but in changes within literary form, which itself is then seen to have an historical content. The canonical example is Georg Lukács's analysis of the rise of the historical novel, whose eclipse of the historical drama is not a matter of fashion but rather a function of the changing organization of society in the wake of the bourgeois revolutions.

Where is the unconscious in all this? Despite Jameson's abundant references to post-Freudian psychoanalysis, the interpretive levels beyond the initial one are not hidden intentions that reside secretly in the mind of the artist, but rather entailments of the original act. We are dealing, then, not with the Freudian unconscious, but with the Hegelian one. In the *Phenomenology of Spirit* (1807), the unconscious is simply everything entailed or presupposed by an action that is not present to consciousness in that action. The distinction between the Hegelian and the Freudian unconscious can be seen most starkly in Hegel's few words in *Phenomenology of Spirit* on *Oedipus Rex*, where *das Unbewusste*, unusually nominalized, as opposed to the more common, adjectival *bewusstlos*, is simply the unknown that is nonetheless part of the deed. When, in his study of the great modernist painter and

writer Wyndham Lewis, Jameson discovers the absent cause of Lewis's proto-fascism and the latent center of his novels—their political unconscious—to be Marxism, this is because Lewis's petty-bourgeois class consciousness, which is central to Lewis's work but which Lewis himself understands not as class consciousness but rather as a kind of meritocratic privilege, logically presupposes working-class consciousness, and is unnecessary and unthinkable without it. Lewis is not aware of that entailment and cannot be said to repress it in any psychological sense. Any Freudian "return of the repressed"—the fact, for example, that social revolution continually reappears in Lewis's work—would then have nothing to do with hidden aspects of the text or of Lewis's psyche, but would rather illustrate the Hegelian "ruse of reason": the fact that logical entailments are real entailments.

(*See also* Chapter 4, Marxism; Chapter 22, Identity Studies; Class; Jameson, Fredric; Production; Semiotic Square; *and* Surface Reading)

Nicholas Brown, *University of Illinois, Chicago (United States)*

Further Reading

Best, Stephen, and Sharon Marcus. "Surface Reading: An Introduction." *Representations* 108.1 (Fall 2009): 1–21.

Jameson, Fredric. *The Political Unconscious: Narrative as a Socially Symbolic Act.* Ithaca: Cornell, 1981.

Jameson, Fredric. *Fables of Aggression: Wyndham Lewis, the Modernist as Fascist.* Berkeley: University of California Press, 1979.

Lukács, Georg. *The Historical Novel* [1937]. Trans. Hannah Mitchel and Stanley Mitchell. Lincoln: University of Nebraska Press, 1983.

Pop Culture

Pop culture is, at one and the same time, a commonly used term everyone knows the meaning of, and a surprisingly complicated analytic and critical term, whose primary import for literary and cultural theory has been its expansion of the range of texts and practices studied and explored within the human sciences. Often associated with the field of cultural studies, the study of pop culture has challenged the legitimacy and self-certainty of areas of study linked to canons and elite forms of culture, and enriched our understanding of the operations of power and agency in and through culture.

The most familiar use of the term pop culture identifies it with the entertainment produced through and by commercial media (television, film, the music industry, etc.) that have the economic and technological capacity to reach large, demographically diverse, and geographically dispersed audiences. Popularity is measured, in this case, by patterns of consumption: it refers to the things we buy (or watch, or listen to, etc.). A somewhat different use of pop culture defines it in terms not of consumption but of production: popular culture is what "the people" make or do for themselves. This definition fits fairly closely with the anthropological definition of culture as "the practices of everyday life" or of folk culture linked to specific communities and communicated from generation to generation.

Both of these definitions understand pop culture as a space of diverse and expansive activities. However, they also position pop culture in relation to power in a specific way that has fast become established. This is despite efforts by scholars to undo the presumption that commercial culture is ipso facto ideological (communicating the values and belief system of capitalist society), while the pop culture of everyday life is the site (at least potentially) of agency in and against this self-same ideology. To avoid producing a definition of pop culture that falls too clearly on the side of celebrating the folk or denigrating the masses, it is best understood as the communicative practices of everyday life (where "communicative practices" comprise all those activities concerned with the production of meaning: talking, writing, social rituals such as eating, shopping, dancing, music, visual culture, sports, fashion, etc.) that are shared among many members of a society, including and especially those who aren't especially socially, economically, or politically powerful. This definition accomplishes three things: (1) it signals the inclusion of mass media alongside, and even within, the practices of everyday life, without determining in advance what relationship it has to those practices; (2) it emphasizes the *meaningful* nature of pop culture—meaningful in the sense that it is important, as well as in the sense that it is concerned with the production of sense and social value; and (3) it highlights the issue of power that always and overtly dogs the production of culture in pop culture.

(*See also* Chapter 11, Cultural Studies; Chapter 16, Pop Culture; Eco, Umberto; *and* Hall, Stuart)

Imre Szeman, *University of Waterloo (Canada)*

Further Reading

Fiske, John. *Understanding Popular Culture.* Second ed. London: Routledge, 2010.

Hall, Stuart. "Cultural Studies and Its Theoretical Legacies." In *Cultural Studies.* Ed. Lawrence Grossberg, Cary Nelson, and Paula Treichler. London: Routledge, 1992. 277–94.

McRobbie, Angela. *The Uses of Cultural Studies.* London: Sage, 2005.

Possible Worlds (*See* Chapter 3, Narrative and Narratology)

Postcolonialism

Postcolonialism commonly refers today to the political, cultural, and economic condition of countries formerly colonized by European powers, as well as the academic study of European colonization and its impacts. In the early decades of postcolonial scholarship, arguments over terminology in the field often revolved around the nature of the "post-" in "postcolonialism," and whether it should refer more narrowly to post-independence conditions, or rather to post-invasion cultural relationships more broadly. Debates today have shifted focus, with wider acceptance of an expansive understanding of the field's potential scope. Postcolonialism includes studies of the imperial conquests and colonial settlements that began in the fifteenth century up through the accession of former colonies to independent statehood in the mid-twentieth century and beyond. Accordingly, postcolonial scholarship is animated by a wide range of questions: How might comparative studies of colonialisms better elucidate linkages and shifts between "pre-modern" and "modern" forms of domination? How do various forms of colonization come to assume or promote particular modes sociopolitical organization (such as nation-states), and of what consequence are these structures today? How has globalization shifted political and economic power relationships? Does the term "postcolonial" adequately channel our critical attention today, or do we risk overlooking new modes of agency, relationship, and oppression by projecting past configurations onto a different historical moment with its own particular characteristics?

As a field of study, postcolonialism spans a number of humanities and social science disciplines, and scholarship in this area varies in method and focus. The term postcolonialism itself also takes on different meanings in relation to other synonyms and contrasting terms. If colonialism designates at once an ideology or logic and also a structure of power, postcolonialism represents both attempts to critique or refute colonialist worldviews and projects and also shifts in this structure itself. Postcoloniality is a synonym for postcolonialism that emphasizes the critical, rather than descriptive, stance taken by anti-colonial thinkers, while neocolonialism designates structures of power that reinstate older colonial modes of exploitation and cultural conquest but in new and different forms. The term decolonialism, most commonly found in Latin American studies, also shares much with postcolonialism, but is used by scholars to highlight the specific contributions of non-Western peoples to the critique of colonialism and elaboration of new ways of thinking beyond the European frameworks of capitalism and communism. Postcolonialism is thus perhaps best thought of as a constellation of critical questions and approaches to colonial and postcolonial life, a dynamic field of investigation animated by a common concern for political progress and social justice, but a wide range of emphases and methodologies.

(*See also* Chapter 4, Marxism; Chapter 13, Race and Postcolonial Studies; Chapter 17, Comparativisms; Chapter 22, Identity Studies; Chapter 27, Antitheory; Colonialism; Decolonization; Globalization; Hybridity; Intersectionality; Rights; Spivak, Gayatryi; *and* Subaltern)

Nicole Simek, *Whitman College*
(United States)

Further Reading
Loomba, Ania, Suvir Kaul, Matti Bunzl, Antoinette Burton, and Jed Esty, eds. *Postcolonial Studies and Beyond*. Durham: Duke University Press, 2005.
Sian, Katy P., ed. *Conversations in Postcolonial Thought*. New York: Palgrave Macmillan, 2014.

Postcritique

Critique is the practice of detailed analysis of what is given or assumed and is often treated as synonymous with literary and cultural theory. What do Marxist, feminist, and postcolonial theorists all have in common? They set out to critique common sense assumptions and cultural norms by denaturalizing, demystifying, or deconstructing them. The term "postcritique" articulates a dissatisfaction with critique as the dominant practice of literary and cultural theory and a drive to theorize alternative practices. There are three basic dimensions to postcritique: historical, evaluative, and innovative. Like any other term making use of the prefix "post-," postcritique suggests we have entered a distinct *historical* moment. In this case, that moment is the one after the dominance of critique. Thus, postcritique would mark a shift away from critique as the primary method of literary and cultural theory. However, since it still includes the term "critique" in its name, it acknowledges critique's persistent influence. Postcritique also signifies an *evaluative* assessment of critique. Critique itself has become the common sense of literary and cultural theory in this view, and we must understand that critique has its own cognitive and affective commitments. It has its own emotional payoffs, such as the feeling of intellectual superiority or revelatory success when the ordinary is revealed to be extraordinary. Postcritique thus evaluates critique as a genre with the same kinds of rhetorical, cultural, and political convictions found propping up the objects of critique. Finally, postcritique inaugurates an *innovative* agenda in which literary and cultural theorists attempt to identify alternative methods and dispositions beyond that of critique as we know it. If critics are no longer exclusively or predominantly critical, then what other forms of intellectual work can they perform? Rita Felski, perhaps the most prominent proponent of postcritique, suggests that postcritics read for recognition, enchantment, knowledge, and shock. She argues that literary and cultural theorists are important not only for the critical work they do but also for their roles as curators, conveyers, and composers. The goal of postcritique is not to become uncritical. Instead, it is best understood as the state of criticism after critique has become second nature, freeing theorists to develop other modes of thinking even while they continue to practice this vital discipline. The critique/postcritique discussion has implications for the significance of the humanities more broadly. Steeped in the language and practices of deconstruction, critique is framed by postcritics as negative in ethos and practice and thus perhaps not as well equipped to provide a rationale for the positive value of the humanities. For its advocates, postcritique offers positive language and methods from which to make a case for why the humanities matter at a moment when higher education faces threats from forces such as privatization and utilitarianism.

(*See also* Chapter 27, Antitheory; Critique; Cultural Critique; *and* Surface Reading)

Matthew Mullins, *Southeastern Baptist Theological Seminary (United States)*

Further Reading
Di Leo, Jeffrey R. *Criticism After Critique: Aesthetics, Literature, and the Political*. New York: Palgrave, 2014.

Felski, Rita, and Elizabeth S. Anker, eds. *Critique and Postcritique*. Durham: Duke University Press, 2017.

Latour, Bruno. "Why Has Critique Run Out of Steam? From Matters of Fact to Matters of Concern." *Critical Inquiry* 30.2 (Winter 2004): 225–58.

Post-Fordism

The term post-Fordism is a periodizing term that seeks to designate the transition away from Fordism. Theories of post-Fordism generally assert that Fordism, the dominant capitalist system after the Second World War, experienced a large-scale crisis in the 1970s. At this point, in order to manage this crisis, capitalism departed from the structural logic that formerly defined Fordist economies. In order to maintain a new "long wave" of growth, a principle that theories of post-Fordism adopt from Neo-Schumpeterian economics, it was necessary to address the crisis of economies based on Fordist mass production. National protectionism gradually gave way to global interrelation and interdependence, national currencies were severed from their backing systems (the Gold Standard in the United States) and transformed into international, floating currencies, and systems of production became increasingly decentralized. In the context of cultural theory, such as in the work of David Harvey, the term post-Fordism is often used as an alternative to other periodizing terms, such as "post-industrial society" or "postmodernity."

One key concept in theories of post-Fordism is that of "flexible specialization," which seeks to indicate the departure from centralized Fordist and Taylorist economic organization and the gradual move toward a necessary diversification of modes of production and circulation. In the European context, such as in the work of Paolo Virno or Christian Marazzi, the term post-Fordism is often mobilized to indicate the rapid virtualization and abstraction of capitalism and capitalist systems after the 1970s. In order to highlight capitalism's increasing diversification and decentralization, Virno famously describes post-Fordism as "the communism of capital." However, a crucial focus of theoretical examinations of post-Fordism in this context is the effect of the gradual severing of production and value from real capital, labor, and the real economy, a change which replaces former protectionist and relatively stable national systems of production and accumulation with more volatile systems. Theorists of post-Fordism, therefore, are also interested in the social and political effects of this economic transition.

Deeply influenced by the work of the French regulation school, theories of post-Fordism maintain that capitalism does not operate based on economic equilibria but that its history can instead be traced by capitalism's perpetual tendency toward crises that require transformation. Consequently, the term post-Fordism methodologically seeks to express not only a shift in capitalism itself but also an analytical focus on the important role that the social dimension plays in the regulation of capitalism. The value and utility of the term post-Fordism for cultural theorists lies to no small degree in this methodological foundation, since the term is wedded to the conviction that the regulation of capitalism ought to be understood as a matter of social regulation. Understanding capitalism's management of the crisis of Fordism and the transition into a post-Fordist regime of accumulation requires a detailed understanding of the role of the capitalism's social dimension in this process. This, in turn, indicates the importance of the cultural realm for our ability to understand capitalism's social regulation.

(*See also* Chapter 12, Postmodernism; Control; *and* Network Society)

Mathias Nilges, *St. Francis Xavier University (Canada)*

Further Reading

Amin, Ash. *Post-Fordism: A Reader.* London: Blackwell, 1994.

Gielen, Pascal. *The Murmuring of the Artistic Multitude: Global Art, Politics and Post-Fordism.* Amsterdam: Valiz, 2010.

Virno, Paolo. *A Grammar of the Multitude: For an Analysis of Contemporary Forms of Life.* Boston: Semiotext(e), 2004.

Posthumanism

Posthumanism refers to a number of critical trends that seek to displace the traditional human (and humanist) self as the center of inquiry, as the measure of all things. While the prefix "post-" in posthumanism does not simply means "after," if we take "after" to signal a clean, complete break with humanism, posthumanism does name a new body of knowledge at odds with humanism, the human, and the tradition of liberal rights. Thinking about posthumanism through a consideration of the "post" highlights the necessity of thinking *with and against* humanism. The fields of biotechnology and animal studies, which take interest in the transformation or decentering of what we think of as "human," have fueled today's posthumanist Zeitgeist.

There are several strands of thought called posthumanist. Biotechnological posthumanism takes an interest in the perfection of the human, in the etymological sense of "completing" human nature, helping humans realize their full potential. Gene therapy, cosmetic surgeries, and pharmaceutical solutions promise to perfect humanity by technological means. Operating on the plane of immanence, posthumanists refuse to settle for what *is*. They do not accept old age, or rather the effects of aging. Cosmetic surgeries are made available to a larger body of people, while Viagra and other drugs reconfigure prior understandings of sexuality. It is, however, gene therapy, along with cloning, which has set off alarm-bells among liberal humanists who see biotechnology as threatening to change humanity at the ontological level. On this view, posthumanism endangers human agency and self-determination. It represents a negative departure from humanist goals.

Other critics celebrate rather than fear these changes, however, which they name transhumanism in order to stress the ways human agency persists rather than declines with these advances in technology. Giving primacy to rationality, transhumanism privileges and elevates the mind while the body is devalued and thematized as a limitation, whose vulnerability technological innovation seeks to reduce if not eliminate. Yet taking a pro- or an anti-technology stance on the question is not the only option. Rather than embracing the humanist goals of individual perfection and self-determination, posthumanism, some argue, should radically question and redefine what it means to be human in the first place. For such critics, posthumanism should be different from transhumanism, which is a repetition of humanism through technological means.

Decoupling transhumanism and posthumanism becomes a precondition for conceiving an alternative form of posthumanism, a "critical" posthumanism that explores the full potential of a non-humancentric perspective. Decentering the human means downgrading man's privileged status in the humanist order of things, in the hierarchy that places humans at the pinnacle, above animals, plants, and inanimate matter. Posthumanism avows a new reality; it invites us to adjust our understanding of human sovereignty—to rewrite the story of the human. This new story tells us that humans are no longer—and perhaps never were—masterful knowers of nature, deploying the tools of science solely for their advantage and progress. Rather, the new posthumanist narrative reconceives the human as fundamentally relational and dependent, constituted by technologies and interspecies contacts.

(*See also* Biotechnology; Chapter 8, Rhetoric; Chapter 23, Materialisms; Chapter 24, Posthumanism; Cyborg; Environmental Humanities; Haraway, Donna; Humanimal; New Materialisms; *and* Transhumanism)

Zahi Zalloua, *Whitman College (United States)*

Further Reading

Derrida, Jacques. *The Animal that Therefore I Am* [2006]. Trans. David Willis. New York: Fordham University Press, 2008.

Haraway, Donna. "A Cyborg Manifesto: Science, Technology, and Socialist-Feminism in the Late Twentieth Century." In *Manifestly Haraway.* Ed. Donna Haraway. Minneapolis: University of Minnesota Press, 2016. 3–90.

Wolfe, Cary. *What is Posthumanism?* Minneapolis: University of Minnesota Press, 2010.

Postmodernism

Postmodernism is a dominant cultural tendency during the second half of the twentieth century in the advanced industrial societies of the West, with analogues and echoes in other regions of the globe. As a cultural dominant, postmodernism favors surfaces over depths, fragmentation over wholeness, plurality over unity, dispersal over concentration, and play over seriousness. Its hallmarks include a proliferation of images and mass-mediated simulations, flattening reality into depthless screens; a weakened sense of historicity; a "schizophrenic" fragmentation of subjectivity, yielding disjointed moments of intensity instead of continuity of experience; a new technological sublime, arising not from machine-age technologies of speed and power but rather from electronic media; and a distinctive new mutation of the experience of space, calling for new skills of orientation and navigation. Postmodern culture has sometimes been associated with the Cold War era (1947–91), and sometimes with the neoliberal economic order that emerged in the late seventies, but it coincides with neither of these periods, predating the emergence of neoliberalism and lingering on beyond the end of the Cold War into the nineties and later. It has also been associated with the belated reception and domestication of Continental theory by the Anglophone world from the sixties through the eighties. The "Americanization" of theory, however, is not so much a cause of postmodernism as a symptom of it; the *post* of postmodernism is *not* identical with the *post* of post-structuralism.

As the term itself indicates, postmodernism's crucial relation is with its predecessor, *modernism*. The postmodern attitude is one of skepticism toward the master narratives that sustained the project of modernity: narratives of rationalization, of secularization and the disenchantment of the world, and of technological progress. These narratives had run disastrously aground in the historical catastrophes of the thirties and forties. However, postmodernism is not a reactionary *anti*-modernism, and its relation to modernism is not one of simple rejection, but a complex dialogue.

There are at least two different types of cultural expression embraced by the umbrella term postmodernism. The first, a *neo-avant-gardist* type, extends and amplifies the experiments of radical modernist-era avant-gardists—Alfred Jarry, Raymond Roussel, Marcel Duchamp, the Dadaists, Gertrude Stein—who had been effaced or sidelined by canonical high modernism. The other is a *populist* postmodernism that defies modernism's strictures against mass culture and breaks down the "great divide" between elite and popular art. Belonging to the first type are such phenomena as the *nouveau roman,* metafiction and surfiction; conceptualism in visual art; the OuLiPo circle and language writing; performance art; and the deconstructivist architecture of Peter Eisenman, Zaha Hadid and the early Frank Gehry. The second type includes magical realism, postmodern historical fiction, and cyberpunk science fiction; pop art in the 1960s and the revival of figurative painting in the 1980s; Beat poetry and poetry slams; minimalism in music; and the allusive, metaphorical and avowedly entertaining architecture of Robert Venturi, Michael Graves, and the later Gehry. Though apparently incompatible, the two strains are reconciled in what Charles Jencks identified as the practice of *double-coding,* and they mingle in the hybrid genre that Larry McCaffery dubbed *Avant-Pop.*

(*See also* Baudrillard, Jean; Chapter 6, Historicisms; Chapter 12, Postmodernism; Chapter 18, Translation; Chapter 20, Digital Humanities; Chapter 23, Materialisms; Jameson, Fredric; Lyotard, Jean-François; Modernism; *and* Reflexivity)

Brian McHale, *The Ohio State University (United States)*

Further Reading
Jameson, Fredric. *Postmodernism; or, The Cultural Logic of Late Capitalism.* Durham: Duke University Press, 1991.
Jencks, Charles. *What Is Post-Modernism?* London: Academy Editions/New York: St. Martin's Press, 1986.

McHale, Brian. *The Cambridge Introduction to Postmodernism.* New York: Cambridge University Press, 2015.

Post-structuralism (*See* Barthes, Roland; Baudrillard, Jean; Chapter 5, Post-structuralism; Delueze, Gilles; Derrida, Jacques; Kristeva, Julia; Lacan, Jacques; Pluralism; Postmodernism; Posttheory; *and* Theory)

Posttheory

Posttheory is a term that was first used in the mid-1990s to reference a range of frustrations with the state of literary and cultural theory. At the time, there was growing resistance to deconstruction in particular, and post-structuralism in general. This work was pejoratively termed at the time as "high theory," "grand theory," and a bit later "sky-high theory" and "theoreticism." The emerging wave of interest in cultural and other "studies" in the 1990s was one of the sources of this antagonism toward this so-called high theory. But there were others including "anti-theorists" who rejected both "theory" and "studies."

In peaceful moments, these various "studies" were defined in opposition to "high" theory as "low" theory. In more antagonistic ones, the term "theory" was entirely rejected in favor of "studies" or some other -ism such as "New Historicism," which Fredric Jameson famously claims in *Postmodernism, or The Cultural Logic of Late Capitalism* (1991) "proves to open up a whole *post*-theoretical set of operations that retain the discursive conquest of a range of heterogeneous materials while quietly abandoning the theoretical component that once justified that enlargement."

One of the major areas of contention was the allegation that "theory" could be reduced to a method, whereas "studies" could not. Another was over the alleged apolitical or non-political character of "high" theory. Still another was over its allegedly ahistorical or non-historical character. And textbooks at the time on "How to Do Theory" did not help the cause of theory as they furthered the belief that theory was as sort of game played through following a prescribed set of rules (or a fixed set of methods).

In retrospect, the emergence of a multitude of studies in the 1990s including race, class, ethnic, sexuality, and gender studies was not the end of theory or the first chapter of a new posttheory generation as some speculated at the time, but rather a move toward a more robust and mature sense of theory. The fact that twenty-five years later there is still interest in what is "post-" or "after" theory is a testament to both the resolve of antitheorists, and the strength and efficacy of theory as a means to make sense of not just literature and culture but also many other aspects of the world including politics, society, and institutions.

As such, the other meaning of "post-theory" is simply what is next for theory and theorists. Jeffrey R. Di Leo and Christian Moraru saw this back in mid-1990s when they described posttheory in several articles as "a pragmatic approach to theory which leads [the posttheorist] to assess various theoretical models on the basis of the sociocultural and political understanding that these models bring about." Posttheory was described more as involving theorists who were much less obsessed with *how* they accomplished the study of the object or subject at hand than *why* they were pursuing it. In other words, method for the posttheorist took a back-seat to things such as public interest, social and political activism, and ethics. Thus, "posttheory" in this sense is a trend in theory that continues to this day, namely, to do theory with an eye toward making the world a better place, rather than avoiding it or trying to deny its existence. It is seen, for example, in the progressive of work of committed contemporary theorists like Judith Butler, Henry Giroux, and Slavoj Žižek.

(*See also* Antitheory; Chapter 27, Antitheory; Introduction, Theory in the New Millenium; *and* Theory)

Jeffrey R. Di Leo, *University of Houston-Victoria (United States)*

Further Reading

Birns, Nicholas. *Theory after Theory: An Intellectual History of Literary Theory from 1950 to the Early Twenty-first Century.* Buffalo: Broadview Press, 2010.

Di Leo, Jeffrey R., and Christian Moraru. "Posttheory Postscriptum." *symplokē* 3.1 (1995): 119–22.

Di Leo, Jeffrey R., and Christian Moraru. "Posttheory, Cultural Studies, and the Classroom: Fragments of a New Pedagogical Discourse." In *Class Issues: Pedagogy, Cultural Studies and the Public Sphere.* Ed. Amitava Kumar. New York: New York University Press, 1997. 237–46.

Eagleton, Terry. *After Theory.* New York: Basic Books, 2003.

Elliott, Jane, and Derek Attridge, eds. *Theory after "Theory."* New York: Routledge, 2011.

Power-Knowledge

Power-Knowledge is a term most associated with the French philosopher and historian Michel Foucault. In French the terms are *le savoir* and *le pouvoir*, distinguished respectively from *la connaissance* and *la puissance*. With the knowledge words, Foucault is stressing overall systems of knowledge in contrast to individual things we know; with the power words he is emphasizing ability and the positive capacity of power rather than just brute force or might. The power-knowledge term emerges in his work of the early 1970s, and is a development from his work of the late

1960s, where he was principally focused on knowledge. Foucault does not say that power and knowledge are the same, but is interested in the relation between them. How does having knowledge increase someone's ability to achieve something, to set the terms of debate, to assert authority over another? Much of Foucault's work looks at institutions where certain people—judges, doctors, psychiatrists, prison-warders, teachers—have power over others, both because of their institutional position but also because of their specialized knowledge. Conversely, holding power enables certain types of claims to be upheld, others disqualified, to dictate what is taken to be true or valid. Power makes use of knowledge, and reproduces it.

Examples in Foucault's work are multiple. In 1971, he was one of the key figures in the Group for Information on Prisons (GIP), an organization set up to demand better information about what was going on inside French prisons. They initially claimed they were not trying to reform the prison, but to know what took place inside their closed walls. The French state did not allow access to this knowledge, which was a means of asserting and preserving its power. Only with information—which they gleaned from questionnaires smuggled into and out of prisons, from ex-prisoners, prisoners' families, from whistle-blowers in the prison service and so on—would the GIP and the French public be able to assess things. Another crucial aspect of the GIP's work was to give prisoners a voice—something denied to them by the system. As soon as ex-prisoners were able to take over, the GIP folded, to be replaced by the Comité d'action prisonniers. In Foucault's subsequent 1975 book *Discipline and Punish: The Birth of the Prison*, among other themes was the relation between the specialized knowledges of criminology, the law and penal psychiatry and the power relations of the prison, the army

and society more generally. In *The History of Sexuality* he is concerned with how the practice of confession produces knowledge and the power relations inherent in the relation.

Foucault's ideas on power and knowledge have been enormously influential in the humanities and social sciences. His stress on what he calls the micro-physics of power is significant, in that he decenters power from a dominant position, and stresses the power relations that circulate throughout society. In his late work he moved away from the term power-knowledge, and stressed other terms such as governmentality—the relation between political power and a population. In his final works he looked at what he called technologies of the self—the ways in which people shape themselves and make themselves into a subject. Nonetheless, the relation between power and knowledge, often with the third term of truth, remained a theme of his work until his death.

(*See also* Chapter 12, Postmodernism; Chapter 15, Biopower and Biopolitics; Disciplinary Society; Discipline; *and* Foucault, Michel)

Stuart Elden, *University of Warwick (United Kingdom)*

Further Reading

Elden, Stuart. *Foucault: The Birth of Power*. Cambridge: Polity, 2017.

Foucault, Michel. *Power/Knowledge: Selected Interviews and Other Writings 1972-1977*. Ed. Colin Gordon. Trans. Coling Gordon, Leo Marshall, John Mepham, and Kate Soper. New York: Pantheon, 1980.

O'Farrell, Clare. *Michel Foucault*. London: Sage, 2005.

Prague School of Linguistics

Members of the Prague school of linguistics (or Prague Linguistic Circle) included

Jan Mukarovsky, Roman Jakobson, and Niko-lay Trubetskoy. With the rise to power of Sta-lin in the Soviet Union, formalist studies were discouraged politically, which meant that lin-guists with strong formalist interests had to resettle; some chose Prague as their base of operations. The Prague school emphasized the study of contrastive elements of language and focused on studies of phonetics and the phoneme. The discovery of the distinctive feature is a celebrated outcome of the Prague school, given Jakobson's membership at the time. Mukarovsky argued that structuralist thinking necessitated attention to an interplay of forces that were in tension and harmony. Where disturbances in equilibrium existed, repeated synthesis was called for. Apparently, he had the arts in mind. In Anton Bruckner's symphonies, equilibrium is constantly being upended and restored, sometimes rather awk-wardly, which has the function of threatening the synthesis even while it is coming about. Another aesthetic principle of the Prague school was the functionalist understanding of how automated processes of significa-tion were being foregrounded with deviant or defamiliarizing elements in order to call attention to the constructedness of norms. In British Restoration drama, norms are constantly being subverted by the actions of characters whom one would imagine should be the upholders of such norms. The Prague school saw art as autonomous and commu-nicative from a semiotic point of view. Franz Kline's abstract expressionist paintings could be taken for autonomous visual signs as well as the communication of subjective expres-sion in the absence of a concrete referent.

(*See also* Chapter 2, Structuralism and Semiotics; *and* Chapter 3, Narrative and Narratology)

Herman Rapaport, *Wake Forest University (United States)*

Further Reading

Dubois, Jean, Mathée Giacomo, Louis Guespin, Christiane Marcellesi, Jean-Baptiste Marcellesi, and Jean-Pierre Mével, eds. *Dictionnaire de linguistique*. Paris: Larousse, 1973.

Presence

Presence (from Modern French *présence*, from Latin *praesentia* "a being present") as a theoretical and conceptual formation, a tra-dition of thought and epistemological turn, has come to influence and inform several branches of understanding in our studies of the humanities. It is a mode of representation, post-representation, materiality and post-ma-teriality—an access to how the past lives in the present and, as Ethan Kleinberg argues, "a return to a relationship with the past pred-icated on our unmediated access to actual things that we can feel and touch and that bring us into contact with the past."

Presence challenges our enframing of understanding, the process of "meanification" and its vexed negotiations with constructiv-ism. Presence is a state of pre-narration; it is also implicated in post-narration. All forms of representation bear the promise of a pres-ence engendered by an absence. This absence can be conscious when the subject chooses to put something at the other end of the line or, without an alarm to the subject, the absence can simmer unwarily in the backyard and then ambush with a meaning under circum-stances where factors required to judge its legitimacy are too feeble to question it. Pres-ence succeeds in introducing a tension in the way we perceive the limits of representability. The relationship that presence is seen to have with the past is problematized by the way we define the past in relation to the present.

Although the history of presence—not that it has a very long genealogical history—goes back to Martin Heidegger and Hans-Georg Gadamer, it, however, comes to a fuller and variegated life through a trio in Jean-Luc Nancy's *The Birth to Presence* (1993), Hans Gumbrecht's *Production of Presence: What Meaning Cannot Convey* (2004) and Ranjan Ghosh and Ethan Kleinberg's edited volume *Presence* (2013). Whether it be Derrida's critique of truth as against Husserl's phenomenological structures of consciousness and presence (the complicated matrices in his idea of différance) or the problematic emerging out of mimesis as against representation that has its fraught stakes in Friedrich Nietzsche and Martin Heidegger (see his notion of *Anwesen, Vorstellung* and *Darstellung,* "onto-theo-logical" figuration of being, unconcealment as the "coming-into-appearance") or Gadamer's understanding of the "event of truth," "speaking" in relation to being, "hermeneutic listening" (his engagement with Paul Celan) and the aesthetics of wholeness and participation or Jean-Luc Nancy's "coming into presence as sense-ing," as transimminence, a complicated negotiation with Hegel's *Aufhebung,* the idea of the "taking place" and negativity or the idea of leap (*Sprung*) as seen by Heidegger, Nancy and Derrida in contrastive merit, presence has found its presence in ways that are wide-ranging but dominantly affiliated to philosophical-literary-aesthetic-linguistic frames. However, Ghosh and Kleinberg's *Presence* volume has reconfigured and seriously extended the domain of presence studies beyond its philosophical origins, by reinvigorating disciplines as varied and divergent as sociology, history, education, aesthetics, photography, memory, media studies, cultural and political theory. So the presence-principle or presence-poetics need to be appropriated further as a possibility of "critical thinking," as a way of diversifying our humanistic thinking, intensifying our hopes for the survival of the humanities.

(*See also* Archi-Trace; Chapter 1, Early Theory; Chapter 5, Post-structuralism; Chapter 9, Deconstruction; Derrida, Jacques; Deconstruction; Différance; Gadamer, Hans-Georg; Heidegger, Martin; Levinas, Emmanuel; Nancy, Jean-Luc; Subjectivity; *and* Supplement)

Ranjan Ghosh, *University of North Bengal (India)*

Further Reading
Ghosh, Ranjan, and Ethan Kleinberg, eds. *Presence: Philosophy, History, and Cultural Theory for the Twenty-First Century.* Ithaca: Cornell University Press, 2013.
Gumbretch, Hans Ulrich. *Production of Presence.* Stanford: Stanford University Press, 2004.
Nancy, Jean-Luc. *The Birth to Presence.* Trans. Brian Holmes. Stanford: Stanford University Press, 1993.

Primordial Discord

This term really derives more from Jacques Lacan than traced back to Sigmund Freud, although *Totem and Taboo* (1913) tells a fable about the primordial discord of the primal horde and the primal father as the hallmark of the human species' creation of civilization. One day, the previously humiliated and repressed sons band together to overpower the primal father of the horde, and after murdering him to gain their access to the females, they institute the law against incest and the law of obedience to the patriarchy, taking upon the tribe the necessity to honor the dead father's word even more than when he lived. It is in this Freudian text that Lacan finds the defense mechanism for linking the trauma and resulting anxiety of the child's fantasized primal scene of the parents making love, which appears more like violence, with its core wish of killing the father and possessing the mother exclusively. The mirror phase internalizes and re-projects the primordial discord of the horde into the aggressively self-dividing and self-destructive formation of the superego. In the mirror phase, which marks the period of breakage between the Imaginary and Symbolic phases, the infant between 6 and 18 months, typically identifies with what he perceives is his whole and unsupported mirror image, the ideal and perfect imago, ego as wished for based on the aesthetic image of the body at rest. At this early point, the infant does not identify with an Other per se, because it not yet a subject fully in language. The libido is still largely self-directed, but less to the separate body-parts of mouth, anus, or genitals, and more to this specular phantasm of the body's aesthetic completeness and satisfactory stasis.

As the mirror stage comes to an end, brought about by the interjection of the father's "no" cutting off the child from its completion in the fantasy (for boys the crisis of castration and for girls the beginning of the Oedipal Complex), the infant discovers and confronts its own prematurity (or continuing essential helplessness), as the child now knows that it cannot stand without support, usually that of the mother, whose total possession has been denied by the father. The internal conflict between the wholeness of the mirror reflection and the consequent fractured psyche results in the turning initially aggressive and libidinal tendencies both further inward, completing the formation of the unconscious, and further outward, hence creating in the newly formed subject of language, particularly of the language of negation, the desire for the Other, the patriarchal, god-like figure perceived by a subject with his acquisition of language.

It is the shift from narcissistic object choice to an external object of desire that helps to characterize the discord of the mirror stage, as the perceived wholeness of being endures fragmentation. That shattering links to Melanie Klein's concept of the paranoid phase, in which the infant separates out good and bad objects from himself, displacing both on the figure of the mother, and governed by a feeling of omnipotence over both. For Klein, the omnipotence is replaced by the deflation of the depressive position through aggression toward the good object. This journey, for Klein, is considered necessary for the development of a healthy adult.

Kristeva's work also considers the Freudian concept of the murder of the father as the act which creates the social code through the advent of language. If so, this reverses Freud's assertions in *Totem and Taboo*, but instead making the murder of the father that which cures primordial discord by reconstituting the subject's ego in language and action.

(*See also* Chapter 7, Psychoanalytic Theory; Chapter 22, Identity Studies; Lacan, Jacques; Libidinal; Mirror Stage; Oedipus Complex; *and* Other, The)

Gina Masucci MacKenzie, *Holy Family University (United States)*

Further Reading

Freud, Sigmund. *Totem and Taboo* [1913]. Trans. James Strachey. New York: W. W. Norton and Company, 1990.
Lacan, Jacques. *Écrits* [1966]. Trans. Bruce Fink. New York: Norton, 2007.

Print Capitalism

The idea of "print capitalism" comes from Benedict Anderson's influential 1983 book, *Imagined Communities*. It refers in a minimal sense to the practices of capitalists whose commodities are printed works; however, more expansively, Anderson takes those practices as an integral force in the development of discrete nations. One passage neatly encapsulates his point: "What, in a positive sense, made the new communities imaginable was a half-fortuitous, but explosive, interaction between a system of production and productive relations (capitalism), a technology of communications (print), and the fatality of human linguistic diversity." For Anderson, nations are imagined communities that could only develop with print capitalism's spread of uniform printed texts in vernacular languages. The book was the first modern mass-produced industrial commodity; print capitalists chased and developed new printing technologies in such a way that, having saturated the market for Latin works, they had no choice really but to develop and expand markets for vernacular texts. The rise of vernacular reading is in Anderson's account inseparable from print capitalists' efforts to secure profits and grow their trade. This trade was in turn beneficiary and engine of several interrelated developments, including the spread of literacy and everyday reading for work and leisure, and expanding urban populations and density reliant on broadside printing, daily newspaper, advertising, job notices and so on. Changed mentalities and capacities follow also. These include the rise of Protestant theologies that privileged personal engagement with the Bible (displacing Catholic mediation of scripture by authorities trained in traditional languages of devotion), and the spread of enfranchised democratization, as people come to experience themselves as informed participants in national civic projects such as voting, going on strike, protesting political developments or inertias, and even, Anderson maintains, revolutions for national sovereignty and independence in Latin America and elsewhere. Print capitalism is thus at the heart of sweeping and integral social transformations in Anderson's work, although naturally one can debate its level of importance or determining force in any given instance. One of the outcomes that most fascinates Anderson and those influenced by his work is the supposed spread of homogenous, "empty," neutral time, which we come to accept in part because of print-capitalist forms, especially the newspaper and the novel. The experience of homogenous time is defined by simultaneity, as we imagine ourselves as participating in common activities that are synchronously undertaken by others who are not in our immediate community. For Anderson, such an experience of time, inculcated in regular readers of newspapers and novels, is integral to the development of the nation. As habitual reading becomes a practice, first for elites and then for relatively large swaths of the population, people become accustomed to thinking of themselves as sharing a language along with various affinities that come from reading the same news and following the same novelistic plotting of lives in terms of already-lived pasts and anticipated futures. Through such means print capitalism is said to have helped set the stage for consolidating state apparatuses that emerged later to define and police the boundaries of emergent nations—and to fight for their sovereignty.

(*See also* Capitalism; Chapter 22, Identity Studies; Homogeneous, Empty Time; Print Culture; Reading; *and* Sovereignty)

Sarah Brouillette, *Carleton University (Canada)*

Further Reading

Anderson, Benedict. *Imagined Communities: Reflections on the Origin and Spread of Nationalism*. London: Verso, 1983.

Reed, Christopher. *Gutenberg in Shanghai: Chinese Print Capitalism, 1876-1937*. Vancouver: University of Britsh Columbia Press, 2004.

Print Culture

The study of print culture centers on the materiality of the printed word in relation to its cultural contexts. It encompasses the writing, editing, production, circulation, reading, and preservation of printed texts. Print culture studies developed from the interdisciplinary field of book history, which was established during the 1980s under the stimulus of Elizabeth Eisenstein's *The Printing Press as an Agent of Change* (1979). The traditional methods of textual scholarship and bibliography have been transformed through the insights of book history, with its theories about textuality, about the influence of the material form of a text on the way that it is interpreted, about the institutions of literary culture, and about the lifecycle of the text and its transmission from author to reader. In turn, the expanding range of research in the field led scholars to seek a new name to describe it.

"Print culture" is, in one way, a broader term than "book history," since it brings books into relationship with more ephemeral forms such as periodicals, pamphlets, posters, postcards and even websites. At the same time, print culture studies has a narrower chronological scope, since it focuses on the post-Gutenberg period, whereas book history extends backward to examine medieval manuscripts.

Print culture histories often begin with a focus on the visual dimensions of a text—typography, page design, illustration, and cover art—together with its material dimensions such as paper and printing processes. These, together with paratextual components such as notes, bibliographies, and prefaces, make up what Jerome McGann has called the "bibliographic code" of a text, as opposed to its "linguistic code" (the words making up the text). If a broader socialized context is invoked, the bibliographic code can also include aspects such as publisher, price, print run, and distribution. In this way, the study of print culture opens out into analysis of the literary marketplace and the networks of editors, publishers, agents, and reviewers who influence the final form of the printed text and the way it is circulated and received. Finally, print culture research can extend into considerations of audience, exploring the kinds of readership addressed and constituted by different types of printed materials, and seeking to recover information about readers' interactions with particular publications.

Some of the most influential books in this field center on rereadings of canonical texts in a series of publication contexts. George Bornstein in *Material Modernism: The Politics of the Page* (2001) analyzes poems that exist in multiple versions, showing how, for example, a poem by Yeats printed in a newspaper had much greater political resonance than its later instantiations in volumes of Yeats' work. Study of the commercial side of print enterprises has also generated surprising insights: revealing the vigorous activity of Romantic and Victorian authors in promoting sales of their work, or the unexpected appearance of experimental modernist texts in glossy magazines and later in cheap paperback reprints. This kind of work shows how the study of print culture can dramatically change conventional narratives of literary history.

(*See also* Chapter 11, Cultural Studies; Chapter 22, Identity Studies; Chapter 23, Materialisms; Cultural Materialism; *and* Print Capitalism)

Faye Hammill, *University of Glasgow*
(United Kingdom)
Mark Hussey, *Pace University*
(United States)

Further Reading

Hammill, Faye, and Mark Hussey. *Modernism's Print Cultures*. London: Bloomsbury, 2016.

Howsam, Leslie. *Old Books and New Histories: An Orientation to Studies in Book and Print Culture*. Toronto: University of Toronto Press, 2006.

McGann, Jerome. *The Textual Condition*. Princeton: Princeton University Press, 1991.

Private Property

"Property," the core concept of the compound "private property," connotes ownership, both broadly and in the particularity of language. The root of property, "proper," refers to intrinsic attributes, qualities, or characteristics that belong to a discreet entity. In some contexts, property is nearly synonymous with land, but "property" entails possession and demarcation within land's continuous expanse. Historically, tribes occupying land conceived of it as communal, and those who would resist the idea of property declared land a bounty given in common to all. Consequently, "private" property identifies a loss (privation) and withdrawal from the communal whole, with the remainder subtracted. At the same time, "private" indicates a claim to the exclusivity of land formerly open to access, which in being sectioned off is marked as an exception, a single thing. Boundaries secured by civil authority enforced the separation, implying a difference and deference between the propertied and the propertyless, permitting only the propertied to participate in social institutions and their regulation. Although land is not the only kind of property, privatization developed from Acts of Enclosure in the seventeenth and eighteenth centuries. To increase prospects for marketable production and thereby add to the coffers of a weakening economy, landowners were encouraged to expand their existing properties by annexing land once held in common. As tribes grew into nations, communal land yielded to distinctions of ownership in rank and property. A perception of property as a barrier against struggles for exclusive possession and consumption of resources justified these social divisions. To escape the threat of continuous war, people exchanged individual power for a sovereign authority established to defend privately held possessions. Later theories identified property as a natural right, returning sovereignty to the people. Land became "proper" by cultivation and harvesting, combining with the action of the worker to form a right to ownership. Although enclosure secured the land and the means of production for the landed, it expelled the people who had shared resources in common and prevented access to the now privately owned productive spaces. Ineligible to own property laborers, women and servants became the property of owners and entered social circulation as marketable items. Property divisions became class divisions. As ownership consolidated and fixed property and its products into commodities for trade, civil authority developed to regulate the market and secure property from pilfering by the poor. Landowners, on the other hand, received their portions from inheritance or royal patronage, linking them with power and further distancing themselves from the landless. Those who formerly worked the land and had no means to own property brought their labor power to the market. In separating their labor from its object, the produce of the land, abstract labor circulated as capital investment for owners of production, who would in turn extract productivity, the life force of the laborer, for capital accumulation. Property morphs from land and its material goods to representations of product value in currency, and extends further as immaterial projections of credit on investment.

(*See also* Capitalism; Chapter 22, Identity Studies; Community; *and* Rights)

Mary Evans, *University at Albany, SUNY*
(United States)

Further Reading

Locke, John. "Of Property." In *Two Treatises of Government* [1689]. Ed. Peter Laslett. Cambridge: Cambridge University Press, 1988. Bk. II. Ch. V; 285–302.

Marx, Karl. *Capital* [1867]. Vol. I. Trans. Ben Fowkes. New York: Penguin Books, 1971. Chs. 27–28; 877–904.

Pocock, J. G. A. "Authority and Property." In *Virtue, Commerce, and History*. Ed. J. G. A. Pocock. Cambridge: Cambridge University Press, 1985. 51–72.

Private Sphere (*See* Public Sphere)

Production (and Reproduction)

The concepts of production and reproduction are at the very heart of the Marxist theoretical problematic. Production includes not only material things, but also ideas, institutions, cultural practices, and even nature itself. Moreover, Giles Deleuze and Félix Guattari in *Anti-Oedipus* (1972) expand the notion of production to encompass desire and the unconscious. Karl Marx argues in the Introduction to the *Grundrisse* manuscripts (1857) that the notion of "production in general"—as in the Aristotelian notion of *poiesis* (making)—is an abstraction: "Whenever we speak of production, then, what is meant is always production at a definite stage of social development—production by social individuals."

In Preface to *A Contribution to the Critique of Political Economy* (1859), Marx fur-

ther maintains that every historical society takes the form of a specific "mode of production," composed of a "base" (*Basis*)—made up of the forces (raw materials, labor processes, technology, knowledge, and so forth) and social relations of production—and a "superstructure" (*Überbau*) of legal, political, social, and cultural institutions, the latter forming what Louis Althusser names the Repressive and Ideological State Apparatuses (RSAs and ISAs). The relationship of determination between the base and superstructure has been, as Raymond Williams attests in *Marxism and Literature* (1977), a highly contested area of debate. In *The Political Unconscious* (1981), Fredric Jameson builds upon the work of Althusserian structuralism to articulate three models of this relationship, which he terms mechanical (reflexive), expressive (dialectical), and structural causalities.

Ernest Mandel in his Introduction to Marx's *Capital*, Volume I (1867), maintains that in the capitalist mode of production, which we still inhabit today, the "process of production is at one and the same time a process of production of value, a process of production of surplus value, a process of production of capital, and a process of production and constant reproduction of the basic antagonistic social relations." Political struggle thus becomes centered on such concerns as the control of the forces of production, the length and intensity of the working period, and the remuneration, or wages, for labor performed.

In Chapter 23, Marx further argues that "every social process of production is at the same time a process of reproduction" and "if production has a capitalist form, so too will reproduction." Reproduction refers to all those things necessary for the continuity of any mode of production, including not only labor power and the bodies, skills, and knowledge of workers at the site of production, but also the reigning ideologies, norms, values, institutions, and interpellated subjectivities of the society as a whole. In his contribution to the collective volume, *Reading Capital* (1966), Étienne Balibar analyzes the inseparable multiple levels—economic, legal-political, and ideological—on which reproduction takes place, and Althusser expands upon these insights in his unfinished book, *On the Reproduction of Capitalism* (1995). The transition from one mode of production to another similarly entails a reorganization of activities on all these levels.

Later feminist theorists have pointed out that the overemphasis in certain strands of Marxism on industrial production has resulted in an undervaluation of the indispensable work of social reproduction that takes place in other locations and is very often performed by women. One result was the International Wages for Housework and other social wage campaigns that began in the early 1970s. More recently, Kathi Weeks has pointed out both the functionalism plaguing these analyses and the fact that fundamental changes in the present, including the blurring of the distinctions between production and reproduction and their sites, call for a rethinking of strategies: "not only is reproductive labor more clearly productive today, as evidenced by its many waged forms, but productive labor is increasingly reproductive in the sense that it often creates not only strictly economic goods and services but also social landscapes, communicative contexts, and cultural forms."

(*See also* Althusser, Louis; Apparatus; Base and Superstructure; Benjamin, Walter; Bourgeois; Capitalism; Chapter 2, Structuralism and Semiotics; Chapter 4, Marxism; Chapter 5, Post-structuralism; Chapter 9, Deconstruction; Chapter 10, Feminism; Chapter 11, Cultural Studies; Chapter 12, Postmodernism; Chapter 15, Biopower and Biopolitics; Chapter 19, Media Studies; Consumer Society; Control; Cultural Capital; Cultural Materialism; Feminist Materialism; Labor; Marx, Karl; Material Culture; Multitude; Network Society; Pop Culture; Post-Fordism; Revolution; *and* Seriality)

Phillip E. Wegner, *University of Florida (United States)*

Further Reading

Althusser, Louis, Étienne Balibar, Roger Esablet, Pierre Macherey, and Jacques Rancière. *Reading Capital: The Complete Edition*. Trans. Ben Brewster and David Fernbach. London: Verso, 2015.

Marx, Karl. *Capital: A Critique of Political Economy* [1867]. Volume I. Trans. Ben Fowkes. New York: Penguin, 1990.

Weeks, Kathi. *The Problem with Work: Feminism, Marxism, Antiwork Politics, and Postwork Imaginaries*. Durham: Duke University Press, 2011.

Professor

If the most salient trait of a professor is thought—theoretically informed analysis, the production of theory itself—isn't it interesting to look at the corollary, that professors also seek *freedom from thinking*?

Akin to their monastic forebears, professors seek the freedom to focus. They push to the periphery matters central to the lives of others. They often partly or fully withdraw from civic or domestic responsibility. To relieve them of quotidian cares, scholar-monks and nuns relied on novices, other monks and nuns, serfs and slaves, as well as the favor of princes and merchants. Like Thomas Jefferson, scholar-clerics generally declined to think about the contradictions involved in pondering ethics or justice while relying on systematic, institutionalized injustice to do it.

The twenty-first-century professoriate is little improved. Since the 1970s, research-intensive faculty have been complicit in throwing teaching-intensive faculty out of the tenure system, and inventing such new nontenurable titles for them as "lecturer," "instructor," "adjunct," "visiting fellow," "clinical professor," or "professor of the practice."

It is by now the unthinking common sense of research faculty that they "deserve" tenure for their work, but the 300 percent larger group of teaching-intensive faculty does not. While common, this nonsensical belief defies fact and history: past and present, tenure protects faculty who focus on teaching as much as faculty who focus on research. (Hence, tenure for school teachers. That survives in good health due to the superior militance, courage, and solidarity of the majority female K-12 workforce.) The tenured research faculty pitched in to dismantle the tenure system for everyone else, trading their acquiescence to the exploitation of others for even more freedom from having to think—about almost everything, that is, except their research.

Nearly all the issues that research faculty choose to ignore are reflexive. The faculty's implication in the wrong side of class struggle? The role of their labor in reproducing an unjust society? Gendered segmentation of compensation by discipline? The apartheid structure of the profession, in which 3/4 of faculty are not professors? Corporate-sponsored questionable research? The professoriate's managerial responsibility to oversee, hire and fire staff, students, nontenurable faculty, outside contractors and so forth? Critical, reflexive thought about the university is rare.

What this means: Our most professionalized thinkers have demanded—and won—freedom from thinking about the profession itself. It is a profession that has deprofessionalized itself. By outsourcing their pro-

fessional responsibilities to administrators (and not fighting to get them back), today's research professor wants the privileges of the profession without the obligations. Today's most prominent scholars in many disciplines lack basic insight into the critical discourse on education known to any well-trained schoolteacher—such as the fairly obvious role of the university in reproducing a class society. Most research-intensive professors represent higher education uncritically, subjectively, and personally. They commonly imagine their position in the education and class system as an unalloyed good, theory and research be damned. They identify the prestige of their institutions with their worth as human beings.

Even straightforward issues, such as the wholesale substitution of student labor for faculty labor, and the related deskilling of teaching, consistently mystify otherwise sophisticated thinkers. The most elite of research faculty, those who teach doctoral students, are tellingly unable to make the simple connection between their own complicity in hiring battalions of temporary contract faculty to the inability of their PhD graduates to find tenure track jobs. Unlike nurses, sanitation workers and civil servants, big-brained research faculty are seemingly unable to understand their labor system or the practices of solidarity required to change it.

This state of unthinking likely owes much to the fact that research faculty are hobbled by their privilege. But our most fortunate colleagues didn't get confused entirely on their own. They've had plenty of help. For decades journalists, administrators, conventional economists, and the amateur data fiddlers at major professional organizations created an entire pseudoscience around a mythical "market" in academic jobs. The whole discourse was founded on a ludicrous conceit, the so-called oversupply of persons with doctorates, when anybody working at a Ford plant can tell you the real issue was, and remains, the administrative restructuring of those jobs into piecework, thereby enabling the hiring of cheaper teachers without doctorates. (Yes, it is unimaginably irresponsible but true that the era universally erroneously characterized as suffering an "oversupply" of PhDs has seen the percentage of faculty with doctorates steadily drop! That's no oversupply; that's coordinated restructuring of demand by management.) Calculating the "market" in tenure track positions—without accounting for the structural casualization of those positions, and for the new kinds of nontenurable, part-time and staff-instructor jobs that emerged—has been a pathetic waste of millions in salary at our "professional" associations.

Perhaps the most interesting question regarding the unthinking of the research faculty is why they beg so hard to be fooled, and fooled again, by obliging administrators and confused association staff.

One view is that the research faculty need an alibi for inaction. In a system evolving to benefit them at the expense of their one-time colleagues, their silence and active complicity is required, and usually freely given. Tenured scholars enjoy the convenient delusion that their helplessness is an inevitability, not a choice. It is their preference to believe that despite their identity as professionals, they have no ability, and thus no obligation, to maintain the standards of the profession for present and future colleagues.

Tenured faculty salve their survivors' guilt with courteous distant sympathy. They witness but do not see.

Who will teach the professors to think again? To reflect on the obligations of a professional to a profession? To be decent human beings who practice workplace democracy rather than medieval hierarchy?

Perhaps once again history will ask more from the wounded, the lost, the scorned and disenfranchised, the un-professors whose material circumstances force them to do actual thinking. They may revolt. Possibly then research faculty will amble in the direction of justice—though well behind the intellectual leadership of their subordinates, wondering what the fuss was about.

(*See also* Chapter 25, University Studies; Labor; *and* University)

Marc Bousquet, *Emory University (United States)*

Further Reading

Bousquet, Marc. *How the University Works: Higher Education and the Low-Wage Nation.* New York: New York University Press, 2008.

Di Leo, Jeffrey R. *Higher Education under Late Capitalism: Identity, Conduct, and the Neoliberal Condition.* New York: Palgrave, 2017.

Rhoades, Gary, and Sheila Slaughter. *Academic Capitalism and the New Economy.* Baltimore: Johns Hopkins University Press, 2009.

Psychoanalysis

In *The Question of Lay Analysis* (1926), Freud contrasts medical training with the cultural competence he presents as a prerequisite for psychoanalysts. His ideal curriculum includes "the history of civilization, mythology, the psychology of religion, and literature (*Literaturwissenschaft*)." Thus *Literaturwissenschaft* conflates literary expertise and a science of literature. If literature and the humanities are essential to the training of analysts, the science of literature will have to be perfomative, thus take into account the practice of interpretation. A general hermeneutics encompasses the literary field and sexual problems common to all human beings.

Since Sophocles gave shape to the myth of Oedipus, culture has provided examples, characters, situations, and even jokes that refine individual diagnoses. An awareness of the chronicles of gods and heroes will be brought to bear on the understanding of transgenerational traumas. Hence culture is not just a marker of distinction; it implies a knowledge that is in touch with the Unconscious. The Unconscious can be defined as a knowledge that does not know itself, which is what our dreams confirm provided we know how to interpret them. Although we are not aware of the fact, because we believe in their singularity, our dreams belong to culture, a term combining our personal engagement with formalized modes of fiction and the values that constitute a whole civilization.

For Freud, the unconscious is explained by the fact that humans are not at ease with culture. They resent it: culture limits our urges to enjoy wildly, to murder, to have sex with forbidden relatives or out of bounds objects. If culture multiplies frustrations, interdictions, deprivations, and also sublimations, it should be defended, otherwise anarchy reigns. People should share ideals constituted by the arts, science, or even sports, all of which generate identifications valid for all, even the underprivileged. Freud broached the links between politics and ideology, noting that subjects and subjected classes alike willingly agree to their own alienation. We must distinguish all the more between ideals and illusions, the latter mostly found among religious doctrines.

Religious illusion helps culture in so far as it lends credibility to the law. It is easier to follow the interdiction to kill one's neighbor if this law is ascribed to God's will. Whoever participates in culture accepts more readily to limit the murderous and libidinal effects of the drives. Despite his innate pessimism, Freud kept his faith in the Enlightenment because it was the moment when science began to dispel religious illusions. Science is not an illusion, he states, which indirectly justifies the need to launch a new "science of literature." This is an insight shared by Lacan; when he baptized *Scilicet* the journal that was to propagate his teachings, he used a Latin word meaning all at once "namely," "to wit," and "you are allowed to know"—three terms sketching the program of psychoanalysis.

(*See also* Castration; Chapter 1, Early Theory; Chapter 7, Psychoanalytic Theory; Deferred Action; Desire; Drive; Fantasy; Hysteria; Jouissance; Libidinal; Mirror Stage; Mourning; Oedipus Complex; objet petit a; Other, The; Phallocentrism; Primordial Discord; Psychoanalysis; Sublimation; Symptom; Trauma; Uncanny; *and* Unconscious, The)

Jean-Michel Rabaté, *University of Pennsylvania (United States)*

Further Reading

Rabaté, Jean-Michel. *The Cambridge Introduction to Literature and Psychoanalysis,* Cambridge: Cambridge University Press, 2014.

Roudinesco, Elisabeth. *Freud in His Time and Ours.* Cambridge: Harvard University Press, 2016.

Zaretsky, Eli. *Political Freud: A History.* New York: Columbia University Press, 2015.

Public Intellectual

In the West, the term "public intellectual" fuses together two words usually held to be different from each other, if not opposed to one another. An "intellectual" is someone identified as possessing both specialized knowledge and fluency in a specific abstract discourse. Members of the "public" are, in contradistinction, associated with more pragmatic interests, and regarded as having in common only generalized knowledge. A "public intellectual" is thus an individual who makes a specific intervention into public life that brings specialized knowledge and abstract principles to bear on a public event, speaking from a position of authority. Most particularly, these interventions are seen to be moments of "speaking truth to power"—an underlying assumption is that something is ethically amiss in the public world, and intellectuals have a responsibility, armed with their knowledge and eloquence, to speak out. An inaugural instance of "public intellectualism" was the Dreyfus Affair in France (1894–1906), in which Emile Zola, André Gide, Marcel Proust, and Anatole France spoke out against the state's case.

In the late 1960s, in the midst of the Vietnam War, Noam Chomsky noted that intellectuals bore a specific responsibility to "expose the lies of governments, to analyze actions according to their causes and motives and often hidden intentions." However, he noted that many academics had gone over to the other side, betrayed their critical and ethical commitments to the truth, and become apologists for the state. Those intellectuals who had not were dismissed by the state and its allies as "unreasonable, ideological types" who delivered "harangues on 'the power structure'" (we see the same sort of co-opting of academic intellectuals during the financial meltdown of 2008, as well-represented in the documentary film "Inside Job"). The battle then, as now, is around claims to truth, and the specific ways public opinion is shaped by various agents.

Today we find the persistence of what has been called "classic" public intellectualism within hybrid types of interventions in various media. Tei-Nehisi Coates' long essay in *The Atlantic*, "The Case for Reparations (2014)," and Angela Davis and Keeanga-Yamahtta Taylor's commentary on the election of Donald Trump to the Presidency are two good examples. Each of these instances brings academic knowledge into the public in ways that seek to change opinion and action based on a specific kind of intellectual appraisal that is otherwise unavailable to the general public.

A new sociological perspective widens the scope of inquiry beyond looking at a specific social group or type ("intellectuals") and focuses instead on a "sociology of interventions." Influenced by the work of Pierre Bourdieu and others, the study of "interventions" looks at the various kinds of enabling conditions that obtain when interventions can be made—it seeks to understand how diverse and heterogeneous agents, media, and resources can come together to interrupt and counteract dominant discourses and apparatuses. This could be a welcomed corrective for too exclusive a focus on a special group of people—it helps us understand how "interventions" actually come about and can have effect.

(*See also* Bourdieu, Pierre; *and* Said, Edward)

David Palumbo Liu, *Stanford University (United States)*

Further Reading

Chomsky, Noam. "The Responsibility of Intellectuals." *New York Review of Books* (23 February 1967). https://chomsky.info/19670223/

Eyal, Gil, and Larissa Buchholz. "From the Sociology of Intellectuals to the Sociology of Interventions." *Annual Review of Sociology* 36 (2010): 117–37.

Said, Edward W. *Representations of the Intellectual*. New York: Vintage Books, 1994.

Public Sphere

Contemporary interest in the public sphere among cultural studies scholars and literary critics received its major impetus from the publication of Jürgen Habermas's *The Structural Transformation of the Public Sphere: An Inquiry into a Category of Bourgeois Society* (1962). According to Habermas, the bourgeois public sphere, a form of society crucial for democratic self-government, emerged in the eighteenth century. It depended on the ascendency of print culture, the invention of the liberal republican state, and the hegemony of capitalism, a complex of developments that still define the character of Western modernity. Habermas describes the part played by newly commodified forms of literature—especially newspapers and novels—in the redistribution of legitimating power between the state and its citizens or subjects. For the first time, public opinion assumes a primary role in the legitimation of state power and the creation of policy. The public sphere, ideally free from state control and the self-interested calculations of the marketplace, provided the site where ideas could be freely expressed and impartially judged and where public opinion could be formed and mobilized. The public sphere's rational, disinterested functioning played a necessary though mediated role in the formation of state policy and stood as the hallmark of self-governing in a liberal democratic state.

Critics soon drew attention to the exclusivity of the public sphere that Habermas described, despite its pretensions to universality. The ideal of an abstract rationality in discourse actually privileged a distinctly Euro-American form of masculinity, ruthless, calculating, and impersonal. Partiality, emotion, and the power of sympathy as well as the particular perspectives of nondominant identities were excluded.

The private sphere, including a redefined bourgeois "domesticity," became the place where liberal society attempted to confine nondominant gendered, racial, and sexual identities. The middle-class home, presided over by a sympathetic woman, usually imagined to be white, was idealized as a haven in a heartless world, softening and balancing a coldly pragmatic mode of public argument, the ruthlessly calculating institutions of state policy, and the heartless competition of the capitalist marketplace in which men acted and from which women and other marked identities were, until recently, largely excluded. In the 1980s, however, feminist critics reinterpreted the private sphere as a powerful force in its own right, a locus of political persuasion based primarily not on abstract rationality, but on sentimentality and passionate advocacy. Jane Tompkins, for example, in *Sensational Designs: The Cultural Work of American Fiction, 1790-1860* (1986), reinterpreted Harriet Beecher Stowe's *Uncle Tom's Cabin* (1852), long dismissed as sentimental pabulum, as a revolutionary work of "sentimental power" and feminist rebellion. The public and private spheres could no longer be thought of as simply distinct and separate. To grasp the conflicted heterogeneities that liberal appeals to universality often mask, one must attend to a multitude of distinct and contending public spheres where an assortment of particular identities and divisive issues of gender, sexuality, class, and race demanded a hearing. The foregrounding of perspectival particularities rather than an idealized and disembodied impartiality calls universality itself into question.

(*See also* Chapter 22, Identity Studies; Cultural Critique; Epistolary Novel; Habermas, Jürgen; *and* Secularism)

John Michael, *University of Rochester (United States)*

Further Reading

Calhoun, Craig J., ed. *Habermas and the Public Sphere*. Cambridge: MIT Press, 1992.

Davidson, Cathy N., and Jessamyn Hatcher, eds. *No More Separate Spheres!: A Next Wave American Studies Reader*. Durham: Duke University Press, 2002.

Habermas, Jürgen. *The Structural Transformation of the Public Sphere: An Inquiry into a Category of Bourgeois Society* [1962]. Trans. Thomas Burger and Frederick Lawrence. Cambridge: MIT Press, 1989.

Robbins, Bruce, ed. *The Phantom Public Sphere*. Minneapolis: University of Minnesota Press, 1993.

Q

Queer Theory

Queer theory, a term first coined by Teresa de Lauretis in 1990, describes a body of inquiry that seeks to interrogate sex, gender, and sexuality in a way that destabilizes binary oppositions within and among those categories. While the knowledges produced under the guise of queer theory are diverse and varied, they all share an interest in challenging views of identity categories as static, undermining attempts to essentialize gender and sexuality, and centering the socially constructed nature of sex, gender, and sexuality.

Like many of the schools of thought that fall under the general heading of critical theory, queer theory emerges out of a particular political moment and set of social conditions. The AIDS crisis of the 1980s, the rise of postmodernism within the academy, and debates within feminism about the nature of sexuality all lead to the crystallization of queer theory as an identifiable body of literature. Queer theory follows women's studies and lesbian and gay studies in the tradition of challenging hierarchies based on sex and gender, however, it differs from both women's studies and lesbian and gay studies in its insistence that all identity categories are socially constituted and therefore open to challenge and reinvention.

Queer theory is used to ask questions about a number of different issues, including kinship, time and space, bodies, sexualities, affect, and borders. Theorists such as Eli Clare, Jack Halberstam, Judith Butler, and Gayle Rubin use queer theory to question uncritical social links between physical bodies, gender, and sexuality. Judith Butler, in particular, articulates a theory of gender as *performative*, socially constituted, and constantly reinforced, which is now considered to be one of the hallmark contributions of queer theory. Scholars such as Jasbir Puar, Martin F. Manalansan IV, and Siobhan Somerville use queer theory transnationally, thinking about the ways in which national borders and nationalist identities both reinforce and are reinforced by gendered regulations. Feminist writers such as Sara Ahmed, Suzanna Walters, and Biddy Martin apply queer theory to more practical questions, thinking explicitly about the political outcomes that may be possible when queer theory is applied to activist concerns.

Those who use queer theory as the basis for their own scholarship often praise its ability to challenge established social norms, disrupt identity categories, and undermine systems that reproduce inequality. Critics of queer theory, however, claim that the postmodern turn toward destabilizing identity ignores the very real social consequences (e.g., racism and homophobia) that people face because of their identity categories, and creates a color-blind "queerness" that becomes tacitly coded as male and white. Ultimately, like all schools of inquiry, queer theory has the potential to prompt social change and radical new world-views, but is not immune to critique or free of problematic deployments.

(*See also* Binary Opposition; Chapter 1, Early Theory; Chapter 10, Feminism; Chapter 23, Materialisms; Chapter 24, Post-humanism; Chapter 26, Affect Studies; Butler, Judith; Capacity; Gender; Interpellation; *and* Sexuality)

Jae Basiliere, *Grand Valley State University (United States)*

Further Reading

Ahmed, Sara. *Queer Phenomenology: Orientations, Objects, Others*. Durham: Duke University Press, 2006.

Clare, Eli. *Exile and Pride: Disability, Queerness, and Liberation*. Second ed. Durham: Duke University Press, 2015.

Hall, Donald E., and Annamarie Jagose, eds. *The Routledge Queer Studies Reader*. New York: Routledge, 2013.

Weed, Elizabeth, and Naomi Schor, eds. *Feminism Meets Queer Theory*. Bloomington: Indiana University Press, 1996.

R

Race

Unlike class, ethnic, and gender categories, which in one form or another go back for thousands of years, race as a concept is judged by most scholars, such as George Fredrickson in *Racism: A Short History* (2015), to be a product of the modern period. But there are some dissenters, such as Benjamin Isaac, *The Invention of Racism in Classical Antiquity* (2004), who contend that race or proto-race can indeed be found in pre-modernity, indeed as far back as ancient Greece and Rome.

In the uncontroversial modern sense, "race" appears in various European languages in early modernity as a noun that eventually stabilizes semantically around the demarcation of human groups identified by their continental origins, physical appearance, and putative cognitive and characterological traits. The number of basic races identified in academic discourse was usually three to five. Europeans, Africans, and Asians were almost always recognized; Native Americans were sometimes identified separately and sometimes subsumed under Asians; Asians were sometimes split into different groups. However, some theorists proposed vastly higher numbers of races, reflecting not just the standard taxonomical disputes between "lumpers" and "splitters," but the fuzziness of the concept itself.

Race has been conceptualized in a bewildering number of ways (cultural, theological, biological), depending on background intellectual frameworks that have shifted over time. However, the common theme running through these variants has almost always been racial hierarchy, with "whites" being depicted (in modernity) as the superior race. Thus, the history of race (as the titles of the Fredrickson and Isaac texts indicate) is in large measure also the history of racism.

The postwar revulsion against Nazism, and the global anti-colonial movement, produced an intellectual climate in which not merely racism but (biological) race itself increasingly came to be regarded by the scientific community as discredited. It was pointed out that the human race displays a continuum of traits in which there are no "natural" breaks; that there are no "racial" chromosomes underlying a clear-cut racial polymorphism homologous to sexual dimorphism; and that there is far greater genetic variation within than between groups denominated as "races." Moreover, "race" is not an innocent concept but one that, in the form of racist ideologies, has rationalized conquest, genocide, and slavery. Accordingly, racial eliminativists have argued that we should drop the term from our vocabulary altogether, as both non-referring and pernicious, and just use "ethnicity."

However, anti-eliminativists have demurred. Naturalistic anti-eliminativists have insisted that population genetics shows that the traditional continental "racial" groupings do indeed mark real intra-human biological differences, though not (they are quick to emphasize) with any implications for differential cognitive ability and character traits, as in traditional racism. On the other hand, social constructionist anti-eliminativists have contended that while race has no biological reality, it does undeniably have a social reality (races as "social constructs"). So the claim is that we need to retain the term—suitably transformed referentially—in order to understand the social dynamics of racist societies and to track racial injustices. Critical race theory and critical whiteness studies are generally constructionist in their assumptions.

(*See also* Chapter 8, Rhetoric; Chapter 13, Race and Postcolonial Studies; Chapter 22, Identity Studies; Chapter 27, Antitheory; Cultural Wars; Ethnicity; Hybridity; Intersectionality; Minority; Multiculturalism; Performativity; *and* Whiteness)

Charles Mills, *Graduate Center, City University of New York (United States)*

Further Reading
Back, Les, and John Solomos, eds. *Theories of Race and Racism: A Reader*. Second ed. New York: Routledge, 2009.

Rancière, Jacques

Jacques Rancière (born 1940), like Friedrich Nietzsche, purveys "untimely" thoughts. One such is his claim that we need a politics that does not look for consensus and a concord among citizens, but seeks *dissensus* instead, articulates a medley of impertinent voices that oppose the political status quo. In the fractious twenty-first century, this idea of politics, and the goals of politics, will strike some as thoroughly unwanted—surely we need more harmony, not less. But the step forward into the twenty-first century requires looking back to the past, to the age when dissenting voices (and indeed, everything) finally spoke up as

a clamorous democracy. Here begins literary theory's interest in Rancière. In his account of the "aesthetic regime" (roughly dating from the nineteenth century), everything speaks. Mundane lives, prosaic objects—the stuff of the world—are deemed *important*: this is his claim for Balzac, and for Flaubert. Neither reproduces the classical condescension that considered only nobles fit for loftier topics, and baser topics fit only for comedy. This is the "egalitarian" politics of literature—it amounts to the indifference with which writers treated subjects, and indeed matter. Balzac does not exclude any "matter" from his novels—this is his democracy. Emma Bovary deserves Flaubert's stylistic attentions as much as any duchess—this is his. But this indifference, this egalitarian disrespect of genre hierarchies and stylistic norms, threatens the dignity of literature-as-art. Whence the claims Rancière makes in respect of aesthetic theory: assuredly, art and literature achieved certain "autonomy." It did become possible, from philosophy's standpoint, and in terms of what Schlegel called "theory," to identify art as such. But that's only part of the story. For, impelled by its own democratic drive, art bled over into nonart. How could literature claim that it was art, distinct from other domains of life, while inviting the voices and sheer stuff that "life" implies into its own pages? How could Flaubert claim to be an absolute stylist and yet write with such attention to Emma's prosaic ecstasies? Literature knew this "contradiction," as Rancière puts it, and it deeply informed its aesthetics and politics. Literary scholars have greeted Rancière's exploration of that contradiction with keen attention. He offers important readings of Balzac, Stendhal, Flaubert, and Mallarmé, among others. Theorists have inspected Rancière's often polemical critiques of alternative aesthetic philosophies (like those of Badiou and Jean-François Lyotard) with equally keen interest. Rancière focuses on literature, largely French but not exclusively so, yet he also explores other art forms, and does not neglect contemporary art. Rancière is polemical here too, his untimely point being that contemporary art understands itself better when it acknowledges its debt to the political and aesthetic contradictions of the past. Equally untimely, however, is the notion that Balzac and Flaubert are our political and aesthetic contemporaries. The strange thought is that Rancière, by the same token, achieves his critical presence in the twenty-first century (and in the present volume) by profiling much of his own theory by way of a reinvestment in writers of the past.

(*See also* Chapter 16, Pop Culture; *and* Subjectivity)

Brian O'Keeffe, *Barnard College*
(United States)

Further Reading

David, Olivier. *Rancière Now: Current Perspectives on Jacques Rancière*. Malden: Polity Press, 2013.

Rancière, Jacques. *Mute Speech: Literature, Critical Theory, and Politics* [1988]. Trans. James Swenson. New York: Columbia University Press, 2011.

Rancière, Jacques. *Dissensus: On Politics and Aesthetics*. Trans. Steven Corcoran. New York: Continuum Books, 2010.

Reader-response Criticism (*See* Reading)

Reading

Twentieth-century critical theory advanced understandings of reading by shifting attention from texts to readers. This countered prior views of reading as the simple retrieval of messages from written works—dating to the low literacy rates and scarcity of books prior to the Industrial Revolution. In that earlier period, elite minorities of "writers" penned works for the masses, with less-educated "readers" (often listeners) regarded as passive for lack of product. But this didn't mean that the "everyday culture" of readers lacked agency, as Michel de Certeau has noted. Lingering in the background was the idea of hermeneutics, long practiced in the interpretation of religious writings.

Hermeneutics saw a revival in the early 1900s, prompted in part by Edmund Husserl's phenomenology and its focus on the individual's experience of the world. Later, scholars such as Stanley Fish and Wolfgang Iser introduced what would be termed "reader-response" theory in proposing a dialogical relationship between text and audience. In his groundbreaking *The Act of Reading* (1976), Iser argued that what readers brought to a text was just as important as an author's intended meaning. Soon Elaine Showalter and Edward Said, among others, would extend this notion in describing how women and non-westerners read contrary meanings into works.

Complimenting modern hermeneutics were evolving theories of language, notably the structuralism of Ferdinand de Saussure. Asserting that words were more than mere lexicological labels, de Saussure wrote that such "signs" also evidenced "collective social interaction." This gave reading a constructed and variable character as a marker of human difference. In the 1970s and 1980s, post-structuralism took matters of variability further, with Roland Barthes and Jacques Derrida questioning both the stability of established meanings and the capacity of the subject to know itself. Looking beyond the printed page, Barthes famously applied these methods in "reading" to everything from professional wrestling to car advertising.

Delving deeper into the reader's mind, the linguistically-informed psychoanalysis of Jacques Lacan explored the unconscious, describing the subject itself as an effect of language. In 1973, Laura Mulvey applied Lacanian principles in formulating the desiring "gaze" through which viewers read themselves into movies and television programs. The field of narratology further examined people's fondness for stories, desires for closure, and tendencies to identify with characters. Often these theories critiqued latent ideologies within media texts, exposing their programs of economic exploitation (Marxism), patriarchy (feminism), elitism (cultural studies), binary reason (deconstruction), imperialism (postcolonialism), and heteronormativity (queer theory). Such workings of discursive power would be summarized historically in the "genealogical" analyses of Michel Foucault.

Contentions over reading continued in the 2000s, with traditionalists asserting that failing schools, digital culture, and rising immigration were undermining reading competency in many nations. In response, proponents of "multiple literacies" have drawn upon theory by such scholars as Judith Butler (performativity), Gilles Deleuze (flexibility), and Homi K. Bhabha (hybridity) in calling for diverse views of communicative transactions. Finally, heightened awareness of learning differences such as dyslexia has prompted disability activists like Lennard J. Davis to advocate more inclusive definitions of what it means to read in a technological global society.

(*See also* Barthes, Roland; Chapter 3, Narrative and Narratology; Chapter 8, Rhetoric; Fish, Stanley; Close Reading; Hermeneutics; Phenomenology; *and* Surface Reading)

David Trend, *University of California, Irvine (United States)*

Further Reading

Barthes, Roland. *Image/Music/Text*. Trans. Stephen Heath. New York: Hill & Wang, 1978.

Iser, Wolfgang. *The Act of Reading: A Theory of Aesthetic Response*. Baltimore: Johns Hopkins University Press, 1978.

Reception Theory

Contrary to narratives of genius or self-containment, theories of reception challenge us to think of the agency of authorship as distributed and dialogic. They analyze how various forms of objects communicate by design—addressing their presents, questioning their pasts, posing future problems.

Differences in reception theories often sort along how one defines what counts as a message as well as limits to whom or what a message is directed toward. Clustered around these defining lines are broader questions of how explicit powers or implicit hierarchies structure the style, meaning, and acceptability of a given message for a given situation. A test case is the differing valences of reception for the study of "information" versus "culture." In 1948, Claude Shannon developed a mathematical theory of communication that measured how the "entropy" in a message produced not only a quantifiable uncertainty of meaning but also a random variability in reception. Shannon's model has been pivotal for computer science, information theory, and media studies in which reception is increasingly conceptualized as a network of human and nonhuman actors. Stuart Hall, a British cultural theorist and sociologist, defined reception as a process of semiotic struggle over the "politics of signification." Hall differentiates between three "positions" of reception occupied by cultural workers: the professional class, who broadcast "dominant-hegemonic" codes with relative autonomy; the negotiators, who adapt "grand significations" to more restricted situations (resulting in contradictory messages); and the "oppositional," who decode/recode dominant forms of communication into alternative frameworks.

Many theories of reception blend structural languages of information or signifiers with the more formal, qualitative, and judgmental languages of aesthetics. During the early 1960s and early 1970s, a group of German literary critics and philosophers at the University of Constance combined elements of the hermeneutic philosophy of Hans-Georg Gadamer, the linguistic formalism of Roman Jakobson, and the historiographic theory of R. G. Collingwood to develop what Hans Robert Jauss coined "reception aesthetics." Though sometimes conflated with "reader-response theory" (advocated by his colleague, Wolfgang Iser), Jauss's theory of reception was distinct in that it relied on a three-part structure of form, interpretation, and experience, each of which informs the other: the mediation of received ideas about social reality and convention through aesthetic forms; the combination of critical methods to produce new discursive paradigms; and the analysis of the social and aesthetic effects of a range of phenomena, from "high" literature to mass media. Jauss saw "reception aesthetics" as a way through critical impasses between more positivistic takes on how art embodies a sociohistorical reality and a-historical, structuralist notions of self-sufficient aesthetic objects.

"Reception" is often shorthand for how a text is read by publics and opinion-makers over time. But no reading strategy or model of expertise is value-neutral. A survey of responses to Shakespeare's *Twelfth Night* (containing a cross-dressing messenger named Viola) might approach an interpretive *con*sensus of what performances of the play have meant for past and present audiences while also revealing a critical *dis*sensus around how language and dramatic form engage notions of sexuality and gender over time. These critical responses are filtered too through how individual performances responded to spatial, political, and economic constraints. Historians have similarly considered reception as a complex social, institutional, and aesthetic process by which our access to events or facts is mediated, particularly when those events or facts are presented by way of phrases, plots, figures, or characters one finds also in literature.

Consistent across these paradigms is a notion that a reader or observer is always participating in the production of the things they perceive, value, and explain to others. Reception serves as an infinitely malleable hinge around which competing priorities about what a message should or could mean bend, gather, or come apart.

(*See also* Chapter 8, Rhetoric; Chapter 11, Cultural Studies; Chapter 19, Media Studies; Emotion; Gadamer, Hans-Georg; *and* Hall, Stuart)

Christopher Patrick Miller, *University of California, Berkeley (United States)*

Further Reading

Hall, Stuart, Dorothy Hobson, Andrew Lowe, and Paul Willis, eds. *Culture, Media, Language: Working Papers in Cultural Studies, 1972–1979*. New York: Routledge, 2006.

Holub, Robert C. *Reception Theory: A Critical Introduction*. New York: Methuen, 1984.

Jauss, Hans Robert. *Aesthetic Experience and Literary Hermeneutics*. Trans. Michael Shaw. Minneapolis: University of Minnesota Press, 1982.

Staiger, Janet. *Media Reception Studies*. New York: New York University Press, 2005.

Thompson, Martyn P. "Reception Theory and the Interpretation of Historical Meaning." *History and Theory* 32.3 (1993): 248–72.

Reflexivity

Reflexivity refers to works of literature that self-consciously reflect upon their own artifice. Although isolated examples of self-referentiality recur throughout literary history, reflexivity is most closely associated with late modernist and postmodernist narratives of the twentieth and twenty-first centuries. Unlike traditional literary forms, which strive for verisimilitude, or a faithful representation of reality, reflexive literary forms draw attention to their own status as text by foregrounding language and form. Some emphasize the actual materiality of the text, the book as physical object. For example, *Willie Masters' Lonesome Wife* (1968) by William H. Gass uses four different page stocks and page colors as well as varying font sizes and types, photographs, and other visual components to remind readers that we hold words, not a world, in our laps as we read. Although sometimes criticized as superficial fun and games, more often than not self-reflexive literary devices constitute strategic means to a serious end. Most traditional literature reflects a realist aesthetic and the foundational assumptions out of which that aesthetic grows. It assumes that language transparently and unproblematically represents the objective world of fact and experience. By contrast, contemporary reflexive literature reflects an irrealist aesthetic and the post-structuralist assumption that the only world available to us is a mediated world that does not exist independently of our symbol systems. The defamiliarizing hallmarks of contemporary reflexive fiction—cartoonlike characters, "black" humor, the self-conscious foregrounding of literary devices, purposeful intertextuality and pastiche, the upending of realistic conventions with fabulism and "magic realism," for example—subvert the circuit of identification between text and reader, reminding the reader that fiction, like "reality," is always already mediated by our symbol systems. In this way, postmodernist reflexivity turns the tables on classical realism by reversing its working assumption that literature holds a mirror up to nature when quite the opposite may be the case. The made up story is not a mirror held up to the world so much as a model of that world, which human beings have largely constructed and which they apprehend through a scrim of simulations. Viewed from the perspective of world-making, then, contemporary reflexive literature becomes much more than anarchistic linguistic play, rendering a world made accessible through the very medium used to construct it. In short, the object of recent reflexive literature is never solely itself, but also mediated reality, the worded world we occupy and which we can access only through language. Primarily associated with fiction, which is sometimes called metafiction, reflexivity occurs in the work of such writers as John Barth, Thomas Pynchon, Vladimir Nabokov, Ronald Sukenick, Raymond Federman, Kathy Acker, Italo Calvino, Julio Cortázar, Colson Whitehead, Carole Maso, Jennifer Egan, Flann O'Brien, Ishmael Reed, Haruki Murakami, David Foster Wallace, and many others. Reflexivity may also be found in contemporary poetry (e.g., the L*A*N*G*U*A*G*E poets), drama (e.g., the plays of Bertolt Brecht, Samuel Beckett, and Karen Finley), and film (e.g., the films of Jean-Luc Godard, Quentin Tarantino, and David Lynch).

(*See also* Chapter 12, Postmodernism; Chapter 16, Pop Culture; *and* Postmodern)

Charles Harris, *Illinois State University (United States)*

Further Reading

Barth, John. "The Literature of Exhaustion [1967]." In *The Friday Book: Essays and Other Nonfiction*. New York: Putnam's, 1984. 62–76.

Barth, John. *Lost in the Funhouse*. Garden
    City: Doubleday, 1968.
Hutcheon, Linda. *Narcissistic Narrative:
    The Metafictional Paradox*. New York:
    Methuen, 1984.

Reification (*See* Thing Theory; *and*
Martin Heidegger)

Remixology

Remixology is a remix or recombination
of two perfectly good preexisting words:
"remix" and "logos." The term "remix" is
generally understood to refer to the practice of recombining media content—popular
songs, films, television programs, texts, web
data—to fabricate a new work. Although initially popularized with digital audio, made
widely available over the internet, and heard
on dance floors across the globe, the practice
is not limited to either digital media or popular music; and its effects have reverberated
backward and forward through time forcing a
critical reconsideration of long-standing cultural assumptions regarding content creation:
originality, authorship, intellectual property,
and plagiarism.

The Greek word λόγος or "logos" is typically appended to the backend of a word in
order to designate "the science of" or "the
study of." Consequently, terms like "biology"
and "sociology" are commonly defined as
"the science of life" and "the study of society." Following this procedure, combining or
mashing up the terms "remix" and "logos"
would, at least superficially, signify "the science or study of remix." This expectation,
although entirely reasonable, proceeds from
a significant and historic reconfiguration or
remix of the meaning of the word λόγος. If
we take a deep cut in the language and literature of the ancient Greeks, we find that
the word λόγος initially meant "discourse"

or "word." In other words, it was the word
for word. Understood as discourse or word,
λόγος signifies not just "talking about stuff,"
but the means by which something—in this
case, what has been called "remix"—comes
to be manifest and exhibited such that it can
be determined to be the object of investigation and debate.

Remix has been discursively situated in
terms of a debate between two opposing factions. On one side there are the plagiarists,
copyleftists, and remix fans and prosumers,
those individuals and organizations who celebrate remix and other cut-up, mash-up, and
collage practices as new and original ways for
creating and distributing media content. On
the opposing side are the critics. According
to this group, the sampling and recombining
of preexisting material is nothing more than
a cheap and easy way of recycling the work
of others, perpetrated by what are arguably
talentless hacks who really have nothing new
to say. Despite their many differences, both
sides of this debate are fueled by and seek
to protect the same underlying values: originality, innovation, uniqueness, artistry, creativity, hard work, and so on. Remixology
deliberately targets these shared and often
unquestioned underlying values in an effort
to deconstruct the existing conceptual system
and fabricate a new axiology—a theory of
moral and aesthetic value—that can respond
to the opportunities and challenges of the
twenty-first century.

(*See also* Chapter 8, Rhetoric; Chapter 12,
Postmodernism; Chapter 20, Digital Humanities; *and* Postmodernism)

David J. Gunkel, *Northern Illinois University*
(United States)

Further Reading

Amerika, Mark. *remixthebook*. Minneapolis:
    University of Minnesota Press, 2011.

Gunkel, David J. *Of Remixology: Ethics and Aesthetics After Remix*. Cambridge: MIT Press, 2016.

Navas, Eduardo. *Remix Theory: The Aesthetics of Sampling*. Wien: Springer, 2012.

Sinnreich, Aram. *Mashed Up: Music, Technology, and the Rise of Configurable Culture*. Amherst: University of Massachusetts Press, 2010.

Repetition

In any system governed by repetition nothing is older or more original, and nothing newer or more recent than repetition. In such systems repetition always therefore arrives from the future, as Martin Heidegger explained.

In literature and culture, the topic of repetition develops innocently enough. In rhetoric, in design, and in architecture, it is associated with rhythm, pattern, and structure, and so contributes to a poetics of emphasis and contrast, for example, in the figure of antimetabole in John Milton's *Paradise Lost* (1667): "The mind is its own place, and in itself can make a heaven of hell, a hell of heaven." Yet, the chiasmic structure, which this antimetabole instantiates, informs the architecture of the entire poem.

It becomes more difficult to contain let alone control repetition in philosophy after G. W. F. Hegel. The philosophy of history, as well as the history of philosophy, implies both progress and repetition in a teleological movement through which the *Geist* (spirit, mind) improves itself toward the establishment of an ethical state. Karl Marx and Friedrich Engels both refer to Hegel in their observation that revolutionary progress takes as many missteps (e.g., the repetition of high tragedy in shallow farce) as it does genuine social developments. Repetition thereafter tends to be regarded as a source of frustration wherever one might be looking toward development, progress, or change.

Sigmund Freud similarly identifies the *Wiederholungszwang* (repetition compulsion) as a neurotic block to the psychoanalytic aim in bringing repressed, especially traumatic, memories to consciousness. The patient tends to unconsciously repeat (act out) the traumatic situation instead of remembering (working through) and then moving on.

In one of Jacques Lacan's main divergences from Freud he identifies the "repetition automatism" (*automatisme de répétition*) as a general characteristic of the unconscious and not, therefore, something from which a subject will ever be free. It is now more a matter of distinguishing between types of repetition, for example, between the repetition automatism, which characterizes the psyche in terms of signifiers substituting for other signifiers, and repetition during psychoanalytic treatment.

Lacan's psychoanalytic theory, which is uniquely attentive to structural relations in the literary text, adopts the linguistic principle, formulated by Roman Jakobson, by which the poetic function projects the paradigmatic (metaphorical) axis onto the syntagmatic (metonymic) one. By pairing these forms of repetition-in-variation with the mechanics of condensation and displacement, as explained in Freud's theory of dreams, Lacan could formulate a theory of desire-in-language that continues to influence diverse readings of literary, cultural and political discourses.

Contemporary theories of trauma, performatives, the postmodern condition, and electronic media all emerge from considerations of repetition in continental theory, from the 1950s onwards. Repetition becomes a main interest not only in theories of language, which evidently operates by repetition, but also with then emerging theories of communication based on mathematical and engineering principles and focused on ideas of performance and performativity. Gilles Deleuze and Jacques Derrida each independently develop an approach to repetition paired inextricably with a concept of difference, which in each case undergoes a necessary conceptual alteration, by which a *difference* of a certain kind (e.g., a difference from self) is indistinguishable from a repetition of the same. The question is no longer addressed to a distinction between origin and novelty, on one hand, and repetition and duplication, on the other. Rather it throws into crisis the decidability in knowing whether a given repetition is empty, mechanical, regulative, even oppressive, or whether it is liberating and productive of change.

Deleuze rediscovers in the writings of Søren Kierkegaard and Friedrich Nietzsche (among others) forceful versions of repetition that encourage him to identify them as philosophers of the future. Kierkegaard opposes repetition (*Gjentagelsen*) to Platonic recollection (*anamnesis*), thus opposing to the theory of eternal forms a philosophy projected toward the yet unwritten future. And Nietzsche formulates one of his most enduring philosophical principles around a concept of repetition in the "eternal recurrence (*Wiederkehr*) of the same."

Beneath such nuanced and diverse concepts of repetition, Derrida's coinage iterability (*Itérabilité*), meaning the ability to repeat/be repeated, points toward the otherwise inaccessible conditions on which a repetition of any kind is possible. Derrida draws from both the Latin *iterum*, "again," and the Sanskrit *itara*, "the other," and thus combines repetition with alterity in a formulation dependent upon an accidental interlingual correspondence that exemplifies the condition it describes. Understood as a productive force, an *ability*, iterability mobilizes associations between difference, repetition, and chance, in several reformulations of presiding philosophical distinctions, between, for example, speech and writing, form and matter, philosophy and literature, constative and performative, and so on, the entire field now understood to be governed by a general iterability.

(*See also* Archi-Trace; Chapter 5, Post-structuralism; Chapter 9, Deconstruction; Deleuze, Gilles; Derrida, Jacques; Freud, Sigmund; Hegel, G. W. F.; Heidegger, Martin; Lacan, Jacques; Memory; Nietzsche, Friedrich; Origin; Seriality; Trauma; Uncanny, The; *and* Vitalism)

John W. P. Phillips, *National University of Singapore (Singapore)*

Further Reading

Deleuze, Gilles. *Difference and Repetition* [1968]. Trans. Paul Patton. New York: Columbia University Press, 1993.

Derrida, Jacques. *Margins of Philosophy* [1972]. Trans. Alan Bass. Chicago: University of Chicago Press, 1982.

Lacan, Jacques. *The Four Fundamental Concepts of Psycho-Analysis, 1954-1955*. Ed. Jacques-Alain Miller. Trans. Alan Sheridan. New York: Norton, 1978.

Reproduction (*See* Production)

Resistance

Resistance has been taken up in literary and cultural theory in several ways. Scholarship of resistance discusses political and cultural resistance to colonial occupation, imperialism, and white supremacy. Such a perspective has analyzed, in turn, the ways that the self and society are also colonized. Frantz Fanon, Amilcar Cabral, and Paolo Freire exemplify this thinking.

In cultural studies, resistance largely refers to the process of engaging in cultural struggle by locating oppositional cultural forms and seeking to change consciousness and discourse toward the end of replacing oppressive meanings with emancipatory ones. Such cultural struggle is frequently understood in the tradition of Antonio Gramsci as part of a broader political and economic struggle by the oppressed to forge a new hegemony. In the Gramscian tradition developed by Stuart Hall, radical democracy theorists and others, a new social order depends not just on the seizure of state power but on the transformation of minds, common sense, and civil society by educative work. A great deal of the scholarship of resistance analyzes the role of informal and formal education in the process of locating oppressive and oppositional meanings that can form the basis for new culture and social action. British cultural studies of youth in the 1970s and 1980s, such as that of Paul Willis, Angela McRobbie, and Dick Hebdige, examined how youth made meanings and resisted meanings and institutions that positioned them symbolically in subordinate ways. Willis's working-class "lads" detailed in his ethnography *Learning to Labor* (1977), for example, acted oppositionally in schools that imposed middle class cultural norms, forging a collective culture yet inadvertently becoming complicit in their own oppression of being punished in school and limited in the economy. Henry Giroux's *Theory and Resistance in Education* (1983) and *Teachers as Intellectuals* (1988) were significant contributions to the scholarship on resistance by highlighting the role of teachers and other cultural workers in helping youth to interpret and theorize oppositional acts and make sense of them in terms of the broader social forces that produced the contexts informing those acts. In this view, opposition is not necessarily always resistance but theorizing opposition can be the basis for resistance. Resistance requires acts of theorizing that can be taught and learned. Critical cultural workers can help youth theorize experience

and the social context as the basis for projects of social intervention.

Much scholarship on media culture in the 1980s and 1990s focused on the possibilities of interpreting media texts to locate "resistant readings." John Fiske's *Power Plays, Power Works* (1993) was an influential and representative work of this sort. Fiske described, for example, as an act of resistance, homeless men in a homeless shelter identifying with the criminals rather than the police while watching the film *Die Hard*. Debate in cultural studies in this period concerned where resistance could be found—in the representation, in the interpretation, in the theoretical and pedagogical intervention.

This era also saw the development of debates about the possibilities of resistance in the wake of post-structural scholarship embracing a "death of the subject." Foucault, Deleuze and Guatarri, and Butler, among others, suggested a shift from ideology to discourse and a shift from the autonomous subject to a nonessential self formed through the process of identification. The nonessential subject has no core or authentic prior subjectivity but rather is self-formed through the process of identification with existing discourses—sets of meanings. The nonessential subject produced by discourse could not resist discourse by stepping outside of it but rather through repetition with a difference. Judith Butler's discussion about Jenny Livingston's film *Paris is Burning* illustrates the post-structural shift in locating resistance. Gay and transgender black men in New York in the 1980s competed in drag balls in which participants aspired to simulate women. As film and theorists discussed, the performance of femininity highlighted the constructedness of gender. By repeating dominant gender and racial tropes, the participants produced new meanings about gender and race that called the dominant meanings into question. The activists, The Yes Men, employ strategies of resistance in which they impersonate corporate executives and heads of NGOs in mass media to amplify the oppressive and exploitative behaviors of these institutions. Such resistance through repetition with a difference in this case publicized and criticized powerful economic and political organizations by amplifying how, for example, particular corporations profit through human destruction. Resistance as an aspect of cultural struggle should always be thought of, not as an end in itself, but rather as a precondition for the enactment of a new normative, egalitarian and emancipatory, political and ethical vision.

(*See also* Chapter 6, Historicisms; Chapter 9, Deconstruction; Chapter 11, Cultural Studies; Chapter 13, Race and Postcolonial Studies; Chapter 15, Biopower and Biopolitics; Chapter 19, Media Studies; Chapter 21, Late Capitalism; Chapter 23, Materialisms; Chapter 27, Antitheory; Decolonization; Finance; Foucault, Michel; Hall, Stuart; Negri, Antonio; *and* Subculture)

Kenneth J. Saltman, *University of Massachusetts, Dartmouth (United States)*

Further Reading

Freire, Paulo. *Pedagogy of the Oppressed.* New York: Continuum, 1972.

Giroux, Henry. *Theory and Resistance in Education.* Westport: Bergin and Garvey, 1983.

Gramsci, Antonio. *Selections from the Prison Notebooks.* New York: International Publishers, 1989.

Hall, Stuart. "Culture, Resistance, and Struggle." In *Cultural Studies 1983: A Theoretical History.* Eds. Jennifer Daryl Slack and Lawrence Grossberg. Raleigh-Durham: Duke University Press, 2016. 180–206.

Saltman, Kenneth. *The Politics of Education: A Critical Introduction.* New York: Routledge, 2016.

Revisionism

Revisionism is a practice of developing self-consciousness and historical awareness. It recognizes what appears as universal human impulse to recreate present conditions in response—negative or positive—to time-honored tendencies, desires, curiosities—that recapitulate themselves from age to age. These reconstrued texts are presented as reborn while simultaneously acknowledging the past from which they stem. A strong preoccupation with literary or other traditions and their influences marks revisionism.

Though focusing on the poetic context, Harold Bloom offers a significant way for thinking about the issues of influence and how texts relate to one another. For Bloom, influence "means that there are no texts, but only relationships between texts" and that "these relationships depend upon a critical act, a misreading or misprision, that one poet performs upon another, and that does not differ in kind from the necessary critical acts performed by every strong reader upon every text he encounters."

I think it is just as important to think about relationships within texts and not just between texts. For instance, Henry James's *Golden Bowl* (1904) is an enactment of revisionism with the text's distinct narrative split between The Prince and The Princess, with the latter half acknowledging and correcting the first half. Maggie Verver corrects the flaw in the original design James's gives her. In his preface to the text, James explains that the Prince and Princess's "chronicle strikes me as quite of the stuff to keep up from forgetting that absolutely no refinement of ingenuity or of precaution need be dreamed of as wasted in that most exquisite of all good causes the appeal to variety, the appeal to incalculability, the appeal to a high refinement and a handsome wholeness of effect." We need both volumes—they create something like a Hegelian dialectic, that continual movement toward a realization of self-consciousness, which informs not just James' writing process, but all writing as it works through and within the literary tradition. James even addresses his initial aversion to the term *revision*: "I had attached to it [revision], in a brooding spirit, the idea of re-writing. . . . I had thought of re-writing as so difficult, and even so absurd, as to be impossible—having also indeed, for that matter, thought of re-reading in the same light." However, revision is more of an act of participation in tradition while seeking to create something new (though a problematic word in and of itself). Specifically, via Bloom's notion of "image of voice," we can see revisionism at work, as in how he reads Whitman in "When Lilacs in the Dooryard Bloom'd," the famous elegy for Lincoln, subsuming and containing in the image of the lilac sprig he breaks off, the entire pastoral elegy tradition, as summed up in Milton's *Lycidas*; with this single image of those voices, Whitman, as Bloom reads him, trumps his poetic predecessors even as he appears to fulfill them.

Bloom and other revisionists comment on the canon and the necessity of tradition. Bloom in particular asks: "What happens if one tries to write, or to teach, or to think, or even to read without the sense of a tradition?" Nothing can happen, as tradition and revision based on tradition are inescapable. Bloom projects, however, that if there is to ever be a break in the continuity of tradition, it will be linked to the "religion of the Liberated Woman"—this matters for how we should think about reading and teaching in academia now. How does the academy now, in a wildly different political, social, and cultural climate, present texts to students in a meaningful way that illustrates both the past and how it is reshaped in the current moment.

(*See also* Canon; Chapter 5, Post-structuralism; *and* Tradition)

Colleen Kropp, *Temple University (United States)*

Further Reading
Bloom, Harold. *The Daemon Knows: Literary Greatness and the American Sublime.* New York: Spiegel & Grau, 2015.
Bloom, Harold. *A Map of Misreading.* Oxford: Oxford University Press, New York, 2003.

Revolution

Originally defined as the orbital motion of astronomical bodies, in its current meaning of a major sociopolitical or economic change, *revolution* dates from the early modern period. Raymond Williams speculates that this later usage stemmed from the similarity of the terms revolution and *revolt*, and because any uprising of the powerless would appear, to those formerly in power, as a revolving in which positions are inverted. In literary and cultural studies, Marxist understandings of revolution predominate: a change in control over the means of economic production reflected in the rise of new social, political, and cultural forms. For Marxism, revolutions entail the seizure of production and the state by the exploited class, and the subsequent transformation of both into a historically new society. Revolutions are conditioned by objective historical factors, but are ultimately achieved through the subjective agency of the masses. Marx's analyses of revolutionary struggles in texts like *The Communist Manifesto* (1848) and *The Eighteenth Brumaire of Louis Bonaparte* (1852) articulate a conceptual lexicon that theorists and historians have used to reevaluate a range of historical revolutions, particularly those carried out by people of color: C. L. R. James's *The Black Jacobins* (1938), a study of the Haitian Revolution, and Frantz Fanon's *The Wretched of the Earth* (1961), dealing with African anti-colonial struggles, have been especially influential in postcolonial studies, African American studies, and studies of the Black Atlantic. Alternative Marxist concepts of revolution shift emphasis from violent class struggle to long-term social and cultural change: for example, Antonio Gramsci's "war of position" and Williams's "long revolution." Marx, it's well known, analyzed past revolutions without describing the specific form that communist society, following the future proletarian revolution, should or would take. This Marxist designation of the communist future as unforeseeable from within the present influences cultural theorists of negative utopianism—such as Walter Benjamin and Fredric Jameson—who variously see the future as a principle of alterity never defined or predicted, but nonetheless inspiring transformative revolutionary ambition in the present.

Marx rarely addressed aesthetics, but *The Eighteenth Brumaire* opens with his influential analysis of the aesthetic self-presentations of bourgeois and proletarian revolutionary movements. Marxist aesthetic theorists have often approached artistic production in relation to the changing dynamics of revolutionary periods: Leon Trotsky's *Literature and Revolution* (1924) traces the emergence of radical ideas in Russian literature leading up to 1917, and Georg Lukács's *The Historical Novel* (1937) theorizes the genre through its formal reflection of historical changes catalyzed by the English and French Revolutions. Literary scholars have used Marxian understandings of specific revolutionary periods to analyze canonical writers: Christopher Hill connected Milton to radical ideas of the English Revolution, and critics have long read

English Romanticism for aesthetic responses to the American, French, and Industrial Revolutions: Marilyn Butler, Marjorie Levinson, Alan Liu, and David Simpson have authored important examples. Finally, Americanists like Alan Wald, Barbara Foley, and Michael Denning have established the influence of Marxism and its revolutionary ideas not only on proletarian literature in the 1930s, but also on US cultural production more broadly.

(*See also* Anti-Humanism; Chapter 4, Marxism; Hegemony; Humanism; Negri, Antonio; Political Unconscious; Repetition; Russian Formalism; *and* Terror)

Nathaniel Mills, *University of Minnesota (United States)*

Further Reading

Fanon, Frantz. *The Wretched of the Earth* [1961]. New York: Grove Press, 2004.

James, C. L. R. *The Black Jacobins: Toussaint L'Ouverture and the San Domingo Revolution* [1938]. New York: Vintage, 1989.

Marx, Karl, and Friedrich Engels. *The Communist Manifesto* [1848]. Trans. Samuel Moore. Rvsd. and ed. David McLellan. New York: Oxford University Press, 1992.

Marx, Karl. *The Eighteenth Brumaire of Louis Bonaparte* [1852]. New York: International Publishers, 1994.

Rhetoric

Rhetoric is one of the most confused and misunderstood terms in our political lexicon. In common parlance, it tends to mean one of two things: fluff or deception. Both definitions disparage rhetoric as a charade and, as such, capture something honest about Americans' experiences with the chicanery that masquerades as political discourse today. But really, rhetoric is the skillful use of language and other symbols to get things done. Anytime we build a relationship or a community or a team, anytime we pump up the troops for war or persuade them to put down their arms for peace, anytime we rally people for change, we use rhetoric. Anytime we speak the truth, we use rhetoric. We use rhetoric to express ourselves. We use rhetoric to change minds. We use rhetoric to alter behaviors. We use rhetoric all the time. Rhetoric is the basic building block of social life.

In political discourse, the word rhetoric is rarely used without the diminutive "mere"— "mere rhetoric." Yet, for much of Western history, rhetoric was not considered to be "mere" at all. In ancient Greece, rhetoric was the first of the liberal arts, and for millennia it has been understood to mean the things people say to persuade or advocate change. Generally speaking, rhetoric means symbolic action aimed at changing minds, changing motives, and changing worlds. Rhetoric is therefore more than mere fluff and deception. Who we are as citizens is constituted through rhetoric; directed at an audience, rhetoric orients self toward other. Humans are social creatures, yet our experiences are subjective, limited by our bodies, our culture, and our language. Though Ralph Waldo Emerson once imagined a transcendent, omnipotent Eye that could see all, we have no such eyes. Our vision is bounded. Everyone is an other to us: some others we draw close, some others we ignore, some others we push far away, some others we refuse to recognize as human. In turn, our relationships are contingent upon our ability and our willingness to engage the other, to see the other as a fellow. Rhetoric matters in our daily lives because how we talk to strangers, to our friends and families, to our enemies, and to the public will affect the composition of those relationships. In the political realm, how we talk influences our ability to make good decisions and resolve conflicts. If our language allows us to identify with the other, peace is possible (but not guaranteed); if our language demonizes the other, then the road to violence is paved (though we need not walk it). Our rhetorical practices—how we go about trying to persuade others and advocate change— influence the character of our personal relationships and also our politics. In this way, rhetoric is foundational to democracy.

(*See also* Aristotelianism; Chapter 1, Early Theory; Chapter 3, Narrative and Narratology; Chapter 8, Rhetoric; Close Reading; de Man, Paul; Figuration; Fish, Stanley; Irony; Persuasion; Sophist; Structuralism; Terror; *and* Trope)

Jeremy David Engels, *Penn State University (United States)*

Further Reading

Engels, Jeremy. *The Politics of Resentment: A Genealogy*. University Park: The Pennsylvania State University Press, 2015.

Fontana, Benedetto, Cary J. Nederman, and Gary Remer, eds. *Talking Democracy: Historical Perspectives on Democracy and Rhetoric*. University Park: The Pennsylvania State University Press, 2005.

McDorman, Todd F., and David M. Timmerman, eds. *Rhetoric and Democracy: Pedagogical and Political Practices*. East Lansing: Michigan State University Press, 2008.

Rhetorical Narratology (*See* Chapter 3, Narrative and Narratology)

Ricoeur, Paul

Paul Ricoeur (1913–2005) is one of the principle figures associated with the expansion of hermeneutics, or the theory of interpretation, in the twentieth century. Ricoeur made critical contributions to theories of symbol, metaphor, narrative, imagination, memory, and translation.

Ricoeur's first engagement with literary theory came in the early work *The Symbolism of Evil* (1969). Ricoeur concluded this work with the argument that symbols, particularly religious symbols, give rise to thought. By this idea, Ricoeur meant that, contra the Cartesian notion that understanding comes through expunging thinking as much as possible of the symbolic register to come to clear and distinct ideas, genuine understanding starts with the symbolic and moves to the level of philosophical reflection. "The task," he argued, "is, starting from symbols, to elaborate existential concepts—that is to say, not only structures of reflection but structures of existence, insofar as existence is the being of man."

In *Interpretation Theory* (1976) and *The Rule of Metaphor* (1981), Ricoeur advanced the idea of a semantic theory of metaphor. Building on the ideas of I. A. Richards, Philip Wheelwright, and others, Ricoeur argued that a metaphor works, not through substitution of one word for another, but at the level of complete utterance. A metaphor functions, he argued, on the basis of a "semantic impertinence" in the relation between subject and predicate: "The metaphorical interpretation presupposes a literal interpretation which self-destructs in a significant contradiction. It is this process of self-destruction or transformation which imposes a sort of twist on the words, an extension of meaning thanks to which we can make sense where a literal interpretation would be literally nonsensical." Thus, metaphors create new meanings and deeper understandings due to the tension between a literal, nonsensical, predication, and a new, figurative interpretation.

Surely, Ricoeur's most important and lasting contribution to literary theory is his work on narrative. In the three volumes of *Time and Narrative* (1984, 1985, 1988), he argued that what metaphor does at the level of the utterance fictional narrative does at the level of the work as a whole, that is, suspend a literal meaning in order to unleash new figurative meanings. A work of fiction, Ricoeur demonstrated, opens a world "in front of" itself, a set of possibilities the reader is invited to inhabit over the course of the reading. In engaging the work, the reader brings her own world—the set of presuppositions she holds about reality—to be questioned by the world of the text. Through the mechanism of the "threefold mimesis," the act of reading involves the imaginative engagement with the world projected by the text (mimesis$_1$), bringing it into contact with the reader's own world (mimesis$_2$), with the possibility of having her world transformed, or refigured, by the work (mimesis$_3$). In this way, the fictional work has the potential of informing the reader's own self-understanding, leading to Ricoeur's later interests in the notion of narrative identity.

In the last few decades, Ricoeur's thought has come under criticism for failing to address feminist scholarship and critical race theory. Nonetheless, his ideas continue to influence work in continental philosophy, religious and biblical studies, rhetoric, and narrative theory.

(*See also* Assujettissement; Chapter 3, Narrative and Narratology; Chapter 18, Translation; Hermeneutics; Ideology; *and* Subject)

W. David Hall, *Centre College (United States)*

Further Reading

Hahn, Lewis E., ed. *The Philosophy of Paul Ricoeur*. Chicago: Open Court, 1995.

Joy, Morny, ed. *Paul Ricoeur and Narrative: Context and Contestation*. Calgary: University of Calgary, 1997.

Kemp, T. Peter, and David Rasmussen, eds. *The Narrative Path: The Later Works of Paul Ricoeur*. Cambridge: MIT Press, 1989.

Rights

In 1966, the US Supreme Court ruled in *Miranda v. Arizona* that suspects must be verbally informed of their Constitutional rights to legal representation and against self-incrimination. In 1967, the popular television police drama *Dragnet* began including the new Miranda warnings in its scripts, inaugurating one of the signal features of crime stories today. Sgt. Joe Friday notified his arrestees: "You have the right to remain silent. Anything you say can and will be used against you in a court of law. You have the right to an attorney. . . ." By 2000, the Miranda warning had become such a common police story trope that when the Supreme Court reaffirmed the ruling, judges and legal scholars credited popular culture with saving the rights, since TV viewers assume that the rights are constitutionally guaranteed. Some even credit the international norm of a right to a fair trial to the globalization of American television.

The case of Miranda warnings is a dramatic example of the normative social work that literature and culture do in popularizing ideas about rights. Ordinarily, literature works in more subtle ways to establish, reinforce, or challenge social norms of behavior. For example, Edward Said argued that the nineteenth-century bourgeois novel showed readers what they could do, where they could go, who they could become, and how they should be treated. In *Human Rights, Inc.* (2007), I argue that the *Bildungsroman* (the coming-of-age novel) has been a primary story form through which human rights law has been normalized, for better and worse, around the world. The *Bildungsroman* was used in British and French colonial schools to teach native children how to be good subjects and citizens, and the genre is often reworked strategically by authors from minority groups who have been excluded from the full benefits of citizenship in Europe and the United States for making human rights claims for social and political inclusion. The burgeoning field of literature and human rights has identified numerous roles that storytelling plays in the protection, promotion, and violation of people's rights.

The Miranda warnings cover a person's right to be represented in a court of law; much scholarly work on culture and rights is about an assumed right to be represented in literature—or, a right to one's own story. Many postcolonial, minority studies, and feminist scholars argue that the right to political representation is closely related to the general logic of representation in literature. Thus, for example, in the mid-twentieth century, Indian and African peoples—like women and ethnic minority activists in the United States and Europe—demanded full rights to political representation while also insisting on their inclusion in literary canons and the worlds they represent. The right to literary representation subtends the current essentialist identitarian discourse about cultural appropriation, which maintains that groups of people have an absolute right not to be represented in literature by people from other identity groups. In some ways, this development shows the risks of rights in a neo-liberalized global and moral economy, where individual rights are treated as forms of private property, properly belonging to one person or group and not to others.

(*See also* Bare Life; Chapter 10, Feminism; Chapter 22, Identity Studies; Chapter 25, University Studies; Humanimal; Identity Politics; Intersectionality; Neoliberalism; *and* Sovereignty)

Joseph R. Slaughter, *Columbia University (United States)*

Further Reading

Lionnet, Françoise. "'Logiques méstises':
Cultural Appropriation and Postcolonial
Representations." *College Literature*.
19.3/20.1 (1993): 100–20.

Mezey, Naomi. "Approaches to the Cultural
Study of Law: Law as Culture." *Yale Journal of Law and the Humanities* 13 (2001):
35–67.

Slaughter, Joseph R. *Human Rights, Inc.:
The World Novel, Narrative Form, and
International Law.* New York: Fordham
University Press, 2007.

Rorty, Richard

Richard Rorty (1931–2007) was the most
famous, if not the most important, American philosopher of the late twentieth century. Rorty broke from the orthodoxy of
Anglo-American academic philosophy, in
which he was trained, to champion a revisionist approach that blended the pragmatism of
John Dewey with the existentialism of Martin
Heidegger and the anti-metaphysical views of
Wilfrid Sellars and W. V. O. Quine. His work,
in particular, spurred a massive revival of
interest in the classic American pragmatism
of Charles Sanders Peirce, William James,
and Dewey.

Rorty's philosophical position is radically
anti-foundationalist and essentially rhetorical. In the book that announced his break
from positivism, *Philosophy and the Mirror
of Nature* (1979), he denies that there is any
external standard—either a mind-independent reality or the dictates of reason—that
secures the "truth" of human assertions.
Rather, truth is a matter of communal agreement. Such agreements are utterly contingent and might dissolve at any time; they are
attained through the historical and communicative processes that constitute communities. Of course, communities also harbor

many disagreements. Whether enough "solidarity" exists to keep the community from
descending into civil war is primarily a matter of sentiment, of loyalty and attachment
to fellow citizens, not of reason. Similarly,
powerful stories and striking images and
metaphors are much more effective than
arguments in forming people's beliefs, values, and commitments.

For the academic philosophers he often
scorned, Rorty was a relativist and irrationalist. His reply was often a refusal to
debate them on their own terms. We need
a different picture, a different story, a different set of images and metaphors, he
claimed, not the endless repetition of a
tired set of debates about realism against
anti-realism. He often denied being a relativist, because he believed we are capable of
judging whether one state of affairs is better than another. But he also, provocatively,
called himself "ethnocentric," because the
accidental fact of his having been born an
American dictated his preference (which
could not be rationally grounded) for a certain vision of liberal democracy.

Already notorious by the middle 1980s
for the philosophical debates he engendered, Rorty became a public figure when
he adopted Dewey's slogan: "the priority of
democracy to philosophy." Much of Rorty's
later writing was political—and appeared
in nonacademic publications. He described
himself as a "postmodern bourgeois liberal"
and delighted in tweaking both the left and
the right with his stolidly liberal views. True
to his philosophical positions, he claimed that
liberalism was not grounded in some order of
reasons or any other form of necessity. Liberal democracy was a contingent historical
creation. Thus, he saw himself as agreeing
substantively with the accounts of liberal
democracy found in John Rawls and Jürgen
Habermas, but disagreed with their efforts to

"ground" their politics theoretically. Against their Kantian efforts, he adopted a Humean ethics based on sentiment. Rorty's was, as he put it, a "bleeding heart liberalism," based on sympathy for the less fortunate and the general desire to alleviate suffering wherever it rears its ugly head. His denunciations of the depredations of our current world (best accessed in the volume *Philosophy and Social Hope* [2000]) are powerful and moving—and the source of his standing as a public intellectual.

The priority of democracy to philosophy meant that allegiance to a vision of a fully democratic society should trump any allegiance to philosophy. Rather, philosophy should be placed at the service of the political vision. Fairly often, Rorty claims that philosophy is irrelevant to politics and that his own philosophical views have no political impact either for or against a commitment to democracy. On the other hand, he does recognize that his political views are, for the most part, radically consequentialist. When he does offer arguments (as contrasted to appeals to sentiments), they are based on claims that arranging society this way as opposed to that will lead to better outcomes, where better outcomes are identified in relation to alleviating suffering or enabling the well-being of the largest number. But he always returns to the assertion that, first, we have to care about others' well-being. The primary political problem, as he sees it, is to extend the circle of people we care about, outward from the family to the nation and then to the globe.

While Rorty is a figure philosophers love to hate, literary critics have a more complicated relation to him. He is an ally in their attempts to open up academic philosophy to wider perspectives and in their skepticism about reason. But his liberalism is distasteful to many of them, as are his pointed critiques of an "identity politics" that he found counterproductive for his own political hopes.

(*See also* Chapter 8, Rhetoric; Chapter 12, Postmodernism; Neopragmatism; *and* Text)

John McGowan, *University of North Carolina, Chapel Hill (United States)*

Further Reading
Brandom, Robert B., ed. *Rorty and His Critics*. Malden: Blackwell, 2000.

Rorty, Richard. *Philosophy and the Mirror of Nature*. Princeton: Princeton University Press, 1979.

Rorty, Richard. *Contingency, Irony, and Solidarity*. Cambridge: Cambridge University Press, 1989.

Rorty, Richard. *Philosophy and Social Hope*. New York: Penguin, 2000.

Russian Formalism

The study of literature as a formal system made up of combinative structures and devices, such as tropes, that constitute an illusion of mimesis: realistic depiction. Russian formalism considered itself to be a scientific investigation of what one could call literature as a signifying technology. The school treated literature and art in terms of autonomous systems whose content was the effect of the whole and not its cause. Like the New Critics, the Russian Formalists were opposed to the idea that a work is like a box that contains or stores an object (the contents) that one simply retrieves. Also similar to the New Critics, the Russian Formalists saw literary works in terms of devices that had the function of calling attention to themselves as extraordinary as opposed to ordinary, normative, or typical. Fyodor Dostoyevsky's Underground Man is not a typical social subject, which is why as a device, made up of rhetorical devices, he exposes the horrors of what people accepted as normal Russian existence. Art opposes itself to "the way things are" and in that sense has revolutionary potential. Major figures associated with Russian formalism include Viktor Shklovsky, Roman Jakobson, Yuri Tynianov, Boris Eichenbaum, and Vladimir Propp. Russian formalism and the Prague School are closely related, given that the Prague School was in some sense an exilic continuation of the former.

(*See also* Chapter 2, Structuralism and Semiotics; Chapter 3, Narrative and Narratology; Formalism; *and* Prague School)

Herman Rapaport, *Wake Forest University (United States)*

Further Reading

Dubois, Jean, Mathée Giacomo, Louis Guespin, Christiane Marcellesi, Jean-Baptiste Marcellesi, and Jean-Pierre Mével, eds. *Dictionnaire de linguistique.* Paris: Larousse, 1973.

S

Said, Edward

The late Edward W. Said is best known for his 1978 book *Orientalism*, a groundbreaking study of modern Western attitudes toward Eastern, especially Middle Eastern people and cultures, whose beginnings trace back to Greco-Roman antiquity and Medieval Christendom. This book inaugurates "post-colonialist" criticism. Said shows here how the West defines itself by invoking the world beyond its borders as the immature, often feminized "Orient" and, in the redemptive name of maturation and manhood, justifies that "inferior" world's colonization. *Orientalism* remains Said's most significant contribution to an understanding of the fraught contemporary occasion, particularly in the aftermath of September 12, 2001.

However, *Culture and Imperialism* (1993) elaborates this critical understanding. This book's oppositional readings put into subversive play the triumphalist narrative of Second World War. Said's contrapuntal diagnosis characterizes the demographics of the postwar world as bearing witness to an occasion that has "produced more refugees, migrants, displaced persons, and exiles than ever before in history, most of them as an accompaniment to and, ironically enough, as afterthoughts of great post-colonial and imperial conflicts." This occasion, he emphasizes, is marked by vast populations of nomads who exist "between the old and the new, between the old empire and the new states," and, as such, they

articulate "the tensions, irresolutions, and contradictions in the overlapping territories shown on the cultural map of imperialism." This break, an interregnum in Western history, manifests a radically different civilization, an exilic polis on the move as it makes, unmakes, and remakes the future.

Acknowledging the "massive dislocations, waste, misery, and horrors endured in our century's migrations and mutilated lives," Said then writes that, nevertheless, "it is no exaggeration to say that liberation as an intellectual mission, born in the resistance and opposition to the confinements and ravages of imperialism, has now shifted from the settled, established, and domesticated dynamics of culture to its unhoused, decentered, and exilic energies." As Said puts this estrangement (recalling his prior reference to Gerard Manly Hopkins), "From this perspective then all things are indeed counter, original, spare, strange," and then adds almost parenthetically, "From this perspective also, one can see "the complete consort dancing together" contrapuntally," as T. S. Eliot's *Four Quartets* (1943) views things from its utopian, albeit religious perspective.

Invoking Theodor Adorno's *Minima Moralia* (1951) on "damaged life," Said concludes that this new exilic resistance inheres in the nonexistent—*spectral*—existence to which the émigré has been reduced by dominant culture, which itself becomes the pervasive dominant mode of consciousness for all. "The emigre consciousness—a mind of winter in Wallace Stevens's phrase—discovers in its marginality that "a gaze averted from the beaten track, a hatred of brutality, a search for fresh concepts not yet encompassed by the general pattern is the last hope of thought." Relocated in this paradoxical context of *Culture and Imperialism*, *Orientalism* and *The Question of Palestine* (1979) undergo a sea change. Said's worldly critique of the West's perennial Orientalist representation appears now in masterful counterpoint as a luminous fruitful universality.

(*See also* Chapter 13, Race and Postcolonial Studies; Chapter 22, Identity Studies; Migration; Orientalism; Origin; Other, The; Philology; Secularism; Spivak, Gayatri; *and* Worldhood)

William Spanos, *Binghamton University (United States)*

Further Reading

Mufti, Aamir. "Critical Secularism: A Reintroduction for Perilous Times." *boundary 2* 31.2 (2004): 1–9.

Radhakrishnan, Rajagopalan. *A Said Dictionary*. New York: Blackwell, 2012.

Spanos, William V. *The Legacy of Edward W. Said*. Urbana: University of Illinois Press, 2009.

Saussure, Ferdinand de

Ferdinand de Saussure (1857–1913) was a foundational figure in the field of general linguistics and of the general social-psychological science of signs of all kinds—*semiology*—that he envisaged, but never fully developed. In his semiological account of language, Saussure postulated an abstract language system—*la langue*—as the principle object of study of the science of linguistics. The various versions of the posthumously published *Course in General Linguistics* (1916) are based on notes compiled by some of the students who attended Saussure's Geneva courses in general linguistics (1907–11). Saussure grounded his general linguistics in the language system (*la langue*). Saussure abstracted this theoretical construct from the "complex," "multiform," and "heteroclite" diversity of speech practices that Saussure called *le langage*, based on the premise that the theoretical point of view constructs the object of study. However, it is important to note that the structuralist interpretation of Saussure first laid down by the editorial shaping of the students' notes by Charles Bally and Albert Sechehaye in the first edition of *Course in General Linguistics* has been questioned in recent decades. More nuanced readings by Michel Arrivé, Paul Bouissac, Simon Bouquet, Roy Harris, Ruqaiya Hasan, E. F. Konrad Koerner, Beata Stawarska, Carol Sanders, and Paul Thibault show a more complex and problematic thinker of continuing relevance. The critical editions of important Saussurean texts such as *Course in General Linguistics* (e.g., Rudolf Engler, Robert Godel, and Tullio de Mauro), *The Germanic Legends* (Anna Marinetti and Marcello Meli), *The Harvard Manuscripts* (e.g., Roman Jakobson, Herman Parret), the *Phonetics* (Maria Pia Marchese), and *Writings in General Linguistics* (Bouquet and Engler) are also central.

According to Saussure, the language system (*la langue*) has both an individual aspect and a social aspect. The individual aspect (*la langue individuelle*) consists in the store of verbal images in the brain of the individual. The social aspect is a relatively homogeneous system of signs, which Saussure described as the "totality of socially ratified associations" of a speech community. For Saussure, "the linguistic reality" combines the agencies of time and the language community ("the speaking mass") to stabilize the system of values in the language system (*la langue*). Linguistic signs are formed in the minds of individual speakers, but are ratified by the collective social dynamics of *la masse parlante* ("the speaking mass") in the language system. The language system is a social-semiological institution; its differentially defined values constrain and regiment the linguistic behaviors of individual speaking subjects.

Saussure placed the individual's articulatory activity outside of the language system in the domain of "speech" (*la parole*). In *Course in General Linguistics*, Saussure made the following twofold distinction: "1. Usage of the general faculty in view of language (*le langage*) (phonation etc.) 2. Also: individual usage of the code of the language system (*la langue*) according to individual thought." In eschewing a naturalistic grounding of language in human neuro-biology and embodied experience in order to set up an autonomous domain of enquiry called general linguistics, Saussure created the premises for a linguistic science in which meaning and cognition are equated with abstract semantic and cognitive functions and verbal pattern in opposition to the purportedly mechanistic and executory functions of the physical body.

Within the language system, Saussure distinguished two distinct spheres that serve to generate "a certain order of values," which he theorized as syntagmatic and associative relations, respectively, in *Course in General Linguistics*. Syntagmatic and associative relations, Saussure argued, are "indispensable to the workings of the language system (*la langue*)" and constitute "two forms of mental activity." Syntagmatic relations are *in praesentia;* they rest on two or more terms equally present in an effective series that is founded on the linear character of the language system (*la langue*). On that basis, they occur as sequential arrangements in acts of speech (*la parole*). On the other hand, associative relations unite terms *in absentia* in a virtual mnemonic series outside of discourse, in memory.

Saussure operates a dual substance theory that assumes two domains: the psychic domain of individual mind where linguistic signs are formed through the association of signifiers with their signifieds and the domains of unformed and inert nonlinguistic "thought" and "sound" on which signs operate. The linguistic sign is a psychic construct consisting of the relation between a signifier (acoustic image) and a signified (concept). The nonlinguistic domains of "thought" and "sound" are inherently inert and formless. Linguistic signs segment and structure the domains of "thought" and "sound" according to the differentially defined phonic and conceptual terms comprising the language system (*la langue*). The system of differences is an unconscious psychic reality which nonetheless influences the conscious operation of sign-making in *la parole*.

In the final section of his essay "The Double Essence of Language," Saussure introduced the idea of "integration or postmeditation-reflection." The process of reflection takes the unconscious facts of the purely negative opposition of differential values in the language system and projects it to a higher level of knowing, which is positive and active in character. Reflection re-organizes the lower level facts into a higher level structure that yields an explicit and positive understanding of the mind's activity, which is actively to differentiate, rather than mechanically and passively to register purely negative differences. According to Saussure, linguistic signs do not have fixed, predetermined values. Their value is an emergent consequence of the incessant flux of the activity of sign-making. Our explicit understanding of the value of a given sign at a given moment is an emergent outcome of the process of integration or postmeditation-reflection. Saussure concludes his extended meditation on the "dual essence of language" in pointing out that the value of a sign is not fixed in advance, but arises according to how "the reciprocal and relative aspect of these signs change from moment to moment in an infinite manner" as a result of the contextualizing activity of the sets of signs made present or absent at a given moment in the process of creating signs.

(*See also* Alterity; Binary Opposition; Chapter 2, Structuralism and Semiotics; Chapter 5, Post-structuralism; Chapter 12, Postmodernism; Différance; Langage; Langue; Parole; Semiotics; Sign; *and* Signifier and Signified)

Paul J. Thibault, *University of Agder, Kristiansand (Norway)*

Further Reading

Sanders, Carol, ed. *The Cambridge Companion to Saussure*. Cambridge: Cambridge University Press, 2004.

Saussure, Ferdinand de. *Cours de Linguistique Générale* [1916]. Eds. Charles Bally and Albert Sechehaye. Paris: Payot, 1971.

Saussure, Ferdinand de. *Course in General Linguistics* [1916]. Eds. Charles Bally and Albert Sechehaye. Trans. W. Baskin. Glasgow: Fontana/Collins, 1977.

Saussure, Ferdinand de. *Écrits de Linguistique Générale par Ferdinand de Saussure*. Eds. Simon Bouquet and Rudolf Engler. Paris: Gallimard, 2002.

Saussure, Ferdinand de. *Writings in General Linguistics by Ferdinand de Saussure* [2002]. Eds. Simon Bouquet and Rudolf Engler. Trans. Carol Sanders and Matthew Pires. Oxford: Oxford University Press, 2006.

Science and Literature (*See* Actor Network Theory; Biotechnology; Canguilhem, Georges; Chapter 20, Digital Humanities; Critical Climate; Cyberculture; Cybernetics; Cyborg; Environmental Humanties; Episteme; Haraway, Donna; Machine; Neuroscience; Ontology; Posthumanism; Psychoanalysis; Scientific Method; Social Constructionism; Systems Theory; *and* Transhumanism)

Scientific Method

Modern Western science has been defined by its experimental method. But Western science began as philosophy, in which case Western ideas of scientific method have been interwoven with philosophical method.

Classical Greek science was dominated by the *strong foundational* model based on two avenues to truth: *noetic* (a priori, conceptual) and *empirical* (aposteriori, observational). Foundational ideas and principles are supposed to be necessarily true (directly grasped *noetically*) whereas empirical facts, being observational, are contingent on experience. Ideally, empirical beliefs would be grounded in necessary ideas as their underlying principles.

As "the science of God," medieval theology declared revealed truths foundational, but theological dogmas proved more politically than noetically necessary. Modern rationalist metaphysics claimed conceptual necessity, but withered when David Hume's empiricism denied the necessity of logic and mathematics to principles of experience. Immanuel Kant reconstructed necessary knowledge of the world through the "transcendental deduction" of the principles necessary to explain knowledge and experience, restoring the twofold scientific methodology of foundational theory and observation. With the rise of modern science, however, "scientific method" came to mean experimental empiricism.

For all the technological success of natural science, the details of its method proved elusive. Francis Bacon and J. S. Mill wrongly associated experimentalism with induction (generalization) from experience, until

William Whewell, Charles Peirce and others, showed that natural science progresses by hypothesizing theoretical explanations, deducing consequences, and checking them experimentally. Moreover, fascination with Newtonian physics prompted a doubly problematic separation of scientific method from foundational theory, that is, from ontology and epistemology.

First, causation was oversimplified. For some, mechanistic physics rendered obsolete Aristotle's formal, material, and final causes as explanatory principles, as if modeling mechanical forces is the sole aim of science. This truncation of scientific explanation has proven inadequate to quantum physics, biology, and sciences of complexity, which require extensive theoretical modeling far beyond observation.

Second, methodology was oversimplified. The Positivists sought "the unity of the sciences" under the rubric of verification—as if data-collection provides a clear standard of verification or falsification. By the end of the mid-twentieth century, however, philosophers believed that scientific progress depends on science's theory-laden web of beliefs, and that adjustments to data follow whatever explanatory preferences one brings to the data. No one empirical method, it seems, demarcates scientific theory from foundational theorizing and its prejudices.

Aside from positivism, nineteenth-century German philosophers followed Kant by theorizing the conditions of knowledge (epistemology), experience (phenomenology), and understanding (hermeneutics), giving rise to a pluralism of sciences and methods that distinguished sciences of culture (e.g., humanities or *Geisteswissenschaften*) and nature (e.g., *Naturwissenschaften*), and sciences of natural laws (*Gesetzeswissenschaften*) and historical facts (*Ereigniswissenschaften*). Elsewhere, Peirce and Ferdinand de Saussure independently founded sciences of signs (semiotics, semiology), while Peirce and Edmund Husserl independently theorized the internal structure of experience (phenomenology). These neo-foundational sciences employed transcendental theorizing while differentiating the methods of different sciences. In the United States, the Stanford school of the "disunity of science" has articulated a methodological pluralism from an analytic perspective.

(*See also* Persuasion; Theory; *and* Tradition)

Horace Fairlamb, *University of Houston-Victoria (United States)*

Further Readings

Bird, Alexander. *Philosophy of Science.* Montreal: McGill-Queen's University Press, 1998.

Galison, Peter, and David J. Stump. *The Disunity of Science.* Stanford: Stanford Press, 1996.

Losee, John. *A Historical Introduction to the Philosophy of Science.* Oxford: Oxford University Press, 1993.

Secularism

Generally understood, secularism is a nonreligious way of understanding and inhabiting the world. In his 1896 book on the subject, George Jacob Holyoake, to whom the coinage of the term secularism is attributed, describes secularism in the following words:

> Secularism is a code of duty pertaining to this life, founded on considerations purely human, and intended mainly for those who find theology indefinite or inadequate, unreliable or unbelievable. Its essential principles are three: (1) The improvement of this life by material means; (2) That science is the available Providence of man; and (3) That it is good to do good. Whether

there be other good or not, the good of the present life is good, and it is good to seek that good.

This definition of secularism, of course, draws on the long history of philosophical debates within the Western and other traditions between universal theological explanations of the world and its nonreligious and rational understanding by individuals and groups. By focusing on "this life" and reason and science as the tools to understanding and functioning of material life, the secularists privilege reason over metaphysical explanation of things. Secularism in this sense is not necessarily anti-religion, but rather a philosophy and practice that defends the human right to exist and practice life without the mandates and dictates of an established state and official religion.

Secularism also emphasizes our actions in this world and their worldly consequences in opposition to consequences of our actions in an afterlife. Thus, in this sense reason guides peoples' ethics and good conduct as related to living in the world and working for the world in a material sense rather than working toward the rewards of material life in a metaphysical hereafter.

In his discussion of secularism, Holyoake also asserts the importance of free thought: thought can only be free if it is not circumscribed through religious injunction or fear of reprisals. This focus on the freedom of thought and its free expression, without the fear of law, is essential to developing a secular society. Thus, secularism does not attempt to erase religion, but rather attempts to create a public sphere where people who think or act without religious interpretation of the world have the right to think freely and express their opinions and live without fear of state oppression and reprisals.

In a nutshell, secularism is a mode of thought and action that privileges a rational understanding of the world, freedom to inquire freely, and freedom to express one's thoughts without fear of reprisals and religious sanction.

In the current usage of the term, Charles Taylor discusses secularism as a practice in which the religion does not necessarily fall away at the cost of science and rational thought but rather becomes one of many ways of thinking and living a moral life.

For Edward Said in *The Word, the Text, and the Critic* (1983), secularism in literary criticism, which he terms secular criticism, "deals with local and worldly situations, and that it is constitutively opposed to the production of massive, hermetic systems." In Said's sense then secularity is not just related to distancing oneself from any single religious mode of thinking but rather producing works of critical scholarship that do not owe their emergence to any single, overbearing systemic affiliation or sense of loyalty. In this sense, then, secular criticism would be open to different modes of seeing texts and would also be open to reading texts within their material and ideological "worldly" context.

(*See also* Anti-Humanism; Chapter 8, Rhetoric; Chapter 15, Biopower and Biopolitics; Chapter 19, Media Studies; Englightenment; Habermas, Jürgen; Humanism; Political Theology; *and* Said, Edward)

Masood Raja, *University of North Texas (United States)*

Further Reading
Holyoake, George Jacob. *English Secularism: A Confession of Belief*. Chicago: Open Court Publishing Company, 1896.
Said, Edward. *The World, the Text, and the Critic*. Cambridge: Harvard University Press, 1983.
Taylor, Charles. *A Secular Age*. Cambridge: Harvard University Press, 2007.

Self

In the context of semiotics, the referent and meaning of the word *self* are highly variable. It is a commonplace term implicitly connected to fundamental disputes. In a field such as semiotics, theorists often devise a technical vocabulary. This is manifestly true of such authors as Charles S. Peirce, Ferdinand de Saussure, A. J. Greimas, Émile Benveniste, and Julia Kristeva. Sometimes this vocabulary draws heavily upon another discipline (e.g., linguistics), while sometimes it involves coining new words specifically for the study of signs. Of course, the investigation of signs can no more dispense with such commonplace words a sign, meaning, and self than the science of linguistics cannot dispense with such words as language, word, and grammar. There is however a crucial difference between, say, the words *sign* and *self* as they appear in semiotic discourse. For the most part, *sign* is explicitly given a technical meaning, whereas the *self* is used in a more or less commonplace way. The implications of a theory for our understanding of the self however are often noted, although as often as not without elaborating a formally semiotic "theory" of the self. Moreover, the terms by which what is commonly called the *self* is identified might be either technical or quasi-technical ones. This is clearly the case here, since *subject* and its cognates (especially *subjectivity*) tend to be more commonly used than *self*.

While the expression "death of the subject" is ambiguous, it often refers to the rejection of a supposedly sovereign self who endows meaningless sounds or inscriptions with significance. As a transcendental condition of human experience, such a subject has been taken as ahistoric, sometimes as a consciousness completely transparent to itself. In semiotics, however, the subject is never equated with either a being outside of time or a consciousness transparent to itself.

Whatever the semiotic self is, it is not the Cartesian or sovereign subject. In both Peirce's semeiotic and Saussure's *semiologie* as well as structuralist and post-structuralists developments, the link between subjectivity and sovereignty is severed.

From a modernist perspective, the self is the explicans whereas signs (or semiosis, i.e., sign- processes or -functions) are the explicanda. Selves endow signs with whatever meaning they possess. From a broadly postmodern perspective, however, it is just the reverse. Signs are constitutive of selves. That is, the self is not a principle of explanation but a phenomenon or range of phenomena to be explained. Peirce goes so far as to claim, "the mind *is* a sign" in the process of developing and "my language is my sum total of myself." What most sign theorists reject is any conception of a self supposed to exist anterior to, and independent of, exchanges of signs. Whatever the self is, it is a being constituted by its use of, and reliance upon, signs. The term *subject* is most often used to designate a divided being.

Both Michel Foucault and Jacques Derrida are explicit in their commitment to subjectivity in some sense. Neither takes the death of the subject to be an unqualified repudiation or rejection of subjectivity. As Foucault contends, a distinction is needed. On the one hand, he is emphatic: "I do indeed believe that there is no sovereign, founding subject, a universal form of subject to be found everywhere." On the other, he believes that "the subject is constituted through the practices of subjection, or, ... through practices of liberation, of liberty." Or, as Derrida puts it, the "subject is absolutely indispensable. I don't destroy the subject. I situate it." As Peirce and Foucault do, Derrida situates the subject in the play of signs and, by implication, in the varying contexts of rival histories. As pragmatists and other theorists suggest no less than Foucault, the subject is a variable function, not an immutable form.

(*See also* Alterity; Assujettissement; Cartesianism; Chapter 1, Early Theory; Chapter 14, Ecocriticism; Chapter 22, Identity Studies; Derrida, Jacques; Foucault, Michel; Intersubjectivity; Lacan, Jacques; Other, The; Peirce, Charles; Saussure, Ferdinand de; Semiotics; Subject; *and* Subjectivity)

Vincent Colapietro, *Pennsylvania State University (United States)*

Further Reading
Colapietro, Vincent. *Peirce's Approach to the Self: A Semiotic Perspective on Human Subjectivity*. Albany, NY: State University of New York Press, 1989.
Silverman, Kaja. *The Subject of Semiotics*. Oxford: Oxford University Press, 1984.
Singer, Milton. *Man's Glass Essence: Explorations in Semiotic Anthropology*. Bloomington: Indiana University Press, 1984.
Wiley, Norbert. *The Semiotic Self*. Chicago: University of Chicago, 1995.

Semiotics

Semiotics is a general theory of signs connecting in the mind the system of language to the study of cultural phenomena. As methodology of the scholarship in (and beyond) the humanities, semiotics has reorganized the structure of traditional linguistics with the use of signs to create a significant new field. The formal (and informal) view of the semiotic world has extended the fictional signs of literature with cultural codes, and *vice versa*. In literature, the new meanings and messages deal with the novelty of symbolism. Following the Sapir-Whorf hypothesis, the terra incognita of literary semiotics advances language not only to linguistics, but also to cultural studies as a branch of "lingüiculture."

The formal directions of contemporary semiotics are derived from two major figures inspiring semiotic "schools." The "structural" linguistics of Ferdinand de Saussure's *Course in General Linguistics* (1916), published in his posthumous lectures, laid out the principles of "semiology" to establish the Paris School (Roland Barthes, A. J. Greimas, Julia Kristeva, Tzvetan Todorov, Claude Lévi-Strauss). Saussure's linguistic concept or sign-image (*signifié*) refers to the object (*signified*). The task of the interpreter (inquirer, reader) is to "intellectually" analyze the figurative structure of the linguistic word. Roman Jakobson expanded the sign-internal model into the rhetoric markedness of metaphor and metonymy, synchrony and diachrony. Saussure's system of demonstrative or appellative function were incorporated by Jakobson with the "emotive" or "expressive" function to deal with the persuasive rhetoric of poetic art.

The comprehensive model of philosopher Charles S. Peirce introduced three categories to shape the quasi-formal doctrine of logical semiotics. Extracted from the *Collected Papers* (and other posthumous editions), Peirce's logical categories of firstness, secondness, and thirdness broadened into the medium of linguistic genres. The icon (firstness), index (secondness), and symbol (thirdness) are the suggestive, indicative, and imperative modality of the linguistic sign. Peirce widened the categories into a variety of terms, such as tone, token, and type; image, diagram, and metaphor; desire, effort, and purpose; instinct, experience, and habit; quality, relation, and representation; abduction, induction, and deduction; and others. Peirce's evolutionary terminology generalized semiotics into all areas of investigation, including art.

While the sign suggests emotional firstness and the object suggests secondness,

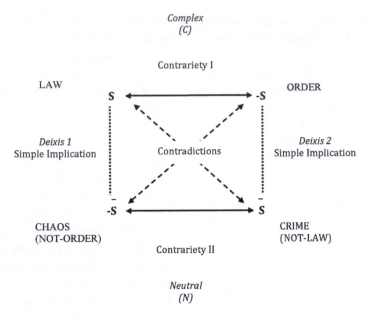

FIGURE 3: Greimas's Semiotic Square.

thirdness is the sign-external sign of "interpretant." The interpretant would be received by the interpreters, reacting to the received sign with new objects, changing the sign into the interpretant-sign. The emotional, energetic, and final interpretant-signs are the reactive effects of the sign upon the "general" interpreter (inquirer, reader, speaker). When the sign *standing for* the object is understood, the interpreter responds to the community of other interpreters in "reagent" signs. The sign's feeling (firstness), opinion (secondness), and argument (thirdness) constitutes the sign-action of received signs in Peirce's "semiosis." Under the aegis of Umberto Eco, the circle of semioticians at the University of Bologna characterized Peirce's literary sign as "open" to multiple interpretations. Eco's *A Theory of Semiotics* (1976) considered the literary sign as a "magic spell" treasuring the art of rule-breaking to make the ambiguous message that *"communicates too much and therefore does not communicate at all."* For Eco, literature has the "particular semiotic status," which "seems to acquire a new status as a *super sign-function.*"

(*See also* Barthes, Roland; Chapter 2, Structuralism and Semiotics; Chapter 19, Media Studies; Diagram; Eco, Umberto; Kristeva, Julia; Langage; Langue; Parole; Peirce, Charles Sanders; Saussure, Ferdinand de; Self; Sign; *and* Signifier and Signified)

Dinda L. Gorlée, *Wittgenstein Archives, University of Bergen (Norway)*

Further Reading

Anderson, Myrdene, and Dinda L. Gorlée. "Duologue in the Familiar and the Strange: Translatability, Translating, Translation." In *Semiotics 2010*. Eds. Karen Haworth, Jason Hogue, and Leonard G. Brocchi. Ontario: Legas Publishing, 2011. 221–32.

Eco, Umberto. *A Theory of Semiotics*. Bloomington: Indiana University Press, 1976.

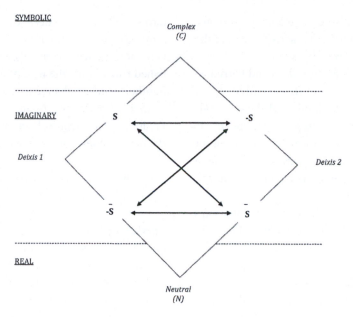

SYMBOLIC

Complex
(C)

IMAGINARY

S

-S

Deixis 1

Deixis 2

-S

S

REAL

Neutral
(N)

FIGURE 4: Greimas's Semiotic Square with Lacan's Three Orders.

Innis, Robert E., ed. *Semiotics: An Introductory Anthology.* Bloomington: Indiana University Press, 1985.

Semiotic Square

Fredric Jameson describes the semiotic square developed by the French linguist and structuralist theorist, A. J. Greimas, as "the supreme achievement of Greimasian semiotics." Greimas first introduces the square in his essay, coauthored with François Rastier, "The Interaction of Semiotic Constraints" (1968), although, as Ronald Schleiffer demonstrates, it already implicitly underlies Greimas's earlier major intervention, *Sémantique structurale: Recherche de méthode* (1966). The square became of great significance for Greimas's subsequent research, and has been deployed throughout Jameson's project, beginning with *The Prisonhouse of Language* (1972).

Greimas's semiotic square is derived from the square of opposition formulated by Aristotle in *De Interpretatione* in order to present formally the set of logical relationships that develop around any concept. According to Greimas, a concept—take "law" for example, indicated in the square by "S"—presupposes two primary relationships: first, that of logical contradiction, or simple negation (not-law, or crime, indicated by the barred "S"); and second, contrariety, or dialectical contradiction—which in this case would be expressed by the notion of "order" ("–S"). Greimas further maintains that the latter term in the contrariety produces its own logical contradiction (disorder/chaos, barred "–S"), and the four terms together suggest another pair of deixical relationships, termed "simple implication."

Greimas then goes beyond Aristotle in a way that makes the square an extraordinarily productive tool for reading narrative texts. Greimas maintains that all narratives offer a deep mediation upon a concept or concepts, as well as a staging of their various relationships. Thus, Greimas concludes, we can always uncover in a narrative not only a presentation of the four internal terms of any square, but also concrete manifestations, often in the form of a character system, of the relationships formed between the two contrarieties (S and –S; barred –S and barred S) and the two implications (S and barred –S; –S and barred S). (The joining of the two logical contradictions or simple negations resists anything more than a formal presentation for the simple fact that they are self-consuming artifacts, a collision of matter and anti-matter, or concept and not-concept.)

A significant shift occurs in Jameson's use of the square, first evident in his 1977 review essay of Louis Marin's *Utopiques: jeux d'espace* (1973), from an emphasis on the narrative manifestation of the topmost contrariety, which Greimas labels the Complex term (C), to the lower, or Neutral (N). The consequences of this shift becomes especially evident when the three planes formed by the square—those of the Complex, the two slots formed by the joining of the implications, and the Neutral—are identified "with" (*avec*) Jacques Lacan's three orders of, respectively, the Symbolic, the Imaginary, and the Real.

The effect is to transform the square from a device for mapping narrative and ideological closure—as Jameson deploys it, for example, in *The Political Unconscious* (1981)—to a way of formally presenting the emergence in any concrete situation, narrative or historical, of the unexpected or uncounted new. The latter is what Alain Badiou refers to in *L'éthique* (1998) as an *event*, located on the "void" of any situation. The Complex term "names" the event that occupies this void of the Real. Such a shift of attention thereby effects a transvaluation of the Neutral from the term for the "radical evil," monstrous Other threatening the continuity of the ideal or Symbolic order, designated by the Complex term, to a name for the radically new. The square thus also offers a way of formally presenting what occurs in the language game Jean-François Lyotard

terms in *The Postmodern Condition* (1984), *paralogy*, a way of achieving not merely "a new move (a new argument) within the established rules," but "the invention of new rules, in other words, a change to a new game."

(*See also* Badiou, Alain; Event; Jameson, Fredric; Lacan, Jacques; Lyotard, Jean-François; Political Unconscious; *and* Semiotics)

Phillip E. Wegner, *University of Florida (United States)*

Further Reading
Greimas, A. J. *On Meaning: Selected Writings in Semiotic Theory.* Trans. Paul J. Perron and Frank H. Collins. Minneapolis: University of Minnesota Press, 1987.
Jameson, Fredric. *The Ideologies of Theory.* New York: Verso, 2008.
Wegner, Phillip E. *Periodizing Jameson: Dialectics, the University, and the Desire for Narrative.* Evanston: Northwestern University Press, 2014.

Seriality

Seriality is a formal property and/or organizational principle that is commonly associated with ongoing narratives, recurring patterns, and periodic publication schedules. As a narrative form, seriality is perhaps most readily associated today with TV—especially the recent explosion of narratively complex television series, which inherit and adapt strategies from twentieth-century film and radio serials and popular serialized literature of the nineteenth century. Outside of popular culture, seriality also characterizes a variety of tendencies or attitudes in modern art, exemplified by conceptual artists such as Sol LeWitt, Pop artists like Andy Warhol and Roy Lichtenstein, or the twelve-tone music of Arnold Schönberg; in each of these cases, seriality refers less to narrative continuity than to aesthetic modularity and material repetition of visual, acoustic, or other elements. Critical discussions of seriality tend to focus either on popular/narrative or on artistic/nonnarrative expressions, thus suggesting a split between "high" and "low" forms; however, there are blurrings and borrowings on both sides: for example, pop art appropriates serialized comics and popular culture generally, while the discontinuous, episodic forms of sitcoms and procedural crime shows embody the modular and quasi-industrial repetition that characterizes so much postWar gallery art. At the root of seriality in all of these forms is an interplay, highlighted by Umberto Eco, between repetition and variation (or innovation).

Seen in terms of this formal interplay, seriality is pervasive across literary and cultural traditions, from the Homeric epics to J. S. Bach's *Goldberg Variations* and beyond. However, serial forms have proliferated at an unprecedented rate since the nineteenth century, when technological advances like the steam-powered printing press enabled serialized publication to dominate the literary marketplace. As Roger Hagedorn has argued, nineteenth-century *feuilletons*, penny dreadfuls, and dime novels attest to close relations between seriality and media-technical innovation: serialized stories "serve to *promote the medium in which they appear*" and thus "to develop the commercial exploitation of a specific medium." Moreover, this explosion of serialized culture corresponds to advances in serialized production more generally; the steam engine not only enabled the daily newspaper but also promoted deskilled factory work, leading eventually to the Taylor/Ford assembly line. Thus, both narrative and nonnarrative forms of seriality find impetus in industrialization; Eugène Sue and Donald Judd alike owe debts to industrial technologies, which are inextricable from capitalism. According to Karl Marx, capital operates according to serialized processes of its own (not just factory production but the process of repetition and variation expressed abstractly as M-C-M' chains of value-production). This grounding of modern seriality in industrial capitalism helps explain the suspicion and scorn heaped on the "culture industry" by the likes of Horkheimer and Adorno, but it also points to the necessity to regard seriality not just as a formal property of cultural objects but as a social phenomenon that is central to the contemporary lifeworld: both our collective identities (such as "the nation," according to Benedict Anderson, or gender for Iris Marion Young) and modern subjectivity itself (in Jean-Paul Sartre's pessimistic view) can be seen as products and expressions of seriality.

(*See also* Chapter 2, Narrative and Narratology; Chapter 15, Biopower and Biopolitics; *and* Chapter 22, Identity Studies)

Shane Denson, *Stanford University (United States)*

Further Reading

Allen, Rob, and Thijs van den Berg, eds. *Serialization in Popular Culture*. New York: Routledge, 2014.

Denson, Shane, and Andreas Jahn-Sudmann, eds. *Digital Seriality*. Special issue. *Eludamos: Journal for Computer Game Culture* 8.1 (2014). http://www.eludamos.org/index.php/eludamos/issue/view/vol8no1.

Kelleter, Frank, ed. *Media of Serial Narrative*. Columbus: Ohio State University Press, 2017.

Sexuality

The term *sexuality* can be understood as an individual's sexual desire for certain types of bodies and the acts that constitute one's sex practices. Historically, the term *sex* has been inextricable from "sexuality" despite the limitations of the former; while "sex" referred to either an act of physical intercourse or the biological signifiers of male and female difference, sexuality no longer relies on the gender binary and thus the separation between the two words must be noted. The use of "sex" can be traced to the fourteenth century in England, but "sexuality" was not articulated as a concept until the nineteenth century.

The politics of sexuality are often linked to ideas of oppression and liberation. Sigmund Freud's theories of desire and the erotic located sexuality as an intrinsic property embodied from childhood onward. Psychoanalytic ideas of sexuality have been critiqued for being too abstract and reliant on normative ideas of gender. Through Freud's work and the studies of early sex theorists like Alfred Kinsey, it is evident that sexuality was thought to be a discourse that required regulation by professionals in the areas of medicine and the law. In *The History of Sexuality* (1976), Michel Foucault dissects the ways that desire and normativity have been read in terms of normalcy and abnormality. Foucault identified how the church, as well as the medical field and the academy, put forth ideologies of sexuality that were thereby mediated by the power of those respective institutions and their points of convergence. Similar research revealed that normative sexual behaviors had been elevated in sex and gender studies in order to reinforce the productive properties of sex practices while demonizing nonnormative sexualities. This served the practical function of creating a rhetoric of sexual criminology so that ostensibly aberrant sexualities could be policed in the juridical sense as well as within societal consciousness.

In the twentieth century, feminist theorist Judith Butler called attention to the problematic nature of prescriptive gendered and sexual norms in *Gender Trouble*. Butler reiterated that reproductive sex was not the correct property through which to measure and define sexuality. Butler identified the collapsibility of gender as a social construct, thereby revealing the potential for new schools of thought about sex practices and sexual identities. Where Foucault was able to historicize the categories of sex and sexuality, Butler gave the praxis for dismantling binary and regulatory ideas of human sexuality. This gave rise to queer sexuality studies in the late twentieth and twenty-first centuries that explores non-gender conforming bodies and nonbinary sex practices. Sex and gender studies scholars continue to note the various matrices of sexuality inscribed through body politics and power structures that are informed by, but not confined to, biological determinants.

(*See also* Binary Opposition; Chapter 1, Early Theory; Butler, Judith; Chapter 7, Psychoanalytic Theory; Chapter 10, Feminism; Chapter 15, Biopower and Biopolitics; Foucault, Michel; Freud, Sigmund; Gender; Irigaray, Luce; *and* Queer Theory)

Rita Mookerjee, *Florida State University*
(United States)

Further Reading

Butler, Judith. *Bodies That Matter: On the Discursive Limits of Sex*. New York: Routledge, 2011.

Butler, Judith. *Undoing Gender*. New York: Routledge, 2004.

Foucault, Michel. *The History of Sexuality, Volume 1* [1976]. Trans. Robert Hurley. New York: Vintage Books, 1978.

Sign

The sign is the fundamental unit of semiotics. A sign consists of anything that stands for something other than itself in some aspect. The signification of the sign reflects the aspect most prominent in the sign, directing the sign-interpreter to the meaning. The signs may be linguistic or nonlinguistic, natural or artificial signs, or classified into specific categories. The sign is not a single or unique communicator, but subject to cultural transformations of sign-and-object. See "symptom," "enemy," "hero and slave," and other signs used in biological, medical, psychological, social, political, philosophical, religious, and other semiotic fields. Signs are always in metaphorical or cultural crisis.

The literary sign involves the reader to substitute the living (physical) thing to refer to the object, both represented by the written (vocal) sign. The sign has the formal structure of the abstract schema, substituting the feeling or event of the object in language. The genres of diary, poem, essay, theater play, or film are understood as literary signs by the sign-receivers. The significant word-clue or mythical image evokes the emotion, opinion, and judgment of the sign-receivers. The literary sign imprints the sign-information on the reader's memory, symbolizing the pleasure, instruction, or reflection of the text.

In structuralist semiology, Ferdinand de Saussure's linguistic sign is not the transparent union of "a thing and its name" but the "arbitrary concept" of the sign-image (signifier, *signifié*) with its object (signified, *signified*). Language (*langue*) is not a neutral code, but constitutes the abstract code of signifier with the underlying signified to signify the process of speech. The word is the fundamental unit of Saussure's figurative speech (*parole*). By deciphering the word, the effect suggests its meaning. Structuralism reconstructed postwar France's intellectual power, as in the writings of Roland Barthes, Algirdas Julien Greimas, Michel Foucault, Jacques Lacan, Jacques Derrida, Claude Lévi- Strauss, Julia Kristeva, and others who inspired sociocultural thought in the second half of the twentieth century. French structur-

alism textualized the philosophical, sexual, political, religious, and mythological signs of self and otherness engaged in contemporary society. The text-signs play with public texts struggling with private identity, like signifier and signified.

In Charles S. Peirce's logical semiotics, anything can be a sign, but distinguished from the *semiotic sign*, that is the union of thing (sign), referee (object), and received sign (interpretant). The sign is produced by the sign-maker (author) for transmission to other interpreters to receive meaningful sign-relations (interpretant). The communication and interpretation imply Peirce's "semiosis." Semiosis is the mediation of the infinite chain of interpretations (interpretant-signs) of sign with object. Peirce's *logical sign* consists of three categories: icon (firstness), index (secondness), and symbol (thirdness) to construct the mimetic, deictic, and conventional logic of suggestive tone, indicative token, and imperative type. Firstness is looked at individually "in itself," secondness is compared with outside characters, and thirdness is regarded as totality or unity. Charles Morris continued Peirce's classification in behavioral signs of designative, appraisive, and prescriptive actions. Umberto Eco's literary narratives argued about the open and closed signs of metaphor, the two images of the metaphor signified through the semiosis of the readers' interpretants.

The literary semiotician Juri Lotman viewed the literary sign of Russian culture as a highly explosive substance. Exiled from Russia to Estonia and founder of the Moscow-Tartu school, Lotman criticized the horror of being caught in the sign-image (*signifié*) and object (*signified*). Reversing the political code of "collective" and "individual" signs in official "honor" and "glory," he chose the third option: the apocalyptic world of the "semiosphere," with signs circulating in different cultural environments. Lotman's culture clash of the literary signs in "norm" and "deviation," "fool" and "madman," and "personal" and "alien" overthrew established Russian rules.

(*See also* Archi-Trace; Chapter 2, Structuralism and Semiotics; Eco, Umberto; Langage; Langue; Parole; Peirce, Charles Sanders; Saussure, Ferdinand de; Self; Semiotics; Sign; Signifier and Signified; *and* Structuralism)

Dinda L. Gorlée, *Wittgenstein Archives, University of Bergen (Norway)*

Further Reading

Eco, Umberto. *The Role of the Reader: Explorations in the Semiotics of Texts*. Bloomington: Indiana University Press, 1976.

Johansen, Jørgen Dines. *Dialogic Semiosis: An Essay on Signs and Meaning*. Bloomington: Indiana University Press, 1993.

Lotman, Juri. *Culture and Explosion*. Berlin: De Gruyter Mouton, 2009.

Scholes, Robert. *Semiotics and Interpretation*. New Haven: Yale University Press, 1982.

Signifier and Signified

In the semiotics of Ferdinand de Saussure the signifier and signified are what make up the sign. The signifier is that dimension of the sign that expresses. The signified is what is expressed. The signifier, moreover, has to be perceptible as some sort of entity, as something that stands for something else. Deer tracks in the snow, for example, can be taken as a semiotic mark for deer that had been present at some time in the past. As the signified, the deer are absent. Indeed, the chief characteristic of the signified is its absence, that the signifier, which is present, indicates to us something that is not there. But what

about addressing things that are present, such as talking about a cup that is right there in front of us? The cup is not absent. In such a case, we have direct reference in which the signified is replaced by the referent as concrete object. The physical cup substitutes itself for the word cup; however, the signified, which is ideational (the idea of cup) persists in that the physical cup is but one of any number of objects that could fulfill the idea of what it would mean for us to say with accuracy "that is a cup." This concerns a certain Platonism wherein the signified is akin to the pure forms and concrete referents are akin to debased representations of these forms. In practice we tend to reverse this Platonic hierarchy by thinking that the idea (the signified) is inferior to the actual object or entity before us. The actual cup on the table before me is superior, more real, than the fuzzy idea I would otherwise have of it and therefore takes priority. But in the absence of a signified—an idea of what cups are—we would be dealing with all sorts of physical objects as referents in the absence of being able to identify them as cups as opposed to pots, jars, or basins. The physical referent doesn't determine meaning; rather, it embodies it. Saussure didn't concern himself with ostensive reference in this way; rather, he saw the signified as an effect of the system of signifiers. But here too the signified takes priority over the referent in that it determines what referents are as phenomena. If we look across various languages, we will quickly encounter signifieds that don't translate from one language into another. This indicates that signifieds aren't Platonic universals but what some call quai-transcendentals. In other words, these signifieds function *as if* they were universals, which they are not, given the fact that they are but the products of a particular system.

(*See also* Chapter 2, Structuralism and Semiotics; Langage; Langue; Parole; Platonism;

Saussure, Ferdinand de; Semiotics; Sign; *and* Signifier and Signified)

Herman Rapaport, *Wake Forest University (United States)*

Further Reading

Nöth, Winfried. *Handbook of Semiotics*. Bloomington: Indiana University Press, 1990.

Saussure, Ferdinand de. *Course in General Linguistics* [1916]. Eds. Charles Bally and Albert Sechehaye. Trans. Roy Harris. Chicago: Open Court, 1998.

Social Construct (*See* Social Constructionism)

Social Constructionism

Social constructionism and *social constructivism* concern human experience, thought, and artifacts insofar as they reflect the influence of social context. These terms are sometimes distinguished, though their philosophical interest is largely the same, as discussed below.

Anticipations of social construction can be found in Greek philosophers—such as Parmenides, Xenophanes, and the Sophists—who argued for the cultural relativity of knowledge. The modern epoch of philosophical constructionism began with David Hume's relativization of morality to local social norms and with Immanuel Kant's theory that the mind constructs reality out of necessary and universal categories. Kant was succeeded by more relativist versions (Johann G. Herder, Wihelm von Humbolt), which made meaning and value contingent upon local features of social context such as language, culture, and history. Linguistic relativism was later radicalized in the Sapir-Worf hypothesis.

Charles Peirce sought to accommodate both the objectively grounded aspects of experience and the socially constructed aspects. His phenomenology and semiotics distinguish the effects of natural force on experience from the socially constructed interpretation of its representations. Since Peirce, others have defended this middle ground between objectivism and relativism, while others have gravitated toward the extremes.

Natural science has been the bulwark of anti-constructivist objectivism. Positivism in particular attempted to escape social construction through the objective grounds of verificationism. But radical objectivism largely collapsed when Thomas Kuhn showed the influence of institutional assumptions on standards of scientific justification. Since Kuhn, the "strong programme" of the Edinburgh School of the sociology of knowledge has explored in depth the social construction of science.

More than nature's facts, normativity and meaning have been subject to social constructivist interpretations in social science, which—in the twentieth century—strenuously sought to avoid ethnocentrism. In American philosophy, Pragmatists such as Josiah Royce, George H. Mead, Charles Cooley, and John Dewey emphasized the social dimensions of learning and selfhood. In Europe, phenomenology took subjectivity to be the window on human reality. Edmund Husserl's late work on the Lifeworld and Alfred Schutz' social phenomenology inspired further explorations of social construction, leading to Peter Berger and Thomas Luckmann's landmark *The Social Construction of Reality* (1966). Typically, sociologists do not deny objectivist constraints on experience, but rather show the ways and extent to which knowledge and competence depend on social knowledge and interaction.

"Postmodern" theorists and social critics, however, have prompted more ambitious claims about the extent of knowledge's social construction. Inspired by Karl Marx, Friedrich Nietzsche, and Sigmund Freud, Continental theorists challenged traditional claims about the stability of meaning in interpretation. At the same time, Michel Foucault explored what might be called the deep social construction of knowledge and value. Championed by Leftist critics of power in Europe and by neopragmatists in the United States, the assumption of radical cultural relativism became widespread.

Against the epistemic radicalism of the postmoderns, more mainstream philosophers of social construction (e.g., John Searle, Alvin Goldman) have argued for the reconciliation of objective constraints on meaning, value, and knowledge while acknowledging the deeply socially constructed nature of reality.

(*See also* Actor Network Theory; Antitheory; Chapter 10, Feminism; Chapter 12, Postmodernism; Chapter 13, Race and Postcolonial Studies; Chapter 23, Materialisms; Chapter 27, Antitheory; Gender; Identity Politics; Performativity; Race; Sexuality; *and* Whiteness)

Horace Fairlamb, *University of Houston-Victoria (United States)*

Further Reading

Berger, Peter, and Thomas Luckmann. *The Social Construction of Reality* [1966]. New York: Anchor, 1967.

Burr, Vivien. *Social Constructionism*. Abington: Routledge, 2015.

Gergen, Kenneth J. *An Invitation to Social Construction*. Thousand Oaks: Sage, 2015.

Sophist

The term "sophist" refers primarily to a number of intellectuals who taught in Greek city-states in the late fifth and fourth centuries BCE, although there was also a second sophistic movement in the Roman Empire. The root of the Greek word *sophist* is *sophia* (wisdom), but in ancient Athens there was considerable dispute as to whether the sophists were wise or not, as well as who counted as a sophist. Today we commonly include figures such as Protagoras, Gorgias, Hippias, Prodicus, Thrasymachus, and Antiphon in a list of sophists. However, the nature of sophistry was a matter of considerable dispute among their contemporaries and later fourth century BCE writers such as Plato.

While early on, "sophist" is used to praise others who are wise, authors such as Isocrates and Plato contrast the sophist with those who pursue wisdom in some more authentic sense. Thus the term as it has come down to us today possesses negative connotations of someone who only pretends to be wise but is not, by being read through the lenses of their critics. Plato especially took pains to distinguish his mentor Socrates and the practice of philosophy from sophistry, as Aristophanes's *Clouds* had presented Socrates as one of the sophists. Plato presents the trial and death of Socrates in 399 BCE as in part due to a failure to distinguish Socrates's philosophical activities from sophistry. Isocrates criticizes the sophists on quite different grounds, for being occupied with trivial matters instead of significant political problems that needed to be addressed.

The sophists themselves, however, offered intellectual theories that supported their practices, although many of their texts have been lost. For example, Protagoras said that the human being is the measure of all, arguing for the position of relativism in which human experience is the measure of truth. Gorgias's essay "On Non-Being" may be read as a parody of Parmenidean thought, but also much more seriously as a demonstration that language is not closely linked to the nature of reality itself and so may be freed from obligation to the truth. Other sophists, such as Hippias, were polymaths who studied what today would fall under the category of natural science.

Plato's criticisms of the sophists were numerous. His dialogues are critical of their willingness to take payment in exchange for teaching virtue, while not actually making their students more virtuous. Gorgias taught rhetoric, or how to persuade others, but according to Plato's *Gorgias* lacked the political skill to improve others on the basis of genuine knowledge. Still, Plato's presentation is not always entirely negative: he presents Protagoras as possessing a challenging set of intellectual ideas in both *Theaetetus* and *Protagoras*. Prodicus is treated with a degree of respect for his ideas about the correct use of language. To examine the sophists and their place in the Greek world also requires exploring how different intellectuals took up key questions about language, rhetoric, truth, and the nature of the human person.

(*See also* Chapter 8, Rhetoric)

Marina McCoy, *Boston College*
(United States)

Further Reading
Kerferd, G. B. *The Sophistic Movement.* Cambridge: Cambridge University Press, 1981.
Schiappa, Edward. *Protagoras and Logos: A Study in Greek Philosophy and Rhetoric.* Second ed. Columbia: University of South Carolina Press, 2003.
Sprague, Rosamund Kent, ed. *The Older Sophists: A Complete Translation by Several Hands of the Fragments in Die Fragmente Der Vorsokratiker, Edited by Diels-Kranz. With a New Edition of Antiphon of Euthydemus.* Columbia: University of South Carolina Press, 1972.

Sound

Those inclined to consult this entry likely know that on August 29, 1952, at a Woodstock *avant la lettre*, David Tudor "premiered" John Cage's "4'33"" a piece wherein nothing (to listen to) and everything (to listen to) became synonymous. Long regarded as a, if not *the*, fundamental rattling of Western "music," the animating logic of "4'33"" was perhaps most succinctly stated when, in responding to Gary Moore's question about whether Cage's "Water Walk" was music, Cage reasoned thus: "I consider music the production of sound, and since in the piece you will hear I produce sounds, I will call it music." Call indeed. However, what both "Water Walk" and "4'33"" left buried in the mix is the question with which this entry must open, namely, what is the rattling of sound that attends the rattling of Western music? This is where "sound" is today.

The temptation is strong to now stop executing keyboard strokes leaving the entry, in effect, blank. Were the task of transferring a durational structure to a spatial expanse be less daunting, there might be no better way of rattling Western sound than to evoke it, to listen for it, precisely in the silence of missing words. "Sound" as the empty entry in a *Zuhandenheit* manual on literary and critical theory.

While not immediately obvious, the event of the empty entry does indeed gesture directly toward where matters stand in the field of Sound Studies, that is, the academic discipline that has assigned itself the task of making sense of sound. A strong current within this initiative treats sound empirically, that is, as the sort of object (whether physiological, physical or psychological) that can have a history, and that is tied in some direct way to the human ear and the faculty of hearing. While it may be true that listening is impossible without hearing, and hearing can take place in the absence of listening, this current concentrates on detailing the facts of how hearing happens or doesn't. Brilliant work here has been done on the matter of "deafness," non-cochlear hearing, and noise abatement.

The empirical or historicist current has not defined itself against theory, but it can be distinguished from those who have harkened to Walter Benjamin's proposition that perception is reading. Although not typically situated within Sound Studies, the scandal of the new musicology lay precisely in its insistence that musical sounds "said" something. For example, music could say, "sexual violence." Or, restated with sufficient range, that sounds can be read, not by being reduced to linguistic messages, but by transporting us to the very limits of legibility. Here making sense of sound means not that it is given as the referent *for* a reading, but that it is a problem that arises *in* reading. It is less an object that, for example, cinema studies might expand to attend to, than a catachresis for what materializes when listening takes place in the absence of a subject who either hears or hears differently.

(*See also* Chapter 12, Postmodernism; *and* Chapter 20, Digital Humanities)

John Mowitt, *University of Leeds (United Kingdom)*

Further Reading

Barrett, G. Douglas. *After Sound: Toward a Critical Music*. London: Bloomsbury, 2016.

Bijsterveld, Karin. *Mechanical Sound: Technology, Culture and Public Problems of Noise in the Twentieth Century*. Cambridge: MIT Press, 2008.

Chion, Michel. *Sound: An Acoulogical Treatise* [1998, 2010]. Second ed. Trans. James A. Steintrager. Durham: Duke University Press, 2016.

Mills, Mara. *On the Phone: Deafness and Communication Engineering*. Durham: Duke University Press, 2017.

Sovereignty

Sovereignty is a concept, usually associated with the rise of the nation-state that defines how authority, power, and legitimacy are configured within a given political order. In the *King's Two Bodies* (1957), Ernst Kantorowicz showed how the power of the monarch was predicated on a relation between the monarch's natural body, which is physical and subject to death, and his "spiritual" body, which is immortal and allows for the possibility of succession. Although it focuses on divine right forms of sovereignty, Kantorowicz's account explains a key feature of modern conceptions as well: sovereignty entails a relation between an unconditional source of legitimacy (i.e., a source without any other authority that precedes or supersedes its capacities), and a real manifestation of that authority. In the case of the monarch, whose authority was founded on God, the real manifestation was the monarch himself. With the waning of divine right conceptions of sovereignty after the democratic revolutions of the late eighteenth and early nineteenth century, the relation between the source of legitimacy and its real manifestation becomes less assured.

In one of the founding texts of political sovereignty, *Leviathan* (1651), English philosopher Thomas Hobbes developed a theory of civil society as founded on a social contract—an agreement between individuals to cede some of their natural rights in return for the right to have individual and social conflicts regulated by a sovereign author-ity. The civil society that emerges from this social contract constitutes a new body poli-tic, one composed of the tacit consent of the governed to be regulated by law. Yet, the *form* that the body politic takes remains undeter-mined because the consent of the governed can always be withdrawn, and a different sov-ereign instituted. Hobbes's theory of sover-eignty, therefore, exposes an important aspect of its modern exigency: whereas in the era of divine right the sovereign was authorized by an already given foundation (God), the modern sovereign must first create or invent this foundation. While natural right tended to replace God as the ground of legitimacy in popular forms of sovereignty, recent political theory has reemphasized the extent to which any pre-given source of authority continues to function, in effect, as a theological concept.

This idea was advanced in Carl Schmitt's *Political Theology* (1922), which argues that one must recognize that the political order is based not on law, but instead on an *exception* to the law—on something extralegal that is only retrospectively constituted within the juridical or political order as its foundation. For Schmitt, this took the form of the sov-ereign's right to decide when the legal order can be suspended, as in a state of emergency. Recent critical theory has extended the con-sequences of the idea that sovereign power is grounded in something extralegal or outside the law: George Bataille, for example, argues that since sovereignty is grounded on "noth-ing," its modern concept exceeds questions of both utility and political power. Drawing on the history of political sovereignty, Gior-gio Agamben claims that the establishment of political power in the exception has led to the progressive normalization of the state of exception, where the legal order is suspended in the name of defending that order. Jacques Derrida suggests in "Force of Law: The 'Mys-

tical Foundation of Authority'" (1990) and elsewhere that the *aporia* of sovereignty—the fact that sovereignty is haunted by the specter of something unconditional that precedes it—undermines its exercise from within. Michael Hardt and Antonio Negri argue in *Empire* that the modern age is witnessing a mutation in the concept of sovereignty that detaches its exer-cise from the nation-state, installing it in the post-national power of global capitalism. As more traditional conceptions of sovereignty have been challenged, however, new forms of political theology that base sovereignty on a natural or divine order have reemerged.

(*See also* Agamben, Giorgio; Bare Life; Biopolitics; Chapter 5, Post-structuralism; Chapter 15, Biopower and Biopolitics; Chap-ter 24, Posthumanism; Democracy; Derrida, Jacques; Negri, Antonio; Political Theology; Private Property; *and* Rights)

Kir Kuiken, *University at Albany, SUNY, (United States)*

Further Reading
Hobbes, Thomas. *Leviathan* [1651]. Ed. J. C. A. Gaskin. Oxford: Oxford Univer-sity Press, 1996.
Jackson, Robert. *Sovereignty: The Evolu-tion of an Idea*. Cambridge: Polity Press, 2007.
Schmitt, Carl. *Political Theology: Four Chapter on the Concept of Sovereignty* [1922]. Trans. George Schwab. Chicago: University of Chicago Press, 1985.

Speculative Realism

Since its codification in 2007 at a conference held at Goldsmiths College, speculative real-ism soon evolved into a sprawling and polem-ical philosophy that came to prominence with the publication of Levi Bryant, Nick Srnicek, and Graham Harman's edited collection *The*

Speculative Turn: Continental Materialism and Realism (2011). Because many of the speculative realists continue to develop their ideas on their individual blogs and other online formats, the field expands rapidly while these theorists actively engage and contest each other's new formulations. Because of these ongoing debates, the primary area of consensus within speculative realism derives from the philosophies it reacts against.

Speculative realism challenges philosophies of access, or philosophies that privilege human-centered understanding of the world. Graham Harman, one of the most prominent speculative realists, argues that metaphysical philosophies of access since Immanuel Kant wrongly focus on the way in which the world appears to a human subject; instead, he argues, the objective of philosophy ought to consist of an investigation into the reality of the world-in-itself, or a philosophical return to the study of *essence*.

For Harman, a philosophical study of the world-in-itself must be performed at the level of the things-in-themselves; Harman calls this brand of speculative realism "object-oriented philosophy" (also referred to as "object-oriented ontology"). Object-oriented philosophy locates an inherently "withdrawn" essence within objects: the *real* object recedes from observation and from other objects, and what we encounter instead are *sensual* objects that enter into relation with our perception and other objects by way of their surface qualities (color, texture, etc.). Object-oriented philosophy poses a philosophical model in which all objects and entities relate and interact, but they retain a fundamentally inaccessible essence.

In the wake of Harman's object-oriented philosophy, Levi Bryant popularized the term *flat ontology* in his book *The Democracy of Objects* (2011). Bryant's flat ontology asserts that all entities, things, and objects are equal in ontological status; while some objects or entities may exert greater influence on their surroundings, all objects and entities are equally "real"; in staking this claim, Bryant seeks to destabilize philosophies of access by decentering the human from what he calls "the center of being."

Speculative realism also contests post-Kantian philosophies of access by critiquing what Quentin Meillassoux deems "correlationism." Correlationism is the tendency of philosophies of access to describe and define worldly phenomena in terms of how they relate or appear to the human. Speculative realism instead prioritizes anti-correlationism, which seeks to ascertain phenomena as they exist in themselves without the subjective mediation of the human observer.

Timothy Morton adopts speculative realism to address pressing ecological concerns. In *The Ecological Thought* (2010), Morton borrows from Harman's object-oriented philosophy to claim that all ontologies—human, nonhuman, object—"intertangle" in a mesh of relations in which nothing exists independently. In order to confront the problem of climate change, he argues that we must rethink our relation to the world and the nonhuman entities with whom we share it. For Morton, anthropocentric philosophies of access are inadequate to address the reality of a world in very real danger.

(*See also* Chapter 23, Materialisms; Hyperobject; Materialism; New Materialisms; Object; Object-Oriented Philosophy; *and* Thing Theory)

T. J. Martinson, *Indiana University, Bloomington (United States)*

Further Reading

Bogost, Ian. *Alien Phenomenology: Or, What It's Like To Be a Thing*. Minneapolis: University of Minnesota Press, 2012.

Harman, Graham. *Guerrilla Metaphysics: Phenomenology and the Carpentry of Things*. Chicago: Open Court, 2005.

Shaviro, Steven. *The Universe of Things.* Minneapolis: University of Minnesota Press, 2014.

Speech (*See* Archi-trace; *and* Derrida, Jacques)

Spivak, Gayatri Chakravorty

It is perhaps most helpful to explain Gayatri Chakravorty Spivak (born 1942) in contrast to Edward Said, since both were key figures who in the late 1970s pioneered what came to be known as postcolonial studies. Both Said and Spivak were viewed as theorists schooled in French structuralism and post-structuralism. Said's "Abecedarium Culturae" was a major exposition of various French theories and their interrelations that for the first time made French theory accessible to Anglo-American audiences. Spivak's introduction to her translation of Jacques Derrida's *De la grammatologie* had a similar impact. By the late 1970s, progressive leftist critics in the United States were debating among themselves whether to follow in the footsteps of Foucault or Derrida, opting for the former after the appearance of Said's *Orientalism* which studied the effects of imperialist impositions of power in the context of how Western bureaucratic inscriptions of culture constructed their colonized objects of investigation from a disciplinary position of omniscient, detached superiority known as orientalism. Spivak, as it happened, was a student and follower of Paul de Man at whose behest she got the opportunity to do the translation of Derrida's breakthrough philosophical study, *De la grammatologie* (1967), wherein ethnocentrism was under attack. In her work, one has been able to see a certain double scene of deconstruction at work insofar as she has allied herself both to de Manian and Der-

ridean modes of analysis, the former more classically tropological than the latter, given Derrida's avant-gardist conceptualization of new tropes, such as triggering, the double session, erasure, dissemination, the faux bond, and so forth. In fact, both Spivak and Said have been quite Eurocentric in terms of their training. The foundations of Said's thinking stem from Erich Auerbach's perception that what we often take to be objective representations are, in fact, a nexus of political contradictions that are being hegemonically resolved by means of cultural depictions that are not transparently propagandistic. Spivak's thinking stems from Karl Marx and Friedrich Engels's conviction that imperialism is the expression of capital-logic, which is predicated on boundless global expansionism. That capitalism is the pitiless ripping apart of the social relation, as Marx and Engels said, pertains not only to the West but even more so to the regions that the West has colonized. What Spivak has called epistemic violence includes what Said called orientalism, though for Spivak it speaks more directly to the brutal oppression and exploitation of colonized social subjects viewed as mere instruments of labor and not as social beings per se. Whereas Said stressed the epistemic violence done to the orient in the name of Western enlightenment, Spivak has presumed this in favor of considering how colonized societies have internalized capitalist exploitation and corrupted Western values, on the one hand, while also continuing to live within frameworks one might call nativist that are themselves complex, contradictory, and in many ways exploitative. From this perspective, Said is more Manichean than Spivak who appreciates Western/Non-Western relations in terms of complex overlays or interfaces characterized at various junctures by not only figural aporias but also the disruptive interference of different discourse formations that can't be rationalized. Spivak has often referred to "catachresis" as a figure of sustained contradiction though she has also defined it as a figure of displacement whereby an abuse occurs. Aporia stems from the hermeneutics of Paul de Man which emphasized textual gridlock, something that in Spivak translates into social impasses. From a Derridean orientation, Spivak borrows the conceptual reverse and displace technique whereby an inferior term replaces a superior one, hence dislocating the structure that the original duality had upheld. Her invocation of strategic essentialism circa 1990 was intended to call into question the structural superiority of anti-essentialism in academic discourse. In Derrida the well-known reversal of the voice/writing distinction is indicative of a revolution wherein a subjected concept subverts its master and brings a whole order crashing down. Spivak participates in that revolutionary spirit. Spivak's work is voluminous and could be subdivided into the following categories: writings on education, literature, culture, subalterns, non-subaltern minorities, and notions of world (globalization, the planet, etc.). Unlike de Man or Derrida, Spivak has been very sensitive to the complicity of the critic in the abuses he or she critiques. Rather than pontificate from the heights of the Ivory Tower, she would rather see academics work directly as activists in terms of improving the lives of subalterns, as she herself has done for many years. Spivak has been critical of Western academics who have turned postcolonialism into a sort of orientalism that disavows the very colonialist strategies it implements. In that sense, she has been very critical of how institutional power is flexed through discourses advanced by people whose lives as Western professional figures contradict their stated views, analyses, and commitments.

(*See also* Chapter 4, Marxism; Chapter 13, Race and Postcolonial Studies; Chapter 17, Comparativisms; Chapter 22, Identity Studies; Chapter 26, Affect Studies; Essentialism; Hybridity; Postcolonialism; *and* Subaltern)

Herman Rapaport, *Wake Forest University (United States)*

Further Reading

Morton, Stephen. *Gayatri Spivak: Ethics, Subalternity, and the Critique of Postcolonial Reason.* London: Routledge, 2006.

Ray, Sangeeta. *Gayatri Chakravorty Spivak: In Other Words.* Oxford: Wiley-Blackwell, 2009.

Sanders, Mark. *Gayatri Chakravorty Spivak: Live Theory.* London: Bloomsbury, 2006.

Story (*See* Chapter 3, Narrative and Narratology)

Structuralism

The study and privileging of linguistic structures and their rules as distinct logical formations underlying signification. As in linguistics, structuralists look for rules that govern relationships that when enacted as specific operations comprise a mode of signifying production. Structualism presupposes that systems as a whole precede their parts. This is reminiscent of the study of ecology that begins with the whole as a complex set of interrelating systems. Structuralism in general applies the principle of binary opposition by showing how difference functions as a means of organizing and relating elements of a system. In *The Fashion System* (1967), Roland Barthes notices that clothing corresponds to the Saussurean language/speech distinction. It is institutional (just as language is), but it is also worn by specific people in specific ways that express *themselves*, hence its analogy to speech. People choose clothes not unlike they choose words to speak; however, these choices are governed by syntax. An ensemble isn't complete without shoes, just as a sentence isn't complete without the direct object that it requires. Clothing is also referential. Uniforms reference the type of vocation one is in. Gender is communicated through clothing, and so on. Here, of course, difference is uppermost. Clothing ensembles have a syntax, which enables and restricts how items of clothing can be exchanged, for example, one pair of shoes for another. Obviously, an evening dress won't tolerate army boots. This intolerance concerns a fundamental difference or opposition between fashion and mere clothing, the aesthetic and the pragmatic. Fashion is governed by highly refined cultural rules of exclusion and inclusion, whereas mere clothing is largely governed by "the world," as Barthes puts it. In other words, clothing is merely ruled by the weather. One would wear army boots with an evening dress if it were wet and muddy outside and one couldn't manage in ordinary shoes, which are now being excluded by natural conditions. Evidently, nature versus culture, the practical versus the aesthetic are divides observed by Barthes in this instance. He notes that the relationship among vestments that one wears is syntactic whereas the connotative aspect of vestments speaks to semantics. Here the syntactic/sematic difference commonplace to language is applied. The raincoat has to fit the ensemble stylistically to count as fashion (i.e., it has to conform to a stylistic system of relations that by definition turn a blind eye to the practical in order to satisfy the condition of being fashionable) but it also has to fit the requirements of being out in rainy weather which also has rules and requirements. How the coat is cut, of what materials it is made, how detailed it is, what color it is, whether it references coats of the past considered traditional, and so on

belongs to a connotative register that Barthes calls rhetorical. Barthes claims that clothing/fashion is negotiated in terms of the real (the world outside), the rhetorical (what one is uttering by wearing a particular outfit), and the written (fashion commentary and display in magazines or on television). In fashion, Barthes says, there is a continuous invention of new signs, which reflects the arbitrariness of the fashion-sign; however, this arbitrariness is oligarchal, the exclusive authority of a "fashion-group" that produces new signs and promotes them by means of fashion writing in the media. "Fashion does not evolve, it changes." Not one system but several, fashion is structurally authoritarian. Here we find out what kind of structure we are dealing with in terms of social dictate: of who or what is in control of operating the system. Foundational to such a system is the difference between fashion-group and fashion user, a difference that is dialectical insofar as the user mediates those in authority who are in the role of producers, not consumers. That the overall structure of the fashion system survives all the changes and upsets comprising historical, economic, and cultural developments speaks to its power as a signifying system in light of human desires and needs.

(*See also* Althusser, Louis; American Structuralism; Binary Opposition; Chapter 2, Structuralism and Semiotics; Chapter 4, Marxism; Chapter 5, Post-structuralism; Chapter 6, Historicisms; Barthes, Roland; Formalism; Foucault, Michel; Lacan, Jacques; Lévi-Strauss, Claude; *and* Saussure, Ferdinand de)

Herman Rapaport, *Wake Forest University*
(United States)

Further Reading
Barthes, Roland. *The Fashion System* [1967]. Trans. Matthew Ward and Richard Howard. Berkeley: University of California, 1990.

Structural Linguistics (*See* American Structuralism)

Subaltern

Originally, the term subaltern applied to the junior ranks of British army signifying the first three officer ranks: second lieutenant, lieutenant, and captain, all of whom were considered the ranks subordinated to field officers and officers of higher rank. In many postcolonial armies following the British tradition, for example, it is still believed that a "subaltern should only be seen, not heard." The term subaltern in this sense refers to human subjects who are neither heard nor allowed a chance to speak for themselves.

The current philosophical usage of the term can be attributed to Antonio Gramsci who occasionally refers to the subordinate groups as *classi suablterne*, *classi subordinate*, and *classi strumntali*, which can be translated, respectively, as the subaltern class, the subordinate class, and the instrumental class. In all its connotations, the subaltern class performs the everyday menial jobs, is subordinated to the dominant class, and, if we go by its British usage, has no voice of its own. In sum, then, a subaltern individual or class can be any individual or group that has either no agency in his or her own person or no representation in terms of being represented by another.

By far the most important engagement with the concept of the subaltern is provided in Gaytari Spivak's famous essay "Can the Subaltern Speak?" In her seminal essay, Spivak attempts to answer one important question: Can the intellectuals assume that the subaltern can speak for his or herself and thus does not need representation? Although mostly misread, the conclusion, that she later retracts as being hasty, is not necessarily on the subaltern's ability to speak, but rather that even when the subaltern leaves a message with her body, the interlocutors will miss reading the sign. Spivak, thus, concludes that the intellectuals cannot just assume that the subaltern can speak for herself, for that would lead them to relinquish their responsibility to represent the subaltern.

The debates launched by this seminal essay also enabled a field of subaltern studies, especially in India, where the Subaltern Studies Collective took it upon itself to recover the subaltern and silenced histories and has produced, so far, ten volumes of history that tell the story of suablternized cultures, individuals, and political moments all offered against the mainstream national narrative of India.

On the whole, one could say that subaltern subjectivity (individual or collective) is always the one that is either erased or sidelined by the dominant discourse, and in order to offer a more comprehensive critique of the dominant classes and regimes, the subaltern histories and narratives need to be retrieved and articulated, thus complicating and, at times, revising the dominant and normalized history.

(*See also* Chapter 4, Marxism; Chapter 13, Race and Postcolonial Studies; Chapter 22, Identity Studies; Chapter 26, Affect Studies; Chapter 27, Antitheory; Gramsci, Louis; Spivak, Gayatri; *and* Subjectivity)

Masood Raja, *University of North Texas (United States)*

Further Reading

Gramsci, Antonio. *Selections from the Prison Notebooks*. Trans. Quintin Hoare and Geoffrey Nowell Smith. New York: International Publishers, 1971.

Spivak, Gayatri Chakravorty. "Can the Subaltern Speak?" In *Marxism and the Interpretation of Culture*. Eds. Cary Nelson and Lawrence Grossberg. Banistoke: Macmillan, 1988. 271–315.

Subculture

A subculture is "a *relatively diffuse* social network having a *shared identity, distinctive meanings* around certain ideas, practices, and objects, and a sense of *marginalization* from or *resistance* to a perceived 'conventional' society." Subcultures have diffuse, symbolic boundaries and a shared identity, but little formal organization or stable "membership." Subculturists share distinctive ideas—for example, about how to live a fulfilling, authentic life; meaningful practices, such as punk and heavy metal mosh pits; and significant objects, as with skinheads' braces and steel-toed boots. Participants commonly distinguish themselves from "mainstream" society, perceived as controlling, conformist, oppressive, and/or unfulfilling, though subcultures never fully separate from the imagined mainstream. Authorities, including religious, political, civic, and media leaders, may stigmatize them as folk devils, blaming them for a variety of social ills and instigating a moral panic.

The most prominent, widely-known, and well-studied subcultures include skinhead, punk, heavy metal, hip hop, Goth, rave, straight edge, Riot Grrrl, and a variety of other music-related social networks. Other examples include graffiti writers, skaters, Kustom Kars, Juggalos, parkour, Kink, bike messengers, gamers, and tattoo/body modification cultures. Most have a global presence, appearing with localized nuances in many countries, and the advent of digital cultures offers new opportunities for translocal connections. While generally associated with youth, subcultural participation can span the life course. Even as direct participation declines for many older subculturists, scene values and experiences can profoundly impact leisure, politics, friendships, and work and career well into adulthood.

Scholars have used "subculture" or similar ideas to theorize deviant groups throughout the twentieth century. Chicago School theorists of the 1920s through the 1940s saw crime and social disorganization as *social* problems (rather than individual pathologies) arising from rapid urbanization that disrupted the natural equilibrium of communities. Deviant subcultures (and/or gangs) often arose among marginalized youth struggling with poverty and racial and ethnic discrimination. Early functionalists suggested that blocked status opportunities—the inability, for structural reasons, to achieve societal goals such as wealth—led some to seek alternative/deviant paths to success. In the 1960s, "contracultures" and "countercultures" described the variety of youth rebellions, including the hippies, who questioned a broad spectrum of social values. In the 1970s and 1980s, UK scholars at Birmingham's Centre for Contemporary Cultural Studies (CCCS) studied mods, rockers, skinheads and other post-War youth groupings through a neo-Marxist lens; working-class youth, especially young men, offered symbolic resistance to the class structure via their "spectacular" style. While they created meaningful communities and critiqued dominant social conventions via their shocking styles, they only minimally impacted wider systems of inequality. Reacting to the limits of the CCCS theories, post-subculture theorists suggested that subcultures—as distinct, relatively stable, class- and style-based groupings—no longer exist, proposing the concept of "scene" as a replacement. Scenes—or similarly, "neo-tribes"—bring people together into diverse, temporary, pleasure-oriented, and largely apolitical gatherings, the 1990s rave scene being an archetypal example. However, many contemporary scholars continue to find the concept useful, seeing subcultural participation as a pragmatic strategy enabling adherents to feel a sense of authenticity, collectively affirm deviant status, critique dominant norms and power relations, and create alternative communities and lifeways.

Importantly, subculture signifies more than simply any social subgroup; some degree of marginalization, resistance, and/or deviance distinguishes Goths from book or wine tasting clubs. Yet subcultures overlap with a variety of other social groupings, including gangs, countercultures, lifestyles, new religious movements, lifestyle movements, and fan cultures.

(*See also* Chapter 11, Cultural Studies; Chapter 27, Antitheory; Culture; *and* Cyberculture)

Ross Haenfler, *Grinnell College* *(United States)*

Further Reading
Gelder, Ken. *The Subcultures Reader*. Second ed. New York: Routledge, 2005.
Haenfler, Ross. *Subcultures: The Basics*. New York: Routledge, 2014.
Williams, J. Patrick. *Subcultural Theory: Traditions and Concepts*. Malden: Polity, 2011.

Subject

The word subject comes from the Latin *subicio*, "to throw under." In theory, this kernel of meaning is manifested in both the active and the passive senses of the word. When we speak of the active "subject," we often mean something like what we designate when we speak of the "subject" of a sentence: the agent, the one who does the doing, that is, the one who throws other persons and things (objects) under its control. In its most refined philosophical version, this subject reaches its apotheosis in the Cartesian *cogito*, that round, impenetrable ball of self-determination that lies at the heart of most Western philosophy from Rene Descartes through Immanuel Kant and continuing on to Jean-Paul Sartre and the existentialists' concern with authenticity. While this version of subjectivity is seldom encountered in its pure form, especially in our postmodern world, it nonetheless is active in a variety of current theoretical discourses that are concerned with agency, with resistance to objectification, and with self-determination. Thus, the active subject remains at the heart of many political and ethical discourses from feminism and gender studies, to postcolonialism, to Michel Foucault's ethics of self-formation, even if these same discourses often problematize what it means to be a subject and seek to probe its gendered, racialized, and ideological assumptions. Nonetheless, the active subject lurks wherever we have discourses concerned with being the "thrower" and not simply the "thrown."

Of course, since Martin Heidegger, we have all been only too aware of our "thrownness." The subject is always the subjected, the seemingly autonomous actor who is in fact the product of complex processes of "subjectivation." This is the divided subject, the subject that knows not what it says. There are many versions of this subject: the most prominent are those grouped under what Paul Ricoeur famously labeled "the hermeneutics of suspicion": Karl Marx, Friedrich Nietzsche, and Sigmund Freud. In each of these discourses, consciousness, to paraphrase Fredric Jameson, is not master in its own house. The subject who thinks he is throwing together original meanings and projects is actually the object of forces beyond his control. He is subjected. In Marx and his descendants, the seeming autonomy of the subject is undermined by the class nature of society, by the economic forces that situate us, shape our desires, and offer us certain delimited options. "Yes, man makes history, but never out of whole cloth."

For Nietzsche, the autonomous subject is constantly seeking post-facto rationalizations for his own will to power, his quasi-instinctual desire to dominate, and his *ressentiment* toward all who would seek to limit his powers, who would have more power and vitality than him. For Freud, it is our desire that shapes us and that desire is not freely chosen, indeed, it is not even conscious.

Yet, while these active and passive senses of subjectivity appear to be mutually exclusive, in practice they are generally much more nuanced, and one might even say dialectical. The Sartrean subject, though often stigmatized as such, is never really autonomous because its freedom only exists in "situation." The Marxian and Niezschean subject, though mystified as to its own intents, seeks through discourse to come to clarity and to act in the world. The Freudian subject seeks to render the unconscious conscious while recognizing the interminable nature of that task.

(*See also* Agency; Assujettissement; Butler, Judith; Cartesianism; Chapter 1, Early Theory; Chapter 2, Structuralism and Semiotics; Chapter 7, Psychoanalytic Theory; Chapter 10, Feminism; Chapter 15, Biopower and Biopolitics; Chapter 22, Identity Studies; Chapter 23, Materialisms; Chapter 24, Posthumanism; Chapter 26, Affect Studies; Double Consciousness; Foucault, Michel; Freud, Sigmund; Heidegger, Martin; Intersubjectivity; Kant, Immanuel; Lacan, Jacques; Marx, Karl; Nietzsche, Friedrich; Self; Subjectivism; Subjectivity; Symbolic Agency; *and* Žižek, Slavoj)

Paul Allen Miller, *University of South Carolina (United States)*

Further Reading
Foucault, Michel. *L'Herméneutique du sub-jet: Cours au Collège de France.* 1981-82. Ed. Frédéric Gros. Paris: Gallimard/Seuil, 2001.

Jameson, Fredric. "Imaginary and Symbolic in Lacan." In *The Ideologies of Theory*, Vol. One. Minneapolis: University of Minnesota Press, 1988. 75–115.
Sartre, Jean-Paul. *Le sursis. Jean-Paul Sartre: Oeuvres romanesques.* Eds. Michel Contat et Michel Rybalka. Paris: Gallimard, 1981.

Subjectivation (*See* Assujettissement)

Subjectivism

The methodological innovation of Cartesian doubt instantiated subjectivism as a point of departure for post-Enlightenment knowledge claims. Historically, subjectivism asserts that reality is an artifact of mind. It stands against religious dogmatisms and scientific empiricisms that locate the grounds for knowledge claims in divine ordination or natural fact respectively. Contrary to transcendental faiths and faith in empirical truths, subjectivism, attributes our grasp of reality to consciousness, exclusive of any other métiers of worldliness. Subjectivism might therefore be deemed to be metaphysical in a way that is radically ungrounded. But it is also arguable that subjectivism does not preclude the relevance of empirical perception. Rather, consciousness of perception is dispositive for grasping reality in a multiplicity of modalities.

On this basis, subjectivism is, of course, susceptible to the charge of anthropocentrism. But this is a weak criticism, since mind must be interested first and foremost in the species that it minds. Such criticism is further mitigated by more modern theorizations of the subject. While the sixteenth-century advent of subjectivism appears to privilege mind above world in the most absolute terms, nineteenth-century Hegelianism makes plain that there is no authority of mind that is not, at the same time, arousing cognizance of the sensorium as its perceptual ground. This acknowledgment inspires the inference that subjectivism presupposes the interdependency of perception and mindful action.

The significance of this point is made more starkly apparent if we consider the often misunderstood notion of subjectivism thought to be epitomized in Søren Kierkegaard's pronouncement: "Subjectivity is truth." As Kierkegaard makes clear, he is not speaking exclusively of perceptual or experiential subjectivity. Rather, he is concerned primarily with what some call "existential" subjectivity. In *Concluding Postcript* (1846), Kierkegaard admonishes his reader that "the task of becoming subjective is assigned to every person." The task then is intrinsically ethical: knowing entails some doing. So subjectivism is neither pure interiority of mind nor some species of panpsychism. Nor is it merely the repository of perceptions.

This view of the ethical nature of subjectivism is, however, at odds with more commonplace assumptions. Typically, ethical subjectivism is believed to inhere independently in mind. Subjectivists are said to privilege images over stimuli, reasons over causes. In other words, ethical subjectivism presupposes a subject possessed of an active will. This is opposed to the notion of a divine willing subject, whereby we defer to an external or objective determination. By such deference, ethical subjectivism is deemed to put moral agents on a slippery slope toward moral relativism. Nevertheless, if Kierkegaard points the way for thinking about subjectivism, it might make sense to treat subjectivism as necessarily reciprocating with inputs rather than thinking of it exclusively as a source of outputs. This approach avoids the mistake of subscribing to a subjectivism that is rendered as intractably absolutist as conventionally conceived objectivism, its putative antagonist. Thinking of subjectivism as inextricable from what the subject perceives to be true in actual perceptions preserves the possibility of a *normative ethical relativism*. Such a stance would be predicated on ongoing exchanges of opinion among self-knowingly corrigible subjects. Otherwise, mere moral disagreement would prevail among epistemically autonomous, stubbornly emotivist subjects.

(*See also* Cartesianism; *and* Idealism)

Alan Singer, *Temple University*
(United States)

Further Reading

Double, Richard. *Metaethical Subjectivism*. London: Routledge, 2017.

Frankel, Ellen, Fred Miller, and Jeffrey Paul, eds. *Objectivism, Subjectivism and Relativism in Ethics*. Cambridge: Cambridge University Press, 2008.

Sobel, David. *From Valuing to Value: A Defense of Subjectivism*. Oxford: Oxford University Press, 2017.

Subjectivity

Subjectivity has long been a question for scholars, and one could do worse by starting in the modern era with the work of Rene Descartes and Immanuel Kant. Cartesian-Kantian subjectivity is grounded internally. The consciousness encounters outside forces but ultimately an internal mechanism controls any and all thoughts and decisions. Husserl pushes the consciousness outward by collapsing the distance between the interior and exterior world. The "reality" of the exterior world is a phenomenon in the mind, which actively "intends" or creates that reality. For Edmund Husserl the subject remains the center, and, despite its more intimate connection to exterior world, will always remain in a position of transcendence to that world. Martin Heidegger radicalizes this final attempt to internalize the subject by inserting the subject into the "thrownness" of a groundless temporality that exceeds the subject, situating it within history and the outside world. The subject is still susceptible to knowledge it has already accumulated when making decisions, but Heidegger pressures this accumulated knowledge by treating it as a hermeneutical "forestructure" to be destructured at the very moment an intended train of thought is about to reach its presumed goal. Jacques Derrida pushes this potential further, refusing the subject any ontological internal presence or unity. Instead the subject is a "play of différance" that does not stand outside of representation. Gilles Deleuze, perhaps, takes this one step further and identifies the subject as "multiple," as a "rhizome" transformed by nomadic movements and exterior "affects" that "transpierce" the body—making it increasingly heterogeneous and always in the process of becoming. Fanon would be one of the first to racialize this Western metaphysics of subjectivity by situating it within the violence of the colonial contest. Black subjectivity, in the eyes of White colonial culture, has no ontological worth, and as such does not exist. Racial struggle against White and colonial imperialism thus takes the form of a struggle for ontological recognition and intersubjective equality. In her critique of gendered subjectivity Judith Butler offers the innovative conception of "performativity" to this equation. Gender is constituted as a "performative act" "within theatrical contexts." Sedgewick takes Derrida's deconstructive maneuver that identity is formed on the basis of an unequally culturally weighted exclusion of disavowed potentials (male has nothing internally present that makes it male; male is "male" because it manufactures itself through the constant and often abusive exclusion of "female") to reveal how the same action generates the cultural predominance of "heterosexuality." Louis Althusser takes a dimmer view, characterizing subjectivity as a manipulative process generated by ideology and ideological State apparatuses. The subject is in fact integral to ideological power, and is constituted as the primary instrument of a "problematic field" that "predetermines the questions" (and equally the answers) than an inquirer can investigate. Michel Foucault complicates these mechanisms by which the State and other manipulative forces "discipline" the individual, transforming citizens into "docile bodies" that are economically productive and active, but equally obedient and politically innocuous. Although Foucault subscribed like Heidegger to a concept of a groundless subject capable of extraordinary freedoms, he spent the bulk of his research on the widespread and sheer force of power relations impacting and limiting human freedom in the modern world.

More recently, theorists like Alain Badiou redefine the subject as an entity that comes into being in and through its very break from an established order or reality. For Badiou the "multiple subject" previously celebrated by others is not revolutionary enough. What defines a subject is an encounter with a singular "truth-event" not defined by an existing structure, one that "induces" a subject through the encounter with this event, thereby generating "hitherto unknown possibilities." One is therefore only a subject when continually exceeding one's own multiple being. In a similar fashion Rancière distinguishes a politically agential subject as "the part of no part" arising through the act of "naming a wrong." The activity of naming a wrong is not accomplished by an existing identity given a part within the system, but by an "appearance" of a non-position denied existence by the inherent inequality found in any system. The planetary events of climate change, species extinction, and the transiting of life from the Holocene into the "Anthropocene" era have introduced the most historically significant challenges to theoretical engagements with subjectivity.

Developing the work of scientist Paul Crutzen, Dipesh Chakrabarty identifies the Anthropocene human as a "geological force," affecting the entirety of planetary life—a massive-scale capacity never encountered in any previous historical age. Prior to this, certain ecocritics warned of the misguided ideal of forming human subjects on the basis of their ability to transcend the supposed limitations of nature. Recent efforts point toward the need to deconstruct this lethally de-linked and supposedly sovereign subjectivity, rethinking the human as an "inhabitant." Perhaps Foucault, despite his dedication to unearthing the many ways in which human subjectivity is normalized by vast policing forces, offers the most constructive criticism for thinking subjectivity. In his concern for how ideas are set up and utilized, he directs our attention to ontological questions now more pressing for humanity than ever before: "How is this subjectivity deployed?"; "Who has the right to speak?"; and finally, to exercise the human of all vestige of subjective hubris, "What matters who's speaking?"

(*See also* Althusser, Louis; Assujettissement; Badiou, Alain; Butler, Judith; Cartesianism; Chapter 10, Feminism; Chapter 12, Postmodernism; Chapter 15, Biopower and Biopolitics; Chapter 22, Identity Studies; Chapter 24, Posthumanism; Deleuze, Gilles; Derrida, Jacques; Double Consciousness; Foucault, Michel; Heidegger, Martin; Husserl, Edmund; Intersubjectivity; Kant, Immanuel; Lacan, Jacques; Negri, Antonio; Self; Subject; *and* Žižek, Slavoj)

Robert P. Marzec, *Purdue University*
(United States)

Further Reading

Hall, Donald. *Subjectivity*. The New Critical Idiom. New York: Routledge, 2004.

Mansfield, Nick. *Subjectivity: Theories of the Self from Freud to Haraway*. New York: New York University Press, 2000.

Sublimation

Sublimation as a concept in Sigmund Freud's oeuvre is perhaps the most well-known concept while the least written about. Many have lamented the lost metapsychological papers (of which sublimation was to be among the key subjects) given that we are left with merely a few fragments that begin with his *Three Essays on the Theory of Sexuality* (1905), through the work *On Narcissism* (1913), his reworking of the model of the mind in *The Ego and the Id* (1923), and some key remarks in the late work, *Civilization and Its Discontents* (1930). Sublimation is seen as an achievement that follows from the repression of the Oedipus complex that crowns the child's efforts of intense sexual research and the attempted satisfaction of incestuous desire. Nevertheless, Freud is clear that whatever gains sublimation might provide for an individual or culture, it is nonetheless a defense—close to reaction-formation and idealization, using the mechanism of displacement and neutralization—and can only work for a small fraction of one's sexual drive life, including, only for a small fraction of human beings. This is because one must tolerate the frustration and delay necessary for artistic or scientific work that requires a change in aim, namely sexual satisfaction.

While this defense structure is the basic model for sublimation, the mechanisms by which it is achieved were always elusive to Freud. During the later work, the main question for him seemed to concern how sublimation worked in the service of Eros and against the death drive. What needed to be understood was how sublimation uniquely manages to get around the barrier of repression: the sexual desire remains repressed, hidden from the artist or scientist while nevertheless fueling and directing his work, and yet, was able to meet a kind of satisfaction. In *Civilization and Its Discontents*, Freud writes,

> Sublimation of instinct is an especially conspicuous feature of cultural development; it is what makes it possible for higher psychical activities, scientific, artistic or ideological, to play such an important part in civilized life. If one were to yield to a first impression, one would say that sublimation is a vicissitude which has been forced upon the instincts entirely by civilization. . . . It is not easy to understand how it can become possible to deprive an instinct of satisfaction. Nor is doing so without danger. If the loss is not compensated for economically, one can be certain that serious disorders will ensue.

Freud is always cautious when discussing sublimation seemingly because of the fragility of its construction. Should a "sublimation" fail to continue functioning it would immediately release a destructiveness which was always already there, seen most clearly in the ideals that direct a given intellectual pursuit which have the character of a "thou shalt." Perhaps here it is important to turn to one of Freud's greatest readers, the French psychoanalyst Jacques Lacan.

In his important seminar during 1959–60 titled "The Ethics of Psychoanalysis" Jacques Lacan reworked what he called the problem of sublimation as the other side of any ethical feeling. Sublimation for Lacan couldn't simply be doing this or that artistic or intellectual activity if it was to play such an important cultural role. But what is the role that it plays, and how? Lacan shows us how sublimation differs from other defenses in so far as it changes our relationship to the object (not just the drive or the ego), liberating that object from mere narcissistic use, and giving the object a dignity beyond itself—what he calls elevating the object to the level of *Das Ding*. In the same way that language liberates us from the world of mere things, sublimation follows a path where Lacan says a certain "respect for emptiness" is given new light, allowing us to resituate ourselves, perhaps more ethically. Sublimation is a creation that allows us to approach the loss or lack at the very center of being. Reframing sublimation in this quasi-existential light allowed for many novel ways of looking at the "vital effects" of an intellectual or artistic achievement and its continuing cultural value.

(*See also* Chapter 7, Psychoanalytic Theory; Freud, Sigmund; Lacan, Jacques; objet petit a; *and* Psychoanalysis)

Jamieson Webster, *Eugene Lang College at The New School (United States)*

Further Reading

Freud, Sigmund. *Civilization and Its Discontents* [1930]. *The Standard Edition of the Complete Psychological Works of Sigmund Freud*. Volume XXI (1927-1931). Trans. James Strachey. London: Hogarth, 1966–74. 57–146.

Lacan, Jacques. *The Seminar of Jaques Lacan Book VII: The Ethics of Psychoanalysis, 1959-60*. Ed. Jacques-Alain Miller. Trans. Dennis Porter. New York: Norton, 1997.

Superstructure (*See* Base and Superstructure)

Supplement

In everyday discourse, a supplement refers to something added to an original. For this reason, it is typically considered secondary and extrinsic to that which is deemed more natural and intrinsic. Writing, for example, is said to supplement speech. If we take speaking to be originary, capable of accounting for the presence of things, due to its claims of spontaneity and immediacy (I can always clarify what I mean on the spot), writing becomes derivative, always lagging behind, removed from the presence of things, and can only stand in for speech as a poor substitute (an orphan, detached from the paternal logos or voice). Writing adds to speech to the extent that it increases the reach of my communication (I am no longer limited to the face-to-face encounter). Writing also augments the possibility of misinterpretation (because of my lack of proximity, I am not available for immediate clarification).

And yet, at times, the supplement surprises. It can prove more adequate than the original. Writing my ideas down might allow me to give a fuller and more accurate account of my position than if I had to account for it on the spot (especially if I became anxiety stricken). Writing thus supplements speech in two ways: it not only adds to the original purity of speech (with varying degrees of success; it can be a useful or superfluous addition) but also risks replacing speech, becoming more desirable than speech, threating, in turn, speech's claims of completeness and priority. Jacques Derrida was particularly attentive to this ambivalence at the heart of the supplement, which he compared to a *pharmakon*, the Greek term for both poison and cure. The supplement complicates any straightforward distinction between the outside and the inside, the accidental and the intrinsic. It wreaks havoc on the natural order of things. It unsettles the desire for purity and originality. The supplement is perhaps best understood as a logic, a way of thinking about binary oppositions. It corrodes the meaning of existing terms (like speech and writing), or short-circuits their representational economy.

Theory can be said to occupy the position of the supplement in relation to philosophy and literary criticism. Theory supplements philosophy to the extent that its interdisciplinary focus (its fondness for psychoanalysis, politics, literature, linguistics, etc.) adds to philosophy's project of rendering the world knowable (or at the very least, it can account for the limits of human knowing). Yet theory's excessive questioning and the way it takes seriously the challenges of psychoanalysis (which shows us that the knower is a split subject internally divided by unconscious drives and desires) puts it fundamentally at odds with philosophy's values of autonomy and comprehension. Likewise, while the dismissive gesture, "I don't do theory," suggests that theory is extrinsic to the labor of literary criticism, theory is never a mere addition, a mere supplement to a preexisting, authorized or legitimate reading. If it is to be conceived as a supplement, then it is a "dangerous supplement," a supplement that, in Derrida's words, productively alters its source, revealing that theory was never *after* reading.

(*See also* Chapter 9, Deconstruction; Deconstruction; Différance; Dissemination; Derrida, Jacques; *and* Writing)

Zahi Zalloua, *Whitman College (United States)*

Further Reading

Derrida, Jacques. *Of Grammatology* [1967]. Trans. Gayatri Spivak. Baltimore: Johns Hopkins University Press, 1974.

Derrida, Jacques. *The Truth in Painting* [1978]. Trans. Geoff Bennington and Ian McLeod. Chicago: University of Chicago Press, 1987.

Surface Reading

In an introduction to their co-edited special issue of *Representations* (2009), entitled "The Way We Read Now," Stephen Best and Sharon Marcus observe that over the last decade, scholars have begun to turn their attention toward the "surface" of literary and cultural texts. Best and Marcus's "surface reading" has since become one of the most influential—and controversial—critical concepts of the twenty-first century, sparking debate over the relations between history and form, empirical observation and critical interpretation, and academic scholarship and political agency.

Best and Marcus present the recent turn to surface as an alternative to the depth hermeneutics that have long animated literary and cultural studies, emblematized by Fredric Jameson's "symptomatic reading," which assumes that "the most interesting aspect of a text is what it represses." Because symptomatic readers construe meaning to be "latent" and "concealed," they focus on the text's absences, elisions and contradictions, "looking past the surface" to "plumb hidden depths." By contrast, surface readers aim for an "accurate" or "neutral" account of "what is evident, perceptible, apprehensible in texts; what is neither hidden nor hiding." Best and Marcus understand "surface" capaciously. It can refer to the materiality of the literary or cultural object, for instance its "linguistic density," or to the reader's bodily, affective, or ethical responsiveness. Surface reading thus embraces a broad array of critical practices: new and old formalisms, cognitive science, affect studies, critical description, history of the book, as well as "distant reading" and other data-driven approaches.

Converging with Heather Love's contemporaneous notion of the "descriptive turn," Best and Marcus place special importance on "describ[ing] texts accurately." They also draw attention to recent scholarly ventures in what Marcus has previously called "just reading"—modes of analysis that take literary language and representation to mean what it says, rather than stand in for something else. Countering deeply held critical commitments toward suspicion and critique, surface reading has resonated with a wide audience of scholars who, following Bruno Latour, believe that an engrained emphasis on ideological demystification has obscured much of what is most resonant in cultural texts, and prevented literary critics from offering objective analysis.

What has most troubled critics about surface reading, however, is the question of politics. Though Best and Marcus draw support from aesthetic and formalist approaches, they insist that surface reading has a political orientation grounded in the present. Arguing that ideology critique has lost its necessity in an age defined by the blatant horrors and abuses of the Bush regime, they claim that surface readers are skeptical of the "heroic" notions of the symptomatic reader's revolutionary agency. Yet the politics of surface reading remains vague: Best and Marcus oscillate between references to "political realism" and "minimal critical agency," on the one hand, and to more utopian invocations of a "freedom in attentiveness" on the other.

Not surprisingly, scholars working especially within Marxist, postcolonial and feminist critical traditions have claimed that surface reading cannot adequately confront the historical structures of oppression sedimented within cultural texts. In addition, some have shown that Best and Marcus ignore symptomatic reading's power to illuminate the textual surface. Following these debates, surface reading's most significant result may not be its articulation of a new post-critical method, such as Rita Felski has proposed, but its reinvigoration of critique as the analytical mode best suited to engage the whole of the cultural object, its surfaces and depths.

(*See also* Antitheory; Chapter 12, Postmodernism; Chapter 16, Pop Culture; Chapter 23,

Materialisms; Chapter 23, Antitheory; Reading; *and* Postcritique)

Jason M. Baskin, *University of Exeter (United Kingdom)*

Further Reading

Bartolovich, Crystal. "Marxism, Surface Reading—and Milton." *PMLA* 127.1 (2012): 115–21.

Best, Stephen, and Sharon Marcus. "Surface Reading: An Introduction." *Representations* 108.1 (2009): 1–21.

Rooney, Ellen. "Live Free or Describe: The Reading Effect and the Persistence of Form." *differences* 21.3 (2010): 112–39.

Surveillance

Surveillance means very literally "to watch over." It describes a series of activities that are meant to secure political and moral boundaries. Before the advent of modernity, surveillance was carried formally and informally by political and religious leaders seeking to squash dissent and blasphemy. Augustine's *Confessions* (400 CE) represented a breakthrough in religious self-observation while Norbert Elias describes the court society in early modern Europe as a place where those close to power learned to watch over each other and themselves. When Jane Jacobs described the safety of urban communities as being guaranteed by "eyes on the street," she thought of mutual, informal surveillance in a positive way.

The work of Michel Foucault set up a new historical frame in which we could understand discipline and punish as part of an apparatus of power, incarnated most effectively in Jeremy Bentham's Panopticon prison design. Foucault's theory of power allowed him to link army, prison, and classroom as disciplinary spaces where bodies in grids made conformity and difference legible and punishable, he presented a fully developed, noneconomic and non-metaphysical method of understanding not just politics, but identity itself. Significantly, Foucault never talked about property or the surveillance of slaves and the counting of bodies in terms of discipline or punish.

Americans have always been ambivalent about the interlocking relationship between privacy and surveillance. Casting the Communist bloc as a tightly surveilled world with no rights to privacy, J. Edgar Hoover wiretapped American citizens, from Martin Luther King, Jr. to Clark Kerr. Colin Powell's presentation to the United Nations of satellite footage of Saddam Hussein's WMD (Weapons of Mass Destruction) installations was presaged by Phillip Noyce's 1992 *Patriot Games*, a film that assumes that satellite imagery is able to capture the curves of an IRA terrorist in the desert as providing reliable forensic evidence for the American military's targeting of an alleged Libyan terrorist training camp.

Liberal democracies and their culture industries are able to tolerate high levels of invasion of privacy. Mark Andrejevic made an important link between reality television, entertainment, and surveillance technologies. When George Orwell's dystopic novel, *1984* (1949) can be mined for infotainment, audiences are ready to watch and be watched in unprecedented ways. The culture industry has been able to make surveillance natural and entertaining at the same time.

Neoliberalism has made our inner lives as tightly monitored and managed as anything external to us. With the rise of social media, ubiquitous and mobile computing, surveillance is built into everything we touch. Despite the warnings about privacy and profits, there has been no stampede away from Google or Facebook. The algorithm rather than the camera or window controls what we see online and who sees us as well. In a deindustrializing world, information gathered about us is the gold for which social media companies are hungry. Wearables and the Internet of Things are other ways for surveillant technologies to penetrate more deeply into what was formerly thought of as private life. Privacy panics about 'security' are not adequate responses to a world in which surveillant technologies are built into the infrastructure of social media itself. From the point of the view of future historians, Airbnb and Uber may be surveillance platforms masquerading as a vacation rental service and a ride-hailing app. We need new ways to think and talk about surveillance.

(*See also* Chapter 5, Post-structuralism; Disciplinary Society; Discipline; *and* Foucault, Michel)

Catherine Liu, *University of California, Irvine (United States)*

Further Reading

Andrejevic, Mark. *Reality TV: The Work of Being Watched*. New York: Rowman and Littlefield, 2003.

Browne, Simone. *Dark Matters: On the Surveillance of Blackness*. Durham: Duke University Press, 2015.

Foucault, Michel. *Discipline and Punish: The Birth of the Prison* [1975]. Trans. Alan Sheridan. New York: Vintage Books, 1995.

Symbolic Agency

In literary theory and cultural studies, the question of agency emerges on two related fronts: (1) the relationship between individual agency and the symbolic field; and (2) the relationship between power and the symbolic field. The first front interrogates the ways in which subjective agency is created, constrained, and/or determined by shared and personal systems of signification. To what extent is the subject free to impose his or her agency on and through images and symbols, and to what extent do shared systems of signification and meaning always already sculpt and channel the subject's behavior? The second front interrogates the ways in which systems of signification and meaning may enact, reproduce, challenge, or undermine relationships of power—the various human struggles over agency and between agents. To what extent is the seemingly neutral symbolic field always already favoring the agency of some individuals or groups of others? To what extent can symbolic acts and objects transform these power relationships? And what kind of more equitable or just relationships might the symbolic field support?

For example, Pierre Bourdieu argues that taste should be read as the performance of class position, determined by relative social capital and closely guarded cultural competencies, rather than as an act of idiosyncratic choice. An experience of individual agency is revealed as a highly determined enactment of social power. Dick Hebdige examines the ways in which members of subordinated social groups selectively misread dominant cultural texts in ways that reflect their experiences of exclusion and exploitation. A practice of seemingly submissive cultural consumption is revealed as an enactment of resistant agency. And members of the Frankfurt school argue that the bending and breaking of stylistic rules, characteristic of bourgeois conceptions of artistic genius, should be read as structural expressions of individual anomie that are ultimately at odds with bourgeois class interests. An act of elitist cultural production is revealed as an expression of politically subversive agency.

Cultural studies' rejection of positivist models of agency that imagine a self-transparent subject using the neutral tool of language to transmit pure, objective ideas has led to the incorporation of a number of theories—particularly Marx's theory of ideology and Gramsci's theory of hegemony—that emphasize how symbolic structures may mislead subjects into misrecognizing obedience as freedom. But more recent incorporations go even further in undermining the notion of free human agency. For example, Jacques Lacan's psychoanalytic theory asserts that truth emerges only when the unconscious speaks—when the individual ego loses control in failures, slips, mistakes, and dreams. Postcolonial and feminist thinkers such as Edward Said and Judith Butler point out that the notion of the self-transparent subject has historically gone hand in hand with the oppressive de-subjectification of others. And for Deleuze and Guattari, the notion of the individual subject is itself an imposition of power that should be exploded into a multiplicity of vectors and forces that can be apprehended only as a body without organs. At the extreme end, these lines of inquiry may lead toward theories such as Dawkins' meme theory, in which agency becomes the purview of cultural signifiers themselves, for which human beings are secondary hosts at best.

While these more recent developments in the question of symbolic agency may seem to shrink the space of freedom for cultural producers, consumers and analysts to the point of disappearance, the opposite is (also) the case: They open up more broadly than ever the space for exploring what an equitable, just, and more liberated social relationship might be, and what cultural artifacts might facilitate, reflect, and/or occasion its arrival.

(*See also* Agency; Adorno, Theodor W.; Bourdieu, Pierre; Chapter 7, Psychoanalytic Theory; Hegemony; Ideology; *and* Subject)

Charles Wells, *Wilfrid Laurier University (Canada)*

Further Reading

Bourdieu, Pierre, and Richard Nice. "The Aristocracy of Culture." *Media, Culture & Society* 2.3 (1980): 225–54.

Fiske, John. *Understanding Popular Culture.* Second ed. New York: Routledge, 2010.

Horkheimer, Max, and Theodor W. Adorno. "The Culture Industry: Enlightenment as Mass Deception." In *Dialectic of Enlightenment* [1944/1947]. Trans. John Cumming. New York: Verso, 1999. 120–167.

Symptom

The term symptom has nuanced meanings, but essentially refers to a substitution-formation created at the moment when repressed material attempts to return from the unconscious to the conscious. That substitution can be either a reaction, frequently taking the form of an "acting-out," or a compromise to alleviate the stress of the return.

Sigmund Freud's concept of the symptom begins with the case study of Anna O, hence characterizing symptoms as hysterical affects. For Freud's hysterics, the symptom is a compromise allowing for mediation between the return of the repressed and daily life. From this idea, Jacques Lacan will theorize the symptom as ever hovering between the Symbolic and the Real, in a position which inhibits heteronormative jouissance, but grants access to unsanctioned kinds (perversions).

For Freud, the symptoms of obsessional neurosis are different than those of the hysteric. Neurotic symptoms are reaction formations, acting as protection against the returning material. Melanie Klein goes on to contend that neurosis itself is a mediating or protective force working against an over-stimulating superego. The obsessional patients repeated acts of purification or expiation continue until the unconscious wish breaks out fully in the pattern of the obsessional action itself.

Both Lacan and Žižek fight against the notion of the control of the superego by positing the symptom as something a subject can potentially embrace as a gateway from the Symbolic into the Real. For Lacan, that would mean engaging in the process of radical Symbolic disassociation, turning the symptom into the sinthome, allowing a person to escape the signifying structure of the Symbolic and the order of the Other. For Julia Kristeva, the process of ridding oneself of the pressure of the symptom is the process of abjection, which entails the physical devastation of bodily fluids as if the outpouring of a psychic material (linked to the mother) and now to a new type of self-ownership.

For Lacan, once the symptom becomes the sinthome, through a self-mutilating rupture, the Lacanian subject can enter the Real. As Lacan explains, the symptom is a mechanism for taking pleasure in one's own unconscious, while containing its worst effects. Žižek's dictum "enjoy your symptom" is not quite as damning as the Lacanian process of self-nomination as self-destitution, but it indicates that the subject need not be "cured" as would be the Freudian demand, but instead should revel in the potentially painful uniqueness of the symptom itself.

For Freud, Lacan and many of their followers, the symptom precedes treatment and transference. Melanie Klein theorizes that treatment itself can produce symptoms, while temporary or transitory in nature, that are necessary for the process of the patient. Controversially, Lacan states that "woman is a symptom" implying that woman, as a category, carries with it the same functions as any symptom. From that, both woman and symptom are metaphors, linguistic creations that serve to communicate the unconscious to the conscious, but as linguistic functions are constructs of the Other. Both the categorization of woman and symptom are bound by the paternal function of the Symbolic, but women, the pluralized individualized notion, is not so strictly bound.

(*See also* Chapter 7, Psychoanalytic Theory; Freud, Sigmund; Hysteria; Kristeva, Julia; Lacan, Jacques; Overdetermination; Trauma; *and* Žižek, Slavoj)

Gina Masucci MacKenzie, *Holy Family University (United States)*

Further Reading

Freud, Sigmund. *Inhibitions, Symptoms and Anxiety* [1926]. New York: W. W. Norton and Company, 1990.

Lacan, Jacques. *Anxiety. The Seminar of Jacques Lacan, Book X* [1962–63]. Trans. Jacques-Alain Miller. Malden: Polity Press, 2016.

Žižek, Slavoj. *Enjoy Your Symptom: Jacques Lacan in Hollywood and Out.* New York: Routledge, 2007.

Synchronic and Diachronic

Synchronic is the present or fixed state of a linguistic system in its entirety as a fixed configuration. Diachronic is the temporal execution of language whereby the state of a system is in play and subject to change. Synchrony relates to the equilibrium and homeostasis of a system that is subject to diachronic transformation as a particular system undergoes changes that disrupt, modify, or merely complement an immediately prior synchronic state. Complex systems are made up of subsystems that are synchronically configured in ways that may or may not be affected by transformations within other systems within the whole. The use of new slang words, for example, may transform language use semantically but not syntactically. James Joyce's *Finnegans Wake* (1939) is an extreme example of interlingual hybridization, defamiliarizing homophonic substitution, and weird word play, though for the most part the syntax of its sentences are recognizable as English, not Gaelic, Japanese, or Hebrew. Without synchronic systems and subsystems (including the bits of stories being retold in many variants), the text would have been completely undecipherable. The fact that one considers *Finnegans Wake* to be a novel and not a psychotic rant or arbitrary word salad speaks to sufficient homeostasis required to identify the work as continuous with other literary works, however experimental they may be. Yet, *Finnegans Wake* has to be considered in terms of a "break" with even avant-gardist tradition, given that no text before or since has pushed interlingual hybridity to such an extreme. Diachronically the work represents a radical break in which difference and differentiatedness take on significance as a means of construing meaning that contrasts with such practices in the case of prior literary works. This is largely typical of much avant-garde art in which new works are supposed to break hermeneutically with the past in ways that challenge modes of analysis and evaluation.

(*See also* Chapter 2, Structuralism and Semiotics; Chapter 3, Narrative and Narratology; Chapter 5, Post-structuralism; Chapter 22, Identity Studies; Lévi-Strauss, Claude; Saussure, Ferdinand de; *and* Structuralism)

Herman Rapaport, *Wake Forest University* *(United States)*

Further Reading
Saussure, Ferdinand de. *Course in General Linguistics* [1916]. Eds. Charles Bally and Albert Sechehaye. Trans. Roy Harris. Chicago: Open Court, 1998.

Systems Theory

Systems theory is the overarching term for several theories arising after the World Wars, which consider organization in terms of function, communication, and information. While its origin is in science and engineering, systems theory is interdisciplinary and its influence has migrated into the social sciences and the humanities. Hence, it has been applied to a wide variety of phenomena such as biological, communication, economic, meteorological, managerial, and social systems. It includes cybernetics and second-order cybernetics; dynamical systems theory; social systems theory; and chaos and complexity theory. It is most often concerned with the behavior of complex and nonlinear, that is non-predictable, systems as they occur in nature, technology, and society.

A system is more structured than its environment: a system orders its world. But, a mere aggregate of elements does not constitute a system by itself. For a collection of components to be considered a system they must be organized in a meaningful way; they must perform a function; that function could not be performed by the individual components themselves; and the function the system performs contributes to the existence of the whole system. A system, then, is a set of dynamic formal relations between elements which form an integrated whole. What a system does determines what it is; hence, to think in terms of systems is to think of the world in terms of function and organization.

Systems theory had an important origin in Claude Shannon's information theory, which used the concepts of information and noise to measure communication in networks. This abstraction means that similar behavior can be observed across diverse systems. Another key moment was the coining of *cybernetics* by Norbert Weiner (1948), who used his experience with radio communication systems in the war to provide a definition: "the entire field of control and communication theory, whether in the machine or in the animal." Weiner sought to establish a vocabulary through which a general theory of scientific, social, and systemic phenomena could be articulated. He proposed an "essential unity" of questions concerning communication and control in biological, technological, and human systems. A similar approach was adopted by Ludwig von Bertalanffy's attempt to find "isomorphisms" (similarities) between complex systems in his "General Systems Theory." Subsequent, important, applications of the systems approach have been Gregory Bateson who applied second-order cybernetics to anthropology and developed an "ecology of mind" in which he explored the complex interrelationships of cognition with its environment and Niklas Luhmann who proposed a radical reconfiguration of Sociology by proposing that modern society is a complex system comprised of other social systems such as law, economy, science, and art.

The cultural impact of systems theory became prevalent in the 1960s against the horizon of new technologies in computation and communication that facilitated its methods. This included the use of systems thinking to plan international policy in America with Project RAND and Stafford Beer's audacious attempt with the *Cybersyn* project to run Chile's socialist economy under President Allende (1971–73) through systems principles and a network of telecommunications linked to central control and command units. Counter cultural movements, such as Stewart Brand's *Whole Earth* catalogue, also considered systems both in terms of

authoritarian structures to be resisted and as alternative forms of social organization and living involving collaboration with ecological systems. Artists moving beyond the legacy of high modernism, such as those using new media, conceptualism, performance, and other strategies, also frequently invoked ideas of system to describe the move away from single artworks into multiple, distributed and time-based practices. This was named systems aesthetics by the curator and art historian Jack Burnham.

Systems thinking presents a serious challenge to the primacy of humans who are conceived of as just one system among many other biological, social, and technological ones. Hence, its legacy today is found in those discourses, such as posthumanism, contemporary neuroscience, artificial intelligence/life and those cultural practices that attempt to have a purchase on a world of increasingly complexity.

(*See also* Chapter 9, Deconstruction; Chapter 24, Posthumanism; Cybernetics; Machine; *and* Posthumanism)

Francis Halsall, *National College of Art and Design, Dublin (Ireland) and University of the Free State, Bloemfontaine (South Africa)*

Further Reading
Halsall, Francis. *Systems of Art.* Oxford: Peter Lang, 2008.
Ramage, Magnus, and Karen Shipp, eds. *Systems Thinkers.* London: Springer, 2009.
Ridd, Thomas. *Rise of the Machines: The Lost History of Cybernetics.* London: Scribe Publications, 2016.

T

Taste

Taste is the human behavioral practice of evaluation and judgment regarding interactions of the body and mind with the material world. Taste functions on at least two levels: those of the individual and of the social. Individual taste operates as a set of personal likes or dislikes that is often determined by both biological and cultural forces. A person's aversion to a particular animal or vegetable food may be encoded in their DNA as a survival mechanism, while the choice of one's reproductive partner could be influenced by the values and norms of their culture. Taste operates on the social level as a self-organizing evolving human system composed of networks of behavioral-choice interactions that determine gradients of value for material objects and human behavior. A society may prefer a certain type of food to another, and the "Taste of the town" could determine an acting style, narrative form, or behavioral vogue.

Taste is often associated with aesthetics, or the question of what is beautiful. Social networks of taste emerge as evaluative responses to aesthetic production, meaning any material good produced by a society upon which the expenditure of labor time would be superfluous to the production of materials necessary for the immediate or sustained subsistence of that society. Instead of containing strictly use value, the object would command additional value (in diverse forms) for the expenditure of a portion of society's labor on adding "beauty" to an object. The earliest known aesthetically produced material objects are jewelry from well over one-hundred-thousand years ago, signifying that social organization in certain prehistoric groups had allotted precious labor time to produce objects with aesthetic qualities. After periods of primitive accumulation, as society became more complex with the advent of large-scale farming and urban centers, and as more people had more leisure time as a consequence of the evolutionary success of social organization, aesthetic production became commercialized and institutionalized as it begun to cater to the tastes of consumers.

Commodification of aesthetic production and the role art as technology plays in disseminating culture manifested in new forms of knowledge regarding how networks of taste determine the value of material objects. Specialized knowledge and usage of these networks of value allow practitioners access to symbolic capital (literally to possess symbols of capital) in forms used by their particular society. Thus taste becomes an integral element in the knowledge of cultural codes used to differentiate between aesthetic objects in order to further an individual's accumulation of symbolic capital. Statuary arrangement representing favored politicians, mansion-house frescoes and representative painting, lavish spectacle-type meals, knowledge of literature and philosophy, and picturesque landscape gardening are all ways that symbolic capital is deployed to convert the knowledge of cultural codes into social power. The possession of resources spent on aesthetic production becomes a symbol of an individual's or group's capacity for taste, which translates to economic power in their society.

(*See also* Bourdieu, Pierre; Chapter 2, Structuralism and Semiotics; Chapter 16, Pop Culture; Chapter 19, Media Studies; Chapter 22, Identity Studies; Chapter 27, Antitheory; Class; Cultural Capital; *and* Symbolic Agency)

Michael Amrozowicz, *University at Albany (United States)*

Further Reading

Bourdieu, Pierre. *Distinction: A Social Critique of the Judgement of Taste* [1979]. Trans. Richard Nice. Cambridge: Harvard University Press, 1984.

Gigante, Denise. *Taste: A Literary History*. New Haven: Yale University Press, 2005.

Ryan, Michael J. *A Taste for the Beautiful: The Evolution of Attraction*. Princeton: Princeton University Press, 2018.

Tellability (*See* Chapter 3, Narrative and Narratology)

Terror

Terror is one of a handful of terms that have emerged as an important locus for engaged literary and cultural theory in the new millennium. The events of September 11, 2001, and the subsequent "War on Terror" launched by US president George W. Bush (2001–09), established a new social and political context for theorists worldwide. However, like many terms in contemporary theory, its roots can be traced back to ancient thought.

In his *Rhetoric*, Aristotle uses the term *phobos* for "a sort of pain or agitation derived from imagination of a future or painful evil."

For him, the evil is always near at hand, and the persons threatened are ourselves. Often translated as "terror"—but also as "fear" and "horror"—*phobos* is the effect upon us when, for example, the story of Oedipus is recounted. Hans-Georg Gadamer has noted in *Truth and Method* (1960) that translation of *phobos* as "fear" gives it a "far too subjective ring." For Gadamer, terror "is not just a state of mind, but a cold shudder that makes one's blood run cold, that makes one shiver." The linguist George Lakoff though pushes back on Gadamer's affective analysis in "Beyond the *War on Terror*" (2011). For Lakoff, "terror is an emotion, a state of mind," albeit one that can be extended indefinitely. "Because extreme fear can be provoked at any time," comments Lakoff, "terror cannot be ended."

The events of September 11 were a wake-up call for theorists to reassess the prevailing discourse on terror and its related term, "terrorism," with Jacques Derrida commenting in an interview with Giovanna Borradori in *Philosophy in a Time of Terror* (2003) that "the prevailing discourse, that of the media and the official rhetoric, relies too readily on received concepts" of these and related terms. Concepts like "terror" and "terrorism" used to describe the "event" of September 11 "are the products of a 'dogmatic slumber' from which only a new philosophical reflection can awaken us, a reflection *on* philosophy, most notably political philosophy and its heritage." To be sure, philosophical work on the concept "terror" and "terrorism," that is, the use of terror as a means of coercion, has been reawakened in the new millennium.

Though much of the work on terror and terrorism comes from historians and social scientists interested in tracing, examining, and comparing its various forms, for example, international, ethnonationalist, revolutionary, leftist, religious, and others dating back to the ancient world, and social and political philosophers seeking accounts of its nature and conditions, there is a wide range of interesting work from literary and cultural theorists too. Recent theoretical work examines terror in conjunction with American exceptionalism (e.g., William V. Spanos, "Terror and American Exceptionalism" [2012]), neoliberalism (e.g., Henry Giroux, *The Terror of Neoliberalism* [2004]), education (e.g., Jeffrey R. Di Leo, et al., *Neoliberalism, Education, and Terrorism* [2014]), rhetoric (e.g., Marc Redfield, *The Rhetoric of Terror* [2009]), literature (e.g., Ann Keniston, et al., *Literature after 9/11* [2008]), the media (W. J. T. Mitchell, *Cloning Terror* [2011]), and culture (Jeffrey Melnick, *9/11 Culture* [2009]) in an effort to provide some insight into use of this ubiquitous concept in the new millennium. Work in these areas often overlaps with related theoretical work on trauma, testimony, witnessing, resistance, and security. And, there are also emerging fields of terrorism studies (see Lisa Stampnitzky, *Disciplining Terror* [2013]), and critical terrorism studies (see Richard Jackson, Lee Jarvis, Jeroen Gunning, and Marie Breen Smyth, *Terrorism: A Critical Introduction* [2011]). In sum, the study of terror is a growing multi- and interdisciplinary endeavor involving scholars from both the humanities and the social sciences that complements the engaged work done by those inside and outside of the academy who are seeking ways both to eliminate it and prevent its spread throughout the world.

(*See also* Chapter 26, Affect Studies; Emotions; Event; Introduction: Theory in the New Millennium; Trauma; *and* Resistance)

Jeffrey R. Di Leo, *University of Houston-Victoria (United States)*

Further Reading
Borradori, Giovanna. *Philosophy in a Time of Terror: Dialogues with Jürgen Habermas and Jacques Derrida.* Chicago: University of Chicago Press, 2003.

Di Leo, Jeffrey R., Henry A. Giroux, Sophia A. McClennen, and Kenneth J. Saltman, *Neoliberalism, Education, and Terrorism: Contemporary Dialogues.* New York: Routledge, 2014.

Di Leo, Jeffrey R., and Uppinder Mehan, eds. *Terror, Theory and the Humanities.* Ann Arbor: Open Humanities Press, 2012.

Mitchell, W. J. T. *Cloning Terror: The War of Images, 9/11 to the Present.* Chicago: University of Chicago Press, 2011.

Redfield, Marc. *The Rhetoric of Terror: Reflections on 9/11 and the War on Terror.* New York: Fordham, 2009.

Text

By the time Jacques Derrida proclaimed "il n'y a pas de hors-text" in 1972, it felt almost impossible to conduct literary and cultural criticism without using the term. By the 1970s, "text" had become ubiquitous in not just cultural and literary theory, but also in a variety of other disciplines. But it was—and still is—used in a number of different, even conflicting, senses. Derrida's pronouncement and the work of his structuralist predecessors served as an important reminder too that depictions of text have been in circulation since Greek antiquity, whereas contemporary usage of the term tended to make distinctions among related ones such as work, artifact, and artistic production, the classical usage of the term did not.

The first use of *textus*, the Latin root of text, is by Quintilian in *Institutio oratoria* (95 CE). Here it is used as a metaphor that regards an instance of language use as a woven tissue or texture. The term's history though is a long and convoluted one, and complicated even more by the various twentieth-century theories of text that are not limited to linguistic or written entities. In addition, philosophers from Aristotle in his *Physics* (fourth century BC) to Ludwig Wittgenstein in his *Philosophical Investigations* (1953) have argued for the impossibility of defining the concept of text. Nevertheless, depictions of it can be generally divided into two distinct groups: the classical and the contemporary depictions.

Broadly speaking, there are four main characteristics of the classical depiction of text: (1) Autonomy—text is isolated from the whole of signification; (2) Stability—text has a perfectly stable and unchanging aspect; (3) Coherence—text is totally coherent and definable; and (4) Identity—text has an entirely determinate identity. Given this wide range of characteristics, it should not be surprising to learn then that greatly differing ideas of criticism such as reader-response, hermeneutic, and New Criticism share the same fundamental depiction of text. Additionally, specific classical depictions of text can vary widely in their metaphysics as well just as long as they fundamentally concur that text involves some level of autonomy, stability, coherence, and determinate identity. From the Stoics through the mid to late twentieth century, versions of this depiction have been championed from thinkers ranging from the New Critics including Monroe Beardsley and W. K. Wimsatt to reader-response critics such as Roman Ingarden, Wolfgang Iser, and Stanley Fish.

Contemporary depictions of text tend to define themselves in direct opposition to classical depictions of text. Thus, again broadly speaking, the contemporary depiction of text also has four main characteristics: (1) Non-Autonomy—text is regarded as coextensive or integrated with the whole of signification; (2) Non-Stability—text is *unstable* and *changing*; (3) Non-Coherence—text exemplifies a total lack of coherence and definability; and (4) Non-Identity—text has an indeterminate identity. Like the classical depiction, the contemporary depiction of text

supports a wide range of critical positions and ideas concerning the metaphysics of text. The common ground among these differing positions on text and textuality will be the relative lack of autonomy, stability, coherence, and identity afforded to their fundamental depiction of text. The contemporary depiction of text can be traced from the semiotics of Ferdinand de Saussure and Yuri Lotman through the work of thinkers as diverse as Roland Barthes, Mikhail Bakhtin, Michel Foucault, Louis Hjelmslev, Julia Kristeva, and Derrida.

While most theories of text do not entirely correspond to either of these depictions, most will more or less accurately fit under one depiction or the other. Still, there are a number of well-known depictions, for example, by Umberto Eco and Richard Rorty, which share characteristics of both depictions, and attempt to mediate them. While expansion of interest and use of the term can be attributed in large part to the twentieth-century's linguistic turn, critical discussion of text has waned in the new millennium—awaiting its next and inevitable wave of interest.

(*See also* Barthes, Roland; Chapter 2, Structuralism and Semiotics; Chapter 3, Narrative and Narratology; Chapter 4, Marxism; Chapter 5, Post-structuralism; Chapter 6, Historicism; Chapter 8, Rhetoric; Chapter 14, Ecocriticism; Chapter 18, Translation; Chapter 20, Digital Humanities; Close Reading; Derrida, Jacques; Feminist Theory; Fish, Stanley; Gadamer, Hans-Georg; Genre; Hermeneutics; Interpretation; Intertextuality; Levinas, Emmanuel; Liminality; Print Culture; Reading; Thing Theory; *and* Translation)

Jeffrey R. Di Leo, *University of Houston-Victoria (United States)*

Further Reading
Barthes, Roland. "From Work to Text"
   [1971]. In *The Rustle of Language*. Trans.

Richard Howard. New York: Hill and Wang, 1986. 56–64.

Derrida, Jacques. *Dissemination* [1972]. Trans. Barbara Johnson. Chicago: University of Chicago Press, 1981.

Di Leo, Jeffrey R. "Text." In *The Oxford Encyclopedia of Aesthetics*. Ed. Michael Kelly. Second ed. New York: Oxford University Press, 2014. Vol. 6: 129–34.

Eco, Umberto. *A Theory of Semiotics.* Bloomington: Indiana University Press, 1976.

Mowitt, John. *Text, the Genealogy of an Antidisciplinary Object.* Durham: Duke University Press, 1992.

Rorty, Richard. "Texts and Lumps." In *Objectivity, Relativism and Truth: Philosophical Papers, Volume 1.* Cambridge: Cambridge University Press, 1991. 78–92.

Thanatopolitics

Thanatopolitics—a politics of death—stands in opposition to biopolitics and its affirmative instantiations of "life itself"; it is the resistant and rhetorical counterpart to the dialectics and reductive ontologies of biopolitical life. In Michel Foucault's work, since the nineteenth-century biopolitics progressively displaced the sovereign's power "to take life or let live." Operating through multiplex neoliberal networks, biopolitics today is the postsovereign state power "to make live and let die," which seizes on the life of the population as its means and its end, its object and objective. Thanatopolitics would contest the ontologization of life and the powers that "make live," which disavow the corollary power that "lets die" in the name of life.

If biopolitics is a productive power that necessitates or silently calls for death as the consequence of "making live," then thanatopolitics is not merely the lethal underside of biopolitics but is itself a productive power in the voices of those who biopolitical power "lets die." Thanatopolitics asks: how might those deaths—collateral damages, negative externalities, opportunity costs—productively disaffirm the regime of a neoliberal biopolitics that condemns to death? How might those deaths rise up, and haunt, the spaces of biopolitical production, to critically disaffirm the ways in which biopolitics not only occasions but also tolerates a certain threshold of death as its modus operandi? Such a perspective would call into question the implicit decisions, and covert cultivation of death, in the biopolitical logics that determine and distinguish those who are worthy of life, those who shall be made to live, from those who are permitted to perish.

In concrete terms, thanatopolitics might imagine the ways in which the actions of the suicide bomber are rhetorically productive, and make a claim, striking at the heart of neoliberal capital and technologies; but at the same time, it would honor the voices of Western soldiers who commit suicide, and would refuse to dismiss these deaths as a consequence of "pre-existing" mental health conditions, substance abuse, or "failed relationships," as the Pentagon has done. Indeed, soldier suicides oftentimes offer a critique of the neoliberal biopolitical regime in whose name they have served, and which in the end has proven unlivable, as many soldier suicide notes attest.

Such a perspective might, as well, consider the willingness to die of hunger-striking inmates held in the inhuman conditions of prolonged solitary confinement, and it might hear in this willingness not simply a loss of hope but rather a hope that is steadfast for more humane forms of treatment. In these cases, the biopolitical state often intervenes to keep inmates alive, through forced-feeding and other measures, against their will and despite legally binding Do No Resuscitate orders. Here, what is intolerable to the state is less the living, who can be administrated, but the dead, whose posthumous claim threaten to disrupt the system.

Reckoning with the dead, then, is the effort to account for our own complicity in a regime that delivers death to some in the name of prosperity and life for others. Thanatopolitics would expose the fault-lines of biopolitical logics. It would attend to the rhetorical conditions in which the dead, the dying, and the dispossessed might rise up and speak. This is not to exalt suicide or other violent forms of biopolitical death, but to better understand the force of these events and to demonstrate how the biopolitical conception of life is deeply duplicitous, and ultimately represents a failed, illegible, and hypocritical form of ethical and political life.

(*See also* Agamben, Giorgio; Bare Life; Biopolitics; Capacity; Chapter 15, Biopower and Biopolitics; Chapter 23, Materialisms; Control; Cyborg; Foucault, Michel; *and* Labor)

Stuart J. Murray, *Carleton University (Canada)*

Further Reading

Bargu, Banu. *Starve and Immolate: The Politics of Human Weapons*. New York: Columbia University Press, 2014.

Esposito, Roberto. *Bíos: Biopolitics and Philosophy*. Minneapolis: University of Minnesota Press, 2008.

Murray, Stuart J. "Thanatopolitics: On the Use of Death for Mobilizing Political Life." *Polygraph: An International Journal of Politics and Culture* 18 (2006): 191–215.

Murray, Stuart J. "Thanatopolitics: Reading in Agamben a Rejoinder to Biopolitical Life." *Communication and Critical/Cultural Studies* 5.2 (2008): 203–07.

Theory

Over the course of the contemporary period, theory has accumulated six different meanings, each of which entails distinct critical receptions. First, theory refers loosely to the gamut of more than a dozen well-known contemporary schools and movements from Marxism and formalism to structuralism and post-structuralism to postcolonial and gender theory. That is to say, it names the broad field and is synonymous in some instances with criticism. Starting in the 1980s and persisting to the present, scholars dedicated single-mindedly to moral and formal analysis of canonical literary works have waged a campaign against such variegated, purportedly ill-focused, often politicized theory. Second, theory designates general principles and procedures—methods—as well as the self-reflection employed in all areas of literary and cultural studies. A small but vigorous skirmish against such theory has been enjoined by neopragmatists, who oppose quests for ultimate truths, foundational principles, and foolproof scientific methods. Third, theory is widely considered a toolbox of flexible, useful, and contingent devices and concepts, judged for their productivity and innovation. The critique of such pragmatic theory, small in scale, has come from various defenders of objective interpretation, ranging from curmudgeons seeking to return to the old days before the rise of contemporary theory to defenders of rigorous formalism to more challenging rules-based hermeneuticists. Fourth, theory denotes professional common sense—what goes without saying and what every specialist knows—so that everyone in the field has a theory, although some people don't realize it. But equating theory with professionally configured common sense paradoxically ends up diluting its historical specificity and its conflicts. Fifth, theory signifies more narrowly structuralism and post-structuralism, the works of Lévi-Strauss,

Jacques Lacan, Roland Barthes, Michel Foucault, Gilles Deleuze, Jacques Derrida, Julia Kristeva, and company. This is frequently called high or grand theory, with low (or vernacular) theory and posttheory arriving after French structuralism and post-structuralism particularly with the rise of cultural studies. Opposition has come to such briefly triumphant high theory from not only conservative formalist-oriented scholars, but also a broad array of contending liberal and left theorists, indicting it (typically deconstruction) for philosophical idealism, nominalism, and obscurantism, charges made famous by certain Marxists, feminists, critical race theorists, plus cultural studies scholars. Yet the persistence of post-structuralism has appeared in its continuous and widespread use past its two-decade-long hegemony during the 1970s and 1980s, most notably through the ongoing influence in the twenty-first century of Foucault, Deleuze, and Derrida. Sixth, theory names the historically new, postmodern mode of discourse that breaches long-standing disciplinary borders, fusing literary criticism, linguistics, philosophy, psychoanalysis, anthropology, sociology, history, and politics. This cross-disciplinary pastiche is, not surprisingly, subject to the broad critique of postmodernism, especially for its undermining the hard-won autonomy of academic disciplines developed during the modern era.

(*See also* Antitheory; Chapter 27, Antitheory; Introduction, Theory in the New Millennium; *and* Posttheory)

Vincent B. Leitch, *University of Oklahoma*
(United States)

Further Reading

Culler, Jonathan. *Literary Theory: A Very Short Introduction*. Second ed. New York: Oxford University Press, 2011.

Groden, Michael, Martin Kreiswirth, and Imre Szeman, eds. *Johns Hopkins Guide to Literary Theory and Criticism*. Second

ed. Baltimore: Johns Hopkins University Press, 2005.

Leitch, Vincent B. *Literary Criticism in the Twenty-First Century: Theory Renaissance*. London: Bloomsbury, 2014.

Ryan, Michael, ed. *The Encyclopedia of Literary and Cultural Theory*. 3 vols. Malden: Wiley-Blackwell, 2011.

Womack, Kenneth. "Selected Bibliography of Theory and Criticism." In *Norton Anthology of Theory and Criticism*. Second ed. General ed., Vincent B. Leitch. New York: W. W. Norton, 2010. 2655–88.

Thing Theory

Thing theory was coined in an eponymous essay that appeared as the introduction to a special issue of *Critical Inquiry* (2001) titled *Things*. That essay and that volume helped to energize a new engagement with objects and materiality across disciplines (from art history and literary studies to anthropology and sociology). Part of the point, though, was to call attention to the place of "things" in European and American poetry of the twentieth century; to the place of thingness and things within social and cultural theory; and to the distinction between the object and the thing in philosophy (above all Martin Heidegger), psychoanalysis (Jacques Lacan), and deconstruction (Jacques Derrida). Thing theory can be understood as one branch of *new materialism* insofar as it focuses on the object world once overlooked by the critical attention to the subject, language, and the image, as by a highly textual(ist) understanding of culture. But it proposes its own scheme for differentiating between object and thing, or an object and its thingness, which is irreducible to the object form (be that thingness physical or metaphysical—a tactile sensation, for instance, or a symbolic aura—some *thing* about that object that compels your attention). The *thing* names a subject/object relation. The subject can be an individual or a group, and an object can appear in the subject position; from a magnet's point of view (if you will) the only thing that matters about a toy truck is the iron that compels the magnet: it is a thing that renders the object form superfluous (except insofar as it provides the source of the thing).

Critics have not felt bound by thing theory's overarching schema while nonetheless making significant use of the theory's lexicon. The *meta-object* is an object that seems to investigate objecthood, the object world more generally, and its own status as an object. *Misuse value* consists of some new value emerging from an object's displacement from routine systems or networks of use. From a thing-theoretical perspective you would ask how a literary text portrays the object world: the mutual transformations of subject and object, or the dynamics of a particular *object culture*—the objects through which a culture or subculture helps to sustain its coherence, and the systems through which those objects gain or lose value or significance. Art appears as the source of a *redemptive reification* that interrupts reification-as-usual (be this the result of the commodity form, of science or philosophy, or of the habits of quotidian perception). It is the inherent doubleness of the object (both object and thing) that the commodity form (use value/exchange value) appropriates and sublimates. The event of redemptive reification, then, appears as a desublimation that discloses what inheres in the object as thing.

Unlike other related theoretical pursuits (object-oriented ontology, speculative realism, metaphysical materialism), thing theory sustains a focus on history and culture—convinced that the event of the thing asserts itself, however unexpectedly, within a particular scene of engagement.

(*See also* Benjamin, Walter; Chapter 22, Identity Studies; Chapter 23, Materialisms;

Cybernetics; Heidegger, Martin; Material Culture; Materialism; New Materialisms; *and* Objects)

Bill Brown, *University of Chicago (United States)*

Further Reading

Benjamin, Walter. "Surrealism: The Last Snapshot of the European Intelligentsia [1929]." In *Selected Writings, Volume Two: 1927-1934*. Trans. Edmund Jephcott. Eds. Michael W. Jennings, Howard Eiland, and Gary Smith. Cambridge: Harvard University Press, 1999. 207–21.

Brown, Bill. *Other Things*. Chicago: University of Chicago Press, 2014.

Heidegger, Martin. "The Thing [1951]." In *Poetry, Language, Thought*. Trans. Albert Hofstadter. New York: HarperCollins, 1971. 161–84.

Trace (*See* Archi-trace)

Tradition

The image embedded in the etymology of the word *tradition* is that of handing something down or "giving" (*datio, onis*) it over (*trans*). *Trado, tradere* in Latin means to hand over, deliver, transmit. The nature of knowledge in humanities disciplines as "traditional" is to be based on transmission of ideas and discourse through time and space within and across cultures. Such handing over or transfer is an ineluctable condition of making sense. Acknowledging tradition, accordingly, is tantamount to recognizing the social and historical predicament of human knowing. Historical context determines the sense and purport of all our intelligible terms. A heritage from the past always operates in any concrete realization of knowledge by existing human beings in some specific historical-cultural situation.

Hans-Georg Gadamer in *Truth and Method* (1960) delivered a penetrating speculative reflection on the notion of tradition that is still path-breaking in its contemporary relevance. Gadamer rehabilitated tradition, along with authority and prejudice, as constitutive of knowledge per se. He theorized tradition as not just an accumulation of antiquities, but as a vital and dynamic mediation of any apprehension of truth and as intrinsic to understanding in the present. The scientific approach to knowledge in the spirit of the Enlightenment had tried to sever true knowing from its dependency on tradition in an attempt to refound knowledge on the basis of what can be tested and verified by oneself and one's contemporaries alone. This scientific method endeavored to make knowledge independent of all that was handed down from one's forbears. But Gadamer, drawing on Martin Heidegger's analysis of the existential grounds of understanding as projecting into the future possibilities of being that emerge from the past, exposes the illusoriness of this endeavor. He brings out the interpretive and historical bases of understanding in existing individuals and in the open, ongoing event of truth as a disclosure of their being.

This perspective on knowledge as grounded in tradition can trace its origins to Latin rhetorical antiquity. It was revived in Italian Renaissance humanism (Pico, Bruno, Salutati, etc.). Such a genealogy for human wisdom as traditional offers an alternative to the modern secular model of knowing based on empirical, experimental method in the natural sciences taken as the universal paradigm for all types of knowing. It was revived again in the eighteenth century by Giambattista Vico, who rediscovered humanities tradition in opposition to the Cartesian scientific method. The approach to knowing through tradition develops further in the spirit of the humanities as *Geisteswissenschaften* or "sciences of the spirit" reaching further high-points of speculative acumen in German Idealism and in contemporary philosophical hermeneutics.

Tradition is demonstrably fundamental to knowledge and interpretive practices in areas such as Scriptural interpretation, legal judgment, and philological study. It opens a historical perspective on these types of knowledge, which are inextricably historical in nature. There can be no unequivocally given object in these domains and throughout humanities disciplines because facts need to be constructed by interpretation on the basis of experience by human subjects. Tradition is always a selection and shaping of the unlimited materials handed over to us by the past. Indeed, as Thomas Kuhn has shown, science, too, evolves and is bound to tradition for its intelligibility, however much it strives to escape from or to dissimulate this condition.

"Tradition" thus recognizes the continuity of culture with a past that precedes and conditions it, but also with a future that shapes all knowledge and consciousness as a horizon of sense. A crucial medium of this transmission in history is human language. Language is the bearer of a destiny in which our past turns itself toward and into our future. Human beings are given to and from themselves through tradition as expressed in language as the medium of their cultural-historical being.

(*See also* Cartesianism; Chapter 1, Early Theory; Chapter 6, Historicisms; Chapter 18, Translation; Gadamer, Hans-Georg; Heidegger, Martin; *and* Scientific Method)

William Franke, *Vanderbilt University (United States)*

Further Reading

Gadamer, Hans-Georg. *Truth and Method* [1960]. Second ed. Trans. rvsd. Joel Weinsheimer and Donald G. Marshall. London: Continuum, 1998.

Grassi, Ernesto. *Rhetoric as Philosophy: The Humanist Tradition* [1980]. Trans. John Michael Krois and Azizeh Azodi. Carbondale: Southern Illinois University Press, 2001.

Vico, Giambattista. *The New Science of Giambattista Vico* [1744]. Third. ed. Trans. Thomas Goddard Bergin and Max Harold Fisch. Ithaca: Cornell University Press, 1976.

Transhumanism

Though popularized by Julian Huxley in the late 1950s, transhumanism arose from the intellectual ferment of the early-twentieth century—a hodgepodge of Russian cosmism, Italian futurism, and British eugenics, which is to say science fiction, technophilia, and biopolitics. The term has subsequently become a catch-all for a not entirely coherent set of ideas, practices, and values centering around the evolutionary destiny of the human species. This destiny, as Huxley asserts in his 1957 article "Transhumanism," is one which humans are in a unique position to shape: science, he claims, is the means by which the Hobbesian yoke will be shrugged off; no longer burdened with hunger, disease, poverty, and ignorance, people will at last be free to pursue their true "cosmic duty"— namely, self-realization and general social uplift. Needless-to-say, transhumanism is an aspirational ideology, implicitly critical of the status quo and the injustice of complacency itself.

Transhumanism in general is marked by this sort of strong ethical imperative—an imperative, on the one hand, to unlock one's own potential as a living being and, on the other, to alleviate the suffering of others. For Huxley, as for predecessors J. B. S. Haldane and J. D. Bernal, this double-project implies the necessity of eugenics—the active selection of "desirable" human traits and, conversely, the elimination of "defective" ones. Whereas Huxley ultimately conceives of eugenics as a prerequisite to enhanced consciousness—that is to say, the "new kind of existence" he imagines, however idyllic, is still very much terrestrial—others, like Haldane and Bernal, see it as a prerequisite for interplanetary travel. In this they echo not only the cosmist fascination with space exploration, but also the futurist fetishization of technologies associated with speed, power, and dynamism. These two implied trajectories of transhumanism may in fact be one and the same, as Freeman Dyson opines: "To explore the possibilities of mental experience will be as great a challenge as the exploration of the physical universe."

Modern-day transhumanism (often styled h+) reflects its origins in Huxley's vision— and more generally in cosmism, futurism, and eugenics—but shifts the emphasis away from belief in the *inherent*, evolutionarily conditioned potential of the species; rather, it embraces emergent technologies that promise liberation of one sort or another from fixed human identities. This sort of utopianism sets transhumanism apart from other forms of posthumanism, which are quicker to acknowledge darker possibilities. While there exist ecological and spiritual forms of transhumanism, the main current primarily concerns itself with scientific developments associated with the technological singularity: cryonics and radical life extension, artificial intelligence, neural enhancement, prosthetics, cyborgization, and various nano- and biotechnologies. These and similar technologies hold the promise of effectively eliminating or mooting strong distinctions between, for example, male and female, child and adult, human and machine, living and nonliving, and so on. Transhumanists in this regard are existential early adopters, beta-testing the future before it arrives.

(*See also* Biotechnology; Chapter 8, Rhetoric; Chapter 23, Materialisms; Chapter 24, Posthumanism; Cyborg; Environmental Humanities; Haraway, Donna; Humanimal; New Materialisms; *and* Posthumanism)

Keith Leslie Johnson, *College of William & Mary (United States)*

Further Reading

Bostrom, Nick, and Julian Savulescu. "Human Enhancement Ethics: The State of the Debate." In *Human Enhancement.* Eds. Julian Savulescu and Nick Bostrom. Oxford: Oxford University Press, 2009. 1–22.

Moravec, Hans. *Robot: Mere Machine to Transcendent Mind.* Oxford: Oxford University Press, 1999.

More, Max. "The Philosophy of Transhumanism." In *The Transhumanist Reader: Classical and Contemporary Essays on the Science, Technology, and Philosophy of the Human Future.* Eds. Max More and Natasha Vita-More. Chichester: Wiley-Blackwell, 2013. 3–17.

Translation

Translation, Umberto Eco declared, is the art of almost saying the same thing. This is not an exercise in damning with faint praise, but a way to appreciate the relative success of translation—no translation can exactly reproduce an original text, nor, arguably, should it try to. Translation bridges linguistic differences, but doesn't erase them. Good translations "foreignize" themselves, allowing the other text to register as foreign—the text is an invited guest, rather than an assimilated entity. Already, translation profiles itself as an ethical activity: respectful of otherness, diplomatically concerned to find common ground. Yet the saying "translator traitor" serves as a reminder that infidelity is translation's stock-in-trade; when such infidelity is deemed inevitable, what emerges is the notion of the "untranslatable." For some, the over-preoccupation with occasions where translation is defeated risks demeaning translation's many successes. For others, inspecting the limits of translation prompt theoretically compelling questions: can there be immunity from translation? Does translation leave something intact? Is there something proper and idiomatic to an original work that remains so, despite the activities of translation? These questions are all the more significant because translation is frequently declared to be violent. Walter Benjamin, for example, speaks of an "extreme conscientiousness with utmost brutality." But quarantining texts denies them other readerships, and indeed that special future Benjamin describes as a "living on" in translation. The real question, however, is whether one can cherish the idiomatic (like cherishing one's mother tongue), while also appreciating the importance of translation. Can one simultaneously resist and appeal for translation? In the English translation of Derrida's "Des tours de Babel" (1987), for instance, the French is preserved so that the pun on "detour" and multiple towers is maintained. In a text about translation, Derrida enacts his authorial entitlement to speak French, forcing the English reader to invoke his title and speak French. Derrida permits and forbids translation, while inviting us to revisit the story of the tower of Babel. God forbids the ideal translation that would allow the world's peoples to speak transparently to each other, to speak in the same idiom. Everything would be translatable, because nothing would ever need the services of translation. Yet while God dooms the world to linguistic confusion, He permits translation so that it may watch over the arrogant impositions of linguistic hegemony. Still, it is not wrong to aspire to a universal language, or vocabulary, a common ground that we might all share. Is this not the aspiration of the universal declaration of human rights? Isn't this the tower we still wish to build? Babel names our greatest aspiration and arrogance. It names a necessary confusion. Translation must speak in the name of all the languages of the other, resist the imposition of majoritarian lingua francas, while simultaneously speaking on behalf of the one idiom. For the world after Babel still needs to recover a meaning of Babel that implies commonality—our values, our human fellowship, our planet. "Babel" remains the keyword for everything that orients translation to its vital task to come.

(*See also* Benjamin, Walter; Chapter 10, Feminism; Chapter 17, Comparativisms; Chapter 18, Translation; Deconstruction; Derrida, Jacques; Eco, Umberto; Figuration; Gadamer, Hans-Georg; Hermeneutics; Phenomenology; *and* Semiotics)

Brian O'Keeffe, *Barnard College (United States)*

Further Reading

Benjamin, Walter. "Translation—For and Against." In *Selected Writings, Volume 3, 1935-1938*. Ed. Howard Eiland and Michael W. Jennings. Trans. Edmund Jephcott. Cambridge: The Belknap Press of Harvard University Press, 2002. 249–252.

Derrida, Jacques. "Des tours de Babel [1987]." In *Psyche: Inventions of the Other, Volume 1*. Trans. Joseph F. Graham. Stanford: Stanford University Press, 2007. 191–225.

Eco, Umberto. *Experiences in Translation*. Trans. Alastair McEwen. Toronto: University of Toronto Press, 2008.

Transnational

Transnational approaches explore how the emergence of culture, whether in the sense of individual cultural products and larger cultural formations, is determined by encounters and exchanges across national borders. These approaches contest the long-standing assumption in the humanities that the nation-state is the natural framework for understanding culture, and that culture is ultimately the self-expression of a nation's people. Against this view, which is historically associated with nationalistic ideologies emerging in the nineteenth and early-twentieth centuries, transnational scholarship insists on the primacy of interaction across borders. Contesting the norms of national purity and fixity, they advocate a new critical vocabulary for the humanities centered on notions of cross-border mobility, plurality, and hybridization.

The transnational "turn" in cultural and literary studies is associated with the process of globalization, especially as it accelerated following the collapse of the bi-polar world order of the Cold War around 1990. Where globalization is primarily defined as an increase in international flows of capital, goods, labor, and information, transnational approaches analyze the impact of such flows on contemporary culture and chart the parallel globalization of the cultural field. However, rather than encouraging an exclusive focus on the global present, globalization has also increased our understanding of how the cultural productions of the past, not least the periods of discovery, colonialization, and imperialism, were equally shaped by cross-border interactions and encounters. In this sense, transnational studies reveals the idea of pristine, self-contained cultures to be a nationalistic myth and highlights the intercultural conversations at the heart of national canons.

Transnational perspectives have a profound impact on our perception of the space of culture. Where the nation-state paradigm tended to see the world as made up of segregated cultural silos, the transnational paradigm sees it instead as defined by movements, connections, and exchanges. Typically, it privileges geographical locales beneath (cities, provinces, sub-national regions) or above the nation (supranational regions, continents, hemispheres), using these non-national spaces to challenge the critical predominance of the nation while also developing new critical practices based on links across political borders. Further, while globalization often involves the idea of a center that benefits from unequal economic exchanges with an underprivileged periphery, transnational studies recognizes that this logic is also present in the cultural field, yet at the same time highlights how interactions across borders are complex and often multidirectional. This is the case, for example, when the normative cultural forms of the center are appropriated and transformed in peripheral locations and then exported back to the center in a process that slowly renegotiates the cultural balance of power.

Unlike older forms of comparativism focused on the differences and similarities between distinctive national traditions, transnational studies emphasizes the interconnectedness of these traditions. At the level of analysis, transnational criticism recovers the traces of cross-border exchange, emphasizing the pervasive intermingling of the local and the global and bringing to light the flows of migration and mobility underneath the alleged cultural purity of nation-states.

(*See also* Capitalism; Chapter 10, Feminism; Chapter 17, Comparativisms; Colonialism; Diaspora; Global Media; Globalization; Hybridity; Migration; Pluralism; *and* Queer Theory)

Jesper Gulddal, *University of Newcastle (Australia)*

Further Reading

Goyal, Yogita. *The Cambridge Companion to American Transnational Literature.* Cambridge: Cambridge University Press, 2017.

Jay, Paul. *Global Matters*: *The Transnational Turn in Literary Studies*. Ithaca: Cornell University Press, 2010.

Trauma

Psychological trauma describes an injury to the psyche caused by a horrific event. In the nineteenth-century, through the work of psychiatrists such as Pierre Janet, the idea of psychic trauma or mental "wounding" gained prominence. Janet pioneered research into dissociation as it manifested in cases of hysteria. Hysterics, as traumatized individuals, were unable to integrate their traumatic experiences and exhibited detachment or emotional numbness. For Janet, this dissociation was a symptom of psychic weakness. Josef Breuer and Sigmund Freud, however, advanced the idea that dissociation in hysteria is a defensive mechanism that causes the mind to split, relegating traumatic experiences to the unconscious. For Breuer and Freud, these experiences, or the memory of them, act like a foreign body (*Fremdkörper*) lodged within the hysteric. This alien agent can only be ousted if the hysteric remembers their trauma in all its affective intensity while simultaneously describing it in words. Talking, accompanied by traumatic affect, therefore forms the hysteric's cure.

Freud further investigates the role of processes of representation in mitigating trauma in "Beyond the Pleasure Principle" (1920), where he ceases to conceive of trauma as memory considering it instead as that which cannot be remembered. Trauma becomes what Cathy Caruth would later describe as a "missed" or "unclaimed" experience. This experience is compulsively repeated by the traumatized individual through actions and in nightmares. It can be relived through transference in analysis and then worked through via interpretation. Recently, Catherine Malabou has argued that psychoanalytic conceptions of trauma inspired by Freud repress neurology and fixate on memory, rendering them outdated. The emotionally pared psyche of those she calls the "new wounded" is incapable of transference making the interpretative endeavors of psychoanalysis redundant.

Freud's conception of trauma as an experience resistant to memorialization, prefigured post-traumatic stress disorder (PTSD) which was first defined in 1980 in the *Diagnostic and Statistical Manual of Mental Disorders*. This condition was initially primarily linked with Vietnam combat veterans. Symptoms of PTSD include repeated, intense sensory or visual reexperiencing of a traumatic event, such as flashbacks and nightmares. Echoing Freud's ideas concerning the repetition of distressing occurrences in the present as a traumatic acting out, this reexperiencing manifests a pathological immediacy. The trauma is not felt as a thing past, remaining unknown to memory.

The Real, one of Jacques Lacan's three registers of psychic reality along with the Imaginary and the Symbolic, is also associated with unknowability and linked with trauma. The Real, a reality related to maternal plenitude, was first conceived by Lacan as inexpressible by the subject from within language in the Symbolic. He called it "troumatique," a traumatic void. The Real as unsayable, as beyond representation, has provided a template for conceptualizing historical traumatic events in Modernity. Georges Didi-Huberman, for example, refers to the crematoria at Auschwitz-Birkenau in 1944 as a Real. Drawing on Lacan's later seminars, Bracha L. Ettinger developed the idea of the Matrixial to describe how, through aesthetic practices, the Real as traumatic experience can resonate in the present through affective encounters. Griselda Pollock recognizes the increasing concern with affect in contemporary critical thinking as symptomatic of the pressures of today's traumatic times and perceives aesthetic processes of the kind described by Ettinger as providing a means by which the trauma of others can be affectively recognized and, potentially, partly processed.

(*See also* Chapter 7, Psychoanalytic Theory; Deferred Action; Freud, Sigmund; Hysteria; Lacan, Jacques; Memory; Psychoanalysis; Repetition; Terror; *and* White, Hayden)

Nicholas Chare, *Université de Montréal (Canada)*

Further Reading

Caruth, Cathy. *Unclaimed Experience: Trauma, Narrative, and History*. Baltimore: Johns Hopkins University Press, 1996.

Malabou, Catherine. *The New Wounded: From Neurosis to Brain Damage* [2007]. Trans. Steven Miller. New York: Fordham University Press, 2012.

Pollock, Griselda. *After-affects/After-images: Trauma and Aesthetic Transformation in the Virtual Feminist Museum*. Manchester: Manchester University Press, 2013.

Trope

The term *trope* has been much debated since it made its way into the English language in the sixteenth century, and no clear consensus has resulted from that debate. Deriving from the Greek *tropos* ("turn," "change," "direction"), the word has been enlisted in a variety of discourses, to serve a variety of purposes. In the medieval Christian tradition, it denotes a gesture through which liturgical texts are amplified, or expanded; it may also refer to the way that texts are set to music. Contemporary popular culture has adopted the term, using it to mean a hackneyed plot device in film and other narrative forms. Still broader usage designates a trope as any kind of easily recognizable convention or cliché, from a figure of speech, to a character type, to a twist of plot. In rhetoric and literary studies, use of the word has clustered around the notions of "turn" or "change of direction" that the Greek etymon displays. In the main, it is employed to denote a figure of speech wherein a word or a phrase is used in a new way, one that changes or gives new direction to its standard, commonly accepted meaning. Certain theorists have attempted to define the term more closely. Kenneth Burke, for instance, spoke of "four master tropes": metaphor, metonymy, synecdoche, and irony. Harold Bloom adds hyperbole and metalepsis to that list of master tropes. In the system of taxonomy that M. H. Abrams proposes, the term identifies one of the two categories of figurative language, "figures of thought." Those latter figures entail a decided change of meaning, while the category from which they are distinguished, "figures of speech," wagers upon word order instead. Abrams concedes that the distinction is not a "sharp" one, and that critics do not always agree about it. Richard Lanham argues that any single definition of "trope" would be prescriptive, and thus counterproductive. He opts for a more ample and flexible definition of the term, hinging upon change of meaning. Like Abrams, he insists on the difference between that change of meaning and a more mundane change of conventional word order. In a pragmatic perspective, Lanham's approach makes a good deal of sense. For the very notion of the trope as a figure of change or difference has something powerfully untamed about it that deserves to be respected and preserved—and in the face of that phenomenon, undue efforts at domestication have foundered over the years, as if inevitably. Thus, it is undoubtedly best to think of a trope as a second-order figure, one wherein language takes a new turn in order to respond to new expressive needs. It is useful to point out that in that very process, language comments upon itself, foregrounding its fundamental agility, versatility, and malleability. In other words, despite the vexed nature of the term, it is legitimate to see tropes as privileged signifiers, ones wherein the drama of meaning is put on stage and caused to perform.

(*See also* Chapter 8, Rhetoric; Chapter 9, Deconstruction; Irony; de Man, Paul; New Criticism; Rhetoric; Russian Formalism; *and* White, Hayden)

Warren Motte, *University of Colorado (United States)*

Further Reading

Abrams, M. H. *A Glossary of Literary Terms.* New York: Holt, Rinehart and Winston, 1971.

Bloom, Harold. *A Map of Misreading.* New York: Oxford University Press, 1975.

Burke, Kenneth. *A Grammar of Motives.* Berkeley: University of California Press, 1969.

Lanham, Richard A. *A Handlist of Rhetorical Terms.* Berkeley: University of California Press, 1969.

U

Uncanny, The

The uncanny is a complex concept that applies to something familiar or "homely" that appears to be alien, maybe even eerie, and evokes the human response of not only discomfort and fear, but sometimes simultaneous pleasure. It can involve, for example, seeing, hearing, or reading about something customary yet strange. Harold Bloom describes it as the "negative sublime." On a basic level, it easily applies to the supernatural, fantastic, occult, magical, and grotesque, characterized by such phenomena as demons, ghosts, spirits, automata, and lifelike figures. Freud's 1919 essay "The Uncanny" ("Das Unheimliche") is credited with bringing the sensation into people's consciousness and ultimately making it into a major concept. By applying a psychoanalytic approach to the term, Freud contends that an uncanny situation evokes an uneasy response of uncertainty and ambivalence because it entails the return of the repressed. He cites as support the observation of the German philosopher Friedrich von Schiller, who describes the term as referring to something that ought to have remained hidden but has been revealed. Freud also looks at motifs that can evoke the uncanny, such as doubling (e.g., alter-egos, doppelgangers); unexplainable repetitions; the death drive; and the lack of differentiation between reality and imagination, the past and the present (e.g., déjà vu), and the living and the dead. He relates it to the animistic, "primitive" ideas that have their genesis "in the childhood of the individual or the race" that have been "surmounted," claiming they return during the uncanny response to a happening and make us fearfully think that these repressed beliefs are true, such as that the dead have the power to return and impact the lives of the living; we have "the omnipotence of thought" to make events happen if we wish them; and recurring phenomena have a mystical significance and do not happen coincidentally. His ideas about the concept underlie a theory of fiction, for he argues that uncanny events happen far less often in real life than they do in literature, where an author can create a realistic atmosphere yet introduce unrealistic, fantastic elements that seem real because he or she doesn't explain them for some time, or not until the very end of the work. As long as the uncertainty remains, so does the uncanny effect. If too much unease is created, however, it can lead to rejection and repulsion.

Scholars have clarified that even psychoanalysis and deconstruction, two developments in the twentieth century, are uncanny in nature: both make the familiar (respectively one's inner self and a text's meaning) more uncertain and bring to the surface unsettling hidden elements. What started out as a relatively obscure concept has gained prominence through the decades and developed beyond its original application to psychology, genre studies (especially fantastic, gothic, and horror literature), and aesthetics. It now relates as well, for example, to literary theory, religion, philosophy, architecture, anthropology, sociology, visual arts, robotics, technology, and film, cultural, queer, and postcolonial studies. It has expanded from denoting the supernatural to evoking a more existential meaning of anxiety and alienation from society and from oneself; estrangement; homelessness (both literal and figurative); and ambivalence, especially in literature of Western culture and with regard to social, cultural, political, and ethical issues. Martin Jay calls it "one of the most supercharged words in our current critical vocabulary."

(*See also* Chapter 7, Psychoanalytic Theory; Chapter 9, Deconstruction; Freud, Sigmund; *and* Psychoanalysis)

Carolyn E. Brown, *University of San Francisco (United States)*

Further Reading

Jay, Martin. "The Uncanny Nineties." In *Cultural Semantics: Keywords of Our Time.* Amherst: University of Massachusetts Press, 1989. 157–64.

Masschelein, Anneleen. *The Unconcept: The Freudian Uncanny in Late Twentieth-Century Theory.* Albany: State University of New York Press, 2011.

Royle, Nicholas. *The Uncanny: An Introduction.* New York: Manchester University Press, 2002.

Unconscious

Although the notion of the unconscious is generally associated with Sigmund Freud and the discipline of psychoanalysis, it was already widely employed by philosophers and creative writers during the eighteenth century, as was demonstrated for example by Lancelot Law Whyte. However, when Freud singled out the unconscious as one of the cornerstones of his psychoanalytic edifice, he provided it with a new meaning, and it is this particular conceptualization that has

left a lasting imprint on literary and cultural studies. In sum, for Freud the unconscious is a repository of repressed representations, an active dynamic force that does not stop imposing itself upon and thereby disrupting the human conscious experience, and a scene of unknown knowledge that can nonetheless be accessed and rendered intelligible through specific techniques of interpretation. On many occasions, Freud himself argued how this unconscious not only conditions a broad array of clinical symptoms, but also is equally at work in sociocultural phenomena and in products of the human creative imagination. Likewise, he showed how psychoanalytic techniques of interpretation can be employed beneficially to reveal the latent knowledge and hidden thought processes permeating works of art as well as common social constructions such as group-formation, religious belief systems, and political ideologies.

In the wake of Freud's groundbreaking contributions, psychoanalysts, literary and cultural theorists developed a new paradigm of interpretation that came to be known as "psychoanalytic criticism," although the protocol and its object were not always as uniform as the term may suggest. Whereas some authors, such as Marie Bonaparte, heavily relied on a psycho-biographical method (explaining the contents of literary works with reference to unresolved infantile conflicts in the life history of the author), others favored a strictly thematic approach, looking for the unconscious by identifying recurrent implicit themes in an author's oeuvre, or in semantically similar cultural manifestations. The latter approach became exceptionally popular during the 1950s by the virtue of Claude Lévi-Strauss's structuralist anthropology, in which human beings, their social settings, and their cultural productions are being depicted as animated by deep linguistic structures of which they themselves are profoundly unaware, and even more so on account of Jacques Lacan's thesis that "the unconscious is structured like a language." During the 1960s, this type of structuralist psychoanalytic criticism influenced a great many forms of social critique, including the Marxist political analyses of Louis Althusser and Étienne Balibar, who were primarily geared toward unraveling the unconscious historical forces behind ideological texts and configurations.

In the twenty-first century, psychoanalytic criticism in literary and cultural studies persists in all its forms, yet it is by no means as popular and widespread as it once was. This is partly the result of the emergence of alternative interpretive frameworks in literary theory—such as semiotics, reception theory, and phenomenological criticism—which leave little room for the unconscious in the text, partly owing to the gradual decline of literary theory itself, yet perhaps most of all due to the massive influence of Jacques Derrida's deconstructionist method which, although it constantly engages with psychoanalysis, tends to expose psychoanalytic criticism as a self-serving method of interpretation. Whenever psychoanalysis claims to find something meaningful, Derrida suggested in the opening lines of his trenchant critique of Lacan's reading of Edgar Allan Poe's "The Purloined Letter," it only ever finds itself, thus confirming its own meaningfulness rather than validating some meaningful aspect of the text.

(*See also* Althusser, Louis; Chapter 5, Post-structuralism; Chapter 7, Psychoanalytic Theory; Chapter 10, Feminism; Chapter 22, Identity Studies; Deferred Action; Desire; Fantasy; Freud, Sigmund; Hysteria; Ideology; Lacan, Jacques; Lévi-Strauss, Claude; Political Unconscious; Psychoanalysis; Repetition; Symptom; *and* Žižek, Slavoj)

Dany Nobus, *Brunel University London (United Kingdom)*

Further Reading

Ellman, Maud, ed. *Psychoanalytic Literary Criticism*. London: Routledge, 2013.

Marcus, Laura, and Ankhi Mukherjee, eds. *A Concise Companion to Psychoanalysis, Literature and Culture*. Malden: Wiley-Blackwell, 2014.

Wright, Elizabeth. *Psychoanalytic Criticism*. London: Routledge, 2013.

University

The university is the site of *higher* education. It is also the site of contestation over curriculum, funding, working conditions, and a host of other metaprofessional concerns such as collegiality, affiliation, tenure, prestige, privilege, and academic freedom and identity.

Up until the 1990s, the study of higher education was by and large carried out by specialists in the fields of sociology and education. However, crises about decreasing university funding and increasing student debt coupled with rising pressure to run universities more like businesses or corporations brought many literary and cultural scholars into the conversation.

Prior to the rise of cultural studies in the late 1980s and 1990s, discussion of the metaprofessional dimensions of the university were nowhere as dominant as they are in the new millennium. Literature professors used to write about literature, and philosophers about philosophy. But over the last twenty years the hot topics at scholarly meetings of literature and language professionals are often the job market, academic publishing, tenure, and the fate of the university. The publication of books like Bruce Wilshire's *The Moral Collapse of the University: Professionalism, Purity, and Alienation* (1990), David Damrosch's *We Scholars: Changing the Culture of the University* (1995), Stanley Fish's *Professional Correctness: Literary Studies and Political Change* (1996), and Bill Readings's

The University in Ruins (1996) intensified economic and political discussion of the academy by humanities scholars.

By the early 2000s, the phrase "corporate university" came to be the central signifier for everything that is wrong with universities in America. Excellent books such as Derek Bok's *Universities in the Marketplace* (2003) and David Kirp's *Shakespeare, Einstein, and the Bottom Line* (2003) brought home this point. And Frank Donoghue put the scare into everyone by boldly predicting in *The Last Professors: The Corporate University and the Fate of the University* (2008), "professors have only been around for the last eighty years," don't count on them being around for the next eighty. Added to this metaprofessional conversation were concerns about online education, for example, David Noble in *Digital Diploma Mills: The Automation of Higher Education* (2001), the increasing reliance on adjunct labor, for example, Marc Bousquet in *How the University Works: Higher Education and the Low-Wage Nation* (2006), public university funding, for example, Christopher Newfield, *Unmaking the Public University: The Forty-Year Assault on the Middle Class* (2008), and rising student debt, for example, Jeffrey J. Williams in a series of articles dating back to 2006. The latter terms this critically-inspired work on the university of late as "critical university studies," though "university" and "metaprofessional" studies is also used, drawing on the affiliation of work in this area with cultural studies.

More recent work, such as Jeffrey R. Di Leo's *Corporate Humanities in Higher Education: Moving Beyond the Neoliberal Academy* (2013) and *Higher Education under Late Capitalism: Identity, Conduct, and the Neoliberal Condition* (2017) situates the university within the context of neoliberalism, identifying the ways it has recalibrated academic identity—and proposing ways out of this condition. Finally, work by Henry Giroux in a number of studies including *Neoliberalism's War on Higher Education* (2014) shows how neoliberal policies have radically reshaped the mission and practice of higher education, and have shortchanged a generation of young people.

These and other studies of the university by literary and cultural theorists share a relationship with more traditional work in the philosophy of education—work that dates back to Plato's theories of education. The difference though between work in the philosophical tradition about education and contemporary critical work on the university is that the latter is fighting for a less managed, corporate, and neoliberal version of higher education—something that previous generations of educational theorists and thinkers did not have to contend with, but contemporary scholars do.

(*See also* Chapter 25, University Studies; Chapter 27, Antitheory; Debt; Labor; Neoliberalism; *and* Professor)

Jeffrey R. Di Leo, *University of Houston-Victoria (United States)*

Further Reading

Bousquet, Marc. *How the University Works: Higher Education and the Low-Wage Nation.* New York: New York University Press, 2008.

Di Leo, Jeffrey R. *Higher Education under Late Capitalism: Identity, Conduct, and the Neoliberal Condition.* New York: Palgrave, 2017.

Di Leo, Jeffrey R. *Corporate Humanities in Higher Education: Moving Beyond the Neoliberal Academy.* New York: Palgrave, 2013.

Newfield, Christopher. *The Great Mistake: How We Wrecked Public Universities and How We Can Fix Them.* Baltimore: Johns Hopkins University Press, 2016.

Unnatural Narratology (*See* Chapter 3, Narrative and Narratology)

V

Violence

Violence is not some abstract concept or theoretical problem. It represents a violation in the very conditions that constitute what it means to be human as such. Violence is always an attack upon a person's dignity, their sense of selfhood, and their future. It is nothing less than the desecration of one's position in the world. It is a denial and outright assault on the very qualities that we claim makes us considered members of this social fellowship and shared union called "civilization." In this regard, we might say violence is both an ontological crime, insomuch as it seeks to destroy the image we give to ourselves as valued individuals, and a form of political ruination, which stabs at the heart of human togetherness that emerges from the ethical desire for worldly belonging.

In order for violence to be accepted there is a need for normalization. Such normalization depends upon immunization, like a surgical strike penetrating the body with such ruthless efficiency we no longer see it as being violence. While we might see the cruelty as something that is painful, we can reason beyond this, hence beyond the violence itself, for some greater political good. The violence in this regard is overlaid with a certain metaphysical cloak whose mask of mastery covers over the desecrated body with a virtuous blood soaked robe. But we also know that violence is always mediated by expressed dichotomies of permissible and impermissible actions. Some forms of violence or what we prefer to call force or collateral damages can be fully reasoned, while others clearly go beyond the tolerance threshold.

What defines the human condition is not simply that we live with a capacity to be wounded. We also have the capacity to think and imagine better worlds. So this is what is really at stake here. To accept violence is to normalize the wounds that tear apart the bodies of the living. That is why violence is so pernicious, especially as it becomes justified and more socially accepted. Through the subtle intimacy of its performance, it brings everything into its orbit such that the future can only appear to us as something that is violently fated. Every scar left upon the body of the individual is another cut into the flesh of the earth.

But the temporality to violence also works in another just as insidious and intellectually colonizing direction. Not only does violence beget violence, continuously, endlessly. As we also know, the memory of violence can also have such a hold over us that the ways we come to read the past are filtered through the most brutal lens. The very concept "humanity" is subject to this historical assay. While the term has a complex and politically fraught history, we know that it really becomes significant after the horrors of the Second World War, especially when confronting the reality of the Holocaust. Humanity in this regard emerges as an ethical and juridical problem out of the realization of the very worst that humans were capable of doing to one another.

This should raise profound questions for us, both in terms of dealing with the torturous legacy of human affliction and the continued capacity for us to violate the bodies of others; alongside the way, we are to respond to these tragic conditions so that we might rethink the very concept of humanity in more affirmative, spiritual, and dignified terms.

(*See also* Agamben, Giorgio; Benjamin, Walter; Bourdieu, Pierre; Butler, Judith; Chapter 9, Deconstruction; Chapter 10, Feminism; Chapter 15, Biopower and Biopolitics; Chapter 19, Media Studies; Chapter 21, Late Capitalism; Deleuze, Gilles; Derrida, Jacques; Force; Foucault, Michel; Infrastructure; Negri, Antonio; Orientalism; Patriarchy; Said, Edward; Whiteness; *and* Žižek, Slavoj)

Brad Evans, *University of Bristol*
(United Kingdom)

Further Reading

Evans, Brad, and Natasha Lennard, eds. *Violence: Humans in Dark Times*. San Francisco: City Lights, 2018.

Evans, Brad, and Terrell Carver, eds. *Histories of Violence: Post-War Critical Thought*. London: Zed Books, 2017.

Evans, Brad, and Henry Giroux. *Disposable Futures: The Seduction of Violence in the Age of Spectacle*. San Francisco: City Lights, 2016.

Vitalism

In the broad sense, vitalism is a metaphysical doctrine, descending from Aristotle and Galen, centered on the claim that the essential foundation of organic nature lies in some metaphysical substance (named variously "life," "vital force," "entelechy," etc.) that cannot be reduced to mechanical causality or to merely material processes describable by chemistry or physics. In maximalist versions of the doctrine, this substance also grounds nonorganic and inanimate nature, or even nature as a whole. In the narrow sense, "vitalism" refers principally to a modern formation that begins as resistance to the Cartesian and then Newtonian project of applying mechanical principles exhaustively to the explanation of organic phenomena. The eighteenth-century manifestations of vitalism (from Caspar Friedrich Wolff to Johann Friedrich Blumenbach to Marie François Xavier Bichat to cultural figures such as Johann Gottfried Herder and Johann Wolfgang von Goethe) nourished the development of Counter-Enlightenment and romanticism with the notion of a spiritualized organic life force. The late-nineteenth and early-twentieth-century forms of vitalism, in turn, contested positivism, as articulated by Hippolyte Taine, Auguste Comte, and Ernest Renan. In German, these later forms of vitalism—which in philosophy (e.g., in Wilhelm Dilthey and Wilhelm Windelband) arose out of and contested also neo-Kantian formalist rationality—are collectively known as *Lebensphilosophie* ("philosophy of life"). *Lebensphilosophie* developed, under the influence of Friedrich Nietzsche, in discourses that raised "life" (*Leben*) and the immediacy of "lived experience" (*Erlebnis*) to the status of an irrationalist, subjectivist absolute. The most prominent vitalist in life science in the twentieth century was Hans Driesch. The most rigorous vitalist in twentieth-century philosophy was Henri Bergson, whose international popularity extended from the 1890s through the First World War, then faded gradually in the 1920s and 1930s, and especially after the Second World War.

Beginning with *Time and Free Will* in 1889, Bergson distinguished between the radically temporal character of subjective experience, which he described as the qualitative dimension of intensities, and the spatial character of the world of objects, which he conceived as the quantitative dimension of extension. In so doing, he situated the vital dimension in the qualitative intensities of consciousness, and argued against the application of the languages of names and numbers (and mathematization more broadly) to this un-nameable core of experience. In *Matter and Memory* (1896), Bergson extended this insight into an elaboration on perception and memory, reserving for the latter in its "pure" form the role of spiritual life. In *Creative Evolution* (1907), Bergson developed this vitalist position into a theory of the *élan vital* or "vital force" in evolution. Through the Second World War, a broad number of appropriations of Bergson were undertaken by both left (e.g., Georges Sorel and other syndicalists, Georg Simmel, Walter Lippmann, Walter Benjamin) and right-wing thinkers (e.g., the early T. E. Hulme, Charles Péguy, the early Jacques Maritain). The ease with which vitalism as *Lebensphilosophie* (e.g., in Ludwig Klages and Oswald Spengler) was appropriated by fascism and national socialism continues to render it politically suspect to this day, although Bergson's own political intentions did not go in this direction and the political implications of Bergsonism remain under discussion.

Having been thrust aside by phenomenology, existentialism, and then structuralism, Bergson—and with him the vitalist tradition—was re-enlivened by the post-structuralism of Gilles Deleuze, who devoted to Bergson an early essay, "Bergson's Conception of Difference" (1956) and an important book, *Bergsonism* (1966), as well as sections of his other works. Deleuze's repetition and displacement of Bergsonian vitalism remains an important component of contemporary theory, especially in affect studies (e.g., in Brian Massumi) and in Lacanian and post-Lacanian theory (Slavoj Žižek and Alain Badiou).

(*See also* Badiou, Alain; Canguilhem, Georges; Chapter 15, Biopower and Biopolitics; Chapter 23, Materialisms; Chapter 26, Affect Studies; Deleuze, Gilles; New Materialisms; *and* Žižek, Slavoj)

Jeffrey S. Librett, *University of Oregon (United States)*

Further Reading

Burwick, Frederick, and Paul Douglass. *The Crisis in Modernism: Bergson and the Vitalist Controversy*. Cambridge: Cambridge University Press 1992.

Guerlac, Suzanne. *Thinking in Time: An Introduction to Henri Bergson*. Ithaca: Cornell University Press, 2006.

Pearson, Keith Ansell. *Germinal Life: The Difference and Repetition of Deleuze*. New York: Routledge, 1999.

White, Hayden

Hayden White (1928–2018) was the leading theorist of historical studies of the late twentieth and twenty-first centuries as well as a highly influential figure in literary theory and narratology. White began his academic career as a medievalist and intellectual historian at the University of Rochester, where he co-wrote, with Wilson Coates, two books on the evolution of liberal humanism in Western Europe (1966, 1970). However, by the time he was named Professor of the History of Consciousness at the University of California, Santa Cruz in the late 1970s, White would be known less as an historian than as a thinker and provocateur whose style of thought resonated with the major currents of critical theory, including structuralism, post-structuralism, and postmodernism. His magnum opus, *Metahistory: The Historical Imagination in Nineteenth-Century Europe*, published in 1973, revolutionized the debate around philosophy of history. It challenged the idea of a scientific historiography and infused the subject with a tropological and narratological understanding that went far beyond all previous efforts. Along with its companion volume, *Tropics of Discourse: Essays in Cultural Criticism* (1978), *Metahistory* created a new and urgent dialogue between literary studies and historiography, a dialogue widely resisted by historians, who felt that the rapprochement between historical writing and literary forms erased the dividing line between fact and fiction. White's 1987 collection, *The Content*

of the Form: Narrative Discourse and Historical Representation, moved even further in the direction of literary theory, revealing important affinities between historiography and the nascent field of narratology.

At the heart of White's thought is the idea that "all stories are fictions"; that is, all stories are composed of conventional, culturally conditioned plot types (an idea White derives from Northrop Frye's "archetypes"). Because stories preexist the historical data to which they are applied—stories are *made*, not found—it is impossible for a narrative to correspond to historical reality. Unlike disparate facts, narratives are thus not subject to scientific verification. Just as for Immanuel Kant perceptual reality is constructed by our cognitive apparatus, White held that historical reality is constructed by narrative and discursive forms, which are themselves underwritten by linguistic tropes (the fourfold system adapted from Italian philosopher Giambattista Vico: Metonymy, Metaphor, Synecdoche, Irony). White called the process by which historical data are transformed into history "emplotment" (a term he coined), meaning that the historical data are shaped by the aesthetic and moral proclivities of the historian. Stories are not mere vessels that contain historical data; they reflect ethical and ideological *choices*. Thus, any pretense to an "objective" historiography—the scientific ideal of a value-neutral account of the facts—reveals a bad-faith misunderstanding of narrative and of the very process of historical writing, which inevitably involves "choosing the past": (re)interpreting the past in light of contemporary projects, thereby creating ever new meanings in and connections with the present (here the influence of Friedrich Nietzsche and Sartrean existentialism becomes abundantly apparent, but also Erich Auerbach's notion of "*figura*"). White thus opposed any concept of the "fixity" of the past.

White published two more collections of essays, *Figural Realism: Studies in the Mimesis Effect* (1999) and *The Practical Past* (2014), in which he fleshed out and refined his ideas but also responded to the challenge of Holocaust historiography, which, since 1990, had become the site of neuralgic debates concerning the problem of representation of traumatic or "limit" events. An anthology of White's uncollected articles (edited by Robert Doran) was published in 2010 under the title *The Fiction of Narrative: Essays on History, Literature, and Theory, 1957–2007*.

(*See also* Chapter 3, Narrative and Narratology; Chapter 6, Historicisms; Ethnicity; *and* Figuration)

Robert Doran, *University of Rochester (United States)*

Further Reading

Doran, Robert, ed. *Philosophy of History After Hayden White*. London: Bloomsbury, 2013.

Paul, Herman. *Hayden White: The Historical Imagination*. London: Polity Press, 2011.

White, Hayden. *Metahistory: The Historical Imagination in Nineteenth-Century Europe* [1973]. Fortieth anniversary ed. Baltimore: Johns Hopkins University Press, 2014.

Whiteness

Like other racial signifiers, "whiteness" can refer to a myriad of contexts and hold a variety of meanings. Also, like "race," whiteness is not a transhistorical category but a social construct. Designations of who is "white," and significations of "whiteness," change over time and differ both between and within geographical contexts. "Whiteness" in the United States, for example, can refer to both a person of European descent and also one of Middle Eastern descent, though such designations by the state may not hold in the day-to-day existence of its citizenry. Thus, one critical aspect of "whiteness" studies is that "whiteness" is not a homogenous category. "Whiteness" can contain a vast array of meanings, from the invisible center of identity politics to structural or individualized manifestations of white privilege. Advantages in education, employment, and incarceration rate are ways in which white privilege operates at a systemic level, while white privilege at the individual level would feature the avoidance of microaggressions or stereotypes. What is more, "whiteness" can signify violence and terror and be considered constitutive of colonialism, and by proxy, capitalism. The latter meaning of "whiteness" suggests that a distinction should be made between "whiteness" as racial signifier and "white supremacy" as institutionalized racial privilege. "White supremacy" then operates immanently within capitalist social relations, thus making "white supremacy" a societal power relation that functions globally.

Major works in the field focus on the construct of the "white working class," while other works focus on the assimilation of various groups from Europe into "whiteness." The former analyses typically think through the reasons why the working class has historically divided itself from other races while not coalescing around class solidarity. Analyses interested in assimilation, on the other hand, look to legal status of immigrant populations along with archival materials to understand the ways in which these groups were considered "white" or "foreign" in the context of the United States. Such groups include the Irish, Jews, Germans, and Italians. This focus on assimilation of various ethnic groups, however, can lead to a potential pitfall in terms of reinscribing racial essentialism, if not racism itself.

Critics of "whiteness" scholarship have pointed out potential issues with assimilationist works in which the latter will "invent" whiteness and then potentially see it everywhere, thereby reifying a social construct and divesting the category itself from any meaningful coherence. Another critique of such scholarship is that it potentially leaves out other systems of oppression including class, gender, sexual orientation, and ableness, thus theorizing "whiteness" on its own without acknowledgment of systems of power with which it is always entangled. In spite of these criticisms, "whiteness" scholarship has usefully created a category of thought that had traditionally been overlooked. Despite its limitations, "whiteness" and "whiteness" studies have opened up race theory and other studies of systemized oppression in fruitful and significant ways, and the possibility remains for further exploration of these modes of analysis.

(*See also* Chapter 11, Cultural Studies; Chapter 22, Identity Studies; Colonialism; Race; *and* Social Constructionism)

Steven Delmagori, *University at Albany (United States)*

Further Reading

Frankenburg, Ruth. *White Women, Race Matters: The Social Construction of Whiteness*. Minneapolis: University of Minnesota Press, 1993.

Ignatiev, Noel. *How the Irish Became White* [1995]. New York: Routledge, 2008.

Roediger, David. *The Wages of Whiteness: Race and the Making of the American Working Class* [1991]. New York: Verso, 2007.

Williams, Raymond

Using a singular description to place Raymond Williams (1921–88) is difficult and, more importantly, misleadingly reductive. He was an author, academic, cultural theorist, literary critic, political analyst, public intellectual, socialist, and a leading figure of the New Left. Williams was the son of working-class parents from a Welsh border village, an adult education tutor, a Cambridge professor, and, according to Terry Eagleton, was and was not a Marxist. From such unique positions, he established a new mode of critical analysis, cultural materialism, grounded in a concept of culture which positions cultural practice as part of an active, dynamic, historical process. His work consistently draws attention to two strands within cultural forms: the contingent and the subjunctive. The former figures history as driven by human action while the latter looks for moments which ask what alternatives are possible and how. From here, Williams developed a number of enduring theoretical concepts: he identified a "structure of feeling," what he described as "the area of interaction between the official consciousness of an epoch . . . and the whole process of actually living its consequences"; he insisted upon viewing culture as "ordinary," as everyday and (potentially at least) democratic, being constantly made and remade; and he formulated three forces or tensions within the development of cultural forms: the residual (preexisting and traditional), the dominant (central and defining), and the emergent (new and challenging). All of these give a glimpse into his relevance and influence as well as providing a way of analyzing and critiquing cultural transformation, placing a primary focus on culture as, what Williams notably called, "a whole way of life," something made and lived. In works such as *Culture and Society* (1958) and *The Long Revolution* (1961) he embarked on what would be a prolonged analysis of cultural development viewed through, and ingrained within, the transformations of industrial capitalism and capitalist society. He was influenced by Antonio Gramsci and the concept of cultural hegemony, writing in opposition to the methods of vulgar or mechanical Marxism which fail to place due emphasis on the dynamic nature of cultural production. As Stuart Hall has noted, Williams played an integral role in the development of (a politically engaged) cultural studies. And he theorized the distinctive and decisive experiences of class, region, and community during an extended engagement with questions of form, realism, and modernism; these were all themes which he drew upon and expertly marshaled in his impressive debut novel, *Border Country* (1960). In *Towards 2000* (1983), published five years before his death, Williams offered a prescient analysis of "nomad capitalism" and labeled as "Plan X" the political and economic project of social management now commonly understood as neoliberalism; for Williams, this was a new form of capitalism which aimed to "grasp" and "control" the future. He envisioned a powerful alternative: a radically new kind of politics coalescing around the disarmament, environment, and feminist movements. Cultural practice would, of course, play a defining role in this and Williams' methodological approach offers a radical kind of critical analysis, one foregrounding the material processes and relations of culture itself.

(*See also* Base and Superstructure; Chapter 4, Marxism; Chapter 11, Cultural Studies; Chapter 14, Ecocriticism; Chapter 21, Late Capitalism; Chapter 22, Identity Studies; Chapter 26, Affect Studies; Cultural Critique; Cultural Materialism; Cultural Studies; Culture; Emotions; Hegemony; Production (and Reproduction); *and* Revolution)

Phil O'Brien, *University of Manchester (United Kingdom)*

Further Reading
Williams, Raymond. *Politics and Letters: Interviews with New Left Review*. London: Verso, 1979.
Williams, Raymond. *Towards 2000*. London: Chatto & Windus, 1983.
Williams, Raymond. *Border Country*. London: Chatto & Windus, 1960.

Worldhood

The current meaning of the word "worldhood" can best be understood when it is considered in the context of Martin Heidegger's effort to think the relationship between world (*Welt*) and earth (*Erde*). According to Heidegger, in the Western (ontotheological) tradition, these two terms have been invariably seen as a hierarchized binary, in which the world or worldhood has been projected as the opposite of the earth. In this Western tradition, especially since the third (anthropological) phase bearing witness to the ascendency of man (anthropos) as sovereign over all the surveys, the earth, to oversimplify, has come to be seen as raw material to be *shaped* by man as maker (*homo faber*). At the liminal point of this late shaping ontological process, Heidegger wrote in his paradigm-changing essay, "The Question Concerning of Technology" (1954), humans, pursuing the imperative of "challenging the earth" endemic to the anthropological phase, have reduced all of its phenomena to *Bestand*: "standing reserve" or, to emphasize the violence of this epochal reduction, "disposable reserve." And, in the process of the "worlding of the earth," he ominously points out, humans themselves have become a category of the disposable. This Heideggerian prophecy of the ominous reduction of the earth to a worldhood understood as disposable reserve, not incidentally, constitutes the genealogical origin of the postmodern critical initiative, from Hannah Arendt through Michel Foucault to Giorgio Agamben, that is bearing witness to the biopoliticization of the political realm, an initiative of the worlding process that, as Agamben has put it, is culminating in the reduction of human life (*bios*) to bare life (*nuda vida*), life that can be killed without the killing being called murder.

From Heidegger's radical genealogical perspective, on the other hand, world (the making or structuration that renders the earth habitable) and earth (the infinitely finite and irreparable temporality of being) do not constitute a binary opposition the imperative of which is a war to the end. These "opposites" are indissolubly related and, in Heidegger's language, *always already* exist in the rift (*das Riss*) between the two. Or, to appropriate another important but still remarkably invisible Heideggerian term, world and earth exist together in an *Auseinandersetzung*—a never ceasing loving strife. In the errant process of this loving strife, each pole—world and earth—maintain the agonic identities history has given them, but unlike the binarist Friend/foe version of the agon, in which the World is empowered to domesticate (to at-home; i.e., to world) the errant wilderness of the earth—these are always enriched: already deepened and expanded.

To put this loving strife and its consequences alternatively, when the world threatens to reduce the unfathomable and always potential earth to standing or disposable reserve, the earth, which is ontologically untamable, resists, not overtly, but by passively *concealing* "itself." And in so doing, the earth also paradoxically produces an occasion the human imperative of which is to unconceal its spectral concealment. This phenomenological rhythm of concealment/unconcealment that is fundamental to the indissoluble affiliation between world and earth, not incidentally, is, as I read it, the *raison d'etre* of Heidegger's urgent (though still unheeded) call to postmodern humanity to retrieve the pre-Socratic Greek understanding of truth, *a-letheia*, which was reduced to a useful apparatus capture by the imperial Romans, who, intent on colonizing the earth in the name of the sovereign center City, read the errant but always potential Greek version to adequaetio intellectus et rei: the adequation of mind and thing: correctness. For the early Greeks, *a-letheia*—un-concealing (or un-forgetting)—like the loving agonic affiliation between world and earth (*Welt und Erde*), was a never-ending temporal process that enhanced the humanness of the human species and at the same time protected the human from becoming de-humanized: disposable reserve or bare life that, as in Nazi world of concentration camps, could be killed with impunity.

This brief diagnosis of the world of anthropological modernity, it is important to add, was not only Heidegger's. Limiting it to such a controversial figure would make it all too easy to dismiss the indissoluble world-earth relation as a further example of the German's impenetrable philosophical rambling or, worse yet, to identify it with his alleged reactionary Nazism. The fact is that the above diagnosis is also, despite it's variations, that of a substantial number of prominent globally-oriented "left" intellectuals—the late Edward Said, Hannah Arendt, and Michel Foucault, and contemporaries, including

Giorgio Agamben, Alain Badiou, Jacques Rancière, Slavoj Žižek, and Judith Butler, for example, all of whom make decisive note of the waning of the worldhood of the world in its modern nation-state form, acknowledge the *Interregnum*, the in-between time, as the occasion of their dislocated existence. And in one way or another, they call for a world-hood that, in its loving strife between world and earth, is adequate to the onto-political Imperatives of the Interregnum which has unconcealed abiding onto-political rift that affiliates the world and the earth.

The present liminal global occasion has borne decisive witness to the irremediable decline of the nation-state system that had hitherto characterized the sovereign world-hood of the world. Given this glaring reality that has returned Western humanity to its beginnings—and, not incidentally, the omi-nous folly of the Donald Trump phenomenon: its astonishing indifference to this patent real-ity—this growing recognition of the indissolu-ble affiliation of the world and earth has come to be experienced viscerally by a vast global population as an urgent question in which sur-vival of the humanity of the human species is at stake. We humans must attune ourselves to this difficult but promising eventual question.

(*See also* Agamben, Giorgio; Foucault, Michel; Heidegger, Martin; *and* Said, Edward)

William Spanos, *Binghamton University (United States)*

Further Reading

Agamben, Giorgio, *Homo Sacer: Sover-eign Power and Bare Life* [1995]. Trans. Daniel Heller-Roazen. Stanford: Stanford University Press, 1998.

Heidegger, Martin. "The Question Con-cerning Technology [1954]." In *Basic Writings*. Ed. David Farrell Krell. New York: Harper and Row, 1977.

Heidegger, Martin. "The Origin of the Work of Art [1950]." Trans. Albert Hofstadter. *Poetry, Language, Thought*. New York: HarperCollins Perennial, 2001.

Worldliness

Worldliness in literary and cultural theory is a confluence of three flows. First, "world" refers, since at least the age of Johann Wolfgang von Goethe, to a possible geographical scope for literary production. For Goethe, "world literature" named the idea of a form of cultural production that escaped the linguistic and political boundaries of the nation, that addressed itself to, and drew influence from, questions that exceeded beyond the scope of any local necessity. In the last decades the debates inaugurated by the idea of world literature have extended into method, with various partisans taking up for or against the idea of world literature on the grounds that it (positively) forces critics to think the history of literature beyond the boundaries of Europe and North America, or that it (negatively) leads to an oversimplified and epistemologically overconfident take on literatures written outside the hegemony, thereby reproducing the structures it sought initially to avoid. These debates about the scope of "world" in literature touched briefly, in the early 2000s, on questions of world-systems and of computational analysis, whose scope was taken as a figure for worldliness more generally.

The second flow of "world" involves its history in philosophy, where it functions, in the work of Martin Heidegger and Jean-Luc Nancy, as a site for the investigation of the ground of human living. These attempts to think the world, which both thinkers oppose to the planet or the globe, push hard on our intuitions about part-whole relations, since the world, considered as a ground for being, is neither part of the world, nor its whole, but something like a substrate or a condition of possibility for wholeness itself. In analytic philosophy, worldliness appears in any number of discussions about the value of logical statements and the standing of social practices like lying or the writing of fiction. Particular attention has been paid to ideas of "possible worlds," and the ways in which such worlds—which are of course emblematic in fiction—invite us to test the limits of our sense of the actual world, and encourage us to consider the philosophical or political consequences of the imagination.

The analytic interest in possible worlds overlaps with a third field, namely the study of the role worldliness plays in the production of the work of art. In what ways do such works present themselves as worlds—not simply as representations of worlds (in the way novels represent to us various realistic or possible realities), but as structures whose grounding qualities, whose very wholeness, constitute formal responses to, or commentaries on, the kinds of worldliness that interested Heidegger or Nancy? In what ways, that is, could we think of worldliness not as something that simply determines *how* one produces or studies literature (our first flow), or as something that addresses a certain set of philosophical concerns (our second flow), but as an active form of social practice embodied in the work of art, and, indeed, the work of art's relation to itself as a work at all?

(*See also* Chapter 17, Comparativisms; Heidegger, Martin; Nancy, Jean-Luc; *and* Worldhood)

Eric Hayot, *Pennsylvania State University*
(United States)

Further Reading

Damrosch, David. *What Is World Literature?* Princeton: Princeton University Press, 2003.

Nancy, Jean-Luc. *The Sense of the World* [1993]. Trans. Jeffrey S. Librett. Minneapolis: University of Minnesota Press, 1997.

Rubenstein, Mary-Jane. *Worlds Without End: The Many Lives of the Multiverse*. New York: Columbia University Press, 2014.

Writing

Writing is arguably one of the most significant and essential inventions of humankind. A technological medium with a material history, it has greatly expanded the human capacity for memory, provided an indispensable resource to the development of law and science, and laid the foundations for much of Western metaphysical thinking. First appearing around 3200 BCE in ancient Sumer as a pictographic script representing physical objects through imitative portraits, it eventually evolved into symbolic logograms and phonetic signs. Historically, most writing systems have entailed different mixtures and refinements of all three types. For example, in China logography developed into a complex system containing thousands of symbols, while in ancient Greece, a phonetic script emerged with unique signs for each vowel. According to critics such as Marshall McLuhan and Robert Logan, these differences in writing systems played a central role in shaping the intellectual lives of their respective cultures. Regardless of form, however, what all writing systems hold in common is that they must be taught and learned consciously. Unlike speech, which can be acquired unconsciously by humans during a certain period of early brain development, learning to write demands the subject's mental engagement with language as an object and formal structure. As a consequence, Walter Ong and Eric Havelock have argued, writing restructures the mind. By altering the subject's relationship to language, by "technologizing the word," writing separates the knower from the known, gives rise to grammar, and provides new ways of organizing and maintaining the contents of the mind.

In the context of Western philosophy and critical theory, the medium of writing has proven crucial, while at the same time being consistently devalued in its relationship to speech. Plato criticizes writing as a dangerous drug (*pharmakon*), asserting that it weakens memory and detaches thought from the speaker. At the same time, Plato's conception of truth as "writing in the soul," his emphasis on analytic reasoning, and his critique of the oral traditions of the poet, point to a highly literate relationship to knowledge. Jacques Derrida shows that many of the key texts in the metaphysical tradition involve this mode of duplicity, denigrating writing as secondary and subordinate to speech, on the one hand, while repeatedly drawing on literate metaphors and conceptions of language to articulate an understanding of truth. This symptom of Western thought could be said to be a direct consequence of its attachment to the alphabet, which presents writing as an encoding of sound. It is thus particularly noteworthy that Derrida's project of deconstruction emerges precisely at a time when the more-than-two-thousand-year hegemony of handwriting and print was being displaced by media such as the radio, tape-recorder, television, and computer. The timing recalls Ong's claim that the critique of a medium cannot begin until its dominance has already passed. At the same time, it is worth mentioning that even if writing as a consciously applied sign system is disappearing from the sphere of human communication, it nonetheless persists, in the rudimentary form of inscription or trace, as the material basis of storage in even the most advanced media technologies.

(*See also* Archi-trace; Chapter 1, Early Theory; Chapter 5, Post-structuralism; Chapter 9, Deconstruction; Deconstruction; Différance; Dissemination; Metaphysics; Origin; Platonism; Presence; Supplement; *and* Text)

Matthew Schilleman, *University of Massachusetts, Amherst (United States)*

Further Reading
Derrida, Jacques. *Of Grammatology* [1967]. Trans. Gayatri Spivak. Baltimore: Johns Hopkins University Press, 1974.
Logan, Robert K. *The Alphabet Effect: The Impact of the Phonetic Alphabet on the Development of Western Civilization.* New York: St. Martin's Press, 1987.
Ong, Walter J., and John Hartley. *Orality and Literacy: The Technologizing of the Word.* London: Routledge, 2012.

Z

Žižek, Slavoj

Ever since his 1989 *Sublime Object of Ideology*, Slovenian philosopher and cultural theorist Slavoj Žižek (born 1949) has argued for the necessity of leftists to become better readers of ideology. To that end Žižek infuses standard Marxist thought with German idealism and Lacanian psychoanalysis. Against the twin deceptive attitudes of pessimism and optimism—postmodern pessimism about the prospects of transformative critique and optimism about the end of history à la Fukuyama, about, that is, the fantasy of a post-ideological stance—Žižek vigorously insists ideology is not a totalizing force, that critique's negativity still has an urgent role to play in today's society.

Whereas postmodern thinkers like Michel Foucault did away altogether with the seemingly defunct language of ideology, replacing it with the more protean notion of power, Žižek pursues a post-Althusserian revival of ideology, seeking to rescue the concept from hermeneutic oblivion. Ideology, for Žižek, operates most frequently at the level of the unconscious, soliciting and securing our libidinal investment. Going beyond the common identification ideology with false consciousness or misrecognition "They do not know it, but they are doing it,"—as Marx famously puts it in *Das Capital*—Žižek rewrites this saying completely, reconfiguring its psychoanalytic bases and implications by highlighting the problem of disavowal: "They know that, in their activity, they are following an illusion, but still they are doing it." Žižek's critical task consists of exposing such a disavowal on the part of the allegedly post-ideological subject of late capitalism.

To truly intervene in the symbolic order, Žižek frequently turns to the Lacanian notion of the act. Unlike a *passage à l'acte*—which is not a genuine political act, but more often than not a sign of frustration and impotence—the act succeeds in changing the coordinates of one's social being. It transforms the subject ontologically—you are no longer the same as before. The act subverts the Symbolic, enacting a momentary eclipsing or *aphanisis* of the subject. As a locus of negativity, the act touches the Real. It reveals the "non-all" (*pas-tout*) of symbolic reality.

Žižek critically reinterprets the Lacanian logic of the feminine "non-all" as referring to the ways a subject's enjoyment (*jouissance*) is organized (so that this feminine subject need *not* be anatomically female). Whereas the masculine logic of exception takes there to be a sovereign subject who has unlimited enjoyment, who stands outside the law of castration that governs social symbolic existence, the feminine logic, by contrast, sees no exception to the law of castration. It declines the illusion of an uncastrated Man (and with it the possibility of absolute enjoyment), but at the same time takes castration to be "non-all," never complete, or whole. For Žižek, the "non-all" articulates the logic of the Real, pointing to what is irreducible to a society's symbolic representation of reality. It gives the lie to any culture's phantasmatic and ideological pretention of wholeness, not only reorienting us to the harshness of being (the reality of the Real), but also compelling us to take an interpretive stance appropriate to a being understood as *a becoming* (a being that lacks), to a social reality that never coincides with the Real. In short, the "non-all" helps Žižek theorize subjectivity, and the signifying order, differently, underscoring the dynamism and mutability of ontology and the need for a skeptical mode of critique that engages and pursues subjectivity and language in their incompleteness, that introduces an infectious doubt about what passes for natural and stable in our social reality.

(*See also* Chapter 24, Posthumanism; Dialectic; Enlightenment; Fantasy; Ideology; Interpellation; Jouissance; Subject; *and* Violence)

Zahi Zalloua, *Whitman College (United States)*

Further Reading
Johnston, Adrian. *Žižek's Ontology: A Transcendental Materialist Theory of Subjectivity*. Evanston: Northwestern University Press, 2008.
Žižek, Slavoj. *How to Read Lacan*. New York: Norton, 2006.
Žižek, Slavoj. *Less Than Nothing: Hegel and the Shadow of Dialectical Materialism*. New York: Verso, 2012.

NAME INDEX

SUBJECT INDEX